A DICTIONARY OF
AMERICAN
PROVERBS

A DICTIONARY OF
AMERICAN
PROVERBS

WOLFGANG MIEDER

EDITOR IN CHIEF

STEWART A. KINGSBURY

KELSIE B. HARDER

EDITORS

NEW YORK   OXFORD
OXFORD UNIVERSITY PRESS
1992

Oxford University Press

Oxford   New York   Toronto
Delhi   Bombay   Calcutta   Madras   Karachi
Petaling Jaya   Singapore   Hong Kong   Tokyo
Nairobi   Dar es Salaam   Cape Town
Melbourne   Auckland

and associated companies in
Berlin   Ibadan

Copyright © 1992 by Oxford University Press, Inc.

Published by Oxford University Press, Inc.,
200 Madison Avenue, New York, New York 10016

Oxford is a registered trademark of Oxford University Press

Library of Congress Cataloging-in-Publication Data
A Dictionary of American proverbs / Wolfgang Mieder, editor in chief ;
Stewart A. Kingsbury and Kelsie B. Harder, editors.
p. cm.   Includes bibliographical references.
ISBN 0-19-505399-0
1. Proverbs, American—Dictionaries.   I. Mieder, Wolfgang.
II. Kingsbury, Stewart A.   III. Harder, Kelsie B.
PN6426.D53   1992
398.9'21'0973—dc20   91-15508

1 3 5 7 9 8 6 4 2
Printed in the United States of America
on acid-free paper

This book is dedicated to

MARGARET M. BRYANT

Chairperson of the Committee on Proverbial Sayings
of the American Dialect Society,
1945–1985

CONTENTS

PREFACE

A Dictionary of American Proverbs is a comprehensive record of proverbs collected during field research that took place in the contiguous United States and parts of Canada, especially Ontario and the Maritime Provinces. It is the first major proverb compilation in the English language based on actual field research, a painstaking collecting endeavor that was carried out by dozens of scholars under the direction of Margaret M. Bryant, to whom this dictionary is respectfully dedicated. As chairperson of the Committee on Proverbial Sayings of the American Dialect Society from 1945 to 1985, she mobilized her colleagues throughout North America to collect approximately 150,000 citation slips of proverbial texts from the 1940s to the end of the 1970s. Her classic monograph, *Proverbs and How to Collect Them* (Greensboro, N.C.: American Dialect Society, 1945), established the guidelines for this massive collecting task. She also wrote short essays for regional language and folklore journals that encouraged people to collect proverbs in oral use. (See the Bibliography at the end of this volume.)

It took forty years of active collecting to complete this extensive project, which yielded almost 150,000 citation slips of proverbs, proverbial expressions, proverbial comparisons, superstitions, weather signs, and wellerisms, and yet another ten years to sort and edit the approximately 75,000 citation slips containing true proverbs. Not counting the many duplicates, this dictionary includes about 15,000 proverbs and their variants in actual use in American speech.

Close to fifty years of work have gone into this elaborate project. In the meantime, Margaret M. Bryant has reached the venerable age of ninety, as can be seen from her recently published autobiography, *A Story of Achievement* (Tokyo: Kenkyusha, 1990). May this proverb dictionary be a very special gift to her on her ninety-first birthday on 3 December 1991. She was the impetus and driving force behind this extraordinary project, and we as editors consider it a privilege and honor to have brought her work to fruition.

We thank the following scholars of American language and folklore, who assisted in amassing this unique collection: Owen S. Adams, Harold B. Allen, Frances M. Barbour, Mac E. Barrick, Ernest W. Baughman, F. W. Bradley, Frederic G. Cassidy, L. W. Collins, Ernest R. Cox, Levette Davidson, Audrey Duckert, Byrd H. Granger, Herbert Halpert, Wayland D. Hand, Muriel J. Hughes, Thelma G. James,

Richard Jente, Lorena E. Kemp, Marjorie M. Kimmerle, William E. Koch, James B. McMillan, Mamie Meredith, Randall Mills, Thomas M. Pearce, Henry A. Person, Louise Pound, Terry K. Pratt, Vance Randolph, W. Edson Richmond, J. Willis Russel, Samuel J. Sackett, G. M. Story, Archer Taylor, Harold W. Thompson, Bartlett Jere Whiting, and Roy M. Wiles. We also thank all the American Dialect Society field researchers and scholars for their invaluable efforts and time spent on this project.

We express our deep appreciation to our colleagues at Northern Michigan University who provided technical assistance during the many years that were required for the preparation of this dictionary: Donald Schlientz, whose knowledge of computer science enabled us to create a raw data base out of the thousands of oral proverb citation slips; Billie L. Schuller, who wrote software and designed and implemented the administrative data base; and Sheila Johnson, Eileen Patterson, Margaret Goodrich, and Christopher A. Jahnke, who helped trace the many historical references and edit entries. Thanks are also due to Janet Sobiesky of the University of Vermont for her editorial assistance and support.

The financial support of Northern Michigan University and Oxford University Press is gratefully acknowledged by us. We thank Stephen Chasteen, Claude Conyers, and John A. Simpson of Oxford University Press for their special editorial assistance. Finally, we do want to thank our wives, Barbara Mieder, Mildred Kingsbury, and Louise Harder, for supporting us throughout the years of work that it took to create this massive reference book.

It is our hope that *A Dictionary of American Proverbs* will be an invaluable reference book for serious paremiologists (i.e., proverb scholars) and paremiographers (i.e., proverb collectors). We also hope it will serve as a major research tool for cultural historians, folklorists, linguists, anthropologists, sociologists, psychologists, scholars of English and American literature, and many others. However, it is above all a "popular" book, containing the rich proverbial wisdom of the American people. May this *Dictionary of American Proverbs* therefore serve scholars and all those who are fascinated by language and folklore.

W.M.   S.A.K.   K.B.H.

INTRODUCTION

The title of this dictionary quite naturally leads to the question of what makes a proverb particularly "American." Even a cursory glance through the following pages will show that such internationally disseminated proverbs as *One hand washes the other* and *Time flies* are included. The same is true for such Biblical proverbs as *Man does not live by bread alone* (Deuteronomy 8.3; Matthew 4.4) and *The love of money is the root of all evil* (1 Timothy 6.10), which are current in many languages and cultures. And there are, of course, many proverbs in this collection that are of British origin, being registered for the first time in the works of Geoffrey Chaucer, William Shakespeare, Charles Dickens, and other British authors.

For all such proverbs, whether international, Biblical, or British, it must be kept in mind that, while they are not of American origin, they are certainly in common use in North America. They are thus "American" proverbs in that the population uses them frequently as concisely expressed, traditional bits of wisdom. As such, they surely belong in a dictionary of American proverbs. Historically, many of the proverbs in this collection appear in British sources dating as far back as the Middle Ages as well as in the seventeenth-century writings of early English-speaking settlers of North America.

Yet, a mere second glance into this dictionary reveals many proverbs that are recorded only in American literary sources. Early examples are the proverbs attributed to Benjamin Franklin and Ralph Waldo Emerson that have, over time, become traditional. While many of the American proverbs that appear herein are also registered in earlier historical collections of proverbs from written sources, there are literally thousands of proverbs and their variants listed in this dictionary that have never been recorded before. The six proverbs listed under the headword *car* serve as a clear example of this fact:

1. A car in every garage and a chicken in every pot.
2. Don't count your new cars before they're built.
3. If in the car you like to court, change your car to a davenport.
4. If you can't drive your car, park it.
5. It's the empty car that makes the most noise.
6. You can't judge a car by its paint job.

Not one of these texts has been recorded before, and each is clearly an American variant of an older proverb or an absolutely new American proverb. Because there are thousands of such proverbs in the present collection, it can be stated unequivocally that the American culture has a unique proverb lore. The value of this dictionary thus lies in its registration of *both* traditional English-language proverbs *and* new, indigenous American proverbs. It should be noted, however, that this dictionary is restricted to those proverbs that were in fact collected under the aegis of the American Dialect Society from the 1940s to the end of the 1970s. It therefore cannot claim to include every proverb used by North Americans and certainly not every proverb ever recorded in the English language.

Because we wanted to make this collection a "pure" one, limited to a single volume, we have included only true proverbs, which might be defined in general terms as concise statements of apparent truths that have common currency. We have excluded proverbial expressions, proverbial comparisons, superstitions, wellerisms, and idioms. Even so, some texts given herein may be questioned as true proverbs, because of their complexity of language or style. However, we decided to err on the side of inclusion rather than exclusion, since only a more "liberal" view of what constitutes a proverb will advance the lexicographical status of paremiography (i.e., collection of proverbs).

Still other texts given herein may be questioned on grounds of the negative views that they reflect. Just as we have included proverbs in dialect when the texts were so recorded, we have not shied away from listing those ill-conceived proverbs that are clearly misogynistic or that are ethnically and racially derogatory. Such negative and stereotypical texts unfortunately do exist, and we believe that scholarly honesty and objectivity justify and demand their inclusion in this comprehensive dictionary. We wish, nevertheless, to advise readers that we have included them not to condone them but rather to show that proverbial wisdom definitely can be misguided and misused.

Turning now to the more pragmatic aspects of this dictionary, we offer the following guidelines to its organization and use.

Order of Entries. It will be noted that we have followed the standard lexicographical method of listing proverbs in alphabetical order according to their most significant key word. Thus, the proverb *A new broom sweeps clean* is listed under the headword *broom,* following the proverb *A bad broom leaves a dirty room* and preceding the proverb *An old broom is better than a new one.*

Variants. Immediately after each proverb are listed all the variants, tagged *Vars.,* found throughout the United States and Canada. For *A new broom sweeps clean,* nine variants are listed:

Vars.: (a) A new broom never sweeps clean. **(b)** A new broom sweeps clean, but an old broom knows all the corners. **(c)** A new broom sweeps clean, but an old one gets in the corners. **(d)** A new broom sweeps clean, but an old one knows where the dirt is. **(e)** A new broom sweeps clean, but an old one scrapes better. **(f)** A new broom sweeps clean, but the old broom knows the corners. **(g)** A new broom sweeps clean; the old one knows the corners best. **(h)** A new broom sweeps the cleanest. **(i)** A new broom sweeps well.

Informants' Comments. When available, we have included short comments provided by informants that may help to clarify the meaning of a text that is particularly obscure. Such explanatory comments, tagged *Infm.,* are unfortunately quite rare, since few remarks by informants were recorded on citation slips by field workers. Occasionally, we have added an editorial comment after the tag *Infm.,* to call attention either to a foreign-language source or to a proverb with a similar meaning that appears under another headword.

Recorded Distribution. Because all the proverbs in this dictionary were collected from oral sources, we are able to show for the first time in a major English-language paremiographical reference work the recorded distribution of the proverbs and their variants in North America. This information follows the tag *Rec. dist.* When a proverb was found in use in more than five regions (i.e., states and provinces) of the United States and Canada, we have indicated its general distribution thus:

Rec. dist.: U.S., Can.

When a proverb was found in use in five or fewer regions, we have indicated the specific regions by giving abbreviations of the names of states and provinces, thus:

Rec. dist.: N.Y., Ont., Vt.

It should be noted that such a listing simply indicates that the proverb was recorded by field workers in New York, Ontario, and Vermont; it does not exclude the possibility that the proverb occurs in other regions of the United States and Canada. (See the Bibliography for citations of published regional and ethnic collections.)

We want to stress that our notation of recorded distribution is unique in Anglo-American paremiographical lexicography. It is a direct result of the fact that this collection is based on field research rather than on the usual method of compiling proverb dictionaries of this magnitude from written sources alone.

History of Use and Sources of Data. Because we wanted this dictionary to be a work of historical reference as well as a record of oral tradition, we have provided basic information on written sources. Wherever possible, we have cited the date, author, and title of the earliest known British and/or American written sources of each proverb. These citations follow the tag *1st cit.* We have, further, given sources of such data by citing one or more of the six standard Anglo-American proverb collections used in our research:

> Stevenson, *The Macmillan (Home) Book of Proverbs, Maxims and Familiar Phrases* (1948)
> Taylor & Whiting, *A Dictionary of American Proverbs and Proverbial Phrases, 1820–1880* (1958)
> Wilson, *The Oxford Dictionary of English Proverbs*, 3d ed. (1970)
> Whiting, *Early American Proverbs and Proverbial Phrases* (1977)
> Simpson, *The Concise Oxford Dictionary of Proverbs* (1982)
> Whiting, *Modern Proverbs and Proverbial Sayings* (1989)

(See the Bibliography for complete citations of these and many other English-language proverb collections.) References to these six twentieth-century collections follow the tag *20c. coll.* and are given in the following order: source of data of earliest British written use; source of data of earliest American written use; other collections in which the proverb is registered, listed in chronological order of earliest recorded written use.

Thus, under the headword *broom*, after the notation of recorded distribution of the proverb *A new broom sweeps clean*, the reader will find the following citations:

> **1st cit.:** 1542 *Unpublished Poems from the Blage MS*, ed. Muir; US1752 Clinton in *Letters and Papers of Cadwallader Colden*, N.Y.Hist.Soc. *Collections* (1917–37). **20c. coll.:** ODEP 564, Whiting 47, *CODP* 161, Sevenson 246:12, T&W 44, Whiting*(MP)* 75.

These citations require interpretation. They indicate (1) that the earliest known British written source of the proverb is dated 1542 and is cited in *The Oxford Dictionary of English Proverbs (ODEP)* on page 564; (2) that the earliest known American written source of the proverb is dated 1752 and is cited in *Early American Proverbs and Proverbial Phrases* (Whiting) on page 47; and (3) that the proverb is also registered in *The Concise Oxford Dictionary of Proverbs (CODP)*, *The Macmillan (Home) Book of Proverbs, Maxims and Familiar Phrases* (Stevenson), *A Dictionary of American Proverbs and Proverbial Phrases, 1820–1880* (T&W), and *Modern Proverbs and Proverbial Phrases* (Whiting*[MP]*).

We have cited foreign sources only when an English translator is listed in one of the six collections used in our research, as, for example, in the case of "1620 Cervantes, *Don Quixote,* tr. Shelton." However, when Stevenson, for example, cites Latin, Greek, Biblical, or other foreign sources in their original languages without giving a British or American source, we have cited Stevenson as the first American written source, given as "US1948 Stevenson, *Home Book of Proverbs,*" with the appropriate page number. (The Bibliography contains a section on international proverb collections that include English-language proverbs.)

Names of authors and titles of the earliest British and American sources usually are given in the forms in which they appear in the six collections we used as references, although where titles were so abbreviated as to be unintelligible, we have expanded them appropriately. In any case, we obviously could not list all the additional historical references that these six dictionaries amass for each proverb. The result would have been a multivolume proverb dictionary superseding all of them. Historically interested proverb scholars will have easy access to these standard reference works. Our dictionary will, however, give them an immediate idea of the first occurrence of a proverb in British and/or American written sources as well as its recorded distribution in the United States and Canada. (See the Bibliography for studies concerning the use and function of proverbs in American literature.) Regarding the many American proverbs lacking historical references (i.e., those proverbs registered herein for the first time), we can say only that they were current between the mid-1940s and the end of the 1970s.

Cross-references. Where appropriate, cross-references are made to proverbs that contain the key word of the entry in view but that are registered elsewhere because their own key word is different. For example, at the end of the entry for *broom* the following cross-reference appears:

SEE ALSO All TRASH goes before the broom.

The reader is thus alerted that this proverb can be found under the headword *trash* and is directed to look there for further information.

ABBREVIATIONS

adj.	adjective	Mass.	Massachusetts
adv.	adverb	Md.	Maryland
a.k.a.	also known as	Mich.	Michigan
Ala.	Alabama	Minn.	Minnesota
Am.	American	Miss.	Mississippi
antiq.	antiquarian	Mont.	Montana
Apr.	April	MS	manuscript
Ariz.	Arizona	n.	noun
Ark.	Arkansas	N.C.	North Carolina
Aug.	August	N.Dak.	North Dakota
ca	circa	Nebr.	Nebraska
Calif.	California	Nev.	Nevada
Can.	Canada	N.H.	New Hampshire
CODP	*The Concise Oxford Dictionary of Proverbs*	N.J.	New Jersey
		N.Mex.	New Mexico
col.	colonel, colonial	Nov.	November
coll.	collection, college	N.Y.	New York
Colo.	Colorado	Oct.	October
comm.	commission	ODEP	*The Oxford Dictionary of English Proverbs*
Dec.	December		
Del.	Delaware	Okla.	Oklahoma
doc.	document, documentary	Ont.	Ontario
ed.	edited by, edition	Oreg.	Oregon
E.E.T.S.	Early English Text Society	Pa.	Pennsylvania
Feb.	February	P.E.I.	Prince Edward Island
1st cit.	first citation	phil.	philosophical, philological
Fla.	Florida	PRAlmanac	*Poor Richard's Almanac*
Ga.	Georgia	prep.	preposition
gen.	general	pron.	pronoun
hist.	historical, history	pseud.	pseudonym
Ill.	Illinois	publ.	publication(s), publishing
Ind.	Indiana	quart.	quarterly
Jan.	January	rec. dist.	recorded distribution
Kans.	Kansas	rev.	revised
Ky.	Kentucky	R.I.	Rhode Island
La.	Louisiana	S.C.	South Carolina
mag.	magazine	S.Dak.	South Dakota
Mal.Soc.	International Maledicta Society	Sept.	September
		ser.	series
Mar.	March	soc.	society

Stevenson	*The Macmillan (Home) Book of Proverbs, Maxims and Familiar Phrases*	v.	verb
		Va.	Virginia
		var(s).	variant(s)
S.T.S.	Scottish Text Society	Vt.	Vermont
Tenn.	Tennessee	Wash.	Washington
Tex.	Texas	Whiting	*Early American Proverbs and Proverbial Phrases*
tr.	translated by		
T.T.	Tudor Translations	Whiting*(MP)*	*Modern Proverbs and Proverbial Sayings*
T&W	*A Dictionary of American Proverbs and Proverbial Phrases*		
		Wis.	Wisconsin
20c. coll.	twentieth-century collection(s)	W.Va.	West Virginia
		Wyo.	Wyoming
U.S.	United States		

A DICTIONARY OF
AMERICAN
PROVERBS

A

A **1.** If you say A, they'll make you say B. *Var.:* Never say A without saying B. *Rec. dist.:* Ill. *Infm.:* Never start something you don't want to finish. *1st cit.:* US1837 Neal, *Charcoal Sketches* (1840). *20c. coll.:* T&W 1.

2. In our alphabet B comes after A. *Rec. dist.:* Miss. *Infm.:* You have something out of order. Do everything in order.

ability **1.** Ability is of little account without opportunity. *Rec. dist.:* Wis.

2. Ability is the poor man's wealth. *Rec. dist.:* N.J., N.C., Ont.

3. Ability, not luck, conquers. *Rec. dist.:* N.C.

4. Ability will enable a man to get to the top, but character will keep him from falling. *Rec. dist.:* Miss., N.Y.

5. Ability will see a chance and snatch it; who has a match will find a place to strike it. *Rec. dist.:* N.Y. *1st cit.:* US1924 Guiterman, *Poet's Proverbs.* *20c. coll.:* Stevenson 1:4.

6. From each according to his abilities, to each according to his needs. *Rec. dist.:* Miss., N.Y. *1st cit.:* 1875 Marx, *Critique of Gotha Program.* *20c. coll.:* Stevenson 2:1.

7. Most men don't lack the will but the ability. *Rec. dist.:* Ill.

8. There are many rare abilities in the world that fortune never brings to life. *Rec. dist.:* Calif., N.C.

SEE ALSO They are the weakest, however strong, who have no CONFIDENCE in their own ability. / The greatest ability is DEPENDABILITY. / True GENEROSITY is the ability to accept ingratitude. / Like a postage stamp a man's VALUE depends upon his ability to stick to a thing till he gets there.

able He who would not when he could is not able when he would. *Rec. dist.:* N.Y. *1st cit.:* ca1000 in *Anglia* (1889); US1743 Franklin, *PRAlmanac.* *20c. coll.:* CODP 245, Stevenson 1724:2.

abolishment SEE ISOLATION means abolishment.

absence **1.** A little absence does much good. *Rec. dist.:* Miss.

2. Absence cools moderate passions but inflames violent ones. *Rec. dist.:* Miss., N.Y., Wis. *1st cit.:* US1948 Stevenson, *Home Book of Proverbs.* *20c. coll.:* Stevenson 4:7.

3. Absence is love's foe: far from the eyes, far from the heart. *Rec. dist.:* Wis. *Infm.:* Cf. "Far from the eye, far from the heart."

4. Absence is the mother of disillusion. *Rec. dist.:* Wis.

5. Absence kills a little love but makes the big ones grow. *Rec. dist.:* Wis.

6. Absence makes the heart grow fonder. *Vars.:* **(a)** Absence makes the heart grow fonder, but don't stay away too long. **(b)** Absence makes the heart grow fonder, but presence brings better results. **(c)** Absence makes the heart grow fonder; distance makes affections wander. **(d)** Absence makes the heart grow fonder for somebody else. **(e)** Absence makes the heart wander. **(f)** Absence makes the mind go wander. *Rec. dist.:* U.S., Can. *1st cit.:* ca1850 Bayly, *Isle of Beauty;* US1755 *Papers of Benjamin Franklin,* ed. Labaree (1959). *20c. coll.:* ODEP 1, Whiting 2, CODP 1, T&W 2, Whiting(MP) 2.

7. Absence of body is better than presence of mind in time of danger. *Rec. dist.:* N.C.

8. Absence sharpens love; presence strengthens it. *Var.:* Absence hinders love; presence strengthens it. *Rec. dist.:* Wis. *1st cit.:* 1557 Tottle, *Songs and Sonnets.* *20c. coll.:* ODEP 1, Stevenson 4:8.

9. Long absence changes friends. *Rec. dist.:* N.Y., Oreg. *1st cit.:* 1611 Cotgrave, *Dictionary of French and English Tongues.* *20c. coll.:* Stevenson 5:14.

absent **1.** He that is long absent is soon forgotten. *Vars.:* **(a)** He that is absent is soon forgotten. **(b)** Long absence, soon forgotten. **(c)** Long absent, soon forgotten. *Rec. dist.:* U.S., Can. *1st cit.:* 1565 Wever, *Lusty Juventus.* *20c. coll.:* ODEP 478, Stevenson 5:14.

2. Speak not evil of the absent; it is unjust. *Rec. dist.*: N.Y. *1st cit.*: US1763 Ames, *Almanacs,* ed. Briggs (1891). *20c. coll.*: Whiting 2, Stevenson 3:3, Whiting*(MP)* 2.

3. The absent are always in the wrong. *Vars.*: **(a)** The absent are always at fault. **(b)** When you are absent you are never right. *Rec. dist.*: Ind., N.Y. *1st cit.*: ca1440 Lydgate, *Fall of Princes;* US1801 *Diary of Gouverneur Morris,* ed. Morris (1939). *20c. coll.*: ODEP 1, Whiting 2, Stevenson 3:8, Whiting*(MP)* 2.

4. The absent are never without fault nor the present without excuse. *Rec. dist.*: N.Y. *1st cit.*: 1616 Draxe, *Bibliotheca Scholastica in Anglia* (1918); US1736 Franklin, *PRAlmanac. 20c. coll.*: ODEP 1, Stevenson 3:6.

SEE ALSO FRIENDS, though absent, are still present.

absolute There are no absolutes that are livable. *Rec. dist.*: Miss.

abstinence Abstinence is the best medicine. *Rec. dist.*: N.Y. *1st cit.*: 1842 Percival, *Tamil Proverbs. 20c. coll.*: Stevenson 573:1.

absurdity Even absurdity has a champion to defend it, for error is always talkative. *Rec. dist.*: Ill.

abundance 1. Abundance is a trouble, but competency brings delight. *Rec. dist.*: Mich.

2. Abundance, like want, can ruin character. *Var.*: It is not want, but abundance, that makes avarice. *Rec. dist.*: Ga., N.J. *1st cit.*: ca1533 Bellenden, *History of Rome. 20c. coll.*: ODEP 2.

3. Abundance, like want, ruins many. *Var.*: Abundance, like want, ruins man. *Rec. dist.*: Ind., Mich., N.Y. 1st cit.: 1766 *Goody Two-Shoes. 20c. coll.*: ODEP 2.

4. Abundance of money ruins youth. *Rec. dist.*: Wis. *1st cit.*: 1611 Cotgrave, *Dictionary of French and English Tongues. 20c. coll.*: ODEP 2.

5. Out of the abundance of the heart the mouth speaks. *Var.*: Out of the fullness of the heart the mouth speaks. *Rec. dist.*: Calif., Mich., N.Y., Ont., Oreg. *1st cit.*: ca1389 Chaucer, *Parson's Tale;* USca1645 Cotton in *Complete Writings of Roger Williams* (1963). *20c. coll.*:

Stevenson 1111:10, Whiting 2, T&W 2, Whiting*(MP)* 2.

abuse *(n.)* **1.** Abuse does not take away use. *Rec. dist.*: Wis.

2. The abuse of the best thing is the worst. *Rec. dist.*: Mich. *1st cit.*: 1639 Clarke, *Paroemiologia. 20c. coll.*: ODEP 49, Stevenson 6:7.

abuse *(v.)* He who abuses others must not be peeved by the actions of others. *Var.*: If you abuse others, you can't squawk if you are given a taste of your own medicine. *Rec. dist.*: Ill., N.Y.

SEE ALSO USE it, but don't abuse it.

abusive *SEE* Abusive LANGUAGE is abuse of language.

accept Who accepts nothing has nothing to return. *Rec. dist.*: N.Y. *Infm.*: Fielding's proverb: "To whom nothing is given, of him nothing is required." *1st cit.*: 1734 Fielding, *Joseph Andrews. 20c. coll.*: Stevenson 1701:10.

accident 1. Accident is a word not to be found in the divine vocabulary. *Rec. dist.*: Wis.

2. Accident is commonly the parent of disorder. *Rec. dist.*: N.Y.

3. Accident is the mother of invention. *Rec. dist.*: Mich., Miss., N.Y.

4. Accidents will happen in the best-regulated families. *Vars.*: **(a)** Accidents happen in the best of families. **(b)** Accidents will happen in the best of families. **(c)** Accidents will occur in the best of places. *Rec. dist.*: U.S., Can. *1st cit.*: 1763 Colman, *Deuce Is In Him;* US1815 Humphreys, *Yankey in England. 20c. coll.*: ODEP 2, Whiting 2, *CODP* 1, Stevenson 7:4, T&W 2, Whiting*(MP)* 3.

5. It takes less time to avoid an accident than it does to report it. *Rec. dist.*: N.C.

6. One accident is one too many. *Rec. dist.*: Ont.

7. Your first accident may be your last. *Rec. dist.*: Miss.

SEE ALSO TIME saved at the cost of an accident is no saving.

accompany *SEE* They are never alone who are accompanied by noble THOUGHT.

accomplice The accomplice is as bad as the thief. *Var.:* The receiver is as bad as the thief. *Rec. dist.:* Calif. *1st cit.:* 1623 Wodroephe, *The Spared Hours of a Soldier.* *20c. coll.:* ODEP 667, Stevenson 2300:8.

account 1. Always keep exact accounts. *Rec. dist.:* Mich.

2. Brief account is the best. *Rec. dist.:* Minn.

3. Short accounts make long friends. *Rec. dist.:* N.Mex., Ohio, Tex. *1st cit.:* 1537 Whitford, *Werke for Householders.* *20c. coll.:* ODEP 728, Stevenson 1943:12.

4. We must give an account of our idle words. *Rec. dist.:* N.Y.

accounting There is no accounting for taste. *Rec. dist.:* U.S., Can. *1st cit.:* 1599 Minsheu, *Dialogues in Spanish;* US1808 Barker, *Tears and Smiles.* *20c. coll.:* ODEP 2, Whiting 2, CODP 1, Stevenson 2282:5, T&W 2, Whiting(MP) 3.

accumulate You never accumulate if you don't speculate. *Rec. dist.:* N.Y. *1st cit.:* US1941 Dodge, *Death and Taxes.* *20c. coll.:* Stevenson 931:2.

accusation Accusation is proof when malice and power sit in judge. *Var.:* Accusing is proving, where malice and power sit in judge. *Rec. dist.:* Ill., Mich.

accuse 1. He that accuses all convicts only one. *Var.:* He who accuses too many accuses himself. *Rec. dist.:* N.J., N.Dak., Wis.

2. Never accuse others to excuse yourself. *Rec. dist.:* Kans., Ohio.

3. When the foxes pack the jury box, the chicken is always found guilty as accused. *Rec. dist.:* Ill. *Infm.:* The ODEP proverb: "A fox should not be on the jury of the goose's trial." *1st cit.:* 1732 Fuller, *Gnomologia.* *20c. coll.:* ODEP 285.

See also Who EXCUSES himself accuses himself.

ache There's nothing to an ache. *Rec. dist.:* Ont.

See also Every HEART has its own ache.

achieve Still achieving, still pursuing. *Rec. dist.:* Minn.

See also Some are born great, some achieve GREATNESS, and some have greatness thrust upon them.

achievement Achievement is one percent aspiration and ninety-nine percent perspiration. *Rec. dist.:* N.Y. *Infm.:* A variant of Thomas Edison's saying, "Genius is one percent inspiration and ninety-nine percent perspiration."

aching Aching teeth are ill tenants. *Rec. dist.:* Ont. *1st cit.:* 1659 Howell, *Paroimiografia (English Proverbs).* *20c. coll.:* ODEP 2.

acorn Acorns were good till bread was found. *Rec. dist.:* Ill. *1st cit.:* ca1580 Sidney, *Arcadia.* *20c. coll.:* ODEP 3, Stevenson 233:3.

See also Great OAKS from little acorns grow. / Even a blind PIG occasionally picks up an acorn.

acquaintance 1. Acquaintance with evil blinds us to its dangers. *Rec. dist.:* Mich., N.C.

2. Acquaintances soften prejudices. *Rec. dist.:* N.Y.

3. If a man does not make new acquaintances as he advances through life, he will soon find himself alone. *Rec. dist.:* N.Y., Utah.

4. Many acquaintances but few friends. *Rec. dist.:* Wis. *1st cit.:* ca1565 Wager, *Enough Good as Feast.* *20c. coll.:* ODEP 291.

5. Of chance acquaintance beware. *Var.:* Sudden short acquaintances bring repentance. *Rec. dist.:* Ind., N.Y., N.C., Oreg. *Infm.:* The ODEP proverb: "Short acquaintance brings repentance." *1st cit.:* 1670 Ray, *English Proverbs;* US1774 Ames, *Almanacs,* ed. Briggs (1891). *20c. coll.:* ODEP 727, Whiting 3, Stevenson 10:5.

6. The more acquaintances, the more danger. *Rec. dist.:* N.Y., N.C. *1st cit.:* 1732 Fuller, *Gnomologia.* *20c. coll.:* Stevenson 10:3.

acquiescence The first step toward enjoyment of the human lot is acquiescence. *Rec. dist.:* N.C.

acquire What we acquire without sweat we give away without regret. *Rec. dist.:* Ill.

acre *See* An acre of PERFORMANCE is worth the whole world of promises.

act *(n.)* **1.** Acts indicate intentions. *Rec. dist.:* Ill., N.Y., N.C.

2. An evil act has a witness in the heart. *Rec. dist.:* Mich., N.Y., N.C.

3. Nip the act while in the bud. *Rec. dist.:* Ind.

4. One foolish act may undo a man, and a timely one make his fortune. *Rec. dist.:* Mich.

5. Sow an act, reap a habit. *Var.:* Sow a thought, reap an act. *Rec. dist.:* Ill., Vt. *1st cit.:* ca1640 Taylor, *Sermons;* US1921 Trine, *Life's Law. 20c. coll.:* Stevenson 1048:6.

6. The best way to keep acts in memory is to refresh them with new ones. *Rec. dist.:* Ohio. *1st cit.:* 1625 Bacon, *Apophthegms. 20c. coll.:* Stevenson 10:17.

See also The EVENT proves the act. / Do not neglect to perform acts of GOODNESS just because they are small. / GOODWILL, like a good name, is won by many acts and lost by one. / We JUDGE others by their acts, but ourselves by our intentions. / An act of KINDNESS is well repaid.

act *(v.)* **1.** Act as if it were impossible to fail. *Rec. dist.:* Calif.

2. Act first and think afterwards. *Rec. dist.:* Ont.

3. Act so in the valley that you need not fear those who stand on the hill. *Rec. dist.:* N.Y., Ont.

4. Act well at the moment, and you have performed a good act for eternity. *Rec. dist.:* Ohio.

5. Act what you are and not what you aren't. *Rec. dist.:* Calif.

6. He acts well who acts quickly. *Rec. dist.:* Ill., N.Y.

7. He who acts through another acts through himself. *Rec. dist.:* N.Y., N.C.

8. To act is easy, but to understand is hard. *Rec. dist.:* Ohio.

See also Against CRITICISM a man can neither protest nor defend; he must act in spite of it. / HOME is where you act the worst and are treated the best. / HONOR and shame from no condition rise. Act well your part; there all the honor lies. / Be sure you know the ROAD before you act as guide. / THINK—then act.

acting After the acting, wishing is in vain. *Rec. dist.:* N.Y.

action **1.** A bad action leaves a worse hangover. *Rec. dist.:* Ill.

2. A man's actions are motion pictures of his beliefs. *Rec. dist.:* Ind., N.J.

3. Action is itself the best remedy for morbid thoughts. *Var.:* A good relief for grief is action. *Rec. dist.:* N.C., Ont.

4. Action is our chief joy. *Rec. dist.:* Miss., N.Y.

5. Action is the basis of success. *Var.:* Success is action—a journey, not a destination. *Rec. dist.:* Kans.

6. Action is the proper fruit of knowledge. *Vars.:* (a) Action must be founded on intelligence. (b) Action must be founded on knowledge. (c) Good actions are founded on intelligence, but a fool may blunder into proper conduct. *Rec. dist.:* Ill., Ind., Miss., N.Y., Vt. *1st cit.:* 1732 Fuller, *Gnomologia. 20c. coll.:* Stevenson 11:4.

7. Action is worry's worst enemy. *Rec. dist.:* Ind.

8. Action without study is fatal; study without action is fatal. *Rec. dist.:* Kans.

9. Action without thought is like shooting without aim. *Rec. dist.:* Iowa.

10. Actions and reactions are equal. *Vars.:* (a) Every action has an opposite and equal reaction. (b) Every action has an opposite reaction. (c) To every action there is always an opposed and equal reaction. *Rec. dist.:* Ill., Mich., N.Y. *1st cit.:* US1834 *Journals of Ralph Waldo Emerson,* eds. Emerson and Forbes (1909–1914). *20c. coll.:* T&W 3.

11. Actions and words are the windows through which the heart is seen. *Rec. dist.:* Kans.

12. Actions, looks, and words are steps from the alphabet by which you spell character. *Rec. dist.:* La., N.C.

13. Actions measured by time seldom prove better by repentance. *Rec. dist.:* Mich.

14. Actions speak louder than words. *Vars.:* **(a)** Actions lie louder than words. **(b)** Actions speak louder than words but not nearly as often. **(c)** Words don't mean a thing; it's the action that counts. *Rec. dist.:* U.S., Can. *1st cit.:* 1628 Pym, *Debate on a Message from Charles I;* US1692 Bulkeley, *Will and Doom,* ed. Hoadly, Conn.Hist.Soc. *Collections* (1895). *20c. coll.:* ODEP 3, Whiting 3, *CODP* 1, Stevenson 2616:11, T&W 3, Whiting(MP) 4.

15. Bad actions lead to worse reactions. *Rec. dist.:* Ill.

16. Brave actions never want a trumpet. *Rec. dist.:* Miss., Wis. *1st cit.:* 1732 Fuller, *Gnomologia. 20c. coll.:* Stevenson 11:5.

17. By united action we stand, by divided action we fall. *Rec. dist.:* Ill. *Infm.:* Cf. "United we stand, divided we fall."

18. For the sake of one good action a hundred evil ones should be forgotten. *Rec. dist.:* Miss., N.Y.

19. Good actions give strength to ourselves and inspire good actions in others. *Rec. dist.:* N.C.

20. Good actions speak for themselves; they need no tin horn. *Rec. dist.:* Ill. *1st cit.:* US1816 Fidfaddy, *Adventures of Uncle Sam. 20c. coll.:* Whiting 3.

21. Great actions speak great minds. *Rec. dist.:* Ind. *1st cit.:* 1647 Fletcher, *The Prophetess. 20c. coll.:* Stevenson 11:3.

22. In great action men show themselves as they ought to be, in small action as they are. *Rec. dist.:* N.J., N.C.

23. It is not the action but the intention that is good or bad. *Rec. dist.:* Wis. *1st cit.:* 1841 Lane, *Thousand and One Nights. 20c. coll.:* Stevenson 1252:8.

24. It is only in action that you have the power to grow. *Rec. dist.:* N.C.

25. Let your actions be equal to your promises. *Rec. dist.:* Mont., N.J., Oreg.

26. Man's actions show his character. *Rec. dist.:* La.

27. Men's actions are not to be judged at first sight. *Rec. dist.:* Ont.

28. Never repent a good action. *Rec. dist.:* N.Y.

29. Only the actions of the great smell sweet and blossom in the dust. *Rec. dist.:* N.Y.

30. Suit the actions to the word. *Vars.:* **(a)** Fit the action to the word, the word to the action. **(b)** Suit the action to the word, the word to the action. *Rec. dist.:* Minn., N.Y., Utah. *1st cit.:* 1600 Shakespeare, *Hamlet. 20c. coll.:* Stevenson 12:2.

31. That action is best which procures the greatest good for the majority. *Rec. dist.:* Ont.

32. The actions of a fool cannot serve as a precedent. *Rec. dist.:* Miss.

33. The fame of men's good actions seldom goes beyond their own doors, but their evil actions are carried to a thousand miles. *Rec. dist.:* Ind.

34. Vicious actions are not hurtful because they are forbidden, but forbidden because they are hurtful. *Rec. dist.:* N.Y.

35. We are remembered by our good actions, not by our good intentions. *Rec. dist.:* Ill.

36. Your one good action excuses a dozen bad ones. *Rec. dist.:* Ill.

SEE ALSO He who ABUSES others must not be peeved by the actions of others. / You can always tell a DRUNKARD by his actions. / HOPE inspires action, the true way to success. / PEACE is good will in action. / WORDS may show a man's wit, but actions his meaning.

active SEE Active MINDS that think and study, like swift brooks, are seldom muddy.

actor One actor cannot make a play. *Rec. dist.:* Calif., Miss.

Adam 1. Adam ate the apple, and our teeth still ache. *Rec. dist.:* Wis.

2. In Adam's fall we sinned all. *Rec. dist.:* Ill., Miss. *1st cit.:* USca1687 Harris, *New England Primer. 20c. coll.:* Stevenson 13:8.

3. We're all Adam's children; silk makes the difference. *Vars.:* **(a)** We're all Adam's children. **(b)** We are all sons and daughters of

Adam. *Rec. dist.:* Ill. *1st cit.:* ca1497 *Fulgens and Lucres;* US1964 Burgess, *Eve.* *20c. coll.:* ODEP 3, Whiting*(MP)* 5, Stevenson 64:6.

4. When Adam delved and Eve span, who was then the gentleman? *Rec. dist.:* N.Y. *1st cit.:* ca1340 Hampole, *Religious Pieces* from *Thornton MS 79,* E.E.T.S. (1867); US1764 Thacher, *Sentiments in Pamphlets of American Revolution,* ed. Bailyn (1965). *20c. coll.:* ODEP 3, Whiting 4, *CODP* 1, Stevenson 944:14, T&W 4, Whiting*(MP)* 5.

add *SEE* HAPPINESS adds and multiplies as we divide it with others. / Add LITTLE to little and there will be a great heap. / If you have WIT and learning, add to it wisdom and modesty.

addition **1.** Addition is the miser's sum of happiness. *Rec. dist.:* Ill.

2. An addition to a family is often a subtraction. *Rec. dist.:* Ill.

administration *SEE* No SCHOOL ever rises above its administration.

admiration Admiration is the daughter of ignorance. *Rec. dist.:* Ill. *1st cit.:* 1642 Fuller, *Holy State;* US1736 Franklin, *PRAlmanac.* *20c. coll.:* Stevenson 15:8.

SEE ALSO FLATTERY is not a proof of true admiration.

admire If what men most admire they would despise, 'twould look like mankind were growing wise. *Rec. dist.:* N.Y. *1st cit.:* US1735 Franklin, *PRAlmanac.* *20c. coll.:* Stevenson 2534:3.

SEE ALSO A BACHELOR is to be admired; a spinster is to be pitied. / A FOOL always finds another fool to admire.

admonish Admonish, but pursue not unto death him who has injured you. *Rec. dist.:* Minn.

adore The ignorant always adore what they cannot understand. *Var.:* Things not understood are admired. *Rec. dist.:* Miss. *1st cit.:* 1732 Fuller, *Gnomologia.* *20c. coll.:* Stevenson 15:8.

adult **1.** An adult is only one who has ceased to grow vertically and started to grow horizontally. *Rec. dist.:* Oreg.

2. The difference between adults and children is that adults don't ask questions. *Rec. dist.:* N.C.

advance Not to advance is to recede. *Vars.:* (a) He who does not advance recedes. (b) Life never stands still: if you don't advance, you recede. (c) Not to advance is to go back. *Rec. dist.:* Ill., Miss.

advantage **1.** Every advantage has its disadvantage. *Rec. dist.:* Ind., Minn., N.Y.

2. He who derives the advantage ought to sustain the burden. *Var.:* He who receives the advantage ought also to suffer the burden. *Rec. dist.:* Ill., N.C.

3. Take advantage of the little opportunities and you won't need to wait for the big one. *Rec. dist.:* N.C.

SEE ALSO BIG men are usually little men who took advantage of opportunity. / CALMNESS is a great advantage. / When FORTUNE smiles, take the advantage.

adventure Who seeks adventure finds blows. *Rec. dist.:* Ind.

adversity **1.** A dose of adversity is often as needful as a dose of medicine. *Rec. dist.:* Utah.

2. Adversity does best discover virtue. *Rec. dist.:* Miss. *1st cit.:* 1574 Bale, *Pageant of Popes,* tr. Studley; US1739 Ames, *Almanacs,* ed. Briggs (1891). *20c. coll.:* ODEP 4, Whiting 4, Stevenson 1903:12.

3. Adversity flatters no man. *Rec. dist.:* Utah. *1st cit.:* 1732 Fuller, *Gnomologia.* *20c. coll.:* Stevenson 18:2.

4. Adversity has no friends. *Rec. dist.:* Ill.

5. Adversity is the diamond dust heaven polishes its jewels with. *Rec. dist.:* Wis.

6. Adversity is the first path to truth. *Rec. dist.:* Ind. *1st cit.:* 1823 Byron, *Don Juan.* *20c. coll.:* Stevenson 18:10.

7. Adversity is the parent of virtue. *Rec. dist.:* Miss.

8. Adversity is the prosperity of the great. *Rec. dist.:* Calif.

9. Adversity is the stuff that shows whether you are what you thought you were. *Rec. dist.:* Ky., Minn., Tenn.

10. Adversity is the test of friendship. *Rec. dist.:* Minn. *Infm.:* Cf. the proverb "Adversity is the touchstone of friendship." *1st cit.:* US1775 *Journal of Nicholas Cresswell, 1774–1777. 20c. coll.:* Whiting 4.

11. Adversity is the true school of the mind. *Rec. dist.:* Miss.

12. Adversity makes a man wise, but not rich. *Vars.:* **(a)** Adversity makes a man wise. **(b)** Adversity makes us wise until next time. *Rec. dist.:* U.S., Can. *Infm.:* Shakespeare, *Henry VI,* "The wind in a man's face makes him wise. Vexation gives wisdom." *1st cit.:* 1574 Bale, *Pageant of Popes,* tr. Studley; US1739 Ames, *Almanacs,* ed. Briggs (1891). *20c. coll.:* ODEP 4, Whiting 4.

13. Adversity makes men; prosperity, monsters. *Rec. dist.:* Ill.

14. Adversity makes strange bedfellows. *Rec. dist.:* N.Y. *Infm.:* Cf. misfortune, politics, and poverty. *1st cit.:* 1611 Shakespeare, *Tempest. 20c. coll.:* ODEP 535, CODP 2.

15. Adversity stimulates endurance. *Rec. dist.:* Tex.

16. Adversity tries virtue. *Rec. dist.:* Ill., Miss.

17. Adversity willingly undergone is the greatest virtue. *Rec. dist.:* Mich.

18. If you faint in the days of adversity, your strength is small. *Rec. dist.:* Ont. *1st cit.:* US1948 Stevenson, *Home Book of Proverbs. 20c. coll.:* Stevenson 18:5.

19. Many can bear adversity, but few contempt. *Var.:* We can bear adversity but not self-contempt. *Rec. dist.:* Ill., Ohio.

SEE ALSO Gold is tried by fire, BRAVE men by adversity. / There is no EDUCATION like adversity. / A FRIEND is best found in adversity. / He that speaks well in PROSPERITY will shrink in adversity. / PROSPERITY discovers vice, adversity virtue. / He who does not TIRE, tires adversity.

advertise 1. Don't advertise what you can't fulfill. *Rec. dist.:* Minn.

2. It pays to advertise. *Rec. dist.:* U.S., Can. *Infm.:* Archer Taylor calls this proverb "truly American."

advice 1. Advice after mischief is taken like medicine after death. *Rec. dist.:* Ill. *1st cit.:* US1948 Stevenson, *Home Book of Proverbs. 20c. coll.:* Stevenson 22:7.

2. Advice comes too late when a thing is done. *Vars.:* **(a)** Advice should precede the act. **(b)** Poor servants ask advice after the accident has happened. *Rec. dist.:* U.S., Can. *1st cit.:* 1592 Delamothe, *Treasure of French Tongue. 20c. coll.:* ODEP 4, Stevenson 22:7.

3. Advice is cheap. *Vars.:* **(a)** Nothing is given as freely as advice. **(b)** People give nothing as freely as advice. *Rec. dist.:* Ark., Ill., Ind., N.Y. *1st cit.:* US1948 Stevenson, *Home Book of Proverbs. 20c. coll.:* Stevenson 21:8.

4. Advice is least heeded when most needed. *Var.:* Advice, when most needed, is least heeded. *Rec. dist.:* Ky., Miss., Tenn. *1st cit.:* US1948 Stevenson, *Home Book of Proverbs. 20c. coll.:* Stevenson 20:2.

5. Advice is not a popular thing to give. *Rec. dist.:* Calif., N.Y.

6. Advice is often judged by results and not by intentions. *Rec. dist.:* Calif. *1st cit.:* US1948 Stevenson, *Home Book of Proverbs. 20c. coll.:* Stevenson 20:8.

7. Advice is something the wise don't need and the fools won't take. *Rec. dist.:* U.S., Can. *Infm.:* Cf. fool. *1st cit.:* US1758 Franklin, *PRAlmanac. 20c. coll.:* Stevenson 22:3.

8. Advice, like water, takes the form of the vessel it is poured into. *Rec. dist.:* Ind.

9. Advice that ain't paid for ain't no good. *Rec. dist.:* N.Y. *1st cit.:* 1546 Heywood, *Dialogue of Proverbs,* ed. Habernicht (1963); US1853 Haliburton, *Sam Slick's Wise Saws. 20c. coll.:* ODEP 78, T&W 4.

10. Advice to a fool goes in one ear and out the other. *Rec. dist.:* Miss., N.Y.

11. Advice to all, security for none. *Var.:* Give advice to all, but be security for none. *Rec. dist.:* Ind.

12. Advice whispered is worthless. *Rec. dist.:* Miss., N.Y. *1st cit.:* 1732 Fuller, *Gnomologia. 20c. coll.:* Stevenson 20:17.

13. After-advice is fool's advice. *Rec. dist.:* Miss.

14. Ask advice, but use your own common sense. *Rec. dist.:* Miss.

15. Ask advice of your equals, help from your superiors. *Rec. dist.:* Mich., Miss.

16. Free advice is worth just what you paid for it. *Var.:* Free advice may cost heavily. *Rec. dist.:* Ky., Miss., Tenn.

17. Give neither salt nor advice till you are asked for it. *Var.:* The best advice—don't give any. *Rec. dist.:* Ill., Ky., Tenn. *1st cit.:* 1523 Erasmus, *Adagia,* tr. Taverner; US1757 Franklin, *PRAlmanac.* *20c. coll.:* Stevenson 20:14.

18. Good advice is beyond price. *Rec. dist.:* Ky., Wis. *1st cit.:* 1522 Erasmus, *Colloquia,* tr. Taverner. *20c. coll.:* Stevenson 20:15.

19. Good advice never comes too late. *Rec. dist.:* Miss. *1st cit.:* US1948 Stevenson, *Home Book of Proverbs.* *20c. coll.:* Stevenson 22:7

20. He asks advice in vain who will not follow it. *Var.:* In vain he asks advice that will not follow it. *Rec. dist.:* Miss. *1st cit.:* 1611 Cotgrave, *Dictionary of French and English Tongues.* *20c. coll.:* Stevenson 20:12.

21. He who can take advice is sometimes superior to those who give it. *Rec. dist.:* Oreg.

22. He who follows his own advice must take the consequences. *Rec. dist.:* Miss.

23. He who gives advice is a bigger fool than he who takes it. *Rec. dist.:* Miss. *1st cit.:* 1893 Wilde, *Portrait of Mr. W. H.;* US1940 Thompson, *Body, Boots, and Britches.* *20c. coll.:* Stevenson 23:2.

24. If you can't take advice, you can't be helped. *Var.:* He who won't be advised cannot be helped. *Rec. dist.:* Ill., Miss.

25. If you ever want to get advice on raising children, ask an old maid or bachelor. *Var.:* You can always get advice on raising children from an old maid or a bachelor who never had any. *Rec. dist.:* N.Y., N.C.

26. If you want good advice, consult an old man. *Var.:* If you want foolish advice, consult an old man. *Rec. dist.:* Miss., N.Y. *1st cit.:* ca1386 Chaucer, *Tale of Melibee.* *20c. coll.:* ODEP 4.

27. It is easier to give advice than to take it. *Rec. dist.:* Ind., Minn. *1st cit.:* US1948 Stevenson, *Home Book of Proverbs.* *20c. coll.:* Stevenson 22:15.

28. Less advice and more hands. *Var.:* What the poor need is less advice and more helping hands. *Rec. dist.:* Calif., N.Y.

29. Many people take advice as they do medicine: fling it away at the moment the doctor's back is turned. *Rec. dist.:* Ill., Miss.

30. Many receive advice, but only the wise profit from it. *Vars.:* **(a)** Fools need advice most, but wise men only are the better for it. **(b)** Many receive advice, but few profit from it. *Rec. dist.:* Miss., N.Y. *1st cit.:* 1539 Publilius Syrus, *Sententiae,* tr. Taverner; US1758 Franklin, *PRAlmanac.* *20c. coll.:* Stevenson 22:3.

31. Never trust the advice of a man in difficulties. *Vars.:* **(a)** Beware of the advice of unfortunates. **(b)** Distrust interested advice. *Rec. dist.:* Miss., N.Y. *1st cit.:* US1948 Stevenson, *Home Book of Proverbs.* *20c. coll.:* Stevenson 21:13.

32. Take your own advice; you'll be too busy to bore others with it. *Rec. dist.:* Miss.

33. The advice of fools is worthless. *Rec. dist.:* Mich.

34. The best advice I know in life is don't give too much. *Rec. dist.:* Minn., N.J. *Infm.:* Whatever advice you give, be brief. *1st cit.:* US1948 Stevenson, *Home Book of Proverbs.* *20c. coll.:* Stevenson 21:4.

35. The kind of advice we do not like to take often turns out to be the best. *Rec. dist.:* Calif.

36. There's no advice like father's—even if you don't take it. *Var.:* You'll come out good if you obey the advice of your father and mother. *Rec. dist.:* Ariz., N.Y.

37. Unasked-for advice smells bad. *Rec. dist.:* Md.

38. We hate those who will not take our advice and despise those who do. *Rec. dist.:* Ariz., Wis.

39. We may give advice, but we cannot give conduct. *Rec. dist.:* Ill., Ind., N.Y. *1st cit.:* 1782 Wesley, *Sermons;* US1736 Franklin,

PRAlmanac. **20c. coll.:** *ODEP* 4, Whiting 4, Stevenson 21:11.

40. We should never be too proud to take advice. ***Rec. dist.:*** Miss.

41. When the rats want advice, they never ask the mice. ***Rec. dist.:*** Ind.

SEE ALSO AGE gives good advice when it is no longer able to give bad example. / Every FOOL wants to give advice. / He is a FOOL that takes a fool's advice. / A no-account WIFE takes advice from everyone but her husband.

advise **1.** Advise not what is pleasant but what is useful. ***Rec. dist.:*** Mich. ***1st cit.:*** US1948 Stevenson, *Home Book of Proverbs.* **20c. coll.:** Stevenson 22:11.

2. Never advise a man to the halter or altar. ***Rec. dist.:*** Ill. ***1st cit.:*** 1640 Herbert, *Outlandish Proverbs (Jacula Prudentum)* in *Works,* ed. Hutchinson (1941). **20c. coll.:** *ODEP* 4.

adviser **1.** Advisers are not payers. ***Rec. dist.:*** Miss.

2. Advisers get away with it. They never have to pay the penalty for their advice. ***Rec. dist.:*** Ill.

3. An adviser may give you a helping hand to the poorhouse. ***Rec. dist.:*** Ill.

SEE ALSO An empty STOMACH is not a good political adviser.

advising Advising is easier than helping. ***Rec. dist.:*** Calif., Wis.

affair **1.** Affairs sleep soundly when fortune is present. ***Rec. dist.:*** Miss.

2. Don't meddle in others' affairs. ***Var.:*** Don't meddle in others' affairs—you'll get your nose scraped. ***Rec. dist.:*** Ohio.

3. In the affairs of this world men are saved, not by faith, but by the want of it. ***Rec. dist.:*** Ind.

4. One cannot manage too many affairs. ***Rec. dist.:*** Miss.

5. There are no small steps in great affairs. ***Rec. dist.:*** Ind.

SEE ALSO FOOLS are wise men in the affairs of women.

affectation **1.** Affectation in dress implies a flaw in understanding. ***Rec. dist.:*** Mich.

2. Affectation is a greater enemy to the face than small pox. ***Rec. dist.:*** N.Y. ***1st cit.:*** 1711 Steele, *Spectator.* **20c. coll.:** Stevenson 23:8.

3. Affectation is at best a deformity. ***Rec. dist.:*** Mich.

affection **1.** Affection is the broadest base of a good life. ***Rec. dist.:*** Calif.

2. Don't be too free with your affections, for when true love strikes, the spark will be dimmed. ***Rec. dist.:*** N.Y.

3. Talk not of wasted affection; affection is never wasted. ***Rec. dist.:*** N.Y. ***1st cit.:*** US1847 Longfellow, *Evangeline.* **20c. coll.:** Stevenson 23:10.

4. The ardor of parental affection consumes the heart with its fire. ***Rec. dist.:*** Mich.

affliction **1.** Affliction is the wholesome sort of virtue. ***Rec. dist.:*** Miss. ***1st cit.:*** US1701 *Diary of Samuel Sewall, 1674–1729,* Mass. Hist.Soc. *Collections* (1878–82). **20c. coll.:** Whiting 5.

2. Afflictions are sometimes blessings in disguise. ***Var.:*** Afflictions are best blessings in disguise. ***Rec. dist.:*** Ill., Miss. ***1st cit.:*** 1747 Mallet, *Amyntor and Theodora.* **20c. coll.:** Stevenson 19:4.

3. Afflictions are the good man's treasure—but he'd rather buy it than bear it. ***Rec. dist.:*** Ill.

affront *SEE* INSULTS and affronts are innocent where men are worthless. / As sore places meet most rubs, PROUD folks meet most affronts.

afraid **1.** Be not afraid; be only afraid of standing still. ***Rec. dist.:*** Ohio.

2. Don't be afraid of opposition; remember, a kite rises against the wind. ***Rec. dist.:*** Ont.

3. Don't be afraid of tomorrow; look what could happen today. ***Rec. dist.:*** Miss.

4. He who is afraid of doing too much always does too little. ***Rec. dist.:*** Calif., La., N.Y.

5. Nobody would be afraid if he could help it. ***Rec. dist.:*** Ill.

SEE ALSO Don't be afraid of a DOG that barks. / He THREATENS who is afraid.

after *See* After a hundred years we shall all be BALD. / After the DANGER everyone is wise. / After us the DELUGE. / After ME, you come first. / After MEAT comes mustard.

afterthought *See* FORETHOUGHT is better than afterthought.

afterward *See* A BUDGET is a method of worrying before you spend as well as afterward.

again *See* What used to BE will be again. / BOWING to a dwarf will not prevent your standing erect again. / A LOUSE not killed is sure to bite again. / If at first you don't SUCCEED, try, try again.

age *(lifespan)* **1.** Age and marriage tame man and beast. *Rec. dist.:* Ill., N.Y. *1st cit.:* 1623 Camden, *Remaines Concerning Britaine.* *20c. coll.:* ODEP 7, Stevenson 37:8.

2. Age before beauty. *Vars.:* **(a)** Age before beauty; beauty before the beast. **(b)** Age before beauty; grace before meat. **(c)** Age before beauty; pearls before the swine. **(d)** Age before honesty. *Rec. dist.:* U.S., Can. *1st cit.:* US1843 Robb, *Streaks of Squatter Life.* *20c. coll.:* T&W 4, Whiting(MP) 6.

3. Age breeds aches. *Rec. dist.:* Ill. *1st cit.:* 1596 Barington, *Metamorphosis of Ajax.* *20c. coll.:* Stevenson 37:4.

4. Age gives good advice when it is no longer able to give bad example. *Var.:* When a man gets too old to set a bad example, he begins to give advice. *Rec. dist.:* N.Y., Ont. *1st cit.:* US1828 *Journals of Ralph Waldo Emerson,* eds. Emerson and Forbes (1909–14). *20c. coll.:* T&W 4.

5. Age is like love: it cannot hide. *Rec. dist.:* Ky., Tenn.

6. Age is no excuse for foolishness. *Rec. dist.:* Wash.

7. Age is venerable in a man and would be in a woman if she ever became old. *Rec. dist.:* Wis. *Infm.:* Found in *Punch.*

8. Age lasts; youth devours. *Rec. dist.:* Miss.

9. Age makes a man white but not better. *Rec. dist.:* Minn., Wis.

10. Age mellows some people; others it makes rotten. *Rec. dist.:* Ark.

11. Age needs a critic, youth a model. *Rec. dist.:* Ind.

12. Age should think and youth should do. *Rec. dist.:* Wis. *1st cit.:* 1864 Thompson, *Sales Attici.* *20c. coll.:* Stevenson 42:3.

13. Age writes in the sand. *Rec. dist.:* N.Y.

14. At 20 years of age the will reigns, at 30 the wit, at 40 the judgment. *Rec. dist.:* Ill. *1st cit.:* 1640 Herbert, *Outlandish Proverbs (Jacula Prudentum)* in *Works,* ed. Hutchinson (1941); US1741 Franklin, *PRAlmanac.* *20c. coll.:* Stevenson 27:6.

15. For age and want, save while you may, for no morning lasts all day. *Rec. dist.:* N.Y., Oreg.

16. From middle age on everything of interest is either illegal, immoral, or fattening. *Var.:* Everything in life that is good is either illegal, immoral, or fattening. *Rec. dist.:* N.Y., Wis.

17. In telling age of another multiply by two; in telling your own age divide by two. *Rec. dist.:* Miss., N.Y.

18. The surest sign of age is loneliness. *Rec. dist.:* N.Y. *1st cit.:* US1868 Alcott, *Tablets.* *20c. coll.:* Stevenson 1449:1.

19. The warnings of age are the weapons of youth. *Rec. dist.:* Miss.

20. Who honors not age is not worthy of it. *Rec. dist.:* Miss.

21. With age comes wisdom. *Rec. dist.:* U.S., Can. *1st cit.:* 1523 Erasmus, *Adagia,* tr. Taverner; US1867 Richardson, *Beyond the Mississippi, 1857–1867.* *20c. coll.:* Stevenson 36:1, T&W 4.

See also A DIPLOMAT is a man who always remembers a woman's birthday but never her age. / EDUCATION is the best provision for old age. / The EXCESSES of our youth are draughts upon our old age. / IDLENESS in youth makes way for a painful and miserable old age. / OLD age comes uncalled. / OLD age is honorable. / OLD age is the night of life, as night is the old age of day. / All the PASSIONS are extinguished with old age; self-love never dies. / SENSE comes with age. / A tart TEMPER never mellows with age. / If YOUTH knew and age could do. / In YOUTH we run into difficulties; in old age difficulties run into us. / Reckless YOUTH makes rueful age. / YOUTH and age can never agree. / YOUTH is a blunder, manhood a struggle, old age a regret. / YOUTH is full of vitamins; age is full of germs. / YOUTH longs and manhood strives, but age remembers. / YOUTH supplies us with colors, age with canvas.

age *(era)* **1.** Each age has its own follies, as its majority is made up of foolish young people. *Rec. dist.:* N.Y. *1st cit.:* US1843 Emerson, *Carlyle's Past and Present.* *20c. coll.:* Stevenson 839:3.

2. Every age wants its playthings. *Rec. dist.:* Miss. *1st cit.:* US1948 Stevenson, *Home Book of Proverbs.* *20c. coll.:* Stevenson 46:3.

3. The golden age never was the present age. *Var.:* The golden age is before, not behind us. *Rec. dist.:* Ill., N.Y. *1st cit.:* 1732 Fuller, *Gnomologia;* US1750 Franklin, *PRAlmanac.* *20c. coll.:* ODEP 316, Stevenson 47:5.

SEE ALSO The DEITIES of one age are the bywords of the next. / An HOUR may destroy what was an age in building.

aged The aged knows; the young supposes. *Rec. dist.:* Md.

agent A press agent is a man who hitches his braggin' to a star. *Rec. dist.:* Ind.

SEE ALSO De littler de STATION, de bigger de agent.

agree Agree, for the law is costly. *Rec. dist.:* N.C. *1st cit.:* ca1607 Middleton, *Family of Love.* *20c. coll.:* ODEP 7, Stevenson 1359:8.

SEE ALSO Two DOGS over one bone seldom agree. / YOUTH and age can never agree.

agreeable Make yourself agreeable to all. *Rec. dist.:* Mich.

SEE ALSO To see an old FRIEND is as agreeable as a good meal.

agriculture Agriculture is the most certain source of wealth. *Rec. dist.:* La., Mich.

ague An ague in spring is physic for the king. *Rec. dist.:* Miss., N.Y. *1st cit.:* 1650

Weldon, *Court and Character of King James I.* *20c. coll.:* ODEP 7, Stevenson 49:5.

ahead He who looks behind will never get ahead. *Var.:* Look ahead or you won't get ahead. *Rec. dist.:* Iowa, Minn.

SEE ALSO It is no DISGRACE to fall down—the disgrace is in not getting up and going ahead. / Be sure you are RIGHT, then go ahead.

aid SEE GOD aids him who changes.

ail It's good for what ails you, and if nothing ails you, it's good for that, too. *Rec. dist.:* Ind., Mich. *Infm.:* It applies to a variety of situations from encouragement to do hard work to drinking whiskey.

aim *(n.)* **1.** A man without aim is like a clock without hands, as useless if it turns as if it stands. *Rec. dist.:* Ill., N.C.

2. Better to fail in a high aim than to succeed in a low one. *Rec. dist.:* N.Y.

3. It is better to have an aim and miss it than to hit and not have an aim. *Rec. dist.:* N.C.

4. The aim is useless without the way. *Rec. dist.:* Oreg.

5. The higher the aim the higher the fall. *Rec. dist.:* N.C.

aim *(v.)* **1.** Aim at the stars, but keep your feet on the ground. *Rec. dist.:* Ont.

2. Aim high and you will succeed. *Rec. dist.:* Miss.

3. Aim high, time flies. *Rec. dist.:* Ont.

4. Always aim at what becomes you. *Rec. dist.:* Mich.

5. Better aim at the moon than shoot into the well. *Rec. dist.:* Ind.

6. If you aims to do a favor, go de whole hog. Don't never do nothing half way. *Rec. dist.:* Miss.

ain't **1.** Ain't ain't right. *Rec. dist.:* Oreg.

2. If you aren't what you ain't, then you ain't what you are. *Rec. dist.:* Fla., Iowa. *Infm.:* Said of people putting on airs.

SEE ALSO The old gray MARE ain't what she used to be. / A little bit of POWDER and a little bit of paint makes a woman look like what she ain't.

air 1. Foul air slays like a sword. *Rec. dist.:* Wis.

2. Fresh air and sunshine and plenty of grace slam the door in the doctor's face. *Rec. dist.:* Minn.

3. Hot air thawed out many a cold reception. *Rec. dist.:* N.Dak.

SEE ALSO The BALLOON with the most air makes the loudest noise when it bursts. / A feather in the hand is better than a BIRD in the air. / Air CASTLES are good; now put foundations under them. / Don't build your CASTLES in the air. It's liable to rain and wash them away. / You can't build CASTLES in the air and live in them. / A man cannot LIVE on air. / A straw VOTE only shows which way the hot air blows.

alarming SEE People are willing to BELIEVE alarming things to keep from believing what they don't want to.

alchemy No alchemy likes saving. *Rec. dist.:* Ill.

alcohol 1. Alcohol and driving don't mix. *Rec. dist.:* U.S., Can. *Infm:* Popularized in America by auto vehicle safety departments of state and federal governmental agencies.

2. Alcohol will preserve anything but a secret. *Rec. dist.:* N.J.

3. All alcohol shows the inner man. *Rec. dist.:* Ariz.

SEE ALSO DIGNITY is one thing that can't be preserved in alcohol. / Mix GUNPOWDER and alcohol, you won't be around long at all.

ale 1. Good ale is meat, drink, and cloth. *Rec. dist.:* Miss., N.Y. *1st cit.:* 1602 Carew, *Survey of Cornwall.* *20c. coll.:* ODEP 8, Stevenson 50:11.

2. When the ale is in, wit is out. *Var.:* Ale in, wit out. *Rec. dist.:* N.Y., Wis. *1st cit.:* ca1386 Chaucer, *Pardoner's Tale.* *20c. coll.:* ODEP 8, Stevenson 2523:7.

SEE ALSO It is better to have BEANS and bacon in peace than cakes and ale in fear.

alert Alert in the beginning, negligent in the end. *Rec. dist.:* Mich.

all 1. All are not hunters that blow the horn. *Rec. dist.:* N.Y.

2. All between the cradle and the coffin is uncertain. *Rec. dist.:* Mich., N.Y.

3. All covet; all lose. *Rec. dist.:* U.S., Can. *1st cit.:* 1297 Robert of Gloucester, *Chronicles;* US1738 Franklin, *PRAlmanac.* *20c. coll.:* ODEP 9, Whiting 8.

4. All for love and the world well lost. *Rec. dist.:* N.Y. *1st cit.:* 1678 Dryden, *All for Love and the World Well Lost (Prologue).* *20c. coll.:* Stevenson 1462:7.

5. All for one, one for all. *Vars.:* **(a)** All for one and one for all. **(b)** All for one—and I'm the one. **(c)** Everyone for himself, and God for all. *Rec. dist.:* U.S., Can. *1st cit.:* US1948 Stevenson, *Home Book of Proverbs.* *20c. coll.:* Stevenson 1717:13.

6. All good things come from heaven. *Rec. dist.:* N.J.

7. All is fair in love and war. *Rec. dist.:* U.S., Can. *1st cit.:* US1835 Kennedy, *Horse-Shoe Robinson.* *20c. coll.:* Stevenson 1461:13, T&W 5, Whiting(MP) 8.

8. All is not grist that goes to the mill. *Var.:* All is not grist that goes to his mill. *Rec. dist.:* Ont. *1st cit.:* 1583 Calvin, *Calvin on Deuteronomy,* tr. Golding; US1913 Dreiser, *Traveler.* *20c. coll.:* ODEP 339, CODP 102, Stevenson, 1042:11, Whiting(MP) 9.

9. All's well that ends well. *Rec. dist.:* U.S., Can. *1st cit.:* ca1300 *Proverbs of Hending;* US1705 *Correspondence Between William Penn and James Logan, 1700–1705,* ed. Armstrong, Hist.Soc. Penn. *Memoirs* (1870). *20c. coll.:* ODEP 879, Whiting 7, CODP 244, Stevenson 678:7, T&W 6, Whiting(MP) 9.

10. All or nothing at all. *Rec. dist.:* Ill., Wis. *1st cit.:* US1940 Reilly, *Dead Can.* *20c. coll.:* Whiting(MP) 9.

11. All that exists in this world is beautiful. *Rec. dist.:* R.I.

12. All that glitters is not gold. *Var.:* All that shines is not silver. *Rec. dist.:* U.S., Can. *1st cit.:* ca1220 *Hali Meidenhad,* E.E.T.S.; US1636 Howes in *Winthrop Papers, 1498–1649,* Mass.Hist.Soc. *Collections* (1929–47). *20c. coll.:*

ODEP 316, *CODP* 92, Stevenson 990:13, Whiting 181, T&W 155, Whiting*(MP)* 9.

13. All that goes up must come down. *Rec. dist.:* U.S., Can. *1st cit.:* US1939 Wilder, *By Shores of Silver Lake.* *20c. coll.:* CODP 236.

14. All things come to him who waits. *Rec. dist.:* Mich., N.C., Ohio. *1st cit.:* ca1530 Barclay, *Eclogues,* E.E.T.S. (1927). *20c. coll.:* CODP 3.

15. All things have an end. *Rec. dist.:* U.S., Can. *1st cit.:* ca1440 *Partonope of Blois,* E.E.T.S. *20c. coll.:* CODP 3.

16. All things work together for good. *Rec. dist.:* Ont.

17. It takes all sorts to make up the world. *Rec. dist.:* U.S., Can. *1st cit.:* 1620 Cervantes, *Don Quixote,* tr. Shelton; US1906 Twain, *Eruption.* *20c. coll.:* ODEP 11, CODP 3, Stevenson 2628:8, Whiting*(MP)* 584.

18. Make all you can, save all you can, give all you can. *Rec. dist.:* Kans.

19. Venture not all in one boat. *Rec. dist.:* Minn., N.Y.

See also All asses do not go on four feet. / All is for the best. / He who denies all confesses all. / All is lost that is poured into a cracked dish. / All may do what has by man been done. / All are presumed good until they are found in a fault. / Let us all hang together or hang separately. / Hear all and say nothing. / It's all in knowing how. / Love all, trust few. / Love conquers all. / All men are created equal. / He that would please all and himself too takes more in hand than he is like to do. / All roads lead to Rome.

alley   1. Every alley has its own tin can. *Rec. dist.:* N.J.

2. It is a long alley that has no turning. *Var.:* It's a long alley that has no ash barrels. *Rec. dist.:* Ind., N.Dak.

alluring If you want to be alluring, don't chase your young man. *Rec. dist.:* N.Y.

almanac   1. The almanac writer makes the almanac, but God makes the weather. *Rec. dist.:* Nebr.

2. With the old almanac and the old year, leave your vices, though ever so dear. *Rec. dist.:* N.Y.

almost   1. Almost made it never made the grade. *Rec. dist.:* Ill.

2. Almost never killed a fly. *Rec. dist.:* Ill., Miss., N.Y.

3. Almost was never hanged. *Rec. dist.:* La., N.C. *1st cit.:* 1639 Clarke, *Paroemiologia.* *20c. coll.:* ODEP 12, Stevenson 53:2.

4. Men who tell you almost nothing but the truth tell you almost nothing. *Rec. dist.:* N.Y.

5. 'Most kill bird don't make stew. *Rec. dist.:* S.C.

See also Confidence of success is almost success.

alms   1. A friar who asks alms for God's sake begs for two. *Var.:* He that seeks alms for God's sake begs for two. *Rec. dist.:* N.Y., Wis.

2. Alms are the golden key that opens the gates of heaven. *Rec. dist.:* Ill.

3. Alms are the salt of riches—but don't rub the salt into the poor man's wound. *Rec. dist.:* Ill.

4. Better to give me nothing than stolen alms. *Rec. dist.:* Ind.

5. No one becomes poor through giving alms. *Var.:* You shall not lose by giving alms. *Rec. dist.:* Ill., Mich. *1st cit.:* 1640 Herbert, *Outlandish Proverbs (Jacula Prudentum)* in *Works,* ed. Hutchinson (1941); US1757 Franklin, *PRAlmanac.* *20c. coll.:* ODEP 12, Stevenson 53:10.

6. The little alms are the good alms. *Rec. dist.:* N.Y.

7. Who gives himself with his alms feeds three: himself, his hungering neighbor, and me. *Rec. dist.:* Ky., Minn., Tenn.

alone   1. Better alone than in bad company. *Var.:* It is better to be alone than in bad company. *Rec. dist.:* U.S., Can. *1st cit.:* 1678 Ray, *Scottish Proverbs.* *20c. coll.:* Stevenson 55:6.

2. Call him not alone who dies side by side with gallant men. *Rec. dist.:* N.Y.

3. Leave well enough alone. *Rec. dist.:* N.Y.

1st cit.: 1840 Russell, *London Times.* *20c. coll.:* Stevenson 54:10.

4. Man can't live in this world alone. *Vars.:* **(a)** It is not good that man should be alone. **(b)** None goes his way alone. **(c)** Not even in paradise can a man live alone. *Rec. dist.:* N.C., Okla. *1st cit.:* ca1386 Chaucer, *Tale of Melibee.* *20c. coll.:* Stevenson 55:1.

5. Those are never alone who are accompanied by noble thoughts. *Rec. dist.:* Calif., Minn.

6. When alone, we have our thoughts to watch; when in the family, our tempers; when in society, our tongues. *Var.:* When alone we have our thoughts to watch. *Rec. dist.:* Ont., Wis.

SEE ALSO You will only GROW when you are alone. / LAUGH and the world laughs with you; cry and you cry alone. / MAN cannot live by bread alone. / MISFORTUNES seldom come alone. / A man is RICH in proportion to the number of things which he can afford to let alone. / An empty SACK won't stand alone. / He TRAVELS fastest who travels alone.

along A little along is better than a long none. *Var.:* Better little than none. *Rec. dist.:* Ont.

alphabet SEE When in ANGER, say the alphabet.

alter SEE CIRCUMSTANCES alter cases. / Alter IDEAS and you alter the world.

always *(n.)* Always is a long time. *Rec. dist.:* Ill.

always *(adv.)* SEE He who is AFRAID of doing too much always does too little. / The CUSTOMER is always right. / Once a DRUNKARD, always a drunkard. / Once a FOOL, always a fool. / The GRASS is always greener on the other side of the fence. / A man with no HAIR seems always to get the haircut. / The HEART that loves is always young. / Always in a HURRY, always behind. / Once a KNAVE, always a knave. / Always ROOM for one more. / Once a THIEF, always a thief. / The UNEXPECTED always happens. / Always a VALLEY before a hill.

amateur An amateur is a person who plays a game for the fun of it. *Rec. dist.:* N.C.

SEE ALSO Every ARTIST was first an amateur.

ambassador An ambassador is a good man sent abroad to lie for his country. *Rec. dist.:* Ill. *1st cit.:* 1616 "Wotton" in *Dictionary of National Biography.* *20c. coll.:* Stevenson 56:3.

SEE ALSO Your TONGUE is your ambassador.

ambition **1.** A man without ambition is like a woman without looks. *Rec. dist.:* N.Y. *1st cit.:* US1900 Harris, *Montes the Matador.* *20c. coll.:* Stevenson 58:1.

2. Ambition and fleas jump high. *Rec. dist.:* Wis.

3. Ambition destroys its possessor. *Rec. dist.:* Ohio. *1st cit.:* 1592 Lyly, *Midas.* *20c. coll.:* ODEP 13, Stevenson 57:2.

4. Ambition has no rest. *Rec. dist.:* Ind. *1st cit.:* US1948 Stevenson, *Home Book of Proverbs.* *20c. coll.:* Stevenson 59:2.

5. Ambition is no cure for love. *Rec. dist.:* Miss. *1st cit.:* 1805 Scott, *Lay of the Last Minstrel.* *20c. coll.:* Stevenson 58:8.

6. Ambition is not the voice of little people. *Rec. dist.:* Kans.

7. Ambition is putting a ladder against the sky. *Rec. dist.:* Wis.

8. Ambition is the incentive that makes purpose great and achievement greater. *Rec. dist.:* N.Y.

9. Ambition is the last infirmity of noble minds. *Rec. dist.:* Ill.

10. Ambition is torment enough for an enemy. *Rec. dist.:* Mich. *1st cit.:* 1574 Guazzo, *Civile Conversation,* tr. Pettie, T.T. (1925). *20c. coll.:* Stevenson 57:9.

11. Ambition knows no obstacles. *Rec. dist.:* Fla.

12. Ambition obeys no laws. *Rec. dist.:* Ill., Vt.

13. Ambition often spends foolishly what avarice has collected wickedly. *Rec. dist.:* N.Y.

14. Be content and do not heed the goadings of ambitions. *Rec. dist.:* Minn.

15. Fling away ambition; by that sin fell the angels. *Rec. dist.:* Ill.

16. Great ambitions forgotten because of lack of ambition are pipe dreams. *Rec. dist.:* Ind.

17. Great ambitions fulfilled are proof of a noble life. *Rec. dist.:* Ind.

18. Great ambitions make great men. *Rec. dist.:* Ind.

19. He who sits on the tack of ambition will surely rise to success. *Rec. dist.:* Miss.

20. It is a laudable ambition that aims at being better than his neighbors. *Rec. dist.:* N.Y. *1st cit.:* US1749 Franklin, *PRAlmanac.* *20c. coll.:* Stevenson 57:7.

21. Man's ambition knows no bars; with vision he carves his way through hardships to the stars. *Rec. dist.:* N.C.

22. Nothing humbler than ambition when it is about to climb. *Rec. dist.:* Wis. *1st cit.:* US1753 Franklin, *PRAlmanac.* *20c. coll.:* Stevenson 57:4.

23. Ride your ambition in the skies. *Rec. dist.:* Ala.

SEE ALSO Many WANTS attend those who have many ambitions.

ambitious **1.** Ambitious is like hunting for fleas. *Rec. dist.:* Ill.

2. An ambitious person is always dangerous. *Rec. dist.:* N.J.

3. The ambitious bullfrog puffed and puffed until he burst. *Rec. dist.:* Ill. *Infm.:* An ambitious person often becomes self-important.

amends A plaster is but small amends for a broken head. *Rec. dist.:* Ark.

SEE ALSO LITTLE said is soonest mended.

America **1.** America is a tune. It must be sung together. *Rec. dist.:* Wis.

2. America means opportunity, freedom, and power. *Rec. dist.:* N.Y.

3. Never sell America short. *Rec. dist.:* Mich., N.Y. *1st cit.:* ca1866 "J.S.Morgan" in *Dictionary of American Biography.* *20c. coll.:* Stevenson 60:4.

4. See America first. *Rec. dist.:* Colo., Mich. *1st cit.:* US1910 Advertising slogan for the Great Northern Railway promoting the development of Glacier National Park. *20c. coll.:* Stevenson 59:11.

American **1.** Americans in unity and unity in Americans. *Rec. dist.:* N.Y. *1st cit.:* US1768 Dickinson, *Liberty Song.* *20c. coll.:* Stevenson 59:9.

2. Good Americans, when they die, go to Paris. *Rec. dist.:* Ill., N.Y. *1st cit.:* US1858 Holmes, *Autocrat of the Breakfast-Table.* *20c. coll.:* ODEP 13, T&W 6, Whiting(MP) 11.

3. It is a striking coincidence that the word American ends in can. *Rec. dist.:* Wis.

amiable That you may be beloved, be amiable. *Rec. dist.:* Mich., N.Y.

amiss Avoid what you see amiss in others. *Rec. dist.:* Mich.

amusement When men are rightly occupied, their amusement grows out of their work. *Rec. dist.:* Vt.

SEE ALSO HELL is populated with the victims of harmless amusements.

anarchy Anarchy is a condition in which everyone is free, so that no one can do as one would like to do. *Rec. dist.:* N.Dak.

ancestor *SEE* Most people consider THRIFT a fine virtue in ancestors.

ancestry Noble ancestry makes a poor dish at the table. *Rec. dist.:* Wis. *1st cit.:* 1855 Bohn, *Handbook of Proverbs.* *20c. coll.:* Stevenson 62:7.

anchor **1.** Good riding at two anchors, for if one breaks the other may hold. *Rec. dist.:* Mich. *1st cit.:* 1546 Heywood, *Dialogue of Proverbs,* ed. Habernicht (1963). *20c. coll.:* Stevenson 65:5.

2. Never cast an anchor in shifting sand. *Rec. dist.:* Ohio.

SEE ALSO A BABE is a mother's anchor: she cannot swing from her moorings. / A bad SHIP never casts anchor in port. / VICE makes virtue look well to its anchor.

ancient The ancients tell us what is best, but we must learn of the moderns what is fittest. *Rec. dist.:* N.Y. *1st cit.:* US1738 Franklin, *PRAlmanac.* *20c. coll.:* Stevenson 74:5.

and *See* If "ifs" and "ands" were pots and pans, there would be no need for tinkers.

anecdote A short anecdote is often a tall tale. *Rec. dist.:* Ohio.

angel 1. Always being up in the air and harping doesn't make one an angel. *Rec. dist.:* Ky.

2. An angel on the street, a devil at home. *Rec. dist.:* N.Y., Wis. *1st cit.:* US1940 Thompson, *Body, Boots, and Britches.* *20c. coll.:* Stevenson 1211:2.

3. An angel on top but a devil underneath. *Rec. dist.:* N.Y. *1st cit.:* 1604 Shakespeare, *Measure for Measure.* *20c. coll.:* Stevenson 1211:3.

4. Angels could do no more. *Vars.:* **(a)** Do your best and bury the rest. Angels can't do better. **(b)** He who does his best, angels can do no more. **(c)** Whoever does the best his circumstances allows, does well; angels could do no more. *Rec. dist.:* Ind., Minn., N.Y. *1st cit.:* US1948 Stevenson, *Home Book of Proverbs.* *20c. coll.:* Stevenson 172:8.

5. Angels playing the "liar" in heaven practiced lying while they preached on earth. *Rec. dist.:* Minn.

6. Angels take care of fools and drunkards. *Rec. dist.:* Kans.

7. Little angels grow into big devils. *Rec. dist.:* Kans.

8. Men are not angels. *Rec. dist.:* N.Y., S.C. *1st cit.:* 1548 Hall, *Chronicle of Lancastre and York.* *20c. coll.:* ODEP 524, Stevenson 1516:10.

9. Only angels wear wings. *Rec. dist.:* N.C.

10. Speak of angels and you'll hear the rustling of their wings. *Rec. dist.:* U.S., Can. *1st cit.:* 1902 Lean, *Collectanea.* *20c. coll.:* ODEP 804, Stevenson 568:9.

11. When a girl whistles, an angel cries. *Rec. dist.:* N.Y.

12. Young angel, old devil; young devil, old angel. *Rec. dist.:* Wash. *1st cit.:* 1732 Fuller, *Gnomologia.* *20c. coll.:* Stevenson 45:7.

See also A babe is an angel whose wings decrease as her legs increase. / The devils in the world shout loud and strong, but the angels outvote them. / Fools rush in where angels fear to tread. / He that has a good wife has an angel at his side; he that has a bad one has a devil at his elbow.

anger 1. A good remedy for anger is delay. *Var.:* The greatest remedy for anger is delay. *Rec. dist.:* Ind., Kans.

2. Anger and folly walk cheek by jowl; repentance treads on both their heads. *Rec. dist.:* N.Y. *1st cit.:* US1741 Franklin, *PRAlmanac.* *20c. coll.:* Stevenson 70:6.

3. Anger and haste hinder good counsel. *Rec. dist.:* Mich., N.Y. *1st cit.:* 1562 Brooke, *Romeus and Juliet.* *20c. coll.:* ODEP 13, Stevenson 67:12.

4. Anger and love give bad counsel. *Rec. dist.:* Miss. *1st cit.:* 1562 Brooke, *Romeus and Juliet.* *20c. coll.:* ODEP 13, Stevenson 67:12.

5. Anger begins with folly and ends with prayer. *Var.:* The beginning of anger is madness, the end repentance. *Rec. dist.:* Miss. *1st cit.:* 1732 Fuller, *Gnomologia.* *20c. coll.:* Stevenson 70:6.

6. Anger dies quickly in a good man. *Rec. dist.:* Miss. *1st cit.:* ca1526 Erasmus, *Dicta Sapientum,* tr. Berthelet. *20c. coll.:* ODEP 13, Stevenson 69:10.

7. Anger edges valor. *Rec. dist.:* Miss.

8. Anger grows old fast. *Rec. dist.:* Miss.

9. Anger improves nothing but the arch of a cat's back. *Rec. dist.:* Minn., Miss.

10. Anger is a brief madness, but it can do damage that lasts forever. *Var.:* Anger is short madness. *Rec. dist.:* Ill., N.Y., Ohio. *1st cit.:* ca1200 *Ancrene Riwle,* ed. Morton, Camden Soc. (1853); US1652 *Complete Writings of Roger Williams* (1963). *20c. coll.:* ODEP 13, Whiting 9, Stevenson 68:11.

11. Anger is a stone cast at a wasp's nest. *Var.:* Anger is a stone thrown into a hornet's nest. *Rec. dist.:* Ill., Kans.

12. Anger is a sworn enemy. *Rec. dist.:* Miss.

13. Anger is a wind that blows out the light of the mind. *Var.:* Anger blows out the lamp of the mind. *Rec. dist.:* N.Y., Oreg.

14. Anger is like a ruin which breaks itself

upon what it falls. *Rec. dist.:* Mich. *1st cit.:* US1948 Stevenson, *Home Book of Proverbs.* *20c. coll.:* Stevenson 70:8.

15. Anger is never without reason. *Var.:* Anger is never without reason, but seldom a good one. *Rec. dist.:* Ill., Wis. *1st cit.:* US1753 Franklin, *PRAlmanac.* *20c. coll.:* Stevenson 68:2.

16. Anger is often more hurtful than the injury that caused it. *Rec. dist.:* Wis. *1st cit.:* 1732 Fuller, *Gnomologia.* *20c. coll.:* Stevenson 71:2.

17. Anger is the fever and frenzy of the soul. *Rec. dist.:* Ill. *1st cit.:* 1732 Fuller, *Gnomologia.* *20c. coll.:* Stevenson 68:4.

18. Anger makes a rich man hated and a poor man scorned. *Rec. dist.:* Miss., N.Y. *1st cit.:* 1732 Fuller, *Gnomologia.* *20c. coll.:* Stevenson 68:4.

19. Anger makes dull men witty but keeps them poor. *Rec. dist.:* Calif., Miss., N.Y. *1st cit.:* 1625 Bacon, *Apophthegms.* *20c. coll.:* Stevenson 70:9.

20. Anger profits nobody. *Rec. dist.:* Miss., N.Y.

21. Anger punishes itself. *Rec. dist.:* Ala. *1st cit.:* 1580 Lyly, *Euphues and His England.* *20c. coll.:* ODEP 14.

22. Anger shows the character of man. *Rec. dist.:* Miss., N.Y.

23. Anger warms the invention but overheats the oven. *Rec. dist.:* N.Y. *1st cit.:* 1673 Halifax, *Maxims;* US1757 Franklin, *PRAlmanac.* *20c. coll.:* Stevenson 70:9.

24. Anger's final resting place is the bosom of fools. *Rec. dist.:* Ill. *1st cit.:* 1732 Fuller, *Gnomologia.* *20c. coll.:* Stevenson 68:4.

25. Avoid anger and you will not sin. *Rec. dist.:* N.Y. *1st cit.:* US1948 Stevenson, *Home Book of Proverbs.* *20c. coll.:* Stevenson 69:3.

26. Be master of your anger. *Rec. dist.:* Ill.

27. Beware of him who is slow to anger; he is angry for something and will not be pleased for nothing. *Rec. dist.:* Miss., N.Y. *1st cit.:* 1578 Florio, *Firste Fruites;* US1753 Franklin, *PRAlmanac.* *20c. coll.:* Stevenson 68:1.

28. Beware the anger of a patient man. *Rec. dist.:* Miss. *1st cit.:* 1578 Florio, *Firste Fruites.* *20c. coll.:* Stevenson 68:1.

29. Dread the anger of a cornered sheep. *Rec. dist.:* Ill.

30. He overcomes a stout enemy who overcomes his own anger. *Rec. dist.:* Miss.

31. He that is slow to anger is better than the mighty. *Var.:* He that is slow to anger is better than the mighty, and he that rules his spirit is better than he that rules the city. *Rec. dist.:* Ind., N.Y., Oreg., Wis. *1st cit.:* US1948 Stevenson, *Home Book of Proverbs.* *20c. coll.:* Stevenson 69:6.

32. It is not the father's anger but his silence his son dreads. *Rec. dist.:* Calif., Wis.

33. Kill your anger while it's hot. *Rec. dist.:* Wis.

34. Let not the sun set on your anger. *Rec. dist.:* U.S., Can.

35. Sleep with your anger. *Var.:* When angry, sleep on it. *Rec. dist.:* Miss.

36. Suppressing a moment of anger may save a day of sorrow. *Rec. dist.:* Ohio. *1st cit.:* US1938 Champion, *Racial Proverbs.* *20c. coll.:* Stevenson 69:9.

37. Whatever is begun in anger ends in shame. *Rec. dist.:* Ill. *1st cit.:* US1734 Franklin, *PRAlmanac.* *20c. coll.:* Stevenson 70:6.

38. When in anger, say the alphabet. *Rec. dist.:* N.Y. *1st cit.:* US1948 Stevenson, *Home Book of Proverbs.* *20c. coll.:* Stevenson 67:12.

angry 1. An angry man opens his mouth and shuts his eyes. *Var.:* When a man is angry, he opens his mouth and shuts his eyes. *Rec. dist.:* Ala., Ill., Minn., N.Y.

2. Every minute you are angry you lose sixty seconds of happiness. *Rec. dist.:* Ky., Tenn.

3. He that is angry is seldom at ease. *Rec. dist.:* N.Y.

4. If you're angry count to ten. *Vars.:* **(a)** At anger count to ten. **(b)** If angry count to ten before you say anything bad. If you get the same impulse, count to ten again. **(c)** If you're angry count to ten, if very angry count to ten again. **(d)** When in anger count to ten before you speak. *Rec. dist.:* U.S., Can. *1st cit.:* 1592 Shakespeare, *Richard III;* US1786 *Papers of Thomas Jefferson,* ed. Boyd (1950). *20c. coll.:* ODEP 14, Whiting 432, Whiting*(MP)* 615.

5. To be angry is to punish yourself for another's sins. *Var.:* To be angry is to punish myself for another's fault. *Rec. dist.:* Ill., Wis. *1st cit.:* US1948 Stevenson, *Home Book of Proverbs. 20c. coll.:* Stevenson 71:2.

6. Two things a man should never get angry at: what he can help and what he cannot help. *Rec. dist.:* N.Y. *1st cit.:* 1732 Fuller, *Gnomologia. 20c. coll.:* Stevenson 68:5.

SEE ALSO The angry BEGGAR gets a stone instead of a handout. / He is a FOOL who cannot be angry but a wise man who will not.

animal **1.** Animals can speak at night. *Rec. dist.:* Kans.

2. Be kind to dumb animals. *Var.:* Be kind to animals. *Rec. dist.:* Ariz., Mich., Miss.

3. Even in animals there exists the spirit of their sires. *Rec. dist.:* Ind.

4. It is the trapped animal that makes the most noise. *Rec. dist.:* N.Y.

5. There are wild animals, but wild hunters, too. *Rec. dist.:* N.Y.

animation Without animation man is naught. *Rec. dist.:* N.Y.

annoyance Put up with small annoyances to gain great results. *Rec. dist.:* Ill.

another If it's not one thing, it's another. *Rec. dist.:* Calif., Miss., N.Y.
SEE ALSO Another DAY, another dollar.

answer *(n.)* **1.** A soft answer turns away wrath. *Vars.:* (a) A soft answer breaks ire. (b) A soft answer turns away wrath, but grievous words stir anger. (c) A soft answer turns away wrath but has little effect on a door-to-door salesman. *Rec. dist.:* U.S., Can. *1st cit.:* 1382 *Wyclif, Bible, Proverbs 15:1;* US1642 *Trelawny Papers* in *Documentary History of State of Maine,* ed. Baxter (1884). *20c. coll.:* ODEP 750, Whiting 9, CODP 206, Stevenson 72:13, Whiting*(MP)* 12.

2. Give a civil answer to a civil question. *Rec.*

dist.: N.Y., N.C. *1st cit.:* US1853 Haliburton, *Sam Slick's Wise Saws. 20c. coll.:* T&W 6, Whiting*(MP)* 12.

3. No answer is also an answer. *Rec. dist.:* Calif., Miss.

4. Short answers save trouble. *Rec. dist.:* N.Y. *1st cit.:* US1869 Alcott, *Little Women. 20c. coll.:* T&W 6.

5. The shortest answer is doing. *Rec. dist.:* Minn., N.Y. *1st cit.:* 1640 Herbert, *Outlandish Proverbs (Jacula Prudentum)* in *Works,* ed. Hutchinson (1941). *20c. coll.:* ODEP 728, Stevenson 73:7.

6. There's no answer to a fool's question. *Rec. dist.:* Ariz.

SEE ALSO Every ARGUMENT has its answer. / Never take NO for an answer. / Silly QUESTION, silly answer. / 'Tis not every QUESTION that deserves an answer. / 'Tis better to ask some of the QUESTIONS than to know all the answers. / Weighty QUESTIONS ask for deliberate answers. / SILENCE is the best answer to the stupid. / Speak kind WORDS, and you will hear kind answers.

answer *(v.)* Who answers suddenly knows little. *Rec. dist.:* Wis.
SEE ALSO A FOOL can ask more questions in a minute than a wise man can answer in an hour. / Answer a FOOL according to his folly.

ant **1.** A coconut shell full of water is an ocean to an ant. *Rec. dist.:* Calif., Utah. *1st cit.:* US1938 Champion, *Racial Proverbs. 20c. coll.:* Stevenson 73:14.

2. An ant may work its heart out, but it can't make money. *Rec. dist.:* Ill.

3. Ants follow fat. *Rec. dist.:* Ariz.

4. Ants live safely till they have gotten wings. *Rec. dist.:* N.Y. *1st cit.:* 1584 Lyly, *Campaspe;* US1853 Willis, *Fun Jottings. 20c. coll.:* ODEP 15, T&W 7, Stevenson 74:2.

5. Ants never lend; ants never borrow. *Rec. dist.:* Utah.

6. Any spoke will lead the ant to the hub. *Rec. dist.:* N.Y. *1st cit.:* US1934 Stout, *Fer-de-Lance. 20c. coll.:* Stevenson 2201:4.

7. Consider the ant, you sluggard, and be wise. *Vars.:* **(a)** Consider the ant rather than the sluggard and be wise. **(b)** Go to the ant, you sluggard; consider her way and be wise. *Rec. dist.:* Ariz., Calif., Kans., R.I. *1st cit.:* 1709 Dykes, *English Proverbs.* *20c. coll.:* Stevenson 74:1.

8. None preaches better than the ant, and she says nothing. *Rec. dist.:* Ark., Ill., Miss.

anticipation **1.** The dawn of anticipation forms a most soothing pillow for a restless head. *Rec. dist.:* Wis.

2. There's more joy in anticipation than in realization. *Vars.:* **(a)** Anticipation is better than realization. **(b)** Anticipation is twice the joy of realization. **(c)** The realization is never as great as anticipation. *Rec. dist.:* Calif., Miss., Ohio. *1st cit.:* 1928 McNeile, *Female.* *20c. coll.:* Whiting(MP) 12.

antique To admire the antique is not to admire the old but the natural. *Rec. dist.:* Ill.

antiquity **1.** Antiquity is not always the mark of verity. *Rec. dist.:* Ill. *1st cit.:* 1732 Fuller, *Gnomologia.* *20c. coll.:* Stevenson 74:6.

2. To look back on antiquity is one thing, to go back to it another. *Rec. dist.:* Ill. *1st cit.:* 1820 Colton, *Lacon.* *20c. coll.:* Stevenson 75:4.

3. With a mirror of brass you can adjust your hat, but with antiquity for a mirror you can predict the rise and fall of the empire. *Rec. dist.:* Utah.

anvil **1.** A good anvil does not fear the hammer. *Rec. dist.:* Ohio. *1st cit.:* US1948 Stevenson, *Home Book of Proverbs.* *20c. coll.:* Stevenson 75:8.

2. If you are an anvil, hold still; if you are a hammer, strike hard. *Var.:* When you are an anvil, hold still; when you are a hammer, strike your fell. *Rec. dist.:* Ill. *1st cit.:* 1591 Florio, *Second Fruites;* US1758 Franklin, *PRAlmanac.* *20c. coll.:* ODEP 15, Whiting 10, Stevenson 76:3.

3. Some men are born anvils, others are born hammers. *Var.:* In this world a man must be born an anvil or a hammer. *Rec. dist.:* Ill. *1st*

cit.: US1948 Stevenson, *Home Book of Proverbs.* *20c. coll.:* Stevenson 76:6.

4. The anvil fears no blows. *Rec. dist.:* Miss., N.Y. *1st cit.:* 1609 Harward, Unpublished manuscript in Trinity College Library, Cambridge. *20c. coll.:* ODEP 15, Stevenson 76:9.

5. The anvil lasts longer than the hammer. *Rec. dist.:* Ill.

6. The old anvil laughs at many hammers. *Rec. dist.:* Ohio.

anxiety **1.** Anxiety attends increase of wealth. *Rec. dist.:* Mich.

2. On anxiety street there are plenty of neighbors. *Rec. dist.:* Ont.

any *SEE* Any PORT in a storm. / Any man can be a SAILOR on a calm sea. / Any TIME means no time.

anybody *SEE* A little DIRT never hurt anyone.

anything **1.** Anything for a novelty. *Rec. dist.:* Mich., N.Y. *1st cit.:* US1815 Paulding, *Bucktails.* *20c. coll.:* Stevenson 1702:5.

2. Anything for a quiet life. *Var.:* Anything for a little peace and quiet. *Rec. dist.:* Calif., Mich., N.Y., Ont. *1st cit.:* 1662 Middleton, *Anything for a Quiet Life;* US1928 Goodwin, *When Dead.* *20c. coll.:* ODEP 15, Whiting(MP) 12.

3. Anything is better than nothing. *Rec. dist.:* Ind. *1st cit.:* US1949 Flockridge, *Dishonest.* *20c. coll.:* Whiting(MP) 12.

4. Call me anything but late for dinner. *Rec. dist.:* Ind., Mich.

5. If anything can go wrong, it will. *Rec. dist.:* Mich., N.Y. *Infm.:* Known as "Murphy's Law," which has many variations. *1st cit.:* US1949 Nichols, *Murphy's Law.* *20c. coll.:* CODP 4.

SEE ALSO You can BUY anything except day and night. / Don't DO anything I wouldn't do. / Never DO anything yourself you can get somebody else to do. / You can DO anything you want to if you want to bad enough. / When you buy FRIENDS with anything but friendship, they do not stay bought long. /

He who never made a MISTAKE never made anything. / If you don't SAY anything, you won't be called on to repeat it.

anytime 1. Anytime is tea time. *Rec. dist.:* Ont.

2. Anytime means no time. *Rec. dist.:* Ill. *1st cit.:* 1721 Kelly, *Scottish Proverbs;* US1871 Jones, *Life of Jefferson S. Batkins. 20c. coll.:* ODEP 198, T&W 373.

anyway *SEE* If you WORRY, you die; if you don't worry, you die anyway.

ape *(n.)* 1. An ape is an ape, a varlet is a varlet, though they be clad in silk and scarlet. *Rec. dist.:* Ill. *1st cit.:* ca1536 Erasmus, *Pilgrim's Pure Devotion. 20c. coll.:* ODEP 16, CODP 5, Stevenson 77:5.

2. An ape is never so like an ape as when he wears a doctor's cape. *Rec. dist.:* N.Y. *1st cit.:* 1732 Fuller, *Gnomologia. 20c. coll.:* Stevenson 78:1. 78:1.

3. The ape clasps her young so long that at last she kills them. *Rec. dist.:* Ill. *1st cit.:* 1670 Ray, *English Proverbs;* US1723 *New England Courant, Writings of Benjamin Franklin. 20c. coll.:* Stevenson 77:4, Whiting 10.

4. The higher the ape goes the more he shows his tail. *Var.:* The higher the monkey goes the more he shows his tail. *Rec. dist.:* Mich., Minn., N.Y. *1st cit.:* ca1594 Bacon, *Promus;* US1738 *Colonial Records of Georgia,* ed. Chandler, in *Original Papers, 1735–1752 (1910–16). 20c. coll.:* ODEP 372, Whiting 294, CODP 111, Stevenson 77:1, Whiting(MP) 420.

ape *(v.)* *SEE* PRIDE often apes humility.

apologizing Apologizing—a very desperate habit—one that is rarely cured. *Rec. dist.:* N.Y. *1st cit.:* US1858 Holmes, *Professor of the Breakfast-Table. 20c. coll.:* Stevenson 78:6.

apology 1. Apologies don't never make nothin' no better. *Var.:* No 'poligy ain't gwine to make ha'r come back whar de b'iling water hit. *Rec. dist.:* N.Y., Wis. *1st cit.:* US1856 Whitcher, *Widow Bedott Papers. 20c. coll.:* T&W 7, Stevenson 78:5.

2. Apologies only account for that which they alter. *Rec. dist.:* Calif.

3. Apology is only egotism wrong side out. *Rec. dist.:* N.Y.

apostate An apostate is like a leper. *Rec. dist.:* Miss.

apparel 1. Apparel makes the man. *Var.:* The apparel often proclaims the man. *Rec. dist.:* U.S., Can. *1st cit.:* ca1500 Wressel, *Proverbs at Leconfield;* US1783 *Writings of George Washington,* ed. Fitzpatrick (1931–44). *20c. coll.:* ODEP 16, Whiting 75, Stevenson 367:3.

2. As costly your apparel as your purse can bear. *Rec. dist.:* Ariz.

appear To appear so does not prove a thing to be really so. *Rec. dist.:* Mich.

SEE ALSO BE what you appear to be. / A CARD which never appears neither wins nor loses. / Talk about the DEVIL and his imps will appear. / What is done in the NIGHT appears in the day.

appearance 1. Appearance passes away; truth abides. *Rec. dist.:* Minn.

2. Appearances are deceiving. *Vars.:* (a) Appearance is deceiving. (b) Appearances are deceptive. (c) We are deceived by fair appearance. *Rec. dist.:* U.S., Can. *1st cit.:* 1666 Torriano, *Select Italian Proverbs;* US1759 *Papers of Benjamin Franklin,* ed. Labaree (1959). *20c. coll.:* CODP 5, Whiting 10, Stevenson 83:3, T&W 7, Whiting(MP) 13.

3. Appearances go a great ways. *Vars.:* (a) Appearances are important. (b) 'Tis a great matter to keep up appearances. *Rec. dist.:* Ill. *1st cit.:* 1763 Churchill, *Night;* US1843 Thompson, *Chronicles of Pineville. 20c. coll.:* Stevenson 83:4, T&W 7.

4. Compliment an old hag on her lovely appearance, and she'll take you at your word. *Rec. dist.:* Ill.

5. Don't trust the weak appearance of the wolf or the disappearance of the cat; they'll both make a comeback. *Rec. dist.:* Ill.

6. Judge not according to appearances. *Vars.:* (a) Don't judge according to appearance, but judge righteous judgment. (b) Don't judge men's wealth or piety by their Sunday appearance. (c) Never judge from appearances. *Rec. dist.:* U.S., Can. *1st cit.:* 1526 Tyndale,

New Testament, John 7:24; US1751 Franklin, *PRAlmanac.* *20c. coll.:* ODEP 415, Stevenson 83:3, Whiting 10, T&W 7, Whiting*(MP)* 14.

7. Merit in appearance is more often rewarded than merit itself. *Rec. dist.:* Ill.

8. Wonderful in appearance are the horns of a cow beyond the seas. *Rec. dist.:* Minn.

appetite **1.** A waiting appetite kindles many a spite. *Rec. dist.:* N.Y., N.C. *1st cit.:* 1875 Cheales, *Proverbial Folk-Lore.* *20c. coll.:* Stevenson 84:8.

2. Always rise from the table with an appetite and you'll never sit down without one. *Rec. dist.:* Ill. *1st cit.:* 1558 Bullein, *The Government of Health;* US1693 Penn, *Some Fruits of Solitude.* *20c. coll.:* Stevenson 84:2.

3. Appetite don't regulate the time of day. *Rec. dist.:* N.Y., N.C.

4. Appetite furnishes the best sauce. *Vars.:* **(a)** A good appetite does not want sauce. **(b)** A good appetite is the best sauce. **(c)** Appetite is the sauce of good eating. *Rec. dist.:* U.S., Can. *1st cit.:* ca1375 Barbour, *Actes and Life of Robert Bruce,* E.E.T.S. (1870–89); US1846 Melville, *Typee* (1923). *20c. coll.:* Stevenson 1201:12, T&W 7.

5. For a good appetite there is no hard bread. *Var.:* To a true appetite there is no hard bread. *Rec. dist.:* Calif., N.C. *1st cit.:* US1948 Stevenson, *Home Book of Proverbs.* *20c. coll.:* Stevenson 84:4.

6. He who cheats his appetite avoids debt. *Rec. dist.:* Miss. *1st cit.:* US1875 Scarborough, *Chinese Proverbs.* *20c. coll.:* Stevenson 83:13.

7. Moderate your appetite so that with a little you may be content. *Rec. dist.:* Mich.

8. New dishes beget new appetites. *Rec. dist.:* Ill. *1st cit.:* 1616 Draxe, *Bibliotheca Scholastica* in *Anglia* (1918). *20c. coll.:* Stevenson 83:12.

9. The appetite comes while eating. *Vars.:* **(a)** The appetite came with eating. The more he had of her, the more he wanted. **(b)** The appetite grows on what it feeds on. *Rec. dist.:* Calif., Ill., Wis. *1st cit.:* ca1594 Bacon, *Promus;* US1867 Richardson, *Beyond the Mississippi, 1857–1867.* *20c. coll.:* ODEP 16, T&W

7, CODP 5, Stevenson 84:19, Whiting*(MP)* 14.

SEE ALSO A small BOY is an appetite with skin drawn over it. / It is easier to feed two HUNGRY people than one with a coming appetite.

applause **1.** Go on deserving applause and you will be sure to meet with it. *Rec. dist.:* N.Y. *1st cit.:* US1787 Jefferson, Letter to J. W. Eppes in *Family Letters of Thomas Jefferson,* ed. Betts and Baer (1966). *20c. coll.:* Stevenson 85:9.

2. Mankind bestows more applause on her destroyer than on her benefactor. *Rec. dist.:* Wis.

3. The applause that pleases the weak mind is but a spur to the strong one. *Var.:* Applause is the spur of noble deeds. *Rec. dist.:* Kans., Miss. *1st cit.:* 1820 Colton, *Lacon.* *20c. coll.:* Stevenson 85:7.

apple **1.** Adam ate the apple, and our teeth still ache. *Rec. dist.:* Wis.

2. An apple a day keeps the doctor away. *Vars.:* **(a)** A green apple a day buys the doctor's coupe. **(b)** An apple a day keeps the doctor away; an onion a day keeps everyone away. **(c)** An apple a day keeps the doctor away, but ladies, if the doctor is out, stay away from the fruit. **(d)** An apple a day keeps the doctor away; more apples than one keeps him on the run. **(e)** An apple a day keeps the fingers sticky. **(f)** An apple a day makes 365 a year. **(g)** An apple a day puts the dentist to flight. **(h)** An apple a day stores the lead away. **(i)** An apple a day the doctor to pay. **(j)** Six green apples a day make the doctor stay. *Rec. dist.:* U.S., Can. *1st cit.:* ca1630 *The Soddered Citizen;* US1913 Wright, *Rustic Speech.* *20c. coll.:* CODP 5, Stevenson 86:1, Whiting*(MP)* 14.

3. An apple never falls far from the tree. *Var.:* An apple doesn't roll far from the tree. *Rec. dist.:* U.S., Can. *1st cit.:* US1839 Emerson, "Letters to Ralph Rusk" in *Letters of Ralph Waldo Emerson,* ed. Rusk (1939). *20c. coll.:* CODP 5, Stevenson 1135:9, T&W 8, Whiting*(MP)* 14.

4. Apples are golden in the morning, silver at noon, and lead at night. *Rec. dist.:* Minn.

5. Eat an apple going to bed, make the doctor beg his bread. *Vars.:* **(a)** Ait a happle avore gwain to bed, un' you'll make the doctor beg his bread. **(b)** Eat an apple going to bed, knock the doctor on the head. **(c)** Eat an apple on going to bed and you'll keep the doctor from earning his bread. **(d)** If you want to be sick or want to be dead, eat an apple and go to bed. *Rec. dist.:* N.Y., S.C. *1st cit.:* ca1630 *The Soddered Citizen. 20c. coll.:* ODEP 17, CODP 5, Stevenson 86:1.

6. Green apples are better than none. *Rec. dist.:* Miss.

7. Handsome apples are sometimes sour. *Rec. dist.:* Ind.

8. If you don't like my apples, don't shake my tree. *Rec. dist.:* N.J.

9. If you eat rotten apples in the barrel, you will continue eating the rotten apples. *Rec. dist.:* Calif.

10. It makes a lot of difference whose apples are getting frozen. *Rec. dist.:* Iowa.

11. Many a rosy apple is rotten to the core. *Var.:* A goodly apple is often rotten at the core. *Rec. dist.:* U.S., Can. *1st cit.:* ca1275 *Proverbs of Alfred. 20c. coll.:* Stevenson 88:3.

12. One bad apple spoils the lot. *Vars.:* **(a)** A rotten apple doesn't make the whole barrel bad. **(b)** It takes only one bad apple to spoil the lot. **(c)** One bad apple can spoil the box. **(d)** One rotten apple can spoil a lot of good ones. **(e)** One rotten apple can spoil a whole barrel full. **(f)** One rotten apple can spoil the whole bunch. **(g)** One rotten apple destroys the barrel. **(h)** One rotten apple in the bushel is enough to spoil the rest. **(i)** One rotten apple will spoil a bushel. **(j)** The rotten apple injures its companion. **(k)** The rotten apple will spoil his companion. **(l)** The rotten apple will spoil his fellow. *Rec. dist.:* U.S., Can. *1st cit.:* 1340 *Ayenbite of Inwit,* E.E.T.S. (1866); US1736 Franklin, *PRAlmanac. 20c. coll.:* ODEP 648, CODP 194, Whiting 11, Whiting(MP) 15.

13. Reach for the high apples first; you can get the low ones any time. *Rec. dist.:* Miss.

14. Save the apples for when you are hungry. *Rec. dist.:* Miss.

15. Shake the barrel and the big apples will come to the top. *Rec. dist.:* Ky., Tenn. *Infm.:* In times of stress those who can do things show their worth.

16. Sour green apples sometimes turn into pretty nice pie. *Rec. dist.:* Minn.

17. The apple of your eye at sixteen is sauce in your eye at twenty. *Rec. dist.:* Ill. *Infm.:* Love becomes disillusion with maturity.

18. The apple of your eye is the core of your trouble. *Rec. dist.:* Kans., Minn.

19. The apples on the other side of the wall are the sweetest. *Var.:* The apple in the other person's yard is sweetest. *Rec. dist.:* Calif., Ill.

20. The best apple is taken by the pig. *Rec. dist.:* Ill., N.J.

21. The fairest apple hangs on the highest bough. *Rec. dist.:* Tex. *1st cit.:* 1678 Ray, *Scottish Proverbs. 20c. coll.:* Stevenson 87:4.

22. The reddest apple may have a worm in it. *Var.:* What's the good of a fair apple if it has a worm in its heart? *Rec. dist.:* Colo., N.Y. *1st cit.:* US1935 Davis, *Terror. 20c. coll.:* Whiting(MP) 15.

23. There's a bad apple in every box. *Var.:* You'll find a bad apple in every pile. *Rec. dist.:* Miss., Wash. *Infm.:* Where there's something good, there's something bad. *1st cit.:* US1960 Masterson, *Hammer. 20c. coll.:* Whiting(MP) 15.

24. When the apple gets ripe, it's likely to fall. *Rec. dist.:* N.Y. *Infm.:* In old age one can expect death.

SEE ALSO We are born believing a man bears BELIEFS as a tree bears apples. / There is little CHOICE in a barrel of rotten apples. / To the IMMATURE, all apples are green. / Apple PIE without cheese is like a kiss without a squeeze. / It is a good apple TREE that has the most clubs under it.

application SEE A docile DISPOSITION will with application surmount every difficulty. /

INSPIRATION for writing is mostly the application of the seat of the pants to the seat of the chair.

apply SEE Desperate CURES to desperate ills apply. / What's good for the DEVIL applies to his imp.

appreciate 1. One never appreciates what he has until he has lost it. *Rec. dist.:* Miss.

2. The thing that often occurs is never much appreciated. *Rec. dist.:* N.Y.

SEE ALSO A man never appreciates ASHES until he slips on the ice. / The BEST things are often least appreciated.

appreciation SEE Dark DAYS and storms heighten the appreciation of sunshine.

approve Approve not of him who commends all you say. *Rec. dist.:* N.Y. *1st cit.:* US1735 Franklin, *PRAlmanac.* *20c. coll.:* Stevenson 827:12.

April 1. A cold April and a wet May fill the barn with grain and hay. *Rec. dist.:* N.Y. *1st cit.:* 1659 Howell, *Paroimiografia (Spanish Proverbs).* *20c. coll.:* ODEP 132.

2. April borrows three days of March, and they are ill. *Rec. dist.:* Wis. *1st cit.:* 1670 Ray, *English Proverbs;* US1824 Doddridge, *Notes on Settlement and Indian Wars of Virginia and Pennsylvania, 1763–1783,* eds. Ritenour and Lindsey (1912). *20c. coll.:* ODEP 511, Whiting 11, Stevenson 1525:12.

3. April showers bring May flowers. *Var.:* March winds and April showers always bring May flowers. *Rec. dist.:* U.S., Can. *1st cit.:* ca1430 Lydgate, *Reason and Sensuality;* US1671 Russell in *Colonial American Poetry,* ed. Silverman (1968). *20c. coll.:* ODEP 17, Whiting 11, CODP 6, Stevenson 88:8, Whiting(MP) 16.

4. April wet or April dry always brings a head of rye. *Rec. dist.:* Ind.

5. If you put me in in April, I'll come when I will. Put me in in May and I'll come right away. *Rec. dist.:* N.Y.

6. No April is so good that it won't snow on a farmer's hat. *Rec. dist.:* Ohio.

7. Oh, the lovely fickleness of an April day. *Rec. dist.:* Wis. *Infm.:* You can't tell what kind of weather you are going to have in April. *1st cit.:* 1594 Shakespeare, *Two Gentlemen of Verona.* *20c. coll.:* Stevenson 89:3.

8. Sharp April kills the pig. *Rec. dist.:* Calif.

9. Till April is dead, change not a thread. *Rec. dist.:* Calif., Wis. *1st cit.:* 1869 Inwards, *Weather Lore.* *20c. coll.:* Stevenson 1103:2. 1103:2.

10. Wet April brings milk to the cows and sheep. *Rec. dist.:* Miss. *Infm.:* Cf. "A cold April and a wet May.. ."

11. When April blows his horn, it's good for hay and corn. *Rec. dist.:* Wis. *Infm.:* This is not always true. *1st cit.:* 1670 Ray, *English Proverbs.* *20c. coll.:* Stevenson 89:2.

apron A wet apron means a drunken husband. *Rec. dist.:* N.J. *Infm.:* The wife has to wash clothes to earn the living for the family.

SEE ALSO Only the witless one expects the BLACKSMITH to wear a white silk apron. / When a CHILD is little, it pulls at your apron strings. When it gets older, it pulls at your heart strings.

arch A triumphal arch should be built out of bricks so that the people will have something convenient to throw at the hero after he passes through. *Rec. dist.:* N.Y. *Infm.:* Attributed to humorist Finley Peter Dunne, creator of the "Mr. Dooley" character in the 1920s.

archer The archer that shoots badly has a lie already. *Rec. dist.:* Miss.

architect 1. All are architects of fate working in these walls of time. *Rec. dist.:* Minn.

2. Every man is the architect of his own fortune. *Rec. dist.:* Calif., Minn., Wis. *1st cit.:* 1533 Udall, *Flowers for Latine Speakyng.* *20c. coll.:* ODEP 230, CODP 68, Stevenson 870:2.

are 1. If you aren't what you ain't, then you ain't what you are. *Rec. dist.:* Fla., Iowa.

2. It is worth a financial loss to find out what some people are. *Rec. dist.:* N.C.

3. Not what you are but what you should be. *Rec. dist.:* Ohio.

4. Things are as they are and not what they ought to be. *Rec. dist.:* Ohio.

5. We are what we are by eternal law. *Rec. dist.:* N.C.

6. What you are—what you are lies with you. *Var.:* What you are now, you are becoming. *Rec. dist.:* N.C., Wash.

SEE ALSO Show me your FRIENDS, and I'll tell you what you are.

argue **1.** Never argue with a man who talks loud; you couldn't convince him of anything. *Rec. dist.:* Ky., Tenn.

2. The man who loves to argue is left without friends. *Rec. dist.:* Ill.

3. What you argue you will soon believe, even if you don't believe it. *Rec. dist.:* N.C.

4. When you argue with a fool, make sure he isn't similarly engaged. *Rec. dist.:* Ill., Kans., N.J., Wis.

argument **1.** Every argument has its answer. *Rec. dist.:* Miss., N.C.

2. In argument men need light, not heat. *Rec. dist.:* Minn.

3. It is a rare thing to win an argument and the other fellow's respect. *Rec. dist.:* Oreg.

4. It is easy as pie to get into an argument and hard as hell to get out. *Rec. dist.:* Ill.

5. It is impossible to defeat an ignorant man in an argument. *Rec. dist.:* N.Y.

6. It takes two to start an argument. *Var.:* It takes two to make an argument. *Rec. dist.:* Miss., Wis. *1st cit.:* 1706 Stevens, *Spanish and English Dictionary;* US1750 *New Weekly Post Boy* in *Newspaper Extracts.* *20c. coll.:* ODEP 852, Whiting 459, Stevenson 91:10, T&W 389, Whiting(MP) 653.

7. No argument will convince a woman or a stubborn ass. *Var.:* Arguing rarely ever convinces anyone. *Rec. dist.:* Ill., N.C.

8. Some people think that the louder they shout the more persuasive their argument is. *Rec. dist.:* N.C.

9. The best way to win an argument is to avoid it. *Rec. dist.:* Ind.

10. The easiest way to lose ground in an argument is to throw mud. *Rec. dist.:* Iowa.

11. The friction of argument produces more heat than light. *Rec. dist.:* Miss. *1st cit.:* 1860 Eliot, *Mill on the Floss.* *20c. coll.:* Stevenson 92:6.

12. The more arguments you win, the less friends you will have. *Rec. dist.:* Ill.

13. The only thing a heated argument ever produced is coolness. *Vars.:* **(a)** Heated arguments cause much coolness. **(b)** Heated arguments do not warm the fireside. *Rec. dist.:* Colo., N.C.

14. The weaker the argument, the stronger the words. *Var.:* Soft words and hard argument. *Rec. dist.:* Wash.

15. There are always two sides to every argument—his and the wrong side. *Var.:* There are three sides to every argument: your tale, my tale, and the truth. *Rec. dist.:* Ill., N.Y. *1st cit.:* US1942 Michel, *The X-ray Murders.* *20c. coll.:* Stevenson 91:14, Whiting(MP) 564.

16. There is no good arguing with the inevitable; the only argument available with the east wind is to put on your overcoat. *Rec. dist.:* N.Y. *1st cit.:* US1887 Lowell, "Democracy" in *Democracy and Other Addresses.* *20c. coll.:* Stevenson 91:13.

17. When the argument flares up, the wise man quenches it by silence. *Rec. dist.:* Ill.

SEE ALSO Where there is no CONTRADICTION, there is no argument. / A single FACT is worth a shipload of argument. / FORCE is no argument. / The HEART has arguments with which the understanding is unacquainted. / NECESSITY is the argument of tyrants and the creed of slaves. / A WAGER is a fool's argument. / A gentle WORD will make the argument stand.

aristocracy Even the workhouses have their aristocracy. *Rec. dist.:* N.C.

arm **1.** An arm and money require good hands. *Rec. dist.:* Wis. *Infm.:* An arm is not much good without a hand on the end of it. Money is not much good without good hands to handle it.

2. Don't stretch out your arm farther than the sleeve will reach. *Var.:* Stretch your arm no farther than your sleeve will reach. *Rec. dist.:* Miss., Ohio. *1st cit.:* 1541 Bullinger,

Christian State of Matrimony, tr. Coverdale. *20c. coll.: ODEP* 780, *CODP* 215, Stevenson 93:8.

3. Keep your broken arm in your sleeve. *Rec. dist.:* Wis. *Infm.:* Don't show people how badly you have been hurt.

4. The paleface's arm is no longer than his word. *Rec. dist.:* N.J.

5. To hoist one's arm is, of course, painful. *Rec. dist.:* N.Y.

SEE ALSO A good CAUSE makes a stout heart and a strong arm. / The best place to find a helping HAND is at the end of your arm. / KINGS have long arms. / PROVIDENCE requires three things of us before it will help us—a stout heart, a strong arm, and a stiff upper lip.

armful An armful of weeds is worth an ear of corn. *Rec. dist.:* Ill.

armor The best armor is to keep out of gunshot. *Rec. dist.:* Miss.

arms 1. Arms without laws produce slavery. *Rec. dist.:* Mich.

2. Arms, women, and locks should be looked at daily. *Rec. dist.:* Wis.

3. Good arms are half the battle. *Rec. dist.:* Ill.

army 1. A headless army fights badly. *Rec. dist.:* N.Y.

2. A singing army and a singing people can't be defeated. *Rec. dist.:* Ind.

3. An army travels on its stomach. *Vars.:* **(a)** An army goes on its belly. **(b)** An army marches on its stomach. *Rec. dist.:* U.S., Can. *Infm.:* An army must be fed to keep on fighting. *1st cit.:* 1904 *Windsor Mag. 20c. coll.: ODEP* 18, *CODP* 6, Whiting*(MP)* 17.

4. It's an ill army when the devil carries the colors. *Rec. dist.:* Oreg.

5. The army knows how to gain a victory but not how to make proper use of it. *Rec. dist.:* N.C.

6. The army of the unemployed prefer alms to arms, hard-earned bread to bullets. *Rec. dist.:* Ill.

7. Your soul may belong to God, but your ass belongs to the army. *Rec. dist.:* N.J. *Infm.:* Said to new recruits in the army.

SEE ALSO A great WAR leaves the country with three armies: an army of cripples, an army of mourners, and an army of thieves.

arrest There's no arrest for the wary. *Rec. dist.:* Wis. *Infm.:* If a person watches, he will be safe from arrest.

arrive SEE MISFORTUNE arrives on horseback but departs on foot.

arrogance 1. Arrogance is a kingdom without a crown. *Rec. dist.:* Miss.

2. The weed of arrogance grows on a dunghill. *Var.:* Arrogance is a weed that grows mostly on a dunghill. *Rec. dist.:* Ill., Mich.

arrow 1. Blunt arrows kill nothing but friendship. *Rec. dist.:* Minn.

2. He that will steal an arrow will steal a horse. *Rec. dist.:* Oreg.

3. Watch out for the returning arrow. *Rec. dist.:* Ohio.

SEE ALSO Draw not your BOW before your arrow is fixed. / The TONGUE wounds more than the arrow.

art 1. All arts are brothers; each is a light to others. *Var.:* All arts are one; all branches on one tree, all fingers, as it were, upon one hand. *Rec. dist.:* N.Y. *1st cit.:* 1847 Story, *Contemporary Criticisms. 20c. coll.:* Stevenson 97:6.

2. All the art lies in making the best of a bad market. *Rec. dist.:* Wash.

3. Art and science have no enemies but those who are ignorant. *Rec. dist.:* Mich.

4. Art for art's sake. *Rec. dist.:* Minn., N.Dak. *1st cit.:* 1875 Swinburne, *Essays and Studies. 20c. coll.:* Stevenson 95:15.

5. Art has no enemy but ignorance. *Rec. dist.:* N.Y.

6. Art imitates nature. *Var.:* All art is but an imitation of nature. *Rec. dist.:* Ill., Minn.

7. Art improves nature. *Rec. dist.:* N.Y. *1st cit.:* 1563 Rainoldes, *Foundation of Rhetoric. 20c. coll.: ODEP* 19, Stevenson 98:4.

8. Art is a jealous mistress, and if a man have

a genius for painting, poetry, music, architecture, or philosophy, he will make a bad husband and an ill provider. **Vars.:** **(a)** Art is a jealous mistress. **(b)** Art is an absolute mistress; she will not be coquetted with or slighted. **Rec. dist.:** N.Y. **1st cit.:** US1860 Emerson, "Wealth" in *Conduct of Life*. **20c. coll.:** Stevenson 95:16.

9. Art is long, life is short. **Rec. dist.:** Ill., N.Y. **1st cit.:** ca1380 Chaucer, *Parliament of Foules;* US1713 Wise, *Churches Quarrel Espoused,* ed. Cook, Scholars' Facsimiles and Reprints (1966). **20c. coll.:** *ODEP* 19, Whiting 13, *CODP* 6, Stevenson 97:9, Whiting*(MP)* 20.

10. Art is power. **Rec. dist.:** N.Y. **1st cit.:** US1839 Longfellow, *Hyperion*. **20c. coll.:** Stevenson 95:13.

11. Art is the right hand of nature. **Rec. dist.:** N.Y., N.C.

12. Art may err, but nature cannot miss. **Rec. dist.:** Miss. **1st cit.:** 1699 Dryden, *Cock and the Fox;* US1841 Emerson, *Essays*. **20c. coll.:** Stevenson 98:2.

13. He that sips many arts drinks none. **Rec. dist.:** Miss., N.Y.

14. He who has an art has a place anywhere. **Rec. dist.:** N.Y. **1st cit.:** 1855 Bohn, *Handbook of Proverbs*. **20c. coll.:** Stevenson 2358:4.

15. It's not art but heart that wins. **Rec. dist.:** Minn.

16. It is not strength but art that obtains the prize. **Rec. dist.:** N.Y.

17. Never judge a work of art by its defects. **Rec. dist.:** Miss.

18. New arts destroy the old. **Rec. dist.:** Wis.

19. Reply with art to gravity and with gravity to art. **Rec. dist.:** Ill.

20. The art of life is the art of avoiding pain. **Rec. dist.:** N.Y.

21. The art of writing is the art of applying the seat of the pants to the seat of the chair. **Var.:** Inspiration for writing is mostly the application of the seat of the pants to the seat of the chair. **Rec. dist.:** N.Y.

22. The best art conceals art. **Var.:** Art consists in concealing art. **Rec. dist.:** Ill., Miss., N.Y. **1st cit.:** ca1581 Sidney, *Apology for Poetry*. **20c. coll.:** *ODEP* 19, Stevenson 96:10.

23. The great art of life is to play for much and stake little. **Rec. dist.:** Mich.

24. The greatest art is the art of life. **Var.:** The finest art, the most difficult to learn, is the art of living. **Rec. dist.:** Ill., N.Y.

25. They may not know just what art is, but they know what they want. **Rec. dist.:** N.Y. **1st cit.:** US1940 McGinley, *Go On, You Scintillate*. **20c. coll.:** Stevenson 97:4.

SEE ALSO The DEVIL is master of all the arts. / DIPLOMACY is the art of letting someone else have your way. / FINANCE is the art of using other people's money to acquire some for yourself. / LOVE is the master of all arts. / TACT is the art of making a point without making an enemy.

artist **1.** A great artist can paint a great picture on a small canvas. **Rec. dist.:** N.Y. **1st cit.:** US1896 Warner, *Washington Irving*. **20c. coll.:** Stevenson 99:11.

2. A man may be an artist though he lacks the necessary tools. **Rec. dist.:** Ill.

3. An artist gains fame and fortune—after he is dead. **Rec. dist.:** Ill.

4. Artists are always young. **Rec. dist.:** N.Y. **1st cit.:** 1842 Ossoli, Letter to W. H. Channing. **20c. coll.:** Stevenson 99:7.

5. Every artist was first an amateur. **Rec. dist.:** Ill., N.Y. **1st cit.:** US1875 Emerson, *Progress of Culture*. **20c. coll.:** Stevenson 99:3.

6. The artist lives on fame, but he prefers bread and cheese. **Rec. dist.:** Ill.

7. The artist must be behind in his own art. **Rec. dist.:** Mich.

8. The artist needs no religion beyond his work. **Rec. dist.:** Ill., N.Y.

9. The artist never dies. **Rec. dist.:** Ill. **1st cit.:** US1844 Longfellow, *Nuremburg*. **20c. coll.:** Stevenson 99:5.

10. The good artist is a successful failure. **Rec. dist.:** Ill.

ascend SEE It is easier to DESCEND than ascend.

ashamed *SEE* Who is not ashamed to BEG, soon is not ashamed to steal. / Never DO anything of which you are ashamed. / Be always ashamed to catch yourself IDLE.

ashes 1. A man never appreciates ashes until he slips on the ice. *Rec. dist.:* Miss.

2. Ashes tell no tales. *Var.:* Dead men and ashes tell no tales. *Rec. dist.:* Utah, Wash.

3. Ashes to ashes and dust to dust. *Vars.:* (a) Ashes to ashes and dust to dust, show me a woman that a poor man can trust. (b) Ashes to ashes, dust to dust, if algebra doesn't get you, geometry must. (c) Ashes to ashes, dust to dust, if heaven doesn't get you the other place must. (d) Ashes to ashes, dust to dust, if the Lord doesn't get you, the devil must. (e) Ashes to ashes, dust to dust, never seen a woman a man can trust. *Rec. dist.:* U.S., Can.

ask 1. Ask, and it shall be given you; seek, and you shall find; knock, and it shall be opened unto you. *Vars.:* (a) Ask and have. (b) Ask and learn. (c) Ask and you'll find out. (d) By asking one learns. (e) Them as asks, gits; them as don't ask, don't git. *Rec. dist.:* U.S., Can. *1st cit.:* ca1475 *Mankind;* US1755 Franklin, *PRAlmanac.* *20c. coll.:* ODEP 20, Whiting 13, CODP 199, Stevenson 100:5.

2. Ask me no questions and I'll tell you no lies. *Var.:* Ask me no questions and I'll tell you no fibs. *Rec. dist.:* U.S., Can. *1st cit.:* 1773 Goldsmith, *She Stoops to Conquer;* US1775 *Correspondence Between John Adams and Mercy Warren,* Mass.Hist.Soc. *Collections* (1878). *20c. coll.:* ODEP 20, Whiting 353, CODP 7, T&W 300, Whiting(MP) 519.

3. Ask much to get little. *Rec. dist.:* Miss. *1st cit.:* 1539 Taverner, *Proverbs of Erasmus.* *20c. coll.:* ODEP 20, Stevenson 100:1.

4. Don't ask a blind man the way to the city. *Rec. dist.:* Ill.

5. It costs nothing to ask. *Vars.:* (a) Asking costs little. (b) Asking costs nothing. (c) Asking is free and so is refusing. (d) Lose nothing for asking. (e) There is no harm in asking. (f) You lose nothing by asking, and there is a chance to gain something lasting. *Rec. dist.:* U.S., Can. *1st cit.:* 1586 Guazzo, *Civile Conversation,* tr. Pettie, T.T. (1925). *20c. coll.:* ODEP 485, Stevenson 99:13.

6. It is better to ask twice than to go wrong once. *Var.:* Better ask twice than lose yourself once. *Rec. dist.:* Miss., N.J.

   SEE ALSO He asks ADVICE in vain who will not follow it. / He is the greatest FOOL who asks for what he can't have.

asleep All are not asleep who have their eyes shut. *Var.:* Every shut eye ain't asleep. *Rec. dist.:* N.Y.

aspiration The loftier your aspirations, the greater the possible disaster. *Rec. dist.:* N.C.

ass *(animal)* 1. All asses do not go on four feet. *Rec. dist.:* Wis. *1st cit.:* 1869 Henderson, *Latin Proverbs.* *20c. coll.:* Stevenson 104:4.

2. An ass covered with gold is more respected than an ass covered with a pack saddle. *Rec. dist.:* Ill., N.Y. *1st cit.:* 1732 Fuller, *Gnomologia.* *20c. coll.:* Stevenson 104:1.

3. An ass is an ass, though laden with gold. *Rec. dist.:* Oreg.

4. An ass is none the wiser by calling him "doctor." *Rec. dist.:* Minn.

5. An ass thinks himself a scholar because he is loaded with books. *Var.:* The ass is not learned though he may be loaded with books. *Rec. dist.:* Ill., Miss.

6. An ass to an ass is beautiful. *Rec. dist.:* Ill.

7. Better ride an ass that carries me than a horse that throws me. *Rec. dist.:* N.J., N.Y. *1st cit.:* 1640 Herbert, *Outlandish Proverbs (Jacula Prudentum)* in *Works,* ed. Hutchinson (1941). *20c. coll.:* Stevenson 104:5.

8. Even an ass will not fall twice in the same quick sand. *Rec. dist.:* Wis.

9. Even if the ass is laden with gold, he will seek his food among the thorns. *Rec. dist.:* N.Y., Oreg. *1st cit.:* 1581 Whitney, *Choice of Emblems;* US1911 Goldman, *Proverbs of Sages.* *20c. coll.:* ODEP 22, Stevenson 104:11.

10. Every ass loves to hear himself bray. *Var.:* Even an ass loves to hear himself bray. *Rec. dist.:* Ill., Wis. *1st cit.:* 1732 Fuller, *Gnomologia.* *20c. coll.:* Stevenson 106:7.

11. Every ass thinks himself worthy to stand

with the king's horses. *Rec. dist.:* Mich. *1st cit.:* 1639 Clarke, *Paroemiologia.* *20c. coll.:* Stevenson 102:12.

12. He that makes himself an ass must not complain if men ride him. *Vars.:* **(a)** If you make yourself an ass, don't complain if people ride you. **(b)** Make yourself an ass and everyone will lay a sack on you. *Rec. dist.:* Ala., Ga., Ill., Miss., N.Y. *1st cit.:* 1732 Fuller, *Gnomologia;* US1869 Spurgeon, *John Ploughman's Talks.* *20c. coll.:* Stevenson 104:2.

13. He who scrubs the head of an ass wastes his soap. *Rec. dist.:* Ariz. *1st cit.:* 1578 Florio, *First Fruites.* *20c. coll.:* ODEP 868, Stevenson 103:4.

14. If an ass goes traveling, he'll not come back a horse. *Rec. dist.:* Ill. *1st cit.:* 1732 Fuller, *Gnomologia.* *20c. coll.:* ODEP 21, Stevenson 2363:4.

15. Jest with an ass and he will slap you in the face with his tail. *Rec. dist.:* Mich. *1st cit.:* 1855 Bohn, *Handbook of Proverbs.* *20c. coll.:* Stevenson 102:5.

16. Never kick an ass and turn your back. *Rec. dist.:* R.I.

17. Nobody can lead an ass from water. *Rec. dist.:* Minn.

18. The ass carries the hay and eats it too. *Rec. dist.:* N.Y.

19. The ass knows in whose face he brays. *Rec. dist.:* N.Y. *1st cit.:* 1853 Trench, *Lessons In Proverbs;* US1867 Richardson, *Beyond the Mississippi, 1857–1867.* *20c. coll.:* ODEP 21, T&W 10, Stevenson 106:11.

20. There are a great many asses without long ears. *Var.:* One ass calls another long ears. *Rec. dist.:* N.Y. *1st cit.:* ca1540 Bale, *Kynge Johan,* Mal.Soc. *20c. coll.:* ODEP 21, Stevenson 1840:11.

21. There is no ass but brays. *Rec. dist.:* N.C. *1st cit.:* US1745 *Papers of Sir William Johnson,* ed. Sullivan (1921–65). *20c. coll.:* Whiting 14.

22. When all men say you are an ass, it is high time to bray. *Rec. dist.:* Ill., Mich. *1st cit.:* 1616 Draxe, *Bibliotheca Scholastica* in *Anglia* (1918). *20c. coll.:* ODEP 10.

23. When one names the ass, he comes running. *Rec. dist.:* N.Dak.

SEE ALSO The OX knows his owner, and the ass his master's crib. / SAILORS get their money like horses but spend it like asses. / A mere SCHOLAR, a mere ass. / A good SERVANT should have the back of an ass, the tongue of a sheep, and the snout of a swine.

ass *(buttocks)* Why are there more horses' asses than there are horses? *Var.:* Why is it there are more horses' asses than there are horses? *Rec. dist.:* N.Y., Wis.

SEE ALSO If FROGS had wings, they wouldn't bump their asses on rocks.

assembly A learned assembly is a living library. *Rec. dist.:* Ill.

assent Never assent merely to please. *Rec. dist.:* Mich.

assert SEE LAW is whatever is boldly asserted and plausibly maintained.

assertion Mere assertion is no proof. *Rec. dist.:* Ill.

asset SEE COURTESY is a business asset—a gain and never a loss.

assiduity Assiduity produces glory and fame. *Rec. dist.:* Mich.

assistance **1.** Give assistance, not advice, in a crisis. *Rec. dist.:* Ark.

2. Mutual assistance in despair will make the ugly world more fair. *Rec. dist.:* Ill.

asthma **1.** Never confuse asthma with passion. *Rec. dist.:* Ind.

2. The only cure for asthma's a casket. *Rec. dist.:* S.C.

astray SEE It is better to turn BACK than to go astray. / The best-laid PLANS of mice and men often go astray.

atheist **1.** A frightened atheist half believes in God. *Rec. dist.:* Ill.

2. An atheist is a man who has no invisible means of support. *Rec. dist.:* Miss.

3. Atheists go one point beyond devils, for they believe and tremble. *Rec. dist.:* Mich. *1st cit.:* 1629 Adams, *Sermons.* *20c. coll.:* ODEP 23, Stevenson 107:8.

4. Better a square-shooting atheist than a false Christian. *Rec. dist.:* Ill.

5. Every village has at least one atheist. *Rec. dist.:* Ill.

6. Fair weather atheists turn to God in a pinch. *Rec. dist.:* Ill.

7. There are no atheists in a fox-hole. *Rec. dist.:* Ariz., N.Y. *1st cit.:* US1944 Cummings, *Sermon* (on Bataan, The Philippines) in *N.Y. Times,* 13 Apr. *20c. coll.:* Stevenson 107:4.

8. Virtue in distress and vice in triumph make atheists of mankind. *Rec. dist.:* Ill.

athlete It does not take an athlete to jump from the frying pan into the fire. *Rec. dist.:* Ohio.

attack A bold attack is half the battle. *Rec. dist.:* Kans.

attempt *(n.)* **1.** A bold attempt is half success. *Rec. dist.:* Ohio.

2. The first attempt is the most difficult. *Rec. dist.:* Miss.

attempt *(v.)* **1.** Attempt not too hastily nor pursue too eagerly. *Rec. dist.:* Mich.

2. Before you attempt consider what you can perform. *Rec. dist.:* Mich.

SEE ALSO He FAILS not who attempts not.

attempting Attempting too little and succeeding is better than trying too much and failing. *Rec. dist.:* N.Dak.

attend *SEE* Attend no AUCTIONS if you have no money.

attention **1.** Attention is the mother of memory. *Var.:* Attention is the stuff memory is made of. *Rec. dist.:* Ind., Minn.

2. Everybody wants a little cheap attention once in a while. *Rec. dist.:* S.C.

3. Too much attention to the pigskin doesn't help the sheepskin. *Rec. dist.:* N.Y.

attitude **1.** An optimistic attitude is half of success. *Rec. dist.:* Ill.

2. Attitudes don't prove nothing. *Rec. dist.:* N.Y. *1st cit.:* US1866 Boucicault, *Flying Scud* in *Forbidden Fruit and Other Plays,* eds. Nicoll and Cloak (1940). *20c. coll.:* T&W 10.

3. Our attitude toward the world today will determine our attitude toward the world tomorrow. *Rec. dist.:* N.C.

4. The mental attitude often depends upon the gastronomic aptitude. *Rec. dist.:* Minn.

SEE ALSO Your whole DESTINY is involved in the attitude you take toward your sin.

attract She most attracts who longest can refuse. *Rec. dist.:* Ala.

SEE ALSO LITTLE things attract light minds. / OPPOSITES attract each other.

auction **1.** At an auction keep your mouth shut. *Rec. dist.:* Ill., Wis.

2. Attend no auctions if you have no money. *Rec. dist.:* Miss.

audience Many people call a doctor when they want an audience. *Rec. dist.:* S.Dak.

author **1.** Choose an author as you choose a friend. *Rec. dist.:* Wis. *Infm.:* Found in Lawson, *World's Best Proverbs* (1926).

2. Like author, like book. *Rec. dist.:* Ill. *1st cit.:* 1611 Cotgrave, *Dictionary of French and English Tongues.* *20c. coll.:* ODEP 23.

authority **1.** Authority can serve no good purpose unless it is rightly exercised. *Rec. dist.:* Ohio.

2. Authority without wisdom is like a heavy axe without an edge: fitter to bruise than to polish. *Rec. dist.:* N.Y. *1st cit.:* USca1670 Bradstreet, *Meditations Divine and Moral.* *20c. coll.:* Stevenson 108:5.

automobile *SEE* HUSBANDS are like automobiles: if you take care of them you don't have to be getting new ones all the time.

avarice **1.** Avarice and happiness never saw each other. How, then, should they become acquainted? *Rec. dist.:* N.Y. *1st cit.:* US1734 Franklin, *PRAlmanac.* *20c. coll.:* Stevenson 109:11.

2. Avarice generally miscalculates and as generally deceives. *Rec. dist.:* Mich.

3. Avarice is never satisfied. *Rec. dist.:* Ill.

4. Avarice is the root of all evil. *Rec. dist.:* Miss. *1st cit.:* US1948 Stevenson, *Home Book of Proverbs.* *20c. coll.:* Stevenson 109:12.

5. Avarice loses all in seeking to gain all. *Rec. dist.:* Ill. *1st cit.:* US1948 Stevenson, *Home Book of Proverbs.* *20c. coll.:* Stevenson 109:13.

6. Avarice overreaches itself. *Rec. dist.:* Ill.

7. The wretch whom avarice bids to pinch and spare, starves, steals, and pilfers to enrich an heir. *Rec. dist.:* Ill.

See also GAMBLING is the son of avarice and the father of despair. / POVERTY wants some things, luxury many things, avarice all things.

avenge Don't avenge every insult—you'll have no time to do anything else. *Rec. dist.:* Ill.

average *See* The INTELLIGENCE of the average individual reaches its lowest ebb when he enters a railroad station.

aversion An aversion to women is like an aversion to life. *Rec. dist.:* Miss.

avoid *See* Avoid ANGER and you will not sin. / Avoid EVIL and it will avoid you.

award A lean award is better than a fat judgment. *Rec. dist.:* Ill. *1st cit.:* US1753 Franklin, *PRAlmanac.* *20c. coll.:* Whiting 14.

away *See* Three may keep COUNSEL if two be away. / What a DAY may bring a day may take away. / The best way to keep a FRIEND is not to give him away.

axe **1.** A dull axe may still cut. *Rec. dist.:* Ill.

2. Don't take the axe out of the carpenter's hand. *Rec. dist.:* Minn.

3. It's a bad axe that hasn't a keen edge. *Rec. dist.:* Ill.

4. Let every fellow grind his own axe. *Rec. dist.:* N.Y.

5. Little axe cuts down big tree. *Rec. dist.:* S.C.

B

B *See* In our alphabet B comes after A. / If you don't C sharp, you'll B flat.

babbling *(n.)* *See* SILENCE is not always a sign of wisdom, but babbling is ever a folly.

babbling *(adj.)* *See* A babbling BROOK makes much noise.

babe 1. A babe in the house is a wellspring of pleasure. *Rec. dist.:* N.Y., N.C., S.C. *1st cit.:* 1840 Tupper, "Of Education." *20c. coll.:* Stevenson 112:2.

2. A babe is a mother's anchor: she cannot swing from her moorings. *Rec. dist.:* Ariz.

3. A babe is an angel whose wings decrease as her legs increase. *Rec. dist.:* Wis.

4. Babes get minks the same way minks get babes. *Rec. dist.:* Kans.

5. From the mouths of babes come words of wisdom. *Var.:* Out of the mouths of babes and sucklings come great truths. *Rec. dist.:* U.S., Can.

baby 1. Babies are one crop that never fails in Kansas. *Rec. dist.:* Kans.

2. Don't throw out the baby with the bathwater. *Rec. dist.:* Fla., Miss., N.Y. *1st cit.:* 1853 Carlyle, *Nigger Question;* US1925 Nevinson, *More Changes. 20c. coll.:* ODEP 220, CODP 225, Stevenson 112:3, Whiting(MP) 24.

3. Every baby born into the world is a finer one than the last. *Rec. dist.:* Ohio.

4. Folks that tend babies mustn't have pins about them. *Rec. dist.:* Ill. *1st cit.:* US1845 Judd, *Margaret. 20c. coll.:* T&W 13.

5. It's the crying baby that gets the milk. *Rec. dist.:* Calif.

6. The baby who always gets carried will never learn to walk. *Rec. dist.:* Ariz.

Bacchus Bacchus has drowned more than Neptune and has killed more than Mars. *Rec. dist.:* N.Y., S.C.

bachelor 1. A bachelor is a man who didn't have a car when he was in college. *Rec. dist.:* Oreg.

2. A bachelor is a man who has never made the same mistake once. *Rec. dist.:* Ill., N.Dak.

3. A bachelor is a souvenir of some woman who has found a better deal at the last minute. *Rec. dist.:* Oreg.

4. A bachelor is to be admired; a spinster is to be pitied. *Rec. dist.:* Oreg.

5. A bachelor oftentimes has more children than the father of many. *Rec. dist.:* Oreg.

6. A lewd bachelor makes a jealous husband. *Rec. dist.:* Calif., Ill. *1st cit.:* 1707 Mapletoft, *Select Proverbs. 20c. coll.:* ODEP 457, Stevenson 112:6.

7. An old bachelor is a poor critter. *Rec. dist.:* N.Y., S.C. *1st cit.:* US1862 Browne, *Artemus Ward: His Book. 20c. coll.:* Stevenson 112:9.

8. An old bachelor is fussy because he has never had a wife to fuss at him. *Rec. dist.:* N.C.

9. An old bachelor is only half of a pair of scissors. *Rec. dist.:* Wis. *1st cit.:* US1781 Partridge in Duane, *Letters to Benjamin Franklin from his Family and Friends* (1859). *20c. coll.:* Whiting 16.

10. Bachelors' wives and maids' children are always well taught. *Rec. dist.:* Mich., Miss. *1st cit.:* 1546 Heywood, *Dialogue of Proverbs,* ed. Habernicht (1963); US1790 *Belknap Papers,* Mass.Hist.Soc. *Collections* (1877). *20c. coll.:* Whiting 16, Stevenson 113:2, T&W 13.

11. Happy bachelors are likely to be happy husbands. *Rec. dist.:* Miss.

12. If you hate storm and strife, lead a bachelor's life. *Rec. dist.:* Ill.

13. Old bachelors and old maids are either too good or too bad. *Rec. dist.:* Wis.

14. Rather keep bachelor's hall in hell than go to board in heaven. *Rec. dist.:* N.Y. *1st cit.:* US1746 *Papers of Sir William Johnson,* ed.

Sullivan (1921–65). **20c. coll.:** Whiting 16, Whiting(MP) 25.

15. The tone of a bachelor's voice sounds good when it has a ring in it. **Rec. dist.:** Minn.

16. There's a funny smell in a bachelor's house. **Rec. dist.:** Ill.

back *(n.)* **1.** Bare is a back without a brother behind it. **Rec. dist.:** Calif., Mich., Miss.

2. God fits the back to the burden. **Vars.: (a)** Eby back is fitted to de bu'den. **(b)** Every back has its pack. **(c)** The back is shaped to the load. **Rec. dist.:** U.S., Can. **1st cit.:** 1822 Cobbett, *Rural Rides;* US1792 Rumsey in *William & Mary Coll. Quart.* (1916). **20c. coll.:** ODEP 312, CODP 94, Whiting 17, Stevenson 981:1, T&W 13.

3. If you must strike a man from behind, slap him on the back. **Rec. dist.:** Colo., Ill.

4. It's a poor back that can't press its own shirt. **Rec. dist.:** Vt.

5. Nothing goes over the devil's back that doesn't come back under the devil's belly. **Vars.: (a)** Nothing goes over the back but that comes out under the belly. **(b)** Nothing goes over the back but that comes under the belly. **(c)** What goes over an eel's back will come under its belly someday. **(d)** What goes over the debbil's back buckles under his belly. **(e)** What goes over the duck's back will come out under his belly. **(f)** What goes under a frog's belly never goes over his back. **(g)** What you win over the devil's back, you reap under his belly. **(h)** Whatever goes over the devil's back comes back under his belly. **Rec. dist.:** U.S., Can. **1st cit.:** 1582 Gosson, *Plays Confuted;* US1940 Rawlings, *Benny and Bird Dogs.* **20c. coll.:** CODP 100, Stevenson 564:6.

6. Some tasks require a strong back and a weak mind. **Vars.: (a)** A strong back and a weak mind. **(b)** Tasks require a strong back and a weak mind. **(c)** The mind is strong, but the back is weak. **Rec. dist.:** Calif., Minn., Miss., N.Y., Oreg.

7. The back of one is the face of another. **Rec. dist.:** Oreg.

8. Turn your back and someone will steal your scone. **Rec. dist.:** Ont., Tex. **Infm.:** A scone is a Scottish biscuit.

9. You scratch my back; I'll scratch yours. **Rec. dist.:** U.S., Can. **1st cit.:** 1605 Montaigne, tr. Florio; US1862 Browne, *Artemus Ward: His Book.* **20c. coll.:** Stevenson 2045:12, T&W 13, Whiting(MP) 25, ODEP 706.

See also Never kick an ASS and turn your back. / To carry CARE into your bed is to sleep with a pack on your back. / Lying rides upon DEBT's back. / A neglected DUTY returns tomorrow with seven others at its back. / He's my FRIEND that speaks well of me behind my back. / A wicked HERO will turn his back to an innocent coward. / LADIES in slacks should not turn their backs. / A PATCH on your coat and money in your pocket is better and more creditable than a writ on your back and no money to take it off. / Better to have a PATCH on your back than a rip on your back. / A STAB in the back is worse than a kick in the face. / If it were not for the STOMACH, the back would wear gold. / The last STRAW will break the camel's back. / Man's TONGUE is soft and bone does lack, yet a stroke therewith may break a man's back.

back *(v.)* *See* Back the WIND and front the sun.

back *(adv.)* **1.** If you look back, you'll soon be going that way. **Rec. dist.:** Ky.

2. It is better to turn back than to go astray. **Rec. dist.:** Ill., N.J.

See also A bad DOLLAR always comes back. / Be slow to take a GIFT: most men give to be paid back. / Bad MONEY always comes back. / The hands of TIME will never turn back.

backbite *See* VANITY backbites more than malice.

backbone It don't take backbone to belly up to a bar. **Rec. dist.:** Oreg.

backslider The way of the backslider is full of splinters. **Rec. dist.:** Miss.

backward *See* To be CONTENT, look backward on those who possess less than yourself, not forward on those who possess more.

backwards No one can walk backwards into the future. **Rec. dist.:** Ind.

backyard **1.** First clean out your own backyard. *Rec. dist.:* Ala., Ga.

2. First determine whether your own backyard is in order. *Rec. dist.:* Oreg. *Infm.:* Cf. "Sweep before your own door..."

3. If you haven't much to do, start cleaning your own backyard. *Rec. dist.:* Vt.

4. Stay in your own backyard. *Rec. dist.:* N.Y.

bacon **1.** If you have no bacon, you must be content with cabbage. *Rec. dist.:* Ill.

2. The flavor of frying bacon beats orange blossoms. *Rec. dist.:* Ind.

SEE ALSO It is better to have BEANS and bacon in peace than cakes and ale in fear.

bad *(n.)* **1.** Bad is called good when worse happens. *Var.:* Bad is never good until worse happens. *Rec. dist.:* N.Dak., N.J.

2. He who looks for bad will find it. *Rec. dist.:* Ind.

3. The bad which is well known is better than the good unknown. *Rec. dist.:* Calif.

4. There is no quarrel between the good and the bad, but only between the bad and the bad. *Rec. dist.:* N.Y.

SEE ALSO Better do little GOOD than a great deal bad.

bad *(adj.)* **1.** A bad deed never dies. *Var.:* A bad thing never dies. *Rec. dist.:* N.Y., S.C.

2. Bad company is the devil's net. *Rec. dist.:* N.Y.

3. Bad men leave their mark wherever they go. *Rec. dist.:* N.Y., S.C.

4. From the day you were born till you ride in a hearse, there's nothing so bad but it might have been worse. *Vars.:* **(a)** Ain't nuthin' so bad but it might be wuss. **(b)** It's never so bad that it can't be worse. **(c)** Nothing so bad but it might have been worse. **(d)** One is never so badly off but that he can find another who is worse. **(e)** There is nothing so bad that it can't be worse. *Rec. dist.:* U.S., Can. *1st cit.:* 1769 Wesley, *Journal,* ed. Curnock (1909, 1938); US1917 Lincoln, *Extricating Obadiah.* *20c. coll.:* ODEP 580, CODP 165, Stevenson 2635:13, Whiting(*MP*) 453.

5. If there were no bad people, there would be no good lawyers. *Rec. dist.:* N.Y., S.C.

6. It ain't half so bad if you can afford it. *Rec. dist.:* Tex.

7. Nothing is ever as bad as you think it is going to be, and nothing is ever as good as you think it is going to be. *Rec. dist.:* Kans., Ont., W.Va.

8. There is no man so bad but he secretly respects the good. *Rec. dist.:* N.Y., S.C. *1st cit.:* 1733 Pope, *Essay on Man;* US1747 Franklin, *PRAlmanac.* *20c. coll.:* Stevenson 1001:9.

9. There is nothing so bad in which there is not something good. *Rec. dist.:* N.Y., S.C. *1st cit.:* 1599 Shakespeare, *Henry V.* *20c. coll.:* ODEP 581, Stevenson 1000:2.

10. Things are never as bad as they seem. *Var.:* It's not as bad as it seems. *Rec. dist.:* Oreg.

11. When things are bad, they get good; and when they are good, they get bad. *Rec. dist.:* Kans.

SEE ALSO Unasked-for ADVICE smells bad. / There's a bad APPLE in every box. / It is a bad BARGAIN when both are losers. / It's a bad BARGAIN that can't run both ways. / It's a bad BARGAIN to sell the bird on the bough. / Make the best of a bad BARGAIN. / Once a bad BOY and always a bad boy. / Bad BOYS make bad men. / A bad BUSH is better than the open field. / BUSYBODIES never want a bad day. / A bad DAUGHTER-IN-LAW is worse than a thousand devils. / A bad DAY never has a good night. / Bad to do EVIL, but worse to boast of it. / Bad HEARING makes bad rehearsing. / A bad HUSBAND cannot be a good man. / It is as bad to believe a LIE as to tell one. / Bad LUCK is bad management. / Bad MONEY drives out good. / A bad PADLOCK invites a picklock. / A bad PENNY always comes back. / A bad REAPER never got a good sickle. / A bad SHIFT is better than none. / A bad YEAR is kinder than the poor man's neighbor.

badly There is no fault in a thing we want badly. *Rec. dist.:* Calif., N.Y.

badman When a badman dies, he either goes to hell or to the Pecos. *Rec. dist.:* N.Mex., Tex.

bag 1. A bag full of flour and a purse full of money are the best relatives in the world. *Rec. dist.:* N.Y.

2. An empty bag cannot stand. *Vars.:* **(a)** It takes a full bag to stand alone. **(b)** It's hard for an empty bag to stand upright. **(c)** You never see an empty bag stand up. *Rec. dist.:* U.S., Can. *1st cit.:* 1642 Torriano, *Select Italian Proverbs;* US1740 Franklin, *PRAlmanac. 20c. coll.:* ODEP 220, CODP 64, Whiting 18, Stevenson 115:10.

bagpipe *SEE* A customary RULER is the devil's bagpipe which the world does run after.

bairn *SEE* Old WIVES and bairns make fools of physicians.

bait *(n.)* 1. A little bait catches a large fish. *Rec. dist.:* Ill.

2. Better shun the bait than struggle on the hook. *Rec. dist.:* Ill.

3. It's the bait that lures, not the fisherman or the reel. *Rec. dist.:* Ill.

4. The bait hides the hook. *Rec. dist.:* U.S., Can. *1st cit.:* 1539 Frontinus, *Stratagems of War,* tr. Morysine; US1906 Bierce, *Devil's Dictionary. 20c. coll.:* ODEP 27, Stevenson 819:9.

5. Without bait you can't catch fish. *Rec. dist.:* Ill. *1st cit.:* 1583 Greene, *Works of Robert Greene. 20c. coll.:* Stevenson 819:9.

SEE ALSO BEAUTY without grace is the hook without the bait. / It is a silly FISH that is caught twice with the same bait. / HOPE and a red rag are bait for men and mackerel.

bait *(v.)* Bait the hook well; the fish will bite. *Rec. dist.:* Ont.

baiter Baiters are not choosers. *Rec. dist.:* Okla. *Infm.:* The proverb "Beggars cannot be choosers" has been altered to conform to another situation of baiting (teasing) others.

bake 1. As they brew, so let them bake. *Rec. dist.:* U.S., Can. *1st cit.:* ca1300 *Cursor Mundi,* E.E.T.S. (1874–92). *20c. coll.:* ODEP 85, CODP 26, Stevenson 240:9.

2. It's easy to bake when the meal is beside you. *Rec. dist.:* N.Y., Ont. *1st cit.:* ca1628 Carmichaell, *Proverbs in Scots,* ed. Anderson (1957). *20c. coll.:* ODEP 28.

SEE ALSO All BREAD is not baked in one oven.

baker Good bakers always make plenty of dough. *Rec. dist.:* Colo., N.Y.

SEE ALSO Never spare the parson's WINE, nor the baker's pudding.

balance The balance doesn't distinguish between gold or lead. *Rec. dist.:* Ill. *1st cit.:* 1640 Herbert, *Outlandish Proverbs (Jacula Prudentum)* in *Works,* ed. Hutchinson (1941). *20c. coll.:* ODEP 28, Stevenson 988:9.

SEE ALSO WORDS and deeds are not weighed in the same balance.

bald After a hundred years we shall all be bald. *Rec. dist.:* Calif.

SEE ALSO A bald HEAD is soon shaven. / A bald HEAD needs a new wig.

bald-headed *SEE* The bald-headed BARBER preaches the miracles of hair tonic.

baldness There is no cure for baldness; the bald-headed barber is the proof. *Rec. dist.:* Calif., N.Y.

balloon The balloon with the most air makes the loudest noise when it bursts. *Rec. dist.:* Ind.

baloney No matter how you slice it, it's still baloney. *Rec. dist.:* U.S., Can. *1st cit.:* US1931 Taylor, *Cape Cod Mystery. 20c. coll.:* Whiting(MP) 29.

banana If you want roasted bananas, you must burn your fingers first. *Rec. dist.:* N.Y.

SEE ALSO MAN is like a banana: when he leaves the bunch, he gets skinned.

bandwagon Don't monkey with the bandwagon if you can't play the horn. *Var.:* Don't monkey with the bandwagon unless you like music. *Rec. dist.:* Calif., N.Y.

bank Banks have no heart. *Rec. dist.:* N.Y., S.C. *1st cit.:* US1853 Boker, *Bankrupt in Glaucus and Other Plays,* ed. Bradley (1940). *20c. coll.:* T&W 16.

SEE ALSO A DOLLAR in the bank is worth two in the hand.

bankbook   A bankbook is the greedy man's Bible. *Rec. dist.:* N.Y.

bankroll   *See* You cannot mate YOUTH with age unless age has a big bankroll.

bankrupt   *See* A BEGGAR can never be bankrupt.

banquet   He that banquets every day never makes a good meal. *Rec. dist.:* N.Y., S.C.

bar   **1.** The man on the sober side of the bar is the one that gets the money. *Rec. dist.:* Oreg.

2. The bars do not make the officer. *Rec. dist.:* Oreg. *Infm.:*"Bars" refers to military insignia.

See also It don't take BACKBONE to belly up to a bar. / When BEAUTY is at the bar, blind men make the best jury.

barber   **1.** A barber learns to shave by shaving fools. *Rec. dist.:* Calif., Ill., N.J., N.Y. *1st cit.:* 1611 Cotgrave, *Dictionary of French and English Tongues.* *20c. coll.:* ODEP 29, Stevenson 2084:15.

2. He is a sorry barber that has but one comb. *Rec. dist.:* Calif., N.J.

3. Some barbers are top-notchers. *Rec. dist.:* Minn. *Infm.:* The double meaning indicates that some are poor barbers leaving "notches on the top of the head" as opposed to some who are first-rate.

4. The bad barber leaves neither hair nor skin. *Rec. dist.:* Ill.

5. The bald-headed barber preaches the miracles of hair tonic. *Rec. dist.:* Ill.

6. The barber shows you the mirror, but it's too late to raise a squawk. *Rec. dist.:* Ill. *Infm.:* "Squawk" means a complaint.

7. The barber's tongue never stops wagging. *Rec. dist.:* Ill.

See also Beware of the young DOCTOR and the old barber. / The TAILORS and barbers go halves with God Almighty.

bare   *See* It's hard to take BREECHES off of bare hips. / Better a bare FOOT than no foot at all. / The GIFT without the giver is bare.

barefooted   **1.** He that waits for a dead man's shoes may long go barefooted. *Var.:* He that waits for dead men's shoes will go long enough barefooted. *Rec. dist.:* Colo., Tex.

2. He who scatters thorns should not go barefooted. *Vars.:* **(a)** Barefooted men should not tread thorns. **(b)** He that sows thorns should never go barefooted. **(c)** He who goes barefooted shouldn't plant briars. *Rec. dist.:* U.S., Can. *1st cit.:* ca1594 Bacon, *Promus;* US1736 Franklin, *PRAlmanac.* *20c. coll.:* ODEP 30, Stevenson 2303:7.

bargain   **1.** A bargain is a bargain. *Rec. dist.:* U.S., Can. *1st cit.:* 1553 Wilson, *Arte of Rhetorique* (1585); US1705 *Diary of Samuel Sewall, 1674–1729,* Mass.Hist.Soc. *Collections* (1878–82). *20c. coll.:* ODEP 30, Whiting 20, Stevenson 121:14, T&W 16, Whiting(MP) 30.

2. A bargain is a pinch-purse. *Var.:* A good bargain is a pick-purse. *Rec. dist.:* Ill. *1st cit.:* 1611 Cotgrave, *Dictionary of French and English Tongues.* *20c. coll.:* ODEP 30, Stevenson 121:1.

3. A bargain is not a bargain unless you can use the product. *Var.:* A bargain isn't a bargain unless it's something you need. *Rec. dist.:* Minn., Tex.

4. A bargain is usually worth no more than you pay for it. *Rec. dist.:* Kans.

5. A bargain usually costs you more in the end. *Rec. dist.:* Fla., N.Dak.

6. Beware of too great a bargain. *Rec. dist.:* N.Y., S.C.

7. If you make a bad bargain, hug it the tighter. *Rec. dist.:* N.Y., S.C.

8. It always takes two to make a bargain. *Vars.:* **(a)** If it takes two to make a bargain, it should take two to break it. **(b)** If it takes two to make a bargain, it takes two to break it. **(c)** It takes two to make a bargain. **(d)** It takes two to make a bargain an' one mo' ter see dat it done all right. **(e)** It takes two to make a bargain, but one usually gets it. **(f)** There are two folks' votes to the unmaking of a bargain, as to the making of one. *Rec. dist.:* U.S., Can. *1st cit.:* 1579 Lyly, *Euphues, Anatomy of Wit* in *Works,* ed. Bond (1902); US1851 Stowe, *Uncle Tom's Cabin* (1910). *20c. coll.:* ODEP 852,

CODP 234, Stevenson 120:15, T&W 16, Whiting*(MP)* 653.

9. It is a bad bargain when both are losers. *Rec. dist.:* U.S., Can. *1st cit.:* 1578 Whetstone, *Promos and Cassandra.* *20c. coll.:* ODEP 397, Stevenson 121:11.

10. It's a bad bargain that can't run both ways. *Rec. dist.:* Ind., Oreg.

11. It's a bad bargain to sell the bird on the bough. *Rec. dist.:* Ind.

12. Make the best of a bad bargain. *Rec. dist.:* Calif., Colo., Mich., N.Y., S.C. *1st cit.:* 1923 Crowley, *Confessions,* ed. Symonds (1969); US1703 *Correspondence Between William Penn and James Logan, 1700–1705,* ed. Armstrong, Hist.Soc. Penn. *Memoirs* (1870, 1872). *20c. coll.:* Whiting 29, Whiting*(MP)* 44.

13. More words than one go to a bargain. *Rec. dist.:* Tex. *1st cit.:* 1580 Munday, *Zelauto.* *20c. coll.:* ODEP 544.

14. Never look an auto bargain under the hood. *Rec. dist.:* Ariz.

15. Never make a bargain with the devil on a dark day. *Rec. dist.:* N.Y.

16. On a good bargain think twice. *Var.:* At a great bargain pause awhile. *Rec. dist.:* U.S., Can. *1st cit.:* 1640 Herbert, *Outlandish Proverbs (Jacula Prudentum)* in *Works,* ed. Hutchinson (1941); US1739 Franklin, *PRAlmanac.* *20c. coll.:* ODEP 317, Stevenson 121:13.

SEE ALSO NECESSITY never made a good bargain.

bargaining Bargaining has neither friends nor relations. *Rec. dist.:* Calif., Colo., N.Y.

bark *(n.)* A dog's bark is worse than his bite. *Vars.:* (a) His bark is louder than his bite. (b) His bark is worse than his bite. (c) His bite isn't as bad as his bark. *Rec. dist.:* U.S., Can. *1st cit.:* 1663 *Lauderdale Papers* (1884); US1841 *Letters of James Fenimore Cooper,* ed. Beard (1960–68). *20c. coll.:* ODEP 30, Whiting 20, Stevenson 613:12, Whiting*(MP)* 31.

bark *(v.)* SEE A barking DOG never bites. / An old DOG does not bark in vain. / Don't be afraid of a DOG that barks. / One DOG barks at nothing; the rest bark at him. / You cannot RUN and bark at the same time. / All are not THIEVES that dogs bark at.

barkers The greatest barkers are not the greatest biters. *Rec. dist.:* Mich., Okla., Tex. *1st cit.:* 1387 Higden, *Polychronicon,* tr. Trevisa. *20c. coll.:* ODEP 30, Stevenson 614:2.

barking A barking dog never bites. *Vars.:* (a) A barking cur never bites. (b) Barking dogs don't bite. (c) Barking dogs seldom bite. *Rec. dist.:* U.S., Can. *1st cit.:* ca1275 *Proverbs of Alfred,* tr. Skeat; US1929 *Alice in the Delighted States.* *20c. coll.:* ODEP 31, Whiting*(MP)* 173, *CODP* 9, Stevenson 614:2.

barn **1.** A barn, a fence, and a woman always need mending. *Rec. dist.:* Vt.

2. A barn is the foundation of a farm. *Rec. dist.:* N.Y., S.C., Va.

3. A big barn: the man is boss. *Rec. dist.:* Ohio.

4. Better a barn filled than a bed. *Rec. dist.:* Minn. *1st cit.:* 1716 Ward, *Female Policy.* *20c. coll.:* Stevenson 123:7.

5. Do not pull down your barns to build greater ones. *Rec. dist.:* Kans., N.Y.

6. Don't shut the barn door after the horse is stolen. *Rec. dist.:* U.S., Can. *1st cit.:* ca1350 *Douce MS 52,* ed. Förster, Erlangen (1906); US1886 Stevenson, *Kidnapped.* *20c. coll.:* ODEP 730, *CODP* 211, Stevenson 2204:8.

7. Round Robin Hood's barn makes a tedious yarn. *Rec. dist.:* Calif., N.Y. *Infm.:* "Round Robin Hood's barn" refers to circumlocution. *1st cit.:* US1779 *Mason Weems: His Works and His Ways,* ed. Skeel (1929). *20c. coll.:* Whiting 365, T&W 308, Whiting*(MP)* 532.

8. The barn is never so full that you can't slap in a bundle at the door. *Rec. dist.:* Ill.

barrel **1.** An empty barrel makes the most noise. *Rec. dist.:* U.S., Can. *Infm.:* Varied from such as "An empty wagon makes the most noise." Cf. vessel. *1st cit.:* ca1430 Lydgate, *Pilgrimage of Man,* E.E.T.S.; US1931 Tully, *Blood on the Moon.* *20c. coll.:* CODP 64, ODEP 220, Stevenson 676:17, Whiting*(MP)* 661.

2. The barrel always smells of the herring. *Rec. dist.:* Ill.

3. The barrel is as strong as its hoops. *Rec. dist.:* Ill., Kans.

4. Thirteen staves and never a hoop will not make a barrel. *Rec. dist.:* Colo., Ga., N.Y.

5. You cannot take more out of a barrel than you put into it. *Rec. dist.:* Ariz.

barren A barren sow was never good to pigs. *Rec. dist.:* Ala., Ga. *1st cit.:* ca1628 Carmichaell, *Proverbs in Scots,* ed. Anderson (1957). *20c. coll.:* ODEP 31, Stevenson 2175:8.

bashful 1. At the table it becomes no one to be bashful. *Rec. dist.:* Wis. *Infm.:* Stevenson cites the only source as Plautus, *Trinummus* (ca194 B.C.E..) *1st cit.:* US1948 Stevenson, *Home Book of Proverbs.* *20c. coll.:* Stevenson 1525:9.

2. It is only the bashful that lose. *Rec. dist.:* N.Y.

bashfulness 1. Bashfulness is a great hindrance to a man. *Rec. dist.:* Mich.

2. Bashfulness is no use to the needy. *Rec. dist.:* N.Y. *Infm.:* The poor cannot afford to be bashful. *1st cit.:* 1539 *Proverbs of Erasmus,* tr. Taverner. *20c. coll.:* ODEP 31, Stevenson 1849:1.

basket 1. A birch-bark basket may be fair to see, but just to make one does not spoil a tree. *Rec. dist.:* Ind.

2. He that makes one basket can make one hundred. *Rec. dist.:* Vt., Wis.
  SEE ALSO Don't put all your EGGS in one basket.

bastard A bastard looks like his father. *Rec. dist.:* Calif., N.Y.

battery A battery that won't produce light will ring a doorbell. *Rec. dist.:* Calif., Colo., N.Y.

battle 1. It is not the trumpeters that fight the battles. *Rec. dist.:* N.Y.

2. The bigger the battle, the bigger the booty. *Rec. dist.:* Md.

3. The harder the battle, the sweeter the victory. *Rec. dist.:* R.I.

4. The real battle of life isn't just winning

your spurs, it's keeping them bright and shining. *Rec. dist.:* Calif., Colo., Tex. *1st cit.:* ca1425 Lydgate, *Assembly of Gods;* US1912 Burroughs, *Princess of Mars.* *20c. coll.:* ODEP 892, Whiting(MP) 589.

bawl A bawl becomes a beller when the tongue is stickin' out. *Rec. dist.:* Colo., Tex.

bawling SEE A bawling COW soon forgets her own calf.

be 1. Be that which you would make others. *Rec. dist.:* Ont. *Infm.:* Varied in form, such as "Be what you would seem to be."

2. Be what you appear to be. *Var.:* Be yourself. *Rec. dist.:* U.S., Can. *1st cit.:* ca1377 Langland, *Piers Plowman,* ed. Skeat, E.E.T.S. (1867); US1744 Franklin, *PRAlmanac.* *20c. coll.:* ODEP 33, Stevenson 2056:7, CODP 10.

3. Sometimes you be, and sometimes you be not. *Rec. dist.:* N.Y., S.C.

4. To be, or not to be. *Rec. dist.:* Ky., N.Dak., Tenn. *Infm.:* Often used to indicate mere indecision rather than suicide. *1st cit.:* 1600 Shakespeare, *Hamlet.* *20c. coll.:* Stevenson 2241:1.

5. We ain't what we want to be, and we ain't what we are gonna be, but we ain't what we waz. *Rec. dist.:* Miss. *Infm.:* From Negro dialect collection of Judge Harris Dickinson, novelist from Vicksburg, Miss.

6. What used to be will be again. *Rec. dist.:* Ill.

7. What will be will be. *Var.:* What is to be will be, and what shouldn't be may happen. *Rec. dist.:* Ill., Miss. *1st cit.:* US1928 Williams, *Crouching.* *20c. coll.:* Whiting(MP) 684.

beak It's better to be the beak of a hen than the tail of an ox. *Rec. dist.:* Miss.

beam Cast the beam out of your own eye before you try to cast the mote from the eyes of your neighbor. *Rec. dist.:* Ky., Tenn. *Infm.:* Cf. Matt. 7:3. *1st cit.:* ca1390 Chaucer, *Reeve's Tale.* *20c. coll.:* ODEP 545, Stevenson 780:2.

bean 1. When the beans get too thick, the pot burns. *Rec. dist.:* N.Mex., Tex.

2. Beans ain't beans without sow belly. *Rec. dist.:* Kans.

3. It is better to have beans and bacon in peace than cakes and ale in fear. *Rec. dist.:* Minn., N.Y.

bear *(n.)* **1.** Time to catch bears is when they're out. *Vars.:* **(a)** The time to shoot bears is when they are around. **(b)** You must first catch the bear before you can draw a ring through his nose and make him dance. *Rec. dist.:* Kans., Vt.

2. When wrestlin' a bear, never grab for his tail. *Rec. dist.:* Minn.

bear *(v.)* **1.** Every man must bear his own burden. *Rec. dist.:* N.Y.

2. We must bear and forbear. *Var.:* You must take two bears to live with you—bear and forbear. *Rec. dist.:* Minn., N.Y., S.C. *1st cit.:* 1573 Tusser, *Husbandry;* US1637 *New English Canaan of Thomas Morton,* ed. Adams, Jr., Publ. Prince Soc. (1883). *20c. coll.:* Whiting 312, *CODP* 10, *ODEP* 34, Stevenson 863:11, T&W 20.

beard **1.** He who has a beard buys himself a comb. *Rec. dist.:* Ill.

2. If the beard were all, the goat might preach. *Vars.:* **(a)** If a beard were a sign of smartness, the goat would be Socrates. **(b)** The beard does not make the doctor or philosopher. *Rec. dist.:* Ill., Wis. *1st cit.:* 1662 Fuller, *History of the Worthies of England. 20c. coll.:* Stevenson 131:7.

beast **1.** A willful beast must have his own way. *Rec. dist.:* Ohio.

2. Every beast but man keeps to a single dish. *Rec. dist.:* Ill.

3. The wild beast becomes timid and tame when he makes love to his mate. *Rec. dist.:* Ill.

4. There is no beast so savage that it sports with its mate. *Rec. dist.:* Calif.

beat **1.** If you can't beat them, join them. *Var.:* If you can't lick 'em, join 'em. *Rec. dist.:* Colo., Kans., Mich. *1st cit.:* 1979 Lessing, *Shikasta;* US1941 Reynolds, *Wounded Don't Cry. 20c. coll.:* *CODP* 10.

2. You can't beat somebody with nobody. *Rec. dist.:* N.Y., S.C.

beaten The beaten road is the safest. *Rec. dist.:* Tex.

beau **1.** A dirty bread tray keeps beaus away. *Rec. dist.:* Ill.

2. No beaus go where the cobwebs grow. *Var.:* Where the sunflowers grow, the beaus never go. *Rec. dist.:* U.S., Can.

beautiful **1.** Everything that is striking and beautiful is not good, but everything that is honest and good is beautiful. *Rec. dist.:* N.C.

2. It hurts to be beautiful. *Rec. dist.:* Wis.

3. Nothing is beautiful from every point of view. *Rec. dist.:* Oreg.

beauty **1.** Beauty and folly are old companions. *Rec. dist.:* N.Y., S.C. *1st cit.:* US1734 Franklin, *PRAlmanac. 20c. coll.:* Whiting 23, Stevenson 136:10.

2. Beauty comes from the soul. *Rec. dist.:* Wis.

3. Beauty comes from within. *Rec. dist.:* Vt.

4. Beauty doesn't make the pot boil. *Vars.:* **(a)** Beauty is a fine thing, but you can't live on it. **(b)** Beauty never boiled a pot. **(c)** Beauty won't buy groceries. **(d)** One can't live on beauty alone. *Rec. dist.:* Ky., Nebr., N.Y., Tenn. *1st cit.:* US1860 Haliburton, *Season-Ticket. 20c. coll.:* T&W 21.

5. Beauty draws more than oxen. *Var.:* Beauty draws smoke. *Rec. dist.:* Ark. *1st cit.:* 1591 Florio, *Second Fruites;* US1860 Longfellow, *Saga of King Olaf. 20c. coll.:* *ODEP* 37, Stevenson 138:8, Whiting(MP) 36.

6. Beauty has no brains. *Var.:* Beauty and brains don't mix. *Rec. dist.:* Calif., Oreg.

7. Beauty is a fading flower. *Rec. dist.:* Calif., Colo., Wis. *1st cit.:* 1563 Rainoldes, *Foundation of Rhetoric;* US1740 Franklin, *PRAlmanac. 20c. coll.:* *ODEP* 37, Stevenson 140:9.

8. Beauty is a good client. *Rec. dist.:* N.Dak.

9. Beauty is a good letter of introduction. *Rec. dist.:* Ind.

10. Beauty is as beauty does. *Rec. dist.:* U.S., Can. *1st cit.:* 1580 Munday, *Sunday Examples;*

US1741 Franklin, *PRAlmanac*. *20c. coll.*: *ODEP* 348, Stevenson 138:3, *CODP* 106.

11. Beauty is its own excuse for being. *Rec. dist.*: N.Y., S.C. *1st cit.*: US1846 Emerson, *Rhodora*. *20c. coll.*: Stevenson 133:11.

12. Beauty is its own reward. *Rec. dist.*: Iowa.

13. Beauty is loved without knowing anything; ugliness hated without being to blame. *Rec. dist.*: Miss.

14. Beauty is no inheritance. *Rec. dist.*: Tex. *1st cit.*: 1616 Draxe, *Bibliotheca Scholastica* in *Anglia* (1918). *20c. coll.*: *ODEP* 38, Stevenson 136:2.

15. Beauty is no longer amiable than while virtue adorns it. *Rec. dist.*: N.Y., S.C.

16. Beauty is one of God's gifts. *Rec. dist.*: Calif. *1st cit.*: 1578 Florio, *Firste Fruites*. *20c. coll.*: Stevenson 133:8.

17. Beauty is only skin-deep. *Vars.*: **(a)** Beauty is but skin-deep; common sense is thicker than water. **(b)** Beauty is only skin-deep; goodness goes to the bone. **(c)** Beauty is only skin-deep; ugly is to the bone. Beauty lasts only a day; ugly holds its own. **(d)** Beauty is skin-deep; it is the size of the heart that counts. **(e)** Beauty's only skin-deep, but ugly goes to the bone. *Rec. dist.*: U.S., Can. *1st cit.*: 1616 Davies of Hereford, *Select Second Husband;* US1710 Dummer in *William & Mary Coll. Quart.* (1967). *20c. coll.*: *ODEP* 38, Whiting 23, *CODP* 11, Stevenson 140:4.

18. Beauty is power: a smile is its sword. *Rec. dist.*: Oreg.

19. Beauty is the bloom of youth. *Rec. dist.*: N.Y., S.C.

20. Beauty is the flower of life, but virtue is the fruit. *Rec. dist.*: Mich.

21. Beauty is the mark God set upon virtue. *Rec. dist.*: Calif., Colo., N.Y. *1st cit.*: US1849 Emerson, "Beauty" in *Nature Addresses and Lectures*. *20c. coll.*: Stevenson 139:7.

22. Beauty is truth, truth beauty. *Var.*: Beauty is not always truth, nor truth beauty. *Rec. dist.*: U.S., Can. *1st cit.*: 1819 Keats, "Ode on a Grecian Urn." *20c. coll.*: Stevenson 134:2.

23. Beauty is vain. *Rec. dist.*: Calif.

24. Beauty is worse than wine: it intoxicates both the holder and the beholder. *Rec. dist.*: Ill.

25. Beauty is yet the pleasing trickery that cheats half the world. *Rec. dist.*: N.Y., S.C.

26. Beauty, like supreme dominion, is but supported by opinion. *Rec. dist.*: N.Y., S.C.

27. Beauty, like truth, is never so glorious as when it goes plainest. *Rec. dist.*: Oreg.

28. Beauty opens locked doors. *Rec. dist.*: Ind.

29. Beauty provokes thieves sooner than gold. *Rec. dist.*: Minn. *1st cit.*: 1599 Shakespeare, *As You Like It. 20c. coll.*: Stevenson 138:2.

30. Beauty seen is never lost. *Rec. dist.*: N.Y., S.C.

31. Beauty soon fades, but virtue lives forever. *Rec. dist.*: Wis.

32. Beauty vanishes; virtue endures. *Rec. dist.*: Calif.

33. Beauty walks while angels sleep. *Rec. dist.*: Ky., Tenn.

34. Beauty without grace is the hook without the bait. *Rec. dist.*: N.Y.

35. Beauty without honesty is like poison kept in a box of gold. *Rec. dist.*: Mich.

36. Beauty without virtue is a rose without fragrance. *Rec. dist.*: Ill., Ind., Wis. *1st cit.*: 1732 Fuller, *Gnomologia. 20c. coll.*: Stevenson 136:4.

37. Beauty's tears are only skin-deep. *Rec. dist.*: Calif., Oreg.

38. She who is a beauty is half married. *Var.*: She who is born beautiful is half married. *Rec. dist.*: Ill., N.Y., Vt. *1st cit.*: 1732 Fuller, *Gnomologia. 20c. coll.*: Stevenson 134:8.

39. Smoke follows beauty. *Var.*: Fire follows beauty. *Rec. dist.*: Ark., Ind., Kans.

40. The only lasting beauty is the worthwhile sparkle that glows through. *Rec. dist.*: Kans.

41. There was never a beauty without aid. *Rec. dist.*: N.Y., Oreg.

42. There's no beauty like the beauty of the soul. *Rec. dist.*: N.C.

43. To see beauty you must have beauty in your soul. *Rec. dist.:* Okla.

44. When beauty is at the bar, blind men make the best jury. *Rec. dist.:* Wis.

45. Where beauty is, there will be love. *Rec. dist.:* N.J.

46. Where there is great beauty, there is great wickedness. *Rec. dist.:* Ariz.

SEE ALSO FAVOR is deceitful, and beauty is vain.

beaver From beavers, bees should learn to mend their ways. A bee works; a beaver works and plays. *Rec. dist.:* N.Y.

bed **1.** A bed of stones with friends is better than a bed of down with those we do not love. *Rec. dist.:* N.Y.

2. As one makes his bed, so must he lie. *Vars.:* (a) After making your bed you must lie in it. (b) If you make your bed hard, you can turn over ofener. (c) Lie in your bed the way you made it. (d) You made your bed; now lie in it. *Rec. dist.:* U.S., Can. *1st cit.:* ca1590 Harvey, *Marginalia;* US1908 Lincoln, *Cy Whittaker's Place.* *20c. coll.:* ODEP 502, Whiting*(MP)* 37, CODP 143, Stevenson 142:5.

3. Early to bed and early to rise makes a man healthy, wealthy, and wise. *Rec. dist.:* U.S., Can. *1st cit.:* 1496 *Treatise on Fishing with an Angle;* USca1700 Saffin, *His Book,* ed. Hazard (1928). *20c. coll.:* ODEP 211, Whiting 24, CODP 62, Stevenson 1995:7, T&W 21, Whiting*(MP)* 37.

4. He that goes to bed thirsty, rises healthy. *Rec. dist.:* N.J.

5. Never go to bed with a misunderstanding. *Rec. dist.:* Ind.

6. No one gets out of bed to sleep on the floor. *Rec. dist.:* N.J.

7. Rather go to bed supperless than run in debt for a breakfast. *Rec. dist.:* Ill.

8. Too much bed makes a dull head. *Rec. dist.:* Ky., Tenn.

SEE ALSO She who wishes to keep ahead of her NEIGHBOR must go to bed at sundown and get up at dawn.

bedfellow SEE MISFORTUNES cause queer bedfellows. / POLITICS makes strange bedfellows. / WEALTH and content are not always bedfellows.

bee **1.** A bee was never caught in a shower. *Rec. dist.:* N.Y., S.C. *1st cit.:* 1893 Inwards, *Weather Lore.* *20c. coll.:* Stevenson 145:6.

2. From the same flower the bee extracts honey and the wasp gall. *Rec. dist.:* Ill.

3. Hit takes a bee fer ter git de sweetness out'n de hoar-houn blossom. *Rec. dist.:* N.Y., S.C. *Infm.:* The dialect form comes from Joel Chandler Harris. *1st cit.:* US1880 Harris, *Plantation Proverbs* in *Uncle Remus, His Songs and His Sayings.* *20c. coll.:* Stevenson 145:3.

4. If a bee didn't have a sting, he couldn't keep his honey. *Rec. dist.:* Ill., N.J. *1st cit.:* 1580 Lyly, *Euphues and His England,* ed. Arber (1868). *20c. coll.:* Stevenson 145:10.

5. If a bee stings you once, it's the bee's fault; if a bee stings you twice, it's your own damn fault. *Rec. dist.:* Kans.

6. If you let the bee be, the bee will let you be. *Rec. dist.:* Vt.

7. It's the roving bee that gathers honey. *Rec. dist.:* Ind.

8. Mighty po' bee dat don't make mo' honey dan he want. *Rec. dist.:* Ala., Ga. *Infm.:* The dialect form is from Joel Chandler Harris. *1st cit.:* US1880 Harris, *Plantation Proverbs* in *Uncle Remus, His Songs and His Sayings.* *20c. coll.:* Stevenson 144:5.

9. No bees, no honey; no work, no money. *Rec. dist.:* Ohio. *Infm.:* Stevenson traces "No bees, no honey" to Sappho, *Fragments* (ca610 B.C.E.), but cites no Br. or U.S. sources. *1st cit.:* US1948 Stevenson, *Home Book of Proverbs.* *20c. coll.:* Stevenson 1159:4.

10. Old bees yield no honey. *Rec. dist.:* Ill., N.Y., Tex. *1st cit.:* 1633 Draxe, *Bibliotheca Scholastica* in *Anglia* (1918). *20c. coll.:* Stevenson 144:9.

11. The bee that makes the honey doesn't stand around the hive, and the man who makes the money has to worry, work, and strive. *Var.:* The bee that gets the honey doesn't hang around the hive. *Rec. dist.:* Ill., N.C.

12. The bee works in the summer and eats honey all winter. *Rec. dist.:* Ill. *1st cit.:* 1732 Fuller, *Gnomologia*. *20c. coll.:* Stevenson 145:2.

13. The drone bee dies soon after the wedding night. *Rec. dist.:* Vt. *Infm.:* Don't be just a drone-type worker, or you will die from boredom and overwork.

14. When the bee sucks, it makes honey; when the spider, poison. *Rec. dist.:* Vt. *1st cit.:* ca1542 Wyatt, *Poems,* ed. Muir. *20c. coll.:* ODEP 39, Stevenson 145:4.

15. Where there are bees, there is honey. *Rec. dist.:* Ind., N.Y., S.C. *1st cit.:* 1616 Draxe, *Bibliotheca Scholastica* in *Anglia* (1918); US1748 *Word* in *Colonial Currency,* ed. Davis, Publ. Prince Soc. (1910–11). *20c. coll.:* ODEP 39, Whiting 26, Stevenson 144:8, Whiting*(MP)* 39.

16. While honey lies in every flower, it takes a bee to get the honey out. *Rec. dist.:* N.Y., S.C.

SEE ALSO From BEAVERS, bees should learn to mend their ways. A bee works; a beaver works and plays. / BOYS avoid the bees that stung 'em.

beer **1.** Beer before wine, you'll feel fine; wine before beer, you'll feel queer. *Var.:* Wine on beer brings good cheer; beer on wine is not so fine. *Rec. dist.:* Pa., Wis. *1st cit.:* 1586 Evans, *Withals Dictionary Revised.* *20c. coll.:* Stevenson 146:12.

2. Beer is cheer. *Rec. dist.:* Wis.

3. Beer on whiskey, mighty risky; whiskey on beer, never fear. *Rec. dist.:* U.S., Can. *1st cit.:* US1957 Cheever, *Wapshot Chronicles.* *20c. coll.:* Whiting*(MP)* 40.

4. They who drink beer think beer. *Rec. dist.:* Wis. *1st cit.:* 1958 Browne, *Death;* US1818 Irving, *Sketch Book: Stratford.* *20c. coll.:* Whiting*(MP)* 40, Stevenson 147:2., T&W 23.

5. You must drink beer of your own brewing, no matter how bitter. *Rec. dist.:* Ill. *Infm.:* Related to "As he brews, so shall he drink."

1st cit.: ca1390 Gower, *Confessio Amantis,* E.E.T.S. (1900). *20c. coll.:* Stevenson 240:7.

SEE ALSO BLAB is not cheer; froth is not beer. / Going FISHING without beer makes the day last a year. / LIFE is not wholly beer and skittles.

before *(adv.)* Look before or you'll find yourself behind. *Rec. dist.:* Miss. *1st cit.:* 1640 Herbert, *Outlandish Proverbs (Jacula Prudentum)* in *Works,* ed. Hutchinson (1941); US1735 Franklin, *PRAlmanac.* *20c. coll.:* ODEP 484, Stevenson 865:14.

SEE ALSO Coming EVENTS cast their shadows before.

before *(conj.)* *SEE* It is always DARKEST before dawn. / FINGERS were made before knives and forks. / Conquer your GRIEVANCES before they conquer you. / HEAR twice before you speak once. / Don't HIT before you look. / Don't get off the LADDER before you reach the ground. / MEASURE twice before you cut once. / Never spend your MONEY before you have it. / Be sure you know the ROAD before you act as guide. / Learn to SAY before you sing. / SIT before you fall. / You have to learn to WALK before you can run. / Never say "WHOOPEE" before you jump.

before *(prep.)* *SEE* AGE before beauty. / Before HONOR is humility. / Everyone has his LOT and a wide world before him. / PRIDE comes before a fall.

befriend When befriended, remember it; when you befriend, forget it. *Rec. dist.:* Miss. *Infm.:* Stevenson traces this proverb to Chilon of Lacedemon, one of the seven sages of Greece in *Apophthegms* (ca600 B.C.E..). *1st cit.:* US1740 Franklin, *PRAlmanac.* *20c. coll.:* Stevenson 170:1.

beg **1.** Better to beg than to steal, but better to work than to beg. *Rec. dist.:* N.Y., S.C., Wis. *1st cit.:* 1568 *Lazarillo de Tormes,* tr. Rowland, ed. Crofts. *20c. coll.:* ODEP 40, Stevenson 150:3.

2. He who begs timidly, courts refusal. *Rec. dist.:* Ont.

3. Who is not ashamed to beg, soon is not ashamed to steal. *Rec. dist.:* Miss.

SEE ALSO Neither beg of him who has been a BEGGAR nor serve him who has been a servant. / To BORROW or beg or get one's own, it is the very worst world that ever was known.

beget   *SEE* A LIE begets a lie, until they become a generation.

beggar   1. A beggar can never be bankrupt. *Rec. dist.:* Ill., N.Y., S.C. *1st cit.:* 1616 Withals, *Dictionary of French and English Tongues.* *20c. coll.:* ODEP 41, Stevenson 149:9.

2. A beggar ennobled does not know his own kinsman. *Rec. dist.:* Wis.

3. Beggar is jealous of beggar. *Rec. dist.:* Wis. *1st cit.:* ca1350 *Douce MS 52,* ed. Förster, Erlangen (1906). *20c. coll.:* Stevenson 148:12.

4. Beggars can't be choosers. *Rec. dist.:* U.S., Can. *1st cit.:* 1546 Heywood, *Dialogue of Proverbs,* ed. Habernicht (1963); USca1719 *Secret Diary of William Byrd of Westover 1739–1742,* ed. Woodfin (1942). *20c. coll.:* ODEP 42, Whiting 26, *CODP* 12, Stevenson 149:2, T&W 24, Whiting(MP) 41.

5. Give a beggar a horse and he'll ride it to death. *Vars.:* (a) Put a beggar on a horse, and he will ride to the devil. (b) Set a beggar on horseback, and he'll ride to ruin. (c) Sit a beggar on horseback, and he'll ride to the death. *Rec. dist.:* U.S., Can. *1st cit.:* 1576 Pettie, *Petite Palace of Pleasure,* ed. Gollancz (1908); US1684 Randolph in *Mather Papers,* Mass. Hist.Soc. *Collections* (1868). *20c. coll.:* ODEP 41, Whiting 26, *CODP* 11, Stevenson 150:10, T&W 24, Whiting(MP) 41.

6. I had rather be a beggar and spend my last dollar like a king, than be a king and spend my money like a beggar. *Rec. dist.:* N.Y., S.C. *1st cit.:* US1877 Ingersoll, *Liberty of Man, Woman and Child.* *20c. coll.:* Stevenson 1308:4.

7. It is better to be a beggar than a fool. *Rec. dist.:* Wis. *1st cit.:* 1678 Ray, *English Proverbs.* *20c. coll.:* Stevenson 149:13.

8. Neither beg of him who has been a beggar nor serve him who has been a servant. *Rec. dist.:* N.Y., S.C. *1st cit.:* 1706 Stevens, *New Spanish and English Dictionary.* *20c. coll.:* ODEP 40, Stevenson 2077:8.

9. One day a beggar, the next a thief. *Rec. dist.:* Wis.

10. Sue a beggar, and you'll get a louse. *Rec. dist.:* Ind. *1st cit.:* 1583 Melbancke, *Philotimus;* US1769 Woodmason, *Carolina Backcountry on Eve of the Revolution, Journal of Charles Woodmason,* ed. Hooker (1953). *20c. coll.:* ODEP 784, Whiting 27, Stevenson 148:4, Whiting(MP) 41.

11. The angry beggar gets a stone instead of a handout. *Rec. dist.:* N.Y., S.C.

12. The beggar is never out of his way. *Rec. dist.:* N.J., N.Y. *1st cit.:* 1575 Still(?), *Gammer Gurtons Nedle.* *20c. coll.:* ODEP 41, Stevenson 1476:6.

13. The beggar may sing before the thief. *Rec. dist.:* Okla. *1st cit.:* ca1377 Langland, *Piers Plowman,* ed. Skeat, E.E.T.S. (1867). *20c. coll.:* ODEP 41, Stevenson 1851:6.

14. The beggar who becomes rich has the pride of Lucifer. *Rec. dist.:* Ill.

15. The beggar's wallet has no bottom. *Var.:* A beggar's wallet is a mile to the bottom. *Rec. dist.:* Ill., Minn., N.Y., S.C. *1st cit.:* 1539 *Proverbs of Erasmus,* tr. Taverner. *20c. coll.:* ODEP 42, Stevenson 148:1.

16. They are but beggars that can count their worth. *Rec. dist.:* Ky., Tenn.

SEE ALSO Who DAINTIES love, shall beggars prove. / A DOLLAR a day keeps the beggar away. / A young IDLER, an old beggar. / The POOR have little; beggars none; the rich too much; enough, not one. / PRIDE is as loud a beggar as want, and a great deal more saucy. / If WISHES were horses, beggars might ride.

beggarly   *SEE* One PATCH is comely, but patch upon patch is beggarly.

beggary   Aspiring beggary is wretchedness itself. *Rec. dist.:* Miss.

SEE ALSO IDLENESS is the key of beggary.

begging   What is got by begging is deeply bought. *Rec. dist.:* Ill.

SEE ALSO BORROWING isn't much better than begging.

begin   1. Begin in time to finish without hurry. *Rec. dist.:* Ont.

2. Begin nothing until you have considered how it is to be finished. *Rec. dist.:* Mich. *1st cit.:* ca1405 *Castle of Perseverance. 20c. coll.:* ODEP 220, Stevenson 151:8.

3. Better begin as you can hold out. *Rec. dist.:* Maine.

4. Better never begin than never make an end. *Rec. dist.:* N.Y., W.Va. *1st cit.:* 1509 Barclay, *Ship of Fools,* ed. Jamieson in *Eclogues,* E.E.T.S. (1874); US1921 O'Neill, *Anna Christie. 20c. coll.:* ODEP 54, Stevenson 154:4.

5. Never begin anything on Friday that you are not able to finish that day. *Rec. dist.:* Calif., Miss., N.Y.

6. Well begun is half done. *Rec. dist.:* U.S., Can. *1st cit.:* ca1415 *Middle English Sermons,* E.E.T.S.; US1931 Taylor, *Cape Cod Mystery. 20c. coll.:* CODP 244, Whiting(MP) 41, ODEP 877, Stevenson 152:10.

7. Whenever you begins to git along good, de niggers will back-cap you. *Rec. dist.:* Miss. *Infm.:* "Back-cap" is dialect for pulling the cap over your eyes. From Negro dialect collection of Judge Harris Dickinson, novelist from Vicksburg, Miss.

SEE ALSO As soon as man is BORN, he begins to die. / CHARITY begins at home. / Some men DIE before they begin to live. / One begins by being a DUPE; one ends by being a rascal. / A JOURNEY of a thousand miles begins with one step. / LIFE and misery begin together. / LIFE begins at forty. / When a MAN marries, his troubles begin; when a man dies, his trouble ends. / The highest TOWERS begin from the ground.

beginning 1. A bad beginning makes a good ending. *Var.:* A poor beginning makes a good ending. *Rec. dist.:* U.S., Can. *1st cit.:* ca1374 Chaucer, *Troilus and Criseyde;* US1755 *Writings of George Washington,* ed. Fitzpatrick (1931–44). *20c. coll.:* Stevenson 153:9, Whiting 27, Whiting(MP) 41.

2. A good beginning is half the task. *Vars.:* (a) A good beginning is half the battle. (b) A good beginning is half the business. *Rec. dist.:* U.S., Can. *Infm.:* Cf. begin. *1st cit.:* ca1415 *Middle English Sermons,* E.E.T.S. *20c. coll.:* CODP 244, ODEP 877, Stevenson 152:10.

3. A good beginning makes a good ending. *Rec. dist.:* U.S., Can. *1st cit.:* ca1300 *Proverbs of Hending;* US1624 *Winthrop Papers 1498–1649,* Mass.Hist.Soc. *Collections* (1929–47). *20c. coll.:* ODEP 317, Whiting 27, CODP 97, Stevenson 156:3, T&W 24, Whiting(MP) 42.

4. All great things had a small beginning. *Var.:* From small beginnings come great things. *Rec. dist.:* U.S., Can. *1st cit.:* 1609 Harward, Unpublished manuscript in Library of Trinity College, Cambridge; USca1656 Bradford, *History of Plymouth Plantation,* ed. Ford (1912). *20c. coll.:* ODEP 42, Whiting 27, Stevenson 1035:15.

5. Beware of beginnings. *Rec. dist.:* Vt. *1st cit.:* 1611 Cotgrave, *Dictionary of French and English Tongues. 20c. coll.:* ODEP 57.

6. Everything must have a beginning. *Rec. dist.:* Ill., N.Y. *1st cit.:* ca1374 Chaucer, *Troilus and Criseyde;* US1750 *Almanacs of Roger Sherman, 1750–1761,* ed. Paltsits, Am.Antiq.Soc. *Proceedings* (1907). *20c. coll.:* ODEP 232, Whiting 135, Whiting(MP) 205.

7. The beginning is not everything. *Rec. dist.:* U.S., Can.

8. The beginning is the hardest. *Rec. dist.:* N.Y., N.C., S.C., Wis. *1st cit.:* ca1500 *15c. School Book,* ed. Nelson; US1758 Carroll, *Correspondence* in Rowland, *Life of Charles Carroll of Carrolton* (1898). *20c. coll.:* ODEP 42, Whiting 27, Stevenson 152:2.

9. The golden rule of life is, make a beginning. *Rec. dist.:* N.Y.

10. There must be a beginning and an end to a thing. *Rec. dist.:* N.Y., N.C., S.C. *Infm.:* Stevenson traces the proverb to Sallust's *Ad Caesarem Senem.* No Br. or U.S. sources cited. *1st cit.:* US1948 Stevenson, *Home Book of Proverbs. 20c. coll.:* Stevenson 156:1.

SEE ALSO EATING and scratching, it's all in the beginning. / The end of PASSION is the beginning of repentance.

behave SEE It is being KNOWN that makes us behave.

behavior 1. Behavior is a mirror in which everyone shows his image. *Rec. dist.:* N.Y. *Infm.:* Stevenson traces the proverb to Goethe's

Elective Affinities (1809). No Br. or U.S. sources cited. *1st cit.:* US1948 Stevenson, *Home Book of Proverbs. 20c. coll.:* Stevenson 157:1.

2. Behavior that is regarded agreeable in one is very rude in another. *Rec. dist.:* N.C.

3. Good behavior is the last refuge of mediocrity. *Rec. dist.:* N.Y., S.C. *Infm.:* Stevenson cites *Meditations in Wall Street* (1940) as source. *1st cit.:* US1948 Stevenson, *Home Book of Proverbs. 20c. coll.:* Stevenson 157:7.

behind *(adv.)* SEE Look BEFORE or you'll find yourself behind. / If you can't be the bell COW, fall in behind. / He who FOLLOWS is always behind. / Always in a HURRY, always behind. / Slow are the STEPS of those who leave their hearts behind.

behind *(prep.)* SEE Behind every GREAT man there is a great woman.

being True worth is in being, not seeming. *Rec. dist.:* N.Y., N.C., S.C.

SEE ALSO You may sometimes be much in the WRONG in owning your being in the right.

belfry SEE It is by the VICAR's skirts that the devil climbs into the belfry.

belief We are born believing a man bears beliefs as a tree bears apples. *Rec. dist.:* N.Y., S.C. *1st cit.:* US1860 Emerson, "Worship" in *Conduct of Life. 20c. coll.:* Stevenson 162:3.

SEE ALSO A man's ACTIONS are motion pictures of his beliefs.

believe **1.** Believe and conquer. *Rec. dist.:* N.Dak., Oreg.

2. Believe only half of what you see and nothing you hear. *Vars.:* **(a)** Believe not half you hear, and repeat not half you believe. **(b)** Believe nothing you hear and half you see. **(c)** Don't believe anything you hear nor half what you read. **(d)** You can only believe half of what you hear. *Rec. dist.:* U.S., Can. *1st cit.:* ca1205 Layamon, *Brut,* Soc. Antiquaries (1847); US1770 Carroll, Letter, 4 Sept., in *Md.Mag.Hist.* (1918). *20c. coll.:* ODEP 43, CODP 12, Stevenson 161:10.

3. Believe well and have well. *Rec. dist.:* Ind., Tex. *1st cit.:* 1546 Heywood, *Dialogue of Prov-*

erbs, ed. Habernicht (1963). *20c. coll.:* ODEP 43, Stevenson 162:4.

4. He who believes easily is easily deceived. *Rec. dist.:* N.J.

5. He who believes has power to do. *Rec. dist.:* Oreg.

6. He who does not believe finds others will not believe him. *Rec. dist.:* Calif., Ind.

7. It is better to believe that a man possesses good qualities than to assert that he does not. *Rec. dist.:* Ind.

8. It is easier to believe than to doubt. *Rec. dist.:* N.Y., S.C. *1st cit.:* US1926 Martin, *Meaning of a Liberal Education. 20c. coll.:* Stevenson 162:13.

9. It is easy to believe what you want to. *Vars.:* **(a)** Men believe what they will to believe. **(b)** We believe what we wish, and wish what we believe is good for us. **(c)** We soon believe what we desire. *Rec. dist.:* U.S., Can. *1st cit.:* ca1386 Chaucer, *Tale of Melibee;* US1753 *Almanacs of Roger Sherman, 1750–1761,* ed. Paltsits, Am.Antiq.Soc. *Proceedings* (1907). *20c. coll.:* ODEP 43, Whiting 27, Stevenson 161:6, Whiting*(MP)* 42.

10. It makes no difference what a man believes if he is honest. *Rec. dist.:* Ind.

11. Men are most apt to believe what they least understand. *Var.:* We are prone to believe what we don't understand. *Rec. dist.:* Ill., Ind., N.C. *Infm.:* Stevenson traces the proverb to Tacitus, *Histories* (ca104). *1st cit.:* US1948 Stevenson, *Home Book of Proverbs. 20c. coll.:* Stevenson 162:20.

12. Never believe the impossible. *Rec. dist.:* Ont.

13. People are willing to believe alarming things to keep from believing what they don't want to. *Rec. dist.:* Miss.

SEE ALSO BLESSED are they that have not seen and yet have believed. / The more a man DREAMS, the less he believes. / What the EYES see the heart believes. / He who KNOWS all believes. / Believe every man a LIAR until he proves himself true. / If you are going to tell a LIE, tell it big enough so that no one will believe you. / It is as bad to believe a LIE as to tell one.

believer **1.** A believer is a songless bird in a cage. *Rec. dist.:* N.Y., S.C. **1st cit.:** US1873 Ingersoll, Speech, Chicago, 21 Dec. **20c. coll.:** Stevenson 162:10.

2. Quick believers need broad shoulders. *Rec. dist.:* Mich. **1st cit.:** 1640 Herbert, *Outlandish Proverbs (Jacula Prudentum)* in *Works,* ed. Hutchinson (1941). **20c. coll.:** ODEP 660, Stevenson 162:16.

believing Believing has a core of unbelieving. *Rec. dist.:* N.Y., S.C. **1st cit.:** USca1866 Buchanan, *Songs of Seeking.* **20c. coll.:** Stevenson 162:10.

SEE ALSO SEEING is believing.

belittle Belittle others and be little. *Rec. dist.:* Ont.

bell *(n.)* **1.** A bell, once rung, cannot be rerung. *Rec. dist.:* N.Y., S.C. *Infm.:* Refers to the sound of the first ringing of the bell; the sound cannot be recalled.

2. A cracked bell can never sound well. *Rec. dist.:* U.S., Can. **1st cit.:** 1629 Adams, *Sermons* (1861). **20c. coll.:** ODEP 153, Stevenson 163:3.

3. As the bell is, so is the clapper. *Rec. dist.:* Mich.

4. If you hear one bell only, you hear but one sound. *Rec. dist.:* Ill.

5. The bell sends others to church but itself never minds the sermon. *Rec. dist.:* N.Y., S.C. **1st cit.:** 1557 North, *Diall of Princes;* US1754 Franklin, *PRAlmanac.* **20c. coll.:** ODEP 44, Stevenson 164:1.

6. The dinner bell is always in tune. *Rec. dist.:* N.J.

7. The loudest bell does not always have the sweetest tone. *Rec. dist.:* Kans.

bell *(adj.)* SEE If you can't be the bell COW, fall in behind.

beller SEE A BAWL becomes a beller when the tongue is stickin' out.

belly **1.** A full belly makes a brave heart. *Rec. dist.:* N.Y., S.C.

2. It's better a belly burst than good food waste. *Rec. dist.:* N.J. **1st cit.:** ca1628 Carmichaell, *Proverbs in Scots,* ed. Anderson (1957). **20c. coll.:** ODEP 52, Stevenson 166:6, Whiting(MP) 43.

3. Lean belly never feeds a fat brain. *Rec. dist.:* Ill.

4. When the belly is full, the bones are at rest. *Rec. dist.:* Okla. **1st cit.:** ca1495 Medwall, *Nature.* **20c. coll.:** ODEP 45, Stevenson 167:12.

SEE ALSO Nothing goes over the devil's BACK that doesn't come back under the devil's belly. / BEANS ain't beans without sow belly. / A growing BOY has a wolf in his belly. / There's many witty men whose BRAINS can't fill their bellies. / It's a good STORY that fills the belly.

beloved If you'd be belov'd, make yourself amiable. *Rec. dist.:* Miss., N.Y., N.C.

below SEE He who thinks his PLACE below him will certainly be below his place.

belt Below the belt all men are brothers. *Rec. dist.:* N.Y.

bend **1.** Bend the rod while it's hot. *Rec. dist.:* Ont.

2. Bend the twig while it is still green. *Vars.:* **(a)** Bend the willow while it's young. **(b)** Best to bend it while a twig. **(c)** Easy matter to bend a twig; hard matter to bend an oak. *Rec. dist.:* U.S., Can. **1st cit.:** 1543 Hardyng, *English Chronicle in Metre.* **20c. coll.:** ODEP 46, Stevenson 2371:4.

3. Better bend the neck than bruise the forehead. *Rec. dist.:* Ont.

4. It is better to bend than break. *Var.:* Better bent than broken. *Rec. dist.:* U.S., Can. **1st cit.:** ca1374 Chaucer, *Troilus and Criseyde;* US1865 Swain in *Ruffin Papers,* ed. Hamilton (1920). **20c. coll.:** ODEP 52, Whiting 28, Stevenson 169:3, T&W 25, Whiting(MP) 43.

SEE ALSO A BOW too much bent will break. / HEARTS don't break, they bend and wither. / REEDS will bend, but iron will not. / As the TREE is bent, so the tree is inclined. / As the TWIG is bent, so grows the tree.

bending Much bending breaks the bow; much unbending, the mind. *Rec. dist.:* Minn.

benefactor See Mankind bestows more AP-PLAUSE on the destroyer than on her benefactor.

benefit 1. Benefits, like flowers, please most when they are fresh. *Rec. dist.:* Ill. *1st cit.:* 1640 Herbert, *Outlandish Proverbs (Jacula Prudentum)* in *Works,* ed. Hutchinson (1941). *20c. coll.:* ODEP 46, Stevenson 170:4.

2. Benefits turn poison in bad minds. *Rec. dist.:* Ill.

3. The last benefit is the most remembered. *Rec. dist.:* Ill. *1st cit.:* 1732 Fuller, *Gnomologia. 20c. coll.:* Stevenson 170:4.

4. We should never remember the benefits we have conferred nor forget the favors received. *Rec. dist.:* N.J. *1st cit.:* US1740 Franklin, *PRAlmanac. 20c. coll.:* Stevenson 170:1.

5. When you accept a benefit, you sell your freedom. *Rec. dist.:* Ill. *1st cit.:* 1539 Publilius Syrus, *Sententiae,* tr. Taverner; US1768 *Writings of John Dickinson, 1764–1777,* ed. Ford, Hist. Soc. Penn. *Memoirs* (1895). *20c. coll.:* ODEP 46, Whiting 28, Stevenson 170:8.

6. When you confer a benefit on a worthy man, you oblige all men. *Rec. dist.:* Ill. *1st cit.:* 1539 Publilius Syrus, *Sententiae,* tr. Taverner. *20c. coll.:* Stevenson 170:9.

See also Write INJURIES in dust, benefits in marble. / QUIET people, whether wise or dull, get the benefit of the doubt.

Bermudas If the Bermudas let you pass, you must beware of Hatteras. *Rec. dist.:* N.Y., S.C. *Infm.:* Sailors along the Atlantic coast know these places for their violent storms and shipwrecks. *1st cit.:* US1830 Ames, *Mariner's Sketches. 20c. coll.:* Whiting 29, ODEP 46, Stevenson 2047:1, T&W 25.

berry 1. Berries white, take flight; berries red, never dread. *Rec. dist.:* Wash.

2. Pick your berries so the thorns won't stick you. *Rec. dist.:* N.J.

3. The blacker the berry, the sweeter the juice. *Var.:* The darker the berry, the sweeter the juice. *Rec. dist.:* Calif., Colo., Ill., Oreg.

4. The time to pick berries is when they're ripe. *Rec. dist.:* Vt.

berth A gutter berth, or maybe the paddy wagon, are fated for the man who loves to quaff each flagon. *Rec. dist.:* Calif. *Infm.:* Heard in a temperance lecture by Lamar Johnson.

best *(n.)* 1. All is for the best. *Vars.:* (a) All for the best. (b) All that happens, happens for the best. (c) All things happen for the best. (d) Everything happens for the best. (e) Everything that happens, happens for the best. (f) Everything will turn out for the best. *Rec. dist.:* U.S., Can. *1st cit.:* ca1388 Chaucer, *Frankeleyn's Tale;* US1751 Franklin, *PRAlmanac. 20c. coll.:* Stevenson 173:2, CODP 13, T&W 26.

2. Do your best and leave the rest with God. *Vars.:* (a) He who does his best does well; angels can do no more. (b) He who does the best he can does well. *Rec. dist.:* U.S., Can. *1st cit.:* 1597 Shakespeare, *Henry IV, Part I;* US1875 Twain, *He Done His Level Best. 20c. coll.:* Stevenson 172:8, Whiting(MP) 44.

3. Everything is best when it is ended. *Var.:* Whatever is, is best. *Rec. dist.:* N.Y. *1st cit.:* US1850 Judd, *Richard Edney and Governor's Family. 20c. coll.:* T&W 26.

4. For he who always does his best, his best will better grow; but he who shirks or slights his task, he lets the better go. *Rec. dist.:* Ill.

5. Give to the world your best, and it will come back to you. *Rec. dist.:* Calif., Ind., Iowa, Nebr.

6. Good, better, best: never let it rest, until your good is better and your better, best. *Rec. dist.:* Calif., Mich., N.Y.

7. Hope for the best, but prepare for the worst. *Var.:* Look for the best, and expect the worst. *Rec. dist.:* U.S., Can. *1st cit.:* 1565 Norton and Sackville, *Gorboduc;* US1813 *Correspondence of John Jay,* ed. Johnston (1893). *20c. coll.:* ODEP 384, Whiting 29, CODP 114, Stevenson 1166:8, Whiting(MP) 44.

8. If you wish to see the best in others, show the best of yourself. *Rec. dist.:* N.Y.

9. The best is cheapest in the end. *Var.:* The

best is cheapest. *Rec. dist.:* N.Y., N.C. *1st cit.:* 1523 Fitzherbert, *Boke of Husbandry;* US1637 *New English Canaan of Thomas Morton,* ed. Adams, Jr., Publ. Prince Soc. (1883). *20c. coll.:* ODEP 48, Whiting 29, Stevenson 327:10.

10. The best is usually saved for last. *Rec. dist.:* N.Y. *1st cit.:* US1972 MacDonald, *Long Lavender Look. 20c. coll.:* Whiting(MP) 44.

SEE ALSO If WORSE comes to worst, make the best of it.

best *(adj.)* **1.** May the best day we have seen be the worst we have to come. *Rec. dist.:* N.Y., Wis.

2. The best men are molded of their faults. *Rec. dist.:* N.C.

3. The best things are often least appreciated. *Rec. dist.:* Kans., N.Y.

4. The best things in life are free. *Rec. dist.:* U.S., Can. *1st cit.:* US1940 Darby, *Death Conducts a Tour. 20c. coll.:* Whiting(MP) 618.

SEE ALSO The best ADVICE I know in life is don't give too much. / The best APPLE is taken by the pig. / The best ARMOR is to keep out of gunshot. / Every DOCTOR thinks his pills the best. / The FOOL well dressed is at his best. / The quickest GENEROSITY is the best. / HOME is where you act the worst and are treated the best. / HONESTY is the best policy. / He who KNOWS most knows best how little he knows. / He who LAUGHS last laughs best. / A sudden LIE has the best luck. / He who LIVES longest who lives best. / MOTHER knows best. / Mother's LOVE is best of all. / A little NONSENSE now and then is relished by the best of men. / The worst PASSIONS have their root in the best. / The best PHYSICIANS are Dr. Diet, Dr. Quiet, and Dr. Merryman. / Old SHOES wear best. / That SUIT is best that best fits me. / You may TALK too much on the best of subjects. / The best way to get out of TROUBLE is not to get in it. / A short VISIT is best.

bet *(n.)* A bet's a bet. *Rec. dist.:* U.S., Can. *1st cit.:* US1857 Bennett, *Border Rover. 20c. coll.:* T&W 26.

bet *(v.)* **1.** Bet a heap and begin to weep. *Rec. dist.:* Ind.

2. Bet 'em high and sleep on the streets. *Rec. dist.:* Calif.

betray If anyone betrays you once, it's his fault; if he betrays you twice, it's your fault. *Rec. dist.:* Minn.

SEE ALSO Those who betray their FRIENDS must not expect others to keep faith with them. / Many are betrayed with a KISS. / When KNAVES betray each other, one can scarce be blamed or the other pitied.

better Man's no better than he thinks he is. *Rec. dist.:* Mich., Minn.

SEE ALSO AGE makes a man white but not better. / Better ALONE than in bad company. / Better to BEG than to steal, but better to work than to beg. / The BIGGER the man, the better the mark. / An old BROOM is better than a new one. / Better BUY than borrow. / The better the DAY, the better the deed. / Better be DEAD than out of fashion. / DEMOCRACY is better than tyranny. / It is better to DIE kicking than to be kicked dying. / Old brag is a good DOG, but hold fast is a better one. / Better be ENVIED than pitied. / The older the FIDDLE, the better the tune. / Better a little FIRE to warm us than a big one to burn us. / Better a big FISH in a little puddle than a little fish in a big puddle. / It is better to be thought a FOOL than to open your mouth and let the world know it. / One FOOT is better than two crutches. / All GARDENERS know better than the others. / It is better to GIVE than to receive. / The GOOD that is, is better than the good that was. / The less GOVERNMENT we have, the better. / HALF a glass is better than none. / HALF a loaf is better than none. / It is better to be a HAS-BEEN than a never-was. / Better to HAVE than wish. / One good HEAD is better than a thousand strong hands. / Two HEADS are better than one. / A big HEART is better than a big house. / The uglier the man, the better the HUSBAND. / The IDEAL we embrace is our better self. / Better be IDLE than badly employed. / It is better to take many INJURIES than to give one. / It is better to bear a single INJURY in silence than to provoke a thousand by flying into a rage. / Better lose a JEST than a friend. / It is better to be LAME than always seated. / It is better to hear the LARK sing than the mouse cheep. / LEARN well and know better. / Better to LEAVE than to take. / Lean LIBERTY is better than fat slavery. / It is better to be lied about than to LIE. / It is better to LIE a little than to be unhappy much. / A LITTLE along is better than a long none. / Better to LIVE well than long. / LOVE sought is good, but love given unsought is better. / If there is anything better than being loved, it is LOVING. / Better a MOUSE in the pot than no flesh at all. / A PATCH is better than a hole. / PLUCK is better than luck. / A POOR man is better than a liar. / Better be POOR and live than rich and perish. / Better be POOR than wicked. / It often happens that a bad PUN goes further than a better one. / Open REBUKE is better than secret love. / It is better to be RIGHT than in the majority. / SAY well is good, but do well is better. / Better cut the SHOE than pinch the foot. / Better be a SHREW than a sheep. / A live SOLDIER is better than a dead hero. / Better three hours too SOON than a minute too late. / The SOONER the better. / SORROW is better than laughter. / Better a TOOTH out than always aching. / The TRUTH is better than a lie. / A boy is better UNBORN than untaught. / To be UNKNOWN is better than to be ill-known. / Better UNTAUGHT than ill taught.

beware SEE Of chance ACQUAINTANCE beware. / Let the BUYER beware. / Beware of little EXPENSES. / Beware of those who get FAMILIAR quickly. / Beware the FLATTERER. / When the FOX preaches, beware of your geese. / Beware the FURY of a patient man. / Beware of the GREEKS bearing gifts. / Beware the man with only one GUN. / Beware of him who has nothing to LOSE.

Bible 1. A knowledge of the Bible without a college course is more valuable than a college course without the Bible. *Rec. dist.:* N.C.

2. Be careful how you live: you may be the only Bible some people will ever read. *Rec. dist.:* Wis.

3. I'd rather be your Bible than your horse. *Rec. dist.:* Ariz.

4. The Bible is printed in 610 different languages and read in none. *Rec. dist.:* Ill.

SEE ALSO A BANKBOOK is the greedy man's Bible. / Even the DEVIL will swear on a stack of Bibles.

biddy It is hard to be biddy and lady too. *Rec. dist.:* N.Y., S.C. *Infm.:* It's hard to be the maid and hostess at the same time.

big 1. A big head means a big headache. *Rec. dist.:* W.Va.

2. A man is as big as the things that make him mad. *Rec. dist.:* Ont.

3. Big men are usually little men who took advantage of opportunity. *Rec. dist.:* Calif., Colo.

4. The big ones don't always get away. *Rec. dist.:* Ind. *Infm.:* Sometimes a person is lucky and gets what he or she wants.

5. When they're big enough, they're old enough. *Var.:* If they are old enough, they're big enough—and if they are big enough, they're old enough. *Rec. dist.:* Mich., Oreg., Wash. *Infm.:* Applications are varied, but usually biological. The variant often has a sexual connotation for young adults. *1st cit.:* US1935 Davis, *Honey in the Horn.* *20c. coll.:* Whiting(MP) 45.

SEE ALSO Better a big FISH in a little puddle than a little fish in a big puddle. / Lose a small FISH to catch a big one. / A big HEART is better than a big house. / There's no HOUSE built big enough for two families. / "IF" is a little word, yet it is so big you can't get around or over it. / If you are going to tell a LIE, tell it big enough so that no one will believe you. / A RAINBOW is big enough for everyone to look at. / If you feel you're too SMALL to do big things, then do big things in a small way. / Big WORDS seldom go with good deeds.

big-bellied SEE A SHIP under sail and a big-bellied woman are the handsomest two things that can be seen in common.

bigamy Bigamy is having one wife too many; monogamy is the same. *Rec. dist.:* Wis.

bigger 1. The bigger the better. *Rec. dist.:* Calif., Mich.

2. The bigger the man, the better the mark.

Rec. dist.: N.Y., S.C. **1st cit.:** 1894 Northall, *Folk-Phrases;* US1940 Case, *Do Not Disturb.* **20c. coll.:** ODEP 59, Stevenson 1033:2.

3. The bigger the man, the smaller he becomes. *Rec. dist.:* Ind.

4. The bigger the man's head gets, the easier it is to fill his shoes. *Rec. dist.:* Colo., Ind.

5. The bigger the rock, the bigger the splash. *Rec. dist.:* Okla.

6. The bigger the tree, the harder she falls. *Rec. dist.:* Ohio.

7. The bigger they come, the harder they fall. *Rec. dist.:* U.S., Can. *Infm.:* Attributed to world heavyweight boxer Robert Fitzsimmons before his fight with Jeffries. **1st cit.:** 1493 Parker, *Dives and Pauper;* US1902 *National Police Gazette,* Sept. 6. **20c. coll.:** CODP 18, Stevenson 749:2, Whiting*(MP)* 45.

biggest **1.** It is always the biggest one that gets away. *Rec. dist.:* Ind., Miss.

2. 'Tain't the biggest an' de strongest dat does de mostest in dis world. *Rec. dist.:* Mass. *Infm.:* Dialect wording is from Joel C. Harris' *Uncle Remus and His Friends.*

SEE ALSO The fellow who blows his HORN the loudest is likely in the biggest fog. / The biggest LIAR in the world is the man who starts out by saying, "They say."

bill *(account)* SEE For most people LIFE is one bill after another.

bill *(animal)* SEE Nothing ruins a DUCK but his bill.

bind SEE WILLOWS are weak, but they bind other wood.

binding SEE WOMEN are like books: too much gilding makes men suspicious that the binding is the most important part.

biography A good biography is never written until after the person is dead. *Rec. dist.:* N.C.

bird **1.** A bird in the hand is better than two in the bush. *Rec. dist.:* Ky., Tenn. **1st cit.:** ca1470 *Harleian MS.* **20c. coll.:** Stevenson 182:6.

2. A bird in the hand is worth two in the bush. *Vars.:* **(a)** A bird in a cage is worth two in a bush. **(b)** A bird in the hand is worth a flock in the sagebrush. **(c)** A bird in the hand is worth a hundred flying. **(d)** A bird in the hand is worth more than two in the bush. **(e)** A bird in the hand is worth ten in the bush. **(f)** A bird in the hand is worth what it will bring. **(g)** A bird in the sack is worth two on the wing. **(h)** A bird on the platter is worth two in the hand. **(i)** A girl had in bed is worth two in the car. **(j)** One bird in the cage is worth two in the bush. *Rec. dist.:* U.S., Can. **1st cit.:** ca1450 Capgrave, *Life of St. Katherine;* USca1700 *Poems of Edward Taylor,* ed. Stanford (1960). **20c. coll.:** ODEP 59, Whiting 31, Stevenson 182:6, T&W 27, Whiting*(MP)* 47.

3. A bird is known by his note and a man by his talk. *Var.:* As a bird is known by his note, so is a man by his discourse. *Rec. dist.:* Ill., Ind., Mich., Wis. **1st cit.:** 1579 Gosson, *School of Abuse;* US1929 Wallace, *Ringer.* **20c. coll.:** ODEP 59, Stevenson 177:8, Whiting*(MP)* 48.

4. A bird may be ever so small, yet it always seeks a nest of its own. *Rec. dist.:* Wis.

5. A bird never flies so far that his tail doesn't follow. *Var.:* A bird never flies so far its "tale" doesn't follow it. *Rec. dist.:* Ark., Ind., Ky., Tenn.

6. A feather in the hand is better than a bird in the air. *Rec. dist.:* N.Y. **1st cit.:** 1640 Herbert, *Outlandish Proverbs (Jacula Prudentum)* in *Works,* ed. Hutchinson (1941). **20c. coll.:** ODEP 251.

7. A mockingbird has no voice of its own. *Rec. dist.:* S.C. **1st cit.:** US1855 Haliburton, *Nature and Human Nature* (1855). **20c. coll.:** T&W 27.

8. As a bird wanders from its nest, so a man wanders from his home. *Rec. dist.:* Vt.

9. As the old bird sings, so the young ones twitter. *Rec. dist.:* Ind.

10. Bad bird, bad eggs. *Rec. dist.:* Ind. *Infm.:* More common form is "Such a bird, such a nest." **1st cit.:** 1586 Guazzo, *Civile Conversation,* tr. Pettie, T.T. (1925). **20c. coll.:** Stevenson 178:3.

11. Better one bird in the bush than two in the tree. *Rec. dist.:* Calif., Colo.

12. Birds of a feather flock together. *Vars.:* **(a)** Birds of a color flock together. **(b)** Birds of a feather will fly together. *Rec. dist.:* U.S., Can. *1st cit.:* 1545 Turner, *Rescuing of the Romish Fox;* US1674 Josselyn, *Account of Two Voyages to New England. 20c. coll.:* ODEP 60, Whiting 31, *CODP* 20, Stevenson 1430:3, T&W 28, Whiting*(MP)* 49.

13. Each bird likes his own nest best. *Rec. dist.:* U.S., Can. *1st cit.:* ca1594 Bacon, *Promus. 20c. coll.:* ODEP 60, Stevenson 178:5.

14. Every bird is known by its feathers. *Rec. dist.:* Ind.

15. Every bird likes to hear himself sing. *Rec. dist.:* U.S., Can. *1st cit.:* 1659 Howell, *English Proverbs. 20c. coll.:* Stevenson 178:10.

16. Every high-flying bird must at some time light. *Rec. dist.:* U.S., Can.

17. Faraway birds have fine feathers. *Rec. dist.:* N.Y. *Infm.:* Cf. "Faraway hills are green." *1st cit.:* US1794 *Philadelphia Gazette* in Calendar, *American Annual Register for 1796* (1797). *20c. coll.:* Whiting 32.

18. Frightening a bird is not the way to catch it. *Rec. dist.:* Okla. *1st cit.:* ca1594 Bacon, *Promus. 20c. coll.:* ODEP 291, Stevenson 177:7.

19. Hasty bird makes hasty nest. *Rec. dist.:* S.C.

20. Hit takes two birds fer to make a nes'. *Rec. dist.:* N.Y., S.C. *Infm.:* Dialect form is by Joel C. Harris. *1st cit.:* US1880 Harris, *Plantation Proverbs* in *Uncle Remus, His Songs and His Sayings. 20c. coll.:* Stevenson 1151:11.

21. It is the beautiful bird which gets caged. *Rec. dist.:* Ill.

22. It's an ill bird that fowls its own nest. *Vars.:* **(a)** It's a mean bird that dirties its own nest. **(b)** It's a poor bird that will dirty its own nest. *Rec. dist.:* U.S., Can. *1st cit.:* ca1250 *Owl and Nightingale;* US1666 Alsop, *Character of Province of Maryland,* ed. Mereness (1902). *20c. coll.:* ODEP 397, Whiting 32, *CODP* 119, Stevenson 179:5, T&W 28, Whiting*(MP)* 49.

23. Little bird, little nest. *Rec. dist.:* Tex. *1st cit.:* 1616 Draxe, *Bibliotheca Scholastica* in *Anglia* (1918). *20c. coll.:* ODEP 469, Stevenson 177:6.

24. Little birds in their nests agree. *Rec. dist.:* Mich., N.Y., S.C. *Infm.:* Said to children when they are quarreling. *1st cit.:* 1715 Watts, *Divine Songs;* US1941 Wilder, *Little Town on the Prairie. 20c. coll.:* *CODP* 19, Stevenson 177:6.

25. Little by little the bird builds his nest. *Rec. dist.:* Oreg. *Infm.:* Said to children to teach them patience.

26. 'Most kill bird don't make stew. *Vars.:* **(a)** 'Mos' kill bird don't make soup. **(b)** 'Mos' kill bird ent mek stew. *Rec. dist.:* Miss., N.Y., S.C. *Infm.:* You get no good out of something you almost do.

27. The bird that can sing and won't sing should be made to sing. *Rec. dist.:* Ky., Tenn. *1st cit.:* 1678 Ray, *English Proverbs;* US1796 Cobbett, *Porcupine's Works. 20c. coll.:* ODEP 469, Whiting 31, *CODP* 20, Stevenson 180:6, Whiting*(MP)* 49.

28. The early bird catches the worm. *Vars.:* **(a)** It is not the early bird that catches the worm, but the smart one. **(b)** The early bird befouls its nest. **(c)** The early bird catches the worm—but who wants worms? *Rec. dist.:* U.S., Can. *1st cit.:* 1636 Camden, *Remaines Concerning Britaine;* US1853 Haliburton, *Sam Slick's Wise Saws. 20c. coll.:* ODEP 211, Stevenson 180:11, *CODP* 62, T&W 28, Whiting*(MP)* 49.

29. The hit bird flutters. *Var.:* A wounded bird will flutter. *Rec. dist.:* Ariz., Kans. *1st cit.:* 1721 Kelly, *Scottish Proverbs. 20c. coll.:* *CODP* 19.

30. There are no birds in last year's nest. *Var.:* Never look for birds of this year in the nests of the last. *Rec. dist.:* Kans., Wis. *1st cit.:* 1620 Cervantes, *Don Quixote,* tr. Shelton; US1845 Longfellow, *It Is Not Always May. 20c. coll.:* ODEP 60, *CODP* 19, Stevenson 177:4.

31. There is more than one way to kill a bird. *Rec. dist.:* Fla., Iowa.

32. There never was a bird who flew so high but what he came down again. *Vars.:* **(a)** A bird may fly high, but he must come down for water. **(b)** A bird never flew so high but it will fly just as low. **(c)** A bird never flies so high but someone can tame it. **(d)** A bird never flies so high that he doesn't know how to light. **(e)** A bird never flies so high that it doesn't touch the ground. **(f)** A bird never flies too high but what he has to light for water. *Rec. dist.:* U.S., Can.

33. Two birds in the bush are still two birds in the bush. *Rec. dist.:* Ariz., Kans. *Infm.:* You are unsuccessful even though you have tried. *1st cit.:* US1941 Marlett, *Death Has a Thousand Doors. 20c. coll.:* Stevenson 181:3.

34. Two birds of prey seldom hunt together. *Rec. dist.:* Ariz.

35. You can't keep the birds from flying over your head, but you can keep them from building a nest in your hair. *Vars.:* **(a)** Though the bird may fly over your head, let it not make its nest in you hair. **(b)** We can't keep the birds from flying over us, but we can keep them from building nests in our hair. **(c)** You cannot prevent the birds of sorrow from flying over your head, but you can prevent them from building nests in your hair. *Rec. dist.:* U.S., Can.

36. You cannot catch old birds with chaff. *Var.:* Old birds only laugh when you try to catch them with chaff. *Rec. dist.:* U.S., Can. *1st cit.:* 1481 Caxton, *Reynard the Fox;* US1755 *Colonial Virginia Satirist,* ed. Davis, Am. Phil.Soc. *Transactions* (1967). *20c. coll.:* ODEP 110, Whiting 33, CODP 33, Stevenson 180:7, T&W 29, Whiting(MP) 50.

See also A fine CAGE won't feed the hungry bird. / CHICKEN ain't nothin' but a bird. / The EAGLE suffers the little bird to sing. / Fine FEATHERS do not make fine birds. / You can't put new FEATHERS on a bird. / GOD sends every bird its food, but He does not throw it into the nest. / Spoken WORDS are like flown birds: neither can be recalled.

birth 1. A man of high birth may be of low worth, and vice versa. *Rec. dist.:* Ill.

2. Birth is much, but breeding is more. *Var.:* Birth is much; breeding is more. *Rec. dist.:* Okla., R.I. *1st cit.:* 1613 Stephens, *Cynthia's Revenge 20c. coll.:* ODEP 61, Stevenson 239:4.

3. No man can help his birth. *Rec. dist.:* Ill. *Infm.:* Stevenson traces the proverb to Mid-

rash: *Leviticus Rabbah* (ca450). *1st cit.:* US1948 Stevenson, *Home Book of Proverbs. 20c. coll.:* Stevenson 185:3.

See also True NOBILITY lies in worth, not birth.

birthright See SCHOLARS are wont to sell their birthright for a mess of learning.

biscuit Burned biscuits will not make a warm house. *Rec. dist.:* N.C.

See also De one dat drap de CRUTCH de bes gits de mos' biscuits.

bishop Nobody is born learned; bishops are made of men. *Rec. dist.:* Ill.

bit *(amount)* **1.** A bit in the morning is better than nothing all day. *Rec. dist.:* Oreg. *1st cit.:* 1678 Ray, *English Proverbs. 20c. coll.:* Stevenson 236:9.

2. Every little bit added to what you have makes just a little bit more. *Rec. dist.:* Ill.

3. Every little bit counts. *Rec. dist.:* N.Y.

4. Every little bit helps. *Rec. dist.:* U.S., Can. *1st cit.:* 1923 Fletcher, *Charing Cross Mystery;* US1787 Hazard in *Belknap Papers,* Mass. Hist.Soc. *Collections* (1877, 1891). *20c. coll.:* Whiting 264, T&W 225, Whiting(MP) 379.

See also A little bit of POWDER and a little bit of paint make a woman look like what she ain't. / A WOMAN knows a bit more than Satan.

bit *(horse)* A golden bit does not make the horse any better. *Rec. dist.:* Ill. *Infm.:* Stevenson traces the proverb to Seneca, *Ad Lucilium* (ca64). *1st cit.:* US1948 Stevenson, *Home Book of Proverbs. 20c. coll.:* Stevenson 990:8.

bitch The hasty bitch brings forth blind puppies. *Rec. dist.:* N.Y., S.C. *1st cit.:* 1556 More, *Utopia,* tr. Robinson; US1755 Franklin, *PRAlmanac. 20c. coll.:* ODEP 356, Whiting 34, Stevenson 1080:11.

bite *(n.)* Never make two bites at a cherry. *Rec. dist.:* N.Y., S.C. *1st cit.:* 1666 Torriano, *Common Place of Italian Proverbs;* US1843 *Letters of James Kirk-Paulding,* ed. Aderman (1962). *20c. coll.:* ODEP 849, Whiting 34, Stevenson 190:1, T&W 30, Whiting(MP) 53.

SEE ALSO A dog's BARK is worse than his bite. / The hair of the DOG is good for the bite.

bite *(v.)* **1.** Don't bite the hand that feeds you. *Var.:* Don't bite the hand that butters your bread. *Rec. dist.:* U.S., Can. *1st cit.:* 1711 Addison, *Spectator*, ed. Bond; US1893 Twain, *Pudd'nhead Wilson's Calendar.* *20c. coll.:* ODEP 62, Stevenson 1242:9.

2. Never bite on another man's game. *Rec. dist.:* Kans.

SEE ALSO A barking DOG never bites. / A man may cause even his own DOG to bite him. / A wagging-tailed DOG never bites. / The mad DOG bites his master. / When a DOG bites a man, that is not news; but when a man bites a dog, that is news. / All DOGS bite the bitten dog. / In every country DOGS bite. / The ELBOW is near, but try and bite it. / Bait the HOOK well and the fish will bite. / A LOUSE not killed is sure to bite again.

biter The biter is sometimes bit. *Rec. dist.:* Ill. *1st cit.:* 1693 D'Urfey, *Richmond Heiress*; US1780 Sargent, *Loyalist Poetry of the Revolution* (1857). *20c. coll.:* ODEP 62, Whiting 34, Stevenson 189:5, T&W 30, Whiting(MP) 53.

SEE ALSO The greatest BARKERS are not the greatest biters. / It always makes the DEVIL laugh to see the biter bitten.

biting SEE REVENGE is like biting a dog because he bit you.

bitten **1.** A man once bitten by a snake will jump at the sight of a rope in his path. *Rec. dist.:* Tex.

2. Once bitten, twice shy. *Var.:* Once bit, twice shy. *Rec. dist.:* U.S., Can. *1st cit.:* 1853 Surtees, *Sponge's Sporting Tour*; US1906 Mitchell, *New York Idea.* *20c. coll.:* ODEP 594, Stevenson 725:8, CODP 169, Whiting(MP) 53.

SEE ALSO You can look at TEETH and not be bitten.

bitter *(n.)* **1.** Every bitter has its sweet. *Vars.:* **(a)** Every bitter has its sweet, or, rather, every sweet has its bitter. **(b)** Where there's a sweet, there's always a bitter. *Rec. dist.:* U.S., Can. *1st cit.:* 1576 Pettie, *Petite Palace of Pleasure*, ed. Gollancz (1908). *20c. coll.:* Stevenson 2260:9.

2. The bitter must come before the sweet. *Rec. dist.:* N.C. *1st cit.:* ca1374 Chaucer, *Troilus and Criseyde*; US1938 Champion, *Racial Proverbs.* *20c. coll.:* Stevenson 2259:4.

3. Who has bitter in his mouth spits not at all sweet. *Rec. dist.:* Ill. *1st cit.:* 1640 Herbert, *Outlandish Proverbs (Jacula Prudentum)* in *Works*, ed. Hutchinson (1941). *20c. coll.:* ODEP 63, Stevenson 2260:3.

4. You have to take the bitter with the sweet. *Vars.:* **(a)** Always take the bitter with the better. **(b)** We must take the bitter with the better. *Rec. dist.:* U.S., Can. *1st cit.:* 1546 Heywood, *Proverbs in the Englishe Tongue*; US1778 *Writings of George Washington*, ed. Fitzpatrick (1931–44). *20c. coll.:* Stevenson 2260:9, Whiting 34, Whiting(MP) 53.

SEE ALSO We know the SWEET when we have tasted the bitter.

bitter *(adj.)* **1.** Bitter is the bread of charity. *Rec. dist.:* N.Y., S.C.

2. That which was bitter to endure may be sweet to remember. *Vars.:* **(a)** What is bitter to stand against today may be sweet to remember tomorrow. **(b)** What may be bitter today may be sweet to remember tomorrow. *Rec. dist.:* Ala., Ga., N.J., Ont. *1st cit.:* 1732 Fuller, *Gnomologia.* *20c. coll.:* Stevenson 2261:4.

SEE ALSO The weed of CRIME bears bitter fruit. / DEFEAT isn't bitter if you don't swallow it. / HUNGER sweetens what is bitter.

bitterest Those who have not tasted the bitterest of life's bitters can never appreciate the sweetest of life's sweets. *Rec. dist.:* Ariz. *1st cit.:* ca1374 Chaucer, *Troilus and Criseyde*; US1938 Champion, *Racial Proverbs.* *20c. coll.:* Stevenson 2259:4.

SEE ALSO An injured FRIEND is the bitterest of foes.

blab Blab is not cheer; froth is not beer. *Rec. dist.:* Minn., Wis.

black *(n.)* **1.** Black is black and white is white. *Rec. dist.:* Kans. *Infm.:* Be exact. *1st cit.:* 1528 Roy and Barlow, *Read Me and Be Not Wroth.* *20c. coll.:* ODEP 64, Stevenson 2194:3.

2. Black will take no other hue. *Rec. dist.:* Okla. *1st cit.:* ca1540 Bale, *Kinge Johan.* *20c. coll.:* ODEP 65, Stevenson 191:10.

3. Two blacks don't make a white. *Rec. dist.:* U.S., Can. *1st cit.:* 1721 Kelly, *Scottish Proverbs.* *20c. coll.:* *ODEP* 849, *CODP* 233, Whiting*(MP)* 54.

black *(adj.)* From the black man keep your wife; with a red man beware your knife. *Rec. dist.:* Colo., N.Y., S.C.
SEE ALSO If you want to keep a BOY out of the mud, blacken his boots. / CROWS are black the world over. / The DEVIL is not as black as he is painted. / A black HEN always lays a white egg. / No LIES are white; they are all black. / White LIES are but ushers to the black ones. / He who touches PITCH will get black. / The POT calls the kettle black. / You can't rub on a black POT without getting black on you. / There is a black SHEEP in every flock. / A black SHOE makes a blithe heart. / All WOMEN and cats are black in darkness.

blackberry Rather eat blackberries than rabbits: they are less fatiguing to overtake. *Rec. dist.:* N.Y.

blackbird One for the blackbird, one for the crow, one for the cutworm, and one for to grow. *Rec. dist.:* N.Y.

blacker *SEE* The blacker the BERRY, the sweeter the juice.

blackest When things look blackest, happiness is often just around the corner. *Rec. dist.:* Ind.

blacksmith **1.** Only the witless one expects the blacksmith to wear a white silk apron. *Rec. dist.:* N.Y., S.C. *1st cit.:* 1732 Fuller, *Gnomologia.* *20c. coll.:* Stevenson 2146:12.

2. The blacksmith's horse and the shoemaker's family always go unshod. *Var.:* The blacksmith's horses are always shod the worst. *Rec. dist.:* N.Y., Pa., S.C.

blade *SEE* Every blade of GRASS has its share of the dews of heaven.

blame *(n.)* **1.** Blame is safer than praise. *Rec. dist.:* N.Y., S.C. *1st cit.:* US1841 Emerson, "Compensation" in *Essays.* *20c. coll.:* Stevenson 457:7.

2. Blame is the lazy man's wages. *Rec. dist.:* Ill.

SEE ALSO If you wish PRAISE, die; if you wish blame, marry.

blame *(v.)* **1.** Avoid that which you blame in others. *Rec. dist.:* Mich.

2. When fools make mistakes, they blame it on Providence. *Rec. dist.:* Miss.
SEE ALSO Blame not others for the FAULTS that are in you. / The losing HORSE blames the saddle.

blame-all Blame-all and praise-all are two blockheads. *Rec. dist.:* N.Y., S.C. *1st cit.:* US1734 Franklin, *PRAlmanac.* *20c. coll.:* Stevenson 457:7.

blamed *SEE* When KNAVES betray each other, one can scarce be blamed or the other pitied. / TRUTH may be blamed, but never shamed. / No one was ever blamed for TRYING.

blanket **1.** Don't rush off in the heat of the day without your blanket. *Rec. dist.:* Ind. *Infm.:* Said to one who makes a hurried call (visit).

2. The Indian usually comes back to his blanket. *Rec. dist.:* Calif., Colo., N.Mex., Oreg. *Infm.:* An educated Indian returns to his native culture despite his wealth or education.

blasphemy There is only one blasphemy, and that is injustice. *Rec. dist.:* Ill.

blast *SEE* The REED does blow at every blast. / SORROW remains when joy is but a blast.

blaze The blaze of glory is the firebrand of the mind. *Rec. dist.:* Mich.

bleed *SEE* PAPER bleeds little.

bless **1.** Bless them which persecute you; bless and curse not. *Rec. dist.:* N.Y., Wis. *Infm.:* Cf. Rom. 12:14.

2. He who blesses most is blessed. *Rec. dist.:* N.Y. *1st cit.:* 1733 Pope, *Essay on Man;* US1858 Whittier, *Lines for Agricultural Exhibition at Amesbury.* *20c. coll.:* Stevenson 196:7.

blessed **1.** Blessed are they that have not seen and yet have believed. *Rec. dist.:* R.I. *Infm.:* Cf. John 20:29. *1st cit.:* US1948 Stevenson, *Home Book of Proverbs.* *20c. coll.:* Stevenson 162:9.

2. Blessed are they who expect nothing, for they shall not be disappointed. *Rec. dist.:* Ind., Wis. *1st cit.:* 1727 Pope, Letter to Gay, 6 Oct.

in *Works* (1824); US1739 Franklin, *PRAlmanac*. *20c. coll.: ODEP* 66, *CODP* 20, Stevenson 721:16, Whiting*(MP)* 453.

3. Blessed is he who takes himself seriously. *Rec. dist.:* Ohio.

4. Blessed is the man who, having nothing to say, says nothing. *Rec. dist.:* Md., Okla. *1st cit.:* 1879 Eliot, *Impressions of Theophrastus Such*. *20c. coll.:* Stevenson 2186:7.

5. To be blessed is not easy. *Rec. dist.:* N.Y. *1st cit.:* 1939 Frank, *The Bridegroom Cometh*. *20c. coll.:* Stevenson 1000:11.

SEE ALSO Blessed are the horned HANDS of toil. / Blessed are the HAPPINESS makers. / Blessed are they that hear the WORD of God and keep it.

blessing **1.** Blessings brighten as they take their flight. *Rec. dist.:* Oreg. *1st cit.:* 1732 Fuller, *Gnomologia;* US1873 Coolidge, *What Katy Did*. *20c. coll.: CODP* 21, Stevenson 196:4.

2. Don't beg a blessing of a wooden god. *Rec. dist.:* Ill.

3. Everything depends on God's blessing. *Rec. dist.:* Kans.

4. Most blessings in disguise are painfully slow in unmasking. *Rec. dist.:* Vt.

5. The blessing of earth is toil. *Rec. dist.:* Minn.

SEE ALSO A national DEBT, if it is not excessive, will be to us a national blessing. / An honest HEART being the first blessing, a knowing head is the second. / TEMPTATION is a blessing in disguise. / WISDOM is ever a blessing; education is sometimes a curse.

blind *(n.)* **1.** In the land of the blind, the one-eyed are kings. *Var.:* In the land of the blind, the one-eyes are kings. *Rec. dist.:* U.S., Can. *1st cit.:* ca1522 Skelton, *Why Come Ye Nat to Courte*. *20c. coll.: ODEP* 428, *CODP* 43, Stevenson 197:8.

2. The blind are bold, but they stumble and fall. *Rec. dist.:* Calif., Colo.

blind *(v.)* SEE INTEREST blinds some people, enlightens others.

blind *(adj.)* **1.** A blind man can see his mouth. *Rec. dist.:* Miss.

2. A blind man is no judge of colors. *Vars.:* **(a)** A blind man can judge no colors. **(b)** A blind man should not judge colors. *Rec. dist.:* Ind., N.Y. *1st cit.:* ca1374 Chaucer, *Troilus and Criseyde*. *20c. coll.: ODEP* 68, Stevenson 197:7.

3. A blind man loses his staff only once. *Rec. dist.:* Ind.

4. A blind man may sometimes shoot a crow by accident. *Rec. dist.:* Ill. *1st cit.:* ca1384 Chaucer, *House of Fame*. *20c. coll.: ODEP* 67, Stevenson 198:9.

5. A blind man needs no looking glass. *Var.:* A blind man will not thank you for a looking glass. *Rec. dist.:* N.Y., Ont. *1st cit.:* 1732 Fuller, *Gnomologia*. *20c. coll.:* Stevenson 198:2.

6. Better blind than burned. *Rec. dist.:* Ohio. *1st cit.:* 1640 Herbert, *Outlandish Proverbs (Jacula Prudentum)* in *Works,* ed. Hutchinson (1941). *20c. coll.:* Stevenson 198:5.

7. If the blind lead the blind, both shall fall into the ditch. *Var.:* When the blind lead the blind, they all go head over heels into the ditch. *Rec. dist.:* U.S., Can. *1st cit.:* 897 Alfred, *Gregory's Pastoral Care,* ed. Sweet, E.E.T.S. (1871); US1733 *Writings of Samuel Johnson, President of King's College,* ed. Schneider (1929). *20c. coll.: CODP* 21, *ODEP* 67, Whiting 35, Stevenson 198:11, Whiting*(MP)* 55.

8. It is worse to be blind than bald. *Rec. dist.:* Minn.

9. The blind man's peck should be well measured. *Rec. dist.:* N.Y. *1st cit.:* 1832 Henderson, *Scottish Proverbs*. *20c. coll.: ODEP* 68, Stevenson 198:4.

10. The blind man's wife needs no painting. *Rec. dist.:* N.Y., S.C. *1st cit.:* 1659 Howell, *Paroimiografia (Spanish Proverbs);* US1736 Franklin, *PRAlmanac*. *20c. coll.: CODP* 21, Stevenson 2496:5.

11. There are none so blind as those who cannot see. *Vars.:* **(a)** None are so blind as those who refuse to see. **(b)** None so deaf as those who will not hear; none so blind as those who will not see. **(c)** There are none so blind as those who will not see. *Rec. dist.:* U.S., Can. *1st cit.:* 1546 Heywood, *Dialogue* *of Proverbs,* ed. Habernicht (1963); US1713 *Works of Thomas Chalkley.* **20c. coll.:** *ODEP* 67, Whiting 35, *CODP* 21, Stevenson 198:10, Whiting*(MP)* 56.

12. We all have our blind spots. *Rec. dist.:* Ill.

SEE ALSO When BEAUTY is at the bar, blind men make the best jury. / A blind DOG won't bark at the moon. / ENVY is blind. / GOD builds a nest for the blind bird. / The blind HORSE is fittest for the mill. / A deaf HUSBAND and a blind wife are always a happy couple. / JUSTICE is blind. / KINDNESS is language which the deaf can hear and the blind can see. / LOVE is blind. / One-eyed MULE can't be handled on the blind side. / It doesn't matter if the OX is blind; load the wagon and apply the line. / A PEBBLE and a diamond are alike to a blind man. / Even a blind PIG occasionally picks up an acorn.

blinded *SEE* Never think yourself so BRILLIANT that you are blinded by your own light.

bliss **1.** A moment of bliss; lifetime of sorrow. *Rec. dist.:* N.Y., Ohio.

2. Every one to his bliss. *Rec. dist.:* Minn.

3. There is eternal bliss in a momentary kiss. *Rec. dist.:* Ill.

4. Who falls from all he knows of bliss cares little into what abyss. *Rec. dist.:* Miss.

SEE ALSO IGNORANCE is bliss. / Where IGNORANCE is bliss, 'tis folly to be wise.

blister If you get burnt you got to sit on the blister. *Vars.:* **(a)** He burned his own blister; now let him sit on it. **(b)** If one of my youngins married and got himself blistered, he'd have to sit on the blister. **(c)** If you burn your bottom, you will have to sit on your blisters. **(d)** If you get burnt, sit on the blister. **(e)** The fellow who burns his seat must sit in the blisters. *Rec. dist.:* U.S., Can.

SEE ALSO LIFE is short and full o' blisters.

blithe *SEE* A blithe HEART makes a blooming visage. / A black SHOE makes a blithe heart.

block **1.** Don't be stumbling blocks but stepping-stones. *Rec. dist.:* Miss.

2. The only difference between stumbling blocks and stepping-stones is the way you use them. *Rec. dist.:* Ont., Wis.

SEE ALSO BUSINESS is to grown men what blocks are to children.

blockhead **1.** A learned blockhead is a greater blockhead than an ignorant one. *Rec. dist.:* N.Y. **1st cit.:** US1734 Franklin, *PRAlmanac.* **20c. coll.:** Stevenson 1376:2.

2. He who has to deal with a blockhead has need of much brains. *Rec. dist.:* Mich.

blonde **1.** A blonde needs just enough perfume for you to know that she's around. *Rec. dist.:* N.C.

2. Blondes aren't the only people who are light-headed. *Rec. dist.:* Ohio.

SEE ALSO GENTLEMEN prefer blondes.

blood **1.** Blood and whiskey run together. *Rec. dist.:* Ky., Tenn.

2. Blood asks blood, and death must death requite. *Rec. dist.:* N.C. **1st cit.:** ca1449 Lydgate, *Minor Poems,* E.E.T.S.; US1764 *Paxton Papers,* ed. Dunbar (1957). **20c. coll.:** *CODP* 22, Whiting 36, *ODEP* 69, Stevenson 202:6, T&W 33, Whiting*(MP)* 57.

3. Blood boils without fire. *Rec. dist.:* Ky., Tenn. **1st cit.:** US1844 Stephens, *High Life in New York.* **20c. coll.:** T&W 34.

4. Blood follows the veins. *Rec. dist.:* Ky., Tenn.

5. Blood is inherited and virtue acquired. *Rec. dist.:* Ill.

6. Blood is thicker than water. *Var.:* Blood is thicker than water, but sometimes it runs mighty thin. *Rec. dist.:* U.S., Can. **1st cit.:** ca1412 Lydgate, *Troy Book,* E.E.T.S.; US1821 Simpson, *Journal of Athabasca Department, 1820–21,* ed. Rich, Champlain Soc. *Publications* (1938). **20c. coll.:** *CODP* 22, Whiting 36, *ODEP* 68, Stevenson 202:7, T&W 33, Whiting*(MP)* 56.

7. Blood will tell. *Var.:* Game to the backbone—blood will tell. *Rec. dist.:* Md., N.Y., S.C. **1st cit.:** ca1489 *Foure Sonnes of Aymon,* tr. Caxton; US1850 Boker, *World a Mask* in *Glaucus and Other Plays,* ed. Bradley (1940). **20c. coll.:** Stevenson 201:17, T&W 33, Whiting*(MP)* 57.

8. Human blood is all one color. *Rec. dist.:* Ill., N.Y., N.Dak., Wis.

9. New blood tells. *Rec. dist.:* Ala., Ga.

10. The blood of the martyrs is the seed of the church. *Rec. dist.:* N.Y. *1st cit.:* 1560 Pilkington, *Aggeus the Prophet;* US1747 Skith, *History of First Settlement of Virginia. 20c. coll.:* ODEP 69, Whiting 36, *CODP* 22, Stevenson 1544:11, T&W 33, Whiting*(MP)* 57.

11. The blood remembers what the mind has never known. *Rec. dist.:* Calif., Colo., S.C.

12. You can't get blood out of a turnip. *Var.:* You can't get blood out of a turnip, but you can wring the devil out of the top. *Rec. dist.:* U.S., Can. *1st cit.:* 1666 Torriano, *Common Place of Italian Proverbs;* US1800 *Letters from William Cobbett to Edward Thornton,* ed. Cole (1937). *20c. coll.:* ODEP 869, Whiting 36, *CODP* 21, Stevenson 203:8, T&W 34, Whiting*(MP)* 57.

See also BUSINESS is the blood of our national life. / The smaller the DRINK, the clearer the head, the cooler the blood. / GASOLINE and whisky usually mix with blood on the highway. / The STAIN of wine is like the stain of blood.

bloom *See* BEAUTY is the bloom of youth.

blooming *See* A blithe HEART makes a blooming visage.

blossom *See* Those who cling must grasp BRANCHES, not blossoms. / You can't eat the FRUIT while the tree is in blossom. / HOME is the blossom of which heaven is the fruit. / HOPE is the blossom of happiness. / A LIE will give blossom but no fruit. / A TREE with beautiful blossom does not always yield the best fruit.

blot Cleaning a blot with dirty fingers only makes a greater smear. *Rec. dist.:* Ill. *1st cit.:* 1732 Fuller, *Gnomologia. 20c. coll.:* Stevenson 204:1.

blow *(n.)* **1.** A blow from a lover is as sweet as eating raisins. *Rec. dist.:* Ind.

2. He who returns the first blow is the man who begins the quarrel. *Rec. dist.:* Ohio.

3. Strike the first blow; it's as good as two. *Rec. dist.:* Ill., N.Y. *1st cit.:* 1640 Herbert, *Outlandish Proverbs (Jacula Prudentum)* in *Works,*

ed. Hutchinson (1941); US1763 Bernard, *Documentary History of Maine: Baxter Manuscripts,* ed. Baxter (1869–1916). *20c. coll.:* ODEP 261, Whiting 37, Stevenson 204:13, Whiting*(MP)* 58.

4. The blow falls more lightly if you expect it. *Rec. dist.:* Ill.

5. The first blow does not fell the tree. *Rec. dist.:* N.Y.

6. 'Tis the second blow that makes the fray. *Var.:* It takes two blows to make a battle. *Rec. dist.:* Mich., Wis. *1st cit.:* 1589 Bacon, *Advertisement Touching the Controversies of the Church of England,* ed. Burgoyne. *20c. coll.:* ODEP 261, Stevenson 204:3.

blow *(v.)* *See* One who blows a HORN will never blow a vault. / The fellow who blows his HORN the loudest is likely in the biggest fog. / All are not HUNTERS who blow the horn. / The STEAM that blows the whistle will never turn the wheel. / An ill WIND blows no good. / Whatever way the WIND does blow, some hearts are glad to have it so.

blue *(n.)* **1.** The blue of heaven is larger than the clouds. *Rec. dist.:* N.C.

2. True blue will never stain. *Var.:* True blue will never stain, but dirty red will dye again. *Rec. dist.:* N.Dak., Okla. *1st cit.:* 1579 Lyly, *Euphues, Anatomy of Wit;* US1802 Irving, *Letters of Jonathan Oldstyle,* ed. Williams (1941). *20c. coll.:* ODEP 841, Whiting 37, Stevenson 205:6.

blue *(adj.)* *See* Blue EYES, true eyes. / A green SALESMAN will sell more than a blue one.

bluejay The bluejay never screams for nothing. *Rec. dist.:* Minn.

blueberry A blueberry is red when it is green. *Rec. dist.:* Kans.

bluff *See* The hardest TUMBLE a man can take is the fall off his own bluff.

bluffing If you're caught bluffing, you lose the pot. *Rec. dist.:* Ohio.

blunder Brooding over blunders is the biggest blunder. *Rec. dist.:* N.C.

blush *(n.)* **1.** A blush is beautiful but often inconvenient. *Rec. dist.:* Wis. *Infm.:* Stevenson cites Goldoni, *Pamela* (ca1770). *1st cit.:* US1948 Stevenson, *Home Book of Proverbs.* *20c. coll.:* Stevenson 207:2.

2. A blush on the face is better than a blot on the heart. *Rec. dist.:* N.C.

blush *(v.)* The man that blushes is not quite a brute. *Rec. dist.:* N.Y. *1st cit.:* 1745 Young, *Night Thoughts.* *20c. coll.:* Stevenson 206:9.

SEE ALSO Many a FLOWER is born to blush unseen. / Do GOOD by stealth and blush to find it fame.

blushing Blushing is virtue's color. *Var.:* Blushing is the color of virtue. *Rec. dist.:* Ill., N.Dak. *1st cit.:* 1519 Horman, *Vulgaria* (1926 ed.) *20c. coll.:* ODEP 71, Stevenson 206:9.

board **1.** Elm boards will warp around your neck before you can get them from the mill. *Rec. dist.:* Ill.

2. The longer the board, the better the teeter. *Var.:* A long board for a good teeter. *Rec. dist.:* Utah, Wash.

boast *(n.)* Great boast, small roast. *Rec. dist.:* Ill. *1st cit.:* ca1532 Copland, *Spyttel House;* US1869 Spurgeon, *John Ploughman's Talks.* *20c. coll.:* ODEP 333, Stevenson 208:7.

boast *(v.)* **1.** Do not boast of a thing until it is done. *Var.:* The man who boasts boosts himself into the company of liars. *Rec. dist.:* Ohio.

2. Such as boast much usually fall much. *Rec. dist.:* Mich.

SEE ALSO One should live to BUILD, not to boast.

boaster **1.** A boaster and a liar are much about the same thing. *Var.:* Boasters are cousins to liars. *Rec. dist.:* Ill., Ind., N.J. *1st cit.:* ca1374 Chaucer, *Troilus and Criseyde.* *20c. coll.:* Stevenson 208:6.

2. Great boaster, little doer. *Rec. dist.:* Wis. *1st cit.:* 1869 Henderson, *Latin Proverbs.* *20c. coll.:* Stevenson 209:1.

boasting **1.** Of boasting be more than of a bomb afraid, merit should be as modest as a maid. *Rec. dist.:* N.Y., S.C.

2. Where boasting ends, there dignity begins. *Rec. dist.:* Iowa. *1st cit.:* 1745 Young, *Night Thoughts.* *20c. coll.:* Stevenson 209:7.

boat **1.** Don't complain of the boat that carries you over safely. *Rec. dist.:* Vt.

2. Every person should row his own boat. *Rec. dist.:* Ill. *1st cit.:* US1829 Turner in *Papers of Thomas Ruffin,* ed. Hamilton (1918–20). *20c. coll.:* Whiting 38, T&W 35.

3. Little boats should stay close to shore. *Vars.:* **(a)** Great boats may venture more, but little boats should keep near shore. **(b)** Great estates may venture more, but little boats shall keep near shore. **(c)** Larger boats may venture more, but little boats should stay near shore. **(d)** Little boats must hug the shore; larger ships may venture more. **(e)** Little boats should stay near shore. **(f)** Vessels large may venture more, but little boats should keep to shore. *Rec. dist.:* U.S., Can. *1st cit.:* 1678 Ray, *English Proverbs;* US1751 Franklin, *PRAlmanac.* *20c. coll.:* Stevenson 2100:15, Whiting 38.

4. Sit still in the boat that carries you across deep water. *Rec. dist.:* N.C.

5. You can't go far in a rowboat without oars. *Rec. dist.:* Ill., N.Y. *1st cit.:* 1573 Sanford, *Garden of Pleasure.* *20c. coll.:* ODEP 71, Stevenson 210:1.

SEE ALSO Venture not ALL in one boat. / He that takes the DEVIL into his boat must carry him over the sound. / When the WATER's high, the boat's high.

body **1.** A deformed body may have a beautiful soul. *Rec. dist.:* Wis.

2. A strong body makes the mind strong. *Rec. dist.:* Ala., Ga. *1st cit.:* US1785 *Papers of Thomas Jefferson,* ed. Boyd (1950). *20c. coll.:* Whiting 290, Stevenson 1583:4.

3. Idle bodies are generally busybodies. *Rec. dist.:* N.J.

4. Little bodies have great souls. *Rec. dist.:* Ind. *1st cit.:* 1599 Shakespeare, *Henry V.* *20c. coll.:* ODEP 469, Stevenson 2173:12.

5. Old in body, young in spirit. *Rec. dist.:* N.C.

6. The larger the body, the bigger the heart. *Rec. dist.:* Kans.

7. The weaker the body, the stronger the mind. *Rec. dist.:* Wash.

8. Though the body may be imprisoned, the soul can be free. *Rec. dist.:* Wis.

9. Ya have to summer an' winter a body before ya can git to know 'em. *Rec. dist.:* Vt.

SEE ALSO COURAGE conquers all things; it even gives strength to the body. / A HOUSE without woman and firelight is like a body without soul or spirit. / INDUSTRY keeps the body healthy, the mind clear, the heart whole, and the purse full. / It's a poor pair of LEGS that will stand around and see the body bruised. / PAIN wastes the body, pleasures the understanding.

boil *(n.)* Everybody thinks the boil on his own neck is the biggest. *Rec. dist.:* Wash.

boil *(v.)* We boil at different degrees. *Rec. dist.:* Ill. **1st cit.:** US1870 Emerson, "Eloquence" in *Essays.* **20c. coll.:** Stevenson 2291:3.

SEE ALSO BEAUTY doesn't make the pot boil. / A KETTLE rattles most before it boils. / MONEY makes the pot boil. / A watched POT never boils. / The POT boils best on its own hearth.

boiling *SEE* The BUSY man has few idle visitors: to the boiling pot the flies come not. / The KETTLE's singing; 'twill soon be boiling.

bold **1.** Be bold, everywhere be bold, but be not bowled over. *Rec. dist.:* N.Y.

2. He was a bold man who first ate an oyster. *Rec. dist.:* N.Y. **1st cit.:** 1655 Moffett, *Health's Improvement.* **20c. coll.:** ODEP 72, Stevenson 1735:10.

SEE ALSO A bold ATTEMPT is half success. / The BLIND are bold, but they stumble and fall. / CARDS and dice is like all in life; dey ever falls well for bold players.

boldly **1.** Do boldly what you do at all. *Rec. dist.:* N.C.

2. He who talks boldly is quick to run away. *Rec. dist.:* R.I.

boldness Boldness does not always succeed. *Rec. dist.:* Mich.

bolt It takes a lot of bolts to hold a car together, but only one nut to scatter it all over the highway. *Rec. dist.:* Kans.

SEE ALSO A FOOL's bolt is soon shot.

bomb *SEE* People who live in STRAW houses shouldn't throw bombs.

bond The bonds of matrimony are like financial bonds: if the interest is not kept up, they become worthless. *Rec. dist.:* Ill.

SEE ALSO A kind FACE needs no bond.

bondage Disguise our bondage as we will, 'tis woman that rules us still. *Rec. dist.:* N.J. **1st cit.:** 1690 Vanbrugh, *Provok'd Wife.* **20c. coll.:** Stevenson 2583:8.

bone **1.** Gnaw the bone which has fallen to your lot. *Rec. dist.:* Ill. **1st cit.:** 1678 Ray, *Adagia Hebraica.* **20c. coll.:** Stevenson 415:4.

2. He that carries a bone will fetch one. *Rec. dist.:* Ariz., Md., Wis. **1st cit.:** 1830 Forby, *Vocabulary of East Anglia.* **20c. coll.:** CODP 58.

3. The closer to the bone, the sweeter the meat. *Vars.:* **(a)** The nearer the bone, the sweeter the flesh. **(b)** The nearer the bone, the sweeter the meat. *Rec. dist.:* U.S., Can. **1st cit.:** ca1398 Bartholomew, *On Properties of Things,* tr. Trevisa; US1778 Cooper in *Writings of Benjamin Franklin,* ed. Smyth (1905–07). **20c. coll.:** CODP 168, Whiting 40, ODEP 557, Stevenson 832:13, Whiting(MP) 63.

4. The sweetest meat is closest the bone. *Rec. dist.:* Kans., N.Y. **1st cit.:** 1662 Fuller, *History of the Worthies of England;* US1957 Erskine, *Pink.* **20c. coll.:** ODEP 557, Stevenson 832:13, Whiting(MP) 63.

5. What is bred in the bone will come out in the flesh. *Vars.:* **(a)** Bred in the bone will come out in the flesh. **(b)** What is bred in the bone will not out of the flesh. **(c)** What is bred in the bone will out in the flesh. **(d)** What is bred in the bone will tell. **(e)** What is bred in the bone won't out in the flesh. **(f)** What's bred in the bone stays there. **(g)** What's bred in the bones can't be beaten out with a stick. *Rec. dist.:* U.S., Can. **1st cit.:** ca1290 *Political Songs,* ed. Wright; US1637 *New English Canaan of Thomas Morton,* ed. Adams, Jr., Publ. Prince Soc. (1883). **20c. coll.:** Stevenson 238:7, Whiting 40, ODEP 83, CODP 25, T&W 37, Whiting(MP) 64.

6. What's in the bone is in the marrow. *Var.:* What's in the marrow can't be knocked out of the bone. *Rec. dist.:* Ill., Ky. **1st cit.:** 1485 Malory, *Morte d'Arthur;* US1637 *New English Canaan of Thomas Morton,* ed. Adams, Jr.,

Publ. Prince Soc. (1883). *20c. coll.*: *ODEP* 83, Whiting 40, *CODP* 25, Stevenson 238:7, T&W 37, Whiting *(MP)* 64.

SEE ALSO A COWARDLY man don't tote no broke bones. / A DOG that will fetch a bone will carry one. / A DOG will not cry if you beat him with a bone. / A DOG with a bone knows no friend. / A good DOG deserves a good bone. / A lazy DOG finds no bone. / Into the mouth of a bad DOG often falls a good bone. / Satisfy a DOG with a bone and a woman with a lie. / The DOG that trots about finds the bone. / Two DOGS over one bone seldom agree. / A sound HEART is the life of the flesh, but envy the rottenness of the bone. / NAMES break no bones. / A broken SPIRIT dries the bones. / STICKS and stones may break my bones, but names will never hurt me. / Soft WORDS break no bones.

bonnet Be ready with your bonnet but slow with your purse. *Rec. dist.*: N.Y.

book 1. A book is like a garden carried in the pocket. *Rec. dist.*: Minn.

2. A book may be as great a thing as a battle. *Rec. dist.*: Ill.

3. A book that remains shut is but a block. *Var.*: A book that is shut is but a block. *Rec. dist.*: N.Y., S.C. *1st cit.*: 1732 Fuller, *Gnomologia*. *20c. coll.*: Stevenson 217:8.

4. A closed book does not produce a learned man. *Rec. dist.*: Ill.

5. A fancy cover doesn't make a fancy book. *Rec. dist.*: Ill.

6. A few books well chosen are of more use than a great library. *Rec. dist.*: Mich.

7. A good book is the best of friends, the same today and forever. *Vars.*: **(a)** A good book is a great friend. **(b)** A good book is the best companion. *Rec. dist.*: Ind., N.C. *1st cit.*: 1838 Tupper, "Of Reading" in *Proverbial Philosophy;* US1807 Irving, *Salmagundi* in *Works of Washington Irving* (1873). *20c. coll.*: Stevenson 218:2, Whiting 40.

8. A man without books is like a king without money. *Rec. dist.*: Ohio.

9. A wicked book is the wickeder because it cannot repent. *Rec. dist.*: Ill. *1st cit.*: 1732 Fuller, *Gnomologia*. *20c. coll.*: Stevenson 218:8.

10. An old book wears well. *Rec. dist.*: Ky.

11. Beware of the man of one book. *Var.*: God protect us from him who has read but one book. *Rec. dist.*: Wis. *1st cit.*: 1642 Torriano, *Select Italian Proverbs*. *20c. coll.*: *ODEP* 58, Stevenson 215:6.

12. Book larnin spiles a man ef he's got mother wit; and ef he ain't got that, et don't do him no good. *Rec. dist.*: N.Y. *Infm.*: "Spiles" means "spoils." *1st cit.*: US1846 Hooper, *Some Adventures of Captain Simon Suggs*. *20c. coll.*: T&W 38.

13. Books alone can never teach the use of books. *Rec. dist.*: Mich.

14. Books and friends should be few and good. *Vars.*: **(a)** Books, like friends, should be few and well chosen. **(b)** Choose your books as you choose your friends. **(c)** Choose your friends like your books: few but choice. *Rec. dist.*: U.S., Can. *1st cit.*: 1820 Colton, *Lacon*. *20c. coll.*: Stevenson 218:2.

15. Books are doors to wide new ways. *Rec. dist.*: Minn.

16. Books are our cheapest friends. *Rec. dist.*: N.C.

17. Books are ships that pass through the vast seas of time. *Rec. dist.*: N.C.

18. Books are the windows through which we see the world. *Rec. dist.*: Calif.

19. Books breed like flies and die as fast. *Rec. dist.*: Ohio.

20. Books do not exhaust words, nor words thoughts. *Rec. dist.*: Minn.

21. Books give not wisdom where none was before. *Rec. dist.*: Ill.

22. Everything is not in books. *Rec. dist.*: N.C.

23. Good books are friends who are always ready to talk to us. *Rec. dist.*: Ind.

24. Good books are the nourishment of youth. *Rec. dist.*: Minn.

25. He that gains well and spends well needs no account book. *Rec. dist.*: Ind.

26. It is a tie between men to have read the same book. *Rec. dist.*: N.Y. *1st cit.*: US1864 *Journals of Ralph Waldo Emerson*, eds. Emerson and Forbes (1909–14). *20c. coll.*: Stevenson 1938:8.

27. Old books are old friends. *Rec. dist.*: Kans.

28. Read much but not too many books. *Rec. dist.:* Ill.

29. Some books leave us free and some books make us free. *Rec. dist.:* S.C. *1st cit.:* US1839 *Journals of Ralph Waldo Emerson,* 22 Dec. *20c. coll.:* Stevenson 217:5.

30. Something is learned every time a book is opened. *Rec. dist.:* Ind.

31. The best part of a book is not the thought it contains but the thought it suggests. *Rec. dist.:* Vt.

32. The man who doesn't read good books has no advantage over the man who can't read them. *Rec. dist.:* Ky., N.Y., Tenn.

33. The two most useful books in married life are the cookbook and the checkbook. *Rec. dist.:* Colo.

34. To open a book brings profit. *Rec. dist.:* Oreg.

35. Too many books make us ignorant. *Rec. dist.:* Ill.

36. Too many books spoil the student. *Rec. dist.:* N.Y., S.C.

37. You are known by the books you read. *Rec. dist.:* Miss.

38. You can't judge a book by its cover. *Vars.:* (a) Don't judge a book by its cover. (b) Never judge a book by its cover. (c) You can't tell a book by its cover. (d) You cannot judge a book by its binding. *Rec. dist.:* U.S., Can. *1st cit.:* 1954 Gardiner, *Murder in Haste;* US1929 *American Speech. 20c. coll.:* Whiting (MP) 65, CODP 23, Stevenson 83:3.

SEE ALSO A HOME without books is like a house without windows. / 'Tis the good READER that makes the book good. / There is no worse ROBBER than a bad book. / The true UNIVERSITY is a collection of books. / YEARS know more than books.

boomerang He who throws boomerangs should learn to duck. *Rec. dist.:* Calif.

booster A booster won't knock and a knocker won't boost. *Rec. dist.:* Colo.

boosting There's no boosting a man up the ladder unless he's willing to climb. *Rec. dist.:* Ky., Tenn.

boot *SEE* A LIE can go a mile before the truth can put its boots on. / A LIE can go around the world and back while the truth is lacing up its boots. / If you want to keep a BOY out of the mud, blacken his boots.

bootstrap Don't try to pull youself up by your own bootstraps. *Rec. dist.:* Ill., Ky., Ont., Tenn.

booze You can tell a man who boozes by the company he chooses. *Rec. dist.:* Ind.

bore (*n.*) **1.** A bore is a guy who is here today and here tomorrow. *Rec. dist.:* Ind.

2. It takes a bore to know a bore. *Rec. dist.:* N.Y.

3. The man who disagrees with you is a bore. *Rec. dist.:* Ill.

bore (*v.*) *SEE* Take your own ADVICE; you'll be too busy to bore others with it.

born **1.** A man is not completely born until he is dead. *Rec. dist.:* N.Y., S.C. *1st cit.:* US1756 Franklin, *Letter to Miss Hubbard. 20c. coll.:* Stevenson 523:11.

2. As soon as man is born, he begins to die. *Rec. dist.:* Calif., Colo., N.Y., S.C. *1st cit.:* 1576 Pettie, *Petite Palace of Pleasure,* ed. Gollancz (1908). *20c. coll.:* ODEP 752, Stevenson 524:6.

3. Every man born is not dead yet. *Rec. dist.:* N.C.

4. He who is born round cannot die square. *Rec. dist.:* N.Y.

5. We weep when we are born, not when we die. *Var.:* When you're born, you're done for. *Rec. dist.:* N.Y., S.C. *1st cit.:* UScа1880 Aldrich, *Metempsychosis. 20c. coll.:* Stevenson 523:14.

SEE ALSO From the day you were born till you ride in a hearse, there's nothing so BAD but it might have been worse. / We are born CRYING, live complaining, and die disappointed. / Many a FLOWER is born to blush unseen. / He who is born a FOOL is never cured. / A GENIUS is born, not made. / Some are born great, some achieve GREATNESS, and some have greatness thrust upon them. / HEROES are made, not born. / All MEN are born free and equal. / It is better to be NOBLY remembered than to be nobly born. / The

NOBLY born must nobly do. / Every man is not born with a silver SPOON in his mouth. / There's a SUCKER born every minute. / There is no man born into the world whose WORK is not born with him.

borrow *(n.)* **1.** Borrow and borrow adds up to sorrow. *Rec. dist.:* Kans. *1st cit.:* US1880 Sill, *Baker's Duzzen uv Wise Sawz.* *20c. coll.:* Stevenson 393:15.

2. Borrow will not pay debt. *Rec. dist.:* N.Y.

borrow *(v.)* **1.** One who borrows brews his own trouble. *Rec. dist.:* Ont.

2. To borrow or beg or get one's own, it is the very worst world that ever was known. *Rec. dist.:* Ont.

SEE ALSO Better BUY than borrow. / If you want to keep a FRIEND, never borrow, never lend. / TODAY must borrow nothing of to-morrow.

borrowed SEE Borrowed CLOTHES never fit.

borrower **1.** A good borrower makes a poor lender. *Rec. dist.:* N.Dak.

2. Neither a borrower nor a lender be. *Rec. dist.:* U.S., Can. *1st cit.:* 1600 Shakespeare, *Hamlet.* *20c. coll.:* Stevenson 224:11.

3. The borrower is a slave to the lender, the security to both. *Rec. dist.:* U.S., Can. *Infm.:* Cf. Prov.22:7. *1st cit.:* US1757 Franklin, *PRAlmanac.* *20c. coll.:* Stevenson 224:9.

4. The borrower runs in his own debt. *Rec. dist.:* N.Y. *1st cit.:* US1839 *Works of Ralph Waldo Emerson,* ed. Cabot. *20c. coll.:* T&W 39.

borrowing **1.** Beware of borrowing: it brings care by night and disgrace by day. *Rec. dist.:* N.Y.

2. Borrowing is the mother of trouble. *Rec. dist.:* N.Dak.

3. Borrowing isn't much better than beg-ging. *Rec. dist.:* Oreg. *Infm.:* Stevenson cites the only source as Lessing, *Nathan der Weise* (1779). *1st cit.:* US1948 Stevenson, *Home Book of Proverbs.* *20c. coll.:* Stevenson 223:6.

4. He that goes a-borrowing goes a-sorrow-ing. *Vars.:* **(a)** Borrowing brings sorrowing. **(b)** Them ez borrows, sorrows. *Rec. dist.:*

U.S., Can. *1st cit.:* ca1470 *Reliquiae Antiquae* in *Harleian MS;* US1743 Franklin, *PRAl-manac.* *20c. coll.:* ODEP 314, Whiting 42, CODP 96, Stevenson 223:11.

SEE ALSO DISPUTING and borrowing cause grief and sorrowing.

bosom A wise man's bosom is his trouble's tomb. *Rec. dist.:* N.Y.

boss *(n.)* **1.** If you work for two bosses, you must lie to one of them. *Rec. dist.:* Ill.

2. The fellow who doesn't need a boss is often the one selected to be one. *Rec. dist.:* N.Y.

3. The one who knows how will always find a place in life, but the one who knows why will be his boss. *Rec. dist.:* Okla.

SEE ALSO Be an EMPLOYEE and work eight hours; be a boss and your work is never done.

boss *(v.)* SEE No one can expect to LEAD others until he has learned to boss himself.

both SEE Never CHOOSE between two good things; take 'em both. / When two QUARREL, both are to blame.

bother SEE Never INTERFERE with nothin' that don't bother you.

bottle **1.** Save your bottles; it may rain whiskey. *Rec. dist.:* Kans.

2. You can't tell what's in the bottle by the label. *Rec. dist.:* Okla.

3. You don't count the bottle, but you count what's in it. *Rec. dist.:* N.Y.

SEE ALSO Getting KISSES out of a woman is like getting olives out of a bottle: the first may be devilish difficult, but the rest come easy. / It is with narrow-souled PEOPLE as with narrow-necked bottles: the less they have in them, the more noise they make in pouring out. / Don't pour new WINE in old bottles. / The WINE of life comes not from battles, but from bottles.

bottom **1.** If you're on the bottom, there's only one way to go—up. *Rec. dist.:* Calif., Colo., Minn.

2. Never let the bottom of your purse or your mind be seen. *Rec. dist.:* Ill.

3. The bottom of the ladder is crowded; there's plenty of room at the top. *Rec. dist.:* Ala., Ga.

SEE ALSO Every ALLEY has a can with a rusty bottom. / The BEGGAR'S wallet has no bottom. / Never tear a BUILDING down from the bottom up. / Better SPARE at the brim than at the bottom. / TRUTH keeps the bottom of her well. / Let every TUB stand on its own bottom.

bough 1. The boughs that bear most hang lowest. *Rec. dist.:* Ill. *1st cit.:* 1655 Fuller, *Church-History of Britain.* *20c. coll.:* ODEP 77, Stevenson 1196:14.

2. The rottenest bough cracks first. *Rec. dist.:* Miss.

bought (*v.*) What is bought is cheaper than a gift. *Rec. dist.:* Miss. *1st cit.:* 1678 Ray, *English Proverbs.* *20c. coll.:* Stevenson 953:6.

SEE ALSO LOVE can neither be bought nor sold; its only price is love. / REVENGE is dearly bought at the price of liberty. / An ounce of WIT that is bought is worth a pound that is taught.

bought (*adj.*) Well bought is half sold. *Rec. dist.:* Vt.

SEE ALSO Bought FRIENDS are not friends indeed. / When you buy FRIENDS with anything other than friendship, they do not stay bought long. / Bought SENSE is the best sense. / Bought WISDOM is the best if you don't pay too dear for it.

bounce (*n.*) SEE The harder the FALL, the higher the bounce.

bound He that is bound must obey. *Rec. dist.:* Vt. *1st cit.:* ca1205 Layamon, *Brut,* Soc. Antiquaries (1847). *20c. coll.:* ODEP 78, Stevenson 1708:10.

SEE ALSO We are bound to be HONEST, but not to be rich. / No one is bound to do what is IMPOSSIBLE.

bounty Bounty is more commended than imitated. *Rec. dist.:* Mich.

bow (*n.*) 1. A bow too much bent will break. *Var.:* When the bow is too much bent, it breaks. *Rec. dist.:* Okla., Tex., Vt. *1st cit.:* ca1500 *Bannatyne MS*; US1770 Paterson, *Glimpses of Colonial Society at Princeton College*

1766–1773, ed. Mills (1903). *20c. coll.:* ODEP 78, Whiting 42, Stevenson 226:3.

2. Draw not your bow before your arrow is fixed. *Rec. dist.:* Mich. *1st cit.:* 1732 Fuller, *Gnomologia.* *20c. coll.:* Stevenson 226:8.

SEE ALSO It's good to have two STRINGS to one's bow.

bow (*v.*) Better bow than break. *Rec. dist.:* Okla. *1st cit.:* ca1374 Chaucer, *Troilus and Criseyde.* *20c. coll.:* ODEP 52, Stevenson 169:3.

bowing Bowing to a dwarf will not prevent your standing erect again. *Rec. dist.:* W.Va.

bowl (*n.*) The empty bowl makes the most noise. *Rec. dist.:* Vt. *1st cit.:* 1547 Baldwin, *Treatise on Morall Phylosophie;* US1645 Cotton in *Complete Writings of Roger Williams* (1963). *20c. coll.:* ODEP 220, Whiting 464, Stevenson 676:17, T&W 391, Whiting(MP) 658.

SEE ALSO LIFE is but a bowl of cherries. / When the SPOON want anything, it batter go ter de bowl.

bowl (*v.*) SEE Be BOLD, everywhere be bold, but be not bowled over.

box 1. Two empty packing boxes make the most noise, but the squeaky wheel gets the grease. *Rec. dist.:* Wis.

2. You must empty the box before you can fill it again. *Rec. dist.:* N.Y.

SEE ALSO There's a bad APPLE in every box. / The old BREAD goes out of the box first. / A little KEY may unlock a box wherein lies a bunch of keys. / Precious OINTMENTS come in small boxes.

boy 1. A bad boy goes like a top—only when he's whipped. *Rec. dist.:* Ill. *Infm.:* Old-fashioned tops had a whipcord wrapped around the top to start the top spinning. A bad boy will only go when whipped. *1st cit.:* 1732 Fuller, *Gnomologia.* *20c. coll.:* Stevenson 228:8.

2. A boy can't do a man's work. *Rec. dist.:* Ill., Ky., Tenn.

3. A boy is better unborn than untaught. *Rec. dist.:* Wis. *Infm.:* A more common form is "Better unborn than untaught." *1st cit.:* ca1275 *Proverbs of Alfred,* tr. Skeat. *20c. coll.:* ODEP 56.

4. A boy is like a fountain—useful as long as there's something in him. *Rec. dist.:* Colo., N.Y.

5. A boy should ask, and a girl deny. *Rec. dist.:* Ohio, S.C.

6. A boy's best friend is his mother. *Rec. dist.:* Ill.

7. A growing boy has a wolf in his belly. *Rec. dist.:* N.Y., S.C.

8. A small boy is an appetite with skin drawn over it. *Rec. dist.:* N.Y., S.C.

9. Bad boys make bad men. *Rec. dist.:* N.Y., Oreg.

10. Boys and books do not mix. *Rec. dist.:* Ill.

11. Boys avoid the bees that stung 'em. *Rec. dist.:* Ill., Ind.

12. Boys seldom make passes for girls who wear glasses. *Var.:* Boys seldom make passes at girls wearing glasses. *Rec. dist.:* U.S., Can. *Infm.:* Ogden Nash used this proverbial saying in his English classes at the University of Wisconsin.

13. Boys who drive with one hand usually end up in church: some of them walk down the aisle, some of them are carried. *Rec. dist.:* Ill.

14. Boys will be boys. *Rec. dist.:* U.S., Can. *1st cit.:* 1589 *Censure of Martin Junior. Marprelate Tracts,* ed. Pierce; US1837 Neal, *Charcoal Sketches* (1840). *20c. coll.:* ODEP 79, T&W 40, CODP 24, Stevenson 228:14, Whiting*(MP)* 69.

15. Building boys is better than mending men. *Rec. dist.:* Colo.

16. Don't send a boy to do a man's job. *Vars.:* **(a)** Don't send a boy to the market when you have a man. **(b)** Don't send a boy to the mill when you have a man. **(c)** Don't send a boy to the well when you have a man. *Rec. dist.:* U.S., Can. *Infm.:* Often used by card players when failing to take a trick with a low card. *1st cit.:* 1932 Dawes, *Lawless;* US1931 Fowler, *Great. 20c. coll.:* Whiting*(MP)* 70, Stevenson 229:2.

17. Every time a boy goes wrong, a good man dies. *Var.:* A good man dies when a boy goes wrong. *Rec. dist.:* N.J., N.Dak.

18. Geese on the mill pond, ducks on the ocean; boys can't get married till the girls take a notion. *Rec. dist.:* Miss.

19. If boys were meant to smoke, they'd have chimneys on their heads. *Rec. dist.:* Colo., Ohio.

20. If you want to get a boy, run away from him. *Var.:* The more a girl runs, the harder a boy chases. *Rec. dist.:* Kans., N.C.

21. If you want to keep a boy out of the mud, blacken his boots. *Rec. dist.:* Ky., Tenn.

22. It is a wise boy that knows that he isn't. *Rec. dist.:* N.Y.

23. Little boys are made of rats and snails and puppy-dog tails. *Vars.:* **(a)** Boys are made of rats and snails and puppy-dog tails, and girls are made of sugar and spice and everything nice—but doesn't a girl have a taste for roughness to marry a boy? **(b)** Boys are made of snails and whales and puppy-dog tails. Girls are made of sugar and spice and everything nice. **(c)** Little boys are made of rats and snails and puppy-dog tails. Little girls are made of sugar and spice and everything nice. **(d)** What are little boys made of? Frogs and snails and puppy-dogs' tails, that's what little boys are made of. *Rec. dist.:* U.S., Can. *1st cit.:* ca1820 Southey, *What All the World Is Made Of. 20c. coll.:* Stevenson 228:13.

24. Little boys who play with matches get their fingers burned. *Rec. dist.:* Calif., N.Y., Wis. *1st cit.:* US1848 Lowell, *Biglow Papers* (1893). *20c. coll.:* T&W 40.

25. Old boys have their playthings as well as young ones; the difference is only in the price. *Rec. dist.:* N.Y.

26. Once a bad boy and always a bad boy. *Rec. dist.:* Kans.

27. One boy's a boy; two boys, a half a boy; three boys, no boy at all. *Vars.:* **(a)** One boy's a boy; two boys a half a boy; three boys no boy. **(b)** One boy by himself is a pretty good boy; two boys together are only half a boy; and three together are no boy at all. **(c)** One boy for a whole boy; two boys a half boy;

three boys no boy at all. *Rec. dist.:* U.S., Can. *Infm.:* The more boys that help the less work they do. *1st cit.:* ca1930 Thompson, *Country Calendar;* US1971 *New York Times,* 31 Jan. *20c. coll.: CODP* 24.

28. Some boys grow with responsibility—others just swell. *Rec. dist.:* Colo., Minn.

29. The boy is father to the man. *Vars.:* (a) As the boy is such is the man. (b) In the boy see the man. (c) The boy makes the man. *Rec. dist.:* Ill., Ind., R.I. *1st cit.:* 1671 Milton, *Paradise Regained;* US1857 Melville, *Confidence-Man. 20c. coll.:* Stevenson 339:9, T&W 40.

30. The boy of today will be the man of tomorrow. *Rec. dist.:* Colo., N.C.

31. The boy who does a stroke and stops will never a great man be. *Rec. dist.:* Kans.

32. The boys won't go where the cobwebs grow. *Rec. dist.:* Oreg. *Infm.:* Cf. beau.

33. The least boy always carries the greatest fiddle. *Rec. dist.:* Mich. *Infm.:* All lay the load on those who are least able to bear it. *1st cit.:* 1670 Ray, *English Proverbs;* US1880 Spurgeon, *John Ploughman's Pictures. 20c. coll.:* Stevenson 1037:1.

34. Windy boys live stormy lives. *Rec. dist.:* Colo.

35. You can lead a boy to college, but you can't make him think. *Rec. dist.:* Miss., N.Y., Oreg.

36. You can take a boy out of the country, but you can't take the country out of the boy. *Vars.:* (a) You can take a boy out of Brooklyn, but you can never get Brooklyn out of the boy. (b) You can take the boy away from the city, but you can't take the city away from the boy. (c) You can take the boy out of the farm, but you can't take the farm out of the boy. (d) You can take the farmer out of the country, but you can't take the country out of the farmer. (e) You can take the girl out of the country, but you can't take the country out of the girl. (f) You can take the man out of the country, but you can't take the country out of the man. *Rec. dist.:* Ill., Ind., N.Y.

37. You can tell a lot about the size of a boy

by what he loses his head over. *Rec. dist.:* U.S., Can.

SEE ALSO An old MAN is twice a boy. / All WORK and no play makes Jack a dull boy.

brag *(n.)* **1.** Brag is a dog that everybody hates but nobody fears. *Rec. dist.:* Miss. *1st cit.:* US1853 Haliburton, *Sam Slick's Wise Saws. 20c. coll.:* Stevenson 229:6.

2. Old brag is a good dog, but hold fast is a better one. *Vars.:* (a) Brag is a good dog, an' hold fast is a better one—but what do you say to a cross of the two? (b) Old brag is a good dog, but hold fast is better. *Rec. dist.:* Ind., Md., Miss., Wis. *1st cit.:* 1580 Munday, *Zelauto;* US1835 Kennedy, *Horse-Shoe Robinson. 20c. coll.: CODP* 24, T&W 41, Stevenson 229:6, Whiting*(MP)* 70.

3. Self brag, half scandal. *Rec. dist.:* Ill., Ind.

4. With every brag, the tighter the balloon; the tighter the balloon, the louder the bang. *Rec. dist.:* Ill.

brag *(v.)* They brag most that can do least. *Rec. dist.:* Ill.

braggart **1.** All are not braggarts that blow the horn. *Rec. dist.:* Ill.

2. Great braggarts are little doers. *Var.:* Great braggers, little doers. *Rec. dist.:* Ill. *1st cit.:* 1509 Barclay, *Ship of Fools,* ed. Jamieson in *Eclogues,* E.E.T.S. (1874). *20c. coll.:* Stevenson 229:5, *ODEP* 332.

brain **1.** All the brains are not in one head. *Rec. dist.:* N.Y.

2. An idle brain is the devil's workshop. *Vars.:* (a) An empty brain is the devil's shop. (b) An idle brain is the devil's work-house. *Rec. dist.:* U.S., Can. *1st cit.:* ca1602 Perkins, *Treatise of Callings* in *Works* (1608). *20c. coll.: ODEP* 395, *CODP* 118, Stevenson 230:2, Whiting*(MP)* 70.

3. Brain is worth more than brawn. *Rec. dist.:* Ill., S.C.

4. Half a brain is too much for him who says little. *Rec. dist.:* Ill.

5. If the brain sows not corn, it plants thistles. *Rec. dist.:* Vt. *1st cit.:* 1640 Herbert, *Outlandish*

Proverbs (Jacula Prudentum) in *Works,* ed. Hutchinson (1941). *20c. coll.:* Stevenson 230:5.

6. Most brains reflect but the crown of a hat. *Rec. dist.:* N.Y., S.C. *1st cit.:* US1848 Lowell, *Fable for Critics. 20c. coll.:* Stevenson 230:7.

7. No brains, no feelings. *Var.:* Where there are no brains, there is no feeling. *Rec. dist.:* Ariz., Okla.

8. Some people have brains, and then there are others. *Rec. dist.:* N.Y.

9. The less the brains, the bigger the hat. *Rec. dist.:* Ind.

10. There's many witty men whose brains can't fill their bellies. *Rec. dist.:* Colo.

11. Use your brain and save your heels. *Vars.:* **(a)** Make your brain save your heels. **(b)** What the brain can't do, the heels have to do. *Rec. dist.:* Ill., Kans., Oreg.

12. Using our brains is often wiser than depending on our strength. *Rec. dist.:* Wis.

13. We need brain more than belly food. *Rec. dist.:* W.Va.

14. You can borrow brains, but you can't borrow character. *Rec. dist.:* Wis.

15. You don't need brains if you have luck. *Rec. dist.:* Oreg.
SEE ALSO BEAUTY has no brains. / You can't grow HAIR and brains in the same head. / The HEART has eyes that the brain knows nothing of. / If you've good LOOKS, you don't need any brains. / A SLIP of the tongue is no fault of the brain.

bramble **1.** A bramble does not produce grapes. *Rec. dist.:* N.Y.

2. He who sows brambles reaps thorns. *Rec. dist.:* N.Y.

bran If you mix with the bran, the cows will eat you. *Rec. dist.:* Ark., Kans.

branch **1.** The branch of the willow breaks not from the snow. *Rec. dist.:* Oreg.

2. The highest branch is not the safest roost. *Rec. dist.:* N.Dak., Vt. *1st cit.:* 1563 *Mirror for Magistrates,* ed. Campbell. *20c. coll.:* ODEP 373, Stevenson 1032:2.

3. Those who cling must grasp branches, not blossoms. *Rec. dist.:* N.Y.
SEE ALSO A crooked TREE will never straighten its branches. / He who loves the TREE loves the branch.

brandy Brandy is lead in the morning, silver at noon, gold at night. *Rec. dist.:* Ill.

brass Brass is some people's gold. *Rec. dist.:* Ill.

brave *(n.)* **1.** None but the brave deserve the fair. *Rec. dist.:* U.S., Can. *1st cit.:* 1697 Dryden, *Poems* (1958). *20c. coll.:* CODP 24.

2. The brave and the wise can both pity and excuse when cowards and fools show no mercy. *Rec. dist.:* N.Y.

3. The brave are born from the brave and good. *Rec. dist.:* Ind.
SEE ALSO FORTUNE favors the brave.

brave *(adj.)* **1.** Be brave, not ferocious. *Rec. dist.:* Mich.

2. Gold is tried by fire, brave men by adversity. *Rec. dist.:* N.Y.

3. It is easy to be brave from a safe distance. *Rec. dist.:* Oreg.

4. The brave man has no country but mankind. *Rec. dist.:* Ill.

5. The brave man holds honor far more precious than life. *Rec. dist.:* Ont.

6. The brave man is daring enough to forgive an injury. *Rec. dist.:* Ill.

7. 'Tis more brave to live than to die. *Rec. dist.:* Ill., Oreg., Vt.
SEE ALSO Brave ACTIONS never want a trumpet. / A full BELLY makes a brave heart.

bravery **1.** Bravery is not lasting. *Rec. dist.:* Ill.

2. True bravery is without witness. *Rec. dist.:* Wis.
SEE ALSO The greatest TEST of true bravery is fear to offend.

bray SEE Every ASS loves to hear himself bray. / When all men say you are an ASS, it is high time to bray.

braying The braying of a jackass never reaches heaven. *Rec. dist.:* Ind., R.I. *1st cit.:* 1802 Wolcot, *Lord Bard and his Motions* in *Works* (1816). *20c. coll.:* ODEP 81.

bread 1. All bread is not baked in one oven. *Rec. dist.:* Ind.

2. Bread always falls buttered side down. *Var.:* There never was a piece of bread so broad and wide, but what if it fell, it would fall on the buttered side. *Rec. dist.:* U.S., Can. *1st cit.:* 1834 Smith, *Major Downing;* US1867 Richardson, *Beyond Mississippi. 20c. coll.:* Stevenson 235:5, *CODP* 25, *ODEP* 81, T&W 41, Whiting*(MP)* 71.

3. Bread is the staff of life. *Rec. dist.:* U.S., Can. *1st cit.:* 1638 Penkethman, *Artachthos;* USca1687 Cotton in Alden, *Collections of American Epitaphs and Inscriptions* (1814). *20c. coll.:* ODEP 81, Whiting 43, Stevenson 234:1, Whiting*(MP)* 71.

4. Bread today is better than cake tomorrow. *Var.:* Our bread today is better than a hundred in the air. *Rec. dist.:* Ind., Oreg.

5. Cast your bread upon the water; it will return to you a hundredfold. *Vars.:* **(a)** Bread cast upon the water returns a hundredfold. **(b)** Cast your bread upon the water, and in a few days it will come back buttered. **(c)** Cast your bread upon the water, and it will come back buttered. **(d)** Cast your bread upon the waters, and it will come back sandwiches. *Rec. dist.:* U.S., Can. *Infm.:* Cf. Eccl. 11:1. *1st cit.:* 1682 Browne, *Christian Morals. 20c. coll.:* Stevenson 232:1.

6. Don't butter your bread on both sides. *Rec. dist.:* U.S., Can. *1st cit.:* 1678 Ray, *English Proverbs;* US1738 Stephens, *Journal of Proceedings in Georgia* in *Georgia Records* (1906, 1908). *20c. coll.:* Stevenson 235:4, Whiting 44, T&W 41, Whiting*(MP)* 71.

7. Dry bread at home is better than roast meat abroad. *Vars.:* **(a)** A crust of bread in peace is better than a feast in contention. **(b)** Better is a slice of bread and garlic eaten at one's own table than a thousand dishes eaten under another's roof. **(c)** Dry bread is better with love than fried chicken with fear and trembling. *Rec. dist.:* U.S., Can. *1st cit.:* ca1389

Chaucer, *Parson's Tale. 20c. coll.:* Stevenson 577:9, *ODEP* 206.

8. Eat bread and drink water, and you will live a long life. *Rec. dist.:* Ill.

9. Eaten bread is soon forgotten. *Rec. dist.:* U.S., Can. *1st cit.:* 1591 Minsheu, *Spanish Grammar. 20c. coll.:* Stevenson 234:3.

10. For a piece of bread a man will transgress. *Rec. dist.:* Vt.

11. Give me yesterday's bread, this day's fish, and last year's cider. *Rec. dist.:* N.Y., S.C.

12. He is rich enough that lacks not bread. *Rec. dist.:* N.J.

13. He who burns bread must hunger dread. *Rec. dist.:* Ill.

14. If they can't eat bread, let them eat cake. *Rec. dist.:* N.J., N.C. *Infm.:* Attributed to Marie Antoinette by Rousseau, ca1768. *1st cit.:* US1948 Stevenson, *Home Book of Proverbs. 20c. coll.:* Stevenson 274:5.

15. If you hate a man, eat his bread; and if you love him, do the same. *Rec. dist.:* Wis.

16. If you have bread, don't look for cake. *Rec. dist.:* Ill. *Infm.:* Stevenson cites Cervantes, *Don Quixote* (1615) as source. *1st cit.:* US1948 Stevenson, *Home Book of Proverbs. 20c. coll.:* Stevenson 231:6.

17. If you have two loaves of bread, sell one and buy a lily. *Rec. dist.:* Iowa.

18. In want of bread, it is well to have seniitas. *Rec. dist.:* Calif. *Infm.: Seniitas* are a Mexican biscuit-like bran preparation, eaten like crackers or bread.

19. It is better to have bread left over than run short of wine. *Rec. dist.:* N.C.

20. It is hard to pay for bread that has been eaten. *Rec. dist.:* Kans., Wis.

21. It just takes a piece of bread to show what is in some folks. *Rec. dist.:* N.Y. *Infm.:* A good host should serve good bread.

22. It will never, never go to make two breads from one dough. *Rec. dist.:* N.Y., N.C.

23. Let him that earns the bread eat it. *Rec. dist.:* N.C., Okla., Tex.

24. Never eat the bread of charity if you can avoid it. *Rec. dist.:* Ariz.

25. The old bread goes out of the box first. *Rec. dist.:* Ill.

26. The whiter the bread, the sooner you're dead. *Rec. dist.:* Ill.

27. Who goes for a day into the forest should take bread for a week. *Rec. dist.:* Wis.

28. Whose bread I eat, his song I sing. *Rec. dist.:* Ark., Fla., Iowa, Kans.

29. Work for your bread if you get your cheese for nothing. *Rec. dist.:* N.Y.

30. You buttered your bread; now eat it. *Var.:* You've buttered your bread; now lie in it. *Rec. dist.:* Ind.

31. You can't eat the same bread twice. *Rec. dist.:* Kans.

SEE ALSO For a good APPETITE there is no hard bread. / BITTER is the bread of charity. / One man's DEATH is another man's bread. / The DOG doesn't get bread every time he wags his tail. / When FAMINE must be fed, crumbs are as good as bread. / HUNGER never saw bad bread / The HUNGRY man often talks of bread. / Because KITTENS may be born in an oven, that does not make them loaves of bread. / Where there's no LAW, there's no bread. / LAWYERS earn their bread in the sweat of their browbeating. / MAN cannot live by bread alone. / A man of many TRADES begs his bread on Sunday. / Hard WORK is not easy, and dry bread is not greasy.

breadth SEE There's only a hair's breadth between a HERO and a fool.

break *(n.)* Mend the first break, kill the first snake, and conquer everything you undertake. *Rec. dist.:* N.Y., S.C.

SEE ALSO Never give a SUCKER an even break.

break *(v.)* SEE It is better to BEND than break. / Better BOW than break. / Neither an EGG nor an ego is any good until you break it. / If the GOAT would not jump around, she wouldn't break her leg. / HEARTS don't break, they bend and wither. / LUCK and glass break easily. / He who is to break his NECK finds the stairs in the dark. / You can't have an OMELETTE unless you break the egg. / Never break your SHIN on a stool that is not in your way. / STICKS and stones may break my bones, but names will never hurt me. / Man's TONGUE is soft and bone does lack, yet a stroke therewith may break a man's back. / WEIGHT can break a bridge.

breakfast *(n.)* After breakfast sit awhile; after supper walk a mile. *Rec. dist.:* Colo., Mich., N.Y.

SEE ALSO Rather go to BED supperless than run in debt for a breakfast. / HOPE is a good breakfast, but it is a bad supper. / A KISS and a drink of water is but a tasteless breakfast. / LAUGH before breakfast, cry before sunset.

breakfast *(v.)* SEE PRIDE breakfasted with plenty, dined with poverty, and supped with infamy.

breath **1.** It's better to have bad breath than no breath at all. *Rec. dist.:* Kans.

2. Keep one's breath to cool one's soup. *Vars.:* **(a)** Save your breath to blow your coffee. **(b)** Save your breath to cool your broth or to groan with when you get home. **(c)** Save your breath to cool your broth. **(d)** Save your breath to cool your porridge. *Rec. dist.:* U.S., Can. *1st cit.:* 1580 Munday, *Zelauto;* US1783 Williams, *Journal of John Penrose, Seaman,* ed. Dickason (1969). *20c. coll.:* ODEP 418, Whiting 44, Stevenson 237:5, T&W 42, Whiting(MP) 72.

3. The first breath is the beginning of death. *Rec. dist.:* N.J. *1st cit.:* 1576 Pettie, *Petite Palace of Pleasure,* ed. Gollancz (1908). *20c. coll.:* ODEP 261, Stevenson 237:7.

SEE ALSO Weigh well your WORDS before you give them breath.

bred He is not well bred that cannot bear ill breeding in others. *Rec. dist.:* N.Y. *1st cit.:* US1748 Franklin, *PRAlmanac. 20c. coll.:* Stevenson 239:2.

SEE ALSO What is bred in the BONE will come out in the flesh.

breeches It's hard to take breeches off of bare hips. *Rec. dist.:* Colo. *Infm.:* Refers to an impossibility. *1st cit.:* 1818 Scott, *Rob Roy.* *20c. coll.:* Stevenson 238:6.

SEE ALSO When LADIES wear the breeches, their petticoats ought to be long enough to hide 'em. / He that is conscious of a STINK in his breeches is jealous of every wrinkle in another's nose.

breed *(n.)* Breed is stronger than pasture. *Rec. dist.:* Utah, Wis. *1st cit.:* 1917 Bridge, *Cheshire Proverbs. 20c. coll.:* Stevenson 239:8.

breed *(v.)* SEE FAMILIARITY breeds contempt. / Too much FORCE breeds suspicion. / IDLENESS breeds trouble. / INVENTION breeds invention. / A shady LANE breeds mud. / LEISURE breeds lust. / A little NEGLECT may breed great mischief. / If you breed a PARTRIDGE, you'll get a partridge. / Old SINS breed new shame. / Little WRONGS breed great evils.

breeding 1. A man's own good breeding is the best security against other people's ill manners. *Rec. dist.:* N.J. *1st cit.:* 1750 Lord Chesterfield, Letter, 9 Feb. in *Letters to His Son. 20c. coll.:* Stevenson 239:1.

2. Good breeding carries along with it a dignity. *Rec. dist.:* Mich.

SEE ALSO BIRTH is much, but breeding is more. / KNOWLEDGE is nothing when good breeding is lacking.

breeks A good pair of breeks will cast down an old coat. *Rec. dist.:* Colo. *Infm.:* "Breeks" means breeches.

brevity 1. Brevity is the soul of wit. *Rec. dist.:* U.S., Can. *1st cit.:* 1600 Shakespeare, *Hamlet;* US1804 Brackenridge, *Modern Chivalry, 1792–1815,* ed. Newlin (1937). *20c. coll.:* ODEP 84, Whiting 45, CODP 25, Stevenson 240:4.

2. Brevity makes the master. *Rec. dist.:* Ill.

brew As you brew, so must you drink. *Vars.:* (a) As they brew, so let them bake. (b) As you brew, so bake. *Rec. dist.:* Mich., N.Y., N.C., Tex. *1st cit.:* 1264 *English Lyrics of the XIIIth Century,* ed. Brown (1932); US1937 Forbes, *Paradise. 20c. coll.:* CODP 26, Whiting(MP) 73, ODEP 85, Stevenson 240:10.

SEE ALSO Too many COOKS spoil the brew.

bribe Avoid all bribes. *Rec. dist.:* Mich.

brick You can't make bricks without straw. *Rec. dist.:* Ark., Kans. *1st cit.:* 1614 Adams, *Heaven and Earth Reconciled;* USca1700 Saffin, *His Book,* ed. Hazard (1928). *20c. coll.:* ODEP 85, Whiting 45, CODP 26, Stevenson 243:2, Whiting(MP) 74.

bride 1. A rich bride goes young to the church. *Rec. dist.:* Wis.

2. A sad bride makes a glad wife. *Rec. dist.:* Ill.

3. All brides are child brides in their mother's eyes. *Rec. dist.:* N.Y.

4. Happy is the bride the sun shines on. *Vars.:* (a) Blessed be the bride the sun shines on; cursed be the bride the rain falls on. (b) Blessed is the bride that the sun shines on. (c) Blessed is the bride that the sun shines on; blessed is the corpse that the rain rains on. (d) Blessed is the bride the sun shines on; blessed is the corpse the rain falls on. (e) Happy is the bride on a sunny day; happy is the corpse on a rainy day. (f) Happy is the bride that the sun shines on. (g) Happy is the bride that the sun shines on; blessed are the dead that the rain falls on. (h) Happy is the bride the sun shines on; blessed is the corpse the rain falls on. (i) Happy is the bride the sun shines on; sorry is the bride the rain rains on. *Rec. dist.:* U.S., Can. *1st cit.:* 1601 Shakespeare, *Twelfth Night. 20c. coll.:* ODEP 85, CODP 26, Stevenson 243:9, Whiting(MP) 74.

5. It's a poor bride who cannot help some. *Rec. dist.:* Vt.

6. June brides, January mothers. *Rec. dist.:* N.Y.

SEE ALSO Always a BRIDESMAID but never a bride.

bridesmaid Always a bridesmaid but never a bride. *Vars.:* (a) If you are three times a bridesmaid, you will never be a bride. (b) If you serve three times as a bridesmaid, you'll never marry. (c) Often a bridesmaid but never a bride. (d) Three times a bridesmaid but never a bride. (e) Three times a bridesmaid, never a bride. *Rec. dist.:* U.S., Can. *1st cit.:*

US1954 Barkley, *That Reminds Me. 20c. coll.:* Whiting*(MP)* 74.

bridge 1. Don't burn your bridges behind you. *Vars.:* **(a)** Don't burn your bridges before you. **(b)** Fearlessness burns its bridges behind; fear, the bridges before. *Rec. dist.:* U.S., Can. *Infm.:* A common tactic of a retreating army. The proverb means "Beware of making final, irrevocable decisions in a hurry." *1st cit.:* 1923 Crowley, *Confessions,* ed. Symonds (1969); US1924 Munday, *Om. 20c. coll.:* Whiting*(MP)* 75.

2. Don't cross the bridge till you come to it. *Vars.:* **(a)** Cross that bridge when you get there. **(b)** Don't cross the bridge before you reach it. **(c)** Don't cross your bridges before you come to them. **(d)** Don't cross your bridges before you consult your dentist. *Rec. dist.:* U.S., Can. *1st cit.:* 1895 Addy, *Household Tales;* US1850 Longfellow, *Journal* in *Life. 20c. coll.:* ODEP 156, CODP 45, Stevenson 244:11, T&W 43, Whiting*(MP)* 75.

3. It is a good thing to make a bridge of gold to a flying enemy. *Rec. dist.:* Miss., Oreg. *1st cit.:* 1576 Lambarde, *Perambulation of Kent;* US1809 *Port Folio. 20c. coll.:* ODEP 316, Whiting 46, CODP 26, Stevenson 684:9, Whiting*(MP)* 75.

4. It is sometimes best to burn your bridges behind you. *Rec. dist.:* U.S., Can. *Infm.:* Make a clean break with the whole matter. *1st cit.:* 1923 Crowley, *Confessions,* ed. Symonds (1969); US1924 Munday, *Om. 20c. coll.:* Whiting*(MP)* 75.

5. Praise the bridge that carries you over. *Vars.:* **(a)** Always speak well of a bridge that has carried you safely over. **(b)** Let every man praise the bridge he goes over. **(c)** Praise the bridge that takes the wagon over. **(d)** Praise the bridge which carries you safely over. **(e)** Speak well of the bridge which carries you safely over. **(f)** You got to stick to the bridge that carries you across. *Rec. dist.:* U.S., Can. *1st cit.:* 1678 Ray, *English Proverbs;* US1769 *Journals of John Montresor,* ed. Scull, N.Y.Hist.Soc. *Collections* (1881). *20c. coll.:* ODEP 644, CODP 210, Whiting 46, Stevenson 244:13, T&W 43.

SEE ALSO Where there's a RIVER there's a bridge. / WORRY never crossed a bridge.

bridle *SEE* A scary HORSE needs a stout bridle.

brief It is better to be brief than tedious. *Rec. dist.:* Ind. *1st cit.:* 1592 Shakespeare, *Richard III. 20c. coll.:* Stevenson 240:5.

SEE ALSO Long PAINS are light ones; cruel ones are brief.

bright If you try to make some people see the bright side, they will complain that it hurts their eyes. *Rec. dist.:* N.Y.

SEE ALSO Through rose-colored GLASSES the world is always bright. / The used KEY is always bright.

brighten *SEE* BLESSINGS brighten as they take their flight.

brightest *SEE* The FIRE burns brightest on one's own hearth. / The love of LIBERTY burns brightest in a dungeon. / The LIGHT that shines farthest shines brightest at home.

brilliant Never think yourself so brilliant that you are blinded by your own light. *Rec. dist.:* Ala., Ga.

brim Better spare at the brim than at the bottom. *Var.:* Spare at the brim, not at the bottom. *Rec. dist.:* Mich., N.Y., Tex. *1st cit.:* 1523 Fitzherbert, *Boke of Husbandry,* English Dialect Soc. *20c. coll.:* ODEP 55.

bring Whoever brings finds the door wide open for his reception—except when he brings trouble. *Rec. dist.:* Ill.

SEE ALSO From the CEMETERY no one is brought back. / He that has no CHILDREN brings them up well. / What a DAY may bring a day may take away. / Desire nothing that would bring DISGRACE. / Nothing can bring you PEACE but yourself. / The UNINVITED should bring their own stool. / The WORST of a thing is what it will bring.

broad *SEE* The path of INIQUITY is broad and smooth: you just let go and slide.

broke When you's broke, dat's de time to ack stylish, so folks won't know you're broke. *Rec. dist.:* Miss., N.Y. *Infm.:* From Negro dialect collection of Judge Harris Dickinson, novelist from Vicksburg, Miss.

broken Nothing seems quite as good as new after being broken. *Rec. dist.:* Ont.

SEE ALSO Bad CUSTOMS are better broken than kept up. / EGGS and oaths are easily broken. / Straight FOLKS never make broken promises. / A man's HEART at thirty is either steeled or broken. / Nobody dies of a broken HEART. / A PITCHER that goes to the well too often is liable to be broken. / A bád PROMISE is better broken than kept. / All PROMISES are either broken or kept. / PROMISES are like piecrust: they are made to be broken. / Never trust a broken STAFF.

broker A broker is a man who runs your fortune into a shoestring. *Rec. dist.:* N.Y. *Infm.:* In the Great Depression some bankrupt rich sold shoestrings on the street.

bronco 1. No man can ride a bronco if he ain't split up the middle. *Rec. dist.:* N.Mex., Tex.

2. The toughest broncs is always them you've rode some other place. *Rec. dist.:* N.Mex.

brook 1. A babbling brook makes much noise. *Rec. dist.:* Calif.

2. Little brooks make great rivers. *Rec. dist.:* Colo.

3. The brook would lose its song if you removed the rocks. *Rec. dist.:* Calif., Colo.

4. The shallow brook warbles, while the still water is deep. *Rec. dist.:* N.Y.

SEE ALSO Deep RIVERS move with silent majesty; shallow brooks are noisy.

broom 1. A bad broom leaves a dirty room. *Rec. dist.:* Wis. *1st cit.:* 1917 Bridge, *Cheshire Proverbs.* *20c. coll.:* Stevenson 246:8.

2. A new broom sweeps clean. *Vars.:* **(a)** A new broom never sweeps clean. **(b)** A new broom sweeps clean, but an old broom knows all the corners. **(c)** A new broom sweeps clean, but an old one gets in the corners. **(d)** A new broom sweeps clean, but an old one knows where the dirt is. **(e)** A new broom sweeps clean, but an old one scrapes better. **(f)** A new broom sweeps clean, but the old

broom knows the corners. **(g)** A new broom sweeps clean; the old one knows the corners best. **(h)** A new broom sweeps the cleanest. **(i)** A new broom sweeps well. *Rec. dist.:* U.S., Can. *1st cit.:* 1542 *Unpublished Poems from the Blage MS,* ed. Muir; US1752 Clinton in *Letters and Papers of Cadwallader Colden,* N.Y.Hist.Soc. *Collections* (1917–37). *20c. coll.:* ODEP 564, Whiting 47, *CODP* 161, Stevenson 246:12, T&W 44, Whiting(MP) 75.

3. An old broom is better than a new one. *Rec. dist.:* Mich.

4. An old broom knows the corners of a house. *Var.:* An old broom knows where the dirt is. *Rec. dist.:* U.S., Can.

SEE ALSO All TRASH goes before the broom.

broth Good broth may be made in an old pot. *Rec. dist.:* N.J. *1st cit.:* 1601 Chamber, *Treatise Against Judicial Astrologie;* US1880 Spurgeon, *John Ploughman's Pictures.* *20c. coll.:* ODEP 318, Stevenson 421:1.

SEE ALSO Every COOK praises his own broth. / Too many COOKS spoil the broth. / As well to eat the DEVIL as drink his broth.

brother 1. A brother may not be a friend, but a friend will always be a brother. *Rec. dist.:* N.Y. *1st cit.:* US1752 Franklin, *PRAlmanac.* *20c. coll.:* Stevenson 895:1.

2. A brother offended is harder to be won than a strong city. *Rec. dist.:* N.Y.

3. Between two brothers have two witnesses and a voting. *Rec. dist.:* Mich.

4. Brothers are like hands and feet. *Rec. dist.:* W.Va.

5. Help your brother's boat across. *Rec. dist.:* Vt.

6. Take-it-easy and live-long are brothers. *Rec. dist.:* Miss.

7. To a brother's virtues be kind; to his faults be a little blind. *Rec. dist.:* N.J.

8. We can live without a brother, but not without a friend. *Rec. dist.:* Ill.

9. When you fight with a brother or sister, you're only hurting yourself, because they are a part of you. *Rec. dist.:* N.Y.

SEE ALSO There is a DESTINY that makes us

brothers. / A FATHER's a treasure; a brother's a comfort; a friend is both. / Better a NEIGHBOR near than a brother far. / The WRATH of brothers is the wrath of devils.

brotherly *See* Brotherly LOVE for brotherly love, but cheese for money.

brow *See* A dull-edged PLOW furrows your brow.

bruise *See* If you can't make every EDGE cut, you can sure make it bruise. / Better bend the NECK than bruise the forehead.

brush *See* A HAIR on the head is worth two in the brush.

brute The man that blushes is not quite a brute. *Rec. dist.:* N.J. *1st cit.:* 1745 Young, *Night Thoughts.* *20c. coll.:* Stevenson 206:9.

bubble *See* LIFE is a bubble on the stream.

buck *(n.)* The older the buck, the stiffer the horn. *Rec. dist.:* Vt.

buck *(v.)* The harder they buck, the easier they gentle. *Rec. dist.:* Tex.

bucket Big buckets can be filled at small streams. *Rec. dist.:* Kans.
  See also When the BUDS start on the trees, it is time to gather the buckets. / A DROP in the bucket each day will fill your life with happiness some day. / A WELL without a bucket is no good.

bud When the buds start on the trees, it is time to gather the buckets. *Rec. dist.:* Vt.

budget A budget is a method of worrying before you spend as well as afterward. *Vars.:* (a) A budget is something to worry about before you spend your money. (b) In budget making you worry before you spend as well as afterward. *Rec. dist.:* Iowa, N.Dak., Oreg.

bug 1. Bugs are bugs whether they bite or not. *Rec. dist.:* Ill.

2. If you fool with a tumble-turd bug, you are apt to be spattered. *Rec. dist.:* Miss.

3. 'Twix de bug en de bee-martin 'tain't hard ter tell w'ich gwineter git kitch. *Rec. dist.:* N.Y. *Infm.:* The dialect form is from Joel Chandler Harris. *1st cit.:* US1880 Harris, *Plantation Proverbs* in *Uncle Remus, His Songs and His Sayings.* *20c. coll.:* Stevenson 251:6.

build 1. If you build according to advice of Tom, Dick, and Harry, you'll build a crazy house where no man will tarry. *Rec. dist.:* Ill.

2. One should live to build, not to boast. *Rec. dist.:* Colo.

3. When we build, let us think that we build forever. *Rec. dist.:* Miss.
  See also Do not pull down your BARNS to build greater ones. / Little by little the BIRD builds his nest. / FOOLS build houses for wise men to live in. / Build not up a FORTUNE on the labor of others. / First build your HOUSE and then think of the furniture. / One can't shingle the HOUSE before one builds it. / To save one LIFE is better than to build a seven-story pagoda. / MEN build houses; women build homes.

builder *See* The great WALL stands; the builder is gone.

building Never tear a building down from the bottom up. *Rec. dist.:* N.Y., S.C.

built *See* An HOUR may destroy what was an age in building. / ROME was not built in a day. / Through WISDOM is a house built, and by understanding it is established.

bull 1. A little bull goes a long way. *Rec. dist.:* Calif., Colo., Ill., N.Y. *Infm.:* Bull refers to exaggerated, facetious speech.

2. A mad bull is not to be tied up with a packthread. *Rec. dist.:* Mich. *1st cit.:* 1732 Fuller, *Gnomologia.* *20c. coll.:* Stevenson 254:4.

3. Bulls with short horns stand close to the bar. *Var.:* Bucks with short horns stand close to the bar. *Rec. dist.:* Ind. *Infm.:* Found near men's urinals.

4. If you play with the bull, you will get a horn in the arse. *Rec. dist.:* Colo., Iowa.

5. It makes a lot of difference whose bull gores the ox. *Rec. dist.:* Ill., N.Y. *1st cit.:* US1845 Cooper, *Chainbearer.* *20c. coll.:* T&W 47.

6. The bull must remember that he once was a calf. *Rec. dist.:* N.Dak.

7. When a bull once takes hold, nothing can make him let go. *Var.:* When a bull takes hold, neither heaven nor hell can make him let go. *Rec. dist.:* Oreg., Tex.

8. You can't grow a two-year-old bull in a day. *Rec. dist.:* Colo., Tex.

bullet **1.** Bullets through the heart make a dead echo. *Rec. dist.:* Calif., Colo. *1st cit.:* 1942 Heym, *Hostages*. *20c. coll.:* Stevenson 255:6.

2. Every bullet has its billet. *Rec. dist.:* Ill., N.Y. *1st cit.:* 1575 Gascoigne, *Posies;* US1840 Cooper, *Pathfinder*. *20c. coll.:* ODEP 90, T&W 47, *CODP* 27, Stevenson 255:5, Whiting(*MP*) 80.

bully **1.** A bully is always a coward. *Rec. dist.:* Ill., Ind. *1st cit.:* 1817 Edgeworth, *Harrington and Ormond;* US1853 Haliburton, *Sam Slick's Wise Saws*. *20c. coll.:* ODEP 90, *CODP* 27, Stevenson 255:8, Whiting(*MP*) 80.

2. The bully bags a lion at a distance but runs when a mule starts kicking. *Rec. dist.:* Ill.

bump *(n.)* There are a lot of bumps on the road to easy street. *Rec. dist.:* N.Y.

bump *(v.)* SEE If FROGS had wings, they wouldn't bump their asses on rocks.

bunch SEE A little KEY may unlock a box wherein lies a bunch of keys. / One STICK is easier broken than a bunch. / A family TREE is valuable when it produces good timber and not just a bunch of nuts.

bundle SEE SOULS are not saved in bundles.

bungling SEE IGNORANCE and bungling with love are better than wisdom and skill without.

burden *(n.)* **1.** A burden becomes lightest when it is well borne. *Rec. dist.:* Miss. *Infm.:* Stevenson cites Ovid, *Amores* (ca13 B.C.E..). *1st cit.:* US1948 Stevenson, *Home Book of Proverbs*. *20c. coll.:* Stevenson 257:12.

2. A burden which one chooses is not felt. *Var.:* A chosen burden is never felt. *Rec. dist.:* Mich., N.J. *1st cit.:* 1855 Bohn, *Handbook of Proverbs*. *20c. coll.:* Stevenson 256:4.

3. A voluntary burden is no burden. *Rec. dist.:* N.Y.

4. Bear one another's burdens. *Rec. dist.:* N.Y.

Infm.: Cf. Galat. 6:2. *1st cit.:* US1948 Stevenson, *Home Book of Proverbs*. *20c. coll.:* Stevenson 257:2.

5. Every man thinks his own burden the heaviest. *Rec. dist.:* Miss., N.Y., S.C. *1st cit.:* 1611 Cotgrave, *Dictionary of French and English Tongues*. *20c. coll.:* Stevenson 256:7.

6. Everyone lays the burden on the willing horse. *Rec. dist.:* Ind., Mich., N.Y.

7. Heavy burdens kill little people, but they make great ones. *Rec. dist.:* Ind.

8. Impose not a burden on others which you cannot bear yourself. *Rec. dist.:* Mich.

9. Only they who have borne burdens understand sympathy. *Rec. dist.:* N.Y.

10. Other people's burdens killed the ass. *Rec. dist.:* Ill. *Infm.:* Stevenson cites Cervantes, *Don Quixote* (1615). *1st cit.:* US1948 Stevenson, *Home Book of Proverbs*. *20c. coll.:* Stevenson 256:5.

11. The burden is light on the shoulders of another. *Rec. dist.:* Miss. ——

12. The greater the burdens, the brighter the crown. *Rec. dist.:* Ill.

13. When we lift the burdens of others, we are developing strength to bear our own. *Rec. dist.:* N.C.

14. Your neighbor's burden is always light. *Rec. dist.:* Ill.

SEE ALSO He who derives the ADVANTAGE ought to sustain the burden. / God fits the BACK to the burden. / LOVE makes all burdens light. / The STRENGTH will with the burden grow. / No one knows the WEIGHT of another's burden.

burden *(v.)* SEE Do not burden today's STRENGTH with tomorrow's load.

burial SEE The only LOT most men do not grumble at is their burial lot.

burial ground SEE A LIBRARY is but the soul's burial ground.

burn What won't burn needn't be blown. *Rec. dist.:* Pa. *Infm.:* Refers to cooling coffee or soup by blowing on it.

SEE ALSO If you want roasted BANANAS, you

must burn your fingers first. / When the BEANS get too thick, the pot burns. / If you get burnt, you got to sit on the BLISTER. / He who burns BREAD must hunger dread. / A watched FIRE never burns. / Better a little FIRE to warm us than a big one to burn us. / FIRE doesn't burn without a flame. / FIRE kept closest burns best of all. / The FIRE you kindle for your enemy often burns yourself more than him. / The love of LIBERTY burns brightest in a dungeon. / Old LOVE burns low when new love breaks. / It's no use crabbing at the SMOKE when the barn's burning down.

burned 1. Once burned, twice shy. *Vars.:* (a) Once burned, twice cautious. (b) Once burnt, twice shy. *Rec. dist.:* U.S., Can. *1st cit.:* US1949 Sterling, *Dead Sure.* *20c. coll.:* Whiting(MP) 81.

2. We got to be burned 'fore we learn. *Rec. dist.:* S.C.

SEE ALSO A burnt CHILD dreads the fire. / A burned LIGHT will never shine.

burning *SEE* Seldom poke another's FIRE, or you may rouse his burning ire.

burp Better to burp and bear the shame than swallow the burp and bear the pain. *Rec. dist.:* Ky., Ont., Vt.

bury *SEE* Bury CAN'T and you'll find will. / Every man should have a fair-sized CEMETERY in which to bury the faults of his friends. / Two good DAYS for a man in this life: when he weds, and when he buries his wife. / To withhold TRUTH is to bury gold.

bus *SEE* The DEVIL never misses the bus.

bush 1. A bad bush is better than the open field. *Rec. dist.:* U.S., Can. *1st cit.:* ca1300 *Proverbs of Hending* in *Anglia.* *20c. coll.:* ODEP 25, Stevenson 259:5.

2. It's a low bush that the sun never shines on. *Rec. dist.:* N.Y., S.C. *1st cit.:* US1942 Lasswell, *Suds in Your Eye.* *20c. coll.:* Stevenson 259:1.

SEE ALSO A BIRD in the hand is better than two in the bush. / There's more than one way to beat the DEVIL around the bush. / Good WINE needs no bush.

bushel *SEE* A handful of common SENSE is worth a bushel of learning.

business 1. A business with an income at its heels always furnishes oil for its own wheels. *Rec. dist.:* N.Y.

2. A shady business never yields a sunny life. *Rec. dist.:* N.C.

3. Business before pleasure. *Var.:* Pleasure first and business after. *Rec. dist.:* U.S., Can. *1st cit.:* 1640 *Grobiana's Nuptials* in *Bodley MS 30;* US1767 *Diary and Letters of Thomas Hutchinson,* ed. P. Hutchinson (1883, 1886). *20c. coll.:* ODEP 93, Whiting 51, CODP 28, Stevenson 263:1, T&W 48, Whiting(MP) 82.

4. Business goes where it is invited and stays where it is well treated. *Rec. dist.:* Ill.

5. Business is business. *Var.:* Business is business, and love is love. *Rec. dist.:* U.S., Can. *1st cit.:* 1797 Colman, *Heir at Law;* US1857 Melville, *Confidence-Man.* *20c. coll.:* ODEP 93, T&W 48, Stevenson 261:8, Whiting(MP) 82.

6. Business is like a car: it will not run by itself, except downhill. *Rec. dist.:* Oreg.

7. Business is like a wheelbarrow: it stands still until somebody pushes it. *Rec. dist.:* Ill.

8. Business is never so healthy as when, like a chicken, it must do a certain amount of scratching for what it gets. *Rec. dist.:* Kans.

9. Business is the blood of our national life. *Rec. dist.:* N.Y. *1st cit.:* 1672 Codrington, *Select Proverbs.* *20c. coll.:* ODEP 93.

10. Business is to grown men what blocks are to children. *Rec. dist.:* Ind. *Infm.:* Stevenson cites St. Augustine, *Confessions* (397). *1st cit.:* US1948 Stevenson, *Home Book of Proverbs.* *20c. coll.:* Stevenson 260:4.

11. Business makes a man as well as tries him. *Rec. dist.:* Mich. *1st cit.:* 1855 Bohn, *Handbook of Proverbs.* *20c. coll.:* Stevenson 261:3.

12. Business makes strange bedfellows. *Rec. dist.:* N.Y.

13. Business neglected is business lost. *Rec. dist.:* U.S., Can.

14. Business whets the appetite and gives a relish to pleasure. *Rec. dist.:* Mich.

15. Do not meddle with business you know nothing about. *Rec. dist.:* Utah.

16. Do right in your business; the rest will take care of you. *Rec. dist.:* Calif.

17. Do the business at hand first. *Rec. dist.:* N.C.

18. Drive your business or it will drive you. *Var.:* Drive your business; let not that it drive you. *Rec. dist.:* U.S., Can. *1st cit.:* 1672 Codrington, *Select Proverbs;* US1738 Franklin, *PRAlmanac. 20c. coll.:* ODEP 204, Stevenson 261:10, Whiting 51.

19. Everybody ought to know his own business the best. *Rec. dist.:* Ohio. *1st cit.:* 1566 Painter, *Palace of Pleasure,* ed. Jacobs (1890). *20c. coll.:* ODEP 230, Stevenson 263:7.

20. Everybody's business is nobody's business. *Var.:* What is everybody's business is nobody's business. *Rec. dist.:* U.S., Can. *1st cit.:* 1611 Cotgrave, *Dictionary of French and English Tongues;* US1629 *The Thomas Hutchinson Papers,* Publ. Prince Soc. (1865). *20c. coll.:* ODEP 231, Whiting 51, Stevenson 260:6.

21. He who tends his own business has a good one. *Vars.:* **(a)** The man who minds his own business generally has a good one. **(b)** The man who minds his own business will always have business to mind. *Rec. dist.:* Ind.

22. If you want to do good business, do it with strangers, not your relatives. *Rec. dist.:* N.C.

23. If you would have your business done, go; if not, send. *Rec. dist.:* Ill., Ind., Ohio. *1st cit.:* US1743 Franklin, *PRAlmanac. 20c. coll.:* Whiting 51.

24. It costs less to retain the business of an old customer than it does to get two new ones. *Rec. dist.:* Ind.

25. It's a woman's business to get married as soon as possible, and a man's to keep unmarried as long as he can. *Rec. dist.:* Wis.

26. Let nobody know your business. *Rec. dist.:* Miss., N.Y.

27. Make it your business to know yourself. *Rec. dist.:* Utah.

28. Mind no business but your own. *Vars.:* **(a)** Always mind your own business and the other fellow will take care of his. **(b)** He that minds not his own business shall never mind mine. **(c)** Tend to your own business and you won't have time to tend to someone else's. **(d)** The eleventh commandment: mind your own business. **(e)** To mind one's own business is sometimes hard to acquire. *Rec. dist.:* U.S., Can. *1st cit.:* 1530 Palsgrave, *Lesclarcissement de la langue Francoyse,* ed. Genin (1852); US1793 *Connecticut Courant* in *William & Mary Coll. Quart.* (1951). *20c. coll.:* ODEP 533, Whiting 51, Stevenson 263:8, T&W 49.

29. No monkey business wanted around here. *Rec. dist.:* Ind., Mich., Tex.

30. Take care of your business and your business will take care of you. *Var.:* Keep your shop and your shop will keep you. *Rec. dist.:* Ill., N.Y. *1st cit.:* 1605 Chapman, Jonson, Marston, *Eastward Ho;* US1652 Shepard, *Hints. 20c. coll.:* ODEP 419, Whiting 392.

31. Tell everybody your business and the devil will do it for you. *Rec. dist.:* Ala., Ga., N.C.

32. The business of America is business. *Rec. dist.:* Wis.

33. Those that have much business must have much pardon. *Rec. dist.:* N.Y., S.C.

34. When you have business with a wolf, look out for trouble. *Rec. dist.:* Vt.

35. Where business and pleasure clash, then let the business go smash. *Rec. dist.:* Ill.

36. Where business starts, friendship ends. *Rec. dist.:* Calif., N.Y.

37. You can't mix business and pleasure. *Rec. dist.:* Mich., N.Y., S.C. *1st cit.:* 1913 Fletcher, *Secret;* US1931 Whitfield, *Death in a Bowl. 20c. coll.:* Whiting(MP) 82.

SEE ALSO COMPETITION is the spice of business. / COURTESY is a business asset—a gain and never a loss. / The DEVIL always tends to his own business. / A DINNER lubricates business. / What ain't your DUTY ain't your business. / Live up to your good INTENTIONS and put the devil out of business. / If LOVE interferes with your business, quit your business.

/ A NEIGHBOR is a person who knows more about your business than you do. / When PLEASURE is the business of life, it ceases to be pleasure. / PUNCTUALITY is the soul of business. / WAR is a business that ruins those who succeed in it.

bust *(n.)* Marble busts are made of those who "raised Cain," not corn. *Rec. dist.:* Ind.

bust *(v.)* SEE A HEAD that is as hard as rock will burst into pieces.

busy 1. The busiest thing in the world is idle curiosity. *Rec. dist.:* Ill., W.Va.

2. The busy man has few idle visitors: to the boiling pot the flies come not. *Rec. dist.:* Ill.
SEE ALSO HAIR never grows on a busy street.

busybodies Busybodies never want a bad day. *Rec. dist.:* Ind., N.C., Tex.

butcher 1. Better to pay the butcher than the doctor. *Rec. dist.:* N.Y., S.C.

2. Watch the butcher when he weighs the roast; otherwise you'll buy his hand. *Rec. dist.:* N.Y.

butler 1. The lazy butler takes eight steps to avoid one, but if he covers up his master's missteps, he is never fired. *Rec. dist.:* Ill.

2. Your butler is always a gentleman; your neighbor's butler is a thief. *Rec. dist.:* Ill.

butter *(n.)* You don't have to eat a whole tub of butter to get the taste. *Rec. dist.:* Wash.
SEE ALSO There are more ways to kill a DOG than by choking him to death on hot butter. / They that have no other MEAT gladly bread and butter eat. / The same SUN that will melt butter will harden clay.

butter *(v.)* SEE Fair WORDS butter no cabbage.

buttered SEE BREAD always falls buttered side down.

butterfly Butterflies store no money. *Rec. dist.:* N.Y.

buttonhole If you miss the first buttonhole, you will not succeed in buttoning up your coat. *Rec. dist.:* Miss. *Infm.:* Stevenson cites

Goethe, *Sprüche in Prosa. 1st cit.:* US1948 Stevenson, *Home Book of Proverbs. 20c. coll.:* Stevenson 154:2.

buy *(n.)* 1. A lot of "good buys" in Wall Street turn out to be "farewells." *Rec. dist.:* N.Dak.

2. Better a bad buy than a good loan. *Rec. dist.:* N.Y.

buy *(v.)* 1. Better buy than borrow. *Rec. dist.:* U.S., Can. *1st cit.:* 1539 Taverner, *Proverbs of Erasmus. 20c. coll.:* ODEP 52, Stevenson 223:4.

2. Buy what you can and save what you earn. *Rec. dist.:* N.C.

3. Buy what you do not need and you will soon need what you cannot buy. *Vars.:* **(a)** Buy what you do not want and you will sell what you cannot spare. **(b)** Buy what you have no need of and ere long you shall sell your necessaries. **(c)** He who buys what he does not need steals from himself. **(d)** He who buys what he does not need will someday need what he does not buy. *Rec. dist.:* U.S., Can. *1st cit.:* US1738 Franklin, *PRAlmanac. 20c. coll.:* Stevenson 269:14.

4. Buy while you can get it. *Rec. dist.:* Ky., Tenn.

5. If you buy everything, the result will be that you sell everything. *Rec. dist.:* Oreg. *1st cit.:* US1738 Franklin, *PRAlmanac. 20c. coll.:* Stevenson 269:14.

6. Never buy anything before you see it. *Rec. dist.:* N.C.

7. Never buy what you do not want because it is cheap. *Rec. dist.:* N.Y., N.C., S.C.

8. You can buy anything except day and night. *Rec. dist.:* N.Y.
SEE ALSO Why buy the COW when you can get the milk free? / A FRIEND whom you can buy can be bought from you. / When you buy FRIENDS with anything other than friendship, they do not stay bought long. / A man may buy GOLD too dear. / GOLD and iron are good to buy gold and iron. / GOLD will not buy everything. / We cannot buy a quart of GOODWILL, a pound of love, or a yard of

patience. / He that will slight my HORSE will buy my horse. / He that speaks ill of the MARE will buy her. / Ask your PURSE what you should buy. / Buy the TRUTH, but never sell it. / TRY it before you buy it.

buyer 1. Let the buyer beware. *Rec. dist.:* Ill. *1st cit.:* 1523 Fitzherbert, *Boke of Husbandry;* US1758 Eliot, *Essays on Field Husbandry in New England, 1748–1762,* eds. Carman and Tugwell (1934). *20c. coll.:* ODEP 96, Whiting 52, *CODP* 28, Stevenson 268:13, Whiting*(MP)* 86.

2. The buyer needs a thousand eyes; the seller wants but one. *Vars.:* **(a)** The buyer has need of a hundred eyes; the seller, not one. **(b)** The buyer has need of a thousand eyes; the seller wants but one. **(c)** The seller needs but one eye; the buyer, a hundred. *Rec. dist.:* Ill., Mich., N.J., N.Y. *1st cit.:* 1640 Herbert, *Outlandish Proverbs (Jacula Prudentum)* in *Works,* ed. Hutchinson (1941); US1745 Franklin, *PRAlmanac. 20c. coll.:* CODP 29, Stevenson 269:8.

buying *See* MONEY isn't worth a thing except to use in buying something. / Many have been ruined by buying good PENNYWORTHS. / Many a man thinks he is buying PLEASURE when he is really selling himself a slave to it.

buzz The buzz of a mosquito can drown out the ocean's roar. *Rec. dist.:* Calif.

buzz saw Don't monkey with the buzz saw. *Rec. dist.:* U.S., Can.

buzzard 1. A buzzard never makes a good hawk. *Rec. dist.:* Miss.

2. Buzzards fly high but roost on the ground. *Rec. dist.:* Miss.

3. Don't go to a buzzard's nest to find a dove. *Rec. dist.:* Ill.

4. Puttin' feathers on a buzzard won't make it no eagle. *Rec. dist.:* Nebr.

by and by Hard by the road called "by and by" there stands a house called "never." *Vars.:* **(a)** By the street of "by and by" one arrives at the house of never. **(b)** The road of "by and by" leads to the town of never. *Rec. dist.:* Ind., Miss., Wis.

bygones Let bygones be bygones. *Rec. dist.:* U.S., Can. *1st cit.:* 1577 Pitscottie, *Chronicle of Scotland;* US1710 *Diary of Cotton Mather,* ed. Ford, Mass.Hist.Soc. *Collections* (1911). *20c. coll.:* ODEP 96, Stevenson 270:5, Whiting 52, T&W 51, Whiting*(MP)* 86.

bystander 1. The innocent bystander often gets beaten up. *Rec. dist.:* Ill.

2. To the bystander no work is too hard. *Rec. dist.:* Ill.

C

C If you don't C sharp, you'll B flat. *Rec. dist.*: N.Mex.

cabbage *(n.)* If they ask you for cabbages, don't give them peas. *Rec. dist.*: Ill.
SEE ALSO Fair WORDS butter no cabbage.

cabbage *(adj.)* SEE Two HEADS are better than one, even if one is a cabbage head.

cable SEE HABITS are first cobwebs, then cables.

caboose SEE Every TRAIN has a caboose.

cackle SEE A good HEN does not cackle in your house and lay in another's. / A HEN that doesn't cackle doesn't lay. / 'Tis not the HEN that cackles most that lays the most eggs. / Hungry ROOSTER never cackles when he scratches up a worm.

cackling *(n.)* SEE He that would have EGGS must endure the cackling of hens.

cackling *(adj.)* SEE A cackling HEN doesn't always lay.

cadaver The cadaver is always right. *Rec. dist.*: N.Y.

Caesar **1.** Caesar's wife must be above suspicion. *Var.*: A man's grammar, like Caesar's wife, must not only be pure, but above suspicion. *Rec. dist.*: Ill., N.Y., S.C. *1st cit.*: 1580 Lyly, *Euphues and His England,* ed. Arber (1868); US1778 *Newspaper Extracts Relating to New Jersey,* ed. Stryker (1901–17). *20c. coll.*: ODEP 97, Whiting 53, CODP 30, Stevenson 271:7, T&W 52, Whiting*(MP)* 87.

2. Render unto Caesar the things which are Caesar's. *Rec. dist.*: Idaho, Ill., Tenn. *1st cit.*: 1601 Barlow, *Sermon at Paul's Cross;* US1680 *Letters of John Randolph,* ed. Dudley (1834). *20c. coll.*: ODEP 671, Whiting 53, Stevenson 272:6, Whiting*(MP)* 88.

cage **1.** A fine cage won't feed the hungry bird. *Var.*: A fine cage won't feed the bird. *Rec. dist.*: Ill., Vt. *1st cit.*: ca1389 Chaucer, *Maunciple's Tale.* *20c. coll.*: Stevenson 177:5.

2. A golden cage is still a cage. *Rec. dist.*: Oreg.
SEE ALSO It is the beautiful BIRD which gets caged. / A NIGHTINGALE won't sing in a cage. / Stone WALLS do not a prison make, nor iron bars a cage.

cagey SEE Any GIRL can handle the beast in a man if she's cagey enough.

cake **1.** Give a bit of your cake to one who is going to eat pie. *Rec. dist.*: Miss. *Infm.*: One is hoping for a favor in return.

2. When one has no flour, one bakes no cakes. *Rec. dist.*: N.Y.

3. You can't have your cake and eat it too. *Var.*: You can't eat your cake and have it too. *Rec. dist.*: U.S., Can. *1st cit.*: 1546 Heywood, *Dialogue of Proverbs,* ed. Habernicht (1963); US1742 *Colonial Records of Georgia,* ed. Chandler, in *Original Papers, 1735–1752* (1910–16). *20c. coll.*: ODEP 215, Whiting 53, CODP 109, Stevenson 274:2, T&W 52 Whiting*(MP)* 88.

calamity **1.** A calamity is often a blessing in disguise. *Rec. dist.*: Wis.

2. Calamity and prosperity are the touchstones of integrity. *Rec. dist.*: N.Y. *1st cit.*: US1752 Franklin, *PRAlmanac.* *20c. coll.*: Stevenson 1904:6.

3. Calamity is often a friend in disguise. *Rec. dist.*: Ill., Wis.

4. Calamity is the touchstone of a brave mind. *Var.*: Calamity is the test of a brave mind. *Rec. dist.*: Ill., Ohio. *1st cit.*: 1602 Marston, *Antonio's Revenge.* *20c. coll.*: ODEP 98, Stevenson 275:1.

5. Calamity is virtue's opportunity. *Rec. dist.*: Ohio. *1st cit.*: US1948 Stevenson, *Home Book of Proverbs.* *20c. coll.*: Stevenson 275:12.

6. Every calamity may be overcome by patience. *Rec. dist.*: Mich.

7. It were no virtue to bear calamities if we did not feel them. *Rec. dist.*: Mich.
SEE ALSO May HOPE be the physician when calamity is the disease.

79

calendar 1. Learned men make the calendar, but God makes the weather. *Rec. dist.:* Wis.

2. No one needs a calendar to die. *Rec. dist.:* Vt.

SEE ALSO DEATH keeps no calendar.

calf 1. A bawling calf soon forgets its mother. *Rec. dist.:* Alaska.

2. A blattin' calf is soon weaned. *Rec. dist.:* N.Y.

3. A lean calf forgets to skip. *Rec. dist.:* Ill.

4. Give a calf enough rope and it will hang itself. *Var.:* Give a calf all the rope it wants and it will hang itself. *Rec. dist.:* U.S., Can.

5. Newborn calves don't fear tigers. *Rec. dist.:* N.Y.

6. Only a suckin' calf don't have to worry about grass. *Rec. dist.:* N.Mex.

7. You can't ever tell what a lousy calf will come to be. *Vars.:* (a) You never can tell how a mangy calf will come out in the spring. (b) You never know the luck of a lousy calf. *Rec. dist.:* U.S., Can. *1st cit.:* US1836 *Col. Crockett's Exploits in Texas.* *20c. coll.:* T&W 231.

SEE ALSO A bawling COW soon forgets her own calf. / If you love de COW, you must love de calf. / Many a good COW has a bad calf. / Salt the COW to get the calf. / The COW has forgotten she was once a calf.

call *(n.)* *SEE* FAME is a bugle call blown past a crumbling wall.

call *(v.)* 1. Many are called but few are chosen. *Rec. dist.:* U.S., Can. *1st cit.:* US1871 Jones, *Life of Jefferson S. Batkins.* *20c. coll.:* T&W 237, Stevenson 348:4.

2. No man can call again yesterday. *Rec. dist.:* Oreg.

SEE ALSO DEEP calls unto deep. / Don't call a DOG while you're holding a stick in your hand. / You can call a DOG without kicking him. / FRIENDS are lost by calling often and calling seldom. / It takes a LIAR to call someone a liar. / He who pays the PIPER may call the tune. / The POT calls the kettle black. / SPEAK when you are spoken to; come when you are called.

calling *SEE* He that has a TRADE has an estate, and he that has a calling has an office of profit and honor.

calm *(n.)* There is always a calm before a storm. *Var.:* It's the calm before a storm. *Rec. dist.:* U.S., Can. *1st cit.:* ca1200 *Ancrene Riwle,* ed. Morton, Camden Soc. (1853); US1754 *Works of William Smith, D.D.* (1803). *20c. coll.:* ODEP 6, Whiting 54, CODP 2, Stevenson 2222:2, T&W 54.

SEE ALSO After the STORM comes the calm. / A vow made in the storm is forgotten in the calm.

calm *(adj.)* *SEE* GOD promises a safe landing, but not a calm passage. / Anyone can hold the HELM when the sea is calm. / Every man is a PILOT in a calm sea. / Any man can be a SAILOR on a calm sea.

calmest *SEE* The calmest HUSBANDS take the stormiest wives.

calmness 1. Calmness is a great advantage. *Rec. dist.:* Kans.

2. Calmness is but a lull before the storm. *Rec. dist.:* N.Y. *1st cit.:* ca1200 *Ancrene Riwle,* ed. Morton, Camden Soc. (1853); US1754 *Works of William Smith, D.D.* (1803). *20c. coll.:* ODEP 6, Whiting 54, CODP 2, Stevenson 2222:2, T&W 54.

calumny 1. Act uprightly and despise calumny; dirt may stick to a mud wall but not to a polished marble. *Rec. dist.:* N.Y., S.C. *1st cit.:* US1757 Franklin, *PRAlmanac.* *20c. coll.:* Stevenson 277:2.

2. Calumny is like coal—it either burns you or besmirches you. *Rec. dist.:* Ariz.

3. Calumny will soil virtue itself. *Rec. dist.:* Ill.

4. To persevere in one's duty and be silent is the best answer to calumny. *Rec. dist.:* N.Y., S.C. *1st cit.:* 1607 Jonson, *Volpone.* *20c. coll.:* Stevenson 277:4.

calvaries Our crosses are hewn from different trees, but we all must have our calvaries. *Rec. dist.:* N.Y., S.C. *1st cit.:* US1948 Stevenson, *Home Book of Proverbs.* *20c. coll.:* Stevenson 460:8.

camel **1.** If the camel once gets his nose in the tent his body will soon follow. *Rec. dist.:* Ill., Oreg.

2. It is easier for a camel to go through the eye of a needle than it is for a rich man to enter the kingdom of heaven. *Rec. dist.:* U.S., Can. *1st cit.:* 1534 Lupset, *Treatise on Dying Well;* US1754 *Works of William Smith, D.D.* (1803). *20c. coll.:* ODEP 559, Whiting 54, Stevenson 278:9, T&W 54, Whiting*(MP)* 89.

camera A camera in the hand is worth two in the alley. *Rec. dist.:* Ohio. *Infm.:* Always have your camera at hand, or you may miss a good picture.

can *(n.)* An empty can makes a lot of noise. *Vars.:* **(a)** Empty cans make the loudest noise. **(b)** Empty cans rattle the most. **(c)** Empty tin cans make the most noise. **(d)** The emptiest can makes the most noise. *Rec. dist.:* U.S., Can.

can *(v.)* **1.** Bury can't and you'll find will. *Rec. dist.:* Nebr., N.C.

2. Can't died in the cornfield. *Vars.:* **(a)** Can't died in the poorhouse. **(b)** I can't died in the poorhouse. *Rec. dist.:* Ohio, Okla.

3. Can't is a liar. *Rec. dist.:* N.Y.

4. Can't is a sluggard, too lazy to work. *Rec. dist.:* Ill.

5. Can't is un-American. *Rec. dist.:* Minn.

6. Can't never could. *Vars.:* **(a)** Can't never could do nothing. **(b)** Can't never did anything. **(c)** Can't never did anything; I don't want to will do less. **(d)** Can't never got anyone anyplace. **(e)** Don't ever say can't: can't never did anything. **(f)** I can't never did anything; I'll try has done wonders. *Rec. dist.:* U.S.

7. Can't was a coward. *Rec. dist.:* N.C.

8. Don't put your can't before your horses. *Rec. dist.:* Ill.

9. He can who thinks he can. *Var.:* They can because they think they can. *Rec. dist.:* U.S., Can.

10. He who can does; he who can't teaches. *Rec. dist.:* Calif., Mich., N.Y. *1st cit.:* 1903

Shaw, *Man and Superman.* *20c. coll.:* CODP 30, Whiting*(MP)* 90.

11. He who makes us do what we can is a friend. *Rec. dist.:* Oreg.

12. I can't means I won't. *Rec. dist.:* N.J.

13. If you can't, don't hinder. *Rec. dist.:* Oreg.

14. Multitudes can't because they think they can't. *Rec. dist.:* N.C.

15. Never say can't. *Rec. dist.:* N.Y.

16. There's no such word as "can't." *Rec. dist.:* Fla., Ind. *1st cit.:* US1900 Pidgin, *Quincy A. Sawyer.* *20c. coll.:* Whiting*(MP)* 700.

17. They who cannot as they would must do as they can. *Rec. dist.:* Okla., Tex.

18. Those who can't, criticize. *Rec. dist.:* N.Y., S.C.

19. Those who think they can't are generally right. *Rec. dist.:* N.J.

SEE ALSO GET what you can, and what you get, hold; 'tis the stone that will turn all your lead into gold. / Most of our HAPPINESS in this world consists in possessing what others can't get. / There are three kinds of PEOPLE: the wills, the won'ts, and the can'ts. / SUCCESS comes in cans, failure in can'ts. / You can't TAKE it with you. / Those can WIN who think they can. / If YOUTH but knew and age but could do.

candle **1.** Don't burn the candle at both ends. *Vars.:* **(a)** Don't burn your candle at both ends. **(b)** Never light your candle at both ends. **(c)** You cannot burn your candle at both ends. *Rec. dist.:* U.S., Can. *1st cit.:* ca1594 Bacon, *Promus;* US1798 *Codman Letters* in *Exposition of Claims of William Vans on Estate of John Codman* (1837). *20c. coll.:* ODEP 91, Stevenson 79:10, Whiting 55, Whiting *(MP)* 90.

2. Don't hide a candle under a bush. *Rec. dist.:* Ill., Ind., Kans., Ky. *1st cit.:* 1574 Guazzo, *Civile Conversation,* tr. Pettie, T.T. (1925); US1840 Cooper, *Pathfinder.* *20c. coll.:* Stevenson 281:3, T&W 220, Whiting*(MP)* 373.

3. How far this little candle throws its beam, so shines a good deed in this naughty world. *Rec. dist.:* Ohio.

4. It is a poor sport that is not worth the candle. *Rec. dist.:* Alaska, Ill., Okla. *1st cit.:* US1643 *Complete Writings of Roger Williams* (1963). *20c. coll.:* Whiting 55, T&W 54.

5. It's always better to light a candle than to curse the darkness. *Var.:* It is better to light one little candle than to stumble around in the dark. *Rec. dist.:* Ariz., Ind., N.Dak., R.I.

6. The candle does not give light to itself. *Rec. dist.:* Ill.

7. The darker the night, the brighter the candle. *Rec. dist.:* Ohio.

8. The smallest candle fills a mile with its rays, and the papillae of a man run out to every star. *Rec. dist.:* N.Y., S.C. *1st cit.:* US1860 Emerson, "Fate" in *Conduct of Life. 20c. coll.:* Stevenson 280:1.

9. To light your candle from mine won't take any off my brilliance. *Rec. dist.:* Ohio.

10. When candles are out, all cats are gray. *Rec. dist.:* Mich.

11. When the candles are all out, all women are fair. *Rec. dist.:* Fla.

SEE ALSO All the DARKNESS in the world cannot put out a single candle. / The morning DAYLIGHT appears plainer when you put out your candle. / If you have KNOWLEDGE, you should let others light their candle by it.

candlelight   Don't pick women or horses by candlelight. *Vars.:* **(a)** Choose neither a woman nor linen by candlelight. **(b)** Fine linen, girls, and gold so bright, choose not to take by candlelight. *Rec. dist.:* Ill., N.Y., S.C. *1st cit.:* 1573 Sanford, *Garden of Pleasure;* US1737 Franklin, *PRAlmanac. 20c. coll.:* ODEP 122, CODP 37, Stevenson 280:3.

candor   **1.** Candor breeds hatred. *Rec. dist.:* Ill.

2. Candor once went further boldly and in smiles, but it crept home in tatters and tears. *Rec. dist.:* N.Y., S.C. *1st cit.:* US1906 *Poor Richard Jr.'s Almanac. 20c. coll.:* Stevenson 2193:11.

3. Candor will lose you some friends, but not as many as deceit. *Rec. dist.:* Miss.

4. Women confess their small faults that their candor may cover great ones. *Rec. dist.:* Ill.

candy   Candy is dandy, but liquor is quicker. *Rec. dist.:* U.S., Can. *1st cit.:* US1931 Nash, *Reflections on Ice-Breaking. 20c. coll.:* Stevenson 632:4.

canoe   **1.** Paddle your own canoe. *Vars.:* **(a)** Love many, hate few, learn to paddle your own canoe. **(b)** Love many, trust few, always paddle your own canoe. **(c)** You'll have to learn to paddle your own canoe. *Rec. dist.:* U.S., Can. *1st cit.:* 1844 Marryat, *Settlers in Canada;* US1802 Dow, *History of Cosmopolite or Lorenzo Dow's Journal* (1848). *20c. coll.:* ODEP 606, Whiting 55, Stevenson 1235:14, T&W 55, Whiting(MP) 91.

2. Paddling your own canoe is good exercise. *Rec. dist.:* Ill.

cap   If the cap fits, wear it. *Var.:* If the cap fits, put it on. *Rec. dist.:* U.S., Can. *1st cit.:* 1600 Breton, *Pasquil's Foolscap;* US1738 Stephens, *Journal of Proceedings in Georgia* in *Georgia Records* (1906, 1908). *20c. coll.:* ODEP 101, Whiting 56, CODP 31, Stevenson 283:10, T&W 55, Whiting(MP) 91.

SEE ALSO If all FOOLS wore white caps, we'd all look like geese.

capital   SEE Your CREDIT is worth more than your capital. / Great PROFITS on small capital are after all small. / WORK is the only capital that never misses dividends.

captain   **1.** A captain of industry is nothing but a buck private to his wife. *Rec. dist.:* Ill.

2. Two captains will sink a ship. *Var.:* Two captains will wreck a ship. *Rec. dist.:* Wash.

car   **1.** A car in every garage and a chicken in every pot. *Rec. dist.:* Minn.

2. Don't count your new cars before they're built. *Rec. dist.:* N.Y.

3. If in the car you like to court, change your car to a davenport. *Var.:* If parking on the highway is your sport, then trade your car for a davenport. *Rec. dist.:* N.C.

4. If you can't drive your car, park it. *Rec. dist.:* N.C.

5. It's the empty car that makes the most noise. *Rec. dist.:* Ill.

6. You can't judge a car by its paint job. **Rec. dist.:** Ill.

SEE ALSO BUSINESS is like a car: it will not run by itself, except downhill.

carcass Where the carcass is, there will the eagles be gathered. **Vars.: (a)** For wheresoever the carcass is, there will the eagles be gathered together. **(b)** Where carcasses are, eagles will gather; and where good lawns are, much people flock thither. **(c)** Where the carcass is, the buzzards gather. **(d)** Where the carcass is, there the ravens will collect together. **Rec. dist.:** U.S., Can. *1st cit.:* 1550 Udall, *Discourse;* US1654 Johnson, *Wonder-Working* in *Providence of Sions Savior in New England,* ed. Poole, Andover, Mass. (1867). **20c. coll.:** ODEP 102, Whiting 57, CODP 31, T&W 56, Whiting*(MP)* 91.

card **1.** A card which never appears neither wins nor loses. **Rec. dist.:** N.Y.

2. Cards and dice is like all in life; dey ever falls well for bold players. **Rec. dist.:** S.C.

3. Cards are the devil's tools. **Rec. dist.:** N.Dak. *1st cit.:* 1676 *Poor Robin's Almanac.* **20c. coll.:** ODEP 102.

4. Lucky at cards, unlucky in love. **Rec. dist.:** U.S., Can. *1st cit.:* 1738 Swift, *Collection of Genteel and Ingenious Conversation;* US1801 Trumbull, *Season in New York 1801: Letters of Harriet and Maria Trumbull,* ed. Morgan (1969). **20c. coll.:** ODEP 496, Whiting 57, CODP 142, Stevenson 1493:4, Whiting*(MP)* 92.

5. Many can pack cards that cannot play. **Var.:** Many carry cards that cannot play. **Rec. dist.:** Mich., N.Y. *1st cit.:* 1597 Bacon, "Of Cunning" in *Essays.* **20c. coll.:** Stevenson 285:5, ODEP 606.

6. The cards beat all the players, be they ever so skillful. **Rec. dist.:** N.J., S.C. *1st cit.:* US1844 Emerson, "Nominalist and Realist" in *Essays.* **20c. coll.:** Stevenson 286:4.

7. When cards begin, friendship ends. **Rec. dist.:** N.C.

SEE ALSO A clear CONSCIENCE is a coat of mail.

care *(n.)* **1.** A man does not die of care. **Rec. dist.:** Ill.

2. An ounce of care is worth a pound of cure. **Rec. dist.:** N.C. *1st cit.:* 1599 Porter, *Two Angry Women of Abington.* **20c. coll.:** Stevenson 288:4.

3. Another's cares will not rob you of sleep. **Rec. dist.:** Ill.

4. Black care rarely sits behind a rider whose pace is fast enough. **Rec. dist.:** N.Y., S.C. *1st cit.:* 1603 *Montaigne's Essays,* tr. Florio; US1888 Roosevelt, *Ranch Life.* **20c. coll.:** ODEP 43, Stevenson 287:14.

5. Care and not the fine stables makes the good horse. **Rec. dist.:** N.J.

6. Care is beauty's thief. **Rec. dist.:** Ill. *1st cit.:* ca1630 Marmion, *Cupid and Psyche.* **20c. coll.:** Stevenson 287:12.

7. Care killed the cat. **Var.:** Care will kill the cat, yet there's no living without it. **Rec. dist.:** U.S., Can. *1st cit.:* 1585–1616 *Shirburn Ballads;* US1824 *Tales of an American Landlord.* **20c. coll.:** ODEP 103, Whiting 57, CODP 31, Stevenson 288:6, Whiting*(MP)* 93.

8. Care saves wear. **Rec. dist.:** N.Y. **Infm.:** Refers to care for automobiles and other equipment that needs periodic maintenance.

9. Good care prevents accidents. **Rec. dist.:** N.Mex. **Infm.:** Refers to care of your automobile.

10. Good care takes the head off danger. **Rec. dist.:** N.J.

11. He that speaks without care shall remember with sorrow. **Rec. dist.:** Wis.

12. Leave your cares to the wind. **Rec. dist.:** N.C. *1st cit.:* 1601 Jonson, *Every Man in His Humour.* **20c. coll.:** ODEP 349, Stevenson 288:3.

13. Light cares speak; great ones are dumb. **Rec. dist.:** Ill. *1st cit.:* 1587 Hughes, *Misfortunes of Arthur.* **20c. coll.:** Stevenson 1041:9.

14. Many cares make the head white. **Rec. dist.:** Ill. *1st cit.:* 1530 Palsgrave, *Acolastus,* ed. Carver, E.E.T.S. (1937). **20c. coll.:** ODEP 102, Stevenson 287:12.

15. Petty cares wear the soul out drop by drop. **Rec. dist.:** Ill.

16. To carry care into your bed is to sleep with a pack on your back. **Rec. dist.:** Wis. *1st* *cit.:* 1594 Shakespeare, *Romeo and Juliet;* US1853 Haliburton, *Sam Slick's Wise Saws.* **20c. coll.:** Stevenson 289:1.

17. Want of care does more harm than want of knowledge. ***Rec. dist.:*** Ill., N.Y., Okla., S.C. ***1st cit.:*** 1732 Fuller, *Gnomologia;* US1746 Franklin, *PRAlmanac.* **20c. coll.:** Stevenson 289:7.

18. When everyone takes care of himself, care is taken of all. ***Rec. dist.:*** Mich.

SEE ALSO If you take care of your CHARACTER, your reputation will take care of itself. / Sew your CLOTHES upon your back; care and trouble you'll never lack. / DRINK does not drown care, but waters it and makes it grow faster. / Little GOODS, little care. / Take care of your PENNIES, and the dollars will take care of themselves. / He who SINGS drives away his cares. / Take care of TODAY, and tomorrow will take care of itself. / Let TOMORROW take care of itself. / He that takes a WIFE takes care. / Handle with care WOMEN and glass.

care *(v.)* **1.** Care not for that which you can never possess. ***Rec. dist.:*** Mich.

2. Don't care lost his corn patch. ***Rec. dist.:*** N.Y.

3. To care is to share. ***Rec. dist.:*** N.C.

SEE ALSO It's amazing how much GOOD you can do if you don't care who gets the credit. / To KNOW is to care.

career **1.** A career never takes the place of a home where love reigns. ***Rec. dist.:*** N.C.

2. A man with a crooked career never ends well. ***Rec. dist.:*** Vt.

SEE ALSO A CARESS is better than a career. / A little INTEGRITY is better than any career.

careful **1.** Be careful but not full of care. ***Rec. dist.:*** N.J.

2. It is better to be careful than sorry. ***Rec. dist.:*** Ohio.

carefully Do what you do carefully. ***Rec. dist.:*** N.Y.

careless **1.** A careless watch invites the vigilant foe. ***Rec. dist.:*** Ill.

2. Careless hurry may cause endless regret. ***Rec. dist.:*** Ont.

3. Careless men come to a sudden and sorry end. ***Rec. dist.:*** Ill.

4. Careless shepherds make many a feast for the wolf. ***Rec. dist.:*** Ill. ***1st cit.:*** US1948 Stevenson, *Home Book of Proverbs.* **20c. coll.:** Stevenson 2089:5.

5. Such as are careless of themselves are seldom mindful of others. ***Rec. dist.:*** Mich.

caress A caress is better than a career. ***Rec. dist.:*** N.Y., S.C. ***1st cit.:*** US1930 Marbury, *Interview on Careers for Women.* **20c. coll.:** Stevenson 1468:12.

carnally He that lives carnally won't live eternally. ***Rec. dist.:*** N.Y., S.C.

carpenter **1.** A carpenter is known by his chips. ***Var.:*** Like carpenter, like chips. ***Rec. dist.:*** U.S., Can. ***1st cit.:*** 1546 Heywood, *Dialogue of Proverbs,* ed. Habernicht (1963). **20c. coll.:** ODEP 103, Stevenson 289:11.

2. A lazy carpenter fights with his tools. ***Rec. dist.:*** N.Y.

3. He's not the best carpenter that makes the most chips. ***Var.:*** It's not the best carpenter who makes the most chips. ***Rec. dist.:*** U.S., Can. ***1st cit.:*** 1609 Harward, Unpublished manuscript in Trinity College Library, Cambridge University; US1924 Guiterman, *Poet's Proverbs.* **20c. coll.:** ODEP 47, Stevenson 289:10.

SEE ALSO The DOOR of the carpenter is loose.

carriage I envied my neighbor's carriage until I met the man who had no feet. ***Rec. dist.:*** Oreg.

carrion **1.** The carrion which the eagle has left feeds the crow. ***Rec. dist.:*** Ill.

2. Where the carrion is, there the eagles gather. ***Rec. dist.:*** Ill.

carry SEE Better ride an ASS that carries me than a horse that throws me. / Praise the BRIDGE that carries you over. / It is one thing to plan a DEED and another to carry it out. / A DOG that will fetch a bone will carry one. / A GRUDGE is the heaviest load one can carry. / Thin ICE carries no weight. / It's not the LOAD that breaks you down, it's the way you carry it. / Let him who deserves the PALM carry it. / Let every PEDDLER carry his own pack. / One can RUN only as fast as his legs will carry him. / Every SIN carries its own punishment. / He that's carried down the STREAM need not row. / It is easier to make a SUGGESTION than to carry it out. / A WISE man always carries his umbrella.

cart 1. An empty cart rattles loudest. *Var.:* An empty cart rattles louder than a full one. *Rec. dist.:* Ind., Miss.

2. An unhappy man's cart is easy to overthrow. *Rec. dist.:* N.Y. *1st cit.:* ca1628 Carmichaell, *Proverbs in Scots,* ed. Anderson (1957). *20c. coll.:* ODEP 854.

3. Don't put the cart before the horse. *Var.:* Don't get the carriage before the horse. *Rec. dist.:* U.S., Can. *1st cit.:* 1340 *Ayenbite of Inwit,* E.E.T.S. (1866); US1676 *Letters of John Randolph,* ed. Dudley (1834). *20c. coll.:* ODEP 104, Whiting 58, Stevenson 290:9, T&W 56, Whiting(MP) 93.

4. It ain't the noisiest cart that's easiest upset. *Rec. dist.:* N.Y., S.C. *1st cit.:* US1853 Haliburton, *Sam Slick's Wise Saws* (1860). *20c. coll.:* T&W 56, Stevenson 290:7.

5. It's easier to dump the cart than to load it. *Rec. dist.:* Wis.

6. The best cart may overthrow. *Rec. dist.:* N.Y. *1st cit.:* 1546 Heywood, *Dialogue of Proverbs,* ed. Habernicht (1963). *20c. coll.:* ODEP 47, Stevenson 290:8.

7. To make the cart go, you must grease the wheels. *Rec. dist.:* Ill.
    SEE ALSO Keep the RAKE near the scythe, and the cart near the rake. / A little STONE may upset a large cart. / The worst WHEEL of a cart makes the most noise.

carver From the very spoon the carver has carved, he'll have to swallow hot mustard. *Rec. dist.:* Ohio.

case 1. A case well stated is half tried. *Rec. dist.:* Ill.

2. He who knows only his side of a case knows little of that. *Rec. dist.:* Ill.

3. Some people are born in the objective case. *Rec. dist.:* Miss.
    SEE ALSO CIRCUMSTANCES alter cases.

cash 1. Cash, and plenty of it, is the life-blood of the nation. *Rec. dist.:* Ill.

2. Cash before virtue: there is time enough to be good. *Rec. dist.:* Ill.

3. Cash begets cash as credit begets creditors. *Rec. dist.:* Ill.

4. Take the cash, and let the credit go. *Rec. dist.:* Ind., Minn. *1st cit.:* 1859 Omar Khayyam, *Rubaiyat,* tr. Fitzgerald. *20c. coll.:* Stevenson 452:1.
    SEE ALSO The reason the DEVIL buys so many of us so cheaply is that he offers cash.

cask 1. A cask and an ill custom must be broken. *Rec. dist.:* N.Y.

2. Empty casks make the most noise. *Rec. dist.:* Vt. *1st cit.:* ca1430 Lydgate, *Pilgrimage of Man,* E.E.T.S. (1899); US1676 *Complete Writings of Roger Williams* (1963). *20c. coll.:* CODP 64, Whiting 59, ODEP 220, Stevenson 676:17, T&W 391.

3. Every cask smells of the wine it contains. *Rec. dist.:* Ill., Vt. *1st cit.:* 1509 Barclay, *Ship of Fools,* ed. Jamieson in *Eclogues,* E.E.T.S. (1874). *20c. coll.:* ODEP 105.

4. When the cask is full, the mother-in-law gets drunk. *Rec. dist.:* Ill.

cast SEE Cast your BREAD upon the water; it will return to you a hundredfold. / The DIE is cast. / Cast no DIRT in the well that gives you water. / Don't cast your PEARLS before swine. / Let him that is without SIN cast the first stone.

castle 1. Air castles are good; now put foundations under them. *Var.:* Build foundations under your castles in the air. *Rec. dist.:* Minn., Oreg. *1st cit.:* US1854 Thoreau, *Walden.* *20c. coll.:* Stevenson 292:10.

2. Air castles are good to have in an earthquake. *Rec. dist.:* Minn.

3. Don't build your castles in the air. It's liable to rain and wash them away. *Rec. dist.:* U.S., Can. *1st cit.:* 1566 Painter, *Palace of Pleasure,* ed. Jacobs (1890); US1634 Wood, *New-England's Prospects,* Publ. Prince Soc. (1865). *20c. coll.:* ODEP 107, Whiting 59, T&W 57, Whiting(MP) 94.

4. Easy to keep the castle that was never besieged. *Rec. dist.:* N.Y. *1st cit.:* ca1628 Carmichaell, *Proverbs in Scots,* ed. Anderson (1957). *20c. coll.: ODEP* 213, Stevenson 292:8.

5. You can't build castles in the air and live in them. *Var.:* Castles in the air are all right until you try to move into them. *Rec. dist.:* Ill., N.Y., S.C., Wis.

SEE ALSO A man's HOME is his castle.

casualty The first casualty when war comes is truth. *Rec. dist.:* N.Y., S.C.

cat **1.** A bad cat deserves a bad rat. *Rec. dist.:* Ohio.

2. A cat has nine lives. *Vars.:* **(a)** A cat has nine lives; a woman has nine cat's lives. **(b)** A cat has nine lives, but a frog croaks every night. *Rec. dist.:* U.S., Can. *1st cit.:* 1546 Heywood, *Dialogue of Proverbs,* ed. Habernicht (1963); US1709 Lawson, *New Voyage to Carolina,* ed. Lefler (1967). *20c. coll.: ODEP* 108, Whiting 61, Stevenson 294:1, T&W 58, Whiting(MP) 96.

3. A cat may look at a king. *Vars.:* **(a)** A cat can look at a king, but it would rather look at a mouse or a bird. **(b)** A cat has a right to look at a king, a much better right to look at a lesser thing. **(c)** The cat may look at a king, they say, but would rather look at a mouse any day. **(d)** The cat may look at the queen. *Rec. dist.:* U.S., Can. *1st cit.:* 1546 Heywood, *Dialogue of Proverbs,* ed. Habernicht (1963); US1788 Todd, *Life and Letters of Joel Barlow* (1886). *20c. coll.: ODEP* 109, Whiting 61, *CODP* 32, Stevenson 296:8, T&W 58, Whiting(MP) 97.

4. A cat with a silver collar is none the better mouser. *Rec. dist.:* Miss.

5. A cat's courting is noisy. *Rec. dist.:* N.Y.

6. A cornered cat becomes as fierce as a lion. *Rec. dist.:* Ill. *1st cit.:* 1620 Cervantes, *Don Quixote,* tr. Shelton. *20c. coll.:* Stevenson 299:7.

7. A lost cat always comes back. *Var.:* The old cat always comes back. *Rec. dist.:* Ky.

8. A singed cat dreads the fire. *Rec. dist.:* U.S., Can. *1st cit.:* ca1450 *Tale of Beryn.* *20c. coll.:* Stevenson 727:1.

9. All cats are black at night. *Vars.:* **(a)** All cats are gray in the dark. **(b)** All cats look alike in the dark. **(c)** At night all cats are gray. **(d)** By night all cats look gray. **(e)** In the dark all cats are gray. **(f)** When candles are out, all cats are gray. *Rec. dist.:* U.S., Can. *1st cit.:* 1546 Heywood, *Dialogue of Proverbs,* ed. Habernicht (1963); US1745 *Papers of Benjamin Franklin,* ed. Labaree (1959). *20c. coll.: ODEP* 111, Whiting 60, *CODP* 33, Stevenson 487:15.

10. Cat after kind. *Vars.:* **(a)** Cats after kind sweet milk will lap. **(b)** For a good mouse hunt, it's cat after kind. *Rec. dist.:* U.S., Can. *1st cit.:* 1546 Heywood, *Dialogue of Proverbs,* ed. Habernicht (1963); US1791 "Thoughts on Proverbs" in *Universal Asylum.* *20c. coll.:* Stevenson 297:1, Whiting 61, *ODEP* 107.

11. Cats hide their claws. *Rec. dist.:* N.Dak., Okla., Tex. *1st cit.:* 1609 Dekker, *Raven's Almanac.* *20c. coll.: ODEP* 111, Stevenson 295:10.

12. Don't expect three legs on a cat when you know he has four. *Rec. dist.:* Ariz.

13. He who plays with a cat must expect to be scratched. *Rec. dist.:* Vt. *1st cit.:* 1710 Palmer, *Moral Essays on English, Scotch, and Foreign Proverbs.* *20c. coll.:* Stevenson 298:8.

14. If you can't feed the cats, you must feed the rats. *Rec. dist.:* Ill.

15. It is in his own interest that the cat purrs. *Rec. dist.:* Wis.

16. Keep no more cats than will catch mice. *Var.:* Keep no more cats than will catch fire. *Rec. dist.:* Mich. *1st cit.:* 1673 Dare, *Counsellor Manners.* *20c. coll.: ODEP* 417, Stevenson 299:2.

17. Let a cat have kittens and they'll learn to catch mice. *Rec. dist.:* Kans.

18. Let every cat cover up his own stink. *Rec. dist.:* N.C.

19. Muffled cats are not good mousers. *Rec. dist.:* Okla.

20. One of the most startling differences between a cat and a lie is that a cat has only nine lives. *Rec. dist.:* Iowa, N.Y., S.C.

21. Scalded cats fear even cold water. *Rec. dist.:* N.Y., S.C. *1st cit.:* 1561 Hoby, *Courtier,*

T.T.; USca1680 Radisson, *Voyages of Radisson,* ed. Scull in Publ. Prince Soc. *20c. coll.:* ODEP 703, Whiting 62, Stevenson 727:3, Whiting*(MP)* 98.

22. Sleeping cats catch no mice. *Rec. dist.:* Calif., Ky., Pa.

23. The cat in gloves catches no mice. *Vars.:* **(a)** Cats that wear gloves catch no mice. **(b)** Handle your tools without mittens: the cat in gloves catches no mice. *Rec. dist.:* U.S., Can. *1st cit.:* 1573 Sanford, *Garden of Pleasure;* US1754 Franklin, *PRAlmanac. 20c. coll.:* ODEP 108, Whiting 61, CODP 32, Stevenson 293:8.

24. The cat is a good friend, but she scratches. *Rec. dist.:* Ill.

25. The cat is honest when the meat is out of her reach. *Rec. dist.:* Ill. *1st cit.:* 1732 Fuller, *Gnomologia. 20c. coll.:* Stevenson 295:11.

26. The cat is mighty dignified until the dog comes by. *Var.:* Cat mighty dignified till dog come by. *Rec. dist.:* Ill., Tex.

27. The cat that would eat fish must wet her feet. *Vars.:* **(a)** The cat loves fish but dares not wet his feet. **(b)** The cat would eat fish, but she will not wet her feet. *Rec. dist.:* U.S., Can. *1st cit.:* ca1225 *Trinity MS O,* ed. Förster in *English Studies* 31. *20c. coll.:* ODEP 109, CODP 33, Stevenson 300:4, Whiting*(MP)* 97.

28. The crying cat always gets the scratch. *Rec. dist.:* N.Y., S.C.

29. The son of the cat pursues the rat. *Var.:* That that comes of a cat will catch mice. *Rec. dist.:* Ohio, Okla. *1st cit.:* 1678 Ray, *English Proverbs. 20c. coll.:* Stevenson 297:1.

30. There's just one way to rub a cat's fur. *Rec. dist.:* Ind.

31. There's more than one way to skin a cat without tearing the hide. *Vars.:* **(a)** More than one way to kill a cat besides choking him with butter. **(b)** More than one way to kill a cat besides skinning him. **(c)** More than one way to skin a cat. **(d)** There are more ways than one to kill a cat. **(e)** There are more ways to kill a cat besides choking him to death. **(f)** There is more than one way to kill a cat. **(g)** There is more than one way to kill a cat

besides choking him on cream. *Rec. dist.:* U.S., Can. *1st cit.:* 1678 Ray, *English Proverbs;* US1839 *John Smith's Letters. 20c. coll.:* ODEP 872, T&W 396, CODP 242, Stevenson 297:5, Whiting*(MP)* 670.

32. To a good cat a good rat. *Rec. dist.:* Del., Ill., Ind. *1st cit.:* 1668 Davenant, *The Man's the Master. 20c. coll.:* Stevenson 296:1.

33. Wait till we see how the cat jumps. *Var.:* Wait and see which way the cat hops. *Rec. dist.:* U.S., Can. *1st cit.:* 1825 Woodworth, *The Forest Rose;* US1811 Jackson, *Massachusetts Merchants, 1765–1844,* ed. Porter (1937). *20c. coll.:* ODEP 108, Whiting 62, T&W 60.

34. What is in the cat will come out in the kitten. *Rec. dist.:* Mich.

35. When the cat is full, then the milk tastes sour. *Rec. dist.:* N.J.

36. While the cat's away, the mice will play. *Vars.:* **(a)** Rats will play while the cat's away. **(b)** The cat is absent, the mice dance. *Rec. dist.:* U.S., Can. *1st cit.:* ca1470 *Harleian MS 3362* in *Anglia;* US1802 *Port Folio. 20c. coll.:* ODEP 109, Whiting 63, CODP 32, Stevenson 301:2, Whiting*(MP)* 102.

37. Who'll bell the cat? *Rec. dist.:* Ky., N.Dak. *1st cit.:* ca1377 Langland, *Piers Plowman;* US1797 Cobbett, *Porcupine Works. 20c. coll.:* ODEP 44, Stevenson 297:7, Whiting 62, T&W 60, Whiting*(MP)* 99.

38. You will never find a cat on a cold hearth. *Rec. dist.:* Md.

SEE ALSO ANGER improves nothing but the arch of a cat's back. / CARE killed the cat. / CURIOSITY killed the cat. / Good LIQUOR will make a cat speak. / SELFISHNESS is harder to kill than a cat. / SYMPATHY killed a cat. / A WOMAN, a cat, and a chimney should never leave the house.

catch 1. Catch before hanging. *Rec. dist.:* N.Y. *1st cit.:* US1818 Royal, *Letters from Alabama, 1817–1822,* ed. Griffeth (1969). *20c. coll.:* Whiting 63, Whiting*(MP)* 103.

2. It's catch as catch can. *Var.:* Catch when catch can. *Rec. dist.:* U.S., Can. *1st cit.:* ca1390 Gower, *Confessio Amantis,* E.E.T.S. (1900); US1721 Wise, *Word of Comfort to Melancholy*

Country. **20c. coll.:** *ODEP* 111, Whiting 63, Stevenson 302:13, Whiting*(MP)* 103.

3. Once caught, twice shy. **Rec. dist.:** Ill.

SEE ALSO Time to catch BEARS is when they're out. / Frightening a BIRD is not the way to catch it. / The early BIRD catches the worm. / Sleeping CATS catch no mice. / The last CHICKEN is the hardest to catch. / Cows can't catch no rabbits. / A man in DEBT is caught in a net. / If the DOG hadn't stopped to lift his leg, he'd have caught the rabbit. / The foremost DOG catches the hare. / A DROWNING man will catch at a straw. / EAGLES don't catch flies. / An EEL held by the tail is not yet caught. / A FISH wouldn't get caught if he kept his mouth shut. / Big FISH are caught with little hooks. / It is a silly FISH that is caught twice with the same bait. / There are better FISH in the sea than have ever been caught. / You can catch more FLIES with molasses than vinegar. / Long runs the FOX, but at last is caught. / The sleeping FOX catches no poultry. / Old FOXES are not easily caught. / The hasty HAND catches frogs for fish. / HARM watch, harm catch. / HURRY is only good for catching flies. / It doesn't pay to HURRY, as you pass up more than you catch. / Be ashamed to catch yourself IDLE. / LAUGHING is catching. / A LIAR is sooner caught than a cripple. / A closed MOUTH catches no flies. / Those who mess with POLITICS are bound to catch smut. / Make not your SAUCE till you have caught the fish. / When the SKY falls, we shall catch larks. / Set a SPRAT to catch a mackerel. / It takes a THIEF to catch a thief.

cattle **1.** Don't rush the cattle. **Rec. dist.:** Ind. **1st cit.:** 1822 Scott, *Pirate;* US1922 Fletcher, *Ravensdene.* **20c. coll.:** *ODEP* 394, Whiting*(MP)* 103, Stevenson 1226:7.

2. He who has fat cattle shall himself be fat. **Rec. dist.:** Minn.

cause **1.** A bad cause will ever be supported by bad means and bad men. **Rec. dist.:** N.Y., S.C. **1st cit.:** US1776 Paine, *The Crisis* in *Complete Writings of Thomas Paine,* ed. Foner (1945). **20c. coll.:** Stevenson 303:14.

2. A good cause finds weapons to defend it. **Rec. dist.:** Ill.

3. A good cause makes a stout heart and a strong arm. **Rec. dist.:** Wis. **1st cit.:** 1732 Fuller, *Gnomologia.* **20c. coll.:** Stevenson 304:4.

4. A man is a lion in his own cause. **Rec. dist.:** Tex. **1st cit.:** 1641 Fergusson, *Scottish Proverbs.* **20c. coll.:** *ODEP* 504, Stevenson 304:1.

5. Great causes are never tried on their merits. **Rec. dist.:** N.Y., S.C. **1st cit.:** US1844 Emerson, "Nature" in *Essays.* **20c. coll.:** Stevenson 307:7.

6. It is an ill cause that none dare speak in. **Rec. dist.:** Mich., R.I. **1st cit.:** 1639 Clarke, *Paroemiologia;* US1834 Loomis, "Proverbs in Farmer's Almanac" in *Western Folklore* (1956). **20c. coll.:** Stevenson 303:14, T&W 62.

7. Men are blind in their own cause. **Rec. dist.:** Okla., Tex.

8. Nothing ever comes to pass without a cause. **Rec. dist.:** Mass. **1st cit.:** 1546 Heywood, *Dialogue of Proverbs,* ed. Habernicht (1963). **20c. coll.:** *ODEP* 67.

9. The best cause requires a good pleader. **Rec. dist.:** Ill.

10. The man with the worst cause makes the most noise. **Rec. dist.:** Ill. **1st cit.:** 1732 Fuller, *Gnomologia.* **20c. coll.:** Stevenson 303:14.

11. They never fail who die in a great cause. **Rec. dist.:** Ill. **1st cit.:** 1820 Byron, *Marino Faliero.* **20c. coll.:** Stevenson 303:7.

SEE ALSO He who is no FRIEND to the good cause is no friend of mine.

caution **1.** Caution is the best keeper of a castle. **Rec. dist.:** Mich.

2. Caution is the downfall to ambition. **Rec. dist.:** Ky.

3. Caution is the parent of safety. **Vars.:** **(a)** Caution is the eldest child of wisdom. **(b)** Distrust and caution are the parents of security. **Rec. dist.:** N.J., Ohio. **1st cit.:** US1733 Franklin, *PRAlmanac.* **20c. coll.:** Stevenson 306:5.

4. Caution never brings regrets. **Rec. dist.:** N.Y.

5. Don't throw caution to the wind. **Rec. dist.:** N.Y. **1st cit.:** US1965 Grebanier, *Great Shakespeare.* **20c. coll.:** Whiting*(MP)* 103.

SEE ALSO Young COURAGE and old caution are a strong pair.

cautious **1.** Be cautious but polite. *Rec. dist.:* Mich.

2. Cautious men conceal knowledge, and the hearts of fools publish folly. *Rec. dist.:* Ind.

3. The cautious seldom cry. *Rec. dist.:* Ohio.

4. The cautious seldom err. *Rec. dist.:* Iowa, N.J., Vt.

cease *SEE* WONDERS will never cease.

celibacy *SEE* Eternal VIGILANCE is the price of celibacy.

cellar January's blossoms fill no man's cellar. *Rec. dist.:* Kans.

cemetery **1.** Every man should have a fair-sized cemetery in which to bury the faults of his friends. *Rec. dist.:* Ill., Oreg.

2. From the cemetery no one is brought back. *Rec. dist.:* Ill.

3. The cemeteries are filled with people who thought the world couldn't get along without them. *Rec. dist.:* Kans.

censor It is the censors who inhibit the earth. *Rec. dist.:* Minn.

censure Censure is a tax which those who fill eminent situations must expect to pay. *Var.:* Censure is the tax a man pays to the public for being eminent. *Rec. dist.:* Mich., N.J. *1st cit.:* 1714 Swift, *Thoughts on Various Subjects.* *20c. coll.:* Stevenson 1033:3.

cent **1.** Dere's come a day when you can't lay up a cent. *Rec. dist.:* Miss.

2. Some days you can't make a cent and the next day you spend it. *Rec. dist.:* Vt.

ceremony **1.** A man without ceremony has need of great merit in its place. *Rec. dist.:* N.Y., S.C. *1st cit.:* 1732 Fuller, *Gnomologia;* US1745 Franklin, *PRAlmanac.* *20c. coll.:* Stevenson 308:11.

2. Ceremony is not civility, nor civility ceremony. *Rec. dist.:* N.Y., S.C. *1st cit.:* US1752 Franklin, *PRAlmanac.* *20c. coll.:* Stevenson 308:10.

3. Excessive ceremony is a blind for bad morals. *Rec. dist.:* Ill.

SEE ALSO DEATH observes no ceremony.

certain **1.** Be certain and on the level; to trust on chance is to dance with the devil. *Rec. dist.:* Ill.

2. Nothing is certain except death and taxes. *Vars.:* **(a)** In this world nothing is certain but death and taxes. **(b)** The only thing certain in life is death and taxes. **(c)** There is nothing more certain than death and nothing more uncertain than the hour of death. *Rec. dist.:* U.S., Can. *1st cit.:* 1726 Defoe, *Political History of the Devil;* US1789 *Writings of Benjamin Franklin,* ed. Smyth (1905–07). *20c. coll.:* CODP 164, Whiting 98, ODEP 580, Stevenson 2248:16, T&W 95, Whiting*(MP)* 158.

3. Nothing is positively certain but uncertainty. *Vars.:* **(a)** Nothing is certain but the unexpected. **(b)** Nothing is certain but the unforeseen. *Rec. dist.:* N.Y. *1st cit.:* 1594 Barnfield, *Shepherd's Content;* US1910 Henry, *Venturers.* *20c. coll.:* Stevenson 309:7, ODEP 580, CODP 164, Whiting*(MP)* 453.

4. That is sufficiently certain which can be made certain. *Rec. dist.:* N.C.

certainty **1.** Certainty is better than hope. *Rec. dist.:* Ohio.

2. Never quit certainty for hope. *Rec. dist.:* Mich. *1st cit.:* 1855 Bohn, *Handbook of Proverbs.* *20c. coll.:* Stevenson 309:4.

cesspool A clean cesspool is better than a typhus serum. *Rec. dist.:* Vt.

chaff *SEE* You cannot catch old BIRDS with chaff.

chain **1.** A chain is no stronger than its weakest link. *Vars.:* **(a)** A chain is as strong as its weakest link. **(b)** A chain is only as strong as its weakest link. **(c)** The strength of a chain is its weakest link. *Rec. dist.:* U.S., Can. *1st cit.:* 1856 Kingsley, *Life and Works;* US1930 Braden, *McCarthy.* *20c. coll.:* ODEP 113, Whiting*(MP)* 104, CODP 34, Stevenson 309:8.

2. Chains of gold are stronger than chains of iron. *Rec. dist.:* Ill., Okla. *1st cit.:* 1574 Guazzo, *Civile Conversation,* tr. Pettie, T.T. (1925). *20c. coll.:* Stevenson 309:9.

3. If you resent your chains, you are half free. *Rec. dist.:* Ill.

4. Men rattle their chains to show that they

are free. *Rec. dist.:* Oreg. *Infm.:* Stevenson notes it is an anonymous English proverb. *1st cit.:* US1948 Stevenson, *Home Book of Proverbs.* *20c. coll.:* Stevenson 310:2.

SEE ALSO To a vicious DOG a short chain. / SUCCESS is a chain of gold—but it is a chain.

chair 1. Easy chair: the hardest one to find empty. *Rec. dist.:* Wis.

2. If you try to sit on two chairs, you'll sit on the floor. *Rec. dist.:* Kans.

3. We have chairs and ears for chums. *Rec. dist.:* N.J.

SEE ALSO He who wants CONTENT can't find it in an easy chair. / You can't keep TROUBLE from coming in, but you needn't give it a chair to sit in. / WORRY is like a rocking chair: both give you something to do, but neither gets you anywhere.

chaise SEE The RICH ride in chaises; the poor walk with God.

chambers Empty chambers make foolish maids. *Rec. dist.:* Ind.

champion A champion is always a fair mark. *Rec. dist.:* N.Y., S.C.

chance 1. Blind chance sweeps the world along. *Rec. dist.:* Ill. *1st cit.:* US1948 Stevenson, *Home Book of Proverbs.* *20c. coll.:* Stevenson 311:6.

2. Chance contrives better than we ourselves. *Rec. dist.:* Ill., Ind. *1st cit.:* US1948 Stevenson, *Home Book of Proverbs.* *20c. coll.:* Stevenson 311:9.

3. Chance dispenses life with unequal justice. *Rec. dist.:* Ill.

4. Chance is the fool's name for fate. *Rec. dist.:* Ohio.

5. Chances rule men, and not men chances. *Rec. dist.:* Ind. *Infm.:* Stevenson attributes the citation to Herodotus, ca445 B.C.E.., in *History.* *20c. coll.:* Stevenson 311:6.

6. Do it well, for you may not get a second chance. *Rec. dist.:* Ind.

7. Keep a cool head and bide your time: a chance is bound to come. *Rec. dist.:* N.C.

8. Many a man who takes a chance would be mighty glad to put it back. *Rec. dist.:* N.Dak.

9. Moses took a chance. *Var.:* Columbus took a chance. *Rec. dist.:* Ind., Oreg.

10. Never lose a chance of doing a good deed. *Rec. dist.:* Minn.

11. Never take a chance till the odds are in your favor. *Rec. dist.:* N.Y.

12. Something has to be left to chance. *Rec. dist.:* Ill. *1st cit.:* 1903 Russell, *Overdue.* *20c. coll.:* ODEP 454, Stevenson 312:5.

13. The more you lean on somebody else, the leaner are your chances of success. *Rec. dist.:* Del., Ill.

14. Whom chance often passes by, it finds at last. *Rec. dist.:* Ill.

SEE ALSO One's chances for HAPPINESS are what he makes them. / A girl who's wearing PAINT has a better chance than one who ain't. / One man's WEAKNESS is another man's chance.

change *(n.)* 1. Be sure you can better your condition before you make a change. *Rec. dist.:* Kans.

2. Change of fortune hurts a wise man no more than a change of the moon. *Rec. dist.:* N.Y., S.C. *1st cit.:* US1756 Franklin, *PRAlmanac.* *20c. coll.:* Stevenson 871:10.

3. Change of pasture makes fat calves. *Rec. dist.:* Ill. *1st cit.:* 1541 Bullinger, *Christian State of Matrimony,* tr. Coverdale (1543). *20c. coll.:* ODEP 114.

4. Change of scenery makes for health. *Rec. dist.:* Ill.

5. In this world nothing is permanent except change. *Rec. dist.:* Iowa. *1st cit.:* US1948 Stevenson, *Home Book of Proverbs.* *20c. coll.:* Stevenson 315:5.

6. Many changes can take place on a spring day. *Rec. dist.:* Miss.

7. Popularity is glory's small change. *Rec. dist.:* Oreg.

8. There is a certain relief in change, even though it be from bad to worse. *Rec. dist.:* N.Y. *1st cit.:* US1824 Irving, "Preface" in *Tales of a Traveller.* *20c. coll.:* Stevenson 313:6.

9. To an optimist every change is a change for the better. *Rec. dist.:* Ill.

10. We are very apt not to notice little changes in those we see every day. *Rec. dist.*: N.C.

SEE ALSO Change of WEATHER is a discourse of fools.

change *(v.)* **1.** All things change, and we with them. *Var.*: Times change and we change with them. *Rec. dist.*: U.S., Can. *1st cit.*: 1579 Lyly, *Euphues, Anatomy of Wit,* ed. Arber (1868); US1877 Longfellow, *Keramos.* *20c. coll.*: ODEP 825, Stevenson 315:5, *CODP* 227, Whiting*(MP)* 628.

2. Bear, and blame not, what you cannot change. *Rec. dist.*: Mich.

3. Change seldom, for changes are inconvenient. *Rec. dist.*: Mich.

4. No change in circumstances will change a defect in character. *Rec. dist.*: N.Y.

5. The more it changes, the more it remains the same. *Rec. dist.*: N.Y., Ohio. *1st cit.*: 1903 Shaw, *The Revolutionist's Handbook.* *20c. coll.*: Stevenson 314:7.

6. The nature of things doesn't change. *Rec. dist.*: Tex.

SEE ALSO You may change the CLOTHES; you cannot change the man. / GOD aids him who changes. / HONORS change manners. / Don't change HORSES in the middle of the stream. / A LEOPARD can't change his spots. / It's a woman's PRIVILEGE to change her mind. / TIME changes ever, but the heart of man never. / TIME changes everything. / A WISE man changes his mind; a fool never does. / A WOLF may change his mind but never his fur.

changing **1.** Sit tight: you may do worse by changing your position. *Rec. dist.*: Ill.

2. We do not always gain by changing. *Rec. dist.*: Ill.

3. When you're through changing, you're through. *Rec. dist.*: Utah, Wis.

SEE ALSO Be slow in choosing a FRIEND, but slower in changing him.

channel We are all channel swimmers, swimming the channel of life. *Rec. dist.*: Miss.

SEE ALSO All great MINDS run in the same channel.

chaos Chaos always precedes order. *Rec. dist.*: Minn.

chapel *SEE* Where GOD has his church, the devil will have his chapel. / There are no reserved SEATS in the halls of fame or the chapels of faith.

chaperon **1.** Chaperons are necessary evils. *Rec. dist.*: Miss.

2. The best chaperon a girl can have is to be in love with another fellow. *Rec. dist.*: Miss.

character **1.** A brave and gentle character is often found under the humblest garb. *Rec. dist.*: Minn.

2. A character, like a kettle, once mended, always needs mending. *Rec. dist.*: Ill.

3. Avoid bad characters. *Rec. dist.*: Mich.

4. Character and hard work go together in nine cases out of ten. *Rec. dist.*: N.C.

5. Character is destiny. *Rec. dist.*: Ind. *Infm.*: Mullach attributes this version of the proverb to Heracleitus in the former's work *Fragments of Greek Philosophy.* *1st cit.*: US1948 Stevenson, *Home Book of Proverbs.* *20c. coll.*: Stevenson 317:2.

6. Character is much easier kept than recovered. *Rec. dist.*: N.Y., S.C. *1st cit.*: US1776 Paine, *The Crisis* in *Complete Writings of Thomas Paine,* ed. Foner (1945). *20c. coll.*: Stevenson 319:1.

7. Character is the cornerstone of success. *Rec. dist.*: Ohio.

8. Character is the diamond that scratches every other stone. *Rec. dist.*: Wis. *1st cit.*: 1902 Hulme, *Proverb Lore.* *20c. coll.*: Stevenson 317:2.

9. Character is what we are; reputation is what others think we are. *Var.*: Character is what you are; reputation, what people think. *Rec. dist.*: Kans., N.Y., S.C.

10. Character is what you are in the dark when no one is around. *Rec. dist.*: N.C. *1st cit.*: ca1883 Moody, "Character" in *Sermons.* *20c. coll.*: Stevenson 317:2.

11. Character, like embroidery, is made stitch by stitch. *Rec. dist.*: Ind.

12. Character, not happiness, is the end of life. *Rec. dist.*: Ill.

13. If you take care of your character, your

reputation will take care of itself. *Rec. dist.:* Kans.

14. It takes a lifetime to build up a character, but you can lose it in a very short time. *Var.:* A man will take a lifetime to build a good character and then destroy it by a single misstep. *Rec. dist.:* Fla., Ill.

15. Like a fence, character cannot be strengthened by whitewash. *Rec. dist.:* Ind.

16. Man's character is no better than he is. *Rec. dist.:* Ohio.

17. Man's only real possession is his character. *Rec. dist.:* Minn.

18. Our character is our will; for what we will we are. *Rec. dist.:* Utah.

19. Strong character depends not so much upon chances as upon choices. *Rec. dist.:* Minn.

20. The man that makes a character makes foes. *Rec. dist.:* N.Y., S.C. *Infm.:* The man who gains fame. *1st cit.:* ca1757 Young, "To Mr. Pope" in *Works.* *20c. coll.:* Stevenson 1033:5.

21. There is no gain in subtracting from your character to add to your popularity. *Rec. dist.:* Ind.

22. We pass for what we are; character teaches above our wills. *Rec. dist.:* N.Y., S.C.

23. You can tell the character of a woman by the house she keeps. *Rec. dist.:* Ky., Minn.

24. You cannot build character and courage by taking away man's initiative and independence. *Rec. dist.:* Ariz.

25. You cannot dream yourself into a character; you must forge one out for yourself. *Rec. dist.:* Nebr.

SEE ALSO Man's ACTIONS show his character. / DREAMS retain the infirmities of our character. / A PAT on the back will build character if applied low enough, hard enough, and often enough.

charity **1.** Charity begins at home. *Vars.:* **(a)** Charity begins at home and spreads abroad. **(b)** Charity begins at home and usually stays there. **(c)** Charity begins at home but should not end there. **(d)** Charity begins in the home but does not end at home. **(e)** Charity should begin at home, but it should not stay there. *Rec. dist.:* U.S., Can. *1st cit.:* ca1380 Wyclif, *Of Prelates* in *English Works,* E.E.T.S. (1880); US1628 Hawes, *Winthrop Papers, 1498–1649,* Mass.Hist.Soc. *Collections* (1863–92). *20c. coll.:* ODEP 115, Whiting 66, *CODP* 34, Stevenson 322:4, T&W 65, Whiting(MP) 105.

2. Charity covers a multitude of sins. *Var.:* Charity covers a multitude of faults. *Rec. dist.:* U.S., Can. *1st cit.:* ca1633 Herbert, *Priest to the Temple* in *Works,* ed. Hutchinson (1941); USca1645 Cotton in *Complete Writings of Roger Williams* (1963). *20c. coll.:* ODEP 115, Whiting 67, Stevenson 321:4, T&W 230, Whiting(MP) 106.

3. Charity gives itself rich; covetousness hoards itself poor. *Rec. dist.:* Ohio. *Infm.:* Stevenson notes this is a German version of "Tithe and be rich." *1st cit.:* 1640 Herbert, *Outlandish Proverbs (Jacula Prudentum)* in *Works,* ed. Hutchinson (1941). *20c. coll.:* Stevenson 321:2.

4. Charity is a rarity. *Rec. dist.:* N.C. *1st cit.:* ca1634 Barrow, *Extemporaneous Replies.* *20c. coll.:* Stevenson 320:3.

5. Charity is a virtue of the heart and not of the hand. *Rec. dist.:* Oreg. *1st cit.:* 1713 Addison, *The Guardian.* *20c. coll.:* Stevenson 321:7.

6. Charity is friendship in common, and friendship is charity enclosed. *Rec. dist.:* Mich.

7. Charity is not a bone you throw to a dog but a bone you share with a dog. *Rec. dist.:* N.Y.

8. Charity is the father of sacrifice. *Rec. dist.:* S.C.

9. He that feeds upon charity has a cold dinner and no supper. *Rec. dist.:* N.J.

10. He that has no charity deserves no mercy. *Rec. dist.:* Ill.

11. He who depends on charity soon learns to fast. *Rec. dist.:* Ill.

12. Proportion your charity to the strength of your estate, or God will proportion your estate to the weakness of your charity. *Rec. dist.:* N.Y., S.C. *1st cit.:* US1757 Franklin, *PRAlmanac.* *20c. coll.:* Stevenson 320:10.

13. The best charity is justice to all. *Rec. dist.:* Ill.

14. The roots of charity are always green. *Rec. dist.:* N.Y.

15. Wanted: not charity but a fair chance. *Rec. dist.:* Wis.

16. What you give in charity in this world you take with you after death. *Rec. dist.:* N.C.

charm **1.** An ounce of charm is worth a pound of lure. *Rec. dist.:* Ky.

2. As charms are nonsense, nonsense is a charm. *Rec. dist.:* N.Y., S.C.

3. Charm strikes the sight, but merit wins the soul. *Rec. dist.:* Ind., Miss. *1st cit.:* 1712 Pope, *Rape of the Lock.* *20c. coll.:* Stevenson 323:4.
SEE ALSO MODESTY has more charm than beauty. / MUSIC has charm to soothe the savage breast.

chase *(n.)* **1.** The chase is better than the kill. *Rec. dist.:* Ky. *1st cit.:* US1965 Disney, *Shadow of a Man.* *20c. coll.:* Whiting*(MP)* 106.

2. The chase of gain is rich in hate. *Rec. dist.:* Ind.

chase *(v.)* *SEE* If you want to be ALLURING, don't chase your young man.

chaste Chaste is she whom no one has asked. *Rec. dist.:* Ill. *1st cit.:* 1695 Congreve, *Love for Love.* *20c. coll.:* Stevenson 325:4.

chastise *SEE* The LORD chastises his own.

chastity **1.** By no art can chastity, once injured, be made whole. *Rec. dist.:* Ill.

2. Chastity is a virtue with some, with the majority almost a vice. *Rec. dist.:* N.Y. *1st cit.:* US1920 Huneker, *Painted Veils.* *20c. coll.:* Stevenson 324:11.
SEE ALSO THRIFT is to a man what chastity is to a woman.

chattering Chattering won't make the pot boil. *Rec. dist.:* N.Y., S.C.

cheap **1.** All things are cheap to the saving, dear to the wasteful. *Rec. dist.:* N.Y., S.C.

2. Cheap goods always prove expensive. *Rec. dist.:* Ill.

3. Cheap things are not good, good things are not cheap. *Rec. dist.:* Ill. *1st cit.:* US1875

Scarborough, *Chinese Proverbs.* *20c. coll.:* Stevenson 327:2.

4. Cheapest is dearest. *Rec. dist.:* Ill., N.J.

5. Cheapest is the dearest labor. *Rec. dist.:* N.Y., S.C. *1st cit.:* US1841 Emerson, "Compensation" in *Essays.* *20c. coll.:* Stevenson 327:10.

6. Dear is cheap; cheap is dear. *Rec. dist.:* Ill. *1st cit.:* 1640 Herbert, *Outlandish Proverbs (Jacula Prudentum)* in *Works,* ed. Hutchinson (1941). *20c. coll.:* Stevenson 327:1, *ODEP* 173.

7. Two can live as cheap as one. *Vars.:* **(a)** Two can live as cheap as one, if one's a horse and the other is a sparrow. **(b)** Two can live cheaper than one. *Rec. dist.:* U.S., Can. *1st cit.:* US1921 Lardner, *Big Town.* *20c. coll.:* Whiting*(MP)* 654.
SEE ALSO What is BOUGHT is cheaper than a gift. / Never BUY what you do not want because it is cheap. / Make not your FRIEND too cheap to you, nor yourself too dear to him. / LIQUOR never hurt a cheap man. / You cannot make a cheap PALACE. / TALK is cheap. / VIRTUE and honesty are cheap at any price.

cheapness Cheapness moves to laughter; dearness, to tears. *Rec. dist.:* Vt.

cheat He who cheats another cheats himself most. *Var.:* He is most cheated who cheats himself. *Rec. dist.:* N.J., N.C., Minn.
SEE ALSO He who cheats his APPETITE avoids debt.

cheated **1.** If you would not be cheated, ask the price at three shops. *Rec. dist.:* N.Y.

2. It is better to be cheated than not to trust. *Rec. dist.:* N.Y.

3. The surest way to be cheated is to think one's self more clever than other people. *Rec. dist.:* Minn.

cheater **1.** A skillful cheater needs no assistance. *Rec. dist.:* Ill.

2. Cheaters never prosper. *Vars.:* **(a)** A cheater never wins; a winner never cheats. **(b)** Cheaters never win. **(c)** Cheaters never win and winners never cheat. **(d)** Cheating people don't prosper. **(e)** Cheating play never thrives. *Rec. dist.:* U.S., Can. *1st cit.:* 1903 Lean, *Collecta-*

nea; US1805 Parkinson, *Tour in America in 1798–1800.* **20c. coll.:** *CODP* 35, Whiting 68, Stevenson 328:1.

3. The cheater finally winds up by cheating himself. **Rec. dist.:** Ill.

cheating The cheating wife doubts the chastity of all women. **Rec. dist.:** Ill.

cheer Small cheer and great welcome make a merry feast. **Rec. dist.:** N.J. **1st cit.:** 1593 Shakespeare, *Comedy of Errors.* **20c. coll.:** Stevenson 330:3.

SEE ALSO CHRISTMAS comes but once a year. / WELCOME is the best of cheer.

cheerful A cheerful look makes a dish a feast. **Rec. dist.:** Ill. **1st cit.:** ca1477 Caxton, *Booke of Curteseye.* **20c. coll.:** Stevenson 329:10, *ODEP* 117.

SEE ALSO The Lord loves the cheerful GIVER. / A merry HEART makes a cheerful countenance.

cheerfulness **1.** Cheerfulness, helpfulness, and honesty are fine, good companions to take with you through life. **Rec. dist.:** Minn.

2. Cheerfulness is perfectly consistent with piety. **Rec. dist.:** Mich.

3. Cheerfulness is the principal ingredient in health. **Rec. dist.:** Wis. **1st cit.:** 1756 Murphy, *Apprentice;* US1870 Emerson, "Success" in *Society and Solitude.* **20c. coll.:** Stevenson 1099:8.

4. Constant cheerfulness is a sign of true wisdom. **Rec. dist.:** Ala.

5. So of cheerfulness or of good temper, the more it is spent, the more of it remains. **Rec. dist.:** N.Y., S.C.

SEE ALSO An hour's INDUSTRY will do more to produce cheerfulness than a month's moaning.

cheese **1.** After cheese comes nothing. **Rec. dist.:** Ill. **1st cit.:** 1609 Harward, Unpublished manuscript in Trinity College Library, Cambridge. **20c. coll.:** *ODEP* 6.

2. Cheese and bread make the cheeks red. **Rec. dist.:** Ill. **1st cit.:** US1948 Stevenson, *Home Book of Proverbs.* **20c. coll.:** Stevenson 331:7.

3. Cheese and salt meat should be sparingly eat. **Rec. dist.:** Ill., N.Y., S.C. **1st cit.:** US1733 Franklin, *PRAlmanac.* **20c. coll.:** Stevenson 331:7.

4. Cheese digests all things but itself. **Rec. dist.:** Ill. **1st cit.:** ca1566 Harvey, *Marginalia.* **20c. coll.:** *ODEP* 117, Stevenson 331:1.

5. Cheese is wholesome when it is given with a sparing hand. **Rec. dist.:** Ill. **1st cit.:** US1948 Stevenson, *Home Book of Proverbs.* **20c. coll.:** Stevenson 331:7.

6. It takes two old women to make a cheese: one to hold and the other to squeeze. **Rec. dist.:** Maine, Mass.

7. The king's cheese goes half away in parings. **Var.:** The king's cheese is half wasted in parings; but no matter, 'tis made of the people's milk. **Rec. dist.:** Mich., N.Y., S.C. **1st cit.:** 1659 Howell, *Paroimiographia.* **20c. coll.:** *ODEP* 427.

8. The miser's cheese is wholesomest. **Rec. dist.:** N.Y., S.C. **1st cit.:** US1737 Franklin, *PRAlmanac.* **20c. coll.:** Stevenson 330:13.

9. Where there's cheese, there's always mice. **Rec. dist.:** N.C.

SEE ALSO A KISS without a squeeze is like a piece of pie without a piece of cheese.

cherish SEE Cherish some FLOWER, be it ever so lowly.

cherry **1.** Life is but a bowl of cherries. **Rec. dist.:** U.S., Can. **1st cit.:** US1933 Holt, *Dark Lady.* **20c. coll.:** Whiting(*MP*) 371.

2. Stolen cherries are the sweetest. **Rec. dist.:** N.Y., S.C.

3. The higher you climb the cherry tree, the sweeter you find the cherries. **Rec. dist.:** Iowa.

4. Those that eat cherries with great persons shall have their eyes squirted out with stones. **Rec. dist.:** Okla.

SEE ALSO Never make two BITES at a cherry. / DISGRACES are like cherries: one draws another.

chest Little chests may hold great treasures. **Rec. dist.:** Nebr.

chew You can chew it even if you can't swaller it. **Rec. dist.:** N.Y., S.C.

SEE ALSO PILLS are to be swallowed, not chewed. / It's allers best for a man to chew his own TOBAKKER.

chick *SEE* Remember, a HEN can scratch for a dozen chicks as easily as for one.

chicken 1. Chicken ain't nothin' but a bird. *Rec. dist.:* Miss.

2. Chickens today, feathers tomorrow. *Rec. dist.:* Ind.

3. Chickens will always come home to roost. *Vars.:* **(a)** Bad chickens come home to roost. **(b)** Chickens come home to roost. **(c)** His chickens have come home to roost. *Rec. dist.:* U.S. *1st cit.:* ca1389 Chaucer, *Parson's Tale;* US1871 Jones, *Life of Jefferson S. Batkins.* **20c. coll.:** ODEP 162, T&W 67, CODP 47, Stevenson 332:17, Whiting*(MP)* 108–09.

4. Don't count your chickens before they are hatched. *Vars.:* **(a)** Don't count your chickens before they hatch. **(b)** Never count your chickens before they are hatched. *Rec. dist.:* U.S., Can. *1st cit.:* 1510 Howell, *New Sonnets;* US1821 Loomis, "Proverbs in Farmer's Almanac" in *Western Folklore* (1956). **20c. coll.:** ODEP 42, CODP 43, Whiting 69, Stevenson 332:8, T&W 67, Whiting*(MP)* 109.

5. It is better to be a live chicken than a dead one. *Rec. dist.:* Tex.

6. It's a mighty poor chicken that can't scratch up his own food. *Rec. dist.:* Miss.

7. Keep your chickens in your own backyard. *Rec. dist.:* N.Y.

8. The last chicken is the hardest to catch. *Rec. dist.:* Ind.

9. There are more ways to kill a chicken than to kiss him to death. *Rec. dist.:* Miss.

SEE ALSO CHILDREN, chickens, and women never have enough. / A howlin' COYOTE ain't stealin' no chickens. / CURSES, like chickens, come home to roost. / From fried EGGS come no chickens. / A STINGY man gives an egg to get a chicken. / The WORM is always wrong when it argues with the chicken.

chide Chide not severely nor punish hastily. *Rec. dist.:* Mich., S.C.

chief Too many chiefs and not enough braves. *Rec. dist.:* Kans. *1st cit.:* US1974 Webster, *Burial in Portugal.* **20c. coll.:** Whiting*(MP)* 110.

child 1. A bitten child dreads a dog. *Rec. dist.:* Ind.

2. A burnt child dreads the fire. *Vars.:* **(a)** A burned child dreads the fire. **(b)** A burned child dreads the flames. **(c)** A burned child won't go near the stove. **(d)** A burnt child avoids the fire. **(e)** A burnt child is afraid of the fire. *Rec. dist.:* U.S. *1st cit.:* ca1300 *Proverbs of Hendling* in *Reliquiae Antiquae,* eds. Wright and Halliwell (1841); US1755 *Papers of Sir William Johnson,* ed. Sullivan (1921–65). **20c. coll.:** ODEP 92, Whiting 69, CODP 27, Stevenson 727:2, T&W 68, Whiting*(MP)* 110.

3. A child and a fool imagine twenty shillings and twenty years can never be spent. *Rec. dist.:* Ind.

4. A child learns to talk in about two years, but it takes about sixty years for him to learn to keep his mouth shut. *Rec. dist.:* Minn.

5. A child must learn to crawl before it can walk. *Rec. dist.:* U.S., Can. *1st cit.:* ca1350 *Douce MS 52,* ed. Förster (1906); US1733 *Jonathan Belcher Papers,* Mass.Hist.Soc. *Collections* (1893–94). **20c. coll.:** ODEP 120, Whiting 70, Stevenson 722:14.

6. A child needs love the most when he deserves it the least. *Rec. dist.:* Ariz.

7. A child that won't hear will feel. *Rec. dist.:* Ohio.

8. A child without parents is like a ship without a rudder. *Rec. dist.:* N.Y.

9. A child's spirit is easily broken and difficult to heal. *Rec. dist.:* Minn., N.Y.

10. A lot of a child's welfare can be done with a razor strap. *Rec. dist.:* Oreg.

11. A man among children will be long a child. *Var.:* A man among children will long be a child; a child among men will soon be a man. *Rec. dist.:* Wis.

12. Even a child makes himself known by his doings. *Rec. dist.:* Ohio.

13. Give a child his will and whelp his fill,

and neither will thrive. *Rec. dist.:* Mich. *1st cit.:* 1303 Manning, *Handlyng Synne;* US1880 Spurgeon, *John Ploughman's Pictures.* *20c. coll.:* Stevenson 336:5, *ODEP* 302.

14. If a child cuts its finger, it has cut its mother's heart. *Rec. dist.:* Wis.

15. It is a wise child that knows its own father. *Rec. dist.:* U.S., Can. *1st cit.:* 1584 Withals, *Dictionary;* US1723 *New England Courant, Writings of Benjamin Franklin* (1956). *20c. coll.:* *ODEP* 899, Whiting 70, *CODP* 247, Stevenson 770:8, T&W 68, Whiting*(MP)* 111.

16. Never argue with a child or a fool. *Rec. dist.:* N.J.

17. Once a man, twice a child. *Rec. dist.:* U.S., Can. *1st cit.:* 1527 Longland, *Sermons;* US1650 *Works of Anne Bradstreet,* ed. Ellis (1932). *20c. coll.:* *ODEP* 591, Whiting 70, Stevenson 26:1, T&W 68.

18. Teach a child to hold his tongue: he will learn fast enough to speak. *Rec. dist.:* N.Y., S.C., Vt.

19. The child is father of the man. *Rec. dist.:* U.S., Can. *1st cit.:* 1807 Wordsworth, "My Heart Leaps Up" in *Poems* (1952); US1853 Baldwin, *Flush Times of Alabama and Mississippi* (1854). *20c. coll.:* *ODEP* 119, T&W 68, *CODP* 36, Stevenson 339:9, Whiting*(MP)* 111.

20. The future of a child is the work of the mother. *Rec. dist.:* Wis.

21. The great man is he who does not lose his child's heart. *Rec. dist.:* N.J.

22. The hardest job a child faces is that of learning manners without seeing any. *Rec. dist.:* Ill.

23. There are four things every child needs. He needs an abundance of love, plenty of good nourishing food, lots of soap and water, and after that some good healthy neglect. *Rec. dist.:* Kans.

24. To a child, all weather is cold. *Rec. dist.:* Wis. *1st cit.:* 1640 Herbert, *Outlandish Proverbs (Jacula Prudentum)* in *Works,* ed. Hutchinson (1941). *20c. coll.:* *ODEP* 118, Stevenson 338:1.

25. To spoil a child is to kill it. *Rec. dist.:* N.Dak.

26. Train up a child in the right way; when he is old he will not depart from it. *Vars.:* **(a)** Teach a child the way in which he shall go, and he will not depart thereof. **(b)** Train a child in the way he should go, and walk there yourself once in a while. **(c)** Train a child in the way he should go, and when he is old he will not depart from it. *Rec. dist.:* U.S., Can. *1st cit.:* US1866 Boucicault, *Flying Scud* in *Forbidden Fruit and Other Plays,* eds. Nicoll and Cloak (1940). *20c. coll.:* T&W 68, Stevenson 340:1.

27. What a child does at home, it will do abroad. *Var.:* Teach children to behave at home, and they will know how to everywhere else. *Rec. dist.:* N.C.

28. When a child is little, it pulls at your apron strings. When it gets older, it pulls at your heart strings. *Rec. dist.:* Kans., Okla.

29. With seven nurses a child will be without eyes. *Rec. dist.:* Wis.

30. You can always tell a youngest child, but you can't tell him much. *Rec. dist.:* Fla., Iowa.

SEE ALSO No MOTHER has a homely child. / PREJUDICE is the child of ignorance. / Spare the ROD and spoil the child. / How sharper than a SERPENT's tooth is a thankless child. / The SHOEMAKER's child goes barefoot. / If you want the TRUTH, ask a child.

childhood **1.** Childhood should be happy and carefree. *Rec. dist.:* Mich.

2. Childhood shows the man as morning shows the day. *Rec. dist.:* Ill.

3. We can forget our childhood, but we cannot deny it. *Rec. dist.:* Calif.

children **1.** Children and fools have merry lives. *Rec. dist.:* Okla. *1st cit.:* 1639 Clarke, *Paroemiologia.* *20c. coll.:* *ODEP* 120, Stevenson 342:7.

2. Children and fools speak the truth. *Vars.:* **(a)** Children and crazy people speak the truth. **(b)** Children and drunkards speak the truth. **(c)** Children, fools, and drunkards tell the truth. *Rec. dist.:* U.S., Can. *1st cit.:* 1537 Hayes in *State Papers of Henry VIII;* US1785 *Letters of Rev. William Gordon, Historian of American Revolution,* Mass.Hist.Soc. *Collections* (1929–

30). **20c. coll.:** *ODEP* 119, Whiting 71, *CODP* 36, Stevenson 342:9, Whiting*(MP)* 111.

3. Children and princes will quarrel for trifles. **Rec. dist.:** N.Y., S.C.

4. Children are love made visible. **Rec. dist.:** N.Y.

5. Children are poor men's riches. **Rec. dist.:** U.S., Can. **1st cit.:** 1541 Bullinger, *Christian State of Matrimony,* tr. Coverdale; US1750 Tilghman in *Md.Mag.Hist.* (1938). **20c. coll.:** *ODEP* 120, Whiting 71, Stevenson 341:3.

6. Children are so happy because they live a day at a time. **Rec. dist.:** Minn.

7. Children are the keys of paradise. **Rec. dist.:** N.Y., S.C. **1st cit.:** 1851 Stoddard, *Children's Prayer.* **20c. coll.:** Stevenson 341:9.

8. Children are to be seen and not heard. **Vars.:** **(a)** Little boys should be seen and not heard. **(b)** Little children should be seen and not heard. **(c)** Little folk should be seen and not heard. **Rec. dist.:** U.S., Can. **1st cit.:** ca1400 Mirkus, *Mirk's Festival,* E.E.T.S. (1905); US1788 *Diary of John Quincy Adams,* Mass. Hist.Soc. *Collections* (1902). **20c. coll.:** *ODEP* 120, Whiting 71, *CODP* 36, Stevenson 335:4, T&W 68, Whiting*(MP)* 112.

9. Children are what their mothers are. **Rec. dist.:** Kans.

10. Children can teach old folks. **Rec. dist.:** N.C.

11. Children, chickens, and women never have enough. **Rec. dist.:** Wis.

12. Children: one is one, two is fun, three is a houseful. **Rec. dist.:** N.Y.

13. Don't slap your children in the face, for the Lord prepared a better place. **Rec. dist.:** N.Y.

14. Go not with bad children. **Rec. dist.:** Okla.

15. He that has no children brings them up well. **Var.:** He that has no children does bring them up well. **Rec. dist.:** Del., Ill. **1st cit.:** 1573 Sanford, *Garden of Pleasure.* **20c. coll.:** *ODEP* 120, Stevenson 337:1.

16. It takes children to make a happy home. **Rec. dist.:** N.C.

17. Late children, early orphans. **Rec. dist.:** Miss., N.J., Wis. **1st cit.:** 1659 Howell, *Paroimiographia (Spanish Proverbs);* US1742 Franklin, *PRAlmanac.* **20c. coll.:** *ODEP* 443, Whiting 70, Stevenson 338:2.

18. Little children have big ears. **Rec. dist.:** U.S., Can. **1st cit.:** 1732 Fuller, *Gnomologia.* **20c. coll.:** Stevenson 338:3.

19. Little children, little troubles; big children, big troubles. **Rec. dist.:** N.Y. **1st cit.:** 1640 Herbert, *Outlandish Proverbs (Jacula Prudentum)* in *Works,* ed. Hutchinson (1941). **20c. coll.:** Stevenson 342:4.

20. Little children step on your toes; big children step on your heart. **Var.:** When your children are small they tread on your toes; and that you don't mind, but when they grow up they tread on your heart, and then it hurts. **Rec. dist.:** U.S., Can.

21. Send the children to town and you'll have to go yourself. **Rec. dist.:** Wash.

22. Undutiful children make wretched parents. **Rec. dist.:** Mich.

23. What children hear at home soon flies abroad. **Rec. dist.:** Ind., R.I. **1st cit.:** 1611 Cotgrave, *Dictionary of French and English Tongues.* **20c. coll.:** *ODEP* 120, Stevenson 336:2.

24. When children stand quiet, they have done some harm. **Vars.:** **(a)** A quiet child is plotting mischief, or has done it. **(b)** When children are doing nothing, they're doing mischief. **Rec. dist.:** U.S., Can. **1st cit.:** 1640 Herbert, *Outlandish Proverbs (Jacula Prudentum)* in *Works,* ed. Hutchinson (1941); US1860 Emerson, *Conduct of Life.* **20c. coll.:** *ODEP* 121, Stevenson 335:5.

SEE ALSO We're all ADAM's children; silk makes the difference. / Men fear DEATH as children do going in the dark. / The DEVIL could not be everywhere so he made children. / HOME is the father's kingdom, the children's paradise, the mother's world. / Old MAIDS fancy nobody knows how to bring up children but them. / MEN are but children of a larger growth. / The RICH get richer, and the poor have children. / A WISE man has wise children.

chill Yuh might as well die wid de chills ez wid de fever. **Rec. dist.:** Tex.

chimney 1. A smoky chimney and a scolding wife are two bad companions. *Rec. dist.:* Ill.

2. Every chimney smells of smoke. *Rec. dist.:* Ill.

3. It's easier to build two chimneys than to keep one in fuel. *Var.:* It is easier to build two chimneys than to keep one in boil. *Rec. dist.:* U.S., Can. *1st cit.:* 1640 Herbert, *Outlandish Proverbs (Jacula Prudentum)* in *Works,* ed. Hutchinson (1941); US1758 Franklin, *PRAlmanac. 20c. coll.: ODEP* 89, Whiting 71.

4. When a chimney smokes the meal is being cooked. *Rec. dist.:* Ill.
SEE ALSO A WOMAN, a cat, and a chimney should never leave the house.

chin 1. Don't lead with your chin. *Rec. dist.:* U.S., Can. *1st cit.:* US1950 Gardner, *Musical. 20c. coll.:* Whiting*(MP)* 112.

2. Keep your chin up. *Rec. dist.:* U.S., Can. *1st cit.:* 1942 Taylor, *Six Iron Spiders. 20c. coll.:* Stevenson 345:9, Whiting*(MP)* 112.

china China and reputations are alike: easily cracked but not easily mended. *Rec. dist.:* Vt.

chip 1. A chip on the shoulder has broken the life of many a man. *Rec. dist.:* Minn.

2. A chip on the shoulder is a good indication of wood higher up. *Var.:* Anybody who has a chip on the shoulder shows that there is wood above it. *Rec. dist.:* U.S., Can.

3. Let the chips fall where they may. *Var.:* Hew to the mark; let the chips fall where they may. *Rec. dist.:* U.S. *1st cit.:* US1880 Conklin, Nomination speech for U.S. Grant at Republican National Convention, Chicago, Ill., 5 June. *20c. coll.:* Stevenson 345:11.

4. Look not too high lest a chip fall in your eye. *Rec. dist.:* Okla., Tex. *1st cit.:* ca1330 Mannyng, *Langtoft's Chronicles. 20c. coll.: ODEP* 371, Stevenson 345:10.
SEE ALSO A CARPENTER is known by his chips. / He's not the best CARPENTER that makes the most chips. / You can tell a WOODSMAN by his chips.

choice 1. He that has a choice has trouble. *Rec. dist.:* Ind.

2. Never try to change the choice of a woman's heart. *Rec. dist.:* N.Y.

3. Of what use is it to pretend there is a choice when there is none? *Rec. dist.:* Vt.

4. The burden of one's own choice is not felt. *Rec. dist.:* Ill. *1st cit.:* 1707 Mapletoft, *Select Proverbs. 20c. coll.: ODEP* 92.

5. The obvious choice is usually a quick regret. *Rec. dist.:* N.Y., S.C.

6. There is little choice in a barrel of rotten apples. *Vars.:* (a) No choice in rotten apples. (b) 'Tain't no choice in rotten apples. (c) There is a small choice in rotten apples. (d) There is small choice in rotten apples. *Rec. dist.:* U.S., Can. *1st cit.:* 1594 Shakespeare, *Taming of the Shrew;* US1931 Wells, *Umbrella. 20c. coll.: ODEP* 121, Whiting*(MP)* 114, Stevenson 348:9.

7. There's no choice among stinking fish. *Rec. dist.:* Ill. *1st cit.:* 1732 Fuller, *Gnomologia. 20c. coll.:* Stevenson 348:9.
SEE ALSO FATE gives you parents; choice gives us friends. / Choose your FRIENDS like your books—few but choice. / Choose your LOVE, then love your choice.

choke *SEE* There are more ways to kill a DOG than by choking him to death on hot butter. / GOD grips but does not choke.

choose Never choose between two good things; take 'em both. *Rec. dist.:* Oreg.
SEE ALSO Choose an AUTHOR as you choose a friend. / Many are CALLED but few are chosen. / Choose the lesser of two EVILS. / You cannot choose your FATHER, but you choose your father's son. / Choose not FRIENDS by outward show, for feathers float while pearls lie low.

chooser *SEE* BEGGARS can't be choosers.

choosing *SEE* Be slow in choosing a FRIEND, but slower in changing him.

Christian 1. A Christian is God Almighty's gentleman. *Rec. dist.:* N.Y., S.C. *1st cit.:* 1827 Hare, *Guesses at Truth. 20c. coll.:* Stevenson 350:2.

2. Christians are like green tea: you don't

know its strength until it is put in hot water. *Rec. dist.:* N.C.

3. If it's wrong for a Christian to do something, then it's surely wrong for a sinner to do the same thing. *Rec. dist.:* N.C.

4. It costs something to be a Christian, but it costs more to be a sinner. *Rec. dist.:* N.C.

5. It is far more Christian to praise a thornbush for its roses than to damn a rosebush for its thorns. *Rec. dist.:* Minn.

Christmas 1. A green Christmas, a white Easter. *Vars.:* (a) A green Christmas makes a white Easter; a white Christmas makes a green Easter. (b) A warm Christmas means a cold Easter. (c) A white Christmas brings forth a green Easter. *Rec. dist.:* U.S., Can. *1st cit.:* 1931 *London Times,* 8 Jan. *20c. coll.:* ODEP 337.

2. A green Christmas means a fat graveyard. *Vars.:* (a) A green Christmas, a full churchyard. (b) A green Christmas brings forth a fat graveyard. (c) A green Christmas fills the churchyard. (d) Green Christmas and a fruitful graveyard. (e) Green Christmas, bigger graveyards. (f) Green Christmas, fat graveyard. (g) Green Christmas makes a fat churchyard. *Rec. dist.:* U.S., Can. *1st cit.:* 1635 Swan, *Speculum Mundi;* US1794 *Journal of Elizabeth Drinker from 1759–1807,* ed. Biddle (1889). *20c. coll.:* ODEP 337, Whiting 72, CODP 102, Stevenson 350:11, T&W 69, Whiting(MP) 114.

3. Christmas comes but once a year. *Vars.:* (a) Christmas comes but once a year, but when it does, it brings good cheer. (b) Christmas comes but once a year; why not celebrate it while it's here? *Rec. dist.:* U.S., Can. *1st cit.:* 1573 Tusser, *Hundreth Good Pointes of Husbandrie;* US1823 Cooper, *Pioneers. 20c. coll.:* ODEP 123, T&W 69, Stevenson 351:1, Whiting(MP) 114.
    See also While THANKSGIVING has its foundation on Plymouth Rock, Christmas rests upon the rock of ages.

chuck Ground chucks get to be riders; riders get to be ground chucks. *Rec. dist.:* N.Y.

church 1. A church debt is the devil's salary. *Rec. dist.:* Ill.

2. A church is God between four walls. *Rec. dist.:* Ill. *1st cit.:* US1948 Stevenson, *Home Book of Proverbs. 20c. coll.:* Stevenson 352:3.

3. Better to come late to church than never. *Rec. dist.:* N.J., Wis.

4. Church is not out 'til they sing. *Rec. dist.:* Okla.

5. Floating church members make a sinking church. *Rec. dist.:* Wis.

6. He who rings the church bells is safe. *Rec. dist.:* Calif.

7. If you go to church for an evil purpose, you go to God's house on the devil's errand. *Rec. dist.:* Ill.

8. New churches and new bars are well patronized. *Rec. dist.:* Ill.

9. Right church but wrong pew. *Rec. dist.:* U.S.

10. The nearer the church, the farther from God. *Var.:* He who is near the church is often far from God. *Rec. dist.:* Ill., N.J., Oreg., Wis. *1st cit.:* ca1303 Mannyng, *Handlyng Synne;* US1803 Davis, *Travels in U.S., 1798–1802. 20c. coll.:* ODEP 557, Whiting 72, CODP 159, Stevenson 351:4, Whiting(MP) 115.

11. There is no life in a church that does not produce praying members. *Rec. dist.:* N.C.

12. When the church of God is in people's hearts, it will get into their schedule. *Rec. dist.:* N.C.

13. You can't build a church with stumbling blocks. *Rec. dist.:* Minn.
    See also A rich BRIDE goes young to the church. / Many bring their CLOTHES to church rather than themselves. / Where GOD has his church, the devil will have his chapel. / All are not SAINTS that go to church.

churchyard A piece of churchyard fits everybody. *Rec. dist.:* N.J. *1st cit.:* 1640 Herbert, *Outlandish Proverbs (Jacula Prudentum)* in *Works,* ed. Hutchinson (1941). *20c. coll.:* ODEP 124, Stevenson 353:11.

SEE ALSO Many good PURPOSES lie in the churchyard.

churl Stroke a churl and he'll scratch; strike him and he'll submit. *Rec. dist.:* Minn.

cider 1. Cider makes the belly wider. *Rec. dist.:* Wis.

2. Never praise your cider or your horse. *Rec. dist.:* Ind. *1st cit.:* US1736 Franklin, *PRAlmanac.* *20c. coll.:* Whiting 73.

cigar You can't make a cigar out of a pig's tail. *Rec. dist.:* Vt.

cigarette Every cigarette is another nail in your coffin. *Var.:* A cigarette is a nail in our coffin. *Rec. dist.:* Ind.

cinch 1. A light cinch is best. *Rec. dist.:* Oreg.

2. Best draw a tight cinch. *Rec. dist.:* Oreg.
SEE ALSO LIFE is hard by the yard, but by the inch life's a cinch.

cinder It's too late to throw water on the cinder when the house is burned down. *Rec. dist.:* N.Y.

Cinderella Cinderella's coach turns to a pumpkin. *Rec. dist.:* Ohio.

circle Circles, though small, are yet complete. *Rec. dist.:* N.Y.
SEE ALSO CONCEIT is as natural to the human mind as a center is to a circle. / The WHEEL comes full circle.

circumstance 1. Be not discouraged by adverse circumstances. *Rec. dist.:* Minn.

2. Circumstances alter cases. *Rec. dist.:* U.S., Can. *1st cit.:* 1678 Rymer, *Tragedies of the Last Age;* US1776 Heath, *Memoirs of Major General William Heath* (1798). *20c. coll.:* ODEP 124, Whiting 73, CODP 37, Stevenson 356:8, T&W 70, Whiting(MP) 16.

3. New circumstances, new controls. *Rec. dist.:* Mich.

circus SEE Don't let the SIDESHOW run away with the circus.

citizen A good citizen owes his life to his country. *Rec. dist.:* N.Dak.
SEE ALSO The DISGRACE of the city is the fault of the citizens.

city 1. A city that sits on a hill cannot be hid. *Var.:* A city that is set on a hill cannot be hid. *Rec. dist.:* R.I. *Infm.:* Cf. Matt. 5:14. *1st cit.:* US1689 Bulkeley, *People's Right to Election,* Conn.Hist.Soc. *Collections* (1860). *20c. coll.:* Whiting 74, Stevenson 358:9.

2. It's not the city that ruins the man, but the life. *Rec. dist.:* N.C.

3. The city for wealth, the country for health. *Rec. dist.:* Mich.

4. The city is recruited from the country. *Rec. dist.:* N.Y., S.C. *1st cit.:* US1844 Emerson, "Manners" in *Essays.* *20c. coll.:* Stevenson 359:14.

5. The city slicker does not always flicker. *Rec. dist.:* Oreg. *Infm.:* The city dweller does not always dupe the country dweller.
SEE ALSO He that can take REST is greater than he that can take cities.

civil 1. A civil denial is better than a rude grant. *Rec. dist.:* N.Y.

2. Be civil to all, sociable to many, familiar with few. *Rec. dist.:* Ill.

3. Be civil to every man; you know not who may prove to be your friend. *Rec. dist.:* Minn.

4. Civil language costs little and does good. *Rec. dist.:* Ind.

civility 1. Civility is a kind of charm that attracts the love of all men. *Rec. dist.:* Mich.

2. Nothing costs less than civility. *Var.:* Civility costs nothing and buys everything. *Rec. dist.:* Ill. *1st cit.:* 1706 Stevens, *New Spanish and English Dictionary.* *20c. coll.:* ODEP 125, Stevenson 440:2, CODP 37.

civilization 1. Civilization and profits go hand in hand. *Rec. dist.:* N.Y., S.C. *1st cit.:* US1920 Coolidge, Speech, New York, 27 Nov. *20c. coll.:* Stevenson 360:5.

2. Civilization begins at home. *Rec. dist.:* N.Y., S.C. *1st cit.:* US1883 James, *Siege of London.* *20c. coll.:* Stevenson 360:10.

3. Civilization degrades the many to exalt the few. *Rec. dist.:* N.Y., S.C. *1st cit.:* US1868 Alcott, "Pursuits" in *Table Talk.* *20c. coll.:* Stevenson 360:4.

clad SEE The TAILOR's wife is worst clad.

class *See* The WORLD is made up of two classes, the hunters and the hunted.

claw *See* CATS hide their claws. / The older the CRAB, the tougher his claws.

clay **1.** The clay replies not to the potter. *Rec. dist.:* Ill.

2. Unless the clay is well pounded, no pitcher can be made. *Rec. dist.:* Ill.

3. We are clay in the hands of the potter. *Rec. dist.:* Ill., Ind. *1st cit.:* US1948 Stevenson, *Home Book of Proverbs.* *20c. coll.:* Stevenson 1508:12.

4. We, like clay, are molded. *Rec. dist.:* Wis.

5. We're all of common clay. *Rec. dist.:* Ill.

clean *(v.)* **1.** Clean around your own back door before you clean around someone else's. *Var.:* Clean out your own backyard. *Rec. dist.:* Ky.

2. Clean as you go. *Rec. dist.:* N.Y., S.C.
See also Don't clean your FISH before you catch it.

clean *(adj.)* **1.** Above all things, keep clean; it is not necessary to be a pig in order to raise one. *Rec. dist.:* N.Y., S.C.

2. One keep clean is worth ten make cleans. *Rec. dist.:* Ill.

3. There's no one so clean that somebody doesn't think they're dirty. *Rec. dist.:* Minn., Vt.
See also A new BROOM sweeps clean. / A clean CONSCIENCE is a good pillow. / A clean HAND needs no washing. / Dirty HANDS make clean money. / Have not only clean HANDS, but clean minds. / A hungry NIGGER makes a clean dish. / One clean SHEET will not soil another. / Don't throw away your dirty WATER until you get clean.

cleaning Saturday's cleaning will not last through Sunday, but Sunday's will last all week. *Rec. dist.:* N.C.

cleanliness **1.** Cleanliness is akin to godliness. *Var.:* Cleanliness is godliness, so why go to church? *Rec. dist.:* U.S., Can. *1st cit.:* 1605 Bacon, *Advancement of Learning;* US1806 *Monthly Anthology and Boston Review* (1804–

07). *20c. coll.:* ODEP 125, Whiting 74, *CODP* 38, Stevenson 361:5, T&W 71, Whiting(*MP*) 118.

2. Cleanliness is the poor man's luxury. *Rec. dist.:* N.C.

clear *See* After CLOUDS, clear weather.

clemency Clemency is the brightest jewel in a crown. *Rec. dist.:* Mich.

clerk The greatest clerks are not always the wisest men. *Rec. dist.:* Mich., Okla. *1st cit.:* ca1390 Chaucer, *Reeve's Tale.* *20c. coll.:* ODEP 126, Stevenson 364:12.

clever **1.** He who knows others is clever; he who knows himself is enlightened. *Rec. dist.:* Vt.

2. He who would be too clever makes a fool of himself. *Rec. dist.:* Ill.

3. It is not clever to play but to stop playing. *Rec. dist.:* N.C.
See also The cleverest DOCTOR cannot save himself. / FLATTERERS are clever mind readers: they tell us exactly what we think.

cleverness **1.** Cleverness does not take the place of knowledge. *Rec. dist.:* Ill.

2. Cleverness is serviceable for everything, sufficient for nothing. *Rec. dist.:* Ill. *1st cit.:* US1948 Stevenson, *Home Book of Proverbs.* *20c. coll.:* Stevenson 365:1.

3. What's the use of cleverness, if foolishness serves? *Rec. dist.:* Ill.

climate **1.** Change your climate, not your mind. *Rec. dist.:* Mich.

2. The only perfect climate is in bed. *Rec. dist.:* Ill.

3. We may achieve climate, but weather is thrust upon us. *Rec. dist.:* N.Y., S.C., Wis.

climb *(n.)* The higher the climb, the broader the view. *Rec. dist.:* Ill.

climb *(v.)* **1.** Climb not too high lest the fall be greater. *Vars.:* **(a)** Climb not for highest lest the fall be greater. **(b)** He who climbs too high is near a fall. **(c)** One who climbs high falls low. **(d)** The higher you climb, the harder you fall. **(e)** Those who climb high often have a fall. **Rec. dist.:** U.S., Can. **1st cit.:** ca1300 *Proverbs of Hendyng,* ed. Schleich; US1928 Small, *Master.* **20c. coll.:** *ODEP* 357, Whiting*(MP)* 119.

2. He climbs highest who helps another up. **Rec. dist.:** N.J.

3. He that climbs the tall tree has a right to the fruit. **Rec. dist.:** U.S., Can.

4. It is harder to climb the mountain than to climb down. **Rec. dist.:** Wis.

5. Who never climbed never fell. **Rec. dist.:** N.J., Tex., Vt. **1st cit.:** 1546 Heywood, *Dialogue of Proverbs,* ed. Habernicht (1963); USca1870 Whittier, *To James T. Fields.* **20c. coll.:** *ODEP* 562, Stevenson 747:10.

SEE ALSO Nothing humbler than AMBITION when it is about to climb. / Don't waste time looking at the HILL—climb it. / A good NEIGHBOR is a fellow who smiles at you over the back fence but doesn't climb it. / Big POSSUM climb little tree. / Every ROAD has hills to be climbed. / Never climb a crooked TREE. / He who climbs to the top of a WALL should not kick over his ladder, as he might wish sometime to climb down again. / Who never WINS can rarely lose; who never climbs as rarely falls.

climber Hasty climbers have sudden falls. **Rec. dist.:** N.J. **1st cit.:** 1563 *Mirror for Magistrates,* ed. Campbell. **20c. coll.:** *ODEP* 357, Stevenson 746:17.

clip SEE The LORD knows when to clip our wings.

clique A clique is a friendship gone to seed. **Rec. dist.:** Minn.

cloak **1.** Have not the cloak to be made when it begins to rain. **Rec. dist.:** Mich. **1st cit.:** ca1595 *Edward III, Reign of King,* Shakespeare Apocrypha (1908). **20c. coll.:** *ODEP* 127, Stevenson 866:1.

2. Under a good cloak may be a bad man. **Rec. dist.:** Ill.

3. You can't make a good cloak out of bad cloth. **Rec. dist.:** Ill.

SEE ALSO Though the SUN shines, leave not your cloak at home.

clock **1.** A clock that stands still is better than one that goes wrong. **Rec. dist.:** Ill.

2. A fellow who works by the clock never earns the price of a watch. **Rec. dist.:** Okla.

3. An alarm clock will wake a man, but he has to get up by himself. **Rec. dist.:** Minn.

4. Even a stopped clock is right twice a day. **Rec. dist.:** Ill.

5. God's clock strikes on time. **Rec. dist.:** N.C.

6. Look at the clock and see how the minutes fly; you shall be a man by and by. **Rec. dist.:** Kans.

7. The clock of the tongue should be set by the dials of the heart. **Rec. dist.:** Mich.

8. The man who watches the clock generally remains one of the hands. **Vars.:** **(a)** He who watches the clock will only be a hand. **(b)** The man that continuously watches the clock never becomes the man of the hour. **Rec. dist.:** U.S. **1st cit.:** US1940 Thompson, *Body, Boots, and Britches.* **20c. coll.:** Stevenson 367:1.

9. Two clocks don't run alike; two men don't think alike. **Rec. dist.:** Ohio.

10. Women's clocks will walk with every wind. **Rec. dist.:** N.C.

SEE ALSO A man without AIM is like a clock without hands, as useless if it turns as if it stands.

close *(adj.)* Close counts only in horseshoes. **Rec. dist.:** Mich., Ohio.

SEE ALSO Little BOATS should stay close to shore. / The closer to the BONE, the sweeter the meat. / FIRE kept closest burns best of all.

close *(adv.)* SEE SIN may be clasped so close we cannot see its face.

closely SEE Closely GATHERED, widely scattered.

closet SEE No man is qualified to remove the SKELETON from his own closet. / There's a SKELETON in every family closet.

closing **1.** No need closing the door after the horse is stolen. **Var.:** No use closing the stable after the horse is gone. **Rec. dist.:** Ill., Miss. **1st cit.:** ca1350 *Douce MS 52,* ed. Förster (1906); US1745 *Correspondence During Law's*

Governorship of Connecticut, 1741–1750, Conn. Hist.Soc. *Collections* (1907–14). *20c. coll.: ODEP* 730, Stevenson 2204:8, Whiting 414, *CODP* 211, T&W 109, Whiting*(MP)* 182.

cloth **1.** Cut the coat according to the cloth. *Vars.:* **(a)** You must cut your coat according to your cloth. **(b)** You must cut your garment according to the cloth. *Rec. dist.:* U.S. *1st cit.:* 1546 Heywood, *Dialogue of Proverbs,* ed. Habernicht (1963); US1720 *Letters of Robert Carter,* ed. Wright (1940). *20c. coll.: ODEP* 164, Whiting 77, *CODP* 47, Stevenson 373:4, T&W 74, Whiting*(MP)* 120.

2. It is a bad cloth indeed that will take no color. *Rec. dist.:* Okla. *1st cit.:* 1546 Heywood, *Dialogue of Proverbs,* ed. Habernicht (1963). *20c. coll.: ODEP* 25, Stevenson 368:10.

3. Measure your cloth ten times; you can cut it but once. *Rec. dist.:* Ohio. *1st cit.:* 1853 Trench, *Lessons in Proverbs.* *20c. coll.: ODEP* 521.

4. No man puts a piece of new cloth unto an old garment. *Var.:* Don't patch an old garment with a new piece of cloth. *Rec. dist.:* N.C.
SEE ALSO You can't make a good CLOAK out of bad cloth. / Cut your SAIL according to your cloth.

clothe SEE DROWSINESS shall clothe a man with rags. / A good INTENTION clothes itself with sudden power.

clothes **1.** A fellow feels considerably like the clothes he wears. *Rec. dist.:* N.C.

2. Borrowed clothes never fit. *Rec. dist.:* Minn., Vt.

3. Clothes don't make the man. *Vars.:* **(a)** Clothes and looks don't make the person. **(b)** Clothes don't change the person. **(c)** Clothes don't make the man, but it sure helps. **(d)** Clothes don't make the man, but they sure dress up one that is. **(e)** Clothes don't make the mind. **(f)** Clothes don't make the woman, but they help. **(g)** Clothes may make the man, but his backbone grows from childhood. *Rec. dist.:* U.S., Can. *1st cit.:* ca1500 *Proverbs at Leconfield* in *Antiquarian Repertory,* ed. Grose (1909); US1783 *Writings of George Washington,*

ed. Fitzpatrick (1931–44). *20c. coll.: ODEP* 16, Whiting 75, Stevenson 367:5, T&W 73, Whiting*(MP)* 120.

4. Clothes speak for men, making or closing their opportunities. *Rec. dist.:* N.C.

5. Dirty clothes are washed at home. *Rec. dist.:* N.Y.

6. Don't throw out old clothes before you get new ones. *Rec. dist.:* Miss.

7. Fine clothes do not make the gentleman, except when he travels abroad. *Rec. dist.:* Ill.

8. Fine clothes may disguise, silly words will disclose a fool. *Rec. dist.:* Ill.

9. Good clothes open all doors. *Var.:* Swank clothes open all doors. *Rec. dist.:* Ohio. *1st cit.:* 1732 Fuller, *Gnomologia;* US1870 *Journals of Ralph Waldo Emerson,* eds. Emerson and Forbes (1909–14). *20c. coll.:* Stevenson 368:4.

10. He who was born first has the greatest number of old clothes. *Rec. dist.:* N.Y., S.C. *1st cit.:* US1849 Thoreau, *Week on Concord and Merrimack Rivers.* *20c. coll.:* Stevenson 369:6.

11. In clothes we value novelty, in men old age. *Rec. dist.:* N.Y.

12. It is not the clothes that count, but the things the clothes cover. *Rec. dist.:* Ill.

13. Many bring their clothes to church rather than themselves. *Rec. dist.:* Wis.

14. Sew your clothes upon your back; care and trouble you'll never lack. *Rec. dist.:* Ky., Minn.

15. Some clothes catch everything except men and money. *Rec. dist.:* N.C.

16. The best-fitting clothes wear out the fastest. *Rec. dist.:* Wis.

17. The putting on of the clothes is not the taking off of them. *Rec. dist.:* Minn.

18. Through tattered clothes small vices do appear. *Rec. dist.:* Minn.

19. You may change the clothes; you cannot change the man. *Rec. dist.:* Oreg.
SEE ALSO COMMON sense is genius dressed in its working clothes. / TROUBLE is merely opportunity in work clothes.

clothing Don't spread your clothing near the quiet brook. *Rec. dist.:* N.Y.

cloud 1. After clouds, clear weather. *Vars.:* **(a)** After clouds comes clear weather. **(b)** After clouds, a clear sun. *Rec. dist.:* N.Y. *1st cit.:* ca1400 *Tale of Beryn.* *20c. coll.:* ODEP 6, Stevenson 370:5.

2. Black clouds thunder a great deal but rain little. *Rec. dist.:* Ill.

3. Every cloud has a silver lining. *Vars.:* **(a)** Behind each cloud is a silver lining. **(b)** Look upon the brightest side of every cloud. **(c)** The darkest cloud has a silver lining. **(d)** The inner side of every cloud is bright and shining. *Rec. dist.:* U.S., Can. *1st cit.:* 1634 Milton, *Comus;* US1863 Locke, *Struggle of Petroleum V. Nasby* (1880). *20c. coll.:* ODEP 128, T&W 73, CODP 39, Stevenson 370:4, Whiting*(MP)* 121.

4. Every cloud is not a sign of a storm. *Var.:* All clouds bring not rain. *Rec. dist.:* Wis. *1st cit.:* 1584 Withals, *Short Dictionary;* US1796 *Works of Fisher Ames,* ed. Ames (1854). *20c. coll.:* ODEP 128, Whiting 75, Stevenson 369:12.

5. He that pries into the clouds may be struck with a thunderbolt. *Rec. dist.:* Mich. *1st cit.:* 1597 *Politeuphuia Wits Commonwealth.* *20c. coll.:* ODEP 647, Stevenson 4772:6.

6. One cloud is enough to eclipse all the sun. *Rec. dist.:* Wis. *1st cit.:* 1732 Fuller, *Gnomologia.* *20c. coll.:* Stevenson 369:11.

7. Somewhere behind the clouds the sun is shining. *Var.:* The sun is always shining behind the clouds. *Rec. dist.:* Ind., Ohio, Vt.

8. The higher the clouds, the fairer the weather. *Rec. dist.:* Vt., Wis.

9. What is one man's cloud is another man's sunshine. *Rec. dist.:* N.J.

SEE ALSO We never appreciate the SUNSHINE and the rainbow until the storm clouds hang low.

cloudy Cloudy mornings may turn to clear evenings. *Rec. dist.:* Tex. *1st cit.:* ca1200 *Ancrene Riwle,* ed. Morton, Camden Soc. (1853). *20c. coll.:* ODEP 128.

clout Change not a clout till May be out. *Rec. dist.:* N.Y. *1st cit.:* 1706 Stevens, *New Spanish and English Dictionary.* *20c. coll.:* ODEP 106, CODP 32.

clown 1. A clown who strikes it rich disowns his own parents. *Rec. dist.:* Ill.

2. Clowns are best in their own company, but gentlemen are best everywhere. *Rec. dist.:* Wis. *1st cit.:* 1732 Fuller, *Gnomologia.* *20c. coll.:* Stevenson 371:2.

3. Crowning a clown won't make him a king. *Rec. dist.:* Ind.

4. Give a clown your finger and he'll take your whole hand. *Rec. dist.:* Mich., Okla., R.I. *1st cit.:* 1640 Herbert, *Outlandish Proverbs (Jacula Prudentum)* in *Works,* ed. Hutchinson (1941). *20c. coll.:* ODEP 302, Stevenson 371:3.

club Best clubs are found under a hickory tree. *Rec. dist.:* Ohio.
SEE ALSO The WORLD does not grow better by force or by the policeman's club.

clumsy SEE Clumsy JESTING is no joke.

coal 1. Coal doesn't shine around diamonds. *Rec. dist.:* Kans.

2. The man who carries coal to Newcastle will pour water on a drowned mouse. *Rec. dist.:* Ill.

coarse SEE Under the coarsest RIND, the sweetest meat.

coat 1. A smart coat is a good letter of introduction. *Rec. dist.:* N.J.

2. If the coat fits, put it on. *Rec. dist.:* Minn., Oreg., Vt.

3. It is not the gay coat that makes the gentleman. *Rec. dist.:* Okla., R.I., Tex., Vt. *1st cit.:* 1615 Goddard, *Nest of Wasps;* US1815 *Port Folio.* *20c. coll.:* ODEP 129, Whiting 77, Stevenson 373:7, T&W 72, Whiting*(MP)* 120.

4. It's the coat that makes the man, not the pants. *Rec. dist.:* Kans.

5. One should turn his coat according to the weather. *Rec. dist.:* Calif. *1st cit.:* 1546 Heywood, *Dialogue of Proverbs,* ed. Habernicht (1963); US1835 Kennedy, *Horseshoe Robinson.* *20c. coll.:* Stevenson 373:3, T&W 74.

6. The coat and pants do all the work, and the vest gets all the gravy. *Rec. dist.:* Ohio.

7. When a man's coat is threadbare, it is easy to peck a hole in it. *Rec. dist.:* Oreg. *1st cit.:* 1639 Clarke, *Paroemiologia.* *20c. coll.:* Stevenson 457:19.

8. You can't always tell what is under a worn coat. *Rec. dist.:* N.C.

9. You can't make a good coat out of bad wool. *Var.:* You can't make a good coat out of poor cloth. *Rec. dist.:* Oreg.

10. You must cut your coat according to your cloth. *Var.:* Cut the coat according to the cloth. *Rec. dist.:* U.S., Can. *1st cit.:* 1546 Heywood, *Dialogue of Proverbs,* ed. Habernicht (1963); US1720 *Letters of Robert Carter,* ed. Wright (1940). *20c. coll.:* ODEP 164, Whiting 77, CODP 47, Stevenson 373:4, T&W 74, Whiting*(MP)* 123.

SEE ALSO If you miss the first BUTTONHOLE, you will not succeed in buttoning up your coat. / A clear CONSCIENCE is a coat of mail. / Rather than run into DEBT, wear your old coat. / Better a good DINNER than a fine coat. / Don't JUDGE a man by the coat he wears. / The SHIRT is nearer than the coat. / A WISE man carries his coat on a dry day.

cob SEE De PIG dat runs off wid de year er corn gits little mo' dan de cob.

cobbler 1. A cobbler's child is always the worst shod. *Vars.:* **(a)** Cobbler's children never wear shoes. **(b)** The cobbler's children go unshod. *Rec. dist.:* Maine, Wis. *1st cit.:* 1546 Heywood, *Dialogue of Proverbs,* ed. Habernicht (1963); US1965 Ransome, *Alias His Wife.* *20c. coll.:* ODEP 543, Whiting*(MP)* 561, CODP 202.

2. All cobblers go barefoot. *Rec. dist.:* Ill.

3. Let the cobbler stick to his last. *Rec. dist.:* U.S., Can. *1st cit.:* 1539 Taverner, *Proverbs of Erasmus;* US1647 Ward, *Simple Cobler of Aggawam in America,* ed. Wroth (1937). *20c. coll.:* ODEP 130, Whiting 78, CODP 39, Stevenson 2098:4, T&W 75, Whiting*(MP)* 124.

4. The richer the cobbler, the blacker his thumb. *Rec. dist.:* Mich. *1st cit.:* 1579 Gosson, *Ephemerides.* *20c. coll.:* ODEP 373.

cobweb Where cobwebs grow, beaus don't go. *Vars.:* **(a)** Beaus don't go where cobwebs grow. **(b)** The boys won't go where the cobwebs grow. **(c)** When cobwebs grow, no love goes. **(d)** Where cobwebs grow, beaus never go. **(e)** Where cobwebs grow, no beaus go; a dirty bread tray keeps beaus away. **(f)** Where the cobweb grows, there comes no beaus. *Rec. dist.:* U.S. *1st cit.:* US1940 Thompson, *Body, Boots, and Britches.* *20c. coll.:* Stevenson 1194:3.

SEE ALSO HABITS are first cobwebs, then cables.

cock 1. A cock is mighty in his own backyard. *Vars.:* **(a)** A good cock will crow on any dung heap. **(b)** Every cock crows the loudest upon his own dunghill. *Rec. dist.:* U.S. *1st cit.:* ca1200 *Ancrene Riwle,* ed. Morton, Camden Soc. (1853); US1634 Wood, *New-England's Prospects,* Publ. Prince Soc. (1865). *20c. coll.:* ODEP 130, Whiting 79, CODP 39, Stevenson 375:9, Whiting*(MP)* 124.

2. As the old cock crows, the young cock learns. *Vars.:* **(a)** As the old cock crows, so the young bird chirrups. **(b)** The old cock crows; the young ones learn. **(c)** The young cock crows as he hears the old one. *Rec. dist.:* U.S., Can. *1st cit.:* ca1350 *Douce MS 52,* ed. Förster (1906); US1809 Cunningham, *Correspondence Between John Adams and William Cunningham* (1823). *20c. coll.:* ODEP 588, Whiting 78, Stevenson 374:9, T&W 75.

3. If you are a cock, crow; if a hen, lay eggs. *Rec. dist.:* Oreg.

4. The cock crows at sunrise to tell us to rise. *Vars.:* **(a)** Cocks crow in the morning to tell us to rise, for he who lies late will never be wise. **(b)** The cock does crow to let us know if we be wise 'tis time to rise. *Rec. dist.:* U.S., Can. *1st cit.:* 1846 Denham, *Proverbs Relating to Weather.* *20c. coll.:* Stevenson 374:8.

SEE ALSO It is a sad house where the HEN crows louder than the cock.

cockerel Young cockerels ever crow the loudest. *Rec. dist.:* Vt.

coffee 1. Coffee boiled is coffee spoiled. *Rec. dist.:* Ind.

2. Good coffee should be black as sin, strong as the devil, and hot as hell. *Var.:* Coffee

should be fresh as spring, hot as hell, strong as a lover's arms. *Rec. dist.:* Minn., Miss.

coffer SEE It is better to have a FRIEND in the market than money in one's coffer.

coffin SEE Every CIGARETTE is another nail in your coffin.

coin A coin is the best friend. *Rec. dist.:* Wis.
  SEE ALSO Those who try to DECEIVE may expect to be paid in their own coin. / A FLIRT gets paid in her own coin.

coincidence SEE It is a striking coincidence that the word AMERICAN ends in can.

cold *(n.)* **1.** Cold and cunning come from the north, but cunning sans wisdom is nothing worth. *Rec. dist.:* N.Y., S.C. *1st cit.:* 1659 Howell, *Paroimiographia (French Proverbs);* US1743 Franklin, *PRAlmanac.* *20c. coll.:* ODEP 133, Stevenson 469:13.

2. Cold in the head is better than nothing. *Rec. dist.:* Wis.

3. Feed a cold and starve a fever. *Vars.:* **(a)** If you stuff a cold, you'll have to starve a fever. **(b)** Stuff a cold and starve a fever. **(c)** Stuff a cold, starve a fever. *Rec. dist.:* U.S., Can. *1st cit.:* 1574 Withals, *Short Dictionary;* USca1864 Twain, *Sketches Old and New.* *20c. coll.:* ODEP 783, Stevenson 795:8, *CODP* 78, T&W 76, Whiting(MP) 126.

4. When day is lengthened, cold strengthens. *Vars.:* **(a)** As the days begin to lengthen, the cold begins to strengthen. **(b)** As the days grow longer, the cold gets stronger. **(c)** When the days begin to lengthen, the cold begins to strengthen. *Rec. dist.:* U.S., Can. *1st cit.:* 1631 Pellham, *God's Power;* US1850 Judd, *Richard Edney and Governer's Family.* *20c. coll.:* ODEP 169, T&W 93, *CODP* 48, Stevenson 494:7, Whiting(MP) 153.
  SEE ALSO PRIDE costs more than hunger, thirst, or cold.

cold *(adj.)* SEE You will never find a CAT on a cold hearth. / To a CHILD, all weather is cold. / A DEAD man feels no cold. / A cold HAND, a warm heart. / LOVE grows cold when it is not mixed with good works. / De PROUDNESS in a man don't count w'en his head's

cold. / The colder the WIND, the warmer the hearth.

collar SEE A CAT with a silver collar is none the better mouser. / Can't tell a DOG by its collar.

collector **1.** Collectors meet many men of promise. *Rec. dist.:* Utah.

2. When the bill collector knocks at the door, love flies out the window. *Rec. dist.:* Kans.

college **1.** Colleges hate geniuses, just as convents hate saints. *Rec. dist.:* N.Y., S.C. *1st cit.:* US1870 Emerson, "Public and Private Education" in *Uncollected Lectures.* *20c. coll.:* Stevenson 378:13.

2. There is no greater college than the college of hard knocks. *Rec. dist.:* Tex.
  SEE ALSO A BACHELOR is a man who didn't have a car when he was in college. / You can lead a STUDENT to college, but you cannot make him think.

color **1.** All colors will agree in the dark. *Rec. dist.:* Utah. *1st cit.:* 1597 Bacon, "Of Unity in Religion" in *Essays,* ed. Arber. *20c. coll.:* Stevenson 488:1.

2. Everything is according to the color of the glass with which one views it. *Rec. dist.:* Calif., N.Y.

3. Never wear more than three colors at once. *Rec. dist.:* Utah.

4. To the color-blind, all colors are alike. *Rec. dist.:* Ill.
  SEE ALSO A BLIND man is no judge of colors. / Human BLOOD is all one color. / TRUTH fears no color.

colt **1.** A colt is worth nothing if it does not break its halter. *Rec. dist.:* Ill.

2. Many a shabby colt makes a fine horse. *Vars.:* **(a)** A shabby colt often makes a fine horse. **(b)** Ragged colts make fine horses. **(c)** The wildest colts make the best horses if they are properly broken and handled. *Rec. dist.:* U.S., Can. *1st cit.:* 1520 Whittington, *Vulgaria;* USca1776 Flynt in *Life and Letters of Paine Wingate* (1930). *20c. coll.:* ODEP 662, Whiting 80, Stevenson 380:8.

3. The colt can't pace if the mare trots. *Rec. dist.:* Wash.

4. The wilder the colt, the better the horse. *Rec. dist.:* N.Mex.

5. You may break a colt but not an old horse. *Rec. dist.:* N.Y.

Columbus Columbus took a chance. *Rec. dist.:* Oreg.

comb *(n.)* SEE He who has a BEARD buys himself a comb. / EXPERIENCE is a comb which fate gives to a man when his hair is all gone.

comb *(v.)* Don't comb your hair if you are bald. *Var.:* Never comb a bald head. *Rec. dist.:* N.Y.
SEE ALSO Wash a DOG, comb a dog: still a dog.

come SEE Go DAY, come day, God send Sunday. / May the best DAY we have seen be the worst we have to come. / EASY come, easy go. / FIRST come, first served. / From LABOR there shall come forth rest. / The MISFORTUNES hardest to bear are those which never come. / When you ain't got no MONEY, well, you needn't come around.

coming Coming down is easier than going up. *Rec. dist.:* Ala.

command *(n.)* **1.** Always obey the second command. *Rec. dist.:* N.Y.

2. Command wants no equal. *Rec. dist.:* N.Y.

3. No one has a finer command of a language than he who keeps his mouth shut. *Rec. dist.:* Kans.

command *(v.)* **1.** If you can't command yourself, you can't command others. *Rec. dist.:* Ill. *1st cit.:* ca1510 Stanbridge, *Vulgaria;* US1850 Melville, *White-Jacket.* **20c. coll.:** ODEP 137, Stevenson 2060:5, T&W 78.

2. If you command wisely, you are willingly obeyed. *Rec. dist.:* Minn. *1st cit.:* 1732 Fuller, *Gnomologia.* **20c. coll.:** Stevenson 381:12.

3. If you wish to command, learn to obey. *Rec. dist.:* Minn. *1st cit.:* ca1510 Stanbridge, *Vulgaria;* US1734 Franklin, *PRAlmanac.* **20c. coll.:** ODEP 137, Whiting 320, Stevenson 2060:5, T&W 78, Whiting(MP) 128.

SEE ALSO Keep COOL and you command everybody. / He who DEMANDS does not command. / Some must FOLLOW and some command. / RICHES serve a wise man but command a fool.

commander Too many commanders cause confusion in the ranks. *Rec. dist.:* Ill.

commandment When one has broken the tenth commandment, the others are not of much account. *Rec. dist.:* N.Y., S.C. *1st cit.:* US1893 Twain, *Pudd'nhead Wilson's Calendar.* **20c. coll.:** Stevenson 383:2.

commence He who commences many things finishes but few. *Rec. dist.:* Can. *1st cit.:* 1666 Torriano, *Common Place of Italian Proverbs.* **20c. coll.:** ODEP 42, Stevenson 153:4.

commend SEE It's safer to commend the DEAD than the living. / Reprove your FRIEND privately; commend him publicly. / A man shall be commended by his WISDOM.

commensurate SEE The HOLE and the patch should be commensurate.

commerce Commerce flourishes by circumstances precarious. *Rec. dist.:* Mich.

common SEE When two FRIENDS have a common purse, one sings and the other weeps. / The common HORSE is worst shod. / NEWSPAPERS are the schoolmaster of the common people.

common sense **1.** A handful of common sense is worth a bushelful of learning. *Rec. dist.:* Minn., N.Y.

2. Common sense is always worth more than cunning. *Rec. dist.:* Kans.

3. Common sense is genius dressed in its working clothes. *Rec. dist.:* Ind.

4. Common sense is the growth of all countries. *Rec. dist.:* Mich.

5. Common sense is the rarest thing in the world and the most valuable. *Rec. dist.:* Md.

6. Common sense is very uncommon with a lot of people. *Rec. dist.:* Kans.

7. Fine sense and exalted sense are not half so useful as common sense. *Rec. dist.:* Mich.

8. Nothing astonishes men so much as common sense and plain dealing. *Rec. dist.:* N.Y., S.C.

9. Where common sense is wanting, everything is wanting. *Rec. dist.:* Ill.

SEE ALSO One pound of LEARNING requires ten pounds of common sense to use it.

communication 1. Evil communications corrupt good manners. *Rec. dist.:* Mich., N.Y. *1st cit.:* ca1425 Arderne, *Treatises of Fistula,* E.E.T.S. (1910); US1649 Conn.Hist.Soc. *Collections* (1860). *20c. coll.:* CODP 70, Whiting 81, ODEP 232, Stevenson 390:5, T&W 78, Whiting*(MP)* 128.

2. There are three types of communication: telephone, telegraph, and tell a woman. *Vars.:* **(a)** Three quickest ways of communication: telephone, telegraph, and tell a woman. **(b)** Ways of communication, telephone, telegraph, and tell a woman. *Rec. dist.:* Alaska, Iowa, Mich.

companion 1. A good companion makes good company. *Var.:* Good companion, good company. *Rec. dist.:* Calif., Kans.

2. A good companion makes heaven out of hell. *Rec. dist.:* Minn.

3. A man knows his companions in a long journey and a small inn. *Rec. dist.:* Mich. *1st cit.:* 1706 Stevens, *New Spanish and English Dictionary. 20c. coll.:* ODEP 138, Stevenson 386:11.

4. A wicked companion invites us all to hell. *Rec. dist.:* Alaska.

5. Bad companions corrupt good morals. *Rec. dist.:* Oreg.

6. Best companions are innocence and health. *Rec. dist.:* N.C.

7. Everybody's companion is nobody's friend. *Rec. dist.:* N.J.

8. No companion can be better for us than gratitude in the darkness. *Rec. dist.:* Miss.

9. Show me your companions, and I'll tell you who you are. *Rec. dist.:* N.Y. *Infm.:* Form of proverb varies. Cf. company. *1st cit.:* 1541 Bullinger, *Christian State of Matrimony,* tr. Coverdale (1543); US1854 Melville, *Complete Short Stories. 20c. coll.:* ODEP 138, CODP 40, Stevenson 386:6.

10. Your companions are your mirrors and show you yourself. *Rec. dist.:* Kans.

company 1. A man in vicious company is among his enemies. *Rec. dist.:* Ill.

2. A man is known by the company that he organized. *Rec. dist.:* Ill.

3. Cheerful company shortens the miles. *Vars.:* **(a)** Good company upon the road is shortest cut. **(b)** Pleasant company shortens the miles. *Rec. dist.:* U.S., Can. *1st cit.:* 1653 Walton, *Compleat Angler. 20c. coll.:* Stevenson 385:1.

4. Company in distress makes trouble less. *Rec. dist.:* S.C. *1st cit.:* ca1349 Rolle, *Meditations on the Passion. 20c. coll.:* ODEP 138, Stevenson 1592:12.

5. Company in misery makes it light. *Rec. dist.:* Ill., Okla. *1st cit.:* ca1349 Rolle, *Meditations on the Passion. 20c. coll.:* ODEP 138.

6. Company on Monday, company all week. *Rec. dist.:* Vt., Wash.

7. Fish and company smell after three days. *Vars.:* **(a)** Company is like fish: after three days they stink. **(b)** Fish and company spoil in three days. *Rec. dist.:* U.S., Can. *1st cit.:* 1580 Lyly, *Euphues and His England,* ed. Arber (1868); US1736 Franklin, *PRAlmanac. 20c. coll.:* ODEP 287, Whiting 154, Stevenson 1045:8, CODP 83, Whiting*(MP)* 274.

8. Folks go to hell to find exciting company. *Rec. dist.:* Ill. *1st cit.:* 1613 Wither, *Abuses. 20c. coll.:* ODEP 366.

9. Having finished the meal, the company leaves. *Rec. dist.:* Calif.

10. If you have company, just put another cup of water in the gravy. *Rec. dist.:* Ind.

11. Keep good company and you shall be of the number. *Rec. dist.:* Kans. *1st cit.:* 1477 Dictes and Sayenges of Philosophirs, tr. Rivers (1877). *20c. coll.:* ODEP 417.

12. Keep not ill company lest you increase the number. *Rec. dist.:* Vt. *1st cit.:* 1581 Guazzo, *Civile Conversation,* tr. Pettie, T.T. (1925). *20c. coll.:* ODEP 417.

13. One is known by the company he keeps.

Vars.: **(a)** A girl is known by the company she keeps. **(b)** A person is counted by the company he keeps. **(c)** We know a man by the company he keeps. **(d)** You can judge a man by the company he keeps. **(e)** You can tell a man who boozes by the company he chooses. *Rec. dist.:* U.S., Can. *1st cit.:* 1541 Bullinger, *Christian State of Matrimony,* tr. Coverdale; US1737 Stephens, *Journal of Proceedings in Georgia* in *Georgia Records* (1906, 1908). *20c. coll.:* ODEP 138, Whiting 81, *CODP* 40, Stevenson 386:6, T&W 78.

14. Show me your company, and I'll tell you who you are. *Var.:* Tell me your company, and I will tell you what you are. *Rec. dist.:* U.S. *1st cit.:* 1541 Bullinger, *Christian State of Matrimony,* tr. Coverdale (1543); US1737 Stephens, *Journal of Proceedings in Georgia* in *Georgia Records* (1906, 1908). *20c. coll.:* ODEP 138, Whiting 81, Stevenson 386:6.

15. The company makes the feast. *Rec. dist.:* N.Y., S.C. *1st cit.:* 1653 Walton, *Compleat Angler.* *20c. coll.:* ODEP 138, *CODP* 40, Stevenson 578:5.

16. The smaller the company, the greater the feast. *Rec. dist.:* Ill.

17. Two is company, three is a crowd. *Vars.:* **(a)** One is company, two is a crowd, four's too many, and five's not allowed. **(b)** One is company, two is a crowd, three is too many, four's not allowed. **(c)** Two's company, three's a crowd, four on a sidewalk is not allowed. *Rec. dist.:* U.S., Can. *1st cit.:* 1706 Stevens, *New Spanish and English Dictionary;* US1860 Haliburton, *Season-Ticket.* *20c. coll.:* ODEP 851, T&W 388, *CODP* 233, Stevenson 386:1, Whiting*(MP)* 654.

18. Who keeps company with a wolf learns to howl. *Var.:* Who keeps company with a wolf will learn to howl. *Rec. dist.:* U.S., Can. *1st cit.:* 1579 Tomson, *Calvin's Sermons on Epistles of Timothie and Titus.* *20c. coll.:* ODEP 419, Stevenson 2554:7.

19. You are judged not by the company you keep but by the company which keeps you. *Rec. dist.:* Vt.

SEE ALSO Better ALONE than in bad company. / A good COMPANION makes good company. / DEATH keeps no company. / A DOG in the kitchen desires no company. / EDUCATION begins a gentleman; conversation completes him. / In a long JOURNEY and a small inn, one knows one's company. / MISERY loves company. / No ROAD is long with good company. / The STRONG and the weak cannot keep company.

comparison **1.** Comparisons are odious. *Rec. dist.:* U.S., Can. *1st cit.:* ca1440 Lydgate, *Minor Poems,* E.E.T.S. (1866); US1652 Bradford, *Dialogue or Third Conference,* ed. Deane (1870). *20c. coll.:* ODEP 138, Whiting 82, *CODP* 41, Stevenson 390:9, T&W 78, Whiting*(MP)* 129.

2. Comparisons make enemies of our friends. *Rec. dist.:* Ill. *1st cit.:* ca1400 Lydgate, *Bochas.* *20c. coll.:* Stevenson 391:1.

3. Nothing is good or bad but by comparison. *Rec. dist.:* Ill. *1st cit.:* 1732 Fuller, *Gnomologia.* *20c. coll.:* Stevenson 391:2.

compassion Compassion will cure more than condemnation. *Rec. dist.:* N.Y., S.C.

compete Compete not with persons who have means beyond your reach. *Rec. dist.:* Mich.

competition **1.** Competition increases the desire. *Var.:* Competition increases desire. *Rec. dist.:* Ill.

2. Competition is the life of trade. *Var.:* Competition is the soul of trade. *Rec. dist.:* Ill., N.Mex., R.I. *1st cit.:* 1903 Lean, *Collectanea;* US1903 McFaul, *Ike Glidden.* *20c. coll.:* Stevenson 395:1, Whiting*(MP)* 129.

3. Competition is the spice of business. *Var.:* Competition is the spice of life. *Rec. dist.:* Minn.

4. Competition makes a horse race. *Rec. dist.:* Ill. *1st cit.:* US1948 Stevenson, *Home Book of Proverbs.* *20c. coll.:* Stevenson 1179:5.

5. The only competition worthy of a wise man is with himself. *Rec. dist.:* Ill. *1st cit.:* 1846 Jameson, "Washington Allston" in *Memoirs and Essays.* *20c. coll.:* Stevenson 395:10.

complacency Complacency is more persuasive than anger. *Rec. dist.:* Mich.

complain They complain most who suffer least. *Var.:* One who complains the most suffers less. *Rec. dist.:* Kans., N.C.

SEE ALSO No GREAT man ever complains of want of opportunity. / All complain for want of MEMORY, but none for want of judgment.

complaining *SEE* We are born CRYING, live complaining, and die disappointed.

complaint 1. Constant complaints never get pity. *Var.:* He that always complains is never pitied. *Rec. dist.:* Mich., N.J.

2. Everyone has a complaint of some kind. *Rec. dist.:* N.C.

3. Those who are free with complaints have little else to offer. *Rec. dist.:* Vt.

complaisance Complaisance obliges while it reprimands. *Rec. dist.:* Mich.

complete *SEE* He that has not got a WIFE is not yet a complete man.

compliment 1. Compliments cost nothing, but many pay dear for them. *Rec. dist.:* N.Y.

2. Exchanging compliments is intellectual back scratching. *Rec. dist.:* Minn.

3. Not even a school teacher notices bad grammar in a compliment. *Rec. dist.:* N.Dak.

4. There's compliments you can return and there's compliments you can't. *Rec. dist.:* N.Y., S.C.

5. Vain compliments are mere equivocations. *Rec. dist.:* Mich.

SEE ALSO To be TRUSTED is a greater compliment than to be loved.

comply He that complies against his will is of his own opinion still. *Rec. dist.:* U.S., Can. *1st cit.:* 1678 Butler, *Hudibras.* *20c. coll.:* ODEP 139, CODP 41, Stevenson 1719:10.

compromise 1. Compromise makes a good umbrella but a poor roof. *Rec. dist.:* N.Y., S.C. *1st cit.:* US1884 Lowell, "Democracy," speech at Birmingham, England. *20c. coll.:* Stevenson 397:3.

2. Every compromise is surrender and invites new demands. *Rec. dist.:* N.Y., S.C. *1st cit.:*

US1849 Emerson, *American Civilization.* *20c. coll.:* Stevenson 396:15.

SEE ALSO The WORLD runs by compromises.

conceal *SEE* A LIE is the most difficult thing in the world permanently to conceal. / What SOBERNESS conceals, drunkenness reveals.

concealment *SEE* TRUTH fears nothing but concealment. / A VICE lives and thrives by concealment.

conceit 1. Conceit grows as natural as the hair on one's head but is longer in coming out. *Rec. dist.:* N.Y., S.C. *1st cit.:* US1853 Haliburton, *Sam Slick's Wise Saws.* *20c. coll.:* Stevenson 398:6.

2. Conceit is as natural to the human mind as a center is to a circle. *Rec. dist.:* Ind.

3. Conceit is like mustard plaster: it hurts no one but yourself. *Rec. dist.:* Wis.

4. Conceit is nature's gift to small men to make up for that which they don't have. *Var.:* Conceit is God's gift to little men. *Rec. dist.:* N.Y., S.C., Wis. *1st cit.:* 1600 Shakespeare, *Hamlet;* USca1925 Barton, *Conceit.* *20c. coll.:* Stevenson 398:16.

5. Conceit is the most incurable disease that is known to the human soul. *Rec. dist.:* Ill. *1st cit.:* US1887 Beecher, *Proverbs from Plymouth Pulpit.* *20c. coll.:* Stevenson 397:14.

6. Conceit is the self-satisfaction of a jackass. *Rec. dist.:* Kans.

7. Conceit may puff a man up but never props him up. *Rec. dist.:* Ohio.

8. If conceit were consumption, we would have a green graveyard all year round. *Rec. dist.:* Md.

9. Self-conceit may lead to self-destruction. *Rec. dist.:* Nebr.

SEE ALSO IGNORANCE is the mother of conceit.

conceited Every man has a right to be conceited until he is successful. *Var.:* Every man has a right to be conceited. *Rec. dist.:* N.Y. *1st cit.:* 1831 Disraeli, *Young Duke.* *20c. coll.:* Stevenson 398:2.

concession Concessions may gain ground. *Rec. dist.:* Ill.

conclusion *SEE* DESPAIR is the conclusion of fools. / The only EXERCISE some people get is jumping to conclusions.

condemn 1. Men often condemn others for what they see no wrong in doing themselves. *Rec. dist.:* Minn.

2. People condemn what they do not understand. *Vars.:* (a) Men condemn because they do not understand. (b) Never condemn what you do not understand. *Rec. dist.:* Ill., Ind., Mich. *1st cit.:* 1869 Henderson, "Cicero" in *Latin Proverbs.* *20c. coll.:* Stevenson 1220:3.
   SEE ALSO The FOX condemns the trap, not himself.

condemned No man should be condemned unheard. *Rec. dist.:* N.C.
   SEE ALSO The JUDGE is condemned when the guilty man is acquitted.

condition 1. Be sure you can better your condition before you make a change. *Rec. dist.:* Kans.

2. Condition is 90 percent of the game. *Rec. dist.:* Ind.

3. Conditions make; conditions break. *Rec. dist.:* Ill.

4. If a man thinks about his physical or moral condition, he generally finds he is ill. *Rec. dist.:* N.J.

conduct *(n.)* 1. Conduct has the loudest tongue. *Rec. dist.:* N.Y.

2. Pursue in health that conduct which you promise in sickness. *Rec. dist.:* N.Y.
   SEE ALSO We may give ADVICE, but we cannot give conduct. / COURAGE without conduct is like a ship without ballast. / Depend not on FORTUNE but on conduct.

conduct *(v.)* *SEE* Too many people conduct their LIFE on the cafeteria style—self-service.

confess Confess and be hanged. *Rec. dist.:* U.S., Can. *1st cit.:* ca1592 Marlowe, *Jew of Malta;* US1966 Fagyas, *Widowmaker.* *20c. coll.:* ODEP 139, Whiting(MP) 129, CODP 41, Stevenson 399:11.
   SEE ALSO QUOTATION confesses inferiority.

confessed *SEE* A FAULT confessed is half forgiven.

confession 1. A generous confession disarms slander. *Rec. dist.:* Ill. *1st cit.:* 1732 Fuller, *Gnomologia.* *20c. coll.:* Stevenson 399:9.

2. An honest confession is good for the soul. *Vars.:* (a) Confession is good for the soul. (b) Confession is good for the soul but bad for the reputation. (c) Honest confession is good for the soul. (d) True confession is good for the soul. *Rec. dist.:* U.S., Can. *1st cit.:* 1615 Welde, *Janua Linguarum;* USca1856 Thompson, *Elephant Club.* *20c. coll.:* ODEP 599, T&W 78, CODP 41, Stevenson 399:8, Whiting(MP) 129.

3. Confession is a luxury of the weak. *Rec. dist.:* Ill.

confidant Have but a few confidants; the fewer the better. *Rec. dist.:* Utah.

confide 1. Confide not in him who has deceived you. *Rec. dist.:* N.Y.

2. God save me from those I confide in. *Rec. dist.:* Ill.
   SEE ALSO None are DECEIVED but they that confide.

confidence 1. Confidence begets confidence. *Var.:* Love begets love as confidence begets confidence. *Rec. dist.:* Ill. *1st cit.:* US1948 Stevenson, *Home Book of Proverbs.* *20c. coll.:* Stevenson 1476:13.

2. Confidence is a plant of slow growth. *Rec. dist.:* Ill., Ohio. *1st cit.:* 1776 Earl of Chatham, Speech to House of Commons, 14 Jan.; US1794 *Letters of William Lee, 1766–1783,* ed. Ford, (1891). *20c. coll.:* ODEP 139, Whiting 82, Stevenson 400:8.

3. Confidence of success is almost success. *Rec. dist.:* Wis.

4. False confidence often leads to disaster. *Rec. dist.:* Alaska, Wis.

5. They are the weakest, however strong, who have no confidence in their own ability. *Rec. dist.:* Wis.

confine *SEE* Confine your TONGUE, lest it confine you.

conflict   There never was a conflict without a woman. *Rec. dist.:* Wis. *1st cit.:* 1639 Clarke, *Paroemiologia. 20c. coll.:* ODEP 867, Stevenson 2587:1.

confound   *See* It takes the FOOLISH to confound the wise.

conquer   **1.** He conquers twice who conquers himself. *Var.:* He conquers twice who overcomes himself. *Rec. dist.:* N.J., Ont. *1st cit.:* 1539 Publilius Syrus, *Sententiae,* tr. Taverner. *20c. coll.:* ODEP 860, Stevenson 2061:4.

2. He conquers who endures. *Rec. dist.:* Ind., Oreg. *1st cit.:* 1869 Henderson, *Latin Proverbs. 20c. coll.:* Stevenson 683:7.

3. He that conquers himself conquers an enemy. *Rec. dist.:* Calif.

4. He that conquers must fight. *Rec. dist.:* Okla., Tex. *1st cit.:* 1732 Fuller, *Gnomologia. 20c. coll.:* Stevenson 403:3.

5. He who conquers himself conquers the world. *Var.:* He conquers the world who conquers himself. *Rec. dist.:* Ala., Ga., Ont. *1st cit.:* 1709 Dykes, *English Proverbs. 20c. coll.:* Stevenson 2061:2.

6. The man who conquers sticks to his guns. *Rec. dist.:* Ill.

7. They conquer who believe they can. *Var.:* To conquer, you must believe you can. *Rec. dist.:* Ill., Oreg. *1st cit.:* US1870 Emerson, *Society and Solitude. 20c. coll.:* Stevenson 402:8.

8. To conquer others, you must first conquer yourself. *Rec. dist.:* Ill. *1st cit.:* 1590 Spenser, *Faerie Queene;* US1813 Lucas, *Document Transcriptions of War of 1812,* ed. Knopf (1957–59). *20c. coll.:* Stevenson 2060:5, Whiting 320.
   See also COURAGE conquers all things; it even gives strength to the body. / DIVIDE and conquer. / Conquer your GRIEVANCES before they conquer you. / KINDNESS is the noblest weapon to conquer with. / KNOWLEDGE conquered by labor becomes a possession. / LABOR conquers all things. / LOVE conquers all. / PATIENCE and time conquer all things. / TRUTH shall conquer all.

conquered   Pity the conquered; you might be beaten yourself some day. *Rec. dist.:* Ill.

conqueror   **1.** No man is such a conqueror as the man who has defeated himself. *Rec. dist.:* N.Y., S.C. *1st cit.:* US1887 Beecher, *Proverbs from Plymouth Pulpit. 20c. coll.:* Stevenson 2061:4.

2. The conqueror is always right, the conquered always wrong. *Rec. dist.:* Ill.

conquest   *See* Real GLORY springs from the silent conquest of ourselves.

conscience   **1.** A bad conscience is an accuser, judge, witness, and hangman. *Rec. dist.:* Miss.

2. A clean conscience is a good pillow. *Rec. dist.:* Okla. *1st cit.:* 1902 Hulme, *Proverb Lore. 20c. coll.:* Stevenson 407:11.

3. A clean conscience is better than a clean face. *Rec. dist.:* Okla.

4. A clear conscience can bear any trouble. *Rec. dist.:* Minn. *1st cit.:* 1732 Fuller, *Gnomologia. 20c. coll.:* Stevenson 407:7.

5. A clear conscience fears no accuser. *Rec. dist.:* Ill., Mich. *1st cit.:* 1580 Lyly, *Euphues and His England. 20c. coll.:* Stevenson 407:7, ODEP 140.

6. A clear conscience is a coat of mail. *Vars.:* **(a)** A clear conscience is a sure card. **(b)** A clear conscience is a wall of brass. *Rec. dist.:* Ill., N.Y. *1st cit.:* 1523 Erasmus, *Adagia,* tr. Taverner. *20c. coll.:* Stevenson 407:7.

7. A clear conscience is God's greatest gift. *Rec. dist.:* Kans. *1st cit.:* 1732 Fuller, *Gnomologia. 20c. coll.:* Stevenson 407:5.

8. A guilty conscience needs no accuser. *Vars.:* **(a)** A guilty conscience is its own accuser. **(b)** A guilty conscience needs no condemner. *Rec. dist.:* U.S., Can. *1st cit.:* ca1390 Chaucer, *Prologue to Canon's Yeoman's Tale;* US1755 Bailey, *Journal of Frontier Missionary, Rev. Jacob Bailey,* ed. Bartlett (1853). *20c. coll.:* CODP 103, Whiting 82, ODEP 340, Stevenson 1046:4, Whiting(MP) 130.

9. A guilty conscience never feels secure. *Rec. dist.:* Utah.

10. An evil conscience breaks many a man's neck. *Rec. dist.:* Ill. *1st cit.:* 1732 Fuller, *Gnomologia. 20c. coll.:* Stevenson 408:1.

11. An evil conscience is the most unquiet companion. *Rec. dist.:* Mich.

12. Conscience gets a lot of credit that belongs to cold feet. *Rec. dist.:* Ind., N.Dak.

13. Conscience is an anticipation of the opinions of others. *Rec. dist.:* N.C. *1st cit.:* 1836 Taylor, *Statesman.* *20c. coll.:* Stevenson 405:4.

14. Conscience is God's presence in man. *Rec. dist.:* R.I. *1st cit.:* 1756 Swedenborg, *Arcana Caelestia,* tr. Noble. *20c. coll.:* Stevenson 404:20.

15. Conscience is the court of justice. *Rec. dist.:* Ill.

16. Conscience makes cowards of us all. *Rec. dist.:* Ill., Minn. *1st cit.:* 1600 Shakespeare, *Hamlet.* *20c. coll.:* CODP 41, Stevenson 408:11.

17. Keep conscience clear, then never fear. *Rec. dist.:* N.Y., S.C.

18. Let your conscience be your guide. *Rec. dist.:* U.S.

19. There is a Sunday conscience as well as a Sunday coat. *Rec. dist.:* Minn. *Infm.:* You don't wear a Sunday coat during the rest of the week.

20. There is no hell like a bad conscience. *Rec. dist.:* Ind. *1st cit.:* 1590 Lodge, *Rosalynde.* *20c. coll.:* Stevenson 408:4.

21. What you take lightly on your conscience you'll feel heavily on your back. *Rec. dist.:* Ill.

22. You can't kid your conscience. *Rec. dist.:* Wash.

23. You cannot hide from your conscience. *Rec. dist.:* N.C.

SEE ALSO Don't find PLEASURE without conscience.

conscious *SEE* The greatest of FAULTS is to be conscious of none.

consciousness The consciousness of duty performed gives us music at midnight. *Rec. dist.:* N.Y.

consent *SEE* SILENCE gives consent.

conservative Men are conservative after dinner. *Rec. dist.:* N.Y., S.C. *1st cit.:* US1844 Emerson, *New England Reformers.* *20c. coll.:* Stevenson 409:9.

consider He who considers too much will perform little. *Rec. dist.:* N.Y., S.C.

SEE ALSO Consider the ANT, you sluggard, and be wise.

consideration **1.** Consideration gets as many victories as rashness. *Rec. dist.:* Ill.

2. Consideration is due to all things. *Rec. dist.:* Mich.

3. Few envy the consideration enjoyed by the oldest inhabitant. *Rec. dist.:* N.Y., S.C. *1st cit.:* US1870 Emerson, *Society and Solitude.* *20c. coll.:* Stevenson 27:3.

consistency **1.** Consistency is a jewel. *Rec. dist.:* Ill., Minn. *1st cit.:* US1867 Richardson, *Beyond the Mississippi.* *20c. coll.:* T&W 79, Stevenson 410:9.

2. Consistency is the hobgoblin of little minds. *Var.:* A foolish consistency is the hobgoblin of little minds. *Rec. dist.:* Ohio, Okla. *1st cit.:* US1841 Emerson, "Self-Reliance" in *Essays.* *20c. coll.:* Stevenson 410:7.

console Seek not to be consoled but to console. *Rec. dist.:* N.C.

conspicuous Some people are conspicuous by their presence, and others by their absence. *Rec. dist.:* Ill.

constancy Constancy is the foundation of all virtues. *Rec. dist.:* Ill., Mich.

constant There is nothing constant but inconsistency. *Rec. dist.:* N.C.

Constitution The Constitution rides behind, and the big stick rides before. *Rec. dist.:* N.Y., S.C. *1st cit.:* US1905 Irwin, *Ballad of Grizzly Gulch.* *20c. coll.:* Stevenson 411:14.

consultation Premature consultation is but the remembrance of sorrow. *Rec. dist.:* Miss.

contagious *SEE* COURTESY is contagious.

contempt **1.** Contempt is the best return for scurrility. *Rec. dist.:* Mich.

2. Contempt of a man is the sharpest reproof. *Var.:* Contempt is the sharpest reproof. *Rec. dist.:* Ill., Tex. *1st cit.:* 1885 Bohn, *Handbook of Proverbs.* *20c. coll.:* Stevenson 412:9.

3. Contempt will sooner kill an injury than

revenge. *Rec. dist.:* Ill. *1st cit.:* 1885 Bohn, *Handbook of Proverbs.* *20c. coll.:* Stevenson 412:9.

4. Contempt with familiarity does grow. *Rec. dist.:* Oreg.

5. What our contempt does often hurl from us we wish ours again. *Rec. dist.:* Wis.

SEE ALSO FAMILIARITY breeds contempt. / PRIDE that dines on vanity sups on contempt.

contemptible There is none more contemptible than a man that is a fortune hunter. *Rec. dist.:* Miss.

content *(n.)* **1.** Better little with content than much with contention. *Rec. dist.:* N.Y.

2. Content in the humblest dwelling is better than care in the most splendid palace. *Rec. dist.:* Mich.

3. Content is more than a kingdom. *Rec. dist.:* Okla. *1st cit.:* ca1560 Lupton, *Money.* *20c. coll.:* ODEP 142, Stevenson 414:3.

4. Content makes poor men rich; discontent makes rich men poor. *Rec. dist.:* Ill., Ind., Miss. *1st cit.:* 1566 Gascoigne, *Jocasta;* US1749 Franklin, *PRAlmanac.* *20c. coll.:* ODEP 141, Stevenson 414:7.

5. He who wants content can't find it in an easy chair. *Rec. dist.:* Ind. *1st cit.:* 1732 Fuller, *Gnomologia.* *20c. coll.:* Stevenson 413:10.

6. In the voyage of life, may content be our fellow passenger. *Rec. dist.:* Minn.

content *(adj.)* **1.** A contented mind is a continual feast. *Rec. dist.:* Ill. *1st cit.:* 1586 Warner, *Albion's England.* *20c. coll.:* Stevenson 413:1, ODEP 142.

2. Be content with your lot. *Vars.:* **(a)** Be content in your lot; one cannot be first in everything. **(b)** Be content with what you have. **(c)** Be contented with your lot. *Rec. dist.:* N.C. *1st cit.:* 1583 Melbancke, *Philotimus.* *20c. coll.:* ODEP 142, Stevenson 414:1.

3. He who is content has enough. *Rec. dist.:* Mich., Minn., N.Y. *1st cit.:* ca1560 Lupton, *Money;* US1758 Franklin, *PRAlmanac.* *20c. coll.:* ODEP 225, Stevenson 413:6.

4. No man is content with his own lot. *Rec. dist.:* Ill. *1st cit.:* 1539 Publilius Syrus, *Senten-*

tiae, tr. Taverner. *20c. coll.:* ODEP 570, Stevenson 415:1.

5. To be content, look backward on those who possess less than yourself, not forward on those who possess more. *Rec. dist.:* N.Y., S.C. *1st cit.:* US1757 Franklin, *PRAlmanac.* *20c. coll.:* Stevenson 413:6.

6. To be content with little is true happiness. *Rec. dist.:* Ill. *1st cit.:* ca1566 *Bugbears;* US1747 Franklin, *PRAlmanac.* *20c. coll.:* ODEP 141, Stevenson 413:4.

SEE ALSO LIVE freely and die content. / Full STOMACH, contented heart.

contention **1.** In a hundred ells of contention, there is not an inch of love. *Rec. dist.:* Mich. *1st cit.:* 1640 Herbert, *Outlandish Proverbs (Jacula Prudentum)* in *Works,* ed. Hutchinson (1941). *20c. coll.:* ODEP 416, Stevenson 416:1.

2. Religious contention is the devil's harvest. *Rec. dist.:* Utah.

contentment **1.** Contentment is better than riches. *Rec. dist.:* Kans., Oreg. *1st cit.:* 1566 Gascoigne, *Jocasta;* US1753 Hume in *Va.Mag.Hist.* (1912). *20c. coll.:* ODEP 141, Whiting 83, Stevenson 414:7.

2. Contentment is to the mind as light to the eye. *Rec. dist.:* Mich.

3. Contentment is worn as a crown of sleepy heads. *Rec. dist.:* N.Y., S.C. *1st cit.:* US1940 *Meditations in Wall Street.* *20c. coll.:* Stevenson 415:2.

contest Mighty contests rise from trivial things. *Rec. dist.:* R.I. *1st cit.:* 1712 Pope, *Rape of the Lock.* *20c. coll.:* Stevenson 1035:1.

continuity Continuity is the father of success. *Rec. dist.:* Ill.

contract *(n.)* **1.** A contract founded in evil or against morality is void. *Rec. dist.:* Mich.

2. A verbal contract isn't worth the paper it's written on. *Rec. dist.:* Ohio.

3. Contracts should never be undertaken unless they can be strictly performed. *Rec. dist.:* Mich.

contract *(v.)* *SEE* It is a thousand times easier to contract a new HABIT than to get rid of an old one.

contradict Contradict with respect and be complaisant without fawning. *Rec. dist.:* Mich.

contradiction 1. Contradiction begets heat. *Rec. dist.:* Mich.

2. Where there is no contradiction, there is no argument. *Rec. dist.:* Md.

SEE ALSO A WOMAN is the greatest contradiction of all. / WOMEN at lust are a contradiction.

contrivance 1. Contrivance is as good as hard work. *Rec. dist.:* Vt.

2. Hard living makes contrivance. *Rec. dist.:* S.C.

control To control others, learn first to control yourself. *Var.:* Be sure you can control yourself before attempting to conquer others. *Rec. dist.:* Fla., Minn.

SEE ALSO You can't control your LOVE. / We cannot control the NEWS we get, but we can control the news we start. / Control your PASSION or it will control you. / He that corrects not YOUTH controls not age.

controversy Controversy should ever be free from the prejudices of sect and party. *Rec. dist.:* Mich.

conveniences Conveniences have their inconveniences, and comforts their crosses. *Rec. dist.:* Mich. *1st cit.:* 1565 Hall, *Court of Virtue;* US1733 Franklin, *PRAlmanac.* *20c. coll.:* ODEP 228, Whiting 83, Stevenson 392:16.

convention Men like conventions because men made them. *Rec. dist.:* N.J.

conversation 1. Conversation, however light, should never approach the confines of impurity. *Rec. dist.:* Mich.

2. Conversation is the music of the mind. *Rec. dist.:* Mich.

3. The conversation of a woman is worth all the libraries in the world. *Rec. dist.:* Wis.

4. When there is a gap in the conversation, don't put your foot into it. *Rec. dist.:* Kans.

5. Your conversation is the mirror of your thoughts. *Var.:* A man's conversation is the mirror of his thoughts. *Rec. dist.:* Ill.

SEE ALSO A FOOL is known by his conversation. / The WIT of conversation consists more in finding it in others than showing a great deal yourself. / WIT is the salt of converstion, not the food.

conversational Conversational floodgates are always open. *Rec. dist.:* N.Y.

converse 1. Converse so as to please others, not in order to please yourself. *Rec. dist.:* Mich.

2. He that converses not knows nothing. *Rec. dist.:* Mich. *1st cit.:* 1594 Shakespeare, *Two Gentlemen of Verona.* *20c. coll.:* ODEP 142.

convert You have not converted a man because you have silenced him. *Rec. dist.:* Ind.

convict Only a convict likes to be stopped in the middle of a sentence. *Rec. dist.:* N.J.

conviction Not he who has many ideas but he who has one conviction may become a great man. *Rec. dist.:* Ill.

convince Convince a man against his will, he is of the same opinion still. *Vars.:* **(a)** A man convinced against his will is of his own opinion still. **(b)** Convince a fool against his will; he's of the same opinion still. **(c)** Convince a person against his will, and he will be of the same opinion still. **(d)** Persuade a man against his will; he's of the same opinion still. *Rec. dist.:* U.S., Can. *1st cit.:* 1678 Butler, *Hudibras.* *20c. coll.:* ODEP 139, CODP 41, Stevenson 1719:10.

cook *(n.)* 1. A cook is no better than her stove. *Rec. dist.:* Wis.

2. All are not cooks who sport white caps and carry long knives. *Var.:* Not everyone who carries a long knife is a cook. *Rec. dist.:* Ill.

3. Every cook knows to lick her own fingers. *Rec. dist.:* Ill.

4. Every cook praises his own broth. *Var.:* Every cook praises his own stew. *Rec. dist.:* Mich., Tex., Vt.

5. He's an ill cook that can't lick his own fingers. *Rec. dist.:* Okla., Tex. *1st cit.:* ca1510 Stanbridge, *Vulgaria;* US1692 Bulkeley, *Will and Doom,* ed. Hoadly, Conn.Hist.Soc. *Collections* (1895). *20c. coll.:* ODEP 143, Whiting 83, Stevenson 419:1.

6. One cook's a cook, two cooks are half a cook, and three cooks are no cook at all. *Rec. dist.:* Ohio.

7. Pity on the cook who can't get enough to eat. *Rec. dist.:* Ohio.

8. The cook that's with you in the morning is against you in the afternoon. *Rec. dist.:* Ill.

9. Too many cooks spoil the broth. *Vars.:* **(a)** Too many cooks spoil the brew. **(b)** Too many cooks spoil the broth, but in numbers there is strength. **(c)** Too many cooks spoil the pie. **(d)** Too many cooks spoil the stew. *Rec. dist.:* U.S., Can. *1st cit.:* 1575 Gascoigne, *Life of Sir P. Carew;* USca1700 Hubbard, *General History of New England* (1865). *20c. coll.:* ODEP 831, Whiting 83, CODP 228, Stevenson 419:5, T&W 79, Whiting(*MP*) 130.

SEE ALSO A three years' DROUGHT will not starve a cook. / A good FIRE makes a good cook. / GOD sends meat, and the devil sends cooks. / HUNGER makes the best cook. / The MUSES starve in a cook's shop.

cook *(v.)* SEE If you cook your own GOOSE, you will have to eat it. / The GOOSE is never cooked till the fire is hottest.

cookie Cookie today, crumb tomorrow. *Rec. dist.:* Wash.

cool *(v.)* SEE ABSENCE cools moderate passions but inflames violent ones. / Keep one's BREATH to cool one's soup.

cool *(adj.)* **1.** A man should study ever to keep cool. *Rec. dist.:* N.Y., S.C.

2. Keep cool and you command everybody. *Rec. dist.:* Miss. *1st cit.:* US1850 Emerson, "Social Aims" in *Lectures. 20c. coll.:* Stevenson 2061:7.

3. Play it cool, but don't freeze up. *Rec. dist.:* Kans.

SEE ALSO As a rule, man's a FOOL: when it's hot, he wants it cool; when it's cool, he wants it hot—always wanting what is not. / He that

has many IRONS in the fire will have some of them cool. / Cool WORDS scald not a tongue.

coon **1.** A young coon for running, but an old coon for cunning. *Rec. dist.:* Fla.

2. You can't get all your coons up one tree. *Rec. dist.:* Fla., Okla. *1st cit.:* US1938 Rawlings, *Yearling. 20c. coll.:* Whiting(*MP*) 131.

cooperation **1.** Cooperation is the natural law of progress. *Rec. dist.:* Utah.

2. Cooperation isn't letting the other fellow do all the work. *Rec. dist.:* N.Y.

3. If you don't believe in cooperation, watch what happens to a wagon when one wheel comes off. *Rec. dist.:* Ohio.

4. If you think cooperation is unnecessary, just try running your car a while on three wheels. *Rec. dist.:* Ohio.

copy *(n.)* Too many people are carbon copies. *Rec. dist.:* N.Dak.

copy *(v.)* SEE Make your LIFE; don't copy it.

cord SEE String your PEARLS on a strong cord.

core SEE Many a rosy APPLE is rotten to the core.

corkscrew **1.** A corkscrew never pulled one out of a hole. *Rec. dist.:* Oreg.

2. Corkscrews have sunk more people than corkjackets will ever save. *Rec. dist.:* Tex.

corn **1.** A full ear of corn will bend its head; an empty ear will stand upright. *Rec. dist.:* Ohio.

2. Corn makes mo' at de mill dan it does in de crib. *Rec. dist.:* N.Y., S.C.

3. Corn should be knee high by the Fourth of July. *Rec. dist.:* Vt.

4. Don't measure my corn by your bushel. *Vars.:* **(a)** Don't measure my corn by your half-bushel. **(b)** Never judge others' corn by your own half-bushel. *Rec. dist.:* U.S., Can. *1st cit.:* 1623 Painter, *Chaucer New Painted;* US1676 *Complete Writings of Roger Williams* (1963). *20c. coll.:* ODEP 521, Whiting 84, Stevenson 422:7, T&W 81, Whiting(*MP*) 132.

5. Don't shuck your corn till the hogs come home. *Rec. dist.:* Tenn.

6. Even the corn has ears. *Vars.:* **(a)** Don't tell your family secrets in the cornfield: remember that corn has ears. **(b)** Never tell tales in a garden, 'cause corn has ears and potatoes have eyes. *Rec. dist.:* U.S., Can.

7. If the corn's not shelled, drive on. *Rec. dist.:* Miss.

8. If you plant corn, buy a grinder. *Rec. dist.:* Minn.

9. If you want to raise corn, plant corn seed, not cotton seed. *Rec. dist.:* S.C.

10. In planting corn, four kernels to a hill: one for the blackbird, one for the crow, one for the cutworm, and one to grow. *Rec. dist.:* Minn.

11. More corn grows in crooked rows. *Rec. dist.:* Kans.

12. Plow deep while sluggards sleep, and you will have corn to sell and to keep. *Vars.:* **(a)** Plow deep and you will have plenty of corn. **(b)** Plow deeply and you will have plenty of corn. *Rec. dist.:* U.S., Can. *1st cit.:* 1659 Howell, *Paroimiografia (Spanish Proverbs);* US1756 Franklin, *PRAlmanac. 20c. coll.:* ODEP 634, Whiting 400, Stevenson 1816:18, Whiting(MP) 575.

13. The more you take care of corn and politics, the better they grow up. *Rec. dist.:* N.J.

14. There's no corn without chaff. *Rec. dist.:* Ill.

15. Thunder in March, corn to parch. *Rec. dist.:* Wis.

16. You can't grind corn with the water that has passed. *Rec. dist.:* Utah.

17. You can't have the ear unless you plant the corn. *Rec. dist.:* Miss.

18. You cannot cut corn unless there is corn to cut. *Rec. dist.:* Wis.

SEE ALSO Don't CARE lost his corn patch. / CROW an' corn can't grow in de same fiel'. / Don't muzzle the OX when he treads out the corn. / De PIG dat runs off wid de year er corn gits little mo' dan de cob. / PRAYER, worn knees, and a rusty hoe never raised a crop of corn. / An armful of WEEDS is worth an ear of corn.

corncrib An empty corncrib needs no roof. *Rec. dist.:* Minn.

corner **1.** Brighten the corner wherever you are. *Rec. dist.:* N.Y.

2. Do the corners first, and the middle will take care of itself. *Var.:* When you are washing windows, do the corners first and the center will take care of itself. *Rec. dist.:* Ill.

3. Every house has its dirty corner. *Rec. dist.:* N.J.

4. If you want to live on the square, don't cut the corners. *Rec. dist.:* Utah.

5. Take time in turning a corner. *Rec. dist.:* Okla. *1st cit.:* US1948 Stevenson, *Home Book of Proverbs. 20c. coll.:* Stevenson 306:5.

6. We should always keep a spare corner in our head to give passing hospitality to our friends' opinions. *Rec. dist.:* Ala.

SEE ALSO It is better to DWELL in the corner of a housetop than with a brawling woman in a wide house. / TRUTH seeks no corner. / Every WOMAN keeps a corner in her heart where she is always twenty-one.

cornpone Cornpone, hog jaw, and salt are fit for a king. *Rec. dist.:* Ky.

corpse **1.** Blessed is the corpse the rain falls on. *Var.:* Happy is the corpse the rain rains on. *Rec. dist.:* U.S., Can. *Infm.:* Cf. bride. *1st cit.:* 1601 Shakespeare, *Twelfth Night;* US1925 Fitzgerald, *Great Gatsby. 20c. coll.:* ODEP 85, CODP 49, Stevenson 505:8, Whiting(MP) 74.

2. Don't count your corpses before they're cold. *Rec. dist.:* N.Y.

3. I'd rather be scared a minute than be a corpse the rest of my life. *Rec. dist.:* Miss.

4. Three times a pallbearer, once a corpse. *Rec. dist.:* Alaska.

5. Where the corpse is, there the vultures gather. *Rec. dist.:* Ill., Ohio, Wis.

SEE ALSO Better be called a COWARD than a corpse.

correct *(v.)* SEE By others' FAULTS wise men correct their own. / He that corrects not YOUTH controls not age.

correct *(adj.)* SEE It's much easier to be CRITICAL than correct.

correction 1. Correction does much, but encouragement everything. *Rec. dist.:* Wis.

2. Correction is good when administered in time. *Rec. dist.:* Ill.

corrupt SEE Evil COMMUNICATIONS corrupt good manners. / Bad COMPANIONS corrupt good morals.

corruption Corruption will find a dozen alibis for its evil deeds. *Rec. dist.:* Ill.

cost *(n.)* 1. He that counts all costs will never put a plow in the earth. *Rec. dist.:* N.Y. *1st cit.:* ca1628 Carmichaell, *Proverbs in Scots,* ed. Anderson (1957). *20c. coll.:* ODEP 148.

2. The cost often spoils the relish. *Rec. dist.:* Ill., Mich., Oreg.

3. The cost takes away the taste. *Rec. dist.:* Ill.

cost *(v.)* 1. What costs, counts. *Rec. dist.:* Vt.

2. What costs little is little respected. *Rec. dist.:* Ill. *1st cit.:* 1620 Cervantes, *Don Quixote,* tr. Shelton. *20c. coll.:* ODEP 145, Stevenson 427:7.

SEE ALSO It costs nothing to ASK. / Nothing costs less than CIVILITY. / COURTESY costs nothing. / There is nothing that costs so little nor goes so far as COURTESY. / What you get without EFFORT is worth what it costs. / It doesn't cost anything to be KIND. / A LOVE letter sometimes costs more than a three-cent stamp. / POLITENESS costs nothing and gains everything. / Remember the POOR; it costs nothing. / A SMILE costs nothing, but gives much. / Courteous SPEECH is much valued and costs little. / A good WORD for a bad one is worth much and costs little.

costly SEE AGREE, for the law is costly.

cottage Wide is the door of the little cottage. *Rec. dist.:* Miss.

SEE ALSO LOVE lives in a cottage as well as in courts.

cotton 1. A lot of good cotton stalks get chopped up for associating with weeds. *Rec. dist.:* Ark.

2. More cotton will grow in a crooked row than in a straight acre. *Rec. dist.:* Tex.

SEE ALSO If you want to raise CORN, plant corn seed, not cotton seed. / DIRT shows the quickest on the cleanest cotton. / A GIRL with cotton stockings never sees a mouse.

counsel *(n.)* 1. Counsel after action is like rain after harvest. *Rec. dist.:* Ill.

2. Counsel in the heart of man is like deep water. *Rec. dist.:* Ohio.

3. Counsel must be followed, not praised. *Rec. dist.:* N.Dak. *1st cit.:* 1580 Lyly, *Euphues and His England,* ed. Arber (1868). *20c. coll.:* ODEP 146.

4. Do not darken counsel with words without knowledge. *Rec. dist.:* Minn.

5. Evil counsel marches with seven-league boots. *Rec. dist.:* Ill.

6. Examine well the counsel that favors your desires. *Rec. dist.:* N.Y.

7. Good counsel brings good fruit. *Rec. dist.:* Ill.

8. Good counsel is a pearl beyond price. *Rec. dist.:* Ill. *1st cit.:* 1606 Day, *Isle of Guls;* US1734 Franklin, *PRAlmanac. 20c. coll.:* ODEP 318, Stevenson 431:7.

9. Good counsel is cast away upon the self-conceited. *Rec. dist.:* N.Y.

10. Good counsel never comes too late. *Rec. dist.:* U.S., Can. *1st cit.:* 1633 Jonson, *Tale of a Tub;* US1734 Franklin, *PRAlmanac. 20c. coll.:* ODEP 318, Stevenson 431:7.

11. If the counsel is good, take it, even from a fool. *Var.:* If the counsel be good, it matters not who gave it. *Rec. dist.:* Ill., Mich. *1st cit.:* ca1640 *Countrym. Commonw.;* US1734 Franklin, *PRAlmanac. 20c. coll.:* ODEP 146, Stevenson 431:7.

12. Take counsel in wine but resolve afterwards in water. *Rec. dist.:* N.Y., S.C. *1st cit.:* 1640 Herbert, *Outlandish Proverbs (Jacula Prudentum)* in *Works,* ed. Hutchinson (1941). *20c. coll.:* ODEP 147, Stevenson 430:10.

13. The wise man keeps his own counsel. *Rec. dist.:* Vt. *1st cit.:* 1598 Shakespeare, *Much Ado About Nothing. 20c. coll.:* ODEP 418.

14. Three may keep counsel if two be away. *Var.:* Two may keep counsel when the third's

away. *Rec. dist.:* U.S., Can. *1st cit.:* ca1370 Chaucer, *Romance of Rose,* ed. Skeat (1894); US1735 Franklin, *PRAlmanac.* *20c. coll.:* ODEP 417, *CODP* 224, Stevenson 431:3, Whiting*(MP)* 654.

15. Where no counsel is, the people fall. *Var.:* Where no counsel is, the people fall, but in the multitude of counselors there is safety. *Rec. dist.:* Minn.

SEE ALSO A FOOL may give a wise man counsel.

counsel *(v.)* He that will not be counseled cannot be helped. *Var.:* They that won't be counseled can't be helped. *Rec. dist.:* Miss., Okla., Tex., Vt. *1st cit.:* 1621 Robinson, *Adagia in Latin and English;* US1747 Franklin, *PRAlmanac.* *20c. coll.:* ODEP 147, Whiting 85.

counselor Good counselors lack no clients. *Rec. dist.:* N.Y.

count *(n.)* Wrong count is no payment. *Rec. dist.:* Ill., Wash.

count *(v.)* **1.** Don't count yourself too many. *Rec. dist.:* N.C.

2. What counts most is what you've got under your hat. *Rec. dist.:* Ga.

SEE ALSO If you're ANGRY count to ten. / Every little BIT counts. / Don't count your CHICKENS before they are hatched. / It is not what we DO but how we do it that counts. / Don't count FISH till on dry land. / It's not what you HAVE in life that counts, but what you are. / You can't count the HEIFER 'fore she's born. / It's not what you KNOW that counts; it's how you use what you know. / It's not the number of hours you STUDY that counts, but how you study. / Count no man SUCCESSFUL until he is dead. / We do not count a man's YEARS until he has nothing else to count.

countenance The countenance is the index of the mind. *Rec. dist.:* Ill., Vt.

country **1.** A country, to be loved, must be lovely. *Rec. dist.:* Minn. *1st cit.:* 1790 Burke, *Reflections on French Revolution.* *20c. coll.:* Stevenson 1758:8.

2. A man's country is where the things he loves are most respected. *Rec. dist.:* Kans.

3. Countries are not more numerous than customs. *Rec. dist.:* Minn.

4. Every country has its own customs. *Var.:* So many countries, so many customs. *Rec. dist.:* Wis. *1st cit.:* ca1100 *Anglo-Saxon Gnomic Verses,* ed. Grein; US1783 *American Wanderer Through Europe.* *20c. coll.:* ODEP 147, Whiting 85, Stevenson 433:5, T&W 82, Whiting*(MP)* 133.

5. Every country has the government it deserves. *Rec. dist.:* Wis.

6. Go to the country to hear the news of the town. *Rec. dist.:* Ind., Mich., Miss. *1st cit.:* 1678 Ray, *English Proverbs;* US1740 Franklin, *PRAlmanac.* *20c. coll.:* ODEP 307, Stevenson 434:3, *CODP* 93.

7. In the country one does not lose faith. *Rec. dist.:* Fla.

8. It's sweet to die for one's country. *Rec. dist.:* N.C. *1st cit.:* US1797 Callendar *Annual Register.* *20c. coll.:* Whiting 85, Stevenson 1760:7.

9. Let's keep this a country where every man is entitled to scratch his own itch. *Rec. dist.:* N.Mex.

10. My country, right or wrong. *Rec. dist.:* Minn. *1st cit.:* 1706 Stevens, *New Spanish and English Dictionary;* US1816 Decatur, Toast at Norfolk, Va. *20c. coll.:* ODEP 147, Stevenson 1758:12.

11. Now is the time for all good men to come to the aid of their country. *Rec. dist.:* U.S., Can. *1st cit.:* US1867 Weller, *Typing Test* for first typewriter, Milwaukee, Wis. *20c. coll.:* Stevenson 1748:4.

12. The man without a country is an exile from life and hope. *Rec. dist.:* Ill.

13. You can get the man out of the country, but you can't get the country out of the man. *Vars.:* **(a)** Now you can take a boy out of the country, but you can't take the country out of the boy. **(b)** You can get the girl out of the country, but you can't get the country out of the girl. **(c)** You can take the farmer out of the country, but you can't take the country out of the farmer. *Rec. dist.:* U.S., Can.

SEE ALSO DYING once, even for one's coun-

try, is once too often. / A PROPHET is without
honor in his own country. / In every country
the SUN rises in the morning.

couple 1. A deaf husband and a blind wife
are always a happy couple. *Rec. dist.:* Ohio.
1st cit.: 1578 Florio, *Firste Fruites;* US1940
Thompson, *Body, Boots, and Britches.* *20c. coll.:*
CODP 50.

2. Every couple is not a pair. *Rec. dist.:* Ind.
1st cit.: 1875 Cheales, *Proverbial Folk-Lore.* *20c.
coll.:* *ODEP* 148, Stevenson 1531:7.

3. Most men and women are merely one
couple more. *Rec. dist.:* N.Y., S.C. *1st cit.:*
1614 Jonson, *Bartholomew Fair;* US1860
Emerson, "Fate" in *Conduct of Life.* *20c. coll.:*
Stevenson 1207:2.

4. The higher the mountain, the cooler the
breeze; the younger the couple, the tighter
they squeeze. *Rec. dist.:* Miss.

SEE ALSO There isn't much to talk about at
some PARTIES until after one or two couples
leave.

courage 1. A great part of courage is the
courage of having done the thing before. *Rec.
dist.:* N.Y., S.C. *1st cit.:* US1870 Emerson,
"Courage" in *Society and Solitude.* *20c. coll.:*
Stevenson 434:9.

2. A man of courage is never in need of
weapons. *Rec. dist.:* Ill. *1st cit.:* 1678 Ray,
Scottish Proverbs. *20c. coll.:* Stevenson 436:13.

3. Against fortune, oppose courage; against
passion, reason. *Rec. dist.:* Mich.

4. Courage comes through suffering. *Rec. dist.:*
N.C.

5. Courage conquers all things; it even gives
strength to the body. *Rec. dist.:* Wis.

6. Courage is a virtue the young cannot spare;
to lose it is to grow old before the time. *Rec.
dist.:* N.C.

7. Courage is always safer than cowardice.
Rec. dist.: Utah.

8. Courage is fear that has said its prayers.
Rec. dist.: Oreg., Wis.

9. Courage without conduct is like a ship
without ballast. *Rec. dist.:* N.Y.

10. Fearless courage is the foundation of vic-

tory. *Rec. dist.:* Ill. *1st cit.:* US1948 Stevenson,
Home Book of Proverbs. *20c. coll.:* Stevenson
436:10.

11. Few persons have courage enough to appear as good as they really are. *Rec. dist.:*
N.Y., S.C.

12. Few there are who have courage enough
to own their faults or resolution enough to
amend them. *Rec. dist.:* N.Y., S.C.

13. Good courage breaks bad luck. *Rec. dist.:*
Ill.

14. Have the courage not to adopt another's
courage. *Rec. dist.:* N.Y., S.C. *1st cit.:* US1870
Emerson, "Courage" in *Society and Solitude.*
20c. coll.: Stevenson 435:11.

15. He who loses his wealth loses much; he
who loses even one friend loses more; but he
that loses his courage loses all. *Var.:* He who
loses wealth loses much; he who loses a friend
loses more; but he that loses courage loses all.
Rec. dist.: Ill., N.J., Ohio. *1st cit.:* 1785 Goethe,
Xenien. *20c. coll.:* Stevenson 1455:10.

16. It requires more courage not to fight than
to fight. *Rec. dist.:* N.Y., S.C.

17. Keep your courage up and it will keep
you up. *Rec. dist.:* N.Dak.

18. One man with courage makes a majority.
Rec. dist.: N.J.

19. The courage of the tiger is one, and of the
horse, another. *Rec. dist.:* N.Y., S.C. *1st cit.:*
US1870 Emerson, "Courage" in *Society and
Solitude.* *20c. coll.:* Stevenson 435:11.

20. Young courage and old caution are a strong
pair. *Rec. dist.:* Wis.

SEE ALSO There is no arguing a COWARD
into courage. / FORTUNE can take away riches
but not courage.

courageous 1. A courageous foe is better
than a cowardly friend. *Rec. dist.:* N.Y., Ont.

2. It is easier to act courageous than to be
courageous. *Rec. dist.:* N.C.

3. One courageous thought will put to flight
a host of troubles. *Rec. dist.:* U.S., Can.

4. The world belongs to the courageous. *Rec.
dist.:* N.J.

course Steer a middle course. *Rec. dist.:* Minn.
SEE ALSO HUNGER is the first course to a good dinner. / A RIVER runs its course.

court *(n.)* He that would rise at court must begin creeping. *Rec. dist.:* N.Y., S.C. *1st cit.:* 1539 Taverner, *Proverbs of Erasmus;* US1757 Franklin, *PRAlmanac.* *20c. coll.:* ODEP 210, Whiting 85, Stevenson 439:4.
SEE ALSO LOVE lives in cottages as well as in courts.

court *(v.)* Always to court and never to wed is the happiest life that ever was led. *Rec. dist.:* N.Y., S.C. *1st cit.:* 1822 Campbell, *Maid's Remonstrances;* US1940 Thompson, *Body, Boots, and Britches.* *20c. coll.:* Stevenson 2594:8.

courteous 1. Be courteous with all but intimate with few, and let those be well tried before you give them your confidence. *Rec. dist.:* Kans.

2. He who is courteous to all is not courteous at all. *Rec. dist.:* Ohio.

courtesy 1. A little courtesy will go a long way. *Rec. dist.:* Minn.

2. Courtesy begins in the home. *Rec. dist.:* Okla. *1st cit.:* 1941 Wren, *Uniform of Glory.* *20c. coll.:* Stevenson 441:9.

3. Courtesy costs nothing. *Rec. dist.:* Ill. *1st cit.:* US1837 *Works of Ralph Waldo Emerson,* ed. Cabot. *20c. coll.:* T&W 82.

4. Courtesy is a business asset—a gain and never a loss. *Rec. dist.:* Wis.

5. Courtesy is contagious. *Rec. dist.:* Kans.

6. Courtesy is cumbersome to them that know it not. *Rec. dist.:* Vt. *1st cit.:* ca1628 Carmichaell, *Proverbs in Scots,* ed. Anderson (1957); US1853 Haliburton, *Sam Slick's Wise Saws.* *20c. coll.:* ODEP 149, Stevenson 440:3.

7. Courtesy is appropriate for gentlemen and necessary for thieves. *Rec. dist.:* N.C.

8. Courtesy is like oil on troubled waters. *Rec. dist.:* Kans.

9. Courtesy is one habit that never goes out of style. *Rec. dist.:* N.Y.

10. Courtesy is one of the best peacemakers. *Rec. dist.:* N.Y.

11. Courtesy is the password to safety. *Rec. dist.:* Utah.

12. Courtesy on one side only never lasts long. *Rec. dist.:* Mich. *1st cit.:* 1611 Cotgrave, *Dictionary of French and English Tongues.* *20c. coll.:* ODEP 149, Stevenson 440:6.

13. Courtesy opens many doors. *Rec. dist.:* Wis.

14. Courtesy pays. *Rec. dist.:* Ohio.

15. Courtesy pays compound interest. *Rec. dist.:* Ill., Kans., Ohio.

16. He who sows courtesy reaps friendship. *Rec. dist.:* Miss.

17. Life is not so short but that there is always time for courtesy. *Rec. dist.:* Okla., Wis.

18. The fox is all courtesy and all craft. *Rec. dist.:* Ill.

19. The small courtesies sweeten life, the greater ennoble it. *Rec. dist.:* Minn.

20. There is nothing that costs so little nor goes so far as courtesy. *Rec. dist.:* Nebr.

21. Too much courtesy, too much craft. *Rec. dist.:* Ill., Ohio. *1st cit.:* 1576 Pettie, *Petite Palace of Pleasure,* ed. Gollancz (1908); US1735 Franklin, *PRAlmanac.* *20c. coll.:* ODEP 293, Whiting 85.

courting A cat's courting is noisy. *Rec. dist.:* Oreg.

courtroom Hell and the courtroom are always open. *Rec. dist.:* Ill.

courtship A courtship is a man's pursuit of a woman until she catches him. *Rec. dist.:* Ohio.

cousin Call me cousin, but cozen me not. *Rec. dist.:* Mich. *1st cit.:* ca1552 "Dice and Play" in *Manifest Det.* *20c. coll.:* ODEP 149, Stevenson 441:11.

cover *(n.)* SEE You can't judge a BOOK by its cover. / You can never tell what's in a PACKAGE by its cover. / Every POT has its cover.

cover *(v.)* That which covers you discovers you. *Rec. dist.:* Mich. *1st cit.:* 1620 Cervantes, *Don Quixote,* tr. Shelton (1908). *20c. coll.:* ODEP 150.
SEE ALSO Let one HAT cover one face.

covered There is nothing covered that shall not be revealed, nor hidden that shall not be known. *Rec. dist.:* N.Y.

SEE ALSO The best way to save FACE is to keep it covered.

covet 1. Covet not that which belongs to others. *Rec. dist.:* Mich. *1st cit.:* US1948 Stevenson, *Home Book of Proverbs.* *20c. coll.:* Stevenson 442:2.

2. Covet nothing overmuch. *Rec. dist.:* Ill.
SEE ALSO ALL covet; all lose.

covetous 1. A covetous man does nothing that he should till he dies. *Rec. dist.:* Ont. *1st cit.:* 1550 Taverner, *Proverbs of Erasmus.* *20c. coll.:* Stevenson 443:4.

2. The covetous are poor givers. *Rec. dist.:* Alaska.

3. The covetous man is his own tormentor. *Rec. dist.:* Mich.

4. The world is too small for the covetous. *Rec. dist.:* Ill.

covetousness 1. Covetousness is harder to cure than cancer. *Rec. dist.:* N.Y.

2. Poverty wants many things, but covetousness all. *Rec. dist.:* N.Y., S.C. *1st cit.:* ca1560 Lupton, *Money.* *20c. coll.:* ODEP 639.

cow 1. A bawling cow soon forgets her own calf. *Vars.:* (a) A bawling cow will forget her calf. (b) A bellowing cow soon forgets her calf. (c) The cow that bawls the loudest soonest forgets her calf. *Rec. dist.:* U.S., Can. *1st cit.:* ca1330 Wright, *Political Songs,* Camden Soc. (1839). *20c. coll.:* ODEP 66, CODP 12, Stevenson 448:1.

2. A cow is a very good animal in the field, but we turn her out of a garden. *Rec. dist.:* Miss.

3. A cow needs her tail more than once in fly time. *Vars.:* (a) Cows don't know the good of the tail till fly time. (b) Every cow needs a tail in fly time. *Rec. dist.:* Ky., Ohio, Vt.

4. A cursed cow has short horns. *Var.:* Cussed cows have short horns. *Rec. dist.:* U.S., Can. *1st cit.:* ca1475 Chaucer, *Eight Goodly Questions* in Bell's *Chaucer;* US1733 Jonathan Belcher

Papers, Mass.Hist.Soc. *Collections* (1893–94). *20c. coll.:* ODEP 162, Whiting 86, Stevenson 446:5, T&W 82.

5. A promised cow doesn't fatten. *Rec. dist.:* N.J.

6. An old cow needs her tail more than once. *Rec. dist.:* Ill.

7. Cows can't catch no rabbits. *Rec. dist.:* Miss. *Infm.:* Usually form is in the affirmative to show poor judgment. *1st cit.:* 1611 Cotgrave, *Dictionary of French and English Tongues.* *20c. coll.:* ODEP 151, Stevenson 445:5.

8. Cows prefer the grass on the other side of the fence. *Rec. dist.:* Vt.

9. Don't swallow the cow and worry with the tail. *Rec. dist.:* Ohio. *1st cit.:* 1659 Howell, *Paroimiografia (English Proverbs);* US1746 *Letters and Papers of Cadwallader Colden,* N.Y.Hist.Soc. *Collections* (1917–37). *20c. coll.:* ODEP 791, Whiting 86, CODP 218, Whiting(MP) 135.

10. Faraway cows have long horns. *Vars.:* (a) Cows far away have long horns. (b) Faraway cows wear long horns. (c) The next man's cows have the longest horns. *Rec. dist.:* N.Y. *1st cit.:* 1922 Joyce, *Ulysses;* US1934 Lincoln, *February Hill.* *20c. coll.:* Whiting(MP) 135.

11. Holstein cows go round the world. *Rec. dist.:* Wis.

12. If you can't be the bell cow, fall in behind. *Rec. dist.:* Ill.

13. If you love de cow, you must love de calf. *Rec. dist.:* S.C.

14. It isn't the cow that lows the most that will milk the most. *Vars.:* (a) 'Taint always the bell cow that gives the most milk. (b) The cow that moos the most gives the least milk. *Rec. dist.:* Vt., Wis.

15. Let him that owns the cow take her by the tail. *Rec. dist.:* Okla.

16. Lick by lick the cow ate the grindstone. *Rec. dist.:* Tex.

17. Many a good cow has a bad calf. *Rec. dist.:* Tex. *1st cit.:* 1520 Whittington, *Vulgaria;* US1816 *Letters of James Fenimore Cooper,* ed.

Beard (1960–68). *20c. coll.: ODEP* 318, Whiting 86.

18. Night brings the cows home. *Rec. dist.:* N.J.

19. Salt the cow to get the calf. *Vars.:* **(a)** Feed the cow nubbins to catch the calf. **(b)** Pet the cow to get the calf. *Rec. dist.:* Ill., Ind., N.C., Wash.

20. The cow gives a good pail of milk and then kicks it over. *Rec. dist.:* Oreg. *1st cit.:* 1546 Heywood, *Dialogue of Proverbs,* ed. Habernicht (1963). *20c. coll.: ODEP* 151.

21. The cow has forgotten she was once a calf. *Rec. dist.:* Oreg.

22. The cow knows not the value of her tail till she has lost it. *Rec. dist.:* U.S., Can. *1st cit.:* 1611 Cotgrave, *Dictionary of French and English Tongues.* *20c. coll.: ODEP* 150, Stevenson 2639:5.

23. The cow must graze where she is tied. *Rec. dist.:* R.I.

24. The cross cow holds up her milk. *Rec. dist.:* N.Y., S.C. *1st cit.:* US1870 Emerson, "Clubs" in *Society and Solitude.* *20c. coll.:* Stevenson 445:7.

25. The leanest cow has the loudest low. *Rec. dist.:* Minn.

26. The more cows, the less milk. *Rec. dist.:* Tex.

27. The world is your cow, but you have to do the milking. *Rec. dist.:* N.Y.

28. 'Tis a lean cow that gives milk. *Rec. dist.:* Vt.

29. When the cow is stolen, they lock the barn. *Rec. dist.:* Minn.

30. Why buy the cow when you can get the milk free? *Vars.:* **(a)** Don't buy a cow to get a glass of milk. **(b)** Who'd keep a cow when he may have a quart of milk for a penny? **(c)** Why buy a cow when the milk is so cheap? **(d)** You don't need to buy a cow just because you like milk. *Rec. dist.:* U.S., Can. *Infm.:* Elvis Presley's usual response to "Why aren't you married?" *1st cit.:* 1659 Howell, *Letter of Advice;* US1927 Powys, *Mr. Weston's Good*

Wine. *20c. coll.: ODEP* 151, *CODP* 44, Stevenson 448:8, Whiting*(MP)* 135.

31. Women, cows, and hens should not run. *Rec. dist.:* N.C.

32. You cannot sell the cow and have the milk. *Var.:* If you sell the cow, you sell the milk too. *Rec. dist.:* Ill., Ind., N.J. *1st cit.:* ca1628 Carmichaell, *Proverbs in Scots,* ed. Anderson (1957). *20c. coll.: ODEP* 713, Stevenson 1229:8.

SEE ALSO The GNAT is small, to be sure, but she is not the servant of the cow. / If you can't get a HORSE, ride a cow. / When the HORSE is dead, the cow gets fat. / It doesn't depend upon SIZE, or a cow would catch a rabbit. / Aim for a STAR even though you hit a cow on a hillside.

coward **1.** A coward is much more exposed to quarrels than a man of spirit. *Rec. dist.:* N.Y., S.C. *1st cit.:* US1785 Jefferson, Letter to James Monroe in *Family Letters of Thomas Jefferson,* eds. Betts and Bean (1966). *20c. coll.:* Stevenson 449:2.

2. A live coward is better than a dead hero. *Var.:* Better to be a live coward than a dead hero. *Rec. dist.:* Ill., Ind., Wis. *1st cit.:* US1942 McCarthy, *Company She Keeps.* *20c. coll.:* Stevenson 1418:3, Whiting*(MP)* 135.

3. Any coward can fight a battle when he is sure of winning. *Rec. dist.:* Minn.

4. Better be a coward than foolhardy. *Rec. dist.:* Ill., Ind., Wis.

5. Better be called a coward than a corpse. *Rec. dist.:* Oreg.

6. Cowards call themselves cautious and misers thrifty. *Rec. dist.:* Ill.

7. Even the devil hates a coward. *Rec. dist.:* Ind.

8. Every man that is capable of doing a secret injury is a coward. *Rec. dist.:* Mich.

9. None but cowards lie. *Rec. dist.:* Ind.

10. One coward makes ten. *Rec. dist.:* Ill.

11. The coward dies many times. *Vars.:* **(a)** A coward dies a thousand deaths. **(b)** Cowards die daily, the brave but once. **(c)** Cowards die many a death, but the valiant die but one. **(d)** Cowards die many times. **(e)** Cowards die many times before their death. **(f)** Cowards die many times before their death; the valiant taste of death but once. **(g)** The coward dies a thousand deaths, the brave but one. *Rec. dist.:* U.S., Can. *1st cit.:* 1596 Drayton, *Mortimeriados.* *20c. coll.:* ODEP 151, CODP 44, Stevenson 449:10.

12. The coward shoots with shut eyes. *Rec. dist.:* N.J.

13. The gods hate a coward but love a brave soul. *Rec. dist.:* Oreg.

14. The Lord hates a coward. *Var.:* God hates a coward. *Rec. dist.:* Vt., Wash.

15. There is no arguing a coward into courage. *Rec. dist.:* Vt.

SEE ALSO A BULLY is always a coward. / CONSCIENCE makes cowards of us all.

cowardice **1.** Bootless speed when cowardice pursues and valor flies. *Rec. dist.:* N.C.

2. Cowardice is infectious. *Rec. dist.:* N.C.

cowardly **1.** A cowardly heart makes swift-runnin' feet. *Rec. dist.:* N.Y.

2. A cowardly man don't tote no broke bones. *Rec. dist.:* N.Y. *Infm.:* Tote means carry, i.e., have.

cowboy *SEE* There's no such thing as a HORSE that can't be rode or a cowboy that can't be throwed.

coy *SEE* Great MERIT is coy, as well as great pride.

coyote **1.** A howlin' coyote ain't stealin' no chickens. *Rec. dist.:* N.Mex.

2. Even a coyote will fight when you have him cornered. *Rec. dist.:* Iowa.

crab **1.** He who goes with crabs learns to walk backwards. *Rec. dist.:* Ohio.

2. The older the crab, the tougher his claws. *Rec. dist.:* Ont.

crab apple Crab apples make good jelly, too. *Rec. dist.:* Miss.

crabgrass It's a mighty dry year when the crabgrass fails. *Rec. dist.:* Okla.

crab tree Plant the crab tree where you will, it never will bear pippins. *Rec. dist.:* N.Y., Vt. *1st cit.:* 1579 Lyly, *Euphues, Anatomy of Wit*, ed. Arber (1868). *20c. coll.:* ODEP 152.

crack *SEE* He that will eat the KERNEL must crack the nut.

cracked A cracked plate always lasts longer than a new one. *Vars.:* **(a)** A cracked plate may last as long as a sound one. **(b)** The cracked pot lasts the longest. **(c)** The cracked saucer lasts longest. *Rec. dist.:* N.Y., Ont.

SEE ALSO A cracked BELL can never sound well. / All is lost that is poured into a cracked DISH. / GLASS, china, and reputations are easily cracked and never well mended.

crackling As the crackling of thorns under a pot, so the laughter of a fool. *Rec. dist.:* Utah.

cradle **1.** Pretty in the cradle, homely at the table. *Vars.:* **(a)** Cute in the cradle, homely at the table. **(b)** Homely in the cradle, pretty at the table. *Rec. dist.:* Minn., Ohio.

2. The cradle empty blesses us more than the cradle full. *Rec. dist.:* N.Y., S.C. *1st cit.:* US1887 Beecher, *Proverbs from Plymouth Pulpit.* *20c. coll.:* Stevenson 450:9.

3. What is learned in the cradle lasts to the grave. *Rec. dist.:* Ill., Ohio.

SEE ALSO The HAND that rocks the cradle is the hand that rules the world.

craft **1.** Of all crafts, to be an honest man is the master craft. *Rec. dist.:* Kans. *1st cit.:* 1732 Fuller, *Gnomologia.* *20c. coll.:* Stevenson 282:4.

2. Think no shame of your craft. *Rec. dist.:* Ill.

SEE ALSO Too much COURTESY, too much craft. / A grain of PRUDENCE is worth a pound of craft.

crank It takes a crank to start the wheel. *Rec. dist.:* Vt.

crave *SEE* It is PRIDE, not nature, that craves much. / SPARE and have is better than spend and crave.

craving Shameless craving must have shameless refusing. *Rec. dist.:* Mich. *1st cit.:* ca1546 Heywood, *Dialogue of Proverbs*, ed.

Habernicht (1963). **20c. coll.:** *ODEP* 720, Stevenson 149:3.

craw *SEE* A HEN with biddies never burst her craw.

crawl One must crawl before he walks. **Vars.:** **(a)** A child must learn to crawl before it can learn to walk. **(b)** You have to crawl before you can walk. **Rec. dist.:** U.S., Can. **1st cit.:** ca1350 *Douce MS 52*, ed. Förster (1906); US1737 *Jonathan Belcher Papers,* Mass.Hist.Soc. *Collections* (1893–94). **20c. coll.:** *ODEP* 120, Whiting 70, *CODP* 240, Whiting*(MP)* 138.

crazy A crazy man thinks everyone crazy but himself. **Rec. dist.:** Ont.

creaking *SEE* A creaking DOOR never falls from its hinges. / The creaking HINGE gets the oil.

cream **1.** Cream always comes to the top. **Rec. dist.:** Ind. **1st cit.:** US1841 Emerson, "Manners" in *Essays.* **20c. coll.:** Stevenson 451:10.

2. Don't expect to enjoy the cream of life if you keep your milk of human kindness bottled up. **Rec. dist.:** Utah.

3. It is not well for a man to pray cream and live skim milk. **Rec. dist.:** Ohio.

4. Put cream and sugar on a fly and it tastes very much like a black raspberry. **Rec. dist.:** N.Y., S.C.

5. You can whip our cream, but you can't beat our milk. **Rec. dist.:** Ill.
SEE ALSO EVERYTHING is not all peaches and cream.

create If you would create something, you must be something. **Rec. dist.:** Oreg.
SEE ALSO All MEN are created equal.

creator Remember your creator in the days of your youth. **Rec. dist.:** Ohio. **1st cit.:** US1948 Stevenson, *Home Book of Proverbs.* **20c. coll.:** Stevenson 2661:12.

creature *SEE* KINDNESS is seldom thrown away, be it given to the highest or lowliest of creatures.

credit **1.** A man who gives credit loses friends, money, and customers. **Rec. dist.:** N.C.

2. Credit is better than ready money. **Rec. dist.:** Ind.

3. Credit is suspicion asleep. **Rec. dist.:** Ill.

4. Credit makes enemies. **Rec. dist.:** Ind., Wis.

5. Do not take credit that is due to others. **Rec. dist.:** Kans.

6. Give credit to whom credit is due. **Rec. dist.:** Wis. **1st cit.:** US1777 *Letters of Samuel Adams,* 29 Oct., Mass.Hist.Soc. *Collections* (1917). **20c. coll.:** *CODP* 45, Whiting*(MP)* 137.

7. He who drinks on credit gets double drunk. **Rec. dist.:** Okla.

8. It's amazing how much good you can do if you don't care who gets the credit. **Var.:** You can get anything done if you don't care who gets the credit for it. **Rec. dist.:** Kans., Wis.

9. Lost credit is like a broken mirror. **Rec. dist.:** Ill.

10. No man's credit is as good as his money. **Rec. dist.:** N.Y., S.C. **1st cit.:** 1926 Howe, *Sinner Sermons.* **20c. coll.:** Stevenson 452:1.

11. Shake not the credit of others in endeavoring to establish your own. **Rec. dist.:** Mich.

12. The other face of credit is debt. **Rec. dist.:** Ill.

13. Your credit is worth more than your capital. **Rec. dist.:** Kans.
SEE ALSO Only aim to do your DUTY, and mankind will give you credit where you fail.

creditor **1.** Creditors have better memories than debtors. **Rec. dist.:** U.S., Can. **1st cit.:** 1659 Howell, *Paroimiografia (Spanish Proverbs);* US1736 Franklin, *PRAlmanac.* **20c. coll.:** *ODEP* 154, Whiting 87, Stevenson 530:12.

2. The creditors are a superstitious sect, great observers of set days and times. **Rec. dist.:** Ill., N.Y., S.C. **1st cit.:** US1737 Franklin, *PRAlmanac.* **20c. coll.:** Stevenson 223:3.

credulity Credulity is not a crime. **Rec. dist.:** N.Y., S.C. **1st cit.:** US1794 Paine, *Age of Reason* in *Writings of Thomas Paine,* ed. Foner (1945). **20c. coll.:** Stevenson 452:13.

credulous Credulous men are the prey of crafty ones. *Rec. dist.:* Mich.

creed Creeds for the credulous. *Rec. dist.:* N.Y., S.C. *1st cit.:* US1897 Sherman, *The Goal. 20c. coll.:* Stevenson 435:5.

See also Good DEEDS are better than creeds.

creep 1. Creep and creep beats hop and sleep. *Rec. dist.:* Ill.

2. You must creep before you can crawl. *Vars.:* (a) Creep before you leap. (b) Creep before you walk. (c) First creep, then go. (d) Learn to creep before you run. (e) Learn to creep before you walk. *Rec. dist.:* U.S., Can. *1st cit.:* ca1350 *Douce MS 52*, ed. Förster (1906); US1733 *Jonathan Belcher Papers*, Mass.Hist.Soc. Collections (1893–94). *20c. coll.:* ODEP 120, Whiting 70, *CODP* 240, Stevenson 722:14, Whiting*(MP)* 138.

See also LOVE will creep where it cannot go.

crew There's always three crews on a job: one coming, one working, and one leaving. *Rec. dist.:* Wash.

crib *See* CORN makes mo' at de mill dan it does in de crib.

crime 1. Crime doesn't pay. *Var.:* Crime doesn't pay like it used to. *Rec. dist.:* U.S., Can. *Infm.:* A slogan of the FBI and the famous cartoon character Dick Tracy. *1st cit.:* US1927 Martin, *Mosaic. 20c. coll.:* Whiting*(MP)* 139, Stevenson 453:11.

2. Crime is the root of all evil. *Rec. dist.:* N.Y.

3. Crime must be concealed by crime. *Rec. dist.:* Ill. *1st cit.:* US1948 Stevenson, *Home Book of Proverbs. 20c. coll.:* Stevenson 453:7

4. Crimes, like virtues, have their own rewards. *Rec. dist.:* N.J. *1st cit.:* 1702 Farquhar, *Inconstant. 20c. coll.:* Stevenson 453:12.

5. From one crime learn the nature of all. *Rec. dist.:* N.J.

6. He acts the third crime that defends the first. *Rec. dist.:* Ill.

7. He that carries a small crime easily, will carry it on when it comes to be an ox. *Rec. dist.:* N.Y., S.C.

8. If you commit a crime in the mind, you may transmit it into action. *Rec. dist.:* Ill.

9. If you share your friend's crime, you make it your own. *Rec. dist.:* Ill.

10. It is unlawful to overcome crime by crime. *Rec. dist.:* Ill.

11. Large habits become small crimes. *Rec. dist.:* N.Y.

12. No crime is founded upon reason. *Rec. dist.:* Ill.

13. Petty crimes are punished; great ones are rewarded. *Rec. dist.:* Ill.

14. The greater the man, the greater the crime. *Rec. dist.:* Ill. *1st cit.:* 1596 Shakespeare, *Edward III*, Shakespeare Apocrypha (1908). *20c. coll.:* ODEP 336, Stevenson 1032:9.

15. The weed of crime bears bitter fruit. *Var.:* The tree of crime bears bitter fruit. *Rec. dist.:* Ind., Ohio, Oreg.

16. What greater crime than loss of time? *Rec. dist.:* N.J.

17. When you have committed a crime, the whole world is a looking glass. *Var.:* Commit a crime and the earth is made of glass. *Rec. dist.:* Ind., N.Y., S.C.

18. Whenever a man commits a crime, God finds a witness. *Rec. dist.:* N.Y., S.C.

See also IGNORANCE is the father of crime. / POVERTY is no crime. / POVERTY is the mother of crime; want of sense is the father.

criminal 1. Mercy to the criminal may be cruelty to the people. *Rec. dist.:* Utah. *1st cit.:* 1711 Addison, *Spectator. 20c. coll.:* ODEP 526.

2. Once a criminal always a criminal. *Rec. dist.:* Ind.

cripple 1. Associate with cripples and you learn to limp. *Rec. dist.:* Alaska. *1st cit.:* ca1535 Elyot, *Education;* US1970 Masterson, *Death of Me Yet. 20c. coll.:* ODEP 210, Whiting*(MP)* 139.

2. It's ill halting before a cripple. *Rec. dist.:* Ind. *1st cit.:* ca1374 Chaucer, *Troilus and Criseyde. 20c. coll.:* ODEP 345, Stevenson 455:1.

See also A LIAR is sooner caught than a cripple.

critic 1. Make each day a critic on the last. *Rec. dist.:* N.J.

2. Man's most severe critic is himself. *Rec. dist.:* Iowa.

3. No critic has ever settled anything. *Rec. dist.:* N.Y., S.C. *1st cit.:* 1913 Huneker, *Pathos of Distance.* *20c. coll.:* Stevenson 456:12.

4. The public is the only critic whose opinion is worth anything at all. *Rec. dist.:* N.Y., S.C. *1st cit.:* US1870 Twain, *General Reply.* *20c. coll.:* Stevenson 457:4.

5. There's no statue built for critics. *Rec. dist.:* Miss.

critical It's much easier to be critical than correct. *Rec. dist.:* Ill., Ky., N.Y. *1st cit.:* 1860 Disraeli, Speech to House of Commons, 24 Jan. *20c. coll.:* Stevenson 458:1.

criticism 1. Against criticism a man can neither protest nor defend; he must act in spite of it. *Rec. dist.:* Miss.

2. Criticism is something you can avoid by saying nothing, doing nothing, and being nothing. *Rec. dist.:* R.I.

3. Criticism should rectify errors or improve the judgment. *Rec. dist.:* Mich.

4. The best place for criticism is in front of your mirror. *Rec. dist.:* Ind., N.Mex.

5. The most destructive criticism is indifference. *Rec. dist.:* N.Dak.

6. You do not get a man's most effective criticism until you provoke him. *Rec. dist.:* N.Y., S.C.

criticize 1. It ill behooves the best of us to criticize the rest of us. *Rec. dist.:* Oreg.

2. Unless you can do better, don't criticize. *Rec. dist.:* Utah.
See also Don't criticize a man's GAIT until you are in his shoes.

croak *See* FROGS do not croak in running water.

crook 1. A crook thinks every man is a crook. *Rec. dist.:* Ill.

2. Give a crook enough rope and he'll hang himself. *Rec. dist.:* Okla.

3. It is not easy to straighten in the oak the crook that grew in the sapling. *Rec. dist.:* N.Dak., Ohio.

4. It takes a crook to catch a crook. *Rec. dist.:* Ind., Kans.

5. No crook finds a jail nice enough to suit him. *Rec. dist.:* Ill.

6. Once a crook, always a crook. *Rec. dist.:* Oreg.

crooked 1. A crooked stick will cast a crooked shadow. *Rec. dist.:* U.S., Can. *1st cit.:* 1640 Herbert, *Outlandish Proverbs (Jacula Prudentum)* in *Works,* ed. Hutchinson (1941). *20c. coll.:* ODEP 769, Stevenson 458:11.

2. A man with a crooked career never ends well. *Rec. dist.:* N.Y.

3. Crooked furrows grow straight grain. *Rec. dist.:* Ont.

4. He that scoffs at the crooked had need go very upright himself. *Rec. dist.:* Mich.

crop 1. Don't reap your crop before you have planted it. *Rec. dist.:* Ohio.

2. When the crops are poorest, the crows are the peskiest. *Rec. dist.:* Ohio.
See also BABIES are one crop that never fails in Kansas. / The FARMER tickles the land and the crops tickle him. / Wild OATS are a sure crop and a big yield for the seed.

cross *(n.)* 1. After crosses and losses, men grow humbler and wiser. *Rec. dist.:* N.Y.

2. Crosses are the ladders to heaven. *Var.:* Crosses are ladders that lead to heaven, but few of us want to climb. *Rec. dist.:* Ill. *1st cit.:* 1616 Draxe, *Bibliotheca Scholastica* in *Anglia* (1918). *20c. coll.:* ODEP 156, CODP 45, Stevenson 459:7.

3. No cross, no crown. *Rec. dist.:* Okla., Tex., Vt. *1st cit.:* 1609 Bretnor, *Almanac*; US1809 Weems, *Life of Gen. Francis Marion* (1815). *20c. coll.:* ODEP 568, Whiting 88, Stevenson 460:7.

4. To everyone his own cross is heaviest. *Rec. dist.:* Ill. *1st cit.:* 1611 Cotgrave, *Dictionary of French and English Tongues.* *20c. coll.:* Stevenson 256:7.

5. When we suffer a great loss, we must bear our cross. *Rec. dist.:* Ill.

6. Where the cross is, there is light. *Rec. dist.:* Utah.

cross *(v.)*   SEE Don't cross the BRIDGE till you come to it. / To learn about one's DISPOSITION, we must cross him. / No RACE is won or lost until the line is crossed.

crow *(n.)*   **1.** A crow does not pull out the eye of another crow. *Vars.:* **(a)** A crow doesn't pick out the eye of another crow. **(b)** Crows are smart enough not to peck out each other's eyes. *Rec. dist.:* Ill. *1st cit.:* 1573 Sanford, *Garden of Pleasure.* *20c. coll.:* ODEP 359, CODP 109, Stevenson 462:5.

2. A crow in a cage won't talk like a parrot. *Rec. dist.:* N.Y.

3. A crow is no whiter for being washed. *Var.:* A crow is never the whiter for often washing. *Rec. dist.:* Mich., Miss., Ohio. *1st cit.:* 1578 Yver, *Courtlie Controversies of Cupids Cantles,* tr. Wotton. *20c. coll.:* ODEP 156, Stevenson 463:3.

4. A dish of crow won't gag you if you've got a strong stomach. *Rec. dist.:* Ohio.

5. Crow an' corn can't grow in de same fiel'. *Rec. dist.:* N.Y. *1st cit.:* US1880 Harris, "Plantation Proverbs" in *Uncle Remus, His Songs and His Sayings* (1881). *20c. coll.:* Stevenson 462:8.

6. Crow's feet are always on the ground. *Rec. dist.:* Ohio.

7. Crows are black the world over. *Var.:* Crows are black all the world over. *Rec. dist.:* Ill. *1st cit.:* US1875 Scarborough, *Chinese Proverbs.* *20c. coll.:* Stevenson 463:5.

8. Crows weep for the dead lamb and then devour him. *Rec. dist.:* Ill.

9. Each old crow thinks her young are the blackest. *Vars.:* **(a)** Each crow thinks its own little crow is the blackest. **(b)** Every crow thinks her baby is blackest. **(c)** Every crow thinks her own bird the blackest. **(d)** Every crow thinks his own the whitest. **(e)** Every crow thinks his wing is blackest. **(f)** Every mother crow thinks hers the whitest. **(g)** The crow thinks her own bird the fairest. *Rec. dist.:* U.S., Can. *1st cit.:* 1513 Virgil, *Aeneid,* tr. Douglas; US1639 Howes in *Winthrop Papers, 1498–1649,* Mass.Hist.Soc. *Collections* (1929–47). *20c. coll.:* ODEP 156, Whiting 88, Stevenson 462:4.

10. From a crow's beak comes a crow's voice. *Rec. dist.:* N.C.

crow *(v.)*   **1.** Don't crow unless you've something to crow about. *Rec. dist.:* Miss.

2. Never crow till you're out of the woods. *Var.:* Don' crow till yuh git out o' de woods; dey might be uh beah behin' de las' tree. *Rec. dist.:* N.Y., Ont.

SEE ALSO As the old COCK crows, the young cock learns. / If you are a COCK, crow; if a hen, lay eggs. / The COCK crows at sunrise to tell us to rise. / The ROOSTER can crow, but it's the hen that delivers the goods.

crowd   **1.** A crowd is not company. *Rec. dist.:* U.S., Can. *1st cit.:* 1625 Bacon, "Friendship" in *Essays,* ed. Arber (1897). *20c. coll.:* ODEP 157, Stevenson 463:11.

2. The man who follows the crowd often follows his doom. *Rec. dist.:* Ill.

3. When three is a crowd, adding one will often thin it out. *Rec. dist.:* N.Y.

SEE ALSO Two is company; three is a crowd.

crowded   SEE FEAST and your halls are crowded.

crowing   SEE A whistling GIRL and a crowing hen always end in the devil's den.

crown   **1.** A crown is no cure for a headache. *Vars.:* **(a)** A crown will not cure the headache, nor a golden slipper the gout. **(b)** The royal crown cures not the headache. *Rec. dist.:* U.S., Can. *1st cit.:* ca1580 Sidney, *Arcadia;* US1757 Franklin, *PRAlmanac.* *20c. coll.:* ODEP 157, Stevenson 464:9.

2. Uneasy is the head that wears the crown. *Vars.:* **(a)** Heavy is the head that wears the crown. **(b)** Uneasy lies the head that wears the crown. *Rec. dist.:* U.S., Can. *1st cit.:* 1597 Shakespeare, *Henry IV, Part 2.* *20c. coll.:* Stevenson 464:12.

SEE ALSO The greater the BURDENS, the brighter the crown. / No CROSS, no crown.

crowning Crowning a clown won't make him a king. *Rec. dist.:* Ind.

cruel SEE Better no RULE than a cruel rule.

cruelty Cruelty to a female is the crime of a monster. *Rec. dist.:* Mich.

crumb SEE Rich men's TABLES have few crumbs.

crumble SEE WALLS of sand are sure to crumble.

crush SEE A stout HEART crushes ill luck. / The boneless TONGUE, so small and weak, can crush and kill.

crust 1. It takes dough to have crust. *Rec. dist.:* Oreg.

2. It's a poor crust that can't grease its own plate. *Rec. dist.:* Vt.

SEE ALSO PROMISES are like piecrust: they are made to be broken.

crutch De one dat drap de crutch de bes gits de mos' biscuits. *Rec. dist.:* N.Y., Tex. *Infm.:* The crippled servant who appears the most helpless gets the most biscuits (i.e., by dropping his crutch).

SEE ALSO LITERATURE is a bad crutch but a good walking stick.

cry *(n.)* Great cry but little wool. *Rec. dist.:* N.H., N.J., R.I. *1st cit.:* ca1475 Fortescue, *Governance of England;* US1686 Dunton, *Letters from New England,* Publ. Prince Soc. (1867). *20c. coll.:* ODEP 333, Whiting 88, CODP 156, Stevenson 465:14, T&W 86, Whiting*(MP)* 142.

cry *(v.)* 1. Don't cry "holloa" till you're out of the wood. *Rec. dist.:* Ont. *1st cit.:* 1792 D'Arblay (a.k.a. Burney), *Diary;* US1770 Papers of Benjamin Franklin, ed. Labaree (1959). *20c. coll.:* ODEP 345, Whiting 495, Stevenson 2591:2, CODP 105, T&W 411, Whiting*(MP)* 696.

2. Don't cry over spilt milk. *Vars.:* **(a)** Don't cry over spilled milk. **(b)** Nay, 'tis no use crying for spilt milk. **(c)** Never cry over spilt milk. **(d)** No weeping for shed milk. **(e)** There's no use to cry over spilled milk. *Rec. dist.:* U.S., Can. *1st cit.:* 1659 Howell, *Paroimiografia (English Proverbs);* US1757 Papers of Henry Laurens, ed. Hamer (1968). *20c. coll.:* ODEP

159, Whiting 289, *CODP* 46, Stevenson 1573:9, T&W 243, Whiting*(MP)* 411.

3. Don't cry till you are hurt. *Rec. dist.:* U.S., Can. *1st cit.:* 1548 *Reliquiae Antiquae* (1843). *20c. coll.:* ODEP 158, Stevenson 466:1.

4. He who cries in bed will soon be dead. *Rec. dist.:* W.Va.

5. Those who cry the hardest are not always the most hurt. *Rec. dist.:* N.Y.

6. You must never cry so hard about your hard luck that you can't hear opportunity knocking. *Rec. dist.:* Kans.

SEE ALSO A DOG will not cry if you beat him with a bone. / When a GIRL whistles, the angels cry. / It is better to LAUGH than to cry. / LAUGH and the world laughs with you; cry and you cry alone. / LAUGH before breakfast, cry before sunset. / Never cry WOLF when not in danger.

crying 1. We are born crying, live complaining, and die disappointed. *Rec. dist.:* Wis.

2. You can't see the sun when you're crying. *Rec. dist.:* Ont.

cuckold The cuckold is the last that knows of it. *Rec. dist.:* Ill. *1st cit.:* 1604 Marston, *What You Will. 20c. coll.:* ODEP 159, Stevenson 467:5.

cuckoo The cuckoo of summer is the scald crow of winter. *Rec. dist.:* Minn.

cuffing SEE The TONGUE offends, and the ears get the cuffing.

cultivate SEE Cultivate FRIENDS who pray for you, not prey upon you. / Soil and FRIENDSHIP must be cultivated. / Every man should cultivate his own GARDEN.

culture Culture is one thing, and varnish is another. *Rec. dist.:* N.Y., S.C.

cunning *(n.)* 1. Cunning is more than strength. *Rec. dist.:* S.C. *1st cit.:* 1736 Bailey, "Wiles" in *Dictionary. 20c. coll.:* Stevenson 470:6.

2. Cunning is the ape of wisdom. *Rec. dist.:* Mich. *1st cit.:* 1732 Fuller, *Gnomologia. 20c. coll.:* Stevenson 469:6.

3. Cunning is the dwarf of wisdom. *Rec. dist.:*

Wis. *1st cit.:* 1732 Fuller, *Gnomologia.* *20c. coll.:* Stevenson 469:6.

4. Cunning often outwits itself. *Rec. dist.:* Ind.

5. The greatest cunning is to have none at all. *Rec. dist.:* Ill.

6. Too much cunning overreaches itself. *Rec. dist.:* Ohio, Utah.

SEE ALSO COMMON SENSE is always worth more than cunning.

cunning *(adj.)* **1.** A cunning man is overmatched by a cunning man and a half. *Var.:* Don't think so much of your own cunning as to forget other men's; a cunning man is overmatched by a cunning man and a half. *Rec. dist.:* Ill., N.Y., S.C. *1st cit.:* US1754 Franklin, *PRAlmanac.* *20c. coll.:* Stevenson 469:9.

2. A cunning man overreaches no one so much as himself. *Rec. dist.:* Ont.

3. One man may be more cunning than another but not more cunning than everybody else. *Rec. dist.:* Calif., N.Y., S.C. *1st cit.:* US1734 Franklin, *PRAlmanac.* *20c. coll.:* Stevenson 469:13.

4. The cunning man steals a horse; the wise man lets him alone. *Rec. dist.:* N.Y., S.C. *1st cit.:* US1735 Franklin, *PRAlmanac.* *20c. coll.:* Stevenson 856:8.

SEE ALSO It is a cunning part to play the FOOL well.

cup **1.** A full cup must be carried steadily. *Vars.:* (a) A full cup needs a steady hand. (b) When the cup is full, carry it even. *Rec. dist.:* U.S., Can. *1st cit.:* ca1025 *Durham Proverbs;* US1836 *Works of Ralph Waldo Emerson,* ed. Cabot. *20c. coll.:* CODP 88, Stevenson 471:4, ODEP 160, T&W 87.

2. A rose leaf on the "beaker's brim" causes the overflow of the cup. *Rec. dist.:* Oreg.

3. The last drop wobbles; the cup flows over. *Var.:* The last drop makes the cup run over. *Rec. dist.:* N.J., Okla., Tex. *1st cit.:* 1655 Fuller, *Church-History of Britain.* *20c. coll.:* CODP 128.

4. The optimist's cup is half full; the pessimist's cup is half empty. *Rec. dist.:* Oreg.

5. When the cup of happiness overflows, disaster follows. *Rec. dist.:* Ariz.

6. While drinking from one cup, look not into another. *Var.:* No man, while drinking one cup, should have his eye on another. *Rec. dist.:* N.J., Wis.

7. You can't escape the hemlock cup. *Rec. dist.:* Oreg.

SEE ALSO LIFE is not a cup to be drained but a measure to be filled. / There is many a SLIP 'twixt cup and lip.

Cupid Cupid is a blind gunner. *Rec. dist.:* N.J., Wis. *1st cit.:* 1699 Farquhar, *Love and a Bottle.* *20c. coll.:* Stevenson 471:5.

cur A mischievous cur must be tied short. *Rec. dist.:* N.Y. *1st cit.:* 1592 Delamothe, *Treasury of French Tongue.* *20c. coll.:* ODEP 162.

cure *(n.)* **1.** A pound of cure will not pay an ounce of debt. *Rec. dist.:* N.Y.

2. As a cure for worry, work is better than whiskey. *Rec. dist.:* Utah.

3. Desperate cures to desperate ills apply. *Var.:* A desperate disease must have a desperate cure. *Rec. dist.:* Ill., Oreg. *1st cit.:* 1539 Taverner, *Proverbs of Erasmus;* US1646 Winslow, *Hypocrisie Unmasked,* ed. Chapin, Providence (1916). *20c. coll.:* ODEP 178, Whiting 110, Stevenson 1951:4, T&W 56.

4. Easy to get a thousand prescriptions, hard to obtain a cure. *Rec. dist.:* Ind.

5. It is part of the cure to wish to be cured. *Rec. dist.:* N.Y. *1st cit.:* 1567 Pickering, *Horestes.* *20c. coll.:* ODEP 611, Stevenson 1558:2.

6. The best cure for drunkenness is, while sober, to see a drunken man. *Rec. dist.:* N.J., Ohio.

7. The cure may be worse than the disease. *Rec. dist.:* U.S., Can. *1st cit.:* 1582 Mulcaster, *Elementary;* US1633 Howes in *Winthrop Papers, 1498–1649,* Mass.Hist.Soc. *Collections* (1929–47). *20c. coll.:* ODEP 671, Whiting 360, Stevenson 1952:6, Whiting(MP) 144.

8. There is no cure for the firewater's burn. *Rec. dist.:* N.J.

9. There is no greater cure for misery than hard work. *Rec. dist.:* Ind.

SEE ALSO AMBITION is no cure for love. / A

CROWN is no cure for a headache. / An ounce of PREVENTION is worth a pound of cure.

cure *(v.)* **1.** What can't be cured must be endured. *Rec. dist.:* U.S., Can. *1st cit.:* ca1377 Langland, *Piers Plowman,* ed. Skeat, E.E.T.S. (1867); US1698 *Diary of Samuel Sewall, 1674–1729,* Mass.Hist.Soc. *Collections* (1878–82). *20c. coll.:* ODEP 161, Whiting 90, *CODP* 46, Stevenson 683:12, T&W 87, Whiting*(MP)* 144.

SEE ALSO A DISEASE known is half cured. / If the DOCTOR cures, the sun sees it; if he kills, the earth hides it. / People should cure their own FAULTS before finding faults in others. / He who is born a FOOL is never cured. / The day you MARRY it is either kill or cure. / PATIENCE cures many an old complaint. / PHYSICIANS kill more than they cure. / PRIDE and the gout are seldom cured throughout.

curiosity **1.** Curiosity has a spiteful way of turning back on the curious. *Rec. dist.:* N.Y., S.C. *1st cit.:* US1943 Disney, *Crimson Friday.* *20c. coll.:* Stevenson 472:7.

2. Curiosity killed the cat. *Vars.:* **(a)** Curiosity killed the cat, but satisfaction brought it back. **(b)** Curiosity killed the cat; satisfaction cured her. **(c)** Too much curiosity killed the cat. *Rec. dist.:* U.S., Can. *1st cit.:* US1909 Henry, *Schools and Schools.* *20c. coll.:* Stevenson 472:9, *CODP* 46, Whiting*(MP)* 144.

3. Foolish curiosity and vanity often lead to misfortune. *Rec. dist.:* Kans., N.C.

currycomb A currycomb is equal to half feed. *Rec. dist.:* Miss.

curse *(n.)* **1.** Curses, like chickens, come home to roost. *Rec. dist.:* U.S., Can. *1st cit.:* ca1275 *Proverbs of Alfred,* E.E.T.S. (1872); US1855 Haliburton, *Nature and Human Nature.* *20c. coll.:* ODEP 162, T&W 88, *CODP* 47, Stevenson 473:11, Whiting*(MP)* 108–09.

2. Curses never put men in hearses, but lying tongues have dug many graves. *Rec. dist.:* Ill.

3. The curse sticks to the tongue of the curser. *Rec. dist.:* Ill. *1st cit.:* ca1389 Chaucer, *Parson's Tale.* *20c. coll.:* Stevenson 473:11.

SEE ALSO LOVE can be a blessing or a curse.

/ A light PURSE is a heavy curse. / WORK is not the curse, but drudgery is.

curse *(v.)* **1.** If you curse others, you will be cursed. *Rec. dist.:* N.C.

2. The man who curses prays to the devil. *Rec. dist.:* Ill.

cushion Them that never had a cushion never need one. *Rec. dist.:* Minn. *1st cit.:* 1859 Eliot, *Adam Bede.* *20c. coll.:* Stevenson 1496:9.

custom **1.** As times are, so are the customs. *Rec. dist.:* Ill.

2. Bad customs are better broke than kept up. *Var.:* Bad customs, like good cakes, should be broken. *Rec. dist.:* Tex., Vt. *1st cit.:* 1611 Cotgrave, *Dictionary of French and English Tongues;* US1765 *Legal Papers of John Adams,* eds. Wroth and Zobel (1965). *20c. coll.:* ODEP 25, Whiting 91, Stevenson 475:5.

3. Choose that which is best and custom will make it most agreeable. *Rec. dist.:* Ohio.

4. Compliance with bad customs argues cowardice and ends in loss of character. *Rec. dist.:* Mich.

5. Consent to common custom, but not to common folly. *Rec. dist.:* Mich.

6. Custom is a master that makes a slave of reason. *Rec. dist.:* Ill.

7. Custom is a second nature. *Var.:* Custom is almost second nature. *Rec. dist.:* Tex., Utah. *1st cit.:* ca1390 Gower, *Confessio Amantis.* *20c. coll.:* ODEP 162.

8. Custom is a tyrant. *Rec. dist.:* Ill. *1st cit.:* 1574 Guazzo, *Civile Conversation,* tr. Pettie, T.T. (1925). *20c. coll.:* Stevenson 476:11.

9. Custom is mummified by habit and glorified by law. *Rec. dist.:* Ill.

10. Custom is the great guide. *Rec. dist.:* Ill.

11. Custom is the reason of fools. *Rec. dist.:* Ill.

12. Custom surpasses nature. *Rec. dist.:* Mich.

13. Customs are more honored in the breach than the observance. *Rec. dist.:* Ill. *1st cit.:* 1600 Shakespeare, *Hamlet.* *20c. coll.:* ODEP 25, Stevenson 476:3.

14. Customs are stronger than laws. *Rec. dist.:*

N.J. *1st cit.:* 1640 Herbert, *Outlandish Proverbs (Jacula Prudentum)* in *Works,* ed. Hutchinson (1941). *20c. coll.:* Stevenson 475:7.

15. Ill customs grow apace. *Rec. dist.:* Mich. *1st cit.:* US1742 Franklin, *PRAlmanac. 20c. coll.:* Stevenson 476:1.

See also Every COUNTRY has its own customs. / The YOUNG are slaves to novelty, the old to customs.

customer **1.** It's better to handle a tough customer with kid gloves. *Rec. dist.:* Ill.

2. No matter how shoddy the goods, you can always find a customer. *Rec. dist.:* Ill.

3. The customer is always right. *Rec. dist.:* U.S., Can. *1st cit.:* US1928 Sandburg, *Good Morning, America. 20c. coll.: CODP* 47, Stevenson 477:9, Whiting*(MP)* 145.

cut *(n.)* **1.** A gaping cut always leaves a scar. *Rec. dist.:* N.Y.

2. A short cut is often the wrong cut. *Rec. dist.:* Oreg., R.I.

cut *(v.)* *See* A dull AXE may still cut. / You must cut your COAT according to your cloth. / You cannot cut CORN unless there is corn to cut. / If you can't make every EDGE cut, you can sure make it bruise. / MEASURE twice before you cut once. / Don't cut off your NOSE to spite your face. / A dull SAW cuts deepest. / Don't cut the SHEET to mend a dishcloth. / Better cut the SHOE than pinch the foot. / It's easy to STEAL from a cut loaf. / Let not your TONGUE cut your throat. / They who play with edged TOOLS must expect to be cut.

D

dab Raw dabs make fat lads. *Rec. dist.:* Ill. *1st cit.:* 1678 Ray, *Proverbs (Scottish)*. *20c. coll.:* Stevenson 769:16.

dainties Who dainties love, shall beggars prove. *Rec. dist.:* Calif. *1st cit.:* 1573 Tusser, *Hundreth Good Pointes of Husbandrie;* US1749 Franklin, *PRAlmanac*. *20c. coll.:* ODEP 165, Whiting 92, Stevenson 479:10.

dainty *See* Too much PLENTY makes mouths dainty.

dairy You don't have to buy a dairy just because you want a glass of milk. *Var.:* You don't have to buy a cow just because you want a glass of milk. *Rec. dist.:* Wash.

daisy Daisies won't tell. *Rec. dist.:* Calif., Ill., Ind., Kans.

dam Where the dam is lowest the water first flows over. *Rec. dist.:* Ill.

damned *See* LIFE is just one damned thing after another.

dance *(n.)* What you lose in the dance, you make up in the turn about. *Rec. dist.:* Vt.
See also The PARROT has fine feathers, but he doesn't go to the dance. / A morning's RAIN is like an old woman's dance: it doesn't last long.

dance *(v.)* **1.** He dances well to whom fortune pipes. *Rec. dist.:* Can. *1st cit.:* ca1390 Chaucer, *Prologue to Reeve's Tale*. *20c. coll.:* ODEP 166, Stevenson 483:9.

2. If you don't know how to dance, you say that the drum is bad. *Rec. dist.:* N.Y.

3. If you want to dance, you must pay the fiddler. *Vars.:* **(a)** He who dances must pay the fiddler. **(b)** He who dances pays the fiddler. **(c)** He who dances shall pay the fiddler. **(d)** If you dance, you must pay the piper. **(e)** If you're going to dance, you must pay the fiddler. **(f)** The dancer must pay the fiddler. **(g)** The dancer must pay the piper. **(h)** The ones that dance have to pay the fiddler. **(i)** They who dance must pay the fiddler. **(j)**

Those who dance must pay the fiddler. **(k)** You may dance, but, remember, the fiddler is always to pay. *Rec. dist.:* U.S., Can. *1st cit.:* 1638 Taylor, *Taylor's Feast;* US1740 *Jonathan Belcher Papers,* Mass.Hist.Soc. *Collections* (1893–94). *20c. coll.:* ODEP 615, Whiting 149, CODP 48, Stevenson 1798:9, T&W 131, Whiting(MP) 495.

4. When you go to dance, take heed whom you take by the hand. *Rec. dist.:* Okla. *1st cit.:* 1621 Robinson, *Adagia in Latin and English*. *20c. coll.:* ODEP 166, Stevenson 481:1.

5. You can't dance at two weddings with one pair of feet. *Rec. dist.:* Calif.

dancing You need more than dancing shoes to be a dancer. *Rec. dist.:* Ill.

danger **1.** A common danger causes common action. *Rec. dist.:* Ill.

2. A danger foreseen is half avoided. *Rec. dist.:* Calif., Ill., Ind. *1st cit.:* 1611 Cotgrave, *Dictionary of French and English Tongues;* US1754 *Diary of Ebenezer Parkman,* ed. Wallett, Am.Antiq.Soc. *Proceedings* (1961–66). *20c. coll.:* Stevenson 483:15, Whiting 93, Whiting(MP) 149.

3. After the danger everyone is wise. *Rec. dist.:* Calif. *1st cit.:* 1523 Erasmus, *Adagia,* tr. Taverner. *20c. coll.:* Stevenson 2540:3.

4. Better face danger than be always in fear. *Rec. dist.:* Ill., Mich. *1st cit.:* 1542 Erasmus, *Apophthegms,* tr. Udall. *20c. coll.:* ODEP 167, Stevenson 485:7.

5. Danger begets caution. *Rec. dist.:* Ind.

6. Danger is next neighbor to security. *Rec. dist.:* Ill. *1st cit.:* 1607 *Dobson's Dry Bobs;* US1875 Scarborough, *Chinese Proverbs*. *20c. coll.:* ODEP 167, Stevenson 484:4.

7. Danger past, God is forgotten. *Rec. dist.:* Okla., Tex., Vt. *1st cit.:* 1571 Read, *Lord Burghley and Queen Elizabeth*. *20c. coll.:* ODEP 167, Stevenson 485:6.

8. Dangers are conquered by dangers. *Rec. dist.:* Ill. *1st cit.:* 1539 Publilius Syrus, *Senten-*

tiae, tr. Taverner. **20c. coll.:** *ODEP* 167, Stevenson 485:3.

9. He that loves danger shall perish therein. **Var.:** He who seeks danger will perish in its quest. **Rec. dist.:** Calif., Ill., R.I. **1st cit.:** ca1386 Chaucer, *Tale of Melibee.* **20c. coll.:** Stevenson 483:12.

10. Sweet is danger. **Rec. dist.:** Ill. **1st cit.:** 1579 Lyly, *Euphues, Anatomy of Wit;* US1753 Franklin, *PRAlmanac.* **20c. coll.:** Stevenson 484:7.

11. The more danger, the more honor. **Rec. dist.:** Okla. **1st cit.:** ca1534 Bouchiev, *Boke Huon de Bordeuxe,* E.E.T.S.; US1792 Brackenridge, *Modern Chivalry,* ed. Newlin (1937). **20c. coll.:** *ODEP* 641, Whiting 93, *CODP* 113, Stevenson 483:13.

12. There is danger in the absence of fear. **Rec. dist.:** Minn.

13. When danger is near, keep out of the way. **Rec. dist.:** N.Y.

SEE ALSO Out of DEBT, out of danger. / There is DELIGHT in danger and danger in delight. / When we have GOLD, we are in fear; when we have money, we are in danger. / NAUGHT is never in danger.

dangerous It's dangerous to dig pits for other folks; you'll fall in yourself. **Rec. dist.:** Ill. **1st cit.:** 1509 Barclay, *Ship of Fools,* ed. Jamieson in *Eclogues,* E.E.T.S. (1874); US1608 Wingfield, *Discourse,* Am.Antiq.Soc. *Transactions* (1860). **20c. coll.:** *ODEP* 187, Stevenson 1799:10, Whiting 339, Whiting(MP) 496.

SEE ALSO All DELAYS are dangerous in war. / DELAYS have dangerous ends. / An educated FOOL is dangerous. / A little KNOWLEDGE is a dangerous thing. / He who is always PRAYING has a dangerous life. / Sudden WEALTH is dangerous.

dangerously Great men live dangerously; small men don't take chances. **Rec. dist.:** N.Y.

dare *(n.)* **1.** A man that will take a dare will take a penny from a dead man's eye. **Rec. dist.:** Okla. **1st cit.:** US1836, *Col. Crockett's Exploits in Texas.* **20c. coll.:** T&W 280, Whiting(MP) 483.

2. Anybody that would take a dare would kill a sheep and eat the hair. **Rec. dist.:** Nebr.

dare *(v.)* **1.** Nothing dared, nothing gained. **Rec. dist.:** N.C. **Infm.:** A variation of "Nothing ventured, nothing gained."

2. Who dares wins. **Rec. dist.:** N.Y., S.C.

SEE ALSO Who dares NOTHING need hope for nothing. / Dare to be TRUE; nothing can need a lie.

darer Darer goes first. **Var.:** Darers go first. **Rec. dist.:** Ohio.

dark *(n.)* What goes on in the dark must come out in the light. **Rec. dist.:** N.J. **1st cit.:** ca1390 Gower, *Confessio Amantis,* E.E.T.S. (1900). **20c. coll.:** Stevenson 537:9.

SEE ALSO CHARACTER is what you are in the dark when no one is around. / Men fear DEATH as children do going in the dark. / FAITH is working in the dark. / He who is to break his NECK finds the stairs in the dark. / When we can't make light of our TROUBLES, we can keep them in the dark.

dark *(adj.)* **1.** It is always dark just under a lamp. **Vars.:** **(a)** It is always darkest under the lantern. **(b)** It is dark at the foot of a lighthouse. **Rec. dist.:** Ala., N.C. **1st cit.:** US1902 Belasco and Long, *Darling of the Gods.* **20c. coll.:** Stevenson 486:8.

2. It is always darkest before dawn. **Vars.:** **(a)** It's always dark before the sun shines. **(b)** It's always darkest just before dawn. **(c)** The darkest hour is just before dawn. **(d)** When the night is darkest, dawn's nearest. **Rec. dist.:** U.S., Can. **1st cit.:** 1650 Fuller, *Pisgah Sight of Palestine;* US1889 Stevenson, *Letters of R. L. Stevenson.* **20c. coll.:** *ODEP* 168, Stevenson 489:16, *CODP* 48.

SEE ALSO Some DAYS are darker than others. / The darkest HOUR has no more minutes in it than the brightest. / The darkest HOUR in any man's life is when he sits down to plan to get money without earning it.

darkness **1.** All the darkness in the world cannot put out a single candle. **Rec. dist.:** Calif., N.Y.

2. Darkness and light cannot dwell together. **Rec. dist.:** N.C.

3. Darkness has no shame. **Rec. dist.:** Ill.

4. Darkness is the owl's desire. **Rec. dist.:** Minn.

SEE ALSO It's always better to light a CAN-DLE than to curse the darkness.

darling Better an old man's darling than a young man's slave. *Vars.:* **(a)** I had rather be a poor man's darling than a rich man's slave. **(b)** It is better to be an old man's darling than a young man's slave. *Rec. dist.:* U.S., Can. *1st cit.:* 1546 Heywood, *Dialogue of Proverbs,* ed. Habernicht (1963). *20c. coll.:* ODEP 51, CODP 14, Stevenson 1542:8.

SEE ALSO A WIFE is a young man's slave and an old man's darling.

dash SEE A man's DESTINY is always dashed. / Follow not TRUTH too near the heels lest it dash out your teeth.

date SEE Bad LUCK can't be dated.

daughter **1.** A diamond daughter turns to glass as a wife. *Rec. dist.:* N.J.

2. An undutiful daughter will prove an unmanageable wife. *Rec. dist.:* N.J. *1st cit.:* 1862 Hislop, *Proverbs of Scotland;* US1752 Franklin, *PRAlmanac. 20c. coll.:* Stevenson 488:8.

3. Daughters are brittle ware. *Rec. dist.:* Ill.

4. Deacons' daughters and ministers' sons are the biggest devils that ever run. *Rec. dist.:* Vt. *1st cit.:* US1855 Haliburton, *Nature and Human Nature. 20c. coll.:* T&W 94, Whiting(MP) 413.

5. First a daughter, then a son, and the family's well begun. *Rec. dist.:* N.Y.

6. He that would the daughter win would with the mother begin. *Vars.:* **(a)** He who would the daughter win with the mother must begin. **(b)** Sweet-talk the old lady to get the daughter. **(c)** Who the daughter would win with mama must begin. *Rec. dist.:* U.S., Can. *1st cit.:* 1578 Wotton, *Courtlie Controversie of Cupids Cantels. 20c. coll.:* ODEP 168, Stevenson 1628:2.

7. It is harder to marry a daughter well then to bring her up well. *Rec. dist.:* N.Dak. *1st cit.:* 1732 Fuller, *Gnomologia. 20c. coll.:* Stevenson 499:10.

8. The daughter of a spry old woman makes a poor housekeeper. *Rec. dist.:* Miss.

SEE ALSO Observe the MOTHER and take the daughter. / Marry your SON when you please and your daughter when you can. / My son's

my SON till he gets him a wife; my daughter's my daughter all of her life.

daughter-in-law **1.** A bad daughter-in-law is worse than a thousand devils. *Rec. dist.:* Calif., N.Y.

2. Daughters-in-law become mothers-in-law. *Rec. dist.:* Alaska.

SEE ALSO The MOTHER-IN-LAW remembers not that she was a daughter-in-law.

dawn Get up with the dawn and you can sleep until noon. *Rec. dist.:* R.I.

SEE ALSO It is always DARKEST before dawn. / The big POSSUM walks just before the dawn.

day **1.** A bad day never has a good night. *Var.:* It is never a bad day that has a good night. *Rec. dist.:* Ill., N.J., R.I., Vt. *1st cit.:* 1581 Lupton, *Siugila. 20c. coll.:* ODEP 25, Stevenson 1686:12.

2. A day lost is never found. *Rec. dist.:* Okla.

3. A day off is usually followed by an off day. *Rec. dist.:* N.Dak.

4. A day to come seems longer than a year that is gone. *Rec. dist.:* N.Y., S.C. *1st cit.:* 1732 Fuller, *Gnomologia. 20c. coll.:* Stevenson 490:15.

5. A wise man's day is worth a fool's life. *Rec. dist.:* Ohio.

6. Another day, another dollar. *Var.:* A new day, a new dollar. *Rec. dist.:* U.S. *1st cit.:* US1957 Erskine, *Pink Hotel. 20c. coll.:* Whiting(MP) 151.

7. As the day lengthens, the cold strengthens. *Rec. dist.:* N.Y., S.C. *1st cit.:* 1631 Pellham, *God's Power;* US1850 Judd, *Richard Edney and Governor's Family. 20c. coll.:* ODEP 169, T&W 93, Stevenson 494:7, Whiting(MP) 153.

8. Count each day that comes by gift of chance so much to the good. *Rec. dist.:* Calif., N.Y.

9. Dark days and storms heighten the appreciation of sunshine. *Rec. dist.:* Calif., N.Y.

10. Dere's come a day when you can't lay up a cent. *Rec. dist.:* Miss., N.Y.

11. Do not wait for a rainy day to fix your roof. *Rec. dist.:* Minn.

12. Drunken days have their tomorrow. *Rec.*

dist.: Ill. *1st cit.:* 1875 Smiles, *Thrift.* *20c. coll.:* ODEP 206, Stevenson 637:8.

13. Each day compel yourself to do something you would rather not do. *Rec. dist.:* Minn.

14. Every day has its night, every weal its woe. *Rec. dist.:* N.Y., S.C. *1st cit.:* 1846 Denham, *Proverbs.* *20c. coll.:* Stevenson 1687:2.

15. Go day, come day, God send Sunday. *Vars.:* **(a)** Day come, day go, God send Sunday. **(b)** Let every day provide for itself and God send Sunday. *Rec. dist.:* Ga., Ky., Vt. *1st cit.:* 1616 Draxe, *Bibliotheca Scholastica in Anglia* (1918); US1931 Tully, *Blood on the Moon.* *20c. coll.:* ODEP 134, Whiting(MP) 153.

16. It's a long day that has no ending. *Rec. dist.:* Minn.

17. Keep the weekdays honest and it will be easy to keep the Sabbath holy. *Rec. dist.:* Minn.

18. Live each day as though it were the last. *Var.:* Every day should be passed as if it were the last. *Rec. dist.:* Ind., Vt.

19. Live only for this day and you ruin tomorrow. *Rec. dist.:* Wis.

20. Many individuals shorten their days by lengthening their nights. *Rec. dist.:* Vt.

21. May the best day we have seen be the worst we have to come. *Rec. dist.:* Wis.

22. No day is over until the sun has set. *Rec. dist.:* Fla. *1st cit.:* 1639 Clarke, *Paroemiologia.* *20c. coll.:* Stevenson 490:9.

23. No day passes without some grief. *Rec. dist.:* R.I. *1st cit.:* 1616 Withals, *Short Dictionary.* *20c. coll.:* ODEP 169, Stevenson 491:2.

24. No day without a deed to crown it. *Vars.:* **(a)** Count the day lost whose low-descending sun views from your hand no worthy action done. **(b)** No day should pass without something being done. *Rec. dist.:* Calif., Ohio.

25. Nothing is harder to endure than a succession of good days. *Rec. dist.:* N.J.

26. On a hot day muffle yourself to move. *Rec. dist.:* Wis.

27. Praise a fine day at night. *Var.:* Praise not the day before the night. *Rec. dist.:* Wis. *1st cit.:* ca1350 *Douce MS 52,* ed. Förster (1906);

US1940 Thayer, *Guilty.* *20c. coll.:* ODEP 643, Stevenson 526:9, Whiting(MP) 154.

28. Pray each day that you might live; live each day that you pray. *Rec. dist.:* Vt.

29. Save your pennies for a rainy day. *Vars.:* **(a)** Put something away for a rainy day. **(b)** Save for a rainy day. **(c)** Save for a rainy day, 'cause there are clouds in the sky. **(d)** Save it for a rainy day. **(e)** Save your money for a rainy day. *Rec. dist.:* U.S., Can. *1st cit.:* ca1566 *Bugbears;* US1753 *Papers of Benjamin Franklin,* ed. Labaree (1959). *20c. coll.:* ODEP 663, Whiting 96, Stevenson 491:8, T&W 93, Whiting(MP) 154.

30. Some days are darker than others. *Rec. dist.:* Ill.

31. Some days it's not even worth getting up. *Rec. dist.:* Fla.

32. Some days you can't make a dollar. *Rec. dist.:* Fla.

33. Take each day as it comes. *Rec. dist.:* Calif., N.Y.

34. The best days are the first to flee. *Rec. dist.:* Ohio.

35. The better the day, the better the deed. *Rec. dist.:* U.S., Can. *1st cit.:* 1607 Middleton, *Michaelmas Terme;* US1677 Hubbard, *History of Indian Wars in New England,* ed. Drake, Roxbury, Mass. (1865). *20c. coll.:* ODEP 52, Whiting 95, CODP 16, Stevenson 492:3, T&W 93, Whiting(MP) 153.

36. The day has but one eye; the night has a thousand. *Vars.:* **(a)** The day has eyes; the night has ears. **(b)** The night has a thousand eyes and the day but one. *Rec. dist.:* Miss., Ohio.

37. The day never becomes brighter by finding fault with the sun. *Rec. dist.:* N.J.

38. The day that makes us happy makes us wise. *Rec. dist.:* Okla.

39. The good old days were once the present, too. *Rec. dist.:* Tenn.

40. The longest day will come to an end. *Vars.:* **(a)** Be the day never so long, at length comes the evensong. **(b)** Long as the day may be, the night comes at last. **(c)** The longest day will have an end. *Rec. dist.:* U.S., Can. *1st cit.:* ca1390 Gower, *Confessio Amantis,* E.E.T.S. (1900); US1969 Hale, *Life in the Studio.* *20c. coll.:* ODEP 482, Stevenson 494:10, Whiting*(MP)* 153.

41. The most utterly lost of all days is that on which you have not laughed. *Rec. dist.:* Ill.

42. The next day is never so good as the day before. *Rec. dist.:* Calif., Ohio. *1st cit.:* 1539 Publilius Syrus, *Sententiae,* tr. Taverner. *20c. coll.:* Stevenson 2341:1.

43. There are more days than sausage. *Rec. dist.:* N.Dak. *Infm.:* There's not enough food for the number of days.

44. Two good days for a man in this life: when he weds, and when he buries his wife. *Rec. dist.:* Calif., N.Y.

45. What a day may bring a day may take away. *Var.:* What a day may bring forth a night may take away. *Rec. dist.:* N.C., Okla., Tex. *1st cit.:* 1592 Delamothe, *Treasury of French Tongue.* *20c. coll.:* ODEP 169, Stevenson 491:1.

46. When a man prays one day and steals six, the great spirit thunders and the evil one laughs. *Rec. dist.:* N.J.

47. Who goes for a day into the forest should take bread for a week. *Rec. dist.:* Wis.

48. You can tell the day by the morning. *Rec. dist.:* R.I. *1st cit.:* 1574 Guazzo, *Civile Conversation,* tr. Pettie, T.T. (1925). *20c. coll.:* Stevenson 1624:6.

See also For AGE and want, save while you may, for no morning lasts all day. / Suppressing a moment of ANGER may save a day of sorrow. / An APPLE a day keeps the doctor away. / From the day you were born till you ride in a hearse, there's nothing so BAD but it might have been worse. / A BIT in the morning is better than nothing all day. / BUSYBODIES never want a bad day. / Many CHANGES can take place on a spring day. / CHILDHOOD shows the man as morning shows the day. / Do a good DEED every day. / Every DOG has his day. / People who DREAM all night don't work all day. / He who DRINKS and walks away lives to drink another day. / A continual

DROPPING on a very rainy day and a contentious woman are alike. / EAT, for some day you will be eaten. / FAIR and softly goes far in a day. / He that FIGHTS and runs away may live to fight another day. / FISH and callers smell in three days. / FRIDAY is the fairest or foulest day. / Every GIRL has her day. / There never was a GOOSE so gray but some gander will wander her way. / LEARN something new every day. / The day you MARRY it is either kill or cure. / A foul MORN turns into a fine day. / What is done in the NIGHT appears in the day. / ROME was not built in a day. / He who SLEEPS late has short days. / He who SMILES when he walks away will live to fight another day. / A SON is a son till he takes a wife; a daughter is a daughter all the days of her life. / The morning SUN never lasts a day. / Boast not of TOMORROW, for you know not what the day may bring forth. / TOMORROW is a new day. / That WOMAN is young that does not look a day older than she says she is. / The YEARS teach much that the days never knew.

daylight The morning daylight appears plainer when you put out your candle. *Rec. dist.:* Calif., N.Y.

See also GOLD, women, and linen should be chosen by daylight.

dead *(n.)* **1.** Bury your own dead. *Rec. dist.:* Fla. *Infm.:* This is a point of honor and standard operating procedure in the military services.

2. It's safer to commend the dead than the living. *Rec. dist.:* Calif., N.Y.

3. Let the dead bury the dead. *Rec. dist.:* Calif., N.Y. *1st cit.:* 1931 Huxley, *What Dare I Think;* US1815 Dow, *History of Cosmopolite.* *20c. coll.:* CODP 49, Whiting 97, Stevenson 502:6, Whiting*(MP)* 156.

4. Speak well of the dead. *Vars.:* **(a)** Don't talk about the dead. **(b)** Never speak ill of the dead. **(c)** Slander not the dead. *Rec. dist.:* U.S., Can. *1st cit.:* 1540 Erasmus, *Flores Sententiarum,* tr. Taverner; US1692 Bulkeley, *Will and Doom,* ed. Hoadly, Conn.Hist.Soc. *Collections* (1895). *20c. coll.:* ODEP 761, Whiting 97, Stevenson 520:7, T&W 94, Whiting*(MP)* 156.

5. The dead are always wrong. *Rec. dist.:* Ohio. *1st cit.:* US1816 Jefferson, *Letter to Samuel Kerchival.* *20c. coll.:* Stevenson 501:12.

6. The dead are soon forgotten. *Rec. dist.:* Calif.

dead *(adj.)* **1.** A dead man feels no cold. *Rec. dist.:* Ill.

2. A dead person is wept for for seven days; a fool, all his life. *Rec. dist.:* Calif., N.Y.

3. Better be dead than out of fashion. *Rec. dist.:* Tex., Vt.

4. Dead men don't walk again. *Rec. dist.:* N.Y.

5. Dead men never bite. *Vars.:* **(a)** Dead men bite not. **(b)** Dead men don't bite. *Rec. dist.:* N.Y. *1st cit.:* 1548 Hall, *Chronicle of Lancastre and York;* US1939 Queen, *Dragon's Teeth.* *20c. coll.:* ODEP 171, Whiting(MP) 393, CODP 49, Stevenson 504:9.

6. Dead men tell no tales. *Vars.:* **(a)** A dead dog tells no tales. **(b)** Dead men and ashes tell no tales. **(c)** Dead men don't talk. **(d)** The dead never tell. **(e)** The dead tell no tales. *Rec. dist.:* U.S., Can. *1st cit.:* ca1592 Bacon, *Of Fasting;* US1797 Cobbett, *Porcupine's Works.* *20c. coll.:* ODEP 171, Whiting 275, CODP 49, Stevenson 505:5, T&W 234, Whiting(MP) 393.

7. It will all be the same after you are dead a hundred years. *Rec. dist.:* Kans.

8. Near dead never filled the kirkyard. *Rec. dist.:* N.Y., S.C.

9. No man is dead till he's dead. *Rec. dist.:* N.Y., S.C. *1st cit.:* 1942 Beeding, *Twelve Disguises.* *20c. coll.:* Stevenson 499:6

10. When we're dead, we're dead for a long time. *Rec. dist.:* Ill. *1st cit.:* US1926 Lardner, *Zone of Quiet.* *20c. coll.:* Stevenson 500:7.

SEE ALSO A man is not completely BORN until he is dead. / Every man BORN is not dead yet. / The whiter the BREAD, the sooner you're dead. / A live COWARD is better than a dead hero. / Plain DEALING is dead, and died without issue. / Call no man HAPPY till he is dead. / Don't give up HOPE till hope is dead. / Don't pay for a dead HORSE. / When the HORSE is dead, the cow gets fat. / A good JAP is a dead Jap. / A LAZY man is no better than a dead

one, but he takes up more room. / There are two good MEN—one dead, the other unborn. / It is better to be a live RABBIT than a dead tiger. / Two can keep a SECRET if one is dead. / Don't pay for a dead man's SHOES. / He that waits for a dead man's SHOES may long go barefoot. / Count no man SUCCESSFUL until he is dead. / Earlier WED, sooner dead.

deaf None so deaf as he who won't hear. *Vars.:* **(a)** No ear is so deaf as one which wishes not hear. **(b)** None are so deaf as they that will not hear. **(c)** None so deaf as those that won't hear. **(d)** None so deaf as those who won't hear. **(e)** There is no one worse deaf than he who does not want to hear. **(f)** There is none so deaf as those who will not hear. **(g)** There's no more deaf man than the man who does not wish to hear. *Rec. dist.:* U.S., Can. *1st cit.:* 1546 Heywood, *Dialogue of Proverbs,* ed. Habernicht (1963); US1766 Parker in *Papers of Benjamin Franklin,* ed. Labaree (1959). *20c. coll.:* ODEP 172, Whiting 98, CODP 49, Stevenson 496:6, Whiting (MP) 157.

SEE ALSO No EAR is deaf to the song that gold sings. / A deaf HUSBAND and a blind wife are always a happy couple. / KINDNESS is language which the deaf can hear and the blind can see. / Hit's a mighty deaf NIGGER dat don't hear de dinner ho'n.

deal *(n.)* SEE If you want to know what a PERSON is, have a business deal with him.

deal *(v.)* Deal small and serve all. *Rec. dist.:* Vt.

SEE ALSO He becomes POOR that deals with a slack hand, but the hand of diligence makes rich.

dealing Plain dealing is dead, and died without issue. *Var.:* Poor plain dealing, dead without issue. *Rec. dist.:* N.Y., S.C. *1st cit.:* 1613 Adams, *White Devil;* US1750 Franklin, *PRAlmanac.* *20c. coll.:* ODEP 629, Stevenson 1805:14.

dear SEE All things are CHEAP to the saving, dear to the wasteful. / With the old year leave your FAULTS, however dear. / Make not your FRIEND too cheap to you, nor yourself too dear to him. / A man's HOUSE is only less dear to him than his honor. / Don't buy at too dear a PRICE.

death 1. After death, the doctor. *Rec. dist.:* Ind., N.J. *1st cit.:* ca1374 Chaucer, *Troilus and Criseyde.* *20c. coll.:* ODEP 6, Stevenson 1349:3.

2. Better death than dishonor. *Rec. dist.:* Calif., N.Y. *1st cit.:* 1932 Dawes, *Lawless;* US1931 Wylie, *Murderer Invisible.* *20c. coll.:* Whiting*(MP)* 158.

3. Death and life are in the power of the tongue. *Rec. dist.:* Minn.

4. Death cannot kill what never dies. *Rec. dist.:* Kans.

5. Death defies the doctor or employs him to do its job. *Var.:* Death defies the doctor. *Rec. dist.:* Ill., Ind., Okla. *1st cit.:* 1609 Shakespeare, *Cymbeline.* *20c. coll.:* Stevenson 512:1, ODEP 173.

6. Death devours lambs as well as sheep. *Rec. dist.:* Ill. *1st cit.:* 1620 Cervantes, *Don Quixote,* tr. Shelton. *20c. coll.:* ODEP 173.

7. Death fiddles and we dance. *Rec. dist.:* Calif., N.Y.

8. Death is a black camel which kneels at every man's gate. *Rec. dist.:* Ill. *1st cit.:* 1853 Trench, *On Lessons in Proverbs;* USca1900 Kenyon, *Black Camel.* *20c. coll.:* Stevenson 499:2.

9. Death is a great leveler. *Rec. dist.:* Ill., Okla. *1st cit.:* 1578 Florio, *Firste Fruites,* ed. Taihoku (1936); USca1656 Bradford, *History of Plymouth Plantation,* ed. Ford (1912). *20c. coll.:* ODEP 174, Whiting 99, CODP 51, Stevenson 513:4, Whiting*(MP)* 159.

10. Death is but death, and all in time shall die. *Rec. dist.:* N.Y., S.C. *1st cit.:* 1600 Shakespeare, *Hamlet;* US1634 Wood, *New-England's Prospects,* Publ. Prince Soc. (1865). *20c. coll.:* ODEP 173, Whiting 99.

11. Death is deaf and will hear no denial. *Rec. dist.:* Mich.

12. Death is no respecter of persons. *Var.:* Death and the grave make no distinction of persons. *Rec. dist.:* N.Y. *1st cit.:* ca1386 Chaucer, *Tale of Man of Law;* US1733 Franklin, *PRAlmanac.* *20c. coll.:* Stevenson 513:7.

13. Death is not chosen. *Rec. dist.:* N.Y.

14. Death is permanent. *Rec. dist.:* Ohio.

15. Death is sometimes a gift. *Rec. dist.:* Wis.

16. Death keeps no calendar. *Vars.:* (a) Death has no calendar. (b) Death has no schedule. *Rec. dist.:* N.Y., Vt. *1st cit.:* 1640 Herbert, *Outlandish Proverbs (Jacula Prudentum) in Works,* ed. Hutchinson (1941). *20c. coll.:* ODEP 174, Stevenson 509:5.

17. Death keeps no company. *Rec. dist.:* Calif., N.Y.

18. Death observes no ceremony. *Rec. dist.:* N.Y., S.C. *1st cit.:* US1717 Wise, *Vindication of the Government of New England Churches.* *20c. coll.:* Stevenson 505:7.

19. Death pays all debts. *Rec. dist.:* Calif., N.Y. *1st cit.:* 1592 Shakespeare, *Richard III;* US1742 *Colonial Records of Georgia,* ed. Chandler, in *Original Papers, 1735–1752* (1910–16). *20c. coll.:* ODEP 174, Whiting 99, CODP 50, Stevenson 508:2, Whiting*(MP)* 158.

20. Death rides with the drinking driver. *Rec. dist.:* Ill.

21. Death to the wolf is life to the lamb. *Rec. dist.:* Ill. *1st cit.:* 1573 Sanford, *Garden of Pleasure.* *20c. coll.:* ODEP 174, Stevenson 2088:1.

22. Death waits for no one. *Rec. dist.:* Ill.

23. Death's a great disguise. *Rec. dist.:* Calif., N.Y.

24. If you fear death, you're already dead. *Rec. dist.:* N.Y., S.C. *1st cit.:* 1534 Lupset, *Treatise, Teaching the Way of Dying Well.* *20c. coll.:* ODEP 251, Stevenson 516:2.

25. Men fear death as children do going in the dark. *Rec. dist.:* Calif., N.Y. *1st cit.:* 1607–12 Bacon, "Death" in *Essays.* *20c. coll.:* ODEP 249, Stevenson 515:3.

26. Nothing is certain except death and taxes. *Vars.:* (a) Death and taxes are the only things certain. (b) Death and taxes are the two things we can't beat. (c) Nothing is certain but death and taxes. (d) Nothing is certain in life but death and taxes. (e) Nothing is so sure as death. (f) Only two things in this life are certain—death and love. (g) There is nothing sure but death and taxes. *Rec. dist.:* U.S., Can.

1st cit.: 1726 Defoe, "Devil" in *History of Apparitions;* US1789 *Writings of Benjamin Franklin,* ed. Smyth (1905–07). *20c. coll.*: *CODP* 164, *ODEP* 580, Whiting 98, Stevenson 2282:10, Whiting*(MP)* 158.

27. Old men go to death, but death comes to young men. *Rec. dist.*: N.Dak. *1st cit.*: 1625 Bacon, *Apophthegms* in *Works,* ed. Chandos. *20c. coll.*: *ODEP* 591, Stevenson 524:10

28. One man's death is another man's bread. *Rec. dist.*: Wis.

29. The death of one dog is the life of another. *Rec. dist.*: Wis.

30. There is no death without a sin. *Rec. dist.*: Wis. *1st cit.*: US1875 Eddy, *Science and Health.* *20c. coll.*: Stevenson 2119:6.

31. There is no way of knowing when death will come; it just does. *Rec. dist.*: N.Y. *1st cit.*: ca1368 Chaucer, *Clerk's Tale.* *20c. coll.*: Stevenson 510:1.

32. When death knocks at your door, you must answer. *Rec. dist.*: Ill.

SEE ALSO ADVICE after mischief is taken like medicine after death. / Give a BEGGAR a horse and he'll ride it to death. / There are more ways to kill a CHICKEN than to kiss him to death. / Every DOOR may be shut but death's door. / Thousands DRINK themselves to death before one dies of thirst. / The FEAR of death is more to be dreaded than death itself. / Never run a free HORSE to death. / Live your own LIFE, for you die your own death. / LUCK is for the few, death for the many. / There is a MEDICINE for all things except death and taxes. / There is a REMEDY for everything but death. / The best way to kill TIME is to work it to death. / All VICTORY ends in the defeat of death. / They who live in WORRY invite death in a hurry.

debt **1.** A man in debt is caught in a net. *Rec. dist.*: Calif., N.Y.

2. A national debt, if it is not excessive, will be to us a national blessing. *Rec. dist.*: Calif., N.Y. *1st cit.*: US1813 Hamilton, Letter to Robert Morris, 30 Apr. *20c. coll.*: Stevenson 530:6.

3. A small debt makes a debtor, a heavy one

an enemy. *Rec. dist.*: Ill. *1st cit.*: 1732 Fuller, *Gnomologia.* *20c. coll.*: Stevenson 531:15.

4. Debt is a hard taskmaster. *Rec. dist.*: Minn.

5. Debt is a rope to your feet. *Rec. dist.*: Minn.

6. Debt is the worst poverty. *Var.*: Debt is the worst kind of poverty. *Rec. dist.*: U.S. *1st cit.*: 1732 Fuller, *Gnomologia;* US1880 Spurgeon, *John Ploughman's Pictures.* *20c. coll.*: Stevenson 530:2.

7. He who pays his debts enriches himself. *Rec. dist.*: Minn. *1st cit.*: 1640 Herbert, *Outlandish Proverbs (Jacula Prudentum)* in *Works,* ed. Hutchinson (1941). *20c. coll.*: Stevenson 530:7.

8. Keep out of debt and you will keep out of trouble. *Rec. dist.*: Vt.

9. Lying rides upon debt's back. *Rec. dist.*: Calif., N.Y. *1st cit.*: 1855 Bohn, *Handbook of Proverbs;* US1741 Franklin, *PRAlmanac.* *20c. coll.*: Stevenson 530:10, Whiting 272, *ODEP* 497.

10. Out of debt is riches enough. *Rec. dist.*: N.Y.

11. Out of debt, out of danger. *Rec. dist.*: Ill., Tex. *1st cit.*: 1551 More, *Utopia,* tr. Robinson; US1772 *Writings of Benjamin Franklin,* ed. Smyth (1905–07). *20c. coll.*: *ODEP* 601, Whiting 100, *CODP* 172, Stevenson 529:14.

12. Pay your debts or lose your friends. *Rec. dist.*: Wis.

13. Rather than run into debt, wear your old coat. *Rec. dist.*: Calif., N.Y.

14. The man in debt is a jump ahead of the sheriff. *Rec. dist.*: Ill.

15. Without debt, without care. *Rec. dist.*: N.Y.

16. You can run into debt, but you have to crawl out. *Rec. dist.*: Ohio.

SEE ALSO Rather go to BED supperless than run in debt for a breakfast. / The other face of CREDIT is debt. / He that DIES pays all debts. / INDUSTRY pays debts, while despair increases them. / It is better to PAY and have a little left than to have much and be always in debt. / TITHING is simply payment of an honest debt.

debtor SEE CREDITORS have better memories than debtors.

decay Decay belongs to every thief. *Rec. dist.:* Mich.

deceit 1. Deceit is a lie which wears a smile. *Rec. dist.:* Minn.

2. Deceit is a spider's web that traps the deceiver. *Rec. dist.:* Ill.

SEE ALSO CANDOR will lose you some friends, but not as many as deceit. / TYRANNY breeds deceit.

deceitful SEE APPEARANCES are deceiving. / FAVOR is deceitful, and beauty is vain.

deceive 1. Deceive not yourselves. *Var.:* It's the easiest thing in the world for a man to deceive himself. *Rec. dist.:* N.Y., S.C.

2. He is not deceived who is knowingly deceived. *Rec. dist.:* N.Y., S.C.

3. If the same man deceives us twice, we deserve ruin. *Rec. dist.:* N.Y., S.C. *1st cit.:* 1720 Kelly, *Scottish Proverbs.* *20c. coll.:* Stevenson 533:3.

4. It is an ill thing to be deceived, but worse to deceive. *Rec. dist.:* Can.

5. Men are never so easily deceived as when they are plotting to deceive others. *Rec. dist.:* Mich. *1st cit.:* 1578 Florio, *Firste Fruites.* *20c. coll.:* Stevenson 533:12.

6. Never deceive, and then you may boldly withstand. *Rec. dist.:* N.J.

7. None are deceived but they that confide. *Rec. dist.:* Calif., N.Y. *1st cit.:* US1740 Franklin, *PRAlmanac.* *20c. coll.:* Stevenson 532:13.

8. Take heed that no man deceive you. *Rec. dist.:* N.Y., S.C.

9. The people are deceived by names, but not by things. *Rec. dist.:* N.C.

10. Those who try to deceive may expect to be paid in their own coin. *Rec. dist.:* Kans.

SEE ALSO He who BELIEVES easily is easily deceived. / LOOKS often deceive. / A true SERVANT will deceive his master never. / Pleasing WORDS and bad deeds deceive both the wise and the simple.

deceiving SEE LIARS begin by imposing on others, but end by deceiving themselves.

deception There is no way of insuring deception against detection. *Rec. dist.:* Ind. *Infm.:* A military axiom when attempting infiltration or using decoy.

decide We cannot decide what may happen to us, but we can decide what happens in us. *Rec. dist.:* N.C.

decision A quick decision may speed you into disaster. *Rec. dist.:* Ill. *1st cit.:* US1875 Longfellow, *Masque of Pandora.* *20c. coll.:* Stevenson 535:3.

decrease SEE A man's PRIDE in what he knows decreases as his knowledge grows.

decree SEE Four THINGS cannot be brought back: a word spoken, an arrow discharged, the divine decree, and past time.

deed 1. A bad deed never dies. *Var.:* A good deed never dies. *Rec. dist.:* Calif., N.C.

2. A good deed bears a blessing for its fruit. *Rec. dist.:* Ill.

3. A good deed comes back a thousand fold. *Rec. dist.:* N.C.

4. A good deed is never forgotten. *Rec. dist.:* Calif., N.C., Wash.

5. A good deed may spring from a bad source. *Rec. dist.:* Okla.

6. Bad deeds follow you; the good ones flee. *Rec. dist.:* N.C.

7. Deed done is well begun. *Rec. dist.:* Ala.

8. Deeds are fruits; words are but leaves. *Rec. dist.:* La., Mich., N.J., Vt. *1st cit.:* 1616 Draxe, *Bibliotheca Scholastica* in *Anglia* (1918). *20c. coll.:* ODEP 175, Stevenson 2614:7.

9. Deeds are love, not fine words. *Var.:* Deeds are love. *Rec. dist.:* Calif., Miss.

10. Deeds are masculine; words are feminine. *Rec. dist.:* N.C. *1st cit.:* 1573 Sanford, *Garden of Pleasure.* *20c. coll.:* ODEP 175, Stevenson 1617:4.

11. Deeds, not words. *Var.:* Few words, many deeds. *Rec. dist.:* U.S. *1st cit.:* 1591 Shakespeare, *Henry VI, Part I;* US1656 Brewster in *Winthrop Papers,* Mass.Hist.Soc. *Collections* (1863–92). *20c. coll.:* ODEP 175, Whiting 101, Stevenson 2614:9, Whiting(MP) 160.

12. Deeds speak louder than words. *Vars.:* (a) Deeds are greater than words. (b) Deeds are mightier than words are, actions mightier than boasting. *Rec. dist.:* Ill., Kans. *Infm.:* Cf. action. *1st cit.:* 1939 Stuart, *Dead Men Sing No Songs;* US1855 Longfellow, *Song of Hiawatha.* *20c. coll.:* Whiting*(MP)* 160, Stevenson 2616:1

13. Do a good deed every day. *Rec. dist.:* Calif., N.Y.

14. Evil deeds do not prosper. *Rec. dist.:* Calif., N.Y.

15. Good deeds are better than creeds. *Var.:* Judge men by their deeds, not be their creeds. *Rec. dist.:* N.Y.

16. Good deeds are easily forgotten, bad deeds never. *Rec. dist.:* Ind.

17. Great deeds are reserved for great souls. *Var.:* Great soul, great deed. *Rec. dist.:* Ill., Utah.

18. It is one thing to plan a deed and another to carry it out. *Rec. dist.:* Ill.

19. Judge a man by his deeds, not by his words. *Rec. dist.:* N.Y. *1st cit.:* 1477 *Dictes and Sayenges of Philosophirs,* tr. Rivers. *20c. coll.:* Stevenson 2617:1.

20. Longer than deeds lives the word. *Rec. dist.:* Pa.

21. One good deed deserves another. *Var.:* One good deed brings forth another. *Rec. dist.:* U.S., Can. *Infm.:* Stevenson traces this varied form back to Sophocles' *Oedipus at Colonus* (ca408 B.C.E.). *1st cit.:* US1948 Stevenson, *Home Book of Proverbs.* *20c. coll.:* Stevenson 540:5.

22. Our greatest deeds we do unknowingly. *Rec. dist.:* Minn.

23. The deed will praise itself. *Rec. dist.:* Minn.

24. We live in deeds, not years. *Rec. dist.:* Minn. *1st cit.:* 1799 Sheridan, *Pizarro.* *20c. coll.:* Stevenson 539:3.

25. Wicked deeds will not stay hid. *Rec. dist.:* N.C.

SEE ALSO The better the DAY, the better the deed. / The best REWARD of a kindly deed is the knowledge of having done it. / The THOUGHT is the father to the deed. / A man of WORDS and not of deeds is like a garden full of weeds. / Big WORDS seldom go with good deeds. / WORDS and deeds are not weighed in the same balance.

deep *(n.)* Deep calls unto deep. *Rec. dist.:* Calif., N.Y. *Infm.:* Stevenson cites ca350 B.C.E.. *Old Testament: Psalms* 42:7. *1st cit.:* US1948 Stevenson, *Home Book of Proverbs.* *20c. coll.:* Stevenson 2048:12.

deep *(adj.)* *SEE* The narrower the EDGE, the deeper the cut. / The best FISHING is in the deepest water. / He who has crossed the FORD knows how deep it is. / A great SHIP asks for deeper water. / Still WATER runs deep. / Deepest WOUNDS are often inflicted by praise.

deep *(adv.)* *SEE* Plow your FURROWS deep while sluggards sleep, and you shall have corn to sell and to keep. / Fairest GEMS lie deepest. / Don't set your PLOW too deep.

deer *SEE* TIGERS and deer do not stroll together.

defeat 1. Defeat is a tonic to a brave man. *Rec. dist.:* N.J.

2. Defeat isn't bitter if you don't swallow it. *Rec. dist.:* Calif., Miss., Okla.

3. It is defeat that turns bones to flint; it is defeat that turns gristle to muscle; it is defeat that makes men invincible. *Rec. dist.:* Calif., N.Y. *1st cit.:* US1862 Beecher, *Royal Truths.* *20c. coll.:* Stevenson 545:4.

4. There is no defeat except from within. *Rec. dist.:* Ind., N.Mex. *1st cit.:* ca1613 Austin, *Perseverance Conquers All.* *20c. coll.:* Stevenson 545:2.

SEE ALSO A man learns little from VICTORY but much from defeat.

defect 1. Do not publish people's defects. *Rec. dist.:* Utah.

2. Great defects belong only to great men. *Rec. dist.:* Mich.

defendant If the defendant is silent the jury will think him guilty. *Rec. dist.:* N.Y.

defense 1. The best defense is a good offense. *Rec. dist.:* N.Y. *1st cit.:* 1931 Grierson, *Jackdaw Mystery;* US1795 Drayton in Gibbs,

Memoirs of Administration of Washington and John Adams (1846). **20c. coll.:** Whiting*(MP)* 21, Whiting 101, *ODEP* 7.

2. Millions for defense but not a cent for tribute. **Rec. dist.:** Calif., N.Y. **1st cit.:** 1798 Harper, Toast at dinner given by U.S. Congress in honor of John Marshall, 18 June 1798. **20c. coll.:** Stevenson 545:5.

SEE ALSO Against LOVE and fortune there is no defense. / A good OFFENSE is the best defense.

defer SEE Defer not till TOMORROW to be wise: tomorrow's sun to you may never rise.

deferred SEE HOPE deferred makes the heart sick.

deformed SEE A deformed BODY may have a beautiful soul.

deities The deities of one age are the by-words of the next. **Rec. dist.:** Calif., N.Y.

delay *(n.)* **1.** All delays are dangerous in war. **Rec. dist.:** Calif., N.Y.

2. Delay breeds loss. **Rec. dist.:** N.C.

3. Delay is dangerous. **Rec. dist.:** U.S., Can. **1st cit.:** ca1300 *Havelok the Dane;* US1636 Hewson in *Winthrop Papers, 1498–1649,* Mass.Hist.Soc. *Collections* (1929–47). **20c. coll.:** *ODEP* 176, Whiting 101, *CODP* 50, Stevenson 546:7, T&W 96, Whiting*(MP)* 160.

4. Delay of justice is the stepmother of misfortune. **Rec. dist.:** N.C.

5. Delays are dangerous, but they make things sure. **Rec. dist.:** Ill.

6. Delays are often more injurious than direct injustice. **Rec. dist.:** N.Y.

7. Delays have dangerous ends. **Rec. dist.:** N.Y., S.C. **1st cit.:** 1591 Shakespeare, *Henry VI, Part I.* **20c. coll.:** *ODEP* 176, Stevenson 546:7.

8. Delays increase desires and sometimes extinguish them. **Rec. dist.:** Ill. **1st cit.:** 1732 Fuller, *Gnomologia.* **20c. coll.:** Stevenson 546:2.

9. To delay may mean to forget. **Rec. dist.:** Calif., N.Y.

SEE ALSO A good remedy for ANGER is delay.

delay *(v.)* You may delay, but time will not. **Rec. dist.:** Miss., Ont.

delayed SEE JUSTICE delayed is justice denied.

deliberate **1.** Deliberate long on that which you can do but once. **Rec. dist.:** Miss. **1st cit.:** 1539 Publilius Syrus, *Sententiae,* tr. Taverner. **20c. coll.:** Stevenson 547:12.

2. Deliberate slowly; execute promptly. **Rec. dist.:** Ill. **1st cit.:** 1856 Cahier, *Quelques Six Milles Proverbes.* **20c. coll.:** Stevenson 547:12.

deliberating Deliberating is not delaying. **Rec. dist.:** N.Y. **1st cit.:** 1732 Fuller, *Gnomologia.* **20c. coll.:** Stevenson 547:11.

delight **1.** Never find your delight in another's misfortune. **Rec. dist.:** Utah. **1st cit.:** 1756 Burke, "On the Sublime and Beautiful" in *Philosophical Inquiry.* **20c. coll.:** Stevenson 1596:7.

2. The delights of the flesh are the despair of the soul. **Rec. dist.:** Ill.

3. There is delight in danger and danger in delight. **Rec. dist.:** Calif., N.Y.

SEE ALSO DILIGENCE brings delight. / RAINBOW at night, sailor's delight; rainbow at morning, sailors take warning. / RED sky at night, sailor's delight; red sky in the morning, sailors take warning.

Delilah There is no leaping from Delilah's lap into Abraham's bosom. **Rec. dist.:** Wis.

delivery Delivery makes the deed valid. **Rec. dist.:** Mich.

deluge After us the deluge. **Rec. dist.:** Calif., N.Y. **1st cit.:** 1876 Burnaby, "Introduction" in *Ride to Khiva;* US1865 Sedley, *Marion Rooke.* **20c. coll.:** *ODEP* 6, T&W 97, Stevenson 548:14.

demand *(n.)* **1.** Inordinate demands should meet with bold denials. **Rec. dist.:** Mich.

2. Where the demand is a jest, the fittest answer is a scoff. **Rec. dist.:** Mich. **1st cit.:** 1597 *Politeuphuia Wits Commonwealth.* **20c. coll.:** *ODEP* 177.

demand *(v.)* He who demands does not command. **Rec. dist.:** Oreg.

SEE ALSO Who demands JUSTICE must administer justice.

democracy 1. Democracy is better than tyranny. *Rec. dist.:* Wis. *1st cit.:* US1948 Stevenson, *Home Book of Proverbs.* *20c. coll.:* Stevenson 550:7.

2. Democracy means not lack of control but self-control. *Rec. dist.:* Minn.

3. The price of democracy is mediocracy [sic]. *Rec. dist.:* Ohio.

democratic The Democratic party is like a man riding backward in a carriage: it never sees a thing until it has gone by. *Rec. dist.:* Calif., N.Y. *1st cit.:* USca1870 Butler, *Epigram.* *20c. coll.:* Stevenson 551:1.

demonstration Demonstration is the best mode of instruction. *Rec. dist.:* N.Y.

denied *See* JUSTICE delayed is justice denied.

denomination Denominations fight while the devil laughs. *Rec. dist.:* Ind.

dentist You can't blame a dentist for looking down at the mouth. *Rec. dist.:* Minn. *Infm.:* Refers to high dental costs while the dentist has an irrefutable advantage, i.e. "to look down the throat."

deny 1. Deny self for self's sake. *Rec. dist.:* N.Y., S.C. *1st cit.:* US1735 Franklin, *PRAlmanac.* *20c. coll.:* Stevenson 2058:1.

2. He who denies all confesses all. *Rec. dist.:* N.Y.
See also We can forget our CHILDHOOD, but we cannot deny it.

depart *See* MISFORTUNE arrives on horseback but departs on foot.

departure The sooner the departure, the quicker the return. *Rec. dist.:* Pa.

depend *See* All GOVERNMENTS depend on the goodwill of the people. / It all depends on whose OX is gored. / What we SEE depends mainly on what we look for. / WORK as if everything depended on you; pray as if everything depended on God.

dependability The greatest ability is dependability. *Rec. dist.:* Calif., N.Y.

dependence The bitter bread of dependence is hard to chew. *Rec. dist.:* Ill.

dependent The dependent man must dine late and eat the leftovers. *Rec. dist.:* Ill. *1st cit.:* 1707 Mapletoft, *Select Proverbs.* *20c. coll.:* ODEP 177.

depth 1. Never venture out of your depth till you can swim. *Rec. dist.:* Wis. *1st cit.:* 1855 Bohn, *Handbook of Proverbs.* *20c. coll.:* Stevenson 1912:10.

2. You can't tell the depth of the well by the length of the handle on the pump. *Vars.:* (a) You can't tell the depth of the well by the length of the puddle on the pump. (b) You can't tell the depth of the well by the length of the pump handle. (c) You cannot tell the depth of the well by the length of the handle of the pump. *Rec. dist.:* U.S. *1st cit.:* US1940 Thompson, *Body, Boots, and Britches.* *20c. coll.:* Stevenson 2479:8.

3. You will never know the depth of a man until he opens his mouth. *Rec. dist.:* Ohio.

Derbyshire Derbyshire-born and Derbyshire-bred, strong in the arm and thick in the head. *Rec. dist.:* Calif., N.Y. *1st cit.:* 1852 Notes and Queries. *20c. coll.:* CODP 253.

descend It is easier to descend than ascend. *Rec. dist.:* Tex. *1st cit.:* 1605 Camden, *Remaines Concerning Britaine.* *20c. coll.:* Stevenson 746:13, ODEP 177.

descent 1. He who boasts of his descent is like a potato: the best part is underground. *Rec. dist.:* Utah.

2. The descent to hell is easy. *Rec. dist.:* R.I. *1st cit.:* 1513 Virgil, *Aeneid,* tr. Douglas. *20c. coll.:* ODEP 177.

desert *(n.)* *See* All SUNSHINE makes a desert.

desert *(v.)* *See* Never trust a FRIEND who deserts you in a pinch.

desertion Desertion is the better part of valor. *Rec. dist.:* Ohio. *Infm.:* A variation on "Discretion is the better part of valor."

deserve First deserve and then desire. *Rec. dist.:* Okla., R.I., Tex., Utah. *1st cit.:* ca1575 Pilkington, *Nehemiah.* *20c. coll.:* ODEP 262, Stevenson 552:2.
See also None but the BRAVE deserve the

fair. / Every COUNTRY has the government it deserves. / One good DEED deserves another. / A good DOG deserves a good bone. / Each HUSBAND gets the infidelity he deserves. / One KINDNESS deserves another. / Deserve SUCCESS and it will come. / He deserves not SWEET that will not taste of sour. / Most men get as good a WIFE as they deserve.

desire *(n.)* **1.** All earnest desires are prayers. *Rec. dist.:* Minn.

2. Desires are nourished by delays. *Rec. dist.:* Ill. *1st cit.:* 1601 Lyly, *Love's Met.* **20c. coll.:** Stevenson 553:1.

3. He who lives in either desire or fear can never enjoy his possessions. *Rec. dist.:* N.C.

4. It is easier to suppress the just desire than to satisfy all that follows it. *Rec. dist.:* Ohio.
SEE ALSO COMPETITION increases the desire.

desire *(v.)* Desire nothing that would bring disgrace. *Rec. dist.:* La.
SEE ALSO First DESERVE and then desire. / A DOG in the kitchen desires no company. / He is RICH who does not desire more.

despair **1.** Despair blunts the edge of industry. *Rec. dist.:* Mich.

2. Despair is the conclusion of fools. *Rec. dist.:* Calif., N.Y.

desperate *SEE* Desperate CURES to desperate ills apply. / Desperate EVILS require desperate remedies.

despise **1.** It is easy to despise what you cannot get. *Var.:* It's easy to despise what you cannot see. *Rec. dist.:* Calif., Ind., Ky., N.J., Ohio. *Infm.:* Stevenson cites Gracian's *Oraculo Manual* (1647). *1st cit.:* US1948 Stevenson, *Home Book of Proverbs.* **20c. coll.:** Stevenson 1021:2.

2. Men despise what they do not understand. *Rec. dist.:* W.Va.

3. There are many who prefer to despise and belittle that which is beyond their reach. *Var.:* There are many who pretend to despise that which is beyond their reach. *Rec. dist.:* U.S., Can.
SEE ALSO If what men most ADMIRE they

would despise, 'twould look like mankind were growing wise.

despised That which is despised is often the most useful. *Rec. dist.:* Mich.
SEE ALSO Better a man be FEARED than despised. / Small HELPS are not despised.

destination He who uses his tongue will reach his destination. *Rec. dist.:* R.I.

destiny **1.** A man's destiny is always dashed. *Rec. dist.:* Calif., N.Y.

2. Destiny leads the willing but drags the unwilling. *Rec. dist.:* Ill. *1st cit.:* 1732 Fuller, *Gnomologia.* **20c. coll.:** Stevenson 556:3.

3. He whose destiny is to be hanged will never be drowned. *Rec. dist.:* Minn. *1st cit.:* ca1503 Barclay, *Castle Labor;* USca1731 Cook, *History of Col. Nathaniel Bacon's Rebellion,* Am. Antiq. Soc. *Proceedings* (1934). **20c. coll.:** ODEP 75, CODP 23, Whiting 41, Stevenson 1066:2, T&W 39, Whiting(MP) 68.

4. There is a destiny that makes us brothers. *Rec. dist.:* Calif., N.Y.

5. You can't fight destiny; submit to it. *Rec. dist.:* Ill. *Infm.:* Stevenson cites Sophocles' *Antigone* (ca441 B.C.E.). *1st cit.:* US1948 Stevenson, *Home Book of Proverbs.* **20c. coll.:** Stevenson 556:6.

6. Your whole destiny is involved in the attitude you take toward your sin. *Rec. dist.:* Calif., N.Y.
SEE ALSO CHARACTER is destiny. / MARRIAGE and hanging go by destiny.

destroy *SEE* PROSPERITY destroys fools and endangers the wise. / The TONGUE destroys a greater horde than does the sword. / One TREE can make a million matches, and one match can destroy a million trees.

destruction *SEE* Self-CONCEIT may lead to self-destruction.

detail Details are not ends in themselves. *Rec. dist.:* N.C.

detection *SEE* There is no way of insuring DECEPTION against detection.

determination *SEE* No TERMINATION without determination.

determine *See* It's not the GALE but the set of the sail that determines the way you go.

determined A determined fellow can do more with a rusty monkey wrench than a lot of people can with a machine shop. *Rec. dist.:* Calif., N.Y.

detraction Detraction is a weed that only grows on dunghills. *Rec. dist.:* Ill.

devil **1.** As well to eat the devil as drink his broth. *Vars.:* **(a)** As well to eat the devil as to drink his broth. **(b)** If it's wrong to eat the devil, it's wrong to drink his broth. *Rec. dist.:* U.S., Can. *1st cit.:* 1545 Brinklow, *Lamentacyon*, E.E.T.S. (1874); US1783 Williams, *Journal of John Penrose, Seaman*, ed. Dickason (1969). *20c. coll.:* ODEP 215, Whiting 106, Stevenson 558:2.

2. Even the devil hates a coward. *Rec. dist.:* Ind.

3. Even the devil will swear on a stack of Bibles. *Rec. dist.:* Calif., N.Y.

4. Fight the devil with his own tools, or fight the devil with fire. *Rec. dist.:* S.C. *1st cit.:* 1926 Taylor, *Heart of Black Papua*; US1866 Smith, *Bill Arp, So Called.* *20c. coll.:* Whiting(MP) 164, T&W 98.

5. Give the devil an inch and he will take an ell. *Rec. dist.:* S.C.

6. Give the devil his dues. *Vars.:* **(a)** Give even the devil his due. **(b)** Give the devil his due. **(c)** Give the devil his due no matter who he is or what he is. **(d)** Give the devil his just dues. **(e)** Render unto the devil his due. **(f)** The devil gets his due. **(g)** The devil will have his due. **(h)** You've got to give the devil his due. *Rec. dist.:* U.S. *1st cit.:* 1589 Lyly, *Pappe with Hatchet*; US1769 Winslow, *American Broadside Verse* (1930). *20c. coll.:* ODEP 304, Whiting 106, CODP 92, Stevenson 568:1, T&W 100, Whiting(MP) 166.

7. Give the devil rope enough and he'll hang himself. *Rec. dist.:* N.C.

8. He must needs go whom the devil drives. *Rec. dist.:* U.S., Can. *1st cit.:* ca1450 Lydgate, *Assembly of Gods*, E.E.T.S. (1896); US1660 *Diary of John Hull* in *Archaeologia Americana,* Am. Antiq. Soc. *Transactions* (1857). *20c. coll.:* CODP 159, Whiting 106, ODEP 180, Stevenson 563:6, T&W 98.

9. He that takes the devil into his boat must carry him over the sound. *Rec. dist.:* Calif., N.Y. *1st cit.:* 1678 Ray, *English Proverbs.* *20c. coll.:* ODEP 802, Stevenson 565:5.

10. It always makes the devil laugh to see the biter bitten. *Rec. dist.:* Calif., N.Y.

11. It's hard to keep out the devil, but it is worse to drive him out. *Var.:* It's hard to keep out the devil, but it is worse to drive him out when he has once got us. *Rec. dist.:* Ont.

12. Never say adieu to the devil until you have met him. *Vars.:* **(a)** Don't bid the devil good morning until you meet him. **(b)** It's time enough to bid the devil good morning when you meet him. *Rec. dist.:* U.S. *1st cit.:* 1892 Blake, *London Daily News.* 5 Aug.; US1967 Dobie, *Some Part of Myself.* *20c. coll.:* Stevenson 557:13, Whiting(MP) 164.

13. Shame the devil and repent of your wickedness. *Rec. dist.:* N.C.

14. Talk about the devil and his imps will appear. *Vars.:* **(a)** Speak of the devil and he always appears. **(b)** Speak of the devil and he jabs you with his pitchfork. **(c)** Speak of the devil and he'll appear. **(d)** Talk of the devil and he is bound to appear. **(e)** Talk of the devil and his imp appears. **(f)** Talk of the devil and his imps will rise out of the ground. **(g)** Think of the devil and he appears. *Rec. dist.:* U.S. *1st cit.:* 1591 Lyly, *Endimion*; US1728 Byrd, *Histories of Dividing Line Betwixt Virginia and North Carolina,* ed. Boyd (1929). *20c. coll.:* ODEP 804, Whiting 106, CODP 120, Stevenson 568:9, T&W 98, Whiting(MP) 165.

15. The devil always tends to his own business. *Rec. dist.:* Calif., N.Y.

16. The devil can cite scripture for his purpose. *Var.:* The devil can quote scripture to his own advantage. *Rec. dist.:* U.S., Can. *1st cit.:* 1573 Bridges, *Supremacy of Christian Princes*; US1691 *Humble Address* in *Andros Tracts,* ed. Whitmore, Publ. Prince Soc. (1868, 1874). *20c. coll.:* ODEP 180, Whiting 103, CODP 51, Stevenson 566:2, T&W 98, Whiting(MP) 161.

17. The devil could not be everywhere so he made children. *Rec. dist.:* Calif., N.Y.

18. The devil goes shares in gaming. *Rec. dist.:* Ala., N.Y. *1st cit.:* 1707 Mapletoft, *Select Proverbs.* *20c. coll.:* ODEP 180, Stevenson 571:2.

19. The devil hawks his wares within the house of God. *Var.:* The devil is a busy bishop in his own diocese. *Rec. dist.:* Ill.

20. The devil I know is better than the devil I don't know. *Var.:* The devil that you do not know may be worse than the devil you do know. *Rec. dist.:* Alaska, Kans., N.Y. *1st cit.:* 1539 Taverner, *Proverbs of Erasmus;* US1934 Livingstone, *Dodd Cases.* *20c. coll.:* ODEP 55, Whiting*(MP)* 161, CODP 16, Stevenson 567:1.

21. The devil is always at the elbow of an idle man. *Rec. dist.:* Ohio.

22. The devil is master of all the arts. *Rec. dist.:* Calif., N.Y.

23. The devil is not always at one door. *Rec. dist.:* N.Y. *1st cit.:* 1592 Delamothe, *Treasure of French Tongue.* *20c. coll.:* ODEP 182.

24. The devil is not as black as he is painted. *Rec. dist.:* U.S., Can. *1st cit.:* 1534 More, *Dialogue of Comfort Against Tribulation;* US1777 Nelson in *Papers of Thomas Jefferson,* ed. Boyd, Princeton, N.J. (1950). *20c. coll.:* CODP 52, Whiting 104, ODEP 182, Stevenson 567:11, T&W 99, Whiting*(MP)* 162.

25. The devil is not idle. *Rec. dist.:* Alaska.

26. The devil never misses the bus. *Rec. dist.:* Calif., N.Y.

27. The devil never sleeps. *Rec. dist.:* Ill. *1st cit.:* US1948 Stevenson, *Home Book of Proverbs.* *20c. coll.:* Stevenson 564:5.

28. The devil never tempts those whom he finds suitably employed. *Rec. dist.:* Ohio.

29. The devil places a pillow for a drunken man to fall on. *Rec. dist.:* N.J.

30. The devil protects his own. *Vars.:* **(a)** The devil is ever kind to his own. **(b)** The devil is fond of his own. **(c)** The devil is good to his own. **(d)** The devil takes care of his own. **(e)** The devil will take care of his own. *Rec. dist.:* U.S., Can. *1st cit.:* 1606 Day, *Isle of Guls;*

US1811 *Letters of Samuel Taggart, Representative in Congress, 1803–14,* ed. Haynes, Am.Antiq.Soc. *Proceedings* (1923). *20c. coll.:* ODEP 181, Whiting 104, CODP 52, Stevenson 559:7, T&W 99, Whiting*(MP)* 163.

31. The devil some mischief finds for idle hands to do. *Vars.:* **(a)** If the devil catch a man idle, he'll set him to work. **(b)** If the devil find a man idle, he'll set him to work. **(c)** The devil finds work for idle hands. **(d)** The devil still some mischief finds for idle hands to do. *Rec. dist.:* U.S., Can. *1st cit.:* ca1386 Chaucer, *Tale of Melibee;* US1808 Adams in Mass. Hist.Soc. *Collections* (1936–41). *20c. coll.:* ODEP 180, Whiting 104, CODP 51, Stevenson 1216:2, T&W 318, Whiting*(MP)* 162.

32. The devil takes only what we give to him. *Rec. dist.:* N.Y.

33. The devil takes the hindmost. *Var.:* The devil take the hindmost. *Rec. dist.:* U.S. *1st cit.:* 1608 Beaumont and Fletcher, *Philaster;* US1742 *Colonial Records of Georgia,* ed. Chandler, in *Original Papers, 1735–1752* (1910–16). *20c. coll.:* ODEP 183, Whiting 104, CODP 52, Stevenson 561:7, T&W 99, Whiting*(MP)* 164.

34. The devils in the world shout loud and strong, but the angels outvote them. *Rec. dist.:* Calif., N.Y.

35. The reason the devil buys so many of us so cheaply is that he offers cash. *Rec. dist.:* Calif., N.Y.

36. There's more than one way to beat the devil around the bush. *Rec. dist.:* Kans., W.Va. *1st cit.:* US1776 *Diary of Col. Landon Carter of Sabine Hall, 1772–1778,* ed. Greene (1965). *20c. coll.:* Whiting 107, T&W 100, Whiting*(MP)* 165.

37. What's good for the devil applies to his imp. *Rec. dist.:* Oreg.

38. When fortune knocks at your door, the devil accompanies it. *Rec. dist.:* N.Dak.

39. When the devil comes, it is too late to pray. *Var.:* There's no use to pray after the devil has you. *Rec. dist.:* Ala., Ill., Oreg.

40. When the devil hungers, he will eat scraps. *Rec. dist.:* Pa.

41. When the devil was sick, a monk was he; when the devil was well, the devil of a monk was he. *Rec. dist.:* U.S., Can. *1st cit.:* 1586 Evans, *Revised Withal's Dictionary;* US1752 Robson, *Account of Residence in Hudson Bay.* *20c. coll.:* ODEP 184, Whiting 105, CODP 53, Stevenson 569:1, T&W 100, Whiting(MP) 164.

42. Where the devil can't go, he sends his grandmother. *Rec. dist.:* Alaska. *1st cit.:* 1853 Trench, *On Lessons in Proverbs. 20c. coll.:* ODEP 180.

43. Where there's money you'll find the devil. *Rec. dist.:* Oreg., Pa.

44. Write on the devil's horns "good angel," and many will believe it. *Rec. dist.:* Calif., N.Y.

45. You can kill the devil by kindness. *Rec. dist.:* Ohio.

SEE ALSO An ANGEL on the street, a devil at home. / Little ANGELS grow into big devils. / Nothing goes over the devil's BACK that doesn't come back under the devil's belly. / An idle BRAIN is the devil's workshop. / Tell everybody your BUSINESS and the devil will do it for you. / Good COFFEE should be black as sin, strong as the devil, and hot as hell. / DISCOURAGEMENT is the devil's most valuable tool. / A whistling GIRL and a crowing hen always end in the devil's den. / GOLD is the devil's fishhook. / Where there is GOLD, there the devil dwells. / Live up to your good INTENTIONS and put the devil out of business. / Young SAINT, old devil. / He must have a long SPOON who sups with the devil. / The devil's TONGUE is sharpest on the backlash. / Tell the TRUTH and shame the devil.

devotion *SEE* There isn't a RASCAL or a thief that doesn't have his devotion.

dexterity Dexterity comes by experience. *Rec. dist.:* Ill.

diamond **1.** A diamond on a dunghill is a precious diamond still. *Rec. dist.:* Ill. *1st cit.:* 1732 Fuller, *Gnomologia. 20c. coll.:* Stevenson 570:10.

2. A fine diamond may be ill set. *Rec. dist.:*

Okla., Tex. *1st cit.:* 1732 Fuller, *Gnomologia.* *20c. coll.:* Stevenson 570:10.

3. Better a diamond with a flaw than a pebble. *Rec. dist.:* Kans., N.J.

4. Diamond cuts diamond. *Rec. dist.:* U.S., Can. *1st cit.:* 1593 Nashe, *Christ's Tears;* US1777 Winslow, *American Broadside Verse,* New Haven, Conn. (1930). *20c. coll.:* ODEP 185, Whiting 108, CODP 53, Stevenson 570:12, T&W 101, Whiting(MP) 166.

5. Diamonds come in small packages. *Rec. dist.:* Ill.

SEE ALSO COAL doesn't shine around diamonds. / True FRIENDS are like diamonds, precious and rare; false ones like autumn leaves, found everywhere. / A PEBBLE and a diamond are alike to a blind man.

dice The best throw upon the dice is to throw them away. *Rec. dist.:* Mich., N.J., N.Y. *1st cit.:* ca1591 Smith, *Sermons of Henry Smith. 20c. coll.:* ODEP 819, Stevenson 571:11.

dictionary The dictionary is the only place where success comes before work. *Rec. dist.:* Kans., N.J.

die (*n.*) The die is cast. *Rec. dist.:* U.S., Can. *1st cit.:* 1548 Patten, *Expedition into Scotland;* US1765 *Letter Book of John Watts, 1762–1765,* N.Y.Hist.Soc. *Collections* (1928). *20c. coll.:* ODEP 186, Whiting 108, Stevenson 572:6, T&W 102, Whiting(MP) 167.

die (*v.*) **1.** A man can only die once. *Vars.:* **(a)** A man can die but once. **(b)** One cannot die twice. *Rec. dist.:* U.S., Can. *1st cit.:* ca1425 "Resurrection" in *Towneley Plays;* US1775 Inman in *Letters of James Murray, Loyalist,* eds. Tiffany and Lesley (1901). *20c. coll.:* ODEP 503, Whiting 109, Stevenson 499:4, T&W 102, Whiting(MP) 168.

2. A man's not ready to die until he's fit to live. *Rec. dist.:* N.C.

3. All men must die. *Rec. dist.:* Nebr. *1st cit.:* 1560 Palfreyman in *Mirror for Magistrates;* US1617 Rolfe in *Va.Mag.Hist.* (1902). *20c. coll.:* ODEP 10, Whiting 109, Stevenson 511:8, T&W 102, Whiting(MP) 167.

4. Better die than turn your back on reason. *Rec. dist.:* Ind.

5. Each man dies as he must. *Rec. dist.:* N.C.

6. He that dies pays all debts. *Rec. dist.:* N.Y. *1st cit.:* 1592 Shakespeare, *Richard III;* US1742 *Colonial Records of Georgia,* ed. Chandler, in *Original Papers, 1735–1752* (1910–16). *20c. coll.:* ODEP 174, Whiting 99, *CODP* 50, Whiting*(MP)* 158.

7. It is better to die kicking than to be kicked dying. *Rec. dist.:* Calif., N.Y.

8. It is better to die young at home than to die old in a hospital. *Rec. dist.:* N.Y.

9. It is not difficult to die well, but it is difficult to live well. *Var.:* It's easy to die right, but it's hard to live right. *Rec. dist.:* Ill., N.C.

10. It matters not how a man dies but how he lives. *Rec. dist.:* N.C.

11. Men don't die who were born to be hanged. *Rec. dist.:* N.C.

12. Never say die. *Rec. dist.:* Calif., N.Y. *1st cit.:* 1837 Dickens, *Pickwick Papers;* US1814 *Diary of F. Palmer, Privateersman, 1813–1815,* Acorn Club *Publications* (1914). *20c. coll.:* ODEP 563, Whiting 109, Stevenson 500:6, Whiting*(MP)* 167.

13. Some die that others may live. *Rec. dist.:* N.C.

14. Some men die before they begin to live. *Rec. dist.:* N.Y.

15. They die well that live well. *Rec. dist.:* N.Y. *1st cit.:* 1579 Spenser, *Shepheardes Calendar. 20c. coll.:* ODEP 186.

16. We die as we live. *Rec. dist.:* N.Y.

17. We leave more to do when we die than we have done. *Rec. dist.:* Minn. *1st cit.:* 1640 Herbert, *Outlandish Proverbs (Jacula Prudentum)* in *Works,* ed. Hutchinson (1941). *20c. coll.:* ODEP 453.

18. When you die, you can't take it with you. *Var.:* No matter how much money you have, when you die, you must leave it. *Rec. dist.:* Ind., Ky., N.C. *1st cit.:* US1855 Jones, *Winkles. 20c. coll.:* T&W 365, Whiting*(MP)* 611.

19. You are never too young to die. *Rec. dist.:* Utah.

20. You might as well die with chills as with fever. *Var.:* You might as well die for an old sheep as a lamb. *Rec. dist.:* N.Y., Tex.

SEE ALSO ANGER dies quickly in a good man. / A BAD deed never dies. / 'Tis more BRAVE to live than to die. / A COVETOUS man does nothing that he should till he dies. / The COWARD dies many times. / DEATH cannot kill what never dies. / A bad DEED never dies. / We must all eat a peck of DIRT before we die. / Do or die. / EAT, drink, and be merry, for tomorrow we may die. / An old FLAME never dies. / FOOLS die young and look sickly. / Men are FOOLS that wish to die. / The GOOD die young. / Eat whole HOG or die. / It's better to die with HONOR than to live in infamy. / Most good LAWYERS live well, work hard, and die poor. / LEARN as you'd live forever; live as you'd die tomorrow. / LIVE and learn; die and forget all. / LIVE freely and die content. / Only those are fit to LIVE who are not afraid to die. / They that LIVE longest must die at last. / They LOVE too much that die for love. / Sooner or later all POLITICIANS die of swallowing their own lies. / A RICH man is happy while he is alive but sorry when he dies. / ROOT, hog, or die. / Whoever steals the neighbor's SHIRT usually dies without his own. / Move an old TREE and it will wither and die. / VIRTUE dies at twelve o'clock at night. / Kind WORDS never die. / The YOUNG may die; the old must die.

diet 1. Diet cures more than the doctor. *Rec. dist.:* Calif., N.Y. *1st cit.:* 1875 Cheales, *Proverbial Folk-Lore. 20c. coll.:* Stevenson 573:1.

2. Simple diet makes healthy children. *Rec. dist.:* Mich.

SEE ALSO He that lives on HOPE has a slender diet. / The best PHYSICIANS are Dr. Diet, Dr. Quiet, and Dr. Merryman.

difference When men come face to face, their differences vanish. *Rec. dist.:* Ind. *1st cit.:* US1875 Scarborough, *Chinese Proverbs. 20c. coll.:* Stevenson 574:2.

SEE ALSO It makes little difference what's on the outside of your HEAD if there's something on the inside. / It is the difference in OPINION that makes good horse races. / The only difference between a RUT and a grave is that a grave is a little longer.

different By different methods different men excel. *Rec. dist.:* N.Y., Oreg., Wis. *1st cit.:* ca1764 Churchill, *Epistle to William Hogarth.* *20c. coll.:* Stevenson 1570:9.

SEE ALSO SAYING and doing are two different things. / Different STROKES for different folks.

difficult 1. All things are difficult before they are easy. *Var.:* Everything is difficult at first. *Rec. dist.:* N.Y. *1st cit.:* 1732 Fuller, *Gnomologia.* *20c. coll.:* Stevenson 574:11.

2. The difficult is done at once; the impossible takes a little longer. *Rec. dist.:* Mich., N.Y. *1st cit.:* 1873 Trollope, *Phineas Redux.* *20c. coll.:* CODP 53.

SEE ALSO The first ATTEMPT is the most difficult. / It is not difficult to DIE well, but it is difficult to live well. / All things are easy to INDUSTRY, all things difficult to sloth.

difficulty 1. Difficulties are things that show what men are. *Rec. dist.:* Ala., N.Y. *1st cit.:* US1948 Stevenson, *Home Book of Proverbs.* *20c. coll.:* Stevenson 574:10.

2. Difficulties relate only to necessity. *Rec. dist.:* Oreg.

3. Difficulty strengthens the mind as labor does the body. *Rec. dist.:* Minn.

4. The best way out of a difficulty is through it. *Rec. dist.:* Minn.

SEE ALSO QUARRELS are easily begun but with difficulty ended.

dig SEE You dig your GRAVE with your teeth. / If you dig a PIT for someone else, you fall into it yourself. / Dig the WELL before you are thirsty.

digest SEE A man must not SWALLOW more than he can digest.

digested SEE Chatted FOOD is half digested.

digestion SEE Unquiet MEALS make ill digestions.

dignity 1. Dignity does not consist in a silk dress. *Rec. dist.:* N.Y.

2. Dignity does not consist in possessing honors but in deserving them. *Rec. dist.:* Mich.

3. Dignity is one thing that can't be preserved in alcohol. *Rec. dist.:* Miss.

diligence 1. Diligence brings delight. *Rec. dist.:* Kans.

2. Diligence is a fair fortune, and industry a good estate. *Rec. dist.:* Mich.

3. Diligence is the mistress of success. *Rec. dist.:* Kans.

4. Diligence is the mother of good luck. *Var.:* Diligence is the mother of good fortune. *Rec. dist.:* U.S., Can. *1st cit.:* 1591 Stepney, *Spanish Schoolmaster;* US1736 Franklin, *PRAlmanac.* *20c. coll.:* CODP 54, Whiting 109.

5. Few things are impossible to diligence and skill. *Rec. dist.:* Ill.

diligent The hand of the diligent shall bear the rule. *Rec. dist.:* Ind. *1st cit.:* ca350 B.C.E., *Old Testament: Proverbs* 10:4. *20c. coll.:* Stevenson 577:6.

dime 1. Dime is money, as the Dutchman says. *Rec. dist.:* Calif., N.Y.

2. Don't hold the dime so near your eye that you can't see the dollar. *Rec. dist.:* Wash.

3. Take care of the dimes and the dollars will take care of themselves. *Rec. dist.:* U.S., Can. *Infm.:* Cf. penny.

dinner 1. A dinner lubricates business. *Rec. dist.:* R.I. *1st cit.:* 1791 Boswell, *Life of Johnson.* *20c. coll.:* Stevenson 580:12.

2. After dinner sit awhile; after supper walk a mile. *Rec. dist.:* U.S., Can. *1st cit.:* 1582 Whetstone, *Heptameron of Civil Discourses;* US1933 Punshon, *Genius.* *20c. coll.:* ODEP 6, CODP 2, Stevenson 1102:8, Whiting(MP) 168.

3. Better a dinner of herbs where love is than a stalled ox and hatred therewith. *Rec. dist.:* Ohio. *1st cit.:* ca1389 Chaucer, *Parson's Tale;* US1849 Thoreau, *Week on Concord and Merrimack Rivers.* *20c. coll.:* Stevenson 577:9.

4. Better a good dinner than a fine coat. *Rec. dist.:* N.Y. *1st cit.:* 1820 D'Israeli, "Curiosities of Literature" in *Philosophy of Proverbs.* *20c. coll.:* Stevenson 578:4.

5. Do not shout dinner till you have your knife in the loaf. *Rec. dist.:* N.J.

SEE ALSO When FLATTERERS meet, Satan goes to dinner. / HUNGER is the first course to a good dinner. / Hit's a mighty deaf NIGGER dat don't hear de dinner ho'n.

diplomacy 1. Diplomacy is the better part of valor. *Rec. dist.:* Kans. **Infm.:** Cf. discretion.

2. Diplomacy is the art of letting someone else have your way. *Rec. dist.:* Calif., N.Y.

3. Diplomacy is to do and say the nastiest thing in the nicest way. *Rec. dist.:* Minn.

diplomat 1. A diplomat is a man who always remembers a woman's birthday but never her age. *Rec. dist.:* Calif., N.Y.

2. A diplomat is a person who can tell you to go to the devil so pleasantly that you are raring to go. *Rec. dist.:* Colo.

dipper SEE Puttin' a HANDLE on the gourd don't make it no dipper.

direction 1. By indirection find direction out. *Rec. dist.:* N.Y. *1st cit.:* 1600 Shakespeare, *Hamlet.* *20c. coll.:* Stevenson 534:3.

2. It's not where we stand but in what direction we are moving. *Rec. dist.:* N.C.
SEE ALSO SPEED will get you nowhere if you are headed in the wrong direction.

dirt 1. A little dirt never hurt anyone. *Rec. dist.:* Miss.

2. Brushin' aginst dirt don't make you any cleaner. *Rec. dist.:* Vt.

3. Cast no dirt in the well that gives you water. *Vars.:* (a) Don't throw dirt into the well that gives you water. (b) Never cast dirt in the fountain that has given you refreshing drink. *Rec. dist.:* N.J., Vt. *1st cit.:* 1593 Shakespeare, *Titus Andronicus;* US1703 *Correspondence Between William Penn and James Logan,* ed. Armstrong, Hist.Soc.Penn. *Memoirs* (1870–72). *20c. coll.:* ODEP 189, Whiting 109, Stevenson 1241:13.

4. Dirt is cheap; it takes money to buy wool. *Rec. dist.:* Vt.

5. Dirt is only matter in the wrong place. *Rec. dist.:* N.J., Ohio.

6. Dirt shows the quickest on the cleanest cotton. *Vars.:* (a) Dirt is dirtiest upon clean white linen. (b) Dirt is dirtiest upon the fairest spot. (c) Dirt show up de quicker' on de cleanes' cotton. *Rec. dist.:* U.S., Can. *1st cit.:* 1855 Bohn, *Handbook of Proverbs.* *20c. coll.:* Stevenson 581:4.

7. Fling dirt enough and some will stick. *Rec. dist.:* N.J. *1st cit.:* 1656 Trepan; US1703 *Correspondence Between William Penn and James Logan, 1700–1705,* ed. Armstrong, Hist.Soc. Penn. *Memoirs* (1870–72). *20c. coll.:* ODEP 189, Whiting 109, CODP 54, Stevenson 277:7.

8. Sweep the dirt from in front of your own door, and don't worry about your neighbor's. *Vars.:* (a) Sweep around your own door and you will find plenty of dirt. (b) Sweep out the dirt from behind your own door before you start to talk about other people. (c) Sweep out the dirt from under your own rug before you start to talk about other people. *Rec. dist.:* U.S., Can. *1st cit.:* 1629 Adams, *Sermons* (1861–62). *20c. coll.:* ODEP 793, CODP 218, Stevenson 617:6.

9. We must all eat a peck of dirt before we die. *Vars.:* (a) Ef you bleedzd ter eat dirt, eat clean dirt. (b) Every man has to eat his peck of dirt. (c) Every man must eat a peck of dirt before he dies. (d) You have to eat a bushel of dirt before you die. (e) You must eat a pint of dirt before you die. (f) You'll eat a peck of dirt before you die. *Rec. dist.:* U.S., Can. *1st cit.:* 1603 Chettle, Dekker, and Haughton, *Patient Grissel.* *20c. coll.:* ODEP 214, CODP 63, Stevenson 581:5.

10. Who deals in dirt has foul fingers. *Rec. dist.:* N.Y. *1st cit.:* 1737 Ramsay, *Scots Proverbs.* *20c. coll.:* ODEP 172, Stevenson 581:3.

11. You can't play in the dirt without getting dirty. *Rec. dist.:* Ky.
SEE ALSO Run with the HOGS and they will rub dirt on you. / Nothing comes without PAIN except dirt and long nails. / SCANDAL will rub out like dirt when it is dry. / He who follows TRUTH too closely will have dirt kicked in his face.

dirty SEE A bad BROOM leaves a dirty room. / Quarrelsome DOGS get dirty coats. / A clean GLOVE often hides a dirty hand. / Dirty HANDS make clean money. / Don't throw away your dirty WATER until you get clean.

disappointed *See* We are born CRYING, live complaining, and die disappointed. / Expect NOTHING and you won't be disappointed.

disappointment Disappointment hurts more than pain. *Rec. dist.:* Wash.

disaster *See* False CONFIDENCE often leads to disaster. / To INQUIRE is neither a disaster nor a disgrace. / Meet SUCCESS like a gentleman and disaster like a man.

disbelieve We easily disbelieve those things which we desire not. *Rec. dist.:* Mich.

disclose *See* Fine CLOTHES may disguise, silly words will disclose a fool.

discontent 1. A man's discontent is his worst evil. *Rec. dist.:* Ill., Mich., Utah. *1st cit.:* 1640 Herbert, *Outlandish Proverbs (Jacula Prudentum)* in *Works,* ed. Hutchinson (1941). *20c. coll.:* ODEP 189, Stevenson 583:3.

2. Discontent is the first step in progress. *Rec. dist.:* Calif., N.Y.

See also CONTENT makes poor men rich; discontent makes rich men poor.

discontented We are never more discontented with others than when we are discontented with ourselves. *Rec. dist.:* R.I.

discouragement Discouragement is the devil's most valuable tool. *Rec. dist.:* Calif., N.Y.

discouraging *See* It is discouraging to be a good NEIGHBOR in a bad neighborhood.

discourse The discourse of flatterers is a rope of honey. *Rec. dist.:* Mich.

discretion 1. An ounce of discretion is worth a pound of wit. *Var.:* An ounce of discretion is worth a pound of knowledge. *Rec. dist.:* U.S., Can. *1st cit.:* 1548 Hall, *Chronicle of Lancastre and York;* US1771 *Diary and Autobiography of John Adams,* ed. Butterfield (1961). *20c. coll.:* ODEP 601, Whiting 323, Stevenson 584:3.

2. Discretion is the better part of valor. *Rec. dist.:* U.S., Can. *1st cit.:* ca1477 Caxton, *Jason,* E.E.T.S.; US1747 Franklin, *PRAlmanac. 20c. coll.:* ODEP 189, Whiting 110, CODP 54, Stevenson 584:6, T&W 103, Whiting(MP) 169.

See also WIT without discretion is a sword in the hand of a fool.

discussion Discussion is the anvil upon which the spark of truth is struck. *Rec. dist.:* Ill. *1st cit.:* 1574 Guazzo, *Civile Conversation,* tr. Pettie, T.T. (1925). *20c. coll.:* Stevenson 91:7.

disease 1. A disease known is half cured. *Rec. dist.:* U.S., Can. *1st cit.:* 1569 Agrippa, *Amorous Tales,* tr. Sanford. *20c. coll.:* ODEP 189, Stevenson 585:13.

2. Cure the disease and kill the patient. *Rec. dist.:* Ill., N.J., Utah. *1st cit.:* 1597 Bacon, "Of Friendship" in *Essays. 20c. coll.:* Stevenson 1952:1.

3. Desperate diseases must have desperate cures. *Var.:* Desperate diseases have desperate remedies. *Rec. dist.:* U.S., Can. *1st cit.:* 1539 Erasmus, *Adages,* tr. Taverner; US1646 Winslow, *Hypocrisie Unmasked,* ed. Chapin, Providence, R.I. (1916). *20c. coll.:* ODEP 178, Whiting 110, CODP 51, Stevenson 1951:5, T&W 103, Whiting(MP) 169.

4. Diseases are the tax on pleasures. *Var.:* Diseases are the interest of pleasures. *Rec. dist.:* Mich., R.I. *1st cit.:* 1616 Withals, *Short Dictionary. 20c. coll.:* ODEP 190, Stevenson 586:14.

See also The CURE may be worse than the disease. / The more DOCTORS, the more diseases. / LOVE is a disease which begins with a fever and ends with a pain. / Sometimes the REMEDY is worse than the disease.

disgrace *(n.)* 1. Desire nothing that would bring disgrace. *Rec. dist.:* Calif., N.Y.

2. Disgraces are like cherries: one draws another. *Rec. dist.:* Ind. *1st cit.:* 1640 Herbert, *Outlandish Proverbs (Jacula Prudentum)* in *Works,* ed. Hutchinson (1941). *20c. coll.:* ODEP 190, Stevenson 587:9.

3. It is no disgrace to ask for an honest quarter. *Rec. dist.:* Utah.

4. It is no disgrace to fall down—the disgrace is in not getting up and going ahead. *Rec. dist.:* Calif., N.Y.

5. It's no disgrace to be poor, but it may as well be. *Vars.:* (a) It is no disgrace to be poor, but a terrible inconvenience. (b) It is no dis-

grace to be poor, but it's mighty unhandy. **(c)** It's awful unhandy to be poor, but it's no disgrace. **(d)** It's no disgrace to be poor, but it's damned inconvenient. **(e)** No disgrace to be poor, but it may as well be. **(f)** To be born poor is no disgrace. *Rec. dist.:* U.S. *1st cit.:* 1591 Florio, *Second Fruites,* ed. Simonini (1953). *20c. coll.:* ODEP 642, CODP 182.

6. The disgrace of the city is the fault of the citizens. *Rec. dist.:* Calif., N.Y.

7. There is no disgrace in honest labor. *Rec. dist.:* Utah.

SEE ALSO To INQUIRE is neither a disaster nor a disgrace. / POVERTY is no disgrace.

disgrace *(v.)* No one can disgrace us but ourselves. *Rec. dist.:* N.Y.

disgraceful It is disgraceful to stumble against the same stone twice. *Rec. dist.:* N.Y. *1st cit.:* 1539 Taverner, *Proverbs of Erasmus. 20c. coll.:* ODEP 783, Stevenson 2232:8.

disguise *(n.)* SEE DEATH's a great disguise. / PRAISE undeserved is scandal in disguise.

disguise *(v.)* SEE Fine CLOTHES may disguise, silly words will disclose a fool. / The VOICE of a pig can't be disguised.

dish *(n.)* **1.** All is lost that is poured into a cracked dish. *Var.:* All's lost that's put in a broken dish. *Rec. dist.:* U.S., Can. *1st cit.:* 1611 Middleton, *Roaring Girl. 20c. coll.:* ODEP 487, Stevenson 588:6.

2. Empty dishes rattle loudly. *Rec. dist.:* Minn. *Infm.:* Cf. barrel, wagon.

3. It's a poor dish wiper that can't get the dishes clean for the dishwasher. *Rec. dist.:* Wash.

SEE ALSO Better a small FISH than an empty dish. / A cheerful LOOK makes a dish a feast. / A hungry NIGGER makes a clean dish. / Even SUGAR itself may spoil a good dish. / WELCOME is the best dish on the table.

dish *(v.)* Don't dish it out if you can't take it. *Rec. dist.:* Ill., Ohio. *1st cit.:* 1936 Hume, *Crime Combine;* US1940 Gardner, *D.A. Goes to Trial. 20c. coll.:* Whiting(MP) 170, Stevenson 957:13.

dishcloth SEE Don't cut the SHEET to mend a dishcloth.

dishonest SEE No matter how SMALL you are, you are too big to be dishonest.

disillusion SEE ABSENCE is the mother of disillusion.

dispose SEE MAN proposes, God disposes.

disposition **1.** A docile disposition will with application surmount every difficulty. *Rec. dist.:* Calif., N.Y.

2. A gentle disposition is like an unruffled stream. *Rec. dist.:* Mich.

3. A loving disposition is never without a ripple. *Rec. dist.:* Ill.

4. Not by years but by disposition is wisdom acquired. *Rec. dist.:* N.Y.

5. To learn about one's disposition, we must cross him. *Rec. dist.:* Ind.

dispute The pain of dispute exceeds by much its utility. *Rec. dist.:* N.Y.

disputing **1.** Between wrangling and disputing, truth is lost. *Rec. dist.:* Ill. *1st cit.:* ca1526 Erasmus, *Dicta Sapientum. 20c. coll.:* ODEP 844.

2. Disputing and borrowing cause grief and sorrowing. *Rec. dist.:* Ill.

3. There is no disputing about tastes. *Rec. dist.:* U.S., Can. *Infm.:* Cf. accounting. *1st cit.:* 1599 Minsheu, *Dictionarie in Spanish and English;* US1786 Hazard in *Belknap Papers,* Mass.Hist.Soc. *Collections* (1877, 1891). *20c. coll.:* ODEP 2, Whiting 111, CODP 1, Stevenson 2282:5, Whiting(MP) 170.

dissatisfaction Dissatisfaction is the father of ambition. *Rec. dist.:* Calif., N.Y.

distance **1.** Distance is the best remedy against an evil-disposed man. *Rec. dist.:* Mich.

2. Distance lends enchantment. *Vars.:* **(a)** Distance adds enchantment. **(b)** Distance ends enchantment. **(c)** Distance lends enchantment to the view. **(d)** Distance plants enchantment. *Rec. dist.:* U.S., Can. *1st cit.:* 1799 Campbell, *Pleasure of Hope;* US1865 Richardson, *Secret Service. 20c. coll.:* CODP 55, T&W 103, Stevenson 591:6, Whiting(MP) 170.

3. The shortest distance between two points is a straight line. *Rec. dist.:* Calif., Ind., N.Y. *Infm.:* Often used in sports to indicate the shortest way to the goal. *1st cit.:* 1942 Lass-well, *Suds in Your Eye.* *20c. coll.:* Stevenson 1433:7.

SEE ALSO It is easy to be BRAVE from a safe distance. / A FRIEND at hand is better than a relative at a distance.

distant SEE Distant FIELDS look greener. / Distant STOVEWOOD is good stovewood.

distress 1. Assuage distress with a smile. *Rec. dist.:* Mich.

2. Two in distress make sorrow less. *Rec. dist.:* Calif., Ohio. *1st cit.:* 1855 Bohn, *Handbook of Proverbs.* *20c. coll.:* Stevenson 1592:12.

SEE ALSO COMPANY in distress makes trouble less.

distrust Wise distrust is the parent of security. *Rec. dist.:* Mich., Vt. *1st cit.:* 1732 Fuller, *Gnomologia;* US1776 *Heath Papers,* Mass. Hist.Soc. *Collections* (1878–1904). *20c. coll.:* Stevenson 592:12, Whiting 111.

ditch 1. Better go around than fall into the ditch. *Var.:* Better go about than fall into the ditch. *Rec. dist.:* U.S., Can. *1st cit.:* 1659 Howell, *Paroimiographia (Spanish Proverbs).* *20c. coll.:* ODEP 56, Stevenson 2468:10.

2. If you dig a ditch for your neighbor, you will fall into it yourself. *Rec. dist.:* Minn. *1st cit.:* 1509 Barclay, *Ship of Fools,* ed. Jamieson in *Eclogues,* E.E.T.S. (1874); US1608 Wingfield, *Discourse,* Am.Antiq.Soc, *Transactions* (1860). *20c. coll.:* ODEP 187, Stevenson 1799:10, Whiting 339, Whiting(MP) 496.

SEE ALSO If the BLIND lead the blind, both shall fall into the ditch. / You can't hold another fellow DOWN in the ditch unless you stay down there with him.

divide Divide and conquer. *Var.:* Divide and rule. *Rec. dist.:* U.S., Can. *1st cit.:* 1605 Hall, *Meditations and Voices Divine and Morall;* US1694 Scottow, *Narrative of Planting of Massachusetts Colony,* Mass.Hist.Soc. *Collections* (1858). *20c. coll.:* ODEP 190, Whiting 112, CODP 55, Stevenson 1014:5, Whiting(MP) 171.

SEE ALSO KNAVES and fools divide the world.

divided A divided man makes an unhappy spirit. *Rec. dist.:* N.C.

SEE ALSO A HOUSE divided against itself cannot stand. / UNITED we stand, divided we fall.

divine SEE To ERR is human; to forgive, divine.

division SEE TRUTH always brings division between right and wrong.

divorce The easiest way to get a divorce is to be married. *Rec. dist.:* Oreg.

do 1. A man can do a lot of things if he has to. *Rec. dist.:* N.C.

2. All may do what has by man been done. *Vars.:* (a) Any man can do what another man has done. (b) What man has done man can do. *Rec. dist.:* U.S., Can. *1st cit.:* 1863 Reade, *Hard Cash;* US1856 Durivage, *Three Brides, Love in a Cottage, and Other Tales.* *20c. coll.:* ODEP 504, T&W 104, CODP 144, Stevenson 539:12, Whiting(MP) 172.

3. Do a thing and have done with it. *Rec. dist.:* Ont.

4. Do as I say, not say I do. *Rec. dist.:* Calif., N.Y.

5. Do as well as you look. *Rec. dist.:* Ohio.

6. Do it well or not at all. *Rec. dist.:* N.Y. Okla. *Infm.:* Varied form. Cf. "Whatever you do . . . ."

7. Do or die. *Rec. dist.:* Calif., N.Y. *1st cit.:* ca1577 Pitscottie; US1819 Peirce, *Rebelliad* (1842). *20c. coll.:* ODEP 192, Whiting 113, Stevenson 537, T&W 104, Whiting(MP) 171.

8. Do something, even if it's wrong. *Rec. dist.:* N.C.

9. Do unto others as you would have them do unto you. *Vars.:* (a) Do as you would be done by. (b) Do it to him before he does it to you. (c) Do others before they do you. (d) Do unto others as others do unto you. (e) Do unto others as though you were the others. (f) Do unto others before they do you. (g) Don't do to others what you would not have done to you. (h) What you do not like done to yourself—do not do to others. *Rec. dist.:* U.S., Can. *1st cit.:* ca901 *Laws of Alfred* in Liebermann, *Gesetze Angelsachsens* (1898); US1668 *Letter Book of Peleg Sanford* (1928).

20c. coll.: *CODP* 56, Whiting 112, *ODEP* 191, Stevenson 2016:6, T&W 104, Whiting*(MP)* 171.

10. Do well, have well. *Rec. dist.:* Mich., N.Y., S.C. *1st cit.:* ca1350 *Douce MS 52,* ed. Förster, (1906). **20c. coll.:** *ODEP* 192, Stevenson 541:5.

11. Do what you do carefully. *Rec. dist.:* Mich.

12. Do what you ought, come what may. *Rec. dist.:* Mich., N.Y. *1st cit.:* 1583 Babington, *Exposition of the Commandments.* **20c. coll.:** *ODEP* 192, Stevenson 540:3.

13. Don't do anything I wouldn't do. *Rec. dist.:* Calif., N.Y.

14. Don't do as I do, but as I say. *Var.:* Don't do as I do, but as I say do. *Rec. dist.:* U.S., Can. *1st cit.:* ca1100 Ker, *Anglo-Saxons;* US1815 Weems, *Life of Benjamin Franklin.* **20c. coll.:** *ODEP* 191, Whiting 155, *CODP* 55, Stevenson 1871:3, Whiting*(MP)* 171.

15. Don't sit around and talk about what you are going to do—do it. *Rec. dist.:* Minn.

16. Eat it up, wear it out, make it do, or do without. *Rec. dist.:* Calif., Ohio.

17. Folks who never do any more than they get paid for never get paid for any more than they do. *Rec. dist.:* Ont., Wash.

18. He who can't do what he wants must want what he can do. *Rec. dist.:* U.S., Can. *1st cit.:* ca1530 *Terence in English,* tr. Bernard; US1778 *Journals and Letters of Francis Asbury,* ed. Potts (1958). **20c. coll.:** *ODEP* 191, Whiting 113, Stevenson 540:8.

19. If we like to do a thing, we do it well. *Rec. dist.:* Ont.

20. If you do what you should not, you must hear what you would not. *Rec. dist.:* Oreg. *1st cit.:* 1578 Florio, *Firste Fruites,* ed. Taihoku (1936). **20c. coll.:** *ODEP* 194.

21. If you don't have anything to do, don't do it here. *Rec. dist.:* Calif., N.Y.

22. If you don't know what to do, don't do anything. *Rec. dist.:* N.C.

23. If you don't you do and if you do you don't, so you might as well. *Rec. dist.:* Ohio. *1st cit.:* ca1825 Dow, *Reflections on Love of God.* **20c. coll.:** Stevenson 537:8.

24. If you mean well, do well. *Rec. dist.:* Ohio.

25. If you want something done and done well, do it yourself. *Vars.:* **(a)** If you want anything well done, do it yourself. **(b)** The best way to get something done is to do it yourself. *Rec. dist.:* U.S., Can. *1st cit.:* 1541 Bullinger, *Christian State of Matrimony,* tr. Coverdale; US1880 Spurgeon, *John Ploughman's Pictures.* **20c. coll.:** *CODP* 240, Stevenson 2063:5.

26. It is not what we do but how we do it that counts. *Var.:* It's not what you do; it's the way you do it. *Rec. dist.:* N.Y., Ohio, Oreg.

27. Many a man has done well at the last hour. *Rec. dist.:* N.C.

28. Mind what you do and how you do it. *Rec. dist.:* Ont.

29. Never do anything of which you are ashamed. *Rec. dist.:* Calif., N.Y.

30. Never do anything yourself you can get somebody else to do. *Rec. dist.:* N.Y. *1st cit.:* US1875 Webster in Emerson, "Quotations and Originality" in *Letters and Social Aims.* **20c. coll.:** Stevenson 2340:7.

31. No one else will do it for you. *Rec. dist.:* Pa.

32. Once done well is twice done. *Rec. dist.:* Calif., N.Y. *1st cit.:* 1606 Day, *Isle of Guls;* US1729 Belcher in *Talcott Papers,* Conn. Hist.Soc. *Collections* (1892, 1896). **20c. coll.:** *ODEP* 878, Whiting 113, Stevenson 536:7.

33. One can only do by doing. *Var.:* We learn to do by doing. *Rec. dist.:* U.S., Can. *1st cit.:* 1640 Herbert, *Outlandish Proverbs (Jacula Prudentum)* in *Works,* ed. Hutchinson (1941). **20c. coll.:** Stevenson 535:7.

34. Self do, self have. *Rec. dist.:* Okla. *1st cit.:* ca1500 *Proverbial Wisdom.* **20c. coll.:** *ODEP* 712, Stevenson 2063:8.

35. What is done cannot be undone. *Rec. dist.:* U.S., Can. *1st cit.:* ca1450 *King Ponthus, PMLA* (1897); US1782 *Diary and Autobiography of John Adams,* ed. Butterfield (1961). **20c. coll.:** *CODP* 58, Whiting 113, *ODEP* 199, Stevenson 543:15, T&W 104, Whiting*(MP)* 172.

36. What's done is done. *Rec. dist.:* U.S. *1st cit.:* 1605 Shakespeare, *Macbeth;* US1782 *Diary and Autobiography of John Adams,* ed. Butterfield (1961). *20c. coll.:* CODP 58, Whiting 113, ODEP 199, Stevenson 543:11, T&W 104, Whiting*(MP)* 172.

37. Whatever you do, do with all your might, for things done by halves are never done right. *Vars.:* **(a)** Do with all your mind and might. **(b)** Things done by halves are never done right. *Rec. dist.:* U.S., Can. *1st cit.:* ca900 B.C.E.. *Old Testament: Ecclesiastes,* 9:10. *20c. coll.:* Stevenson 536:11.

38. Who will do, will do. *Rec. dist.:* N.C.

39. You can do anything you want to if you want to bad enough. *Var.:* A fellow can do anything if he lists. *Rec. dist.:* U.S., Can.

40. You can't tell what a man can do. *Rec. dist.:* N.Y.

41. You don't have to do anything but live till you die. *Rec. dist.:* N.J., N.C.

SEE ALSO AGE should think and youth should do. / BEAUTY is as beauty does. / He who CAN does; he who can't teaches. / If DOUBTFUL, do. / EASY does it. / The EVILS you do two by two you pay for one by one. / FATHER works from sun to sun, but mother's work is never done. / Forbid a FOOL a thing, and that he'll do. / FOOLISH is as foolish does. / Take a FRIEND for what he does, a wife for what she has, and goods for what they are worth. / FRIENDLY is as friendly does. / If you want a thing done, GO; if not, send. / It's the empty GUN that does the mischief. / Pretty HANDS are those that do. / HANDSOME is as handsome does. / It is better to suffer INJUSTICE than to do it. / The JAWBONE does the mischief. / If you want a JOB well done, give it to a busy man. / When the JOB is well done, you can hang up the hammer. / KNAVES imagine nothing can be done without knavery. / LITTLE by little does the trick. / MAN works from sun to sun, but a woman's work is never done. / MONKEY see, monkey do. / NEARLY never did any good. / To do NOTHING is the way to be nothing. / He that would PLEASE all and himself too takes more in hand than he is like to do. / PRETTY is as pretty does. / PROMISE little but do much. / RESPECT a man—he will do the more. / When in ROME, do as the Romans. / Less SAID, more done. / SAY well is good, but do well is better. / SPEAK little; do much. / A TASK well begun is a task half done. / Getting THINGS done is largely a matter of getting things started. / If THINGS were to be done twice, all would be wise. / Never put off until TOMORROW what you can do today. / A WORK ill done must be done twice. / Never look at half-done WORK. / WORK well done makes pleasure more fun. / As YOUNG folks see, the young folks do; as they hear, they say.

doctor **1.** A doctor eases your pain; God cures it. *Rec. dist.:* Kans.

2. A drunken doctor is always smart. *Rec. dist.:* Calif., N.Y.

3. A good doctor treats both the patient and the disease. *Rec. dist.:* Calif.

4. A man who is his own doctor has a fool for his patient. *Rec. dist.:* Ill. *1st cit.:* US1940 Montague, *Broadway Stomach.* *20c. coll.:* Stevenson 599:8.

5. Always tell your doctor and your lawyer the truth. *Rec. dist.:* Nebr. *1st cit.:* 1573 Sanford, *Garden of Pleasure;* US1737 Franklin, *PRAlmanac.* *20c. coll.:* ODEP 371, Whiting 114, Stevenson 593:10.

6. Beware of the young doctor and the old barber. *Rec. dist.:* Minn., N.Y., S.C. *1st cit.:* 1573 Sanford, *Garden of Pleasure;* US1733 Franklin, *PRAlmanac.* *20c. coll.:* ODEP 927, Stevenson 594:7, Whiting*(MP)* 114.

7. Doctors' faults are covered with earth, and rich men's with money. *Vars.:* **(a)** Doctors bury their mistakes. **(b)** The doctor buries his mistakes in the cemetery. **(c)** The doctor's errors are covered by earth. *Rec. dist.:* U.S., Can. *1st cit.:* 1477 *Dictes and Sayenges of Philosophirs,* tr. Rivers; US1931 Edington, *Monk's-Hood Murders.* *20c. coll.:* Stevenson 597:2, Whiting*(MP)* 173.

8. Doctors make the worst patients. *Rec. dist.:* Calif., Okla., Tex., Vt.

9. Every doctor thinks his pills the best. *Rec. dist.:* Wis.

10. Good doctors do not treat themselves. *Rec. dist.:* N.Y.

11. If the doctor cures, the sun sees it; if he kills, the earth hides it. *Rec. dist.:* U.S., Can. *1st cit.:* 1547 Baldwin, *Treatise on Morall Phylosophie.* *20c. coll.:* ODEP 193, Stevenson 597:2.

12. No doctor like a true friend. *Rec. dist.:* N.Y. *1st cit.:* ca1386 Chaucer, *Tale of Melibee.* *20c. coll.:* ODEP 622, Stevenson 891:8.

13. Pay the doctor; praise the Lord. *Rec. dist.:* N.J.

14. The cleverest doctor cannot save himself. *Rec. dist.:* Ind. *1st cit.:* US1875 Scarborough, *Chinese Proverbs.* *20c. coll.:* Stevenson 599:8.

15. The doctor we hear about is always better than the one we know about. *Rec. dist.:* Tenn.

16. The more doctors, the more diseases. *Rec. dist.:* Calif., N.Y.

17. The three doctors Diet, Quiet, and Temperance are the best physicians. *Var.:* Rest, good cheer, and moderate diets are the three best doctors. *Rec. dist.:* Mich., N.Y. *1st cit.:* 1558 Bulleyn, *Government of Health;* US1761 Ames, *Almanacs,* ed. Briggs (1891). *20c. coll.:* ODEP 622, Whiting 114, CODP 56, Stevenson 598:5, Whiting*(MP)* 172.

SEE ALSO Fresh AIR and sunshine and plenty of grace slam the door in the doctor's face. / An APPLE a day keeps the doctor away. / After DEATH, the doctor. / DEATH defies the doctor or employs him to do its job. / DIET cures more than the doctor. / There are more old DRINKERS than old doctors. / He is a FOOL that makes his doctor his heir. / GOD heals and the doctor takes the fee.

doer Ill doers are ill thinkers. *Rec. dist.:* N.Y., Ohio, Okla., Tex. *1st cit.:* ca1568 Ascham, *Scholemaster.* *20c. coll.:* ODEP 398, CODP 70, Stevenson 542:16.

SEE ALSO Great BRAGGARTS are little doers. / Big TALKER, little doer.

dog 1. A bad dog never sees the wolf. *Rec. dist.:* N.Dak. *1st cit.:* 1611 Cotgrave, *Dictionary of French and English Tongues.* *20c. coll.:* ODEP 25, Stevenson 604:7.

2. A barking dog never bites. *Var.:* Dogs that bark don't always bite. *Rec. dist.:* U.S., Can.

1st cit.: ca1275 *Proverbs of Alfred,* tr. Skeat, E.E.T.S. (1907); US1929 Hope, *Alice in the Delighted States.* *20c. coll.:* ODEP 31, CODP 9, Stevenson 614:2, Whiting*(MP)* 173.

3. A barking dog was never a good hunter. *Rec. dist.:* Wis.

4. A beaten dog is afraid of the stick's shadow. *Rec. dist.:* Ind.

5. A blind dog won't bark at the moon. *Rec. dist.:* Ind.

6. A dead dog never bites. *Var.:* Dead dogs never bite. *Rec. dist.:* Ill., Wash. *1st cit.:* 1619 Fletcher, *Custom of the Country.* *20c. coll.:* Stevenson 504:9, Whiting*(MP)* 174.

7. A dead dog tells no tales. *Var.:* Dead dogs carry no tales *Rec. dist.:* Nebr., Ohio.

8. A dog, a woman, and a walnut tree: the more they're beat, the better they be. *Var.:* A woman, a dog, and a walnut tree: the harder you beat 'em, the better they be. *Rec. dist.:* U.S. *1st cit.:* 1581 Guazzo, *Civile Conversation,* tr. Pettie, T.T. (1925); US1836 Haliburton, *Clockmaker* (1839). *20c. coll.:* ODEP 758, CODP 248, T&W 408, Stevenson 2558:5.

9. A dog ain't healthy if he ain't got any fleas. *Rec. dist.:* Vt.

10. A dog has friends because he wags his tail instead of his tongue. *Rec. dist.:* N.C.

11. A dog in the kitchen desires no company. *Rec. dist.:* Ill. *1st cit.:* 1903 Hulme, *Proverb Lore.* *20c. coll.:* Stevenson 615:5.

12. A dog is loved by old and young; he wags his tail and not his tongue. *Rec. dist.:* Kans.

13. A dog is man's best friend. *Var.:* Man's best friend is his dog. *Rec. dist.:* U.S., Can. *1st cit.:* 1709 Pope, Letter to Cromwell, 9 Oct.; US1927 Bridges, *Girl in Black.* *20c. coll.:* Stevenson 607:2, Whiting*(MP)* 174.

14. A dog knows his own master. *Rec. dist.:* Ind.

15. A dog returns to where he has been fed. *Var.:* A dog returns to his own home. *Rec. dist.:* S.C.

16. A dog smells his own tracks first. *Rec. dist.:* Nebr.

17. A dog that has two homes is no good. *Rec. dist.:* Ark., Kans.

18. A dog that will fetch a bone will carry one. *Vars.:* **(a)** A dog that brings a bone will carry one. **(b)** A dog that brings you a bone will also carry it away. **(c)** A dog that will bring a bone will take one away. *Rec. dist.:* U.S., Can. *1st cit.:* 1830 Forby, *Vocabulary of East Anglia;* US1940 Thompson, *Body, Boots, and Britches. 20c. coll.:* ODEP 196, Stevenson 1012:12, *CODP* 58, Whiting*(MP)* 175.

19. A dog will bite or be bit. *Rec. dist.:* N.Y.

20. A dog will down another dog. *Rec. dist.:* S.C.

21. A dog will not cry if you beat him with a bone. *Rec. dist.:* Miss. *1st cit.:* 1659 Howell, *Paroimiografia (English Proverbs). 20c. coll.:* ODEP 196.

22. A dog with a bone knows no friend. *Rec. dist.:* Calif., N.Y. *1st cit.:* ca1225 *Trinity MS O,* ed. Förster in *English Studies. 20c. coll.:* ODEP 195, Stevenson 615:5.

23. A dog with money is addressed, "Mr. Dog." *Rec. dist.:* N.Y.

24. A dog's nose and a maid's knee are always cold. *Rec. dist.:* Wis. *1st cit.:* 1639 Clarke, *Paroemiologia. 20c. coll.:* ODEP 197, Stevenson 603:10.

25. A good dog deserves a good bone. *Rec. dist.:* Ill., Miss., W.Va. *1st cit.:* 1611 Cotgrave, *Dictionary of French and English Tongues. 20c. coll.:* ODEP 318, Stevenson 614:7.

26. A guilty dog always barks. *Rec. dist.:* Ky., Tenn.

27. A lazy dog finds no bone. *Var.:* A lazy dog catches no meat. *Rec. dist.:* Ill., N.C.

28. A little dog will run a lion out of his own yard. *Rec. dist.:* Ky., Tenn.

29. A mad dog neither drinks nor smokes, but it would be rash to conclude that he was therefore a safe and pleasant companion. *Rec. dist.:* Calif., N.Y. *1st cit.:* US1915 Lodge, Speech, U.S. Senate, 6 Jan. *20c. coll.:* Stevenson 608:1.

30. A man may cause even his own dog to bite him. *Var.:* A man may provoke his own dog to bite him. *Rec. dist.:* U.S., Can. *1st cit.:* 1546 Heywood, *Dialogue of Proverbs,* ed. Habernicht (1963). *20c. coll.:* ODEP 196, Stevenson 613:8.

31. A mischievous dog must be tied short. *Rec. dist.:* Fla. *1st cit.:* 1592 Delamothe, *Treasure of French Tongue. 20c. coll.:* ODEP 162, Stevenson 608:6.

32. A scalded dog thinks cold water hot. *Rec. dist.:* Fla. *1st cit.:* 1561 *Courtier,* tr. Hoby, T.T. *20c. coll.:* ODEP 703, Stevenson 727:3.

33. A sleeping dog never bites. *Rec. dist.:* Ky., Tenn.

34. A snappish dog usually has torn ears. *Rec. dist.:* Wis. *1st cit.:* 1611 Cotgrave, *Dictionary of French and English Tongues. 20c. coll.:* Stevenson 604:6.

35. A wagging-tailed dog never bites. *Rec. dist.:* Ill., Ky., Tenn.

36. A wandering dog always returns to a warm hearth. *Rec. dist.:* N.Y.

37. A wise dog knows its master. *Var.:* A dog knows his own master. *Rec. dist.:* N.Y.

38. All dogs bite the bitten dog. *Rec. dist.:* Calif., N.Y. *1st cit.:* US1948 Stevenson, *Home Book of Proverbs. 20c. coll.:* Stevenson 751:1.

39. An old dog bites sore. *Rec. dist.:* Vt. *1st cit.:* 1545 Erasmus, *Adages,* tr. Taverner. *20c. coll.:* ODEP 589, Stevenson 613:7.

40. An old dog does not bark in vain. *Var.:* An old dog does not bark for nothing. *Rec. dist.:* Kans., Nebr., Ohio. *1st cit.:* 1573 *Garden of Pleasure,* tr. Sanford. *20c. coll.:* ODEP 589, Stevenson 612:11.

41. An old dog does not work for nothing. *Rec. dist.:* Ala., Ga., Wis.

42. As the dogs bark, the young ones learn. *Rec. dist.:* Ohio. *1st cit.:* ca1470 Ashby, *Poems,* E.E.T.S. (1899). *20c. coll.:* Stevenson 612:2.

43. At open doors dogs come in. *Rec. dist.:* N.Y. *1st cit.:* ca1200 *Ancrene Riwle,* ed. Morton, Camden Soc. (1853). *20c. coll.:* ODEP 599.

44. Better live dog than dead lion. *Vars.:* **(a)** A live dog is better than a dead lion. **(b)** A live dog is better than a dead lion anytime. **(c)**

A living dog is better than a dead lion. *Rec. dist.:* U.S. *1st cit.:* ca1390 *Minor Poems of Vernon MS,* E.E.T.S. (1892–1901); US1677 Hubbard, *History of Indian Wars in New England,* ed. Drake, Roxbury, Mass. (1865). *20c. coll.:* CODP 136, Whiting 117, ODEP 476, Stevenson 1418:3, T&W 105, Whiting*(MP)* 177.

45. Beware of a silent dog and silent water. *Rec. dist.:* U.S. *1st cit.:* 1585 Robson, *Choice Change. 20c. coll.:* ODEP 58, Stevenson 2464:7.

46. Can't excuse a dog after he bites. *Rec. dist.:* Ky., Tenn.

47. Can't tell a dog by its collar. *Rec. dist.:* Ill.

48. De howlin' dog know w'at he sees. *Rec. dist.:* N.Y., S.C. *1st cit.:* US1880 Harris, *Plantation Proverbs* in *Uncle Remus, His Songs and His Sayings* (1881). *20c. coll.:* Stevenson 606:6.

49. Dog will not eat dog. *Rec. dist.:* Ind., Tex. *1st cit.:* 1543 Turner, *Hunting of Romish Fox;* US1792 Brackenridge, *Modern Chivalry,* ed. Newlin (1937). *20c. coll.:* ODEP 194, Whiting 115, CODP 57, Stevenson 611:9, T&W 106, Whiting*(MP)* 174.

50. Dogs delight to bark and bite for God has made 'em so. *Rec. dist.:* Minn. *1st cit.:* 1720 Watts, *Against Quarrelling and Fighting. 20c. coll.:* Stevenson 336:8.

51. Dogs don't bite at de front gate. *Rec. dist.:* N.Y., S.C. *1st cit.:* US1880 Harris, *Plantation Proverbs* in *Uncle Remus, His Songs and His Sayings* (1881). *20c. coll.:* Stevenson 613:5.

52. Dogs don't kill sheep at home. *Rec. dist.:* Ind.

53. Don't be afraid of a dog that barks. *Rec. dist.:* N.Y.

54. Don't call a dog while you're holding a stick in your hand. *Rec. dist.:* Tex.

55. Don't kick a dog when he is down. *Rec. dist.:* Kans.

56. Every dog has his day. *Vars.:* **(a)** Every dog has his day, and every man his hour. **(b)** Every dog has his day, and the cats their nights. **(c)** Every dog must have his day. **(d)** Every dog will have his day, a bitch two afternoons. *Rec. dist.:* U.S., Can. *1st cit.:* 1545

Erasmus, *Adages,* tr. Taverner; US1777 Sewall in Austin, *Life of Elbridge Gerry* (1828–29). *20c. coll.:* ODEP 195, Whiting 116, CODP 57, Stevenson 609:8, T&W 106, Whiting*(MP)* 175.

57. Every dog is a lion at home. *Vars.:* **(a)** Every dog is brave in his own yard. **(b)** Every dog is stout at his own door. **(c)** Every dog is valiant at his own door. *Rec. dist.:* U.S., Can. *Infm.:* Cf. Torriano in Florio, *Vocabolario Italiano & Inglese* (1659). *1st cit.:* 1568 Tilney, *Duties in Marriage;* US1869 Spurgeon, *John Ploughman's Talks. 20c. coll.:* ODEP 196, Stevenson 602:1.

58. Every dog thinks her puppies are the cutest. *Rec. dist.:* Ill.

59. Fighting dogs never win. *Rec. dist.:* Ky., Tenn.

60. For every dog there is a leash. *Rec. dist.:* N.J.

61. Get out of the way of a mad dog. *Rec. dist.:* Ind.

62. Give a dog a bad name and hang him. *Vars.:* **(a)** Give a dog a bad name and it will stay with him. **(b)** Give a dog a bad name and you may as well shoot him. *Rec. dist.:* U.S., Can. *1st cit.:* 1706 Stevens, *New Spanish-English Dictionary;* US1732 *New England Courant, Writings of Benjamin Franklin* (1956). *20c. coll.:* ODEP 302, Whiting 116, CODP 56, Stevenson 605:8, T&W 106, Whiting*(MP)* 175.

63. Give a dog enough rope and he'll hang himself. *Rec. dist.:* Minn.

64. Give a dog your finger and he'll want your hand. *Rec. dist.:* N.J., N.Y.

65. He who associates with dogs learns to pant. *Rec. dist.:* Ohio.

66. He who has a mind to beat a dog will easily find a stick. *Rec. dist.:* N.Y. *1st cit.:* 1593 Bacon, *Early Works. 20c. coll.:* ODEP 769, CODP 212, Stevenson 608:5.

67. Help the lame dog over the stile. *Rec. dist.:* Tex. *1st cit.:* 1546 Heywood, *Dialogue of Proverbs,* ed. Habernicht (1963). *20c. coll.:* ODEP 368, Stevenson 1129:10.

68. Hungry dogs will eat dirty puddings. *Rec.*

dist.: Ky., N.Y., Tenn. *1st cit.:* 1538 Bale, *Three Laws;* US1777 Danvers, *Downfall of Justice. 20c. coll.:* ODEP 393, Whiting 115, Stevenson 607:1, T&W 106, Whiting*(MP)* 174.

69. If one gets over the dog, one gets over the tail. *Rec. dist.:* Pa.

70. If the dog hadn't stopped to lift his leg, he'd have caught the rabbit. *Vars.:* **(a)** If the dog hadn't stopped to rest, he'd have caught the rabbit. **(b)** If the dog hadn't stopped to shit, he would have caught the rabbit. **(c)** If the dog hadn't stopped to smell the tree, he would have caught the fox. **(d)** If the dog hadn't stopped, it would have caught the rabbit. *Rec. dist.:* Ill., Iowa, Tex.

71. If you lie down with dogs, you'll get up with fleas. *Vars.:* **(a)** He who goes to bed with dogs wakes up with fleas. **(b)** He who lies down with dogs must not be surprised if he gets up with fleas. **(c)** He who lies down with dogs will rise with fleas. **(d)** He who sleeps with dogs gets up with fleas. **(e)** If you lie down with dogs, you must expect to get up with fleas. **(f)** Lay down with dogs, get up with fleas. **(g)** Lie down with dogs, you're liable to get up with fleas. *Rec. dist.:* U.S., Can. *1st cit.:* 1573 Sanford, *Garden of Pleasure;* US1733 Franklin, *PRAlmanac. 20c. coll.:* ODEP 460, Whiting 116, *CODP* 132, Stevenson 610:7, Whiting*(MP)* 176.

72. In every country dogs bite. *Rec. dist.:* N.Y. *1st cit.:* 1640 Herbert, *Outlandish Proverbs (Jacula Prudentum)* in *Works,* ed. Hutchinson (1941). *20c. coll.:* ODEP 197, Stevenson 613:6.

73. Into the mouth of a bad dog often falls a good bone. *Rec. dist.:* N.Y. *1st cit.:* 1592 Delamothe, *Treasure of French Tongue. 20c. coll.:* ODEP 26, Stevenson 615:2.

74. It is best to let a sleeping dog lie. *Var.:* Let the sleeping dog lie. *Rec. dist.:* U.S., Can. *1st cit.:* ca1374 Chaucer, *Troilus and Criseyde;* US1919 Thayer, *Mystery of the 13th Floor. 20c. coll.:* ODEP 456, Whiting*(MP)* 176, *CODP* 205, Stevenson 616:4.

75. It takes a lean dog for a long race. *Rec. dist.:* Ohio. *1st cit.:* 1902 Lean, *Collectanea;*

US1940 Montague, *Broadway Stomach. 20c. coll.:* ODEP 450, Stevenson 1374:9.

76. It's a daft dog that bites himself. *Rec. dist.:* Ohio.

77. It's a poor dog that can't wag its own tail. *Rec. dist.:* Ark., Kans.

78. It's not the size of the dog in the fight, it's the size of the fight in the dog. *Rec. dist.:* Ind., Kans., Vt.

79. Life is a matter of dog eat dog. *Vars.:* **(a)** Dog eat dog. **(b)** It's a hard winter when dog eats dog. **(c)** Let dog eat dog. *Rec. dist.:* U.S. *1st cit.:* 1926 Arnold, *Murder!;* US1749 *Papers of Sir William Johnson,* ed. Sullivan (1921–65). *20c. coll.:* Whiting*(MP)* 174, Whiting 114, T&W 106.

80. Little dogs start the hare, but great ones catch it. *Rec. dist.:* N.Y., S.C. *1st cit.:* 1640 Herbert, *Outlandish Proverbs (Jacula Prudentum)* in *Works,* ed. Hutchinson (1941). *20c. coll.:* Stevenson 1035:10.

81. Mad dogs and Englishmen go out in the noontime sun. *Rec. dist.:* Kans., Mich. *1st cit.:* 1933 Snell, *And Then...One Dark Night;* US1819 Brackenridge, *Voyage to South America. 20c. coll.:* Whiting*(MP)* 177, Whiting 117.

82. Never let the same dog bite you twice. *Rec. dist.:* Md.

83. Never trust a man a dog doesn't like. *Rec. dist.:* Ohio.

84. No sense in keepin' a dog when doin' your own barkin'. *Var.:* I will not keep a dog and bark myself. *Rec. dist.:* Miss., N.Y., Vt. *1st cit.:* 1583 Melbancke, *Philotimus;* US1791 *Thoughts on Proverbs* in *Universal Asylum. 20c. coll.:* ODEP 416, Whiting 117, *CODP* 124, Stevenson 612:14, T&W 106, Whiting*(MP)* 178.

85. Notice a dog and he will leap on your neck. *Rec. dist.:* Wis.

86. Old brag is a good dog, but hold fast is a better one. *Rec. dist.:* Calif., N.Y. *1st cit.:* 1580 Munday, *Zelauto;* US1835 Kennedy, *Horse-Shoe Robinson,* ed. Leisy (1937). *20c. coll.:* ODEP 80, T&W 41, *CODP* 24, Stevenson 229:6, Whiting*(MP)* 70.

87. One dog barks at nothing; the rest bark at him. *Rec. dist.*: Ind.

88. One dog may kill another, but that doesn't stop dogfights. *Rec. dist.*: Tex.

89. One sheep-killing dog kills a good one. *Rec. dist.*: Ohio. *Infm.*: A good dog is often mistaken for a sheep-killing dog. Also means sheep-killing dogs are vicious.

90. Quarreling dogs come halting home. *Rec. dist.*: Okla., Vt. *1st cit.*: 1591 *Troublesome Reign of King John*. *20c. coll.*: ODEP 659, Stevenson 604:6.

91. Quarrelsome dogs get dirty coats. *Rec. dist.*: Calif., N.Y. *1st cit.*: 1659 Howell, *Paromiografia (English Proverbs)*. *20c. coll.*: ODEP 659, Stevenson 604:6.

92. Satisfy a dog with a bone and a woman with a lie. *Rec. dist.*: Calif., N.Y.

93. Short-tailed dog wag his tail same as a long 'un. *Rec. dist.*: Miss.

94. Strike my dog and you strike me. *Rec. dist.*: Ala., Ga. *1st cit.*: 1588 *Discourse Upon the Present State of France*. *20c. coll.*: ODEP 781, Stevenson 607:6.

95. The dog always returns to his vomit. *Vars.*: (a) As a dog returns to his vomit, so a fool returns his folly. (b) The dog has returned to his vomit again, and the sow that was washed to her wallowing in the mire. *Rec. dist.*: Minn., Wis. *1st cit.*: ca1389 Chaucer, *Parson's Tale*; US1636 *Documentary History of State of Maine, Containing Trelawny Papers*, ed. Baxter (1884). *20c. coll.*: CODP 57, Whiting 115, ODEP 196, Stevenson 2438:2, T&W 106, Whiting(MP) 175.

96. The dog doesn't get bread every time he wags his tail. *Rec. dist.*: Calif., N.Y.

97. The dog has four legs, but he does not run on four roads. *Rec. dist.*: N.Y., S.C.

98. The dog in the doghouse barks at his fleas, the dog that hunts does not feel them. *Rec. dist.*: Ill. *1st cit.*: 1894 Hole, *More Memories*. *20c. coll.*: ODEP 196, Stevenson 606:11.

99. The dog in the manger won't eat the oats or let anyone else eat them. *Rec. dist.*: Minn.

1st cit.: ca1390 Gower, *Confessio Amantis*; US1674 Josselyn, *Account of Voyage to New England*. *20c. coll.*: ODEP 195, Whiting 114, T&W 106, Stevenson 601:1, Whiting(MP) 174.

100. The dog that minds not your whistle is good for nothing. *Rec. dist.*: N.Y. *1st cit.*: 1546 Heywood, *Dialogue of Proverbs*, ed. Habernicht (1963); US1952 Hoole, *Simon Suggs*. *20c. coll.*: ODEP 638, Stevenson 606:10, Whiting(MP) 176.

101. The dog that trots about finds the bone. *Rec. dist.*: Calif., N.Y. *1st cit.*: 1843 Borrow, *Bible in Spain*; US1845 Judd, *Margaret*. *20c. coll.*: ODEP 196, T&W 107, Stevenson 614:4.

102. The dog without teeth barks the most. *Rec. dist.*: N.Dak.

103. The foremost dog catches the hare. *Var.*: Maybe the last dog will catch the hare. *Rec. dist.*: N.J., Wis. *Infm.*: The variant form occurred later in Ray, *English Proverbs* (1678). *1st cit.*: 1580 Lyly, *Euphues and His England*. *20c. coll.*: ODEP 196, Stevenson 608:2.

104. The hair of the dog is good for the bite. *Var.*: The hair of the dog is the cure of his bite. *Rec. dist.*: U.S. *1st cit.*: 1546 Heywood, *Dialogue of Proverbs*, ed. Habernicht (1963); USca1820 Tucker, *Essays by Citizen of Virginia*, Georgetown, D.C. (1822). *20c. coll.*: ODEP 343, Whiting 191, Stevenson 1051:4, T&W 166, Whiting(MP) 278.

105. The hit dog is always the one that howls. *Vars.*: (a) A bit dog always barks. (b) A hit dog always howls. (c) Bit dog always hollers. (d) The bit dog always hollers. *Rec. dist.*: U.S.

106. The lean dog is all fleas. *Rec. dist.*: Maine.

107. The mad dog bites his master. *Rec. dist.*: Okla., Tex., Vt. *1st cit.*: 1706 Stevens, *New Spanish and English Dictionary*. *20c. coll.*: ODEP 498, Stevenson 613:3.

108. The saddest dog sometimes wags its tail. *Rec. dist.*: N.J. *1st cit.*: 1578 Florio, *Firste Fruites*. *20c. coll.*: Stevenson 605:9.

109. The silent dog is first to bite. *Rec. dist.*: Vt. *1st cit.*: US1962 *Bangor Daily News*, 19 June. *20c. coll.*: Whiting(MP) 177.

110. The time to befriend a dog is when the dog is down. *Rec. dist.:* Oreg.

111. There are more ways to kill a dog than by choking him to death on hot butter. *Vars.:* **(a)** More ways o' killin' a dog 'sides chokin' him with a dumplin'. **(b)** More ways to kill a dog than choking him with butter. **(c)** There are many ways to kill a dog without choking him on apple butter. **(d)** There are more ways than one of breaking a dog from sucking eggs. **(e)** There are more ways to choke a dog than on butter. **(f)** There are more ways to choke a dog than with butter. **(g)** There are more ways to kill a dog than by choking him on hot butter. **(h)** There are more ways to kill a dog than by choking him on peanut butter. **(i)** There are more ways to kill a dog than choking him on buttermilk. **(j)** There are more ways to kill a dog than to choke him to death with butter. **(k)** There is more ways to kill a dog than by hanging. *Rec. dist.:* U.S., Can. *1st cit.:* 1678 Ray, *English Proverbs;* US1843 Thompson, *Chronicles of Pineville.* *20c. coll.:* ODEP 872, T&W 397, CODP 242, Stevenson 610:3, Whiting*(MP)* 670.

112. 'Tis dog's delight to bark and bite, but little children never. *Rec. dist.:* Minn. *1st cit.:* 1720 Watts, *Against Quarrelling and Fighting.* *20c. coll.:* Stevenson 336:8.

113. To a vicious dog a short chain. *Rec. dist.:* Ill. *1st cit.:* 1623 Camden, *Remaines Concerning Britaine.* *20c. coll.:* Stevenson 608:6.

114. To kill an old dog you must hide your stick. *Rec. dist.:* N.Y.

115. Two dogs fight over a bone while the third always runs away with the bone. *Rec. dist.:* Ind. *1st cit.:* ca1386 Chaucer, *Knight's Tale;* US1766 Parker in *Papers of Benjamin Franklin,* ed. Labaree (1959). *20c. coll.:* ODEP 850, Whiting 118, Stevenson 614:6.

116. Two dogs over one bone seldom agree. *Rec. dist.:* Ind., Vt. *1st cit.:* 1732 Fuller, *Gnomologia;* US1809 Irving, *History of New York by D. Knickerbocker* (1819). *20c. coll.:* Stevenson 615:4, Whiting 118, Whiting*(MP)* 180.

117. Wash a dog, comb a dog: still a dog. *Rec. dist.:* Ark., Kans. *1st cit.:* 1860 Henderson, *Latin Proverbs.* *20c. coll.:* Stevenson 1673:6.

118. When a dog bites a man, that is not news; but when a man bites a dog, that is news. *Rec. dist.:* Calif., N.Y. *1st cit.:* USca1880 Bogart, *N.Y. Sun.* *20c. coll.:* Stevenson 1682:2.

119. When a dog is drowning, everyone offers him drink. *Rec. dist.:* Ill., Okla., Tex., Vt. *1st cit.:* 1611 Cotgrave, *Dictionary of French and English Tongues.* *20c. coll.:* ODEP 195, Stevenson 604:4.

120. Where there's a dog, there's fleas. *Rec. dist.:* Ark., Kans.

121. Who yaps like a dog will be beaten like a dog. *Rec. dist.:* Ill., Ind.

122. You can call a dog without kicking him. *Rec. dist.:* Calif., N.Y. *Infm.:* You don't have to resort to force.

123. You can never tell a dog by his bark. *Rec. dist.:* Oreg.

124. You can tell a dog by his collar. *Rec. dist.:* Ill.

125. You can't keep a good dog down. *Rec. dist.:* Okla. *Infm.:* Cf. "You can't keep a good man down."

126. You can't teach an old dog new tricks. *Vars.:* **(a)** An old dog will learn no new tricks. **(b)** An old dog will learn no tricks. *Rec. dist.:* U.S., Can. *1st cit.:* 1523 Fitzherbert, *Boke of Husbandry;* US1806 *Letters of John Randolph,* ed. Dudley (1834). *20c. coll.:* ODEP 805, Whiting 118, CODP 221, Stevenson 615:6, T&W 105, Whiting*(MP)* 179.

127. You have to be smarter than the dog to teach him tricks. *Rec. dist.:* Oreg., Tex.

SEE ALSO A dog's BARK is worse than his bite. / Old BRAG is a good dog, but hold fast is a better one. / CHARITY is not a bone you throw to a dog but a bone you share with a dog. / A bitten CHILD dreads a dog. / The DEATH of one dog is the life of another. / The fatter the FLEA, the leaner the dog. / A certain amount of FLEAS are good for a dog. / Man's best FRIEND is his dog. / Three faithful FRIENDS: an old wife, an old dog, and ready money. / It's better to have the GOODWILL of a dog than not. / Don't think to hunt two HARES with one dog. / LOVE me, love my dog. / Puppy LOVE leads to a dog's life. / REVENGE is like biting a dog because he bit you. / The TAIL cannot shake the dog. / Look out for the man that does not TALK, and the dog that does not bark. / WOMEN and dogs cause too much strife.

dogfight 1. A dogfight at home is more interesting than a civil war in Asia. *Rec. dist.:* Calif., N.Y.

2. All's fair in a dogfight. *Var.:* All's fair in a dog's fight. *Rec. dist.:* Ill., N.Y.

doghouse The doghouse is no place to keep a sausage. *Rec. dist.:* Ill.

doing 1. Anything worth doing is worth doing well. *Vars.:* (a) A task that's worth doing at all is worth doing well. (b) A thing worth doing is worth doing well. (c) If anything is worth doing, it is worth doing well. (d) Whatever is worth doing at all is worth doing well. *Rec. dist.:* U.S., Can. *1st cit.:* 1746 Chesterfield, Letter, 9 Oct., in *Letters to His Son;* US1780 A. Adams in *Adams Family Correspondence,* ed. Butterfield (1963). *20c. coll.:* ODEP 921, Whiting 113, *CODP* 222, Stevenson 536:3, T&W 104.

2. Doing is better than saying. *Rec. dist.:* N.Y. *1st cit.:* 1633 Draxe, *Bibliotheca Scholastica. 20c. coll.:* Stevenson 2037:4.

3. Doing nothing is doing ill. *Rec. dist.:* Okla. *1st cit.:* 1531 Elyot, *Boke Named the Governor. 20c. coll.:* ODEP 198.

4. Doing things by halves is worthless, for it may be the other half that counts. *Rec. dist.:* N.Mex.

SEE ALSO He who is AFRAID of doing too much always does too little. / The shortest ANSWER is doing. / Even a CHILD makes himself known by his doings. / One can only DO by doing. / Your HAND is never the worse for doing your own work. / LOVE is not merely saying, it is doing. / Without a good REASON for doing a thing, we have a fine reason for leaving it alone. / The REWARD is in the doing. / SAYING and doing are two different things. / Happy's the WOOING that's not long a doing. / WORRYING is often stewing without doing.

dole Life on the dole brings sadness to the soul. *Rec. dist.:* Ill.

SEE ALSO A NATION that lives by the dole shall perish by the dole.

dollar 1. A bad dollar always comes back. *Rec. dist.:* Ind. *Infm.:* Cf. penny.

2. A dollar a day keeps the beggar away. *Rec. dist.:* Ohio.

3. A dollar in the bank is worth two in the hand. *Rec. dist.:* Calif., N.Y.

4. A dollar saved is a dollar earned. *Rec. dist.:* Calif., Ind., Kans., Mass. *Infm.:* Cf. penny. *1st cit.:* US1859 Shillaber, *Knitting-Work. 20c. coll.:* T&W 108.

5. Don't waste ten dollars looking for a dime. *Rec. dist.:* N.Y., S.C.

6. If you keep a dollar in your pocket, you'll never go broke. *Rec. dist.:* N.Y., S.C.

7. Lend a dollar, lose a friend. *Rec. dist.:* Calif., N.J.

8. One dollar in your hand beats the promise of two in somebody else's. *Vars.:* (a) A dollar in the bank is worth two in the hand. (b) A dollar in your pocket is worth two that are spent. (c) A dollar invested is worth two in the pocket. *Rec. dist.:* Calif., Fla., Ohio, Oreg.

9. Save a dollar and keep your worries away. *Rec. dist.:* N.Y.

10. You can't get dollars by pinching nickels. *Rec. dist.:* Tex.

11. Your best friend is your dollar. *Rec. dist.:* Ind. *1st cit.:* US1942 Offord, *Clues to Burn. 20c. coll.:* Stevenson 617:4.

SEE ALSO I had rather be a BEGGAR and spend my last dollar like a king, than be a king and spend my money like a beggar. / Another DAY, another dollar. / Don't hold the DIME so near your eye that you can't see the dollar. / A ten-dollar DUDE may have a two-dollar salary. / The poor FOOL who closes his mouth never makes a dollar. / A quick NICKEL is better than a slow dollar. / PENNIES make dollars. / Take care of your PENNIES and the dollars will take care of themselves.

domestic *SEE* Domestic FRUIT will not grow on a wild tree.

donkey 1. A donkey is but a donkey though laden with gold. *Rec. dist.:* Ill. *Infm.:* Cf. ass.

2. A donkey looks beautiful to a donkey. *Rec. dist.:* Ill. *Infm.:* Cf. ass.

3. A donkey prefers thistles because he is an ass. *Rec. dist.:* Calif., N.Y.

4. A donkey that carries the load is more decent than a lap dog that lives in idle luxury. *Rec. dist.:* Calif., N.Y.

5. Better a donkey that carries me than a horse that throws me. *Rec. dist.:* Ind. *Infm.:* Cf. ass.

6. Don't try to back a donkey through. *Rec. dist.:* Fla.

door **1.** A creaking door never falls from its hinges. *Vars.:* **(a)** A creaking door hangs long on its hinges. **(b)** A creaking door never falls. *Rec. dist.:* U.S., Can. *1st cit.:* 1776 Cogan, *John Buncle, Jr.* *20c. coll.:* ODEP 154, Stevenson 936:15, *CODP* 45.

2. A door must be open or shut. *Rec. dist.:* N.Y. *1st cit.:* 1762 Goldsmith, *Citizen of the World.* *20c. coll.:* ODEP 199, CODP 59, Stevenson 618:5.

3. A sealed door invites a thief. *Rec. dist.:* Oreg.

4. An open door may tempt a saint. *Rec. dist.:* U.S. *1st cit.:* 1659 Howell, *Paroimiographia (Spanish Proverbs).* *20c. coll.:* ODEP 559, Stevenson 618:2.

5. Beware of a door that has many keys. *Rec. dist.:* N.C.

6. Don't knock at a dead man's door and expect an answer. *Rec. dist.:* Ill.

7. Doors have eyes and walls have ears. *Rec. dist.:* Okla. *Infm.:* Popular during World War II.

8. Every door may be shut but death's door. *Rec. dist.:* Calif., N.Y. *1st cit.:* 1609 Shakespeare, *Cymbeline.* *20c. coll.:* ODEP 199, Stevenson 503:6.

9. He that would make a door of gold must drive in a nail every day. *Rec. dist.:* Mich. *1st cit.:* 1640 Herbert, *Outlandish Proverbs (Jacula Prudentum)* in *Works,* ed. Hutchinson (1941). *20c. coll.:* ODEP 199, Stevenson 492:9.

10. He who closes his door to the poor will find the gates of heaven closed. *Rec. dist.:* Wis.

11. Just pushing ahead will open the door to success much quicker than pulling. *Rec. dist.:* Miss.

12. Lock your door and keep your neighbors honest. *Rec. dist.:* Wis.

13. Men shut their doors against the setting sun. *Rec. dist.:* Okla.

14. No need to lock your door till your neighbor pulls his shades down. *Rec. dist.:* Ohio.

15. Sweep in front of your own door first. *Vars.:* **(a)** Before you call someone else dirty, be sure you sweep your own door. **(b)** Clean around your own back door before you clean around someone else's. **(c)** Everyone should sweep before his own door. **(d)** If you want to keep the town clean, sweep before your own door. **(e)** Sweep before your own door before you sweep before others. **(f)** Sweep the dirt from in front of your own door, and don't worry about your neighbor's. *Rec. dist.:* U.S., Can. *1st cit.:* 1629 Adams, *Sermon* (1861–62). *20c. coll.:* ODEP 793, CODP 218, Stevenson 617:6.

16. The back door robs the house. *Rec. dist.:* Ill. *1st cit.:* ca1450 *Proverbs of Good Counsel* in *Book of Precedence,* E.E.T.S.; US1676 *Complete Writings of Roger Williams* (1963). *20c. coll.:* CODP 181, Whiting 119, ODEP 25, Stevenson 618:4.

17. The door of the carpenter is loose. *Rec. dist.:* Calif., N.Y.

18. The door to success is labeled "push." *Rec. dist.:* Wis.

19. The door to the room of success always swings off the hinges of opposition. *Rec. dist.:* Wis.

20. There's no use in closing the barn door after the horse is stolen. *Vars.:* **(a)** Don't lock the barn door after the horse is stolen. **(b)** Don't lock the door after the horse has run away. **(c)** He is a fool who locks the barn door after the horse is stolen. **(d)** It is too late to lock the stable door when the steed is stolen. **(e)** It is too late to shut the stable door when the horse is stolen. **(f)** Lock the stable door before the steed is stolen. **(g)** Never latch the stable door after the horse has gone. **(h)** No need closing the door after the horse is stolen. **(i)** No use in closing the barn door after the horses are out. **(j)** No use to shut your barn door after the mule gets out. **(k)** There's no need of shutting the stable door after the horse is stolen. **(l)** When the horse is stolen, lock the barn door. **(m)** When the steed is stolen, you shut the stable door. *Rec. dist.*: U.S., Can. *1st cit.*: ca1350 *Douce MS 52*, ed. Förster (1906); US1745 *Correspondence During Law's Governorship of Connecticut, 1741–1750*, Conn.Hist.Soc. *Collections* (1907–14). *20c. coll.*: ODEP 730, Whiting 414, *CODP* 211, Stevenson 2204:8, Whiting*(MP)* 182.

21. When one door closes, another one opens. *Var.*: When one door shuts, another opens. *Rec. dist.*: Calif., Ill., N.Y., Oreg. *1st cit.*: 1586 *Lazarillo de Tormes*, tr. Rowland; US1870 McCloskey, *Across the Continent* in *Davy Crockett and Other Plays*, eds. Goldberg and Heffner (1940). *20c. coll.*: ODEP 596, T&W 109, *CODP* 169, Stevenson 618:8.

22. When the door is shut, the work improves. *Rec. dist.*: N.J.

23. When you open a door, you do not know how many rooms lie beyond. *Rec. dist.*: Wis.

24. Wide is the door of the little cottage. *Rec. dist.*: Miss.

See also Fresh AIR and sunshine and plenty of grace slam the door in the doctor's face. / The BARN is never so full that you can't slap in a bundle at the door. / Good CLOTHES open all doors. / COURTESY opens many doors. / The DEVIL is not always at one door. / When fortune knocks at your door, the DEVIL accompanies it. / At open doors DOGS come in. / FORTUNE always leaves one door open in disasters. / FORTUNE knocks once at every door. / When FORTUNE knocks, open the door. / A LOCK on a door keeps honest men honest. / When want comes in at the door, LOVE flies out of the window. / OPPORTUNITY doesn't knock the door down. / One SIN opens the door for another. / SLANDER expires at a good woman's door. / You can shut the door on a THIEF, but you can do nothing about a liar. / A nice WIFE and a back door oft do make a rich man poor. / The doors of WISDOM are never shut. / A WOMAN can throw out the window more than a man can bring in at the door.

doormat If you make yourself a doormat, you will be stepped on. *Rec. dist.*: Minn.

doorstep **1.** Keep your own doorsteps clean. *Vars.*: **(a)** Clean your own doorstep before you clean someone else's. **(b)** Clean your own doorstep before you speak of your neighbor. **(c)** Clean your own dooryard before you clean others'. **(d)** Sweep around your own doorstep first. **(e)** Sweep your own doorstep before you clean someone else's. **(f)** Sweep your own doorstep clean. **(g)** Sweep your own doorstep clean before scowling at others. **(h)** Sweep your own doorstep off first. *Rec. dist.*: Oreg. *1st cit.*: 1930 *London Times*, 25 Mar. *20c. coll.*: ODEP 793.

2. The doorstep of a great house is slippery. *Var.*: Slippery is the flagstone of the grand house door. *Rec. dist.*: Ill.

dose A dose is not worse than a bad cold. *Rec. dist.*: Calif., N.Y.

double *(adj.)* *See* A reconciled FRIEND is a double enemy. / TONGUE double brings trouble.

doubt *(n.)* **1.** A little doubt saves many a mistake. *Rec. dist.*: N.C.

2. Doubt comes in at the window when inquiry is denied at the door. *Rec. dist.*: Minn.

3. Doubt grows up with knowledge. *Rec. dist.*: Utah. *Infm.*: Varied in form. This form is German. Cf. Goethe, *Sprüche in Prosa* (1819). *1st cit.*: US1948 Stevenson, *Home Book of Proverbs*. *20c. coll.*: Stevenson 619:6.

4. Doubts never yet helped a man to live, to grow, or to build. *Rec. dist.*: Tex.

5. Our doubts are traitors. *Rec. dist.*: Minn.

6. When doubt comes in, love goes out. *Rec. dist.*: N.Y., S.C.

7. When doubt is doubted, death is clouted. *Rec. dist.*: Ill.

8. When in doubt, ask. *Vars.*: **(a)** When in doubt, find out. **(b)** When in doubt, look about. *Rec. dist.*: Calif., Ill.

9. When in doubt, hesitate. *Rec. dist.:* Kans.

10. When in doubt, leave it out. *Vars.:* **(a)** If doubtful, don't. **(b)** When in doubt what to do, don't do it. **(c)** When in doubt, do nothing. **(d)** When in doubt, do without. **(e)** When in doubt, don't. **(f)** When in doubt, don't do it. **(g)** When in doubt, say no. *Rec. dist.:* U.S. *1st cit.:* 1917 Bridge, *Cheshire Proverbs;* US1884 Weatherly, *Little Folks Proverb Painting Book.* *20c. coll.:* ODEP 200, CODP 59, Whiting*(MP)* 184.

11. When in doubt, punt. *Rec. dist.:* Ind. *Infm.:* Originated in football.

12. When in doubt, salute. *Rec. dist.:* Ky., Tenn. *Infm.:* Military advice to a young recruit.

13. When in doubt, tell the truth. *Rec. dist.:* Ala., Ill. *1st cit.:* US1893 Twain, *Pudd'nhead Wilson's Calendar. 20c. coll.:* Stevenson 619:11.

SEE ALSO QUIET people, whether wise or dull, get the benefit of the doubt.

doubt *(v.)* **1.** Doubt whom you will, but never doubt yourself. *Rec. dist.:* Minn.

2. He who doubts nothing knows nothing. *Rec. dist.:* Ill.

3. Who never doubted never half believed. *Rec. dist.:* N.C.

SEE ALSO It is easier to BELIEVE than to doubt. / Twin FOOLS: one doubts nothing, the other everything. / Never try to PROVE what nobody doubts.

doubtful If doubtful, do. *Rec. dist.:* Calif., N.Y.

dough It takes dough to have crust. *Rec. dist.:* Oreg.

SEE ALSO It will never, never go to make two BREADS from one dough.

down **1.** A man may be down, but he is never out. *Var.:* A man may be down but not out. *Rec. dist.:* N.Y., N.C. *1st cit.:* USca1925 Leffingwell, slogan of Salvation Army. *20c. coll.:* Stevenson 620:13, Whiting*(MP)* 176.

2. Don't be down on something before you are up on it. *Rec. dist.:* Minn.

3. He that is down need fear no fall. *Var.:* He that is down can fall no lower. *Rec. dist.:* Ill.,

Iowa, N.Y. *1st cit.:* 1539 Publilius Syrus, *Sententiae,* tr. Taverner. *20c. coll.:* Stevenson 748:1.

4. It is easier to pull down than to build up. *Var.:* It's easier to go down than up. *Rec. dist.:* N.Y., S.C. *1st cit.:* 1577 Stanyhurst, *History of Ireland* in Holinshed, *Chronicles. 20c. coll.:* ODEP 655, CODP 185.

5. When a man is down, don't kick him lower. *Rec. dist.:* N.C. *1st cit.:* 1551 Cranmer, *Answer to Gardiner;* US1634 Wood, *New-England's Prospects,* Publ. Prince Soc. (1865). *20c. coll.:* ODEP 374, Whiting 281, Stevenson 1292:8, T&W 207, Whiting*(MP)* 401.

6. When a man is down, everyone runs over him. *Vars.:* **(a)** When a man is down, everyone picks on him. **(b)** When a man is down, everyone steps on him. **(c)** When a man's down, you know, people are inclined to kick him. *Rec. dist.:* U.S., Can. *1st cit.:* 1530 Palsgrave, *Lesclarcissement de la langue Francoyse. 20c. coll.:* ODEP 200.

7. You can't hold another fellow down in the ditch unless you stay down there with him. *Rec. dist.:* Wis.

8. You can't keep a good man down. *Rec. dist.:* U.S., Can. *1st cit.:* 1942 Lasswell, *Suds in Your Eye;* US1900 Carey, Title of popular song. *20c. coll.:* Stevenson 997:4, Whiting *(MP)* 399.

SEE ALSO Rub a HOG and he'll lay down on you. / It is harder to climb the MOUNTAIN than to climb down. / It is easier to PULL down than to build up. / WATER always flows down, not up. / A WORM is about the only thing that does not fall down.

downfall SEE EVIL will be its own downfall. / SECURITY is man's downfall.

downhill When a man is going downhill, everyone gives him a push. *Rec. dist.:* N.Y., S.C. *1st cit.:* 1732 Fuller, *Gnomologia;* US1809 Weems, *Mario. 20c. coll.:* Stevenson 1292:8, Whiting 281, T&W 207.

downstream Anyone can go downstream, but it takes a real man to go upstream. *Rec. dist.:* N.C.

downward SEE The downward ROAD is easy.

dozen SEE ELEVEN don't make a dozen.

draw SEE Do not put your FOOT further than you can draw it back again. / Don't stick out your HAND further than you can draw it back. / Two PEOPLE draw four, and four draw eight.

drawn SEE Drawn WELLS are seldom dry.

dread SEE It is not the father's ANGER but his silence his son dreads. / He who burns BREAD must hunger dread. / A singed CAT dreads the fire. / A burnt CHILD dreads the fire.

dream *(n.)* **1.** A man's dreams are his own. *Rec. dist.:* N.C. *Infm.:* Stevenson cites Petronius, *Fragments*. **1st cit.:** US1948 Stevenson, *Home Book of Proverbs*. **20c. coll.:** Stevenson 623:8.

2. Dreams are what you hope for; reality is what you plan for. *Rec. dist.:* Ala., Ga.

3. Dreams are wishes your heart makes. *Rec. dist.:* Kans.

4. Dreams give wings to fools. *Rec. dist.:* N.Y. **1st cit.:** US1948 Stevenson, *Home Book of Proverbs*. **20c. coll.:** Stevenson 622:2.

5. Dreams go by contraries. *Var.:* Dreams go contrary. *Rec. dist.:* Ill., N.Y., S.C. **1st cit.:** ca1400 *Tale of Beryn*, E.E.T.S. (1909); USca1725 *Secret Diary of William Byrd of Westover, 1739–1741*, ed. Woodfin (1942). **20c. coll.:** ODEP 202, Whiting 120, CODP 60, Stevenson 621:15, T&W 110, Whiting (MP)185.

6. Dreams retain the infirmities of our character. *Rec. dist.:* Ill. **1st cit.:** US1877 Emerson, *Demonology*. **20c. coll.:** Stevenson 622:5.

7. In dreams and in love, nothing is impossible. *Rec. dist.:* N.Y.

8. Love's dreams prove seldom true. *Rec. dist.:* Ill.

9. Only in dreams does happiness of the earth dwell. *Rec. dist.:* Ill.

10. You can make your dreams come true if you wake up and work. *Vars.:* **(a)** Dreaming won't help us accomplish our aims, but work will. **(b)** To make dreams come true, don't oversleep. **(c)** Your dreams won't come true until you wake up. *Rec. dist.:* Kans., N.Y.

SEE ALSO FAILURE isn't the end of dreams, it is only the beginning. / LIFE is but a dream.

dream *(v.)* **1.** People who dream all night don't work all day. *Rec. dist.:* Kans.

2. The more a man dreams, the less he believes. *Rec. dist.:* N.Y., S.C. **1st cit.:** US1920 Mencken, *Prejudices*. **20c. coll.:** Stevenson 623:6.

3. To dream is to see beyond. *Rec. dist.:* N.Y.

dress **1.** Keep a dress seven years and it will come back into style. *Var.:* Keep a dress long enough and it will come back in style. *Rec. dist.:* Ky., Tenn.

2. Love of dress is sure the very curse. *Var.:* Fond of dress is sure a very curse; ere you fancy consult your purse. *Rec. dist.:* Ind., N.Y. **1st cit.:** US1940 Thompson, *Body, Boots, and Britches*. **20c. coll.:** Stevenson 367:7.

dressed The best-dressed woman usually arrives last with the least. *Rec. dist.:* Ont.

SEE ALSO The FOOL well dressed is at his best.

driftwood Driftwood never goes upstream. *Rec. dist.:* Ill.

drink *(n.)* **1.** A man takes a drink and then the drink takes the man. *Var.:* A man takes a drink, the drink takes a drink, the drink takes the man. *Rec. dist.:* Ill., Iowa. **1st cit.:** 1574 Guazzo, *Civile Conversation*, tr. Young. **20c. coll.:** Stevenson 627:13.

2. Drink does not drown care, but waters it and makes it grow faster. *Rec. dist.:* N.Y., S.C.

3. Drink is the curse of the working class. *Rec. dist.:* Ariz.

4. Of all the meat in the world, drink goes down the best. *Rec. dist.:* N.Y., S.C. **1st cit.:** 1721 Kelly, *Scottish Proverbs*. **20c. coll.:** Stevenson 633:8.

5. One drink is good, two is too much, and three is not enough. *Rec. dist.:* N.Y.

6. One drink leads to another. *Rec. dist.:* Okla.

7. One man's drink is another man's poison. *Var.:* One man's poison is another man's drink. *Rec. dist.:* Kans. *Infm.:* Cf. meat.

8. The last drink is always the best. *Rec. dist.:* N.Y.

9. The one who takes a drink now and then is always drunk. *Rec. dist.:* N.C.

10. The smaller the drink, the clearer the head, the cooler the blood. *Rec. dist.:* N.Y. *1st cit.:* US1693 Penn, *Some Fruits of Solitude.* *20c. coll.:* Stevenson 632:6.

11. When the drink is in the many, the wisdom is in the can. *Rec. dist.:* Ariz.

12. You can't take a second drink unless you have taken a first. *Rec. dist.:* Ind.

SEE ALSO WATER is the only drink for a wise man.

drink *(v.)* **1.** Drink like hell and be happy. *Rec. dist.:* N.Y., S.C. *1st cit.:* US1948 Stevenson, *Home Book of Proverbs.* *20c. coll.:* Stevenson 630:2.

2. Drink little that you may drink long. *Rec. dist.:* Idaho, Kans.

3. He who drinks and walks away lives to drink another day. *Rec. dist.:* Ind.

4. He who drinks fast pays slow. *Rec. dist.:* Ill., Oreg.

5. It is all right to drink like a fish if you drink what a fish drinks. *Rec. dist.:* Fla.

6. Nobody should drink but those that can drink. *Rec. dist.:* N.Y.

7. The more you drink, the more you want. *Rec. dist.:* Oreg. *1st cit.:* 1557 North, *Diall of Princes.* *20c. coll.:* ODEP 204.

8. Thousands drink themselves to death before one dies of thirst. *Rec. dist.:* Calif., N.Y.

9. Who has drunk will drink. *Var.:* A man who drank once will drink again. *Rec. dist.:* N.Y.

SEE ALSO He that sips many ARTS drinks none. / They who drink BEER think beer. / As you BREW, so must you drink. / While drinking from one CUP, look not into another. / As well to eat the DEVIL as drink his broth. / If you DRIVE, don't drink; if you drink, don't drive. / EAT, drink, and be merry, for tomorrow we may die. / You can lead a HORSE to water, but you can't make him drink. / He that spills the RUM loses that only; he that drinks it, often loses that and himself. / The still sow drinks the slop. / Those who drink but WATER will have no liquor to buy. / Do not spit into the WELL: you may have to drink out of it. / Drink WINE and have the gout; drink none and have it too.

drinker There are more old drinkers than old doctors. *Var.:* There are more old drunkards than old doctors. *Rec. dist.:* Oreg. *1st cit.:* 1574 Guazzo, *Civile Conversation,* tr. Young; US1736 Franklin, *PRAlmanac.* *20c. coll.:* Stevenson 596:12, Whiting 122.

drinking *(n.)* Drinking and thinking don't mix. *Rec. dist.:* Ind.

drinking *(adj.)* SEE DEATH rides with the drinking driver.

dripping Constant dripping wears away a stone. *Vars.:* **(a)** Constant dripping wears away stone. **(b)** Constant dripping wears away the hardest stone. **(c)** Constant dripping will wear away the stone. **(d)** The constant drip of water will wear away the hardest rock. **(e)** The constant dripping of water will wear away the strongest stone. *Rec. dist.:* U.S., Can. *1st cit.:* ca1200 *Ancrene Riwle,* ed. Morton, Camden Soc. (1853); US1702 Mather, *Magnalia Christi Americana* (1853–55). *20c. coll.:* ODEP 141, Whiting 121, CODP 42, Stevenson 2463:1, T&W 111, Whiting(MP) 186.

drive **1.** Drive safe today and drive tomorrow. *Rec. dist.:* Okla.

2. If you drive, don't drink; if you drink, don't drive. *Rec. dist.:* U.S.

3. You can drive sixty miles a minute, but there ain't no future in it. *Rec. dist.:* Calif., N.Y.

SEE ALSO Drive your BUSINESS or it will drive you. / He must needs go whom the DEVIL drives. / Bad MONEY drives out good. / One NAIL drives out another. / NEEDS must when necessity drives. / If PASSION drives, let reason hold the reins. / He that by the PLOW would thrive, himself must either hold or drive. / He who SINGS drives away his cares. / The WAGON of God drives slowly and well. / A WOMAN can't drive her husband, but she can lead him.

driven SEE A man may be LED, but he can't be driven.

driver The best drivers have wrecks. *Rec. dist.:* Okla.

SEE ALSO DEATH rides with the drinking driver.

drop *(n.)* **1.** A drop in the bucket each day will fill your life with happiness some day. *Rec. dist.:* Calif., N.Y.

2. A little drop may end in a great fall. *Rec. dist.:* N.J. *Infm.:* One drink can lead to one's downfall.

3. Drop by drop and the pitcher is full. *Rec. dist.:* N.Y. *1st cit.:* 1732 Fuller, *Gnomologia.* *20c. coll.:* Stevenson 642:8.

4. Little drops produce a shower. *Rec. dist.:* Ind. *1st cit.:* 1559 *Mirror for Magistrates.* *20c. coll.:* ODEP 509, Stevenson 642:11.

5. Many drops of water make an ocean. *Vars.:* **(a)** Little drops of water, little grains of sand, make a mighty ocean and a pleasant land. **(b)** Little drops of water, little grains of sand, make the mighty ocean and the pleasant lands. **(c)** The whole ocean is made up of little drops. *Rec. dist.:* N.Y., N.C., Ohio, S.C. *1st cit.:* 1845 Carney, *Little Things.* *20c. coll.:* Stevenson 642:11.

6. Many drops of water will sink a ship. *Rec. dist.:* Ill., Kans., Tex., Vt.

7. One drop of liquor makes two drips. *Rec. dist.:* N.Y. *Infm.:* "Drip" refers to a foolish person. The proverb warns against the evil of drink.

8. The falling drops at last will wear the stone. *Vars.:* **(a)** A steady drop knocks a hole in the rock. **(b)** A steady drop makes a hole in a rock. **(c)** The constant drop wears the stone. *Rec. dist.:* Calif., N.Y. *1st cit.:* ca1200 *Ancrene Riwle,* ed. Morton, Camden Soc. (1853); US1702 Mather, *Magnalia Christi Americana* (1853–55). *20c. coll.:* ODEP 141, Whiting 121, CODP 42, Stevenson 2463:1, T&W 111, Whiting(MP) 186.

9. The last drop makes the cup turn over. *Rec. dist.:* U.S., Can. *1st cit.:* 1655 Fuller, *Church-History of Britain.* *20c. coll.:* ODEP 443, CODP 60, Stevenson 2226:2.

SEE ALSO A drop of INK may make a million think.

drop *(v.)* SEE The weakest FRUIT drops earliest to the ground.

dropping **1.** A continual dropping on a very rainy day and a contentious woman are alike. *Rec. dist.:* Calif., N.Y. *1st cit.:* ca1386 Chaucer, *Tale of Melibee;* US1966 Boyle, *With a Pinch of Sin.* *20c. coll.:* ODEP 817, Whiting(MP) 186.

2. Constant dropping wears away the stone. *Vars.:* **(a)** Constant dropping wears away stones. **(b)** Constant dropping wears the stone. **(c)** Continual dropping wears away the stone. **(d)** Continued dropping will wear away a rock. *Rec. dist.:* U.S., Can. *Infm.:* Cf. dripping. *1st cit.:* ca1200 *Ancrene Riwle,* ed. Morton, Camden Soc. (1853); US1702 Mather, *Magnalia Christi Americana* (1853–55). *20c. coll.:* ODEP 141, Whiting 121, CODP 42, Stevenson 2463:1, T&W 111, Whiting(MP) 186.

drought A three years' drought will not starve a cook. *Rec. dist.:* Wis.

drown Don't drown yourself to save a drowning man. *Var.:* Drown not yourself to save a drowning man. *Rec. dist.:* Ont. *1st cit.:* 1732 Fuller, *Gnomologia.* *20c. coll.:* Stevenson 643:4.

drowned SEE BACCHUS has drowned more than Neptune and has killed more than Mars. / You can never HANG a man if he is born to be drowned. / WINE has drowned more men than the sea.

drowning A drowning man will catch at a straw. *Vars.:* **(a)** A drowning man clutches at a thread. **(b)** A drowning man grabs at a straw. *Rec. dist.:* U.S., Can. *1st cit.:* 1534 More, *Dialogue of Comfort Against Tribulation;* US1720 Noyes, Letter in *Colonial Currency,* ed. Davis, Publ. Prince Soc. (1910–11). *20c. coll.:* ODEP 205, Whiting 275, CODP 60, Stevenson 643:5, T&W 233, Whiting(MP) 394.

SEE ALSO A FOOL will ask for a glass of water when he is drowning. / HOPE keeps a man from hanging and drowning himself.

drowsiness Drowsiness shall clothe a man with rags. *Var.:* Drowsiness dresses a man in rags. *Rec. dist.:* Miss., Vt. *Infm.:* Stevenson cites ca350 B.C.E., *Old Testament: Proverbs* 23:21. *1st cit.:* US1948 Stevenson, *Home Book of Proverbs.* *20c. coll.:* Stevenson 2141:6.

drug The drug always does good, if not to the patient at least to the druggist. *Rec. dist.:* Ill.

See also A physician is a man who pours drugs of which he knows little into a body of which he knows less.

drum 1. A hollow drum makes the most noise. *Rec. dist.:* U.S., Can. *Infm.:* Cf. Barrel, tub, wagon, etc.

2. Where drums beat, laws are silent. *Rec. dist.:* Mich. *1st cit.:* 1549 Bullinger, *Treatise Concerning Magistrates.* *20c. coll.:* ODEP 205, Stevenson 643:10.

See also If you don't know how to dance, you say that the drum is bad.

drunk 1. A drunk man and a sleepwalker never get hurt when they fall. *Rec. dist.:* N.C.

2. A drunk man will sober up, but a damn fool never. *Rec. dist.:* Calif., N.Y.

3. Ever drunk, ever dry. *Rec. dist.:* N.Y. *1st cit.:* 1509 Barclay, *Ship of Fools,* ed. Jamieson in *Eclogues,* E.E.T.S. (1874). *20c. coll.:* ODEP 227, Stevenson 635:7.

4. The drunk man is the rich man. *Rec. dist.:* N.C. *Infm.:* Drink makes one feel like he or she is rich.

drunkard 1. A drunkard puts ten times more in his jug than he gets out of it. *Rec. dist.:* Ind.

2. A young drunkard, an old pauper. *Rec. dist.:* N.Y.

3. Once a drunkard, always a drunkard. *Rec. dist.:* Ill.

4. The drunkard's cure is drink again. *Rec. dist.:* Minn.

5. You can always tell a drunkard by his actions. *Rec. dist.:* Calif., N.Y.

drunken 1. A drunken man will get sober, but a fool will never get wise. *Rec. dist.:* Ont.

2. Drunken folks seldom take harm. *Rec. dist.:* Vt. *1st cit.:* 1591 Ariosto, *Orlando Furioso,* tr. Harrington; US1702 Mather, *Magnalia Christi Americana* (1853–55). *20c. coll.:* ODEP 206, Whiting 276, Stevenson 636:2.

3. You can't kill a drunken man. *Rec. dist.:* N.Y.

See also Drunken days have their tomorrow. / A drunken doctor is always smart.

drunkenness 1. Don't add drunkenness to thirst. *Rec. dist.:* Minn., N.Y.

2. Drunkenness is an egg from which all vices are hatched. *Rec. dist.:* N.J., Ont.

3. Drunkenness is voluntary madness. *Rec. dist.:* Ohio, Oreg. *1st cit.:* US1948 Stevenson, *Home Book of Proverbs.* *20c. coll.:* Stevenson 638:11.

See also What soberness conceals, drunkenness reveals.

dry *(v.)* *See* Nothing dries sooner than tears. / There is a time to fish and a time to dry nets.

dry *(adj.)* *See* A pair of good ears will drain dry a hundred tongues. / Don't count fish till on dry land. / It's a dry kettle that has the most spouting. / Keep your powder dry. / The rain that rains on everybody else can't keep you dry. / You never miss the water till the well runs dry. / Drawn wells are seldom dry.

ducat If you want to know what a ducat is worth, borrow one. *Vars.:* **(a)** If you want to know the value of money, try borrowing some. **(b)** If you want to know what money is worth, try borrowing some. *Rec. dist.:* Ill., Ohio. *Infm.:* Cf. money. *1st cit.:* 1659 Howell, *Paroimiographia (Spanish Proverbs).* *20c. coll.:* ODEP 435.

duck 1. A duck never flies so high but that it has to come down for water. *Rec. dist.:* N.Mex. *Infm.:* Cf. bird.

2. A duck won't always paddle in the same gutter. *Rec. dist.:* Miss. *1st cit.:* 1721 Kelly, *Scottish Proverbs.* *20c. coll.:* ODEP 207, Stevenson 644:11.

3. Every duck thinks it is a swan. *Rec. dist.:* Minn.

4. Every mother's duck is a swan. *Rec. dist.:* N.Y.

5. It's better to be a big duck in a little puddle than to be a little duck in a big puddle. *Var.:* Rather be a big duck in a little pond than a little duck in a big one. *Rec. dist.:* U.S.

6. Nothing ruins a duck but his bill. *Vars.:* **(a)** A wise duck takes care of its bill. **(b)** Nothing ruins a duck like his bill. *Rec. dist.:* Ill., N.Y., N.C., S.C.

7. Roasted ducks don't fly into your mouth. *Rec. dist.:* N.Y.

dude   A ten-dollar dude may have a two-dollar salary. *Rec. dist.:* Calif., N.Y.

due *(n.)* **1.** Some pay their dues when due, some others when overdue, and some never do. *Rec. dist.:* Wis.

2. Who loses his due gets no thanks. *Rec. dist.:* Mich. *1st cit.:* 1640 Herbert, *Outlandish Proverbs (Jacula Prudentum)* in *Works,* ed. Hutchinson (1941). *20c. coll.:* ODEP 486.

SEE ALSO Give the DEVIL his dues. / Pay the PIPER his due.

due *(adj.)*   SEE Give CREDIT to whom credit is due. / HONOR to whom honor is due. / WORRY is interest paid on trouble before it falls due.

dull   It is the dull man who is always sure and the sure man who is always dull. *Rec. dist.:* N.Y. *1st cit.:* US1920 Mencken, *Prejudices.* *20c. coll.:* Stevenson 645:10.

SEE ALSO QUIET people, whether wise or dull, get the benefit of the doubt. / A dull SAW cuts deepest. / Dull SCISSORS can't cut straight. / All WORK and no play makes Jack a dull boy.

dumb   **1.** Dumb folks get no lands. *Rec. dist.:* Ont. *1st cit.:* ca1390 Gower, *Confessio Amantis,* E.E.T.S. (1900). *20c. coll.:* ODEP 208, Stevenson 1646:6.

2. Nothing is dumber than a goose. *Rec. dist.:* Kans.

3. There's none so dumb as those who will not learn. *Rec. dist.:* Ind., N.Y.

SEE ALSO Good LISTENING does not mean sitting dumb.

dump   SEE It's easier to dump the CART than to load it.

dunce   **1.** The dunce wonders; the wise man asks. *Rec. dist.:* Ill.

2. The globe-trotting dunce is more stupid than the dunce who stays at home. *Rec. dist.:* Ill.

dungeon   SEE The love of LIBERTY burns brightest in a dungeon.

dupe   One begins by being a dupe; one ends by being a rascal. *Rec. dist.:* Ill. *1st cit.:* US1948 Stevenson, *Home Book of Proverbs.* *20c. coll.:* Stevenson 931:14.

durability   Durability is better than show. *Rec. dist.:* Ill.

durable   Nothing is more durable than a hog's snout. *Rec. dist.:* Ill.

duration   SEE Deepest HAPPINESS is for a short duration.

dust   **1.** A speck of dust may clog the works of a watch. *Rec. dist.:* N.Y., S.C.

2. Every pint of March dust brings a peck of September corn and a pound of 'tober cotton. *Rec. dist.:* Calif., N.Y.

3. He that blows dust fills his own eyes. *Rec. dist.:* Ind., Mich., N.Y., Okla., Vt. *1st cit.:* 1640 Herbert, *Outlandish Proverbs (Jacula Prudentum)* in *Works,* ed. Hutchinson (1941). *20c. coll.:* ODEP 70, Stevenson 1967:2.

4. There is no dust so blinding as gold dust. *Rec. dist.:* N.J. *1st cit.:* 1875 Cheales, *Proverbial Folk-Lore.* *20c. coll.:* Stevenson 987:5.

SEE ALSO Write INJURIES in dust, benefits in marble. / A small RAIN lays a great dust. / SECONDS are the gold dust of time.

Dutchman   Judge a Dutchman by what he means, not by what he says. *Var.:* Take a Dutchman as he means, not as he says. *Rec. dist.:* Ill., Ind.

duty   **1.** A duty should be injurious to no one. *Rec. dist.:* N.C.

2. A neglected duty returns tomorrow with seven others at its back. *Rec. dist.:* Ala., Ga., N.Y.

3. Do your duty and be afraid of none. *Rec. dist.:* N.Y. *1st cit.:* US1749 *Letters and Papers of Cadwallader Colden,* N.Y.Hist.Soc. *Collections* (1917–37). *20c. coll.:* Whiting 124.

4. Duties are ours; events are God's. *Rec. dist.:* Ill.

5. Duty before pleasure. *Rec. dist.:* N.Y., Ohio, Utah, Wis.

6. Duty done is the soul's fireside. *Rec. dist.:* Ind.

7. He who sidesteps duty avoids a gain. *Rec. dist.:* Ohio.

8. Higher duties mean greater responsibilities. *Rec. dist.:* N.C.

9. It is a man's duty to go as far as he can on the right road. *Rec. dist.:* Minn., Utah.

10. Only aim to do your duty, and mankind will give you credit where you fail. *Rec. dist.:* Calif., N.Y.

11. There is not a moment without some duty. *Rec. dist.:* N.J., N.Y.

12. What ain't your duty ain't your business. *Rec. dist.:* Oreg.

dwell It is better to dwell in the corner of a housetop than with a brawling woman in a wide house. *Rec. dist.:* Ala., Ga.

SEE ALSO Where there is GOLD, there the devil dwells. / LOVE cannot dwell with suspicion.

dye *SEE* Bad is the WOOL that cannot be dyed.

dying *(n.)* **1.** Dying is as natural as living. *Rec. dist.:* U.S., Can. *1st cit.:* 1597 Bacon, "Of Death" in *Essays.* *20c. coll.:* Stevenson 523:7.

2. Dying once, even for one's country, is once too often. *Rec. dist.:* N.Y.

3. The dying never weep. *Rec. dist.:* Ohio.

dying *(adj.)* Dying men speak true. *Rec. dist.:* N.Y., S.C. *1st cit.:* 1595 Copley, *Wits, Fits.* *20c. coll.:* ODEP 210.

SEE ALSO Dying FLIES spoil the sweetness of the ointment. / A dying HORSE can kick harder than a normal horse.

dynamite Dynamite comes in small packages. *Rec. dist.:* U.S.

E

each *(pn.)*   To each his own. *Rec. dist.:* U.S. **Infm.:** Similar to "Every man to his own taste." *1st cit.:* US1713 Wise, *Churches Quarrel Espoused,* ed. Cook, Scholar's Facsimile Reprints (1966). *20c. coll.:* Whiting 125, Whiting(MP) 192.

each *(adj.)*   SEE Take each DAY as it comes. / Into each life some RAIN must fall.

eagle   **1.** Attempt not to fly like an eagle with the wings of a wren. *Rec. dist.:* Mich. *1st cit.:* 1909 Hudson, *Afoot in England. 20c. coll.:* Stevenson 2650:1.

2. Eagles don't catch flies. *Rec. dist.:* Colo., N.Y. *1st cit.:* 1574 Guazzo, *Civile Conversation,* tr. Pettie, T.T. (1925); US1645 Wheelwright, *His Writings,* ed. Bell, Publ. Prince Soc. (1876). *20c. coll.:* Stevenson 650:5, Whiting 125, Whiting(MP) 192.

3. Eagles fly alone, but sheep flock together. *Var.:* Eagles sleep alone, but sheep flock together. *Rec. dist.:* Ill., Mich., Wis. *1st cit.:* ca1580 Sidney, *Arcadia. 20c. coll.:* ODEP 211, Stevenson 651:8.

4. Eagles fly high. *Rec. dist.:* Vt.

5. The old age of an eagle is as good as the youth of a sparrow. *Rec. dist.:* Ill., Wis.

6. When the eagle is dead, the crows pick out his eyes. *Rec. dist.:* Ill.

7. Where the carrion is, there the eagles gather. *Var.:* Where the carcass is, there will the eagles be gathered. *Rec. dist.:* Ill., Ind., N.Y. *1st cit.:* ca1566 Curio, *Pasquin in Trance;* US1654 Johnson, *Wonder-Working. 20c. coll.:* ODEP 102, Whiting 57, CODP 31, Stevenson 651:3, T&W 56, Whiting(MP) 91.

SEE ALSO Puttin' FEATHERS on a buzzard don't make it no eagle. / A good SURGEON must have an eagle's eye, a lion's heart, and a lady's hand.

ear *(body)*   **1.** A pair of good ears will drain dry a hundred tongues. *Rec. dist.:* Ill., Minn., N.J., N.Dak. *1st cit.:* 1640 Herbert, *Outlandish Proverbs (Jacula Prudentum)* in *Works,*

ed. Hutchinson (1941); US1753 Franklin, *PRAlmanac. 20c. coll.:* ODEP 607, Stevenson 655:7.

2. An open ear and a closed mouth is the best known substitution for wisdom. *Rec. dist.:* Utah.

3. Give every man your ear but few your voice. *Rec. dist.:* Ill., N.Y., Utah. *1st cit.:* 1600 Shakespeare, *Hamlet. 20c. coll.:* Stevenson 656:1.

4. Have a wide ear and a short tongue. *Rec. dist.:* Minn. *1st cit.:* 1597 *Politeuphuia Wits Commonwealth. 20c. coll.:* ODEP 887, Stevenson 652:1.

5. He who has ears to hear, let him hear. *Rec. dist.:* N.Y., Utah. *1st cit.:* US1948 Stevenson, *Home Book of Proverbs. 20c. coll.:* Stevenson 653:8.

6. Keep your ears open: even a rattlesnake will warn before he bites. *Rec. dist.:* Ark., Ga., Ohio.

7. No ear is deaf to the song that gold sings. *Rec. dist.:* N.Y.

8. No ear is so deaf as one which wishes not to hear. *Rec. dist.:* N.Y.

9. One can't hear one's own ears. *Rec. dist.:* Tex. *1st cit.:* 1738 Swift, *Collection of Genteel and Ingenious Conversation. 20c. coll.:* Stevenson 654:4.

10. What the ear does not hear disturbs not the mind. *Rec. dist.:* Minn. *1st cit.:* US1875 Scarborough, *Chinese Proverbs. 20c. coll.:* Stevenson 738:2.

11. You'll hear a lot of things before your ears drop off. *Rec. dist.:* Ohio.

SEE ALSO It is better to trust the EYE than the ear. / A FOOL talks with his ears stuffed up. / HUNGRY bellies have no ears. / Little PITCHERS have big ears. / You can't make a silk PURSE out of a sow's ear. / You can't tell how far a RABBIT can jump by the length of its ears. / Tune your own UTTERANCE to your own ear. / The WALL has ears, and the plain has eyes.

ear *(corn)* You can't have the ear unless you plant the corn. *Rec. dist.:* Miss.

early *(adj.)* SEE Good LUCK beats early rising.

early *(adv.)* **1.** Because you rise earlier does not mean it will be daylight. *Rec. dist.:* N.Y.

2. Early to rise has virtues three: 'tis healthy, wealthy, and Godly. *Rec. dist.:* N.Y.

3. Better early than late, but better never late. *Rec. dist.:* N.Y., Ont.

4. He who gets up early has gold in his mouth. *Rec. dist.:* Ariz.

5. He who rises early makes progress in his work. *Rec. dist.:* R.I.

6. Rise early, live soberly, and apply yourself with industry. *Rec. dist.:* Mich.

7. They that get the name of rising early may lie in bed all day. *Var.:* One may get up late if one has the name of getting up early. *Rec. dist.:* Miss., N.Y., Ont.

8. To get up early three mornings is equal to one day of time. *Rec. dist.:* Ind.

SEE ALSO The weakest kind of FRUIT drops earliest to the ground. / It early pricks that will be a THORN.

earn SEE Learn a TRADE and earn a living.

earned SEE A PENNY saved is a penny earned.

earning SEE There's more in SAVING than there is in earning.

earth **1.** Earth has no sorrow that heaven cannot heal. *Rec. dist.:* Fla., N.Y. *1st cit.:* ca1852 Moore, *Come, Ye Disconsolate;* US1909 Henry, *Discounters of Money.* *20c. coll.:* Stevenson 2168:5.

2. No one is entitled to more than six feet of earth. *Rec. dist.:* Wis.

3. Six feet of earth makes all men equal. *Vars.:* **(a)** Six feet of earth make all men of one size. **(b)** Six feet underground makes all men equal. *Rec. dist.:* N.Y., Ohio, Wis. *1st cit.:* 1563 *Mirror for Magistrates,* ed. Campbell. *20c. coll.:* ODEP 738, Stevenson 1027:12.

4. The earth provides all things and receives all again. *Rec. dist.:* Ill.

SEE ALSO There are more THINGS than are thought of in heaven and earth. / TRUTH, crushed to earth, will rise again.

ease **1.** Think of ease but work on. *Rec. dist.:* Ohio. *1st cit.:* 1640 Herbert, *Outlandish Proverbs (Jacula Prudentum)* in *Works,* ed. Hutchinson (1941). *20c. coll.:* ODEP 812, Stevenson 2619:4.

2. When you are not at ease with others, others are not at ease with you. *Rec. dist.:* Kans.

3. Would you live with ease, do what you ought and not what you please. *Rec. dist.:* Miss.

SEE ALSO He that is ANGRY is seldom at ease. / Anything worth HAVING is never gotten on a flowery bed of ease.

easily SEE LUCK and glass break easily. / PEOPLE are more easily led than driven.

east **1.** East is east, and west is west, and never the twain shall meet. *Rec. dist.:* U.S. *1st cit.:* ca1900 Kipling, *Ballad of East and West.* *20c. coll.:* Stevenson 659:2.

2. Too far east is west. *Rec. dist.:* Ill., N.J. *1st cit.:* 1664 Butler, *Hudibras.* *20c. coll.:* ODEP 831, Stevenson 658:16.

SEE ALSO East or west, HOME is best.

Easter SEE A green CHRISTMAS, a white Easter.

easy *(adj.)* **1.** A thing easy to get is easy to lose. *Rec. dist.:* Ill., N.Y. *1st cit.:* US1650 Bradstreet, *Tenth Muse.* *20c. coll.:* CODP 63.

2. Easy got, easy gain: short joy, long pain. *Rec. dist.:* Miss.

3. Easy is as easy does. *Rec. dist.:* Ohio, Wis.

4. Nothing is easy to the unwilling. *Rec. dist.:* Ill. *1st cit.:* 1732 Fuller, *Gnomologia;* USca1800 Jefferson, *Writings.* *20c. coll.:* Stevenson 2511:7.

5. Some things seem easy at first, but they are easier said than done. *Rec. dist.:* N.Y., Okla.

6. Take-it-easy and live-long are brothers. *Rec. dist.:* Miss.

SEE ALSO It is easy to be BRAVE from a safe distance. / It's easier to build two CHIMNEYS than to keep one in fuel. / It's much easier to be CRITICAL than correct. / The DESCENT to hell is easy. / It is easy to DESPISE what you cannot get. / All things are DIFFICULT before they are easy. / The easiest way to get a DIVORCE is to be married. / It is easier to pull DOWN than to build up. / To FORGIVE is easy; to forget is impossible. / A FRIEND is easier lost than found. / A GOOD man is seldom uneasy, an ill one never easy. / It is a thousand times easier to contract a new HABIT than to get rid of an old one. / It is easy for a man in HEALTH to preach patience to the sick. / A gentle HEART is tied with an easy thread. / All things are easy to INDUSTRY, all things difficult to sloth. / A LADY is a woman who makes it easy for a man to be a gentleman. / Easy to LEARN, hard to master. / ORDER and method make all things easy. / It is easy to REPEAT but hard to originate. / It is easier SAID than done. / Old SHOES are easy, old friends are best. / SLAVERY is too high a price to pay for easy living. / It's easy to STEAL from a cut loaf.

easy *(adv.)* **1.** Easy come, easy go. *Rec. dist.:* U.S. **1st cit.:** 1832 Warren, *Diary of Late Physician;* US1650 *Works of Anne Bradstreet,* ed. Ellis (1932). **20c. coll.:** *ODEP* 213, Whiting 80, Stevenson 660:5, T&W 77, Whiting(*MP*) 127.

2. Easy does it. *Rec. dist.:* U.S. **1st cit.:** US1908 Young, *Climbing Doom.* **20c. coll.:** Whiting(*MP*) 195.

eat **1.** A man eats so he works. *Rec. dist.:* Ind.

2. Dem what eats kin say grace. *Rec. dist.:* Ga.

3. Don't eat before you set the table. *Rec. dist.:* Ont.

4. Eat at pleasure; drink by measure. *Rec. dist.:* Ill. **1st cit.:** ca1532 Fortescue, *Fortescue Papers.* **20c. coll.:** *ODEP* 214, Stevenson 665:5.

5. Eat, drink, and be merry, for tomorrow we may die. *Var.:* Eat, drink, and be merry, for tomorrow your wife may come home. *Rec. dist.:* U.S., Can. **1st cit.:** 1870 Rossetti, *The Choice* in *The House of Life;* USca1700 Hubbard, *General History of New England* (1848). **20c. coll.:** Stevenson 666:3, Whiting 127, T&W 116, Whiting(*MP*) 195.

6. Eat, for someday you will be eaten. *Rec. dist.:* Fla., Minn.

7. Eat it up, wear it out, make it do, or do without. *Rec. dist.:* Kans.

8. Eat to live; do not live to eat. *Vars.:* **(a)** One should eat to live, not live to eat. **(b)** We must eat to live and not live to eat. *Rec. dist.:* U.S., Can. **1st cit.:** 1387 Higden, *Polychronicon,* tr. Trevisa; US1693 Penn, *Some Fruits of Solitude.* **20c. coll.:** *ODEP* 215, Whiting 127, *CODP* 63, Stevenson 664:12.

9. Eat to please yourself, but dress to please others. *Rec. dist.:* Miss., N.Dak.

10. Eat well, drink well, and do your duty well. *Rec. dist.:* Ill. **1st cit.:** 1609 Lithgow, *Rare Adventures.* **20c. coll.:** Stevenson 663:2.

11. Eat when you are hungry; drink when you are dry. *Rec. dist.:* Calif., N.C. **1st cit.:** 1917 Bridge, *Cheshire Proverbs.* **20c. coll.:** Stevenson 665:1.

12. He that eats till he is sick must fast till he is well. *Rec. dist.:* Ont. **1st cit.:** 1732 Fuller, *Gnomologia.* **20c. coll.:** Stevenson 661:14.

13. He who eats the fastest eats the mostest. *Rec. dist.:* Wash.

14. Tell me what you eat and I will tell you what you are. *Rec. dist.:* Minn., N.Y. **1st cit.:** US1941 Veiller, *Bait for Tiger.* **20c. coll.:** Stevenson 661:4.

15. The more you eat, the more you want. *Rec. dist.:* N.Y., S.C. **1st cit.:** 1738 Swift, *Collection of Genteel and Ingenious Conversation.* **20c. coll.:** Stevenson 664:3.

16. Whoever eats fine at sight eats with greed out of sight. *Rec. dist.:* Ariz.

17. You are what you eat. *Var.:* Man is what he eats. *Rec. dist.:* Ill., Kans. **1st cit.:** US1941 Gray, *Advancing Front of Medicine.* **20c. coll.:** Stevenson 661:4.

SEE ALSO Let him that earns the BREAD eat it. / You can't have your CAKE and eat it too. / As well to eat the DEVIL as drink his broth. / We must all eat a peck of DIRT before we die. / DOG will not eat dog. / Hungry DOGS will eat dirty puddings. / FOOLS make feasts, and wise men eat them. / If you cook your own GOOSE, you will have to eat it. / He that will eat the KERNEL must crack the nut. / They who have no other MEAT gladly bread and butter eat. / There was never a PERSIMMON except there was a possum to eat it. / He who stirs the soup POT eats first. / Eat a peck of SALT with a man before you trust him. / Eat few SUPPERS, and you'll need few medicines. / TAKE all you want, but eat all you take.

eaten   SEE It is hard to pay for BREAD that has been eaten.

eater   1. A good eater is a happy man. *Rec. dist.:* Ill. *1st cit.:* 1831 Disraeli, *Young Duke.* *20c. coll.:* Stevenson 575:6.

2. A swift eater, a swift worker. *Rec. dist.:* Kans.

eating   1. Eating and scratching, it's all in the beginning. *Rec. dist.:* Pa. *Infm.:* Once you start eating, it's hard to stop. *1st cit.:* 1678 Ray, *Scottish Proverbs.* *20c. coll.:* Stevenson 665:13.

2. If it were not for eating, the back might wear gold. *Rec. dist.:* Mich.
   SEE ALSO APPETITE comes while eating. / The PROOF of the pudding is in the eating.

eavesdropper   Eavesdroppers never hear any good of themselves. *Vars.:* **(a)** An eavesdropper never hears anything good about himself. **(b)** Eavesdroppers hear no good of themselves. **(c)** Eavesdroppers never hear good of themselves. **(d)** Eavesdroppers seldom hear any good of themselves. **(e)** When one eavesdrops, he hears no good of himself. *Rec. dist.:* U.S. *1st cit.:* US1860 Harris, *Uncle Remus, His Songs and His Sayings* (1881). *20c. coll.:* T&W 116.

ebb   1. The lowest ebb is the turn of the tide. *Rec. dist.:* Calif.

2. What the ebb takes out, the flood brings in. *Rec. dist.:* Miss. *1st cit.:* 1587 *Mirror for Magistrates.* *20c. coll.:* ODEP 217, Stevenson 2317:9.
   SEE ALSO A FLOW will have an ebb.

echo   There are many echoes in the world, but few voices. *Rec. dist.:* N.J.

eclipse   SEE One CLOUD is enough to eclipse all the sun.

economize   He who does not economize must agonize. *Rec. dist.:* Va.

economizing   Don't start economizing when you are down to your last dollar. *Rec. dist.:* Ill.

economy   1. Economy is a wise expenditure of money, not stinginess. *Rec. dist.:* N.Y.

2. Economy is itself a great income. *Var.:* Economy is a great revenue. *Rec. dist.:* Mich.

3. Economy is the easy chair of old age. *Rec. dist.:* Ill.

4. Economy is the road to wealth. *Rec. dist.:* Ohio.

edge   *(n.)*   1. If you can't make every edge cut, you can sure make it bruise. *Rec. dist.:* La.

2. The finest edge is made with the blunt whetstone. *Rec. dist.:* Minn. *1st cit.:* ca1374 Chaucer, *Troilus and Criseyde.* *20c. coll.:* Stevenson 2484:2.

3. The narrower the edge, the deeper the cut. *Rec. dist.:* N.Y.

4. You can't cut with too keen an edge. *Rec. dist.:* Ill.
   SEE ALSO It's a bad AXE that hasn't a keen edge. / IDLENESS turns the edge of wit. / There's nothin' like too much PREPARATION to dull the sharp edge of a man's honin'.

edge   *(v.)*   SEE ANGER edges valor.

edged   SEE They who play with edged TOOLS must expect to be cut.

educated   It is one thing to get educated and another thing to keep educated. *Rec. dist.:* N.Y.
   SEE ALSO An educated FOOL is dangerous.

education   1. A little education is a dangerous thing. *Rec. dist.:* Ind.

2. Education begins a gentleman; conversation completes him. *Rec. dist.:* N.Y. *1st cit.:* 1732 Fuller, *Gnomologia.* *20c. coll.:* Stevenson 668:4.

3. Education doesn't come by bumping your head against the school house. *Rec. dist.:* N.Y.

4. Education is a gift that none can take away. *Rec. dist.:* Calif.

5. Education is an investment never to be lost nor removed. *Rec. dist.:* Ill.

6. Education is the best provision for old age. *Rec. dist.:* R.I.

7. Education makes the man. *Rec. dist.:* Minn., N.Y. *1st cit.:* 1727 Gay, *Owl, the Swan, and the Farmer* in *Fables.* *20c. coll.:* Stevenson 668:5.

8. Never let your education interfere with your intelligence. *Rec. dist.:* Calif.

9. Silver and gold may tarnish away, but a good education will never decay. *Rec. dist.:* N.Y.

10. There is no education like adversity. *Rec. dist.:* Miss. *1st cit.:* 1880 Disraeli, *Endymion.* *20c. coll.:* Stevenson 18:10.

SEE ALSO GENIUS without education is like silver in the mine. / It is only the IGNORANT that despise education. / NATURE is stronger than education. / Mother WIT is better than book education.

eel 1. An eel held by the tail is not yet caught. *Rec. dist.:* N.Y. *1st cit.:* 1670 Ray, *English Proverbs;* US1837 Neal, *Charcoal Sketches,* 5th ed. (1840). *20c. coll.:* Stevenson 669:6, T&W 117.

2. Let every man skin his own eel. *Rec. dist.:* Calif., Tex. *1st cit.:* US1840 Neal, *Beedle's Sleigh Ride.* *20c. coll.:* Stevenson 669:9, T&W 117.

3. One cannot hunt eels and hares at the same time. *Rec. dist.:* Ohio.

effect We know the effects of many things but the causes of few. *Rec. dist.:* Mich.

effort 1. Earnest effort leads to success. *Rec. dist.:* Kans. *1st cit.:* ca1350 *Douce MS 52,* ed. Förster (1906). *20c. coll.:* Stevenson 2237:3.

2. It takes little effort to watch a man carry a load. *Rec. dist.:* Ind.

3. To give lip service to someone requires very little effort. *Rec. dist.:* N.Y.

4. What you get without effort is worth what it costs. *Rec. dist.:* N.Y.

SEE ALSO Folks spend their HEALTH to acquire wealth and later spend their wealth in an effort to regain their health.

egg 1. A broken egg cannot be put back together *Rec. dist.:* N.Y. *1st cit.:* US1862 *Collected Works of Abraham Lincoln,* eds. Basler and Dunlap (1953). *20c. coll.:* T&W 118.

2. A rotten egg spoils the pudding. *Rec. dist.:* Ark. *1st cit.:* US1948 Stevenson, *Home Book of Proverbs.* *20c. coll.:* Stevenson 1240:3.

3. A stingy man gives an egg to get a chicken. *Rec. dist.:* Miss.

4. An egg today is worth a hen tomorrow. *Vars.:* **(a)** Better an egg today than a hen tomorrow. **(b)** Eggs now are better than chickens tomorrow. *Rec. dist.:* Ill., Ind., Miss., N.Y., Oreg. *1st cit.:* 1659 Howell, *Paroimiografia;* US1734 Franklin, *PRAlmanac.* *20c. coll.:* Stevenson 671:5, Whiting 128.

5. Better an egg in peace than an ox in war. *Rec. dist.:* Okla.

6. Don't count your eggs before they're hatched. *Rec. dist.:* Ark., Kans., Ohio.

7. Don't gather cracked eggs. *Rec. dist.:* N.Dak.

8. Don't put all your eggs in one basket. *Var.:* Don't carry all your eggs in one basket. *Rec. dist.:* U.S., Can. *1st cit.:* 1666 Torriano, *Common Place of Italian Proverbs;* US1838 *Letters of John Fairfield,* ed. Staples (1902). *20c. coll.:* ODEP 218, Stevenson 672:2, CODP 64, T&W 118, Whiting(MP) 198.

9. Eggs and oaths are easily broken. *Rec. dist.:* Ind., N.Y.

10. Eggs can't teach the hen. *Rec. dist.:* Ill.

11. From fried eggs come no chickens. *Rec. dist.:* Oreg.

12. Half an egg is better than the shell. *Rec. dist.:* N.Y. *1st cit.:* 1621 Robinson, *Adagia in Latin and English.* *20c. coll.:* ODEP 344, Stevenson 671:6.

13. He that steals an egg will steal a chicken. *Var.:* He that steals an egg will steal an ox. *Rec. dist.:* Ind.

14. He that would have eggs must endure the cackling of hens. *Rec. dist.:* Wis. *1st cit.:* 1659 Torriano, *Dictionary: English and Italian* in Florio, *Vocabolario Italiano & Inglese;* US1909 Sunderman, *Song of Songs.* *20c. coll.:* ODEP 218, Stevenson 672:3.

15. He who lays a good egg has a right to cackle. *Rec. dist.:* Utah, Wash.

16. If you want an egg, demand an ox. *Rec. dist.:* Minn.

17. 'Tis very hard to shave an egg. *Rec. dist.:* N.J., Okla. *Infm.:* Where nothing is, nothing can be had. *1st cit.:* 1592 Delamothe, *Treasury of the French Tongue.* *20c. coll.:* ODEP 721, Stevenson 670:4.

18. Neither an egg nor an ego is any good until you break it. *Rec. dist.:* N.Y.

19. Other people's eggs have two yolks. *Rec. dist.:* N.Y. *1st cit.:* 1721 Kelly, *Scottish Proverbs.* *20c. coll.:* Stevenson 671:1.

20. The more you stir a rotten egg, the more it stinks. *Rec. dist.:* Ohio.

21. There's always a bad egg in every crowd. *Rec. dist.:* Ind. *1st cit.:* 1855 Hammett, *Wonderful Adventures of Captain Priest.* *20c. coll.:* T&W 118, Stevenson 670:7.

22. Where you lay your egg, pick your grain. *Rec. dist.:* Minn.

23. You can't carry an egg in two baskets. *Rec. dist.:* Wash.

24. You can't spoil a rotten egg. *Vars.:* (a) A rotten egg cannot be spoiled. (b) It's pretty hard to spoil a rotted egg. *Rec. dist.:* Ind., N.J., N.Y. *1st cit.:* US1941 Fitzsimmons and Adams, *This Is Murder.* *20c. coll.:* Stevenson 670:7.

25. You can't tell whether an egg is good by looking at its shell. *Rec. dist.:* Ohio.

26. You can't unscramble eggs. *Var.:* Scrambled eggs can't be unscrambled. *Rec. dist.:* Ill., N.Y., Ohio, Wis. *Infm:* Attributed to J. Pierpont Morgan, ca1905. *1st cit.:* US1928 Apple, *Mr. Chang's Crime Ray.* *20c. coll.:* Stevenson 671:7, T&W 118, Whiting(MP) 197.

SEE ALSO A wild GOOSE never laid a tame egg. / Don't kill the GOOSE that lays the golden egg. / A black HEN always lays a white egg. / Fat HENS lay few eggs. / If you're LUCKY, even your rooster will lay eggs. / You can't have an OMELETTE unless you break the egg. / ROOSTER makes more racket dan de hen w'at lay de aig.

ego SEE The way to a man's HEART is through his ego.

elbow **1.** The elbow is near, but try and bite it. *Rec. dist.:* N.Y.

2. There's no elbow that bends outward. *Rec. dist.:* Ill. *1st cit.:* US1938 Champion, *Racial Proverbs.* *20c. coll.:* Stevenson 674:6.

elbow grease Elbow grease gives the best polish. *Rec. dist.:* N.Y. *1st cit.:* 1672 Marvell, *Rehearsal Transposed;* USca1825 Tyler, *Prose of Royall Tyler,* ed. Peladeau (1972). *20c. coll.:* ODEP 219, Whiting 128, Stevenson 674:7, T&W 119.

elder Respect your elders. *Rec. dist.:* N.Y., Ont., Oreg.

elephant **1.** An elephant is an elephant whether on high or low ground. *Rec. dist.:* Ohio.

2. An elephant is not won with anger. *Rec. dist.:* Ind.

3. An elephant never forgets. *Rec. dist.:* U.S., Can. *Infm.:* Stevenson notes this is probably a variation of the Greek proverb: "The camel never forgets an injury." *1st cit.:* US1937 Martyn, *Blue Ridge.* *20c. coll.:* Stevenson 675:8, Whiting(MP) 199.

4. At home an elephant, abroad a cat. *Rec. dist.:* Ill., Ind.

5. Don't look a gift elephant in the tusk. *Rec. dist.:* N.Mex.

6. Lots of elephants can't be on one flea, but lots of fleas can be on one elephant. *Rec. dist.:* Ohio. *Infm.:* Some things are possible; others aren't.

7. You can't kill an elephant shooting at a mouse hole. *Rec. dist.:* Ind.

8. You can't kill an elephant with bird shot. *Rec. dist.:* N.C., Tex.

eleven Eleven don't make a dozen. *Rec. dist.:* Wash.

ell Give an ell and they'll take a mile. *Rec. dist.:* Ga., Vt.

eloquence **1.** Eloquence is saying the right thing at the right time. *Rec. dist.:* Oreg.

2. Eloquence is the child of knowledge. *Rec. dist.:* Ind.

else No one else will do it for you. *Rec. dist.:* Pa.

employ *SEE* Employ the TIME well if you mean to gain leisure. / None but the WISE man can employ leisure well.

employee **1.** Be an employee and work eight hours; be a boss and your work is never done. *Rec. dist.:* Pa.

2. It is the employee who knows how; it is the employer who knows why. *Rec. dist.:* Iowa.

employer Strike while your employer has a big contract. *Rec. dist.:* Ill.

empty *(v.)* *SEE* You must empty the BOX before you can fill it again.

empty *(adj.)* *SEE* An empty BAG cannot stand. / An empty BARREL makes the most noise. / The empty BOWL makes the most noise. / An empty CAN makes a lot of noise. / Better a small FISH than an empty dish. / Better an empty HOUSE than a bad tenant. / An empty KETTLE makes the most noise. / No one can love his NEIGHBOR on an empty stomach. / An empty PURSE fills the face with wrinkles. / Better an empty PURSE than an empty head. / The empty WAGON makes the most noise.

emulate To emulate is to envy. *Rec. dist.:* Ill.

enable *SEE* ABILITY will enable a man to get to the top, but character will keep him from falling.

enchantment *SEE* DISTANCE lends enchantment.

encouragement *SEE* CORRECTION does much, but encouragement everything.

end *(n.)* **1.** All things come to an end. *Vars.:* **(a)** All things have an end. **(b)** Everything has an end. *Rec. dist.:* U.S., Can. *1st cit.:* ca1374 Chaucer, *Troilus and Criseyde;* USca1680 *Voyages of Radisson,* ed. Scull, Publ. Prince Soc. (1885). *20c. coll.:* ODEP 231, Whiting 130, CODP 3, Stevenson 677:5, T&W 120, Whiting(MP) 617.

2. At the end of the work, you may judge the workman. *Rec. dist.:* Okla.

3. If everyone had his own ends, all would come to a bad end. *Rec. dist.:* Mich.

4. If you play both ends against the middle, the middle will soon fold up. *Rec. dist.:* Ill., Miss., N.Y., Ohio. *1st cit.:* US1928 Maury, *Wars of Godly.* *20c. coll.:* Whiting(MP) 203.

5. In the end, all will mend. *Rec. dist.:* Ind., Ky., Tenn. *1st cit.:* 1659 Howell, *English Proverbs.* *20c. coll.:* Stevenson 679:7.

6. It will all work out in the end. *Rec. dist.:* Calif., Mich., N.Y.

7. The end crowns the work. *Var.:* The end crowns all. *Rec. dist.:* Ariz., Wis. *1st cit.:* 1509 Watson, *Ship of Fools;* US1703 *Correspondence Between William Penn and James Logan, 1700–1705,* ed. Armstrong, Hist.Soc. Penn. *Memoirs* (1870, 1872). *20c. coll.:* CODP 65, Whiting 129, ODEP 220, Stevenson 679:9, Whiting(MP) 200.

8. The end justifies the means. *Rec. dist.:* U.S., Can. *1st cit.:* 1583 Babington, *Exposition of the Commandments;* US1657 Wigglesworth, *Diary.* *20c. coll.:* ODEP 220, Whiting 129, CODP 65, Stevenson 681:11, T&W 120, Whiting(MP) 200.

9. The end of the thief is the gallows. *Rec. dist.:* N.Y.

10. The heavy end of a match is the light end. *Rec. dist.:* Wis.

SEE ALSO Don't burn the CANDLE at both ends. / The longest DAY will come to an end. / DELAYS have dangerous ends. / He who does EVIL comes to an evil end. / A whistling GIRL and a crowing hen always end in the devil's den. / An ill LIFE, an ill end. / A NEEDLE is sharp only at one end. / There's a POT of gold at the end of the rainbow. / When you pick up a STICK at one end, you also pick up the other end. / TRUTH is truth to the end of the reckoning.

end *(v.)* *SEE* ALL's well that ends well. / A good mother's JOB does not end in the house.

ending *SEE* A bad BEGINNING makes a good ending.

endurance SEE ADVERSITY stimulates endurance.

endure **1.** First endure, then pity, then embrace. *Rec. dist.:* Oreg.

2. He that endures is not overcome. *Rec. dist.:* Calif. *1st cit.:* ca1374 Chaucer, *Troilus and Criseyde.* *20c. coll.:* ODEP 221, Stevenson 682:5.
    SEE ALSO He CONQUERS who endures. / What can't be CURED must be endured.

enemy **1.** A common enemy makes friends. *Rec. dist.:* N.Y.

2. A dead enemy is as good as a cold friend. *Rec. dist.:* Ill.

3. A wise enemy is better than a foolish friend. *Rec. dist.:* Iowa. *1st cit.:* 1678 La Fontaine, *Fables,* ed. Thompson (1806). *20c. coll.:* Stevenson 911:10.

4. All men think their enemies ill men. *Rec. dist.:* N.Y.

5. Always forgive your enemies. *Rec. dist.:* Wis.

6. An enemy does not sleep. *Rec. dist.:* N.Y.

7. An enemy may chance to give good counsel. *Rec. dist.:* Ind. *1st cit.:* 1663 Hawkins, *Youth's Behavior.* *20c. coll.:* ODEP 222, Stevenson 685:1.

8. An enemy's mouth seldom speaks well. *Rec. dist.:* Wis. *1st cit.:* 1481 Caxton, *Reynard.* *20c. coll.:* ODEP 222, Stevenson 686:1.

9. Better a certain enemy than a doubtful friend. *Rec. dist.:* Utah.

10. Better an open enemy than a false friend. *Var.:* False friends are worse than open enemies. *Rec. dist.:* Oreg., Wis. *1st cit.:* ca1200 *Ancrene Riwle,* ed. Morton, Camden Soc. (1853); US1740 Franklin, *PRAlmanac.* *20c. coll.:* ODEP 50, Whiting 131, Stevenson 910:3.

11. Beware of enemies reconciled and meat twice boiled. *Rec. dist.:* Mich. *1st cit.:* 1670 Ray, *English Proverbs;* US1733 Franklin, *PRAlmanac.* *20c. coll.:* Stevenson 687:9.

12. Despise not your enemy. *Rec. dist.:* N.Y.

13. Don't believe your enemy even when he's telling the truth. *Rec. dist.:* Ill.

14. Don't try to get even with your enemies;

try to get even with your friends. *Rec. dist.:* Ill.

15. Every man is his own worst enemy. *Var.:* A man's best friend and worst enemy is himself. *Rec. dist.:* Ill., N.Y., S.C. *1st cit.:* 1643 Browne, *Religio Medici.* *20c. coll.:* Stevenson 689:8.

16. Every man's your enemy till he proves your friend. *Rec. dist.:* Minn.

17. From the enemy you learn a lot. *Rec. dist.:* Wis.

18. He that conquers himself conquers an enemy. *Rec. dist.:* N.J., Okla., R.I., Utah.

19. If you have no enemies, it is a sign fortune has forgot you. *Rec. dist.:* Ill. *1st cit.:* 1666 Torriano, *Common Place of Italian Proverbs.* *20c. coll.:* ODEP 221, Stevenson 688:3.

20. It is easier to forgive an enemy than a friend. *Rec. dist.:* Minn.

21. Kill your enemy with kindness. *Rec. dist.:* Ark.

22. Learn even from an enemy. *Rec. dist.:* Ill.

23. Lend money to an enemy and you will gain him, to a friend and you will lose him. *Var.:* If you would make an enemy of a man, lend him money. *Rec. dist.:* Miss., N.C. *1st cit.:* 1813 Ray, *Lusit;* US1740 Franklin, *PRAlmanac.* *20c. coll.:* ODEP 222, Whiting 293, Whiting(MP) 203.

24. Love your enemy—but don't put a gun in his hand. *Rec. dist.:* Ill.

25. Make your enemy your friend. *Rec. dist.:* Wis. *1st cit.:* 1639 Clarke, *Paroemiologia.* *20c. coll.:* ODEP 222, Stevenson 908:2.

26. Never make an enemy when you can keep a friend. *Rec. dist.:* Oreg.

27. Never underestimate an enemy. *Rec. dist.:* Fla., Kans.

28. Once an enemy, always an enemy. *Rec. dist.:* N.Y.

29. One enemy is too much for a man, and a hundred friends are too few. *Rec. dist.:* N.Y., Ohio. *1st cit.:* 1659 Torriano, *Dictionary: English and Italian* in Florio, *Vocabolario Italiano & Inglese.* *20c. coll.:* ODEP 596, Stevenson 909:8.

30. Rejoice not when your enemy falls. *Rec. dist.:* Minn.

31. The enemies of my enemies are my friends. *Rec. dist.:* N.Y.

32. There is no little enemy. *Rec. dist.:* Ill., Minn., Ohio, Wis. *1st cit.:* ca1386 Chaucer, *Tale of Melibee;* US1691 Mather, *Bills of Credit in Colonial Currency.* *20c. coll.:* ODEP 221, Whiting 131, *CODP* 134, Stevenson 685:10.

33. To make enemies, talk; to make friends, listen. *Rec. dist.:* N.Y.

34. We carry our greatest enemies within us. *Rec. dist.:* Wis.

35. You cannot jest an enemy into a friend, but you can jest a friend into an enemy. *Rec. dist.:* Ill., Tex., Wis.

36. You can win your enemy by love. *Rec. dist.:* Ohio.

SEE ALSO ACTION is worry's worst enemy. / ANGER is a sworn enemy. / It is a good thing to make a BRIDGE of gold to a flying enemy. / FAITHFUL are the wounds of a friend, but the kisses of an enemy are deceitful. / The FIRE you kindle for your enemy often burns yourself more than him. / A reconciled FRIEND is a double enemy. / It's hard to make a FRIEND but easy to make an enemy. / Trust not a new FRIEND nor an old enemy. / Speak well of your FRIENDS; of your enemies say nothing. / Your IGNORANCE is your worst enemy. / A JOKE never gains over an enemy but often loses a friend. / He that shows a PASSION tells his enemy where he may hit him. / TRUTH is truth, though spoken by an enemy.

energy The energy we use in getting even might be used in getting ahead. *Rec. dist.:* Calif.

engine Don't race your engine or you'll burn out a bearing. *Rec. dist.:* R.I. *Infm.:* Don't lose your temper; it doesn't pay to get upset.

Englishman Once an Englishman, always an Englishman. *Rec. dist.:* Ohio.

SEE ALSO Mad DOGS and Englishmen go out in the noontime sun.

enjoy 1. Enjoy yourself: it's later than you think. *Rec. dist.:* U.S., Can.

2. He enjoys much who is thankful for a little. *Rec. dist.:* Ont.

SEE ALSO If you would enjoy the FRUIT, pluck not the flower. / Enjoy your ICE CREAM while it's on your plate. / He enjoys LIFE who makes others enjoy it best. / WEALTH is not his that has it, but his that enjoys it.

enjoyable *SEE* IDLENESS is never enjoyable unless there is plenty to do.

enjoyment Enjoyment is a part of living. *Rec. dist.:* Ohio.

SEE ALSO We milk TROUBLE drier than we do enjoyment.

enough 1. Enough is a feast to a hungry man. *Rec. dist.:* N.C.

2. Enough is as good as a feast. *Rec. dist.:* U.S., Can. *1st cit.:* ca1375 Barbour, *Actes and Life of Robert Bruce,* E.E.T.S. (1870–89); USca1656 Bradford, *History of Plymouth Plantation,* ed. Ford (1912). *20c. coll.:* ODEP 224, Whiting 132, *CODP* 66, Stevenson 699:3, T&W 121, Whiting(MP) 203.

3. Enough is enough. *Vars.:* **(a)** Enough is enough and sometimes plenty. **(b)** Enough of a thing is enough, and too much is God's plenty. **(c)** Enough's enough—too much is a dog's bait. *Rec. dist.:* U.S., Can. *1st cit.:* 1546 Heywood, *Dialogue of Proverbs,* ed. Habernicht (1963); US1833 Neal, *Down-Easters.* *20c. coll.:* ODEP 224, T&W 121, Stevenson 699:8., Whiting(MP) 204.

4. Enough is what would satisfy us if the neighbors didn't have any more. *Rec. dist.:* N.Dak.

5. Enough of a good thing is plenty. *Rec. dist.:* Ill. *1st cit.:* 1573 Tusser, "Dinner Matters" in *Five Hundredth Pointes of Good Husbandrie.* *20c. coll.:* Stevenson 699:6.

6. Let well enough alone. *Var.:* Leave well enough alone. *Rec. dist.:* U.S. *1st cit.:* ca1346 Chaucer, *Envoy to Bukton;* US1833 *Correspondence of Andrew Jackson,* ed. Bassett (1926–33). *20c. coll.:* ODEP 453, Whiting 478, *CODP* 131, T&W 399, Whiting(MP) 676.

7. Many have by far too much, but nobody enough. *Rec. dist.:* Vt.

8. More than enough is too much. *Rec. dist.:*

Ill., Okla., Tex. *1st cit.:* 1546 Heywood, *Dialogue of Proverbs,* ed. Habernicht (1963). *20c. coll.:* ODEP 544, Stevenson 700:6.

9. Time enough always proves little enough. *Rec. dist.:* Ohio.

10. To whom a little is not enough, nothing is enough. *Rec. dist.:* N.Y.

11. Too few know when they possess enough, and fewer know how to enjoy it. *Rec. dist.:* N.Y.

SEE ALSO Never think of the FUTURE; it comes soon enough. / No HOUSE was ever big enough for two women. / A long LIFE may not be good enough, but a good life is long enough. / A RAINBOW is big enough for everyone to look at. / Give a man ROPE enough and he'll hang himself.

enter SEE At the workingman's house, HUNGER looks in but dares not enter. / LOVE enters man through his eyes, woman through her ears.

enthusiasm 1. Enthusiasm is that driving force that overcomes all obstacles. *Rec. dist.:* Minn.

2. Nothing great was ever achieved without enthusiasm. *Rec. dist.:* Ohio, Utah, Wis. *1st cit.:* US1841 Emerson, "Circles" in *Essays. 20c. coll.:* Stevenson 701:1.

3. Temper your enthusiasm with judgment. *Rec. dist.:* Kans.

envied Better be envied than pitied. *Rec. dist.:* N.Y., Okla., Tex. *1st cit.:* 1546 Heywood, *Dialogue of Proverbs,* ed. Habernicht (1963); US1639 Winslow in *Thomas Hutchinson Papers,* Publ. Prince Soc. (1865). *20c. coll.:* ODEP 51, Whiting 132, CODP 15, Stevenson 703:5.

environment What a man can be is born with him; what he becomes is a result of his environment. *Rec. dist.:* N.Dak.

envy 1. A friend's envy is worse than an enemy's hatred. *Rec. dist.:* Calif.

2. Envy doesn't enter an empty house. *Rec. dist.:* N.Y.

3. Envy feeds on the living; it ceases when they are dead. *Rec. dist.:* Ill. *1st cit.:* US1948 Stevenson, *Home Book of Proverbs. 20c. coll.:* Stevenson 703:1.

4. Envy has smarting eyes. *Rec. dist.:* Wis.

5. Envy is a kind of praise. *Var.:* Envy is left-handed praise. *Rec. dist.:* Ill., Minn., N.J. *1st cit.:* 1727 Gay, "Hound and Huntsman" in *Fables. 20c. coll.:* Stevenson 702:2.

6. Envy is blind. *Rec. dist.:* N.Y.

7. Envy is destroyed by true friendship. *Rec. dist.:* Fla.

8. Envy is the basest of all enemies. *Rec. dist.:* Mich.

9. Envy is the sincerest form of flattery. *Rec. dist.:* Ill. *1st cit.:* ca1904 Collins, *Aphorisms. 20c. coll.:* Stevenson 702:2.

10. Envy is what inclines us to speak evil of the virtuous rather than of the wicked. *Rec. dist.:* Wis.

11. Envy never dwells in noble souls. *Rec. dist.:* Minn.

12. Envy never has a holiday. *Rec. dist.:* N.J. *1st cit.:* 1605 Bacon, *De Augmentis Scientiarum. 20c. coll.:* Stevenson 701:9.

13. If envy were a rash, the whole town would be ill. *Rec. dist.:* N.C.

14. The dog of envy barks at a celebrity. *Rec. dist.:* Ill.

15. The envious die, but envy never. *Rec. dist.:* Ill. *1st cit.:* ca1523 Froissart, *Cronycles of Englande,* tr. Berners. *20c. coll.:* ODEP 225, Stevenson 701:9.

equal *(n.)* Equals make the best friends. *Rec. dist.:* Kans., Wash.

equal *(adj.)* 1. An equal going is equal to an equal loss. *Rec. dist.:* Wis.

2. In the bathhouse all are equal. *Rec. dist.:* Ill.
SEE ALSO Six feet of EARTH makes all men equal.

equality 1. Equality begins in the grave. *Var.:* He who seeks equality should go to the cemetery. *Rec. dist.:* Ill., N.Y., Ont., S.C., Wis.

2. Equality breeds no war. *Rec. dist.:* Ill. *1st cit.:* US1948 Stevenson, *Home Book of Proverbs. 20c. coll.:* Stevenson 705:5.

equity Equity regards that as done which ought to be done. *Rec. dist.:* Ohio.

eraser They wouldn't make erasers if we all didn't make mistakes. *Rec. dist.:* Ky., Mich., Tenn.

err To err is human; to forgive, divine. *Vars.:* (a) To err is human. (b) To err is human; to forgive is divine. (c) To err is human; to keep it up is folly. (d) To err is human; to persist in it, beastly. *Rec. dist.:* U.S., Can. *1st cit.:* 1539 Vives, *Introduction to Wisdom,* tr. Morrison. *20c. coll.:* ODEP 225, CODP 67, Stevenson 707:18.

SEE ALSO ART may err, but nature cannot miss. / He who TALKS much errs much.

erring Erring is not cheating. *Rec. dist.:* N.Y.

error 1. Admitting error clears the score and proves you wiser than before. *Rec. dist.:* Fla. *1st cit.:* US1924 Guiterman, *Poet's Proverbs.* *20c. coll.:* Stevenson 707:13.

2. Error cannot be defended by error. *Rec. dist.:* Ind.

3. Error is the force that welds men together. *Rec. dist.:* Ohio.

4. Error is worse than ignorance. *Rec. dist.:* Ind., Iowa. *1st cit.:* 1839 Bailey, *Festus, Mountain Sunrise.* *20c. coll.:* Stevenson 706:7.

5. Errors, like straws, float on the surface. *Rec. dist.:* Okla. *1st cit.:* 1678 Dryden, *All for Love and the World Well Lost (Prologue).* *20c. coll.:* Stevenson 706:14.

6. From errors of others a wise man corrects his own. *Rec. dist.:* Ohio. *1st cit.:* US1798 Jefferson, *Letter to Mary Jefferson Eppes.* *20c. coll.:* Stevenson 707:4.

7. Honest error is to be pitied not ridiculed. *Rec. dist.:* Utah.

8. It is great error to make oneself for more than one is or less than one is worth. *Rec. dist.:* Oreg.

9. One error breeds more. *Rec. dist.:* Ill. *1st cit.:* US1840 Haliburton, *Clockmaker* (1849). *20c. coll.:* T&W 121.

SEE ALSO We all err, but only FOOLS continue in error. / IGNORANCE is better than error, but the active fool is a holy terror.

escape SEE You cannot escape your FATE. / The FISH that escapes is the biggest fish of all.

Eskimo Too many Eskimos, too few seals. *Rec. dist.:* N.Dak.

estate 1. Great estates may venture more; little boats must keep near shore. *Rec. dist.:* Ill., Ind., Miss. *Infm.:* Cf. boat. *1st cit.:* US1751 Franklin, *PRAlmanac.* *20c. coll.:* Stevenson 1035:5, Whiting 38.

2. Many estates are spent in getting. *Rec. dist.:* Ohio. *1st cit.:* 1758 Franklin in Arber's *English Garner;* US1733 Franklin, *PRAlmanac.* *20c. coll.:* ODEP 509, Whiting 133, Stevenson 2586:1.

SEE ALSO He that has a TRADE has an estate, and he that has a calling has an office of profit and honor.

eternal SEE HOPE springs eternal in the human breast.

eternally SEE He that LIVES carnally won't live eternally.

eternity 1. Eternity has no gray hairs. *Rec. dist.:* Mich., Wis.

2. We can crowd eternity into an hour or stretch an hour into eternity. *Rec. dist.:* Ariz.

evening 1. A joyous evening often leads to a sorrowful morning. *Rec. dist.:* Minn., N.J.

2. Evening red and morning gray will send the sailor on his way, but evening gray and morning red will bring rain down upon his head. *Vars.:* (a) An evening red and a morning gray is a sign of a fair day. (b) Evening red and morning gray helps the traveler on his way; evening gray and morning red brings down rain upon his head. (c) Evening red and morning gray will send the traveler on his way; evening gray and morning red will heap rain on the traveler's head. (d) When the evening is gray and morning is red, the sailor is sure to have a wet head. *Rec. dist.:* U.S., Can. *1st cit.:* 1584 Withals, *Shorte Dictionarie in Latine and English,* ed. Fleming; US1852 Cary, *Clovernook.* *20c. coll.:* ODEP 227, CODP 189, T&W 122, Stevenson 2474:11, Whiting(MP) 573.

3. The evening brings all home. *Rec. dist.:*

N.Y. *1st cit.*: 1857 Ramsay, *Reminiscences.* **20c. coll.**: *ODEP* 227, Stevenson 711:2.

SEE ALSO An HOUR in the morning is worth two in the evening.

event 1. Coming events cast their shadows before. *Var.*: Coming events cast their shadows before them. *Rec. dist.*: U.S., Can. *1st cit.*: 1803 Campbell, *Lochiel's Warning* in *Poetical Works* (1907); US1845 Cooper, *Chainbearer.* **20c. coll.**: *ODEP* 136, T&W 122, *CODP* 40, Stevenson 711:5, Whiting(*MP*) 204.

2. Great events give scope for great virtues. *Rec. dist.*: Mich.

3. The event proves the act. *Rec. dist.*: N.Y., S.C., Wis. *Infm.*: Stevenson states that George Washington adopted this as his motto ca1775. *1st cit.*: US1948 Stevenson, *Home Book of Proverbs.* **20c. coll.**: Stevenson 711:7.

4. We are not here to lead events but to follow them. *Rec. dist.*: Wis.

every SEE Every AGE wants its playthings. / Every DOG has his day. / If you can't make every EDGE cut, you can sure make it bruise. / For every EVIL under the sun there is a remedy or there is none. / There's a FOOT for every old shoe. / Every HEART has its own ache. / There's a JACK for every Jill. / Every LANE has a turning. / Every MAN can tame a shrew but he that has one. / Every MAN drags water to his own mill. / Every MAN for himself. / Every MAN has his price. / Every MAN has one black patch, and some have two. / Every MAN is a volume if you know how to read him. / Every MAN to his trade. / Every MAN would live long, but no woman would be old. / Every PATH has a puddle. / Every RAG meets its mate. / Every ROAD has hills to be climbed. / Every SHEEP with its like. / Every SIN has its own punishment. / Every UNDERTAKING is only begun with difficulty. / Every WHY has a wherefore. / Every WORD has a meaning.

everybody 1. Everybody to his own taste. *Rec. dist.*: Nebr., R.I. *1st cit.*: 1580 Lyly, *Euphues and His England;* US1767 Hulton, *Letters of a Loyalist Lady.* **20c. coll.**: *ODEP* 230, Whiting 135, *CODP* 68, Stevenson 2281:2, T&W 235, Whiting(*MP*) 395.

2. Everybody to their own notion. *Rec. dist.*: Miss.

3. He labors in vain who tries to please everybody. *Rec. dist.*: Ill., Okla. *1st cit.*: ca1500 *15c. School Book,* ed. Nelson; US1742 *Colonial Records of Georgia,* ed. Chandler, in *Original Papers, 1735–1752* (1910–16). **20c. coll.**: *ODEP* 633, Whiting 134.

SEE ALSO Everybody's BUSINESS is nobody's business.

everyone 1. Everyone can't be first. *Rec. dist.*: Ala.

2. Everyone enjoys himself in his own way. *Rec. dist.*: Ont.

3. Everyone excels in something in which someone fails. *Var.*: Everyone excels in something in which another fails. *Rec. dist.*: Fla., Wis. *1st cit.*: 1508 Erasmus, *Adagia,* tr. Taverner. **20c. coll.**: Stevenson 718:11.

4. Everyone for himself. *Vars.*: **(a)** Every man for himself. **(b)** Everyone for himself, and God for all. *Rec. dist.*: Calif. *1st cit.*: ca1386 Chaucer, *Knight's Tale;* US1706 *Correspondence Between William Penn and James Logan, 1700–1705,* ed. Armstrong, Hist.Soc. Penn. *Memoirs* (1870, 1872). **20c. coll.**: *ODEP* 229, Whiting 134, T&W 235, Whiting(*MP*) 394.

5. Everyone has his lot and a wide world before him. *Rec. dist.*: Ont.

6. Everyone is a master and a servant. *Rec. dist.*: N.Y., S.C.

7. Everyone lives by selling something. *Rec. dist.*: Wis.

8. Everyone prefers his own. *Rec. dist.*: N.J.

9. Everyone speaks for his own interest. *Rec. dist.*: Ont.

10. Everyone to his equal. *Rec. dist.*: N.Y.

SEE ALSO A CRAZY man thinks everyone crazy but himself. / After the DANGER everyone is wise. / When a man is DOWN, everyone runs over him. / When a man is going DOWNHILL, everyone gives him a push. / Where everyone goes the GRASS never grows. / Everyone has his MASTER. / A RAINBOW is big enough for everyone to look at. / Everyone knows where his SHOE pinches.

everything **1.** A place for everything and everything in its place. *Rec. dist.:* U.S., Can. *1st cit.:* 1640 Herbert, *Outlandish Proverbs (Jacula Prudentum)* in *Works,* ed. Hutchinson (1941); US1855 Haliburton, *Nature and Human Nature. 20c. coll.:* ODEP 628, CODP 179, T&W 288, Whiting*(MP)* 499.

2. Could everything be done twice everything would be done better. *Rec. dist.:* N.J.

3. Doing everything is doing nothing. *Rec. dist.:* Minn. *1st cit.:* 1859 Henderson, *Latin Proverbs. 20c. coll.:* Stevenson 544:2.

4. Everything comes to him who waits. *Rec. dist.:* U.S., Can. *1st cit.:* ca1530 Barclay, *Eclogues,* E.E.T.S. (1927); US1863 Longfellow, *Poems* (1960). *20c. coll.:* ODEP 231, CODP 3, Stevenson 2440:10, Whiting*(MP)* 225.

5. Everything does not fall that totters. *Rec. dist.:* Ala. *1st cit.:* 1603 Montaigne, *Essays of Montaigne,* tr. Florio, T.T. *20c. coll.:* ODEP 11, Stevenson 747:12.

6. Everything has a beginning. *Rec. dist.:* Wis. *1st cit.:* ca1374 Chaucer, *Troilus and Criseyde;* US1750 *Almanacs of Roger Sherman, 1750–1761,* ed. Paltsits, Am.Antiq.Soc. *Proceedings* (1907). *20c. coll.:* ODEP 232, Whiting 135, Whiting*(MP)* 205.

7. Everything has its price. *Rec. dist.:* Ill., N.Y. *1st cit.:* US1829 *Journals of Ralph Waldo Emerson,* eds. Emerson and Forbes (1909–14). *20c. coll.:* Stevenson 1878:2, T&W 122.

8. Everything has two sides. *Rec. dist.:* Ill.

9. Everything is funny as long as it is happening to somebody else. *Rec. dist.:* Vt.

10. Everything is good for something. *Rec. dist.:* Ill.

11. Everything is not all peaches and cream. *Rec. dist.:* Wis.

12. Everything is the worse for wear. *Rec. dist.:* Ill. *1st cit.:* 1516 Skelton, *Magnyfycence. 20c. coll.:* ODEP 232.

13. Everything looks blue to the jaundiced eye. *Rec. dist.:* Kans.

14. Everything that goes up must come down. *Var.:* What goes up must come down. *Rec. dist.:* U.S., Can. *1st cit.:* US1929 Pottle, *Sketches. 20c. coll.:* Whiting*(MP)* 257, CODP 236.

15. Everything that is worth having must be paid for. *Rec. dist.:* N.Y. *1st cit.:* US1829 *Journals of Ralph Waldo Emerson,* eds. Emerson and Forbes (1909–1914). *20c. coll.:* T&W 122.

16. Everything will turn out for the best. *Rec. dist.:* Ky., Tenn.

17. Give some people everything you have and they still want the moon. *Var.:* Give some people everything you have and they still want the moon for a cow pasture. *Rec. dist.:* N.Mex.

18. No one has everything. *Var.:* You can't have everything. *Rec. dist.:* N.Y. *1st cit.:* US1930 Private 19022, *Her Privates. 20c. coll.:* Whiting*(MP)* 205.

19. One can get used to everything, even hanging. *Rec. dist.:* Ont.

20. There is a remedy for everything, could we but hit upon it. *Rec. dist.:* Okla., Tex.

21. There's a time and place for everything. *Rec. dist.:* Ky., Ohio. *1st cit.:* 1509 Barclay, *Ship of Fools,* ed. Jamieson in *Eclogues,* E.E.T.S. (1874); US1860 Haliburton, *Season-Ticket. 20c. coll.:* CODP 225, T&W 374, Stevenson 2329:1, Whiting*(MP)* 627.

22. There's everything in a name. *Rec. dist.:* N.C.

23. To know everything is to know nothing. *Rec. dist.:* La.

SEE ALSO CORRECTION does much, but encouragement everything. / Twin FOOLS: one doubts nothing, the other everything. / GOLD will not buy everything. / To a young HEART everything is fun. / There's a LIMIT to everything. / LOOKS aren't everything. / MAIDS want nothing but husbands, and when they have them they want everything. / NECESSITY does everything well. / A WISE man knows his own ignorance; a fool thinks he knows everything.

evidence Hear the evidence before you pass sentence. *Rec. dist.:* N.Y.

evil *(n.)* **1.** Apprehension of evil is often worse than the evil itself. *Rec. dist.:* Mich.

2. Avoid evil and it will avoid you. *Rec. dist.:* N.Y.

3. Bad to do evil, but worse to boast of it. *Rec. dist.:* N.Y. *1st cit.:* 1606 Heywood, *If You Know Not Me.* *20c. coll.:* Stevenson 712:7

4. Cease to do evil, learn to do well. *Rec. dist.:* Ohio.

5. Choose the lesser of two evils. *Vars.:* (a) Of evils we must choose the least. (b) Of two evils, choose the lesser. *Rec. dist.:* U.S., Can. *1st cit.:* ca1374 Chaucer, *Troilus and Criseyde;* US1714 Dudley in *Winthrop Papers,* Mass. Hist.Soc. *Collections* (1863–92). *20c. coll.:* *ODEP* 233, *CODP* 70, Stevenson 716:2, Whiting 136, T&W 122, Whiting*(MP)* 206.

6. Desperate evils require desperate remedies. *Rec. dist.:* Wis.

7. Destroy the seed of evil, or it will grow up to your ruin. *Rec. dist.:* Fla.

8. Do no evil and fear no harm. *Rec. dist.:* N.Y.

9. Do not look for wrong and evil. *Rec. dist.:* Okla.

10. Doing evil is fun, but it costs less to be good. *Rec. dist.:* Ill.

11. Evil is brought on by oneself. *Rec. dist.:* N.Y.

12. Evil is wrought for want of thought. *Rec. dist.:* Ohio.

13. Evil seldom goes alone. *Rec. dist.:* Ill.

14. Evil to him who evil thinks. *Vars.:* (a) Evil on him who evil thinks. (b) Evil to him who evil does. *Rec. dist.:* U.S., Can. *Infm.:* Motto of the Royal Order of the Garter, instituted ca1344 by Edward III of England. *1st cit.:* 1460 Ros, *La Belle Dame;* US1776 Malmedy in *Lee Papers,* N.Y.Hist.Soc. *Collections* (1871–74). *20c. coll.:* *ODEP* 397, Whiting 135, Stevenson 712:16.

15. Evil will be its own downfall. *Rec. dist.:* Kans.

16. Evil won is evil lost. *Rec. dist.:* Kans.

17. For every evil under the sun there is a remedy or there is none. *Rec. dist.:* Wis. *1st cit.:* 1869 Hazlitt, *English Proverbs.* *20c. coll.:* *ODEP* 228, Stevenson 714:4.

18. He who does evil comes to an evil end. *Rec. dist.:* R.I.

19. He who does evil suspects evil on the part of his fellow man. *Rec. dist.:* N.C. *1st cit.:* 1732 Fuller, *Gnomologia.* *20c. coll.:* Stevenson 712:6.

20. He who speaks evil hears worse. *Rec. dist.:* Ill. *1st cit.:* US1948 Stevenson. *Home Book of Proverbs.* *20c. coll.:* Stevenson 2127:10.

21. He who thinks evil wishes it on himself. *Rec. dist.:* N.Y.

22. If a man wishes to know the strength of evil, let him try to abandon it. *Rec. dist.:* Utah.

23. If you help the evil, you hurt the good. *Rec. dist.:* Ala. *1st cit.:* ca1526 Erasmus, *Dicta Sapientum,* tr. Berthelet. *20c. coll.:* *ODEP* 368.

24. In avoiding one evil care must be taken not to fall into another. *Rec. dist.:* N.Y.

25. Keep your tongue from evil. *Rec. dist.:* N.Y., Okla.

26. Money is the root of all evil. *Vars.:* (a) The love of money is the root of all evil. (b) Want of money is the root of all evil. *Rec. dist.:* U.S., Can. *1st cit.:* ca1000 Aelfric, *Homilies;* US1777 Adams, *Adams Family Correspondence,* ed. Butterfield (1963, 1973). *20c. coll.:* *CODP* 153, Whiting 270, T&W 230, Whiting*(MP)* 387.

27. Never do evil for evil. *Rec. dist.:* Ohio.

28. Never do evil hoping that good will come of it. *Rec. dist.:* Calif. *1st cit.:* 1578 Whetstone, *Promos and Cassandra;* US1689 Bulkeley, *People's Right to Election,* Conn.Hist.Soc. *Collections* (1860). *20c. coll.:* *ODEP* 562, Whiting 137, Stevenson 1003:7, Whiting*(MP)* 206.

29. Of two evils, choose the prettier. *Rec. dist.:* Minn. *1st cit.:* ca1374 Chaucer, *Troilus and Criseyde;* US1714 Dudley in *Winthrop Papers,* Mass.Hist.Soc. *Collections* (1863–72). *20c. coll.:* *ODEP* 233, *CODP* 70, Whiting 136, T&W 122, Whiting*(MP)* 206.

30. One does evil enough when one does nothing good. *Rec. dist.:* N.Y. *1st cit.:* 1616 Adams, *Divine Herhal.* *20c. coll.:* *ODEP* 194.

31. One evil breeds another. *Rec. dist.:* Ill. *1st cit.:* US1948 Stevenson, *Home Book of Proverbs.* *20c. coll.:* Stevenson 712:9.

32. Roots of evil bear bitter fruits. *Rec. dist.:* Kans., N.Y.

33. See no evil, hear no evil, speak no evil. *Var.:* Speak no evil, see no evil, and hear no evil. *Rec. dist.:* U.S., Can. *1st cit.:* 1926 *Army and Navy Store Catalogue.* *20c. coll.:* CODP 199.

34. Small evils hatch quick. *Rec. dist.:* Minn.

35. Take the evil with the good. *Rec. dist.:* S.C.

36. That which is evil is soon learned. *Rec. dist.:* Ill. *1st cit.:* 1670 Ray, *English Proverbs.* *20c. coll.:* ODEP 233.

37. The evils you do two by two you pay for one by one. *Rec. dist.:* Ill.

38. We cannot do evil to others without doing it to ourselves. *Rec. dist.:* Kans.

39. Who rewards evil for good, evil shall not depart his house. *Rec. dist.:* Minn. *1st cit.:* US1948 Stevenson, *Home Book of Proverbs.* *20c. coll.:* Stevenson 1003:8.

SEE ALSO AVARICE is the root of all evil. / CHAPERONS are necessary evils. / GOOD is recognized when it goes, and evil when it comes. / IDLENESS is the mother of evil. / A busy MIND breeds no evil. / PROCRASTINATION is the root of all evil. / WOMEN are the root of all evil. / Little WRONGS breed great evils.

evil *(adj.)* **1.** Nothing evil or good lasts a hundred years. *Rec. dist.:* R.I.

2. Nothing is evil but thinking makes it so. *Rec. dist.:* Miss.

3. The track of evil thought is crooked and has no end. *Rec. dist.:* Tex.

evil *(adv.)* Evil gotten, evil spent. *Rec. dist.:* N.Y., Ohio, Tex., Utah. *1st cit.:* ca1377 Langland, *Piers Plowman.* *20c. coll.:* Stevenson 926:2, ODEP 399.

evildoer **1.** Fret not for yourself because of evildoers. *Rec. dist.:* Ohio.

2. The evildoer is ever anxious. *Rec. dist.:* N.C., Wash.

3. The evildoer weeps. *Rec. dist.:* Wash.

ewe The ewes who bleat lose most of their meat. *Rec. dist.:* Ill.

exaggeration An exaggeration is the truth that has lost its temper. *Rec. dist.:* Ill., Minn.

exalt He who exalts himself shall be humbled. *Rec. dist.:* Calif., Minn., N.Y. *1st cit.:* Guazzo, *Civile Conversation,* tr. Pettie, T.T. (1925). *20c. coll.:* Stevenson 1195:12.

examine Examine what is said, not him who speaks. *Rec. dist.:* N.Y., Ohio.

example **1.** A good example is the best sermon. *Var.:* A bad example is the best sermon. *Rec. dist.:* U.S. *1st cit.:* 1732 Fuller, *Gnomologia;* US1747 Franklin, *PRAlmanac.* *20c. coll.:* Stevenson 718:8.

2. Example is better than following it. *Rec. dist.:* Ill.

3. Example is better than precept. *Var.:* Example teaches more than precept. *Rec. dist.:* U.S. *1st cit.:* ca1400 Mirk, *Festival,* E.E.T.S. (1905); US1702 Taylor, *Christographia,* ed. Grabo (1962). *20c. coll.:* ODEP 233, Whiting 137, CODP 71, Stevenson 718:3, T&W 122, Whiting(MP) 206.

4. Example is the strongest part of education. *Rec. dist.:* Wis.

5. Nothing is so infectious as example. *Rec. dist.:* N.Y. *1st cit.:* US1948 Stevenson, *Home Book of Proverbs.* *20c. coll.:* Stevenson 717:14.

excellence Excellence is its own reward. *Rec. dist.:* Ohio.

exception There is an exception to every rule. *Vars.:* **(a)** It's the exception that proves the rule. **(b)** The exception proves the rule. **(c)** There is no rule without an exception. *Rec. dist.:* U.S., Can. *1st cit.:* 1579 *Newes from the North;* US1691 *Fitzhugh and His Chesapeake World, 1676–1701,* ed. Davis, Va.Hist.Soc. *Documents* (1963). *20c. coll.:* ODEP 687, Whiting 137, CODP 71, Stevenson 2014:1, T&W 122, Whiting(MP) 206.

excess **1.** Nothing in excess is best. *Rec. dist.:* Ohio. *1st cit.:* 1508 Erasmus, *Adagia,* tr. Taverner. *20c. coll.:* Stevenson 1603:9.

2. The excesses of our youth are draughts upon our old age. *Rec. dist.:* Mich., N.Y., S.C.

exchange A fair exchange is no robbery. *Vars.:* **(a)** A fair exchange brings no quarrel.

(b) Exchange is no robbery. *Rec. dist.:* U.S. *1st cit.:* 1546 Heywood, *Dialogue of Proverbs,* ed. Habernicht (1963); US1737 *Colonial Records of Georgia,* ed. Chandler, in *Original Papers, 1735–1752* (1910–16). *20c. coll.:* ODEP 234, Whiting 138, *CODP* 71, Stevenson 719:6, T&W 123, Whiting*(MP)* 20.

excuse *(n.)* **1.** A poor excuse is better than none. *Vars.:* **(a)** A bad excuse is better than none. **(b)** A bad excuse is better than none at all. **(c)** A poor excuse is better than none at all. **(d)** Better a bad excuse than none at all. **(e)** Poor excuses are better than none. **(f)** Some excuse is better than none at all. *Rec. dist.:* U.S. *1st cit.:* 1551 Wilson, *Rule of Reason;* US1686 Dunton, *Letters from New England,* Publ. Prince Soc. (1867). *20c. coll.:* ODEP 26, Whiting 138, *CODP* 8, Stevenson 720:7, Whiting*(MP)* 207.

2. Any excuse will serve a tyrant. *Rec. dist.:* Fla.

3. Don't make excuses; make good. *Rec. dist.:* N.Y. *1st cit.:* US1905 Hubbard, *Epigrams.* *20c. coll.:* Stevenson 720:5.

4. He who is good at making excuses is seldom good at anything else. *Var.:* A person good at making excuses is seldom good for anything else. *Rec. dist.:* N.J., N.Y., Ohio, Okla., Oreg.

5. If you have a good excuse, don't use it. *Rec. dist.:* Kans.

6. One excuse is as good as another. *Rec. dist.:* Okla.

See also IGNORANCE is no excuse. / IGNORANCE of the law is no excuse. / A LAZY man always finds excuses. / SUCCESS never needs an excuse.

excuse *(v.)* Who excuses himself accuses himself. *Vars.:* **(a)** If you excuse yourself, you accuse yourself. **(b)** To excuse is to accuse. *Rec. dist.:* Ill., Ind., N.J., R.I. *1st cit.:* 1596 Shakespeare, *King John;* US1919 Haggard, *She and Allan.* *20c. coll.:* ODEP 234, Whiting*(MP)* 207, Stevenson 720:1.

See also Never ACCUSE others to excuse yourself.

execute *See* LAWS too gentle are seldom obeyed; too severe, seldom executed.

execution The execution of the laws is more important than the making of them. *Rec. dist.:* Wis.

exercise *(n.)* The only exercise some people get is jumping to conclusions. *Rec. dist.:* Miss., N.C.

See also Paddling your own CANOE is good exercise.

exhaust *See* What some of us need is more HORSEPOWER and not so much exhaust.

exhausted *See* A FIELD becomes exhausted by constant tillage. / When the OIL is exhausted, the lamp dies out.

exist It is not enough just to exist; you have to live. *Rec. dist.:* Utah.

expect Expect to be treated as you have treated others. *Rec. dist.:* Ill.

See also Those who betray their FRIENDS must not expect others to keep faith with them. / Expect NOTHING and you won't be disappointed.

expectation Expectation always surpasses realization. *Rec. dist.:* Kans., Minn.

expected **1.** Least expected, sure to happen. *Rec. dist.:* Ohio.

2. Long expected comes at last. *Rec. dist.:* Nebr.

See also LITTLE is given, little is expected.

expense **1.** Beware of little expenses. *Var.:* Beware of little expenses: a small leak will sink a great ship. *Rec. dist.:* Miss., N.J., Wis.

2. He is poor whose expenses exceed his income. *Rec. dist.:* N.Y.

3. In hard times the wise man cuts his expenses; the foolish spendthrift cuts his throat. *Rec. dist.:* N.Y.

See also All FLATTERERS live at the expense of those they flatter. / Those who take the PROFITS should also bear the expense.

experience **1.** A thimbleful of experience is worth a tubful of knowledge. *Rec. dist.:* Ky., Tenn.

2. A thorn of experience is worth a wilderness of advice. *Rec. dist.:* Ill.

3. Everyone must learn by experience. *Rec. dist.:* Ill.

4. Experience bought by suffering teaches wisdom. *Rec. dist.:* Ill.

5. Experience is a comb which fate gives to a man when his hair is all gone. *Rec. dist.:* Ind.

6. Experience is a dear school, but fools learn in no other. *Var.:* Experience keeps a dear school, but fools will learn in no other. *Rec. dist.:* U.S. *1st cit.:* 1897 King, *Story of British Army;* US1743 Franklin, *PRAlmanac.* *20c. coll.:* ODEP 235, Whiting 139, CODP 72, Stevenson 723:2.

7. Experience is a dear teacher. *Var.:* Experience is the best teacher, but it charges high tuition fees. *Rec. dist.:* Ill., Iowa, Okla., Vt., Wis.

8. Experience is a hard master but a good teacher. *Vars.:* **(a)** Experience is the best teacher. **(b)** Experience is the greatest teacher. *Rec. dist.:* Ark., N.Y., Ohio. *1st cit.:* 1803 Weems, Letter, 12 Nov.; US1719 *Addition* in *Colonial Currency Reprints, 1682–1751,* ed. Davis, Publ. Prince Soc. (1910–11). *20c. coll.:* CODP 72, Whiting 139, Stevenson 723:3, T&W 123, Whiting*(MP)* 207.

9. Experience is good if not bought too dear. *Var.:* Experience is good if you don't pay too dear for it. *Rec. dist.:* Ill. *1st cit.:* 1732 Fuller, *Gnomologia.* *20c. coll.:* ODEP 234, Stevenson 723:2.

10. Experience is not what happens to a person, but what one does with what happens to him. *Rec. dist.:* Ohio.

11. Experience is something you get when looking for something else. *Rec. dist.:* N.Dak.

12. Experience is the blind man's dog. *Rec. dist.:* Ill.

13. Experience is the father of wisdom and memory the mother. *Rec. dist.:* Ill. *1st cit.:* 1574 Guazzo, *Civile Conversation,* tr. Pettie, T.T. (1925). *20c. coll.:* ODEP 235, CODP 72, Stevenson 722:13.

14. Experience is the mother of knowledge. *Rec. dist.:* N.Y. *1st cit.:* 1539 Taverner, *Garden of Wysedome;* US1788 *American Museum.* *20c. coll.:* ODEP 235, Whiting 139, T&W 123.

15. Experience is the mother of science. *Rec. dist.:* Ohio.

16. Experience is the stuff life is made of. *Rec. dist.:* N.C.

17. Experience is the teacher of fools. *Rec. dist.:* N.Y., Ohio. *1st cit.:* ca1568 Ascham, *Scholemaster.* *20c. coll.:* ODEP 234, CODP 72, Stevenson 724:13.

18. Experience teaches slowly and at the cost of mistakes. *Rec. dist.:* N.Y. *1st cit.:* 1850 Froude, "Party Politics" in *Short Studies on Great Subjects;* USca1656 Bradford, *History of Plymouth Plantation,* ed. Ford (1912). *20c. coll.:* Whiting 139, Stevenson 724:5.

19. Experience teaches wisdom unto fools. *Rec. dist.:* Miss., N.Y., S.C. *1st cit.:* USca1656 Bradford, *History of Plymouth Plantation,* ed. Ford (1912). *20c. coll.:* Whiting 139, Stevenson 724:5.

20. Experience tests the truth. *Rec. dist.:* Ill.

21. Experience without learning is better than learning without experience. *Rec. dist.:* Ill. *1st cit.:* 1707 Mapletoft, *Select Proverbs.* *20c. coll.:* ODEP 235, Stevenson 723:5.

22. Experience without learning is the delusion of fancy. *Rec. dist.:* Mich.

23. Listen to the voice of experience, but also make use of your brains. *Rec. dist.:* Ill.

24. Some folks speak from experience; others, from experience, don't speak. *Rec. dist.:* Wis.

25. Wide experience makes for deep tolerance. *Rec. dist.:* Calif.

26. You must profit from experience. *Rec. dist.:* N.Y.

expression Your expression is the most important thing you can wear. *Var.:* Of all the things you wear, your expression is the most important. *Rec. dist.:* Calif., N.Y.

exterior A fair exterior is a silent recommendation. *Rec. dist.:* Calif., Minn.

SEE ALSO Many a kind HEART beats under a rugged exterior.

extinguish *SEE* A FIRE is never out until the last spark is extinguished. / Kindle not a FIRE that you cannot extinguish.

extreme **1.** Extremes meet. *Rec. dist.:* Ill., N.Y., Okla., Tex. *1st cit.:* 1606 Shakespeare,

Antony and Cleopatra; US1762 *Letter Book of John Watts 1762–1765,* N.Y.Hist.Soc. *Collections* (1928). **20c. coll.:** *ODEP* 235, Whiting 139, *CODP* 73, Stevenson 658:16, T&W 123, Whiting*(MP)* 207.

2. One extreme follows another. **Rec. dist.:** Ohio, R.I. **1st cit.:** 1748 Richardson, *Clarissa.* **20c. coll.:** Stevenson 729:10.

extremity Man's extremity is God's opportunity. **Rec. dist.:** Calif., Minn. **1st cit.:** 1586 Warner, *Albion's England;* US1776 Hodgkins in Wade and Lively, *Glorious Cause, Adventures of Two Officers in Washington's Army* (1958). **20c. coll.:** *ODEP* 507, Whiting 279, *CODP* 144, Stevenson 968:5.

eye **1.** A man may have a thousand eyes, yet if his mind is blank, he cannot see a thing. **Rec. dist.:** Ohio.

2. A rolling eye, a roving heart. **Rec. dist.:** N.Y.

3. A roving eye misses opportunities close by. **Rec. dist.:** Oreg.

4. An eye for an eye, a tooth for a tooth. **Rec. dist.:** U.S., Can. **1st cit.:** US1781 Adams, *Adams Family Correspondence,* ed. Butterfield (1963, 1973). **20c. coll.:** Whiting 139, Stevenson 1966:3, Whiting*(MP)* 207.

5. Bad eyes never see any good. **Var.:** An evil eye can see no good. **Rec. dist.:** Fla.

6. Big eyes mean small stomachs. **Var.:** Big eyes overshadow a small stomach. **Rec. dist.:** Calif., N.Y.

7. Blue eyes, true eyes. **Rec. dist.:** Wis.

8. Calf eyes, calf love. **Rec. dist.:** Fla.

9. Closed eyes cannot see roses; neither can cold hands hold them. **Rec. dist.:** Ohio.

10. Don't fire until you see the white of his eye. **Var.:** Don't shoot till you see the white of his eye. **Rec. dist.:** U.S. **Infm.:** This is the order given at the Battle of Bunker Hill (American Revolution), meaning "Don't shoot until the enemy is within close range."

11. Every shut eye ain't asleep. **Rec. dist.:** Ill., Miss., N.Y., S.C.

12. Four eyes see more than two. **Var.:** Two eyes can see better than one. **Rec. dist.:** Fla.,

Ill., Ky. **1st cit.:** 1592 Delamothe, *Treasury of French Tongue;* US1689 Bulkeley, *People's Right to Election,* Conn.Hist.Soc. *Collections* (1860). **20c. coll.:** *CODP* 37, Whiting 140, Stevenson 730:3, Whiting*(MP)* 208.

13. He that winks with the eye causes sorrow. **Rec. dist.:** Utah. **Infm.:** Usually his own. **1st cit.:** US1948 Stevenson, *Home Book of Proverbs.* **20c. coll.:** Stevenson 2528:1.

14. He who hasn't anything to do pulls his wife's eyes out. **Rec. dist.:** N.Y.

15. However high the eye may rise, it will find the eyebrow above it. **Rec. dist.:** N.J. **Infm.:** There are always those higher than you.

16. If the eye won't admire, the heart won't desire. **Rec. dist.:** Ill. **1st cit.:** 1669 Penn, *No Cross, No Crown.* **20c. coll.:** Stevenson 736:13.

17. It is better to get something in your eye and then wink than to wink and then get something in your eye. **Rec. dist.:** Utah. **Infm.:** If you wink at someone's girl, you may get a fist in your eye.

18. It is better to trust the eye than the ear. **Rec. dist.:** Ind. **1st cit.:** 1539 Taverner, *Proverbs of Erasmus.* **20c. coll.:** Stevenson 737:9.

19. Keep your eyes on the future, never on the past. **Rec. dist.:** Okla.

20. Keep your eyes wide open before marriage, half shut afterwards. **Var.:** Before marriage open your eyes wide; afterwards close them tightly. **Rec. dist.:** Kans., Miss., N.Y., Ohio, Wis. **1st cit.:** US1738 Franklin, *PRAlmanac.* **20c. coll.:** Whiting 140, *ODEP* 419.

21. Keep your mouth shut and your eyes open. **Rec. dist.:** N.Y., Ohio, Pa. **1st cit.:** 1574 Guazzo, *Civile Conversation,* tr. Pettie, T.T. (1925); US1721 Wise, *Word of Comfort to Melancholy Country.* **20c. coll.:** *ODEP* 419, Whiting 140, Stevenson 1636:4.

22. Man was born with two eyes and only one tongue in order that he might see twice as much as he says. **Rec. dist.:** Utah.

23. Never rub your eye but with your elbow. **Rec. dist.:** N.Y. **1st cit.:** 1670 Ray, *English Proverbs.* **20c. coll.:** Stevenson 730:2.

24. No eye like the master's eye. *Rec. dist.:* N.C. *1st cit.:* US1933 Freeman, *Dr. Thorndyke Intervenes. 20c. coll.:* Whiting(MP) 208.

25. One eye has more faith than two ears. *Rec. dist.:* N.Y.

26. Open your eyes to the facts. *Rec. dist.:* N.Y.

27. Our eyes are placed in front because it is more important to look ahead than behind. *Rec. dist.:* Utah.

28. That which catches the eye also catches the penny. *Rec. dist.:* N.C.

29. The eye is not satisfied with seeing. *Var.:* The eye is not satisfied with seeing, nor is the ear filled with hearing. *Rec. dist.:* N.Y., Ohio. *1st cit.:* US1948 Stevenson, *Home Book of Proverbs. 20c. coll.:* Stevenson 737:8.

30. The eye of the master does more than his hand. *Var.:* The eye of a master will do more work than both his hands. *Rec. dist.:* Ill., Miss., Ohio. *1st cit.:* 1843 Carlyle, *Past and Present;* US1744 Franklin, *PRAlmanac. 20c. coll.:* Stevenson 1547:6, Whiting 140, *ODEP* 236, *CODP* 73, T&W 124.

31. The eye that sees all things sees not itself. *Rec. dist.:* Mich., N.Y. *1st cit.:* ca1591 Smith, *Sermons* (1866). *20c. coll.:* *ODEP* 236, Stevenson 735:13.

32. The eyes are bigger than the stomach. *Vars.:* (a) Guard lest the eyes be bigger than the stomach. (b) The eye is bigger than the belly. (c) The eye is bigger than the mouth. *Rec. dist.:* U.S., Can. *1st cit.:* 1580 Lyly, *Euphues and His England. 20c. coll.:* *ODEP* 235, Stevenson 733:12.

33. The eyes are of little use if the mind be blind. *Rec. dist.:* N.C.

34. The eyes are the windows of the soul. *Vars.:* (a) The eyes are the mirror of the mind. (b) The eyes are the mirrors of the soul. *Rec. dist.:* U.S. *1st cit.:* 1545 Goeurot, *Regiment of Life. 20c. coll.:* *ODEP* 235, *CODP* 73, Stevenson 732:11.

35. The master's eye makes the horse fat. *Vars.:* (a) If the owner keeps his eye on the horse, he will fatten. (b) The eye of the master fattens his herd. *Rec. dist.:* Calif., Okla., Vt. *1st cit.:* 1552 Latimer, *5th Sermon, "Lord's Prayer." 20c. coll.:* *ODEP* 517.

36. We see least with borrowed eyes. *Rec. dist.:* Ill.

37. What the eye doesn't see, the heart doesn't grieve for. *Vars.:* (a) If the eyes do not see, the heart will not break. (b) The heart soon forgets what the eye sees not. (c) What the eye can't see, the heart won't crave. (d) What the eye doesn't see, the heart doesn't feel. (e) What the eye sees not, the heart rues not. *Rec. dist.:* U.S., Can. *1st cit.:* 1545 Erasmus, *Adages;* US1692 Bulkeley, *Will and Doom,* ed. Hoadly, Conn.Hist.Soc. *Collections* (1895). *20c. coll.:* *ODEP* 236, Whiting 141, *CODP* 73, Stevenson 736:8, Whiting(MP) 210.

38. What the eyes see, the heart believes. *Rec. dist.:* Ill.

39. Whatever catches our eye long enough will catch us. *Rec. dist.:* Fla.

40. You can look in the eyes but not in the heart. *Rec. dist.:* N.Y.

41. You may know de way, but better keep yo' eyes on de seven stars. *Rec. dist.:* Miss., N.Y., S.C.

SEE ALSO ABSENCE is love's foe: far from the eyes, far from the heart. / The APPLE of your eye at sixteen is sauce in your eye at twenty. / The BUYER needs a thousand eyes; the seller wants but one. / Look not too high lest a CHIP fall in your eye. / ENVY has smarting eyes. / Every GIRL is beautiful in her father's eyes. / The HEART has eyes that the brain knows nothing of. / There is more to HONESTY than meets the eye. / An angry MAN opens his mouth and shuts his eyes. / The NIGHT has a thousand eyes. / With seven NURSES a child will be without eyes. / Hold a PENNY close enough to the eye and it will hide the sun. / A good SURGEON must have an eagle eye, a lion's heart, and a lady's hand. / The WALL has ears, and the plain has eyes. / He who has a fair WIFE needs more than two eyes.

eyesight   1. He who weeps for everybody soon loses his eyesight. *Rec. dist.:* Mich.

2. You may have perfect eyesight and be as blind as a bat. *Rec. dist.:*

eyewitness One eyewitness is better than ten hearsays. *Rec. dist.:* N.Y. *1st cit.:* 1519 Horman, *Vulgaria. 20c. coll.:* ODEP 237, Stevenson 737:12.

F

face *(n.)* **1.** A beautiful face is a silent commendation. *Vars.:* **(a)** A beautiful face is a letter of recommendation. **(b)** A good face is a letter of commendation. **(c)** A pleasant face is the best recommendation you can write. *Rec. dist.:* Fla., N.C., Ohio. *1st cit.:* 1620 Cervantes, *Don Quixote,* tr. Shelton. *20c. coll.:* ODEP 319.

2. A face without a smile is like a lantern without a light. *Rec. dist.:* Miss., N.C.

3. A fair face may hide a foul heart. *Vars.:* **(a)** A fair face may be a foul bargain. **(b)** A fair face often covers a crooked mind. **(c)** Fair face, foul heart. *Rec. dist.:* Fla., Ill. *1st cit.:* 1584 Lyly, *Campaspe.* *20c. coll.:* Stevenson 1208:5.

4. A good face needs no paint. *Vars.:* **(a)** A fair face needs no paint. **(b)** Fair faces need no paint. *Rec. dist.:* Colo., Miss., N.J. *1st cit.:* 1616 Heywood, *Somers Tracts.* *20c. coll.:* Stevenson 738:4.

5. A kind face needs no bond. *Rec. dist.:* Ill. *1st cit.:* 1639 Clarke, *Paroemiologia;* US1666 Alsop, *Character of Province of Maryland,* ed. Mereness (1902). *20c. coll.:* Stevenson 741:2, Whiting 142.

6. A long face makes a long road seem twice as long. *Rec. dist.:* Ont. *1st cit.:* US1775 McDougal in *Naval Documents of American Revolution,* ed. Clark (1964). *20c. coll.:* Whiting 142.

7. A long face shortens your list of friends. *Var.:* A long face shortens your following. *Rec. dist.:* N.Y., Vt.

8. A man with a pockmarked face will laugh at another's freckles. *Rec. dist.:* Colo.

9. A man without a smiling face must not open a shop. *Var.:* Without a smiling face, do not become a merchant. *Rec. dist.:* Calif., N.J., N.Y., Ont.

10. A pretty face has been the downfall of many a man. *Var.:* A pretty face has ruined many a man. *Rec. dist.:* Mich., Minn.

11. A pretty face may hide an empty head. *Rec. dist.:* Wash.

12. Be it ever so homely, there's no face like your own. *Rec. dist.:* Kans., Ohio, Ont.

13. Do not make ugly faces at others until you can improve your own. *Rec. dist.:* Utah.

14. Faces are stubborn things. *Rec. dist.:* Colo.

15. Fair faces go places. *Rec. dist.:* Ill.

16. It matters more what's in a woman's face than what's on it. *Rec. dist.:* Miss.

17. Long faces make short lives. *Rec. dist.:* Kans.

18. May the man be damned and never gain fat who wears two faces under one hat. *Rec. dist.:* N.Y. *1st cit.:* 1855 Bohn, *Handbook of Proverbs.* *20c. coll.:* Stevenson 741:8.

19. Men's faces are not to be trusted. *Rec. dist.:* N.Y. *1st cit.:* US1948 Stevenson, *Home Book of Proverbs.* *20c. coll.:* Stevenson 739:8.

20. Never carry two faces under one hood. *Rec. dist.:* Mich., Ont. *1st cit.:* ca1440 Lydgate, *Minor Poems;* US1669 *New England Memorial,* ed. Lord (1903). *20c. coll.:* Stevenson 741:8, Whiting 143.

21. New face, new fancy. *Rec. dist.:* N.Y.

22. Pretty face, poor fate. *Rec. dist.:* Miss.

23. The best way to save face is to keep it covered. *Rec. dist.:* Kans.

24. The face is a mask; look behind it. *Rec. dist.:* Ill.

25. The face is the index of the mind, but appearances are deceitful. *Rec. dist.:* Minn. *1st cit.:* ca1575 Pilkington, *Nehemiah;* US1702 Taylor, *Christographia,* ed. Grabo (1962). *20c. coll.:* ODEP 237, Stevenson 738:9, Whiting(MP) 211.

26. Turn your face to the sun and the shadows will fall behind you. *Vars.:* **(a)** Always turn your face toward the sunshine. **(b)** If you keep your face turned toward the sun, all the shadows of life will fall behind. **(c)** Keep your face toward the sunshine. **(d)** Keep your face toward the sunshine and the shadows always fall behind you. **(e)** Keep your face toward the sunshine and the shadows will fall behind. **(f)** Stand with your face toward the sunshine and the shadows will fall behind you. *Rec. dist.:* U.S., Can.

27. When men come face to face, their differences vanish. *Rec. dist.:* Ind.

SEE ALSO AFFECTATION is a greater enemy to the face than smallpox. / Fresh AIR and sunshine and plenty of grace slam the door in the doctor's face. / The other face of CREDIT is debt. / Better FAME than face. / It is well that our FAULTS are not written on our faces. / FEMALE is one head with two faces. / FOOLS' names and fools' faces are always seen in public places. / What you wear in your HEART shows in your face. / HUSBANDS are all alike, but they have different faces so you can tell them apart. / Don't cut off your NOSE to spite your face. / Face POWDER may win a man, but it takes baking powder to hold him. / An empty PURSE fills the face with wrinkles. / Wrinkled PURSES make wrinkled faces. / SIN may be clasped so close we cannot see its face. / A SMILE is worth its face value. / SOAP and water will not make a Negro's face white. / Who SPITS against the wind spits in his own face. / A STAB in the back is worse than a kick in the face. / Throw a STONE in the mud and it splashes in your face.

face *(v.)* SEE The hardest JOB a child faces is that of learning manners without seeing any.

fact **1.** A single fact is worth a shipload of argument. *Rec. dist.:* Ill., Miss.

2. Fact is stranger than fiction. *Rec. dist.:* Ohio, Okla. **1st cit.:** 1823 Byron, *Don Juan;* US1853 Haliburton, *Sam Slick's Wise Saws.* **20c. coll.:** ODEP 844, T&W 127:2, CODP 75.

3. Facts are better than theories. *Rec. dist.:* Utah.

4. Facts are facts. *Rec. dist.:* Mich., N.Y. **1st cit.:** US1930 Kennedy, *Corpse Guard Parade.* **20c. coll.:** Whiting(MP) 212.

5. Facts are stubborn things. *Rec. dist.:* Ohio.

1st cit.: 1732 Budgell, *Liberty and Progress;* US1748 Eliot, *Essays in Field Husbandry in New England, 1748–1762,* eds. Carman and Tugwell (1934). **20c. coll.:** ODEP 238, Whiting 143, CODP 238, Stevenson 742:3, Whiting(MP) 212.

6. Facts don't lie. *Rec. dist.:* N.Y., S.C. **1st cit.:** US1748 Eliot, *Essays on Field Husbandry in New England, 1748–1762,* eds. Carman and Tugwell (1934). **20c. coll.:** Whiting 143, Whiting(MP) 212.

7. Get your facts first, and then you can distort them as much as you please. *Rec. dist.:* Wis.

8. It ain't the matter of fact, it's the point of view. *Rec. dist.:* Vt.

9. Let's face the facts and get at the root of trouble. *Rec. dist.:* W.Va. **1st cit.:** 1932 Grierson, *Murder in Mortimer Square;* US1930 Cournos, *Grandmother Martin Is Murdered.* **20c. coll.:** Stevenson 742:17, Whiting(MP) 212.

10. One fact is stronger than a dozen texts or pretexts. *Rec. dist.:* Ill.

SEE ALSO FIGURES are not always facts. / No IDEAL is as good as a fact.

fade We all fade as the leaf. *Rec. dist.:* N.Y. **1st cit.:** 1640 Howell, "To the Prince" in *Dodong's Grove.* **20c. coll.:** Stevenson 1374:2.

SEE ALSO All that's FAIR must fade. / He who comes through the FIRE will not fade in the sun. / Flowers of true FRIENDSHIP never fade.

fail **1.** He fails not who attempts not. *Rec. dist.:* Ill.

2. He who never fails will never grow rich. *Rec. dist.:* N.Y. **1st cit.:** US1869 Spurgeon, *John Ploughman's Talks.* **20c. coll.:** Stevenson 743:13.

3. If one fails, the whole world tramples on him. *Rec. dist.:* Ont.

4. Many men fail because they lack purpose. *Rec. dist.:* N.Y.

SEE ALSO Where FORCE fails, skill and patience will prevail. / FRIENDS and mules fail us in hard places. / When the FRUIT fails, welcome haws. / GOODNESS is the only investment that never fails. / HEAVEN-sent men never fail. / LOVE never fails. / REASON succeeds where force fails. / All SIGNS fail in dry weather. / He who STEALS will always fail. / STRIVE though you fail. / The SUNRISE never failed us yet.

failing We see the failings of others but are blind to our own. *Rec. dist.:* Ill. *1st cit.:* US1948 Stevenson, *Home Book of Proverbs.* *20c. coll.:* Stevenson 779:4.

SEE ALSO PERSEVERANCE is failing nineteen times and succeeding the twentieth.

failure **1.** A man can fail many times, but he isn't a real failure until he begins to blame someone else. *Rec. dist.:* Iowa.

2. Every failure teaches a man something, if he will learn. *Rec. dist.:* N.C.

3. Failure breeds failure. *Rec. dist.:* Ky., Tenn.

4. Failure is failure, however close you come to the goal. *Rec. dist.:* Ariz.

5. Failure is more frequently from want of energy than want of capital. *Rec. dist.:* Wis.

6. Failure is not falling down but staying down. *Rec. dist.:* N.J.

7. Failure isn't the end of dreams, it is only the beginning. *Rec. dist.:* Minn.

8. Failure teaches success. *Rec. dist.:* Fla., Ill., N.J. *1st cit.:* 1902 Balfour, *Life of Stevenson.* *20c. coll.:* ODEP 238.

9. Failures are the stepping-stones to success. *Vars.:* **(a)** Failure is a stepping-stone to greatness. **(b)** Your failures are stepping-stones to success. *Rec. dist.:* Fla., Ill. *1st cit.:* US1948 Stevenson, *Home Book of Proverbs.* *20c. coll.:* Stevenson 743:3.

10. If there were no failures, there would be no successes. *Rec. dist.:* Okla.

11. If we blame others for our failures, we should also give them credit for our successes. *Var.:* When a man blames others for his failures, it's a good idea to credit others with his success. *Rec. dist.:* Kans., Wis.

12. It is better to die than to live a failure. *Rec. dist.:* Calif.

13. Not failure but low aim is a crime. *Rec. dist.:* Ill.

14. Nothing beats a failure but a try. *Rec. dist.:* Md., N.J., Va.

15. Other men's failures can never save you. *Rec. dist.:* Ill.

16. The only failure is to admit failure. *Rec. dist.:* Calif.

17. There is no failure except in no longer trying. *Var.:* There is no failure until you fail to keep trying. *Rec. dist.:* Okla., Ont.

18. We learn something even by our failures. *Rec. dist.:* N.Y., Ont.

SEE ALSO He who is small in FAITH will never be great but in failure. / A true FRIEND worries more over your success than your failure. / It is the part of a good GENERAL to talk of success, not of failure. / Your own HEAD—your own success or failure. / IDLENESS leads to failure. / A selfish SUCCESS is a successful failure. / SUCCESS comes in cans, failures in can'ts. / Nothing beats a TRIAL but a failure.

faint *SEE* Faint HEART never won fair lady.

fainthearted *SEE* FORTUNE is not often on the side of the fainthearted.

fair *(beautiful)* **1.** All that's fair must fade. *Rec. dist.:* Fla.

2. Fair in the cradle, foul in the saddle. *Rec. dist.:* N.Y. *1st cit.:* 1614 Camden, *Remaines Concerning Britaine.* *20c. coll.:* ODEP 238.

3. Fair is foul and foul is fair. *Rec. dist.:* Ohio.

4. If it's long fair, it'll be long foul. *Rec. dist.:* Ont.

SEE ALSO None but the BRAVE deserve the fair. / The higher the CLOUDS, the fairer the weather. / A fair FACE may hide a foul heart. / Fair FEATHERS make fair fowl. / Fair FLOWERS are never left standing by the wayside. / FRIDAY is the fairest or foulest day. / Fairest GEMS lie deepest. / LADIES young and fair have the gift to know it. / In fair WEATHER prepare for foul.

fair *(just)* **1.** Be fair, be good, and be loved. *Rec. dist.:* N.Mex.

2. Fair and softly go far in a day. *Rec. dist.:* Mich.

3. **Fair is fair.** *Rec. dist.:* Mich., N.Y., Vt. *1st cit.:* US1928 Barry, *Corpse on the Bridge.* *20c. coll.:* Whiting*(MP)* 213.

SEE ALSO ALL is fair in love and war. / Wanted: not CHARITY but a fair chance. / Good PLAY is fair play. / SPEAK fair, think what you will. / TURNABOUT is fair play.

fairly SEE A single PENNY fairly got is worth a thousand that are not.

fairy tale If you will it, it will not remain a fairy tale. *Rec. dist.:* N.Y.

faith 1. A proof of faith is obedience. *Rec. dist.:* N.C.

2. All fails when faith fails. *Rec. dist.:* N.Y.

3. Faith begins where reason stops. *Rec. dist.:* Minn., N.Y.

4. Faith can move mountains. *Vars.:* **(a)** Faith moves mountains. **(b)** Faith will move mountains. **(c)** Faith will remove mountains. *Rec. dist.:* U.S., Can. *1st cit.:* 1897 Grand, *Beth Book.* *20c. coll.:* *CODP* 76, Stevenson 745:1.

5. Faith is inward truth daring the unknown. *Rec. dist.:* N.C.

6. Faith is that quality which enables us to believe what we know to be untrue. *Var.:* Faith is believing what you know isn't so. *Rec. dist.:* N.Y., N.Dak.

7. Faith is the vision of the heart. *Rec. dist.:* Miss.

8. Faith is working in the dark. *Rec. dist.:* Kans.

9. Faith laughs at impossibilities. *Rec. dist.:* N.Y.

10. Faith without works is vain hope. *Var.:* Faith without works is dead. *Rec. dist.:* Fla., N.Y. *1st cit.:* ca1389 Chaucer, *Prologue to Second Nonnes Tale* in *Canterbury Tales.* *20c. coll.:* Stevenson 744:13.

11. He who has no faith in others finds no faith in them. *Rec. dist.:* Ohio.

12. He who is small in faith will never be great but in failure. *Rec. dist.:* Fla.

13. If you don't keep faith with man, you can't keep faith with God. *Rec. dist.:* Ill.

14. In the affairs of this world, men are saved not by faith but by the want of it. *Rec. dist.:* Ill.

15. It's easier to lose faith than to find it again. *Rec. dist.:* Ill., Ind.

16. Little men are men of little faith; big men have the faith to move mountains. *Rec. dist.:* Ill.

17. Pin not your faith on another's sleeve. *Rec. dist.:* Fla., Mich., Tex. *1st cit.:* 1548 Hall, *Chronicle of Lancastre and York;* US1734 *Writings of Samuel Johnson, President of King's College,* ed. Schneider (1929). *20c. coll.:* *ODEP* 626, Whiting 143.

18. Respect faith, but doubt is what gets you an education. *Rec. dist.:* Ont.

19. Show your faith by your works. *Rec. dist.:* N.Y.

20. Trust not him that has once broken faith. *Rec. dist.:* N.J., N.C.

SEE ALSO In the COUNTRY one does not lose faith. / FALSEHOOD is the darkness of faith. / Those who betray their FRIENDS must not expect others to keep faith with them. / LOVE asks faith and faith asks firmness. / There are no reserved SEATS in the halls of fame or the chapels of faith.

faithful 1. Better to be faithful than successful. *Rec. dist.:* Kans. *1st cit.:* USca1903 Roosevelt in Riis, *Theodore Roosevelt the Citizen.* *20c. coll.:* Stevenson 746:6.

2. Faithful are the wounds of a friend, but the kisses of an enemy are deceitful. *Var.:* Faithful are the wounds of a friend. *Rec. dist.:* N.Y., Ont. *1st cit.:* 1862 Rossetti, *House to House.* *20c. coll.:* Stevenson 912:5.

3. Faithful in little, faithful in much. *Rec. dist.:* Ont.

SEE ALSO A faithful FRIEND is better than gold. / TRUTH, harsh though it be, is a faithful friend.

faithfulness 1. A little thing is a little thing, but faithfulness in a little thing is a big thing. *Rec. dist.:* Ohio.

2. Faithfulness to duty brings rewards. *Rec. dist.:* Minn.

fall *(n.)* **1.** A late fall means a hard winter. *Rec. dist.:* Vt.

2. Long fall, late spring. *Rec. dist.:* Ont.

SEE ALSO CLIMB not too high lest the fall be greater. / FOLLY has a fall before it. / PRIDE comes before a fall. / A STUMBLE may prevent a fall.

fall *(v.)* **1.** Everything does not fall that totters. *Rec. dist.:* Ala., Ga., N.Y. *1st cit.:* 1603 Montaigne, *Essays,* tr. Florio. *20c. coll.:* ODEP 11.

2. Fall but don't bawl. *Rec. dist.:* Ill.

3. If a man once falls, all will tread on him. *Rec. dist.:* Okla., Tex.

4. It's easier to fall than to get on your feet. *Rec. dist.:* Ill.

5. One may sooner fall than rise. *Rec. dist.:* Fla., Okla., Tex. *1st cit.:* 1616 Draxe, *Bibliotheca Scholastica* in *Anglia* (1918). *20c. coll.:* ODEP 753.

6. The harder you fall, the higher you bounce. *Rec. dist.:* Ill., Wash.

SEE ALSO An APPLE doesn't fall far from its tree. / Even an ASS will not fall twice in the same quicksand. / The BIGGER they come, the harder they fall. / Let the CHIPS fall where they may. / Who never CLIMBED never fell. / Blessed is the CORPSE the rain falls on. / If you can't be the bell COW, fall in behind. / Better go around than fall into the DITCH. / Into the mouth of a bad DOG often falls a good bone. / A creaking DOOR never falls from its hinges. / The higher they FLY, the harder they fall. / A prating FOOL shall fall. / The older the FOOL, the harder he falls. / A HALO only has to fall a few inches to become a noose. / Let JUSTICE be done though the heavens fall. / Hew to the LINE; let the chips fall where they may. / As a man LIVES, so shall he die; as a tree falls, so shall it lie. / He that falls in LOVE with himself will have no rivals. / Even a MONKEY will fall from a tree sometime. / If you dig a PIT for someone else, you fall into it yourself. / Into each life some RAIN must fall. / RAIN falls alike on the just and unjust. / It is better to SIT still than to rise to fall. / He who lays a SNARE for another himself falls into it. / When you think you STAND, take heed—you may fall. / SUCCESS comes in rising every time you fall. / Wish not to TASTE what does not fall to you. / As a TREE falls, so shall it lie. / Those who make TROUBLE for others often fall into it themselves. / UNITED we stand, divided we fall. / It is too late to close the WELL after the goat has fallen in. / A WORM is about the only thing that does not fall down.

falling *(n.)* **1.** By falling we learn to go safely. *Rec. dist.:* Fla.

2. Falling hurts least those who fly low. *Rec. dist.:* Ind., Ont.

3. Falling is easier than rising. *Rec. dist.:* Calif., Fla., N.J.

4. Keeping from falling is better than helping up. *Rec. dist.:* Ont.

5. To keep from falling, keep on climbing. *Rec. dist.:* Ind.

SEE ALSO The falling out of LOVERS is the renewing of love. / Our greatest GLORY consists not in never falling, but in rising every time we fall.

falling *(adj.)* Press not a falling man too hard. *Rec. dist.:* N.Y., Vt.

false *(n.)* An hour perhaps divides the false and truth. *Rec. dist.:* N.Y.

false *(adj.)* False with one can be false with two. *Rec. dist.:* N.Y.

SEE ALSO False FRIENDS are worse than open enemies. / True FRIENDS are like diamonds, precious and rare; false ones like autumn leaves, found everywhere. / MONEY and man a mutual friendship show: man makes false money; money makes man so. / A false REPORT rides post.

falsehood **1.** Falsehood is a nettle that stings those who meddle with it. *Var.:* Falsehood, like a nettle, stings those who meddle with it. *Rec. dist.:* Ill., Ont.

2. Falsehood is a red apple rotten at the core. *Rec. dist.:* Ill.

3. Falsehood is the darkness of faith. *Rec. dist.:* Ill.

4. Falsehood will not bear to be examined in every point of view. *Rec. dist.:* Mich.

5. One falsehood leads to another. *Rec. dist.:* Kans.

SEE ALSO Better suffer for TRUTH than prosper by falsehood.

fame 1. Better fame than face. *Rec. dist.:* Fla. *1st cit.:* 1721 Kelly, *Scottish Proverbs.* *20c. coll.:* ODEP 319.

2. Common fame is often a common liar. *Rec. dist.:* Mich. *1st cit.:* 1594 Lyly, *Mother Bombie;* US1779 *Correspondence of Samuel Webb,* ed. Ford (1897). *20c. coll.:* ODEP 137, Whiting 144.

3. Fame always follows virtuous and glorious actions. *Rec. dist.:* Mich.

4. Fame is a bugle call blown past a crumbling wall. *Rec. dist.:* N.Y., S.C.

5. Fame is better than fortune. *Rec. dist.:* Mich., N.Y., S.C. *1st cit.:* 1721 Kelly, *Scottish Proverbs.* *20c. coll.:* ODEP 319, Whiting(MP) 213.

6. Fame is longer than life. *Rec. dist.:* Ill.

7. Fame is the last infirmity of noble minds. *Rec. dist.:* Ill.

8. Fame one day, zero the next. *Rec. dist.:* Wis. *Infm.:* Used in reference to a sports hero.

9. From fame to infamy is a much-traveled road. *Rec. dist.:* Ill.

10. In seeking fame and profit, depend only on yourself and not others. *Rec. dist.:* N.Y.

11. Some have the fame, and others live in shame. *Rec. dist.:* Ill.

SEE ALSO Do GOOD by stealth and blush to find it fame. / LOVE is better than fame—and money is best of all. / TIME is the sire of fame.

familiar Beware of those who get familiar quickly. *Rec. dist.:* Miss.

familiarity Familiarity breeds contempt. *Vars.:* **(a)** Contempt with familiarity grows. **(b)** Familiarity breeds contempt—and children. **(c)** Too much familiarity breeds contempt. *Rec. dist.:* U.S., Can. *1st cit.:* ca1386 Chaucer, *Tale of Melibee;* USca1680 *Voyages of Radisson,* ed. Scull, Publ. Prince Soc. (1885). *20c. coll.:* ODEP 243, Whiting 144, CODP 76, Stevenson 756:4, T&W 127, Whiting(MP) 213.

family 1. A family is a twosome that grew some. *Rec. dist.:* Miss.

2. Every family has a goddess of mercy. *Rec. dist.:* Ind.

3. In a united family happiness springs up of itself. *Rec. dist.:* Ind.

4. The family who prays together stays together. *Rec. dist.:* Calif., Kans. *1st cit.:* US1948 *St. Joseph Magazine (Oregon).* *20c. coll.:* CODP 76.

5. There's a black sheep in every family. *Var.:* Every large family has at least one black sheep. *Rec. dist.:* U.S., Can. *1st cit.:* 1911 Munro, *Chronicles of Clovis.* *20c. coll.:* Whiting(MP) 555.

6. You can't have a family fuss without the whole town knowing about it. *Rec. dist.:* Miss.

SEE ALSO ACCIDENTS will happen in the best of families. / If you ACT as good as you look, you'll never shame your family. / The family of FOOLS is very old. / You may choose your FRIENDS; your family is thrust upon you. / Big HOUSES have small families, and small houses big families. / If the HUSBAND had every other child, there would be no second child in the family. / THANKS is poor pay on which to keep a family. / When alone, we have our own THOUGHTS to watch; when in the family, our tempers; when in society, our tongues.

famine 1. All's good in a famine. *Rec. dist.:* N.J., N.Y.

2. When famine must be fed, crumbs are as good as bread. *Rec. dist.:* Ind.

SEE ALSO It's either a FEAST or a famine. / More die of FOOD than famine.

fan SEE Don't fan the FLAME that supports the fire.

fancy *(n.)* **1.** Ever let the fancy roam; pleasure never is at home. *Rec. dist.:* Ill.

2. False fancy brings real misery. *Rec. dist.:* Ill.

3. Fancy may bolt bran and think it flour. *Rec. dist.:* N.C. *1st cit.:* 1546 Heywood, *Dialogue of Proverbs,* ed. Habernicht (1963). *20c. coll.:* ODEP 244.

4. Fancy runs most furiously when a guilty conscience drives it. *Rec. dist.:* Ill.

5. For every fancy you consult, consult your purse. *Rec. dist.:* Ill., N.Y.

6. In spring a young man's fancy lightly turns to thoughts of love. *Vars.:* **(a)** In spring a young man's fancy lightly turns to what he's been thinking about all winter. **(b)** In spring a young man's fancy turns to what the woman has been thinking all winter. **(c)** In the spring a young man's fancy turns to love. **(d)** In the spring a young man's fancy turns to thoughts of love. **(e)** Spring turns a young man's fancy to thoughts of love. *Rec. dist.:* U.S., Can. *1st cit.:* 1842 Tennyson, *Locksley Hall.* *20c. coll.:* Stevenson 2203:3.

7. It is the fancy, not the reason of things, that makes us so uneasy. *Rec. dist.:* Ill.

8. One man's fancy, another man's poison. *Rec. dist.:* Fla., N.Y. *Infm.:* Cf. meat.

9. Rule your fancy with your reason, or it will overrule you. *Rec. dist.:* Mich.

fancy *(v.)* SEE The WISEST man is he who does not fancy he is wise at all.

far *(adj.)* SEE Too far EAST is west. / Better a NEIGHBOR near than a brother far.

far *(adv.)* SEE The FRUIT doesn't fall far from the tree. / A HUNGRY man sees far. / The LIGHT that shines farthest shines brightest at home. / LITTLE by little one goes far. / Don't press LUCK too far. / You can't tell how far a RABBIT can jump by the length of its ears. / He who treads SOFTLY goes far. / You can't tell how far a TOAD will jump by the length of its tail.

faraway SEE Faraway COWS have long horns.

fare *(n.)* SEE The fewer to STARE, the better the fare.

fare *(v.)* SEE Go FARTHER and fare worse. / Ill fares the LAND in which money is more than men.

farm You can take the girl away from the farm, but you can't take the farm away from the girl. *Rec. dist.:* U.S. *Infm.:* Cf. boy.

farmer **1.** A farmer has a lot of woes. *Rec. dist.:* Ark., Kans. *Infm.:* A pun on the word "whoa."

2. A farmer on his knees is higher than a gentleman on his legs. *Rec. dist.:* Fla., N.Dak.

3. It's the farmer's care that makes the field bear. *Rec. dist.:* Ill.

4. The farmer feeds them all. *Rec. dist.:* Ont.

5. The farmer tickles the land and the crops tickle him. *Rec. dist.:* Miss.

6. The farmer was the first man, and he will be the last. *Rec. dist.:* Ont.

7. You can take the farmer out of the country, but you can't take the country out of the farmer. *Rec. dist.:* Ill.

SEE ALSO LIME and lime without manure makes the farmer rich and the son poor.

farther **1.** Go farther and fare worse. *Rec. dist.:* Okla., Ont., Tex. *1st cit.:* 1546 Heywood, *Dialogue of Proverbs,* ed. Habernicht (1963); US1819 Welby, *Visit to North America and English Settlements in Illinois.* *20c. coll.:* ODEP 306, Whiting 177, Whiting(MP) 256, T&W 154.

2. He goes farthest that knows not where he is going. *Rec. dist.:* Ill.

SEE ALSO The nearer the CHURCH, the farther from God. / The FASTER they are, the farther they go. / Put your HAND no farther than your sleeve will reach. / Your THOUGHTS go no farther than your vocabulary.

farting SEE A farting HORSE will never tire, and a farting man is the man to hire.

fashion **1.** Better be dead than out of fashion. *Vars.:* **(a)** As good out of the world as out of fashion. **(b)** You're as well out of the world as out of fashion. *Rec. dist.:* U.S., Can. *1st cit.:* 1639 Clarke, *Paroemiologia.* *20c. coll.:* ODEP 602, CODP 15, Stevenson 762:2.

2. No matter how fashions change, a ruffled temper will never be in style. *Rec. dist.:* Miss.

SEE ALSO MONEY in the purse will always be in fashion. / Do not be a SLAVE to fashion.

fast *(n.)* SEE FEAST today makes fast tomorrow.

fast *(v.)* SEE The FOOL that eats till he is sick must fast till he is well.

fast *(adj.)* The faster they are, the farther they go. *Rec. dist.:* Ind.

fast *(adv.)* Get there fastest with the mostest. *Rec. dist.:* U.S., Can. *1st cit.:* 1862 Forrest, *Military Maxims.* *20c. coll.:* Stevenson 983:1.

SEE ALSO He that DRINKS fast pays slow. / Hold fast to that which is GOOD. / Bad NEWS travels fast. / One can RUN only as fast as his legs will carry him. / Wisely and slowly— they STUMBLE that run fast. / He TRAVELS fastest who travels alone. / WALK too fast and stumble over nothing.

fat *(n.)* A man must take the fat with the lean. *Var.:* You have to take the fat with the lean. *Rec. dist.:* U.S. *1st cit.:* 1813 Ray, *English Proverbs;* US1959 Cheever, *Wapshot Chronicles.* *20c. coll.:* ODEP 800, Stevenson 765:16, Whiting(MP) 215.

fat *(adj.)* **1.** Fat people are jolly people. *Rec. dist.:* Miss.

2. It ain't over till the fat lady sings. *Rec. dist.:* Calif., Mich., N.Y. *Infm.:* The original form begins "The opera isn't over...." *1st cit.:* US1978 *Washington Post,* 13 June. *20c. coll.:* CODP 171.

3. It isn't what you like that makes you fat— it's what you eat. *Var.:* It's not what you want that makes you fat, but what you get. *Rec. dist.:* U.S.

4. Nobody loves a fat man. *Rec. dist.:* Ill., N.Y., S.C. *1st cit.:* US1907 Day, *Round-Up.* *20c. coll.:* Stevenson 764:7, Whiting(MP) 396.

SEE ALSO A green CHRISTMAS means a fat graveyard. / A setting HEN never gets fat. / Fat HENS lay few eggs. / Fat HENS make rich soup. / When the HORSE is dead, the cow gets fat. / A fat KITCHEN makes a lean will. / LAUGH and grow fat. / Lean LIBERTY is better than fat slavery. / Change of PASTURE makes a fat calf. / Good PASTURES make fat sheep. / PIGS grow fat where lambs would starve. / Fat SORROW is better than lean sorrow. / Little knows the fat SOW what the lean one thinks. / You need not grease a fat SOW.

fate **1.** Everyone is more or less master of his own fate. *Var.:* Everyone is the maker of his own fate. *Rec. dist.:* N.Y. *1st cit.:* 1888 Henley, *Invictus.* *20c. coll.:* Stevenson 2170:8.

2. Fate can be taken by the horns, like a goat, and pushed in the right direction. *Rec. dist.:* N.Y.

3. Fate gives us parents; choice gives us friends. *Var.:* Fate makes our relatives; choice makes our friends. *Rec. dist.:* Wis.

4. The fates lead the willing man; the unwilling they drag. *Rec. dist.:* Ont. *1st cit.:* 1629 Adams, *Sermons.* *20c. coll.:* ODEP 247.

5. There's no flying from fate. *Rec. dist.:* Ill. *1st cit.:* 1587 Greene, *Alphonsus.* *20c. coll.:* ODEP 271.

6. You cannot escape your fate. *Rec. dist.:* Ont.

SEE ALSO EXPERIENCE is a comb which fate gives to a man when his hair is all gone. / Pretty FACE, poor fate.

father **1.** A father's a treasure; a brother's a comfort; a friend is both. *Rec. dist.:* N.Y., S.C.

2. A miserly father makes a prodigal son. *Rec. dist.:* Wis. *1st cit.:* 1612 Parkes, *The Curtaine-Drawer of the World.* *20c. coll.:* Stevenson 772:5.

3. A thrifty father rarely has thrifty sons. *Rec. dist.:* Miss.

4. Despise not your father when he is old. *Rec. dist.:* Colo.

5. The father is the head, but the mother is the heart. *Rec. dist.:* Kans.

6. Father knows best. *Rec. dist.:* U.S. *1st cit.:* 1958 Christie, *Ordeal;* US1931 Wells, *Horror House.* *20c. coll.:* Whiting(MP) 427.

7. Father works from sun to sun, but mother's work is never done. *Rec. dist.:* Ont. *Infm.:* Cf. man. *1st cit.:* 1570 Baldwin, *Beware the Cat;* US1722 Franklin, *PRAlmanac.* *20c. coll.:* ODEP 909, Whiting 494, Stevenson 2583:9, Whiting(MP) 398.

8. Honor your father and your mother. *Rec. dist.:* U.S., Can. *1st cit.:* 1574 Guazzo, *Civile Conversation,* tr. Pettie, T.T. (1925); US1739 Franklin, *PRAlmanac.* *20c. coll.:* Stevenson 1745:4.

9. It's a wise father who knows his own son. *Var.:* It's a wise father that knows his own children. *Rec. dist.:* U.S., Can. *1st cit.:* 1597

Shakespeare, *Merchant of Venice*. *20c. coll.*: Stevenson 770:8.

10. Like father, like son. *Vars.*: **(a)** As father, as son. **(b)** As father, so the son. **(c)** As mother and father, so is daughter and son. **(d)** As the baker, so the buns; as the father, so the sons. **(e)** Such is the father, such is the son. *Rec. dist.*: U.S., Can. *1st cit.*: ca1340 Rolle, *Psalter;* US1774 Ames, *Almanacs,* ed. Briggs (1891). *20c. coll.*: ODEP 248, Whiting 146, CODP 77, Stevenson 770:12, T&W 128, Whiting*(MP)* 216.

11. Many a good father has a bad son. *Rec. dist.*: Fla. *1st cit.*: 1574 Guazzo, *Civile Conversation,* tr. Pettie, T.T. (1925). *20c. coll.*: Stevenson 770:7.

12. No man is responsible for his father. *Rec. dist.*: Ind.

13. The father is the guest who best becomes the table. *Rec. dist.*: Ont.

14. The father to his desk, the mother to her dishes. *Rec. dist.*: Ill.

15. To become a father is easy, but to be a father is difficult. *Rec. dist.*: Ariz.

16. What's good enough for father is good enough for me. *Rec. dist.*: Fla.

17. When a father praises his son he flatters himself. *Rec. dist.*: Ill.

18. You cannot choose your father, but you choose your father's son. *Rec. dist.*: Miss.

See also No advice like a father's. / A bachelor oftentimes has more children than the father of many. / It is a wise child that knows its own father. / The child is father of the man. / Continuity is the father of success. / Dissatisfaction is the father of ambition. / Experience is the father of wisdom, and memory the mother. / Any fool knows more than his father. / Every girl is beautiful in her father's eyes. / Do not marry an heiress unless her father has been hanged. / Home is the father's kingdom, the children's paradise, the mother's world. / A wise son hears his father's instruction. / A wise son makes a glad father, but a foolish son is the heaviness of his mother. / The thought is the father to the deed. / The wish is father of the thought.

fatten *See* If the owner keeps his eye on the horse, it will fatten.

fault **1.** A fault confessed is half redressed. *Vars.*: **(a)** A fault confessed is half forgiven. **(b)** Confession of a fault makes half amends for it. *Rec. dist.*: U.S., Can. *1st cit.*: 1592 *Arden of Feversham*. *20c. coll.*: ODEP 248, CODP 77, Stevenson 778:9.

2. Avoid great faults by keeping away from small ones. *Rec. dist.*: Ill.

3. Bad men excuse their faults; good men leave them. *Rec. dist.*: Ill., Ohio, Ont.

4. Be not lenient to your own faults. *Rec. dist.*: Ont.

5. Before you flare up at anyone's faults, take time to count ten of your own. *Rec. dist.*: Ont., R.I.

6. Blame not others for the faults that are in you. *Rec. dist.*: N.Y. *1st cit.*: US1875 Scarborough, *Chinese Proverbs*. *20c. coll.*: Stevenson 777:9.

7. By others' faults wise men correct their own. *Rec. dist.*: Ont.

8. Condemn the fault and not the actor of it. *Rec. dist.*: Minn.

9. Don't find fault with what you don't understand. *Rec. dist.*: Wis.

10. Every man has his faults. *Var.*: Great men have great faults. *Rec. dist.*: U.S., Can. *1st cit.*: 1557 Erasmus, *Merry Dialogue,* ed. de Vocht. *20c. coll.*: ODEP 229, Stevenson 773:7.

11. Faults are thick when love is thin. *Var.*: Fault is thick where love is thin. *Rec. dist.*: U.S., Can. *1st cit.*: 1616 Draxe, *Bibliotheca Scholastica* in *Anglia* (1918). *20c. coll.*: ODEP 249.

12. Find faults in yourself before finding faults in others. *Rec. dist.*: Ont.

13. Forgive every man's faults except your own. *Rec. dist.*: Ont.

14. Forgive others' faults by remembering your own. *Rec. dist.*: Ont.

15. Go hide the faults of others and God will veil your own. *Rec. dist.*: Ont.

16. He who does one fault at first and lies to

hide it makes it two. *Vars.:* **(a)** A fault is made worse by endeavoring to conceal it. **(b)** A fault once denied is twice committed. **(c)** Concealing faults is but adding to them. **(d)** Denying a fault doubles it. *Rec. dist.:* U.S., Can. *1st cit.:* 1720 Watts, *Divine Songs.* *20c. coll.:* Stevenson 775:14.

17. He who sees his own faults is too busy to see the faults of others. *Rec. dist.:* Kans.

18. If someone betrays you once, it is his fault. If he betrays you twice, it is your fault. *Var.:* Once betrayed, his fault. If betrayed twice, your fault. *Rec. dist.:* U.S., Can.

19. In every fault there is folly. *Rec. dist.:* N.C., Okla. *1st cit.:* ca1641 Fergusson, *Scottish Proverbs,* ed. Beveridge, S.T.S. (1924). *20c. coll.:* ODEP 228, Stevenson 776:9.

20. It is well that our faults are not written on our faces. *Rec. dist.:* Ont.

21. No man is born without faults, but he is best who has the fewest. *Rec. dist.:* N.Y.

22. Not to repent of a fault is to justify it. *Rec. dist.:* Ont.

23. Our faults are more pardonable than the methods we use to hide them. *Rec. dist.:* N.Y., Oreg.

24. Our greatest faults we soonest see in others. *Var.:* You always see your faults in others. *Rec. dist.:* Calif., Oreg.

25. People should cure their own faults before finding faults in others. *Rec. dist.:* Ont.

26. Rich men have no faults. *Rec. dist.:* Ont.

27. Small faults indulged in are little thieves that let in greater. *Var.:* Small faults let in greater. *Rec. dist.:* N.Y., Ont. *1st cit.:* 1732 Fuller, *Gnomologia;* US1755 Franklin, *PRAlmanac.* *20c. coll.:* Stevenson 774:10.

28. The greatest of faults is to be conscious of none. *Var.:* The greatest fault is to be conscious of none. *Rec. dist.:* U.S., Can. *1st cit.:* 1840 Carlyle, "The Hero" in *On Heroes and Hero-Worship.* *20c. coll.:* Stevenson 777:4.

29. The most faulty always find fault. *Rec. dist.:* Ill.

30. The real fault is to have faults and not try to amend them. *Rec. dist.:* Calif.

31. The way to avoid great faults is to be aware of little ones. *Rec. dist.:* Ind.

32. There is no fault in a thing we want badly. *Rec. dist.:* Fla.

33. We are more agreeable through our faults than through our qualities. *Rec. dist.:* R.I.

34. We easily forget our faults when they are known only to ourselves. *Rec. dist.:* Ont.

35. We see the faults of others but not our own. *Vars.:* **(a)** It is easiest to see the faults of others. **(b)** Man sees all the faults but his own. **(c)** We see the splinter in others' faults, but never the spike in our own. *Rec. dist.:* U.S., Can. *1st cit.:* 1585 Smith, *Sermons.* *20c. coll.:* Stevenson 781:7.

36. We tax our friends with faults but see not our own. *Rec. dist.:* Ont.

37. Wink at small faults. *Rec. dist.:* Ont. *1st cit.:* 1543 Cousin, *Of the Office of Servants.* *20c. coll.:* ODEP 896.

38. With the old year leave your faults, however dear. *Rec. dist.:* N.Y., Ont.

39. Your own faults look as big to the other fellow as his do to you. *Rec. dist.:* N.Y.

SEE ALSO He has sorry FOOD who feeds on the faults of others. / A true FRIEND is one who knows all your faults and loves you still. / You will never have a FRIEND if you must have one without faults. / All are presumed GOOD until they are found in a fault. / LOVE sees no faults. / Where there is no LOVE, all faults are seen. / A SLIP of the tongue is no fault of the mind. / SUSPICION may be no fault, but showing it may be a great one.

fault finding Nothing is easier than fault finding. *Rec. dist.:* Ohio.

faultless He is dead that is faultless. *Var.:* He is lifeless that is faultless. *Rec. dist.:* Ill., Tex., Wis. *1st cit.:* 1546 Heywood, *Dialogue of Proverbs,* ed. Habernicht (1963). *20c. coll.:* ODEP 462.

favor *(n.)* **1.** A favor ill placed is great waste. *Rec. dist.:* Ont. *1st cit.:* US1948 Stevenson, *Home Book of Proverbs.* *20c. coll.:* Stevenson 781:4.

2. A favor to come is better than a hundred received. *Rec. dist.:* Miss.

3. An ounce of favor goes further than a pound of justice. *Rec. dist.:* R.I. *1st cit.:* 1907 Benham, *Book of Quotations, Proverbs, and Household Words.* *20c. coll.:* Stevenson 781:10.

4. Don't ask a man for a favor before he has had his lunch. *Rec. dist.:* Ill.

5. Favor is deceitful, and beauty is vain. *Rec. dist.:* Wis. *1st cit.:* USca1754 "Wall and Garden" in *Mass. Election Sermons, 1670–1775,* ed. Plumstead (1968). *20c. coll.:* Whiting 146.

6. If you accept favors from crooked men, you sell yourself down the river. *Rec. dist.:* Ill., N.Y. *Infm.:* "To sell yourself down the river" means "to betray yourself."

7. If you want a favor done, ask a busy man. *Rec. dist.:* Kans., N.C. *Infm.:* Cf. job.

8. Many will entreat the favor of the prince. *Rec. dist.:* Ont.

9. Small favors are thankfully received. *Vars.:* **(a)** Be thankful of small favors. **(b)** Thank God for little favors. *Rec. dist.:* Calif., Colo., Ill. *1st cit.:* US1906 Lincoln, *Mr. Pratt.* *20c. coll.:* Whiting(MP) 216.

10. The first time is a favor, the second time a rule. *Rec. dist.:* N.C.

SEE ALSO There is no GRACE in a favor that sticks to the fingers. / Make your JOB important; it will return the favor. / KISSING goes by favor.

favor *(v.)* *SEE* FORTUNE favors the brave. / FORTUNE sometimes favors those she afterwards destroys. / To favor the ILL is to injure the good.

favorite **1.** A favorite has no friends. *Rec. dist.:* N.C.

2. Favorites are commonly unfortunate. *Rec. dist.:* Mich. *1st cit.:* 1732 Fuller, *Gnomologia.* *20c. coll.:* Stevenson 438:1.

SEE ALSO DEATH plays no favorites.

fear *(n.)* **1.** A slave to fear creates a hell on earth. *Rec. dist.:* Ill.

2. Don't let fear hold you back. *Rec. dist.:* Colo.

3. Fear always springs from ignorance. *Var.:* Fear springs from ignorance. *Rec. dist.:* Ill., N.Y.

4. Fear brings more pain than does the pain. *Rec. dist.:* Oreg.

5. Fear has many eyes. *Rec. dist.:* N.Y.

6. Fear has torment. *Rec. dist.:* N.C.

7. Fear is a fine spur; so is rage. *Rec. dist.:* Ont.

8. Fear is a great inventor. *Rec. dist.:* N.Y.

9. Fear is stronger than love. *Rec. dist.:* U.S., Can. *1st cit.:* 1621 Robinson, *Adagia in Latin and English.* *20c. coll.:* ODEP 250, Stevenson 785:3.

10. Fear is the beginning of wisdom. *Rec. dist.:* N.Y.

11. Fear is the father of cruelty. *Rec. dist.:* Ill.

12. Fear is the virtue of slaves. *Rec. dist.:* Ont.

13. Fear kills more than illness. *Rec. dist.:* Ill. *1st cit.:* 1892 Surtees, *Mr. Facey Romford's Hounds.* *20c. coll.:* Stevenson 787:4.

14. Fear mothers safety, but it often smothers it. *Rec. dist.:* Ill., Ohio.

15. Fear of the Lord is the beginning of wisdom. *Vars.:* **(a)** Fear of Jehovah is the beginning of knowledge. **(b)** Fear of the Lord is the beginning of knowledge. *Rec. dist.:* U.S., Can. *1st cit.:* 1930 Fielding, *Murder at the Nook;* US1632 Howes in *Winthrop Papers, 1498–1649,* Mass.Hist.Soc. *Collections* (1929–47). *20c. coll.:* Whiting(MP) 217, Whiting 147.

16. If you fear to suffer, you suffer from fear. *Rec. dist.:* N.Y.

17. Men who fear to live are in love with fear. *Rec. dist.:* Ill.

18. The fear of death is more to be dreaded than death itself. *Rec. dist.:* Ill. *1st cit.:* 1594 *King Lear, The Chronicle Historie.* *20c. coll.:* ODEP 250.

19. The fear of God makes the heart shine. *Rec. dist.:* Ill.

20. The fear's greater than the reason for it. *Rec. dist.:* Ont. *1st cit.:* ca1580 Sidney, *Arcadia.* *20c. coll.:* Stevenson 787:7.

21. The only thing we have to fear is fear itself. *Var.:* He who fears has nothing to fear but fear itself. *Rec. dist.:* U.S. *Infm.:* Used by Franklin D. Roosevelt in his first inaugural address (1933). *1st cit.*: 1605 Bacon, *De Augmenta Scientiarum*. *20c. coll.*: Stevenson 783:14.

22. Where there is fear, there is modesty. *Rec. dist.*: N.Y. *1st cit.*: US1948 Stevenson, *Home Book of Proverbs*. *20c. coll.*: Stevenson 1606:2.

23. Where there is fear, there is shame. *Rec. dist.*: N.Y. *1st cit.*: 1641 Milton, *Church Government*. *20c. coll.*: Stevenson 2082:7.

SEE ALSO COURAGE is fear that has said its prayers. / When we have GOLD, we are in fear; when we have more, we are in danger. / POVERTY with security is better than plenty in the midst of fear and uncertainty.

fear *(v.)* **1.** Fear no man, and do justice to all men. *Rec. dist.*: Mich.

2. If you fear that people will know, don't do it. *Rec. dist.*: Ont.

3. We seldom fear what we can laugh at. *Rec. dist.*: Ariz.

SEE ALSO ACT so in the valley that you need not fear those who stand on the hill. / The ANVIL fears no blows. / BEER on whiskey, mighty risky; whiskey on beer, never fear. / Fear not the loss of the BELL more than the loss of the steeple. / Newborn CALVES don't fear tigers. / A burnt CHILD dreads the fire. / A clear CONSCIENCE fears no accuser. / If you fear DEATH, you're already dead. / He that is DOWN need fear no fall. / Fear to do ILL and you need fear nought else. / He that fears LEAVES must not come into a wood. / He who LOVES much fears much. / Do RIGHT and fear no man; don't write and fear no woman. / Do RIGHT and fear not. / TRUTH fears no colors. / The man who fears no TRUTHS has nothing to fear from lies.

feared Better a man be feared than despised. *Rec. dist.*: N.C.

feast *(n.)* **1.** Be first at a feast and last at a fight. *Rec. dist.*: Colo.

2. Feast today makes fast tomorrow. *Var.*: Feast today, fast tomorrow. *Rec. dist.*: Ala., Ga., Ont.

3. It's either a feast or a famine. *Rec. dist.*: U.S., Can. *1st cit.*: 1732 Fuller, *Gnomologia*; US1767 *Commerce of Rhode Island*, Mass.

Hist. Soc. *Collections* (1914–15). *20c. coll.*: ODEP 251, Whiting 147, Stevenson 763:10, Whiting(MP) 217.

4. Keep the feast till feast day. *Rec. dist.*: Mich.

5. Merry is the feast making till we come to the reckoning. *Rec. dist.*: Ont.

SEE ALSO ENOUGH is as good as a feast. / FOOLS make feasts and wise men eat them. / A cheerful LOOK makes a dish a feast. / A contented MIND is a continual feast.

feast *(v.)* Feast and your halls are crowded. *Rec. dist.*: N.Y. *1st cit.*: US1883 Wilcox, "Solitude" in *N.Y. Sun*, 25 Feb. *20c. coll.*: Stevenson 905:6.

feasting Feasting is the physician's harvest. *Rec. dist.*: N.J. *1st cit.*: 1639 Clarke, *Paroemiologia*. *20c. coll.*: Stevenson 789:10.

feather *(n.)* **1.** A feather in the hand is better than a bird in the air. *Rec. dist.*: Ind. *1st cit.*: 1640 Herbert, *Outlandish Proverbs (Jacula Prudentum)* in *Works*, ed. Hutchinson (1941). *20c. coll.*: ODEP 251.

2. A pound of feathers and a pound of iron weigh the same. *Rec. dist.*: N.Y.

3. Fair feathers make fair fowl. *Var.*: Fine feathers make fine fowl. *Rec. dist.*: U.S., Can. *1st cit.*: 1592 Delamothe, *Treasury of French Tongue*; US1783 *Writings of George Washington*, ed. Fitzpatrick (1931–44). *20c. coll.*: ODEP 258, Whiting 148, Stevenson 791:7, T&W 129, Whiting(MP) 217.

4. Feather by feather a goose is plucked. *Rec. dist.*: Ont. *1st cit.*: 1666 Torriano, *Common Place of Italian Proverbs and Phrases*. *20c. coll.*: ODEP 251, Stevenson 792:5.

5. Feathers float, but pearls lie low. *Rec. dist.*: Ont.

6. Fine feathers do not make fine birds. *Vars.*: **(a)** Feathers don't make a bird. **(b)** Fine feathers don't make fine birds. **(c)** It's not the feathers that make the bird. *Rec. dist.*: U.S., Can. *1st cit.*: 1572 Fenton, *Monophylo*; US1783 *Writings of George Washington*, ed. Fitzpatrick (1931–44). *20c. coll.*: ODEP 258, Whiting 148, CODP 80, Stevenson 80:2, Whiting(MP) 217.

7. Puttin' feathers on a buzzard don't make it no eagle. *Rec. dist.*: Nebr.

8. Stroke the feathers the right way. ***Rec. dist.:*** Ont.

9. Where the feathers fly is where the shot hit. ***Rec. dist.:*** Tex.

10. You can't get feathers off a toad. ***Vars.:*** **(a)** You can't pick feathers off a toad. **(b)** You can't take feathers off a toad. ***Rec. dist.:*** Ont. *1st cit.:* 1918 Torr, *Small Talk at Wreyland;* US1929 Peckham, *Murder in Strange House.* *20c. coll.:* Whiting(MP) 217.

11. You can't put new feathers on a bird. ***Rec. dist.:*** Kans.

12. You can't stick a feather in a frog's tail and make a peacock out of it. ***Rec. dist.:*** Ky., Tenn.

SEE ALSO Every BIRD is known by its feathers. / BIRDS of a feather flock together. / CHICKENS today, feathers tomorrow. / Choose not FRIENDS by outward show, for feathers float while pearls lie low. / A setting GOOSE has no feathers on her breast. / The PARROT has fine feathers, but he doesn't go to the dance. / WORDS like feathers are carried away by the wind.

feather *(v.)* *SEE* Feather your own NEST. / He that feathers his NEST must sleep in it. / A SHREWD man feathers his own nest.

February *SEE* February SUN is dearly won.

fee *SEE* GOD heals and the doctor takes the fee.

feed *(n.)* *SEE* A CURRYCOMB is equal to half feed.

feed *(v.)* *SEE* Feed a COLD and starve a fever. / A DOG returns to where he has been fed. / The FARMER feeds them all. / Don't bite the HAND that feeds you. / Don't worry about the old HORSE being poor, just feed him. / Feed a PIG and you'll have a hog.

feeding *SEE* ZEAL is like fire: it needs feeding and watching.

feel Great men never feel great; small men never feel small. ***Rec. dist.:*** N.Y., S.C.

SEE ALSO He that can't HEAR must feel. / If you don't LISTEN, you have to feel. / Hear REASON or she'll make you feel her. / REMORSE is the thing we ought to feel and don't. / It is

only ROGUES who feel the restraint of law. / SICKNESS is felt, but health not at all. / Social TACT is making your company feel at home even though you wish they were. / You're as YOUNG as you feel. / You're as YOUNG as you look, and as old as you feel.

feeling **1.** Feelings are useless without words. ***Rec. dist.:*** Ont.

2. In order to judge another's feelings, remember your own. ***Rec. dist.:*** Mich.

fell The first blow does not fell the tree. ***Rec. dist.:*** N.Y.

SEE ALSO Little STROKES fell great oaks. / When the TREE is felled, everyone goes to it with his hatchet.

fellow **1.** An artful fellow is the devil in a doublet. ***Rec. dist.:*** Mich.

2. Don't kick a fellow when he's down. ***Rec. dist.:*** U.S., Can. *1st cit.:* 1551 Cranmer, *Answer to Gardiner;* US1634 Wood, *New-England's Prospects,* Publ. Prince Soc. (1865). *20c. coll.:* ODEP 374, Whiting 281, T&W 207, Whiting(MP) 401.

3. Never trust a fellow that wears a suit. ***Rec. dist.:*** Ark.

SEE ALSO The best CHAPERON a girl can have is to be in love with another fellow. / A DETERMINED fellow can do more with a rusty monkey wrench than a lot of people can with a machine shop. / Your own FAULTS look as big to the other fellow as his do to you. / The fellow who blows his HORN the loudest is likely in the biggest fog. / A good NEIGHBOR is a fellow who smiles at you over the back fence but doesn't climb it. / Every fellow likes his own PLOW best. / The WISE and the fool have their fellows. / It is better to say a good WORD about a bad fellow than a bad word about a good fellow. / The fellow who WORKS for a song has trouble meeting his notes. / WORTH makes the man, and want of it the fellow.

fellowship *SEE* A HEDGE between keeps fellowship green. / POVERTY makes good fellowship.

female **1.** Female is one head with two faces. ***Rec. dist.:*** Fla.

2. The female of the species is more deadly than the male. *Var.:* The female is the more deadly of the species. *Rec. dist.:* U.S., Can. *1st cit.:* 1911 Kipling, *Female of the Species*. *20c. coll.:* CODP 78, Stevenson 2568:1.

fence *(n.)* **1.** A fence between makes friends more keen. *Rec. dist.:* N.Y.

2. Do not protect yourself by a fence, but rather by friends. *Rec. dist.:* N.Y.

3. Everything worthwhile has a fence around it, but there is always a gate and a key. *Rec. dist.:* N.Y.

4. Fences mean nothing to those who can fly. *Rec. dist.:* Iowa.

5. Good fence: horse high and bull strong. *Rec. dist.:* N.Y., S.C. *1st cit.:* US1950 Gould, *Maine Man*. *20c. coll.:* Whiting(MP) 219.

6. Good fences make good neighbors. *Vars.:* **(a)** Fences make good neighbors. **(b)** Have a good fence and you will keep good neighbors. **(c)** High board fences make good neighbors. *Rec. dist.:* U.S., Can. *1st cit.:* 1640 Rogers, Letter in *Winthrop Papers* (1944); US1815 Brackenridge, *Modern Chivalry*. *20c. coll.:* CODP 98, Whiting 149, Stevenson 1674:13, Whiting(MP) 219.

7. Never climb a fence until you get to the stile. *Rec. dist.:* N.Y., Ont. *1st cit.:* 1599 Porter, *Two Angry Women of Abington*. *20c. coll.:* Stevenson 2377:12.

8. No fence against a flail. *Rec. dist.:* Ont.

9. No fence against gold. *Rec. dist.:* N.Y., S.C.

10. No fence against ill fortune. *Var.:* There is no fence against fortune. *Rec. dist.:* N.C., N.Dak., Okla. *1st cit.:* 1623 Camden, *Remaines Concerning Britaine*. *20c. coll.:* ODEP 253, Stevenson 794:15.

SEE ALSO A *barn*, a fence, and a woman always need mending. / *FIELDS* on the other side of the fence are greener. / The *grass* is always greener on the other side of the fence. / Love your *neighbor*, but do not pull down the fence.

ferry *See* Look at the *river* before you cross with the ferry.

fetch *See* A *dog* that will fetch a bone will carry one. / *Hunger* fetches the wolf out of the woods.

fever *See* You might as well die of the *chills* as the fever. / Feed a *cold* and starve a fever.

few *See* *Books* and friends should be few and good. / Many are *called*, but few are chosen. / He who *commences* many things finishes but few. / A *fool* has few friends. / Many *friends*, few helpers. / There are few who would rather be *hated* than laughed at. / The man who loafs most gets the fewest *loaves*. / *Love* many; hate few; learn to paddle your own canoe. / *Opportunities* are few to the man who cannot make up his mind. / The fewer to *stare*, the better the fare. / Eat few *suppers*, and you'll need few medicines. / *Truth* is heavy; therefore few wear it. / Follow the *wise* few rather than the vulgar many. / Few *words* are best. / To one who understands, few *words* are needed.

fib Those who tell one fib will hardly stop at two. *Rec. dist.:* Miss. *Infm.:* Cf. lie (n.).

fickle *See* *Fortune* is fickle.

fiction *See* *Fact* is stranger than fiction. / *Truth* is stranger than fiction.

fiddle *(n.)* **1.** The fiddle makes the feast. *Rec. dist.:* Ill.

2. The older the fiddle, the better the tune. *Rec. dist.:* Ont.

3. You cannot play a fiddle without a fiddle-stick. *Rec. dist.:* Ont. *1st cit.:* US1851 Riley, *Puddleford Papers*. *20c. coll.:* T&W 131, Whiting(MP) 220.

SEE ALSO *Harmony* is often obtained by playing second fiddle. / There is many a good *tune* played on the old fiddle.

fiddle *(v.)* He who fiddles doesn't dance. *Rec. dist.:* Vt.

fiddler If you can't pay the fiddler, you had better not dance. *Var.:* You must pay the fiddler if you want to dance. *Rec. dist.:* Calif., Iowa. *1st cit.:* 1638 Taylor, *Taylor's Feast* in *Works* (1876); US1740 *Jonathan Belcher Papers*, Mass.Hist.Soc. *Collections* (1893–94). *20c. coll.:*

FIGURE 207

ODEP 615, *CODP* 48, Whiting 149, Stevenson 1798:9, T&W 131 Whiting*(MP)* 495.

SEE ALSO If you want to DANCE, you must pay the fiddler.

fidelity Fidelity is a noble virtue, yet justice is nobler still. *Rec. dist.:* N.Y.

field 1. A field becomes exhausted by constant tillage. *Rec. dist.:* Ont. *Infm.:* Applies to people who are overworked.

2. A field has three needs: good weather, good seed, and a good husbandman. *Rec. dist.:* Miss.

3. Distant fields look greener. *Vars.:* (a) Distant fields look greenest. (b) Far fields look green. (c) Far-off fields look green. (d) Faraway fields look greenest. (e) Other fields always look greener. *Rec. dist.:* U.S., Can. *Infm.:* Cf. hill.

4. Do not neglect your own field and plow your neighbor's. *Rec. dist.:* Utah.

5. Fields on the other side of the fence are greener. *Var.:* Fields on the other side of the fence look greener. *Rec. dist.:* Ont.

6. Out of old fields comes new grain. *Rec. dist.:* S.C.

SEE ALSO CROW an' corn can't grow in de same fiel'. / FLOWERS are always brighter in the next field.

fifty SEE The bottom RAIL gets on top every fifty years.

fig You can't grow figs from thistles. *Vars.:* (a) Figs do not grow on thistles. (b) You can't gather figs from thorns. *Rec. dist.:* Ont. *1st cit.:* 1666 Torriano, *Common Place of Italian Proverbs.* *20c. coll.:* ODEP 331, Stevenson 919:5.

SEE ALSO A fig TREE looking on a fig tree becomes fruitful.

fight *(n.)* 1. It takes two to make a fight. *Rec. dist.:* U.S., Can. *Infm.:* Cf. quarrel. *1st cit.:* 1706 Stevens, *Dictionary in Spanish and English;* US1750 *New York Weekly Post Boy* in *Newspaper Extracts.* *20c. coll.:* ODEP 852, Whiting 459, CODP 234, Stevenson 91:10, T&W 389, Whiting*(MP)* 653.

2. The tougher the fight, the sweeter the triumph. *Rec. dist.:* Oreg.

3. When the fight begins with himself, a man's worth something. *Rec. dist.:* Ont.

SEE ALSO It's not the size of the DOG in the fight, it's the size of the fight in the dog.

fight *(v.)* 1. He who fights and runs away may live to fight another day. *Vars.:* (a) He who fights and runs away may turn and fight another day, but he that is in battle slain will never rise to fight again. (b) He who smiles when he walks away will live to fight another day. *Rec. dist.:* U.S. *1st cit.:* ca1532 *Tales and Quick Answers;* US1774 Willard, *Letters on American Revolution, 1774–1776.* *20c. coll.:* ODEP 256, Whiting 150, CODP 79, Stevenson 800:9, T&W 132, Whiting*(MP)* 222.

2. If you fight for someone, you won't fight with him. *Var.:* If you fight for someone, you won't fight with them. *Rec. dist.:* Ont.

3. No fight, no win. *Rec. dist.:* Ont.

4. You can't keep from getting soiled if you fight with a skunk. *Rec. dist.:* N.C.

SEE ALSO He that CONQUERS must fight. / DENOMINATIONS fight while the devil laughs. / Fight the DEVIL with his own tools, or fight the devil with fire. / Fight FIRE with fire. / Forever and ever it takes a POUND to fight a pound. / It is easier to fight for one's PRINCIPLES than to live up to them. / Even a RAT when cornered will turn and fight. / Never wear your best TROUSERS when you go out to fight for freedom. / A WOMAN fights with her tongue.

figure 1. Be not a figure among ciphers. *Rec. dist.:* Mich.

2. Figures are not always facts. *Rec. dist.:* N.Y., Ont.

3. Figures don't lie. *Vars.:* (a) Figgers can't lie, but liars can figger. (b) Figures don't lie, but sometimes liars figure. (c) Figures lie. (d) Figures never lie, but liars can figure. (e) Figures won't lie. *Rec. dist.:* U.S. *1st cit.:* 1933 Lorac, *Murder in St. John's Wood;* US1739 Fry in *Colonial Currency,* ed. Davis, Publ. Prince Soc. (1910–11). *20c. coll.:* Whiting*(MP)* 222, Whiting 150, T&W 132, Stevenson 802:1.

SEE ALSO The FOOD consumed today shapes your figure tomorrow. / NAUGHT's a naught

and figger's a figger—all for de white man
and none for de nigger.

file SEE Much RUST needs a rough file. /
TIME is a file that wears and makes no noise.

fill SEE You must empty the BOX before you
can fill it again. / LITTLE and often fills the
purse. / Every PEA helps to fill the sack. /
PROMISES fill no sack.

filth 1. He who goes to sleep in filth gets up
dirty. *Rec. dist.:* Ky., Tenn.

2. The more you stir filth, the worse it smells.
Vars.: (a) The more you stir dirt, the worse it
smells. (b) The more you stir dirt, the worse
it stinks. *Rec. dist.:* Ont.

finance Finance is the art of using other people's money to acquire some for yourself. *Rec.
dist.:* Miss.

find SEE A new BROOM sweeps clean, but the
old one finds the corners. / Bury CAN'T and
you'll find will. / He who wants CONTENT
can't find it in an easy chair. / He that would
make a FOOL of himself will find many to help
him. / A FRIEND is easier lost than found. /
GOLD is where you find it. / Do no GOOD and
you shall find no evil. / HAPPINESS is where
you find it. / Real HAPPINESS is found not in
doing the things you like to do, but in liking
the things you have to do. / KNOWLEDGE finds
its price. / Be sure a LIE will find you out. /
LOVE is where you find it. / LOVE will find a
way. / PEACE is found only in the graveyard.
/ SEEK and you shall find; knock and it shall
be opened unto you. / Your SINS will find you
out. / Scratch a SLUGGARD and find a saint. /
Mean SOULS like mean pictures are often found
in good looking frames. / Lost TIME is never
found. / It takes a WISE man to find a wise
man.

finder Finders keepers, losers weepers. *Vars.:*
(a) Finders are keepers. (b) Losers weepers,
finders keepers. *Rec. dist.:* U.S., Can. *1st cit.:*
1824 Moir, *Life of Mansie Wauch;* US1874
Eggleston, *Circuit Rider.* 20c. coll.: ODEP 486,
T&W 133, *CODP* 80, Stevenson 803:5, Whiting*(MP)* 223.

finding Finding is keeping. *Rec. dist.:* Calif.,
N.Y. *1st cit.:* 1595 Cooke, *Country Errors* in

Harley MS 5247. **20c. coll.:** ODEP 259, *CODP*
80.

SEE ALSO There's plenty of HUNTING but
little finding.

fine SEE Fine CLOTHES may disguise, silly
words will disclose a fool. / Many a shabby
COLT makes a fine horse. / DEEDS are love,
not fine words. / FEAR is a fine spur; so is
rage. / Fine FEATHERS do not make fine birds.
/ There is no LIE spun so fine, through which
the truth won't shine. / The MILLS of the gods
grind slowly, but they grind exceedingly fine.

finger 1. Clean your finger before you point
at my spot. *Rec. dist.:* N.J.

2. Don't put your finger in too tight a ring.
Rec. dist.: N.Y.

3. Fingers were made before knives and forks.
Var.: Fingers were made before forks. *Rec.
dist.:* U.S., Can. *1st cit.:* 1567 *Loseley Manuscripts,* ed. Kempe (1836); US1855 Haliburton, *Nature and Human Nature.* 20c. coll.: ODEP
259, T&W 134, *CODP* 80, Stevenson 803:5,
Whiting*(MP)* 223.

4. Five fingers hold more than two forks.
Rec. dist.: Fla.

5. Give him a finger and he will take a hand.
Vars.: (a) Give a clown your finger and he'll
take your whole hand. (b) Give a dog a finger
and he will want a whole hand. *Rec. dist.:*
Calif., N.Y., Ohio, Ont. *1st cit.:* 1640 Herbert, *Outlandish Proverbs (Jacula Prudentum)* in
Works, ed. Hutchinson (1941). 20c. coll.: ODEP
302.

6. If you want your finger bit, stick it in a
possum's mouth. *Rec. dist.:* Fla.

7. The finger hurts more than the nail. *Rec.
dist.:* Colo.

8. The fingers of the housewife do more than
a yoke of oxen. *Rec. dist.:* N.Y., Wis.

9. The moving finger writes and, having
written, moves on. *Rec. dist.:* N.Y. *1st cit.:*
1859 Omar Khayyam, *Rubaiyat,* tr. Fitzgerald. 20c. coll.: Stevenson 804:10.

10. Too many fingers spoil the pie. *Rec. dist.:*
Calif., Colo., Ill., N.Y.

11. When you point one finger at someone

else, you point three at yourself. *Rec. dist.:* Fla.

SEE ALSO If a CHILD cuts its finger, it has cut its mother's heart. / He's an ill COOK that can't lick his own fingers. / A man's best FRIEND is his ten fingers. / FRIENDS you can count on, you can count on your fingers. / There is no GRACE in a favor that sticks to the fingers.

finish SEE Neither a FOOL nor a gentleman should see a thing until it is finished. / Don't START anything you can't finish. / A TASK that is pleasant is soon finished.

fire 1. A dirty fire never made a clean weld. *Rec. dist.:* Ohio.

2. A fair fire makes a room gay. *Rec. dist.:* Ont. *1st cit.:* 1678 Ray, *English Proverbs.* *20c. coll.:* Stevenson 809:4.

3. A fire is never out until the last spark is extinguished. *Rec. dist.:* Ont.

4. A fire scorches from near, a beautiful woman from near and from afar. *Rec. dist.:* Wis.

5. A girl who cannot build a fire will have a lazy husband. *Rec. dist.:* Wis.

6. A good fire makes a good cook. *Var.:* The fire helps the cook. *Rec. dist.:* Fla., Ind.

7. A hidden fire may be discovered by its smoke. *Rec. dist.:* Calif., Utah.

8. A smothered fire may rekindle. *Rec. dist.:* N.J.

9. A watched fire never burns. *Rec. dist.:* Ont.

10. All fires are the same size at the start. *Rec. dist.:* Colo. *Infm.:* Don't let a small fire get out of control.

11. Behold what a fire a little matter kindles. *Rec. dist.:* Ont. *1st cit.:* ca1465 Ashby, *Poems,* E.E.T.S. (1899); US1699 *Diary of Cotton Mather,* ed. Ford, Mass.Hist.Soc. *Collections* (1911–12). *20c. coll.:* Stevenson 806:9, Whiting 153.

12. Better a little fire to warm us than a big one to burn us. *Rec. dist.:* N.Y., Okla., Vt. *1st cit.:* ca1530 Barclay, *Eclogues,* E.E.T.S. (1927). *20c. coll.:* Stevenson 806:8.

13. Can't carry fire in one hand and water in the other. *Rec. dist.:* N.Y. *1st cit.:* 1412 Lydgate, *Troy.* *20c. coll.:* ODEP 104.

14. Covered fire is always stronger. *Rec. dist.:* N.Y.

15. Don't light your fire until you have gathered your sticks. *Rec. dist.:* Ill.

16. Don't play with fire. *Vars.:* (a) He who plays with fire could get burned. (b) If you play with fire, you are bound to get burned. (c) One can't play with fire without being burned. (d) People who play with fire always get burned. (e) Play with fire and you'll get burned. (f) You can't play with fire without getting burned. *Rec. dist.:* U.S., Can. *1st cit.:* 1655 Vaughan, "Garland" in *Silex Scintillans* (1847); US1928 O'Neill, *Strange Interlude.* *20c. coll.:* ODEP 632, Whiting(MP) 226, CODP 179.

17. Fight fire with fire. *Var.:* Fire is put out by fire. *Rec. dist.:* U.S., Can. *1st cit.:* 1607 Shakespeare, *Coriolanus;* US1846 Cooper, *Redskins.* *20c. coll.:* CODP 79, T&W 134, Stevenson 808:5, Whiting(MP) 225.

18. Fire and flax agree not. *Vars.:* (a) Fire and cotton can't live together. (b) Put not fire to flax. *Rec. dist.:* N.Y., Ont. *1st cit.:* ca1386 Chaucer, *Prologue to Wife of Bath's Tale.* *20c. coll.:* ODEP 260, Stevenson 807:6.

19. Fire and water do not mix. *Rec. dist.:* Ont.

20. Fire doesn't burn without a flame. *Rec. dist.:* Ont.

21. Fire is a good servant but a bad master. *Vars.:* (a) Fire and water are good servants but bad masters. (b) Fire is a good servant but a cruel master. *Rec. dist.:* U.S., Can. *1st cit.:* 1580 Lyly, *Euphues and His England;* US1677 Hubbard, *History of Indian Wars in New England,* ed. Drake (1865). *20c. coll.:* ODEP 259, Whiting 153, Stevenson 812:3, Whiting(MP) 225.

22. Fire is not to be quenched with tow. *Rec. dist.:* Ont.

23. Fire is the test of gold. *Var.:* Fire proves the gold. *Rec. dist.:* N.Y., Ont. *1st cit.:* 1576 Pettie, *Petite Palace of Pleasure.* *20c. coll.:* Stevenson 989:6.

24. Fire kept closest burns best of all. *Rec.*

dist.: Ont. *1st cit.:* ca1374 Chaucer, *Troilus and Criseyde.* *20c. coll.:* ODEP 260.

25. He that can make a fire well can end a quarrel. *Rec. dist.:* Ont. *1st cit.:* 1640 Herbert, *Outlandish Proverbs (Jacula Prudentum)* in *Works,* ed. Hutchinson (1941). *20c. coll.:* ODEP 500.

26. He that makes a fire of straw has much smoke but little warmth. *Rec. dist.:* Ont.

27. He who blows in the fire will get sparks in his eyes. *Rec. dist.:* Ohio.

28. He who comes through the fire will not fade in the sun. *Rec. dist.:* N.C., Ont.

29. Hidden fires are always the hottest. *Rec. dist.:* N.Y.

30. It is easy to poke another man's fire. *Rec. dist.:* Fla., N.J.

31. Keep the home fires burning. *Rec. dist.:* U.S.

32. Kindle not a fire that you cannot extinguish. *Rec. dist.:* N.Y., Okla., Ont., Tex. *1st cit.:* 1584 Herodotus, *Euterpe,* tr. Rich, ed. Lang (1888). *20c. coll.:* ODEP 424, Stevenson 810:8.

33. Never stir the fire with a sword. *Rec. dist.:* Tex. *1st cit.:* 1574 Guazzo, *Civile Conversation,* tr. Pettie, T.T. (1925). *20c. coll.:* Stevenson 810:7.

34. No one can scatter his fire indefinitely. *Rec. dist.:* N.Y.

35. Oft fire is without smoke, and peril without show. *Rec. dist.:* Calif., Pa.

36. Old fires are easily rekindled. *Rec. dist.:* Ont.

37. Seldom poke another's fire, or you may rouse his burning ire. *Var.:* You may poke a man's fire after you've known him seven years, and not before. *Rec. dist.:* Ont. *1st cit.:* 1803 Dibin, *Professional Life.* *20c. coll.:* ODEP 637.

38. Soft fire makes sweet malt. *Rec. dist.:* N.Y., Okla. *1st cit.:* ca1530 Hill, *Songs,* ed. Dyboski, E.E. T.S. (1907). *20c. coll.:* ODEP 750, Stevenson 809:3.

39. The fire burns brightest on one's own hearth. *Rec. dist.:* Ont.

40. The fire in the flint shows not until it is struck. *Rec. dist.:* Ill., N.Y., Ont. *1st cit.:* 1579 Lyly, *Euphues, Anatomy of Wit.* *20c. coll.:* Stevenson 809:9.

41. The fire you kindle for your enemy often burns yourself more than him. *Rec. dist.:* Ala., Ga.

42. The nearer the fire, the hotter it is. *Rec. dist.:* Fla. *1st cit.:* ca1374 Chaucer, *Troilus and Criseyde.* *20c. coll.:* Stevenson 811:1.

43. Those who are easily burned should never go near the fire. *Rec. dist.:* Oreg.

44. When the fire burns in the soul, the tongue cannot be silent. *Rec. dist.:* N.C.

45. You can hide the fire, but not the smoke. *Rec. dist.:* Ky., N.Y., S.C., Tenn. *1st cit.:* ca1375 Barbour, *Actes and Life of Robert Bruce,* E.E.T.S. (1870–89); US1880 Harris, *Plantation Proverbs* in *Uncle Remus, His Songs and His Sayings* (1881). *20c. coll.:* Stevenson 811:10.

SEE ALSO A singed CAT dreads the fire. / Don't fan the FLAME that supports the fire. / The GOOSE is never cooked till the fire is hottest. / HATE is a burning fire that may consume the one who hates. / When your neighbor's HOUSE is on fire, beware of your own. / Crooked LOGS make straight fires. / LOVE is the only fire against which there is no insurance. / True LOVE is friendship set on fire. / Three MOVES are as bad as a fire. / SILKS and satins, scarlet and velvet, put out the kitchen fire. / Where there's SMOKE, there's fire. / Just because there's SNOW on the roof, that doesn't mean the fire's out inside. / A little SPARK kindles a great fire. / Little STICKS kindle large fires. / TEMPTATION is the fire that brings up the scum of the heart. / Don't keep all your TONGS in one fire. / WINE and youth are flax upon fire. / Green WOOD makes a hot fire. / ZEAL is like fire, it needs feeding and watching. / ZEAL without knowledge is fire without light.

firefly **1.** Fireflies shine only when in motion. *Rec. dist.:* N.J.

2. The light of the firefly is sufficient for itself only. *Rec. dist.:* Ill.

firewood He who cuts his own firewood has it warm him twice. *Var.:* He who cuts his own firewood warms himself twice. **Rec. dist.:** Ill.

firmness **1.** We usually admire firmness in ourselves but find it darned stubbornness in others. **Rec. dist.:** Wis.

2. When firmness is sufficient, rashness is unnecessary. **Rec. dist.:** Ill.

SEE ALSO LOVE asks faith and faith asks firmness.

first *(n.)* **1.** Be not the first by whom the new is tried. **Var.:** Be not the first to pick up the new nor yet the last to lay down the old. **Rec. dist.:** U.S., Can.

2. First come, first served. **Var.:** First there, first served. **Rec. dist.:** U.S., Can. *1st cit.:* ca1545 Brinkelow, *Complaynt of Roderick Mors;* US1630 *Thomas Hutchinson Papers.* **20c. coll.:** ODEP 262, Whiting 80, CODP 81, Stevenson 815:4, T&W 77, Whiting*(MP)* 128.

3. First gets the worst. **Rec. dist.:** Ky., Tenn.

4. First is worst, second the same, last is best of all the game. **Rec. dist.:** Ont.

5. The first shall be last and the last, first. **Vars.:** **(a)** But many shall be last that are first, and first that are last. **(b)** The last shall be the first. **Rec. dist.:** U.S., Can. *1st cit.:* US1948 Stevenson, *Home Book of Proverbs.* **20c. coll.:** Stevenson 815:7.

SEE ALSO You can't take a second DRINK unless you have taken a first. / He who does one FAULT at first and lies to hide it makes it two. / Be not the first to QUARREL nor the last to make up. / If at first you don't SUCCEED, try, try again.

first *(adj.)* **1.** Everyone can't be first. **Rec. dist.:** Ala., Ga.

2. Put first things first. **Rec. dist.:** U.S. *1st cit.:* 1844 Jackson, *First Things First;* US1941 Eberhart, *House of Storm.* **20c. coll.:** CODP 82, Whiting*(MP)* 618.

3. The first hundred years are the hardest. **Rec. dist.:** Fla. *1st cit.:* 1965 Sharp, *Green Tree in Gedde;* US1928 Thomas, *Raiders of the Deep.* **20c. coll.:** Whiting*(MP)* 707.

SEE ALSO Your first ACCIDENT may be your last. / The first ATTEMPT is the most difficult. / If you miss the first BUTTONHOLE, you will

not succeed in buttoning up your coat. / The FARMER was the first man, and he will be the last. / HEALTH is the first muse. / First IMPRESSIONS are often lasting. / Never judge by first IMPRESSIONS. / JUDGE not of men or things at first sight. / First LOVE, last love, best love. / One always returns to his first LOVE. / It's the first STEP that costs. / There must be a first TIME for everything. / The first essential of a TYPIST is a good eraser. / First WINNER, last loser.

first *(adv.)* **1.** Git there firstest with the mostest. **Rec. dist.:** Nebr. **Infm.:** Cf. fast *(adv.).*

2. He who comes first grinds first. **Rec. dist.:** N.Y. *1st cit.:* ca1386 Chaucer, *Prologue to Wife of Bath's Tale.* **20c. coll.:** ODEP 262, Stevenson 815:4.

SEE ALSO The rottenest BOUGH cracks first. / First a DAUGHTER, then a son, and the family's well begun. / First DESERVE and then desire. / HEAR first and speak afterwards. / What we first LEARN we best ken. / Those whom we LOVE first we seldom wed. / He who stirs the soup POT eats first.

fish *(n.)* **1.** A dead fish can float downstream, but it takes a live one to swim upstream. **Vars.:** **(a)** A dead fish can float down current, but it takes a live one to swim upstream. **(b)** A dead fish floats downstream; a live one goes up. **(c)** An old fish can swim downstream, but it takes a young one to swim upstream. **(d)** Only live fish swim upstream. **Rec. dist.:** N.J., Ohio, Ont., Wash. *1st cit.:* US1930 Rice, *Ballad of Game Fish.* **20c. coll.:** Stevenson 2226:7.

2. A fish never nibbles at the same hook twice. **Rec. dist.:** Ont.

3. A fish wouldn't get caught if it kept its mouth shut. **Vars.:** **(a)** A fish who keeps his mouth shut will never get caught. **(b)** Even a fish sometimes keeps his mouth closed, so that he wouldn't be caught. **(c)** Even a fish wouldn't get in trouble if he kept his mouth shut. **Rec. dist.:** U.S., Can.

4. All fish are not caught with flies. **Rec. dist.:** Ala., Ga., N.Y., N.C., Tex.

5. All's fish that come to his net. **Vars.:** **(a)**

All is not fish that comes to net. **(b)** All's fish that comes to my net. **(c)** Anything is fish in the net. *Rec. dist.:* Fla., Miss., Ohio. *1st cit.:* ca1520 *Ballads from Manuscripts,* Ballad Soc.; US1733 Franklin, *PRAlmanac.* *20c. coll.:* ODEP 264.

6. Better a big fish in a little puddle than a little fish in a big puddle. *Vars.:* **(a)** Better a big fish in a little pond than a little fish in a big pond. **(b)** It is better to be a big fish in a little pond than a little fish in a big pond. **(c)** It is better to be the biggest fish in a small puddle than the smallest fish in a big puddle. *Rec. dist.:* U.S., Can.

7. Better a small fish than an empty dish. *Rec. dist.:* Ill., N.Y. *1st cit.:* 1732 Fuller, *Gnomologia.* *20c. coll.:* Stevenson 235:11.

8. Big fish are caught in a big river. *Rec. dist.:* N.Y.

9. Big fish are caught with little hooks. *Rec. dist.:* Ont.

10. Catch no more fish than you can salt. *Rec. dist.:* N.J.

11. Do not make fish of one and flesh of another. *Var.:* You can't make fish out of one and fowl out of another. *Rec. dist.:* Ont., Tex., Vt. *1st cit.:* 1639 Clarke, *Paroemiologia;* USca1692 *Wullys Papers,* Conn.Hist.Soc. Collections (1924). *20c. coll.:* ODEP 264, Whiting 155, Stevenson 820:10, T&W 136, Whiting(MP) 229.

12. Don't clean your fish before you catch it. *Rec. dist.:* Ont. *1st cit.:* 1721 Kelly, *Scottish Proverbs.* *20c. coll.:* ODEP 341, Stevenson 334:3.

13. Don't count your fish before you get them. *Rec. dist.:* Kans.

14. Don't count your fish until on dry land. *Rec. dist.:* Ill.

15. Every fish is not a sturgeon. *Rec. dist.:* Ill., Ont.

16. Every fish that escapes seems greater than it is. *Rec. dist.:* Ont.

17. Every little fish would become a whale. *Rec. dist.:* Fla.

18. Fish and callers smell in three days. *Vars.:* **(a)** Company is like fish: after three days they stink. **(b)** Fish and visitors smell after three days. **(c)** Fish and visitors smell in three days. **(d)** Fish and visitors stink within three days. *Rec. dist.:* U.S., Can. *1st cit.:* 1580 Lyly, *Euphues and His England;* US1736 Franklin, *PRAlmanac.* *20c. coll.:* ODEP 287, Whiting 154, *CODP* 83, Stevenson 1045:8, Whiting(MP) 274.

19. Fish begin to stink at the head, men at the feet. *Var.:* The fish stinks first in the head. *Rec. dist.:* Ill., Ohio. *1st cit.:* 1574 Guazzo, *Civile Conversation,* tr. Pettie, T.T. (1925); US1674 Josselyn, *Account of Voyage to New England.* *20c. coll.:* ODEP 263, Whiting 154, CODP 82, Stevenson 816:7, Whiting(MP) 227.

20. Fish have no language. *Rec. dist.:* Ont.

21. Fish on the hook is better than ten in the brook. *Rec. dist.:* Minn.

22. Great fishes are caught in great waters. *Rec. dist.:* Ill. *1st cit.:* 1640 Herbert, *Outlandish Proverbs (Jacula Prudentum)* in *Works,* ed. Hutchinson (1941). *20c. coll.:* Stevenson 817:6.

23. He who has the longest nets catches the biggest fish. *Rec. dist.:* Ohio.

24. He who would catch fish must not mind getting wet. *Var.:* You can't catch fish on a dry line. *Rec. dist.:* Mich., N.C.

25. If you catch fish, you're a fisherman. *Rec. dist.:* Ill.

26. It is a silly fish that is caught twice with the same bait. *Rec. dist.:* Nebr., Wis. *1st cit.:* 1732 Fuller, *Gnomologia.* *20c. coll.:* ODEP 734, Stevenson 819:5.

27. It is only the excited fish that jumps at the lure. *Rec. dist.:* Miss.

28. Little fish swim in shallow water. *Rec. dist.:* Ky., Tenn.

29. Lose a small fish to catch a big one. *Var.:* Venture a small fish to catch a great one. *Rec. dist.:* Fla., Tex.

30. No fish was ever so full he wouldn't bite at something. *Rec. dist.:* Minn.

31. Sma' fish are better than nae fish. *Rec. dist.:* Ont.

32. That fish is soon caught who nibbles at

every bait. **Var.:** That fish will soon be caught that nibbles at every bait. **Rec. dist.:** Tex. **1st cit.:** 1732 Fuller, *Gnomologia.* **20c. coll.:** ODEP 265, Stevenson 819:3.

33. The big fish eat the little ones, the little ones eat shrimps, and the shrimps are forced to eat mud. **Var.:** The big fish eat the little ones. **Rec. dist.:** Ill., N.Y. **1st cit.:** ca1200 *Old English Homilies,* E.E.T.S.; US1643 *Complete Writings of Roger Williams* (1963). **20c. coll.:** ODEP 333, CODP 18, Whiting 154, Stevenson 817:2.

34. The fish that escapes is the biggest fish of all. **Rec. dist.:** Miss.

35. The fish that has once felt the hook suspects the crooked metal in every food which is offered. **Rec. dist.:** Ark. **1st cit.:** 1590 Spenser, *Faerie Queene.* **20c. coll.:** Stevenson 727:4.

36. The hasty angler loses the fish. **Rec. dist.:** Ill.

37. The sea is full of other fish. **Vars.: (a)** There are always more fish in the pond. **(b)** There are other fish in the sea. **(c)** There are plenty of other fish in the sea. **(d)** There is always more fish in the ocean, but only one whale. **(e)** There is still better fish left in the pond. **(f)** There's just as good fish in the sea. **(g)** There's more than one fish in the sea. **Rec. dist.:** U.S., Can. **1st cit.:** 1982 Simpson, *Concise Oxford Dictionary of Proverbs;* US1909 Lincoln, *Keziah.* **20c. coll.:** T&W 136, CODP 83, Whiting(MP) 228.

38. There are better fish in the sea than have ever been caught. **Vars.: (a)** As good fish in the sea as ever was caught. **(b)** Better fish in the sea than ever was caught. **(c)** There are as good fish in the sea as ever came out of it. **(d)** There are just as good fish in the sea as have ever been caught. **Rec. dist.:** U.S., Can. **1st cit.:** 1816 Peacock, *Headlong Hall;* US1809 *Port Folio.* **20c. coll.:** ODEP 263, Whiting 155, CODP 83, Stevenson 816:9, Whiting(MP) 228.

39. There's a fish in every sea and a pebble on every beach. **Rec. dist.:** Ill.

See also It's all right to DRINK like a fish if you drink what a fish drinks. / FISHERMEN never see fish stink. / The hasty HAND catches frogs for fish. / Bait the HOOK well and the fish will bite.

fish *(v.)*   **1.** Do not fish in front of a net. **Rec. dist.:** Ont. **1st cit.:** 1546 Heywood, *Dialogue of Proverbs,* ed. Habernicht (1963). **20c. coll.:** ODEP 265.

2. Fish or cut bait. **Var.:** You've got to fish or cut bait. **Rec. dist.:** Ill., Oreg., Vt. **1st cit.:** US1876 Cannon, Debate in House of Representatives in *Congressional Record.* **20c. coll.:** Stevenson 823:7, Whiting(MP) 229.

3. There is a time to fish and a time to dry nets. **Rec. dist.:** Ont.

fisherman   **1.** A dry fisherman and a wet hunter are a sorry sight. **Rec. dist.:** N.Y.

2. A fisherman, once stung, will be wiser. **Rec. dist.:** Fla.

3. Fishermen never see fish stink. **Rec. dist.:** Ala., Ga.

4. Old fishermen never die, they just smell that way. **Rec. dist.:** Colo.

5. While the kingfisher and the oyster are struggling, the fisherman gets both. **Rec. dist.:** Ont.

fishhook   *See* GOLD is the devil's fishhook.

fishing   **1.** Going fishing without beer makes the day last a year. **Rec. dist.:** Kans.

2. It's good fishing in troubled waters. **Var.:** There's always good fishing in muddy waters. **Rec. dist.:** Ill., Okla., Ont., Tex. **1st cit.:** 1568 Grafton, *Chronicle;* US1637 Morton, *New English Canaan.* **20c. coll.:** ODEP 265, Whiting 472, Stevenson 821:6, Whiting(MP) 667.

3. One at a time is good fishing. **Var.:** One at a time is good fishing; two at a time is making a hog of yourself. **Rec. dist.:** Ont.

4. The best fishing is in the deepest water. **Rec. dist.:** Ky., Tenn. **1st cit.:** 1616 Draxe, *Bibliotheca Scholastica* in *Anglia* (1918). **20c. coll.:** ODEP 176.

fist   A closed fist is the lock of heaven, and the open hand is the key of mercy. **Rec. dist.:** Ont.

See also If you have no HAND you can't make a fist.

fit *(v.)* S*EE* If the CAP fits, wear it. / No matter how black the KETTLE, there is always a lid to fit it. / Never tell a LIE till the truth doesn't fit. / If the SHOE fits, put it on. / A STONE that may fit in the wall is never left by the way. / That SUIT is best that best fits me.

fit *(adj.)* S*EE* A man's not ready to DIE until he's fit to live. / The blind HORSE is fittest for the mill. / LEARNING makes a man fit company for himself. / Only those are fit to LIVE who are not afraid to die.

flag A worn flag is an honor to the capital. *Rec. dist.:* N.Y.

flame 1. An old flame is easily kindled. *Rec. dist.:* Ont.

2. An old flame never dies. *Rec. dist.:* Fla.

3. Don't fan the flame that supports the fire. *Rec. dist.:* Ill.

4. The flame is not far from the smoke. *Rec. dist.:* Ill. *1st cit.:* US1948 Stevenson, *Home Book of Proverbs. 20c. coll.:* Stevenson 811:14.

5. The flame of a setting sun tells you there are better days to come. *Var.:* The end of another day has come when you see the flame of the setting sun. *Rec. dist.:* Wis.

S*EE ALSO* The spark of AMBITION lights the flame of achievement. / FIRE doesn't burn without a flame. / A little WIND kindles a big flame.

flannel Stick to your flannels until they stick to you. *Rec. dist.:* Vt.

flare S*EE* Before you flare up at anyone's FAULTS, take time to count ten of your own.

flat S*EE* LIFE is a song, but it often goes flat.

flatter 1. A man that flatters his neighbor spreads a net for his feet. *Rec. dist.:* Ont. *1st cit.:* US1948 Stevenson, *Home Book of Proverbs. 20c. coll.:* Stevenson 811:14.

2. He who flatters me is my enemy; he who reproves me is my teacher. *Rec. dist.:* N.C.

3. If no one flatters you, you flatter yourself. *Rec. dist.:* Ill. *1st cit.:* US1948 Stevenson, *Home Book of Proverbs. 20c. coll.:* Stevenson 829:8.

4. If you reward the chap who flatters you, you are begging for his flattery. *Rec. dist.:* Ill.

5. The man who flatters you is a liar: the greater the flattery, the bigger the liar. *Rec. dist.:* Ill.

S*EE ALSO* If we are VAIN and love to be flattered, we shall become foolish.

flatterer 1. A flatterer has a venal tongue. *Rec. dist.:* Mich.

2. All flatterers live at the expense of those they flatter. *Rec. dist.:* N.Y.

3. Beware the flatterer. *Vars.:* **(a)** Beware of a flatterer—he always has an axe to grind. **(b)** Beware of flatterers—they always have an axe to grind. **(c)** Beware of flatterers. **(d)** Do not trust flatterers. *Rec. dist.:* Fla., Ont. *1st cit.:* ca1386 Chaucer, *Tale of Melibee. 20c. coll.:* Stevenson 827:7.

4. Flatterers are cats that lick before and scratch behind. *Rec. dist.:* Ill.

5. Flatterers are clever mind readers: they tell us exactly what we think. *Rec. dist.:* Ont.

6. If he's your flatterer, he can't be your friend. *Rec. dist.:* N.Y., S.C. *1st cit.:* US1744 Franklin, *PRAlmanac. 20c. coll.:* Stevenson 830:4.

7. The flatterer scratches you where you itch. *Rec. dist.:* Ill.

8. The flatterer's bite is poisonous. *Rec. dist.:* Ill.

9. When flatterers meet, Satan goes to dinner. *Rec. dist.:* Mich. *1st cit.:* 1678 Ray, *English Proverbs. 20c. coll.:* Stevenson 829:12.

S*EE ALSO* A good LISTENER is a silent flatterer.

flattery 1. Be not led by flattery. *Vars.:* **(a)** Be not misled by flattery. **(b)** Beware of foolish flattery. *Rec. dist.:* Ill., Ont.

2. Bold flattery gives an impression of insincerity. *Rec. dist.:* Ont. *1st cit.:* US1948 Stevenson, *Home Book of Proverbs. 20c. coll.:* Stevenson 829:12.

3. Do not let flattery throw you off guard against an enemy. *Rec. dist.:* N.Y.

4. Flattery begets friends, but the truth begets enmity. *Rec. dist.:* N.Y. *1st cit.:* 1581 Guazzo, *Civile Conversation,* tr. Pettie, T.T. (1925). *20c. coll.:* Stevenson 827:11.

5. Flattery butters no parsnips. *Rec. dist.:* Ohio.

6. Flattery is a vice disguised as a virtue. *Rec. dist.:* Ill.

7. Flattery is like an empty tomb on which friendship is inscribed. *Rec. dist.:* Mich.

8. Flattery is not a proof of true admiration. *Rec. dist.:* Kans.

9. Flattery is soft soap, and soft soap is ninety percent lye. *Vars.:* **(a)** Don't use flattery, for flattery is soft soap, and soft soap is ninety percent lye. **(b)** Flattery is soft soap, and all soap is half lye. **(c)** Flattery is soft soap, and soap is ninety percent lye. **(d)** Flattery is soft soap, ninety-five percent lye. *Rec. dist.:* U.S., Can. *1st cit.:* US1840 Neal, *John Beedle's Sleigh Ride.* *20c. coll.:* Stevenson 829:5.

10. Flattery is sweet food to those who can swallow it. *Rec. dist.:* Ill.

11. Flattery is sweet poison. *Rec. dist.:* Ill.

12. Flattery is the bellows that blows up sin. *Rec. dist.:* Ill.

13. Flattery is the food of fools. *Rec. dist.:* Ill., N.Y., Ont. *1st cit.:* 1726 Swift, "Cadenus and Vanessa." *20c. coll.:* Stevenson 830:2.

14. Flattery is the last resort of fools. *Rec. dist.:* N.Y., Ont.

15. Flattery, like perfume, should be smelled, not swallowed. *Var.:* Flattery should be like perfume: it should be sniffed but not swallowed. *Rec. dist.:* Colo., Ont. *1st cit.:* US1858 Shaw, *Josh Billings' Philosophy.* *20c. coll.:* Stevenson 827:7.

16. Flattery makes friends. *Rec. dist.:* Minn.

17. Flattery will get you nowhere. *Vars.:* **(a)** Flattery will get you everywhere. **(b)** Flattery will get you many places. *Rec. dist.:* Fla., Kans. *1st cit.:* US1954 Box, *Death Likes It Hot.* *20c. coll.:* Whiting(MP) 231, T&W 138.

18. He that rewards flattery begs it. *Rec. dist.:* Fla., Ont. *1st cit.:* 1732 Fuller, *Gnomologia.* *20c. coll.:* Stevenson 828:1.

19. The coin that is most current is flattery. *Rec. dist.:* Ill. *1st cit.:* 1732 Fuller, *Gnomologia.* *20c. coll.:* Stevenson 828:13.

20. The most flattering flattery is to be told

you cannot be flattered. *Rec. dist.:* Minn., N.Y.

21. There is flattery in friendship. *Rec. dist.:* Minn.

SEE ALSO IMITATION is the highest form of flattery. / A man is really a SUCCESS when flattery gives him a headache instead of a big head.

flax *SEE* FIRE and flax agree not.

flay *SEE* No man can flay a STONE.

flea 1. A certain amount of fleas are good for a dog. *Var.:* A reasonable amount of fleas is good for a dog—they keep him from broodin' on bein' a dog. *Rec. dist.:* Ind. *1st cit.:* US1899 Wescott, *David Harum.* *20c. coll.:* Stevenson 606:11.

2. Do not flay a flea for hide and tallow. *Rec. dist.:* U.S., Can. *1st cit.:* 1591 Florio, *Second Fruites;* US1803 Davis, *Travels in U.S., 1798–1802.* *20c. coll.:* ODEP 267, Whiting 157, Stevenson 1590:6, T&W 138, Whiting(MP) 231.

3. Even a flea can bite. *Rec. dist.:* Ill., N.Y.

4. Little fleas have lesser fleas. *Rec. dist.:* Ark. *1st cit.:* 1732 Swift, *Poems II.* *20c. coll.:* CODP 18, Stevenson 830:20.

5. The brave flea dares to eat his breakfast on the lip of a lion. *Rec. dist.:* Ill. *1st cit.:* 1599 Shakespeare, *Henry V.* *20c. coll.:* Stevenson 830:18.

6. The fatter the flea, the leaner the dog. *Rec. dist.:* Ill.

SEE ALSO AMBITION is like hunting for fleas. / If you lie down with DOGS, you'll get up with fleas. / Who play wid de PUPPY get bit wid de fleas.

flee He who flees proves himself guilty. *Rec. dist.:* N.Y. *1st cit.:* 1793 Clerk, *Muir's Case.* *20c. coll.:* Stevenson 833:10.

flesh All flesh is grass. *Rec. dist.:* Ill. *1st cit.:* 1871 Loring, *Epitaphs;* US1643 *Complete Writings of Roger Williams.* *20c. coll.:* Whiting 157, Stevenson 832:4, T&W 138, Whiting(MP) 232.

SEE ALSO What is bred in the BONE will come out in the flesh. / An ounce of GRIT is worth a pound of flesh. / A sound HEART is the life of the flesh, but envy the rottenness of the bones. / The SPIRIT is willing but the flesh is weak.

flight SEE BLESSINGS brighten as they take their flight. / One courageous THOUGHT will put to flight a host of troubles.

fling *(n.)* After your fling, watch for the sting. *Rec. dist.:* N.Y. *1st cit.:* 1917 Bridge, *Cheshire Proverbs.* *20c. coll.:* ODEP 6, Stevenson 1965:17.
   SEE ALSO YOUTH will have its fling.

fling *(v.)* SEE The man who flings a STONE up a mountainside may have it rolled back upon himself.

flint Strike a flint and you get fire. *Rec. dist.:* Ill. *1st cit.:* US1840 Cooper, *Pathfinder.* *20c. coll.:* T&W 139.
   SEE ALSO The FIRE in the flint shows not until it is struck.

flirt A flirt gets paid in her own coin. *Rec. dist.:* Kans.

flitting Saturday's flitting is short sitting. *Vars.:* **(a)** A Friday flit is a short sit. **(b)** A Friday's flit is a very short sit. **(c)** A Saturday flit is a short sit. **(d)** Friday flit, short sit. **(e)** Friday flitter, short time sitter. **(f)** Friday flitting means short sitting. **(g)** Move on Saturday, flitting, and short sitting. **(h)** Saturday flit, short sit. *Rec. dist.:* Ohio, Ont. *1st cit.:* 1854 Baker, *Glossary of Northamptonshire Words and Phrases;* US1957 Beck, *Folklore of Maine.* *20c. coll.:* ODEP 699, Whiting(MP) 547.

float SEE FEATHERS float, but pearls lie low. / A dead FISH can float downstream, but it takes a live one to swim upstream.

flock *(n.)* SEE One sickly SHEEP infects the flock and poisons all the rest. / There is a black SHEEP in every flock.

flock *(v.)* SEE BIRDS of a feather flock together. / EAGLES fly alone, but sheep flock together.

flood A May flood never did good. *Rec. dist.:* Wis.
   SEE ALSO What the EBB takes out, the flood brings in.

floodgates SEE CONVERSATIONAL floodgates are always open.

floor A dirty floor means a busy stove. *Rec. dist.:* Colo.
   SEE ALSO If you try to sit on two CHAIRS, you'll sit on the floor.

Florida The Spaniards discovered Florida and the Georgians populated it. *Rec. dist.:* Fla.

flourish To flourish is one thing, to fight another. *Rec. dist.:* Mich.

flow A flow will have an ebb. *Rec. dist.:* N.Y., Tex. *1st cit.:* ca1420 Lydgate, *Troy.* *20c. coll.:* ODEP 269, Stevenson 2317:9.
   SEE ALSO A flow of WORDS is no proof of wisdom.

flower 1. Cherish some flower, be it ever so lowly. *Rec. dist.:* Ont.

2. Fair flowers are never left standing by the wayside. *Rec. dist.:* Ont.

3. Flowers are always brighter in the next field. *Rec. dist.:* Ont.

4. Flowers are the pledges of fruit. *Rec. dist.:* Ill.

5. Flowers bloom in the spring. *Rec. dist.:* N.Y. *1st cit.:* 1578 Florio, *Firste Fruites.* *20c. coll.:* Stevenson 835:10.

6. Flowers leave fragrance in the hand that bestows them. *Rec. dist.:* N.Y., Ohio.

7. Flowers of true friendship never fade. *Rec. dist.:* Ont.

8. Flowers open without choosing the rich man's garden. *Rec. dist.:* Ill.

9. Give me a flower while I live, and don't bother when I'm dead. *Var.:* Give me flowers while I live. *Rec. dist.:* N.Y., Okla.

10. If you don't give flowers water, they die. *Rec. dist.:* Ont.

11. Many a flower is born to blush unseen. *Var.:* Many flowers are born to blush unseen. *Rec. dist.:* Ill., N.Y., N.C., Ont. *1st cit.:* 1570 Gray, *Elegy Written in Country Church-Yard.* *20c. coll.:* Stevenson 1710:2.

12. One flower makes no garland. *Rec. dist.:* Ont. *1st cit.:* 1640 Herbert, *Outlandish Proverbs (Jacula Prudentum)* in *Works,* ed. Hutchinson (1941). *20c. coll.:* ODEP 596, Stevenson 835:12.

13. Painted flowers have no scent. *Rec. dist.:*

Ill., Vt. *1st cit.:* 1869 Henderson, *Latin Proverbs.* *20c. coll.:* Stevenson 98:9.

14. Say it with flowers. *Var.:* Say it with signs—flowers die. *Rec. dist.:* U.S. *1st cit.:* 1941 Marsh, *Death and Dancing Footman;* US1917 O'Keefe, Slogan of Society of American Florists. *20c. coll.:* Stevenson 835:2.

15. The flower of sweetest smell is shy and lowly. *Rec. dist.:* Ont.

16. The handsomest flower is not the sweetest. *Rec. dist.:* N.Y. *1st cit.:* 1855 Bohn, *Handbook of Proverbs.* *20c. coll.:* Stevenson 835:5.

17. The same flowers that adorn a bride are placed on a corpse. *Rec. dist.:* Ill.

18. There is no pathway of flowers leading to glory. *Var.:* No flowery road leads to glory. *Rec. dist.:* Ont.

19. Where the flower is, the honey is also. *Rec. dist.:* N.Y.

SEE ALSO APRIL showers bring May flowers. / BEAUTY is a fading flower. / It is not enough for a GARDENER to love flowers; he must also hate weeds. / GENEROSITY is the flower of justice. / HAPPINESS is a wayside flower growing upon the highways of usefulness. / Kind HEARTS are the gardens, kind thoughts the roots, kind words the flowers, kind deeds the fruits. / To have IDEAS is to gather flowers; to think is to weave them into garlands. / LIFE is the flower of which love is the honey. / PATIENCE is a flower that grows not in every garden. / No SUN, no showers, no summer flowers. / A true WIFE is her husband's flower of beauty.

flutter SEE The hit BIRD flutters.

fly (*n.*) **1.** A fly follows the honey. Rec. dist.: Ky., Tenn. *1st cit.:* ca1400 Hoccleye, *De Regimine Principum.* *20c. coll.:* Stevenson 836:7.

2. A fly may conquer a lion. *Rec. dist.:* Calif. *1st cit.:* US1813 *Letter Books of W. C. Claiborne, 1801–1816,* ed. Rowland (1917). *20c. coll.:* Whiting 159.

3. A person is not a fly. *Rec. dist.:* N.J.

4. Big flies break the spiderweb. *Rec. dist.:* N.Y.

5. Can't kill flies with a spear. *Rec. dist.:* Fla. *1st cit.:* 1678 Ray, *English Proverbs.* *20c. coll.:* Stevenson 1551:7.

6. Dying flies spoil the sweetness of the ointment. *Rec. dist.:* Ont. *1st cit.:* 1833 Lamb, *Poor Relations* US1642 *Winthrop's Journal of New England, 1630–1649,* ed. Hosmer (1908). *20c. coll.:* ODEP 270, Whiting 159, Stevenson 835:17, Whiting(MP) 234.

7. Even a fly has its spleen. *Rec. dist.:* Ont. *1st cit.:* 1580 Lyly, *Euphues and his England.* *20c. coll.:* ODEP 270, Stevenson 836:13.

8. Flies never bother a boiling pot. *Vars.:* (a) A smart fly never lights on a boiling pot. (b) To a boiling pot flies come not. *Rec. dist.:* Ohio. *1st cit.:* 1640 Herbert, *Outlandish Proverbs (Jacula Prudentum)* in *Works,* ed. Hutchinson (1941). *20c. coll.:* ODEP 72.

9. You can catch more flies with molasses than vinegar. *Vars.:* (a) A drop of honey catches more flies than a hogshead of vinegar. (b) A little honey draws a lot of flies. (c) A teaspoon of sugar will catch more flies than a gallon of vinegar. (d) An ounce of honey draws more flies than a gallon of gall. (e) Catch your flies with molasses. (f) Honey catches more flies than vinegar. (g) Honey gathers more flies than vinegar. (h) Molasses catches more flies than vinegar. (i) More flies are caught with honey than with molasses. (j) One can catch more flies with sugar than with vinegar. (k) You can catch more flies with honey than with vinegar. (l) You can catch more flies with love than with vinegar. (m) You can't catch flies with vinegar. *Rec. dist.:* U.S., Can. *1st cit.:* 1666 Torriano, *Common Place of Italian Proverbs;* US1744 Franklin, *PRAlmanac.* *20c. coll.:* CODP 113, Whiting 159, Stevenson 1158:14, T&W 140, Whiting(MP) 234.

SEE ALSO ALMOST never killed a fly. / A COW needs her tail more than once in fly time. / EAGLES don't catch flies. / HURRY is only good for catching flies. / A closed MOUTH catches no flies.

fly (*v., soar*) **1.** He who flies high must keep on flying. *Rec. dist.:* Ky., Tenn.

2. The higher they fly, the harder they fall. *Rec. dist.:* N.Y.

3. You cannot fly with one wing. *Rec. dist.:* Ont. *1st cit.:* US1914 Purdon, *Folk of Furry Farm.* *20c. coll.:* ODEP 60.

SEE ALSO You can't keep the BIRDS from flying over your head, but you can keep them from making a nest in your hair. / A DUCK never flies so high but that it has to come down for water. / EAGLES fly alone, but sheep flock together. / FALLING hurts least those who fly low. / Where the FEATHERS fly is where the shot hit. / Fly your KITE when it's windy. / He that has feathered his NEST may flee when he likes.

fly (v., escape) SEE AIM high, time flies. / Better to bear the ILLS we have than fly to others we know not of. / Fly PLEASURE and it will follow you. / TIME flies.

flying SEE It is a good thing to make a BRIDGE of gold to a flying enemy.

fodder SEE A good HORSE is worth its fodder.

foe 1. A courageous foe is better than a cowardly friend. *Rec. dist.:* N.Y., Ont. *1st cit.:* 1732 Fuller, *Gnomologia.* *20c. coll.:* Stevenson 911:10.

2. A foe to God was never a true friend to man. *Rec. dist.:* N.J.

3. He makes a foe who makes a jest. *Rec. dist.:* Wis. *1st cit.:* US1740 Franklin, *PRAlmanac.* *20c. coll.:* Stevenson 1266:7.

SEE ALSO ABSENCE is love's foe: far from the eyes, far from the heart. / The man that makes a CHARACTER makes foes. / Who overcomes by FORCE has overcome but half his foe. / A rash FRIEND is worse than a foe. / He makes no FRIENDS who never made a foe. / The QUARREL of friends is the opportunity of their foes. / A careless WATCH invites the vigilant foe.

foeman There are worser ills than to face foemen in the fray. *Rec. dist.:* N.Dak.

fog 1. A summer's fog will roast a hog. *Rec. dist.:* Ont.

2. A winter's fog will freeze a dog. *Rec. dist.:* Vt.

SEE ALSO The fellow who blows his HORN the loudest is likely in the biggest fog.

fold (n.) SEE If one SHEEP has left the fold, all the rest will follow. / It is better to keep a

wolf out of the fold than to trust drawing his teeth and talons after he shall have entered.

fold (v.) SEE If you play both ENDS against the middle, the middle will soon fold up.

folk 1. Folks never understand the folks they hate. *Rec. dist.:* N.Y.

2. Good folks are scarce. *Rec. dist.:* Ont.

3. It takes all sorts of folks to make up the world. *Rec. dist.:* Ill. *1st cit.:* 1620 Cervantes, *Don Quixote,* tr. Shelton; US1860 Haliburton, *Season-Ticket.* *20c. coll.:* ODEP 11, T&W 141, Whiting(MP) 583.

4. Little folks are fond of talking about what great folks do. *Rec. dist.:* N.Y.

5. Mad folks and proverbs reveal many truths. *Rec. dist.:* Ill.

6. Poor folks are glad of porridge. *Rec. dist.:* Ont. *1st cit.:* 1576 Fulwell, "Art of Flattery" in *Ars Adulandi.* *20c. coll.:* ODEP 638, Stevenson 1844:9.

7. Straight folk never make broken promises. *Rec. dist.:* Ill.

SEE ALSO When you's BROKE, dat's de time to ack stylish, so folks won't know you're broke. / Folks who never DO any more than they get paid for never get paid for any more than they do. / DRUNKEN folks seldom take harm. / DUMB folks get no land. / Some folks speak from EXPERIENCE; others, from experience, don't speak. / Folks spend their HEALTH to acquire wealth and later spend their wealth in an effort to regain their health. / Some folks enjoy poor HEALTH. / HOME-keeping folks are happiest. / LAZY folks are most efficient. / When the SUN's in the west, lazy folks work the best. / THREATENED folks live the longest: they take numerous precautions. / Folks like the TRUTH that hits their neighbors. / As YOUNG folks see, the young folks do; as they hear, they say.

follow 1. He who follows another is always behind. *Rec. dist.:* Colo., Mich.

2. Some must follow and some command. *Rec. dist.:* Kans.

SEE ALSO You can't follow two PATHS. / Fly PLEASURE and it will follow you. / He is a good PREACHER who follows his own preaching. / If one SHEEP has left the fold, all the rest will follow. / One SHEEP follows another. / SMOKE follows beauty. / SUNSHINE follows rain.

following SEE EXAMPLE is better than following it.

folly 1. A man's folly ought to be his greatest secret. *Rec. dist.:* Calif.

2. Folly and beauty walk hand in hand. *Rec. dist.:* Ill.

3. Folly has a fall before it. *Rec. dist.:* Ont.

4. Folly is an incurable disease. *Rec. dist.:* Ill. *1st cit.:* 1640 Herbert, *Outlandish Proverbs (Jacula Prudentum)* in *Works,* ed. Hutchinson (1941). *20c. coll.:* Stevenson 840:9.

5. It is the ordinary way of the world to keep folly at the helm and wisdom under the hatches. *Rec. dist.:* Ont.

6. No country or age has a monopoly on human folly. *Rec. dist.:* N.Y.

7. Profit by the folly of others. *Var.:* The best plan is to profit by the folly of others. *Rec. dist.:* Ill., Ont.

8. The first degree of folly is to conceit one's self wise, the second to profess it, the third to despise counsel. *Rec. dist.:* Ill. *1st cit.:* 1598 Barckley, *Discourse on the Felicitie of Man.* *20c. coll.:* ODEP 262.

9. The follies of a fool are known to the world and not to himself; the follies of a wise man are known to himself but not to the world. *Rec. dist.:* Ind.

10. The folly of one man is the fortune of another. *Vars.:* (a) One man's folly is another man's fortune. (b) One man's fortune is another man's folly. *Rec. dist.:* U.S., Can. *1st cit.:* 1607 Bacon, "Essay on Fortune" in *Works* (1858). *20c. coll.:* ODEP 273.

11. The shortest follies are the best. *Rec. dist.:* Mich. *Infm.:* Given as an admonition by one of the Duke of Savoy's council in 1589. *1st cit.:* ca1594 Bacon, *Promus.* *20c. coll.:* ODEP 273.

12. What is a poor man's folly is a rich man's gain. *Rec. dist.:* Ind.

13. When folly passes by, reason draws back. *Rec. dist.:* Ill.

SEE ALSO ANGER begins with folly and ends with repentance. / A CAUTIOUS man conceals knowledge, and the heart of fools publishes folly. / A FOOL laughs at his own folly. / Answer a FOOL according to his folly. / FOOLS multiply folly. / One man's FORTUNE is another man's folly. / We are taxed twice as much by our IDLENESS, three times as much by our pride, and four times by our follies. / Where IGNORANCE is bliss, 'tis folly to be wise. / JEALOUSY leads to folly and injustice. / SILENCE is not always a sign of wisdom, but babbling is ever a folly. / SILENCE is wisdom when speaking is folly. / Learn WISDOM by the follies of others. / ZEAL without knowledge is the sister of folly.

fond SEE ABSENCE makes the heart grow fonder.

food 1. Another man's food is sweeter. *Rec. dist.:* Ill.

2. Chatted food is half digested. *Rec. dist.:* Ohio, Wis. *Infm.:* "Chatted food" means food eaten with conversation.

3. Food without hospitality is medicine. *Rec. dist.:* Ohio.

4. Forbidden food is sweetest. *Rec. dist.:* Ont. *Infm.:* Cf. fruit.

5. He has sorry food who feeds on the faults of others. *Rec. dist.:* Ont.

6. More die of food than famine. *Rec. dist.:* N.Y.

7. Never throw away food that will make a pig open his mouth. *Rec. dist.:* Vt.

8. One man's food may be another man's poison. *Rec. dist.:* Ohio. *Infm.:* Cf. meat. *1st cit.:* ca1613 Beaumont and Fletcher, *Love's Cure;* US1940 Gould, "Allergy" in *Physical Culture.* *20c. coll.:* Stevenson 1825:15.

9. The food consumed today shapes your figure tomorrow. *Rec. dist.:* Kans.

10. Who has burnt himself with hot food blows it cold. *Rec. dist.:* Fla.

SEE ALSO There are four things every CHILD needs. He needs an abundance of love, plenty of good nourishing food, lots of soap and water, and after that some good healthy neglect. / FLATTERY is the food of fools. / GOD puts food into clean hands. / GOD sends every bird its food, but he does not throw it into the nest. / PRAYER is food for the soul. / One's own WILL is good food.

fool (*n.*) **1.** A fool always finds a bigger fool to praise him. *Vars.:* **(a)** Fools always find a bigger fool to praise them. **(b)** One fool praises another. *Rec. dist.:* N.J., Ont. *1st cit.:* 1674 Boileau, *L'Art Politique;* US1740 Franklin, *PRAlmanac.* *20c. coll.:* ODEP 275, Stevenson 843:5.

2. A fool always finds a greater fool to admire. *Rec. dist.:* Ind. *1st cit.:* US1797 Cobbett, *Porcupine's Works.* *20c. coll.:* Whiting 160.

3. A fool always talks most when he has the least to say. *Rec. dist.:* Ont.

4. A fool and his money are soon parted. *Vars.:* **(a)** A fool and his gold are soon parted. **(b)** A fool and his money are invited places. **(c)** A fool and his money soon fast. **(d)** A fool and his money soon part. *Rec. dist.:* U.S., Can. *1st cit.:* 1587 Bridges, *Defence of Gov't. of Church of England;* US1699 Ward, *Trip to New England* in Winship, *Boston in 1682 and 1699* (1905). *20c. coll.:* ODEP 273, Whiting 160, CODP 84, Stevenson 853:6, Whiting(MP) 236.

5. A fool and his words are soon parted. *Rec. dist.:* N.J. *1st cit.:* 1763 Shenstone, *On Reserve.* *20c. coll.:* Stevenson 2604:6.

6. A fool believes everything. *Rec. dist.:* N.Y. *1st cit.:* 1579 Calvin, *Sermons.* *20c. coll.:* ODEP 274, Stevenson 851:8.

7. A fool can ask more questions in a minute than a wise man can answer in an hour. *Vars.:* **(a)** A fool can ask more questions in an hour than a wise man can answer in seven years. **(b)** A fool can ask questions that wise men cannot answer. *Rec. dist.:* U.S., Can. *1st cit.:* 1666 Torriano, *Italian Proverbs;* US1690 Further Quaeries in *Andros Tracts*, ed. Whitmore, Publ. Prince Soc. (1868-74). *20c. coll.:* ODEP 274, Whiting 161, T&W 142.

8. A fool demands much, but he's a greater fool that gives it. *Rec. dist.:* N.Y., Wis. *1st cit.:*

1616 Draxe, *Bibliotheca Scholastica* in *Anglia* (1918). *20c. coll.:* ODEP 273, Stevenson 847:7.

9. A fool despises his father's correction, but he that regards reproof grows prudent. *Rec. dist.:* Minn.

10. A fool has few friends. *Rec. dist.:* Ont.

11. A fool has no understanding but that his heart may discover itself. *Rec. dist.:* Ala., Ga.

12. A fool is born every minute. *Var.:* There is a fool born every minute. *Rec. dist.:* Ohio, Ont.

13. A fool is known by his conversation. *Vars.:* **(a)** A fool is known by his multitude of words. **(b)** A fool is known by his speech. *Rec. dist.:* Ark., Ont. *1st cit.:* 1477 *Dictes and Sayenges of the Philosophirs,* tr. Rivers. *20c. coll.:* Stevenson 858:6.

14. A fool is like other men as long as he is silent. *Rec. dist.:* Ohio.

15. A fool laughs at his own folly. *Var.:* Fools laugh at their own sport. *Rec. dist.:* U.S., Can.

16. A fool laughs at his own jokes. *Rec. dist.:* Calif.

17. A fool laughs when others laugh. *Rec. dist.:* La.

18. A fool may give a wise man counsel. *Rec. dist.:* Ind., Tex. *1st cit.:* ca1350 *Ywain & Gawain,* E.E.T.S. (1964). *20c. coll.:* ODEP 274, Stevenson 845:9.

19. A fool may talk, but a wise man speaks. *Rec. dist.:* N.Y.

20. A fool might be counted wise if he kept his mouth shut. *Vars.:* **(a)** A fool who is silent is counted wise. **(b)** A fool, when he is silent, is counted wise. **(c)** Even a fool, when he holds his peace, is counted wise. **(d)** Let a fool hold his tongue, and he can pass for a sage. *Rec. dist.:* U.S., Can. *1st cit.:* 1611 Cotgrave, *Dictionary of French and English Tongues.* *20c. coll.:* Stevenson 850:9.

21. A fool never changes his mind, but a wise man does. *Var.:* A fool will never change his mind, but a wise man will. *Rec. dist.:* Calif.

22. A fool over forty is a fool indeed. *Var.:* A fool at forty will never be wise. *Rec. dist.:* N.Y., Ohio, Ont. *1st cit.:* 1557 Edgeworth,

Sermons. **20c. coll.:** *ODEP* 273, *CODP* 84, Stevenson 33:3.

23. A fool says I can't. A wise man says I'll try. **Rec. dist.:** N.Y., R.I. **1st cit.:** US1940 Thompson, *Body, Boots, and Britches.* **20c. coll.:** Stevenson 854:14.

24. A fool says what he knows; a wise man knows what he says. **Rec. dist.:** N.Y.

25. A fool sees not the same tree that a wise man sees. **Rec. dist.:** Ont.

26. A fool talks when he should be listening. **Rec. dist.:** Ky., Tenn.

27. A fool talks while a wise man thinks. **Rec. dist.:** Ont.

28. A fool talks with his ears stuffed up. **Rec. dist.:** Tex.

29. A fool thinks nothing is right but what he does himself. **Rec. dist.:** Mich.

30. A fool utters all his mind, but a wise man keeps it in till afterwards. **Vars.: (a)** A fool says all he thinks; a wise man thinks and says nothing. **(b)** A fool utters all he knows. **(c)** Only a fool tells all he knows. **Rec. dist.:** Calif., N.Y., N.C., Ont.

31. A fool who keeps his mouth closed fools the whole world. **Rec. dist.:** N.Y.

32. A fool will ask for a glass of water when he is drowning. **Var.:** A fool would ask for a drink if he were drowning. **Rec. dist.:** N.Y., Ohio, Ont.

33. A fool's bolt is soon shot. **Rec. dist.:** N.C.

34. A fool's head never grows white. **Rec. dist.:** Ill., Ind.

35. A fool's mouth is his destruction. **Rec. dist.:** N.Y.

36. A fool's tongue is long enough to cut his throat. **Rec. dist.:** Miss., N.Y., Ohio. **1st cit.:** 1673 Dare, *Counsellor Manners.* **20c. coll.:** *ODEP* 277.

37. A fool's treasure is in his tongue. **Rec. dist.:** Kans.

38. A fool's wrath is presently known, but a prudent man covers his shame. **Var.:** A fool's vexation is presently known, but a prudent man conceals his. **Rec. dist.:** Mich.

39. A man is a stark fool all the while he is angry. **Rec. dist.:** N.Y.

40. A man's a fool till he's 40. **Rec. dist.:** Ky., Ohio, Tenn.

41. A prating fool shall fall. **Rec. dist.:** Ont.

42. A silent fool is a wise fool. **Rec. dist.:** Ont.

43. All men are fools, but the wisest of fools are called philosophers. **Rec. dist.:** Ont.

44. An educated fool is dangerous. **Rec. dist.:** Calif., Ill.

45. Answer a fool according to his folly. **Rec. dist.:** U.S., Can. **1st cit.:** 1589 Nashe, *Works,* ed. Grosart; US1721 Wise, *Friendly Check* in *Colonial Currency,* ed. Davis in Publ. Prince Soc. (1910–11). **20c. coll.:** Stevenson 851:3, Whiting 160, Whiting*(MP)* 235.

46. Any fool knows his mother, but 'tis a wise man that can tell who his father is. **Rec. dist.:** Vt.

47. Any fool knows more than his father. **Rec. dist.:** N.Y.

48. Any fool may make money, but it takes a wise man to keep it. **Vars.: (a)** A fool may make money, but it takes a wise man to spend it. **(b)** Any fool can earn a penny, but it takes a wise man to spend it. **(c)** Any fool can make money, but it takes a wise one to save it. **Rec. dist.:** U.S., Can.

49. Arguing with a fool shows there are two. **Vars.: (a)** If you argue with a fool, that makes two fools arguing. **(b)** When you argue with a fool, make sure he is not doing the same. **(c)** When you argue with a fool, that makes two. **Rec. dist.:** Utah.

50. As a rule, man's a fool: when it's hot, he wants it cool; when it's cool, he wants it hot—always wanting what is not. **Rec. dist.:** Ind., Ohio, Ont.

51. Better a kindly fool than a proud wise man. **Rec. dist.:** N.Y.

52. Better a witty fool than a foolish wit. **Rec. dist.:** Ark., Ohio. **1st cit.:** 1601 Shakespeare, *Twelfth Night.* **20c. coll.:** Stevenson 852:10.

53. Better be a fool and know it than be a damn fool and not know it. **Rec. dist.:** Vt.

54. Better to be a fool with a crowd than a wise man by oneself. *Rec. dist.:* Calif.

55. By rote rule goes many a fool. *Rec. dist.:* Ont.

56. Do not be proud of being a fool. *Rec. dist.:* N.Y.

57. Even a fool can learn. *Rec. dist.:* Calif.

58. Even a fool carries his coat in the rain. *Rec. dist.:* N.Mex.

59. Every fool wants to give advice. *Rec. dist.:* Wis.

60. Every man has a fool in his sleeve. *Rec. dist.:* N.C., Okla. *1st cit.:* 1640 Herbert, *Outlandish Proverbs (Jacula Prudentum)* in *Works,* ed. Hutchinson (1941). *20c. coll.:* ODEP 274, Stevenson 848:3.

61. Fool is he who deals with other fools. *Rec. dist.:* N.Y.

62. Fools and children tell the truth. *Vars.:* **(a)** Fools and children cannot lie. **(b)** Fools and children speak the truth. *Rec. dist.:* Mich., N.Y. *1st cit.:* 1537 Hayes in *State Papers of Henry VIII;* US1936 Clark, *High Wall.* *20c. coll.:* ODEP 119, Whiting(*MP*) 111, CODP 36, Stevenson 342:9.

63. Fools are never uneasy. *Rec. dist.:* Ont.

64. Fools are the worst thieves: they rob you of time and temper. *Rec. dist.:* Ill.

65. Fools are wise men in the affairs of women. *Rec. dist.:* N.Y.

66. Fools build houses for wise men to live in. *Var.:* Fools build houses; wise men buy them. *Rec. dist.:* Ill., Ind. *1st cit.:* 1670 Ray, *English Proverbs;* US1820 Faux, *Memorable Days in America, 1819–1820,* ed. Thwaites (1905). *20c. coll.:* ODEP 278, Whiting 161, CODP 85, Stevenson 189:7, Whiting(*MP*) 236.

67. Fools cannot hold their tongues. *Rec. dist.:* Ont.

68. Fools despise wisdom and instruction. *Rec. dist.:* Ont.

69. Fools die for want of wisdom. *Rec. dist.:* Utah.

70. Fools die young and look sickly. *Rec. dist.:* Ky., Tenn.

71. Fools fall the hardest. *Rec. dist.:* N.Y.

72. Fools fight one another; wise men agree. *Rec. dist.:* Utah.

73. Fools for arguments use wagers. *Rec. dist.:* Wis. *1st cit.:* 1664 Butler, *Hudibras.* *20c. coll.:* Stevenson 930:11.

74. Fools give parties; sensible people go to them. *Rec. dist.:* Md.

75. Fools go in crowds. *Var.:* Fools go in throngs. *Rec. dist.:* N.Y., Ont.

76. Fools grow without watering. *Rec. dist.:* Ky., Okla., Tenn. *1st cit.:* 1640 Herbert, *Outlandish Proverbs (Jacula Prudentum)* in *Works,* ed. Hutchinson (1941). *20c. coll.:* ODEP 278, Stevenson 847:8.

77. Fools make feasts and wise men eat them. *Rec. dist.:* Fla., Ont., Tex. *1st cit.:* 1573 Sanford, *Garden of Pleasure;* US1733 Franklin, *PRAlmanac.* *20c. coll.:* ODEP 278, Whiting 167, Stevenson 791:1.

78. Fools multiply folly. *Rec. dist.:* Ont.

79. Fools' names and fools' faces are always seen in public places. *Vars.:* **(a)** A fool's name appears everywhere. **(b)** A fool's name is seen in many places. **(c)** A fool's name is written everywhere. **(d)** A fool's name, like a fool's face, is always stuck in a public place. **(e)** Fools' names and jackasses are often found in public places. **(f)** Fools' names, like monkeys' faces, are always seen in public places. *Rec. dist.:* U.S., Can. *1st cit.:* US1940 Footner, *Murderer's Vanity.* *20c. coll.:* Stevenson 847:2, Whiting(*MP*) 236.

80. Fools never prosper. *Rec. dist.:* Ont.

81. Fools reflect on what they have said, wise men on what they are going to say. *Rec. dist.:* Utah.

82. Fools rush in where angels fear to tread. *Vars.:* **(a)** Fools dash in where angels fear to tread. **(b)** Fools enter where brave men fear to tread. **(c)** Fools rush in where wise men fear to tread. **(d)** Fools rush in where wise men never tread. **(e)** Fools walk in boldly where angels fear to tread. *Rec. dist.:* U.S., Can. *1st cit.:* 1711 Pope, *Essay on Criticism;* US1789 *Life and Correspondence of James Iredell,* ed. McKee (1857–58). *20c. coll.:* CODP

86, Whiting 161, Stevenson 850:4, Whiting(*MP*) 236.

83. Fools seldom differ. *Rec. dist.:* Ont.

84. Fools set stools for wise men to fall over. *Var.:* Fools set stools for wise men to stumble over. *Rec. dist.:* Ohio, Okla., Tex. *1st cit.:* 1605 Rowley, *When You See Me.* *20c. coll.:* ODEP 278, Stevenson 855:1.

85. Fools think alike, and great minds run in the same channel. *Rec. dist.:* N.Y.

86. Fools tie knots, and wise men loosen them. *Rec. dist.:* Okla. *1st cit.:* 1639 Clarke, *Paroemiologia.* *20c. coll.:* ODEP 278, Stevenson 855:1.

87. Fools try to convince a woman, but wise men persuade her. *Rec. dist.:* N.Y.

88. Fools will be fools still. *Rec. dist.:* Ont. *1st cit.:* 1575 Still(?), *Gammer Gurtons Nedle.* *20c. coll.:* ODEP 279, Stevenson 843:3.

89. Fools will be meddling. *Var.:* Every fool will be a-meddling. *Rec. dist.:* N.Y., Ohio, Ont. *1st cit.:* 1616 Draxe, *Bibliotheca Scholastica in Anglia* (1918). *20c. coll.:* ODEP 279, Stevenson 851:2.

90. Forbid a fool a thing, and that he'll do. *Rec. dist.:* N.C., Okla., Tex., Vt.

91. Give a fool an inch and he'll take a mile. *Var.:* Give a fool an inch and he'll take a yard. *Rec. dist.:* Fla. *1st cit.:* 1639 Fuller, *Holy War;* US1698 Usher in *William & Mary Coll. Quart.* (1950). *20c. coll.:* ODEP 683, CODP 194, Whiting 369, T&W 311, Whiting(*MP*) 537.

92. Give a fool enough rope and he'll hang himself. *Rec. dist.:* N.Y., Okla. *1st cit.:* 1837 Emerson, *Journals.* *20c. coll.:* T&W 198, Whiting(*MP*) 336.

93. Go on, fools, hell's only half full. *Rec. dist.:* Ky., Tenn.

94. He is a fool that kisses the maid when he may kiss the mistress. *Rec. dist.:* Ont. *1st cit.:* 1659 Howell, *Paroimiografia.* *20c. coll.:* ODEP 275, Stevenson 1599:11.

95. He is a fool that makes his doctor his heir. *Rec. dist.:* N.Y., Wis. *1st cit.:* 1539 *Proverbs of Erasmus,* tr. Taverner; US1733 Franklin, *PRAlmanac.* *20c. coll.:* ODEP 275, Whiting 162, Stevenson 596:11.

96. He is a fool that takes a fool's advice. *Rec. dist.:* Ill.

97. He is a fool who cannot be angry, but he is wise who will not. *Rec. dist.:* Ill., Ind., Okla., Wis. *1st cit.:* 1604 Dekker, *Honest Whore* in *Notes & Quaeries.* *20c. coll.:* Stevenson 67:10.

98. He is a fool who cannot conceal his knowledge. *Rec. dist.:* Ind.

99. He is the greatest fool who asks for what he can't have. *Rec. dist.:* Wis. *1st cit.:* US1948 Stevenson, *Home Book of Proverbs.* *20c. coll.:* Stevenson 849:12.

100. He that talks to himself talks to a fool. *Rec. dist.:* Ill., Ind. *1st cit.:* 1721 Kelly, *Scottish Proverbs.* *20c. coll.:* ODEP 804, Stevenson 2278:11.

101. He that teaches himself has a fool for a teacher. *Rec. dist.:* Ind., Wis. *1st cit.:* ca1637 Jonson, *Timber;* US1741 Franklin, *PRAlmanac.* *20c. coll.:* ODEP 806, Whiting 162, Stevenson 2284:6.

102. He that would make a fool of himself will find many to help him. *Rec. dist.:* Ill., N.Dak.

103. He who is born a fool is never cured. *Rec. dist.:* N.Y., Ont., Tex. *1st cit.:* 1642 Torriano, *Select Italian Proverbs.* *20c. coll.:* ODEP 75, Stevenson 843:3.

104. He who knows he is a fool is not a big fool. *Rec. dist.:* N.Y.

105. He who passes judgment on a fool is himself judged to be a fool. *Rec. dist.:* N.Y.

106. He who says little may be a fool or a genius. *Rec. dist.:* N.Y.

107. He who treats himself has a fool for a patient. *Rec. dist.:* N.Y.

108. He who would be too clever makes a fool of himself. *Rec. dist.:* N.Y.

109. He's no fool who parts with what he cannot keep to get what he shall not lose. *Rec. dist.:* Miss.

110. If a fool goes shopping, there is joy among the shopkeepers. *Rec. dist.:* N.Y.

111. If a fool is associated with a wise man all his life, he will perceive the truth as little as a spoon perceives the taste of soup. *Rec. dist.:* Utah.

112. If a fool's tongue is long enough, he will hang himself. *Rec. dist.:* N.Y. *1st cit.:* 1678

Ray, *English Proverbs*. **20c. coll.:** Stevenson 844:12.

113. If all fools wore white caps, we'd all look like geese. **Rec. dist.:** Ky., Tenn. **1st cit.:** 1640 Herbert, *Outlandish Proverbs (Jacula Pruden-tum)* in *Works*, ed. Hutchinson (1941). **20c. coll.:** *ODEP* 279, Stevenson 848:3.

114. If fools went not to market, bad wares would not be sold. **Var.:** If fools did not go to market, the rubbish would not be sold. **Rec. dist.:** Ill., Ont. **1st cit.:** 1611 Cotgrave, *Dictionary of French and English Tongues.* **20c. coll.:** *ODEP* 279.

115. If you play with a fool at home, he will play with you abroad. **Rec. dist.:** Mich., Okla.

116. It is a cunning part to play the fool well. **Var.:** It takes a smart woman to be a fool. **Rec. dist.:** Ind., Ont. **1st cit.:** 1574 Guazzo, *Civile Conversation,* tr. Pettie, T.T. (1925). **20c. coll.:** Stevenson 854:6.

117. It is a fool who loves a woman from afar. **Rec. dist.:** Ind.

118. It is an honor for a man to cease from strife, but every fool will be meddling. **Rec. dist.:** Ala., Ga.

119. It is as sport to a fool to do mischief, but a man of understanding has wisdom. **Rec. dist.:** Ont., Wis. **1st cit.:** US1948 Stevenson, *Home Book of Proverbs.* **20c. coll.:** Stevenson 1587:8.

120. It is better to be thought a fool than to open your mouth and let the world know it. **Vars.: (a)** It is better to be silent and be thought a fool than to speak out and remove all doubt. **(b)** It is better to keep your mouth shut and be thought a fool than to open it and leave no doubt. **(c)** It is better to remain silent and be thought of as a fool than to speak and prove the same. **Rec. dist.:** U.S., Can.

121. It is better to marry a quiet fool than to marry a merry scold. **Rec. dist.:** N.Y.

122. It is ill manners to silence a fool, and it is cruelty to let him go on. **Rec. dist.:** Ill. **1st cit.:** US1741 Franklin, *PRAlmanac.* **20c. coll.:** Stevenson 845:6.

123. It takes a fool to know a fool. **Var.:** Set a fool to catch a fool. **Rec. dist.:** U.S.

124. It takes a smart woman to be a fool. **Rec. dist.:** Md.

125. Lazy fools drop their tools. **Rec. dist.:** N.Y.

126. Let fools talk; knowledge still remains. **Rec. dist.:** Calif.

127. Live a fool, die a fool. **Rec. dist.:** N.Y.

128. Men are fools that wish to die. **Rec. dist.:** Ind.

129. Neither a fool nor a gentleman should see a thing until it is finished. **Rec. dist.:** Ont.

130. Never joke with a fool. **Rec. dist.:** N. Dak.

131. Never judge a fool's work half done. **Rec. dist.:** N.J.

132. Never show a fool a half-done job. **Vars.: (a)** A fool should never see unfinished work. **(b)** Fools and children should never look at unfinished work. **Rec. dist.:** N.Y., Ont. **1st cit.:** 1818 Scott, *Lockhart's Life.* **20c. coll.:** *ODEP* 277, *CODP* 85, Stevenson 848:6.

133. No fool, no fun. **Rec. dist.:** Fla., Kans., S.C.

134. No man is always a fool, but every man is sometimes. **Rec. dist.:** N.Y.

135. None but a fool is always right. **Rec. dist.:** Ohio, Wis.

136. Nothing hides a fool like a closed mouth. **Rec. dist.:** Calif.

137. Once a fool, always a fool. **Rec. dist.:** Ark., Ind., Ont.

138. One fool is enough in a house. **Rec. dist.:** Ont.

139. One fool makes many. **Rec. dist.:** Ill., N.Y., Okla., Tex. **1st cit.:** 1617 Swetnam, *School of Defence;* US1791 *Thoughts on Proverbs* in *Universal Asylum.* **20c. coll.:** *ODEP* 274, Whiting 162, Stevenson 851:9, T&W 142.

140. Only a fool argues with the cook. **Rec. dist.:** Colo.

141. Only a fool dares, but a bigger fool takes the dare. **Rec. dist.:** N.Y., Okla.

142. Only a fool is positive. **Rec. dist.:** Ohio, Okla., Ont.

143. Only a fool makes the same mistake twice. *Rec. dist.:* Ala., Ga.

144. Only a fool never changes his mind. *Var.:* Only fools and dead men never change their minds. *Rec. dist.:* Kans., Ont.

145. Only fools and horses work. *Rec. dist.:* Ohio.

146. Only fools are loafers. *Rec. dist.:* Utah.

147. Only fools speak or fiddle at the table. *Rec. dist.:* N.Mex.

148. Praise a fool and you make him useful. *Rec. dist.:* Ont., Wis.

149. Send a fool to the market, and a fool he'll return. *Rec. dist.:* Okla., Ont., Tex. *1st cit.:* 1586 Whitney, *Choice of Emblems. 20c. coll.:* ODEP 276, Stevenson 853:9.

150. Set a fool to catch a fool. *Rec. dist.:* N.Y.

151. The biggest fool of all fools is the fool that can be fooled by a fool. *Rec. dist.:* Ohio.

152. The family of fools is very old. *Rec. dist.:* Ind., Wis. *1st cit.:* US1735 Franklin, *PRAl-manac. 20c. coll.:* Stevenson 845:6.

153. The fool is busy in everyone's business but his own. *Rec. dist.:* N.Y.

154. The fool must look to the madman. *Rec. dist.:* Calif.

155. The fool that eats till he is sick must fast till he is well. *Rec. dist.:* Ont.

156. The fool wanders; the wise man travels. *Rec. dist.:* Ill., N.Y. *1st cit.:* 1732 Fuller, *Gnomologia. 20c. coll.:* ODEP 276.

157. The fool well dressed is at his best. *Rec. dist.:* Ill.

158. The fool wonders; the wise man asks. *Rec. dist.:* Ind., N.J. *1st cit.:* 1732 Fuller, *Gnomologia. 20c. coll.:* ODEP 276.

159. The fools do more hurt in this world than the rascals. *Rec. dist.:* Ont.

160. The older the fool, the harder he falls. *Rec. dist.:* Ill.

161. The poor fool who closes his mouth never makes a dollar. *Rec. dist.:* Oreg.

162. There is no fool like a learned fool. *Var.:* There is no fool like an educated fool. *Rec. dist.:* Ill., Ind.

163. There is no fool like an old fool. *Vars.:* (a) An old fool is the worst fool. (b) An old fool is worse than a young fool. (c) No fool like an old one. (d) Old fools are the worst. (e) The older the fool, the worse he is. (f) There's never a fool like an old fool. (g) There's no fool like an old fool. (h) There's no fool like an old fool says the young fool. *Rec. dist.:* U.S., Can. *1st cit.:* 1546 Heywood, *Dialogue of Proverbs,* ed. Habernicht (1963); US1876 Twain, *Tom Sawyer. 20c. coll.:* ODEP 276, Stevenson 848:1, *CODP* 84, T&W 142, Whiting*(MP)* 237.

164. Too much prosperity makes most men fools. *Rec. dist.:* Ind.

165. Twin fools: one doubts nothing, the other everything. *Rec. dist.:* Ill.

166. We all err, but only fools continue in error. *Rec. dist.:* N.Y.

167. What a fool does in the end, the wise man does in the beginning. *Rec. dist.:* Minn.

168. What one fool can do, another can. *Rec. dist.:* Ont.

169. When a fool has made up his mind, the market has gone by. *Rec. dist.:* Ohio. *1st cit.:* 1706 Stevens, *New Spanish and English Dictionary. 20c. coll.:* ODEP 274.

170. When a man's a fool, his wife will rule. *Rec. dist.:* Ont.

171. When fools make mistakes, they lay the blame on providence. *Rec. dist.:* Miss.

172. You can fool a fool once, but you can't fool him twice. *Rec. dist.:* N.Y.

SEE ALSO The ACTIONS of a fool cannot serve as a precedent. / A BARBER learns to shave by shaving fools. / It is better to be a BEGGAR than a fool. / A CHILD and a fool imagine twenty shillings and twenty years can never be spent. / Fine CLOTHES may disguise, silly words will disclose a fool. / DREAMS give wings to fools. / A DRUNK man will sober up, but a damn fool never. / EXPERIENCE is a dear school, but fools learn in no other. / FLATTERY is the last resort of fools. / The FOLLIES of a fool are known to the world and not to himself; the follies of a wise man are known to himself but not to the world. / FORTUNE favors fools. / GOLD is the most useless metal in the world, for it is good for plugging teeth and tormenting fools. / He that hides HATRED with lying lips and he that utters slander is a fool. / He that puts trust in his own HEART is a fool. / The HEART of a fool is in his mouth, but the mouth of a wise man is in his heart. / There's only a hair's breadth between a HERO and a fool. / IDLENESS is only the refuge of weak minds, the holiday of fools. / KNAVES are in such repute that honest men are accounted fools. / To LAUGH at a man with sense is the privilege of fools. / 'Tis better to LOSE with a wise man than to win with a fool. / He who forces LOVE where none is found remains a fool the whole year round. / LOVE is not time's fool. / Who busies himself where no PROFIT is found remains a fool the whole year round. / RICHES serve a wise man but command a fool. / SUCCESS makes a fool seem wise. / SUCCESS ruins a fool. / A great TALKER may be no fool, but he is one who relies on him. / It's a TRIFLE that makes a fool laugh. / A white WALL is the fool's writing paper: he writes his name there. / Change of WEATHER is a discourse of fools. / A WHIP for a fool and a rod for a school. / WISDOM is too high for a fool. / A WISE man changes his mind; a fool never does. / A WISE man is nobody's fool. / A WISE man learns by the experiences of others; an ordinary man learns by his own experience; a fool learns by nobody's experiences. / He who thinks he is WISE is a fool; he who knows he is a fool is wise. / It is better to sit with a WISE man in prison than with a fool in paradise. / None so WISE but the fool overtakes him. / Something said by a WISE man may be made fun of by a fool. / The WISE and the fool have their fellows. / You can tell by his WORDS what a fool has in his head. / Only YANKEES and fools predict the weather.

fool (*v.*) Fool me once, shame on you; fool me twice, shame on me. *Var.:* When a man fools me once, shame on him; when he fools me twice, shame on me. *Rec. dist.:* U.S.
SEE ALSO It is FUN to be fooled, but better to know. / You can fool an old HORSE once, but you can't fool him twice. / LIFE is too short to fool with dishonest people. / You can fool some of the PEOPLE all the time, all the people some of the time, but you can't fool all the people all the time. / It is easy to fool the young WOLF.

fooling Fooling others is only fooling yourself. *Rec. dist.:* Colo.

foolish (*n.*) **1.** Foolish is as foolish does. *Rec. dist.:* Calif., R.I.

2. It takes the foolish to confound the wise. *Rec. dist.:* Ont.

3. You can't kid the foolish. *Rec. dist.:* Ont.

foolish (*adj.*) **1.** A foolish man despises his mother. *Rec. dist.:* Ont.

2. A foolish woman knows a foolish man's heart. *Rec. dist.:* Ont.
SEE ALSO PENNY-WISE, pound-foolish. / If we are VAIN and love to be flattered, we shall become foolish.

foolishness **1.** Foolishness grows by itself— no need to sow it. *Rec. dist.:* N.J., N.Y., Ont.

2. The mouth of fools pours out foolishness. *Rec. dist.:* Ont.

foot **1.** A going foot always gets something, if it is only a thorn. *Rec. dist.:* N.J., Ont. *1st cit.:* 1721 Kelly, *Scottish Proverbs*. *20c. coll.:* Stevenson 863:5.

2. Always put your best foot forward. *Vars.:* **(a)** Start off with the best foot. **(b)** Start with the right foot forward. *Rec. dist.:* U.S., Can. *1st cit.:* ca1495 Medwall, *Nature;* US1744 Stephens, *Journal of Proceedings in Georgia* in *Georgia Records* (1906). *20c. coll.:* ODEP 47, Whiting 163, Stevenson 862:12, T&W 143, Whiting(MP) 239.

3. Better a bare foot than none at all. *Rec. dist.:* N.J., Wis. *1st cit.:* 1611 Cotgrave, *Dictionary of French and English Tongues*. *20c. coll.:* ODEP 49, Stevenson 861:5.

4. Better a foot slip than a friend. *Rec. dist.:* N.Y., S.C.

5. Big feet, large understanding. *Rec. dist.:* Ohio.

6. Crows' feet are always on the ground. *Rec. dist.:* Ohio.

7. Do not put your foot further than you can draw it back again. *Rec. dist.:* Ont. *Infm.:* Cf. head.

8. Don't use your feet, use your head. *Rec. dist.:* Ont.

9. Every man should measure himself with his own foot rule. *Rec. dist.:* N.C.

10. Feet were made before wheels. *Rec. dist.:* Ont.

11. He who has one foot in a brothel has the other in the hospital. *Rec. dist.:* N.Y.

12. It's a poor foot that can't shape a stocking. *Rec. dist.:* Ont.

13. Keep your feet on the ground. *Rec. dist.:* Fla. *1st cit.:* 1939 Gribble, *Arsenal Stadium Mystery;* US1931 Wells, *Horror House.* *20c. coll.:* Whiting(MP) 238.

14. Keep your foot on the mark. *Rec. dist.:* Ohio. *Infm.:* Be ready to start.

15. Lift your feet and they'll fall themselves. *Rec. dist.:* Ont.

16. Never start off on the wrong foot. *Rec. dist.:* Ala., Ga.

17. No foot, no horse. *Rec. dist.:* Ont.

18. On an unknown path every foot is slow. *Rec. dist.:* Miss.

19. One foot is better than two crutches. *Rec. dist.:* N.Y., Ont., Wis.

20. Put your foot down where you mean to stand. *Rec. dist.:* N.Dak.

21. Save your foot and grieve your heart. *Rec. dist.:* Ont.

22. Settin' still your foot meets nothing. *Var.:* The foot at rest meets nothing. *Rec. dist.:* Miss., Ont.

23. Stand on your own two feet. *Rec. dist.:* U.S., Can. *1st cit.:* 1582 Fioravanti, *Compendium of Rational Secrets,* tr. Hester; US1791 Jefferson in *Works of John Adams,* ed. Adams (1850–56). *20c. coll.:* ODEP 770, Whiting 164, Whiting(MP) 239.

24. The feet are slow when the head wears snow. *Rec. dist.:* Ont.

25. The longer the foot, the higher the man. *Rec. dist.:* Ohio.

26. There's a foot for every old shoe. *Rec. dist.:* Ont.

27. Though feet should slip, never let the tongue. *Var.:* Better the foot slip than the tongue. *Rec. dist.:* U.S., Can. *1st cit.:* 1573 Sanford, *Garden of Pleasure;* US1734 Franklin, *PRAlmanac.* *20c. coll.:* ODEP 55, Whiting 162, Stevenson 2342:4.

28. To walk one must use his feet. *Rec. dist.:* Ont.

29. Walk on your own feet. *Rec. dist.:* N.Y.

30. We would rather die on our feet than live on our knees. *Rec. dist.:* Ohio.

SEE ALSO AIM at the stars, but keep your feet on the ground. / All ASSES do not go on four feet. / BROTHERS are like hands and feet. / The CAT that would eat fish must wet her feet. / You can't DANCE at two weddings with one pair of feet. / A man that FLATTERS his neighbor spreads a net for his feet. / What you haven't got in your HEAD you have in your feet. / A willing HEART carries a weary pair of feet a long way. / Light of HEART, light of feet. / All HEIRS to some six feet of sod are equal in the world at last. / MISFORTUNE arrives on horseback but departs on foot. / PRIDE goes forth on horseback grand and gay, and comes back on foot and begs its way. / Better cut the SHOE than pinch the foot. / Every SHOE fits not every foot. / The pretty SHOE often pinches the foot. / A SLIP of the foot and you may soon recover, but a slip of the tongue you may never get over. / A SPUR in the head is worth two in the feet. / A small STONE in shoe causes large pain in foot. / Where the WILL is ready the feet are light. / Little WIT in the head makes much work for the feet.

footprints **1.** To leave footprints on the sands of time you must have plenty of sand. *Rec. dist.:* N.Dak.

2. You can't put your footprints in the sands of time by sitting down. *Var.:* Footprints in the sands of time are not made by sitting down. *Rec. dist.:* Colo., N.Dak.

forbear SEE We must BEAR and forbear.

forbid Forbid a thing, and that we do. *Rec. dist.:* Ohio. *1st cit.:* ca1386 Chaucer, *Prologue* to *Wife of Bath's Tale. 20c. coll.: ODEP* 279, Stevenson 1894:4.

forbidden Everything forbidden is sweet. *Rec. dist.:* N.Y. *1st cit.:* 1817 Burckhardt, *Arabic Proverbs. 20c. coll.:* Stevenson 1894:3.

SEE ALSO Forbidden FRUIT is the sweetest.

force *(n.)* **1.** Force is no argument. *Rec. dist.:* Miss.

2. Never do that by force which may be effected by fair means. *Rec. dist.:* Mich.

3. That which had no force in the beginning can gain no strength from the lapse of time. *Rec. dist.:* Ill.

4. There is always room for a man of force, and he makes room for many. *Rec. dist.:* N.J.

5. Too much force breeds suspicion. *Rec. dist.:* Ont.

6. Use force tempered with kindness. *Rec. dist.:* Ont.

7. Where force fails, skill and patience will prevail. *Rec. dist.:* Ont., Wis.

8. Where force prevails, right perishes. *Rec. dist.:* Utah. *1st cit.:* US1774 Jefferson, *Rights of British America. 20c. coll.:* Stevenson 864:8.

9. Who overcomes by force has overcome but half his foe. *Rec. dist.:* Ill.

SEE ALSO PERSISTENCE will accomplish more than force. / REASON succeeds where force fails.

force *(v.)* SEE He who forces LOVE where none is found remains a fool the whole year round.

ford He who has crossed the ford knows how deep it is. *Rec. dist.:* Ind.

forearmed SEE FOREWARNED is forearmed.

forehanded He is forehanded who always has a dish out to catch the rain. *Rec. dist.:* N.Y.

forelock SEE Take OPPORTUNITY by the forelock. / Take TIME by the forelock.

forenoon You can make the forenoon, but God almighty makes the afternoon. *Rec. dist.:* Maine.

foreseen SEE A DANGER foreseen is half avoided.

foresight **1.** Foresight is better than hindsight. *Rec. dist.:* Fla., Ill., N.Y., Okla.

2. If a man's foresight were as good as his hindsight, we would all get somewhere. *Var.:* If your foresight was as good as your hindsight, you would be better off by a damn sight. *Rec. dist.:* Kans., Ohio, Ont.

SEE ALSO HINDSIGHT is better than foresight.

forest SEE It takes all kinds of TREES to make a forest. / He who marries a WOLF often looks toward the forest.

forethought Forethought is better than afterthought. *Rec. dist.:* N.C.

forever SEE When we BUILD, let us think that we build forever. / LONG is not forever. / A NICKNAME lasts forever. / NOTHING can last forever. / WORK as though you were to live forever.

forewarned Forewarned is forearmed. *Var.:* Forewarned, forearmed. *Rec. dist.:* U.S., Can. *1st cit.:* ca1425 Arderne, *Treatises of Fistula,* E.E.T.S. (1910); US1685 Hooke in Belknap, *History of New Hampshire* (1813). *20c. coll.:* ODEP 280, Whiting 164, *CODP* 86, Stevenson 2445:7, T&W 144, Whiting(MP) 239.

forget It is better to forget than to remember and regret. *Rec. dist.:* N.Y.

SEE ALSO We can forget our CHILDHOOD, but we cannot deny it. / A bawling COW soon forgets her own calf. / To DELAY may mean to forget. / We easily forget our FAULTS when they are known only to ourselves. / To FORGIVE is easy; to forget is impossible. / The GOOD you do is not lost, though you forget it. / He who never LEARNS anything never forgets anything. / MAN gets and forgets; woman gives and forgives. / Men apt to PROMISE are apt to forget. / WOMEN forgive injuries, but never forget slights. / To forget a WRONG is the best revenge.

forgetting **1.** Forgetting is regretting. *Rec. dist.:* Ont.

2. Forgetting of a wrong is a mild revenge. *Rec. dist.:* N.C., Tex.

forgive **1.** Forgive and forget. *Rec. dist.:* U.S., Can. *1st cit.:* ca1377 Langland, *Piers Plowman;*

US1653 Keayne, *Apologia of Robert Keayne,* ed. Bailyn (1965). *20c. coll.:* ODEP 281, Whiting 164, T&W 144, Stevenson 869:1, Whiting*(MP)* 239.

2. Forgive others often, but rarely yourself. *Var.:* Forgive yourself nothing and others much. *Rec. dist.:* Ill., Pa. *1st cit.:* 1539 Taverner, *Proverbs of Erasmus. 20c. coll.:* ODEP 281, Stevenson 868:14.

3. Good to forgive, best to forget. *Rec. dist.:* Ont.

4. He who cannot forgive others breaks the bridge over which he must pass himself. *Rec. dist.:* Ill.

5. He who forgives ends the quarrel. *Rec. dist.:* Ohio.

6. He who wishes to be forgiven must forgive. *Rec. dist.:* N.Y. *1st cit.:* US1948 Stevenson, *Home Book of Proverbs. 20c. coll.:* Stevenson 868:4.

7. It is easier to forgive than forget. *Var.:* It is easy to forgive, but hard to forget. *Rec. dist.:* Ind.

8. Those who forgive most will be most forgiven. *Var.:* They who forgive most shall be most forgiven. *Rec. dist.:* Iowa, N.Y.

9. To forgive is easy; to forget is impossible. *Rec. dist.:* Ill.

See also To know ALL is to forgive all. / Always forgive your ENEMIES. / To ERR is human; to forgive, divine. / A small LOVE forgives much, a great love forgives little, and a perfect love forgives all. / MAN gets and forgets; woman gives and forgives. / WOMEN forgive injuries, but never forget slights.

forgiven *See* A good HORSE may be forgiven a kick. / INJURIES may be forgiven but not forgotten.

forgiveness 1. Forgiveness is better than revenge. *Rec. dist.:* Ont.

2. If you want forgiveness, you must be forgiving. *Rec. dist.:* Ill.

See also It is only one step from TOLERANCE to forgiveness.

forgotten Some things are better forgotten. *Rec. dist.:* Ky., Mich., Tenn.

See also He that is long ABSENT is soon forgotten. / Eaten BREAD is soon forgotten. / The COW has forgotten she was once a calf. / The DEAD are soon forgotten. / Good DEEDS are easily forgotten, bad deeds never. / GONE but not forgotten. / An INJURY is sooner forgotten than an insult. / The NEW is what has been forgotten. / The RIVER past, and God forgotten. / Seldom SEEN, soon forgotten. / A WOMAN remembers a kiss long after a man has forgotten.

fork *See* FINGERS were made before knives and forks.

form 1. A homely form oft holds a handsome heart. *Rec. dist.:* Nebr.

2. Good form is the yardstick of society. *Rec. dist.:* N.Y.

3. The outward forms the inward man reveal—we guess the pulp before we cut the peel. *Rec. dist.:* N.Y., S.C.

See also IMITATION is the highest form of flattery.

fort It's easy to hold the fort when it's not attacked. *Rec. dist.:* Ill. *1st cit.:* 1937 Bush, *Eight O'Clock Alibi;* US1932 Turner, *Who Spoke Last. 20c. coll.:* Whiting*(MP)* 240.

fortress A fortress on its guard is not surprised. *Rec. dist.:* Ohio.

fortune 1. A change in fortune hurts a wise man no more than a change of the moon. *Rec. dist.:* Ind., N.Y., Wis. *1st cit.:* US1756 Franklin, *PRAlmanac. 20c. coll.:* Stevenson 871:10.

2. A fortune never passes the second generation. *Rec. dist.:* Ont.

3. A great fortune is slavery. *Vars.:* (a) A great fortune is a great servitude. (b) A great fortune is a great slavery. *Rec. dist.:* Ill. *1st cit.:* US1948 Stevenson, *Home Book of Proverbs. 20c. coll.:* Stevenson 879:6.

4. Better a fortune in a wife than with a wife. *Rec. dist.:* N.J., N.Y.

5. Build not up a fortune on the labor of others. *Rec. dist.:* Ont.

6. Depend not on fortune but on conduct. *Rec. dist.:* Kans.

7. Don't put your fortune in a funnel. **Rec. dist.:** Calif.

8. Fortune always leaves one door open in disasters. **Rec. dist.:** Miss. **1st cit.:** US1948 Stevenson, *Home Book of Proverbs.* **20c. coll.:** Stevenson 871:1.

9. Fortune and misfortune are next-door neighbors. **Rec. dist.:** Ill., N.Y., Ohio.

10. Fortune can take away riches but not courage. **Rec. dist.:** Miss. **1st cit.:** 1566 Seneca, *Medea,* tr. Studley. **20c. coll.:** ODEP 281, Stevenson 875:3.

11. Fortune can take nothing from us but what she gave us. **Var.:** Fortune takes from us nothing but what she has given. **Rec. dist.:** Ill., Ind., Ohio. **1st cit.:** 1666 Torriano, *Common Place of Italian Proverbs and Phrases.* **20c. coll.:** ODEP 281, Stevenson 874:4.

12. Fortune comes to him who seeks her. **Rec. dist.:** N.Y.

13. Fortune doesn't lie at the end of the rainbow, it is found behind some obstacle. **Rec. dist.:** Kans.

14. Fortune favors fools. **Var.:** Fortune always favors fools. **Rec. dist.:** Colo., N.C. **1st cit.:** 1546 Heywood, *Dialogue of Proverbs,* ed. Habernicht (1963); US1928 Gibbons, *Red Knight.* **20c. coll.:** ODEP 281, CODP 86, Stevenson 872:2, Whiting(MP) 240.

15. Fortune favors the brave. **Vars.:** (a) Fortune befriends the bold. (b) Fortune favors the audacious. (c) Fortune favors the bold. (d) Fortune favors the daring. (e) Fortune is on the side of the bold. **Rec. dist.:** U.S. **1st cit.:** ca1374 Chaucer, *Troilus and Criseyde;* US1677 Hubbard, *History of Indian Wars in New England,* ed. Drake (1865). **20c. coll.:** ODEP 282, Whiting 166, CODP 86, Stevenson 878:4, T&W 144, Whiting(MP) 240.

16. Fortune helps him that is willing to help himself. **Var.:** Fortune helps them that help themselves. **Rec. dist.:** Ill., N.Y. **1st cit.:** 1611 Cotgrave, *Dictionary of French and English Tongues;* US1865 Sedley, *Marian.* **20c. coll.:** Stevenson 871:4, T&W 144.

17. Fortune is easy to find but hard to keep. **Var.:** Fortune is more easily gotten than kept.

Rec. dist.: Ill., Tex. **1st cit.:** US1875 Scarborough, *Chinese Proverbs.* **20c. coll.:** Stevenson 948:4.

18. Fortune is fickle. **Rec. dist.:** Ill., Kans., Ont. **1st cit.:** ca1390 Gower, *Confessio Amantis,* E.E.T.S. (1900); US1650 *Works of Anne Bradstreet,* ed. Ellis (1932). **20c. coll.:** ODEP 282, Whiting 166, Stevenson 876:11, Whiting(MP) 240.

19. Fortune is like glass: it breaks when it is brightest. **Rec. dist.:** Ill. **1st cit.:** 1539 Taverner, *Proverbs of Erasmus.* **20c. coll.:** ODEP 282, Stevenson 874:2.

20. Fortune is like price: if you can wait long enough, the price will fall. **Rec. dist.:** Ill.

21. Fortune is not often on the side of the fainthearted. **Rec. dist.:** Kans.

22. Fortune is the companion of virtue. **Rec. dist.:** Ill.

23. Fortune is the good man's prize but the bad man's bane. **Rec. dist.:** Ill.

24. Fortune knocks once at every door. **Var.:** Fortune knocks once at least at every man's gate. **Rec. dist.:** N.Y., Ohio. **1st cit.:** 1567 Fenton, *Bandello;* US1809 *The Port Folio.* **20c. coll.:** ODEP 282, Whiting 166, Stevenson 872:3.

25. Fortune knows neither reason nor law. **Rec. dist.:** Wis. **1st cit.:** US1948 Stevenson, *Home Book of Proverbs.* **20c. coll.:** Stevenson 874:3.

26. Fortune makes friends; misfortune tries them. **Rec. dist.:** Wis.

27. Fortune never comes with both hands full. **Rec. dist.:** Oreg.

28. Fortune sometimes favors those she afterwards destroys. **Rec. dist.:** Ill.

29. If fortune smiles, who doesn't—if fortune doesn't, who does? **Rec. dist.:** Ohio, Ont.

30. Men never think their fortune too great nor their wit too little. **Rec. dist.:** Ont.

31. One man's fortune is another man's folly. **Rec. dist.:** Kans., Ont., Tex.

32. When fortune frowns, friends are few. **Rec. dist.:** Ariz.

33. When fortune knocks, open the door. **Rec.**

dist.: Fla., Ky., N.Y., Tenn. **1st cit.:** 1736 Bailey, *Dictionary*. **20c. coll.:** Stevenson 874:7.

34. When fortune smiles, embrace her. **Rec. dist.:** N.J. **1st cit.:** 1611 Cotgrave, *Dictionary of French and English Tongues*. **20c. coll.:** ODEP 282, Stevenson 874:7.

35. When fortune smiles, take the advantage. **Rec. dist.:** Tex.

36. When fortune smiles, we ride in chase, and when she frowns, we walk away. **Rec. dist.:** Miss.

37. You can't overfill fortune's sacks. **Rec. dist.:** Tex.

SEE ALSO Every man is the ARCHITECT of his own fortune. / He DANCES well to whom fortune pipes. / INDUSTRY is fortune's right hand, and frugality her left. / Against LOVE and fortune there is no defense.

forty *SEE* LIFE begins at forty.

forward He who never goes forward goes backwards. **Rec. dist.:** Wis.

SEE ALSO Always put your best FOOT forward.

foul *(v.)* *SEE* It's an ill BIRD that fouls its own nest.

foul *(adj.)* *SEE* A fair FACE may hide a foul heart. / FRIDAY is the fairest or foulest day. / A foul MORN turns into a fine day. / In fair WEATHER prepare for foul.

foundation **1.** A weak foundation destroys the superstructure. **Rec. dist.:** Mich. **1st cit.:** 1493 Parker, *Dives and Pauper*. **20c. coll.:** ODEP 318, Stevenson 252:3.

2. High things must have low foundations. **Rec. dist.:** Utah. **1st cit.:** 1605, Camden, *Remaines Concerning Britaine*. **20c. coll.:** ODEP 372, Stevenson 252:3.

3. The deeper the foundation the stronger the house. **Rec. dist.:** N.J.

SEE ALSO HUMILITY is the foundation of all virtues.

fount Seek not for fresher founts afar; just drop your bucket where you are. **Rec. dist.:** Ill.

fountain The fountain is clearest at its source. **Rec. dist.:** Tex. **1st cit.:** US1948 Stevenson, *Home Book of Proverbs*. **20c. coll.:** Stevenson 879:11.

SEE ALSO A kind HEART is a fountain of gladness.

four *SEE* The DOG has four legs, but he does not run on four roads. / Four EYES see more than two. / Four HANDS can do more than two.

fowl Black fowl can lay white eggs. **Rec. dist.:** N.Y.

SEE ALSO Fair FEATHERS make fair fowl. / You can't stay up with the midnight OWL and expect to get up with the barnyard fowl.

fox **1.** A fox does not smell his own stench. **Var.:** A fox never catches his own scent. **Rec. dist.:** N.Dak., Ont., Wis.

2. A fox is not caught twice in the same place. **Rec. dist.:** Ont. **1st cit.:** US1948 Stevenson, *Home Book of Proverbs*. **20c. coll.:** Stevenson 881:13.

3. A fox never goes so far but what his tail will follow him. **Rec. dist.:** N.Y.

4. An old fox needs not to be taught tricks. **Rec. dist.:** N.J. **1st cit.:** 1732 Fuller, *Gnomologia*. **20c. coll.:** Stevenson 880:7.

5. Don't put the fox to guard the henhouse. **Rec. dist.:** Mich., N.Y. **1st cit.:** 1589 *Contre-League*, tr. E.A.; US1924 Guiterman, *Poet's Proverbs*. **20c. coll.:** ODEP 285, Stevenson 939:5, Whiting*(MP)* 241.

6. Foxes, when they cannot reach the grapes, say they are not ripe. **Var.:** "Sour grapes," said the fox when he could not reach them. **Rec. dist.:** Okla., Ont., Tex. **1st cit.:** 1484 Caxton, *Fables of Aesop;* US1700 Byrd, *Another Secret Diary*. **20c. coll.:** ODEP 331, Whiting 185, Stevenson 1021:2, T&W 158, Whiting*(MP)* 268.

7. He that will outwit the fox must rise early. **Rec. dist.:** Calif. **1st cit.:** 1616 Draxe, *Bibliotheca Scholastica in Anglia* (1918). **20c. coll.:** ODEP 284.

8. It's the little foxes that spoil the vines. **Var.:** It's the little foxes that spoil the grapes. **Rec. dist.:** Kans., Ont.

9. Long runs the fox, but at last is caught.

Rec. dist.: Ont. *1st cit.:* ca1450 Henryson, *Morall Fabillis of Esope.* *20c. coll.:* ODEP 480, Stevenson 881:3.

10. Old foxes are not easily caught. *Rec. dist.:* Ont. *1st cit.:* 1539 Taverner, *Proverbs of Erasmus.* *20c. coll.:* ODEP 480.

11. Old foxes want no tutors. *Rec. dist.:* Mich. *1st cit.:* 1639 Clarke, *Paroemiologia.* *20c. coll.:* ODEP 589, Stevenson 880:7.

12. The fox barks not when he steals a lamb. *Rec. dist.:* Calif. *1st cit.:* 1591 Shakespeare, *Henry VI.* *20c. coll.:* Stevenson 882:15.

13. The fox changes his skin but not his habits. *Rec. dist.:* Calif., N.Y., S.C. *1st cit.:* 1572 Parinchef, *Extract of Examples;* US1749 Franklin, *PRAlmanac.* *20c. coll.:* ODEP 284, Whiting 167, Stevenson 882:9, Whiting *(MP)* 241.

14. The fox condemns the trap, not himself. *Rec. dist.:* Ont.

15. The fox may grow gray, but never good. *Var.:* Many foxes grow gray, but few grow good. *Rec. dist.:* Ont. *1st cit.:* 1572 Parinchef, *Extract of Examples;* US1749 Franklin, *PRAlmanac.* *20c. coll.:* ODEP 284, Whiting 167, Stevenson 882:9.

16. The sleeping fox catches no poultry. *Vars.:* **(a)** A sleeping fox catches no geese. **(b)** Sleeping fox catches no pork. **(c)** The sleeping fox catches no chickens. **(d)** The sleepy fox catches no poultry. *Rec. dist.:* U.S., Can. *1st cit.:* 1611 Cotgrave, *Dictionary of French and English Tongues;* US1743 Franklin, *PRAlmanac.* *20c. coll.:* ODEP 742, Stevenson 880:9, Whiting 167.

17. The smartest fox is caught at last. *Rec. dist.:* Ill.

18. Though the fox wear silk, he is still a fox. *Rec. dist.:* Ill.

19. When a fox walks lame, old rabbit jumps. *Rec. dist.:* N.Y., S.C.

20. When the fox dies, fowls do not mourn. *Rec. dist.:* Ariz.

21. When the fox preaches, beware of your geese. *Vars.:* **(a)** When the fox preaches, beware of the geese. **(b)** When the fox preaches, take care of your geese. *Rec. dist.:* Ont. *1st cit.:*

ca1460 *Townley Mysteries,* E.E.T.S. (1897). *20c. coll.:* ODEP 285, Stevenson 883:6.

foxhole SEE There are no ATHEISTS in a foxhole.

fragrance SEE FLOWERS leave fragrance in the hand that bestows them.

frailty **1.** Frailty belongs to the nature of man. *Rec. dist.:* Mich.

2. Frailty, your name is woman. *Rec. dist.:* Minn., N.Y. *1st cit.:* 1600 Shakespeare, *Hamlet.* *20c. coll.:* Stevenson 2559:4.

frame SEE Mean SOULS like mean pictures are often found in good looking frames.

fraud **1.** Fraud and cunning are the weapons of the weak. *Rec. dist.:* N.Y., S.C.

2. Fraud is always in a terrible hurry. *Rec. dist.:* Ill. *1st cit.:* 1732 Fuller, *Gnomologia.* *20c. coll.:* Stevenson 886:6.

free **1.** Better free in a foreign land than a serf at home. *Rec. dist.:* Ill.

2. No man is free who cannot command himself. *Rec. dist.:* Mich. *1st cit.:* US1948 Stevenson, *Home Book of Proverbs.* *20c. coll.:* Stevenson 887:8.

SEE ALSO Free ADVICE is worth just what you pay for it. / The BEST things in life are free. / Though the BODY may be imprisoned, the soul can be free. / Why buy the COW when you can get the milk free. / You have to go to the GRAVEYARD to locate guys free from fault. / Never run a free HORSE to death. / It is better POOR and free than rich and a slave. / The TRUTH shall make you free. / The WIND is fresh and free.

freedom **1.** A poor freedom is better than rich slavery. *Rec. dist.:* Mich.

2. Eternal vigilance is the price of freedom. *Rec. dist.:* S.C.

3. Freedom comes before silver and gold. *Rec. dist.:* Oreg.

4. If we lose our freedom, we have nothing else to lose. *Rec. dist.:* Ill. *1st cit.:* ca1430 Lydgate, *Minor Poems.* *20c. coll.:* Stevenson 888:14.

5. Never wear your best trousers when you go out to fight for freedom. *Rec. dist.:* Ont.

6. Who accepts from another sells his freedom. *Rec. dist.:* N.Y.

SEE ALSO There is no FRIENDSHIP without freedom, no freedom without the friendship of brothers.

freely SEE LIVE freely and die content.

freeze SEE Play it COOL, but don't freeze up. / A running RIVER never freezes.

frenzy SEE ZEAL without knowledge is frenzy.

fresh SEE Fresh AIR and sunshine and plenty of grace slam the door in the doctor's face. / Waste not fresh TEARS over old griefs. / The WIND is fresh and free.

fret Fret today, regret tomorrow. *Rec. dist.:* Ont.

friction SEE The friction of ARGUMENT produces more heat than light.

Friday **1.** Every day is not Friday; there is also Thursday. *Rec. dist.:* Wis.

2. Friday and the week are seldom alike. *Rec. dist.:* N.Dak.

3. Friday begun, never done. *Rec. dist.:* Ark.

4. Friday is the fairest or foulest day. *Vars.:* **(a)** Friday is the fairest or foulest. **(b)** Friday is the fairest or foulest day of the week. *Rec. dist.:* U.S. *1st cit.:* 1587 Harrison, *Description of England.* *20c. coll.:* ODEP 288.

5. Never start anything important on Friday. *Var.:* Start a job on Friday and it will never be done. *Rec. dist.:* U.S., Can.

6. Thank God it's Friday. *Rec. dist.:* U.S., Can. *Infm.:* Friday night begins the weekend.

fried SEE From fried EGGS come no chickens.

friend **1.** A boy's best friend is his mother. *Vars.:* **(a)** A girl's best friend is her mother. **(b)** A man's best friend is his mother. *Rec. dist.:* Ill.

2. A faithful friend is better than gold. *Vars.:* **(a)** A faithful friend is as rare as a diamond. **(b)** Friends are better than sacks of gold. **(c)** He that has found a faithful friend has found treasure. *Rec. dist.:* N.Y., N.C., Oreg., Utah.

1st cit.: US1948 Stevenson, *Home Book of Proverbs.* *20c. coll.:* Stevenson 891:8.

3. A faithful friend is the medicine of life. *Rec. dist.:* Mich. *1st cit.:* US1948 Stevenson, *Home Book of Proverbs.* *20c. coll.:* Stevenson 891:8.

4. A friend at hand is better than a relative at a distance. *Rec. dist.:* Ind.

5. A friend by your side can keep you warmer than the richest furs. *Rec. dist.:* Ont.

6. A friend cannot be known in prosperity; an enemy cannot be hidden in adversity. *Rec. dist.:* N.Y.

7. A friend in need is a friend indeed. *Vars.:* **(a)** A friend is never known till a man has need. **(b)** A friend is never known until needed. **(c)** A friend that isn't in need is a friend indeed. **(d)** You find your true friends only in an hour of need. *Rec. dist.:* U.S., Can. *1st cit.:* ca1275 *Proverbs of Alfred,* tr. Skeat; US1640 Winslow in *Winthrop Papers, 1498–1649,* Mass.Hist.Soc. *Collections* (1929). *20c. coll.:* ODEP 289, Whiting 168, CODP 87, Stevenson 902:2, T&W 146, Whiting(MP) 242.

8. A friend in power is a friend lost. *Rec. dist.:* Ont., Wis.

9. A friend in the market is better than money in the purse. *Rec. dist.:* N.Y. *1st cit.:* 1664 Codrington, *Select Proverbs.* *20c. coll.:* ODEP 289.

10. A friend is a present you give yourself. *Rec. dist.:* Okla., Ont.

11. A friend is best found in adversity. *Rec. dist.:* Tex. *1st cit.:* ca1303 Mannyng, *Handlyng Synne;* US1935 Woodthrope, *Shadow on the Downs.* *20c. coll.:* ODEP 289, Whiting(MP) 242.

12. A friend is easier lost than found. *Rec. dist.:* U.S., Can.

13. A friend is not known till he is lost. *Rec. dist.:* N.Y.

14. A friend is not so soon gotten as lost. *Rec. dist.:* Ont., R.I. *1st cit.:* 1599 Porter, *Two Angry Women of Abington.* *20c. coll.:* ODEP 289.

15. A friend is one who can be good company

with you for an hour without saying a word. *Rec. dist.:* W.Va.

16. A friend is to be taken with his faults. *Rec. dist.:* N.Y., S.C.

17. A friend is worth all the hazards we can run. *Rec. dist.:* Oreg.

18. A friend married is a friend lost. *Rec. dist.:* N.Y. *1st cit.:* 1863 Ibsen, *Love's Comedy. 20c. coll.:* Stevenson 915:9.

19. A friend should bear his friend's infirmities. *Rec. dist.:* Ill. *1st cit.:* 1599 Shakespeare, *Julius Caesar. 20c. coll.:* Stevenson 899:1.

20. A friend to all is a friend to none. *Vars.:* **(a)** A friend to everyone is a friend to nobody. **(b)** Everybody's companion is nobody's friend. *Rec. dist.:* U.S., Can. *1st cit.:* 1623 Wodroephe, *Spared Houres of Soldier. 20c. coll.:* ODEP 290, Stevenson 890:6.

21. A friend whom you can buy can be bought from you. *Rec. dist.:* Ill.

22. A friend won with a feather can be lost with a straw. *Rec. dist.:* Calif.

23. A friend's frown is better than a foe's smile. *Rec. dist.:* Ill., Ky., Oreg., Tenn.

24. A good friend is a great treasure. *Rec. dist.:* N.Y. *1st cit.:* 1580 Lyly, *Euphues and His England;* US1744 Franklin, *PRAlmanac. 20c. coll.:* Stevenson 893:5.

25. A good friend is better than a hundred relatives. *Rec. dist.:* N.Y.

26. A good friend is my nearest relation. *Rec. dist.:* N.Y. *1st cit.:* 1611 Cotgrave, *Dictionary of French and English Tongues. 20c. coll.:* ODEP 289, Stevenson 894:5.

27. A good friend never offends. *Rec. dist.:* N.Dak., Ont. *1st cit.:* 1659 Howell, *English Proverbs. 20c. coll.:* Stevenson 896:7.

28. A long spell of illness is apt to point out your best friends. *Rec. dist.:* N.J.

29. A man is known by his friends. *Vars.:* **(a)** You are known by the friends you make. **(b)** You are known by your friends. *Rec. dist.:* Miss., N.Y.

30. A man that has friends must show himself friendly. *Var.:* A man, to have friends, must show himself friendly. *Rec. dist.:* U.S., Can.

31. A man's best friend and worst enemy is himself. *Rec. dist.:* N.J. *1st cit.:* 1831 Hone, *Year-Book. 20c. coll.:* Stevenson 910:2.

32. A man's best friend is his ten fingers. *Rec. dist.:* Ont.

33. A person is reflected in the friends he chooses. *Rec. dist.:* N.Y.

34. A rash friend is worse than a foe. *Rec. dist.:* Ont.

35. A reconciled friend is a double enemy. *Rec. dist.:* Mich., N.Y. *1st cit.:* 1732 Fuller, *Gnomologia. 20c. coll.:* Stevenson 909:11.

36. A rich friend is a treasure. *Rec. dist.:* Ind.

37. A true friend is forever a friend. *Rec. dist.:* N.Dak., N.Y.

38. A true friend is one that steps in when the rest of the world steps out. *Rec. dist.:* Kans.

39. A true friend is one who knows all your faults and loves you still. *Vars.:* **(a)** A friend is a person who knows all about you and likes you anyway. **(b)** A friend is one who knows all your faults and loves you just the same. *Rec. dist.:* Ill., Miss., Wis.

40. A true friend is the wine of life. *Var.:* Friendship is the wine of life. *Rec. dist.:* Ill., Ont.

41. A true friend is your second self. *Vars.:* **(a)** A friend is another self. **(b)** A friend is one's second self. *Rec. dist.:* Minn., N.Y., Okla.

42. A true friend loves at all times. *Var.:* A friend loves at all times. *Rec. dist.:* Ohio, Ont.

43. A true friend worries more over your success than your failure. *Rec. dist.:* N.J.

44. All are not friends that speak us fair. *Rec. dist.:* N.Y. *1st cit.:* ca1350 *How Gode Wyfe Taught Her Daughter. 20c. coll.:* ODEP 291, Stevenson 900:14.

45. Always take a friend with you and you'll have a friend. *Rec. dist.:* Ohio.

46. An injured friend is the bitterest of foes. *Rec. dist.:* N.C., S.C.

47. An old friend do not forsake. *Rec. dist.:* N.Y. *1st cit.:* 1575 Pettie, *Petite Palace of Pleasure.* *20c. coll.:* Stevenson 904:1.

48. An old friend is a mount for a black day. *Rec. dist.:* Ill.

49. An old friend is a new house. *Rec. dist.:* Ark. *1st cit.:* 1640 Herbert, *Outlandish Proverbs (Jacula Prudentum)* in *Works,* ed. Hutchinson (1941). *20c. coll.:* Stevenson 904:6.

50. An old friend wears well. *Var.:* Old friends wear well. *Rec. dist.:* Fla., N.Y., Ont.

51. Ascend a step in choosing a friend. *Rec. dist.:* N.Y.

52. Be a friend to yourself and others will soon be. *Rec. dist.:* N.Y., Wis. *1st cit.:* ca1500 *Early English Carols,* ed. Greene. *20c. coll.:* ODEP 290, Stevenson 891:1.

53. Be a friend to yourself; depend not on others. *Rec. dist.:* Minn.

54. Be kind to your friends: if it weren't for them, you would be a total stranger. *Rec. dist.:* Ind., Kans.

55. Be slow in choosing a friend, but slower in changing him. *Vars.:* (a) Be slow in choosing a friend; be slower in changing. (b) Be slow in choosing a friend, slower in changing. *Rec. dist.:* Ill., Miss., N.Y., Ohio, Oreg. *1st cit.:* US1735 Franklin, *PRAlmanac.* *20c. coll.:* Stevenson 892:1.

56. Before you make a friend, eat a peck of salt with him. *Rec. dist.:* N.J., Okla., Tex. *1st cit.:* ca1500 *15c. School Book,* ed. Nelson. *20c. coll.:* ODEP 40, Stevenson 2030:4.

57. Better have a friend on the road than gold or silver in your purse. *Rec. dist.:* Ont. *1st cit.:* US1948 Stevenson, *Home Book of Proverbs.* *20c. coll.:* Stevenson 890:7.

58. Bought friends are not friends indeed. *Rec. dist.:* Ont., Oreg.

59. Cherish your friend, and temperately admonish your enemy. *Rec. dist.:* Mich.

60. Choose not friends by outward show, for feathers float while pearls lie low. *Rec. dist.:* Ont.

61. Choose your friends like your books— few but choice. *Rec. dist.:* Nebr. *1st cit.:* 1659 Howell, *English Proverbs.* *20c. coll.:* Stevenson 890:3.

62. Contend not with the friend lest you make him an enemy. *Rec. dist.:* Mich.

63. Cultivate friends who pray for you, not prey upon you. *Rec. dist.:* Miss.

64. Do not count too much on friends. *Rec. dist.:* S.C.

65. Don't be a fair-weather friend. *Var.:* Fair-weather friends are not worth having. *Rec. dist.:* U.S., Can. *1st cit.:* 1508 Erasmus, *Adagia,* tr. Taverner; US1773 *New York Gazette* in *Newspaper Extracts.* *20c. coll.:* Stevenson 906:1, Whiting 143, Whiting(MP) 242.

66. Don't trade old friends for new. *Vars.:* (a) Don't trade in old friends for new. (b) Forsake not old friends for new. (c) Keep old friends with the new. (d) Never forsake old friends for new ones. *Rec. dist.:* U.S., Can. *1st cit.:* 1575 Pettie, *Petite Palace of Pleasure.* *20c. coll.:* Stevenson 904:1.

67. Even a new friend can be tiring. *Rec. dist.:* Ariz.

68. Fall not out with a friend for a trifle. *Rec. dist.:* Ill., N.Y. *1st cit.:* 1621 Robinson, *Adagia in Latin and English.* *20c. coll.:* ODEP 242, Stevenson 892:10.

69. Fall sick and you will know who is your friend and who is not. *Rec. dist.:* N.Y.

70. False friends are like autumn leaves, found everywhere. *Rec. dist.:* Ind.

71. False friends are worse than open enemies. *Rec. dist.:* N.Y., Vt. *1st cit.:* 1655 Gurnall, *Christian in Compleat Armour.* *20c. coll.:* Stevenson 910:3.

72. For a good friend, the journey is never too long. *Rec. dist.:* N.Y.

73. Friends and mules fail us in hard places. *Rec. dist.:* Oreg.

74. Friends are lost by calling often and calling seldom. *Rec. dist.:* Ill.

75. Friends are the surest guards for kings; gold in time does wear away. *Rec. dist.:* N.Y.

76. Friends are to be preferred to relatives.

Vars.: (a) Friends are more valuable than relatives. (b) Friends are the best relatives. (c) Friends are the nearest relatives. *Rec. dist.*: U.S., Can. *1st cit.*: 1732 Fuller, *Gnomologia*. *20c. coll.*: ODEP 289, Stevenson 894:5.

77. Friends have all things in common. *Rec. dist.*: N.Y. *1st cit.*: 1546 Hugh, *Troubled Man's Medicine*; US1693 Penn, *Some Fruits of Solitude*. *20c. coll.*: Stevenson 903:4.

78. Friends, if often used, wear out. *Rec. dist.*: Utah.

79. Friends slowly won are long held. *Rec. dist.*: N.Y.

80. Friends tie their purses with spider's thread. *Rec. dist.*: Ill. *1st cit.*: 1659 Howell, *Paroimiografia*. *20c. coll.*: ODEP 291, Stevenson 903:2.

81. Friends will greet where the hills won't meet. *Rec. dist.*: Ont.

82. Friends you can count on, you can count on your fingers. *Rec. dist.*: Tex.

83. Friends, though absent, are still present. *Rec. dist.*: Wis. *1st cit.*: 1580 Lyly, *Euphues and His England*. *20c. coll.*: Stevenson 3:5.

84. Go often to the house of a friend. *Rec. dist.*: Vt.

85. God protect me from my friends; my enemies I know enough to watch. *Vars.*: (a) God protect me from my friends. (b) May the Lord protect me from my friends. (c) Save me from my friends. *Rec. dist.*: U.S. *1st cit.*: 1477 *Dictes and Sayenges of Philosophirs*, tr. Rivers. *20c. coll.*: Stevenson 910:3.

86. Good friends make good neighbors. *Rec. dist.*: N.Y.

87. Have few friends, many acquaintances. *Rec. dist.*: Minn.

88. Have no friends not equal to yourself. *Rec. dist.*: N.Y. *1st cit.*: 1576 Pettie, "Sinorix and Camma" in *Petite Palace of Pleasure*. *20c. coll.*: Stevenson 914:10.

89. Have patience with a friend rather than lose him forever. *Rec. dist.*: Ill.

90. He is a friend that sticks closer than a brother. *Rec. dist.*: Minn., Miss.

91. He is my friend that helps me, and not he that pities me. *Rec. dist.*: R.I.

92. He is no friend who plays double. *Rec. dist.*: Ark.

93. He makes no friends who never made a foe. *Var.*: He makes no friends who makes no foes. *Rec. dist.*: Ala., Ga., Ont., Wis.

94. He never was a friend who has ceased to be one. *Rec. dist.*: Ill., N.J., N.Y. *1st cit.*: 1732 Fuller, *Gnomologia*. *20c. coll.*: Stevenson 895:4.

95. He that has a thousand friends has not a friend to spare. *Rec. dist.*: Ill., N.Y., Ont. *1st cit.*: 1711 Swift, *Journal to Stella*; US1860 Emerson, "Considerations by the Way" in *Conduct of Life*. *20c. coll.*: Stevenson 909:8.

96. He that is neither one thing nor the other has no friends. *Rec. dist.*: Ind., Minn., Ont.

97. He who asks more of a friend than he can bestow deserves to be refused. *Rec. dist.*: N.Y.

98. He who despises a humble friend may be doing an ill turn to himself. *Rec. dist.*: Okla.

99. He who has many friends has no friends. *Rec. dist.*: N.Y.

100. He who is no friend to the good cause is no friend of mine. *Rec. dist.*: Minn., Miss.

101. He who is true to one friend thus proves himself worthy of many. *Rec. dist.*: N.Y.

102. He who makes us do what we can is a friend. *Rec. dist.*: Ont.

103. He who would have friends must show himself friendly. *Rec. dist.*: Ill., Ont.

104. He's my friend who speaks well behind my back. *Rec. dist.*: N.Y.

105. Hold a true friend with both hands. *Rec. dist.*: Ohio.

106. I cannot be your friend and your flatterer, too. *Rec. dist.*: Ill. *1st cit.*: 1550 Crowley, *One & Thirty Epigrams*, E.E.T.S. (1872); US1669 Penn, *No Cross, No Crown*. *20c. coll.*: ODEP 288, Stevenson 897:4.

107. If you have one true friend, you have more than your share. *Rec. dist.*: N.Dak.

108. If you impose on your friends, you will wear out your welcome. *Rec. dist.*: Ohio.

109. If you want a friend, you will have to be one. *Vars.*: (a) If you want a friend, you must first be one. (b) If you want a friend, you will

have to make one. **(c)** In order to have a friend, you must first be one. **(d)** To have a friend, be one. *Rec. dist.:* U.S., Can.

110. If you want to keep a friend, never borrow, never lend. *Var.:* Never borrow, never lend, if you wish to keep a friend. *Rec. dist.:* Kans., Ont.

111. If your friend is honey, do not lick him up altogether. *Rec. dist.:* N.Y.

112. In time of prosperity, friends will be plenty; in time of adversity, not one in twenty. *Rec. dist.:* N.Y. *1st cit.:* ca1526 Erasmus, *Dicta Sapientum,* tr. Berthelet. *20c. coll.:* ODEP 650, Stevenson 907:5.

113. It is better to have a friend in the market than money in one's coffer. *Var.:* It is better to have friends in the market, than money in the bank. *Rec. dist.:* Fla., Wis. *1st cit.:* 1664 Codrington, *Select Proverbs. 20c. coll.:* ODEP 289.

114. It is better to have one friend of great value than to have many friends of little value. *Rec. dist.:* N.Y. *1st cit.:* US1948 Stevenson, *Home Book of Proverbs. 20c. coll.:* Stevenson 890:3.

115. It is easier to visit friends than to live with them. *Rec. dist.:* Ill.

116. It is good to have some friends both in heaven and in hell. *Rec. dist.:* Ill., Wis. *1st cit.:* 1592 Delamothe, *Treasury of the French Tongue. 20c coll.:* ODEP 290, Stevenson 892:14.

117. It takes a year to make a friend. *Rec. dist.:* Ont.

118. It takes half of our lives to learn who our friends are and the other half to keep them. *Rec. dist.:* N.Y.

119. It takes years to make a friend, but minutes to lose one. *Vars.:* **(a)** It takes years to make a friend, but you can lose one in an hour. **(b)** You can hardly make a friend in a year, but you can easily lose one in a minute. *Rec. dist.:* Ind., Ont.

120. It's hard to make a friend but easy to make an enemy. *Rec. dist.:* Wis.

121. It's not lost, what a friend gets. *Var.:* What a friend gets is not lost. *Rec. dist.:* Ont.

1st cit.: 1566 Wager, *Mary Magdalene;* US1933 Gordon, *Shakespeare. 20c. coll.:* ODEP 487, Whiting*(MP)* 243.

122. Keep your friends constantly in repair. *Vars.:* **(a)** A man should keep his friendship in repair. **(b)** Keep your friendship in repair. *Rec. dist.:* N.J., N.Y., Ont.

123. Lend money, lose a friend. *Vars.:* **(a)** A loan often loses itself and the friend. **(b)** A ready way to lose a friend fast is to lend him money. **(c)** An easy way to lose a friend is to loan him money. **(d)** If you want to keep friends, don't loan them any money. **(e)** If you wish to lose a friend, lend him money. **(f)** Lend money to an enemy and you will gain him, to a friend and you will lose him. **(g)** Lending money makes bad friends. **(h)** Loan money to a friend and you lose both. **(i)** Make a loan and lose a friend. **(j)** Never loan money to a friend unless you wish to lose a friend. **(k)** The way to lose a friend is to loan him money. *Rec. dist.:* U.S., Can. *1st cit.:* ca1594 Bacon, *Promus;* US1740 Franklin, *PRAlmanac. 20c. coll.:* ODEP 455, Whiting 293, Stevenson 1385:3, Whiting*(MP)* 416.

124. Let your friends have their peculiarities. *Rec. dist.:* N.J.

125. Little friends sometimes prove to be big friends. *Var.:* Little friends may prove great friends. *Rec. dist.:* Calif., Ind., N.Y., Ont.

126. Make friends with the good if you wish to be like them. *Rec. dist.:* N.Y., N.C. *1st cit.:* US1937 Hart, *Seven Hundred Chinese Proverbs. 20c. coll.:* Stevenson 891:5.

127. Make new friends but keep the old. *Var.:* Make new friends but keep the old, for one is silver and the other gold. *Rec. dist.:* Ark., Ill., N.Y. *1st cit.:* 1575 Pettie, *Petite Palace of Pleasure. 20c. coll.:* Stevenson 904:1.

128. Make no friends with an angry man. *Var.:* Make no friendship with an angry man. *Rec. dist.:* Miss., Ohio.

129. Make not your friend too cheap to you, nor yourself too dear to him. *Rec. dist.:* Ont. *1st cit.:* 1601 Shakespeare, *Twelfth Night. 20c. coll.:* ODEP 290, Stevenson 896:6.

130. Man's best friend is his dog. *Var.:* A dog

is man's best friend. *Rec. dist.:* U.S. *1st cit.:* 1935 Gardiner, *Transatlantic Ghost;* US1927 Bridges, *Girl in Black.* *20c. coll.:* Whiting(MP) 174.

131. Many friends, few helpers. *Var.:* Many kinfolk, few helpers. *Rec. dist.:* Ont. *1st cit.:* US1875 Cheales, *Proverbial Folk-Lore.* *20c. coll.:* Stevenson 890:6.

132. My friends can do no wrong, and my enemies can do no right. *Rec. dist.:* Ill.

133. Never drop the friends you make on the way up; you may need them on the way down. *Rec. dist.:* Calif.

134. Never trust a friend who deserts you in a pinch. *Rec. dist.:* Ont., Utah.

135. New friends are like silver, but old ones are like gold. *Rec. dist.:* Ill.

136. No doctor like a true friend. *Rec. dist.:* N.Y. *1st cit.:* ca1386 Chaucer, *Tale of Melibee.* *20c. coll.:* ODEP 622, Stevenson 891:8.

137. No friend is like an old friend. *Vars.:* (a) There are no friends like old friends. (b) There is no friend like an old friend. *Rec. dist.:* U.S., Can. *1st cit.:* US1942 Young, *Man about the House.* *20c. coll.:* Stevenson 905:3, Whiting(MP) 243.

138. No man can be happy without a friend nor be sure of his friend until he is happy. *Rec. dist.:* N.Y. *1st cit.:* 1732 Fuller, *Gnomologia.* *20c. coll.:* Stevenson 895:4.

139. Often we hold friends by holding our tongues. *Rec. dist.:* Ind.

140. Old friends are best. *Vars.:* (a) New things are the best things, but old friends are the best friends. (b) Old friends are the best, but new ones are the most fun. (c) Old friends, like old wine, are best. (d) Old roads and old friends are the best. (e) Old shoes are easy; old friends are best. (f) Old tunes are sweetest; old friends are surest. (g) When put to the test, old friends are best. *Rec. dist.:* U.S., Can. *1st cit.:* 1565 Hall, *Court of Virtue;* US1766 Franklin, *PRAlmanac.* *20c. coll.:* ODEP 589, Whiting 169, Stevenson 905:1, Whiting(MP) 243.

141. One could live on next to nothing if one's friends could live on less. *Rec. dist.:* N.Y.

142. One does not make friends; one recognizes them. *Rec. dist.:* N.Y.

143. One old friend is better than two new ones. *Rec. dist.:* Ohio.

144. One's best friend is his mirror. *Rec. dist.:* N.Y.

145. Our friends are our mirrors and show us ourselves. *Rec. dist.:* N.Y.

146. Procure not friends in haste, neither part with them in haste. *Rec. dist.:* Wis.

147. Real friends are few and far between. *Rec. dist.:* Ill.

148. Reprove your friend privately; commend him publicly. *Var.:* Admonish your friends in private, praise them in public. *Rec. dist.:* N.Y., Ont.

149. Show me your friends, and I'll tell you what you are. *Var.:* Tell me who your friends are, and I'll tell you who you are. *Rec. dist.:* U.S., Can.

150. Speak well of your friends; of your enemies say nothing. *Rec. dist.:* Kans., N.Y. *1st cit.:* 1707 Mapletoft, *Select Proverbs.* *20c. coll.:* ODEP 761, Stevenson 909:5.

151. Take a friend for what he does, a wife for what she has, and goods for what they are worth. *Rec. dist.:* Ill., Ohio.

152. The best of friends must part. *Rec. dist.:* U.S., Can. *1st cit.:* ca1602 Chapman, *May Day.* *20c. coll.:* ODEP 290, Stevenson 897:12.

153. The best of friends wear out with wrong use. *Rec. dist.:* Ind.

154. The best way to keep a friend is not to give him away. *Var.:* The best way to keep friends is not to give them away. *Rec. dist.:* Ont.

155. The day I break my faith with friends, that day my right to friends ends. *Rec. dist.:* Wis.

156. The friends of the unlucky are far away. *Rec. dist.:* N.J.

157. The time to make friends is before you need them. *Rec. dist.:* Okla.

158. The way to gain a friend is to be one. *Vars.:* **(a)** The best way to have a friend is to be a friend. **(b)** The only way to have a friend is to be one. *Rec. dist.:* U.S. *1st cit.:* US1841 Emerson, "Friendship" in *Essays*. *20c. coll.:* Stevenson 896:3.

159. There is a lot of difference between friends and acquaintances. *Rec. dist.:* N.Y.

160. There is quite a difference between making fast friends and making friends fast. *Rec. dist.:* W.Va.

161. There's forever something new to be found in friends. *Rec. dist.:* Miss.

162. They are rich who have friends. *Vars.:* **(a)** They are rich who have true friends. **(b)** Those who have friends are rich. *Rec. dist.:* Ill., N.Y., Ohio. *1st cit.:* 1608 Shakespeare, *Timon of Athens*. *20c. coll.:* Stevenson 898:6.

163. Think twice before you speak to a friend in need. *Rec. dist.:* Ill.

164. Those who betray their friends must not expect others to keep faith with them. *Rec. dist.:* Ont.

165. Thoughtless friends are often a nuisance. *Rec. dist.:* Ont.

166. Three faithful friends: an old wife, an old dog, and ready money. *Var.:* There are but three faithful friends: an old dog, an old wife, and ready money. *Rec. dist.:* Ill., Ind., Wis. *1st cit.:* US1738 Franklin, *PRAlmanac*. *20c. coll.:* Whiting 169, Stevenson 895:1.

167. To be a friend is to have a friend. *Rec. dist.:* Ill., Ind.

168. To get a friend, close one eye; to keep him, close both. *Rec. dist.:* N.Y.

169. To have friends, never speak out of both sides of your mouth. *Rec. dist.:* Ark.

170. To lose a friend, advise him. *Rec. dist.:* Minn.

171. To see an old friend is as agreeable as a good meal. *Rec. dist.:* Ont.

172. True friends are like diamonds, precious and rare; false ones like autumn leaves, found everywhere. *Var.:* Friends are like jewels. *Rec. dist.:* Ill., Wash., Wis.

173. True friends, like ivy and the wall, both stand together and together fall. *Rec. dist.:* Ont.

174. True friends never run deep. *Rec. dist.:* N.Y.

175. True friends share both the bad and the good. *Rec. dist.:* Wis.

176. Trust not a new friend nor an old enemy. *Rec. dist.:* Tex., Vt. *1st cit.:* 1721 Kelly, *Scottish Proverbs*. *20c. coll.:* ODEP 842.

177. Try your friend before you trust him. *Vars.:* **(a)** First prove your friends before you need them. **(b)** Try your friend ere you trust him. *Rec. dist.:* Okla., Ont., Tex.

178. Value your friends above your opinions. *Rec. dist.:* Ont.

179. We love our friends in spite of, not because of. *Rec. dist.:* N.Y.

180. We tax our friends with faults but see not our own. *Rec. dist.:* Ont.

181. When a friend asks, there is no tomorrow. *Rec. dist.:* Ill. *1st cit.:* 1611 Cotgrave, *Dictionary of French and English Tongues*. *20c. coll.:* ODEP 288, Stevenson 898:3.

182. When friends meet, hearts warm. *Rec. dist.:* Ill., N.Y. *1st cit.:* 1678 Ray, *English Proverbs*. *20c. coll.:* Stevenson 892:16.

183. When two friends have a common purse, one sings and the other weeps. *Rec. dist.:* Ont. *1st cit.:* 1707 Mapletoft, *Select Proverbs*. *20c. coll.:* ODEP 850, Stevenson 903:2.

184. When you buy friends with anything other than friendship, they do not stay bought long. *Rec. dist.:* Ont.

185. Who seeks a faultless friend rests friendless. *Rec. dist.:* Oreg.

186. Without a friend the world is a wilderness. *Var.:* Without friends the world is a wilderness. *Rec. dist.:* N.J., N.Y., Ohio, Ont.

187. You can't live without friends—and quite often you can't live with them. *Rec. dist.:* Ill.

188. You can't trust your best friend. *Rec. dist.:* Ont.

189. You cannot use your friends and have them too. *Rec. dist.:* U.S., Can.

190. You love your friends despite their faults. *Rec. dist.:* N.Y.

191. You may choose your friends; your family is thrust upon you. *Var.:* God sends us our relatives, but we can choose our friends. *Rec. dist.:* U.S., Can. *1st cit.:* 1910 Mizner, *The Cynic's Calendar.* *20c. coll.:* Stevenson 1296:2.

192. You never know the value of friends until you lose them. *Rec. dist.:* Ont.

193. You will never have a friend if you must have one without faults. *Rec. dist.:* Kans., Ont., Oreg.

194. Your best friend is your dollar. *Var.:* Your best friend is your money. *Rec. dist.:* Ind., N.Y.

195. Your best friend is yourself. *Rec. dist.:* N.Y., Okla.

SEE ALSO Long ABSENCE changes friends. / Have many ACQUAINTANCES but few friends. / The more ARGUMENTS you win, the less friends you'll have. / Choose an AUTHOR as you choose a friend. / A good BOOK is the best friend. / Good BOOKS are friends who are always ready to talk to us. / A BROTHER may not be a friend, but a friend will always be a brother. / CANDOR once went further boldly and in smiles, but it crept home in tatters and tears. / Every man should have a fair sized CEMETERY in which to bury the faults of his friends. / Everybody's COMPANION is nobody's friend. / Pay your DEBTS or lose your friends. / Don't try to get even with your ENEMIES; try to get even with your friends. / The ENEMIES of my enemies are my friends. / To make ENEMIES, talk; to make friends, listen. / A common ENEMY makes friends. / Better an open ENEMY than a false friend. / A long FACE shortens your list of friends. / FAITHFUL are the wounds of a friend, but the kisses of an enemy are deceitful. / FLATTERY begets friends, but the truth begets enmity. / A courageous FOE is better than a cowardly friend. / A FOOL has few friends. / Better a FOOT slip than a friend. / FORTUNE makes friends; misfortune tries them. / An INDIAN scalps his enemy while a white man skins his friends. / Better lose a JEST than a friend. / A JOKE never gains over an enemy but often loses a friend. / Go down the LADDER for a wife; go up the ladder for a friend. / He who LAUGHS at others' woes finds few friends and many foes. / A LOAN oft loses both itself and the friend. / There is no better LOOKING GLASS than an old friend. / Your LOOKING GLASS will tell you what none of your friends will. / Good MORALS and good manners are sworn friends. / A full PURSE has many friends. / A RICH man knows not his friends. / SILENCE is a friend that will never betray. / W'en TROUBLE cum, friends run. / TRUTH, harsh though it be, is a faithful friend. / He who loses WEALTH loses much, he who loses even one friend loses more, but he that loses his courage loses all. / It's always fair WEATHER when good friends get together. / Tart WORDS make no friends.

friendliness Friendliness is to do and say the kindest thing in the kindest way. *Rec. dist.:* N.Y.

friendly *(n.)* Friendly is as friendly does. *Rec. dist.:* Miss., Wis.

friendly *(adj.)* **1.** Be friendly and you will never want friends. *Var.:* If you want to have friends, be friendly. *Rec. dist.:* Kans., Miss., Ont.

2. Being friendly doesn't cost anything. *Rec. dist.:* N.Dak.

SEE ALSO For NEIGHBORS to keep a friendly tone is equal to finding a precious stone.

friendship **1.** A blazing friendship goes out in a flash. *Rec. dist.:* Ill.

2. A broken friendship may be soldered but will never be sound. *Vars.:* **(a)** A broken friendship is never mended. **(b)** A patched-up friendship seldom becomes whole again. *Rec. dist.:* N.J., N.Y., Ont. *1st cit.:* ca1526 Erasmus, *Dicta Sapientum,* tr. Berthelet. *20c. coll.:* ODEP 87, Stevenson 914:4.

3. Flowers of true friendship never fade. *Rec. dist.:* Ont.

4. Friendship cannot stand all on one side. *Rec. dist.:* N.Y., S.C. *1st cit.:* ca1641 Fergusson, *Scottish Proverbs,* ed. Beveridge (1924). *20c. coll.:* ODEP 291, Stevenson 913:6.

5. Friendship is a magic weaver. *Rec. dist.:* N.Y.

6. Friendship is a plant that one must often water. *Rec. dist.:* N.Y.

7. Friendship is a silken tie which binds friends together. *Rec. dist.:* Kans.

8. Friendship is a two-way street. *Rec. dist.:* N.Dak.

9. Friendship is an empty word if it only works one way. *Rec. dist.:* N.J.

10. Friendship is like hand-painted china, expensive and rare: when broke it may be mended, but the crack is always there. *Rec. dist.:* Kans.

11. Friendship is love with understanding. *Rec. dist.:* Ill.

12. Friendship is love without wings. *Rec. dist.:* N.Y., Ont. *1st cit.:* 1806 Byron, "Friendship Is Love without Wings." *20c. coll.:* Stevenson 915:12.

13. Friendship is not to be bought at a fair. *Rec. dist.:* N.Y. *1st cit.:* 1732 Fuller, *Gnomologia. 20c. coll.:* Stevenson 914:1.

14. Friendship is to be worked at, not on. *Rec. dist.:* Ohio.

15. Friendship, like persimmons, is good only when ripe. *Rec. dist.:* Nebr.

16. Friendship often ends in love, but love in friendship never. *Var.:* Friendship sometimes turns to love, but love to friendship never. *Rec. dist.:* Miss., Ont. *1st cit.:* 1820 Colton, *Lacon. 20c. coll.:* Stevenson 916:2.

17. It's a poor friendship that needs to be constantly bought. *Rec. dist.:* N.Y.

18. No friendship can survive the gift of gold. *Rec. dist.:* Utah.

19. Nothing spoils friendship sooner than exaggeration of friends. *Rec. dist.:* Fla.

20. Once a torn friendship, a patch can't be sewn. *Var.:* Keep your friendships in repair. *Rec. dist.:* N.Y.

21. Real friendship is a slow grower. *Rec. dist.:* Ohio.

22. Soil and friendship must be cultivated. *Rec. dist.:* Calif., Oreg.

23. Sudden friendship, sure repentance. *Rec. dist.:* N.J., Ont. *1st cit.:* 1678 Ray, *English Proverbs. 20c. coll.:* ODEP 784, Stevenson 915:1.

24. The essence of friendship is not getting, but sharing. *Rec. dist.:* Minn.

25. The only rose without thorns is friendship. *Rec. dist.:* N.Y.

26. There are many kinds of fruit that grow on the tree of life, but none so sweet as friendship. *Rec. dist.:* N.Mex.

27. There is no friendship without freedom, no freedom without the friendship of brothers. *Var.:* There can be no friendship without freedom. *Rec. dist.:* Ill., Ont. *1st cit.:* 1732 Fuller, *Gnomologia. 20c. coll.:* Stevenson 913:10.

28. True friendship is a plant of slow growth. *Rec. dist.:* Ill., N.Y., Ohio, S.C. *1st cit.:* ca1746 Lord Chesterfield, *Letters to His Son;* US1783 Washington, Letter, 15 Jan. *20c. coll.:* Stevenson 912:11.

29. Water your friendships as you water your flowerpots. *Rec. dist.:* Ill.

30. While you seek new friendships, cultivate the old. *Rec. dist.:* Ohio.

31. With women, friendship ends when rivalry begins. *Rec. dist.:* N.J.

SEE ALSO ENVY is destroyed by true friendship. / Let not the GRASS grow on the path of friendship. / True LOVE is friendship set on fire. / MONEY and man a mutual friendship show: man makes false money; money makes man so. / STRIFE makes friendship stronger.

frog   1. Better to be a big frog in a little pool than a little frog in a big pool. *Vars.:* **(a)** It's better to be a big frog in a little puddle than a little frog in a big puddle. **(b)** 'Tis better to be a big frog in a little pond than a little frog in a big pond. *Rec. dist.:* U.S., Can. *Infm.:* Cf. toad. *1st cit.:* US1871 Jones, *Life of Jefferson S. Batkins. 20c. coll.:* T&W 376, Whiting*(MP)* 243.

2. Even a frog would bite if it had teeth. *Rec. dist.:* Ill.

3. Frogs do not croak in running water. *Rec. dist.:* Ont.

4. If frogs had wings, they wouldn't bump their asses on rocks. *Rec. dist.:* N.C., Va.

5. It isn't the frog with the longest legs who can jump the farthest. *Rec. dist.:* Okla.

6. It's a poor frog who doesn't play with his own pond. *Var.:* It's a poor frog that won't holler for his own pond. *Rec. dist.:* Kans., Vt.

7. It's easy to make a frog jump into water when that's what he wants to do. *Rec. dist.:* Ill.

8. Set a frog on a golden stool, away it hops to reach the pool. *Rec. dist.:* Ont.

9. There is more than one frog in the puddle. *Rec. dist.:* Ont.

10. There's more than one way to kill a frog. *Rec. dist.:* Kans.

11. What goes under a frog's belly never goes over his back. *Rec. dist.:* Ill. *Infm.:* Cf. devil.

12. When a frog flies into a passion, the pond knows nothing of his tantrum. *Rec. dist.:* Ill.

13. You can't tell a frog by the size of his jump. *Vars.:* **(a)** Never judge the size of a frog by the length of his jump. **(b)** You can never tell by the looks of a frog how far he can jump. **(c)** You can't tell by looking at a frog how far he'll leap. **(d)** You can't tell by the looks of a frog how far he can jump. *Rec. dist.:* U.S., Can.

frost **1.** The frost hurts not the weeds. *Rec. dist.:* Ont., Wis. *1st cit.:* 1732 Fuller, *Gnomologia. 20c. coll.:* Stevenson 917:4.

2. The frost will bring the pig home. *Rec. dist.:* Ont.

3. They must hunger in frost that will not work in heat. *Rec. dist.:* N.Y., Okla. *1st cit.:* ca1540 Bannatyne MS of Scottish Text Society. *20c. coll.:* ODEP 392, Stevenson 2623:3.

frown He gives little who gives much with a frown; he gives much who gives little with a smile. *Rec. dist.:* N.Y.

SEE ALSO When FORTUNE smiles, we ride in chase, and when she frowns, we walk away. / A FRIEND's frown is better than a fool's smile.

frugality **1.** Frugality is a fair fortune, and industry a good estate. *Rec. dist.:* Mich.

2. Frugality is the mother of all the virtues.

Rec. dist.: Ill. *1st cit.:* US1948 Stevenson, *Home Book of Proverbs. 20c. coll.:* Stevenson 918:9.

3. Frugality when all is spent comes too late. *Rec. dist.:* Ill. *1st cit.:* US1948 Stevenson, *Home Book of Proverbs. 20c. coll.:* Stevenson 918:9.

4. Without frugality none can be rich, and with it, few would be poor. *Rec. dist.:* Mich. *1st cit.:* 1750 Johnson, *Rambler. 20c. coll.:* Stevenson 918:4.

SEE ALSO INDUSTRY is fortune's right hand and frugality her left.

fruit **1.** Better the fruit lost than the tree. *Rec. dist.:* Ill.

2. By their fruits you shall know them. *Rec. dist.:* Ind., S.C. *1st cit.:* ca1389 Chaucer, *Parson's Tale. 20c. coll.:* Stevenson 919:5.

3. Domestic fruit will not grow on a wild tree. *Rec. dist.:* Ont.

4. Forbidden fruit is the sweetest. *Vars.:* **(a)** Forbidden fruit always tastes the sweetest. **(b)** Nothing is so good as forbidden fruits. **(c)** Stolen fruit is always sweeter. *Rec. dist.:* U.S., Can. *1st cit.:* ca1386 Chaucer, *Parson's Tale;* US1893 Twain, *Pudd'nhead Wilson's Calendar. 20c. coll.:* ODEP 279, Stevenson 919:9, CODP 213, Whiting(MP) 244.

5. Fruit is silver in the morning, gold at noon, and lead at night. *Rec. dist.:* N.Dak. *1st cit.:* ca1800 Barrington, *Rules of Health. 20c. coll.:* Stevenson 918:10.

6. He that would have the fruit must climb the tree. *Var.:* He that climbs the tall tree has a right to the fruit. *Rec. dist.:* Wis. *1st cit.:* 1721 Kelly, *Scottish Proverbs;* US1843 Hall, *New Purchase. 20c. coll.:* ODEP 215, T&W 147, CODP 63, Stevenson 2593:4.

7. If you would enjoy its fruit, pluck not the blossom. *Var.:* If you would enjoy the fruit, pluck not the flower. *Rec. dist.:* Mich., Ont.

8. The best fruit is on top of the tree. *Rec. dist.:* Ont.

9. The fruit doesn't fall far from the tree. *Var.:* The fruit falls nearest the branch. *Rec. dist.:* Ill., Ont. *Infm.:* Cf. apple.

10. The fruit of a good tree is also good. *Rec.*

dist.: N.Y. **1st cit.:** ca1525 Tyndale, *Pathway,* Parker Soc. **20c. coll.:** ODEP 319.

11. The redder the fruit, the higher it hangs. *Rec. dist.:* Ont.

12. The weakest fruit drops earliest to the ground. *Var.:* The weakest kind of fruit drops earliest to the ground. *Rec. dist.:* Ill. **1st cit.:** 1597 Shakespeare, *Merchant of Venice.* **20c. coll.:** Stevenson 919:7.

13. When the fruit fails, welcome haws. *Rec. dist.:* Calif., N.Y. **1st cit.:** 1721 Kelly, *Scottish Proverbs;* US1914 Purdon, *Folk of Furry Farm.* **20c. coll.:** ODEP 292, Stevenson 919:3.

14. You can't eat the fruit while the tree is in blossom. *Rec. dist.:* N.C.

15. You can't force a fruit to ripen by beating it with a stick. *Rec. dist.:* Ill.

SEE ALSO ACTION is the proper fruit of knowledge. / DEEDS are fruits; words are but leaves. / Roots of EVIL bear bitter fruits. / There are many kinds of fruit that grow on the tree of life, but none so sweet as FRIEND-SHIP. / Kind HEARTS are the gardens, kind thoughts the roots, kind words the flowers, kind deeds the fruits. / The LABOR of the righteous tends to life, the fruit of the wicked to sin. / The tree of SILENCE bears the fruit of peace. / A rotten TREE bears no fruit. / A TREE is known by its fruit. / A TREE with beautiful blossoms does not always yield the best fruit. / Large TREES give more shade than fruit. / When the VINE is ripe, the fruit will fall.

frying pan **1.** Don't jump from the frying pan into the fire. *Rec. dist.:* U.S., Can. **1st cit.:** 1528 More, *Dyaloge Concerning Heresies* in *Workes* (1557); US1681 *James Claypoole's Letter Book,* ed. Balderton (1967). **20c. coll.:** ODEP 292, Whiting 170, Stevenson 814:1, T&W 147, Whiting(MP) 244.

2. If you hold the frying pan, don't blame it if you burn yourself. *Rec. dist.:* Ill.

fuel SEE It's easier to build two CHIMNEYS than to keep one in fuel.

full *(n.)* The full do not believe the hungry. *Rec. dist.:* Ill. **1st cit.:** 1573 Sanford, *Garden of Pleasure.* **20c. coll.:** ODEP 45.

full *(adj.)* **1.** He that is full of himself is empty. *Rec. dist.:* Mich.

2. It's hard to carry a full cup. *Vars.:* **(a)** A full cup must be carried steadily. **(b)** 'Tis hard to carry a full cup even. *Rec. dist.:* N.Y. **1st cit.:** 1820 Scott, *Monastery.* **20c. coll.:** Stevenson 471:4.

3. What isn't full won't yell. *Rec. dist.:* Ont.

SEE ALSO INDUSTRY keeps the body healthy, the mind clear, the heart whole, and the purse full. / LIFE is short and full o' blisters. / Full STOMACH, contented heart.

fun **1.** All fun is gone when left alone. *Rec. dist.:* Oreg.

2. Always stop to think whether your fun will cause another's unhappiness. *Rec. dist.:* Ont.

3. Everything that's fun is either illegal, immoral, or fattening. *Rec. dist.:* Mich., Minn.

4. Have fun in this life: you'll never get out of it alive. *Var.:* Have fun while you live, because you are going to be dead a long time. *Rec. dist.:* Ky., Tenn., Wis.

5. Have fun while you are young. *Rec. dist.:* N.Y.

6. It is fun to be fooled, but better to know. *Rec. dist.:* Ill.

7. There ain't much fun in physics, but there's a great deal of physics in fun. *Rec. dist.:* Wis.

SEE ALSO CHILDREN: one is one, two is fun, three is a houseful. / Something said by a WISE man may be made fun of by a fool. / WORK well done makes pleasure more fun.

funny Everything is funny as long as it happens to someone else. *Rec. dist.:* N.Y., S.C.

fur SEE A FRIEND by your side can keep you warmer than the richest furs. / A WOLF may change his mind but never his fur.

furnace The furnace that hardens clay will melt gold. *Rec. dist.:* Vt.

furniture **1.** The best furniture in the house is a virtuous woman. *Rec. dist.:* Vt.

2. They don't put marble tops on cheap furniture. *Rec. dist.:* Ohio.

SEE ALSO First build your HOUSE and then think of the furniture.

furrow 1. Crooked furrows grow straight grain. *Rec. dist.:* P.E.I.

2. Plow your furrows deep while sluggards sleep, and you shall have corn to sell and to keep. *Rec. dist.:* Ill., N.Y. *1st cit.:* 1659 Howell, *Paroimiografia;* US1756 Franklin, *PRAlmanac.* *20c. coll.:* ODEP 634, Whiting 400, Stevenson 1239:15, Whiting(MP) 575.

3. To plow a straight furrow, never look back. *Rec. dist.:* Ill.

fury 1. Beware the fury of a patient man. *Rec. dist.:* Ill., N.J., Ohio, Vt. *Infm.:* Cf. anger, wrath. *1st cit.:* 1681 Dryden, *Absalom and Achitophel;* US1865 Richardson, *Secret.* *20c. coll.:* Stevenson 1756:12, T&W 148.

2. Fury is armed with its own madness. *Rec. dist.:* Ill.

3. There is no fury like a woman's fury. *Rec. dist.:* Calif., Colo., N.Y. *1st cit.:* 1696 Cibber, *Love's Last Shift;* US1836 Whittier, *Mogg Megone.* *20c. coll.:* CODP 110, Stevenson 2566:6, Whiting(MP) 302.

fuss 1. Can't have a family fuss without the whole town knowing about it. *Rec. dist.:* Miss.

2. It takes two to make a fuss. *Rec. dist.:* Ky., Tenn. *1st cit.:* 1706 Stevens, *New Spanish and English Dictionary;* US1750 *New York Weekly Post Boy* in *Newspaper Extracts.* *20c. coll.:* ODEP 852, Whiting 459, CODP 234, Stevenson 90:10, T&W 389, Whiting(MP) 655.

future 1. A man without thought of the future must soon have present sorrow. *Rec. dist.:* Ont.

2. Don't mortgage the future for the present. *Rec. dist.:* Ont.

3. Fear not the future: weep not for the past. *Rec. dist.:* N.Y.

4. Invest in the future. *Rec. dist.:* N.Dak.

5. Look to the future and you will always look up. *Rec. dist.:* Kans.

6. Never think of the future; it comes soon enough. *Rec. dist.:* Wis.

7. No one can walk backwards into the future. *Rec. dist.:* Ind.

8. One can never tell what the future will bring. *Rec. dist.:* N.Y.

9. Planning your future saves you from regretting your past. *Rec. dist.:* Ont.

10. The future becomes the present if we fight for it. *Rec. dist.:* Ill., Oreg. *1st cit.:* 1750 Johnson, *Rambler.* *20c. coll.:* Stevenson 1875:2.

11. The future belongs to those who prepare for it. *Rec. dist.:* Ohio.

12. The future gains from present pains. *Rec. dist.:* N.Y.

13. The future is a sealed book. *Rec. dist.:* Ill.

14. The future of a child is the work of the mother. *Rec. dist.:* Wis.

15. The future takes care of itself. *Rec. dist.:* R.I.

16. The man who has no future loses his grip on the present. *Var.:* He who has no future loses his grip on the present. *Rec. dist.:* Ariz., Ill.

17. There is no future like the present. *Rec. dist.:* N.Y.

18. What the future has in store for you depends in large measure on what you have in store for the future. *Rec. dist.:* Utah.

19. When all else is lost, the future still remains. *Rec. dist.:* Ill.

20. You can never plan the future by the past. *Rec. dist.:* Ont. *1st cit.:* 1791 Burke, Letter to a member of the National Assembly. *20c. coll.:* Stevenson 1751:16.

SEE ALSO You can DRIVE sixty miles a minute, but there ain't no future in it. / LIVE for the present; plan for the future. / May the best of your PAST be the worst of your future. / Study the PAST if you would divine the future. / While you glory in the PAST, be busy in the present lest you be caught unprepared in the future. / A man's best REPUTATION for his future is his record of the past. / A YOUNG man looks into the future as an old man into his past.

G

gain *(n.)* **1.** A small gain is worth more than a large promise. *Rec. dist.:* Ont.

2. An evil gain is equal to a loss. *Var.:* Dishonest gains are losses. *Rec. dist.:* Ill., N.J. *1st cit.:* US1755 Franklin, *PRAlmanac. 20c. coll.:* Stevenson 926:11.

3. Every gain must have a loss. *Rec. dist.:* N.Y. *1st cit.:* 1597 Bacon, "Of Seditions and Troubles" in *Essays,* ed. Arber. *20c. coll.:* Stevenson 928:6.

4. Gain bends one's better judgment. *Rec. dist.:* N.Y.

5. Gain cannot be made without some other person's loss. *Rec. dist.:* Ill. *1st cit.:* 1576 Pettie, *Petite Palace of Pleasure,* ed. Gollancz (1908). *20c. coll.:* Stevenson 928:6.

6. Gain is temporary and uncertain, but expense is constant and certain. *Rec. dist.:* Mich.

7. Great gains are not won except by great risks. *Rec. dist.:* N.J.

8. Hope of gain lessens pain. *Rec. dist.:* Miss., N.Y., Ont. *1st cit.:* 1583 Melbancke, *Philotimus;* US1734 Franklin, *PRAlmanac. 20c. coll.:* ODEP 294, Whiting 219, Stevenson 924:6.

9. Ill-gotten gain is no gain at all. *Rec. dist.:* Ark., Ky., Tenn.

10. Ill-gotten gain never does anyone any good. *Rec. dist.:* Ont. *1st cit.:* 1670 Ray, *English Proverbs. 20c. coll.:* Stevenson 926:4.

11. Ill-gotten gains are soon lost. *Rec. dist.:* Fla., Ont. *1st cit.:* 1519 Horman, *Vulgaria. 20c. coll.:* ODEP 398.

12. Light gains make a heavy purse. *Vars.:* **(a)** Light gains make heavy profits. **(b)** Little gains make heavy profits. **(c)** The proverb is true, that light gains make heavy purses; for light gains come often, great gains now and then. *Rec. dist.:* Ind., Okla., Utah. *1st cit.:* 1546 Heywood, *Dialogue of Proverbs,* ed. Habernicht (1963); US1744 Franklin, *PRAlmanac. 20c. coll.:* ODEP 463, Whiting 171, Stevenson 923:13.

13. Little gain, little pain. *Rec. dist.:* Mich., N.Y., Ont.

14. One who does everything for gain does nothing for good. *Rec. dist.:* N.Y.

15. Only that which is honestly got is gain. *Rec. dist.:* Kans., R.I.

16. The chase of gain is rich in hate. *Rec. dist.:* Ind.

17. There are no gains without pains. *Rec. dist.:* U.S., Can. *1st cit.:* 1577 Grange, *Golden Aphroditis;* US1745 Franklin, *PRAlmanac. 20c. coll.:* ODEP 572, Whiting 171, Stevenson 924:6, T&W 149, Whiting(MP) 247.

SEE ALSO What is a poor man's FOLLY is a rich man's gain. / Little LABOR, little gain. / His LOSS is my gain. / No PAINS, no gains; no sweat, no sweet. / No RISK, no gain.

gain *(v.)* Not what I gain, but what I lose. *Rec. dist.:* Ont.

SEE ALSO CONCESSIONS may gain ground. / The way to gain a FRIEND is to be one. / The ground of LIBERTY must be gained by inches. / MONEY lost is never gained. / Employ the TIME well if you mean to gain leisure. / Nothing VENTURED, nothing gained.

gainer No one ought to be a gainer by his own wrongdoing. *Rec. dist.:* Mich.

gait Don't criticize a man's gait until you are in his shoes. *Rec. dist.:* Ont.

gale It's not the gale but the set of the sail that determines the way you go. *Rec. dist.:* N.Y.

SEE ALSO Hoist up the SAIL while the gale does last.

gallant The gallant man needs no drums to rouse him. *Rec. dist.:* N.Y.

SEE ALSO Call him not ALONE who dies side by side with gallant men.

gallows SEE Save a THIEF from the gallows, and he will be the first to cut your throat. / The end of the THIEF is the gallows.

gambler 1. A gambler picks his own pocket. *Rec. dist.:* Calif.

2. All players can't win; no gambler wins in the end. *Rec. dist.:* Ill.

3. The best gambler is the man who doesn't gamble. *Rec. dist.:* Ill.

4. You can tell a gambler by his chips. *Rec. dist.:* Calif.

5. Young gambler—old beggar. *Rec. dist.:* Wis.

gambling 1. Gambling is getting nothing for something. *Rec. dist.:* Ind.

2. Gambling is the son of avarice and the father of despair. *Var.:* Gambling is the son of avarice, the brother of iniquity, and the father of mischief. *Rec. dist.:* Ill., Miss. *1st cit.:* US1783 Washington, Letter to Bushrod Washington, 15 Jan. *20c. coll.:* Stevenson 931:14.

game *(contest)* 1. A game is not won until it has been played. *Rec. dist.:* Ind.

2. Be game, but not everybody's. *Rec. dist.:* N.Dak.

3. First game's a kid's game. *Rec. dist.:* Ont.

4. If he calls it a silly and childish game, that means his wife can beat him at it. *Rec. dist.:* N.Dak.

5. It's a great game if you don't weaken. *Rec. dist.:* Ky., Tenn.

6. The game's not over until the last man strikes out. *Rec. dist.:* Ind., Ky., Ohio, Tenn.

7. The same game does not often succeed twice. *Rec. dist.:* Ont.

8. You can't beat a man at his own game. *Rec. dist.:* U.S. *1st cit.:* US1756 *Papers of Henry Laurens,* ed. Hamer (1968). *20c. coll.:* Whiting 172, T&W 150, Whiting(MP) 248.

9. You might as well have the game as the name. *Var.:* If you have the name, you might as well have the game. *Rec. dist.:* U.S., Can. *1st cit.:* US1836 Haliburton, *Clockmaker.* *20c. coll.:* T&W 257.

SEE ALSO FIRST is worst, second the same, last is best of all the game. / POSSESSION is nine-tenths of the game.

game *(animal)* You cannot kill game by looking at it. *Rec. dist.:* Ohio.

gamester Gamesters and racers never last long. *Rec. dist.:* Mich. *1st cit.:* 1640 Herbert, *Outlandish Proverbs (Jacula Prudentum)* in *Works,* ed. Hutchinson (1941). *20c. coll.:* ODEP 295, Stevenson 931:11.

gaming SEE The DEVIL goes shares in gaming.

gander As is the gander, so is the goose. *Rec. dist.:* Mich., S.C. *1st cit.:* 1732 Fuller, *Gnomologia.* *20c. coll.:* Stevenson 1011:31.

SEE ALSO For every GOOSE there is a gander. / There never was a GOOSE so gray but some gander will wander her way. / What's sauce for the GOOSE is sauce for the gander.

garbage Garbage in, garbage out. *Rec. dist.:* Mich. *Infm.:* Garbage is computer slang for "garbled input." *1st cit.:* 1964 *CIS Glossary of Typesetting & Computer Terms;* US1970 Rhodes, *Inland Ground: An Evocation of the American Middle West.* *20c. coll.:* CODP 90, Whiting(MP) 248.

garden 1. A good garden always has weeds. *Vars.:* **(a)** A good garden may have some weeds. **(b)** No garden without its weeds. *Rec. dist.:* Ind., N.Dak., Ont. *1st cit.:* 1579 Lyly, *Euphues, Anatomy of Wit* in *Works,* ed. Bond (1902); US1942 Morison, *Admiral of Ocean Sea: Life of Christopher Columbus.* *20c. coll.:* ODEP 296, Whiting(MP) 249, Stevenson 394:1.

2. As is the garden, such is the gardener. *Var.:* As is the gardener, so is the garden. *Rec. dist.:* Mich., Ont. *1st cit.:* 1732 Fuller, *Gnomologia.* *20c. coll.:* Stevenson 935:12.

3. Every man should cultivate his own garden. *Rec. dist.:* Ont. *1st cit.:* US1888 James, *The Aspern Papers.* *20c. coll.:* Stevenson 936:7.

4. In the garden more grows than the garden shows. *Rec. dist.:* Ill. *1st cit.:* 1659 Howell, *Paroimiografia (Spanish Proverbs).* *20c. coll.:* Stevenson 935:10.

5. Make a garden or plant, and a man is happy for life. *Rec. dist.:* Nebr.

6. Plant your garden in the ground and not in the moon. *Rec. dist.:* Kans.

7. Sadness is a wall between two gardens. *Rec. dist.:* N.Y.

8. The market is the best garden. *Rec. dist.:* Ont., Utah. *1st cit.:* 1640 Herbert, *Outlandish Proverbs (Jacula Prudentum)* in *Works,* ed. Hutchinson (1941). *20c. coll.:* ODEP 513, Stevenson 935:16.

9. The soul of a man is a garden where, as he sows, so shall he reap. *Rec. dist.:* Ont. *1st cit.:* ca900 Cynewulf, *Christian Anglo-Saxon Poetic Records,* eds. Knapp & Dobbie; US1679 *Fitzhugh & His Chesapeake World,* ed. Davis, Va.Hist.Soc. *Documents* (1963). *20c. coll.:* ODEP 757, Whiting 408, *CODP* 208, Stevenson 2179:4, Whiting(MP) 585.

10. Weed your own garden first. *Rec. dist.:* Ont.

SEE ALSO HAPPINESS grows at our own firesides and is not to be picked in strangers' garden. / Kind HEARTS are the garden, kind thoughts the roots, kind words the flowers, kind deeds the fruits. / A man of WORDS and not of deeds is like a garden full of weeds.

gardener **1.** All gardeners know better than other gardeners. *Rec. dist.:* Wis.

2. It is not enough for a gardener to love flowers; he must also hate weeds. *Rec. dist.:* Kans.

garland SEE One FLOWER makes no garland. / To have IDEAS is to gather flowers; to think is to weave them into garlands.

garment **1.** Borrowed garments never fit. *Rec. dist.:* N.J., N.Y., Ohio. *1st cit.:* 1732 Fuller, *Gnomologia.* *20c. coll.:* ODEP 77, Stevenson 223:10.

2. Never sew a new patch on an old garment. *Rec. dist.:* U.S., Can.

3. Worn-out garments have the newest patches. *Rec. dist.:* Ind.

4. You must cut your garment according to the cloth. *Var.:* Cut the garment to fit the cloth. *Rec. dist.:* Oreg., Vt. *1st cit.:* 1546 Heywood, *Dialogue of Proverbs,* ed. Habernicht

(1963); US1720 *Letters of Robert Carter, 1720–1727,* ed. Wright (1940). *20c. coll.:* CODP 47, Whiting 77, ODEP 164, Stevenson 373:4, T&W 74, Whiting(MP) 123.

SEE ALSO LEISURE is a pretty garment; it won't do to wear it all the time. / The garment of PEACE never fades.

gasoline Gasoline and whiskey usually mix with blood on the highway. *Vars.:* (a) Gasoline and whiskey don't mix. (b) Whiskey and gasoline never mix. *Rec. dist.:* U.S.

gate **1.** A squeaking gate hangs the longest. *Vars.:* (a) A creaking gate hangs long on its hinges. (b) A creaking gate lasts long. (c) A creaking gate swings a long time. *Rec. dist.:* Ohio, Ont. *1st cit.:* 1776 Cogan, *John Buncle, Jr.;* US1928 Freeman, *As Thief in Night.* *20c. coll.:* ODEP 154, Whiting(MP) 249, CODP 45, Stevenson 936:15.

2. Always swing on your own gate. *Rec. dist.:* Ont.

3. An open gate lets stock out. *Rec. dist.:* Ohio.

4. Don't swing on the same gate too long. *Rec. dist.:* Kans.

5. If you don't like my gate, don't swing on it. *Vars.:* (a) Don't swing on my gate if you don't like it. (b) If you don't like my gate, you don't need to swing on it. *Rec. dist.:* Ont.

6. No use to close the gate after the horse is gone. *Vars.:* (a) Always shut the gate after the horse is out. (b) Don't close the gate after the chickens are out. (c) Don't lock the gate after the horses are gone. *Rec. dist.:* Fla., Ind., Ky., Tenn. *1st cit.:* ca1350 *Douce MS 22,* ed. Förster (1906); US1845 Judd, *Margaret.* *20c. coll.:* ODEP 730, T&W 109, Stevenson 2204:8.

SEE ALSO DOGS don't bite at de front gate. / Better once in HEAVEN than ten times at the gate.

gather Closely gathered, widely scattered. *Rec. dist.:* Ont.

SEE ALSO Don't light your FIRE until you have gathered your sticks. / Scatter with one HAND; gather with two. / The HAND that gives, gathers. / We shall never gather HAPPI-

NESS if we try to retain it for ourselves. / A setting HEN gathers no feathers. / Gather ROSEBUDS while you may. / A rolling STONE gathers no moss.

gathering **1.** A close gathering gets a wide scattering. *Var.:* A narrow gathering will take a wide scattering. *Rec. dist.:* Ont.

2. The smaller the gathering, the greater the joy. *Rec. dist.:* N.Y.

gay Be gay today, for tomorrow you may die. *Rec. dist.:* Ohio. *1st cit.:* 1870 Rossetti, "Choice" in *House of Life.* *20c. coll.:* Stevenson 666:4.

SEE ALSO It is not the gay COAT that makes the gentleman.

gear Little gear, less care. *Rec. dist.:* N.Y., S.C. *1st cit.:* 1721 Kelly, *Scottish Proverbs.* *20c. coll.:* ODEP 470, Stevenson 1834:1.

gem **1.** A gem is not polished without rubbing, nor is a man perfect without trials. *Rec. dist.:* Ont.

2. Don't value a gem by its setting. *Var.:* Don't value a gem by what it's set in. *Rec. dist.:* N.J., Ont.

3. Fairest gems lie deepest. *Rec. dist.:* Ill., Ont.

general **1.** Generals die in bed. *Rec. dist.:* Ill.

2. It is the part of a good general to talk of success, not of failure. *Rec. dist.:* N.Y. *1st cit.:* US1948 Stevenson, *Home Book of Proverbs.* *20c. coll.:* Stevenson 938:4.

generalizer A generalizer is a man who learns less and less about more and more until he knows nothing about everything. *Rec. dist.:* R.I.

generation **1.** Generations grow weaker and wiser. *Rec. dist.:* Ill.

2. It takes three generations to make a gentleman. *Rec. dist.:* N.Y. *1st cit.:* 1598 Romei, *Courtier's Academy;* US1823 Cooper, *Pioneers.* *20c. coll.:* CODP 90, T&W 151, ODEP 298, Stevenson 945:6, Whiting(MP) 250.

3. One generation comes, another passes, but the world goes on forever. *Rec. dist.:* Utah.

SEE ALSO A FORTUNE never passes the second generation. / From SHIRTSLEEVES to shirtsleeves in three generations.

generosity **1.** Broad is the shadow of generosity. *Rec. dist.:* Ill., N.J.

2. Generosity is catching: you are generous if your neighbor is generous. *Rec. dist.:* Ill.

3. Generosity is more charitable than wealth. *Rec. dist.:* Ill.

4. Generosity is the flower of justice. *Rec. dist.:* Ill. *1st cit.:* US1850 Hawthorne, *American Notebooks.* *20c. coll.:* Stevenson 938:10.

5. Generosity never impoverished a man, nor robbery enriched him, nor prosperity made him wise. *Rec. dist.:* N.Y.

6. Our generosity should never exceed our abilities. *Rec. dist.:* Ill. *1st cit.:* US1948 Stevenson, *Home Book of Proverbs.* *20c. coll.:* Stevenson 938:11.

7. The quickest generosity is the best. *Var.:* The best generosity is that which is quick. *Rec. dist.:* Ill. *1st cit.:* US1948 Stevenson, *Home Book of Proverbs.* *20c. coll.:* Stevenson 938:9.

8. True generosity is the ability to accept ingratitude. *Rec. dist.:* Ala., Ga., Miss.

generous *(n.)* **1.** The generous can forget they have given, but the grateful can never forget that they have received. *Rec. dist.:* Utah.

2. The generous is always just, and the just is always generous. *Rec. dist.:* Ill.

generous *(adj.)* **1.** Folks is mighty generous wid money what dey ain't got. *Rec. dist.:* Miss.

2. It is easier to be generous than grateful. *Rec. dist.:* Ill.

3. The generous man receives more than he gives. *Rec. dist.:* N.Y.

SEE ALSO Be JUST before you are generous.

genius **1.** A genius does not shout his wisdom from the housetops. *Rec. dist.:* Mont., N.J., Oreg.

2. A genius is born, not made. *Vars.:* **(a)** Genius must be born, never taught. **(b)** Geniuses, like poets, are born, not taught. *Rec. dist.:* U.S.

3. A great genius will sincerely acknowledge his defects. *Rec. dist.:* N.Y.

4. Genius begins great works; labor alone

finishes them. *Rec. dist.*: N.Y. *1st cit.*: US1948 Stevenson, *Home Book of Proverbs*. *20c. coll.*: Stevenson 942:3.

5. Genius does what it must; talent, what it may. *Var.*: Talent does what it can; genius does what it must. *Rec. dist.*: Ill.

6. Genius is akin to madness. *Vars.*: **(a)** A genius is next door to an idiot. **(b)** Genius is a step from insanity, but insanity is not a step from genius. *Rec. dist.*: N.Y., Oreg. *1st cit.*: US1948 Stevenson, *Home Book of Proverbs*. *20c. coll.*: Stevenson 940:9.

7. Genius is one percent inspiration, ninety-nine percent perspiration. *Var.*: Genius is one part inspiration and three parts perspiration. *Rec. dist.*: Ill., N.J., N.Y. *Infm.*: Attributed to Thomas Alva Edison in a newspaper interview. *1st cit.*: US1931 Edison, *Golden Book,* Apr. *20c. coll.*: Stevenson 939:16.

8. Genius is the capacity for taking infinite pains. *Rec. dist.*: N.Y. *1st cit.*: 1858 Carlyle, *Frederick the Great;* US1941 Birney (pseud. Kent), *Jason Burr's First Case*. *20c. coll.*: CODP 90.

9. Genius without education is like silver in the mine. *Var.*: Genius without education is like silver in the moon. *Rec. dist.*: Ill., N.Y., Wis. *1st cit.*: US1750 Franklin, *PRAlmanac*. *20c. coll.*: Stevenson 940:13.

10. Men of genius often bring great misery to the world. *Rec. dist.*: Ont.

11. Where genius, wealth, and strength fail perseverance will succeed. *Rec. dist.*: Ind.

gentility Gentility without ability is worse than beggary. *Rec. dist.*: Mich. *1st cit.*: 1580 Munday, *Zelauto* in *View of Sundry Examples,* Shakespeare Soc. (1851). *20c. coll.*: ODEP 298, Stevenson 942:12.

gentle SEE A gentle HEART is tied with an easy thread. / LAWS too gentle are seldom obeyed; too severe, seldom executed.

gentleman 1. A gentleman is broad and fair; the vulgar are biased and petty. *Rec. dist.*: Ind.

2. A gentleman never makes any noise. *Rec. dist.*: Okla. *1st cit.*: US1844 Emerson, "Manners" in *Essays,* Second Series. *20c. coll.*: Stevenson 943:1.

3. Gentlemen cherish worth; the vulgar cherish dirt. *Rec. dist.*: Fla.

4. Gentlemen prefer blondes. *Rec. dist.*: N.Y. *1st cit.*: US1925 Loos, *Gentlemen Prefer Blondes*. *20c. coll.*: Whiting(MP) 250.

5. He is the best gentleman who is the son of his own deserts. *Rec. dist.*: Ind.

6. It always pays to be a gentleman. *Rec. dist.*: N.Y.

7. Once a gentleman, always a gentleman. *Rec. dist.*: Wis. *1st cit.*: 1857 Dickens, *Little Dorrit*. *20c. coll.*: Stevenson 944:5.

SEE ALSO It is not the gay COAT that makes the gentleman. / EDUCATION begins a gentleman; conversation completes him. / Neither a FOOL nor a gentleman should see a thing until it is finished. / A LADY is a woman who makes it easy for a man to be a gentleman.

gentleness 1. Gentleness and kindness conquer at last. *Rec. dist.*: Ill.

2. Gentleness often disarms the fierce and melts the stubborn. *Rec. dist.*: Mich.

SEE ALSO POWER itself has not one-half the might of gentleness.

gently SEE SPEAK gently: it is better to rule by love than by fear.

German Once a German, always a German. *Rec. dist.*: N.Y.

get 1. Get justly, use soberly, distribute cheerfully, and live contentedly. *Rec. dist.*: Mich.

2. Get what you can, and what you get, hold; 'tis the stone that will turn all your lead into gold. *Rec. dist.*: N.Y., Ohio, S.C. *1st cit.*: US1756 Franklin, *PRAlmanac*. *20c. coll.*: Stevenson 925:3.

3. Ill got, ill spent. *Var.*: Evil gotten, evil spent. *Rec. dist.*: Ind., N.Y., Okla., Tex. *1st cit.*: 1481 Caxton, *Reynard*. *20c. coll.*: ODEP 399, Stevenson 926:1.

4. Since we cannot get what we like, let us like what we can get. *Rec. dist.*: Ont. *1st cit.*: US1948 Stevenson, *Home Book of Proverbs*. *20c. coll.*: Stevenson 415:4.

5. Some guys got it, and some guys ain't got it. *Rec. dist.*: Oreg.

6. Soon got, soon spent. ***Rec. dist.:*** Okla., Tex., Vt. ***1st cit.:*** 1546 Heywood, *Dialogue of Proverbs,* ed. Habernicht (1963). ***20c. coll.:*** *ODEP* 752, Stevenson 924:1, Whiting*(MP)* 251.

7. What you can't get is just what suits you. ***Rec. dist.:*** Ont.

8. What you want, you can't get—what you can get the devil wouldn't have. ***Rec. dist.:*** Miss.

9. You get out of the world just what you put into it. ***Var.:*** We get out of life exactly what we put into it. ***Rec. dist.:*** U.S., Can.

10. You get what you pay for. ***Rec. dist.:*** Kans., Mich.

11. You get what you try for. ***Rec. dist.:*** Vt.

SEE ALSO Get there FASTEST with the mostest. / It's not lost what a FRIEND gets. / Them as HAS, gits. / You can't HOLD what you haven't got in your hand. / You cannot LOSE what you haven't got. / MAN gets and forgets; woman gives and forgives. / The MORE you get the more you want. / You get NOTHING for nothing. / If you breed a PARTRIDGE, you'll get a partridge. / It ain't what you WANTS in dis world, it's what you gits. / Don't skin your WOLVES before you get them.

getting **1.** Get it while the getting's good. ***Rec. dist.:*** Ind.

2. Getting on is largely a matter of getting up each time you are knocked down. ***Rec. dist.:*** Utah.

SEE ALSO If you would be WEALTHY, think of saving as well as getting.

gift **1.** A gift is better than a promise. ***Vars.:*** **(a)** A gift in the hand is better than two promises. **(b)** One gift is worth two promises. ***Rec. dist.:*** N.Y.

2. A gift long waited for is sold, not given. ***Rec. dist.:*** Mich., N.Y. ***1st cit.:*** 1586 Warner, *Albion's England.* ***20c. coll.:*** *ODEP* 301, Stevenson 956:8.

3. A gift today is a treasure tomorrow. ***Rec. dist.:*** Ont.

4. A gift with a kind word is a double gift. ***Rec. dist.:*** N.J., N.C., N.Dak.

5. A man's gift makes room for him. ***Rec. dist.:*** N.Y. ***1st cit.:*** 1732 Fuller, *Gnomologia.* ***20c. coll.:*** *ODEP* 301, Stevenson 951:5.

6. A small gift usually gets small thanks. ***Rec. dist.:*** N.Y.

7. Be slow to take a gift: most men give to be paid back. ***Rec. dist.:*** Miss.

8. Every man loves a man who gives gifts. ***Rec. dist.:*** Ind.

9. It's not the gift that counts, but the thought behind it. ***Rec. dist.:*** N.Y.

10. Life's greatest gift: a year of time. ***Rec. dist.:*** Ohio.

11. Rich gifts wax poor when givers prove unkind. ***Rec. dist.:*** Ill., N.Y. ***1st cit.:*** 1600 Shakespeare, *Hamlet.* ***20c. coll.:*** Stevenson 955:2.

12. The gift bringer always finds an open door. ***Rec. dist.:*** Ill.

13. The gift of an enemy is no better than an injury. ***Rec. dist.:*** Ill.

14. The gift without the giver is bare. ***Rec. dist.:*** U.S.

SEE ALSO What is BOUGHT is cheaper than a gift. / CONCEIT is nature's gift to a small man to make up for that which he does not have. / A clear CONSCIENCE is God's greatest gift. / DEATH is sometimes a gift. / The GIVER makes the gift precious. / Beware the GREEKS bearing gifts. / Don't look a gift HORSE in the mouth. / SPEECH is a gift of all, but thought of few.

girdle SEE All the KEYS hang not at one's girdle.

girl **1.** A girl with cotton stockings never sees a mouse. ***Rec. dist.:*** Ont.

2. A girl worth kissing is not easily kissed. ***Rec. dist.:*** Ohio.

3. A good girl always gets caught; a bad girl knows how to avoid it. ***Rec. dist.:*** Ky., Tenn.

4. A whistling girl and a crowing hen always end in the devil's den. ***Vars.:*** **(a)** A girl who can whistle and a hen that can crow will make their way wherever they go. **(b)** A whistling girl and a cackling hen come to no good end. **(c)** A whistling girl and a crowing hen all come to the same bad end. **(d)** A whistling girl and a crowing hen always come to some bad end. **(e)** A whistling girl and a crowing hen always come to the same bad end. **(f)** A whistling girl and a crowing hen never come to any good end. **(g)** A whistling girl and a crowing hen will come to no good end. **(h)** A whistling girl and an old black sheep are two of the best things a farmer can keep. **(i)** Whistling girls and crowing hens are not the kind that catch the men. *Rec. dist.:* U.S. *1st cit.:* 1721 Kelly, *Scottish Proverbs;* US1930 *Folk-Say,* ed. Botkin. *20c. coll.:* CODP 245, ODEP 155, Stevenson 2505:5, Whiting*(MP)* 305.

5. All are good girls, but where do the bad wives come from? *Rec. dist.:* N.Y.

6. Any girl can handle the beast in a man if she's cagey enough. *Rec. dist.:* Miss.

7. Don't marry a girl who wants strawberries in January. *Rec. dist.:* Ohio.

8. Every girl has her day. *Rec. dist.:* Ky., Tenn.

9. Every girl is beautiful in her father's eyes. *Rec. dist.:* Ill.

10. Girls will be girls. *Rec. dist.:* U.S. *1st cit.:* US1870–73 McCloskey, *Across the Continent* in *Davy Crockett and Other Plays,* eds. Goldberg and Heffner (1940). *20c. coll.:* T&W 152, Whiting*(MP)* 253.

11. It is as easy to love a rich girl as a poor one. *Rec. dist.:* N.J., N.Y. *1st cit.:* US1941 Gruber, *Simon Lash. 20c. coll.:* Stevenson 1465:1.

12. Kissing a girl for the first time is like getting the first olive from a jar: after the first one, they come rolling out. *Rec. dist.:* Okla.

13. Men seldom make passes at girls who wear glasses. *Vars.:* **(a)** Boys seldom make passes at girls wearing glasses. **(b)** Boys seldom make passes for girls who wear glasses. *Rec. dist.:* U.S. *1st cit.:* US1926 Parker, *News Item. 20c. coll.:* Stevenson 961:3.

14. Nothing will ruin an interesting intellectual conversation any quicker than the arrival of a pretty girl. *Rec. dist.:* N.Y.

15. One girl is a girl, two girls are half a girl, and three girls are no girl at all. *Rec. dist.:* Ky.,

Tenn. *Infm.:* Cf. boy. *1st cit.:* ca1930 Thompson, *Country Calendar. 20c. coll.:* CODP 24.

16. The first girl up in the morning is the best-dressed girl that day. *Rec. dist.:* Ill.

17. The girl that thinks no man is good enough for her is right, but she's left. *Var.:* The girl who thinks no man is good enough for her may be right—but she is now often left. *Rec. dist.:* Ill., Ohio.

18. The more a girl runs, the harder a boy chases. *Rec. dist.:* Kans.

19. The whisper of a pretty girl can be heard further than the roar of a lion. *Rec. dist.:* Wis.

20. When a girl whistles, the angels cry. *Rec. dist.:* N.Y.

21. When you get one girl you better try two, cause there ain't no telling what one'll do. *Rec. dist.:* Ala., Ga.

22. You can take the girl out of the country, but you can't take the country out of the girl. *Var.:* You can take a girl off a farm, but you can't take the farm out of a girl. *Rec. dist.:* Ill., Kans.

girlhood Our girlhood determines our womanhood. *Rec. dist.:* Fla.

give **1.** Better to give than lend. *Rec. dist.:* N.Y.

2. Give a little, take a little. *Rec. dist.:* Ont.

3. Give and you shall receive. *Rec. dist.:* Kans. *1st cit.:* 1548 Hall, *Chronicle;* US1948 Stevenson, *Home Book of Proverbs. 20c. coll.:* Stevenson 957:2.

4. He gives twice who gives promptly. *Vars.:* **(a)** He gives doubly who gives happily. **(b)** He gives twice who gives happily. **(c)** He that gives soon gives twice. **(d)** He who gives quickly gives twice. *Rec. dist.:* Ill., N.Y., Wis. *1st cit.:* ca1385 Chaucer, *Legend of Good Women;* US1650 *Letters of John Davenport,* ed. Calder (1937). *20c. coll.:* CODP 92, Whiting 175, ODEP 304, Stevenson 956:3, Whiting*(MP)* 253.

5. He who gives is twice blessed. *Rec. dist.:* Ill., N.Y., Wis.

6. He who gives twice gives without hesitation. *Rec. dist.:* Wis. *1st cit.:* ca1385 Chaucer,

Legend of Good Women. **20c. coll.:** ODEP 304, Stevenson 956:3.

7. It is better to give than to receive. **Vars.:** **(a)** Better to give than to take. **(b)** It is more blessed to give than to receive. **(c)** More blessed to give than to receive. **Rec. dist.:** U.S., Can. **1st cit.:** ca1390 Gower, *Confessio Amantis,* E.E.T.S. (1900); US1647 Ward, *Simple Cobler of Aggawam in America,* ed. Wroth (1937). **20c. coll.:** ODEP 53, Whiting 175, CODP 16, Stevenson 957:2, Whiting*(MP)* 253.

8. It is not only what we give but how we give it that counts. **Rec. dist.:** Ind., N.Y., Wis.

9. Let him who gives nothing be silent, and him who receives speak. **Rec. dist.:** N.Y.

10. Not what we give, but what we share makes us great. **Rec. dist.:** Kans.

11. They who give willingly love to give quickly. **Rec. dist.:** Mich.

12. We give and grow. **Rec. dist.:** Kans.

13. You can't give what you haven't got. **Var.:** No one can give what he has not got. **Rec. dist.:** N.C.

SEE ALSO ADVICE is not a popular thing to give. / We may give ADVICE, but we cannot give conduct. / Give even the DEVIL his due. / A FRIEND is a present you give yourself. / The best way to keep a FRIEND is not to give him away. / GOD gives every bird its food but he does not throw it into the nest. / The HAND that gives, gathers. / To him who HAS shall be given. / Don't give up HOPE till hope is dead. / To the strong is JUSTICE given. / LIBERTY is one thing you can't have unless you give it to others. / LIFE is just; it will give us all we earn. / LITTLE is given, little is expected. / LOVE sought is good, but given unsought is better. / He who gives to the POOR lends to the Lord. / Give a man ROPE enough and he'll hang himself. / SAVE while you have; give while you live. / SILENCE gives consent. / A SMILE costs nothing, but gives much.

giver The Lord loves the cheerful giver. **Vars.:** **(a)** God loves a cheerful giver. **(b)** The Lord loves a cheerful giver. **Rec. dist.:** U.S., Can.

1st cit.: US1809 Weems, *Life of Gen. Francis Marion* (1815). **20c. coll.:** Whiting 179, Stevenson 953:7.

SEE ALSO The GIFT without the giver is bare.

giving **1.** Giving is an honor. **Rec. dist.:** Calif., Miss.

2. Some are always giving; others are always taking. **Rec. dist.:** Kans.

SEE ALSO It's LOVING and giving that make life worth living.

glad Twice glad—when you come and when you go. **Rec. dist.:** Ont.

SEE ALSO Got the same PANTS to get glad in as you had to get sad in. / POOR folks are glad of porridge. / When the STOMACH is full the heart is glad. / Whatever way the WIND does blow, some hearts are glad to have it so.

gladness **1.** A man of gladness seldom falls into madness. **Var.:** A man of gladness falls into madness. **Rec. dist.:** Ill., N.Y. **1st cit.:** 1659 Howell, *Paroimiografia (English Proverbs).* **20c. coll.:** ODEP 305, Stevenson 1072:1.

2. Happiness comes from gladness as light from the sun. **Rec. dist.:** Ont.

3. There is gladness in remembrance. **Rec. dist.:** Ont.

SEE ALSO A kind HEART is a fountain of gladness.

glass **1.** A looking glass never tells a woman she is homely. **Rec. dist.:** Ont.

2. A woman who looks much in the glass spins but little. **Rec. dist.:** Wis.

3. Glass, china, and reputations are easily cracked and never well mended. **Rec. dist.:** Ill. **1st cit.:** US1750 Franklin, *PRAlmanac.* **20c. coll.:** Whiting 176.

4. Half a glass is better than none. **Rec. dist.:** Ont.

5. He that has a head of glass must not throw stones at another. **Rec. dist.:** Ont., Tex. **1st cit.:** ca1374 Chaucer, *Troilus and Criseyde.* **20c. coll.:** ODEP 360, CODP 92, Stevenson 1095:1.

6. People who live in glass houses shouldn't throw stones. **Vars.:** **(a)** Don't throw rocks at glass houses. **(b)** Don't throw stones at your neighbors if your own windows are glass. **(c)** Don't throw stones from glass houses. **(d)** He who lives in a glass house shouldn't throw stones. **(e)** He who lives in a house of glass should not throw stones at other people. **(f)** People in glass houses shouldn't throw stones. **(g)** People who live in brick houses shouldn't throw glass. **(h)** People who live in glass houses should undress in the basement. **(i)** Those who live in glass houses gather no moss. **(j)** Those who live in glass houses should never throw stones. **(k)** Those who live in glass houses should undress in the dark. *Rec. dist.:* U.S., Can. *1st cit.:* 1640 Herbert, *Outlandish Proverbs (Jacula Prudentum)* in *Works,* ed. Hutchinson (1941); US1710 Dummer in *William & Mary Coll. Quart.* (1967). *20c. coll.:* ODEP 360, CODP 92, Whiting 225, Stevenson 1193:2, T&W 194, Whiting*(MP)* 484.

SEE ALSO A BLIND man needs no looking glass. / When you have committed a CRIME, the whole world is a looking glass. / When you incline to drink RUM, fill the glass half with water. / Handle with care WOMEN and glass.

glasses 1. Glasses and lasses are brittle ware. *Rec. dist.:* Ont.

2. He pays for the glasses who breaks them. *Rec. dist.:* Wis.

3. Men seldom make passes at girls who wear glasses. *Vars.:* **(a)** Boys seldom make passes at girls who wear glasses. **(b)** Boys seldom make passes for girls who wear glasses. **(c)** Fellows don't make passes at girls who wear glasses. **(d)** Women who wear glasses will never receive passes. *Rec. dist.:* Ill., Ind., Oreg., Wis. *1st cit.:* US1926 Parker, *News Item. 20c. coll.:* Stevenson 961:3.

4. People who wear glasses shouldn't have too long a nose. *Rec. dist.:* Ind.

5. Through rose colored glasses the world is always bright. *Rec. dist.:* U.S., Can.

glitter SEE All that glitters is not GOLD.

glorious No man e'er was glorious who was not laborious. *Rec. dist.:* Ind., N.Y., S.C.

SEE ALSO BEAUTY, like truth, is never so glorious as when it goes plainest.

glory *(n.)* 1. Glory is a poison, good to be taken in small doses. *Rec. dist.:* Ill.

2. Glory is the fair child of peril. *Rec. dist.:* Ill.

3. Glory paid to our ashes comes too late. *Rec. dist.:* Ill. *1st cit.:* 1659 Lovelace, *Poems. 20c. coll.:* Stevenson 962:11.

4. Hasty glory goes out in a snuff. *Rec. dist.:* N.Dak., Ont. *1st cit.:* 1732 Fuller, *Gnomologia. 20c. coll.:* Stevenson 962:2.

5. Mean men admire wealth, great men seek true glory. *Rec. dist.:* Mich.

6. No flowery road leads to glory. *Var.:* There is no pathway of flowers leading to glory. *Rec. dist.:* Ill., Ont., Wis. *1st cit.:* US1948 Stevenson, *Home Book of Proverbs. 20c. coll.:* Stevenson 962:15.

7. Our greatest glory consists not in never falling, but in rising every time we fall. *Rec. dist.:* Ill., Miss., Ont.

8. Real glory springs from the silent conquest of ourselves. *Rec. dist.:* Miss.

9. Seldom comes glory till a man is dead. *Rec. dist.:* N.Y. *1st cit.:* 1648 Herrick, *Hesperides. 20c. coll.:* Stevenson 962:11.

10. The desire for glory is the torch of the mind. *Rec. dist.:* Ill.

11. The paths of glory lead to the grave. *Var.:* The paths of glory lead but to the grave. *Rec. dist.:* N.J., N.Y., Ohio. *1st cit.:* 1751 Gray, *Elegy Written in a Country Church-Yard. 20c. coll.:* Stevenson 1026:8.

12. The smoke of glory is not worth the smoke of a pipe. *Rec. dist.:* Ill.

13. Unless what we do is useful, our glory is vain. *Rec. dist.:* Ill. *1st cit.:* US1948 Stevenson, *Home Book of Proverbs. 20c. coll.:* Stevenson 2412:5.

14. We rise in glory as we sink in pride. *Rec. dist.:* Ill.

15. When glory comes, memory departs. *Rec. dist.:* Ill.

SEE ALSO A woman's HAIR is her crowning glory. / The greater the OBSTACLE, the more glory in overcoming it. / The WISE shall inherit glory, but shame shall be the promotion of fools.

glory *(v.)* While you glory in the past, be busy in the present lest you be caught unprepared in the future. *Rec. dist.:* Miss.

glove 1. A clean glove often hides a dirty hand. *Rec. dist.:* Ill., Ind., N.Y., Ont., Oreg. *1st cit.:* 1902 Hulme, *Proverb Lore.* *20c. coll.:* Stevenson 79:3.

2. If the glove fits, wear it. *Rec. dist.:* Ont. *Infm.:* Cf. shoe.

3. The steel glove under the silken glove. *Rec. dist.:* Ill., Mich., Ont. *1st cit.:* 1850 Carlyle, *Latter Day Pamphlets.* *20c. coll.:* Stevenson 1058:11.

SEE ALSO The CAT in gloves catches no mice. / The PORCUPINE, whom one must handle gloved, may be respected, but is never loved.

glowworm Glowworms are not lanterns. *Rec. dist.:* Ill.

glutton 1. The glutton is born merely for the purpose of digestion. *Rec. dist.:* Ill.

2. The glutton's god is his belly, and his glory is his shame. *Rec. dist.:* Ill.

gluttony 1. Gluttony kills more than the sword. *Rec. dist.:* Mich., Ont. *1st cit.:* ca1384 Wyclif, *Works,* ed. Arnold; US1754 Ames, *Almanacs,* ed. Briggs (1891). *20c. coll.:* ODEP 306, Whiting 177, Stevenson 965:10.

2. Gluttony makes the body sting as well as the pocket. *Rec. dist.:* Ill.

gnat The gnat is small, to be sure, but she is not the servant of the cow. *Rec. dist.:* N.Y., S.C.

go 1. Go farther and fare worse. *Rec. dist.:* N.Y., S.C. *1st cit.:* 1546 Heywood, *Dialogue of Proverbs,* ed. Habernicht (1963); US1819 Welby, *Visit to North America.* *20c. coll.:* ODEP 306, Whiting 177, Stevenson 967:1, T&W 154, Whiting(MP) 256.

2. Go it while you're young. *Rec. dist.:* N.H.

3. If you can't go over or under, go through. *Rec. dist.:* Ont.

4. If you want a thing done, go; if not, send. *Rec. dist.:* U.S., Can. *1st cit.:* 1666 Torriano, *Common Place of Italian Proverbs;* US1743

Franklin, *PRAlmanac.* *20c. coll.:* ODEP 865, Stevenson 2063:11, T&W 369.

5. Not to go forwards is to go backwards. *Rec. dist.:* Miss., Ohio.

6. Tell me with whom you go, and I'll tell you what you are. *Rec. dist.:* Ont. *1st cit.:* 1581 Guazzo, *Civile Conversation,* tr. Pettie, T.T. (1925). *20c. coll.:* ODEP 807.

SEE ALSO Not to ADVANCE is to go back. / If you look BACK, you'll soon be going that way. / Twice GLAD—when you come and when you go. / Hasty GLORY goes out in a snuff. / Where everyone goes the GRASS never grows. / To go to LAW is to go to sea. / A LITTLE goes a long way. / LOVE goes where it's sent. / LOVE makes the world go round. / LOVE will creep where it cannot go. / MONEY makes the mare go. / MONEY makes the world go around. / A NAIL can go no farther than its head will let it. / PAY as you go. / It's better to be READY and not to go than not to be ready and go. / Be sure you are RIGHT, then go ahead. / Everything that goes UP must come down. / The WORLD is his who has the money to go over it. / Wherever you go you can never get rid of YOURSELF.

goal Do not turn back when you are just at the goal. *Rec. dist.:* Utah.

goat 1. A lame goat takes no siesta. *Rec. dist.:* Ont.

2. An old goat is never the more revered for his beard. *Rec. dist.:* Mich. *1st cit.:* 1732 Fuller, *Gnomologia.* *20c. coll.:* Stevenson 967:16.

3. Don't mistake an old goat for a preacher because of his beard. *Rec. dist.:* Ill.

4. If the goat would not jump around, she wouldn't break her leg. *Rec. dist.:* Ont.

5. No goat ever died of hunger. *Rec. dist.:* Ill.

SEE ALSO It is too late to close the WELL after the goat has fallen in.

God 1. God aids him who changes. *Rec. dist.:* Wis.

2. God builds a nest for the blind bird. *Var.:* God makes a nest for the blind bird. *Rec. dist.:* Ill. *1st cit.:* 1909 *Spectator (London),* 2 Jan. *20c. coll.:* Stevenson 981:4.

3. God fits the back to its burden. *Rec. dist.:* U.S., Can. *1st cit.:* 1822 Cobbett, *Rural Rides;* US1955 Disney, *Room for Murder.* *20c. coll.:* ODEP 312, CODP 94, Stevenson 256:3, Whiting*(MP)* 259.

4. God grips but does not choke. *Rec. dist.:* Calif., N.Y.

5. God heals and the doctor takes the fee. *Var.:* God cures, and the doctor takes the fee. *Rec. dist.:* Ind., Miss., Tex., Wis. *1st cit.:* 1640 Herbert, *Outlandish Proverbs (Jacula Prudentum)* in *Works,* ed. Hutchinson (1941); US1736 Franklin, *PRAlmanac.* *20c. coll.:* ODEP 310, Whiting 178, Stevenson 595:2.

6. God help the rich, for the poor can beg. *Rec. dist.:* Calif., N.Y. *1st cit.:* 1623 Painter, *Chaucer New Painted;* US1922 Taylor, *So-Called Human Race.* *20c. coll.:* ODEP 310, Stevenson 1854:10.

7. God helps those who help themselves. *Vars.:* (a) God helps him who helps himself. (b) God helps those who help themselves, but God help those who get caught helping themselves. (c) God never helps those who are caught helping themselves. *Rec. dist.:* U.S., Can. *1st cit.:* 1545 Erasmus, *Adagia,* tr. Taverner; US1736 Franklin, *PRAlmanac.* *20c. coll.:* CODP 93, Whiting 178, ODEP 310, Stevenson 979:4,11, T&W 154, Whiting*(MP)* 259.

8. God is always opening his hand. *Rec. dist.:* Wis.

9. God is no respecter of persons. *Rec. dist.:* N.Y., S.C. *1st cit.:* US1960 Malleson, *Out for the Kill.* *20c. coll.:* Stevenson 970:6, Whiting*(MP)* 260.

10. God loves the cheerful giver. *Rec. dist.:* Calif. *1st cit.:* US1809 Weems, *Life of Gen. Francis Marion.* *20c. coll.:* Whiting 179, Stevenson 953:7.

11. God made the cities, but the devil himself made the small towns. *Rec. dist.:* Calif. *1st cit.:* 1897 Tennyson, *Memoir II;* US1972 Catton, *Waiting for the Morning Train.* *20c. coll.:* ODEP 311, Stevenson 360:3, Whiting*(MP)* 260.

12. God made the country, and man made the town. *Var.:* God made the country, man made the city. *Rec. dist.:* N.Y. *1st cit.:* ca1783 Cowper, *The Task;* US1972 Catton, *Waiting for the Morning Train.* *20c. coll.:* ODEP 311, CODP 94, Stevenson 360:3, Whiting*(MP)* 260.

13. God never sends mouths but he sends meat. *Var.:* God never sends a mouth but he feeds it. *Rec. dist.:* Ont. *1st cit.:* ca1377 Langland, *Piers Plowman,* ed. Skeat, E.E.T.S. (1867); US1832 Kennedy, *Swallow Barn,* ed. Hubbell (1929). *20c. coll.:* CODP 94, T&W 154, ODEP 311, Stevenson 971:10.

14. God promises a safe landing, but not a calm passage. *Rec. dist.:* Ill., Wis.

15. God puts food into clean hands. *Rec. dist.:* Wis.

16. God restores health, and the physician gets the thanks. *Rec. dist.:* Utah. *1st cit.:* 1640 Herbert, *Outlandish Proverbs (Jacula Prudentum)* in *Works,* ed. Hutchinson (1941); US1736 Franklin, *PRAlmanac.* *20c. coll.:* ODEP 310, Whiting 178, Stevenson 595:2.

17. God sends every bird its food, but he does not throw it into the nest. *Rec. dist.:* Oreg., W.Va., Wis. *1st cit.:* US1940 Thompson, *Body, Boots, and Britches.* *20c. coll.:* Stevenson 980:11.

18. God sends meat, and the devil sends cooks. *Rec. dist.:* U.S., Can. *1st cit.:* ca1542 Boorde, *Compendyons Regyment, or Dyatorye of Healthe,* E.E.T.S. (1870); US1735 Franklin, *PRAlmanac.* *20c. coll.:* ODEP 312, CODP 94, Whiting 179, Stevenson 419:2, Whiting*(MP)* 260.

19. God's mill grinds slowly, but it grinds exceedingly fine. *Rec. dist.:* U.S. *1st cit.:* 1640 Herbert, *Outlandish Proverbs (Jacula Prudentum)* in *Works,* ed. Hutchinson (1941); US1870 Longfellow, *Poems.* *20c. coll.:* CODP 151, Stevenson 1575:11, ODEP 314, Whiting*(MP)* 411.

20. God tempers the wind to the shorn lamb. *Rec. dist.:* U.S. *1st cit.:* 1640 Herbert, *Outlandish Proverbs (Jacula Prudentum)* in *Works,* ed. Hutchinson (1941); US1780 Sewall in *Winslow Papers,* ed. Raymond (1901). *20c. coll.:* CODP 95, Whiting 179, ODEP 312, Stevenson 980:15, T&W 154, Whiting*(MP)* 260.

21. He who leaves God out of his reckoning does not know how to count. *Rec. dist.:* Ill.

22. Nothing with God is accidental. *Rec. dist.:* La., N.Y., Wis.

23. One with God is a majority. *Rec. dist.:* Calif.

24. Pray to God, but keep hammering. *Var.:* Pray to God, but hammer away. *Rec. dist.:* Ill., Wis. *1st cit.:* US1948 Stevenson, *Home Book of Proverbs.* *20c. coll.:* Stevenson 979:7.

25. Trust in God and do something. *Rec. dist.:* Wis.

26. Where God has a church, the devil has a chapel. *Rec. dist.:* N.Y., S.C. *1st cit.:* 1560 Becon, *Catechism.* *20c. coll.:* ODEP 309.

27. Who trusts in God builds well. *Rec. dist.:* Kans., N.J.

SEE ALSO The writer makes the ALMANAC, but God makes the weather. / The nearer the CHURCH, the farther from God. / DANGER past, God is forgotten. / Go hide the FAULTS of others and God will veil your own. / All GOOD comes to an end except the goodness of God. / An HONEST man is the noblest work of God. / LOOK out for others and God will look out for you. / MAN proposes, God disposes. / PARENTS are God's most gifted ministers. / He is POOR that God hates. / REBELLION to tyrants is obedience to God. / The RICH ride in chaises; the poor walk with God. / The most acceptable SERVICE of God is doing good to man. / SPEND and God will send. / For a WEB begun, God sends thread. / WORK as if everything depended on you; pray as if everything depended on God.

god **1.** Even a god, falling in love, could not be wise. *Rec. dist.:* Wis. *1st cit.:* 1539 Publilius Syrus, *Sententiae,* tr. Taverner. *20c. coll.:* ODEP 488.

2. Whom the gods love die young. *Rec. dist.:* U.S., Can. *1st cit.:* 1546 Hugh, *Troubled Man's Medicine;* US1907 Hubbard, *Epigram* in *The Philistine.* *20c. coll.:* ODEP 314, CODP 95, Stevenson 525:3, Whiting(MP) 261.

3. Whom the gods would destroy they first make mad. *Rec. dist.:* U.S. *1st cit.:* 1640 Herbert, *Outlandish Proverbs (Jacula Prudentum)* in *Works,* ed. Hutchinson (1941); US1704 *Correspondence Between William Penn and James Logan, 1700–1705,* ed. Armstrong. *20c. coll.:*

CODP 95, Whiting 180, Stevenson 1500:5, Whiting(MP) 261

SEE ALSO The MILLS of the gods grind slowly, but they grind exceedingly fine. / A WOMAN is a dish for the gods.

godliness SEE CLEANLINESS is akin to godliness.

gold **1.** A man may buy gold too dear. *Rec. dist.:* Miss., Okla., Tex. *1st cit.:* 1546 Heywood, *Dialogue of Proverbs,* ed. Habernicht (1963); US1691 Mather, *Bills of Credit* in *Colonial Currency,* ed. Davis, Publ. Prince Soc. (1910–11). *20c. coll.:* ODEP 95, Whiting 182, CODP 96, Stevenson 988:10.

2. All that glitters is not gold. *Vars.:* **(a)** All is not gold that glitters. **(b)** All that glistens is not gold. **(c)** All that glitters is sold as gold. **(d)** Gold isn't the only thing that glitters. *Rec. dist.:* U.S., Can. *1st cit.:* ca1220 Hali Meidenhad, E.E.T.S. (1866); US1636 Howes in *Winthrop Papers, 1498–1649,* Mass.Hist.Soc. Collections (1929–47). *20c. coll.:* ODEP 316, Whiting 181, CODP 92, Stevenson 990:13, T&W 154, Whiting(MP) 9.

3. An inch of gold cannot buy an inch of time. *Rec. dist.:* N.Y., Oreg.

4. Before gold even kings take off their hats. *Rec. dist.:* Ind.

5. Better whole than patched with gold. *Rec. dist.:* Miss., Ont.

6. Even if it rained gold, a lover would never become rich. *Rec. dist.:* Ind.

7. Gold and iron are good to buy gold and iron. *Rec. dist.:* N.Y. *1st cit.:* US1841 Emerson, "Politics" in *Essays,* First Series. *20c. coll.:* Stevenson 988:1.

8. Gold dust blinds all eyes. *Rec. dist.:* N.Y. *1st cit.:* US1875 Cheales, *Proverbial Folk-Lore.* *20c. coll.:* Stevenson 987:5.

9. Gold is an unseen tyrant. *Rec. dist.:* Ont. *1st cit.:* US1948 Stevenson, *Home Book of Proverbs.* *20c. coll.:* Stevenson 987:7.

10. Gold is proven by touch. *Rec. dist.:* Ont. *1st cit.:* 1592 Shakespeare, *Richard III.* *20c. coll.:* Stevenson 989:6.

11. Gold is tested by fire, men by gold. *Rec.*

dist.: Ont. *1st cit.:* 1666 Torriano, *Common Place of Italian Proverbs;* US1702 Mather, *Magnalia Christi Americana. 20c. coll.: ODEP* 315, Whiting 182, Stevenson 2568:11.

12. Gold is the devil's fishhook. *Rec. dist.:* Ill., Ky.

13. Gold is the most useless metal in the world, for it is good for plugging teeth and tormenting fools. *Rec. dist.:* Ind.

14. Gold is the snare of the soul. *Rec. dist.:* Ind.

15. Gold is wealth in fancy only. *Rec. dist.:* Fla.

16. Gold is where you find it. *Rec. dist.:* U.S., Can.

17. Gold must be tried by fire. *Var.:* Fire proves the gold. *Rec. dist.:* N.Y., Ont. *1st cit.:* ca1500 *15c. School Book,* ed. Nelson; US1702 Mather, *Magnalia Christi Americana. 20c. coll.: ODEP* 315, Whiting 182, Stevenson 989:6.

18. Gold rules the world. *Rec. dist.:* Ill. *1st cit.:* US1948 Stevenson, *Home Book of Proverbs. 20c. coll.:* Stevenson 987:7.

19. Gold will not buy everything. *Rec. dist.:* N.Y., Ont. *1st cit.:* 1576 Pettie, *Petite Palace of Pleasure,* ed. Gollancz (1908). *20c. coll.:* Stevenson 987:7.

20. Gold, women, and linen should be chosen by daylight. *Rec. dist.:* Wis.

21. He that can catch and hold, he is the man of gold. *Rec. dist.:* N.Y.

22. He that has no gold in his purse should have silver on his tongue. *Rec. dist.:* Ont. *1st cit.:* 1611 Cotgrave, *Dictionary of French and English Tongues. 20c. coll.: ODEP* 734, Stevenson 2115:2.

23. In misfortune, gold is dull; in happiness iron is bright. *Var.:* In happiness, iron is bright; in sadness, gold is dull. *Rec. dist.:* Ala., Ont.

24. It is gold that greases the wheel of love. *Rec. dist.:* Ind.

25. Like liberty, gold never stays where it is undervalued. *Rec. dist.:* N.Y. *1st cit.:* US1878 Morrill, Speech in the U.S. Senate, 25 Jan. *20c. coll.:* Stevenson 989:11.

26. Old woman's gold is not ugly. *Rec. dist.:*
Ont., Wis. *1st cit.:* 1732 Fuller, *Gnomologia. 20c. coll.:* Stevenson 989:5.

27. When gold speaks, other tongues are dumb. *Rec. dist.:* Ill. *1st cit.:* 1670 Ray, *English Proverbs. 20c. coll.:* Stevenson 988:8.

28. When gold speaks, everyone is silent. *Rec. dist.:* N.Y. *1st cit.:* 1586 Guazzo, *Civile Conversation,* tr. Pettie, T.T. (1925). *20c. coll.:* Stevenson 988:8.

29. When we have gold, we are in fear; when we have more, we are in danger. *Rec. dist.:* Ill. *1st cit.:* 1616 Draxe, *Bibliotheca Scholastica in Anglia* (1918). *20c. coll.: ODEP* 316, Stevenson 990:4.

30. Where there is gold, there is wealth. *Rec. dist.:* Ont.

31. Where there is gold, there the devil dwells. *Rec. dist.:* Oreg.

SEE ALSO An ASS covered with gold is more respected than an ass covered with a pack saddle. / An ASS is but an ass though laden with gold. / BRASS is some people's gold. / No EAR is deaf to the song that gold sings. / Silver and gold may tarnish away, but a good EDUCATION will never decay. / FIRE is the test of gold. / Better have a FRIEND on the road than gold or silver in your purse. / Make new FRIENDS but keep the old. / GET what you can, and what you get, hold; 'tis the stone that will turn all your lead into gold. / Find HEALTH better than gold. / An HONEST man is worth his weight in gold. / The MORNING hour has gold in its mouth. / SECONDS are the gold dust of time. / If it were not for the STOMACH, the back would wear gold. / SUCCESS is a chain of gold—but it is a chain. / A WORD fitly spoken is like apples of gold in pictures of silver.

golden A golden key opens every door—except that of heaven. *Rec. dist.:* Ill. *1st cit.:* 1580 Lyly, *Euphues and His England,* ed. Arber (1868). *20c. coll.: CODP* 96, Stevenson 988:13.

SEE ALSO A golden CAGE is still a cage. / Set a FROG on a golden stool, away it hops to reach the pool. / Don't kill the GOOSE that lays the golden egg. / SILENCE is golden.

gone Gone but not forgotten. *Rec. dist.:* Ill., Iowa, Kans., R.I.

SEE ALSO Unbidden GUESTS are most welcome when they are gone. / HERE today and gone tomorrow.

good *(n.)* **1.** All good comes to an end except the goodness of God. *Vars.:* **(a)** All good comes to an end—except the goodness of bed. **(b)** All good things must come to an end. *Rec. dist.:* Calif., Ill. *1st cit.:* US1900 Pidgin, *Quincy Adams Sawyer.* *20c. coll.:* Whiting*(MP)* 617.

2. All things work together for good for those who love God. *Var.:* All things work together for good. *Rec. dist.:* Kans., Ont. *1st cit.:* US1948 Stevenson, *Home Book of Proverbs.* *20c. coll.:* Stevenson 992:11.

3. Any good that we do should be done now, for we pass this way but once. *Rec. dist.:* Kans. *1st cit.:* USca1855 Grellet, *Maxim.* *20c. coll.:* Stevenson 995:14.

4. As often as we do good, we sacrifice. *Rec. dist.:* N.Y.

5. Associate with the good and you will be one of them. *Rec. dist.:* N.Y., Ont.

6. Better do little good than a great deal bad. *Var.:* Better do a little good than a great deal of bad. *Rec. dist.:* Calif., Ill.

7. Certain good should never be relinquished for uncertain hopes. *Rec. dist.:* Mich.

8. Do good by stealth and blush to find it fame. *Rec. dist.:* Miss. *1st cit.:* 1733 Pope, *Epilogue to the Satires.* *20c. coll.:* Stevenson 541:10.

9. Do no good and you shall find no evil. *Rec. dist.:* Ill., Oreg.

10. Good and quickly seldom meet. *Rec. dist.:* R.I. *1st cit.:* 1640 Herbert, *Outlandish Proverbs (Jacula Prudentum)* in *Works,* ed. Hutchinson (1941); US1927 Wright, *"Canary" Murder Case.* *20c. coll.:* Stevenson 1083:2, Whiting*(MP)* 262.

11. Good, better, best: never let it rest until your good is better and your better best. *Var.:* Good, better, best: never let them rest till the good is better and the better is best. *Rec. dist.:* U.S.

12. Good comes to some while they are sleeping. *Rec. dist.:* N.Y.

13. Good is recognized when it goes, and evil when it comes. *Rec. dist.:* Calif., Ill., Ohio.

14. Good that comes too late is good as nothing. *Rec. dist.:* Okla., Tex. *1st cit.:* 1732 Fuller, *Gnomologia.* *20c. coll.:* Stevenson 992:10.

15. He injures the good who spares the bad. *Rec. dist.:* Ont.

16. He that worked for the good of others will be honored and loved. *Rec. dist.:* Utah.

17. If you can't say something good about someone, don't say anything at all. *Var.:* If it isn't good, don't say it. *Rec. dist.:* Ga.

18. If you want to win, return good for evil. *Rec. dist.:* Ill. *1st cit.:* 1640 Herbert, *Outlandish Proverbs (Jacula Prudentum)* in *Works,* ed. Hutchinson (1941). *20c. coll.:* ODEP 317.

19. It's amazing how much good you can do if you don't care who gets the credit. *Rec. dist.:* Wis.

20. It's never too late to do good. *Rec. dist.:* Ill.

21. Never pour good after bad. *Rec. dist.:* Calif.

22. No good or evil can last a lifetime. *Rec. dist.:* Calif.

23. One never did repent of doing good. *Rec. dist.:* Wis. *1st cit.:* 1597 Shakespeare, *Merchant of Venice.* *20c. coll.:* Stevenson 996:12.

24. The good die young. *Rec. dist.:* U.S., Can. *1st cit.:* 1697 Defoe, *Character of Dr. Annesley;* US1852 Cary, *Clovernook.* *20c. coll.:* CODP 97, T&W 155, Stevenson 510:3, Whiting*(MP)* 263.

25. The good that is, is better than the good that was. *Rec. dist.:* Ont.

26. The good that men do lives after them. *Rec. dist.:* Kans., N.Y., R.I., S.C. *1st cit.:* 1942 Wells, *You Can't Be Too Careful.* *20c. coll.:* Stevenson 1005:3.

27. The good you do is not lost, though you forget it. *Rec. dist.:* R.I. *1st cit.:* 1732 Fuller, *Gnomologia.* *20c. coll.:* Stevenson 996:4.

28. The good you do to others will always come back to you. *Var.:* The good we confer on others recoils on ourselves. *Rec. dist.:* Miss.

1st cit.: 1948 Stevenson, *Home Book of Proverbs.* *20c. coll.:* Stevenson 996:9.

29. There is no good that does not cost a price. *Rec. dist.:* Kans.

30. To do good is to be good. *Rec. dist.:* Ark., Ont.

31. You will never lose a turn by doing good. *Rec. dist.:* Ont. *1st cit.:* 1642 Torriano, *Select Italian Proverbs.* *20c. coll.:* ODEP 486.

SEE ALSO The BAD which is well known is better than the good unknown. / There is no man so BAD but he secretly respects the good. / There is nothing so BAD in which there is not something good. / If you help the EVIL, you hurt the good. / Take the EVIL with the good. / To favor the ILL is to injure the good. / LISTENERS hear no good of themselves. / Learn the LUXURY of doing good. / The PLEASURE of doing good is the only one that will not wear out. / The most acceptable SERVICE of God is doing good to man. / The SUN never repents of the good he does, nor does he ever demand a recompense. / A man's true WEALTH is the good he does in the world. / An ill WIND blows no good. / No WIND can do him good who steers for no port.

good *(adj.)* **1.** A good man is seldom uneasy, an ill one never easy. *Rec. dist.:* N.Y. *1st cit.:* US1734 Franklin, *PRAlmanac.* *20c. coll.:* Stevenson 1000:9.

2. A man going on and thinking he's no good is no man at all. *Rec. dist.:* N.C.

3. A man is only as good as the worst on his team. *Rec. dist.:* N.C.

4. All are presumed good until they are found in a fault. *Rec. dist.:* N.Y. *1st cit.:* 1640 Herbert, *Outlandish Proverbs (Jacula Prudentum)* in *Works,* ed. Hutchinson (1941). *20c. coll.:* ODEP 646.

5. All good things come to those who wait. *Rec. dist.:* N.Y., W.Va. *1st cit.:* ca1530 Barclay, *Eclogues,* E.E.T.S. (1927); US1863 Longfellow, *Poems* (1960). *20c. coll.:* CODP 3.

6. All that looks good ain't. *Rec. dist.:* N.Y.

7. Anything is good if your idea is good. *Rec. dist.:* Wis.

8. Be good and have fun; but if you're good, you'll not have fun. *Rec. dist.:* Ind.

9. Be good and you will be lonesome. *Rec. dist.:* N.Y. *1st cit.:* US1897 Twain, *Following the Equator.* *20c. coll.:* Stevenson 995:7.

10. Be good; and if you can't be good, be careful. *Rec. dist.:* U.S. *1st cit.:* ca1303 Mannyng, *Handlyng Synne,* E.E.T.S. (1901). *20c. coll.:* CODP 97, Stevenson 995:8, Whiting(MP) 263.

11. Be not simply good; be good for something. *Rec. dist.:* Calif., Kans., N.Y., Ont., Oreg.

12. Being good is the mother of doing good. *Rec. dist.:* Calif., Ill., Ont.

13. By good nature half the misery of human life might be assauged. *Rec. dist.:* Mich.

14. Get good sense and you will not repine at the want of good luck. *Rec. dist.:* Mich.

15. Good men and bad men are each less so than they seem. *Rec. dist.:* N.Y.

16. Good people are not always nice people. *Rec. dist.:* Ill.

17. Good things are seldom cheap. *Rec. dist.:* N.J. *1st cit.:* US1875 Scarborough, *Chinese Proverbs.* *20c. coll.:* Stevenson 327:2.

18. Good things come in small packages. *Vars.:* **(a)** Good goods are done up in small parcels. **(b)** Good goods are done up in small parcels, and so are poisons. **(c)** Good goods make small parcels. *Rec. dist.:* Kans., Miss., N.J., N.Y., Ont. *1st cit.:* 1659 Howell, *Paroimiografia (French Proverbs);* US1961 Mathews, *Very Welcome.* *20c. coll.:* CODP 13, Whiting(MP) 618.

19. Good things soon find a purchaser. *Rec. dist.:* N.J.

20. Hold fast to that which is good. *Rec. dist.:* Ont.

21. If they're good, they're not good-looking; if good-looking, they're not good. *Rec. dist.:* N.Y. *1st cit.:* ca1930 Kummer, *In Dingle-Dongle Bell.* *20c. coll.:* Stevenson 2582:1.

22. If you're good, you're good and lonely. *Rec. dist.:* Ohio. *1st cit.:* US1897 Twain, *Following the Equator.* *20c. coll.:* Stevenson 995:7.

23. 'Tis more to be good than great; to be happy is better than wise. *Rec. dist.:* R.I.

24. Some people are so good that they are no good. *Rec. dist.:* Ont. *1st cit.:* ca1594 Bacon, *Promus*. *20c. coll.:* ODEP 324, Stevenson 992:1.

25. The good man can't be bribed: he is good for nothing. *Rec. dist.:* Ill.

26. There's good and bad in everything. *Rec. dist.:* Calif.

27. Too much of a good thing is worse than none at all. *Rec. dist.:* N.Y. *1st cit.:* ca1390 Chaucer, *Prologue to Canon's Yeoman's Tale;* US1784 Winslow in *Winslow Papers 1776– 1826,* ed. Raymond (1901). *20c. coll.:* ODEP 831, Whiting 302, *CODP* 228, Stevenson 1637:6, T&W 253, Whiting(MP) 620.

28. What is good for one man may not be good for another. *Rec. dist.:* Ky., N.C., Oreg.

29. What's good for one is good for another. *Rec. dist.:* Ill., Oreg.

30. When you are good to others, you are best to yourself. *Rec. dist.:* Ill. *1st cit.:* 1642 Torriano, *Select Italian Proverbs*. *20c. coll.:* ODEP 191.

SEE ALSO For the sake of one good ACTION a hundred evil ones should be forgotten. / Never repent of a good ACTION. / It is not good that the man should be ALONE. / For a good APPETITE there is no hard bread. / On a good BARGAIN think twice. / A good BEGIN-NING makes a good ending. / BOOKS and friends should be few and good. / To a good CAT a good rat. / A good CAUSE makes a stout heart and a strong arm. / You can't make a good COAT out of bad wool. / A good COM-PANION makes good company. / An honest CONFESSION is good for the soul. / The best DEFENSE is a good offense. / What's good for the DEVIL applies to his imp. / DILIGENCE is the mother of good luck. / Better a good DINNER than a fine coat. / A good DOG de-serves a good bone. / You can't keep a good man DOWN. / The FOX may grow gray, but never good. / A good FRIEND never offends. / FRIENDSHIP, like persimmons, is good only when ripe. / What's good for the GOOSE is good for the gander. / One good HEAD is better than a thousand strong hands. / The road to HELL is paved with good intentions. / A good HEN does not cackle in your house and lay in another's. / An overdose of HILAR-ITY does no one any good. / It is a good HORSE who never stumbles. / Good HUMOR is the suspenders that keep our working clothes on. / There never was a good KNIFE made of bad steel. / A good LAWYER, a bad neighbor. / Most good LAWYERS live well, work hard, and die poor. / A good LEADER is also a good follower. / LEARNING makes a good man bet-ter and a bad man worse. / A LIAR should have a good memory. / If you tell a LIE an' stick to it, dat's as good as de truth anyhow. / A long LIFE may not be good enough, but a good life is long enough. / Good LISTENING does not mean sitting dumb. / Better to be a good LOSER than a poor winner. / Good LUCK beats early rising. / Good MANAGEMENT is better than good income. / Good MANNERS are made up of petty sacrifices. / A good MAXIM is never out of season. / A MISS is as good as a mile. / Bad MONEY drives out good. / It is discouraging to be a good NEIGHBOR in a bad neighborhood. / To be a good NEIGH-BOR, take heed to your tongue. / No NEWS is good news. / An OLD man in the house is a good sign. / When the OUTLOOK isn't good, try the uplook. / The good PAYMASTER is lord of another man's purse. / A good RUN is better than a poor stand. / A good RUNNER is never caught. / SAY well is good, but do well is better. / A SCANDAL is something that has to be bad to be good. / A SECRET is either too good to keep or too bad not to tell. / A good SERVANT makes a good master. / One SHOT meat; two shots maybe; three shots no good. / A barren SOW was never good to pigs. / A good START is half the race. / A good TALE is none the worse for being twice told. / He who has not a good TONGUE needs to have good hands. / There is many a good TUNE played on the old fiddle. / A good TURN goes a long way. / One good TURN deserves an-other. / There never was a good WAR or a bad peace. / A good WIFE and health are a man's best wealth. / A good WIFE makes a good husband. / He that has a good WIFE has an angel by his side; he that has a bad one has a devil at his elbow. / Good is the man who refrains from WINE. / It is just as hard to be a good WINNER as to be a good loser. / Good WIVES and good plantations are made by good husbands. / It is better to say a good WORD about a bad fellow than a bad word about a good fellow. / Big WORDS seldom go with good deeds.

goodbye Everyone who says goodbye is not gone. *Vars.:* **(a)** Evahbody say goodnight ain't gone home. **(b)** Every goodbye ain't gone. *Rec. dist.:* N.Y., S.C.

goodness 1. A man's goodness is his only greatness. *Rec. dist.:* Calif.

2. A real man is he whose goodness is a part of himself. *Rec. dist.:* Ill.

3. Do not neglect to perform acts of goodness just because they are little. *Rec. dist.:* Miss.

4. Goodness always enriches the possessor. *Rec. dist.:* Mich.

5. Goodness is the only investment that never fails. *Rec. dist.:* N.Y. *1st cit.:* US1854 Thoreau, *Walden. 20c. coll.:* Stevenson 1006:12.

6. There is no odor so bad as that which arises from goodness tainted. *Rec. dist.:* N.Y. *1st cit.:* US1854 Thoreau, *Walden. 20c. coll.:* Stevenson 1001:17.

SEE ALSO Of IDLENESS comes no goodness. / POLITENESS is to goodness what words are to thought.

goods 1. A man has no more goods than he gets good by. *Rec. dist.:* N.Y. *1st cit.:* 1621 Robinson, *Adagia in Latin and English. 20c. coll.:* ODEP 504, Stevenson 1007:6.

2. After you sell the goods, set down the charge before you put out the fire. *Rec. dist.:* Vt.

3. Don't put all your goods in your shop window. *Rec. dist.:* Calif.

4. Every man can be sold a bill of goods. *Rec. dist.:* Ill.

5. Good goods come in small packages. *Var.:* Good goods are done up in small packages. *Rec. dist.:* Calif. *Infm.:* Cf. thing.

6. Goods well bought are half sold. *Rec. dist.:* Ill.

7. Ill-gotten goods prosper not long. *Var.:* Ill-gotten goods seldom prosper. *Rec. dist.:* Mich., Ont., Tex., Vt. *1st cit.:* 1519 Horman, *Vulgaria. 20c. coll.:* ODEP 398, Stevenson 926:1, Whiting*(MP)* 263.

8. Little goods, little care. *Rec. dist.:* Tex. *1st cit.:* 1663 Draxe, *Bibliotheca Scholastica in Anglia* (1918). *20c. coll.:* Stevenson 1834:1.

9. Sell your goods at market price; keep it not for rats and mice. *Rec. dist.:* Ont.

10. The best goods are the cheapest in the end. *Rec. dist.:* N.Y., S.C.

11. When goods lie a long time, the price is forgotten. *Rec. dist.:* N.Y.

SEE ALSO Take a FRIEND for what he does, a wife for what she has, and goods for what they are worth. / When KNAVES fall out, honest men get their goods; when priests dispute, we come at the truth.

goodwill 1. Goodwill, like a good name, is won by many acts and lost by one. *Var.:* Goodwill, like a good name, is got by many deeds and lost by one. *Rec. dist.:* N.Mex., Wis.

2. Goodwill, like a good woman, is hard to get and easy to lose. *Rec. dist.:* N.Mex., N.Y.

3. It's better to have the goodwill of a dog than not. *Rec. dist.:* Ga.

4. We cannot buy a quart of goodwill, a pound of love, or a yard of patience. *Rec. dist.:* N.Y.

goody-good The goody-good is often good for nothing. *Rec. dist.:* N.Dak.

goose 1. A setting goose has no feathers on her breast. *Vars.:* **(a)** A setting goose gets no feathers. **(b)** A setting goose yields no down. **(c)** A setting goose yields no feathers. *Rec. dist.:* Ill., Kans., Ky., Miss.

2. A setting goose never gets fat. *Rec. dist.:* Ill.

3. A wild goose never laid a tame egg. *Rec. dist.:* Mich., Miss., N.Y., Wis. *1st cit.:* 1855 Bohn, *Handbook of Proverbs. 20c. coll.:* Stevenson 1008:5.

4. All is well and the goose hangs high. *Rec. dist.:* U.S., Can. *1st cit.:* US1863 *Dictionary of Americanisms,* ed. Matthews (1951). *20c. coll.:*

T&W 156, Stevenson 1010:4, Whiting*(MP)* 264.

5. As the old goose yells, so yells the young goose. *Rec. dist.:* Ohio.

6. Don't kill the goose that lays the golden egg. *Vars.:* **(a)** Don't kill the goose that laid the golden egg. **(b)** Kill not the goose that lays the golden egg. *Rec. dist.:* U.S. *1st cit.:* 1484 Caxton, *Aesope;* US1764 Thacher, "Sentiments" in *Pamphlets of American Revolution,* ed. Bailyn (1965). *20c. coll.:* ODEP 422, Whiting 183, Stevenson 1007, T&W 156, Whiting*(MP)* 265.

7. Don't throw away anything a goose can swallow. *Rec. dist.:* Vt.

8. Every man thinks his own geese swans. *Vars.:* **(a)** All his geese are swans. **(b)** Every man thinks his own geese to be swans. *Rec. dist.:* N.Y., Ont., S.C., Tex. *1st cit.:* 1516 Skelton, *Magnyfycence;* US1702 *Correspondence Between William Penn and James Logan, 1700–1705,* ed. Armstrong, Hist.Soc.Penn. Memoirs (1870–72). *20c. coll.:* ODEP 298, Whiting 182, Stevenson 1010:11, T&W 156, Whiting*(MP)* 263.

9. Feather by feather the silly goose is plucked. *Var.:* Feather by feather a goose is plucked. *Rec. dist.:* Ont. *1st cit.:* 1666 Torriano, *Common Place of Italian Proverbs.* *20c. coll.:* ODEP 251, Stevenson 792:5.

10. For every goose there is a gander. *Rec. dist.:* Ill., Kans. *1st cit.:* ca1386 Chaucer, *Prologue to Wife of Bath's Tale.* *20c. coll.:* Stevenson 1011:2.

11. Geese eat all that is before them and kill all that is behind them. *Rec. dist.:* Vt.

12. If you cook your own goose, you will have to eat it. *Rec. dist.:* Ont. *1st cit.:* 1851 "Street Ballad" in Mayhew, *London Labour and London Poor;* US1905 White, *Crimson Blind.* *20c. coll.:* ODEP 143, Whiting*(MP)* 265.

13. Nothing cooks your goose quicker than a boiling temper. *Rec. dist.:* Utah. *1st cit.:* 1851 "Street Ballad" in Mayhew, *London Labour and London Poor;* US1905 White, *Crimson Blind.* *20c. coll.:* ODEP 143, Whiting*(MP)* 265.

14. Nothing is dumber than a goose. *Rec. dist.:* Kans.

15. The goose hangs high. *Rec. dist.:* Ind. *1st cit.:* US1870 Nowland, *Early Reminiscences of Indianapolis.* *20c. coll.:* T&W 156, Stevenson 1010:4, Whiting*(MP)* 264.

16. The goose is never cooked till the fire is hottest. *Rec. dist.:* Ont.

17. There is more than one way to cook a goose. *Rec. dist.:* Kans. *1st cit.:* US1941 Shriber, *Murder Well Done.* *20c. coll.:* Stevenson 2467:5.

18. There's never a goose so old and gray but what a gander would wander her way. *Vars.:* **(a)** Never a goose so gray but some old gander'll come that way. **(b)** There never was a goose so gray but some day, soon or late, a gander came that way and claimed her for his mate. **(c)** There never was a goose so gray but some gander will wander her way. *Rec. dist.:* Ill., Kans., Vt., Wis. *1st cit.:* ca1386 Chaucer, *Prologue to Wife of Bath's Tale.* *20c. coll.:* ODEP 328, Stevenson 1011:2.

19. What's good for the goose is good for the gander. *Vars.:* **(a)** As is the gander, so is the goose. **(b)** Fair for the goose is fair for the gander. **(c)** What is sauce for the goose is sauce for the gander. **(d)** What is wrong for the goose cannot be right for the gander. **(e)** What's fair for the goose is fair for the gander. **(f)** What's good for the goose is sauce for the gander. *Rec. dist.:* U.S., Can. *1st cit.:* 1670 Ray, *English Proverbs;* US1757 *Colonial Virginia Satirist,* ed. Davis (1967). *20c. coll.:* ODEP 699, Whiting 379, CODP 197, Stevenson 2035:4, T&W 318, Whiting*(MP)* 548.

20. You can't fool a goose. *Rec. dist.:* Ont.

SEE ALSO When the FOX preaches, beware of your geese.

gossip *(n.)* **1.** A gossip speaks ill of all and all of her. *Var.:* A gossip speaks ill, and all speak ill of her. *Rec. dist.:* N.Y., Ont. *1st cit.:* 1732 Fuller, *Gnomologia.* *20c. coll.:* Stevenson 1012:2.

2. Gossip is the lifeblood of society. *Rec. dist.:* N.Y. *1st cit.:* US1941 Birney, (pseud. David

Kent), *Jason Burr's First Case*. *20c. coll.:* Stevenson 1012:6.

3. Gossip is vice enjoyed vicariously. *Rec. dist.:* N.Y. *1st cit.:* US1904 Hubbard, *Philistine*. *20c. coll.:* Stevenson 1012:4.

4. Gossip needs no carriage. *Rec. dist.:* Calif.

5. Gossips drink and talk; frogs drink and squawk. *Rec. dist.:* Ill. *1st cit.:* 1640 Herbert, *Outlandish Proverbs (Jacula Prudentum)* in *Works*, ed. Hutchinson (1941). *20c. coll.:* ODEP 329, Stevenson 1012:3.

6. Gossips have a keen sense of rumor. *Rec. dist.:* Mich., Miss.

7. The gossip's mouth costs her nothing, for she never opens it but at another's expense. *Rec. dist.:* N.J.

gossip *(v.)* Whoever gossips to you will gossip of you. *Vars.:* **(a)** Those who bring gossip will carry it. **(b)** Who chatters to you will chatter of you. *Rec. dist.:* Ill.

gossiping Gossiping and lying go together. *Var.:* Gossiping and lying go hand in hand. *Rec. dist.:* Ind., Mich., Ont. *1st cit.:* 1732 Fuller, *Gnomologia*. *20c. coll.:* Stevenson 1012:7.

gourd An empty gourd makes the most noise. *Rec. dist.:* Calif.

SEE ALSO Puttin' a HANDLE on the gourd don't make it no dipper.

gout SEE Drink WINE and have the gout; drink none and have it too.

govern **1.** As soon as there are some to be governed, there are also some to govern. *Rec. dist.:* N.Y. *1st cit.:* 1797 Boucher, *Causes and Consequences of the American Revolution*. *20c. coll.:* Stevenson 1014:6.

2. Govern yourself and you'll be able to govern the world. *Rec. dist.:* Ill., N.C. *1st cit.:* US1948 Stevenson, *Home Book of Proverbs*. *20c. coll.:* Stevenson 2061:4.

3. He is most powerful who governs himself. *Rec. dist.:* N.Y.

4. He is unworthy to govern others who cannot govern himself. *Vars.:* **(a)** He that would govern others must first govern himself. **(b)**

To govern a child is to govern yourself first. *Rec. dist.:* N.Y. *1st cit.:* 1477 *Dictes and Sayenges of the Philosophirs*, tr. Rivers. *20c. coll.:* Stevenson 2060:5.

5. The man who can govern a woman can govern a nation. *Rec. dist.:* N.Y., S.C.

6. Those who can't govern themselves must be governed. *Rec. dist.:* Ill.

SEE ALSO He that can't bear with other people's PASSIONS cannot govern his own.

government **1.** All free governments are party governments. *Rec. dist.:* N.Y. *1st cit.:* US1878 Garfield, Speech, House of Representatives, 18 Jan. *20c. coll.:* Stevenson 1748:3.

2. All governments depend on the goodwill of the people. *Rec. dist.:* N.Y. *1st cit.:* US1780 Adams, Letter to Genet, 15 May, in *Adams Family Correspondence*, ed. Butterfield (1963, 1973). *20c. coll.:* Stevenson 1014:10.

3. Government is the soul of society. *Rec. dist.:* Miss.

4. In rivers and bad government, the lightest things swim at the top. *Rec. dist.:* N.Y. *1st cit.:* US1754 Franklin, *PRAlmanac*. *20c. coll.:* Stevenson 1015:6.

5. Oppressive government is more to be feared than a tiger. *Rec. dist.:* Ohio.

6. People get the government they deserve. *Rec. dist.:* Ill., Wis.

7. That government is best that serves man best. *Rec. dist.:* N.Y.

8. That government is best which governs least. *Vars.:* **(a)** That government is hurt that governs least. **(b)** The best governed are least governed. *Rec. dist.:* Ill. *1st cit.:* US1845 Judd, *Margaret*. *20c. coll.:* T&W 157, Stevenson 1015:5.

9. The best government is that in which the law speaks instead of the lawyer. *Rec. dist.:* N.Y. *1st cit.:* US1852 Byrn, *Repository of Wit and Humor*. *20c. coll.:* Stevenson 1014:3.

10. The government tips when the people rise. *Rec. dist.:* N.Y.

11. The less government we have, the better. *Rec. dist.:* N.Y. *1st cit.:* US1844 Emerson, "Politics" in *Essays*. *20c. coll.:* Stevenson 1015:5.

governor   He is a governor that governs his passions, and he is a servant that serves them. *Rec. dist.:* N.Y.

gown   The gown is his that wears it, and the world his that enjoys it. *Rec. dist.:* Mich. *1st cit.:* 1573 Sanford, *Garden of Pleasure*. *20c. coll.:* ODEP 330, Stevenson 2630:6.

grace *(n.)*   **1.** Grace is a charming sound. *Rec. dist.:* Wis.

2. There is no grace in a favor that sticks to the fingers. *Rec. dist.:* Ont. *1st cit.:* US1834 Loomis, "Proverbs in Farmer's Almanac" in *Western Folklore* (1956). *20c. coll.:* T&W 157.

3. Without grace beauty is an unbaited hook. *Rec. dist.:* Ill.

See also Fresh AIR and sunshine and plenty of grace slam the door in the doctor's face. / LAMBS have the grace to suck kneeling. / Past SHAME, past grace.

grace *(v.)*   *See* Grace your HOUSE, and not let that grace you.

gracious   A gracious woman retains honor. *Var.:* A gracious woman retains honor, and strong men retain riches. *Rec. dist.:* Ont.

graft   *See* POLITICS is the mother of graft.

grain *(crop)*   **1.** By the stubble you may guess the grain. *Rec. dist.:* Ill. *1st cit.:* US1948 Stevenson, *Home Book of Proverbs*. *20c. coll.:* Stevenson 305:7.

2. Don't lock the granary after the grain has been stolen. *Rec. dist.:* Ont.

3. Every grain is not a pearl. *Rec. dist.:* Oreg.

4. Of evil grain no good seed can come. *Rec. dist.:* N.Y. *1st cit.:* 1513 Virgil, *Aeneid*, tr. Douglas. *20c. coll.:* ODEP 233, Stevenson 1135:6.

5. Though one grain fills not the sack, it helps. *Rec. dist.:* Okla. *1st cit.:* ca1542 Boorde, *Compendyons Regyment, or Dyatorye of Healthe*, E.E.T.S. (1870). *20c. coll.:* ODEP 330, Stevenson 1019:8.

6. You can't raise grain by sowing grass. *Rec. dist.:* Miss.

See also A cold APRIL and a wet May fills the barn with grain and hay. / KINDNESS, like grain, increases by sowing. / SORROW is only grain deep.

grain *(custom)*   It goes against the grain. *Rec. dist.:* U.S., Can. *1st cit.:* 1607 Shakespeare, *Coriolanus;* US1675 *Leete* in *Winthrop Papers*, Mass.Hist.Soc. *Collections* (1863–92). *20c. coll.:* ODEP 6, Whiting 184, Stevenson 1019:10, T&W 158, Whiting(MP) 266.

grammar   False grammar does not destroy a deed. *Rec. dist.:* Mich.

granary   *See* Don't lock the granary after the GRAIN has been stolen.

grandchildren   Grandchildren are the interest paid on the original investment. *Rec. dist.:* Iowa.

grandfather   What's good enough for grandfather is good enough for me. *Rec. dist.:* Ont.

grandmother   Do not try to teach your grandmother how to suck eggs. *Rec. dist.:* U.S., Can. *1st cit.:* 1707 Quevedoy Villegas, *Comical Works,* tr. Stevens; US1825 Neal, *Brother Jonathan*. *20c. coll.:* ODEP 806, CODP 221, Stevenson 1020:11, T&W 158, Whiting(MP) 267–68.

grape   **1.** Sour grapes can never make sweet wine. *Rec. dist.:* Ont. *1st cit.:* 1732 Fuller, *Gnomologia*. *20c. coll.:* Stevenson 1022:1.

2. The sweetest grapes hang highest. *Var.:* Sour grapes hang high. *Rec. dist.:* Ill., Ind., N.Y., Ont., R.I. *1st cit.:* 1902 Hulme, *Proverb Lore*. *20c. coll.:* Stevenson 574:9.

3. Winter grape sour whedder you kin reach 'im or not. *Rec. dist.:* N.Y., S.C. *1st cit.:* US1876 Twain, *Tom Sawyer*. *20c. coll.:* Stevenson 1021:2.

See also He who sows THORNS will never reap grapes.

grasp *(n.)*   *See* A man's REACH must exceed his grasp.

grasp *(v.)*   **1.** Grasp a little and you may secure it; grasp too much and you will lose everything. *Rec. dist.:* Ill., Okla., Mich., N.Y. *1st cit.:* ca1205 Layamon, *Brut,* Soc. Antiquaries (1847). *20c. coll.:* ODEP 331, Stevenson 443:12.

2. Grasp no more than the hand will hold. *Rec. dist.*: Ill., Tex. *1st cit.*: 1732 Fuller, *Gnomologia*. *20c. coll.*: Stevenson 443:12.

grass **1.** A trodden path bears no grass. *Rec. dist.*: Ont. *1st cit.*: US1769 Woodmason, *Carolina Backcountry on Eve of the Revolution, Journal of Charles Woodmason*, ed. Hooker (1953). *20c. coll.*: Whiting 186.

2. Don't let any grass grow under your feet. *Rec. dist.*: U.S., Can. *1st cit.*: ca1533 *Ralph Roister Doister*, ed. Arber (1869) ; US1740 *Jonathan Belcher Papers*, Mass.Hist.Soc. *Collections* (1893–94). *20c. coll.*: ODEP 331, Whiting 186, Stevenson 1024:2, T&W 159, Whiting(MP) 269.

3. Every blade of grass has its share of the dews of heaven. *Rec. dist.*: N.Y.

4. Grass doesn't grow on a busy street. *Vars.*: **(a)** Grass don't grow on a busy street. **(b)** Grass grows not upon the highway. **(c)** No grass grows on a busy street. **(d)** You can't grow grass on the beaten track. *Rec. dist.*: U.S. *1st cit.*: 1659 Howell, *Paroimiografia (English Proverbs)*; US1769 Woodmason, *Carolina Backcountry on Eve of the Revolution, Journal of Charles Woodmason*, ed. Hooker (1953). *20c. coll.*: ODEP 331, Whiting 186, Stevenson 1023:4.

5. Grass never grows in a goose pasture. *Rec. dist.*: Ont.

6. Let not the grass grow on the path of friendship. *Rec. dist.*: Ont.

7. More rain, more grass. *Rec. dist.*: N.Y.

8. Rip, roam while the grass is green. *Rec. dist.*: Ill.

9. The grass is always greener on the other side of the fence. *Vars.*: **(a)** Grass always seems greener in foreign fields. **(b)** Grass is always green on the other side of the fence. **(c)** Grass is always greener away from home. **(d)** Grass is always greener in somebody else's backyard. **(e)** Grass is greener in other pastures. **(f)** Grass is greener on the other side of the stream. **(g)** The grass always looks greener on the other side of the fence. **(h)** The grass grows greener on the other side of the pasture. **(i)** The grass is always greener in the next man's yard. **(j)** The grass is always greener on the other man's lawn. **(k)** The grass is always greener on the other side. **(l)** The grass is always greener on the other side of the street. **(m)** The grass is always greener on your neighbor's lawn. **(n)** The grass may be greener across the street, but watch out for the barbed wire. **(o)** The grass on the other side of the fence is always greener. **(p)** The grass over the fence is greener. **(q)** The greenest grass is always on the other side of the fence. **(r)** The other man's grass is always greener. **(s)** Things always look greener on the other side of the street. *Rec. dist.*: U.S. *1st cit.*: 1545 Erasmus, *Adages*, tr. Taverner; US1959 *Bangor Daily News*, 16 June. *20c. coll.*: CODP 100, Whiting(MP) 268.

10. The grass is greenest where the waters lap the shore. *Rec. dist.*: Ariz.

11. The nearer the ground the sweeter the grass. *Rec. dist.*: N.Y., Ont., S.C.

12. Where everyone goes the grass never grows. *Rec. dist.*: Ill., Ont.

13. While the grass grows the horse starves. *Rec. dist.*: N.Y. *1st cit.*: ca1350 *Douce MS 52*, ed. Förster (1906); US1748 Eliot, *Essays on Field Husbandry in New England, 1748–1762*, eds. Carman and Tugwell (1934). *20c. coll.*: ODEP 331, CODP 100, Whiting 186, Stevenson 1023:12, Whiting(MP) 269.

SEE ALSO Only a suckin' CALF don't have to worry about grass. / You can't raise GRAIN by sowing grass.

grateful **1.** Men who are grateful are usually good. *Rec. dist.*: Ill.

2. The grateful man gets more than he asks. *Rec. dist.*: N.Y. *1st cit.*: 1706 Stevens, *New Spanish and English Dictionary*. *20c. coll.*: ODEP 332.

SEE ALSO It's easier to be GENEROUS than grateful.

gratefulness Gratefulness is the poor man's payment. *Rec. dist.*: Ill.

gratitude **1.** Don't overload gratitude, if you do, she'll kick. *Rec. dist.*: N.Y. *1st cit.*: US1741 Franklin, *PRAlmanac*. *20c. coll.*: Stevenson 1025:3.

2. Gratitude and greed do not go together. *Rec. dist.:* N.Y., Ont., Utah.

3. Gratitude is a heavy burden. *Rec. dist.:* Ill. *1st cit.:* 1765 Lord Chesterfield, Letter, 7 Nov., in *Letters to His Son. 20c. coll.:* Stevenson 1025:3.

4. Gratitude is a lively expectation of favors yet to come. *Rec. dist.:* Calif.

5. Gratitude is the memory of the heart. *Rec. dist.:* Ohio. *1st cit.:* US1948 Stevenson, *Home Book of Proverbs. 20c. coll.:* Stevenson 1025:9.

6. Gratitude is the sign of noble souls. *Rec. dist.:* Ill., Ont.

7. Next to ingratitude, the most painful thing to bear is gratitude. *Rec. dist.:* N.Y. *1st cit.:* US1887 Beecher, *Proverbs from Plymouth Pulpit. 20c. coll.:* Stevenson 1025:1.

8. No gratitude from the wicked. *Var.:* No gratitude is received from the wicked. *Rec. dist.:* Ont., Utah.

9. Of all the virtues, gratitude has the shortest memory. *Rec. dist.:* Mich.

SEE ALSO No COMPANION can be better for us than gratitude in the darkness.

grave 1. He who digs a grave for another falls in himself. *Rec. dist.:* N.Y. *1st cit.:* 1509 Barclay, *Ship of Fools,* ed. Jamieson in *Eclogues,* E.E.T.S. (1874); US1608 Wingfield, *Discourse,* Am.Antiq.Soc. *Transactions* (1860). *20c. coll.:* ODEP 187, Whiting 339, Stevenson 1799:10, Whiting(MP) 496.

2. Only in the grave is there rest. *Rec. dist.:* N.Y.

3. The grave levels all distinctions. *Rec. dist.:* Ill., N.Y. *1st cit.:* ca1570 Preston, *Cambyses;* US1782 *Prose of Philip Freneau,* ed. Marsh (1955). *20c. coll.:* ODEP 459, Whiting 187, Stevenson 1026:1.

4. The grave will receive us all. *Rec. dist.:* Mich.

5. When you die, even a grave is comfortable. *Rec. dist.:* N.Y.

6. You dig your grave with your own hands. *Rec. dist.:* U.S. *1st cit.:* 1616 Adams, *Sacrifices of Thankfulness;* US1789 *Columbian Mag. 20c. coll.:* ODEP 187, Whiting 187, Stevenson 965:9, T&W 160, Whiting(MP) 270.

7. You dig your grave with your teeth. *Vars.:*

(a) A man may dig a grave with his teeth. **(b)** Don't dig your grave with your teeth. **(c)** You dig your grave with your fork. *Rec. dist.:* Ohio, S.C. *1st cit.:* US1789 *Columbian Mag. 20c. coll.:* Whiting 187, Whiting(MP) 270.

SEE ALSO EQUALITY begins in the grave. / The paths of GLORY lead to the grave. / If you want REVENGE, then dig two graves. / The only difference between a RUT and a grave is that a grave is a little longer. / The SICKEST is not the nearest to the grave. / There shall be SLEEPING enough in the grave. / TEARS bring nobody back from the grave. / When the TIGER is dead, the stag dances on his grave. / VIRTUE survives the grave.

graveyard You have to go to the graveyard to locate guys free from fault. *Rec. dist.:* N.Y.

SEE ALSO A green CHRISTMAS means a fat graveyard. / If CONCEIT were consumption, we would have a green graveyard all year round.

gravy Better de gravy dan no grease 'tall. *Rec. dist.:* Ga., N.Y. *1st cit.:* US1880 Harris, "Plantation Proverbs" in *Uncle Remus, His Songs and His Sayings* (1881). *20c. coll.:* Stevenson 235:10.

gray Gray hairs are honorable but old maids are abominable. *Rec. dist.:* Ont.

SEE ALSO EVENING red and morning gray will send the sailor on his way, but evening gray and morning red will bring rain down upon his head. / The FOX may grow gray, but never good.

grease *(n.)* If you use a little elbow grease, you will get the job done right. *Rec. dist.:* Ind., N.Y., Ohio, Okla., Ont.

SEE ALSO The WHEEL that does the squeaking is the one that gets the grease.

grease *(v.)* He who greases well drives well. *Rec. dist.:* Kans., Tex. *1st cit.:* 1666 Torriano, *Common Place of Italian Proverbs. 20c. coll.:* ODEP 332.

SEE ALSO It is GOLD that greases the wheel of love. / It's poor PIE that doesn't grease its own tin. / You need not grease a fat SOW. / He who greases his WHEELS helps his oxen.

great *(n.)* **1.** None think the great unhappy. *Rec. dist.:* N.Dak. *1st cit.:* 1728 Young, *Love of Fame. 20c. coll.:* Stevenson 1033:7.

2. Resembling the great in some ways does not make us equally great. *Rec. dist.:* Ont.

3. The great are often selfish in their patronage of those who help them. *Rec. dist.:* Ont.

SEE ALSO You may share the LABORS of the great, but you will not share the spoil. / Many SMALL makes a great.

great *(adj.)* **1.** A great man is what he is because he was what he was. *Rec. dist.:* Miss.

2. Behind every great man there is a great woman. *Rec. dist.:* Miss.

3. Every great man is unique. *Rec. dist.:* N.Y. *1st cit.:* US1841 Emerson, "Self-Reliance" in *Essays.* *20c. coll.:* Stevenson 1029:12.

4. Great men are not always wise. *Rec. dist.:* N.Y., S.C. *1st cit.:* US1948 Stevenson, *Home Book of Proverbs.* *20c. coll.:* Stevenson 1030:5.

5. Great men never feel great; small men never feel small. *Rec. dist.:* N.C.

6. He who will be great among you, let him serve. *Rec. dist.:* Ont.

7. It's great to be great, but it's greater to be human. *Rec. dist.:* Okla.

8. No great man ever complains of want of opportunity. *Rec. dist.:* N.Y.

9. No really great man thought himself so. *Rec. dist.:* Ind. *1st cit.:* 1821 Hazlitt, *Commonplaces.* *20c. coll.:* Stevenson 1031:8.

10. Nothing great was ever achieved without enthusiasm. *Rec. dist.:* Wis.

11. The great man makes the great thing. *Rec. dist.:* N.Y. *1st cit.:* US1837 *Works of Ralph Waldo Emerson,* ed. Cabot. *20c. coll.:* T&W 236, Stevenson 1030:9.

12. The greatest men may ask a foolish question now and then. *Rec. dist.:* Okla.

13. There could be no great ones if there were no little ones. *Rec. dist.:* R.I. *1st cit.:* ca1513 More, *Richard III,* 1821 ed. *20c. coll.:* ODEP 334, Stevenson 1034:4.

SEE ALSO AFFECTATION is a greater enemy to the face than smallpox. / Do not pull down your BARNS to build greater ones. / Great BOASTER, little doer. / The DOORSTEP of a great house is slippery. / Small FAULTS indulged in are little thieves that let in greater. / The greatest of FAULTS is to be conscious of none.

/ Men never think their FORTUNE too great nor their wit too little. / 'Tis more to be GOOD than great; to be happy is better than wise. / A great HEART is never proud. / KINDNESS is greater than law. / Add LITTLE to little and there will be a great heap. / Great LOVE from little things may grow. / Great MERIT is coy, as well as great pride. / All great MINDS run in the same channel. / Little MINDS are tamed and subdued by misfortune, but great minds rise above it. / Great OAKS from little acorns grow. / The greater the OBSTACLE, the more glory in overcoming it. / At a great PENNYWORTH, pause a while. / The greatest RIGHT in the world is the right to be wrong. / To do a great RIGHT, do a little wrong. / A great SHIP asks for deeper water. / The greater the SINNER, the greater the saint. / Better be SMALL and shine than to be great and cast a shadow. / With SMALL men no great thing can be accomplished. / Little STROKES fell great oaks. / The less the TEMPTATION, the greater the sin. / TIME is the greatest healer. / The TONGUE destroys a greater horde than does the sword. / Great TREES keep down little ones. / Of all your TROUBLES great and small, the greatest are those that don't happen at all. / The greater your TROUBLES, the greater is your opportunity to show yourself a man. / Half TRUTH is often a great lie. / The great WALL stands; the builder is gone.

greatness **1.** 'Tis in the mind all genuine greatness lies. *Rec. dist.:* N.Y. *1st cit.:* US1751 Franklin, *PRAlmanac.* *20c. coll.:* Stevenson 1030:9.

2. Greatness is nothing unless it be lasting. *Rec. dist.:* N.Y.

3. If any man seek for greatness, let him forget greatness and seek truth. *Rec. dist.:* Utah.

4. Nothing is more simple than greatness; indeed, to be simple is to be great. *Rec. dist.:* Ont. *1st cit.:* US1840 Emerson, "Literary Ethics" in *Essays.* *20c. coll.:* Stevenson 2115:14.

5. Small is the seed of every greatness. *Rec. dist.:* Ill.

6. Some are born great, some achieve greatness, and some have greatness thrust upon them. *Rec. dist.:* N.Y., Ont. *1st cit.:* 1601

Shakespeare, *Twelfth Night*. **20c. coll.:** Stevenson 1031:9.

7. The first step to greatness is to be honest. **Rec. dist.:** Ill., Ont.

8. The less people speak of their greatness, the more we think of it. **Rec. dist.:** N.Y.

9. True greatness is not in never falling but in rising when you fall. **Rec. dist.:** Ont.

See also FAILURES are the stepping-stones to success.

greed   **1.** Greed breeds contempt. **Rec. dist.:** Wis.

2. Greed killed the wolf. **Rec. dist.:** S.C.

3. Greed oft overreaches itself. **Var.:** Greediness overreaches itself. **Rec. dist.:** Ont.

4. Greed often makes one poor. **Var.:** Greed often makes one poorer. **Rec. dist.:** Ont.

5. Greed to need does surely lead. **Rec. dist.:** Ind.

See also GRATITUDE and greed go not together.

greedy *(n.)*   The greedy never know when they have had enough. **Rec. dist.:** Utah.

greedy *(adj.)*   Greedy folks have long arms. **Rec. dist.:** Ill., Oreg. **1st cit.:** 1721 Kelly, *Scottish Proverbs*. **20c. coll.:** ODEP 336, Stevenson 1039:3.

Greek   **1.** Beware the Greeks bearing gifts. **Var.:** Beware of the gift-bearing Greeks. **Rec. dist.:** U.S., Can. **1st cit.:** 1791 Boswell, "Johnson's Letter, 3 May 1777" in *Life of Samuel Johnson* (1848); US1922 Ostranden, *Ethel Opens the Door*. **20c. coll.:** ODEP 250, CODP 78, Stevenson 1038:8, Whiting*(MP)* 271.

2. When Greek meets Greek, then comes a tug of war. **Rec. dist.:** Ont. **1st cit.:** 1677 Lee, *Rival Queens;* US1804 Irving, *Journals and Notebooks, 1803–1806*, ed. Wright (1969). **20c. coll.:** CODP 102, Whiting 187, ODEP 336, Stevenson 1038:4, T&W 166, Whiting*(MP)* 271.

green   *See* Green APPLES are better than none. / A green CHRISTMAS means a fat graveyard. / Distant FIELDS look greener. / FIELDS on the other side of the fence are greener. / A HEDGE

between keeps fellowship green. / HILLS look green far away. / The other man's PASTURE always looks the greenest. / A green SALESMAN will sell more than a blue one. / Green WOOD makes a hot fire.

greet   *See* FRIENDS will greet where the hills won't meet.

greyhound   The greyhound that starts many hares kills none. **Rec. dist.:** Ill.

grief   **1.** Everyone can master a grief but he that has it. **Rec. dist.:** N.Y. **1st cit.:** 1598 Shakespeare, *Much Ado About Nothing*. **20c. coll.:** Stevenson 1596:3.

2. Great griefs are mute. **Rec. dist.:** Ill. **1st cit.:** 1587 Hughes, *Misfortunes of Arthur*. **20c. coll.:** Stevenson 1041:9.

3. Great griefs are the medicines for our lesser sorrows. **Rec. dist.:** Ohio. **1st cit.:** 1594 Shakespeare, *Rape of Lucrece*. **20c. coll.:** ODEP 338, Stevenson 1041:12.

4. Grief can take care of itself, but to get the full value of joy you must have somebody to divide it with. **Rec. dist.:** N.Y.

5. Grief makes one hour ten. **Rec. dist.:** N.J. **1st cit.:** 1595 Shakespeare, *King Richard II*. **20c. coll.:** Stevenson 1041:15.

6. Grief often treads upon the heels of pleasure. **Rec. dist.:** N.Y. **1st cit.:** US1734 Franklin, *PRAlmanac*. **20c. coll.:** Stevenson 1814:6.

7. Grief pent up will burst the heart. **Rec. dist.:** Ill. **1st cit.:** 1589 *Triumphs Love and Fort.* **20c. coll.:** ODEP 338, Stevenson 1041:2.

8. New griefs awaken the old. **Rec. dist.:** Ill. **1st cit.:** 1732 Fuller, *Gnomologia*. **20c. coll.:** Stevenson 1042:5.

9. Patch grief with proverbs. **Rec. dist.:** Ill., Ont. **1st cit.:** 1598 Shakespeare, *Much Ado About Nothing*. **20c. coll.:** Stevenson 1908:5.

10. Secret griefs are the sharpest. **Rec. dist.:** Ill.

11. The only cure for grief is action. **Rec. dist.:** Ill.

12. There is a limit to grief but not to fear. **Rec. dist.:** Ill.

13. What's gone and what's past help should be past grief. **Rec. dist.:** Oreg. **1st cit.:** 1610

Shakespeare, *Winter's Tale.* **20c. coll.:** Stevenson 684:4.

14. Yield not to grief. *Rec. dist.:* Miss.

SEE ALSO NO DAY passes without some grief. / DISPUTING and borrowing cause grief and sorrowing. / HOPE is grief's best music. / Waste not fresh TEARS over old griefs.

grievance **1.** A bad man may have a good grievance. *Rec. dist.:* Ill.

2. Conquer your grievances before they conquer you. *Rec. dist.:* Ont.

3. Grievances should be slept on before being aired. *Rec. dist.:* N.Y.

grieve SEE What the EYE doesn't see, the heart doesn't grieve for. / He who knows most grieves most for wasted TIME.

grin A pleasant grin will let you in where a knocker was never known. *Var.:* Smile and the world smiles with you, kick and you kick alone; for a cheerful grin will let you in where the kicker was never known. *Rec. dist.:* Iowa, Ont.

grind SEE MILLS won't grind if you give them no water. / The MILL cannot grind with the water that is past. / The MILLS of the gods grind slowly, but they grind exceedingly fine. / One STONE alone cannot grind corn.

grindstone SEE Keep your NOSE to the grindstone. / The man who will not SAVE as he goes keeps his nose to the grindstone.

grist **1.** All is grist that goes to his mill. *Rec. dist.:* Ont., Oreg. **1st cit.:** 1583 Calvin, *On Deuteronomy,* tr. Goulding; US1637 *New English Canaan of Thomas Morton,* ed. Adams, Jr., Publ. Prince Soc. (1883). **20c. coll.:** ODEP 339, Whiting 188, *CODP* 102, Stevenson 1042:11, T&W 162.

2. No grist is ground with the water that is passed. *Rec. dist.:* N.Y. **1st cit.:** 1616 Draxe, *Bibliotheca Scholastica in Anglia* (1918). **20c. coll.:** ODEP 531, *CODP* 151.

grit An ounce of grit is worth a pound of flesh. *Rec. dist.:* Ky.

groan SEE A LAUGH is worth a thousand groans in any market.

groat SEE 'Tis a well spent PENNY that saves a groat.

grouch A grouch is a man who thinks the world is against him—and it is. *Rec. dist.:* Ill.

ground **1.** Fly ten feet above ground and rest six feet under. *Rec. dist.:* N.Mex.

2. The nearer the ground, the sweeter the grass. *Rec. dist.:* N.Y., Ont., S.C.

SEE ALSO AIM at the stars, but keep your feet on the ground. / The weakest FRUIT drops earliest to the ground. / Don't get off the LADDER before you reach the ground. / The ground of LIBERTY must be gained by inches. / He who slings MUD loses ground. / The highest TOWERS begin from the ground. / TRUTH creeps out of the ground.

grow **1.** Letting grow and raising are different. *Rec. dist.:* Ky.

2. We grow like what we think, so let us think of the good, the true, and the beautiful. *Rec. dist.:* Ill.

3. You will only grow when you are alone. *Rec. dist.:* Ind., Okla., Ont.

SEE ALSO ABSENCE kills a little love but makes a big one grow. / Tall oaks from little ACORNS grow. / An ADULT is only one who has ceased to grow vertically and started to grow horizontally. / ANGER grows old fast. / For he who always does his BEST, his best will better grow; but he who shirks or slights his task, he lets the better go. / CONTEMPT with familiarity does grow. / More COTTON will grow in a crooked row than in a straight acre. / CROW an' corn can't grow in de same fiel'. / DRINK does not drown care, but waters it and makes it grow faster. / You can't grow FIGS from thistles. / A FOOL's head never grows white. / FOOLISHNESS grows by itself—no need to sow it. / The FOX may grow gray, but never good. / There are many kinds of fruit that grow on the tree of life, but none so sweet as FRIENDSHIP. / GENERATIONS grow weaker and wiser. / Don't let any GRASS grow under your feet. / GRASS doesn't grow on a busy street. / GRASS never grows in a goose pasture. / HAPPINESS grows at our own firesides and is not to be picked in strangers' gardens. / LAUGH and grow fat. / Great LOVE from little things may grow. / Grow OLD gracefully. / TRUTH never grows old. / Ill WEEDS always grow apace; folly runs a rapid race.

growth   SEE MEN are but children of a larger growth.

grudge (n.)   A grudge is the heaviest load one can carry. *Rec. dist.:* Ont.

grudge (v.)   1. Do not grudge others what you cannot enjoy yourself. *Rec. dist.:* Kans.

2. Grudge not another that which you cannot attain yourself. *Rec. dist.:* Miss.

grumble   The grumbler does not work; the worker does not grumble. *Rec. dist.:* Ont.

SEE ALSO The only LOT most men do not grumble at is their burial lot.

grumbling   Grumbling makes the loaf no larger. *Rec. dist.:* Ill.

grunt   You can't take the grunt out of a pig. *Rec. dist.:* Md., N.J., Ohio.

grunting   The one who does the grunting seldom does the lifting. *Rec. dist.:* Md.

guard (n.)   SEE Do not let FLATTERY throw you off guard against an enemy. / WISE men keep guard on their tongue.

guard (v.)   SEE In company, guard your TONGUE; in solitude, your heart.

guest   1. A constant guest is never welcome. *Rec. dist.:* U.S. *1st cit.:* 1732 Fuller, *Gnomologia.* *20c. coll.:* Stevenson 1045:2.

2. A constant guest will wear out his welcome. *Rec. dist.:* Ky., Miss.

3. An unbidden guest knows not where to sit. *Rec. dist.:* Ont. *1st cit.:* ca1350 *Douce MS 52,* ed. Förster (1906). *20c. coll.:* ODEP 341, Stevenson 1044:10.

4. If you would leave guests merry with cheer, be so yourself, or so at least appear. *Rec. dist.:* N.Y.

5. Show no preference among your guests. *Rec. dist.:* N.Y.

6. Speed the parting guest. *Rec. dist.:* N.Y., Ont. *1st cit.:* 1726 *Odyssey,* tr. Pope; US1930 Williamson, *American Hotel.* *20c. coll.:* Stevenson 1045:4, Whiting(MP) 274.

7. The dinner over, away go the guests. *Rec. dist.:* Miss.

8. The unbidden guest is always a pest. *Var.:* The unbidden guest is a bore and a pest. *Rec. dist.:* Ind.

9. Unbidden guests are most welcome when they are gone. *Var.:* Unbidden guests are welcomest when they are gone. *Rec. dist.:* Ill., Okla., Tex., Vt. *1st cit.:* 1591 Shakespeare, *Henry VI, Part I.* *20c. coll.:* Stevenson 1044:10.

10. Unbidden guests quickly outstay their welcome. *Rec. dist.:* N.Y., Utah.

guide   The guide of life is common sense. *Rec. dist.:* Ont.

SEE ALSO Let your CONSCIENCE be your guide. / Be sure you know the ROAD before you act as guide.

guilt   1. Custom and practice may countenance guilt, but they cannot lessen it. *Rec. dist.:* N.Y.

2. Guilt levels those whom it strains. *Rec. dist.:* Miss.

3. Guilt makes the bravest man a coward. *Rec. dist.:* Ill.

4. Guilt proves the hardest nearest home. *Rec. dist.:* Ill.

5. Guilty men see guilt written on the faces of saints. *Rec. dist.:* Ill.

6. He who denies his guilt doubles his guilt. *Rec. dist.:* N.Y.

7. Secret guilt by silence is betrayed. *Rec. dist.:* N.Y.

8. The guilt and not the gallows makes the shame of evil fellows. *Rec. dist.:* Ill.

SEE ALSO PUNISHMENT is a close attendant to guilt. / The smaller the WRONG, the greater the guilt.

guilty (n.)   1. Better ten guilty than one innocent suffer. *Rec. dist.:* N.Y. *1st cit.:* 1765 Blackstone, *Commentaries on the Laws of England.* *20c. coll.:* Stevenson 1249:3.

2. The guilty flee when no man pursues. *Rec. dist.:* Wis. *1st cit.:* 1937 Barton, *Triumphs of Crime Detection;* US1929 Quinn, *Phantom Fighter, Ten Memoirs of Jules de Grandin.* *20c. coll.:* Stevenson 1046:4, Whiting(MP) 274.

guilty *(adj.)* **1.** A man cannot be declared guilty in his absence. *Rec. dist.:* Miss.

2. The guilty one always runs. *Rec. dist.:* Ky. *1st cit.:* 1937 Barton, *Triumphs of Crime Detection*. *20c. coll.:* Stevenson 1046:4.

SEE ALSO A guilty CONSCIENCE needs no accuser. / The JUDGE is condemned when the guilty man is acquitted.

guinea The jingle of the guinea heals the hurt that honor feels. *Rec. dist.:* Ill.

gull When a gull dives in the sea, there are fish for you and me. *Rec. dist.:* Ill.

gum Some people are born simply to tread on the gum that other people chew. *Rec. dist.:* N.Y.

gumption SEE Where there is great STRENGTH, there ain't apt to be much gumption.

gun **1.** Better a loaded gun than a missed shot. *Rec. dist.:* Calif., N.Y.

2. Beware the man with only one gun. *Rec. dist.:* Colo., N.Mex.

3. It is the unloaded gun that kills many. *Rec. dist.:* Iowa.

4. It's the empty gun that does the mischief. *Rec. dist.:* Ont.

5. Stick to your guns. *Rec. dist.:* U.S. *1st cit.:* 1769 Boswell, *Life of Samuel Johnson;* US1913 Biggers, *Seven Keys to Baldpate.* *20c. coll.:* ODEP 770, Stevenson 1047:1, Whiting(MP) 276.

6. When the guns bark, the law is silent. *Rec. dist.:* N.Y.

7. When your guns are few your words are few. *Rec. dist.:* N.J.

gunner SEE CUPID is a blind gunner.

gunpowder Mix gunpowder and alcohol, you won't be around long at all. *Rec. dist.:* Oreg.

guts No guts, no glory. *Rec. dist.:* Calif.

gutter It's not so bad to fall in the gutter, but it's worse to lay there. *Rec. dist.:* Calif.

SEE ALSO A DUCK won't always paddle in the same gutter.

guy **1.** Do other guys before they do you. *Rec. dist.:* U.S. *1st cit.:* 1843 Dickens, *Martin Chuzzlewit.* *20c. coll.:* Stevenson 2016:1.

2. Some guys got it, and some guys ain't got it. *Rec. dist.:* U.S.

H

habit 1. A habit is first cobwebs, then cables. *Rec. dist.:* Ill., Wis. *1st cit.:* 1933 Phillpotts, *Captain's Curio;* US1873 Aldrich, *Mlle. Olympe Zabriski. 20c. coll.:* Whiting(MP) 277, Stevenson 1048:7, T&W 166.

2. It is a thousand times easier to contract a new habit than to get rid of an old one. *Rec. dist.:* N.J., N.C., Ont.

3. The habit does not make the monk. *Rec. dist.:* Ala. *1st cit.:* 1340 Michel, *Ayenbite of Inwit,* E.E.T.S. (1866). *20c. coll.:* Stevenson 80:2, *ODEP* 152, *CODP* 44, Whiting(MP) 136.

hair 1. A hair on the head is worth two in the brush. *Rec. dist.:* Nebr., Wis.

2. A man with no hair seems always to get the haircut. *Rec. dist.:* Ont.

3. A woman's hair is her crowning glory. *Rec. dist.:* Ind.

4. A woman's hair is long, but her tongue is longer. *Rec. dist.:* Ill., Ind., N.Y., Oreg.

5. Don't comb your hair if you are bald. *Rec. dist.:* Ont.

6. Don't wash your hair before you get the water. *Rec. dist.:* Ont.

7. Gray hairs are death's blossoms. *Var.:* Hoary hairs are death's messengers. *Rec. dist.:* Ill. *1st cit.:* ca1390 Chaucer, *Prologue to Reeve's Tale. 20c. coll.:* *ODEP* 338.

8. Hair by hair the head grows bald. *Rec. dist.:* N.Y.

9. Hair never grows on a busy street. *Rec. dist.:* Ont.

10. It is better to split hairs than split heads. *Rec. dist.:* Ill. *1st cit.:* 1594 Shakespeare, *Love's Labour's Lost;* US1767 *Papers of Lloyd Family of Lloyd's Neck, L.I., N.Y.,* ed. Barck, N.Y.Hist.Soc. *Collections* (1926–27). *20c. coll.:* *ODEP* 164, Whiting 192, Stevenson 1053:5, T&W 167, Whiting(MP) 279.

11. Little hair, much wit. *Rec. dist.:* Ky., Tenn.

12. Long hair, little brains. *Vars.:* **(a)** Hair long, wisdom little. **(b)** Long hair and short sense. *Rec. dist.:* Ill.

13. One hair of a woman draws more than a team of horses. *Rec. dist.:* N.C., Ont.

14. The hair of the dog is good for the bite. *Var.:* The hair of the dog is the cure of his bite. *Rec. dist.:* U.S. *1st cit.:* 1546 Heywood, *Dialogue of Proverbs,* ed. Habernicht (1963); USca1820 Tucker, *Essays by Citizen of Virginia* (1822). *20c. coll.:* *ODEP* 343, Whiting 191, Stevenson 1051:4, Whiting(MP) 278.

15. The smallest hair throws its shadow. *Vars.:* **(a)** Even a single hair casts its shadow. **(b)** The smallest hair casts its shadow on the ground. **(c)** There is no hair so small but has its shadow. *Rec. dist.:* U.S., Can. *1st cit.:* ca1526 Erasmus, *Dicta Sapientum; 20c. coll.:* *ODEP* 343, Stevenson 1052:6.

16. You can't grow hair and brains in the same head. *Rec. dist.:* Wash.

17. You cannot pull hair where there is none. *Rec. dist.:* Maine.

SEE ALSO The bad BARBER leaves neither hair nor skin. / Anybody that would take a DARE would kill a sheep and eat the hair. / ETERNITY has no gray hairs. / Good LUCK disappears like our hair; bad luck lasts like our nails.

half 1. Do nothing by halves. *Rec. dist.:* U.S., Can. *1st cit.:* 1753 Hanway, *Journal of Travels from London to Persia* (1762); US1930 Crooker, *Hollywood Murder Mystery. 20c. coll.:* *ODEP* 562, Whiting(MP) 280, Stevenson 537:14.

2. Do what you do with all your might: things done half are never done right. *Vars.:* **(a)** All that you do, do with your might: things done by halves are never done right. **(b)** Things done by halves are never done right. *Rec. dist.:* U.S., Can. *1st cit.:* 1753 Hanway, *Journal of Travels from London to Persia* (1762); US1793 *Writings of George Washington,* ed. Fitzpatrick (1925). *20c. coll.:* *ODEP* 562,

Whiting 113, Stevenson 537:14, Whiting*(MP)* 280.

3. Half a glass is better than none. *Rec. dist.:* Ont.

4. Half a loaf is better than none. *Rec. dist.:* U.S., Can. *1st cit.:* 1546 Heywood, *Dialogue of Proverbs,* ed. Habernicht (1963); US1693 *Andros Tracts,* ed. Whitmore (1968–74). *20c. coll.: CODP* 104, Whiting 192, *ODEP* 344, Stevenson 235:12, T&W 167, Whiting*(MP)* 280.

5. Half is false of what you hear. *Rec. dist.:* Ill. *1st cit.:* ca1205 Layamon, *Brut,* Soc. Antiquaries (1847); US1770 Carroll, Letter, 4 Sept., in *Md.Mag.Hist.* (1918). *20c. coll.: ODEP* 43, *CODP* 12, Stevenson 161:10, Whiting*(MP)* 42.

6. Never look at half-done work. *Rec. dist.:* Ont.

7. One half the world does not know how the other half lives. *Vars.:* **(a)** Half the world does not know how the other half lives. **(b)** One half of the world knows not how the other half lives. *Rec. dist.:* U.S. *1st cit.:* 1607 Hall, *Holy Observations;* US1755 Franklin, *PRAlmanac. 20c. coll.: CODP* 104, Whiting 192, *ODEP* 344, Whiting*(MP)* 280.

8. The half is better than the whole. *Var.:* Half is more than the whole. *Rec. dist.:* Ill., N.Y. *1st cit.:* 1546 Heywood, *Dialogue of Proverbs,* ed. Habernicht (1963). *20c. coll.:* Stevenson 1056:2, *ODEP* 344, *CODP* 104.

SEE ALSO An old BACHELOR is only half of a pair of scissors. / A good BEGINNING is half the task. / BELIEVE only half of what you see and nothing you hear. / One BOY's a boy; two boys, a half a boy; three boys, no boy at all. / A DISEASE known is half cured. / Well begun is half DONE. / Whatever you DO, do with all your might, for things done by halves are never done right. / Keep your EYES wide open before marriage, half shut afterwards. / A MAN without a wife is but half a man. / The OPTIMIST's cup is half full; the pessimist's cup is half empty. / A good START is half the race. / Half the TRUTH is often a great lie.

half-burnt *SEE* WOOD half-burnt is easily kindled.

half-god When half-gods go, the gods arrive. *Rec. dist.:* N.Y., S.C.

half-truth Don't believe half-truths. *Rec. dist.:* Kans.

half-wit Just the weak-minded, the idiot, and the half-wit can't. *Rec. dist.:* N.C.

hall *SEE* FEAST and your halls are crowded. / There are no reserved SEATS in the halls of fame or the chapels of faith.

halloo Don't halloo till you're out of the woods. *Rec. dist.:* N.Y., S.C. *1st cit.:* 1801 Huntington, *Book of Faith;* US1770 *Papers of Benjamin Franklin,* ed. Labaree (1959). *20c. coll.: CODP* 105, *ODEP* 345, Whiting*(MP)* 696.

halo A halo only has to fall a few inches to become a noose. *Rec. dist.:* Ont., R.I.

halved *SEE* TROUBLE shared is trouble halved.

halving Halving your wants quadruples your wealth. *Rec. dist.:* Ont.

ham A large ham, a large hand. *Rec. dist.:* Ont.

hammer **1.** An old anvil laughs at many broken hammers. *Rec. dist.:* Ohio. *1st cit.:* 1609 Harward, Unpublished manuscript in library of Trinity College, Cambridge; US1869 Spurgeon, *John Ploughman's Talks. 20c. coll.: ODEP* 15, Stevenson 75:8.

2. Heed the hammer: it keeps its head. *Rec. dist.:* Kans.

3. If you are going to use a hammer, build something. *Rec. dist.:* Utah.

SEE ALSO Some men are born ANVILS, others are born hammers. / You can't saw WOOD with a hammer.

hand **1.** A clean glove often hides a dirty hand. *Rec. dist.:* Ill., Ind., N.Y., Ont., Oreg. *1st cit.:* 1902 Hulme, *Proverb Lore. 20c. coll.:* Stevenson 79:3.

2. A clean hand needs no washing. *Var.:* A clean hand wants no washing. *Rec. dist.:* Miss., N.Y., Ont. *1st cit.:* 1732 Fuller, *Gnomologia. 20c. coll.:* Stevenson 1064:5.

3. A cold hand, a warm heart. *Vars.:* **(a)** A cold hand means a warm heart. **(b)** Cold hands and a warm heart means that you have a good sweetheart. **(c)** Cold hands show a warm heart. **(d)** Cold hands, warm heart; dirty feet, no sweetheart. **(e)** Warm hands, cold heart. *Rec. dist.:* U.S., Can. *1st cit.:* 1903 Lean, *Collectanea;* US1928 Snell, *Blue Murder.* *20c. coll.:* CODP 40, ODEP 132, Whiting *(MP)* 282, Stevenson 1062:1.

4. A little thing in hand is worth more than a great thing in prospect. *Rec. dist.:* Ind., Ont.

5. A person with a free hand is one who gives. *Rec. dist.:* N.C.

6. Always lend a helping hand. *Rec. dist.:* U.S. *1st cit.:* 1598 Florio, *World of Words;* US1741 Stephens, *Journal of Proceedings in Georgia* in *Georgia Records* (1904). *20c. coll.:* Stevenson 1060:1, Whiting 196, Whiting*(MP)* 285.

7. Arm and money require good hands. *Rec. dist.:* Wis.

8. Blessed are the horned hands of toil. *Rec. dist.:* Ont., Oreg.

9. Busy hands are happy hands. *Var.:* Busy hands do no mischief. *Rec. dist.:* Ont.

10. Dirty hands make clean money. *Rec. dist.:* Ky., S.C. *1st cit.:* US1940 Thompson, *Body, Boots, and Britches. 20c. coll.:* Stevenson 759:12.

11. Divine are many hands; cursed are many mouths. *Rec. dist.:* Ill.

12. Do the business at hand first. *Rec. dist.:* N.C.

13. Don't bite the hand that feeds you. *Vars.:* **(a)** Despise not the hand that feeds you. **(b)** Don't bite the hand that butters your bread. *Rec. dist.:* U.S., Can. *1st cit.:* 1711 Addison, *Spectator;* US1681 *Winthrop Papers,* Mass. Hist.Soc. *Collections* (1863–92). *20c. coll.:* ODEP 64, Whiting 195, Stevenson 1242:9, Whiting*(MP)* 284.

14. Don't stick out your hand further than you can draw it back. *Rec. dist.:* Miss.

15. Don't stick your hand in boiling water to see if it is hot. *Rec. dist.:* R.I.

16. Don't take your hand off the plow. *Rec. dist.:* Ind., Miss., Ont. *1st cit.:* 1928 Cobb, *Who Opened the Door;* US1747 Rutherford in

Letters and Papers of Cadwallader Colden, N.Y.Hist.Soc. *Collections* (1917–37). *20c. coll.:* Whiting*(MP)* 285, Whiting 196.

17. Empty hands allure no hawks. *Rec. dist.:* Okla. *1st cit.:* ca1390 Chaucer, *Reeve's Tale. 20c. coll.:* ODEP 219, Stevenson 1061:4.

18. Four hands can do more than two. *Rec. dist.:* Ont.

19. Hands off of someone else's man. *Rec. dist.:* N.C.

20. Have not only clean hands, but clean minds. *Rec. dist.:* N.J. *1st cit.:* ca1370 Chaucer, *Romance of Rose. 20c. coll.:* Stevenson 362:5.

21. He becomes poor that deals with a slack hand, but the hand of diligence makes rich. *Var.:* He who works with a slack hand becomes poor. *Rec. dist.:* Ill., Ind., N.Y., Ont. *1st cit.:* US1948 Stevenson, *Home Book of Proverbs. 20c. coll.:* Stevenson 577:6.

22. He has three hands: a right hand, a left hand, and little behind hand. *Rec. dist.:* Vt.

23. He who hits himself with his own hands should not cry. *Rec. dist.:* N.H.

24. He who puts his hand to the plow should never look back. *Rec. dist.:* Ont. *1st cit.:* 1928 Cobb, *Who Opened the Door;* US1774 Rutherford in *Letters and Papers of Cadwallader Colden,* N.Y.Hist.Soc *Collections* (1917–37). *20c. coll.:* Stevenson 1416:2, Whiting*(MP)* 285, Whiting 196.

25. Idle hands are the devil's tools. *Vars.:* **(a)** Idle hands are mischief makers. **(b)** Idle hands are Satan's willing instruments. **(c)** Idle hands create mischief. **(d)** Idle hands get into trouble. **(e)** Satan has some mischief still for idle hands to do. *Rec. dist.:* U.S., Can. *1st cit.:* ca1386 Chaucer, *Tale of Melibee;* US1808 Adams in Mass.Hist.Soc. *Collections* (1936–41). *20c. coll.:* CODP 51, Whiting 104, ODEP 180, Stevenson 1216:2, T&W 318, Whiting*(MP)* 162.

26. If you have no hand, you can't make a fist. *Rec. dist.:* N.Y., Ont.

27. It's the new hand who always gets the short-handled rake. *Rec. dist.:* N.Y.

28. Kiss the hand you cannot bite. *Rec. dist.:*

N.J. *1st cit.:* 1634 Howell, Letter, 28 Feb. *20c. coll.:* Stevenson 1063:1.

29. Life ain't in holding a good hand but in playing a poor hand well. *Rec. dist.:* Tex. *1st cit.:* US1948 Stevenson, *Home Book of Proverbs.* *20c. coll.:* Stevenson 1401:16.

30. Look up, not down; look out, not in; look forward, not back; and lend a hand. *Rec. dist.:* Ill., N.Y., S.C. *1st cit.:* US1871 Hale, *Ten Times One Is Ten.* *20c. coll.:* Stevenson 1726:4.

31. Many hands make light work. *Var.:* By the hands of many a great work is made light. *Rec. dist.:* U.S., Can. *1st cit.:* ca1330 *Sir Beyes,* E.E.T.S. (1885); US1637 Stroughton in *Winthrop Papers, 1498–1649,* Mass.Hist.Soc. *Collections* (1929–47). *20c. coll.:* CODP 146, Whiting 169, ODEP 509, Stevenson 1060:11, T&W 169, Whiting(MP) 283.

32. Many kiss the hand they wish to see cut off. *Var.:* Many kiss the hand they wish to cut off. *Rec. dist.:* N.Y., Okla. *1st cit.:* 1599 Minsheu, *Spanish Dictionary;* US1634 Howell, Letter, 28 Feb. *20c. coll.:* ODEP 430, Stevenson 1063:1.

33. Never let your left hand know what your right hand is doing. *Var.:* Let not your left hand know what your right hand does. *Rec. dist.:* U.S., Can. *1st cit.:* 1925 Hext, *Monster;* US1766 *Extracts from the Itineraries of Ezra Stiles,* ed. Dexter (1916). *20c. coll.:* Whiting(MP) 283, Whiting 194, Stevenson 54:1.

34. Never shake hands with a rattlesnake. *Rec. dist.:* Kans.

35. Nothing enters into a closed hand. *Rec. dist.:* Wis. *1st cit.:* 1641 Fergusson, *Scottish Proverbs.* *20c. coll.:* ODEP 579, Stevenson 1590:1.

36. Nothing is impossible to a willing hand. *Rec. dist.:* Utah.

37. One hand is better than no hand at all. *Rec. dist.:* Fla.

38. One hand scatters what the other saves. *Rec. dist.:* Ont.

39. One hand washes the other. *Vars.:* (a) Let one hand wash the other. (b) One hand has to wash the other. (c) One hand may wash the other, but both the face. (d) One hand washes the other, and both wash the face. *Rec. dist.:* U.S., Can. *1st cit.:* 1573 Sanford, *Garden of Pleasure;* US1836 *Diary of Philip Hone, 1828–1851,* ed. Nevins (1927). *20c. coll.:* CODP 105, Whiting 194, ODEP 347, Stevenson 1059:9, Whiting(MP) 283.

40. Pretty hands are those that do. *Rec. dist.:* Kans., N.Dak.

41. Put your hand no farther than your sleeve will reach. *Rec. dist.:* Okla. *1st cit.:* 1541 Bullinger, *Christian State of Matrimony,* tr. Coverdale. *20c. coll.:* CODP 215, ODEP 780, Stevenson 93:8.

42. Scatter with one hand; gather with two. *Rec. dist.:* N.Y., S.C.

43. Show me your hand and I'll tell you your trade. *Rec. dist.:* Ont.

44. The best place to find a helping hand is at the end of your arm. *Rec. dist.:* N.Y., N.C.

45. The eye of the master does more than his hand. *Rec. dist.:* Ill., Ind., Miss. *1st cit.:* 1876 Banks, *Manchester Man;* US1744 Franklin, *PRAlmanac.* *20c. coll.:* CODP 73, ODEP 236, Whiting 140, T&W 124.

46. The hand is quicker than the eye. *Rec. dist.:* Ind., R.I., Wis.

47. The hand of the diligent shall bear the rule. *Rec. dist.:* Ind. *1st cit.:* US1948 Stevenson, *Home Book of Proverbs.* *20c. coll.:* Stevenson 577:6.

48. The hand that gives, gathers. *Rec. dist.:* Kans., Ont. *1st cit.:* 1659 Howell, *Paroimiografia (English Proverbs).* *20c. coll.:* ODEP 347, Stevenson 958:6.

49. The hand that rocks the cradle is the hand that rules the world. *Var.:* The hand that rocks the cradle rules the world. *Rec. dist.:* U.S., Can. *1st cit.:* ca1881 Wallace, *Jack O'London's Treasure Trove;* US1943 Carson, *Bride Saw Red.* *20c. coll.:* ODEP 347, Stevenson 1061:2, Whiting(MP) 282.

50. The hands that lift the cup that cheers should not be used to shift the gears. *Rec. dist.:* Calif.

51. The hasty hand catches frogs for fish. *Rec. dist.:* Ont.

52. The man with the lazy hand has an empty mouth. *Rec. dist.:* Oreg.

53. The right hand is slave to the left. *Rec. dist.:* Wis.

54. Tie a flying instructor's hands behind him and he couldn't say a word. *Rec. dist.:* Ark., Kans.

55. Too many hands in the pot make poor soup. *Rec. dist.:* Ill., Ind., N.J., Ohio, Ont.

56. Too many hands spoil the pie. *Rec. dist.:* Ky., N.J., Tenn.

57. Two hands are better than one. *Rec. dist.:* N.Y., N.C.

58. When the hand ceases to scatter, the mouth ceases to praise. *Rec. dist.:* Ill.

59. When you get your hand in a bear's mouth, you'd better work easy until you get it out. *Rec. dist.:* N.Y. *1st cit.:* 1696 *Cornish Comedy;* US1761 *Boston Gazette* in *Olden Time Series,* ed. Brooks (1886). *20c. coll.:* ODEP 346, Whiting 196, Stevenson 1437:5, T&W 177, Whiting(MP) 296.

60. White hands cannot hurt. *Rec. dist.:* Ont. *1st cit.:* 1852 Trench, *Lessons in Proverbs.* *20c. coll.:* Stevenson 1059:7.

61. Your hand is never the worse for doing your own work. *Rec. dist.:* Ont. *1st cit.:* 1659 Howell, *Paroimiografia (English Proverbs);* US1746 Franklin, *PRAlmanac.* *20c. coll.:* Stevenson 1061:3.

SEE ALSO Less ADVICE and more hands. / A man without AIM is like a clock without hands, as useless if it turns as if it stands. / A BIRD in the hand is worth two in the bush. / BROTHERS are like hands and feet. / A CAMERA in the hand is worth two in the alley. / CHARITY is a virtue of the heart and not of the hand. / We are CLAY in the hands of the potter. / The man who watches the CLOCK generally remains one of the hands. / Give a DOG your finger and he'll want your hand. / A DOLLAR in the bank is worth two in the hand. / The EYE of the master does more than his hand. / Give him a FINGER and he will take a hand. / FLOWERS leave fragrance in the hand that bestows them. / GOD is always opening his hand. / GOD puts food into clean hands. / You dig your GRAVE with your own hands. / A large HAM, a large hand. / A HANDKERCHIEF dropped is worth two in the hand. / A sinful HEART makes a feeble hand. / IDLENESS and pride tax with a heavier hand than kings and parliaments. / An IDLER is a watch that wants both hands, as useless if it goes as if it stands. / Many a one for LAND takes a fool by the hand. / A PENNY in the hand is worth two in the pot. / He that would PLEASE all and himself too takes more in hand than he is like to do. / The SKIN you love to touch isn't nearly so handy around the house as dishpan hands. / A rugged STONE grows smooth from hand to hand. / A good SURGEON must have an eagle's eye, a lion's heart, and a lady's hand. / The hands of TIME will never turn back. / A long TONGUE has a short hand. / He who has not a good TONGUE needs to have good hands. / A TOOL is but the extension of a man's hand. / WIT without discretion is a sword in the hand of a fool.

handful You may know by the handful the whole sack. *Rec. dist.:* Ont.

SEE ALSO A handful of common SENSE is worth a bushel of learning.

handkerchief **1.** A handkerchief dropped is worth two in the hand. *Rec. dist.:* Miss.

2. A handkerchief is a poor woman's purse. *Rec. dist.:* N.C.

handle *(n.)* **1.** Look for the handle when the pot's in the fire. *Rec. dist.:* Miss.

2. Puttin' a handle on the gourd don't make it no dipper. *Rec. dist.:* Nebr., N.Y., S.C.

3. Take things always by their smooth handle. *Rec. dist.:* Ind., N.Y., S.C. *1st cit.:* 1881 Ainger, *Charles Lamb;* US1787 *Papers of Thomas Jefferson,* ed. Boyd (1950). *20c. coll.:* Stevenson 1065:3, Whiting 197, T&W 170.

SEE ALSO SIN has many tools, but a lie is the handle that fits them all.

handle *(v.)* *SEE* One-eyed MULE can't be handled on the blind side. / Handle your TOOLS without mittens: the cat in gloves catches no mice. / Handle with care WOMEN and glass.

handling *SEE* Our best IMPULSES are too delicate to endure much handling.

handsaw A handsaw is a good thing, but not to shave with. *Rec. dist.:* Ont.

handsome 1. A handsome man has something to start with. *Rec. dist.:* Ill.

2. Handsome is as handsome does. *Vars.:* (a) Handsome is that handsome does. (b) She is handsome that handsome does. *Rec. dist.:* U.S., Can. *1st cit.:* 1580 Munclay, *Sunday Examples;* US1774 Schaw, *Journal of Lady of Quality, 1774–1776,* ed. Andrews (1934). *20c. coll.:* CODP 106, Whiting 197, ODEP 348, Stevenson 539:2, T&W 171, Whiting(*MP*) 286.

3. Marry a handsome man and you marry trouble. *Rec. dist.:* Ill.

SEE ALSO Every mother's CHILD is handsome. / There are no ugly LOVES nor handsome prisons.

handy 1. Be handy as well as ornamental. *Rec. dist.:* Ky., Tenn.

2. Keep a thing for seven years and it will come in handy. *Rec. dist.:* Ont. *1st cit.:* 1541 Bullinger, *Christian State of Matrimony,* tr. Coverdale (1543). *20c. coll.:* ODEP 417, CODP 124, Stevenson 1291:5, Whiting(*MP*) 619.

hang *(execute)* 1. All are not hanged that are condemned. *Rec. dist.:* Ark. *1st cit.:* 1732 Fuller, *Gnomologia. 20c. coll.:* Stevenson 1065:8.

2. Better be half hanged than ill wed. *Rec. dist.:* N.Y. *1st cit.:* 1670 Ray, *English Proverbs. 20c. coll.:* Stevenson 1067:1.

3. If you hang long enough, you get used to it. *Rec. dist.:* Ohio.

4. Let us all hang together or hang separately. *Vars.:* (a) If we don't hang together we will hang separately. (b) We must hang together, or we shall hang separately. (c) We must indeed all hang together, or most assuredly we shall all hang separately. *Rec. dist.:* U.S., Can. *1st cit.:* US1776 Franklin, Retort to John Hancock's address to the Continental Congress in Sparks, *Life of Franklin* (1873). *20c. coll.:* Stevenson 1067:11.

5. Might as well be hanged for a sheep as a lamb. *Rec. dist.:* U.S. *1st cit.:* 1678 Ray, *Somerset;* US1787 *Diary and Autobiography of John Adams,* ed. Butterfield (1961). *20c. coll.:* CODP

106, Whiting 386, *ODEP* 350, Stevenson 1067:4, T&W 324, Whiting(*MP*) 555.

6. The man who's anxious to hang himself will always find a rope. *Rec. dist.:* Ill. *1st cit.:* 1639 Fuller, *Holy War. 20c. coll.:* CODP 194, ODEP 683.

7. You can never hang a man if he is born to be drowned. *Vars.:* (a) Born to be hanged, never be drowned. (b) If I was born to be drowned, I won't be hanged, and if born to be hanged, I'll never be drowned. (c) If you were born to be drowned, you will never be hanged. (d) Men don't die who were born to be hanged. (e) They say a man who is born to be hanged will never be drowned. *Rec. dist.:* U.S. *1st cit.:* ca1503 Barclay, *Gringore's Castle of Labour;* USca1731 Cook, *History of Col. Nathaniel Bacon's Rebellion,* Am. Antiq. Soc. Proceedings (1934). *20c. coll.:* CODP 23, Whiting 41, ODEP 75, Whiting(*MP*) 68.

8. You can't hang a man for an idea. *Var.:* A man can't be hanged for his thoughts. *Rec. dist.:* Ont., Vt. *1st cit.:* US1760 *Papers of Benjamin Franklin,* ed. Labaree (1959). *20c. coll.:* Whiting 198.

SEE ALSO ALMOST was never hanged. / Give a CALF enough rope and he will hang himself. / Give a DOG a bad name and hang him. / We hang little THIEVES and take off our hats to great ones. / Do not MARRY an heiress unless her father has been hanged. / Give a man enough ROPE and he will hang himself. / Give a THIEF enough rope and he will hang himself.

hang *(suspend)* Some hang out more'n they wash. *Rec. dist.:* Vt.

SEE ALSO The redder the FRUIT, the higher it hangs. / All WORDS are pegs to hang ideas on.

hanging 1. Many a good hanging prevents a bad marriage. *Rec. dist.:* Ill. *1st cit.:* 1601 Shakespeare, *Twelfth Night. 20c. coll.:* Stevenson 1536:9.

2. One can get used to everything—even hanging. *Rec. dist.:* Ont.

3. You can put a man to a better use than hanging him. *Rec. dist.:* Ill. *1st cit.:* ca1639

Wotton, *Reliquiae Wottonian* (1651). *20c. coll.:* *ODEP* 921, Stevenson 1067:12.

hanker *SEE* Settin' HENS don't hanker after fresh aigs.

hap Some of us have the hap; some stick in the gap. *Rec. dist.:* N.Y., S.C. *1st cit.:* 1639 Clarke, *Paroemiologia.* *20c. coll.:* *ODEP* 351.

happen 1. Nothin' don't happen till it takes place. *Rec. dist.:* Miss.

2. Nothing ever just happens; everything is caused. *Rec. dist.:* Ohio.

3. Nothing happens from saying so. *Rec. dist.:* N.Y., S.C.

4. Nothing merely happens: things are done. *Rec. dist.:* Ind.

5. What happens twice, happens thrice. *Rec. dist.:* Ont.

6. What has happened once can happen again. *Rec. dist.:* N.J. *1st cit.:* US1815 Walterhouse, *Journal of a Young Man of Massachusetts* in *Magazine of History* (1911). *20c. coll.:* Whiting 198.

7. What's going to happen will happen, and what isn't is liable to happen anyway. *Rec. dist.:* Ill.

8. What is to be will be, whether it ever happens or not. *Var.:* What is to be will be, and what shouldn't be may happen. *Rec. dist.:* Miss.

9. What must happen will happen regardless. *Rec. dist.:* Ill.

10. Whatever happens, take it on the chest. *Rec. dist.:* N.Mex.

SEE ALSO ACCIDENTS will happen in the best-regulated families. / Everything is FUNNY as long as it is happens to someone else. / MISTAKES will happen. / Don't be afraid of TOMORROW; look what could happen today. / It's always the UNEXPECTED that happens.

happening You can't guarantee tomorrow's happenings today. *Rec. dist.:* N.Y.

happiness 1. All happiness is in the mind. *Rec. dist.:* Ill., Okla., Tex. *1st cit.:* 1732 Fuller, *Gnomologia.* *20c. coll.:* Stevenson 1072:16.

2. Blessed are the happiness makers. *Rec. dist.:* N.Y., S.C.

3. Content is happiness. *Rec. dist.:* N.Y. *1st cit.:* ca1566 *Bugbears.* *20c. coll.:* *ODEP* 141, Stevenson 413:9.

4. Deepest happiness is for a short duration. *Rec. dist.:* N.Y. *1st cit.:* 1576 Pettie, *Petite Palace of Pleasure,* ed. Gollancz (1908). *20c. coll.:* Stevenson 1071:5.

5. Happiness adds and multiplies as we divide it with others. *Rec. dist.:* Ind.

6. Happiness comes from gladness as light from the sun. *Rec. dist.:* Ont.

7. Happiness comes to those who give it. *Rec. dist.:* N.Y.

8. Happiness goes on forever. *Rec. dist.:* Ohio.

9. Happiness grows at our own firesides and is not to be picked in strangers' gardens. *Rec. dist.:* Ill. *1st cit.:* ca1840 Jerrold, *Jerrold's Wit.* *20c. coll.:* Stevenson 1070:15.

10. Happiness has no longings. *Rec. dist.:* Mich.

11. Happiness in this world, when it comes, comes incidentally. *Rec. dist.:* N.Y., S.C. *1st cit.:* US1852 Hawthorne, *American Notebooks.* *20c. coll.:* Stevenson 1071:8.

12. Happiness is a butterfly. *Rec. dist.:* Ind.

13. Happiness is a form of courage. *Rec. dist.:* Ind.

14. Happiness is a good that nature sells us. *Rec. dist.:* W.Va.

15. Happiness is a habit. *Rec. dist.:* Kans., N.Y., S.C. *1st cit.:* US1914 Hubbard, *Epigrams.* *20c. coll.:* Stevenson 1070:9.

16. Happiness is a perfume that you cannot pour on others without spilling a little on yourself. *Rec. dist.:* Oreg.

17. Happiness is a wayside flower growing upon the highways of usefulness. *Rec. dist.:* Ont.

18. Happiness is for those who make it and not for those who search for it. *Rec. dist.:* Ont.

19. Happiness is like jam: you can't spread even a little without getting some on yourself. *Rec. dist.:* N.Dak., R.I., Utah.

20. Happiness is more than riches. *Rec. dist.:* Ont.

21. Happiness is never found by pursuing it. *Rec. dist.:* Kans. *1st cit.:* US1852 Hawthorne, *American Notebooks. 20c. coll.:* Stevenson 1071:8.

22. Happiness is not perfect until it is shared. *Rec. dist.:* Ont. *1st cit.:* 1818 Byron, *Don Juan. 20c. coll.:* Stevenson 1071:3.

23. Happiness is the art of never holding in your mind the memory of any unpleasant thing that has passed. *Rec. dist.:* Ala.

24. Happiness is the best reward. *Rec. dist.:* Ala.

25. Happiness is the true measure of success. *Rec. dist.:* N.J.

26. Happiness is to be sought not outside but within. *Rec. dist.:* N.C. *1st cit.:* ca1391 Boethius, *Consolation of Philosophy,* tr. Chaucer, E.E.T.S. (1868). *20c. coll.:* Stevenson 1070:15.

27. Happiness is what you make of it. *Rec. dist.:* Ala. *1st cit.:* US1838 Thoreau, *Journals,* 21 Jan. *20c. coll.:* Stevenson 1070:15.

28. Happiness is where you find it. *Rec. dist.:* U.S.

29. Happiness makes health; health makes more happiness. *Rec. dist.:* Ind., N.Y., Ohio. *1st cit.:* 1712 Addison, *Spectator;* US1852 Curtis, *Lotus Eating: Trenton. 20c. coll.:* Stevenson 1099:8.

30. He who seeks only for applause from without has all his happiness in another's keeping. *Rec. dist.:* Utah.

31. In happiness, iron is bright; in sadness, gold is dull. *Rec. dist.:* Ala., Ont.

32. It is neither wealth nor splendor, but tranquility and occupation, which give happiness. *Rec. dist.:* N.Y., S.C. *1st cit.:* US1788 Jefferson, Letter to Mrs. A. S. Marks in *Writings of Thomas Jefferson,* ed. Bergh (1907). *20c. coll.:* Stevenson 1070:3.

33. Learn, see, do something beautiful every day is a prescription for happiness. *Rec. dist.:* Miss.

34. May your sun of happiness never set. *Rec. dist.:* Ont.

35. Most of our happiness in this world consists in possessing what others can't get. *Rec. dist.:* N.Y., S.C. *1st cit.:* US1874 Shaw (pseud. Josh Billings), *Encyclopedia of Wit and Wisdom. 20c. coll.:* Stevenson 1070:1.

36. Much happiness is overlooked because it doesn't cost anything. *Rec. dist.:* Calif.

37. One does not appreciate happiness unless one has known sorrow. *Rec. dist.:* N.Y.

38. One's chances for happiness are what he makes them. *Rec. dist.:* Miss.

39. Our happiness does not consist in things, but in thoughts. *Rec. dist.:* N.C. *1st cit.:* 1732 Fuller, *Gnomologia. 20c. coll.:* Stevenson 1072:16.

40. Real happiness consists of peace of mind and heart. *Rec. dist.:* N.C. *1st cit.:* US1948 Stevenson, *Home Book of Proverbs. 20c. coll.:* Stevenson 1070:2.

41. Real happiness is found not in doing the things you like to do, but in liking the things you have to do. *Rec. dist.:* Ont.

42. So long as we can lose any happiness we possess some. *Rec. dist.:* N.Y., S.C. *1st cit.:* USca1935 Tarkington, *Looking Forward. 20c. coll.:* Stevenson 1073:8.

43. The way to happiness is through tribulation. *Rec. dist.:* N.Y.

44. There ain't no happiness in this world, so we must be happy without it. *Rec. dist.:* Oreg.

45. There is more happiness in pursuit than possession. *Rec. dist.:* Fla.

46. To fill the hour—that is happiness. *Rec. dist.:* N.Y., S.C. *1st cit.:* US1844 Emerson, "Experience" in *Essays,* Second Series. *20c. coll.:* Stevenson 1071:2.

47. True happiness consists of making others happy. *Var.:* Keeping someone else happy is the secret of happiness. *Rec. dist.:* Ill., N.J., Ont.

48. True happiness is in a contented mind. *Rec. dist.:* Ill. *1st cit.:* ca1566 *Bugbears. 20c. coll.:* ODEP 141, Stevenson 413:9.

49. We shall never gather happiness if we try to retain it for ourselves. *Rec. dist.:* Ont. *1st* *cit.:* 1818 Byron, *Don Juan.* **20c. coll.:** Stevenson 1071:4.

50. When things look blackest, happiness is often right around the corner. **Rec. dist.:** Ind.

51. Without virtue, happiness cannot be. **Rec. dist.:** N.Y., N.C., S.C. **1st cit.:** 1733 Pope, *Essay on Man;* US1750 Franklin, *PRAlmanac.* **20c. coll.:** Stevenson 2434:6.

SEE ALSO Every minute you are ANGRY you lose sixty seconds of happiness. / In a united FAMILY happiness springs up of itself. / HOPE is the blossom of happiness. / KINDNESS brings happiness. / LABOR is the law of happiness. / MONEY can't buy happiness. / SIN and happiness cannot dwell together. / Getting what you go after is called SUCCESS, but liking it while you are getting it is happiness.

happy 1. A happy husband is the happiest of men. **Rec. dist.:** Miss.

2. A happy man will also like his wife, though love may long have passed. **Rec. dist.:** Ind.

3. A poor man can't be happy because a happy man is never poor. **Rec. dist.:** Kans.

4. Call no man happy till he is dead. **Rec. dist.:** Tex. **1st cit.:** 1539 Taverner, *Proverbs of Erasmus.* **20c. coll.:** *CODP* 107, *ODEP* 352, Stevenson 527:2.

5. Call not him the happiest who is the richest. **Rec. dist.:** Mich.

6. Happy is he who is content. **Rec. dist.:** N.Y. **1st cit.:** ca1566 *Bugbears.* **20c. coll.:** *ODEP* 141.

7. Happy is he who is simple. **Rec. dist.:** N.Y., S.C.

8. Happy is he who limits his wants to his necessities. **Rec. dist.:** Mich.

9. Happy is the bride the sun shines on. **Rec. dist.:** U.S. **1st cit.:** 1648 Herrick, *Hesperides;* US1926 Wentworth, *Black Cabinet.* **20c. coll.:** *CODP* 26, *ODEP* 85, Stevenson 243:9, Whiting(*MP*) 74.

10. Happy is the man that finds wisdom and that gets understanding. **Rec. dist.:** N.Y., S.C., Wis. **1st cit.:** US1948 Stevenson, *Home Book of Proverbs.* **20c. coll.:** Stevenson 2537:10.

11. Happy is the man who has a hobby. **Rec. dist.:** Ky., Tenn.

12. Happy men shall have many friends. **Rec. dist.:** Ont.

13. Happy's the wooing that's not long a-doing. **Rec. dist.:** Miss. **1st cit.:** 1576 Edwards, *Paradyse of Devices* in *British Bibliography* (1812); US1734 Franklin, *PRAlmanac.* **20c. coll.:** *ODEP* 913, Whiting 496, Stevenson 2592:1, Whiting(*MP*) 697.

14. He is happiest, be he peasant or king, who finds peace in his home. **Var.:** He is happy who finds peace in his own home. **Rec. dist.:** Ind.

15. He is happy who wants what he has. **Rec. dist.:** N.Y.

16. He is truly happy who makes others happy. **Rec. dist.:** N.Y., Ont.

17. If you want to be happy, make yourself useful. **Rec. dist.:** Ill.

18. It's better to be happy than wise. **Vars.:** **(a)** 'Tis more to be good than great; to be happy is better than wise. **(b)** Better be happy than wise. **(c)** Better happy than wise. **Rec. dist.:** U.S. **1st cit.:** 1546 Heywood, *Dialogue of Proverbs,* ed. Habernicht (1963). **20c. coll.:** *ODEP* 51, Stevenson 1071:11.

19. Man was never so happy as when he was doing something. **Rec. dist.:** N.Y., S.C. **1st cit.:** 1870 Disraeli, *Lothair.* **20c. coll.:** Stevenson 11:1.

20. No man is ever happy unless he thinks himself so. **Rec. dist.:** N.Y., N.C. **1st cit.:** 1732 Fuller, *Gnomologia.* **20c. coll.:** Stevenson 1072:16.

21. One is happy when one is satisfied with one's self. **Rec. dist.:** Fla.

22. People are not always feeling their pulse to see if they are happy. **Rec. dist.:** Miss.

23. The happiest person is the person who thinks the most interesting thoughts. **Rec. dist.:** N.Y., S.C.

24. The happiest place in the world to live is within one's income. **Rec. dist.:** N.Y.

25. The man with peace of mind is blissfully happy. **Rec. dist.:** Ill.

26. There is not a happy home on earth but stands on faith. *Rec. dist.:* Ind.

27. To be happy is to be healthy. *Rec. dist.:* Ind. *1st cit.:* 1712 Addison, *Spectator;* US1852 Curtis, *Lotus-Eating: Trenton.* *20c. coll.:* Stevenson 1099:8.

28. To be happy, make yourself necessary to somebody. *Rec. dist.:* N.J.

29. Whoever is tired of a happy day, let him take a wife. *Rec. dist.:* N.Y.

30. You're truly happy if you make others happy. *Rec. dist.:* N.Y.

SEE ALSO Always to COURT and never to wed is the happiest life that ever was led. / Busy HANDS are happy hands. / The happy HIGHWAY, though never straight, is often scenic. / HOME-keeping folks are the happiest. / The HOURS that make us happy make us wise. / A deaf HUSBAND and a blind wife are always a happy couple. / Motherless HUSBAND makes happy wife. / PRAY and work and you will be happy. / The happiest WIFE is not she that gets the best husband, but she that makes the best of that which she gets.

harbor SEE Slow WIND also brings the ship to harbor.

hard **1.** Don't take it so hard—it might not all be so. *Rec. dist.:* N.C.

2. It is hard to kick against the pricks. *Rec. dist.:* Tex. *1st cit.:* ca1300 *Cursor Mundi,* E.E.T.S. (1874–92); US1637 *John Wheelwright, His Writings,* ed. Bell, Publ. Prince Soc. (1876). *20c. coll.:* ODEP 421, Whiting 347, Stevenson 1293:10, T&W 296, Whiting(MP) 511.

3. Nothing's so hard but search will find it out. *Rec. dist.:* Ont. *1st cit.:* 1648 Herrick, *Seeke and Finde.* *20c. coll.:* Stevenson 2056:5.

4. One hard word brings another. *Rec. dist.:* Ont. *1st cit.:* 1546 Heywood, *Dialogue of Proverbs,* ed. Habernicht (1963). *20c. coll.:* Stevenson 2601:5.

5. The hard word cuts the heart. *Rec. dist.:* Ont. *1st cit.:* 1593 Shakespeare, *Titus Andronicus.* *20c. coll.:* Stevenson 2604:5.

6. The worst of all policies in hard times is to sit down and fold your hands. *Rec. dist.:* Miss.

7. 'Tis hard to carry a full cup even. *Rec. dist.:* N.Y. *1st cit.:* 1721 Kelly, *Scottish Proverbs;* US1836 Emerson, *Works,* ed. Cabot. *20c. coll.:* Stevenson 471:4, T&W 87.

8. To work hard, live hard, die hard, and go to hell after all would be hard indeed. *Rec. dist.:* N.Y., S.C. *1st cit.:* US1840 Dana, *Two Years Before the Mast;* *20c. coll.:* ODEP 917, Stevenson 1075:2, T&W 414.

9. What is hard to bear is sweet to remember. *Rec. dist.:* Vt. *1st cit.:* ca1370 Chaucer, *Romance of Rose,* ed. Skeat (1894). *20c. coll.:* ODEP 353, Stevenson 1952:8.

10. When hard times come in at the door, love goes out at the window. *Rec. dist.:* Kans. *1st cit.:* ca1476 Caxton, *Game Chess;* US1790 *Columbian Mag.* *20c. coll.:* ODEP 642, Whiting 346, *CODP* 181, Stevenson 1481:3, Whiting(MP) 508.

SEE ALSO To ACT is easy, but to understand is hard. / The BEGINNING is the hardest. / The BIGGER they come, the harder they fall. / The older the FOOL, the harder he falls. / GOODWILL, like a good woman, is hard to get and easy to lose. / A HEAD that is as hard as rock will burst into pieces. / Hold your HEAD up if you do die hard. / An old HORSE for a hard road. / ILLNESS which we imagine is often harder to bear than illness which we experience. / Easy to LEARN, hard to master. / It is a task to LEARN, but it is much harder to unlearn. / LIFE is hard by the yard, but by the inch life's a cinch. / MEN and melons are hard to know. / The MISFORTUNES hardest to bear are those which never come. / The harder the NUT the sweeter the kernel. / It is easy to REPEAT but hard to originate. / If your SEAT is hard to sit upon, stand up. / The first STEP is the hardest. / The hardest STEP is over the threshold. / The harder the WIND, the deeper the oak becomes rooted. / It is just as hard to be a good WINNER as to be a good loser. / 'Tis a hard WINTER when one wolf eats another. / Hard WORK is the best investment a man can make. / He has hard WORK indeed who has nothing to do. / Nothing worth having ever comes without a lot of hard WORK. / WORK is not hard unless you prefer doing something else. / The first hundred YEARS are the hardest.

hare 1. A hare is not caught with a drum. *Rec. dist.:* Ind. *1st cit.:* 1399 Langland, *Richard the Redeles;* US1608 Smith, *True Relation of Virginia.* *20c. coll.:* Stevenson 1076:8.

2. Don't think to hunt two hares with one dog. *Rec. dist.:* Ill. *1st cit.:* 1509 Barclay, *Ship of Fools;* US1734 Franklin, *PRAlmanac.* *20c. coll.:* CODP 194, Whiting 198, ODEP 688, Stevenson 1076:5.

3. First catch your hare before you skin it. *Var.:* First catch your hare, then cook it. *Rec. dist.:* N.C., Ont. *1st cit.:* 1801 *Spirit of Farmers' Museum;* US1922 Fox, *Ethel Opens the Door.* *20c. coll.:* CODP 81, Whiting(MP) 287, ODEP 262, Stevenson 1075:14.

4. He who chases two hares catches neither. *Vars.:* (a) He who hunts two hares leaves one and loves the other. (b) If you choose two hares, both will escape you. *Rec. dist.:* Ill., N.Y., Okla. *1st cit.:* 1509 Barclay, *Ship of Fools,* ed. Jamieson in *Eclogues,* E.E.T.S. (1874); US1734 Franklin, *PRAlmanac.* *20c. coll.:* CODP 194, Whiting 198, ODEP 688, Stevenson 1076:5, Whiting(MP) 288.

5. If the hare is to be caught, it must not stay too far ahead of the hound. *Rec. dist.:* Kans.

6. The timid hare dares to pluck the dead lion by the beard. *Rec. dist.:* Ill. *1st cit.:* 1574 Guazzo, *Civile Conversation,* tr. Pettie, T.T. (1925). *20c. coll.:* Stevenson 1435:1, ODEP 354.

SEE ALSO Little DOGS start the hare, but great ones catch it. / Don't run with the HOUND and hold on to the hare.

harm 1. A person can do himself more harm than others. *Rec. dist.:* N.Y.

2. Harm watch, harm catch. *Rec. dist.:* Okla., Ont. *1st cit.:* 1481 Caxton, *Reynard;* USca1838 Emerson, *Works,* ed. Cabot. *20c. coll.:* ODEP 354, Stevenson 1077:11, T&W 172.

3. He who does harm should expect harm. *Rec. dist.:* N.Y.

4. Keep out of harm's way. *Rec. dist.:* Ill. *1st cit.:* 1662 Fuller, *History of the Worthies of England.* *20c. coll.:* Stevenson 1078:3.

5. No harm in trying. *Rec. dist.:* S.C. *1st cit.:* 1934 Gregg, *Execution of Diamond Deutsch;*

US1857 Melville, *Confidence-Man.* *20c. coll.:* Whiting(MP) 288, T&W 172.

6. There is no harm in asking. *Rec. dist.:* Vt.

SEE ALSO When CHILDREN stand quiet, they have done some harm. / Do no EVIL and fear no harm. / LIES do harm only to them that tells 'em. / It's not the WHEEL that makes the most noise that does the most harm.

harmless SEE A necessary LIE is harmless.

harmony 1. Harmony is often obtained by playing second fiddle. *Rec. dist.:* Ont.

2. Harmony seldom makes a headline. *Rec. dist.:* N.Y., S.C. *1st cit.:* US1928 Bent, *Strange Bedfellows.* *20c. coll.:* Stevenson 48:2.

harness 1. Before you go in double harness, look well to the other horse. *Rec. dist.:* Ont.

2. The higher up in the world a man is, the less good harness he puts on. *Rec. dist.:* N.Y., S.C. *1st cit.:* US1864 Browne (pseud. Artemus Ward), *In Canada.* *20c. coll.:* Stevenson 626:6.

harvest 1. Good harvests make men prodigal, bad ones provident. *Rec. dist.:* Mich. *1st cit.:* 1611 Cotgrave, *Dictionary of French and English Tongues.* *20c. coll.:* ODEP 320, Stevenson 1079:6.

2. Man who wants a good harvest will not sow bad seed. *Rec. dist.:* Ind.

3. Pray to God for a good harvest, but continue to hoe. *Rec. dist.:* Wis.

4. Work hard in harvest time. *Rec. dist.:* Ind.

SEE ALSO There is STUBBLE only where harvest has been.

has-been It is better to be a has-been than a never-was. *Var.:* It is better to be a has-been than a might-have-been. *Rec. dist.:* Ill., N.Y., Ohio, S.C.

hash SEE LAST gets the hash.

haste 1. Great haste is not always good spent. *Rec. dist.:* N.C. *1st cit.:* ca1530 Berners, *Boke of Duke Huon of Burdeux,* E.E.T.S. (1882–83). *20c. coll.:* Stevenson 1082:3.

2. Haste is slow. *Rec. dist.:* N.Y. *1st cit.:* US1948 Stevenson, *Home Book of Proverbs.* *20c. coll.:* Stevenson 1083:4.

3. Haste makes waste. *Vars.:* **(a)** Haste not, waste not. **(b)** Rash haste makes waste. *Rec. dist.:* U.S., Can. *1st cit.:* ca1386 Chaucer, *Tale of Melibee;* US1753 Franklin, *PRAlmanac.* *20c. coll.:* CODP 108, Whiting 199, ODEP 356, Stevenson 1082:8, Whiting*(MP)* 289.

4. Haste makes waste, and waste makes want. *Vars.:* **(a)** Haste makes waste; waste makes want; want makes a poor boy a beggar. **(b)** Haste makes waste; waste makes want; want makes strife between a good man and his wife. *Rec. dist.:* Mich. *1st cit.:* 1678 Ray, *English Proverbs;* US1940 Thompson, *Body, Boots, and Britches.* *20c. coll.:* ODEP 356, Stevenson 1082:8.

5. Haste may trip up its own heels. *Rec. dist.:* Ont. *1st cit.:* 1580 Baret, *Alvarie.* *20c. coll.:* Stevenson 1081:1.

6. Haste not, rest not. *Rec. dist.:* N.Y.

7. I am always in haste, but never in a hurry. *Rec. dist.:* Ont. *1st cit.:* 1777 Wesley, *Letter,* 10 Dec. *20c. coll.:* Stevenson 1202:19.

8. Make haste but do not hurry. *Rec. dist.:* Ont. *1st cit.:* ca1374 Chaucer, *Troilus and Criseyde;* US1734 *Jonathan Belcher Papers,* Mass.Hist.Soc. *Collections* (1893–94). *20c. coll.:* CODP 108, Whiting 199, ODEP 501, Stevenson 1081:2, T&W 172.

9. Make haste slowly. *Rec. dist.:* U.S., Can. *1st cit.:* ca1374 Chaucer, *Troilus and Criseyde;* US1734 *Jonathan Belcher Papers,* Mass.Hist.Soc. *Collections* (1893–94). *20c. coll.:* CODP 108, Whiting 199, ODEP 501, Stevenson 1081:2, T&W 172, Whiting*(MP)* 289.

10. Make haste while the sun shines. *Rec. dist.:* Fla., N.Y.

11. More haste, worse speed. *Vars.:* **(a)** Less speed, more haste. **(b)** More haste, less speed. **(c)** More haste, less speed, like the tailor with the long thread. **(d)** Most haste, worst speed. **(e)** The more haste, the worse speed. *Rec. dist.:* U.S., Can. *1st cit.:* ca1350 *Douce MS 52;* US1787 *American Museum.* *20c. coll.:* CODP 108, Whiting 200, ODEP 356, Stevenson 1085:1, T&W 173, Whiting*(MP)* 289.

SEE ALSO ANGER and haste hinder good counsel. / Procure not FRIENDS in haste, nei-ther part with them in haste. / MARRY in haste and repent at leisure.

hasty **1.** A hasty man is seldom out of trouble. *Rec. dist.:* La. *1st cit.:* ca1374 Chaucer, *Troilus and Criseyde;* US1927 VanDine, *Canary Murder Case.* *20c. coll.:* ODEP 357, Stevenson 1082:10, Whiting*(MP)* 396.

2. Be not too hasty to outbid others. *Rec. dist.:* Ont. *1st cit.:* 1664 Codrington, *Select Proverbs.* *20c. coll.:* ODEP 357, Stevenson 1085:6.

3. Hasty climbers have sudden falls. *Rec. dist.:* N.Y. *1st cit.:* ca1300 *Proverbes of Hendyng* in *Antiquarian Repertory,* ed. Grose (1809). *20c. coll.:* ODEP 357, Stevenson 746:17.

4. The hasty hand catches frogs for fish. *Rec. dist.:* Ont.

SEE ALSO Hasty GLORY goes out in a snuff.

hat **1.** A broad hat does not always cover a venerable head. *Rec. dist.:* N.Y. *1st cit.:* 1732 Fuller, *Gnomologia.* *20c. coll.:* Stevenson 80:2.

2. A hat will never be worn without a head. *Rec. dist.:* Ont. *1st cit.:* 1611 Cotgrave, *Dictionary of French and English Tongues.* *20c. coll.:* ODEP 360.

3. Don't talk through your hat. *Var.:* Never talk through your hat. *Rec. dist.:* U.S., Can. *1st cit.:* 1922 Joyce, *Ulysses;* US1904 Harben, *Georgians.* *20c. coll.:* Whiting*(MP)* 291, Stevenson 2277:8.

4. It's the life of an old hat to cock it. *Rec. dist.:* N.Y., S.C. *1st cit.:* US1940 Thompson, *Body, Boots, and Britches.* *20c. coll.:* Stevenson 1087:2.

5. Let one hat cover one face. *Rec. dist.:* Ill.

6. What counts most is what you've got under your hat. *Rec. dist.:* Ga., N.Y. *1st cit.:* 1933 Brown, *Murder at Mocking House;* US1924 Fergusson, *Black Company.* *20c. coll.:* Whiting*(MP)* 291.

SEE ALSO Most BRAINS reflect but the crown of a hat. / May the man be damned and never gain fat who wears two FACES under one hat. / Before GOLD even kings take off their hats. / Use your HEAD for something besides a hat rack. / HOME is where you hang your hat.

hatch *See* Don't count your CHICKENS before they're hatched.

hatchet 1. Do not use a hatchet to remove a fly from your friend's forehead. *Rec. dist.:* Kans. *1st cit.:* US1938 Champion, *Racial Proverbs.* *20c. coll.:* Stevenson 1551:7.

2. Nobody ever forgets where he buried a hatchet. *Rec. dist.:* N.Y., S.C. *1st cit.:* 1919 Rohmer, *Quest of the Sacred Slipper;* US1720 Adams in *History of State of Maine,* ed. Baxter (1869–1916). *20c. coll.:* Whiting*(MP)* 291, Whiting 201, ODEP 92, Stevenson 867:9, T&W 173.

See also When the TREE is fallen, everyone goes to it with his hatchet.

hate *(n.)* 1. Hate from hate is sure to grow. *Rec. dist.:* Ont.

2. Hate is a burning fire that may consume the one who hates. *Rec. dist.:* Ont.

3. Hate likely turns to love. *Rec. dist.:* Miss. *1st cit.:* ca1205 Layamon, *Brut,* Soc. Antiquaries (1847). *20c. coll.:* Stevenson 1088:6.

4. Hate twins to love. *Rec. dist.:* N.C. *1st cit.:* US1956 Lewis, *Jenny.* *20c. coll.:* Whiting*(MP)* 291.

5. The greatest hate comes from the greatest love. *Rec. dist.:* Ill. *1st cit.:* 1579 Lyly, *Euphues, Anatomy of Wit* in *Works,* ed. Bond (1902). *20c. coll.:* ODEP 336, Stevenson 1484:13.

6. There is no medicine for hate. *Rec. dist.:* Ohio.

See also The chase of GAIN is rich in hate. / LOVE and hate are the two closest emotions. / LOVE is akin to hate.

hate *(v.)* 1. He who hates is lost. *Rec. dist.:* N.Y.

2. If you hate a man, eat his bread; and if you love him, do the same. *Rec. dist.:* Wis.

3. If you hate a man, let him live. *Rec. dist.:* N.Y., S.C.

4. It does not matter what a man hates provided he hates something. *Rec. dist.:* N.C. *1st cit.:* ca1880 Butler, *Note-books.* *20c. coll.:* Stevenson 1087:10.

5. Men always hate most what they envy most. *Rec. dist.:* N.Y., S.C.

6. Men hate where they hurt. *Rec. dist.:* Ont. *1st cit.:* 1732 Fuller, *Gnomologia.* *20c. coll.:* Stevenson 1244:5.

7. There are few who would rather be hated than laughed at. *Rec. dist.:* Ont.

8. We hate those whom we have wronged. *Rec. dist.:* Ill. *1st cit.:* 1732 Fuller, *Gnomologia.* *20c. coll.:* Stevenson 1244:5.

9. You may hate the things a person does, but never hate the person. *Rec. dist.:* N.Mex., W.Va. *1st cit.:* 1533 Tyndale, *Enchiridion.* *20c. coll.:* ODEP 358.

See also The gods hate a COWARD but love a brave soul. / He that does ILL hates the light. / LOVE many; hate few; learn to paddle your own canoe.

hatred 1. Hatred is blind, as well as love. *Rec. dist.:* Ill., N.Y. *1st cit.:* 1732 Fuller, *Gnomologia.* *20c. coll.:* ODEP 358, Stevenson 1484:2.

2. Hatred stirs up strife. *Var.:* Hatred stirs up strife, but love covers all sins. *Rec. dist.:* Ont., Wis.

3. He that hides hatred with lying lips and he that utters slander is a fool. *Rec. dist.:* Ont.

4. The hatred of the nearest relatives is the most bitter. *Rec. dist.:* Mich. *1st cit.:* US1948 Stevenson, *Home Book of Proverbs.* *20c. coll.:* Stevenson 1088:16.

Hatteras *See* If the BERMUDAS let you pass, you must beware of Hatteras.

haughty Never be haughty to the humble; never be humble to the haughty. *Rec. dist.:* N.Y., S.C.

have 1. Better to have than to hold. *Vars.:* **(a)** To have is to hold, and to hold is to have not. **(b)** What we have, we hold. **(c)** You can't hold what you haven't got in your hands. *Rec. dist.:* Ont. *1st cit.:* ca1377 Langland, *Piers Plowman,* ed. Skeat, E.E.T.S. (1867); US1936 DePuy, *Long Knife.* *20c. coll.:* Stevenson 1089:11, Whiting*(MP)* 292.

2. Better to have than to wish. *Rec. dist.:* Okla., Tex., Vt. *1st cit.:* ca1530 *Calisto and Melibea.* *20c. coll.:* ODEP 56, Stevenson 1089:9.

3. It is better to have it and not need it than to need it and not have it. *Var.:* It's better to

have and not need than to need and not have. *Rec. dist.:* N.Y., N.C.

4. It is better to have what you cannot love than love what you cannot have. *Rec. dist.:* Ont.

5. It's not what you have but how you use it. *Rec. dist.:* Ind.

6. It's not what you have in life that counts, but what you are. *Rec. dist.:* N.C., S.C.

7. Them as has, gits. *Rec. dist.:* Ill., N.Y., Oreg., S.C. *1st cit.:* 1546 Heywood, *Dialogue of Proverbs,* ed. Habernicht (1963); US1880 Sill, *Baker's Duzzen uv Wize Sawz.* *20c. coll.:* Stevenson 1089:12.

8. Those that have must lose. *Var.:* Them as has must lose, 'cause them as hasn't can't. *Rec. dist.:* Md., Ohio, Tex.

9. To him who has shall be given. *Rec. dist.:* N.Y., S.C. *1st cit.:* 1546 Heywood, *Dialogue of Proverbs,* ed. Habernicht (1963); US1867 Emerson, *Celestial Railroad.* *20c. coll.:* Stevenson 1089:12.

10. We would be better off to have than to have coming. *Rec. dist.:* Ont.

11. Who has not, is not. *Rec. dist.:* Ind.

12. The more we have, the more we want; the more we want, the less we have. *Var.:* The more you have, the more you want. *Rec. dist.:* Ont.

SEE ALSO You can't have your CAKE and eat it too. / Do well, have well. / You cannot LOSE what you haven't got. / Never spend your MONEY before you have it. / He that can have PATIENCE can have what he will. / The POOR you have with you always. / SAVE while you have; give while you live. / SPARE and have is better than spend and crave. / WASTE and want; save and have. / WISE men care not for what they cannot have.

having **1.** Anything worth having is never gotten on a flowery bed of ease. *Rec. dist.:* Ga.

2. Anything worth having is worth keeping. *Rec. dist.:* N.C.

3. If it is worth having, it is worth working for. *Rec. dist.:* Ont.

SEE ALSO Of SAVING comes having.

haw *SEE* When all FRUIT fails, welcome haws.

hawk *SEE* A BUZZARD never makes a good hawk.

hay **1.** Make hay while the sun shines. *Vars.:* **(a)** Gather hay while the sun shines. **(b)** It is good to make hay while the sun shines. **(c)** Make your hay before the fine weather leaves you. *Rec. dist.:* U.S., Can. *1st cit.:* 1509 Barclay, *Ship of Fools,* ed. Jamieson in *Eclogues,* E.E.T.S. (1874); US1637 *New English Canaan of Thomas Morton,* ed. Adams, Jr., Publ. Prince Soc. (1883). *20c. coll.:* ODEP 501, Whiting 202, Stevenson 1092:5, *CODP* 143, T&W 175, Whiting*(MP)* 293.

2. People who live in hay houses shouldn't throw pitchforks. *Rec. dist.:* Ont.

3. You can't make hay where the grass won't grow. *Rec. dist.:* Vt.

SEE ALSO The ASS carries the hay and eats it too. / If there were no RAIN, there'd be no hay to make when the sun shines.

hazard One must see a hazard to avoid it. *Rec. dist.:* Ill.

he He yesterday, I today. *Rec. dist.:* Ont.

head **1.** A bald head is soon shaven. *Rec. dist.:* Miss., N.Y., Ont. *1st cit.:* ca1450 *Reliquiae Antiquae,* eds. Wright and Halliwell (1841–43). *20c. coll.:* ODEP 28, Stevenson 117:5.

2. A bald head needs a new wig. *Rec. dist.:* Ont.

3. A big head has a big ache. *Rec. dist.:* Ind.

4. A good head does not want for hats. *Rec. dist.:* Ind.

5. A head that is as hard as rock will burst into pieces. *Rec. dist.:* Ky., Tenn.

6. A spur in the head is worth two in the heels. *Rec. dist.:* Ind., Miss., Ont. *1st cit.:* 1668 Skippon, *Diary.* *20c. coll.:* ODEP 768, Stevenson 2203:11.

7. A steady head means a good job. *Rec. dist.:* Ont.

8. All too often the only thing time does to the head is to make it whiter and smoother. *Rec. dist.:* Ont.

9. Better be the head of an ass than the tail of a horse. *Rec. dist.:* Ill. *1st cit.:* 1639 Clarke, *Paroemiologia. 20c. coll.:* ODEP 51, Stevenson 1099:6.

10. Big head, little sense. *Vars.:* **(a)** Big head and little wit. **(b)** Big head, little wit; little head, not a bit. **(c)** Little head, little wit; big head, not a bit. **(d)** Muckle head, little wit. **(e)** Small head, little wit; big head, not a bit. *Rec. dist.:* N.C., Ont. *1st cit.:* ca1470 *Mankind;* US1735 *South Carolina Gazette* in Cook, *Literary Influences in Colonial Newspapers* (1912). *20c. coll.:* ODEP 530, Stevenson 1095:9, Whiting(MP) 293.

11. Don't cut off your head with your tongue. *Var.:* Don't let your tongue cut off your head. *Rec. dist.:* Ill., Ont. *1st cit.:* 1616 Draxe, *Bibliotheca Scholastica* in *Anglia* (1918); US1875 Scarborough, *Chinese Proverbs. 20c. coll.:* ODEP 830, Stevenson 2342:1.

12. Don't lose your head; count first to ten. *Rec. dist.:* N.C.

13. Empty heads talk the loudest. *Rec. dist.:* N.Y.

14. Haud your head up and ye'll no stumble. *Rec. dist.:* Ont. *Infm.:* "Haud" is Scottish dialect form of "hold."

15. He that has a head of glass must not throw stones at another. *Rec. dist.:* Ont., Tex. *1st cit.:* ca1374 Chaucer, *Troilus and Criseyde. 20c. coll.:* ODEP 360, Stevenson 1192:8.

16. He that has a head of wax must not walk in the sun. *Vars.:* **(a)** If your head be waxed, do not walk in the sun. **(b)** If your head is wax, don't walk in the sun. *Rec. dist.:* Miss., N.Y., Ont., S.C., Vt. *1st cit.:* 1640 Herbert, *Outlandish Proverbs (Jacula Prudentum)* in *Works,* ed. Hutchinson (1941); US1749 Franklin, *PRAlmanac. 20c. coll.:* ODEP 360, Whiting 203, Stevenson 1095:7.

17. Hold up your head even if your tail does drag in the mud. *Rec. dist.:* Ont.

18. Hold your head up if you do die hard. *Rec. dist.:* Ill.

19. If you're right, you don't need to lose your head; and if you're wrong, you can't afford to. *Rec. dist.:* Ohio.

20. If you don't use your head, you must use your legs. *Vars.:* **(a)** If you don't use your head, you'll have to use your feet. **(b)** If you haven't got it in your head, you've got it in your heel. *Rec. dist.:* Okla., Ont. *1st cit.:* 1828 Carr, *Dialect of Craven. 20c. coll.:* Stevenson 1093:1.

21. If you lose your head, hold your tongue. *Rec. dist.:* Ill. *1st cit.:* 1616 Draxe, *Bibliotheca Scholastica* in *Anglia* (1918). *20c. coll.:* ODEP 830, Stevenson 2349:2.

22. If you put nothing in your head, you will get nothing from it. *Rec. dist.:* Okla. *1st cit.:* 1630 Taylor, *Works;* US1845 Cooper, *Chainbearer. 20c. coll.:* Stevenson 1701:10, T&W 265.

23. It makes little difference what's on the outside of your head if there's something on the inside. *Rec. dist.:* Miss.

24. It takes a level head to win. *Rec. dist.:* Ont.

25. Keep your head high and your nose clean. *Rec. dist.:* Ohio.

26. Keep your head out of the clouds. *Rec. dist.:* Ill., Miss., N.Y. *1st cit.:* ca1205 Layamon, *Brut,* Soc. Antiquaries (1847); USca1656 Bradford, *History of Plymouth Plantation,* ed. Ford (1912). *20c. coll.:* Stevenson 370:3, Whiting 75.

27. Let your head save your heels. *Vars.:* **(a)** Let your head save your feet. **(b)** Make your head save your heels. **(c)** Use your head and save your heels. *Rec. dist.:* U.S., Can. *1st cit.:* 1828 Carr, *Dialect of Craven;* US1895 Jewett, *Life of Nancy. 20c. coll.:* Stevenson 1093:7, Whiting(MP) 296.

28. Never comb a bald head. *Rec. dist.:* Ont.

29. One good head is better than a thousand strong hands. *Rec. dist.:* Ont. *1st cit.:* 1732 Fuller, *Gnomologia. 20c. coll.:* Stevenson 1094:10.

30. Small head, big ideas. *Rec. dist.:* Ont. *1st cit.:* US1735 *South Carolina Gazette* in Cook, *Literary Influences in Colonial Newspapers* (1912). *20c. coll.:* Whiting 203.

31. So many heads, so many wits. *Rec. dist.:* Ohio. *1st cit.:* ca1386 Chaucer, *Squire's Tale. 20c. coll.:* ODEP 525, CODP 149, Stevenson 1722:1.

32. Some have no heads, but all have hearts. *Rec. dist.:* Ont.

33. Stand on your head and the world will be upside down. *Rec. dist.:* Ont.

34. Still head, wise heart. *Rec. dist.:* Ind.

35. The bigger a man's head gets, the easier it is to fill his shoes. *Rec. dist.:* U.S., Can.

36. The stoutest head bears longest out. *Rec. dist.:* Ont.

37. There's no head like an old head. *Rec. dist.:* Ky., Tenn.

38. There is no putting old heads on young shoulders. *Vars.:* **(a)** It is hard to put old heads on young shoulders. **(b)** Old heads cannot fit on young shoulders. **(c)** Old heads don't grow on young shoulders. **(d)** You can't put an old head on young shoulders. *Rec. dist.:* U.S., Can. *1st cit.:* 1591 Smith, *Preparative to Marriage;* US1785 Van Schaack, *Life of Peter Van Schaack* (1842). *20c. coll.:* CODP 167, Whiting 204, ODEP 589, Stevenson 1093:2, T&W 176, Whiting*(MP)* 295.

39. To a wise head, two or three words. *Rec. dist.:* Ont.

40. Two heads are better than one. *Rec. dist.:* U.S., Can. *1st cit.:* ca1390 Gower, *Confessio Amantis,* E.E.T.S. (1900); US1743 *Boston Evening Post* in *Newspaper Extracts,* eds. Nelson and Honeyman, Archives of New Jersey (1894–1923). *20c. coll.:* CODP 233, Whiting 206, Stevenson 1096:1, T&W 177, Whiting*(MP)* 297.

41. Two heads are better than one, even if one is a cabbage head. *Vars.:* **(a)** Two heads are better than one, even if one is a goat head. **(b)** Two heads are better than one, even if one is a pumpkin head. **(c)** Two heads are better than one, even though one may be a sheep's head. *Rec. dist.:* Miss., R.I., Vt., Wis. *1st cit.:* 1864 "Cornish Proverbs" in *Notes & Queries;* US1968 Saxton, *Plant. 20c. coll.:* ODEP 851, Stevenson 1096:1, Whiting*(MP)* 297.

42. Two heads are better than one if one is deceitful. *Rec. dist.:* Vt.

43. Use your head for something besides a hat rack. *Rec. dist.:* Ala., Miss., N.C.

44. We have heads on us for the same reason pins do—to keep us from going too far. *Rec. dist.:* Kans., Ont. *1st cit.:* 1709 Steele, *Tatler;* US1811 Wirt, *Letters of the British Spy* (1832). *20c. coll.:* ODEP 360, Whiting 203, Stevenson 1098:5.

45. We have heads to get money and hearts to spend it. *Rec. dist.:* N.C.

46. Weak heads are often headstrong. *Rec. dist.:* Ont.

47. What you haven't got in your head, you have in your feet. *Rec. dist.:* Ill., N.J., Ohio, Ont., S.C.

48. What your head forgets, your heels must remember. *Rec. dist.:* N.Dak. *1st cit.:* 1869 Hazlitt, *English Proverbs. 20c. coll.:* Stevenson 1095:5.

49. When you can step on your head, it's time to go home. *Rec. dist.:* N.Y., S.C.

50. You mustn't expect a man's head on a boy's shoulders. *Rec. dist.:* Ohio. *1st cit.:* 1591 Smith, *Preparative for Marriage;* US1785 Van Schaack, *Life of Peter Van Schaack* (1842). *20c. coll.:* CODP 167, Whiting 204, ODEP 589, Stevenson 1093:2, T&W 176.

51. Your own head—your own success or failure. *Rec. dist.:* Wis.

SEE ALSO BLONDES aren't the only people who are light-headed. / The FEET are slow when the head wears snow. / A FOOL's head never grows white. / A HAIR in the head is worth two in the brush. / You can't grow HAIR and brains in the same head. / Heed the HAMMER: it keeps its head. / An honest HEART being the first blessing, a knowing head is the second. / If the HEART is right, the head can't be very far wrong. / One good IDEA put to use is worth a hundred buzzing around in the back of your head. / Soft LIVING hardens the head. / A still MOUTH makes a wise head. / OPPORTUNITY is bald on the back of her head; seize her as she passes. / PEOPLE who wouldn't think of talking with their mouths full often speak with their heads empty. / De PROUDNESS in a man don't count w'en his head's cold. / Better an empty PURSE than an empty head. / If a man empties his PURSE into his head, no one can take it from him. / Full

STOMACHS make empty heads. / A still TONGUE makes a wise head. / Keep a good TONGUE in your head.

headache To ease another's headache is to forget one's own. *Rec. dist.:* Utah.

SEE ALSO A CROWN is no cure for a headache. / A man is really a SUCCESS when flattery gives him a headache instead of a big head.

headless SEE A headless ARMY fights badly.

headline SEE HARMONY seldom makes a headline.

heal 1. Before healing others, heal yourself. *Rec. dist.:* N.J. *1st cit.:* US1948 Stevenson, *Home Book of Proverbs.* *20c. coll.:* Stevenson 598:7.

2. One is not so soon healed as hurt. *Rec. dist.:* Mich., R.I., Ont. *1st cit.:* 1599 Porter, *Two Angry Women of Abington,* Percy Soc. (1841). *20c. coll.:* ODEP 361, Stevenson 1950:15.

SEE ALSO EARTH has no sorrow that heaven cannot heal. / GOD heals and the doctor takes the fee. / Gild a JOY and heal a pain. / TIME heals all wounds. / Reopen not a WOUND once healed. / WOUNDS made by words are hard to heal.

health 1. A man too busy to take care of his health is like a mechanic too busy to take care of his tools. *Rec. dist.:* N.Y.

2. A nation's health is a nation's wealth. *Rec. dist.:* Ohio.

3. Find health better than gold. *Rec. dist.:* Ont. *1st cit.:* 1578 Lemnius, *Touchstones of Complexions;* US1718 Chalkley, *Letters in Works of Thomas Chalkley* (1766). *20c. coll.:* ODEP 362, Whiting 206, Stevenson 1100:5.

4. Folks spend their health to acquire wealth and later spend their wealth in an effort to regain their health. *Rec. dist.:* Ont.

5. Give me my health and take my wealth. *Rec. dist.:* N.Y., N.C. *1st cit.:* 1678 Ray, *English Proverbs;* US1718 Chalkley, *Letters in Works of Thomas Chalkley* (1766). *20c. coll.:* Stevenson 1100:5, Whiting 206.

6. Good health and good sense are two of life's greatest blessings. *Rec. dist.:* N.Y., S.C.

1st cit.: US1948 Stevenson, *Home Book of Proverbs.* *20c. coll.:* Stevenson 1101:10.

7. Good health is priceless. *Rec. dist.:* N.C. *1st cit.:* ca1510 *Health and Wealth;* US1718 Chalkley, *Letters in Works of Thomas Chalkley* (1766). *20c. coll.:* ODEP 362, Whiting 206, Stevenson 1100:5.

8. He who has health has hope, and he who has hope has everything. *Rec. dist.:* Wis.

9. Health and money go far. *Rec. dist.:* N.Y. *1st cit.:* 1640 Herbert, *Outlandish Proverbs (Jacula Prudentum)* in *Works,* ed. Hutchinson (1941). *20c. coll.:* Stevenson 1101:3.

10. Health is a call loan. *Rec. dist.:* N.Y., S.C. *1st cit.:* US1858 Shaw (pseud. Josh Billings), *Sayings.* *20c. coll.:* Stevenson 1100:6.

11. Health is not valued till sickness comes. *Rec. dist.:* Ill., N.Y., Ont., S.C. *1st cit.:* 1553 *Respublica,* ed. Magnus, E.E.T.S. (1905); US1747 Franklin, *PRAlmanac.* *20c. coll.:* ODEP 362, Stevenson 1101:7.

12. Health is the first muse. *Rec. dist.:* N.Y., S.C. *1st cit.:* US1875 Emerson, "Inspirations" in *Letters and Social Aims.* *20c. coll.:* Stevenson 1103:7.

13. Health is wealth. *Vars.:* **(a)** All health is better than wealth. **(b)** Good health is more to be desired than wealth. **(c)** Health is the best wealth. **(d)** The first wealth is health. *Rec. dist.:* U.S. *1st cit.:* ca1510 *Health and Wealth;* US1718 Chalkley, *Letters in Works of Thomas Chalkley* (1766). *20c. coll.:* ODEP 362, Stevenson 1100:5.

14. Health is worth more than learning. *Rec. dist.:* N.Y., S.C. *1st cit.:* US1790 Jefferson, Letter to John G. Jefferson. *20c. coll.:* Stevenson 1100:5.

15. If you lack health you lack everything. *Rec. dist.:* Ill., N.Y., S.C. *1st cit.:* 1902 Hulme, *Proverb Lore.* *20c. coll.:* Stevenson 1101:10.

16. It is better to lose health like a spendthrift than to hoard it like a miser. *Rec. dist.:* Utah. *1st cit.:* 1874 Stevenson, *Aes Triplex.* *20c. coll.:* Stevenson 1102:2.

17. It is easy for a man in health to preach patience to the sick. *Rec. dist.:* Ont.

18. Some folks enjoy poor health. *Rec. dist.:* Kans., Ky., Tenn., Vt. *1st cit.:* US1855 Whitcher, *Widow Bedott Papers.* *20c. coll.:* Stevenson 1102:6.

19. We are not so sensible of the greatest health as of the least sickness. *Rec. dist.:* N.Y., S.C., Wis. *1st cit.:* 1732 Fuller, *Gnomologia;* US1747 Franklin, *PRAlmanac.* *20c. coll.:* Stevenson 1101:7.

20. We drink one another's health and spoil our own. *Rec. dist.:* N.Y., S.C. *1st cit.:* 1604 Dekker, *Honest Whore.* *20c. coll.:* Stevenson 635:3.

21. Without health no one is rich. *Rec. dist.:* N.Y.

SEE ALSO Good POSTURE means better health. / SICKNESS is felt, but health not at all. / WEALTH can buy no health. / A good WIFE and health are a man's best wealth.

healthy SEE Early to BED and early to rise makes a man healthy, wealthy, and wise. / To be HAPPY is to be healthy. / INDUSTRY keeps the body healthy, the mind clear, the heart whole, and the purse full.

heap Add little to little and there will be a great heap. *Var.:* Out of many little things a great heap will be formed. *Rec. dist.:* Ill., Ont., Wis. *1st cit.:* ca1303 Mannyng, *Handlyng Synne.* *20c. coll.:* Stevenson 1443:13.

hear **1.** Gently to hear, kindly to judge. *Rec. dist.:* N.C.

2. He that can't hear must feel. *Rec. dist.:* N.C., Ont.

3. Hear all and say nothing. *Var.:* Hear all, see all, say nothing. *Rec. dist.:* Ind., Miss., R.I. *1st cit.:* ca1420 *Peter Idel's Instructions,* E.E.T.S. (1868); US1712 Danforth, *Poems.* *20c. coll.:* ODEP 362, CODP 109, Stevenson 2192:6, Whiting(MP) 206.

4. Hear and be just. *Rec. dist.:* Ind.

5. Hear first and speak afterwards. *Rec. dist.:* Ind.

6. Hear much, speak little. *Rec. dist.:* N.J., N.Y. *1st cit.:* ca1420 *Peter Idel's Instructions,* E.E.T.S. (1868). *20c. coll.:* ODEP 362, CODP 109, Stevenson 2192:7.

7. Hear, see, and be silent. *Rec. dist.:* Ind. *1st cit.:* ca1430 Lydgate, *Minor Poems,* Percy Soc. (1840). *20c. coll.:* ODEP 362, CODP 109, Stevenson 1767:3.

8. Hear twice before you speak once. *Rec. dist.:* Ill., Ont. *1st cit.:* 1855 Bohn, *Handbook of Proverbs.* *20c. coll.:* Stevenson 2192:2.

9. If you heard, then heed. *Rec. dist.:* Calif., N.Y.

10. One hears only what he understands. *Rec. dist.:* Ill.

11. To hear is to obey. *Rec. dist.:* N.Y.

12. What you don't hear will not hurt you. *Rec. dist.:* N.C.

13. What you hear never sounds half so important as what you overhear. *Rec. dist.:* N.Y., Ont.

14. You never hear the one that gets you. *Rec. dist.:* Ind.

SEE ALSO BELIEVE only half of what you see and nothing you hear. / CHILDREN should be seen and not heard. / None so DEAF as he who won't hear. / If you DO what you should not, you must hear what you would not. / No EAR is so deaf as one which wishes not to hear. / EAVESDROPPERS never hear any good of themselves. / He who speaks EVIL hears worse. / See no EVIL, hear no evil, speak no evil. / LISTENERS hear no good of themselves. / LOVERS, travelers, and poets will give money to be heard. / If you want to hear the whole TRUTH about yourself, anger your neighbour.

hearing **1.** Bad hearing makes bad rehearsing. *Rec. dist.:* Ont. *1st cit.:* 1721 Kelly, *Scottish Proverbs.* *20c. coll.:* Stevenson 1105:8.

2. Be silent or speak something worth hearing. *Rec. dist.:* N.Y., Tex. *1st cit.:* 1639 Clarke, *Paroemiologia.* *20c. coll.:* Stevenson 2113:3.

3. It is hard to keep from hearing what you don't want to. *Rec. dist.:* N.C.

hearsay SEE One EYEWITNESS is better than ten hearsays.

hearse SEE From the day you were born till you ride in a hearse, there's nothing SO BAD but it might have been worse. / Don't QUIT till the hearse comes around.

heart 1. A big heart is better than a big house. *Rec. dist.:* Ont.

2. A blithe heart makes a blooming visage. *Rec. dist.:* U.S., Can. *1st cit.:* 1586 Guazzo, *Civile Conversation*, tr. Pettie, T.T. (1925); US1812 Melish, *Travels Through U.S., 1806–1811* (1818). *20c. coll.:* ODEP 68, Whiting 207, Stevenson 1110:3.

3. A broken heart is like broken china: we can mend it, but we can never erase the scars. *Rec. dist.:* Ala.

4. A broken heart mends quickly when repaired. *Rec. dist.:* N.Dak.

5. A cheerful heart is good medicine, but a broken spirit dries up the bones. *Rec. dist.:* N.Y. *1st cit.:* ca1386 Chaucer, *Tale of Melibee*; US1789 *New Letters of Abigail Adams*, ed. Mitchell (1947). *20c. coll.:* Stevenson 1112:7, Whiting 207.

6. A gentle heart is tied with an easy thread. *Rec. dist.:* Calif. *1st cit.:* ca1633 Herbert, *The Glimpse*. *20c. coll.:* ODEP 299, Stevenson 1107:3.

7. A good cause makes a stout heart and a strong arm. *Rec. dist.:* Wis. *1st cit.:* 1732 Fuller, *Gnomologia*. *20c. coll.:* Stevenson 304:4.

8. A good heart cannot lie. *Rec. dist.:* N.Y. *1st cit.:* 1611 Cotgrave, *Dictionary of French and English Tongues*. *20c. coll.:* ODEP 320, Stevenson 1109:8, Whiting(MP) 298.

9. A great heart is never proud. *Rec. dist.:* Ont.

10. A heart without love is a violin without strings. *Rec. dist.:* N.Y.

11. A kind heart is a fountain of gladness. *Rec. dist.:* Ill.

12. A light heart lives long. *Rec. dist.:* Ind., N.J. *1st cit.:* 1594 Shakespeare, *Love's Labour's Lost*. *20c. coll.:* Stevenson 1110:3.

13. A light heart makes light work. *Rec. dist.:* N.Y.

14. A little man may have a large heart. *Rec. dist.:* Ont. *1st cit.:* 1599 Greene, *Sinner of Wakefield*. *20c. coll.:* Stevenson 1106:2.

15. A loving heart is better and stronger than wisdom. *Rec. dist.:* Ky., Tenn.

16. A man's heart at thirty is either steeled or broken. *Rec. dist.:* Ala.

17. A merry heart does good like a medicine. *Rec. dist.:* U.S., Can. *1st cit.:* US1789 *New Letters of Abigail Adams*, ed. Mitchell (1947). *20c. coll.:* Stevenson 1110:3, Whiting 207.

18. A merry heart goes all the day. *Rec. dist.:* Ont. *1st cit.:* 1610 Shakespeare, *Winter's Tale*. *20c. coll.:* Stevenson 1110:3.

19. A merry heart makes a cheerful countenance. *Var.:* A merry heart makes a cheerful countenance, but by sorrow of the heart the spirit is broken. *Rec. dist.:* Ill., N.Y., Oreg. *1st cit.:* 1573 Sanford, *Garden of Pleasure*; US1812 Melish, *Travels Through U.S., 1806–1811* (1818). *20c. coll.:* ODEP 414, Whiting 207, Stevenson 1110:3.

20. A selfish heart desires love for itself; a Christian heart delights to love without return. *Rec. dist.:* Mich., N.C.

21. A sinful heart makes a feeble hand. *Rec. dist.:* Wis.

22. A sound heart is the life of the flesh, but envy the rottenness of the bones. *Rec. dist.:* Ind., Ohio, Ont. *1st cit.:* US1948 Stevenson, *Home Book of Proverbs*. *20c. coll.:* Stevenson 703:8.

23. A stout heart crushes ill luck. *Rec. dist.:* Ont. *1st cit.:* 1564 Edwards, *Damon and Pithias*. *20c. coll.:* ODEP 320, Stevenson 1106:2.

24. A thankful heart is not only the greatest virtue but the parent of all other virtues. *Rec. dist.:* Ind.

25. A willing heart carries a weary pair of feet a long way. *Rec. dist.:* Ont. *1st cit.:* 1640 Herbert, *Outlandish Proverbs (Jacula Prudentum)* in *Works*, ed. Hutchinson (1941). *20c. coll.:* Stevenson 2511:4.

26. All things are false and yet the heart is true. *Rec. dist.:* N.Y.

27. An evil heart can make any doctrine heretical. *Rec. dist.:* Mich.

28. An honest heart being the first blessing, a knowing head is the second. *Rec. dist.:* N.Y., S.C. *1st cit.:* 1785 Jefferson, Letter to Peter Carr. *20c. coll.:* Stevenson 1116:6.

29. As a man thinks in his heart, so is he. *Rec. dist.:* U.S. *1st cit.:* US1948 Stevenson, *Home Book of Proverbs*. *20c. coll.:* Stevenson 2305:15.

30. As the heart makes the home, the teacher makes the child. *Rec. dist.:* Kans.

31. Brave hearts are tender hearts. *Rec. dist.:* Ont.

32. Don' take no mo' tuh yo' haht dan yuh kin kick offen yo' heels. *Rec. dist.:* Tex.

33. Don't use your heart for a cash register. *Rec. dist.:* Utah.

34. Don't wear your heart on your sleeve. *Rec. dist.:* U.S., Can. *1st cit.:* 1605 Shakespeare, *Othello;* USca1891 Gilder, *Strephon and Sardon*. *20c. coll.:* Stevenson 1113:11, Whiting(*MP*) 299.

35. Every heart has its own ache. *Rec. dist.:* Miss., Ont., R.I. *1st cit.:* 1732 Fuller, *Gnomologia*. *20c. coll.:* ODEP 363, Stevenson 1112:8.

36. Faint heart never won fair lady. *Rec. dist.:* U.S., Can. *1st cit.:* 1390 Gower, *Confessio Amantis*, E.E.T.S. (1900); US1777 Livingston in *Correspondence of Samuel Webb*, ed. Ford (1893). *20c. coll.:* ODEP 238, Whiting 207, CODP 75, Stevenson 1108:9, T&W 178, Whiting(*MP*) 298.

37. Have you wealth or have you none, if you lose heart all is gone. *Rec. dist.:* N.Y.

38. He that puts trust in his own heart is a fool. *Rec. dist.:* Wis.

39. Hearts don't break, they bend and wither. *Rec. dist.:* N.Y., S.C. *1st cit.:* US1940 Thompson, *Body, Boots, and Britches*. *20c. coll.:* Stevenson 1114:13.

40. Hearts may agree, though heads differ. *Rec. dist.:* Mich. *1st cit.:* 1602 Shakespeare, *All's Well That Ends Well*. *20c. coll.:* ODEP 364, Stevenson 1116:4.

41. His heart cannot be pure whose tongue is not clean. *Var.:* Who has a clean heart has also a clean tongue. *Rec. dist.:* Wis.

42. Home-keeping hearts are happiest. *Rec. dist.:* Ont. *1st cit.:* US1855 Longfellow, *Song of Hiawatha*. *20c. coll.:* Stevenson 1153:4.

43. Hope springs eternal in the human heart. *Rec. dist.:* U.S. *1st cit.:* 1733 Pope, *Essay on Man;* US1942 Goldman, *Murder Behind the Mike*. *20c. coll.:* CODP 114, Stevenson 1168:2.

44. Humble hearts have humble desires. *Rec. dist.:* Wis. *1st cit.:* 1611 Cotgrave, *Dictionary of French and English Tongues*. *20c. coll.:* ODEP 391, Stevenson 1109:6.

45. If the heart is right, the head can't be very far wrong. *Rec. dist.:* Wis.

46. If your heart fails you, climb not at all. *Rec. dist.:* Calif.

47. In whose heart there is no song, to him the miles are many and long. *Rec. dist.:* Ont.

48. It's a poor heart that never rejoices. *Rec. dist.:* Ill., R.I. *1st cit.:* 1834 Marryat, *Peter Simple;* US1970 Blackburn, *Burry*. *20c. coll.:* CODP 180, ODEP 638, Stevenson 1111:8, Whiting(*MP*) 298.

49. Kind hearts are more than coronets. *Var.:* Kind hearts are more than a corner lot. *Rec. dist.:* Md., Wis. *1st cit.:* 1833 Tennyson, *Lady Clara Vere de Vere*. *20c. coll.:* Stevenson 1107:3.

50. Kind hearts are soonest wronged. *Rec. dist.:* N.Y. *1st cit.:* ca1374 Breton, *Crossing of Proverbs*. *20c. coll.:* ODEP 424, Stevenson 1296:9.

51. Kind hearts are the gardens, kind thoughts the roots, kind words the flowers, kind deeds the fruits. *Rec. dist.:* Ont.

52. Let not your heart with cares be filled, for care has many a victim killed. *Rec. dist.:* N.Y.

53. Let your heart keep pure and the world will, too. *Rec. dist.:* Ont.

54. Let your heart rule your head in matters of affection. *Rec. dist.:* Kans.

55. Light of heart, light of feet. *Rec. dist.:* Ont.

56. Little is much if the heart be but turned toward heaven. *Rec. dist.:* N.Y.

57. Loving hearts find peace in love; clever heads find profit in it. *Rec. dist.:* Ind.

58. Many a heart is caught on the rebound. *Rec. dist.:* Ill. *1st cit.:* 1902 Lean, *Collectanea*. *20c. coll.:* Stevenson 1114:6.

59. Many a kind heart beats under a rugged exterior. *Rec. dist.:* Ont.

60. Nearest the heart comes first out. *Rec. dist.:* Ont. *1st cit.:* 1580 Lyly, *Euphues and His England,* in *Works,* ed. Bond (1902). *20c. coll.:* ODEP 557, Stevenson 1108:10.

61. Nobody dies of a broken heart. *Rec. dist.:* Ind.

62. Out of the abundance of the heart, the mouth speaks. *Rec. dist.:* N.Y., Oreg. *1st cit.:* ca1389 Chaucer, *Parson's Tale;* USca1645 Cotton in *Complete Writings of Roger Williams* (1963). *20c. coll.:* Stevenson 1111:10, Whiting 2, T&W 2, Whiting*(MP)* 2.

63. Some people will put heart into a stone image. *Rec. dist.:* N.C.

64. Temptation is the fire that brings up the scum of the heart. *Rec. dist.:* Ala.

65. The heart has arguments with which the understanding is unacquainted. *Rec. dist.:* N.Y., S.C. *1st cit.:* US1860 Emerson, "Wisdom" in *Conduct of Life. 20c. coll.:* Stevenson 1105:15.

66. The heart has eyes that the brain knows nothing of. *Rec. dist.:* Oreg., R.I., Wis. *1st cit.:* US1913 Parkhurst, "Coming to Truth" in *Sermons. 20c. coll.:* Stevenson 1105:15.

67. The heart has its reasons. *Var.:* The heart has reasons that reason does not understand. *Rec. dist.:* N.Y. *1st cit.:* US1948 Stevenson, *Home Book of Proverbs. 20c. coll.:* Stevenson 1105:15.

68. The heart has no wrinkles. *Rec. dist.:* Ky., Tenn.

69. The heart is the eyes—you must look there. *Rec. dist.:* N.Y.

70. The heart knows its own bitterness. *Rec. dist.:* Ohio. *1st cit.:* US1948 Stevenson, *Home Book of Proverbs. 20c. coll.:* Stevenson 1112:8.

71. The heart of a fool is in his mouth, but the mouth of a wise man is in his heart. *Rec. dist.:* Ill. *1st cit.:* 1477 *Dictes and Sayenges of Philosophirs,* tr. Rivers. *20c. coll.:* Stevenson 856:3.

72. The heart that loves is always young. *Rec. dist.:* Ont.

73. The mother's heart is the child's schoolroom. *Rec. dist.:* Oreg., Utah, Wis.

74. The prayerful heart is the happy heart. *Rec. dist.:* Utah.

75. The quickest way to a man's heart is through his stomach. *Var.:* The way to a man's heart is through his stomach. *Rec. dist.:* U.S., Can. *1st cit.:* 1845 Ford, *Handbook for Travellers in Spain;* US1814 Adams, Letter, 15 Apr., in *Works* (1851). *20c. coll.:* Stevenson 2217:8, *CODP* 242, *ODEP* 871, T&W 179, Whiting*(MP)* 673.

76. The way to a man's heart is through his ego. *Rec. dist.:* Kans.

77. To a brave heart, nothing is impossible. *Rec. dist.:* Kans., N.C., Tex. *1st cit.:* 1509 Hawes, *Passetyme of Pleasure. 20c. coll.:* ODEP 580, Stevenson 1227:1.

78. To a young heart, everything is fun. *Rec. dist.:* Ont.

79. To live in hearts we leave behind is not to die. *Rec. dist.:* N.C. *1st cit.:* 1825 Campbell, *Hallowed Ground. 20c. coll.:* Stevenson 500:2.

80. Two hearts can live cheaper than one. *Rec. dist.:* Ohio.

81. Two hearts never beat the same. *Rec. dist.:* N.C.

82. What the eye does not see, the heart does not feel. *Rec. dist.:* Kans., Tex. *1st cit.:* ca1153 St. Bernard, "All Saints" in *Sermons;* US1692 Bulkeley, *Will and Doom,* ed. Hoadly, Conn.Hist.Soc. *Collections* (1895). *20c. coll.:* ODEP 236, Whiting 141, *CODP* 73, Stevenson 736:8, Whiting*(MP)* 210.

83. What the heart thinks, the tongue speaks. *Rec. dist.:* N.C., R.I., Tex., Vt. *1st cit.:* 1477 *Dictes and Sayenges of Philosophirs,* tr. Rivers; US1938 Champion, *Racial Proverbs. 20c. coll.:* Stevenson 1112:16.

84. What you wear in your heart shows in your face. *Rec. dist.:* Miss.

85. When the heart is afire, some sparks will fly out through the mouth. *Rec. dist.:* Ind. *1st cit.:* 1520 Whittington, *Vulgaria* (1527). *20c. coll.:* ODEP 363, Stevenson 1111:1.

86. When you let your heart show, people are apt to kick it around. *Rec. dist.:* N.C.

87. Where the heart is past hope, the face is past shame. *Rec. dist.:* Mich. *1st cit.:* 1732 Fuller, *Gnomologia.* *20c. coll.:* Stevenson 1111:5.

88. Where the heart is, there will your treasure be also. *Vars.:* **(a)** Where your heart is, there will your treasure be also. **(b)** Where your treasure is, there will your heart be also. *Rec. dist.:* Ill., Ky., Ont., Tenn. *1st cit.:* ca1366 De Lorris, *Romance of the Rose,* tr. Chaucer; US1630 *Winthrop Papers, 1498–1649,* Mass. Hist. Soc. *Collections* (1929–47). *20c. coll.:* Stevenson 1110:10, Whiting 451, T&W 381, Whiting(MP) 642.

89. You are nearer God's heart in a garden than anywhere else on earth. *Rec. dist.:* N.Y.

See also Absence makes the heart grow fonder. / Actions and words are the windows through which the heart is seen. / Banks have no heart. / A blush on the face is better than a blot on the heart. / The larger the body, the bigger the heart. / Bullets through the heart make a dead echo. / Charity is a virtue of the heart and not of the hand. / If a child cuts its finger, it has cut its mother's heart. / When a child is little, it pulls at your apron strings. When it gets older, it pulls at your heart strings. / Little children step on your toes; big children step on your heart. / Dreams are wishes your heart makes. / A rolling eye, a roving heart. / What the eye doesn't see, the heart doesn't grieve for. / You can look in the eyes, but not in the heart. / A fair face may hide a foul heart. / Faith is the vision of the heart. / A fool has no understanding but that his heart may discover itself. / A homely form oft holds a handsome heart. / A cold hand, a warm heart. / Some have no heads, but all have heart. / Many are lighter in the heels than in the heart. / Home is where the heart is. / Hope deferred makes the heart sick. / The way to a man's heart is through his stomach. / All men are poets at heart. / Providence requires three things of us before it will help us: a stout heart, a strong arm, and a stiff upper lip. / A light purse makes a heavy heart. / As the purse is emptied, the heart is filled. / Heated remarks never thaw icy hearts. / A black shoe makes a blithe heart. / Slow are the steps of those who leave their heart behind. / Full stomach, contented heart. / When the stomach is full, the heart is glad. / A good surgeon must have an eagle's eye, a lion's heart, and a lady's hand. / The thoughts of the heart are the wealth of a man. / In company, guard your tongue; in solitude, your heart. / The tongue of the just is a choice silver; the heart of the wicked is little worth. / The tongue's great storehouse is the heart. / The understanding is always the dupe of the heart. / Whatever way the wind does blow, some hearts are glad to have it so. / Every woman keeps a corner in her heart where she is always twenty-one. / Soft words win a hard heart. / The hard words cut the heart.

hearth A hearth is not a hearth unless a woman sits by it. *Rec. dist.:* N.Y., S.C. *1st cit.:* USca1879 Ingersoll, *Home.* *20c. coll.:* Stevenson 1151:11.

See also You will never find a cat on a cold hearth. / The fire burns brightest on one's own hearth. / The pot boils best on its own hearth. / The colder the wind, the warmer the hearth.

heartstring *See* Inaction gnaws the heartstrings.

heat After great heat comes cold. *Rec. dist.:* Ind. *1st cit.:* ca1390 Chaucer(?), *Proverbs.* *20c. coll.:* Stevenson 1116:17.

heaven 1. Better once in heaven than ten times at the gate. *Rec. dist.:* Ont.

2. Everybody that talks about heaven ain't going there. *Rec. dist.:* N.C.

3. Heaven helps those that help themselves. *Var.:* Help yourself and heaven will help you. *Rec. dist.:* U.S., Can. *1st cit.:* 1545 Taverner, *Proverbs of Erasmus;* US1736 Franklin, *PRAlmanac.* *20c. coll.:* CODP 93, ODEP 310, Stevenson 979:11, Whiting 178, Whiting(MP) 259.

4. Heaven is a place prepared for those prepared for it. *Rec. dist.:* Ind.

5. Heaven is above all. *Rec. dist.:* N.Y. *1st cit.:* 1595 Shakespeare, *Richard II.* *20c. coll.:* ODEP 365, Stevenson 1119:10.

6. Heaven is at the feet of mothers. *Rec. dist.:* Ill.

7. Heaven isn't in the next hollow. *Rec. dist.:* Miss., N.C.

8. Heaven keeps them who keep themselves. *Rec. dist.:* Okla.

9. Heaven protects the good man. *Rec. dist.:* N.Dak. *1st cit.:* US1875 Scarborough, *Chinese Proverbs.* *20c. coll.:* Stevenson 1118:10.

10. Heaven sends us good meat, but the devil sends cooks. *Rec. dist.:* S.C.

11. Heaven will mend all. *Rec. dist.:* Ala.

12. Heaven-sent men never fail. *Rec. dist.:* N.C.

13. One path to heaven is to get home by eleven. *Rec. dist.:* Iowa.

14. Some people are too mean for heaven and too good for hell. *Rec. dist.:* N.C.

15. Tears are often the telescope through which men see far into heaven. *Rec. dist.:* Ala., N.Y., S.C. *1st cit.:* US1887 Beecher, *Proverbs from Plymouth Pulpit.* *20c. coll.:* Stevenson 2287:1.

16. The blue of heaven is larger than the clouds. *Rec. dist.:* N.C.

17. The will of heaven is mysterious and not easily discovered. *Rec. dist.:* N.Y.

18. Those who know all about heaven seldom get there. *Rec. dist.:* Calif.

SEE ALSO ADVERSITY is the diamond dust heaven polishes its jewels with. / The BRAYING of a jackass never reaches heaven. / It is easier for a CAMEL to go through the eye of a needle than it is for a rich man to enter the kingdom of heaven. / He who closes his DOOR to the poor will find the gates of heaven closed. / A closed FIST is the lock of heaven, and the open hand is the key of mercy. / It is good to have some FRIENDS both in heaven and in hell. / Every blade of GRASS has its share of the dews of heaven. / HELL is full of good meanings, but heaven is full of good works. / HELL is where heaven ain't. / HOME is the blossom of which heaven is the fruit. / Let JUSTICE be done though the heavens fall. / MARRIAGES are made in heaven. / ORDER is heaven's first law. / Ten measures of TALK were sent down from heaven and women took nine. / Your

TEARS will be bottled up in heaven. / There are more THINGS than are thought of in heaven and earth. / A man's WILL is his heaven. / Use the WORLD, desire heaven.

heavy *SEE* Every man thinks his own BURDEN the heaviest. / A GRUDGE is the heaviest load one can carry. / A light PURSE makes a heavy heart. / Everyone thinks his SACK heaviest. / TRUTH is heavy; therefore few wear it. / Too light for heavy WORK and too heavy for light work.

hedge *(n.)* **1.** A hedge between keeps fellowship green. *Rec. dist.:* Ill. *1st cit.:* 1707 Mapletoft, *Select Proverbs.* *20c. coll.:* ODEP 366, Stevenson 1674:13.

2. A low hedge is easily leaped over. *Rec. dist.:* N.Y., Okla. *1st cit.:* 1611 Gruterus, *Florilegii Ethico-Politici.* *20c. coll.:* ODEP 495, Stevenson 1121:9.

3. Hedges have eyes, and walls have ears. *Rec. dist.:* Ill., Vt. *1st cit.:* ca1225 *Englische Studien* (1902). *20c. coll.:* CODP 79, ODEP 255.

4. Where the hedge is lowest, everyone, including the devil, leaps over. *Rec. dist.:* Ill. *1st cit.:* 1546 Heywood, *Dialogue of Proverbs,* ed. Habernicht (1963). *20c. coll.:* ODEP 366, Stevenson 1121:9.

5. Where the hedge is thin, men will see through it. *Rec. dist.:* Ont.

6. Without a hedge a vineyard is laid waste. *Rec. dist.:* Wis. *1st cit.:* US1948 Stevenson, *Home Book of Proverbs.* *20c. coll.:* Stevenson 1121:5.

hedge *(v.)* *SEE* PROPHESY as you like, but always hedge.

hedgehog Don't kill hedgehogs or porcupines with your bare fists. *Rec. dist.:* Ill.

heed *(n.)* **1.** Pay no heed to the people who say one thing and mean another. *Rec. dist.:* Utah. *1st cit.:* US1875 Scarborough, *Chinese Proverbs.* *20c. coll.:* Stevenson 2189:8.

2. Take heed when you see no need of taking heed. *Rec. dist.:* N.Y.

3. Take heed will surely speed. *Rec. dist.:* Ont.

1st cit.: 1639 Clarke, *Paroemiologia.* **20c. coll.:** *ODEP* 799, Stevenson 306:8.

4. When you think you stand, take heed: you may fall. *Rec. dist.:* Ind., Ky., Miss., Tenn.

5. Who has glass windows must take heed not to throw stones. *Rec. dist.:* N.Y. *1st cit.:* ca1374 Chaucer, *Troilus and Criseyde;* US1736 Franklin, *PRAlmanac.* **20c. coll.:** *CODP* 92, Stevenson 1193:4, *ODEP* 360.

SEE ALSO SPEED does not take heed.

heed *(v.)* SEE If you HEARD, then heed.

heel **1.** Many are lighter in the heels than in the heart. *Rec. dist.:* Ont.

2. Never take more on your heels than you can kick off with your toes. *Rec. dist.:* Fla., N.Y., S.C.

3. Trust not a horse's heel or a dog's tooth. *Rec. dist.:* Miss. *1st cit.:* ca1382 Fordun, *Scotichronicon.* **20c. coll.:** *ODEP* 842, Stevenson 1176:5.

SEE ALSO GRIEF often treads upon the heels of pleasure. / A spur in the HEAD is worth two in the heels. / Let your HEAD save your heels. / POLISH on the heels of shoes is a truer test of thoroughness than shine on the toes. / A good SOLDIER never shines the heels of his shoes. / SORROW treads on the heels of mirth. / One who keeps on his TOES is never down at the heels. / Follow not TRUTH too near the heels lest it dash out your teeth.

heifer You can't count the heifer 'fore she's born. *Rec. dist.:* S.C.

height **1.** People often grow in height at the expense of their brains. *Rec. dist.:* Ill.

2. Without climbing mountains, no one can know the height of heaven. *Rec. dist.:* Ill. *1st cit.:* US1875 Scarborough, *Chinese Proverbs.* **20c. coll.:** Stevenson 1119:17.

heir **1.** All heirs to some six feet of sod are equal in the world at last. *Rec. dist.:* Ont. *1st cit.:* 1659 Howell, *Paroimiografia (Italian Proverbs).* **20c. coll.:** Stevenson 1027:12.

2. Land was never lost for want of an heir. *Rec. dist.:* Ont. *1st cit.:* 1678 Ray, *English Proverbs.* **20c. coll.:** *ODEP* 441, Stevenson 1124:8.

SEE ALSO The man who plants PEARS is planting for his heirs. / The PRODIGAL robs his heir; the miser robs himself.

heiress Do not marry an heiress unless her father has been hanged. *Rec. dist.:* Wis.

hell **1.** Hell and high water wait for no man. *Rec. dist.:* Ohio.

2. Hell if you do, hell if you don't. *Rec. dist.:* N.Y., S.C.

3. Hell is full of good meanings, but heaven is full of good works. *Var.:* Hell is full of good meanings and wishes, but heaven is full of good works. *Rec. dist.:* N.J., Tex. *1st cit.:* 1574 Guevara, *Familiar Epistles,* tr. Hellowes (1584); US1809 *Port Folio.* **20c. coll.:** *CODP* 192, Whiting 209, *ODEP* 367, Stevenson 1128:2.

4. Hell is full of sorry people. *Rec. dist.:* Ohio.

5. Hell is never full: there is always room for one more. *Var.:* Hell and destruction are never full. *Rec. dist.:* Ill. *1st cit.:* 1721 Kelly, *Scottish Proverbs.* **20c. coll.:** *ODEP* 367.

6. Hell's only half full. *Var.:* Hell ain't half full. *Rec. dist.:* Ohio.

7. Hell is populated with the victims of harmless amusements. *Rec. dist.:* N.Y., S.C. *1st cit.:* US1887 Beecher, *Proverbs from Plymouth Pulpit.* **20c. coll.:** Stevenson 62:1.

8. Hell is truth seen too late. *Rec. dist.:* N.J.

9. Hell is where heaven ain't. *Rec. dist.:* Ala. *1st cit.:* 1592 Delamothe, *Treasury of French Tongue.* **20c. coll.:** *ODEP* 367, Stevenson 1120:2.

10. Hell knows no wrath like a woman scorned. *Var.:* Hell has no fury like a woman scorned. *Rec. dist.:* Ill., N.J., Ont., Oreg. *1st cit.:* 1696 Cibber, *Love's Last Shift;* US1940 Coxe, *Glass Triangle.* **20c. coll.:** *CODP* 110, Stevenson 2566:6, Whiting(MP) 302.

11. It is better to be in hell than in the newspapers. *Rec. dist.:* N.J.

12. It's sure hell to be broke. *Var.:* It's hell to be poor. *Rec. dist.:* Tex.

13. People in hell want ice water, too. *Rec. dist.:* U.S.

14. Some people tell us there ain't no hell, but

they never farmed, so how can they tell. *Rec. dist.*: Utah.

15. The hell of women is old age. *Rec. dist.*: Ky. *1st cit.*: US1948 Stevenson, *Home Book of Proverbs*. *20c. coll.*: Stevenson 34:14.

16. The road to hell is paved with good intentions. *Vars.*: **(a)** Hell is paved with good intentions. **(b)** The streets of hell are paved with promises. *Rec. dist.*: U.S., Can. *1st cit.*: 1574 Guevara, *Familiar Epistles,* tr. Hellowes (1584); US1809 *Port Folio.* *20c. coll.*: CODP 192, Whiting 209, ODEP 367, Stevenson 1128:8, Whiting*(MP)* 673.

17. The road to hell is very wide. *Rec. dist.*: N.C.

18. There's no sense you going to hell just because someone else is. *Rec. dist.*: Kans.

19. Until hell is full, no lawyer can be saved. *Rec. dist.*: N.Y.

20. You go to hell for lying the same as stealing. *Rec. dist.*: Kans.

SEE ALSO When a BADMAN dies, he either goes to hell or to the Pecos. / Good COFFEE should be black as sin, strong as the devil, and hot as hell. / It is good to have some FRIENDS both in heaven and in hell. / To work HARD, live hard, die hard, and go to hell after all, would be hard indeed. / WAR is hell. / For WEATHER go to heaven, but for company go to hell.

helm Anyone can hold the helm when the sea is calm. *Rec. dist.*: Ont.

SEE ALSO It is the ordinary way of the world to keep FOLLY at the helm and wisdom under the hatches. / The VESSEL that will not obey her helm will have to obey the rocks.

helmet The safest helmet is virtue. *Rec. dist.*: Ont.

help *(n.)* **1.** A little help is worth a lot of pity. *Rec. dist.*: Iowa.

2. An ounce of help is worth a pound of pity. *Rec. dist.*: N.Y., Ohio, Okla., Ont.

3. Help is fine till it comes to dine. *Rec. dist.*: Calif.

4. Help never comes too late. *Rec. dist.*: Ind.

5. Self-help is the best help. *Rec. dist.*: Ark.,

Kans., N.Y., Ont. *1st cit.*: 1831 Carlyle, *Sartor Resartus.* *20c. coll.*: Stevenson 2063:4.

6. Slow help is no help. *Rec. dist.*: Ill. *1st cit.*: 1852 Trench, *On the Lessons in Proverbs.* *20c. coll.*: Stevenson 1130:10.

7. Small helps are not despised. *Rec. dist.*: Ont.

8. The more the help, the lighter the work. *Rec. dist.*: Ind.

9. There's no help for misfortune but to marry again. *Rec. dist.*: N.Y., S.C. *1st cit.*: US1940 Thompson, *Body, Boots, and Britches.* *20c. coll.*: Stevenson 1543:7.

10. To ask for free help is to spoil the millionaires. *Rec. dist.*: N.C.

help *(v.)* **1.** Help others as they help you. *Rec. dist.*: Ont. *1st cit.*: US1948 Stevenson, *Home Book of Proverbs.* *20c. coll.*: Stevenson 1130:11.

2. Help yourself and heaven will help you. *Rec. dist.*: U.S., Can. *1st cit.*: 1545 Taverner, *Proverbs of Erasmus;* US1736 Franklin, *PRAlmanac.* *20c. coll.*: CODP 93, ODEP 310, Whiting 178, Stevenson 979:10, Whiting*(MP)* 259.

3. If you can't help, don't hinder. *Rec. dist.*: N.Y., R.I.

4. If you don't help yourself, nobody will. *Rec. dist.*: Ky., Tenn.

5. If you help everybody, you help nobody. *Rec. dist.*: Ill.

6. If you would have many to help you, be sure not to need them. *Rec. dist.*: N.Y.

7. Three helping each other is as good as six. *Rec. dist.*: Miss. *1st cit.*: 1640 Herbert, *Outlandish Proverbs (Jacula Prudentum)* in *Works,* ed. Hutchinson (1941). *20c. coll.*: ODEP 816, Stevenson 2311:2.

8. What can't be helped must be endured. *Rec. dist.*: Vt. *1st cit.*: ca1377 Langland, *Piers Plowman;* US1698 *Diary of Samuel Sewall, 1674–1729,* Mass.Hist.Soc. *Collections* (1878–82). *20c. coll.*: CODP 46, Whiting 90, ODEP 161, Stevenson 683:12, T&W 87.

9. You always help yourself by helping others. *Rec. dist.*: N.Y.

SEE ALSO If you can't take ADVICE, you

can't be helped. / Two things a man should never get ANGRY at: what he can help and what he cannot help. / Every little BIT helps. / If you help the EVIL, you hurt the good. / He that would make a FOOL of himself will find many to help him. / He is my FRIEND that helps me and not he that pities me. / GOD helps those that help themselves. / The GREAT are often selfish in their patronage of those who help them. / HEAVEN helps those that help themselves. / Every LITTLE helps. / The LORD helps those who help themselves. / The LORD never helps him who sits on his ass and waits. / SHARE a little, help a lot. / He who greases his WHEELS helps his oxen.

helper SEE Many FRIENDS, few helpers.

helping SEE ADVISING is easier than helping. / Keeping from FALLING is better than helping up.

hen 1. A black hen always lays a white egg. *Var.:* A black hen will lay a white egg. *Rec. dist.:* Ky., Tenn. *1st cit.:* 1611 Cotgrave, *Dictionary of French and English Tongues.* *20c. coll.:* ODEP 64, Stevenson 1131:5.

2. A cackling hen doesn't always lay. *Rec. dist.:* Ky.

3. A crowing hen never lays eggs. *Rec. dist.:* Ky.

4. A good hen does not cackle in your house and lay in another's. *Rec. dist.:* Ala. *1st cit.:* 1732 Fuller, *Gnomologia.* *20c. coll.:* Stevenson 1132:4.

5. A hen is the only animal that can lay around and make money. *Rec. dist.:* Kans.

6. A hen that doesn't cackle doesn't lay. *Rec. dist.:* N.Y. *1st cit.:* 1580 Lyly, *Euphues and His England* in *Works,* ed. Bond (1902). *20c. coll.:* ODEP 369, Stevenson 1132:4.

7. A hen will always go home to roost. *Rec. dist.:* Vt. *1st cit.:* US1871 Jones, *Life of Jefferson S. Batkins.* *20c. coll.:* T&W 67, Whiting(MP) 108.

8. A hen with biddies never burst her craw. *Rec. dist.:* Miss.

9. A setting hen gathers no feathers. *Rec. dist.:*

Ill., Ky., Ont. *1st cit.:* US1845 Judd, *Margaret.* *20c. coll.:* T&W 181.

10. A setting hen never gets fat. *Vars.:* (a) A clucking hen never gets fat. (b) A lame hen never grows fat. (c) A setting hen doesn't get very fat. *Rec. dist.:* U.S., Can.

11. An old hen never grows young. *Rec. dist.:* Ont.

12. Fat hens lay few eggs. *Var.:* Fat hens are aye ill layers. *Rec. dist.:* Ind., Ont.

13. Fat hens make rich soup. *Rec. dist.:* Ont.

14. First hen cackled, first hen laid. *Rec. dist.:* Fla., Miss.

15. It's a poor hen that can't scratch for itself. *Rec. dist.:* Vt.

16. It is a sad house where the hen crows louder than the cock. *Var.:* It is ill with the roost when the hens crow and the cock must remain silent. *Rec. dist.:* Ill., Wis. *1st cit.:* 1573 Sanford, *Garden of Pleasure;* US1734 Franklin, *PRAlmanac.* *20c. coll.:* ODEP 368, Whiting 210, Stevenson 2505:2.

17. It's better to be the beak of a hen than the tail of an ox. *Rec. dist.:* Miss.

18. Nothing can sit still and make a profit except a hen. *Rec. dist.:* Kans.

19. Remember, a hen can scratch for a dozen chicks as easily as for one. *Rec. dist.:* Oreg.

20. Settin' hens don't hanker after fresh aigs. *Rec. dist.:* N.Y., S.C. *1st cit.:* US1880 Harris, "Plantation Proverbs" in *Uncle Remus, His Songs and His Sayings.* *20c. coll.:* Stevenson 1131:10.

21. There's more ways to kill a hen besides choking her. *Rec. dist.:* Ky., Tenn.

22. 'Tis not the hen that cackles most that lays the most eggs. *Rec. dist.:* Ind. *1st cit.:* 1901 Taylor, *Folk-Speech of South Lancashire.* *20c. coll.:* Stevenson 1132:4.

23. Where the hen scratches, there she expects to find a bug. *Var.:* Wherever de hen scratches, dar be duh bug. *Rec. dist.:* Ohio, Vt.

SEE ALSO If you are a COCK, crow; if a hen, lay eggs. / An EGG today is worth a hen tomorrow. / A whistling GIRL and a crowing hen always end in the devil's den. / ROOSTER makes more racket dan de hen w'at lay de aig. / The ROOSTER can crow, but it's the hen that delivers the goods.

herb No herb will cure love. *Rec. dist.:* Mich. *1st cit.:* ca1385 Chaucer, *Legend of Good Women.* *20c. coll.: ODEP* 369.

SEE ALSO Much VIRTUE in herbs, little in men.

here Here today and gone tomorrow. *Var.:* We're here today and gone tomorrow. *Rec. dist.:* Ohio, Okla., N.Y., S.C. *1st cit.:* 1549 Calvin, *Life and Conversion of a Christian Man;* US1843 Haliburton, *Attache or Sam Slick in England. 20c. coll.: ODEP* 370, T&W 182, Stevenson 1133:6, Whiting(*MP*) 633.

hermit 1. The hermit has known many men and has therefore fled to the woods. *Rec. dist.:* Ill.

2. The hermit thinks the sun shines nowhere but in his own cell. *Rec. dist.:* Mich. *1st cit.:* 1732 Fuller, *Gnomologia. 20c. coll.:* Stevenson 1137:2.

hero 1. A wicked hero will turn his back to an innocent coward. *Rec. dist.:* N.Y., S.C. *1st cit.:* US1734 Franklin, *PRAlmanac. 20c. coll.:* Stevenson 1283:12.

2. Heroes are brave for just five minutes longer. *Rec. dist.:* N.Y.

3. Heroes are made, not born. *Rec. dist.:* Ala., Ont., Wis.

4. Heroes today, bums tomorrow. *Var.:* Heroes yesterday, bums today. *Rec. dist.:* N.Y.

5. No man is a hero to his valet. *Vars.:* **(a)** No man is a hero in his hometown. **(b)** No man is a hero to his saddle horse. **(c)** No man is a hero to his wife or his butler. *Rec. dist.:* U.S. *1st cit.:* 1603 Montaigne, *Essays,* tr. Florio; US1801 Taylor in *Papers of John Steele,* ed. Wagstaff (1924). *20c. coll.: CODP* 162, Whiting 279, *ODEP* 570, Stevenson 1137:3, Whiting(*MP*) 399.

6. One cannot always be a hero, but one can always be a man. *Rec. dist.:* N.Y.

7. There's only a hair's breadth between a hero and a fool. *Rec. dist.:* Oreg.

SEE ALSO A live COWARD is better than a dead hero.

herring Don't cry herrings till they are in the net. *Rec. dist.:* Okla., Tex.

hesitate 1. He who hesitates in the case of truth acts ill when he deliberates. *Rec. dist.:* Wis. *1st cit.:* 1539 Publilius Syrus, *Sententiae,* tr. Taverner. *20c. coll.:* Stevenson 1140:1.

2. He who hesitates is last. *Rec. dist.:* Ind., Ohio.

3. He who hesitates is lost. *Var.:* He who hesitates is bossed and usually lost. *Rec. dist.:* U.S. *1st cit.:* 1713 Addison, *Cato;* US1858 Holmes, *Autocrat of the Breakfast-Table. 20c. coll.: ODEP* 909, T&W 409, *CODP* 111, Stevenson 1139:12, Whiting(*MP*) 306.

4. He who hesitates is sometimes saved. *Rec. dist.:* Ind., R.I.

SEE ALSO When in DOUBT, hesitate.

hesitation Hesitation seldom prospers. *Rec. dist.:* Wis.

hew Hew to the line; let the chips fall where they may. *Vars.:* **(a)** Hew straight to the line, and let the chips fall where they will. **(b)** Hew the log and let the chips fall where they may. *Rec. dist.:* Ill., Ky., Oreg. *1st cit.:* ca1923 Crowley, *Confessions of Neister Crowley;* US1880 Conkling, Nomination speech for U.S. Grant at the Republican National Convention, Chicago, Ill., 5 June. *20c. coll.:* Stevenson 345:11, Whiting *(MP)* 377.

hidden There is nothing hidden that is not shown. *Var.:* Nothing comes fairer to light than what has been hidden. *Rec. dist.:* N.C.

SEE ALSO A CITY that sits on a hill cannot be hidden. / Hidden FIRES are always the hottest. / LOVE and smoke cannot be hidden. / A PEARL is often hidden in an ugly shell.

hide *(n.)* 1. Each must carry his own hide to the tanner. *Rec. dist.:* Ont.

2. Let the tail go with the hide. *Rec. dist.:* U.S., Can. *1st cit.:* 1721 Kelly, *Scottish Proverbs;* US1959 Cushman, *Goodbye, Old Dry. 20c. coll.: ODEP* 797, Whiting(*MP*) 611, Stevenson 2268:6.

SEE ALSO The SPUR won't hurt when the hide is thick.

hide *(v.)* **1.** He who hides behind another does not saddle when he pleases. *Var.:* Those who hide know how to find. *Rec. dist.:* Mich.

2. Hide nothing from your minister, physician, and lawyer. *Rec. dist.:* Wis. *1st cit.:* 1573 Sanford, *Garden of Pleasure.* *20c. coll.:* ODEP 371.

3. Them that hides can find. *Var.:* Those who hide know how to find. *Rec. dist.:* U.S., Can. *1st cit.:* ca1400 *Seven Sages of Rome* (1845); US1766 *Writings of Christopher Gadsden, 1764–1805,* ed. Walsh (1966). *20c. coll.:* CODP 111, Whiting 211, ODEP 372, Stevenson 1140:6, Whiting(MP) 307.

SEE ALSO To kill an old DOG you must hide your stick. / A fair FACE may hide a foul heart. / He who does one FAULT at first and lies to hide it makes it two. / Go hide the FAULTS of others and God will veil your own. / He that hides HATRED with lying lips and he that utters slander is a fool. / Don't hide your LIGHT under a bushel. / The SCOFFER is only trying to hide his own conscience. / Hide not your TALENTS: they for use are given.

hider Hiders are good finders. *Var.:* Hiders make the best finders. *Rec. dist.:* N.Y., Ont. *1st cit.:* 1855 Bohn, *Handbook of Proverbs.* *20c. coll.:* Stevenson 1140:6.

high *(adj.)* **1.** It is hard to be high and humble. *Rec. dist.:* Ohio.

2. Seize what is highest and you will possess what is in between. *Rec. dist.:* N.Y.

SEE ALSO The higher the AIM the higher the fall. / Reach for the high APPLES first; you can get the low ones any time. / The higher the CLIMB the broader the view. / The longer the FOOT, the higher the man. / High LIVING, low thinking. / The ripest PEACH is highest on the tree. / The highest TOWERS begin from the ground. / When the WATER's high, the boat's high. / WISDOM is too high for a fool.

high *(adv.)* **1.** The higher they go, the lower they fall. *Rec. dist.:* Tex. *1st cit.:* ca1230 *Hali Meidenhad,* E.E.T.S. (1866); US1955 Knight, *Robineau Look.* *20c. coll.:* ODEP 372, Whiting(MP) 307.

2. The sweetest grapes hang highest. *Rec. dist.:*

Ont. *1st cit.:* 1902 Hulme, *Proverb Lore.* *20c. coll.:* Stevenson 574:9.

SEE ALSO There never was a BIRD who flew so high but what he came down again. / CLIMB not too high lest the fall be the greater. / A DUCK never flies so high but that it has to come down for water. / He who FLIES high must keep on flying. / The redder the FRUIT, the higher it hangs. / It doesn't matter how high you JUMP provided you walk straight when you get down. / LOOK high and fall low. / He who PITCHES too high will not get through his song. / He SITS not sure that sits too high. / SOAR not too high, but stoop to rise.

high-powered SEE High-powered SADDLES ain't half as rare as high-powered hombres in 'em.

highway **1.** The happy highway, though never straight, is often scenic. *Rec. dist.:* Ind.

2. The highway is never about. *Rec. dist.:* Ont. *1st cit.:* 1621 Robinson, *Adagia in Latin and English.* *20c. coll.:* ODEP 373, Stevenson 2468:9.

hilarity **1.** An overdose of hilarity does no one any good. *Rec. dist.:* Ont.

2. Hilarity is a poor substitute for living heroically. *Rec. dist.:* Ont.

hill **1.** Don't climb the hill until you get to it. *Var.:* Don't go over the hill before you come to it. *Rec. dist.:* Ill., N.Y., S.C.

2. Don't waste time looking at the hill—climb it. *Rec. dist.:* Ont.

3. Hills look green far away. *Vars.:* **(a)** Far away the hills are green. **(b)** Far hills are greenest. **(c)** Far hills look the bluest. **(d)** Hills look green that are far away. **(e)** It's the hills far off that are green. *Rec. dist.:* Ill., Ohio, Ont. *1st cit.:* 1887 Caine, *Deemster;* US1959 Cushman, *Goodbye, Old Dry.* *20c. coll.:* CODP 23, Whiting(MP) 307, ODEP 373, Stevenson 591:8.

4. Looking at a hill won't move it. *Rec. dist.:* Ont.

5. No hill too steep, no sand too deep. *Rec. dist.:* Wis.

6. There is no hill without a valley. *Vars.:* **(a)** Always a valley before a hill. **(b)** If you are ever discouraged, remember, first comes a hill, then comes a valley. **(c)** You can't have two hills without a valley. *Rec. dist.:* Ky., Tenn. *1st cit.:* 1583 Melbancke, *Philotimus.* *20c. coll.:* Stevenson 1142:2.

7. To climb steep hills requires slow pace at first. *Rec. dist.:* N.Y.

SEE ALSO ACT so in the valley that you need not fear those who stand on the hill. / A CITY that sits on a hill cannot be hid. / FRIENDS will greet where the hills won't meet. / A HORSE never goes straight up a hill. / Small POTATOES are few in a hill. / The poor POTATOES are all in one hill. / Every ROAD has hills to be climbed. / He that stays in the VALLEY will never get over the hill. / Don't try running WATER up a hill.

hillbilly All hillbillies don't live in the hills. *Rec. dist.:* Ont.

himself **1.** Every man for himself, and the devil for all. *Vars.:* **(a)** Every fellow for himself, and the devil take the hindermost. **(b)** Every man for himself, and the devil take the hindermost. **(c)** Everyone for himself, and God for all. *Rec. dist.:* Miss. *1st cit.:* ca1386 Chaucer, *Knight's Tale;* US1706 *Correspondence Between William Penn and James Logan, 1700–1705,* ed. Armstrong, Hist.Soc. Penn. *Memoirs* (1870, 1872). *20c. coll.:* ODEP 229, Whiting 134, CODP 68, Stevenson 2058:10, T&W 235, Whiting(MP) 394.

2. He that conquers himself conquers an enemy. *Rec. dist.:* R.I.

3. He who is all for himself is often all by himself. *Rec. dist.:* N.J.

4. He who reigns within himself is more than a king. *Rec. dist.:* Ont.

5. The man who does not know himself is a poor judge of the other fellow. *Rec. dist.:* N.Y.

SEE ALSO The cleverest DOCTOR cannot save himself. / He that would make a FOOL of himself will find many to help him. / He who would have FRIENDS must show himself friendly. / GOD helps him who helps himself. / He is unworthy to GOVERN others who cannot govern himself. / He who is a LAW to himself no law does need. / He that falls in LOVE with himself will have no rivals. / To be the MASTER of others, one must first be the master of himself. / The man who loses his OPPORTUNITY loses himself. / He is a good ORATOR who convinces himself. / The man who flings a STONE up a mountainside may have it rolled back upon himself. / He that TALKS to himself talks to a fool. / Every man stamps his VALUE upon himself. / He is not WISE who is not wise for himself. / Man only from himself can suffer WRONG.

hinder *SEE* If you CAN'T, don't hinder. / PRAYER and provender hinder no man's journey. / You can't hinder the WIND from blowing.

hindmost *SEE* The DEVIL takes the hindmost.

hindsight Hindsight is better than foresight. *Vars.:* **(a)** Hindsight is better than foresight by a damn sight. **(b)** If our foresight were as good as our hindsight, we would never make mistakes. **(c)** If your foresight was as good as your hindsight, you would be better off by a damn sight. *Rec. dist.:* Ill. *1st cit.:* 1879 Burdette, *Hawk-Eyes;* US1931 Dyer, *Three Cornered Wound.* *20c. coll.:* Stevenson 865:7, Whiting(MP) 308.

hinge A squeaking hinge lasts the longest. *Var.:* The squeaky hinge swings long. *Rec. dist.:* Ont. *1st cit.:* 1776 Coogan, *John Buncle, Jr.* *20c. coll.:* CODP 45, ODEP 154.

hint A hint is as good as a kick. *Rec. dist.:* N.Y., S.C. *1st cit.:* 1933 Holt, *Dark Lady;* US1825 Neal, *Brother Jonathan.* *20c. coll.:* Whiting(MP) 308, T&W 183.

hip *SEE* It's hard to take BREECHES off of bare hips.

hire *SEE* A WORKMAN is worthy of his hire.

history **1.** History is a fable agreed upon. *Rec. dist.:* N.Y. *1st cit.:* US1948 Stevenson, *Home Book of Proverbs.* *20c. coll.:* Stevenson 1143:15.

2. History is fiction with the truth left out. *Rec. dist.:* Ill.

3. History repeats itself. *Vars.:* **(a)** History always repeats itself. **(b)** History does not repeat itself; historians do. **(c)** History repeats itself every twenty years. **(d)** The worst thing about history is that every time it repeats itself, the price goes up. *Rec. dist.:* U.S., Can. *1st cit.:* 1553 Quintus Crutius, *Rufus Historie,* tr. Brende (1561); US1865 Sedley, *Marian Rooke. 20c. coll.:* ODEP 374, T&W 184, CODP 112, Stevenson 1145:8, Whiting(MP) 308.

4. History teaches by example. *Rec. dist.:* Mich.

5. The history of human opinion is the history of human errors. *Rec. dist.:* Ill.

6. To ignore the facts of history is to repeat them. *Var.:* To ignore the mistakes of history is to repeat them. *Rec. dist.:* Ont.

hit *(n.)* **1.** A hit is as good as a run. *Rec. dist.:* N.Y.

2. A man who tries to get home on a three-base hit is generally thrown out at the plate. *Rec. dist.:* N.J.

3. Hits are the only shots that count. *Rec. dist.:* N.Y.

4. More of a hit than any good wit. *Rec. dist.:* Vt.

hit *(v.)* **1.** Don't hit before you look. *Rec. dist.:* Ont.

2. Hit first; talk afterwards. *Rec. dist.:* Oreg.

3. Never hit a man when he's down. *Vars.:* **(a)** Don't hit a man when he is down. **(b)** Why hit a man when he's down? *Rec. dist.:* U.S., Can. *1st cit.:* 1551 Cranmer, *Answer to Gardiner;* US1943 Farjeon, *Murder at a Police Station. 20c. coll.:* ODEP 374, Stevenson 1146:2, Whiting(MP) 401.

4. Never hit a man when he's drunk. *Rec. dist.:* N.Y., S.C. *1st cit.:* 1551 Cranmer, *Answer to Gardiner;* US1940 Pentecost, *Twenty-Fourth Horse. 20c. coll.:* ODEP 374, Stevenson 1292:8, Whiting(MP) 401.

SEE ALSO Where the FEATHERS fly is where the shot hit.

hit *(adj.)* *SEE* The hit BIRD flutters.

hitch *(n.)* Hitches lead to stitches. *Rec. dist.:* Ont.

hitch *(v.)* *SEE* Hitch your WAGON to a star.

hives *SEE* One man's STRAWBERRIES are another man's hives.

hobby Every man has his hobby. *Rec. dist.:* Mich., N.C. *1st cit.:* 1676 Hale, *Contemplations Moral and Divine;* US1650 *Works of Anne Bradstreet,* ed. Ellis (1932). *20c. coll.:* ODEP 375, Whiting 212, Stevenson 1147:4.

SEE ALSO HAPPY is the man who has a hobby.

hoe You have to hoe a row of corn with a man in order to know him. *Rec. dist.:* N.Y.

SEE ALSO Pray to God for a good HARVEST, but continue to hoe. / Hoe your own ROW.

hog *(n.)* **1.** Eat whole hog or die. *Rec. dist.:* Ga.

2. If you have but one hog, you make him fat; if you have but one sow, you make her a fool. *Rec. dist.:* Ill. *1st cit.:* 1640 Herbert, *Outlandish Proverbs (Jacula Prudentum)* in *Works,* ed. Hutchinson (1941). *20c. coll.:* ODEP 597, Stevenson 2161:18.

3. If you talk with a hog, don't expect anything but a grunt. *Rec. dist.:* Ind. *1st cit.:* 1731 *Poor Robin's Almanac. 20c. coll.:* CODP 72, ODEP 234, Stevenson 1149:1.

4. Live with a hog and you'll grunt like one. *Rec. dist.:* Ky., Tenn.

5. No hog ever grunted the ring out of its nose. *Rec. dist.:* Ont.

6. Rub a hog and he'll lay down on you. *Rec. dist.:* Ky.

7. Run with the hogs and they will rub dirt on you. *Rec. dist.:* Ind.

8. The stillest hog gets the most swill. *Vars.:* **(a)** It's the still hog that drinks the swill. **(b)** The quiet hog drinks the most swill. **(c)** The still hog gets the most swill. *Rec. dist.:* U.S. *1st cit.:* ca1225 *Trinity MS;* US1855 Haliburton, *Nature and Human Nature. 20c. coll.:* ODEP 774, Stevenson 2176:4, T&W 284, Whiting(MP) 584.

9. Wash a hog and it will return to its wallow. *Rec. dist.:* Ill.

10. You can't make a hog without a pig to start with. *Rec. dist.:* N.C.

11. You can't root with the hogs and have a clean nose. *Rec. dist.:* Ark., Kans.

SEE ALSO A summer's FOG will roast a hog. / Feed a PIG and you'll have a hog. / Runt PIG is best hog in litter. / POVERTY makes a hog gentle.

hog *(v.)* Root, hog, or die. *Rec. dist.:* U.S., Can. *1st cit.:* US1834 Crockett, *Life of David Crockett.* *20c. coll.:* T&W 184, Stevenson 1147:9, Whiting*(MP)* 310.

hoist SEE Hoist up the SAIL while the gale does last.

hold *(n.)* The man who is overfond of anything will be unwilling to let go his hold upon it. *Rec. dist.:* N.C.

SEE ALSO When a BULL once takes hold, nothing can make him let go.

hold *(v.)* **1.** Hold fast to that which is good. *Rec. dist.:* Ont.

2. To hold is to have. *Rec. dist.:* N.Y. *1st cit.:* ca1460 "Killing of Abel" in *Towneley Plays,* E.E.T.S. (1897). *20c. coll.:* ODEP 377.

3. What'll hold more will hold less. *Rec. dist.:* Ohio.

4. You can't hold another fellow down in the ditch unless you stay down there with him. *Rec. dist.:* W.Va., Wis.

5. You can't hold what you haven't got in your hand. *Rec. dist.:* Ont.

SEE ALSO Better BEGIN as you can hold out. / Old BRAG is a good dog, but hold fast is a better one. / FOOLS cannot hold their tongues. / Hold a true FRIEND with both hands. / GET what you can, and what you get, hold; 'tis the stone that will turn all your lead into gold. / Better to HAVE than to hold. / Anyone can hold the HELM when the sea is calm. / He that by the PLOW would thrive, himself must either hold or drive. / He cannot SPEAK well that cannot hold his tongue.

hole **1.** A hole is nothing at all, but you can break your neck in it. *Rec. dist.:* Wis.

2. A little hole in your pocket is worse than a big one at the knee. *Rec. dist.:* N.C.

3. A little hole will sink a ship. *Rec. dist.:* N.C.

4. Every man must climb out of his own hole. *Rec. dist.:* Ill.

5. He that peeps through a hole may see what will vex him. *Rec. dist.:* Mich. *1st cit.:* 1706 Stevens, *New Spanish and English Dictionary.* *20c. coll.:* ODEP 618, Stevenson 1149:4.

6. No one can dig up a hole. *Rec. dist.:* N.C.

7. The hole and the patch should be commensurate. *Rec. dist.:* N.Y., S.C.

8. The hole invites the thief. *Rec. dist.:* Ont. *1st cit.:* 1640 Herbert, *Outlandish Proverbs (Jacula Prudentum)* in *Works,* ed. Hutchinson (1941). *20c. coll.:* ODEP 378, Stevenson 1149:6.

9. Where there's a mouse hole there'll soon be a rat hole. *Rec. dist.:* Ont.

10. You can't bore an auger hole with a gimlet. *Rec. dist.:* N.Y. *1st cit.:* US1845 Judd, *Margaret.* *20c. coll.:* T&W 10.

SEE ALSO When a man's COAT is threadbare, it is easy to peck a hole in it. / MONEY burns a hole in the pocket. / The MOUSE that has but one hole is soon caught. / A PATCH is better than a hole. / A PATCH is the sign of thrift, a hole the sign of negligence. / You can't put a round PEG in a square hole. / A SKUNK smells its own hole first. / If WIND blows on you through a hole, say your prayers and mind your soul.

holiday **1.** Every day is not a holiday. *Rec. dist.:* N.Y.

2. 'Tis not a holiday what's not kept holy. *Rec. dist.:* N.Y., S.C. *1st cit.:* US1751 Franklin, *PRAlmanac.* *20c. coll.:* Stevenson 1149:12.

holler Don't holler before you are hurt. *Var.:* Never holler until you're hurt. *Rec. dist.:* N.C., N.Dak., Okla., Ont. *1st cit.:* US1840 Haliburton, *Clockmaker.* *20c. coll.:* T&W 185.

SEE ALSO A hit DOG always hollers. / WORK don't never set aroun' hollerin' fer ole reliable to come to do it.

hollow *(n.)* SEE HEAVEN isn't in the next hollow.

hollow *(adj.)* SEE Hollow LOGS often rattle.

holy *SEE* 'Tis not a HOLIDAY what's not kept holy.

homage *SEE* HYPOCRISY is the homage which vice pays to virtue.

home **1.** A home without books is like a house without windows. *Rec. dist.:* N.C.

2. A man's home is his castle. *Vars.:* **(a)** A man's home is his kingdom. **(b)** A man's own home is his castle. *Rec. dist.:* U.S. *1st cit.:* 1581 Etienne, *Stage of Popish Toys,* tr. G.N.; US1692 Bulkeley, *Will and Doom,* ed. Hoadley, Conn.Hist.Soc. *Collections* (1895). *20c. coll.:* ODEP 389, Whiting 226, CODP 66, Stevenson 1192:1, T&W 193, Whiting(MP) 328.

3. A small home is better than a large mortgage. *Rec. dist.:* Vt.

4. At home everything is easy. *Rec. dist.:* N.Y.

5. East or west, home is best. *Var.:* Travel east and travel west, a man's own home is still the best. *Rec. dist.:* U.S., Can. *1st cit.:* 1859 Kelly, *Proverbs of All Nations;* US1869 Spurgeon, *John Ploughman's Talks. 20c. coll.:* CODP 62, Stevenson 1154:2, ODEP 213, Whiting(MP) 194.

6. Every home is a world in itself. *Rec. dist.:* R.I.

7. Give a home to a child and reap reward. *Rec. dist.:* N.Y.

8. Home is a world of strife shut out, a world of love shut in. *Rec. dist.:* Miss.

9. Home is home, be it ever so homely. *Var.:* Home is home though it be it ever so homely. *Rec. dist.:* U.S. *1st cit.:* 1546 Heywood, *Dialogue of Proverbs,* ed. Habernicht (1963); US1723 Symmes, *Utile Dulci. 20c. coll.:* CODP 112, Whiting 216, ODEP 379, Stevenson 1153:8, T&W 186.

10. Home is the blossom of which heaven is the fruit. *Rec. dist.:* Miss.

11. Home is the father's kingdom, the children's paradise, the mother's world. *Rec. dist.:* Miss.

12. Home is the resort of love, joy, and plenty. *Rec. dist.:* Utah.

13. Home is what we make it. *Rec. dist.:* Kans., N.Y.

14. Home is where the heart is. *Rec. dist.:* U.S., Can. *1st cit.:* US1870 McCloskey, *Davy Crockett and Other Plays,* eds. Goldberg and Heffner (1940). *20c. coll.:* CODP 112, T&W 186, Whiting(MP) 313.

15. Home is where the mortgage is. *Rec. dist.:* Ohio.

16. Home is where you act the worst and are treated the best. *Var.:* Home is where you grumble the most and are treated the best. *Rec. dist.:* Miss., Ont.

17. Home is where you hang your hat. *Rec. dist.:* Ill., Ky., Tenn. *1st cit.:* 1930 Fletcher, *Green Rope;* US1932 Stevens, *Saginaw Paul Bunyan. 20c. coll.:* Whiting(MP) 313.

18. Home is where you make it. *Rec. dist.:* N.C.

19. Home-keeping folks are happiest. *Rec. dist.:* Ont.

20. It isn't a home without a phone. *Rec. dist.:* Ind.

21. One comfortable home is sufficient; any more are added headaches. *Rec. dist.:* N.Y.

22. The longest mile is the last mile home. *Rec. dist.:* Okla.

23. The proof of the home is the nursery. *Rec. dist.:* N.Y., S.C. *1st cit.:* US1906 *Poor Richard Jr.'s Almanac. 20c. coll.:* Stevenson 1153:2.

24. There is not a happy home on earth but stands on faith. *Rec. dist.:* Ind.

25. There's no place like home. *Vars.:* **(a)** Be it ever so humble, there's no place like home. **(b)** There's no place like home, and many a man's glad of it. *Rec. dist.:* U.S., Can. *1st cit.:* 1571 Tusser, *Five Hundredth Pointes of Good Husbandrie;* US1856 Durivage, *Three Brides, Love in a Cottage, and Other Tales. 20c. coll.:* CODP 179, T&W 186, ODEP 629, Stevenson 1153:8, Whiting(MP) 499.

26. You can go home when you can't go anywhere else. *Rec. dist.:* Ill., N.C.

27. You can't come back to a home unless it was a home you left. *Rec. dist.:* Ind.

SEE ALSO A CAREER never takes the place of a home where love reigns. / CHARITY begins at home. / What CHILDREN hear at home soon flies abroad. / CURSES, like chickens, come home to roost. / DOGS don't kill sheep at home. / The FROST will bring the pig home. / He is HAPPIEST, be he peasant or king, who finds peace in his home. / It's not the HOUSE that makes the home, it's the love that is inside. / You can build a HOUSE, but you have to make a home. / Not all HOUSES are homes. / The best of the JOURNEY is getting home. / The LIGHT that shines farthest shines brightest at home. / It takes a heap of LIVING to make a home. / It takes a lot of LOVING to make a home. / NIGHT brings the cows home. / The longer the PATH, the sweeter the way home. / The longest ROAD is sometimes the shortest way home. / SAINT abroad and devil at home. / Where there is no WIFE there is no home. / Go where he will, a WISE man is always at home. / WOMAN's place is in the home. / Many go out for WOOL and come home shorn.

homely SEE A homely FORM oft holds a handsome heart. / A looking GLASS never tells a woman she is homely. / HOME is home, be it ever so homely.

homeward SEE LIFE's a voyage that's homeward bound.

honest 1. An honest citizen is an exile in his own country. *Rec. dist.:* Calif.

2. An honest man is the noblest work of God. *Rec. dist.:* Ind., Ont. *1st cit.:* 1733 Pope, *Essay on Man*. *20c. coll.:* Stevenson 1156:15.

3. An honest man is worth his weight in gold. *Rec. dist.:* Ont. *1st cit.:* ca1495 Medwell, *Nature;* US1699 Chalkley, *Journal* in *Works of Thomas Chalkley* (1766). *20c. coll.:* ODEP 922, Whiting 478, Stevenson 2639:1, T&W 398.

4. Be honest to your own self. *Rec. dist.:* N.Y.

5. Honest men are soon bound. *Rec. dist.:* Mich. *1st cit.:* 1732 Fuller, *Gnomologia*. *20c. coll.:* Stevenson 1157:20.

6. It is better to be an honest man than a rich one. *Rec. dist.:* N.Y., S.C.

7. We are bound to be honest, but not to be rich. *Rec. dist.:* Ont. *1st cit.:* 1678 Ray, *English Proverbs*. *20c. coll.:* Stevenson 1157:1.

SEE ALSO Everything that is striking and BEAUTIFUL is not good, but everything that is

honest and good is beautiful. / Of all CRAFTS, to be an honest man is the master craft. / The first step towards GREATNESS is to be honest. / HONOR lies in honest toil. / When the HOUSE is open, the honest man sins. / KNAVES are in such repute that honest men are accounted fools. / When KNAVES fall out, honest men get their goods; when priests dispute we come at the truth. / A LOCK on a door keeps honest men honest. / LOCKS keep out only honest people. / An honest man's WORD is as good as his bond.

honestly SEE Only that which is honestly got is GAIN.

honesty 1. Don't measure your neighbor's honesty by your own. *Rec. dist.:* Ill.

2. Every man has assurance enough to boast of his honesty—few of their understanding. *Rec. dist.:* N.Y., S.C. *1st cit.:* US1745 Franklin, *PRAlmanac*. *20c. coll.:* Stevenson 1156:1.

3. He that departs with his own honesty for vulgar praise does too dearly buy. *Rec. dist.:* Utah. *1st cit.:* 1612 Jonson, *Epigrams*. *20c. coll.:* Stevenson 1861:4.

4. Honesty is more praised than practiced. *Rec. dist.:* Ill., Ont.

5. Honesty is praised and left to starve. *Rec. dist.:* Ont. *1st cit.:* US1948 Stevenson, *Home Book of Proverbs*. *20c. coll.:* Stevenson 1156:8.

6. Honesty is the best policy. *Var.:* Honesty is the best policy, though it may not pay the largest dividends. *Rec. dist.:* U.S., Can. *1st cit.:* 1605 Sandys, *Europae Speculum;* USca1700 John Saffin, *His Book,* ed. Hazard (1928). *20c. coll.:* CODP 113, Whiting 215, ODEP 380, Stevenson 1155:2, T&W 186, Whiting(MP) 314.

7. Honesty is the first step to greatness. *Rec. dist.:* Ill.

8. Honesty pays. *Rec. dist.:* N.Dak. *1st cit.:* US1876 Nash, *New England Life*. *20c. coll.:* T&W 186, Whiting(MP) 314.

9. Let honesty and industry be your consistent companions. *Rec. dist.:* Ill.

10. No legacy is so rich as honesty. *Rec. dist.:* N.Y., N.C. *1st cit.:* 1602 Shakespeare, *All's*

Well That Ends Well. 20c. coll.: Stevenson 1157:3.

11. Sell honestly, but not honesty. *Rec. dist.:* Ont.

12. There is more to honesty than meets the eye. *Rec. dist.:* R.I.

13. There is no price to honesty. *Rec. dist.:* N.C.

14. Thieves cannot teach honesty. *Rec. dist.:* Ont.

honey **1.** Daub yourself with honey and you will have plenty of flies. *Rec. dist.:* Mich. *1st cit.:* 1620 Cervantes, *Don Quixote,* tr. Shelton. *20c. coll.:* ODEP 381, Stevenson 1158:9.

2. Don't lick the honey off a briar even if it is sweet. *Rec. dist.:* Miss. *1st cit.:* ca1175 *Old English Homilies,* E.E.T.S. (1867–88); US1869 Spurgeon, *John Ploughman's Talks. 20c. coll.:* ODEP 381, Stevenson 1159:7.

3. Eat your honey, but stop when you are full. *Rec. dist.:* N.C. *1st cit.:* ca1386 Chaucer, *Tale of Melibee. 20c. coll.:* Stevenson 2033:12.

4. Honey catches more flies than vinegar. *Vars.:* **(a)** A drop of honey catches more flies than a hogshead of vinegar. **(b)** A spoonful of honey is worth more than a gallon of vinegar. **(c)** Honey attracts more flies than vinegar. **(d)** Honey gathers more flies than vinegar. **(e)** More flies are caught with honey than with vinegar. **(f)** More wasps are caught by honey than by vinegar. **(g)** Tart words make no friends: a spoonful of honey will catch more flies than a gallon of vinegar. **(h)** You can catch more flies with a drop of honey than with a barrel of vinegar. **(i)** You can catch more flies with honey than with vinegar. **(j)** You catch more flies with honey than with vinegar. *Rec. dist.:* U.S., Can. *1st cit.:* 1666 Torriano, *Common Place of Italian Proverbs;* US1744 Franklin, *PRAlmanac. 20c. coll.:* CODP 113, Whiting 159, Stevenson 1158:14, T&W 140, Whiting(MP) 234.

5. Honey is sweet, but bees sting. *Rec. dist.:* Ind. *1st cit.:* 1594 Shakespeare, *Rape of Lucrece;* USca1700 Hubbard, *General History of New England* (1848). *20c. coll.:* ODEP 381, Whiting 218, Stevenson 1159:5.

6. If you have no honey in your pot, have some in your mouth. *Vars.:* **(a)** If you have no money in your purse, you must have honey in your mouth. **(b)** When there's little honey in the jar, have some in the mouth. *Rec. dist.:* N.Y., Ont., S.C. *1st cit.:* 1616 Draxe, *Bibliotheca Scholastica* in *Anglia* (1918); US1753 Franklin, *PRAlmanac. 20c. coll.:* ODEP 381, Stevenson 1158:10.

7. If you want to gather honey, you must bear the stings of bees. *Rec. dist.:* Ill. *1st cit.:* 1721 Kelly, *Scottish Proverbs. 20c. coll.:* ODEP 773, Stevenson 1159:5.

8. It is not with saying "honey, honey" that sweetness comes into the mouth. *Var.:* The mouth is not sweetened by saying "honey," "sugar," and "sugar-plum." *Rec. dist.:* Ont. *1st cit.:* 1853 Trench, *Lessons in Proverbs* (1894). *20c. coll.:* ODEP 702, Stevenson 2259:3.

9. Look for the honey where you see the bee. *Rec. dist.:* Ind. *1st cit.:* 1616 Draxe, *Bibliotheca Scholastica* in *Anglia* (1918); US1748 Ward in *Colonial Currency,* ed. Davis, Publ. Prince Soc. (1910–11). *20c. coll.:* ODEP 39, Whiting 26, Stevenson 144:8, Whiting(MP) 39.

10. Make yourself honey and the flies will devour you. *Rec. dist.:* Ill. *1st cit.:* 1620 Cervantes, *Don Quixote,* tr. Shelton. *20c. coll.:* ODEP 381, Stevenson 1158:9.

11. Nothing but money is sweeter than honey. *Rec. dist.:* Miss., N.Y., S.C., Wis. *1st cit.:* US1735 Franklin, *PRAlmanac. 20c. coll.:* Whiting 293, Stevenson 1613:9.

12. While honey lies in every flower, no doubt, it takes a bee to get the honey out. *Rec. dist.:* N.Y., S.C. *1st cit.:* US1924, Guiterman, *Poet's Proverbs. 20c. coll.:* Stevenson 145:3.

13. You never miss the honey till the bees are gone. *Rec. dist.:* Ont.

SEE ALSO Mighty po' BEE dat don't make mo' honey dan he want. / The BEE that makes the honey doesn't stand around the hive, and the man who makes the money has to worry, work, and strive. / No BEES, no honey; no work, no money. / Old BEES yield no honey. / Where there are BEES, there is honey. / A FLY follows the honey. / A WISE man without work is a bee without honey.

honeymoon 1. The honeymoon is not actually over until we cease to stifle our sighs and begin to stifle our yawns. *Rec. dist.:* N.Y.

2. The honeymoon is over; now the marriage begins. *Rec. dist.:* N.Y., Wis.

honor *(n.)* 1. A gracious woman obtains honor, and strong men obtain riches. *Var.:* A gracious woman retains honor. *Rec. dist.:* N.Y., Ont.

2. All honor's wounds are self-inflicted. *Rec. dist.:* N.Y., S.C. *1st cit.:* USca1900 Carnegie, Epigram. *20c. coll.:* Stevenson 1160:13.

3. Among men of honor a word is a bond. *Rec. dist.:* Ill. *1st cit.:* ca1400 Chaucer, *Book of Duchess;* US1777 *Diary of Col. Landon Carter of Sabine Hall, 1772–1778,* ed. Greene (1965). *20c. coll.:* ODEP 380, Whiting 497, Stevenson 2613:3, T&W 413, Whiting(MP) 699.

4. Be able to see someone else get honor, even if you can't. *Rec. dist.:* N.C.

5. Before honor is humility. *Rec. dist.:* Ont., R.I., Utah. *1st cit.:* US1948 Stevenson, *Home Book of Proverbs. 20c. coll.:* Stevenson 1197:9.

6. Honor and shame from no condition rise. Act well your part; there all the honor lies. *Var.:* Act well thy part; there all honor lies. *Rec. dist.:* Wis. *1st cit.:* 1733 Pope, *Essay on Man. 20c. coll.:* Stevenson 1161:8.

7. Honor exists but for the honorable. *Rec. dist.:* Ind. *1st cit.:* 1539 Publilius Syrus, *Sententiae,* tr. Taverner. *20c. coll.:* Stevenson 1163:12.

8. Honor is of an old immaculate pedigree. *Rec. dist.:* Ont.

9. Honor is the reward of virtue. *Rec. dist.:* Ont. *1st cit.:* 1501–02 *Pageant for Princess Katherine on Marriage with Arthur. 20c. coll.:* ODEP 382, Stevenson 961:14.

10. Honor lies in honest toil. *Var.:* Honor waits at labor's gate. *Rec. dist.:* U.S. *1st cit.:* US1884 Cleveland, Letter accepting presidential nomination, 18 Aug. *20c. coll.:* Stevenson 1331:7.

11. Honor lost, much lost. *Rec. dist.:* N.J.

12. Honor to whom honor is due. *Rec. dist.:* N.Y., N.C., Ont. *1st cit.:* 1894 *Girl's Own Paper,* 6 Jan.; US1777 Adams in *Warren-Adams Letters,* Mass.Hist.Soc. *Collections* (1917). *20c. coll.:* CODP 45, Whiting 218, Stevenson 1163:13.

13. Honor will honor meet. *Rec. dist.:* Okla.

14. Honors change manners. *Rec. dist.:* Ont. *1st cit.:* 1528 Roy and Barlow, *Rede me and be not Wroth,* ed. Arber. *20c. coll.:* ODEP 383, Whiting 218, Stevenson 1164:2.

15. It is an honor not to be crowned. *Rec. dist.:* N.C.

16. It's better to die with honor than to live in infamy. *Rec. dist.:* Ill. *1st cit.:* ca1532 *Tales and Quick Answers. 20c. coll.:* ODEP 52, Stevenson 1420:7.

17. Seek honor first; pleasure always follows. *Rec. dist.:* N.J., N.C.

18. Some are born to honor, and some have honor thrust upon them. *Rec. dist.:* Ohio.

19. The owner should bring honor to the house, not the house to the owner. *Var.:* The place honors not the man; 'tis the man who gives honor to the place. *Rec. dist.:* N.Y., S.C. *1st cit.:* US1948 Stevenson, *Home Book of Proverbs. 20c. coll.:* Stevenson 1189:6.

20. There is honor even among thieves. *Var.:* Honor among thieves. *Rec. dist.:* U.S., Can. *1st cit.:* ca1630 *Soddered Citizen;* US1799 Prentiss, *Life of Late Gen. William Eaton* (1813). *20c. coll.:* CODP 113, Whiting 218, ODEP 382, Stevenson 2296:13, T&W 187, Whiting(MP) 315.

SEE ALSO The BRAVE man holds honor far more precious than life. / GIVING is an honor. / A man's HOUSE is only less dear to him than his honor. / SELF-PRAISE, no honor. / He that has a TRADE has an estate, and he that has a calling has an office of profit and honor.

honor *(v.)* SEE Who honors not AGE is not worthy of it.

honorable SEE OLD age is honorable.

hood SEE Never carry two FACES under one hood.

hook 1. A hook's well lost to catch a salmon. *Rec. dist.:* Ont. *1st cit.:* 1616 Draxe, *Bibliotheca Scholastica in Anglia* (1918). *20c. coll.:* ODEP 383, Stevenson 1164:6.

2. Bait the hook well and the fish will bite. *Rec. dist.*: Ont. *1st cit.*: 1598 Shakespeare, *Much Ado About Nothing.* *20c. coll.*: Stevenson 819:13.

3. The hook without bait catches no fish. *Rec. dist.*: Ill.

SEE ALSO The BAIT hides the hook. / A FISH never nibbles at the same hook twice. / OPPORTUNITIES never nibble twice at the same hook.

hoop SEE Thirteen STAVES and never a hoop will not make a barrel.

hop Don't say "hop" until you've jumped over. *Rec. dist.*: N.Y.

SEE ALSO CREEP and creep beats hop and sleep.

hope *(n.)* **1.** A false-grounded hope is but a waking man's dream. *Rec. dist.*: Mich. *1st cit.*: 1718 Prior, *Solomon.* *20c. coll.*: ODEP 384, Stevenson 1165:6.

2. A good hope is better than a bad possession. *Rec. dist.*: Ill. *1st cit.*: 1732 Fuller, *Gnomologia.* *20c. coll.*: Stevenson 1166:6.

3. A mightier hope abolishes despair. *Rec. dist.*: Ind.

4. A vain hope flatters the heart of a fool. *Rec. dist.*: Mich.

5. Don't feed yourself on false hopes. *Rec. dist.*: Ill.

6. Don't give up hope till hope is dead. *Rec. dist.*: Ont.

7. He that lives on hope has a slender diet. *Rec. dist.*: Ill., N.J., N.Y. *1st cit.*: 1616 Draxe, *Bibliotheca Scholastica* in *Anglia* (1918); US1796 *Papers of Alexander Hamilton,* ed. Lodge (1904). *20c. coll.*: ODEP 475, Whiting 219, Stevenson 1166:11.

8. He that lives upon hope will die fasting. *Rec. dist.*: U.S. *1st cit.*: 1616 Draxe, *Bibliotheca Scholastica* in *Anglia* (1918); US1736 Franklin, *PRAlmanac.* *20c. coll.*: ODEP 475, Whiting 219, Stevenson 1166:11, T&W 188.

9. He who has health has hope, and he who has hope has everything. *Rec. dist.*: Wis.

10. He who has hope has everything. *Rec. dist.*: N.C.

11. Hope and a red rag are baits for men and mackerel. *Rec. dist.*: N.Y., S.C. *1st cit.*: US1742 Franklin, *PRAlmanac.* *20c. coll.*: Stevenson 1167:1.

12. Hope and fear, peace and strife, make up the troubled web of life. *Rec. dist.*: Ont.

13. Hope deferred makes the heart sick. *Var.*: You can't love on hope, and hope deferred makes the heart sick. *Rec. dist.*: U.S., Can. *1st cit.*: ca1395 Wyclif, *Bible;* US1733 *Talcott Papers, Correspondence of Governor of Conn., 1724–1741,* ed. Talcott, Conn.Hist.Soc. *Collections* (1892–96). *20c. coll.*: CODP 114, Whiting 219, ODEP 384, Stevenson 1168:3, T&W 188, Whiting(MP) 317.

14. Hope dies only when you die. *Rec. dist.*: Ohio.

15. Hope inspires action, the true way to success. *Rec. dist.*: Ind.

16. Hope inspires; work wins; success rewards. *Rec. dist.*: Kans.

17. Hope is a good breakfast, but it is a bad supper. *Rec. dist.*: Ill., Wis. *1st cit.*: 1625 Bacon, *Apophthegms.* *20c. coll.*: ODEP 384, CODP 114, Stevenson 1166:12.

18. Hope is a medicine every doctor can dispense without cost to his patient. *Rec. dist.*: Ill.

19. Hope is a slender reed for a stout man to lean on. *Rec. dist.*: N.Y., S.C. *1st cit.*: US1853 Haliburton, *Sam Slick's Wise Saws.* *20c. coll.*: Stevenson 1167:4.

20. Hope is grief's best music. *Rec. dist.*: Ill., Ont. *1st cit.*: 1855 Bohn, *Handbook of Proverbs.* *20c. coll.*: Stevenson 1167:18.

21. Hope is the blossom of happiness. *Rec. dist.*: Ill.

22. Hope is the light of the world. *Rec. dist.*: Wis.

23. Hope is the nurse of misery. *Rec. dist.*: Ohio.

24. Hope is the poor man's bread. *Rec. dist.*: Ill., Wis. *1st cit.*: 1640 Herbert, *Outlandish Proverbs (Jacula Prudentum)* in *Works,* ed. Hutchinson (1941). *20c. coll.*: ODEP 384, Stevenson 1167:18.

25. Hope is the worst of evils, for it prolongs the torment of man. *Rec. dist.*: Calif.

26. Hope keeps a man from hanging and drowning himself. *Rec. dist.:* Ont. *1st cit.:* 1584 Kelly, *Scottish Proverbs. 20c. coll.: ODEP* 384, Stevenson 1167:15.

27. Hope keeps the heart from breaking. *Rec. dist.:* Ill., Tex. *1st cit.:* ca1200 *Ancrene Riwle,* Camden Soc. (1853); US1810 *Kennon Letters* in *Va.Mag.Hist.* (1923–32). *20c. coll.: ODEP* 384, Whiting 219, *CODP* 114, Stevenson 1169:13.

28. Hope paints her palace on the hilltop. *Rec. dist.:* Ont.

29. Hope proves a man deathless. *Rec. dist.:* Ont.

30. Hope runs to infinity. *Rec. dist.:* Ohio.

31. Hope springs eternal in the human breast. *Var.:* Hope rises ever in the human breast. *Rec. dist.:* U.S. *1st cit.:* 1733 Pope, *Essay on Man. 20c. coll.: CODP* 114, Stevenson 1168:2.

32. Hopes delayed hang the heart upon tenterhooks. *Rec. dist.:* Mich. *1st cit.:* 1732 Fuller, *Gnomologia. 20c. coll.:* Stevenson 1168:3.

33. May hope be the physician when calamity is the disease. *Rec. dist.:* Wis.

34. Mighty hopes make us men. *Rec. dist.:* Ill., Ont. *1st cit.:* 1732 Fuller, *Gnomologia. 20c. coll.:* Stevenson 1167:2.

35. The hope for the poor is like tough meat for one who has no teeth. *Rec. dist.:* Calif.

36. The hope of reward sweetens labor. *Rec. dist.:* Ont.

37. The houses hope builds are castles in the air. *Rec. dist.:* Colo. *1st cit.:* US1853 Haliburton, *Sam Slick's Wise Saws. 20c. coll.:* Stevenson 1167:4.

38. There is more delight in hope than in enjoyment; anticipation is greater than realization. *Rec. dist.:* N.Y. *1st cit.:* US1938 Champion, *Racial Proverbs. 20c. coll.:* Stevenson 1166:7.

39. There's no hope for the wicked. *Rec. dist.:* Utah. *1st cit.:* US1948 Stevenson, *Home Book of Proverbs. 20c. coll.:* Stevenson 2491:6.

40. To seek is better than to gain: the fond hope dies as we attain. *Rec. dist.:* Ind.

See also FAITH without works is vain hope.

/ Where there's LIFE there is hope. / PRAYER is a cry of hope.

hope *(v.)* **1.** Do not anxiously hope for what is not yet come; do not vainly regret what is already past. *Rec. dist.:* Ind.

2. He who only hopes is hopeless. *Rec. dist.:* N.Y.

3. Hope and have. *Var.:* Hope well and have well. *Rec. dist.:* Ind., Tex., Vt. *1st cit.:* 1540 Fullonius, *Comedye of Acolastus,* tr. Palsgrave, ed. Carver, E.E.T.S. (1935). *20c. coll.: ODEP* 384, Stevenson 1167:8.

4. Hope to the end. *Rec. dist.:* Ill.

5. To hope is to live. *Rec. dist.:* Ont. *1st cit.:* 1584 Kelly, *Scottish Proverbs. 20c. coll.: ODEP* 384.

See also Hope for the BEST, but prepare for the worst. / DREAMS are what you hope for; reality is what you plan for. / Who dares NOTHING need hope for nothing.

hopeless If things look hopeless, look and see if you aren't facing the wrong direction. *Rec. dist.:* Kans.

See also The only WORK that hurts a man is hopeless work.

hoper Hopers wind up in hell. *Var.:* Hell is paved with good intentions; hopers go to hell. *Rec. dist.:* Miss. *1st cit.:* 1721 Kelly, *Scottish Proverbs;* US1809 *Port Folio. 20c. coll.: ODEP* 384, Whiting 209, Stevenson 1167:11, Whiting(MP) 673.

horehound *See* Hit takes a BEE fer ter git de sweetness out'n de horehound blossom.

horizon The higher you rise, the higher is your horizon. *Rec. dist.:* Calif., Colo.

horn **1.** Horns do sprout and often show; wings come out but you seldom know. *Rec. dist.:* Ohio.

2. One who blows a horn will never blow a vault. *Rec. dist.:* Ont.

3. Speak of Satan and you'll see his horns. *Rec. dist.:* Ont. *1st cit.:* 1591 Lyly, *Endimion;* US1728 Byrd, *Histories of Dividing Line Betwixt Virginia and North Carolina,* ed. Boyd (1929). *20c. coll.: ODEP* 804, Whiting 106, *CODP* 220, Stevenson 568:9, T&W 98, Whiting(MP) 165.

4. The fellow who blows his horn the loudest is likely in the biggest fog. *Rec. dist.:* Ont.

5. The horn of plenty has started many a man on a toot. *Rec. dist.:* Calif.

6. Toot your own horn lest the same be never tooted. *Vars.:* **(a)** He that toots not his own horn, the same shall not be tooted. **(b)** He who does not toot his own horn, that horn will not be tooted. **(c)** He who toots not his own horn, the same does not get tooted. **(d)** If you don't toot your own horn, no one else will toot it for you. **(e)** If you don't toot your own horn, nobody else will. **(f)** Toot your own horn, but deliver the goods. *Rec. dist.:* U.S., Can. *1st cit.:* 1967 Berkley, *Winking at the Brim;* USca1776 Adams in *Warren-Adams Letters,* Mass.Hist.Soc. *Collections* (1917). *20c. coll.:* Whiting*(MP)* 318, Whiting 454, Stevenson 2382:1, T&W 189.

SEE ALSO When APRIL blows his horn, it's good for hay and corn. / The older the BUCK, the stiffer the horn. / Faraway COWS have long horns. / All are not HUNTERS who blow the horn. / Tell an OX by his horns, but a man by his word. / The OX is never weary of carrying its horns.

horse 1. A chestnut horse will die before tiring. *Rec. dist.:* N.Y. *1st cit.:* 1838 Southey, *Doctor. 20c. coll.:* ODEP 118.

2. A dying horse can kick harder than a normal horse. *Rec. dist.:* Ont.

3. A farting horse will never tire, and a farting man is the man to hire. *Rec. dist.:* Vt.

4. A flea-bitten horse never tires. *Rec. dist.:* N.Y. *1st cit.:* 1577 *Heresbach's Husbandrie. 20c. coll.:* ODEP 268, Stevenson 1176:1.

5. A good horse is worth its fodder. *Rec. dist.:* Kans.

6. A good horse may be forgiven a kick. *Rec. dist.:* Ont.

7. A hired horse never tires. *Rec. dist.:* Mich. *1st cit.:* ca1641 Fergusson, *Scottish Proverbs,* ed. Beveridge, S.T.S. (1924). *20c. coll.:* ODEP 374, Stevenson 1183:5.

8. A horse can't pull while kicking. *Rec. dist.:* N.C., Ont.

9. A horse is as old as his teeth. *Rec. dist.:* Ont.

10. A horse never goes straight up a hill. *Rec. dist.:* N.Mex.

11. A lean horse wins the race. *Vars.:* **(a)** A lean horse for a long run, and a long board for a good teeter. **(b)** It takes a lean horse to win a long race. **(c)** Pick a lean horse for a long race. *Rec. dist.:* N.J., R.I., Vt. *1st cit.:* 1935 Martyn, *Nightmare Castle;* US1936 Bradley, *Hiram Hardy at Hardcastle. 20c. coll.:* Stevenson 1374:9, Whiting*(MP)* 322.

12. A man on a galloping horse will never sit it. *Rec. dist.:* Ont.

13. A man without a horse is a man without legs. *Rec. dist.:* Colo.

14. A scary horse needs a stout bridle. *Rec. dist.:* Miss. *1st cit.:* 1539 Taverner, *Proverbs of Erasmus. 20c. coll.:* ODEP 72, Stevenson 1175:2.

15. A short horse is soon curried. *Vars.:* **(a)** A short horse is easy to curry. **(b)** Short horse, soon curried. *Rec. dist.:* U.S., Can. *1st cit.:* ca1350 *Douce MS 52;* US1816 Fidfaddy, *Adventures of Uncle Sam. 20c. coll.:* CODP 202, Whiting 233, ODEP 727, Stevenson 1175:7, T&W 190, Whiting*(MP)* 322.

16. An old horse always knows its way home. *Rec. dist.:* Vt.

17. An old horse for a hard road. *Rec. dist.:* Ont.

18. An old horse slips quicker than a young one. *Rec. dist.:* Ont.

19. Any old horse can fart in the morning, but it takes a good horse to fart at night after a good day's work. *Rec. dist.:* Kans.

20. Better ride a poor horse than go afoot. *Rec. dist.:* N.J.

21. Blind horse don't fall w'en he follers de bit. *Rec. dist.:* N.Y., S.C. *1st cit.:* US1880 Harris, *Plantation Proverbs* in *Uncle Remus, His Songs and His Sayings. 20c. coll.:* Stevenson 1175:5.

22. Don't back the wrong horse. *Rec. dist.:* U.S. *1st cit.:* 1897 Marquis of Salisbury, Speech in the House of Lords, 19 Jan.; US1942

MacInnes, *Assignment in Brittany*. **20c. coll.:** Stevenson 1180:7, Whiting*(MP)* 322.

23. Don't change horses in the middle of the stream. **Vars.:** **(a)** Don't change horses crossing a stream. **(b)** Don't change your horse in the middle of the stream if you want to keep your trousers dry. **(c)** Don't swap horses crossing a stream. **(d)** Don't swap horses in the middle of the road. **(e)** Don't swap horses in the middle of the stream. **(f)** It's no time to swap horses when you are in the middle of the stream. **Rec. dist.:** U.S., Can. **1st cit.:** 1929 Graves, *Good-bye to All That;* US1864 *Collected Works of Abraham Lincoln,* eds. Bassler and Dunlap (1953). **20c. coll.:** CODP 34, ODEP 791, Stevenson 1178:10, T&W 191, Whiting*(MP)* 325.

24. Don't look a gift horse in the mouth. **Vars.:** **(a)** A gift horse should not be looked in the mouth. **(b)** Look not a gift horse in the mouth. **(c)** Never look a gift horse in the eye. **(d)** Never look a gift horse in the mouth. **Rec. dist.:** U.S., Can. **1st cit.:** ca1510 Stanbridge, *Vulgaria,* E.E.T.S. (1931); US1853 Haliburton, *Sam Slick's Wise Saws.* **20c. coll.:** CODP 91, T&W 191, ODEP 301, Stevenson 1182:2, Whiting*(MP)* 324.

25. Don't overwork a willing horse. **Vars.:** **(a)** Don't overwork the willing horse. **(b)** Never overwork a willing horse. **Rec. dist.:** Ont. **1st cit.:** 1477 *Paston Letters,* ed. Gairdner (1872–75); US1924 Bridges, *Red Lodge.* **20c. coll.:** ODEP 768, Whiting*(MP)* 324.

26. Don't pay for a dead horse. **Rec. dist.:** Ont. **1st cit.:** US1732 Byrd, *Progress to the Mines* in *Journey to Land of Eden.* **20c. coll.:** Whiting 224.

27. Don't ride the high horse: the fall, when it comes, is hard. **Rec. dist.:** N.Y., S.C. **1st cit.:** 1721 Kelly, *Scottish Proverbs;* US1787 Smith in *Papers of Thomas Jefferson,* ed. Boyd (1950). **20c. coll.:** ODEP 676, Whiting 224, Stevenson 1173:8, T&W 192, Whiting*(MP)* 323.

28. Don't spur a willing horse. **Vars.:** **(a)** A good horse should be seldom spurred. **(b)** Spur not the willing horse. **Rec. dist.:** Ark., Ill., N.Y. **1st cit.:** 1477 *Paston Letters,* ed. Gairdner (1872–75) ; US1924 Bridges, *Red*

Lodge. **20c. coll.:** ODEP 768, Whiting*(MP)* 324, Stevenson 1182:9.

29. Don't whip the horse that is pulling. **Rec. dist.:** N.C.

30. Don't worry about the old horse being poor—just feed him. **Rec. dist.:** N.C.

31. Every horse is an animal, but not every animal is a horse. **Rec. dist.:** N.C.

32. Every horse thinks his pack heaviest. **Rec. dist.:** U.S. **1st cit.:** 1732 Fuller, *Gnomologia.* **20c. coll.:** Stevenson 256:7, ODEP 231.

33. Everyone lays a burden on the willing horse. **Var.:** All lay the load on the willing horse. **Rec. dist.:** Ark., Ind., N.C., Tex. **1st cit.:** 1546 Heywood, *Dialogue of Proverbs,* ed. Habernicht (1963). **20c. coll.:** ODEP 891, Stevenson 1176:10.

34. Galled horses can't endure the saddle. **Rec. dist.:** Okla. **1st cit.:** ca1384 Wyclif, *Works,* ed. Arnold, E.E.T.S. (1880) ; US1676 *Complete Writings of Roger Williams* (1963). **20c. coll.:** ODEP 586, Whiting 222, Stevenson 1181:8.

35. He that can travel well afoot keeps a good horse. **Rec. dist.:** Ill., N.Y., S.C. **1st cit.:** US1737 Franklin, *PRAlmanac.* **20c. coll.:** Whiting 223, Stevenson 2441:1.

36. He that will slight my horse will buy my horse. **Rec. dist.:** Ont.

37. He who wants to travel far saves his horse. **Rec. dist.:** Ont.

38. Hustle your horse and don't say die. **Rec. dist.:** Ind.

39. If the owner keeps his eye on the horse, it will fatten. **Rec. dist.:** Calif.

40. If you are on a strange horse, get off in the middle of the road. **Rec. dist.:** Ont.

41. If you can get over the horse, you can get over the tail. **Rec. dist.:** Kans.

42. If you can't get a horse, ride a cow. **Var.:** Ef you ent hab hoss to ride, ride cow. **Rec. dist.:** S.C.

43. If you want a good horse, ride the hell out of him. **Rec. dist.:** N.Y.

44. In a hoss trade you gotta know either the hoss or the man. **Rec. dist.:** Vt.

45. It is a good horse who never stumbles. *Var.:* It is a good horse that never stumbles, and a good wife that never grumbles. *Rec. dist.:* N.Y., Okla., Tex., Vt. *1st cit.:* 1530 Palsgrave, *Lesclarcissement de la langue Francoyse,* ed. Genin (1852); US1821 Loomis, "Proverbs in Farmer's Almanac" in *Western Folklore* (1956). *20c. coll.: ODEP* 320, T&W 191, Stevenson 1179:6.

46. It is of little use to whip a dead horse. *Rec. dist.:* N.J., Ont. *1st cit.:* 1770 Wesley, *Letters,* ed. Telford (1931); US1933 Markham, *Inspector Rusby's Finale. 20c. coll.: ODEP* 269, Stevenson 1335:5, Whiting*(MP)* 324.

47. It's a poor horse that doesn't know his oats. *Rec. dist.:* Utah.

48. It takes a young horse to do what an old horse can't. *Rec. dist.:* N.Y., S.C.

49. Lend your horse and you may have back his skin. *Rec. dist.:* Ont. *1st cit.:* 1659 Howell, *Paroimiografia. 20c. coll.: ODEP* 455, Stevenson 1177:9.

50. More than one way to shoe a horse. *Rec. dist.:* Ind.

51. Never run a free horse to death. *Rec. dist.:* U.S. *1st cit.:* 1633 Jonson, *Tale of a Tub;* US1778 *Complete Writings of Thomas Paine,* ed. Foner (1945). *20c. coll.:* Stevenson 1178:5, Whiting 224.

52. One can't shoe a running horse. *Rec. dist.:* Ind.

53. One horse doesn't kick by itself. *Rec. dist.:* Calif.

54. Rub a galled horse and he will kick. *Rec. dist.:* Vt. *1st cit.:* ca1384 Wyclif, *Works,* ed. Arnold, E.E.T.S. (1880); US1676 *Complete Writings of Roger Williams* (1963). *20c. coll.: ODEP* 686, Whiting 222, Stevenson 1181:8.

55. Stick to the old horse that carried you safely across. *Rec. dist.:* N.C.

56. The blind horse is fittest for the mill. *Rec. dist.:* N.Y., S.C. *1st cit.:* 1692 Southerne, *Maid's Last Prayer. 20c. coll.:* Stevenson 1175:5.

57. The borrowed horse has hard feet. *Rec. dist.:* Calif., Colo.

58. The common horse is worst shod. *Rec.*

dist.: Okla. *1st cit.:* 1546 Heywood, *Dialogue of Proverbs,* ed. Habernicht (1963). *20c. coll.: ODEP* 138, Stevenson 1176:11.

59. The horse fed too freely with oats often becomes unruly. *Rec. dist.:* N.Y.

60. The horse knows the way to his own stable. *Rec. dist.:* Ohio.

61. The horse rides the rider. *Rec. dist.:* N.C.

62. The horse that draws best is most whipped. *Rec. dist.:* N.Y.

63. The losing horse blames the saddle. *Rec. dist.:* Ont. *1st cit.:* 1842 Lover, *Handy Andy. 20c. coll.:* Stevenson 1182:6.

64. The willing horse carries the load. *Rec. dist.:* Ont., Utah.

65. The willing horse gets the whip. *Rec. dist.:* Ont.

66. There's no such thing as a horse that can't be rode or a cowboy that can't be throwed. *Rec. dist.:* Kans.

67. Try horse sense instead of horseplay. *Rec. dist.:* Ohio.

68. When the horse is dead, the cow gets fat. *Rec. dist.:* N.Y., S.C.

69. When two ride one horse, one must sit behind. *Var.:* When two men ride the same horse, one has to sit behind. *Rec. dist.:* N.C., Okla., Ont., Wis. *1st cit.:* 1598 Shakespeare, *Much Ado About Nothing;* US1930 Bush, *Dead Man. 20c. coll.: ODEP* 851, *CODP* 233, Stevenson 1181:2, Whiting*(MP)* 652.

70. While one horse pulls and one horse bucks, there is no teamwork. *Rec. dist.:* Colo.

71. You cain't make a runnin' hoss outer a jackass. *Rec. dist.:* Miss.

72. You can fool an old horse once, but you can't fool him twice. *Rec. dist.:* N.C.

73. You can lead a horse to water, but you can't make him drink. *Vars.:* **(a)** One man can lead a horse to water, but ten men can't make him drink. **(b)** One may lead a horse to the river, but twenty cannot make him drink. **(c)** You can lead a horse to a fountain, but you can't make him drink. **(d)** You can lead a horse to the water, but you can't make him drink; you can lead a fool to college, but you can't make him think. **(e)** You can lead a mule to water, but you can't make him drink. **(f)** You can lead your horse to water, but you can't force it to drink. *Rec. dist.:* U.S., Can. *1st cit.:* ca1175 *Old English Homilies*, E.E.T.S. (1867–68); US1692 Bulkeley, *Will and Doom*, ed. Hoadly, Conn.Hist.Soc. *Collections* (1895). *20c. coll.:* CODP 115, Whiting 223, ODEP 449, Stevenson 1179:9, T&W 191, Whiting*(MP)* 322.

74. You can't judge a horse by its harness, nor people by their clothing. *Var.:* Don't judge a horse by its harness. *Rec. dist.:* Ky., N.Y., S.C., Vt. *1st cit.:* 1581 Guazzo, *Civile Conversation*, tr. Pettie, T.T. (1925); US1940 Thompson, *Body, Boots, and Britches*. *20c. coll.:* ODEP 435, Stevenson 82:3.

75. You can't teach an old horse new tricks. *Rec. dist.:* N.J., Ont. *Infm.:* Cf. dog. *1st cit.:* 1530 Fitzherbert, *Boke of Husbandry;* US1806 *Letters of John Randolph*, ed. Shaffer (1970). *20c. coll.:* CODP 221, Whiting 118, ODEP 805, Stevenson 615:6, T&W 105, Whiting *(MP)* 179.

SEE ALSO He that will steal an ARROW will steal a horse. / Better ride an ASS that carries me than a horse that throws me. / If an ASS goes traveling, he'll not come back a horse. / Give a BEGGAR a horse and he'll ride it to death. / The BLACKSMITH's horse and the shoemaker's family always go unshod. / Don't put your CART before the horse. / Many a shabby COLT makes a fine horse. / The wilder the COLT the better the horse. / You may break a COLT but not an old horse. / The CUNNING man steals a horse; the wise man lets him alone. / There's no use in closing the barn DOOR after the horse is stolen. / A NOD is as good as a wink to a blind horse. / It is the difference in OPINION that makes good horse races. / A man in PASSION rides a mad horse. / PEDIGREE won't sell a lame horse. / A man without a RELIGION is a horse without a bridle. / Always put the SADDLE on the right horse. / SAILORS get their money like horses but spend it like asses. / If WISHES were horses, beggars might ride. / It is WIT to pick a lock and steal a horse, but wisdom to let it alone.

/ One hair of a WOMAN draws more than a team of horses.

horseback SEE MISFORTUNE arrives on horseback but departs on foot. / PRIDE goes forth on horseback grand and gay, and comes back on foot and begs its way.

horseflesh They are scared of horseflesh where two ride on a dog. *Rec. dist.:* Mich. *1st cit.:* 1678 Ray, *English Proverbs.* *20c. coll.:* ODEP 703.

horseman A timid horseman does not stay mounted long. *Rec. dist.:* Ind.

horsepower What some of us need is more horsepower and not so much exhaust. *Rec. dist.:* N.Y.

horseshoe **1.** Close ones only count in horseshoes. *Var.:* Close only counts in horseshoes. *Rec. dist.:* Ind.

2. The horseshoe that clatters wants a nail. *Rec. dist.:* N.J.

host **1.** A merry host makes merry guests. *Rec. dist.:* Ill.

2. Don't reckon without your host. *Vars.:* **(a)** He that reckons without his host must reckon again. **(b)** He that reckons without his host will have to reckon again. **(c)** Reckon not without your host. **(d)** Reckoners without their host reckon twice. *Rec. dist.:* U.S., Can. *1st cit.:* ca1489 Caxton, *Blanchardyn;* USca1680 *Voyages of Radisson*, ed. Scull, Publ. Prince Soc. (1885). *20c. coll.:* ODEP 388, Whiting 225, Stevenson 1184:4, T&W 193, Whiting*(MP)* 326.

hostess The fairer the hostess, the fouler the reckoning. *Rec. dist.:* Tex. *1st cit.:* 1611 Cotgrave, *Dictionary of French and English Tongues.* *20c. coll.:* ODEP 241, Stevenson 1184:6.

hot SEE Kill your ANGER while it's hot. / The nearer the FIRE, the hotter it is. / Hidden FIRES are always the hottest. / The GOOSE is never cooked till the fire is hottest. / Don't stick your HAND in boiling water to see if it is hot. / Strike while the IRON is hot. / A hot KITCHEN makes a lean will. / A little POT is soon hot. /

Bend the ROD while it's hot. / Green WOOD makes a hot fire.

hound   1. A hound is worth whistling for. *Rec. dist.:* N.J.

2. A hungry hound thinks not of her whelps. *Rec. dist.:* Miss.

3. A lean hound for a long race. *Rec. dist.:* Ohio, S.C. *Infm.:* Cf. horse. *1st cit.:* US1940 Montague, *Broadway Stomach.* *20c. coll.:* Stevenson 1374:9.

4. Don't get ahead of the hounds. *Rec. dist.:* Ind.

5. Don't run with the hound and hold on to the hare. *Vars.:* **(a)** Don't stay with the rabbits but run with the hounds. **(b)** Run with the fox and hunt with the hounds. *Rec. dist.:* Ill., Tex. *1st cit.:* ca1440 *Jacob's Well,* E.E.T.S. (1900); US1755 Davis, *Colonial Virginia Satirist,* Am. Phil.Soc. *Transactions* (1967). *20c. coll.:* ODEP 689, Whiting 225, CODP 195, Stevenson 1077:10, Whiting*(MP)* 288.

6. It's safer to be a hound than a rabbit. *Rec. dist.:* Ont.

7. The fed hound never hunts. *Rec. dist.:* Wis.
   SEE ALSO If the HARE is to be caught, it must not stay too far ahead of the hound.

hound dog   There's more ways to kill a hound dog than to choke him to death on hot butter. *Rec. dist.:* Ky. *1st cit.:* 1678 Ray, *English Proverbs;* US1855 Kingsley, *Westward Ho! 20c. coll.:* ODEP 872, Stevenson 297:5, CODP 243, Whiting*(MP)* 670.

hour   1. A man has his hours, a dog his day. *Rec. dist.:* N.Y. *1st cit.:* 1525–29 *Godly Queen Hester,* ed. Greg; US1777 Sewall in Austin, *Life of Elbridge Gerry* (1828–29). *20c. coll.:* ODEP 504, Whiting 116, CODP 57, Stevenson 609:8, T&W 106, Whiting*(MP)* 175.

2. All of our sweetest hours fly fastest. *Rec. dist.:* N.Y. *1st cit.:* 1574 Guazzo, *Civile Conversation,* tr. Pettie, T.T. (1925). *20c. coll.:* Stevenson 1187:4.

3. An hour in the morning is worth two in the evening. *Vars.:* **(a)** An hour before breakfast is worth two the rest of the day. **(b)** An hour in the morning is worth two in the

afternoon. **(c)** One hour in the morning is worth two at night. **(d)** One hour today is worth two tomorrow. *Rec. dist.:* U.S. *1st cit.:* 1827 Hone, *Every-day Book. 20c. coll.:* ODEP 389, Stevenson 1187:5.

4. An hour may destroy what was an age in building. *Rec. dist.:* Ill. *1st cit.:* 1732 Fuller, *Gnomologia. 20c. coll.:* Stevenson 1188:3.

5. An hour wasted can never be regained. *Rec. dist.:* Ark., Kans.

6. Everyone has twenty-four hours in his day. *Rec. dist.:* Ind.

7. Hours were made for men, and not men for hours. *Rec. dist.:* N.Y., S.C. *1st cit.:* US1853 Haliburton, *Sam Slick's Wise Saws. 20c. coll.:* Stevenson 1188:1.

8. If you have an hour to spare, don't spend it with someone who hasn't. *Rec. dist.:* Miss.

9. It's better to be an hour too early than a minute too late. *Vars.:* **(a)** Better be an hour early and stand and wait than a minute behind time. **(b)** Better be two hours too soon than two minutes too late. **(c)** Better three hours too soon than a minute too late. **(d)** Better three hours too soon than one minute too late. *Rec. dist.:* N.Y., Ohio, Ont., Utah, Wis.

10. Late hours are bad for one, but they're all right for two. *Rec. dist.:* Wis.

11. Let the last hour be the hardest. *Rec. dist.:* Mich.

12. Many a man has done well at the last hour. *Rec. dist.:* N.C.

13. Pleasant hours fly fast. *Rec. dist.:* Ill. *1st cit.:* 1732 Fuller, *Gnomologia. 20c. coll.:* Stevenson 1187:4.

14. Slowpokes get busy when the hour gets late. *Rec. dist.:* Ont.

15. Some people stay longer in an hour than others in a week. *Rec. dist.:* Miss.

16. Stolen hours are the sweetest. *Rec. dist.:* Ont.

17. The darkest hour has no more minutes in it than the brightest. *Var.:* The darkest hour is only sixty minutes. *Rec. dist.:* Ind.

18. The darkest hour in any man's life is

when he sits down to plan to get money without earning it. *Rec. dist.:* Ont.

19. The darkest hour is just before dawn. *Vars.:* **(a)** The darkest hour comes before dawn. **(b)** The darkest hour is just before day. **(c)** The darkest hour is just before the dawning. **(d)** The darkest hour is nearest the dawn. *Rec. dist.:* U.S. *1st cit.:* 1650 Fuller, *Pisgah Sight of Palestine;* US1776 *Journal of Samuel Curwen, Loyalist,* ed. Oliver (1972). *20c. coll.:* CODP 48, Whiting 225, ODEP 168, Stevenson 489:15, T&W 193, Whiting*(MP)* 327.

20. The hours that make us happy make us wise. *Rec. dist.:* Ont.

21. The only way to save an hour is spend it wisely. *Rec. dist.:* N.C.

22. To fill the hour—that is happiness. *Rec. dist.:* N.Y., S.C. *1st cit.:* US1844 Emerson, "Experience" in *Essays.* *20c. coll.:* Stevenson 1071:2.

SEE ALSO MORNING hour has gold in its mouth. / A sunshining SHOWER never lasts half an hour. / One hour's SLEEP before midnight is worth three after. / It's not the number of hours you STUDY that counts, but how you study. / SUNSHINE and showers make up life's hours.

house 1. A house divided against itself cannot stand. *Var.:* A full house divided don't win no pots. *Rec. dist.:* U.S., Can. *1st cit.:* 1939 Barry, *Avenging Ikon;* US1704 Chalkley, *Journal* in *Works of Thomas Chalkley* (1766). *20c. coll.:* Whiting*(MP)* 328, Whiting 226, Stevenson 1191:4.

2. A house filled with guests is eaten up and ill spoken of. *Rec. dist.:* Mich.

3. A house is best decorated by the presence of friends. *Rec. dist.:* N.Y.

4. A house that is built on sand will surely fall. *Var.:* A house built on sand will soon fall. *Rec. dist.:* Ohio, Okla. *1st cit.:* 1548–49 Udall, *Paraphrase of Erasmus;* US1965 Gralopp, *Boom.* *20c. coll.:* ODEP 698, Whiting*(MP)* 329, Stevenson 253:2.

5. A house without books is like a room without windows. *Rec. dist.:* N.Y., N.C.

6. A house without woman and firelight is

like a body without soul or spirit. *Rec. dist.:* N.Y., S.C. *1st cit.:* US1733 Franklin, *PRAlmanac.* *20c. coll.:* Whiting 226, Stevenson 1151:11.

7. A little house well filled, a little land well tilled, and a little wife well willed are great riches. *Var.:* A small house well filled is better than an empty palace. *Rec. dist.:* Miss., N.Y., S.C. *1st cit.:* US1735 Franklin, *PRAlmanac.* *20c. coll.:* Whiting 226.

8. A man should love his house well but should not ride on the ridge. *Rec. dist.:* N.Y. *1st cit.:* 1546 Heywood, *Dialogue of Proverbs,* ed. Habernicht (1963). *20c. coll.:* ODEP 490, Stevenson 1190:10.

9. A man's house is his safest refuge. *Rec. dist.:* N.H.

10. A man's house is only less dear to him than his honor. *Rec. dist.:* Ont.

11. An empty house needs no roof. *Rec. dist.:* N.C.

12. Be deaf and blind in another man's house. *Rec. dist.:* Miss.

13. Better an empty house than a bad tenant. *Rec. dist.:* Ont. *1st cit.:* 1721 Kelly, *Scottish Proverbs.* *20c. coll.:* ODEP 50.

14. Big houses have small families, and small houses big families. *Rec. dist.:* N.Y.

15. Burn not your house to scare away the mice. *Rec. dist.:* N.J. *1st cit.:* 1615 Adams, *England's Sickness.* *20c. coll.:* ODEP 91, Stevenson 1192:12.

16. Everyone can keep house better than her mother until she tries. *Rec. dist.:* Wis. *1st cit.:* 1732 Fuller, *Gnomologia.* *20c. coll.:* Stevenson 1193:10.

17. First build your house and then think of the furniture. *Rec. dist.:* Wis.

18. Grace your house, and not let that grace you. *Rec. dist.:* N.Y., S.C. *1st cit.:* US1739 Franklin, *PRAlmanac.* *20c. coll.:* Stevenson 1189:6.

19. He who sells a house gets the price of the nails. *Rec. dist.:* N.J.

20. House goes mad when women gad. *Rec.*

dist.: Kans., Wis. *1st cit.:* 1822 Scott, *Nigel.* *20c. coll.:* ODEP 389, Stevenson 2586:12.

21. If everyone swept in front of his house, the whole town would be clean. *Rec. dist.:* Ill., Ind., Ont. *1st cit.:* 1629 Adams, *Sermons in Works. 20c. coll.:* Stevenson 617:6.

22. If you don't live in the house, you don't know when it leaks. *Rec. dist.:* N.Y., S.C.

23. In an orderly house all things are always ready. *Rec. dist.:* Ont. *1st cit.:* 1611 Cotgrave, *Dictionary of French and English Tongues. 20c. coll.:* Stevenson 1189:8.

24. It's a poor house that can't afford one lady. *Rec. dist.:* Kans., N.Y.

25. It's not the house that makes the home, it's the love that is inside. *Rec. dist.:* Ont.

26. Let us put our own house in order. *Rec. dist.:* N.Y. *1st cit.:* 1939 Livingston, *Trackless Death. 20c. coll.:* Whiting(MP) 330, Stevenson 1191:1.

27. Men build houses; women build homes. *Rec. dist.:* Ont. *1st cit.:* US1938 Champion, *Racial Proverbs. 20c. coll.:* Stevenson 1520:3.

28. No house was ever big enough for two women. *Var.:* No home large enough for two women to manage. *Rec. dist.:* Md., Miss., Ont. *1st cit.:* ca1450 *Reliquiae Antiquae,* eds. Wright and Halliwell (1841-43); US1953 Clough, *Grandma. 20c. coll.:* Stevenson 1997:14, Whiting 274, Whiting(MP) 693.

29. Not all houses are homes. *Rec. dist.:* Kans.

30. One can't shingle the house before one builds it. *Rec. dist.:* Wis.

31. Talk is but talk, but it's the money that buys the house. *Rec. dist.:* N.Y.

32. The house is a castle which the king cannot enter. *Rec. dist.:* N.Y., S.C. *1st cit.:* US1856 Emerson, "Wealth" in *English Traits. 20c. coll.:* Stevenson 1191:16.

33. The house without children is a cemetery. *Rec. dist.:* N.Y.

34. The houses hope builds are castles in the air. *Rec. dist.:* N.Y., S.C. *1st cit.:* US1853 Haliburton, *Sam Slick's Wise Saws. 20c. coll.:* Stevenson 1167:4.

35. There's no house built big enough for two families. *Rec. dist.:* Ind., Ky., Tenn. *1st cit.:* US1940 Thompson, *Body, Boots, and Britches. 20c. coll.:* Stevenson 757:12.

36. To a friend's house the trail is never long. *Rec. dist.:* Ont.

37. We each build our house of life from day to day—weak or strong. *Rec. dist.:* Kans.

38. When the house is open, the honest man sins. *Rec. dist.:* Ont.

39. When your neighbor's house is on fire, beware of your own. *Rec. dist.:* Tex., Vt. *1st cit.:* 1519 Horman, *Vulgaria;* US1643 *Winthrop Papers,* Mass.Hist.Soc. *Collections* (1863-92). *20c. coll.:* ODEP 560, Whiting 310, Stevenson 1675:3.

40. With houses and gold men are rarely bold. *Rec. dist.:* Ind.

41. You can build a house, but you have to make a home. *Rec. dist.:* Kans.

SEE ALSO A BABE in the house is a well-spring of pleasure. / Burned BISCUITS will not make a warm house. / The back DOOR robs the house. / The DOORSTEP of a great house is slippery. / One FOOL is enough in a house. / FOOLS build houses for wise men to live in. / People who live in GLASS houses shouldn't throw stones. / A big HEART is better than a big house. / It is a sad house where the HEN crows louder than the cock. / A HOME without books is like a house without windows. / Start HOUSECLEANING in your own house. / At the workingman's house HUNGER looks in but dares not enter. / The HUSBAND is the head of the house, but the wife is the neck and the neck moves the head. / The PAINTER never paints his own house. / The PAPERHANGER never papers his own house. / Better a dry morsel with QUIETNESS than a house full of sacrifice with strife. / Where there is ROOM in the heart, there is room in the house. / Never talk of ROPE in the house of a man who has been hanged. / A SAINT has no value in his own house. / Through WISDOM is a house built, and by understanding it is established. / A YARD is an index to the interior of the house.

housecleaning Start housecleaning in your own house. *Rec. dist.:* N.C.

housekeeper 1. A good housekeeper is always rewarded. *Rec. dist.:* N.Y.

2. The daughter of a spry old woman makes a poor housekeeper. *Rec. dist.:* Miss.

housetop Better to dwell on the housetop than with a contentious woman. *Rec. dist.:* Vt.

housewife 1. The eye of the housewife makes the cat fat. *Rec. dist.:* Ill.

2. The fingers of the housewife do more than a yoke of oxen. *Rec. dist.:* Wis.

3. The real housewife is at once a slave and a lady. *Rec. dist.:* Wis.

howl Never howl till you're hit. *Rec. dist.:* N.Y. *Infm.:* Cf. cry. *1st cit.:* 1548 *Reliquiae Antiquae;* US1930 Mavity, *Other Bullet.* *20c. coll.:* ODEP 158, Whiting*(MP)* 142, Stevenson 466:1.

SEE ALSO The hit DOG is always the one that howls. / Who keeps company with a WOLF learns to howl.

howling SEE A howling COYOTE ain't stealin' no chickens. / De howling DOG know w'at he sees.

hug A hug is energy gone to waste. *Rec. dist.:* Ohio.

SEE ALSO WHISKEY make rabbit hug lion.

human *(n.)* A human learns how to talk early, but how to keep silent late. *Rec. dist.:* N.Y.

human *(adj.)* The human race has improved everything except people. *Rec. dist.:* Ill.

SEE ALSO To ERR is human; to forgive, divine.

humanity Above all nations is humanity. *Rec. dist.:* N.Y., S.C. *1st cit.:* USca1870 Smith, *Aphorism.* *20c. coll.:* Stevenson 1195:10.

humble *(n.)* The humble suffer from the folly of the great. *Rec. dist.:* Ill.

humble *(adj.)* 1. Be humble and obey: you will be giving orders someday. *Rec. dist.:* Kans.

2. The humble man is like the earth which kisses the feet of the king and of the beggar alike. *Rec. dist.:* Ill.

SEE ALSO Never be HAUGHTY to the humble; never be humble to the haughty. / Humble HEARTS have humble desires. / The more NOBLE, the more humble. / A humble POSITION often brings safety.

humbug The greatest humbug is to imagine that wealth makes a man happy. *Rec. dist.:* N.Y.

humility 1. Before honor comes humility. *Var.:* Before honor is humility. *Rec. dist.:* Ont., R.I. *1st cit.:* US1948 Stevenson, *Home Book of Proverbs.* *20c. coll.:* Stevenson 1197:9.

2. Fairest and best adorned is she whose clothing is humility. *Rec. dist.:* N.Y., S.C. *1st cit.:* ca1854 Montgomery, *Humility.* *20c. coll.:* Stevenson 1197:5.

3. Humility is the foundation of all virtues. *Var.:* Humility is the first of virtues—for other people. *Rec. dist.:* Mich., N.Y., S.C. *1st cit.:* US1948 Stevenson, *Home Book of Proverbs.* *20c. coll.:* Stevenson 1196:7.

4. It is not a sign of humility to disclaim against pride. *Rec. dist.:* N.Y., S.C. *1st cit.:* 1732 Fuller, *Gnomologia;* US1749 Franklin, *PRAlmanac.* *20c. coll.:* ODEP 175, Stevenson 1197:4.

5. Too much humility is pride. *Rec. dist.:* Ill. *1st cit.:* 1799 Southey, *St. Gualberto.* *20c. coll.:* Stevenson 1197:4.

SEE ALSO LIFE is a long lesson in humility.

humor 1. Good humor comes from the kitchen. *Rec. dist.:* Miss.

2. Good humor is the suspenders that keep our working clothes on. *Rec. dist.:* Minn.

3. Humor is the spice of life. *Rec. dist.:* Ont.

4. Humor is wit with a rooster's tail feathers stuck in its cap. *Rec. dist.:* N.Y., S.C. *1st cit.:* US1858 Shaw (pseud. Josh Billings), *Proverbial Philosophy.* *20c. coll.:* Stevenson 1197:13.

5. One of the best articles of dress one can put on in the morning is good humor. *Rec. dist.:* Kans. *1st cit.:* ca1855 Thackeray, *On Tailoring and Toilets.* *20c. coll.:* Stevenson 330:10.

hunchback 1. A hunchback cannot see his hunch. *Rec. dist.:* N.Y. *1st cit.:* 1659 Howell, *Paroimiografia (English Proverbs).* *20c. coll.:* ODEP 391.

2. The hunchback only sees the hump of his

neighbor. *Rec. dist.*: Ill. *1st cit.*: 1659 Howell, *Paroimiografia (English Proverbs)*. *20c. coll.*: *ODEP* 391, Stevenson 778:10.

hundred SEE A FAVOR to come is better than a hundred received. / Hundreds would never have known WANT if they had not at first known waste. / It will be all the same in a hundred YEARS. / The first hundred YEARS are the hardest.

hunger 1. At the workingman's house, hunger looks in, but dares not enter. *Rec. dist.*: U.S. *1st cit.*: US1737 Franklin, *PRAlmanac*. *20c. coll.*: Whiting 229, Stevenson 2623:8.

2. Hunger eats through stone walls and builds barricades. *Var.*: Hunger will break through stone walls. *Rec. dist.*: Ill., N.Y. *1st cit.*: ca1350 *Douce MS 52*; US1700 *Poems of Edward Taylor*, ed. Stanford (1960). *20c. coll.*: *ODEP* 392, Whiting 228, Stevenson 1199:16, T&W 195.

3. Hunger fetches the wolf out of the woods. *Rec. dist.*: Okla., Tex. *1st cit.*: 1483 Caxton, *Cato*; US1926 Cabell, *Line*. *20c. coll.*: *CODP* 116, *ODEP* 392, Stevenson 1200:7, Whiting *(MP)* 331.

4. Hunger is a great leveler. *Rec. dist.*: N.Y., S.C. *1st cit.*: 1939 Bayne, *Murder Recalls Van Kill*. *20c. coll.*: Stevenson 1199:2.

5. Hunger is a good kitchen. *Rec. dist.*: Ont. *1st cit.*: ca1540 Melville, "King James the Fifth his Pasquil" in *Bannatyne MS*. *20c. coll.*: *ODEP* 392, Stevenson 1202:2.

6. Hunger is the best pickle. *Rec. dist.*: N.Y., S.C. *1st cit.*: US1750 Franklin, *PRAlmanac*. *20c. coll.*: Stevenson 1201:13.

7. Hunger is the best sauce. *Rec. dist.*: U.S., Can. *1st cit.*: 1530 Barclay, *Eclogues*, E.E.T.S. (1961); US1690 Davis, *Documentary History of Maine Containing Baxter Manuscripts*, ed. Baxter (1869–1916). *20c. coll.*: *CODP* 116, Whiting 228, *ODEP* 392, Stevenson 1201:13, T&W 195, Whiting *(MP)* 331.

8. Hunger is the first course to a good dinner. *Rec. dist.*: Ill.

9. Hunger knows no friend. *Rec. dist.*: Ill. *1st cit.*: 1719 Defoe, *Robinson Crusoe*. *20c. coll.*: *ODEP* 392, Stevenson 1199:7.

10. Hunger made the monkey eat red pepper. *Rec. dist.*: Ky., Tenn.

11. Hunger makes hard beans sweet. *Rec. dist.*: Ill. *1st cit.*: ca1350 *Douce MS 52*. *20c. coll.*: *ODEP* 392, Stevenson 1198:6.

12. Hunger makes the best cook. *Var.*: Hunger is the best cook. *Rec. dist.*: U.S., Can. *1st cit.*: US1869 Spurgeon, *John Ploughman's Talks*. *20c. coll.*: Stevenson 1198:6.

13. Hunger never saw bad bread *Var.*: Hunger never saw bad food. *Rec. dist.*: Ind., Wis. *1st cit.*: 1659 Howell, *Paroimiografia (French Proverbs)*; US1733 Franklin, *PRAlmanac*. *20c. coll.*: Stevenson 1198:6, Whiting 229.

14. Hunger sweetens what is bitter. *Rec. dist.*: Wis. *1st cit.*: US1948 Stevenson, *Home Book of Proverbs*. *20c. coll.*: Stevenson 1201:8.

15. Hunger tames the wild beast. *Rec. dist.*: S.C.

16. Where there is hunger law is not regarded, and where law is not regarded there will be hunger. *Rec. dist.*: N.Y., S.C. *1st cit.*: US1755 Franklin, *PRAlmanac*. *20c. coll.*: Stevenson 1201:1.

SEE ALSO He who burns BREAD must hunger dread. / POVERTY and hunger have many apt pupils. / A winter's THUNDER is a summer's hunger.

hungry *(n.)* SEE The fat OX in the stall gives no thought to the hungry as they pass by.

hungry *(adj.)* 1. A hungry louse bites hard. *Rec. dist.*: W.Va.

2. A hungry man is an angry man. *Var.*: A hungry man, an angry man. *Rec. dist.*: Ill., Ind., Ont. *1st cit.*: ca1641 Fergusson, *Scottish Proverbs*, S.T.S. (1924). *20c. coll.*: *CODP* 116, *ODEP* 393, Stevenson 1201:1, Whiting *(MP)* 396.

3. A hungry man sees far. *Rec. dist.*: Ont. *1st cit.*: 1678 Ray, *English Proverbs*. *20c. coll.*: Stevenson 1200:14.

4. A hungry nigger makes a clean dish. *Rec. dist.*: Miss., N.Y., S.C.

5. A hungry stomach has no ears. *Var.*: Hungry bellies have no ears. *Rec. dist.*: Ill., N.Y., W.Va., Wis. *1st cit.*: USca1770 Hubbard,

General History of New England. 20c. coll.: Whiting 28.

6. Hungry men call the cook lazy. *Rec. dist.:* Mich. *1st cit.:* 1732 Fuller, *Gnomologia. 20c. coll.:* Stevenson 1198:6.

7. Hungry rooster don't cackle w'en he fin' a wum. *Rec. dist.:* N.Y., S.C. *1st cit.:* US1880 Harris, "Plantation Proverbs" in *Uncle Remus, His Songs and His Sayings. 20c. coll.:* Stevenson 1199:18.

8. It is easier to feed two hungry people than one with a coming appetite. *Rec. dist.:* Miss.

9. The hungry man often talks of bread. *Rec. dist.:* Ind.

SEE ALSO Men do not despise a THIEF if he steals to satisfy his soul when it is hungry.

hunt Don't hunt with unwilling hounds. *Rec. dist.:* Ill. *1st cit.:* US1948 Stevenson, *Home Book of Proverbs. 20c. coll.:* Stevenson 1179:9.

SEE ALSO Don't think to hunt two HARES with one dog. / The fed HOUND never hunts.

hunter All are not hunters who blow the horn. *Rec. dist.:* Ill., N.Y., S.C., Ont. *1st cit.:* 1586 Evans, *Withals Dictionary (Revised). 20c. coll.:* ODEP 394, Stevenson 81:3.

SEE ALSO There are wild ANIMALS, but wild hunters, too.

hunting There's plenty of hunting but little finding. *Rec. dist.:* Ont.

hurl SEE What our CONTEMPT does often hurl from us we wish ours again.

hurry *(n.)* **1.** Always in a hurry, always behind. *Rec. dist.:* Ont. *1st cit.:* US1948 Stevenson, *Home Book of Proverbs. 20c. coll.:* Stevenson 1082:2.

2. Careless hurry may cause endless regret. *Rec. dist.:* Ont.

3. Hurry is only good for catching flies. *Rec. dist.:* Ont.

4. Hurry makes waste. *Rec. dist.:* Miss. *Infm.:* Cf. haste. *1st cit.:* ca1386 Chaucer, *Tale of Melibee;* US1735 Franklin, *PRAlmanac. 20c. coll.:* Stevenson 1082:8, Whiting 199, Whiting(MP) 289.

5. Let no one see you in a hurry. *Rec. dist.:*

N.Y., S.C. *1st cit.:* US1948 Stevenson, *Home Book of Proverbs. 20c. coll.:* Stevenson 1202:18.

6. The greater hurry, the worse the speed. *Vars.:* **(a)** More hurry, less speed. **(b)** The more hurry, the less speed. *Rec. dist.:* N.Y., Ohio, Ont. *1st cit.:* ca1350 *Douce MS 52;* US1787 *American Museum. 20c. coll.:* Stevenson 1085:1, Whiting 200, T&W 173, Whiting(MP) 289.

7. The man in a hurry is in a hurry to go nowhere. *Rec. dist.:* Ill.

SEE ALSO BEGIN in time to finish without hurry.

hurry *(v.)* **1.** Don't hurry—start early. *Rec. dist.:* Calif., Colo.

2. It doesn't pay to hurry, as you pass up more than you catch. *Rec. dist.:* Kans.

hurry-up Watch out for the hurry-up man. *Var.:* Look out for the hurry-up man. *Rec. dist.:* N.C.

hurt *(v.)* **1.** He who hurts gets hurt. *Rec. dist.:* Calif. *1st cit.:* 1573 Sanford, *Garden of Pleasure;* US1872 Doolittle, *Chinese Vocabulary. 20c. coll.:* ODEP 394, Stevenson 1244:9.

2. The things which hurt, instruct. *Var.:* What hurts us instructs us. *Rec. dist.:* Ind., N.C., Ont. *1st cit.:* US1744 Franklin, *PRAlmanac. 20c. coll.:* Stevenson 726:6.

3. You always hurt the one you love. *Var.:* We always hurt the ones we love. *Rec. dist.:* N.C.

SEE ALSO It hurts to be BEAUTIFUL. / A COLLEGE education never hurt anyone who was willing to learn something afterwards. / CONCEIT is like mustard plaster: it hurts no one but yourself. / A little DIRT never hurt anyone. / A DRUNK man and a sleepwalker never get hurt when they fall. / If you help the EVIL, you hurt the good. / FALLING hurts least those who fly low. / The FROST hurts not weeds. / White HANDS cannot hurt. / Don't HOLLER before you are hurt. / What one doesn't KNOW won't hurt him. / LIQUOR never hurt a cheap man. / The SPUR won't hurt when the hide is thick. / STICKS and stones can break my bones, but names will never hurt me. / The TRUTH doesn't hurt unless it ought to. /

TRUTH never hurts the teller. / A WORD hurts more than a wound.

hurt *(adj.)*   SEE One is not so soon HEALED as hurt.

hurtful   SEE Vicious ACTIONS are not hurtful because they are forbidden, but forbidden because they are hurtful. / ANGER is often more hurtful than the injury that caused it.

husband   **1.** A bad husband cannot be a good man. *Rec. dist.:* Ind., N.Y. *1st cit.:* US1948 Stevenson, *Home Book of Proverbs.* *20c. coll.:* Stevenson 1203:12.

2. A deaf husband and a blind wife are always a happy couple. *Var.:* To make a happy couple, the husband must be deaf and the wife blind. *Rec. dist.:* Ill., Wis. *1st cit.:* 1578 Florio, *Firste Fruites;* US1940 Thompson, *Body, Boots, and Britches.* *20c. coll.:* CODP 50, Stevenson 1207:10.

3. A good husband makes a good wife. *Rec. dist.:* Miss., N.Y., S.C. *1st cit.:* 1492 *Salomon and Marcolphus,* ed. Duff (1892). *20c. coll.:* ODEP 320, Stevenson 1206:6.

4. Better to have a husband without love than with jealousy. *Rec. dist.:* Miss.

5. Each husband gets the infidelity he deserves. *Var.:* It is their husbands' faults if wives do fall. *Rec. dist.:* N.Y., S.C. *1st cit.:* 1605 Shakespeare, *Othello;* US1942 Popkin, *No Crime for a Lady.* *20c. coll.:* Stevenson 1207:9.

6. Husbands are all alike, but they have different faces so you can tell them apart. *Rec. dist.:* Wis.

7. Husbands are like automobiles: if you take care of them, you don't have to be getting new ones all the time. *Rec. dist.:* Miss.

8. Husban's is as husban's done. *Rec. dist.:* Miss., N.Y., S.C.

9. If the husband had every other child, there would be no second child in the family. *Rec. dist.:* Kans.

10. If you would know a bad husband, look at his wife's countenance. *Rec. dist.:* Mich.

11. Motherless husband makes happy wife. *Rec. dist.:* Ont.

12. Plenty of husbands, but only one mother. *Rec. dist.:* N.Y.

13. The best husbands aren't caught, they're made. *Rec. dist.:* Ohio.

14. The calmest husbands make the stormiest wives. *Rec. dist.:* Ill., Ont. *1st cit.:* 1604 Dekker, *Honest Whore.* *20c. coll.:* Stevenson 1205:10.

15. The husband is the head of the house, but the wife is the neck—and the neck moves the head. *Rec. dist.:* N.C.

16. The husband's the last one to know. *Rec. dist.:* N.Y., S.C. *1st cit.:* 1604 Marston, *What You Will;* US1941 Brown (pseud. Ford), *Murder of a Fifth Columnist.* *20c. coll.:* CODP 116, Stevenson 1204:15, ODEP 159, Whiting(MP) 332.

17. The uglier the man, the better the husband. *Rec. dist.:* N.C.

18. The woman who obeys her husband rules him. *Rec. dist.:* Ont., Utah. *1st cit.:* 1642 Fuller, "Good Wife" in *Holy State.* *20c. coll.:* Stevenson 1206:10.

19. When the husband earns well, the wife spends well. *Rec. dist.:* Wis.

SEE ALSO The LORD makes a man, but the wife makes a husband. / MAIDS want nothing but husbands, and when they have them they want everything. / A reformed RAKE makes the best husband. / A good SON makes a good husband. / SORROW for the husband is like a pain in the elbow, sharp and short. / Never marry a WIDOW unless her first husband was hanged. / A good WIFE makes a good husband. / A light WIFE does make a heavy husband. / A no-account WIFE takes advice from everyone but her husband. / A true WIFE is her husband's better half. / A true WIFE is her husband's flower of beauty. / A true WIFE is her husband's heart's treasure. / The happiest WIFE is not she that gets the best husband, but she that makes the best of that which she gets. / Fat WIVES make lean husbands. / Good WIVES and good plantations are made by good husbands. / A virtuous WOMAN is a source of honor to her husband; a vicious one causes him disgrace. / A woman can't drive her husband, but she can lead him.

husbandry 1. Good husbandry is not bad divinity. *Rec. dist.:* Mich. *1st cit.:* 1678 Ray, *English Proverbs. 20c. coll.:* Stevenson 761:1, *ODEP* 321.

2. Husbandry and letters are the two chief professions. *Rec. dist.:* Ind.

husk The husk often tells what the kernel is. *Rec. dist.:* Ky. *1st cit.:* 1732 Fuller, *Gnomologia. 20c. coll.:* Stevenson 82:2.

hustle All things come to him who hustles while he waits. *Var.:* All things come to him who waits—if he hustles while he's waiting. *Rec. dist.:* Ont.

hut A hut is a palace to a poor man. *Rec. dist.:* Ont.

hyacinths Buy hyacinths to feed the soul. *Var.:* If you have two loaves, sell one and buy hyacinths. *Rec. dist.:* N.Y., S.C. *1st cit.:* 1942 Lasswell, *Suds in Your Eye. 20c. coll.:* Stevenson 2172:2.

hypocrisy 1. Hypocrisy is the homage that vice pays to virtue. *Rec. dist.:* Ill. *1st cit.:* 1732 Fuller, *Gnomologia. 20c. coll.:* Stevenson 1210:1.

2. It is rank hypocrisy to teach virtue and yet to practice vice. *Rec. dist.:* Mich.

3. There is an hypocrisy in vice as well as religion. *Rec. dist.:* N.Y., S.C.

hypocrite 1. A hypocrite deceives no one but himself. *Rec. dist.:* Ark.

2. A hypocrite destroys his neighbor with his mouth. *Rec. dist.:* Ont.

3. A hypocrite is one who feeds a starving man words. *Rec. dist.:* N.J.

4. The hypocrite tributes to God that he may impose on men. *Rec. dist.:* Mich.

5. The hypocrite's mask becomes his face. *Rec. dist.:* Ill.

I

ice 1. In skating over thin ice, our safety is in our speed. *Rec. dist.:* N.Y., S.C. *1st cit.:* US1841 Emerson, "Prudence" in *Essays*. *20c. coll.:* Stevenson 1211:8, Whiting*(MP)* 334.

2. The thinner the ice is, the more anxious is everyone to see whether it will bear. *Rec. dist.:* Ohio.

3. Thin ice and thick ice look the same from a distance. *Rec. dist.:* Ill.

4. Thin ice carries no weight. *Rec. dist.:* Ont.

5. Try the ice before you venture upon it. *Rec. dist.:* N.J., Okla., Ont., Tex., Vt.

SEE ALSO LOVE can melt the ice and the snow of the coldest regions. / PEOPLE in hell want ice water.

ice cream Enjoy your ice cream while it's on your plate. *Rec. dist.:* N.Y., S.C. *1st cit.:* US1942 Wilder, *Skin of Our Teeth*. *20c. coll.:* Stevenson 2325:2.

icebox If the icebox gets on fire, wring the towel. *Rec. dist.:* Ind.

idea 1. Alter ideas and you alter the world. *Rec. dist.:* Ont.

2. An idea that is not dangerous is unworthy to be called an idea at all. *Rec. dist.:* N.Y., S.C. *1st cit.:* US1910 Hubbard, *Dictionary of Epigrams*. *20c. coll.:* Stevenson 1212:12.

3. Good ideas are born in the minds that keep working—lazy minds and good ideas are strangers. *Rec. dist.:* Ind.

4. Ideas are weapons. *Rec. dist.:* Ill.

5. Ideas never work unless you do. *Var.:* Ideas are funny things: they won't work unless you do. *Rec. dist.:* Ill., Miss.

6. It is better to have no ideas than false ones. *Rec. dist.:* Minn.

7. It's with ideas as with pieces of money: those with the least value generally circulate the most. *Rec. dist.:* Ill.

8. Notice that ideas start with "I." *Rec. dist.:* Minn.

9. One good idea put to use is worth a hundred buzzing around in the back of your head. *Rec. dist.:* N.C.

10. To have ideas is to gather flowers; to think is to weave them into garlands. *Rec. dist.:* Ont.

11. You can't just abstract ideas into concrete heads. *Rec. dist.:* Wash.

SEE ALSO Small HEAD, big ideas. / TIMES change and people change their ideas. / All WORDS are pegs to hang ideas on.

ideal 1. No ideal is as good as a fact. *Rec. dist.:* Ont.

2. The ideal is but the truth at a distance. *Rec. dist.:* N.Y.

3. The ideal we embrace is our better self. *Var.:* Our ideals are our better selves. *Rec. dist.:* Ill. *1st cit.:* US1877 Alcott, "Habits" in *Table Talk*. *20c. coll.:* Stevenson 1213:1.

idiocy If idiocy were pain, there would be groaning in every house. *Rec. dist.:* Ill.

idiot 1. A natural idiot is bad enough, but a learned idiot is an intolerable bore. *Rec. dist.:* Ill.

2. An idiot—they happen in the best of families. *Rec. dist.:* N.Y., S.C. *1st cit.:* US1939 Barry, *Philadelphia Story*. *20c. coll.:* Stevenson 7:4.

3. The idiot bakes snow in the oven and expects ice-cream pie. *Rec. dist.:* Ill.

4. The idiot looks at the mirror and sees a scholar. *Rec. dist.:* Ill.

idle 1. Be always ashamed to catch yourself idle. *Vars.:* (a) Be ashamed to catch yourself idle. (b) Never be idle. *Rec. dist.:* Ind. *1st cit.:* US1741 Franklin, *PRAlmanac*. *20c. coll.:* Stevenson 1215:8.

2. Better be idle than badly employed. *Vars.:* (a) Better idle than workin' for nothin'. (b) You're idle if you might be better employed. *Rec. dist.:* Minn. *1st cit.:* 1560 More, "Dedication" in *Defense of Women*. *20c. coll.:* Stevenson 1213:5.

3. Better to sit idle than to work idle. *Var.:* You might as well be idle as work idle. *Rec. dist.:* Ont.

SEE ALSO An idle BRAIN is the devil's workshop. / The DEVIL some mischief finds for idle hands to do. / Idle HANDS are the devil's tools. / An idle WORD is never well-spoken.

idleness 1. Idleness and lust are bosom friends. *Rec. dist.:* Ill. *1st cit.:* ca1389 Chaucer, *Prologue to Second Nonnes Tale* in *Canterbury Tales. 20c. coll.:* Stevenson 1214:3.

2. Idleness and pride tax with a heavier hand than kings and parliaments. *Rec. dist.:* N.Y., S.C. *1st cit.:* US1765 Franklin, Letter on Stamp Act, 11 July. *20c. coll.:* Stevenson 1215:8.

3. Idleness breeds trouble. *Var.:* Trouble springs from idleness. *Rec. dist.:* Ind., Ont. *1st cit.:* US1756 Franklin, *PRAlmanac. 20c. coll.:* Stevenson 1215:8.

4. Idleness goes in rags. *Rec. dist.:* Okla. *1st cit.:* 1732 Fuller, *Gnomologia. 20c. coll.:* Stevenson 1215:16.

5. Idleness in youth makes way for a painful and miserable old age. *Rec. dist.:* N.Y. *1st cit.:* 1564 Bullein, *Dialogue Against Fever Pestilence. 20c. coll.:* ODEP 395.

6. Idleness is hunger's mother, and of theft it is full brother. *Rec. dist.:* Ill. *1st cit.:* 1616 Gainsford, *The Rich Cabinet. 20c. coll.:* Stevenson 1215:16.

7. Idleness is never enjoyable unless there is plenty to do. *Rec. dist.:* Ont.

8. Idleness is only the refuge of weak minds, the holiday of fools. *Rec. dist.:* Ont. *1st cit.:* 1749 Chesterfield, Letter, 20 July, in *Letters to His Son. 20c. coll.:* Stevenson 1215:1.

9. Idleness is the Dead Sea that swallows all virtues. *Rec. dist.:* N.Y., S.C. *1st cit.:* US1757 Franklin, *PRAlmanac. 20c. coll.:* Stevenson 1214:3.

10. Idleness is the greatest prodigality. *Rec. dist.:* Mich. *1st cit.:* 1650 Taylor, *Holy Living;* US1745 Franklin, *PRAlmanac. 20c. coll.:* Stevenson 1215:16, Whiting 231.

11. Idleness is the key of beggary. *Rec. dist.:* Ind. *1st cit.:* 1597 *Politeuphuia Wits Commonwealth. 20c. coll.:* ODEP 396, Stevenson 1215:16.

12. Idleness is the mother of evil. *Vars.:* (a) All sins come out of the house of idleness. (b) Idleness is the mother of all the vices. (c) Idleness is the mother of mischief. (d) Idleness is the mother of want. (e) Idleness is the parent of many vices. (f) Idleness is the root of all evil. *Rec. dist.:* U.S., Can. *1st cit.:* ca1205 Layamon, *Brut,* Soc. Antiquaries (1847); USca1680 *Voyages of Radisson,* ed. Scull, Publ. Prince Soc. (1885). *20c. coll.:* ODEP 396, Whiting 231, *CODP* 118, Stevenson 1214:3, T&W 198, Whiting(MP) 334

13. Idleness is the refuge of weak minds and the holiday of fools. *Rec. dist.:* Ill.

14. Idleness leads to failure. *Rec. dist.:* Miss.

15. Idleness turns the edge of wit. *Rec. dist.:* N.Y. *1st cit.:* 1597 Lyly, *Works,* ed. Bond (1902). *20c. coll.:* ODEP 396.

16. In idleness there is perpetual despair. *Rec. dist.:* Oreg. *1st cit.:* 1737 Green, *The Spleen. 20c. coll.:* Stevenson 1215:3.

17. Of idleness comes no goodness. *Rec. dist.:* R.I. *1st cit.:* 1611 Cotgrave, *Dictionary of French and English Tongues. 20c. coll.:* ODEP 396.

18. Prolonged idleness provides food for vice. *Rec. dist.:* N.Y., S.C. *1st cit.:* ca1389 Chaucer, *Prologue to Second Nonnes Tale* in *Canterbury Tales. 20c. coll.:* Stevenson 1214:3.

19. We are taxed twice as much by our idleness, three times as much by our pride, and four times as much by our folly. *Rec. dist.:* Ill.

SEE ALSO TROUBLE springs from idleness.

idler 1. A young idler, an old beggar. *Rec. dist.:* Ohio.

2. An idler is a watch that wants both hands, as useless if it goes as if it stands. *Rec. dist.:* Ont. *1st cit.:* 1781 Cowper, *Retirement. 20c. coll.:* Stevenson 1215:4.

if 1. If "ifs" and "ands" were pots and pans, there would be no need for tinkers. *Rec. dist.:* Calif., Miss., Nebr. *1st cit.:* 1850 Kingsley, *Alton Locke;* US1945 Wentworth, *Death. 20c. coll.:* CODP 118, ODEP 396, Whiting(MP) 334.

2. "If" is a big stiff. *Rec. dist.:* Ont.

3. "If" is a little word with a big meaning.

Var.: "If" is a small word that sometimes has a large meaning. *Rec. dist.:* Maine, Ont., Wash.

4. "If" is a little word, yet it is so big you can't get around or over it. *Rec. dist.:* N.C.

5. "If" is the longest word ever spoken. *Rec. dist.:* N.C.

6. If it wasn't for the "ifs," you would be rich. *Rec. dist.:* N.C.

7. "Ifs" and "buts" butter no bread. *Rec. dist.:* N.Y., S.C.

ignorance **1.** Better be unborn than untaught, for ignorance is the root of misfortune. *Rec. dist.:* Ont.

2. Double ignorance is where a man is ignorant of his ignorance. *Rec. dist.:* Miss., Wis.

3. If ignorance is bliss, why be otherwise? *Rec. dist.:* U.S.

4. Ignorance and bungling with love are better than wisdom and skill without. *Rec. dist.:* N.Y., S.C.

5. Ignorance and pride grow on the same wood. *Rec. dist.:* Ont.

6. Ignorance breeds impudence. *Rec. dist.:* Ill. *1st cit.:* 1573 Sanford, *Garden of Pleasure.* *20c. coll.:* ODEP 396.

7. Ignorance is a voluntary misfortune. *Rec. dist.:* Ill., Mich.

8. Ignorance is an ungrateful guest. *Rec. dist.:* Wis.

9. Ignorance is better than error, but the active fool is a holy terror. *Var.:* Ignorance is preferable to error. *Rec. dist.:* Ill.

10. Ignorance is bliss. *Rec. dist.:* U.S. *1st cit.:* 1742 Gray, *Poems;* US1852 Cary, *Clovernook.* *20c. coll.:* CODP 118, T&W 198, ODEP 396, Stevenson 1222:3, Whiting*(MP)* 335.

11. Ignorance is blister. *Rec. dist.:* N.Y.

12. Ignorance is no excuse. *Rec. dist.:* Ill., Ind.

13. Ignorance is the father of crime. *Rec. dist.:* Ind.

14. Ignorance is the mother of conceit. *Rec. dist.:* Wis. *1st cit.:* 1573 Sanford, *Garden of Pleasure.* *20c. coll.:* ODEP 396.

15. Ignorance is the mother of superstition. *Rec. dist.:* Mich.

16. Ignorance is the result of neglected opportunities. *Rec. dist.:* Ind.

17. Ignorance is universal. *Rec. dist.:* N.C.

18. Ignorance leads men into a party, and shame keeps them from getting out again. *Rec. dist.:* Ind., N.Y., S.C.

19. Ignorance of one's misfortunes is clear gain. *Rec. dist.:* Minn.

20. Ignorance of the law is no excuse. *Rec. dist.:* U.S., Can. *1st cit.:* 1530 Saint German, *Dialogues in English;* US1755 Sherman, *Almanacs.* *20c. coll.:* ODEP 396, Whiting 231, CODP 119, Stevenson 1369:5, Whiting*(MP)* 335.

21. Laugh and show your ignorance. *Rec. dist.:* N.Y., Ohio, S.C.

22. No one can talk for more than five minutes without exposing the extent of his ignorance. *Rec. dist.:* Ohio.

23. The more we study, the more we discover our ignorance. *Rec. dist.:* Miss., Ont.

24. The quickest way to show ignorance is to talk about something you know nothing about. *Rec. dist.:* Kans.

25. There is nothing more frightful than a bustling ignorance. *Rec. dist.:* Ont.

26. Where ignorance is bliss, 'tis folly to be wise. *Vars.:* **(a)** If ignorance is bliss, 'tis folly to be wise. **(b)** Ignorance is bliss, and we're in seventh heaven. **(c)** Ignorance is bliss; 'tis folly to be wise. *Rec. dist.:* U.S. *1st cit.:* 1742 Gray, *Poems;* US1852 Cary, *Clovernook.* *20c. coll.:* CODP 118, T&W 198, ODEP 396, Stevenson 1222:3.

27. Your ignorance is your worst enemy. *Rec. dist.:* N.Y.

See also FEAR always springs from ignorance. / KNOWLEDGE talks lowly; ignorance talks loudly. / PREJUDICE is the child of ignorance. / A WISE man knows his own ignorance; a fool thinks he knows everything.

ignorant **1.** Being ignorant is not so much shame as being unwilling to learn. *Rec. dist.:* Oreg.

2. He who is ignorant knows not that he is. *Rec. dist.:* Utah.

3. How ignorant are those who men say know it all. *Rec. dist.:* N.C.

4. It ain't the things you don't know that makes you ignorant as much as the things you know that ain't so. *Rec. dist.:* Miss.

5. It is impossible to defeat an ignorant man in argument. *Rec. dist.:* N.Y.

6. It is only the ignorant that despise education. *Rec. dist.:* N.Y.

7. It pays to be ignorant. *Rec. dist.:* N.C.

8. Some are too ignorant to be humble. *Rec. dist.:* Ont.

9. Unlettered men are not always the most ignorant, nor learned men always wise. *Rec. dist.:* Mich.

SEE ALSO A learned BLOCKHEAD is a greater blockhead than an ignorant one.

ill *(n.)*   **1.** Better to bear the ills we have than fly to others we know not of. *Rec. dist.:* Ont.

2. Don't speak ill of yourself; others will do it for you. *Rec. dist.:* Ont.

3. Fear to do ill and you need fear nought else. *Rec. dist.:* N.Y., S.C.

4. For every ill beneath the sun, there is some remedy or none. If there be one, go find it; if not, never mind it. *Var.:* For every ill beneath the sun, there is a remedy or none. *Rec. dist.:* N.C., Ont.

5. He that does ill hates the light. *Rec. dist.:* N.C., Okla. *1st cit.:* ca1250 *Owl and Nightingale.* *20c. coll.:* ODEP 194.

6. He that speaks ill of the mare will buy her. *Rec. dist.:* N.Y., S.C. *1st cit.:* 1659 Howell, *Paroimiografia;* US1742 Franklin, *PRAlmanac.* *20c. coll.:* ODEP 762, Stevenson 268:10, Whiting 283.

7. If you do ill, the joy fades, not the pains; if well, the pain does fade, the joy remains. *Rec. dist.:* N.Y., S.C.

8. It costs more to do ill than well. *Rec. dist.:* Ill., N.Y. *1st cit.:* 1640 Herbert, *Outlandish Proverbs (Jacula Prudentum)* in *Works,* ed. Hutchinson (1941). *20c. coll.:* ODEP 145.

9. Of two ills, choose the least. *Rec. dist.:* Ont. *1st cit.:* ca1374 Chaucer, *Troilus and Criseyde.* *20c. coll.:* ODEP 233.

10. Say no ill of the year till it be past. *Rec. dist.:* Ont. *1st cit.:* 1640 Herbert, *Outlandish Proverbs (Jacula Prudentum)* in *Works,* ed. Hutchinson (1941). *20c. coll.:* ODEP 701.

11. Speak not rather than speak ill. *Rec. dist.:* Ohio.

12. To favor the ill is to injure the good. *Rec. dist.:* Ont.

SEE ALSO Desperate CURES to desperate ills apply. / DOING nothing is doing ill. / A GOSSIP speaks ill of all and all of her. / A man in SUFFERING finds relief in rehearsing his ills.

ill *(adj.)*   **1.** Better ill fed than ill bred. *Rec. dist.:* N.Y.

2. Ill will never speaks well or does well. *Rec. dist.:* Mich. *1st cit.:* ca1400 Chaucer, *Romance of Rose,* ed. Skeat (1894); US1767 Ames, *Almanacs,* ed. Briggs (1891). *20c. coll.:* ODEP 401, Whiting 232.

3. It's ill halting before a cripple. *Rec. dist.:* N.Y.

4. Never do anyone an ill turn. *Rec. dist.:* Ont.

SEE ALSO Ill-gotten GAIN is no gain at all. / A GOOD man is seldom uneasy, an ill one never easy. / Ill-gotten GOODS prosper not long. / A stout HEART crushes ill luck. / Unquiet MEALS make ill digestion. / PRIDE's an ill horse to ride. / It matters not what RELIGION an ill man is of. / It is not a SIN to sell dear, but it is to make ill measure. / No WEATHER's ill if the wind be still. / An ill WIND blows no good. / An ill WOUND, but not an ill name, may be healed.

ill-breeding   SEE He is not WELL bred that cannot bear ill-breeding in others.

ill-doer   Ill-doers are ill-thinkers. *Var.:* Ill-doers are ill-deemers. *Rec. dist.:* N.Y., Tex. *1st cit.:* 1509 Barclay, *Ship of Fools,* ed. Jamieson in *Eclogues,* E.E.T.S. (1874). *20c. coll.:* ODEP 398, CODP 120.

illegal   SEE From middle AGE on everything of interest is either illegal, immoral, or fattening.

illness 1. Illness makes a man a scoundrel. *Rec. dist.:* Wis.

2. Illness which we imagine is often harder to bear than illness which we experience. *Rec. dist.:* Ont.

illusions 1. Don't part with your illusions; when they are gone you may exist, but you have ceased to live. *Rec. dist.:* Ont.

2. It is natural to man to indulge in the illusions of hope. *Rec. dist.:* N.Y., S.C.

I'll warrant ye "I'll warrant ye" goes before rashness. *Rec. dist.:* N.Y., S.C.

imagination 1. Don't let your imagination run away with you. *Rec. dist.:* Ark., Ind., Ohio.

2. Imagination dives deeper and soars higher than nature goes. *Rec. dist.:* Minn.

3. Imagination rules the world. *Rec. dist.:* Miss.

4. Imagination will take you a long ways and then let you fall. *Rec. dist.:* Fla.

See also REALITY never surpasses imagination.

imagine *See* ILLNESS which we imagine is often harder to bear than illness which we experience. / KNAVES imagine nothing can be done without knavery.

imitation Imitation is the highest form of flattery. *Rec. dist.:* U.S., Can. *1st cit.:* 1820 Colton, *Lacon;* US1940 Cameron, *Malice.* *20c. coll.:* CODP 120, ODEP 402, Whiting(MP) 335.

immature To the immature, all apples are green. *Rec. dist.:* N.Y., S.C.

immoral *See* From middle AGE on everything of interest is either illegal, immoral, or fattening.

imp *See* Talk about the DEVIL and his imps will appear.

impatience 1. A little impatience spoils great plans. *Rec. dist.:* N.C.

2. Impatience does not diminish, but increases the evil. *Rec. dist.:* Ill. *1st cit.:* 1732 Fuller, *Gnomologia.* *20c. coll.:* Stevenson 1226:6.

3. Impatience gathers unripe fruit. *Rec. dist.:* Ill.

importance 1. Don't measure your importance by your morning shadow. *Rec. dist.:* Ont.

2. We are often of greater importance in our own eyes than in the eyes of our neighbors. *Rec. dist.:* Kans.

important No matter how important you are, you can catch the measles. *Rec. dist.:* Miss.

See also THINKING is the important thing in life.

impose He who has suffered you to impose on him knows you. *Rec. dist.:* Ont.

imposing *See* LIARS begin by imposing on others, but end by deceiving themselves.

impossible 1. Do not attempt the impossible. *Rec. dist.:* N.Y., N.C., Ont.

2. Impossible is un-American. *Rec. dist.:* Okla.

3. Never believe the impossible. *Rec. dist.:* Ont.

4. No one is bound to do the impossible. *Var.:* No one is bound to do what is impossible. *Rec. dist.:* Ill., N.C.

5. Nothing is impossible. *Vars.:* (a) Nothing is impossible to a willing heart. (b) Nothing is impossible to a willing mind. *Rec. dist.:* Fla., Ind., Ky. *1st cit.:* 1509 Hawes, *Passetyme of Pleasure;* US1940 Rawson, *Headless.* *20c. coll.:* ODEP 580, Whiting(MP) 453.

6. The impossible always happens. *Rec. dist.:* N.Y., S.C.

7. The impossible is possible if true. *Rec. dist.:* Ill.

8. The word "impossible" is not in my dictionary. *Rec. dist.:* N.Y.

See also The DIFFICULT is done at once; the impossible takes a little longer. / Few things are impossible to DILIGENCE and skill. / To FORGIVE is easy; to forget is impossible.

impression 1. First impressions are best. *Rec. dist.:* Ont.

2. First impressions are half the battle. *Rec.*

dist.: Ill. *1st cit.*: 1700 Congreve, *Way of the World. 20c. coll.*: ODEP 262.

3. First impressions are the most lasting. *Vars.*: **(a)** First impressions are often lasting. **(b)** The first impression is a lasting one. **(c)** The first impression is the lasting impression. **(d)** The first impression is the most lasting. *Rec. dist.*: U.S., Can. *1st cit.*: 1700 Congreve, *Way of the World;* US1786 Van Schaack, *Life of Peter Van Schaack* (1842). *20c. coll.*: ODEP 262, Whiting 232 *CODP* 81, Stevenson 1231:8.

4. First impressions rule the mind. *Rec. dist.*: Miss.

5. It is easier to make an impression on an easy chair than to make an impression on the world. *Rec. dist.*: Minn.

6. Never judge by first impressions. *Rec. dist.*: Miss. *1st cit.*: US1929 Fairlie, *Stone. 20c. coll.*: Whiting(MP) 335.

SEE ALSO Bold FLATTERY gives an impression of insincerity. / YOUTH and white paper take any impression.

imprisoned SEE Though the BODY may be imprisoned, the soul can be free.

improve **1.** First improve yourself today; then improve your friends tomorrow. *Rec. dist.*: Ont.

2. If you don't improve today, you'll grow worse tomorrow. *Rec. dist.*: Ill.

3. Try to improve yourself. *Rec. dist.*: Miss.

SEE ALSO INDUSTRY will improve great talents if you have them. / WEALTH does not always improve us.

improvement SEE The biggest ROOM in the world is the room for improvement.

impudent It is better to be impudent than a bootlicker. *Rec. dist.*: Ill.

impulse Our best impulses are too delicate to endure much handling. *Rec. dist.*: N.C.

impunity Impunity always invites to greater crime. *Rec. dist.*: Mich.

inaction Inaction gnaws the heartstrings. *Rec. dist.*: Ont.

inactivity Inactivity breeds ignorance. *Rec. dist.*: N.Y., S.C.

inanity Nothing is endless but inanity. *Rec. dist.*: Ill.

inch **1.** An inch in missing is as bad as a mile. *Vars.*: **(a)** An inch is as good as a mile. **(b)** An inch is good as a mile if it's a miss. *Rec. dist.*: Calif., Okla., Ont., Tex., Vt. *1st cit.*: 1614 Camden, *Remaines Concerning Britaine. 20c. coll.*: ODEP 403.

2. Deviate an inch, lose a thousand miles. *Rec. dist.*: Calif.

3. Give an inch, take a mile. *Vars.*: **(a)** Give a fool an inch and he'll take a mile. **(b)** Give him an inch and he thinks he's a ruler. **(c)** Give him an inch and he'll take a span. **(d)** Give him an inch and he'll take a yard. **(e)** Give him an inch and he'll take an ell. **(f)** Give him an inch, he'll take a yard. **(g)** Give 'em an inch, they'll take a mile. **(h)** Give some people an inch and they will take a mile. *Rec. dist.*: Calif., Nev. *1st cit.*: 1546 Heywood, *Dialogue of Proverbs,* ed. Habernicht (1963); US1680 *Letters of John Randolph,* ed. Dudley (1834). *20c. coll.*: ODEP 303, Whiting 232, Stevenson 1232:3, T&W 198, Whiting(MP) 336.

SEE ALSO A HALO only has to fall a few inches to become a noose. / The ground of LIBERTY must be gained by inches. / LIFE is hard by the yard, but by the inch life's a cinch. / MEN are not to be measured by inches. / An inch of RUBBING saves scrubbing.

incident SEE RELIGION should be a rule of life, not a casual incident of it.

income **1.** Income is measured by output. *Rec. dist.*: Calif.

2. The happiest place in the world to live is within one's income. *Var.*: The only place to live a happy life is within your income. *Rec. dist.*: N.Y., Ohio.

3. The larger the income, the harder it is to live within it. *Rec. dist.*: Miss.

SEE ALSO A BUSINESS with an income at its heels always furnishes oil for its own wheels. / Good MANAGEMENT is better than good income.

inconsistency **1.** Inconsistency is the attendant of a weak mind. *Rec. dist.*: Mich.

2. Inconsistency is the only thing in which men are consistent. *Rec. dist.:* Ill.

increase SEE KNOWLEDGE directs practice, and practice increases knowledge.

incurable SEE CONCEIT is the most incurable disease that is known to the human soul.

indecision Indecision is fatal, so make up your mind. *Rec. dist.:* Kans.

independent He who is independent cannot be greater. *Rec. dist.:* Mich.

index SEE SPEECH is the index of the mind. / A YARD is an index to the interior of the house.

Indian **1.** An Indian, a partridge, and a spruce tree can't be tamed. *Rec. dist.:* N.Y., S.C. *1st cit.:* US1853 Haliburton, *Sam Slick's Wise Saws.* *20c. coll.:* Stevenson 2507:8, T&W 199.

2. An Indian scalps his enemies, while a white man skins his friends. *Rec. dist.:* Kans.

3. Don't be an Indian giver. *Rec. dist.:* U.S. *1st cit.:* US1728 Byrd, *Histories of the Dividing Line Betwixt Virginia and N. Carolina,* ed. Boyd (1929). *20c. coll.:* Whiting 233, T&W 199, Whiting(MP) 336.

4. Maybe the Indians didn't do much for the country, but they didn't mortgage it. *Rec. dist.:* N.Y., S.C.

5. Never trust an Indian. *Rec. dist.:* Kans.

6. The Indian will come back to his blanket. *Rec. dist.:* Oreg.

7. The only good Indian is a dead Indian. *Var.:* The only good Indian is a dead one. *Rec. dist.:* U.S., Can. *1st cit.:* US1868 Cavanaugh in *Congressional Globe,* 28 May. *20c. coll.:* CODP 98, Whiting(MP) 337.

8. White man fool Indian once, shame on white man; white man fool Indian twice, shame on Indian. *Rec. dist.:* Wis.

indifference Do not undertake rashly nor perform with a cold indifference. *Rec. dist.:* Mich.

indigent SEE For one POOR man there are a hundred indigent.

indigestion SEE LOVE never dies of starvation, but often of indigestion.

indirection By indirection find direction out. *Rec. dist.:* N.Y.

indolence Indolence breeds misery. *Rec. dist.:* Ill.

indolent **1.** An indolent man draws his breath but does not eat. *Rec. dist.:* Ill.

2. The indolent makes little headway. *Rec. dist.:* Wis.

indulge SEE Small FAULTS indulged in are little thieves that let in greater.

industrious An industrious man is tempted by one devil, an idle one by seven. *Rec. dist.:* Ill.

industry **1.** All things are easy to industry, all things difficult to sloth. *Vars.:* (a) All things are won by industry. (b) Sloth makes all things difficult, but industry makes all things easy. *Rec. dist.:* N.Y., S.C. *1st cit.:* US1734 Franklin, *PRAlmanac.* *20c. coll.:* Stevenson 1239:13.

2. An hour's industry will do more to produce cheerfulness than a month's moaning. *Rec. dist.:* Ill.

3. In every rank, both great and small, 'tis industry that supports us all. *Rec. dist.:* N.Y., S.C.

4. Industry is fortune's right hand, and frugality her left. *Rec. dist.:* Vt. *1st cit.:* 1651 Hobbes, *Philosophical Rudiments Concerning Government and Society* (1841). *20c. coll.:* ODEP 403.

5. Industry is the greatest conqueror. *Rec. dist.:* N.Y., S.C.

6. Industry is the parent of success. *Rec. dist.:* Kans., Ont.

7. Industry keeps the body healthy, the mind clear, the heart whole, and the purse full. *Rec. dist.:* Ill.

8. Industry need not wish. *Rec. dist.:* U.S., Can. *1st cit.:* US1739 Franklin, *PRAlmanac.* *20c. coll.:* Whiting 233.

9. Industry pays debts, but despair increases them. *Rec. dist.:* Ill., Ind., N.Y. *1st cit.:* US1742 Franklin, *PRAlmanac.* *20c. coll.:* Whiting 233.

10. Industry will improve great talents if you have them. *Rec. dist.:* Ont.

11. Nothing is impossible to industry. *Rec. dist.:* Ill. *1st cit.:* US1948 Stevenson, *Home Book of Proverbs.* *20c. coll.:* Stevenson 1239:13.

12. When industry goes out at the door, poverty comes in at the window. *Rec. dist.:* Ill.
SEE ALSO WANT is the mother of industry.

inequality Inequality is as dear to the American heart as liberty itself. *Rec. dist.:* N.Y., S.C. *1st cit.:* US1896 Howells, "New York Streets" in *Impressions and Experiences.* *20c. coll.:* Stevenson 705:2.
SEE ALSO LOVE levels all inequalities.

infallible No one is infallible. *Rec. dist.:* Okla. *1st cit.:* ca1880 Thompson, Remark. *20c. coll.:* Stevenson 2665:1.

infamy Infamy is the livery of bad deserts. *Rec. dist.:* Mich.
SEE ALSO PRIDE breakfasted with plenty, dined with poverty, and supped with infamy.

infect *SEE* One sickly SHEEP infects the flock and poisons all the rest.

inferior Spurn not an inferior. *Rec. dist.:* N.Y., S.C.

inferiority *SEE* QUOTATION confesses inferiority.

infidelity *SEE* Each HUSBAND gets the infidelity he deserves.

infirmity Deride not any man's infirmities. *Rec. dist.:* Mich.
SEE ALSO A FRIEND should bear his friend's infirmity.

informal Informal's what women always say they're going to be and never are. *Rec. dist.:* Wis.

information **1.** A great part of the information one has was acquired by looking up something and finding something else on the way. *Rec. dist.:* Minn.

2. Don't memorize information; know where to find it. *Rec. dist.:* Wis.

informer **1.** An informer's money has a Judas ring. *Rec. dist.:* Ill.

2. The informer is the worse rogue of the two. *Rec. dist.:* Okla. *1st cit.:* 1732 Fuller, *Gnomologia.* *20c. coll.:* Stevenson 1241:10.

ingratitude **1.** Ingratitude is unpardonable and dries up the fountain of all goodness. *Rec. dist.:* Mich.

2. Ingratitude sometimes brings its own punishment. *Rec. dist.:* Ark.

3. Next to ingratitude, the most painful thing to bear is gratitude. *Rec. dist.:* N.Y., S.C.
SEE ALSO True GENEROSITY is the ability to accept ingratitude.

ingredient There are three ingredients in the good life: learning, earning, and yearning. *Rec. dist.:* Kans.

inherit *SEE* The MEEK shall inherit the earth. / The WISE shall inherit glory, but shame shall be the promotion of fools.

inheritance He who anticipates his inheritance will be the inheritor of beggary. *Rec. dist.:* Mich.
SEE ALSO BEAUTY is no inheritance.

inhuman It is inhuman to bless when one is being cursed. *Rec. dist.:* Wis.

inhumanity Man's inhumanity to man makes countless thousands mourn. *Rec. dist.:* Ont. *1st cit.:* 1788 Burns, "Man Was Made To Mourn." *20c. coll.:* Stevenson 1519:1.

iniquity **1.** He that sows iniquity shall reap vanity. *Rec. dist.:* Ont.

2. The path of iniquity is broad and smooth. *Rec. dist.:* N.Y., S.C.

initiative **1.** A man possessing initiative is a creator. *Rec. dist.:* Minn.

2. Initiative is doing the right thing without being told. *Rec. dist.:* Kans., Ohio.

injure **1.** Folks often injure all they fear and hate all they injure. *Rec. dist.:* Ill. *1st cit.:* 1732 Fuller, *Gnomologia.* *20c. coll.:* Stevenson 1244:5.

2. Injure no man. *Rec. dist.:* Mich. *1st cit.:* US1948 Stevenson, *Home Book of Proverbs.* *20c. coll.:* Stevenson 1245:6.

3. Injure others, injure yourself. *Var.:* You will injure yourself in injuring others. *Rec.*

dist.: Ind., N.Y., Ont. *1st cit.:* 1578 Florio, *Firste Fruites.* *20c. coll.:* Stevenson 1244:9.

SEE ALSO To favor the ILL is to injure the good.

injured SEE An injured FRIEND is the bitterest of foes.

injurious Nothing is more injurious than unoccupied time. *Rec. dist.:* Ont.

injury 1. A small injury often brings great woe. *Rec. dist.:* N.Dak.

2. An injury is sooner forgotten than an insult. *Rec. dist.:* Ont. *1st cit.:* 1746 Chesterfield, Letter, 9 Oct., in *Letters to His Son.* *20c. coll.:* Stevenson 1251:10.

3. Be more ready to forgive than to return an injury. *Rec. dist.:* Kans. *1st cit.:* US1752 Franklin, *PRAlmanac.* *20c. coll.:* Stevenson 1244:10.

4. If you defend an injury, you are almost as bad as the guilty party. *Rec. dist.:* Ill.

5. Injuries may be forgiven, but not forgotten. *Rec. dist.:* N.C., Ont.

6. It costs more to revenge than to bear with injuries. *Rec. dist.:* N.C., Ont. *1st cit.:* 1775 Wilson, *Maxims of Piety.* *20c. coll.:* Stevenson 1244:8.

7. It is better to bear a single injury in silence than to provoke a thousand by flying into a rage. *Rec. dist.:* Ont.

8. It is better to suffer an injury than to inflict one. *Vars.:* (a) It is better to receive than to do an injury. (b) It is better to take many injuries than to give one. (c) It's better to suffer an injury than to commit one. *Rec. dist.:* Ill., N.Y., N.C., S.C. *1st cit.:* US1735 Franklin, *PRAlmanac.* *20c. coll.:* Stevenson 1244:7.

9. No one pretends to hate an injury more than he who offers it. *Rec. dist.:* Mich.

10. Requite injury with kindness. *Rec. dist.:* Ohio, Utah. *1st cit.:* US1948 Stevenson, *Home Book of Proverbs.* *20c. coll.:* Stevenson 1245:3.

11. The best remedy for an injury is to forget it. *Rec. dist.:* Ill., N.Y. *1st cit.:* ca1526 Erasmus, *Dicta Sapientum,* tr. Berthelet. *20c. coll.:* ODEP 670.

12. Write injuries in dust, benefits in marble. *Rec. dist.:* Ill., N.Y.

Var.: Write injuries in dust, but kindness in marble. *Rec. dist.:* Kans., N.Y., S.C. *1st cit.:* ca1513 More, *Richard III;* US1747 Franklin, *PRAlmanac.* *20c. coll.:* ODEP 404, Stevenson 1246:4.

13. You invite future injuries if you revive past ones. *Rec. dist.:* Ill.

SEE ALSO ANGER is often more hurtful than the injury that caused it. / He who puts up with INSULT invites injury. / NEGLECT kills injuries; revenge increases them. / He that teaches a SCORNER does an injury to himself. / WOMEN forgive injury, but never forget slights.

injustice It is better to suffer injustice than to do it. *Var.:* It is more disgraceful to do injustice than to suffer it. *Rec. dist.:* Ind., N.Y., S.C. *1st cit.:* US1850 Emerson, "Plato" in *Representative Men.* *20c. coll.:* Stevenson 1247:1.

SEE ALSO JEALOUSY leads to folly and injustice. / It is not possible to found a lasting POWER upon injustice. / WAR is the sink of all injustice.

ink 1. A drop of ink may make a million think. *Rec. dist.:* N.J., N.Y.

2. The palest ink is better than the finest memory. *Rec. dist.:* Ind.

inn An inn and fresh acquaintances are dangerous. *Rec. dist.:* Mich.

innocence 1. Innocence breeds confidence. *Rec. dist.:* Ill.

2. Innocence is no protection. *Rec. dist.:* Wis. *1st cit.:* 1605 Jonson, *Sejanus;* US1841 Thoreau, *Winter,* 28 Jan. *20c. coll.:* ODEP 404, Stevenson 1247:15.

3. Lost innocence and wasted time are never recovered. *Rec. dist.:* Ont.

innocent 1. An innocent man needs no loudspeaker: his life speaks for itself. *Rec. dist.:* Ill.

2. It is easy to defend the innocent. *Rec. dist.:* Mich. *1st cit.:* 1578 Florio, *Firste Fruites,* ed. Taihoku (1936); US1733 Franklin, *PRAlmanac.* *20c. coll.:* Stevenson 1247:16.

3. Only the innocent die young. *Rec. dist.:* N.Dak.

SEE ALSO An innocent PLOWMAN is more worth than a vicious prince. / The PRAYER of the innocent is never unheard.

innovate To innovate may not reform. *Rec. dist.:* Ont. *1st cit.:* 1796 Burke, *Letter to a Noble Lord. 20c. coll.:* Stevenson 1945:2.

innovation Innovations are dangerous. *Rec. dist.:* Ill.

inquire To inquire is neither a disaster nor a disgrace. *Rec. dist.:* Ill.

insanity SEE RAGE is brief insanity.

insensibility Insensibility is the companion of drunkenness. *Rec. dist.:* Mich.

inside *(n.)* SEE I'd rather be on the OUTSIDE a-looking in than on the inside a-looking out. / Don't be VOGUE on the outside and vague on the inside.

inside *(adv.)* If you are inside, you can't be outside. *Rec. dist.:* Ont.
SEE ALSO It's not the HOUSE that makes the home, it's the love that is inside. / There's more ROOM outside than inside.

inside *(prep.)* SEE Keep your broken ARM inside your sleeve.

insincerity SEE Bold FLATTERY gives an impression of insincerity.

insolence SEE PROSPERITY is the surest breeder of insolence.

insolent The insolent have no friends. *Rec. dist.:* Ill. *1st cit.:* 1732 Fuller, *Gnomologia. 20c. coll.:* Stevenson 1249:12.
SEE ALSO Sudden POWER is apt to be insolent, sudden liberty saucy; that behaves best which has grown gradually.

inspiration 1. Inspiration for writing is mostly the application of the seat of pants to the seat of the chair. *Rec. dist.:* N.Y., S.C. *1st cit.:* US1942 Rich, *We Took to the Woods. 20c. coll.:* Stevenson 1250:1.

2. Three-fourths of inspiration is perspiration. *Vars.:* **(a)** Inspiration is nine-tenths perspiration. **(b)** Inspiration is perspiration. **(c)** Inspiration is three parts perspiration. *Rec. dist.:* Kans., Ont.

SEE ALSO GENIUS is one percent inspiration, ninety-nine percent perspiration.

inspire SEE Good ACTIONS give strength to ourselves and inspire good actions in others.

institution An institution is the lengthened shadow of one man. *Var.:* Institutions are the lengthened shadow of one man. *Rec. dist.:* N.Y.
SEE ALSO MARRIAGE is an institution for the blind.

instruct The things which hurt, instruct. *Var.:* What hurts us instructs us. *Rec. dist.:* Ind., N.C., Ont. *1st cit.:* US1744 Franklin, *PRAlmanac. 20c. coll.:* Stevenson 724:6.

instructed SEE MEN seek less to be instructed than applauded.

instruction 1. Good instruction is better than riches. *Rec. dist.:* N.Y.

2. Hear instruction and be wise and refuse it not. *Rec. dist.:* N.Y.
SEE ALSO DEMONSTRATION is the best mode of instruction. / FOOLS despise wisdom and instruction. / POVERTY and shame shall be to him that refuses instructions, but he that regards reproof shall be honored. / A wise SON hears his father's instructions.

instructor The grand instructor is time. *Rec. dist.:* Ont. *1st cit.:* 1799 Burke, Letter to Sir H. Langrishe, 26 May. *20c. coll.:* Stevenson 2318:7.

insult 1. Don't add insult to injury. *Rec. dist.:* Ill., N.C., Ont., Wis. *1st cit.:* 1748 Moore, *The Foundling;* US1775 Lee, *Naval Documents. 20c. coll.:* ODEP 405, Whiting 234, Stevenson 1251:1, T&W 200, Whiting(MP) 338.

2. He who puts up with insult invites injury. *Rec. dist.:* Ont.

3. Insult begets insult as bugs beget bugs. *Rec. dist.:* Ill.

4. Insults and affronts are innocent where men are worthless. *Rec. dist.:* Miss.
SEE ALSO An INJURY is sooner forgotten than an insult.

integrity 1. A little integrity is better than any career. *Rec. dist.:* N.Y., S.C. *1st cit.:*

US1860 Emerson, "Behavior" in *Conduct of Life*. **20c. coll.:** Stevenson 1156:16.

2. Integrity is praised and starves. ***Rec. dist.:*** Ill.

3. Integrity is the best mantle. ***Rec. dist.:*** Mich.
SEE ALSO CALAMITY and prosperity are the touchstones of integrity.

intellect Intellect is invisible to the man who has none. ***Rec. dist.:*** Ill.

intelligence **1.** A man shall be commended according to his intelligence; but he that is of a distorted understanding shall be despised. ***Rec. dist.:*** N.Y.

2. If you don't claim too much intelligence, people will give you credit for more than you have. ***Rec. dist.:*** N.Y.

3. In a world of fools, intelligence is a fatal handicap. ***Rec. dist.:*** Ill.

4. Intelligence is like a river: the deeper it is, the less noise it makes. ***Rec. dist.:*** Kans.

5. Intelligence is worth more than richness. ***Rec. dist.:*** Fla.

6. Intelligence seeks its own level. ***Rec. dist.:*** Oreg.

7. Never underestimate the intelligence of your enemy. ***Rec. dist.:*** W.Va.

8. The intelligence of the average individual reaches its lowest ebb when he enters a railroad station. ***Rec. dist.:*** Ind.

intelligent An intelligent person is one who knows when to keep his mouth shut. ***Rec. dist.:*** Miss.

intemperance In the current of life, beware of the gulf of intemperance. ***Rec. dist.:*** Mich.

intent SEE A TRUTH that's told with bad intent beats all the lies you can invent.

intention **1.** A good intention clothes itself with sudden power. ***Rec. dist.:*** Ont.

2. Good intentions will not justify evil actions. ***Rec. dist.:*** Mich.

3. Intentions as well as actions must be good to be acceptable. ***Rec. dist.:*** Mich. **1st cit.:** 1841 Lane, *Thousand and One Nights.* **20c. coll.:** Stevenson 1252:8.

4. Live up to your good intentions and put the devil out of business. ***Rec. dist.:*** Ky.

5. The intention denominates the action. ***Rec. dist.:*** Mich. **1st cit.:** 1841 Lane, *Thousand and One Nights.* **20c. coll.:** Stevenson 1252:8.

6. To buy something with the intention of not paying for it is as bad as to steal it. ***Rec. dist.:*** N.C.
SEE ALSO It is not the ACTION but the intention that is good or bad. / ACTS indicate intentions. / The road to HELL is paved with good intentions.

interest *(concern)* **1.** Everyone speaks for his own interest. ***Rec. dist.:*** Ont. **1st cit.:** US1948 Stevenson, *Home Book of Proverbs.* **20c. coll.:** Stevenson 2064:12.

2. He who makes an idol of his interest makes a martyr of his integrity. ***Rec. dist.:*** Mich.

3. Interest blinds some people, enlightens others. ***Rec. dist.:*** N.Y., S.C. **1st cit.:** US1745 Franklin, *PRAlmanac.* **20c. coll.:** Stevenson 2064:5.

4. It is in his own interest that the cat purrs. ***Rec. dist.:*** Wis.

5. When interest is lost, memory is lost. ***Rec. dist.:*** N.Y.

6. Would you persuade, speak of interest, not of reason. ***Rec. dist.:*** N.Y., S.C.
SEE ALSO COURTESY pays compound interest. / WORRY is the interest we pay on trouble before it is due.

interest *(money)* **1.** Interest runs on while you sleep. ***Rec. dist.:*** Miss.

2. Many a man has risen above principle for the sake of interest. ***Rec. dist.:*** Ohio.

3. They who borrow trouble must pay a high rate of interest. ***Rec. dist.:*** Ont.
SEE ALSO An INVESTMENT in knowledge pays the best interest. / 'Tis against some men's PRINCIPLE to pay interest, and seems against others' interest to pay the principal.

interested Be interested and you will be interesting. ***Rec. dist.:*** Ohio.

interfere Never interfere with nothin' that don't bother you. ***Rec. dist.:*** N.Y.

SEE ALSO If LOVE interferes with your business, quit your business.

interior SEE A YARD is an index to the interior of the house.

intimacy 1. Intimacy breeds contempt. *Rec. dist.:* Ind., N.Y.

2. Intimacy has been the course of the deadliest enemy. *Rec. dist.:* Mich.

intimate Make one in a thousand an intimate. *Rec. dist.:* Ont.

intolerable There is nothing so intolerable as a fortunate fool. *Rec. dist.:* Ill.

intolerance Intolerance is the child of ignorance. *Rec. dist.:* Ill.

intoxication 1. Intoxication is a temporary madness. *Rec. dist.:* Ill.

2. Intoxication is not the wine's fault, but the man's. *Rec. dist.:* Ind.

invent SEE MAN is greater than the tools he invents.

invention 1. Invention breeds invention. *Rec. dist.:* N.Y., S.C. *1st cit.:* US1870 Emerson, "Work and Days" in *Society and Solitude. 20c. coll.:* Stevenson 1253:3.

2. One of the greatest labor-saving inventions of today is tomorrow. *Rec. dist.:* Ill.

SEE ALSO ANGER warms the invention but overheats the oven. / NECESSITY is the mother of invention. / POVERTY is the mother of invention.

inventor SEE FEAR is a great inventor.

investment 1. A good investment is the time spent in the Lord's house. *Rec. dist.:* N.C.

2. An investment in knowledge pays the best interest. *Rec. dist.:* N.Y., S.C.

3. Goodness is the only investment that never fails. *Rec. dist.:* N.Y., S.C.

4. The best investment for income is honesty. *Rec. dist.:* Minn.

SEE ALSO EDUCATION is an investment never to be lost nor removed. / Hard WORK is the best investment a man can make.

invincible Invincible in peace and invisible in war. *Rec. dist.:* N.Y., S.C.

invisible SEE INVINCIBLE in peace and invisible in war.

invite SEE BUSINESS goes where it is invited and stays where it is well treated. / The HOLE invites the thief. / A careless WATCH invites the vigilant foe.

inward SEE The outward FORMS the inward man reveal.

inwardly As we are inwardly, so shall we appear outwardly. *Rec. dist.:* N.Y., S.C.

Irish Nothing's too good for the Irish. *Rec. dist.:* Ohio.

iron 1. Don't have too many irons in the fire. *Vars.:* (a) Don't put too many irons in the fire. (b) If you have too many irons in the fire, some of them will burn. (c) Too many irons in the fire. (d) Too many irons in the fire to tend to one. *Rec. dist.:* Calif., Ill., Ky. *1st cit.:* 1549 Paget, *Letter to Somerset;* US1753 Collinson in *Papers of Benjamin Franklin,* ed. Labaree (1959). *20c. coll.:* ODEP 509, Whiting 235, Stevenson 1255:4, T&W 201, Whiting(MP) 339.

2. Iron cuts iron. *Rec. dist.:* Ont. *1st cit.:* 1545 Taverner, *Proverbs of Erasmus. 20c. coll.:* ODEP 406, Stevenson 1255:5.

3. Iron sharpens iron. *Rec. dist.:* R.I. *1st cit.:* 1545 Taverner, *Proverbs of Erasmus;* US1805 William Plumer's *Memorandum of Proceedings in Senate 1803–1807,* ed. Brown (1923). *20c. coll.:* ODEP 406, Whiting 235, Stevenson 1255:5.

4. Strike while the iron is hot. *Vars.:* (a) Beat the iron while it is hot. (b) Forge the iron while it is hot. (c) Not only strike while the iron is hot, but make it hot by striking. (d) Strike when the iron is the hottest. (e) When the iron is hot, it's time to strike. *Rec. dist.:* U.S., Can. *1st cit.:* ca1386 Chaucer, *Tale of Melibee;* US1682 James Claypoole's *Letter Book,* ed. Balderston (1967). *20c. coll.:* CODP 215, Whiting 235, ODEP 781, Stevenson 1256:1, T&W 201, Whiting(MP) 338.

SEE ALSO GOLD and iron are good to buy gold and iron. / In HAPPINESS, iron is bright; in sadness, gold is dull. / REEDS will bend, but iron will not.

is It is just as is and ain't no is-er. *Vars.:* (a) That that is, is. (b) That that is, is; that that is not, is not; that that is, is not that that is not;

that that is not, is not that that is. **Rec. dist.:** Ky., Mich., Tenn.

island SEE The larger the island of KNOWLEDGE, the longer the shoreline of wonder.

isolation Isolation means abolishment. **Rec. dist.:** Kans.

issue SEE Plain DEALING is dead, and died without issue.

itch *(n.)* The itch of pleasure does not itch at all. **Rec. dist.:** Ont.

SEE *ALSO* Let's keep this a COUNTRY where every man is entitled to scratch his own itch.

itch *(v.)* **1.** He who itches for something seldom scratches for it. **Rec. dist.:** Ohio.

2. If you itch for something, scratch for it. **Rec. dist.:** Ky.

SEE *ALSO* Each ORGANISM knows best where it itches. / SCRATCH where it itches.

itching SEE A SORROW is an itching place which is made worse by scratching.

J

Jack 1. A bad Jack may have a bad Jill. *Vars.:* (a) A good Jack makes a good Jill. (b) There is always a Jill as bad as a Jack. *Rec. dist.:* N.J. *1st cit.:* 1732 Fuller, *Gnomologia*. *20c. coll.:* Stevenson 1262:8.

2. For every Jack there is a Jill. *Vars.:* (a) Each Jack shall have his Jill. (b) Every Jack has his Jill. (c) Every Jack has his Jill; if one won't, another will. (d) Every Jack has Jill. (e) Every Jack must have his Jill. (f) Every Jack must have his Jill. Like will to like. *Rec. dist.:* U.S., Can. *1st cit.:* 1594 Shakespeare, *Love's Labour's Lost. 20c. coll.:* Stevenson 1263:1, *ODEP* 407, *CODP* 122.

3. Jack of all trades and master of none. *Vars.:* (a) A Jack of many trades makes a master of none. (b) Better be master of one than Jack of all trades. (c) Better master of one than Jack of all trades. (d) Jack of all trades an' good at none. *Rec. dist.:* U.S., Can. *1st cit.:* 1732 Fuller, *Gnomologia;* US1721 Buckingham, *Specimens of Newspaper Literature. 20c. coll.:* Stevenson 1259:1, Whiting 237, *ODEP* 408, T&W 202, Whiting(*MP*) 341.

4. Jack's as good as his master. *Rec. dist.:* Ont., Wis. *1st cit.:* ca1790 Dibdin, *The Blind Sailor;* US1931 Arlington, *Through. 20c. coll.:* Stevenson 1259:5, *ODEP* 408, *CODP* 122, Whiting(*MP*) 340.

5. There's a Jack for every Jill. *Vars.:* (a) Every Jill has a Jack. (b) There's a Jack for every Jane. (c) There's a Jack for every Jean. (d) There's a Jack for every Jenny. *Rec. dist.:* Ohio, Ont., Wis. *1st cit.:* US1855 Hammett, *Wonderful Adventures of Captain Priest. 20c. coll.:* T&W 202, Whiting(*MP*) 341.

6. There's never a Jack without a Jill. *Vars.:* (a) There's nae so simple a Jack but there's just as simple a Jenny. (b) There's never a Jack but there's a Jill. (c) There's never a Jack but what there's a Jill; if one won't, the other will. (d) There's never a Jennie but there's a Johnny. *Rec. dist.:* U.S., Can. *1st cit.:* 1738 Swift, *Collection of Genteel and Ingenious Conversation;* US1721 "The Little-Compton Scourge" in *New-England Courant. 20c. coll.: ODEP* 408, Whiting 237.

SEE ALSO All WORK and no play makes Jack a dull boy.

jackal A jackal gone on a pilgrimage is incredible news. *Rec. dist.:* Ill.

jackass 1. A jackass makes no progress when he's kicking. *Rec. dist.:* N.Y.

2. Any jackass can make money; it takes a wise man to keep it. *Rec. dist.:* N.Y.

SEE ALSO The BRAYING of a jackass never reaches heaven. / CONCEIT is the self satisfaction of a jackass.

jackdaw A jackdaw is ever found near to a jackdaw. *Rec. dist.:* Ill.

jade Do not wish to be rare like jade or common like stone. *Rec. dist.:* Ohio.

jail He who waits for something to turn up is likely to turn up in jail. *Rec. dist.:* N.Y.

James As James treats God, so God treats James. *Rec. dist.:* N.Y., S.C.

January Never shut out the January sun. *Rec. dist.:* Ont.

Jap A good Jap is a dead Jap. *Var.:* Only good Jap is a dead one. *Rec. dist.:* N.C., Ohio.

jar Women's jars breed men's wars. *Rec. dist.:* Ill. *1st cit.:* US1948 Stevenson, *Home Book of Proverbs. 20c. coll.:* Stevenson 2569:1.

jaundiced SEE EVERYTHING looks blue to the jaundiced eye.

jawbone The jawbone does the mischief. *Rec. dist.:* Ont.

jaybirds Jaybirds don't rob their own nests. *Var.:* Jaybird don't rob his own nes'. *Rec. dist.:* N.J., N.Y., S.C. *1st cit.:* 1818 Scott, *Rob Roy. 20c. coll.:* Stevenson 179:5.

jealous A loving man is always a jealous man. *Rec. dist.:* Ill.

SEE ALSO BEGGAR is jealous of beggar. / He that is conscious of a STINK in his breeches is jealous of every wrinkle in another's nose.

jealousy **1.** Jealousy is a green-eyed monster. *Var.:* Jealousy is a green-eyed monster that feeds on itself. *Rec. dist.:* Ill., N.J. *1st cit.:* 1597 Shakespeare, *Merchant of Venice.* *20c. coll.:* Stevenson 1264:13.

2. Jealousy is a proof of self-love. *Rec. dist.:* Mich. *1st cit.:* US1948 Stevenson, *Home Book of Proverbs.* *20c. coll.:* Stevenson 1264:3.

3. Jealousy leads to folly and injustice. *Rec. dist.:* Ont.

4. Without jealousy, there is no love. *Var.:* Love is never without jealousy. *Rec. dist.:* Ind. *1st cit.:* 1576 Pettie, *Petite Palace of Pleasure;* US1967 McGerr, *Murder.* *20c. coll.:* ODEP 491, Stevenson 1264:8, Whiting(MP) 343.

SEE ALSO Better to have a HUSBAND without love than with jealousy. / LOVE knows no jealousy.

Jehovah Jehovah helps the ones that help themselves. *Rec. dist.:* N.Y., S.C.

jelly SEE CRAB APPLES make good jelly, too.

jest (*n.*) **1.** A jest is no argument, and loud laughter no demonstration. *Rec. dist.:* Mich.

2. A jest is received in good spirit; a jeer breeds ill will. *Rec. dist.:* Ind.

3. A jest's prosperity lies in the ear of him that hears it, never in the tongue of him that makes it. *Rec. dist.:* Minn. *1st cit.:* 1594 Shakespeare, *Love's Labour's Lost.* *20c. coll.:* Stevenson 1268:6.

4. Better lose a jest than a friend. *Rec. dist.:* Ill., Tex. *1st cit.:* 1589 Harvey, *Pierce's Supererogation* in *Works,* ed. Gros. *20c. coll.:* ODEP 54.

5. Half in jest, whole in earnest. *Var.:* Half joking, whole earnest. *Rec. dist.:* Minn.

6. Jests, like sweetmeats, often have sour sauce. *Rec. dist.:* Ont.

7. The worst jests are the true ones. *Var.:* There is no worse jest than a true one. *Rec. dist.:* Ill., Kans. *1st cit.:* 1659 Howell, *Paroimiografia;* USca1665 *Rosburghe Ballads.* *20c. coll.:* ODEP 841, Stevenson 1267:5.

8. True jests breed bad blood. *Rec. dist.:* Ill. *1st cit.:* 1732 Fuller, *Gnomologia.* *20c. coll.:* Stevenson 1266:10.

9. When your jest is at its best, let it rest. *Rec. dist.:* Ill. *1st cit.:* 1640 Herbert, *Outlandish Proverbs (Jacula Prudentum)* in *Works,* ed. Hutchinson (1941). *20c. coll.:* ODEP 452, Stevenson 1267:2, *CODP* 230.

SEE ALSO He makes a FOE who makes a jest. / LIFE is a jest. / There's many a true WORD said in jest.

jest (*v.*) **1.** Do not jest in serious matters. *Rec. dist.:* N.Y., S.C. *1st cit.:* USca1700 Hubbard, *General History of New England.* *20c. coll.:* Whiting 239.

2. Jest with your equals: a fool can't take a joke. *Rec. dist.:* Ill.

3. You cannot jest an enemy into a friend, but you can jest a friend into an enemy. *Rec. dist.:* Ill.

jester **1.** A common jester may have wit but not wisdom. *Rec. dist.:* Wis.

2. Jesters do oft prove prophets. *Rec. dist.:* Ont. *1st cit.:* 1605 Shakespeare, *King Lear.* *20c. coll.:* ODEP 841, Stevenson 1267:5.

3. Men may be pleased with a jester, but they never esteem him. *Rec. dist.:* Mich.

4. The truest jester sounds worst in guilty ears. *Rec. dist.:* Mich. *1st cit.:* 1670 Ray, *English Proverbs.* *20c. coll.:* Stevenson 1265:10.

jesting (*n.*) **1.** Clumsy jesting is no joke. *Rec. dist.:* Ont.

2. Jesting often indicates a want of understanding. *Rec. dist.:* Mich.

jesting (*adj.*) SEE Jesting LIES bring serious sorrows.

Jew A Jew can make a living by selling shoestrings. *Rec. dist.:* N.C.

jewel SEE ADVERSITY is the diamond dust heaven polishes its jewels with. / LOVE is the jewel that wins the world. / SILENCE is a beautiful jewel for a woman. / SILENCE is a rare jewel. / A VIRTUOUS woman is rarer than a precious jewel.

Jill SEE For every JACK there is a Jill.

jingle The jingle of the guinea heals the hurt that honor feels. *Rec. dist.:* Ill.

job 1. A good mother's job does not end in the house. *Rec. dist.:* Ont.

2. A job is an uncomfortable thing to be down on. *Rec. dist.:* Calif., Colo.

3. A job started right is a job half done. *Vars.:* **(a)** A job started is a job half done. **(b)** A job well begun is half done. *Rec. dist.:* Kans., Maine, N.Y.

4. A job well done is worth two half done. *Rec. dist.:* Ind.

5. A job worth doing is worth doing well. *Vars.:* **(a)** A job that is worth doing is worth doing well. **(b)** A job worth doing is a job worth doing well. **(c)** If a job's worth doing, it's worth doing right. *Rec. dist.:* U.S., Can. *1st cit.:* 1746 Chesterfield, Letter, 9 Oct., in *Letters to His Son* (1932); US1931 Jacobs, *Snug.* *20c. coll.:* ODEP 921, CODP 222, Whiting(MP) 619.

6. A man ain't no bigger than the job it takes to give him a swell head. *Rec. dist.:* U.S., Can.

7. Any man with nothing to do has a hard job. *Rec. dist.:* Ky.

8. Better to fall down on the job than to lie down. *Rec. dist.:* Minn.

9. Don't get down on your job because you are not quite up to it. *Rec. dist.:* Minn.

10. Handle the hardest job first. *Rec. dist.:* Ohio.

11. If you want a job well done, give it to a busy man. *Rec. dist.:* Colo.

12. If you wish the job was through, do it now. *Rec. dist.:* Minn.

13. It's a poor job that can't afford one boss. *Rec. dist.:* Kans., Maine, Ohio, Vt.

14. Let us make the best of a bad job. *Rec. dist.:* Wis.

15. Make your job important; it will return the favor. *Rec. dist.:* N.Y.

16. Soft jobs make soft people. *Rec. dist.:* Calif.

17. Start a job on Friday and it will never be finished. *Rec. dist.:* Ont.

18. Stick to your own job. *Rec. dist.:* N.Y., S.C.

19. The hardest job a child faces is that of learning manners without seeing any. *Rec. dist.:* Ill.

20. The hardest job is no job. *Var.:* Doing nothing is the most tiresome job in the world. *Rec. dist.:* N.Y.

21. The hardest job to find is an easy job. *Rec. dist.:* Ohio.

22. The hardest part of the job is the beginning. *Rec. dist.:* Oreg.

23. The other fellow's job is always easier. *Rec. dist.:* Minn.

24. There may be luck in getting a good job, but there's no luck in keeping it. *Rec. dist.:* N.J.

25. Two-thirds of the job is to please the master. *Rec. dist.:* Minn.

26. When the job is well done, you can hang up the hammer. *Rec. dist.:* Ind.

SEE ALSO You can't judge a CAR by its paint job. / SATISFACTION is a result of a job well done. / Don't waste five-dollar TIME on a five-cent job.

Johnny 1. Johnny is as Johnny does. *Rec. dist.:* Wis.

2. What Johnny will not teach himself, Johnny will never learn. *Rec. dist.:* Ont.

join SEE If you can't LICK 'em, jine 'em.

joke *(n.)* 1. A joke never gains over an enemy but often loses a friend. *Rec. dist.:* Mich., Tex., Vt., Wis. *1st cit.:* 1732 Fuller, *Gnomologia.* *20c. coll.:* Stevenson 1268:15.

2. A rich man's joke is always funny. *Rec. dist.:* Minn.

3. Don't carry a joke too far. *Rec. dist.:* Ill. *1st cit.:* US1849 Mayo, *Kaloolah.* *20c. coll.:* T&W 205.

4. Don't tell all of your jokes on one program. *Rec. dist.:* Ohio.

5. He who laughs last just got the joke. *Rec. dist.:* Ohio.

SEE ALSO Clumsy JESTING is no joke. / TRUTH is found in strange places and often slumbers even in a joke.

joke *(v.)* SEE The WEAK may be joked out of everything but their weakness.

joking It's past joking when the head's off. *Rec. dist.:* Ill.

jolly SEE FAT people are jolly people.

journey **1.** A journey of a thousand miles begins with one step. *Var.:* A journey of a thousand miles begins from but a single step. *Rec. dist.:* U.S., Can. *1st cit.:* US1948 Stevenson, *Home Book of Proverbs.* *20c. coll.:* Stevenson 1035:15.

2. In a long journey and a small inn, one knows one's company. *Rec. dist.:* Ind.

3. Journey's end is lover's meeting. *Rec. dist.:* Minn. *1st cit.:* 1601 Shakespeare, *Twelfth Night.* *20c. coll.:* Stevenson 1273:9.

4. The best of the journey is getting home. *Rec. dist.:* Ont.

joy **1.** A joy that's shared is a joy made double. *Rec. dist.:* Okla. *1st cit.:* US1948 Stevenson, *Home Book of Proverbs.* *20c. coll.:* Stevenson 1276:6.

2. After joy comes sorrow. *Rec. dist.:* N.Y. *1st cit.:* 1640 Cervantes, *Exemplary Novels,* tr. Mabbe. *20c. coll.:* Stevenson 1275:7.

3. All the joys in the world can't take one gray hair out of our heads. *Rec. dist.:* Ill.

4. Easy got, easy gain: short joy, long pain. *Rec. dist.:* Miss.

5. Gild a joy and heal a pain. *Rec. dist.:* Ont.

6. Joy and sorrow are next-door neighbors. *Rec. dist.:* Ohio. *1st cit.:* 1869 Henderson, *Latin Proverbs.* *20c. coll.:* Stevenson 1275:7.

7. Joy is kin to sorrow. *Rec. dist.:* N.C.

8. Joy is the best wine. *Rec. dist.:* Ont.

9. Joy which we cannot share with others is only half enjoyed. *Rec. dist.:* Minn.

10. Joys are our wings; our sorrows, our spurs. *Rec. dist.:* Miss.

11. Let your joys be many and your sorrows be few. *Rec. dist.:* R.I.

12. No joy without annoy. *Vars.:* **(a)** There is no joy without affliction. **(b)** There is no joy without alloy. **(c)** There's no joy without alloy: grief is mixed with the keenest bliss. *Rec. dist.:* Minn., N.Y., Oreg., S.C. *1st cit.:* 1592 Delamothe, *Treasury of French Tongue.* *20c. coll.:* ODEP 414, Stevenson 1275:7.

13. One inch of joy surmounts of grief a span, because to laugh is proper to the man. *Rec. dist.:* Wis.

14. Our greatest joys and our greatest sorrows grow on the same vine. *Rec. dist.:* Ont.

15. Shared joys are doubled; shared sorrows are halved. *Var.:* Shared pleasures are doubled; shared griefs are halved. *Rec. dist.:* Ill.

16. Taste the joy that springs from labor. *Rec. dist.:* N.Y., S.C.

17. The future joy makes the past and the present bearable. *Rec. dist.:* Ill.

18. There's more joy in anticipation than in realization. *Rec. dist.:* Miss.

19. There's no joy in anything unless we share it. *Rec. dist.:* Ill.

20. Today's joys may be tomorrow's woes. *Rec. dist.:* N.C.

21. When joy is in the parlor, sorrow is at the kitchen sink. *Rec. dist.:* Ill.

22. Who pleasure gives shall joy receive. *Rec. dist.:* N.Y., S.C.

SEE ALSO ACTION is our chief joy. / If you do ILL, the joy fades, not the pains; if well, the pain does fade, the joy remains. / SORROW remains when joy is but a blast. / SORROWS remembered sweeten present joy. / They that sow in TEARS shall reap in joy. / WEEPING may endure for a night, but joy comes in the morning.

judge *(n.)* **1.** An upright judge has more regard for justice than for man. *Rec. dist.:* Mich.

2. An upright judge regards the law and disregards the lawyers and litigants. *Rec. dist.:* Ill.

3. Judges should have two ears, both alike. *Rec. dist.:* Ill.

4. The best judge knows the least. *Rec. dist.:* Ill.

5. The judge is condemned when the guilty

man is acquitted. *Rec. dist.:* Ont. *1st cit.:* 1732 Fuller, *Gnomologia. 20c. coll.:* Stevenson 1278:6.

6. When you buy judges someone sells justice. *Rec. dist.:* N.Y.

SEE ALSO A BLIND man is no judge of colors.

judge *(v.)* **1.** Don't judge a man by his opinion of himself. *Rec. dist.:* Miss.

2. Don't judge a man by the coat he wears. *Rec. dist.:* Ill., Ky., Tenn.

3. Don't judge others by yourself. *Vars.:* **(a)** Don't judge other people by yourself. **(b)** You can't judge others by yourself. *Rec. dist.:* U.S., Can.

4. Few men would live if all were judged justly. *Rec. dist.:* Ill.

5. He judges best who thinks least. *Rec. dist.:* Calif.

6. He who judges others condemns himself. *Var.:* When you judge others, you condemn yourself. *Rec. dist.:* Ill., N.Y., S.C.

7. If you judge your own case you are judged by a fool. *Rec. dist.:* Ill.

8. Judge a man by his deeds, not by his words. *Rec. dist.:* N.Y.

9. Judge a man by what he does, not by what he says. *Rec. dist.:* N.Y., Okla., S.C.

10. Judge not of men or things at first sight. *Rec. dist.:* Ill.

11. Judge not that you be not judged. *Vars.:* **(a)** Judge and you shall be judged. **(b)** Judge not and you shall not be judged. **(c)** Judge not and you won't be judged. **(d)** Judge not lest you be judged. **(e)** Judge not that you be not judged. **(f)** Judge not that you may not be judged. *Rec. dist.:* U.S., Can. *1st cit.:* 1481 Caxton, *Reynard. 20c. coll.:* CODP 123, Stevenson 1279:3.

12. Judge others by what you do. *Rec. dist.:* N.Y.

13. Judge well yourself before you criticize. *Rec. dist.:* N.Y.

14. Judge yourself by the friends you have. *Var.:* You are judged by the company you keep. *Rec. dist.:* Ind.

15. Never judge before you see. *Rec. dist.:* Ont.

16. We are judged by how we look as well as how we act. *Rec. dist.:* N.C.

17. We judge others by their acts, but ourselves by our intentions. *Rec. dist.:* N.C.

18. You are judged not by what you have but by what you do with that you have. *Var.:* You are judged not by what you have but by what you are. *Rec. dist.:* N.C.

SEE ALSO Judge not according to APPEARANCES. / Never judge a work of ART by its defects. / You can't judge a BOOK by its cover. / Judge a DUTCHMAN by what he means, not by what he says. / Gently to HEAR, kindly to judge. / To really UNDERSTAND a man we must judge him in misfortune.

judgment **1.** Correct judgment is the mind's most resplendent ornament. *Rec. dist.:* Mich.

2. When the judgment is weak, the prejudice is strong. *Rec. dist.:* Ill., N.Y. *1st cit.:* 1769 O'Hara, *Midas. 20c. coll.:* Stevenson 1872:11.

SEE ALSO All complain for want of MEMORY, but none for want of judgment. / Don't let another's OPINION sway your judgment.

jug **1.** The jug goes to the well until it breaks. *Var.:* Many a jug goes to the well, but sometimes gets broken. *Rec. dist.:* N.J., Ont. *Infm.:* Cf. pitcher.

2. The less there is in a jug, the more noise it makes coming out. *Rec. dist.:* Ind., Kans.

3. Whether the stone bumps the jug or the jug bumps the stone, it is bad for the jug. *Rec. dist.:* N.J.

SEE ALSO A DRUNKARD puts ten times more in his jug than he gets out of it. / LIQUOR talks aloud when it gets loose from the jug.

juice *SEE* The blacker the BERRY, the sweeter the juice.

jump *(n.) SEE* You can't tell a FROG by the size of his jump.

jump *(v.)* **1.** Don't jump from the frying pan into the fire. *Rec. dist.:* U.S., Can. *1st cit.:* 1528 More, *Works;* US1681 Claypoole, *Letter Book. 20c. coll.:* ODEP 292, Stevenson 814:1, Whiting 170, Whiting(MP) 244.

2. It doesn't matter how high you jump provided you walk straight when you get down. *Rec. dist.:* N.C.

3. Jump when the wave is on the swell. *Rec. dist.:* N.Y.

SEE ALSO A man once BITTEN by a snake will jump at the sight of a rope in his path. / It is only the excited FISH that jumps at the lure. / It's easy to make a FROG jump into water when that's what he wants to do. / If the GOAT would not jump around, she wouldn't break her leg. / You can't tell how far a RABBIT can jump by the length of its ears. / Never say "WHOOPEE" before you jump.

jury 1. Every man is entitled to be judged by a jury of his peers. *Rec. dist.:* Ill., Miss.

2. Many a wretch has been hanged because the jury men didn't want to miss their supper. *Rec. dist.:* Ill.

SEE ALSO When BEAUTY is at the bar, blind men make the best jury. / If the DEFENDANT is silent the jury will think him guilty.

just 1. Be just and fear not. *Rec. dist.:* Ill. *1st cit.:* 1612 Shakespeare, *Henry VIII.* *20c. coll.:* Stevenson 160:13.

2. Be just before you are generous. *Rec. dist.:* Ohio. *1st cit.:* 1744 Haywood, *The Female Spectator;* US1826 Vans, *Codman Letters.* *20c. coll.:* Stevenson 1289:2, Whiting 242, ODEP 416, CODP 123, Whiting(MP) 346.

3. Be just in your dealings and trust to providence for aid in advancement. *Rec. dist.:* Minn.

4. Be just to all, but trust not all. *Var.:* Be just to all, but never trust all. *Rec. dist.:* Ind., N.Y., Ohio. *1st cit.:* 1855 Bohn, *Handbook of Proverbs.* *20c. coll.:* Stevenson 1283:11.

5. It rains on the just and on the unjust. *Vars.:* **(a)** It rains on the unjust in fodder-pulling time. **(b)** Rain falls on the just and unjust alike. **(c)** The rain falls on the just and the unjust. **(d)** The sun shines on the just and the unjust. *Rec. dist.:* Miss., Ohio, Ont. *1st cit.:* 1522 Latimer, *Sermon;* US1948 Stevenson, *Home Book of Proverbs.* *20c. coll.:* ODEP 787, Stevenson 1284:9.

SEE ALSO HEAR and be just. / LIFE is just; it will give us all we earn. / The TONGUE of the just is a choice silver; the heart of the wicked is little worth.

justice 1. Do justice; love mercy; practice humility. *Rec. dist.:* Mich.

2. If you want justice for yourself, be just to others. *Rec. dist.:* Ill.

3. Justice delayed is justice denied. *Var.:* Justice is not justice if long delayed. *Rec. dist.:* N.J., Ont.

4. Justice exalts a nation. *Rec. dist.:* Minn.

5. Justice goes out the window when profit comes in. *Rec. dist.:* Ill., Miss.

6. Justice has a nose of putty—it is easily broken. *Rec. dist.:* Miss.

7. Justice is blind. *Rec. dist.:* Nebr., N.Y. *1st cit.:* 1663 Dryden, *The Wild Gallant;* US1782 *Correspondence of John Jay,* ed. Johnston (1890–93). *20c. coll.:* Stevenson 1287:5, Whiting 242, Whiting(MP) 346.

8. Let justice be done though the heavens fall. *Rec. dist.:* Ill., Ont. *1st cit.:* 1602 Watson, *A Decacordon of Ten Quodlibeticall Questions Concerning Religion and State.* *20c. coll.:* Stevenson 1286:2.

9. One man's justice is another man's injustice; one man's beauty another man's ugliness; one man's wisdom another's folly. *Rec. dist.:* N.Y. *1st cit.:* US1837 *Works of Ralph Waldo Emerson,* ed. Cabot. *20c. coll.:* T&W 206.

10. The sword of justice has no scabbard. *Rec. dist.:* N.J.

11. To the strong is justice given. *Rec. dist.:* Ind.

12. We all love justice—at our neighbor's expense. *Rec. dist.:* Ill.

13. Who demands justice must administer justice. *Rec. dist.:* Ind.

14. You don't like justice when it is brought home to your own door step. *Rec. dist.:* Ill. *1st cit.:* 1640 Herbert, *Outlandish Proverbs (Jacula Prudentum)* in *Works,* ed. Hutchinson (1941). *20c. coll.:* Stevenson 1287:12, ODEP 416.

SEE ALSO An ounce of FAVOR goes further than a pound of justice. / GENEROSITY is the flower of justice.

justification **1.** The only justification for a business is the service it renders. *Rec. dist.:* Kans.

2. The only justification of rebellion is success. *Rec. dist.:* N.Y., S.C.

justify *SEE* Not to repent of a FAULT is to justify it. / One LIE does not justify another.

justly *SEE* Few men would live if all were JUDGED justly.

K

keen *See* A FENCE between makes friends more keen.

keep *See* Easy to keep the CASTLE that was never besieged. / One is known by the COMPANY he keeps. / Keep your own DOORSTEPS clean. / He's no FOOL who parts with what he cannot keep to get what he shall not lose. / If you want to keep a FRIEND, never borrow, never lend. / The best way to keep a FRIEND is not to give him away. / Make new FRIENDS but keep the old. / Those who betray their FRIENDS must not expect others to keep faith with them. / HOPE keeps a man from hanging and drowning himself. / He that can travel well afoot keeps a good HORSE. / Keep the LAW and keep from the law. / Keep your NOSE to the grindstone. / Keep yourself from the OPPORTUNITY and God will keep you from the sin. / Better keep PEACE than make peace. / Who will not keep a PENNY shall never have many. / Keep your POWDER dry. / A little SAND keeps you from slipping. / Praise the SEA, but keep on land. / Two can keep a SECRET if one is dead. / Keep your SHOP and your shop will keep you. / Keep your SOUL and your shop will keep you. / Keep the STAFF in your own hand. / One SWORD keeps another in its scabbard. / Keep your TEMPER: nobody else wants it. / Keep a THING seven years and it's bound to come in handy. / Keep your TONGUE within your teeth. / Great TREES keep down little ones. / WORK keeps you out of mischief. / You can't keep up with the WORLD by letting it roll by.

keeper *See* FINDERS keepers, losers weepers. / KINGS and bears often worry their keeper.

kept *See* A bad PROMISE is better broken than kept. / All PROMISES are either broken or kept.

kernel **1.** He that will eat the kernel must crack the nut. *Vars.:* **(a)** He that wants the kernel must crack the nut. **(b)** He that would eat the kernel must not complain of cracking the nuts. **(c)** He who would eat the kernel must crack the nut. *Rec. dist.:* Miss., N.Y., Ohio, Ont. *1st cit.:* ca1500 *Antiquarian Reper-*

tory (1809); US1788 *Papers of Thomas Jefferson,* ed. Boyd (1950). *20c. coll.:* ODEP 215, Whiting 243, Stevenson 2623:5.

2. He that will have the kernel must crack the shell. *Rec. dist.:* Okla., Tex. *1st cit.:* ca1500 in *Antiq. Repertory* (1809); US 1779 *Public Papers of George Clinton,* ed. Hastings (1899–1911). *20c. coll.:* ODEP 215, Whiting 243, Stevenson 394:2.

3. The sweetest kernel lies in the hard shell. *Var.:* The harder the nut, the sweeter the kernel. *Rec. dist.:* Ill., Ont.

See also The HUSK often tells what the kernel is.

kettle **1.** A kettle rattles most before it boils. *Rec. dist.:* Colo., N.Y.

2. A watched kettle never boils. *Var.:* If you watch the kettle, it will never boil. *Rec. dist.:* U.S. *Infm.:* Cf. pot. *1st cit.:* 1848 Gaskell, *Mary Barton;* US1940 Boothe, *Europe in Spring.* *20c. coll.:* ODEP 869, CODP 242, Whiting(MP) 507.

3. An empty kettle makes the most noise. *Rec. dist.:* Ind., N.Y., Ohio, Ont.

4. Every kettle has to sit on its own bottom. *Rec. dist.:* Ohio.

5. It's a dry kettle that has the most spouting. *Rec. dist.:* Ind.

6. No matter how black the kettle, there is always a lid to fit it. *Vars.:* **(a)** Every kettle has a lid. **(b)** Never a kettle so crooked but there was a lid to fit it. *Rec. dist.:* Kans., Ohio, Utah.

7. On an old kettle there isn't much to mend. *Rec. dist.:* Ont.

8. Remember the kettle: though up to the neck in hot water, it continues to sing. *Var.:* When in trouble, think of the kettle, which, though up to its neck in hot water, sings. *Rec. dist.:* Ont., Utah.

9. The kettle should not call the pot black. *Vars.:* **(a)** A kettle can't throw up black to the pot. **(b)** The kettle called the pot smutty. **(c)** The kettle can't call the skillet blackbottom.

(d) The kettle can't say to the pot, "you're black." **(e)** The pot can't call the kettle black ass. *Rec. dist.:* Ind., Ky., N.C., Ont., Pa. *1st cit.:* 1620 Cervantes, *Don Quixote,* tr. Shelton; US1807 Irving, *Salmagundi* in *Works of Washington Irving* (1873). *20c. coll.:* ODEP 421, Whiting 344, Stevenson 1840:14, Whiting(MP) 507.

10. The kettle's singing; 'twill soon be boiling. *Rec. dist.:* Miss., Ont.

key 1. A little key may unlock a box wherein lies a bunch of keys. *Rec. dist.:* Ill. *1st cit.:* US1950 Thompson, *Pointed Tower.* *20c. coll.:* Whiting(MP) 348.

2. All the keys hang not at one's girdle. *Rec. dist.:* Tex. *1st cit.:* ca1546 Heywood, *Dialogue of Proverbs,* ed. Habernicht (1963). *20c. coll.:* ODEP 421.

3. Silence is often the key to success. *Rec. dist.:* Ont.

4. The golden key opens every door. *Var.:* A silver key can open an iron lock. *Rec. dist.:* Ill. *1st cit.:* 1580 Lyly, *Euphues and His England.* *20c. coll.:* CODP 96, Stevenson 988:13.

5. The used key is always bright. *Vars.:* **(a)** A used key is the brightest. **(b)** Sloth, like rust, consumes faster than labor wears, while the used key is always bright. *Rec. dist.:* U.S. *1st cit.:* 1561 *Kitt Hath Lost Key* in *Extra Stationers' Co.,* ed. Collier; US1744 Franklin, *PRAlmanac.* *20c. coll.:* ODEP 857, Whiting 243, Stevenson 2411:5.

6. There's a key for every lock. *Rec. dist.:* Ill.

SEE ALSO A closed FIST is the lock of heaven, and the open hand is the key of mercy. / IDLENESS is the key of beggary. / KNOWLEDGE is a treasure, but practice is the key to it.

keyhole Look through a keyhole and your life will be sore. *Rec. dist.:* N.Y.

kick *(n.)* What many of us need most is a good vigorous kick in the seat of the can'ts. *Rec. dist.:* N.Y.

SEE ALSO A HINT is as good as a kick. / A good HORSE may be forgiven a kick. / A STAB in the back is worse than a kick in the face.

kick *(v.)* You needn't kick before you're spurred. *Var.:* Don't kick until you are spurred.

Rec. dist.: Miss., N.Y., Tex., Va. *1st cit.:* US1836 Longstreet, *Georgia Scenes* (1840). *20c. coll.:* T&W 208, Stevenson 1293:8.

SEE ALSO When a man is DOWN, don't kick him lower. / Don't overload GRATITUDE; if you do, she'll kick. / A dying HORSE can kick harder than a normal horse. / MULES don't kick according to rules.

kicked It's better to be kicked around than kicked about. *Rec. dist.:* Ohio.

SEE ALSO It is better to DIE kicking than to be kicked dying.

kicking *SEE* You can call a DOG without kicking him. / A HORSE can't pull while kicking.

kid *(n.)* *SEE* First GAME's a kid's game.

kid *(v.)* You can't kid the foolish. *Rec. dist.:* Ont.

kill There are more ways than one to kill a cat. *Vars.:* **(a)** There are more ways to kill a chicken than to kiss him to death. **(b)** There are more ways to kill a dog than by choking him on peanut butter. **(c)** There are more ways to kill a dog than hanging him. **(d)** There is more than one way to kill a bird. **(e)** There is more than one way to kill a cat besides choking it on apple butter. **(f)** There is more than one way to kill a cat besides soaking him in butter. **(g)** There's more than one way to kill a frog. **(h)** There's more ways than one to kill a dog. **(i)** There's more ways to kill a hen besides choking her. **(j)** There's more ways to kill a hound dog than to choke him to death on hot butter. **(k)** You can kill a hog more ways besides choking him on butter. *Rec. dist.:* U.S. *1st cit.:* 1678 Ray, *English Proverbs;* US1839 *John Smith's Letters,* ed. Smith. *20c. coll.:* ODEP 872, CODP 242, T&W 396, Stevenson 297:5, Whiting(MP) 670.

SEE ALSO ABSENCE kills a little love but makes the big ones grow. / ALMOST never killed a fly. / Heavy BURDENS kill little people, but they make great ones. / CURIOSITY killed the cat. / If the DOCTOR cures, the sun sees it; if he kills, the earth hides it. / To kill an old DOG you must hide your stick. / DOGS don't kill sheep at home. / GLUTTONY kills more than the sword. / Don't kill the GOOSE that lays the golden egg. / No one has ever been killed by KINDNESS. / A LOUSE not killed is sure to bite again. / The day you MARRY, it is either kill or cure. / NEGLECT kills injuries; revenge increases them. / One PAIN kills another. / PHYSICIANS kill more than they cure. / No one will kill SANTA CLAUS. / SYMPATHY killed a cat. / Kill TIME and time will kill you. / The best way to kill TIME is to work it to death. / Tell the TRUTH if it kills you.

killing SEE Killing TIME is not murder, it's suicide.

kin No one claims kin to the fortuneless age. *Rec. dist.:* Minn.

> SEE ALSO POVERTY has no kin.

kind *(n.)* **1.** Each kind attracts its own. *Rec. dist.:* N.Y.

2. It takes all kinds of people to make a world. *Var.:* It takes all sorts of people to make a world. *Rec. dist.:* Ill. *1st cit.:* 1620 Cervantes, *Don Quixote,* tr. Shelton; US1910 Phillpotts, *Tales.* *20c. coll.:* ODEP 11, Stevenson 2628:8, Whiting*(MP)* 583.

> SEE ALSO CAT after kind. / There are three kinds of PEOPLE: the wills, the won'ts, and the can'ts. / All PROGRESS of the best kind is slow. / There are two kinds of WOMEN: those who take what you are and those who take what you have.

kind *(adj.)* **1.** Be kind in all you do and say, that others may be kind to you. *Rec. dist.:* Ont.

2. Be kind to animals. *Rec. dist.:* Ill.

3. Be kind to one another. *Rec. dist.:* N.C. *1st cit.:* 1715 Watts, *Divine and Moral Songs for Children.* *20c. coll.:* Stevenson 2014:7.

4. It doesn't cost anything to be kind. *Var.:* Pleasant words are valued and do not cost much. *Rec. dist.:* N.C.

5. You never lose by being kind. *Rec. dist.:* Calif.

> SEE ALSO A kind FACE needs no bond. / Many a kind HEART beats under a rugged exterior. / A kind WORD goes a long way. / Kind WORDS never die. / Speak kind WORDS and you will hear kind answers. / A bad YEAR is kinder than the poor man's neighbor.

kindle SEE Behold what a FIRE a little matter kindles. / Kindle not a FIRE that you cannot extinguish. / The FIRE you kindle for your enemy often burns yourself more than him. / A little SPARK kindles a great fire. / Little STICKS kindle large fires.

kindled SEE WOOD half-burnt is easily kindled.

kindly SEE KNAVES and nettles are akin: stroke 'em kindly, yet they'll sting.

kindness **1.** A forced kindness deserves no thanks. *Rec. dist.:* U.S. *1st cit.:* 1732 Fuller, *Gnomologia.* *20c. coll.:* Stevenson 1297:1.

2. A kindness is never lost. *Var.:* A kindness is never wasted. *Rec. dist.:* Ill., N.Y., Ohio, Ont. *1st cit.:* US1948 Stevenson, *Home Book of Proverbs.* *20c. coll.:* Stevenson 1296:7.

3. A word of kindness is seldom spoken in vain. *Rec. dist.:* Ont. *1st cit.:* US1852 Cary, *Clovernook.* *20c. coll.:* T&W 412, Whiting*(MP)* 699.

4. An act of kindness is well repaid. *Rec. dist.:* N.C.

5. Be kind and gentle to those who are old, for kindness is dearer and better than gold. *Rec. dist.:* Minn.

6. He that has once done you a kindness will be more ready to do you another than he whom you yourself have obliged. *Rec. dist.:* N.Y.

7. He who plants kindness gathers joy. *Rec. dist.:* Ont.

8. Kindness always begets kindness. *Rec. dist.:* Miss., Ont. *1st cit.:* US1818 Faux, *Memorable Days in America.* *20c. coll.:* Whiting 244, Stevenson 1298:6.

9. Kindness always pays. *Rec. dist.:* N.Y.

10. Kindness brings happiness. *Rec. dist.:* Ont.

11. Kindness does more than violence. *Rec. dist.:* N.Y.

12. Kindness effects more than severity. *Rec. dist.:* Minn., Ont.

13. Kindness is a great peacemaker. *Rec. dist.:* Okla.

14. Kindness is greater than law. *Rec. dist.:*

Ind., Ont. *1st cit.:* US1875 Scarborough, *Chinese Proverbs. 20c. coll.:* Stevenson 1298:3.

15. Kindness is language which the deaf can hear and the blind can see. *Rec. dist.:* Ill. *1st cit.:* US1746 Franklin, *PRAlmanac. 20c. coll.:* Stevenson 1296:12.

16. Kindness is lost upon an ungrateful man. *Rec. dist.:* Miss., Ont.

17. Kindness is more binding than a loan. *Rec. dist.:* N.J.

18. Kindness is seldom thrown away, be it given to the highest or lowliest of creatures. *Rec. dist.:* Wis.

19. Kindness is stronger than force. *Rec. dist.:* Ill.

20. Kindness is the noblest weapon to conquer with. *Rec. dist.:* Ont. *1st cit.:* 1732 Fuller, *Gnomologia. 20c. coll.:* Stevenson 1298:2.

21. Kindness is the sunshine of social life. *Rec. dist.:* N.J.

22. Kindness is to do and say the kindest thing in the kindest way. *Rec. dist.:* Ind.

23. Kindness, like grain, increases by sowing. *Rec. dist.:* Miss., Ont. *1st cit.:* 1855 Bohn, *Handbook of Proverbs. 20c. coll.:* Stevenson 1298:6.

24. Kindness to the just is never lost, but kindness to the wicked is unkindness to yourself. *Rec. dist.:* Ill.

25. Never forget a kindness. *Rec. dist.:* Ill.

26. No one has ever been killed by kindness. *Rec. dist.:* Ind. *1st cit.:* ca1557 *Wealth and Health;* US1716 *Selected Letters of Cotton Mather,* ed. Silverman (1971). *20c. coll.:* ODEP 423, Whiting 244, Stevenson 1297:7, T&W 208, Whiting(MP) 349.

27. One kindness deserves another. *Rec. dist.:* N.C. *1st cit.:* US1948 Stevenson, *Home Book of Proverbs. 20c. coll.:* Stevenson 1245:3.

28. One kindness is the price of another. *Rec. dist.:* Minn. *1st cit.:* 1732 Fuller, *Gnomologia. 20c. coll.:* Stevenson 1245:3.

29. Repay kindness with kindness. *Rec. dist.:* N.C., Ont. *1st cit.:* 1867 Confucius, *Analects* in *Life and Teachings of Confucius,* tr. Legge. *20c. coll.:* Stevenson 1245:3.

30. Tell a miser he's rich and a woman she's old, and you'll get no money of one nor kindness of t'other. *Rec. dist.:* N.Y.

31. There's nothing so kingly as kindness and nothing so royal as truth. *Rec. dist.:* Ky., Ont.

32. Unfading are the gardens of kindness. *Rec. dist.:* Ill.

SEE ALSO Use FORCE tempered with kindness. / POLITENESS is inward kindness outwardly expressed.

king 1. A king is never powerful that has not power on the sea. *Rec. dist.:* Ont.

2. An ignorant king is a crowned ass. *Rec. dist.:* Minn.

3. Bad kings and governors help us if only they are bad enough. *Rec. dist.:* N.Y., S.C. *1st cit.:* US1875 Emerson, *Progress of Culture. 20c. coll.:* Stevenson 1301:5.

4. He who reigns within himself is more than a king. *Rec. dist.:* Ont.

5. I'd rather be king among dogs than be a dog among kings. *Rec. dist.:* Ky.

6. If the king is in the palace, nobody looks at the walls. *Rec. dist.:* N.Y., S.C.

7. Kings and bears often worry their keeper. *Rec. dist.:* Oreg. *1st cit.:* ca1595 Fergusson, *Scottish Proverbs. 20c. coll.:* Stevenson 1301:12.

8. Kings and queens must die, as well as you and I. *Rec. dist.:* Ont.

9. Kings and realms pass away, but time goes on forever. *Rec. dist.:* Ont.

10. Kings can do no wrong. *Vars.:* (a) A king can do no wrong. (b) The king can do no wrong. *Rec. dist.:* N.Y., Ont. *1st cit.:* 1538 Starkey, *England in the Reign of Henry VIII,* E.E.T.S. (1878); US1647 Rynchon in *Winthrop Papers. 20c. coll.:* ODEP 425, CODP 125, Stevenson 1305:10, Whiting(MP) 349.

11. Kings have long arms. *Var.:* Kings have long hands. *Rec. dist.:* Mich., N.Y. *1st cit.:* 1539 Taverner, *Proverbs of Erasmus;* US1752 Franklin, *PRAlmanac. 20c. coll.:* ODEP 428, Whiting 245, CODP 125, Stevenson 1307:10, T&W 208.

12. The king goes as far as he can, not so far as he would. *Rec. dist.:* Mich., N.Y. *1st cit.:*

1706 Stevens, *New Spanish and English Dictionary*. *20c. coll.*: ODEP 425, Stevenson 1307:2.

13. The king is the man who can. *Rec. dist.*: N.J.

14. The king reigns but does not rule. *Rec. dist.*: Ont. *1st cit.*: 1874 Stubbs, *Constitutional History of England. 20c. coll.*: Stevenson 1307:8.

15. The king who fights himself, fights himself. *Rec. dist.*: Ill. *Infm.*: The king himself should not engage in battle.

16. Where nothing is, the king must lose his right. *Rec. dist.*: N.J. *1st cit.*: ca1546 Heywood, *Dialogue of Proverbs,* ed. Habernicht (1963). *20c. coll.*: ODEP 580, Stevenson 1301:13.

17. Where the king is, there is the court. *Rec. dist.*: Mich.

SEE ALSO An AGUE in spring is physic for the king. / I had rather be a BEGGAR and spend my last dollar like a king, than be a king and spend my money like a beggar. / In the land of the BLIND, the one-eyed are kings. / A man without BOOKS is like a king without money. / A CAT may look at a king. / Before GOLD even kings take off their hats. / The HOUSE is a castle which the king cannot enter. / IDLENESS and pride tax with a heavier hand than kings and parliaments. / VIRTUOUS men are kings' treasures.

kingdom A kingdom divided against itself cannot stand. *Rec. dist.*: Ont., Wis. *1st cit.*: ca1440 Lydgate, *Fall of Princes* (1924). *20c. coll.*: ODEP 428.

SEE ALSO ARROGANCE is a kingdom without a crown.

kingfisher While the kingfisher and the oyster are struggling, the fisherman gets both. *Rec. dist.*: Ont.

kingly There is nothing so kingly as kindness and nothing so royal as truth. *Rec. dist.*: Ont.

kinsfolk Many kinsfolk, few friends. *Rec. dist.*: Ont. *1st cit.*: ca1546 Heywood, *Dialogue of Proverbs,* ed. Habernicht (1963). *20c. coll.*: ODEP 510.

kinsman *SEE* A BEGGAR ennobled does not know his own kinsman.

kirk Nearest the kirk, the farthest frae grace. *Rec. dist.*: Ont. *Infm.*: Kirk refers to church. *1st cit.*: ca1303 Mannyng, *Handlyng Synne;* US1803 Davis, *Travels in U.S. 1798–1802. 20c. coll.*: ODEP 557, Whiting 72, Stevenson 351:4, Whiting(MP) 115.

kirkyard *SEE* Near DEAD never filled the kirkyard.

kiss *(n.)* **1.** A kiss and a drink of water is but a tasteless breakfast. *Rec. dist.*: N.Y.

2. A kiss without a squeeze is like a piece of pie without a piece of cheese. *Var.*: Apple pie without cheese is like a kiss without a squeeze. *Rec. dist.*: Ind., Kans., Oreg., Wis.

3. Getting kisses out of a woman is like getting olives out of a bottle: the first may be devilish difficult, but the rest come easy. *Var.*: Kisses are like olives out of a bottle: after the first, the rest come easy. *Rec. dist.*: N.Y., Ohio, S.C.

4. Kisses are the language of love. *Var.*: Kisses are the language of love, so let's talk it over. *Rec. dist.*: Ill.

5. Many are betrayed with a kiss. *Rec. dist.*: Ont.

6. Stolen kisses are the best. *Var.*: Stolen kisses are sweet. *Rec. dist.*: Ky., N.Y. *1st cit.*: 1821 Hunt, *The Indicator. 20c. coll.*: Stevenson 1312:7.

7. There's never been anyone to die because of a kiss, but many a poor soul has died for the lack of one. *Rec. dist.*: N.C.

SEE ALSO A WOMAN remembers a kiss long after a man has forgotten.

kiss *(v.)* **1.** Don't kiss and tell: honor in love is silence. *Rec. dist.*: Ill. *1st cit.*: 1616 Jonson, *Forest;* US1809 Lindsley, *Love and Friendship, or Yankee Notions. 20c. coll.*: ODEP 429, Whiting 246, Stevenson 1312:2, Whiting(MP) 351.

2. If you can kiss the mistress, never kiss the maid. *Rec. dist.*: Ill., Okla., Ont., Tex. *1st cit.*: 1620 Ray, *English Proverbs. 20c. coll.*: ODEP 275, Stevenson 1599:11.

3. Kiss and make up. *Rec. dist.*: Ind., N.C. *1st cit.*: 1338 *Langtoft Chronicles,* tr, Manning; US1930 Ashbrook, *Murder of Cecily Thane. 20c. coll.*: ODEP 429, Whiting(MP) 350, Stevenson 1310:6.

4. She who is kissed by more than one is worthy of being kissed by none. *Rec. dist.:* N.Y.

SEE ALSO He is a FOOL that kisses the maid when he may kiss the mistress. / Many kiss the HAND they wish to see cut off. / It is better to be beaten by your own man than kissed by a STRANGER.

kissing Kissing goes by favor. *Var.:* Kissing goes by power. *Rec. dist.:* Minn., N.Y. *1st cit.:* 1616 Draxe, *Bibliotheca Scholastica in Anglia* (1918); US1739 *Jonathan Belcher Papers,* Mass.Hist.Soc. *Collections* (1893–94). *20c. coll.:* ODEP 430, Whiting 246, CODP 126, Stevenson 1311:1, Whiting*(MP)* 351.

kitchen A fat kitchen makes a lean will. *Vars.:* (a) A fat kitchen makes a lean purse. (b) A hot kitchen makes a lean will. *Rec. dist.:* U.S., Can. *1st cit.:* US1948 Stevenson, *Home Book of Proverbs. 20c. coll.:* Stevenson 764:6.

SEE ALSO A DOG in the kitchen desires no company. / Good HUMOR comes from the kitchen. / HUNGER is a good kitchen. / SILKS and satins, scarlet and velvet put out the kitchen fire.

kite *(bird)* A hungry kite sees a dead horse afar off. *Rec. dist.:* Ill.

kite *(toy)* **1.** Don't fly your kite too high. *Rec. dist.:* Utah.

2. Fly your kite when it's windy. *Rec. dist.:* Ohio, Ont.

3. No kite ever flew so high but what its tail followed it. *Rec. dist.:* Ky.

kitten **1.** Because kittens may be born in an oven, that does not make them loaves of bread. *Rec. dist.:* Miss.

2. For if you burn the kittens, sure the old cat comes their wounds to cure. *Rec. dist.:* Oreg.

3. Wanton kittens may make sober cats. *Rec. dist.:* Mich. *1st cit.:* 1732 Fuller, *Gnomologia. 20c. coll.:* ODEP 866, CODP 241, Stevenson 2444:10.

4. Who ever saw a kitten bring a mouse to the old cat? *Rec. dist.:* Maine. *1st cit.:* 1917 Bridge, *Cheshire Proverbs. 20c. coll.:* Stevenson 294:4.

knave **1.** A knave discovered is the greatest fool. *Rec. dist.:* Mich. *1st cit.:* 1732 Fuller, *Gnomologia. 20c. coll.:* Stevenson 854:4.

2. Knave in grain, a knave of the first rate. *Rec. dist.:* N.Y., S.C. *1st cit.:* 1785 Close, *Classical Dictionary of Vulgar Tongue. 20c. coll.:* Stevenson 1316:7.

3. Knaves and fools divide the world. *Rec. dist.:* Ind., Ont. *1st cit.:* 1659 Gent, *Proverbs English, French, Dutch, Italian and Spanish. 20c. coll.:* ODEP 432, Stevenson 854:1.

4. Knaves and nettles are akin: stroke 'em kindly, yet they'll sting. *Rec. dist.:* N.Y., S.C. *1st cit.:* US1748 Franklin, *PRAlmanac. 20c. coll.:* Whiting 246, Stevenson 1315:16.

5. Knaves are in such repute that honest men are accounted fools. *Rec. dist.:* Ont. *1st cit.:* 1732 Fuller, *Gnomologia. 20c. coll.:* Stevenson 1157:19.

6. Knaves imagine nothing can be done without knavery. *Rec. dist.:* Ont. *1st cit.:* 1732 Fuller, *Gnomologia. 20c. coll.:* Stevenson 1315:17.

7. Once a knave, always a knave. *Rec. dist.:* Ohio, Okla., Ont., Tex. *1st cit.:* ca1566 Curio, *Pasquin in Trance,* tr. W. P. *20c. coll.:* ODEP 594, Stevenson 1316:5.

8. One piece of knave begets another. *Rec. dist.:* Ill.

9. When knaves betray each other, one can scarce be blamed or the other pitied. *Rec. dist.:* N.Y., S.C.

10. When knaves fall out, honest men get their goods; when priests dispute we come at the truth. *Vars.:* (a) When knaves fall out, honest men come by their own. (b) When knaves fall out, honest men get a break. *Rec. dist.:* Ill., N.Y., Okla., S.C., Tex. *1st cit.:* US1742 Franklin, *PRAlmanac. 20c. coll.:* Stevenson 1315:16.

knavery **1.** Knavery is the worst trade. *Var.:* Knavery without luck is the worst trade in the world. *Rec. dist.:* Ont. *1st cit.:* 1732 Fuller, *Gnomologia. 20c. coll.:* Stevenson 1315:17.

2. Knavery may serve a turn, but honesty is best in the end. *Rec. dist.:* Mich. *1st cit.:* 1678 Ray, *English Proverbs,* 2d ed. *20c. coll.:* ODEP 432, Stevenson 1158:1.

3. Love, knavery, and necessity make men good orators. *Rec. dist.:* Ont.

knee **1.** Girls who show their knees know all about the birds and bees. *Rec. dist.:* Ohio.

2. If your knees knock, kneel on them. *Rec. dist.:* N.C.

3. Never get down on your knees: your pants get baggy. *Rec. dist.:* Ind.

4. The human knee is a joint and not an entertainment. *Rec. dist.:* Ind.

SEE ALSO A FARMER on his knees is higher than a gentleman on his legs. / The second WIFE always sits on the right knee. / When a WOMAN throws a man over, he usually lands on his knees to another woman.

knife **1.** Dull knife cuts cheese thinner than a sharp one. *Rec. dist.:* Kans.

2. Not every one who carries a long knife is a cook. *Rec. dist.:* Ariz.

3. One knife sharpens another. *Rec. dist.:* Ill. *1st cit.:* 1578 Yver, *Courtlie Controversies of Cupids Cantles,* tr. Wotton. *20c. coll.:* ODEP 432.

4. There never was a good knife made of bad steel. *Rec. dist.:* Ind., N.Y., S.C. *1st cit.:* US1755 Franklin, *PRAlmanac.* *20c. coll.:* Whiting 246, Stevenson 772:10.

5. Wherever there's a sharp knife there's always a sharpener. *Rec. dist.:* Ohio.

SEE ALSO FINGERS were made before knives and forks.

knock *(n.)* **1.** A knock is as good as a boost. *Rec. dist.:* Ark., Ill. *1st cit.:* US1836 Crockett, *Col. Crockett's Exploits in Texas.* *20c. coll.:* T&W 207, Whiting(MP) 354.

2. Every knock knicks the knocker. *Rec. dist.:* Md.

knock *(v.)* *SEE* ASK, and it shall be given you; seek, and you shall find; knock, and it shall be opened unto you. / When FORTUNE knocks, open the door. / If your KNEES knock, kneel on them. / OPPORTUNITY knocks but once.

knocker **1.** A knocker never wins and a winner never knocks. *Rec. dist.:* Ont.

2. Opportunities seldom knock for knockers. *Rec. dist.:* Miss., N.Y.

SEE ALSO A pleasant GRIN will let you in where a knocker was never known.

knocking Those knocking are always on the outside. *Rec. dist.:* Okla.

SEE ALSO You must never CRY so hard about your hard luck that you can't hear opportunity knocking.

knot **1.** He that doesn't tie a knot may lose his first stitch. *Vars.:* **(a)** Always tie a knot in the end of your thread and you will never lose the first stitch. **(b)** He that doesn't tie a knot may lose his first stitch. **(c)** Knot your thread and save a stitch. *Rec. dist.:* Miss., N.Y. *1st cit.:* 1642 Torriano, *Select Italian Proverbs.* *20c. coll.:* ODEP 798.

2. If a string is in a knot, patience can untie it. *Rec. dist.:* Ohio.

3. If the knot is loose, the string will slip. *Var.:* Where the knot is loose, the string slips. *Rec. dist.:* Ill., Ont. *1st cit.:* 1579 Gosson, *Ephemerides of Phialo.* *20c. coll.:* ODEP 433, Stevenson 1318:6.

4. Knots are more easily tied than untied. *Rec. dist.:* N.J. *1st cit.:* 1614 Webster, *Duchess of Malfi.* *20c. coll.:* Stevenson 1319:1.

5. The knot that is tied in treachery will be loosed by jealousy. *Rec. dist.:* Mich.

6. When one reknots a broken cord, it holds, but one feels the knot. *Rec. dist.:* N.Y.

7. When the knot reaches the comb of the loom, you have to break the thread. *Rec. dist.:* N.Y.

8. When you get married you tie a knot with your tongue that you can't untie with your teeth. *Vars.:* **(a)** Don't tie a knot with your tongue that you can't untie with your teeth. **(b)** You can tie a knot with your tongue you cannot undo with your teeth. *Rec. dist.:* N.C., Ont. *1st cit.:* 1580 Lyly, *Euphues and His England;* US1837 Hall, *Soldier's Bride.* *20c. coll.:* ODEP 821–22, Stevenson 1318:9, T&W 211.

9. When you're down and out, tie a knot in your rope and hang on. *Var.:* When you think you have reached the end of your rope, tie a knot in it and hang on. *Rec. dist.:* Miss., N.Mex.

know 1. All that we know is that we know nothing. *Rec. dist.:* Ill.

2. Better know nothing than half-know many things. *Rec. dist.:* N.Y.

3. He knows enough who knows how to mind his own business. *Rec. dist.:* Ill., N.C.

4. He knows most who speaks least. *Rec. dist.:* Ill., Ind., N.J., N.Y., Ont. *1st cit.:* 1666 Torriano, *Common Place of Italian Proverbs.* *20c. coll.:* ODEP 437.

5. He that knows himself knows others. *Rec. dist.:* Mich., Miss.

6. He that knows least presumes most. *Rec. dist.:* Miss., Ohio.

7. He who knows all believes. *Rec. dist.:* Miss.

8. He who knows does not speak; he who speaks does not know. *Rec. dist.:* Ind., N.Y.

9. He who knows little repeats it. *Rec. dist.:* Minn., N.Y.

10. He who knows little soon tells it. *Rec. dist.:* N.Y.

11. He who knows most knows best how little he knows. *Rec. dist.:* N.Y., Ont., S.C.

12. He who thinks he knows the most knows the least. *Rec. dist.:* Ill.

13. It is better not to know than to be wrong. *Rec. dist.:* Oreg. *1st cit.:* US1751 Franklin, *PRAlmanac.* *20c. coll.:* Stevenson 1324:9.

14. It is good to know much but better to have use of what we know. *Rec. dist.:* Mich., Miss.

15. It isn't how much you know, but what you know. *Rec. dist.:* Kans.

16. It's better to know nothing than to know that it ain't so. *Rec. dist.:* Ky.

17. It's not what you know, but whom you know. *Var.:* It's not whom you know or what you know; it's what you know on whom. *Rec. dist.:* Ind., Kans., N.Y., Okla.

18. It's not what you know that counts; it's how you use what you know. *Rec. dist.:* N.C.

19. Know thyself. *Rec. dist.:* U.S., Can. *1st cit.:* 1387 Higden, *Polychronicon,* tr. Trevisa, Rolls Ser. (1865–86); US1772 *Papers of James Madison,* ed. Hutchinson and Rachal (1962). *20c. coll.:* ODEP 435, Whiting 247, CODP 126, Stevenson 2066:4, Whiting(MP) 355.

20. Most of us know how to say nothing; few of us know when. *Rec. dist.:* N.Y., S.C., Wis.

21. No one knows what will happen to him the next moment. *Rec. dist.:* Ill.

22. Of all cold words of tongue or pen, the worst are these: "I knew him when." *Rec. dist.:* N.Y.

23. People who know themselves best are ashamed of themselves. *Rec. dist.:* Ill.

24. The less we know, the more we suspect. *Rec. dist.:* N.Y., S.C.

25. The more one knows, the more one simplifies. *Rec. dist.:* N.Y.

26. The more that a man knows, the more worth he is. *Rec. dist.:* Ill., N.C.

27. Those who know do not speak; those who speak do not know. *Rec. dist.:* Kans., Ohio. *1st cit.:* US1948 Stevenson, *Home Book of Proverbs.* *20c. coll.:* Stevenson 2113:13.

28. 'Tis better not to know than in knowing err. *Rec. dist.:* Ky., N.J., N.Y. *1st cit.:* US1751 Franklin, *PRAlmanac.* *20c. coll.:* Stevenson 1324:9.

29. To know is nothing at all; to imagine is everything. *Rec. dist.:* Wis.

30. To know is to care. *Rec. dist.:* N.C., Wis.

31. To know what we know and to know what we do not know—that is understanding. *Rec. dist.:* Ind. *1st cit.:* US1854 Thoreau, *Walden.* *20c. coll.:* Stevenson 132:7.

32. We know what we are, but we do not know what we may be. *Rec. dist.:* N.Y. *1st cit.:* 1600 Shakespeare, *Hamlet.* *20c. coll.:* Stevenson 2066:2.

33. What one doesn't know won't hurt him. *Vars.:* (a) What a fellow doesn't know won't hurt him. (b) What a person don't know don't hurt them. (c) What they don't know won't hurt them. (d) What we don't know can't hurt us, but it can make us look pretty

stupid at times. *Rec. dist.:* U.S., Can. *1st cit.:* 1576 Pettie, *Petite Palace of Pleasure,* ed. Gollancz (1908); US1908 Walter, *The Easiest Way.* *20c. coll.:* CODP 126, Stevenson 1329:1, Whiting*(MP)* 356.

34. What we know is the measure of what we see. *Rec. dist.:* Minn.

35. When we don't know it, it won't make us feel hot. *Rec. dist.:* Ind., Pa.

36. You will never know till you try. *Var.:* You can never know what you can do if you don't try. *Rec. dist.:* Ky., N.Y. *1st cit.:* 1829 Marryat, *Life of Frank Mildmay;* US1818 Cobbett, *Year's Residence in America. 20c. coll.:* ODEP 436, CODP 126, Stevenson 2396:14, Whiting*(MP)* 355.

SEE ALSO Who ANSWERS suddenly knows little. / They may not know just what ART is, but they know what they want. / An old BROOM knows the corners of a house. / Everybody ought to know his own BUSINESS the best. / When you open a DOOR, you do not know how many rooms lie beyond. / If you want to know what a DUCAT is worth, borrow one. / It is better to be thought a FOOL than to open your mouth and let the world know it. / It takes a FOOL to know a fool. / He who has crossed the FORD knows how deep it is. / By their FRUITS you shall know them. / The HEART has eyes that the brain knows nothing of. / The HUSBAND's the last one to know. / How IGNORANT are those who men say know it all. / He who has suffered you to IMPOSE on him knows you. / KNOWING that you don't know much is knowing a lot. / KNOWLEDGE is knowing that we cannot know. / LEARN not, know not. / It is only when we forget all our LEARNING that we begin to know. / LOVE knows no jealousy. / A MAN thinks he knows, but a woman knows better. / MOTHER knows best. / NECESSITY knows no law. / A NEIGHBOR is a person who knows more about your business than you do. / He who knows NOTHING never doubts. / He's the best PHYSICIAN that knows the worthlessness of most medicines. / Be sure you know the ROAD before you act as guide. / The ROOSTER crows to let us know; if we are wise, it's time to rise. / Everyone knows where his SHOE pinches. / He who knows how to keep SILENT knows a great deal. / SPECIALISTS are people who know more and more about less and less until they know everything about nothing. / TELL not all you know, and tell only what you know right well. / He that TRAVELS far knows much. / Much WATER goes by the mill the miller knows not of. / He knows the WAY best who went there last. / A WISE man knows his own ignorance; a fool thinks he knows. / He is a WISE man who knows more today than he did yesterday. / A WOMAN conceals what she knows not.

knowing 1. It's all in knowing how. *Rec. dist.:* N.C.

2. Knowing is power. *Rec. dist.:* U.S. *Infm.:* Cf. knowledge.

3. Knowing that you don't know much is knowing a lot. *Rec. dist.:* N.C.

SEE ALSO THINKING is very far from knowing.

knowledge 1. A little knowledge is a dangerous thing. *Rec. dist.:* U.S. *1st cit.:* 1881 Huxley, *Science and Culture. 20c. coll.:* CODP 134.

2. A man can be saved no faster than he gains knowledge. *Rec. dist.:* N.Y., S.C.

3. Concealed knowledge is buried treasure. *Rec. dist.:* Ill., N.J.

4. He that boasts of his own knowledge proclaims his ignorance. *Rec. dist.:* Ill., Kans.

5. He that has knowledge spares his words. *Rec. dist.:* Ala., Ga., Kans.

6. He who has knowledge has force. *Rec. dist.:* N.Y.

7. He who loves correctors loves knowledge. *Rec. dist.:* Ala., Ga., N.Y.

8. If you have knowledge, you should let others light their candles by it. *Rec. dist.:* N.Y., N.C.

9. If you want knowledge, you must toil for it. *Rec. dist.:* N.Y.

10. Increase your knowledge and you increase your griefs. *Rec. dist.:* Ill., N.Y., N.C.

1st cit.: 1869 Henderson, *Latin Proverbs. 20c. coll.:* Stevenson 1321:5.

11. Knowledge and timber shouldn't be much used until they are seasoned. *Rec. dist.:* U.S. *1st cit.:* US1858 Holmes, *Autocrat of the Breakfast-Table. 20c. coll.:* T&W 211.

12. Knowledge and wisdom are far from being one. *Rec. dist.:* N.J., N.Y., Ont., S.C. *1st cit.:* ca1783 Cowper, *The Task. 20c. coll.:* Stevenson 1328:5.

13. Knowledge begins with awareness of self. *Rec. dist.:* Minn., Ont.

14. Knowledge cannot be stolen from us; it cannot be bought or sold. *Rec. dist.:* Ill., Minn.

15. Knowledge comes, but wisdom lingers. *Rec. dist.:* Ill., N.Y., Ont. *1st cit.:* 1842 Tennyson, *Locksley Hall. 20c. coll.:* Stevenson 1328:7.

16. Knowledge comes, knowledge goes; wisdom stays. *Rec. dist.:* N.Y., S.C. *1st cit.:* 1842 Tennyson, *Locksley Hall. 20c. coll.:* Stevenson 1328:7.

17. Knowledge conquered by labor becomes a possession. *Rec. dist.:* N.J., Ont.

18. Knowledge directs practice, and practice increases knowledge. *Rec. dist.:* Ont. *1st cit.:* 1732 Fuller, *Gnomologia. 20c. coll.:* Stevenson 1320:3.

19. Knowledge finds its price. *Rec. dist.:* Ind., Ont. *1st cit.:* US1948 Stevenson, *Home Book of Proverbs. 20c. coll.:* Stevenson 1323:4.

20. Knowledge is a treasure, but practice is the key to it. *Rec. dist.:* Ill., N.Y., Ont.

21. Knowledge is better than riches. *Rec. dist.:* N.Y., Wis.

22. Knowledge is better than wealth. *Rec. dist.:* Fla., N.Y.

23. Knowledge is knowing that we cannot know. *Rec. dist.:* Fla., N.Y., S.C. *1st cit.:* US1850 Emerson, *Montaigne* in *Representative Men. 20c. coll.:* Stevenson 1324:8.

24. Knowledge is nothing when good breeding is lacking. *Rec. dist.:* N.Y., N.C., S.C.

25. Knowledge is proud that he knows so much; wisdom is humble that he knows no more. *Rec. dist.:* Utah.

26. Knowledge is the basis of life. *Rec. dist.:* Ill., Utah.

27. Knowledge is the treasure of the mind. *Rec. dist.:* Ill., Mich., Miss.

28. Knowledge itself is power. *Vars.:* **(a)** Knowledge is power. **(b)** Knowledge is power, and power is success. **(c)** There is no knowledge that is not power. *Rec. dist.:* U.S. *1st cit.:* 1591 Shakespeare, *Henry VI;* US1806 Rush, *Letters,* ed. Butterfield (1951). *20c. coll.:* ODEP 436, Whiting 247, *CODP* 126, Stevenson 1323:2, Whiting*(MP)* 356.

29. Knowledge talks lowly; ignorance talks loudly. *Rec. dist.:* U.S., Can.

30. Much knowledge is gained by listening. *Rec. dist.:* Maine, Ont.

31. One should respect knowledge, but doubt is what gets you an education. *Rec. dist.:* Ala., Ga., Maine.

32. The lamp of knowledge burns brightly. *Rec. dist.:* N.Y.

33. The larger the island of knowledge the longer the shoreline of wonder. *Rec. dist.:* Ont.

34. To be proud of knowledge is to be blind with light; to be proud of virtue is to poison yourself with the antidote. *Var.:* To be proud of knowledge is to be blind with light. *Rec. dist.:* Ill., N.Y., Ont., S.C.

35. To gather knowledge, roam; to use it, bide at home. *Rec. dist.:* Ind., N.Y., S.C.

36. Who keeps the old akindle and adds new knowledge is fit to be a teacher. *Rec. dist.:* Ind.

37. Without knowledge there is no sin or sinner. *Rec. dist.:* Ill., Ind.

SEE ALSO ACTION is the proper fruit of knowledge. / Want of CARE does more harm than want of knowledge. / He is a FOOL who cannot conceal his knowledge. / An INVESTMENT in knowledge pays the best interest. / PATIENCE surpasses knowledge. / A man's PRIDE in what he knows decreases as his knowledge grows. / Let him STUDY who wishes to get knowledge. / The WEIGHT of knowledge is never measured. / WISE men lay up knowledge. / By WORK you get money, by talk you get knowledge. / ZEAL without knowledge is the sister of folly.

known **1.** Better known than trusted. *Rec. dist.:* N.Y. *1st cit.:* ca1560 Huth, *Ancient Ballads* (1867). *20c. coll.:* ODEP 54, Stevenson 2383:1.

2. If you don't want it known, don't do it. *Rec. dist.:* Ind., N.Y., N.C.

3. It is being known that makes us behave. *Rec. dist.:* Ohio.

SEE ALSO The BAD which is well known is better than the good unknown. / One is known by the COMPANY he keeps. / We easily forget our FAULTS when they are known only to ourselves. / A FOOL is known by his conversation. / A pleasant GRIN will let you in where a knocker was never known. / A TREE is known by its fruit. / Hundreds would never have known WANT if they had not at first known waste.

L

label   Don't rely on the label of the bag. *Rec. dist.:* Wis. *1st cit.:* US1885 Spurgeon, *Salt-Cellars. 20c. coll.:* Stevenson 80:3.

labeled   *SEE* The door to SUCCESS is labeled push.

labor *(n.)*   **1.** A mountain in labor brought forth a mouse. *Rec. dist.:* N.C. *1st cit.:* ca1390 Gower, *Confessio Amantis;* US1685 Wisehall in *Hinckley Papers,* Mass.Hist.Soc. *Collections* (1861). *20c. coll.:* ODEP 547, Whiting 299, Stevenson 1629:6, Whiting*(MP)* 428.

2. By labor comes wealth. *Rec. dist.:* N.J.

3. From labor there shall come forth rest. *Rec. dist.:* N.Y., S.C. *1st cit.:* US1845 Longfellow, *To a Child. 20c. coll.:* Stevenson 1330:8.

4. In all labor there is profit. *Rec. dist.:* N.J., N.Y., Ont., S.C. *1st cit.:* US1948 Stevenson, *Home Book of Proverbs. 20c. coll.:* Stevenson 1331:3.

5. Labor brings pleasure, idleness, and pain. *Rec. dist.:* Mich.

6. Labor conquers all things. *Var.:* Labor overcomes all things. *Rec. dist.:* Ill., Ind., Ohio. *1st cit.:* 1573 *Amorous Tales,* tr. Sannford; US1970 Friedrich, *Decline and Fall. 20c. coll.:* ODEP 438, Whiting*(MP)* 357, Stevenson 1334:3.

7. Labor helps, but you get more by luck. *Rec. dist.:* Ill.

8. Labor is light where love does pay. *Rec. dist.:* Wis. *1st cit.:* 1539 Frontinus, *Stratagems of War,* tr. Monsigne. *20c. coll.:* ODEP 438, Stevenson 1332:6.

9. Labor is the law of happiness. *Rec. dist.:* N.Y., S.C. *1st cit.:* USca1881 Stevens, *Life of Mme. de Stael. 20c. coll.:* Stevenson 1330:8.

10. Labor makes life sweet. *Rec. dist.:* Ill., N.Y.

11. Labor warms; sloth harms. *Rec. dist.:* Ill. *1st cit.:* US1948 Stevenson, *Home Book of Proverbs. 20c. coll.:* Stevenson 1330:7.

12. Little labor, little gain. *Vars.:* **(a)** If little labor, little are our gains. **(b)** If little labor, little are your gains. *Rec. dist.:* Ont., Wis.

13. Nothing is denied to well-directed labor, and nothing is attained without it. *Rec. dist.:* Ill., Ind.

14. Seek till you find and you'll never lose your labor. *Rec. dist.:* N.Y. *1st cit.:* 1678 Ray, *English Proverbs;* US1652 *Complete Writings of Roger Williams. 20c. coll.:* ODEP 711, Whiting 249, Stevenson 2056:3.

15. The labor of the righteous tends to life, the fruit of the wicked to sin. *Rec. dist.:* Ill., Ind.

16. The poor man's labor is the rich man's wealth. *Rec. dist.:* N.Y.

17. There is no labor in the labor of love, and there is love in honest labor. *Rec. dist.:* Ill.

18. What you get by your own labor is sweet to the taste. *Rec. dist.:* Ill.

19. You may share the labors of the great, but you will not share the spoil. *Rec. dist.:* Ont.

SEE ALSO CHEAPEST is the dearest labor. / Build not up a FORTUNE on the labor of others. / GENIUS begins great works; labor alone finishes them. / KNOWLEDGE conquered by labor becomes a possession. / LEARNING without thought is labor lost; thought without learning is dangerous. / REST is the sweet sauce of labor. / The hope of REWARD sweetens labor.

labor *(v.)*   **1.** Labor not to be rich. *Rec. dist.:* N.C.

2. Learn to labor and to wait. *Rec. dist.:* Miss., N.Y. *1st cit.:* US1838 Longfellow, *Psalm of Life. 20c. coll.:* Stevenson 1333:2.

3. People labor all their lives to be rich that they might live without labor. *Rec. dist.:* Ill.

4. 'Tis pleasant to labor for those we love. *Rec. dist.:* Iowa.

SEE ALSO He labors in vain who tries to PLEASE everybody.

laborer   **1.** A poor laborer is better than a rich loafer. *Rec. dist.:* Tex.

2. The laborer is worthy of his hire. *Rec. dist.:* Ill., Ont. *1st cit.:* ca1390 Chaucer, *Summoner's Tale;* US1644 *Complete Writings of Roger Williams* (1963). *20c. coll.:* CODP 128, Whiting 249, ODEP 439, Stevenson 1339:9, T&W 212, Whiting*(MP)* 357.

laboring SEE The SLEEP of a laboring man is sweet.

laborious SEE No man e'er was GLORIOUS who was not laborious.

lack SEE There's never been anyone to die because of a KISS, but many a poor soul has died for the lack of one. / What makes LIFE weary is lack of motive.

lad The lazy lad makes a stark old man. *Rec. dist.:* Ont.
SEE ALSO Raw DABS make fat lads.

ladder **1.** Don't get off the ladder before you reach the ground. *Rec. dist.:* Ont.

2. Go down the ladder for a wife; go up the ladder for a friend. *Var.:* Go down the ladder when you pick a wife; go up when you choose a friend. *Rec. dist.:* Ala., Ga., Ill. *1st cit.:* 1678 Ray, *Adagia Hebraica. 20c. coll.:* ODEP 306.

3. He that climbs a ladder must begin at the first round. *Vars.:* **(a)** If one must climb a ladder, one must begin at the lowest rung. **(b)** One begins to climb the ladder from the bottom. *Rec. dist.:* U.S. *1st cit.:* 1710 Palmer, *Moral Essays on English, Scotch, and Foreign Proverbs. 20c. coll.:* ODEP 127.

4. He who climbs to the top of a wall should not kick over his ladder, as he might wish sometime to climb down again. *Rec. dist.:* Ont. *1st cit.:* 1599 Shakespeare, *Julius Caesar. 20c. coll.:* ODEP 421.

5. He who holds the ladder is as bad as the thief. *Rec. dist.:* N.Y., Ohio, Wis.

6. Step by step the ladder is ascended. *Rec. dist.:* Ill., N.Y., Ohio, Okla. *1st cit.:* 1611 Cotgrave, *Dictionary of French and English Tongues. 20c. coll.:* ODEP 773, Stevenson 2212:5.

7. The bottom of the ladder is crowded; there's plenty of room at the top. *Rec. dist.:* Ala., Ga.

8. There's no boosting a man up the ladder unless he's willing to climb. *Rec. dist.:* Ky., Tenn.

9. We build ladders by which we rise. *Rec. dist.:* Miss.
SEE ALSO PUNCTUALITY is the first rung on the ladder of success. / The WORLD is a ladder for some to go up and some down.

lady **1.** A lady is a woman who makes it easy for a man to be a gentleman. *Rec. dist.:* Ill.

2. A lady is known by the product she endorses. *Rec. dist.:* N.Y., S.C. *1st cit.:* US1936 Nash, *First Families, Move Over. 20c. coll.:* Stevenson 1340:14.

3. A lady persuaded against her will is of the same opinion still. *Rec. dist.:* Kans., Ohio.

4. Farfetched and dear bought is a bargain for the ladies. *Rec. dist.:* Mich. *1st cit.:* ca1350 *Douce MS 52;* US1720 Wigglesworth, *Letter in Colonial Currency,* ed. Davis, Publ. Prince Soc. (1910–11). *20c. coll.:* CODP 77, Whiting 144, ODEP 173, Stevenson 1340:9.

5. Keep the ladies busy and that keeps them out of mischief. *Rec. dist.:* N.Y., S.C. *1st cit.:* US1908 O. Henry, *Midsummer Masquerade. 20c. coll.:* Stevenson 1216:2.

6. Ladies don't smoke. *Rec. dist.:* N.C.

7. Ladies in slacks should not turn their backs. *Rec. dist.:* Oreg.

8. Ladies young and fair have the gift to know it. *Rec. dist.:* Kans., N.Y., S.C. *1st cit.:* 1599 Shakespeare, *As You Like It. 20c. coll.:* Stevenson 1340:15.

9. Once a lady, always a lady. *Rec. dist.:* N.Y., S.C.

10. To change the mind is a lady's privilege. *Rec. dist.:* N.Y., S.C. *1st cit.:* ca1500 *Sloane MS 38* in *Early English Carols;* US1871 *Mark Twain's Letters,* ed. Payne (1917). *20c. coll.:* ODEP 909, T&W 410, Stevenson 2578:9, Whiting*(MP)* 694.

11. When a lady says no, she means perhaps; when she says perhaps, she means yes; when she says yes, she is no lady. *Var.:* A lady says no, meaning maybe, and maybe, meaning yes; but when she says yes, she isn't a lady. *Rec. dist.:* N.Y., N.C., S.C.

12. When ladies wear the breeches, their petticoats ought to be long enough to hide 'em. *Rec. dist.:* N.Y., S.C.

13. You mustn't rush a lady. *Rec. dist.:* Ohio.

SEE ALSO It is hard to be BIDDY and lady too. / Faint HEART never won fair lady. / It's a poor HOUSE that can't afford one lady. / A good SURGEON must have an eagle's eye, a lion's heart, and a lady's hand.

lamb 1. Lambs have the grace to suck kneeling. *Rec. dist.:* Ind. *1st cit.:* US1938 Champion, *Racial Proverbs. 20c. coll.:* Stevenson 1341:5.

2. Outwardly a lamb, inwardly a wolf. *Rec. dist.:* N.Y.

3. The bleating lamb is strangled by the wolf. *Rec. dist.:* Colo.

4. The lamb who bites a wolf never bites again. *Rec. dist.:* Ill.

5. The older a lamb becomes, the more sheepish he grows. *Var.:* The older a lamb grows, the more sheepish he becomes. *Rec. dist.:* N.Y., Ohio.

SEE ALSO GOD tempers the wind to the shorn lamb. / MARCH is in like a lion, out like a lamb. / PIGS grow fat where lambs would starve. / Might as well be hanged for a SHEEP as a lamb.

lame *(n.)* Live with the lame and you will limp. *Var.:* Walk with the lame and you limp. *Rec. dist.:* Miss., Ont. *1st cit.:* US1948 Stevenson, *Home Book of Proverbs. 20c. coll.:* Stevenson 389:7.

SEE ALSO The LAND provides for the lame and the lazy. / The LORD provides for the lame and lazy.

lame *(adj.)* **1.** A lame man won't walk with one who is lamer. *Rec. dist.:* N.Y.

2. It is better to be lame than always seated. *Rec. dist.:* Ont.

3. The lame man who keeps the right road outstrips the runner who keeps the wrong one. *Rec. dist.:* N.C.

SEE ALSO A lame GOAT takes no siesta. / PEDIGREE won't sell a lame horse.

lamp *SEE* When the OIL is exhausted the lamp dies out. / A poor man without PATIENCE is like a lamp without oil.

land 1. He who sows his land trusts in God. *Rec. dist.:* Ont. *1st cit.:* 1640 Herbert, *Outlandish Proverbs (Jacula Prudentum)* in *Works,* ed. Hutchinson (1940). *20c. coll.:* Stevenson 2177:3.

2. Ill fares the land in which money is more than men. *Rec. dist.:* Ont. *1st cit.:* 1770 Goldsmith, *Deserted Village. 20c. coll.:* Stevenson 2473:3.

3. Many a one for land takes a fool by the hand. *Rec. dist.:* Ont. *1st cit.:* ca1300 *Proverbs of Hending. 20c. coll.:* ODEP 508.

4. The land provides for the lame and the lazy. *Rec. dist.:* Calif., Colo., N.Y.

5. Who has land has war. *Rec. dist.:* Ont. *1st cit.:* 1579 Calvin, *Thirteen Sermones. 20c. coll.:* ODEP 441, Stevenson 1343:9.

SEE ALSO In the land of the BLIND, the one-eyed are kings. / The FARMER tickles the land, and the crops tickle him. / Don't count FISH till on dry land. / A little HOUSE well filled, a little land well tilled, and a little wife well willed are great riches. / Praise the SEA, but keep on land.

lane 1. A shady lane breeds mud. *Rec. dist.:* N.J., N.Y., Wis.

2. Every lane has a turning. *Rec. dist.:* Ill., Ont.

3. It's a long lane that has no turn. *Vars.:* **(a)** It's a long lane that has no turning. **(b)** It's a long lane that never turns. **(c)** It's a long road that has no turning. **(d)** Long is that lane that has no turning. *Rec. dist.:* U.S., Can. *1st cit.:* 1633 *Stationers' Register,* 8 July; US1778 Paine, *American Crisis* in *Writings of Thomas Paine,* ed. Foner (1945). *20c. coll.:* ODEP 480, Whiting 251, CODP 137, Stevenson 1345:1, T&W 214, Whiting(MP) 360.

language 1. Abusive language is abuse of language. *Rec. dist.:* Miss.

2. Civil language costs little and does good. *Rec. dist.:* Ind.

3. He who is ignorant of foreign languages knows not his own. *Rec. dist.:* Ill. *1st cit.:*

US1948 Stevenson, *Home Book of Proverbs.* **20c. coll.:** Stevenson 1346:4.

4. It often shows a fine command of language to say nothing. *Rec. dist.:* N.Dak.

5. Language is caught, not taught. *Rec. dist.:* Wis.

6. Language is the dress of thought. *Rec. dist.:* Ala. *1st cit.:* 1779 Johnson, "Cowley" in *Lives of Poets.* **20c. coll.:** Stevenson 1346:8.

7. Language is the vehicle of truth. *Rec. dist.:* N.C.

8. The fouler his language, the fouler the man. *Rec. dist.:* Ill.

9. The man who knows two languages is worth two men. *Rec. dist.:* N.Y.

SEE ALSO KINDNESS is language which the deaf can hear and the blind can see. / MONEY is a universal language speaking any tongue. / A SMILE is the same in any language—easily understood.

lantern *SEE* A FACE without a smile is like a lantern without a light.

lap The last lap is the hardest. *Rec. dist.:* Ind., Ky.

larceny Everybody has a little larceny in him. *Rec. dist.:* Wash.

large *SEE* A small GAIN is worth more than a large promise. / A large HAM, a large hand. / The larger the INCOME, the harder it is to live within it. / Make not your SAIL too large for your ship.

lark **1.** It is better to hear the lark sing than the mouse cheep. *Rec. dist.:* Ont. *1st cit.:* 1831 Scott, *Tales of a Grandfather.* **20c. coll.:** Stevenson 1347:6.

2. You can't rise with the lark if you've been on one the night before. *Rec. dist.:* N.Y., N.Dak., S.C.

SEE ALSO If the SKY falls, we shall catch larks.

last *(n., final)* **1.** Last gets the hash. *Rec. dist.:* Ky., Tenn.

2. The last is not the least. *Var.:* Last but not least. *Rec. dist.:* U.S., Can. *1st cit.:* 1580 Lyly, *Euphues and His England* in *Works,* ed. Bond

(1902); US1789 *Diary of William Bentley* (1905–14). **20c. coll.:** ODEP 442, Whiting 252, Stevenson 1348:1, Whiting*(MP)* 361.

SEE ALSO Every BABY born into the world is a finer one than the last. / Live each DAY as though it were the last. / The FARMER was the first man, and he will be the last. / The FIRST shall be last and the last, first. / Long runs the FOX, but at last is caught. / Be not the first to QUARREL nor the last to make up.

last *(n., tool)* *SEE* SHOEMAKER, stick to your last.

last *(v.)* *SEE* A squeaking HINGE lasts the longest. / LOVE lasts seven seconds, the fantasia lasts seven minutes, unhappiness lasts all one's life. / Good LUCK disappears like our hair, bad luck lasts like our nails. / NOTHING can last forever. / QUARRELS never could last long if on one side only lay the wrong. / REGRETS last longer than repentence.

last *(adj.)* That which is last is best. *Var.:* First is worst, second the same, last is best of all the game. *Rec. dist.:* N.Dak. *1st cit.:* 1670 Ray, *Scottish Proverbs.* **20c. coll.:** Stevenson 36:4.

SEE ALSO The last DROP makes the cup run over. / The HUSBAND's the last one to know. / First LOVE, last love, best love. / The last STRAW will break the camel's back.

last *(adv.)* *SEE* He who LAUGHS last laughs best.

lasting *SEE* BRAVERY is not lasting.

latchstring The latchstring is always out. *Rec. dist.:* Mich., N.Y. *1st cit.:* US1874 Eggleston, *Circuit Rider.* **20c. coll.:** T&W 215.

late **1.** Always late, never succeed. *Rec. dist.:* Kans.

2. Better come late to church than never. *Rec. dist.:* Wis.

3. Better late than before anyone has invited you. *Rec. dist.:* Ill., N.Y., S.C.

4. Better late than never. *Vars.:* **(a)** Better late than never, but better never late. **(b)** Better late than never, but better still, never late. **(c)** Better late than never, but better yet, never late. **(d)** Better late than not at all. **(e)** Better to be late than never, but better never late. **(f)**

It's better late than never, but still better never late. *Rec. dist.:* U.S., Can. *1st cit.:* ca1200 *Ancrene Riwle;* US1630 *Winthrop Papers, 1498–1649,* Mass.Hist.Soc. *Collections* (1863–92). *20c. coll.:* ODEP 54, Whiting 252, CODP 15, Stevenson 1348:5, T&W 215, Whiting*(MP)* 361.

5. Better late than sorry. *Rec. dist.:* Ind.

6. Better on time than late. *Rec. dist.:* N.Y., S.C. *1st cit.:* ca1520 *Hickscorner* in Hazlitt, *Old Plays. 20c. coll.:* Stevenson 1349:1.

7. It is too late to cover the well when the child is drowned. *Rec. dist.:* Ill. *1st cit.:* 1732 Fuller, *Gnomologia. 20c. coll.:* Stevenson 1349:8.

8. It is too late to lock the stable door when the steed is stolen. *Rec. dist.:* Wis. *1st cit.:* ca1350 *Douce MS 52;* US1845 Judd, *Margaret. 20c. coll.:* CODP 211, T&W 109, ODEP 730, Stevenson 2204:8.

9. It is too late to throw water on the cinders when the house is burned down. *Rec. dist.:* Ill., N.Y. *1st cit.:* 1575 Gascoigne, *Glasse of Government* in *Works,* ed. Cunliffe (1907–10). *20c. coll.:* ODEP 389, Stevenson 1350:7.

10. It's never too late until it's too late. *Vars.:* **(a)** It is never too late. **(b)** It's never too late to turn over a new leaf. *Rec. dist.:* U.S.

11. It's too late to learn how to box when you're in the ring. *Rec. dist.:* Ill.

12. It's too late to spare when the bottom is bare. *Var.:* Too late to spare when all is spent. *Rec. dist.:* Ill. *1st cit.:* 1539 Taverner, *Proverbs of Erasmus. 20c. coll.:* ODEP 759, Stevenson 2182:3.

See also Advice comes too late when a thing is done. / Enjoy yourself: it's later than you think. / Long FALL, late spring. / It's never too late to do GOOD. / It's better to be an HOUR too early than a minute too late. / It is never too late to LEARN. / What we LEARN early we remember late. / A LITTLE too late is much too late. / It's never too late to MEND. / We get too soon OLD and too late smart. / REPENTANCE is never too late. / He that RISES late must trot all day. / SLOW pokes get busy when the hour gets late. / Better late THRIVE than never do well. / Never too late to WIN.

lathered Well lathered, half shaved. *Rec. dist.:* N.Y., Ont. *1st cit.:* 1732 Fuller, *Gnomologia. 20c. coll.:* Stevenson 2085:4.

laugh *(n.)* **1.** A laugh a day makes the world seem gay. *Rec. dist.:* N.Y.

2. A laugh is worth a thousand groans in any market. *Var.:* One laugh is worth a hundred groans. *Rec. dist.:* Ala., Ga., Ill., Kans., Ont.

3. A loud laugh bespeaks the vacant mind. *Vars.:* **(a)** A loud laugh bespeaks a hollow mind. **(b)** A loud laugh shows a vacant mind. **(c)** The loud laugh betrays the vacant mind. **(d)** The louder the laugh, the more empty the head. *Rec. dist.:* Ill., Kans., N.C., Ohio, Ont. *1st cit.:* 1732 Fuller, *Gnomologia. 20c. coll.:* Stevenson 1352:4.

laugh *(v.)* **1.** Better you laugh than I weep. *Rec. dist.:* N.Y.

2. He who laughs at others' woes finds few friends and many foes. *Rec. dist.:* Ont.

3. He who laughs in his youth cries in his old age. *Rec. dist.:* N.Y.

4. He who laughs last laughs best. *Vars.:* **(a)** He laughs best whose laugh lasts. **(b)** He who laughs first laughs loudest. **(c)** He who laughs last didn't get the point anyway. **(d)** He who laughs last is probably an Englishman. **(e)** He who laughs last laughs longest. *Rec. dist.:* U.S., Can. *1st cit.:* 1546 Heywood, *Dialogue of Proverbs;* US1908 Lincoln, *Cy Whitaker's Place. 20c. coll.:* ODEP 445, Stevenson 1356:1, CODP 129, Whiting*(MP)* 362.

5. It is better to laugh than to cry. *Rec. dist.:* N.Y., Ont., S.C.

6. Laugh and be well. *Rec. dist.:* N.C.

7. Laugh and grow fat. *Rec. dist.:* U.S. *1st cit.:* 1596 Harington, *Metamorphosis of Ajax,* eds. Warlock and Lindsay (1927); US1798 *Journal of Elizabeth Drinker, 1759–1807,* ed. Biddle. *20c. coll.:* ODEP 444, Whiting 252, Stevenson 1352:8, T&W 215, Whiting*(MP)* 362.

8. Laugh and show your ignorance. *Rec. dist.:* N.Y., S.C. *1st cit.:* US1941 Updegraff, *Hills Look Down. 20c. coll.:* Stevenson 1355:12.

9. Laugh and the world laughs with you; cry and you cry alone. *Var.:* Laugh and the world laughs with you; weep and you weep alone. **Rec. dist.:** U.S., Can. **1st cit.:** 1979 Daily Telegraph, 3 Nov.; US1883 Wilcox in N.Y. Sun, 25 Feb. **20c. coll.:** CODP 129, Stevenson 2255:10.

10. Laugh before breakfast, cry before sunset. **Vars.: (a)** Laugh before breakfast, cry before night. **(b)** Laugh before breakfast, cry before supper. **Rec. dist.:** U.S. **1st cit.:** 1530 Palsgrave, Comedye of Acolastus, ed. Carver, E.E. T.S. (1937). **20c. coll.:** ODEP 444, Stevenson 1356:13, Whiting(MP) 362.

11. Laugh in the face of disaster: fate never meddles with mirth. **Rec. dist.:** Ill.

12. Let them laugh that win. **Var.:** The winners laugh; the losers weep. **Rec. dist.:** U.S., Can. **1st cit.:** 1546 Heywood, Dialogue of Proverbs, ed. Habernicht (1963); US1765 Letter Book of John Watts, 1762–1765 N.Y.Hist.Soc. Collections (1928). **20c. coll.:** CODP 129, Whiting 253, ODEP 445, Stevenson 1353:4, T&W 215, Whiting(MP) 362.

13. To laugh at a man with sense is the privilege of fools. **Rec. dist.:** Ala., Ga.

14. To laugh at someone is to be laughed back at. **Rec. dist.:** N.C.

15. When we laugh, everyone sees; when we cry, no one sees. **Rec. dist.:** N.Y., S.C.

SEE ALSO The old ANVIL laughs at many hammers. / The most utterly lost of all DAYS is that in which you have not laughed. / DENOMINATIONS fight while the devil laughs. / It always makes the DEVIL laugh to see the biter bitten. / A FOOL laughs at his own folly. / A FOOL laughs when others laugh. / There are few who would rather be HATED than laughed at. / MONEY makes a man laugh. / It's a TRIFLE that makes fools laugh. / Laugh your TROUBLES away.

laugher A good laugher makes a bad neighbor. **Rec. dist.:** N.Y.

laughing 1. A spoonful of laughing equals a spoonful of crying. **Rec. dist.:** Ind.

2. Always leave them laughing. **Rec. dist.:** Calif.

3. Laughing at the table is the best sauce. **Rec. dist.:** Iowa.

4. Laughing is catching. **Var.:** Laughing is catching; hanging is stretching. **Rec. dist.:** U.S. **1st cit.:** US1858 Hammett, Piney Woods Tavern or Sam Slick in Texas. **20c. coll.:** T&W 215.

laughter 1. A ripple of laughter is worth a flood of tears. **Rec. dist.:** Wis.

2. After laughter, tears. **Var.:** Through laughter come tears. **Rec. dist.:** Kans., S.C.

3. Laughter before sleep, tears when wakened. **Rec. dist.:** Calif.

4. Laughter does not spoil the skin. **Rec. dist.:** Wash.

5. Laughter is the best medicine. **Rec. dist.:** Wis.

6. Laughter is the hiccup of a fool. **Rec. dist.:** Calif., N.Y., Ont., S.C. **1st cit.:** 1670 Ray, English Proverbs. **20c. coll.:** Stevenson 1352:4.

SEE ALSO SORROW is better than laughter. / All TEETH showing is not laughter.

laundress The laundress washes her own smock first. **Rec. dist.:** Ont. **1st cit.:** 1732 Fuller, Gnomologia. **20c. coll.:** Stevenson 2456:1.

law 1. All things obey fixed laws. **Rec. dist.:** Ga., N.Y. **1st cit.:** US1948 Stevenson, Home Book of Proverbs. **20c. coll.:** Stevenson 1362:13.

2. Better no law than laws not enforced. **Rec. dist.:** Ill.

3. Good laws spring from bad morals. **Rec. dist.:** N.Y. **1st cit.:** 1659 Howell, Paroimiografia (French Proverbs); US1652 Complete Writings of Roger Williams. **20c. coll.:** Stevenson 1366:11, Whiting 253.

4. He knows not the law who knows not the reason thereof. **Rec. dist.:** N.J.

5. He who is a law to himself no law does need. **Rec. dist.:** N.C.

6. In a thousand pounds of law there is not one ounce of love. **Var.:** A pennyweight of love is worth a pound of law. **Rec. dist.:** N.Y., Wis. **1st cit.:** 1611 Cotgrave, Dictionary of French and English Tongues. **20c. coll.:** ODEP 815, Stevenson 1360:3.

7. Keep the law and keep from the law. **Rec. dist.:** Ont.

8. Law cannot persuade where it cannot push.

Rec. dist.: N.Y. *1st cit.:* 1732 Fuller, *Gnomologia. 20c. coll.:* Stevenson 1361:12.

9. Law is whatever is boldly asserted and plausibly maintained. *Rec. dist.:* N.Y., S.C. *1st cit.:* USca1800 Burr, Epigram in Parton, *Life and Times of Aaron Burr. 20c. coll.:* Stevenson 1361:8.

10. Law often codifies disorder and makes madness legal. *Rec. dist.:* Ill.

11. Laws are made to be broken. *Rec. dist.:* N.Y. *1st cit.:* US1928 Williams, *Voyage to Pagany. 20c. coll.:* Whiting(MP) 363.

12. Laws are made to be evaded. *Rec. dist.:* Ill. *1st cit.:* US1928 Williams, *Voyage to Pagany. 20c. coll.:* Whiting(MP) 363.

13. Laws are silent when wars are waging. *Rec. dist.:* Calif. *1st cit.:* 1549 Bullinger, *Treatise Concerning Magistrates;* US1692 Bulkeley, *Will and Doom,* ed. Hoadly in Conn.Hist.Soc. *Collections* (1895). *20c. coll.:* ODEP 205, Whiting 254, Stevenson 1359:7, Whiting(MP) 363.

14. Laws catch flies and let hornets go free. *Rec. dist.:* Ill. *1st cit.:* ca1412 Hoccleve, *De Regimine Principum,* E.E.T.S. (1897); US1703 Taylor, *Christographia,* ed. Grabo (1962). *20c. coll.:* ODEP 446, Whiting 253, Stevenson 1358:4.

15. Laws too gentle are seldom obeyed; too severe, seldom executed. *Rec. dist.:* U.S. *1st cit.:* US1756 Franklin, *PRAlmanac. 20c. coll.:* Stevenson 1361:4.

16. Necessity knows no law, but it is intimately acquainted with many lawyers. *Rec. dist.:* N.Y., S.C. *1st cit.:* ca1377 Langland, *Piers Plowman;* US1674 Norton in *Winthrop Papers. 20c. coll.:* ODEP 557, Stevenson 1667:9, Whiting 307, T&W 258, Whiting(MP) 441.

17. No man is above the law, and no man is below it. *Rec. dist.:* N.Y., S.C. *1st cit.:* US1904 Roosevelt, Message to Congress, Jan. *20c. coll.:* Stevenson 1363:8.

18. The greater the number of laws, the more thieves there will be. *Rec. dist.:* Calif.

19. The law is like an axle: you can turn it whichever way you please if you give it plenty of grease. *Rec. dist.:* Miss.

20. The law of love is better than the love of law. *Rec. dist.:* N.Y.

21. The law that codifies evil is the essence of lawlessness. *Rec. dist.:* Ill.

22. The laws of nature are immutable. *Rec. dist.:* Mich.

23. The more laws, the more offenders. *Rec. dist.:* N.Y., Ont., S.C. *1st cit.:* 1573 Sanford, *Garden of Pleasure. 20c. coll.:* ODEP 447, Stevenson 1362:10.

24. There are nine ways to make a law, ten ways to break a law, and eleven ways to live within the law. *Rec. dist.:* N.Y.

25. There is one law for the rich and another for the poor. *Rec. dist.:* U.S., Can. *1st cit.:* 1830 Marryat, *King's Own;* US1846 Hooper, *Some Adventures of Captain Simon Suggs. 20c. coll.:* ODEP 445, T&W 215, Stevenson 1364:4, Whiting(MP) 364.

26. To go to law is to go to sea. *Rec. dist.:* Ont.

27. Where law ends, tyranny begins. *Rec. dist.:* Ill., N.Y. *1st cit.:* 1770 Pitt, Speech, 9 Mar., in *Case of Wilkes. 20c. coll.:* Stevenson 2404:1.

28. Where the law is uncertain, there is no law. *Rec. dist.:* Ont.

29. Where there's no law, there's no bread. *Rec. dist.:* N.Y., S.C. *1st cit.:* US1744 Franklin, *PRAlmanac. 20c. coll.:* Stevenson 1361:4.

30. Who will have law must have money. *Rec. dist.:* N.C. *1st cit.:* ca1460 *Parliment of Birds* in *Early Popular Poetry,* ed. Hazlitt (1864); US1732 *Jonathan Belcher Papers,* Mass.Hist.Soc. *Collections* (1893–94). *20c. coll.:* Stevenson 1372:6, Whiting 253.

SEE ALSO AGREE, for the law is costly. / AMBITION obeys no laws. / The EXECUTION of the laws is more important than the making of them. / FORTUNE knows neither reason nor law. / The best GOVERNMENT is that in which the law speaks instead of the lawyer. / Where there is HUNGER law is not regarded, and where law is not regarded there will be hunger. / LABOR is the law of happiness. / He that gives the laws of LOVE is usually a bachelor. / The MAGISTRATE should obey the law; the people should obey the magistrate. / Ill MAN-

NERS produce good laws. / NECESSITY knows no law. / ORDER is heaven's first law. / POSSESSION is nine points of the law, and self-possession is the other one. / REASON is the life of the law. / It is only ROGUES who feel the restraint of law. / SELF-PRESERVATION is the first law of nature. / WAR is the law of violence, peace the law of love.

lawmaker Lawmakers should not be law-breakers. *Rec. dist.:* Ill., N.J. *1st cit.:* ca1386 Chaucer, *Man of Law's Tale;* US1669 Penn, *No Cross, No Crown. 20c. coll.:* ODEP 446, Stevenson 1364:2.

lawsuit 1. Fond of lawsuits, little wealth; fond of doctors, little health. *Rec. dist.:* Ill.

2. If one family has a lawsuit, ten families are involved. *Rec. dist.:* Ind.

3. Lawsuits were invented to make lawyers rich. *Rec. dist.:* Ill.

4. The longer the lawsuit, the larger the lawyer's fee. *Rec. dist.:* Ill.
SEE ALSO Where there's a WILL, there's a lawsuit.

lawyer 1. A good lawyer, a bad neighbor. *Rec. dist.:* Ind., N.Y., Ont., S.C. *1st cit.:* 1604 Dallington, *View of Fraunce;* US1710 Mather, "An Essay Upon the Good" in *Bonifacius* (1967). *20c. coll.:* ODEP 447, Whiting 255, Stevenson 1370:6.

2. A man who is his own lawyer has a fool for a client. *Rec. dist.:* N.Y. *1st cit.:* 1850 Hunt, *Autobiography;* US1809 *Port Folio. 20c. coll.:* ODEP 146, CODP 130, Stevenson 1370:8, T&W 234, Whiting(MP) 364.

3. Lawyer's gowns are lined with the willfulness of their clients. *Rec. dist.:* Mich. *1st cit.:* 1707 Mapletoft, *Select Proverbs. 20c. coll.:* ODEP 447.

4. Lawyers earn their bread in the sweat of their browbeating. *Rec. dist.:* N.Y., S.C. *1st cit.:* US1920 Huneker, *Painted Veils. 20c. coll.:* Stevenson 1371:7.

5. Lawyers, like painters, can easily change white into black. *Rec. dist.:* Ill.

6. Most good lawyers live well, work hard, and die poor. *Rec. dist.:* N.Y., S.C. *1st cit.:*

US1847 Webster, Speech, Charleston, S.C., 10 May. *20c. coll.:* Stevenson 1372:14.

7. No matter who loses, the lawyer always wins. *Rec. dist.:* Ont.
SEE ALSO If there were no BAD people, there would be no good lawyers. / The best GOVERNMENT is that in which the law speaks instead of the lawyers. / Necessity knows no LAW, but it is intimately acquainted with many lawyers. / LAWSUITS were invented to make lawyers rich. / Always tell your doctor and your lawyer the TRUTH.

lay *SEE* If you are a COCK, crow; if a hen, lay eggs. / Don't kill the GOOSE that lays the golden egg. / A good HEN does not cackle in your house and lay in another's. / A HEN that doesn't cackle doesn't lay. / First HEN cackled, first hen laid. / A small RAIN lays a great dust.

laziness 1. He who knows no laziness will know prosperity. *Rec. dist.:* Kans.

2. Laziness has no boosters but many pals. *Rec. dist.:* Ill.

3. Laziness isn't worth a thing if not well carried out. *Rec. dist.:* Ont.

4. Laziness travels so slow that poverty overtakes him. *Rec. dist.:* Mich., N.Y. *1st cit.:* US1756 Franklin, *PRAlmanac. 20c. coll.:* Whiting 255, Stevenson 2141:6.

lazy 1. A lazy man always finds excuses. *Rec. dist.:* Ala., Ga.

2. A lazy man is no better than a dead one, but he takes up more room. *Rec. dist.:* Ala., Ga.

3. A lazy man will live the longest. *Rec. dist.:* Ont.

4. A lazy man works the hardest. *Rec. dist.:* N.Y., S.C.

5. A lazy person will never try to see the light. *Rec. dist.:* Calif.

6. Lazy folks are most efficient. *Rec. dist.:* Ont.

7. Lazy folks' stomachs don't get tired. *Rec. dist.:* Ont. *1st cit.:* US1880 Harris, *Plantation Proverbs* in *Uncle Remus, His Songs and His Sayings. 20c. coll.:* Stevenson 2217:18.

8. The lazy man goes to his work like a thief to the gallows. *Rec. dist.:* Wis.

9. The lazy man takes the most pain. *Rec. dist.:* W.Va. *1st cit.:* US1735 *Papers of Benjamin Franklin,* ed. Labaree (1959). *20c. coll.:* Whiting 160, Stevenson 2140:10.

SEE ALSO The lazy LAD makes a stark old man. / A man who can't get up to LOAF is too lazy to enjoy it. / A lazy SHEEP thinks its wool heavy.

lead 1. A man may be led, but he can't be driven. *Var.:* People are more easily led than driven. *Rec. dist.:* N.C. *1st cit.:* 1678 Ray, *English Proverbs;* US1727 Myatt in *Letters from Hudson Bay, 1703–1740,* ed. Davies, Hudson Bay Record Soc. (1965). *20c. coll.:* Stevenson 1373:11, Whiting 255, Whiting(MP) 365.

2. No one can expect to lead others until he has learned to boss himself. *Rec. dist.:* N.Y., S.C.

SEE ALSO If the BLIND lead the blind, both shall fall into the ditch. / You can lead a BOY to college, but you can't make him think. / The FATES lead the willing man; the unwilling they drag. / Be not led by FLATTERY. / The paths of GLORY lead but to the grave. / GREED to need does surely lead. / HITCHES lead to stitches. / You can lead a HORSE to water, but you can't make him drink. / IGNORANCE leads men into a party, and shame keeps them from getting out again. / One LIE leads to another. / The man who READS is the man who leads. / The ROAD of by-and-by leads to the town of never. / Easy STREET never leads anywhere. / You can lead a STUDENT to college, but you cannot make him think. / A WOMAN can't drive her husband, but she can lead him.

leader A good leader is also a good follower. *Rec. dist.:* Ind.

leaf 1. A rose leaf on the beaker's brim causes the overflow of the cup. *Rec. dist.:* Oreg.

2. He that fears leaves must not come into a wood. *Rec. dist.:* Okla. *1st cit.:* 1592 Delamothe, *Treasure of French Tongue.* *20c. coll.:* ODEP 251, Stevenson 784:9.

3. Just because there are no leaves on the trees doesn't mean there's no life in the limbs. *Rec. dist.:* Okla.

4. There are leaves to every vine. *Rec. dist.:* N.Y.

5. We all fade as the leaf. *Var.:* We all do fade as a leaf. *Rec. dist.:* Ill., N.Y. *1st cit.:* US1642 Gorton in Winslow, *Hypocrisie Unmasked,* ed. Chapin (1916). *20c. coll.:* Whiting 256, Stevenson 1409:6.

SEE ALSO DEEDS are fruits, words are leaves. / TIME and patience change the mulberry leaf to satin.

leafless *SEE* The WIND blows easily through a leafless tree.

leak *(n.)* Small leaks sink big ships. *Vars.:* **(a)** A little leak will sink a big ship. **(b)** A small leak will sink a great ship. **(c)** Beware of little expenses: a small leak will sink a great ship. *Rec. dist.:* U.S., Can. *1st cit.:* 1616 Adams, *Three Divine Sisters;* US1745 Franklin, *PRAlmanac.* *20c. coll.:* ODEP 450, Whiting 256, Stevenson 1443:6, Whiting(MP) 366.

leak *(v.)* *SEE* If you don't live in the HOUSE, you don't know when it leaks.

lean *(n.)* *SEE* A man must take the FAT with the lean.

lean *(v.)* The more you lean on somebody else, the leaner your chances of success. *Rec. dist.:* Ill.

SEE ALSO HOPE is a slender reed for a stout man to lean on.

lean *(adj.)* *SEE* A lean HORSE wins the race. / A hot KITCHEN makes a lean will. / Lean LIBERTY is better than fat slavery. / The leanest PIGS squeal the most. / Fat SORROW is better than lean sorrow. / Little knows the fat SOW what the lean one thinks. / Fat WIVES make lean husbands.

leaner *SEE* Be a LIFTER, not a leaner.

leap *(n.)* If you take a leap in the dark, you usually land in a pit. *Rec. dist.:* Ill. *1st cit.:* 1690 Vanbrugh, *Provok'd Wife;* US1741 Stephens, *Journal of Proceedings in Georgia* in *Georgia Records* (1906). *20c. coll.:* ODEP 450, Whiting 256, Stevenson 1374:14.

leap *(v.)* *SEE* LOOK before you leap. / THINK twice before you leap.

learn **1.** Easy to learn, hard to master. *Rec. dist.:* Ont. *1st cit.:* US1875 Scarborough, *Chinese Proverbs.* *20c. coll.:* Stevenson 1377:9.

2. He who never learns anything never forgets anything. *Rec. dist.:* N.C. *1st cit.:* 1903 Shaw, *Revolutionist's Handbook.* *20c. coll.:* Stevenson 409:7.

3. In order to learn, we must attend. *Rec. dist.:* Mich.

4. It is a task to learn, but it is much harder to unlearn. *Vars.:* **(a)** One who has learned unlearns with difficulty. **(b)** To learn is hard, but to unlearn is harder. *Rec. dist.:* Ill., Ind., Ont. *1st cit.:* US1948 Stevenson, *Home Book of Proverbs.* *20c. coll.:* Stevenson 1375:5.

5. It is never too late to learn. *Rec. dist.:* U.S. *1st cit.:* ca1530 Barclay, *Eclogues,* E.E.T.S. (1927); US1783 Williams, *Journal of John Penrose, Seaman,* ed. Dickason (1969). *20c. coll.:* ODEP 563, Whiting 257, *CODP* 130, Stevenson 1378:6, Whiting(MP) 361.

6. Learn as you'd live forever; live as you'd die tomorrow. *Rec. dist.:* Ind., N.Y.

7. Learn not, know not. *Rec. dist.:* Ont. *1st cit.:* 1659 Howell, *Paroimiographia (English Proverbs).* *20c. coll.:* Stevenson 1376:10.

8. Learn something new every day. *Rec. dist.:* Ill.

9. Learn to know when you are well off. *Rec. dist.:* S.C. *1st cit.:* US1855 Kingsley, *Westward Ho! 20c. coll.:* Stevenson 1329:11.

10. Learn to unlearn what you have learned to miss. *Rec. dist.:* Ohio.

11. Learn well and know better. *Rec. dist.:* Kans.

12. Lessons hard to learn are sweet to know. *Rec. dist.:* Calif.

13. Men learn while they teach. *Rec. dist.:* N.Y., Ohio, S.C. *1st cit.:* 1732 Fuller, *Gnomologia.* *20c. coll.:* Stevenson 2285:1.

14. We can only learn from our betters. *Rec. dist.:* N.Y., S.C. *1st cit.:* US1940 Adler, *How to Read a Book.* *20c. coll.:* Stevenson 1375:8.

15. We learn by doing, achieve by pursuing. *Rec. dist.:* Ill., Kans., Wis. *1st cit.:* 1589 Nashe, *Anatomy of Absurd.* *20c. coll.:* ODEP 198, Stevenson 535:7.

16. We learn by mistakes. *Rec. dist.:* N.C., Okla.

17. We learn not for school but for life. *Rec. dist.:* Ont. *1st cit.:* US1948 Stevenson, *Home Book of Proverbs.* *20c. coll.:* Stevenson 1378:1.

18. We learn not in school but in life. *Rec. dist.:* Colo.

19. What is well learned is not forgotten. *Rec. dist.:* Miss., N.Y.

20. What we first learn we best ken. *Rec. dist.:* Ont. *1st cit.:* 1721 Kelly, *Scottish Proverbs.* *20c. coll.:* ODEP 262, Stevenson 1379:7.

21. What we learn early we remember late. *Rec. dist.:* Calif. *1st cit.:* ca1320 *Proverbs of Hendying.* *20c. coll.:* Stevenson 1379:7.

22. You are never too wise to learn. *Rec. dist.:* N.C.

23. You can't learn any younger. *Rec. dist.:* Ohio, Ont.

SEE ALSO A BARBER learns to shave by shaving fools. / As the old COCK crows, the young cock learns. / From the ENEMY you learn a lot. / EXPERIENCE is a dear school, but fools learn in no other. / We learn something even by our FAILURES. / What JOHNNIE will not teach himself Johnnie will never learn. / You pay for every LESSON you learn. / LIVE and learn; die and forget all. / You cannot be a true MAN until you learn to obey. / Learn from the MISTAKES of others. / By doing NOTHING, we learn to do ill. / You must learn to STOOP as you go through life. / A man doesn't learn to UNDERSTAND anything unless he loves it. / You have to learn to WALK before you can run. / Learn WISDOM by the follies of others. / A WISE man will learn. / WISE men learn by other men's mistakes; fools insist on learning by their own. / Who keeps company with a WOLF learns to howl.

learned *(n.)* Write with the learned; pronounce with the vulgar. *Rec. dist.:* N.Y., S.C. *1st cit.:* 1678 Ray, *English Proverbs.* *20c. coll.:* Stevenson 2652:3.

learned *(adj.)* **1.** A learned man can be appreciated only by another learned man. *Rec. dist.:* Wis.

2. A learned man is twice born. *Rec. dist.:* Wis.

SEE ALSO A learned ASSEMBLY is a living library. / A closed BOOK does not produce a learned man.

learning 1. A little learning is a bad thing. *Var.:* A little learning is a dangerous thing. *Rec. dist.:* U.S., Can. *1st cit.:* 1711 Pope, *Essay on Criticism;* US1861 Holmes, *Elsie Venner. 20c. coll.: CODP* 131, T&W 217, Stevenson 1377:1, Whiting*(MP)* 366.

2. Advance in learning as you advance in life. *Rec. dist.:* Ill., N.J.

3. It is only when we forget all our learning that we begin to know. *Rec. dist.:* N.Y., S.C. *1st cit.:* US1859 Thoreau, *Autumn. 20c. coll.:* Stevenson 1379:3.

4. Learning has no enemy but ignorance. *Rec. dist.:* Calif. *1st cit.:* 1559 Cunningham, *Cosmographical Glasse;* US1797 Mann, "Life of Debora Sampson" in *Female Review,* ed. Vinton (1866). *20c. coll.:* Stevenson 1327:9, Whiting 257.

5. Learning has no limit. *Rec. dist.:* N.Y.

6. Learning makes a good man better and a bad man worse. *Var.:* Learning makes a good man better and an ill man worse. *Rec. dist.:* Ill., Ont. *1st cit.:* 1612 Charron, *Of Wisdom,* tr. Lennard (1640); US1758 Ames, *Almanacs,* ed. Briggs (1891). *20c. coll.: ODEP* 451, Whiting 257, Stevenson 1376:4.

7. Learning makes a man fit company for himself. *Rec. dist.:* N.Y., Wis. *1st cit.:* 1732 Fuller, *Gnomologia. 20c. coll.:* Stevenson 1377:5.

8. Learning refines and elevates the mind. *Rec. dist.:* Mich.

9. Learning to the studious and riches to the careful. *Var.:* Learning to the studious, riches to the careful, power to the bold, heaven to the virtuous. *Rec. dist.:* Ind. *1st cit.:* 1578 Florio, *Firste Fruites;* US1754 Franklin, *PRAlmanac. 20c. coll.:* Stevenson 1975:5.

10. Learning without thought is labor lost; thought without learning is dangerous. *Rec. dist.:* Wis. *1st cit.:* US1948 Stevenson, *Home Book of Proverbs. 20c. coll.:* Stevenson 1375:12.

11. Like unto like, and learning unto skill. *Rec. dist.:* N.C.

12. Men of learning are plain men. *Rec. dist.:* Ill.

13. Most of the learning in use is of no great use. *Rec. dist.:* N.Y., S.C. *1st cit.:* US1749 Franklin, *PRAlmanac. 20c. coll.:* Stevenson 1376:2.

14. One pound of learning requires ten pounds of common sense to use it. *Var.:* A handful of common sense is worth a bushel of learning. *Rec. dist.:* Iowa, Kans., N.J., Ont., Tenn.

15. Too much learning is worse than no learning at all. *Rec. dist.:* Ky., Tenn.

16. Wear your learning like your watch, in a private pocket. *Rec. dist.:* Ont. *1st cit.:* 1748 Lord Chesterfield, Letter, 22 Feb., in *Letters to His Son. 20c. coll.:* Stevenson 1375:10.

SEE ALSO HEALTH is worth more than learning. / No LICKIN', no learning. / REPETITION is the mother of learning. / There is no royal ROAD to learning. / SCHOLARS are wont to sell their birthright for a mess of learning. / If you have WIT and learning, add to it wisdom and modesty.

leash Undo the leash and loosen the hound. *Rec. dist.:* Ont.

least 1. Least said, soonest mended. *Vars.:* **(a)** Least said, sooner mended. **(b)** The least said is the easiest mended. **(c)** The least said is the soonest mended. **(d)** The least said, the easier mended. **(e)** The least said, the soonest mended. *Rec. dist.:* U.S., Can. *1st cit.:* ca1460 Hazlitt, *Remains of Early Poetry* (1864); US1698 Usher in *William & Mary Coll. Quart.* (1950). *20c. coll.: ODEP* 472, Whiting 257, *CODP* 131, Stevenson 2190:10, T&W 217, Whiting*(MP)* 366.

2. That government is best which governs least. *Rec. dist.:* Ill., N.Y. *1st cit.:* US1845 Judd, *Margaret. 20c. coll.:* T&W 157, Stevenson 1015:5.

SEE ALSO A FOOL always talks most when he has the least to say. / He KNOWS most who speaks least. / Say LITTLE, write less, print least. / The RICHEST man is he who wants least. / The best dressed WOMAN usually arrives with the least.

leather Raw leather will stretch. *Rec. dist.:* Okla. *1st cit.:* 1583 Melbancke, *Philotimus.* *20c. coll.:* ODEP 665, Stevenson 1379:8.

leave 1. Better leave than take. *Rec. dist.:* Ont.

2. Leave well enough alone. *Rec. dist.:* N.Y. *1st cit.:* ca1396 Chaucer, *Envoy to Burton;* US1833 *Correspondence of Andrew Jackson,* ed. Bassett. *20c. coll.:* ODEP 453, Whiting 478, T&W 399, Whiting(MP) 676.

3. Never leave until tomorrow what you can do today. *Var.:* Never leave that till tomorrow which you can do today. *Rec. dist.:* N.Y., Tex. *1st cit.:* ca1386 Chaucer, *Tale of Melibee;* US1690 *Winthrop Papers, 1498–1649,* Mass. Hist.Soc. *Collections* (1863–92). *20c. coll.:* CODP 186, Whiting 446, ODEP 656, Stevenson 2340:6, T&W 377, Whiting(MP) 636.

4. Never leave until you know where you are going. *Rec. dist.:* Kans.

5. When in doubt, leave it out. *Rec. dist.:* Oreg. *1st cit.:* 1884 Weatherly, *Little Folks' Proverb Painting Book.* *20c. coll.:* CODP 59, ODEP 200.

SEE ALSO BAD men leave their mark wherever they go. / With the old year leave your FAULTS, however dear. / FORTUNE always leaves one door open in disasters. / The GIRL that thinks no man is good enough for her is right, but she's left. / If you would leave GUESTS merry with cheer, be so yourself, or so at least appear. / Everything leaves, but LOVE remains. / Always leave the PARTY when you are still having a good time. / Never leave a TASK until it's done. / If you leave your UMBRELLA at home, it is sure to rain. / WOMEN leave peace behind 'em when they go. / The WORLD: we live in it, but leave it we must.

leaven Too little leaven spoils the loaf. *Rec. dist.:* Ont.

leaver A little leaver has the whole lump. *Rec. dist.:* Ind.

left *SEE* Never let your left HAND know what your right hand is doing.

leg 1. It's a poor pair of legs that will stand around and see the body bruised. *Rec. dist.:* Ohio.

2. Stand on your own two legs. *Rec. dist.:* Ont. *1st cit.:* 1582 Fioravanti, *Compendium of Rational Secrets,* tr. Hester; US1653 Keayne, *Apologia of Robert Keayne,* ed. Bailyn (1965). *20c. coll.:* ODEP 770, Whiting 258, Stevenson 1383:4.

3. What yo' laigs fails to do, yo' haid has to do. *Rec. dist.:* S.C.

SEE ALSO A LIE has no legs. / A LIE stands on one leg, truth on two. / You get the RABBIT from the hind legs. / One can RUN only as fast as his legs can carry him.

leisure 1. A life of leisure and a life of laziness are two things. *Rec. dist.:* Ind., Wis. *1st cit.:* 1732 Fuller, *Gnomologia;* US1746 Franklin, *PRAlmanac.* *20c. coll.:* Stevenson 1384:2, Whiting 260.

2. Leisure breeds lust. *Rec. dist.:* Calif. *1st cit.:* US1875 Scarborough, *Chinese Proverbs.* *20c. coll.:* Stevenson 1384:7.

3. Leisure is a pretty garment; it won't do to wear it all the time. *Rec. dist.:* Miss.

4. Leisure is time for doing something useful. *Rec. dist.:* N.J. *1st cit.:* US1758 Franklin, *PRAlmanac.* *20c. coll.:* Stevenson 1384:5.

SEE ALSO There's LUCK in leisure. / MARRY in haste and repent at leisure. / Employ the TIME well if you mean to gain leisure. / None but the WISE man can employ leisure well.

leisurely Done leisurely, done well. *Rec. dist.:* Ill. *1st cit.:* US1875 Scarborough, *Chinese Proverbs.* *20c. coll.:* Stevenson 538:4.

lemon The lemon, after being squeezed, is thrown away. *Rec. dist.:* N.Y.

lend 1. Lend and lose is the game of fools. *Rec. dist.:* Ill. *1st cit.:* 1678 Ray, *English Proverbs.* *20c. coll.:* ODEP 455, Stevenson 1385:5.

2. Them as lends, spends. *Rec. dist.:* N.Y., S.C. *1st cit.:* 1640 Herbert, *Outlandish Proverbs (Jacula Prudentum)* in *Works,* ed. Hutchinson

(1941); US1880 Sill, *Baker's Duzzen uv Wize Sawz*. **20c. coll.:** ODEP 455, Stevenson 393:15.

SEE ALSO DISTANCE lends enchantment. / Lend money to an ENEMY and you will gain him, to a friend and you will lose him. / If you want to keep a FRIEND, never borrow, never lend. / Lend your HORSE and you may have back his skin. / If you would lose a troublesome VISITOR, lend him money.

lender Let the lender beware. **Rec. dist.:** Ill.

SEE ALSO Neither a BORROWER nor a lender be. / The BORROWER is a slave to the lender, the security to both. / Great SPENDERS are bad lenders.

lending SEE Lend MONEY and you get an enemy.

length SEE It's not the length of the PRAYER that is the most important.

lengthen SEE As the DAYS lengthen the cold strengthens. / To lengthen your LIFE, lessen your meals.

lenient SEE Be not lenient to your own FAULTS.

Lent Those have a short Lent who owe money to be paid at Easter. **Rec. dist.:** Ind., Ky., Tenn. **1st cit.:** 1642 Torriano, *Select Italian Proverbs;* US1738 Franklin, *PRAlmanac.* **20c. coll.:** ODEP 728, Whiting 258, Stevenson 223:5.

leopard **1.** A leopard cannot change his spots. **Vars.: (a)** A leopard doesn't change his spots. **(b)** A leopard never changes its spots. **(c)** A leopard won't change its spots. **(d)** The leopard can't change his spots. **(e)** You can't change a leopard's spots. **(f)** You can't change the spots of a leopard. **Rec. dist.:** U.S., Can. **1st cit.:** 1546 Bale, *First Examination of Anne Askewe;* US1652 *Complete Writings of Roger Williams* (1963). **20c. coll.:** CODP 131, Whiting 132, ODEP 456, Stevenson 1673:6, T&W 121, Whiting(MP) 368.

2. The leopard is absent, so they play with the cubs. **Rec. dist.:** Ill.

3. You can't tell a leopard by its spots. **Rec. dist.:** Kans.

less *(n.)* **1.** The less we know, the more we suspect. **Rec. dist.:** N.Y., S.C. **1st cit.:** US1874

Shaw (pseud. Billings), *Encyclopedia of Wit and Wisdom.* **20c. coll.:** Stevenson 2252:4.

2. The less you say, the less you have to take back. **Var.:** The better the less said. **Rec. dist.:** Ark., Kans. **1st cit.:** 1960 Davies, *Papers of Andrew Melmoth;* US1789 *Life and Letters of Simeon Baldwin,* ed. Baldwin (1919). **20c. coll.:** Whiting(MP) 369, Whiting 259.

SEE ALSO The more a man DREAMS, the less he believes. / Say LITTLE, write less, print least. / We can always LIVE on less when we have more to live on.

less *(adj.)* SEE Choose the lesser of two EVILS. / The less GOVERNMENT we have the better. / The less the TEMPTATION, the greater the sin.

less *(adv.)* SEE GOOD men and bad men are each less so than they seem. / Least SAID, soonest mended. / TALK less; listen more.

lessen SEE Hope of GAIN lessens pain. / To lengthen your LIFE, lessen your meals.

lesson **1.** A bought lesson is a good lesson. **Var.:** A bought lesson is the best lesson. **Rec. dist.:** Ill.

2. An evil lesson is soon learned. **Rec. dist.:** Okla. **1st cit.:** 1639 Clarke, *Paroemiologia.* **20c. coll.:** ODEP 233.

3. One of the lessons a woman never learns is never to talk to a drunken or angry man. **Rec. dist.:** Mich., Miss.

4. You pay for every lesson you learn. **Rec. dist.:** N.C.

SEE ALSO Lessons hard to LEARN are sweet to know.

letter **1.** A love letter sometimes costs more than a three-cent stamp. **Rec. dist.:** Calif., N.Y., S.C.

2. Do not close a letter without reading it. **Rec. dist.:** Mich.

3. Letters blush not. **Rec. dist.:** N.Y.

level *(n.)* **1.** It pays to be on the level. **Rec. dist.:** U.S. **1st cit.:** US1875 Burnham, *Three Years.* **20c. coll.:** T&W 218.

2. The level of the woman is the level of the world. **Rec. dist.:** N.C.

SEE ALSO WATER seeks its own level.

level *(v.)* SEE LOVE levels all inequalities.

liar **1.** A fish is caught by the mouth; the liar is caught by his tongue. *Rec. dist.:* Ariz.

2. A liar is sooner caught than a cripple. *Rec. dist.:* Miss., N.C. *1st cit.:* 1732 Fuller, *Gnomologia. 20c. coll.:* Stevenson 1394:1.

3. A liar is worse than a thief. *Rec. dist.:* N.Y., Okla., Ont., Tex. *1st cit.:* 1545 Cato, *Precepts,* tr. Burrant. *20c. coll.:* ODEP 457, Stevenson 1397:6.

4. A liar should have a good memory. *Vars.:* **(a)** A liar needs a good memory. **(b)** In order to be a good liar, one needs to have an excellent memory. **(c)** Liars need good memories to cover up their lies, but people who tell the truth need remember little. **(d)** No man has a good enough memory to be a successful liar. *Rec. dist.:* U.S., Can. *1st cit.:* ca1531 Latimer, *Letters;* US1702 Mather, *Magnalia Christi Americana. 20c. coll.:* ODEP 457, Whiting 259, CODP 132, Stevenson 1395:6, Whiting*(MP)* 369.

5. Believe every man a liar until he proves himself true. *Rec. dist.:* Ont.

6. Each liar loves to hear himself talk. *Rec. dist.:* N.C.

7. It takes a liar to call someone a liar. *Rec. dist.:* Ind.

8. Liars begin by imposing on others but end by deceiving themselves. *Rec. dist.:* Ill., Ont. *1st cit.:* 1611 Shakespeare, *Tempest. 20c. coll.:* ODEP 457.

9. Liars have short wings. *Rec. dist.:* Ill.

10. Liars never prosper. *Rec. dist.:* Ont.

11. No one believes a liar when he tells the truth. *Vars.:* **(a)** A liar is not believed when he speaks the truth. **(b)** A liar won't be believed when he tells the truth. **(c)** If a liar tells the truth, he is also not believed. **(d)** You can't believe a liar even when he tells the truth. *Rec. dist.:* U.S., Can. *1st cit.:* 1477 *Dictes and Sayenges of Philosophirs,* tr. Rivers. *20c. coll.:* ODEP 457, Stevenson 1391:10.

12. Show me a liar and I'll show you a thief. *Rec. dist.:* N.Y., N.C., Okla., Ont., Tex. *1st cit.:* 1615 Adams, *Mystical Bedlam. 20c. coll.:* ODEP 729, Stevenson 1397:6.

13. The biggest liar in the world is the man who starts out by saying, "They say." *Vars.:* **(a)** "They say" is a liar. **(b)** "They say" is a tough old liar. **(c)** "They say" is often a great liar. **(d)** "They say" is the biggest liar in the world. *Rec. dist.:* Ind., N.J., N.C., Ont.

14. There's no liar like an old liar. *Rec. dist.:* N.Y., S.C. *1st cit.:* US1941 Gruber, *Navy Colt. 20c. coll.:* Stevenson 1394:3.

SEE ALSO Tell a LIE once, you are always a liar to that person. / If there were no LISTENERS there would be no liars. / Muddy ROADS call de milepost a liar. / You can shut the door on a THIEF, but you can do nothing about a liar.

liberal Liberal hands make many friends. *Rec. dist.:* Ill.

liberality Liberality consists less in giving much than in giving at the right time. *Var.:* Liberality is not giving largely but wisely. *Rec. dist.:* N.Y., Ont., S.C. *1st cit.:* US1948 Stevenson, *Home Book of Proverbs. 20c. coll.:* Stevenson 1387:6.

liberty **1.** All men love liberty and seem bent on destroying her. *Var.:* All men love liberty. *Rec. dist.:* Ill., Utah.

2. Give me liberty or give me death. *Rec. dist.:* N.Y., Va. *1st cit.:* US1775 Henry, Speech in Virginia House of Delegates, 23 Mar. *20c. coll.:* Stevenson 1387:12.

3. It is dangerous to take liberties with great men. *Rec. dist.:* Mich.

4. Lean liberty is better than fat slavery. *Rec. dist.:* Mich., Ont. *1st cit.:* 1605 Heywood, *If You Know Not Me. 20c. coll.:* ODEP 450, Stevenson 1388:9.

5. Liberty is not license. *Rec. dist.:* Ill. *1st cit.:* 1640 Jonson, *Time Vindicated. 20c. coll.:* ODEP 458, Whiting 259, Stevenson 1389:5, Whiting*(MP)* 369.

6. Liberty is one thing you can't have unless you give it to others. *Rec. dist.:* N.Y., Ohio, S.C. *1st cit.:* US1940 White, Editorial, *Emporia, Kans. Gazette,* 24 Oct. *20c. coll.:* Stevenson 1390:8.

7. Liberty, like charity, must begin at home. *Rec. dist.:* Ill.

8. Like liberty, gold never stays where it is undervalued. *Rec. dist.:* N.Y., S.C. *1st cit.:* US1878 Morrill, Speech, U.S. Senate, 25 Jan. *20c. coll.:* Stevenson 989:1.

9. Little liberties are great offenses. *Rec. dist.:* Ohio.

10. The ground of liberty must be gained by inches. *Rec. dist.:* Ont.

11. The love of liberty burns brightest in a dungeon. *Rec. dist.:* Ill.

12. There is no liberty without security, and no security without unity. *Rec. dist.:* N.Y., S.C. *1st cit.:* US1940 André Maurois (Emile Herzog), Speech at 45th annual convention of the National Association of Manufacturers, New York, 12 Dec. *20c. coll.:* Stevenson 1390:7.

13. Your liberty ends where my nose begins. *Rec. dist.:* N.Mex., N.C.

SEE ALSO REVENGE is dearly bought at the price of liberty. / Sell not VIRTUE to purchase wealth nor liberty to purchase power. / He who marries for WEALTH sells his liberty.

library **1.** A great library is the diary of the human race. *Rec. dist.:* Wis.

2. A library is a repository of medicine for the mind. *Rec. dist.:* N.Y. *1st cit.:* US1948 Stevenson, *Home Book of Proverbs.* *20c. coll.:* Stevenson 1390:16.

3. A library is but the soul's burial ground. *Rec. dist.:* N.Y., S.C. *1st cit.:* USca1887 Beecher, "Oxford" in *Star Papers.* *20c. coll.:* Stevenson 1390:11.

4. Libraries are not made; they grow. *Rec. dist.:* Okla.

lick **1.** Don't lick it till it drops. *Rec. dist.:* Ont.

2. Every lick counts. *Rec. dist.:* Kans.

3. If you can't lick 'em, jine 'em. *Rec. dist.:* N.Mex., N.Y., S.C. *1st cit.:* 1979 Lessing, *Shikasta;* US1941 Reynolds, *Wounded Don't Cry.* *20c. coll.:* CODP 10, Stevenson 1829:6, Whiting(MP) 369.

4. No lickin', no learnin'. *Rec. dist.:* Calif., Colo.

5. You're never licked until you admit it. *Rec. dist.:* Ohio.

SEE ALSO If you play with a PUPPY, he will lick your mouth.

lid There's a lid for every pot. *Vars.:* **(a)** There is a pot to fit every lid. **(b)** There is never a pot too crooked but what there's a lid to fit it. **(c)** There isn't a pan so crooked that there isn't a lid to fit it. *Rec. dist.:* Ariz., Kans., Ohio. *1st cit.:* 1532 More, "Preface" in *Confutation of Tyndale.* *20c. coll.:* Stevenson 1427:6.

lie *(n.)* **1.** A great lie is the best. *Rec. dist.:* Ill.

2. A lie begets a lie until they become a generation. *Rec. dist.:* Ill., Okla., Tex. *1st cit.:* 1534 Udall, *Floures for Latine Speaking;* US1962 *Bangor Daily News,* 16 June. *20c. coll.:* ODEP 460, Stevenson 1397:3, Whiting(MP) 370.

3. A lie can go a mile before the truth can put its boots on. *Var.:* A lie will travel a mile while truth is putting on its boots. *Rec. dist.:* Ill.

4. A lie can go around the world and back while the truth is lacing up its boots. *Var.:* A lie can travel round the world while the truth is tieing up its shoestrings. *Rec. dist.:* Ill., N.C., Ohio, W.Va. *1st cit.:* US1885 Spurgeon, *Salt-Cellars.* *20c. coll.:* Stevenson 2395:5.

5. A lie has no legs. *Vars.:* **(a)** A lie has no legs, but a scandal has wings. **(b)** A lie has no legs to stand on, but it gets places. **(c)** Though a lie has no legs and cannot stand, it has wings and can fly far. *Rec. dist.:* Ill., Wis. *1st cit.:* 1573 Sanford, *Garden of Pleasure.* *20c. coll.:* ODEP 461, Stevenson 1393:11.

6. A lie is like a snowball: the farther you roll it, the bigger it becomes. *Rec. dist.:* N.Y., Wis.

7. A lie is the most difficult thing in the world permanently to conceal. *Rec. dist.:* N.C.

8. A lie runs until it is overtaken by the truth. *Rec. dist.:* Wis. *1st cit.:* 1902 Lean, *Collectanea.* *20c. coll.:* Stevenson 2395:5.

9. A lie stands on one leg, truth on two. *Var.:* A lie only runs on one leg. *Rec. dist.:* U.S., Can. *1st cit.:* 1659 Howell, *Paroimiographia (English Proverbs);* US1735 Franklin, *PRAlmanac.* *20c. coll.:* Stevenson 2395:10, Whiting 259.

10. A lie will give blossom but no fruit. *Rec. dist.:* Ohio.

11. A necessary lie is harmless. *Var.:* A white lie is harmless; so is a necessary one. *Rec. dist.:* Ill., N.C.

12. A sudden lie has best luck. *Rec. dist.:* N.C.

13. A white lie leaves a black spot. *Rec. dist.:* Ill., N.C.

14. Be sure, a lie will find you out. *Rec. dist.:* Ont.

15. Dare to be true; nothing can need a lie. *Rec. dist.:* Minn., Ont. *1st cit.:* ca1633 Herbert, *Church-Porch. 20c. coll.:* Stevenson 1396:5.

16. He that tells a lie must invent twenty more to maintain it. *Rec. dist.:* Ohio. *1st cit.:* 1727 Pope, *Thoughts on Various Subjects. 20c. coll.:* Stevenson 1397:3.

17. If you are going to tell a lie, tell it big enough so that no one will believe you. *Rec. dist.:* N.C.

18. If you believe a lie, it's a truth as far as you are concerned. *Rec. dist.:* Ill.

19. If you tell a lie an' stick to it, dat's as good as de truth anyhow. *Rec. dist.:* N.Y., S.C.

20. It is as bad to believe a lie as to tell one. *Rec. dist.:* N.C.

21. Jesting lies bring serious sorrows. *Rec. dist.:* N.Y., Ont. *1st cit.:* 1855 Bohn, *Handbook of Proverbs. 20c. coll.:* Stevenson 1267:4.

22. Lies do harm only to them that tells 'em. *Rec. dist.:* N.Y., S.C. *1st cit.:* US1941 Updegraff, *Hills Look Down. 20c. coll.:* Stevenson 1392:4.

23. Misunderstanding brings lies to town. *Rec. dist.:* N.J., N.Y. *1st cit.:* 1639 Clarke, *Paroemiologia. 20c. coll.:* ODEP 536, Stevenson 1600:1.

24. Never tell a lie till the truth doesn't fit. *Rec. dist.:* Ont.

25. No lies are white; they are all black. *Rec. dist.:* N.C.

26. One lie does not justify another. *Rec. dist.:* N.C.

27. One lie leads to another. *Rec. dist.:* Calif., Colo., Mich., N.Y. *1st cit.:* 1534 Udall, *Floures for Latine Speaking. 20c. coll.:* ODEP 460, Stevenson 1397:3.

28. One seldom meets a lonely lie. *Rec. dist.:* Ala., Ga., N.Y., N.C.

29. Tell a lie and find the truth. *Rec. dist.:* Okla., Tex. *1st cit.:* ca1594 Bacon, *Promus. 20c. coll.:* ODEP 806, Stevenson 2394:5.

30. Tell a lie once, you are always a liar to that person. *Rec. dist.:* Kans.

31. Telling lies is a fault in a boy, an art in a lover, an accomplishment in a bachelor, and second nature in a married woman. *Rec. dist.:* Minn.

32. The bigger the lie, the more it is believed. *Rec. dist.:* Ill.

33. There are a thousand ways to tell a lie, but only one way to tell the truth. *Rec. dist.:* Ohio.

34. There is no lie, spun so fine, through which the truth won't shine. *Rec. dist.:* Ont.

35. "They say so" is half a lie. *Var.:* "I heard one say so" is half a lie. *Rec. dist.:* N.Y., N.C., Ont., Tex. *1st cit.:* 1666 Torriano, *Common Place of Italian Proverbs;* US1869 Spurgeon, *John Ploughman's Talks. 20c. coll.:* ODEP 809, Stevenson 2018:8.

36. White lies are but the ushers to black ones. *Rec. dist.:* Ont. *1st cit.:* 1785 Paley, *Moral Philosophy. 20c. coll.:* Stevenson 1397:8.

37. White lies save your soul; black lies damage your soul. *Rec. dist.:* Calif.

38. You can get far with a lie, but not come back. *Rec. dist.:* N.Y.

39. You can't live down a lie. *Rec. dist.:* Calif.

SEE ALSO One of the most startling differences between a CAT and a lie is that a cat has only nine lives. / Sooner or later all POLITICIANS die of swallowing their own lies. / Ask me no QUESTIONS, and I'll tell you no lies. / SIN has many tools, but a lie is the handle which fits them all. / Half TRUTH is often a great lie. / The TRUTH is better than a lie.

lie *(v., deceive)* **1.** A man who won't lie to a woman has very little consideration for her feelings. *Rec. dist.:* N.Y.

2. He who lies once is never believed again. *Rec. dist.:* N.Y., Ont.

3. If you lie, you steal. *Rec. dist.:* Ont. *1st cit.:* 1607 West, *Court of Conscience.* **20c. coll.:** ODEP 460, Stevenson 1397:6.

4. It is better to be lied about than to lie. *Rec. dist.:* N.Y., S.C. *1st cit.:* US1901 Hubbard, *Philistine.* **20c. coll.:** Stevenson 1396:5.

5. It is better to lie a little than to be unhappy much. *Rec. dist.:* N.Y., S.C. *1st cit.:* US1902 Belasco and Long, *Darling of the Gods.* **20c. coll.:** Stevenson 1392:6.

SEE ALSO None but COWARDS lie. / He who does one FAULT at first and lies to hide it makes it two. / FIGURES don't lie.

lie *(v., recline, reside)* SEE What you ARE— what you are lies with you. / If you lie down with DOGS, you'll get up with fleas. / As a man LIVES, so shall he die; as a tree falls, so shall it lie. / Where LOVE falls it lies, and even if it be on the manure pile. / 'Tis not in NUMBERS but in unity that our great strength lies. / Don't STAND when you can sit, and don't sit when you can lie down.

life **1.** A good life keeps away wrinkles. *Rec. dist.:* N.Y.

2. A humble life with peace and quiet is better than a splendid one with danger and risk. *Rec. dist.:* N.Y.

3. A libertine's life is not a life of liberty. *Rec. dist.:* Mich. *1st cit.:* 1732 Fuller, *Gnomologia.* **20c. coll.:** Stevenson 1495:4.

4. A long life may not be good enough, but a good life is long enough. *Rec. dist.:* N.Y., S.C. *1st cit.:* US1755 Franklin, *PRAlmanac.* **20c. coll.:** Stevenson 1410:14.

5. An ill life, an ill end. *Rec. dist.:* Ill., N.Y. *1st cit.:* ca1300 *King Alisaunder,* tr. Weber (1810). **20c. coll.:** ODEP 399, Stevenson 1419:11.

6. Don't spend your life reaching for the moon. *Rec. dist.:* N.Y.

7. For a long life be moderate in all things, but don't miss anything. *Rec. dist.:* N.Y.

8. For most people life is one bill after another. *Rec. dist.:* N.Y., S.C. *1st cit.:* US1935 Odets, *Paradise Lost.* **20c. coll.:** Stevenson 1401:6.

9. He enjoys life who makes others enjoy it best. *Rec. dist.:* Ind.

10. He who saves another life adds years to his own. *Rec. dist.:* N.Y. *1st cit.:* US1938 Champion, *Racial Proverbs.* **20c. coll.:** Stevenson 1405:2.

11. Hidden life, happy life. *Rec. dist.:* N.J.

12. If life were a thing that money could buy, the rich would live and the poor would die. *Rec. dist.:* Ont.

13. It's a great life if you don't weaken. *Vars.:* **(a)** It's a great life if you can live through it. **(b)** It's a great life if you don't weaken, but more fun if you do. **(c)** Life is wonderful if you don't weaken. *Rec. dist.:* U.S., Can. *1st cit.:* 1927 Williams, *Crouching Beast;* US1929 Edington, *Studio Murder Mystery.* **20c. coll.:** Whiting*(MP)* 371.

14. Life and misery begin together. *Rec. dist.:* Ont. *1st cit.:* 1732 Fuller, *Gnomologia.* **20c. coll.:** Stevenson 1591:13.

15. Life begins at forty. *Rec. dist.:* U.S. *1st cit.:* US1932 Pitkin, *Life Begins at Forty.* **20c. coll.:** CODP 132.

16. Life can be beautiful. *Rec. dist.:* Calif.

17. Life consists in wishing you had if you didn't and wishing you hadn't if you did. *Rec. dist.:* Miss.

18. Life ends when honor ends. *Rec. dist.:* Calif.

19. Life is a bubble on the stream. *Rec. dist.:* Oreg. *1st cit.:* US1948 Stevenson, *Home Book of Proverbs.* **20c. coll.:** Stevenson 1402:3.

20. Life is a chart as well as a coast, and a little care will keep clear of rocks, reefs, and sandbars. *Rec. dist.:* N.Y., S.C.

21. Life is a comedy to those who think, a tragedy to those who feel. *Rec. dist.:* Ill.

22. Life is a jest. *Rec. dist.:* Ind. *1st cit.:* 1720 Gay, Letter to Alexander Pope in *My Own Epitaph.* **20c. coll.:** Stevenson 1400:5.

23. Life is a light before the wind. *Rec. dist.:* Calif.

24. Life is a long lesson in humility. *Rec. dist.:* Ala., Ga., Wis. *1st cit.:* 1891 Barrie, *Misalliance.* **20c. coll.:** Stevenson 1398:3.

25. Life is a mirror. *Rec. dist.:* Ind.

26. Life is a mystery that death alone may solve. *Rec. dist.:* N.Y., N.C., S.C.

27. Life is a picture, so paint it well. *Rec. dist.:* Ind.

28. Life is a queer proposition. *Rec. dist.:* N.Y., S.C. *1st cit.:* 1907 Cohan, "Life's a Funny Proposition" in *Little Johnny Jones. 20c. coll.:* Stevenson 1402:2.

29. Life is a song, but it often goes flat. *Rec. dist.:* Wis.

30. Life is a theater where the worst people sometimes get the best seats. *Rec. dist.:* Ind.

31. Life is an onion which one peels crying. *Rec. dist.:* Ill., N.Y.

32. Life is but a bowl of cherries. *Rec. dist.:* Ill., Ind., Oreg., Wis. *1st cit.:* 1933 Holt, *Dark Lady.* US1941 Stong, *Other Worlds. 20c. coll.:* Whiting(MP) 371.

33. Life is but a dream. *Rec. dist.:* N.Y.

34. Life is death without real friends, and money can't buy them. *Rec. dist.:* Ill.

35. Life is hard by the yard, but by the inch life's a cinch. *Rec. dist.:* Wis.

36. Life is just; it will give us all we earn. *Rec. dist.:* N.C.

37. Life is just one damned thing after another. *Rec. dist.:* U.S. *1st cit.:* 1929 Whitechurch, *Robbery at Rudwick House;* USca1906 O'Malley, Epigram in Hubbard, *Thousand and One Epigrams. 20c. coll.:* Whiting(MP) 371, Stevenson 1401:6.

38. Life is just one parting after another. *Rec. dist.:* N.Y., S.C. *1st cit.:* US1943 Addis, *Night Over the Wood. 20c. coll.:* Stevenson 1401:6.

39. Life is made up of little things. *Var.:* Life is a great bundle of little things. *Rec. dist.:* N.C., Ont. *1st cit.:* 1902 Lean, *Collectanea. 20c. coll.:* Stevenson 1445:10.

40. Life is no bed of roses. *Rec. dist.:* U.S., Can. *1st cit.:* 1938 Walling, *Corpse with Grimy Glove;* US1780 Duane in *Correspondence of American Revolution,* ed. Sparks (1853). *20c. coll.:* Whiting 24, Whiting(MP) 371.

41. Life is not a cup to be drained, but a measure to be filled. *Rec. dist.:* Miss.

42. Life is not a push from below, but a gift from above. *Rec. dist.:* Wis.

43. Life is not so short but that there is always time enough for courtesy. *Rec. dist.:* Wis.

44. Life is not what you find, it's what you create. *Rec. dist.:* N.J.

45. Life is not wholly beer and skittles. *Rec. dist.:* N.Y., S.C. *1st cit.:* 1836 Dickens, *Pickwick Papers;* US1855 Haliburton, *Nature and Human Nature. 20c. coll.:* ODEP 462, T&W 220, *CODP* 133, Stevenson 1403:4.

46. Life is one long process of getting tired. *Rec. dist.:* N.C. *1st cit.:* ca1900 Butler, *Note Books: Life. 20c. coll.:* Stevenson 1398:7.

47. Life is short and full o' blisters. *Rec. dist.:* Miss.

48. Life is short and sweet. *Rec. dist.:* Ind., Ky., N.Y., Ont. *1st cit.:* 1931 Bailey, *Fortune Speaking;* US1802 *Port Folio. 20c. coll.:* Whiting(MP) 371, Stevenson 1404:4, Whiting 259, T&W 220.

49. Life is short, and time is swift. *Rec. dist.:* N.C.

50. Life is subject to ups and downs. *Rec. dist.:* Ill. *1st cit.:* US1853 Curtis, *Potiphar Papers. 20c. coll.:* T&W 219.

51. Life is swell when you keep well. *Rec. dist.:* Ill.

52. Life is the flower of which love is the honey. *Rec. dist.:* Ind.

53. Life is too short to be little. *Rec. dist.:* Ohio, Ont.

54. Life is too short to fool with dishonest people. *Rec. dist.:* N.C., Ohio.

55. Life is too short to waste time on trifles. *Rec. dist.:* Ill., N.Y., Ohio, S.C.

56. Life is what you make it. *Var.:* One's life is what one makes it. *Rec. dist.:* U.S., Can. *1st cit.:* 1941 Cheyney, *Trap for Bellamy. 20c. coll.:* Stevenson 1402:9.

57. Life isn't life without a wife. *Rec. dist.:* N.J., N.Y., N.Dak., Ohio.

58. Life should be partly cakes and red geraniums. *Rec. dist.:* Wis.

59. Life without memories is like a rare food

that the cook forgot to season. **Rec. dist.:** Calif.

60. Life's a gamble: you win or lose. **Var.:** Life is a lottery: most folks draw blanks. **Rec. dist.:** Ill.

61. Life's a voyage that's homeward bound. **Rec. dist.:** N.Y., S.C. **1st cit.:** US1891 Melville quoted by Cournos, *Modern Plutarch.* **20c. coll.:** Stevenson 1401:7.

62. Life's fairest things are those which seem; the leaf is that of which we dream. **Rec. dist.:** Ind.

63. Life's jes pushin' 'side yo' troubles and lookin' for de light. **Rec. dist.:** Ala., Ga.

64. Life's race is either forward or backward. **Rec. dist.:** Kans.

65. Live as though life were earnest, and life will be so. **Rec. dist.:** Ohio.

66. Live your life, do your work, then take your hat. **Rec. dist.:** N.Y., S.C. **1st cit.:** US1849 Thoreau, *Week on the Concord and Merrimack Rivers.* **20c. coll.:** Stevenson 1421:1.

67. Live your life so that even the undertaker will be sorry when you die. **Rec. dist.:** N.J.

68. Live your own life, for you die your own death. **Rec. dist.:** Kans., Wis.

69. Make your life; don't copy it. **Rec. dist.:** U.S.

70. No life without pain. **Rec. dist.:** N.Y.

71. Nothing is better than a single life. **Rec. dist.:** Utah.

72. Nothing is certain in life but death and taxes. **Vars.:** (a) The only thing certain in life is death and taxes. (b) Two things you must do in life: die and pay taxes. **Rec. dist.:** Ill. **1st cit.:** 1726 Defoe, *History of Devil;* US1789 Franklin, Letter, 13 Nov., in *Writings* (1907). **20c. coll.:** CODP 164, ODEP 580, Stevenson 2248:16, Whiting(*MP*) 158.

73. Plan your life as though you were going to live forever, but live today as if you were going to die tomorrow. **Rec. dist.:** Calif.

74. Quite a life without a wife, worse with one. **Rec. dist.:** N.Y., N.Dak., S.C.

75. Save your life and lose a minute. **Rec. dist.:** N.C., Ont.

76. The great secret of life is to hear lessons and not teach them. **Rec. dist.:** N.Y., S.C.

77. The life you save may be your own. **Rec. dist.:** Calif. **Infm.:** Drive carefully and save your own life.

78. The secret of life is not to do what you like but to like what you do. **Rec. dist.:** U.S., Can.

79. The true value of life cannot be measured in dollars. **Rec. dist.:** Calif., Mich.

80. To a nitwit life is one laugh after another. **Rec. dist.:** N.Y., S.C. **1st cit.:** US1935 Odets, *Paradise Lost.* **20c. coll.:** Stevenson 1401:6.

81. To lengthen your life, lessen your meals. **Rec. dist.:** N.Y., S.C., Utah. **1st cit.:** US1733 Franklin, *PRAlmanac.* **20c. coll.:** Stevenson 660:14.

82. To save one life is better than to build a seven-story pagoda. **Rec. dist.:** Ind.

83. To widen your life without deepening it is only to weaken it. **Rec. dist.:** N.C.

84. Today life is our school; tomorrow our school is life. **Rec. dist.:** Ind.

85. Too many people conduct their life on the cafeteria style—self-service. **Rec. dist.:** W.Va.

86. What makes life weary is lack of motive. **Rec. dist.:** Calif.

87. What you put into someone's life will someday come back into your own. **Rec. dist.:** Okla.

88. When there is life there is love. **Rec. dist.:** Ky., Tenn.

89. Where there's life there is hope. **Vars.:** (a) As long as there is life there is hope. (b) While the sick man has life, there is hope. **Rec. dist.:** U.S., Can. **1st cit.:** 1539 Erasmus, *Adages,* tr. Taverner; US1781 *Correspondence of Samuel B. Webb,* ed. Ford (1893). **20c. coll.:** CODP 133, Whiting 260, ODEP 462, Stevenson 1170:1, T&W 220, Whiting(*MP*) 373.

90. You get out of life what you put into it. **Rec. dist.:** U.S., Can.

91. You have to work the life out of you to keep the life in you. **Rec. dist.:** N.Y.

See also ART is long, life is short. / The ART of life is the art of avoiding pain. / The BEST things in life are free. / BREAD is the staff of life. / Eat BREAD and drink water, and you will live a long life. / A shady BUSINESS never yields a sunny life. / CARDS and dice is like all in life; dey ever falls well for bold players. / CHILDREN and fools have merry lives. / COMPETITION is the life of trade. / Always to COURT and never to wed is the happiest life that ever was led. / The DEATH of one dog is the life of another. / FAME is longer than life. / There are many kinds of fruit that grow on the tree of life but none so sweet as FRIENDSHIP. / Have FUN in this life: you'll never get out of it alive. / The GUIDE of life is common sense. / It's not what you HAVE in life that counts, but what you are. / HOPE and fear, peace and strife, make up the troubled web of life. / HUMOR is the spice of life. / A life of LEISURE and a life of laziness are two things. / MIRTH prolongs life. / MONEY isn't everything in life. / When PLEASURE is the business of life, it ceases to be pleasure. / POUT and you bear life alone. / He who is always PRAYING has a dangerous life. / Into each life some RAIN must fall. / REASON is the life of the law. / STOOP low and it will save you many a bump through life. / You must learn to STOOP as you go through life. / Lightest SUPPERS make long lives. / A wholesome TONGUE is a tree of life. / VARIETY is the spice of life. / YOUTH is not a time of life, it is a state of mind.

lifeblood *See* GOSSIP is the lifeblood of society.

lifeguard *See* The slave's LOVE is the master's lifeguard.

lifeless He is lifeless that is faultless. *Rec. dist.:* N.J., N.Y., Tex., Wis.

lifetime *See* YOUTH comes but once in a lifetime.

lifter Be a lifter, not a leaner. *Rec. dist.:* Colo. *1st cit.:* ca1890 Wilcox, *Lifting and Leaning*. *20c. coll.:* Stevenson 999:4.

lifting *See* The one who does the GRUNTING seldom does the lifting.

light *(n.)* **1.** A burned light will never shine. *Rec. dist.:* N.Y.

2. Don't hide your light under a bushel. *Var.:* Don't hide your light under a bushel basket. *Rec. dist.:* U.S., Can. *1st cit.:* 1379 Daniel, *Uricrisiarum;* US1840 Cooper, *Pathfinder.* **20c. coll.:** ODEP 371, T&W 228, Stevenson 281:3, Whiting(*MP*) 373.

3. Light is bad for sore eyes. *Rec. dist.:* N.Y. *1st cit.:* ca1548 Bale, *Image of Both Churches.* **20c. coll.:** ODEP 463, Stevenson 736:7.

4. The best way to see divine light is to put out your own candle. *Rec. dist.:* Mich., N.C.

5. The light that shines farthest shines brightest at home. *Rec. dist.:* Minn.

6. There's a light in the window for those who look. *Rec. dist.:* N.Y.

7. Travel in the light; rest in the night. *Rec. dist.:* Calif., Colo.

8. Turn the light on the braggart and he will run. *Rec. dist.:* N.Y.

9. Where there is light there is shadow. *Var.:* Every light has its shadow. *Rec. dist.:* N.Y. *1st cit.:* 1578 Florio, *Firste Fruites.* **20c. coll.:** ODEP 228, Stevenson 1422:3.

See also Never think yourself so BRILLIANT that you are blinded by your own light. / HAPPINESS comes from gladness as light from the sun. / HOPE is the light of the world. / He that does ILL hates the light. / A LAZY person will never try to see the light. / LIFE's jes pushin' side yo' troubles and lookin' for de light. / The LOVE light goes out when the gas bill comes in.

light *(v.)* *See* Don't light your FIRE until you have gathered your sticks. / If you have KNOWLEDGE, you should let others light their candles by it.

light *(adj.)* **1.** In rivers and bad government, the lightest things swim at top. *Rec. dist.:* N.Y., S.C.

2. Many are lighter in the heels than in the heart. *Rec. dist.:* Colo.

3. Once light, always light. *Rec. dist.:* N.Y. *See also* A BURDEN becomes lightest when it is well borne. / The BURDEN is light on the shoulders of another. / COMPANY in misery makes it light. / Light GAINS make a heavy purse. / Many HANDS make light work. / Light of HEART, light of feet. / A LOAD becomes light when carefully borne. / LOVE makes all burdens light. / LOVE makes obedience light. / Long PAINS are light ones; cruel ones are brief. / Lightest SUPPERS make long lives. / Where the WILL is ready the feet are light.

light *(adv.)* Come light, go light. *Var.:* Lightly come, lightly go. *Rec. dist.:* N.C., Tex. *1st cit.:* ca1386 Chaucer, *Pardoner's Tale.* *20c. coll.:* CODP 133, Stevenson 927:7.

lightning 1. Lightning never strikes in the same place twice. *Vars.:* (a) Lightning never strikes the same place twice. (b) Lightning never strikes twice in the same place except when it forgets where it struck last. (c) Lightning seldom strikes twice in the same place. *Rec. dist.:* U.S., Can. *1st cit.:* 1860 Myers, *Thrilling Adventures of the Prisoner of the Border;* US1909 Rinehart, *Man in Lower Ten.* *20c. coll.:* CODP 133, T&W 221, Stevenson 1424:12, Whiting*(MP)* 374.

2. When lightning strikes, you have no time to worry. *Rec. dist.:* Fla.

SEE ALSO It's the THUNDER that frights, but the lightning that smites.

like *(n.)* 1. Every like ain't the same. *Rec. dist.:* N.Y., S.C. *1st cit.:* 1587 Bridges, *Defence;* US1694 Josselyn, *Account of Voyage to New England.* *20c. coll.:* ODEP 464, CODP 133, T&W 222, Stevenson 1429:5.

2. Like attracts like. *Rec. dist.:* Utah. *1st cit.:* 1375 "Matthias" in *Scottish Legends,* S.T.S. (1896); US1818 Fessenden, *Ladies Monitor.* *20c. coll.:* ODEP 463, Whiting 262, Stevenson 1431:2, T&W 222, Whiting*(MP)* 375.

3. Like begets like. *Rec. dist.:* Kans. *1st cit.:* US1822 Weems, *Life of William Penn* (1836). *20c. coll.:* ODEP 464, Whiting 262, T&W 222, Whiting*(MP)* 375.

4. The like breeds the like. *Rec. dist.:* N.C. *1st cit.:* 1557 Edgeworth, *Sermons;* US1845

Cooper, *Chainbearer.* *20c. coll.:* ODEP 464, CODP 132, Stevenson 1428:6, T&W 222, Whiting*(MP)* 375.

SEE ALSO Every SHEEP with its like.

like *(v.)* *SEE* Each BIRD likes his own nest best. / If you don't like my GATE, don't swing on it. / Since we cannot GET what we like, let us like what we can get. / LOSE as if you like it, win as if you were used to it. / Every fellow likes his own PLOW best. / The SECRET of life is not to do what you like, but like what you do.

like *(prep.)* *SEE* Like FATHER, like son. / Like MASTER, like man.

liking *SEE* Real HAPPINESS is found not in doing the things you like to do, but in liking the things you have to do.

lily 1. Gild the lily if you will; it remains a lily still. *Rec. dist.:* U.S., Can. *1st cit.:* 1596 Shakespeare, *King John;* US1928 Biggers, *Behind That Curtain.* *20c. coll.:* Stevenson 1339:6, Whiting*(MP)* 376.

2. Lilies don't spring from thistles. *Rec. dist.:* Ohio.

3. Lilies that fester smell far worse than weeds. *Rec. dist.:* Ill. *1st cit.:* 1609 Shakespeare, *Sonnet 94.* *20c. coll.:* Stevenson 1432:7.

4. You can't paint the lily. *Rec. dist.:* Calif. *1st cit.:* 1596 Shakespeare, *King John;* US1928 Biggers, *Behind That Curtain.* *20c. coll.:* Stevenson 1339:6, Whiting*(MP)* 376.

limb Don't cut the limb which bears your weight. *Rec. dist.:* N.C.

lime Lime and lime without manure makes the farmer rich and the son poor. *Rec. dist.:* Ont. *1st cit.:* 1846 Denham, *Proverbs Relating to Weather;* US1795 *Diary and Autobiography of John Adams,* ed. Butterfield (1961). *20c. coll.:* ODEP 465, Whiting 262.

limit There's a limit to everything. *Rec. dist.:* N.Y., Ont.

limitation 1. Know your limitations and go not beyond them. *Rec. dist.:* Ill., N.Y.

2. Men cease to interest us when we find their limitations. *Rec. dist.:* Ill.

3. No man can climb out beyond the limitations of his own character. *Rec. dist.:* Ill.

limp Better to limp on the right road than to speed on the wrong one. *Rec. dist.:* Calif., Colo., N.Y.

line **1.** Hew to the line; let the chips fall where they may. *Vars.:* **(a)** Hew to the line. **(b)** Hew to the mark; let the chips fall where they may. *Rec. dist.:* Ill., N.J., Oreg. *1st cit.:* ca1923 Crowley, *Confessions of Neister Crowley;* US1880 Conkling, Nomination speech for U.S. Grant at the Republican National Convention, Chicago, Ill., 5 June. *20c. coll.:* Stevenson 345:11. Whiting(*MP*) 377.

2. It's a long line that has no turning. *Rec. dist.:* N.Y., S.C. *Infm.:* Cf. lane. *1st cit.:* 1942 Lasswell, *Suds in Your Eye. 20c. coll.:* Stevenson 1433:7.

3. The shortest distance between two points is a straight line. *Rec. dist.:* U.S., Can. *Infm.:* Cf. distance. *1st cit.:* 1942 Lasswell, *Suds in Your Eye. 20c. coll.:* Stevenson 1433:7.

4. The thinnest line is between love and hate. *Rec. dist.:* Kans.

See also It doesn't matter if the ox is blind, load the wagon and apply the line.

linen Don't air your dirty linens in public. *Var.:* Wash your dirty linen at home. *Rec. dist.:* U.S., Can. *1st cit.:* 1867 Trollope, *Last Chronicle of Barsetshire;* US1809 Fessenden, *Pills. 20c. coll.:* ODEP 868, Whiting 262, CODP 241, Stevenson 1434:5, Whiting(*MP*) 377.

See also Gold, women, and linen should be chosen by daylight.

linger He who lingers is lost. *Rec. dist.:* N.Y., S.C.

See also Knowledge comes, but wisdom lingers.

lining Always look for the silver lining. *Rec. dist.:* U.S. *1st cit.:* US1928 Goodwin, *When Dead. 20c. coll.:* Whiting(*MP*) 121.

See also Every cloud has a silver lining.

link *See* A chain is no stronger than its weakest link.

lion **1.** Don't wake a sleeping lion. *Vars.:* **(a)** It is not wise to wake a sleeping lion. **(b)** It's

no good to wake a sleeping lion. *Rec. dist.:* Calif., N.Y., S.C. *1st cit.:* ca1580 Sidney, *Arcadia. 20c. coll.:* ODEP 863, Stevenson 1437:9.

2. It is better to live like a lion for a day than to live like a lamb for a hundred years. *Rec. dist.:* Calif.

See also Better a live dog than a dead lion. / The whisper of a pretty girl can be heard further than the roar of a lion. / March is in like a lion, out like a lamb. / Whiskey make rabbit hug lion.

lip **1.** Even rosy lips must be fed. *Rec. dist.:* Calif. *1st cit.:* 1855 Bohn, *Handbook of Proverbs. 20c. coll.:* Stevenson 1440:6.

2. Keep a stiff upper lip. *Rec. dist.:* U.S., Can. *1st cit.:* 1825 Neal, *Brother Jonathan;* US1815 Thornton, *American Glossary* (1912). *20c. coll.:* ODEP 774, Whiting(*MP*) 379, Whiting 264, Stevenson 1439:15, T&W 225.

3. The lips of the righteous feed many, but fools die for want of wisdom. *Rec. dist.:* N.Y., N.C. *1st cit.:* 1855 Bohn, *Handbook of Proverbs. 20c. coll.:* Stevenson 1440:6.

4. The lips that touch liquor must never touch mine. *Rec. dist.:* N.Y., S.C.

See also He that hides hatred with lying lips and he that utters slander is a fool. / Providence requires three things of us before it will help us: a stout heart, a strong arm, and a stiff upper lip. / A slip of the lip will sink a ship. / There is many a slip twixt cup and lip.

liquor **1.** Good liquor will make a cat speak. *Rec. dist.:* Ill., N.Y., S.C.

2. Liquor never hurt a cheap man. *Rec. dist.:* Ont.

3. Liquor talks mighty loud when it gets loose from the bottle. *Vars.:* **(a)** Liquor talk mighty loud w'en it git loose from de jug. **(b)** Liquor talks aloud when it gets loose from the jug. *Rec. dist.:* N.Y., S.C.

See also Candy is dandy, but liquor is quicker. / Little minds like weak liquor are soon soured. / Those who drink but water will have no liquor to buy.

listen **1.** If you don't listen, you have to feel. *Var.:* If you can't listen, you can feel. *Rec. dist.:* Ill., Kans.

2. Listen at the keyhole and you'll hear bad news about yourself. *Rec. dist.:* Miss., N.Y., S.C. **1st cit.:** 1939 Walling, *Corpse with Blistered Hand;* US1900 Pidgen, *Quincy Adams Sawyer.* **20c. coll.:** Whiting*(MP)* 379.

3. Listen much and speak little. *Rec. dist.:* Calif., Colo.

4. Listen when spoken to. *Rec. dist.:* Mich.

SEE ALSO To make ENEMIES, talk; to make friends, listen. / SAY little and listen much. / STOP, look, listen. / TALK less; listen more.

listener **1.** A good listener is a silent flatterer. *Rec. dist.:* Wis.

2. If there were no listeners, there would be no liars. *Rec. dist.:* Ont.

3. Listen to him who is a good listener himself. *Rec. dist.:* N.Y.

4. Listeners hear no good of themselves. *Vars.:* **(a)** Listeners seldom hear anything good of themselves. **(b)** Listeners seldom hear good of themselves. *Rec. dist.:* U.S., Can. **1st cit.:** 1649 *Mercurius Elenticus;* US1722 *Papers of Benjamin Franklin,* ed. Labaree (1959). **20c. coll.:** ODEP 468, Whiting 264, *CODP* 134, Stevenson 1441:7, T&W 225, Whiting*(MP)* 379.

listening Good listening does not mean sitting dumb. *Rec. dist.:* Ont.

literature **1.** Literature has her quacks no less than medicine. *Rec. dist.:* Wis.

2. Literature is a bad crutch but a good walking stick. *Var.:* Literature is a very good walking stick but a very bad crutch. *Rec. dist.:* Ind., N.Y. **1st cit.:** 1830 Scott, *Lockhart's Life.* **20c. coll.:** ODEP 468, Stevenson 1442:2.

3. Literature is the thought of thinking souls. *Rec. dist.:* Wis. **1st cit.:** 1857 Carlyle, *Memories of the Life of Scott* in *Essays.* **20c. coll.:** Stevenson 1441:9.

litter SEE Don't build the PEN before the litter comes. / WOLVES of the same litter run in the same pack.

little *(n.)* **1.** A little along is better than a long none. *Rec. dist.:* Ont.

2. A little goes a long way. *Rec. dist.:* Calif., Colo., Mich., N.Y. **1st cit.:** 1925 Fletcher,

Secret of Barbican and Other Stories; USca1860 Paul, *Courtship and Adventure of Jonathan Homebred.* **20c. coll.:** Whiting*(MP)* 379, T&W 225.

3. A little is a big percent on nothing. *Rec. dist.:* Miss.

4. A little makes a lot. *Var.:* Many littles make a lot. *Rec. dist.:* N.Y.

5. A little too late is much too late. *Rec. dist.:* N.Y.

6. Add little to little and there will be a great heap. *Rec. dist.:* Ont., Wis. **1st cit.:** 1678 Ray, *English Proverbs.* **20c. coll.:** Stevenson 1443:13.

7. Every little helps. *Rec. dist.:* Ark., Miss., N.Y., N.C., S.C. **1st cit.:** 1791 O'Keefe, *Wild Oats;* US1787 Hazard in *Belknap Papers,* Mass.Hist.Soc. *Collections* (1891). **20c. coll.:** CODP 67, Whiting 264, Stevenson 1445:2, T&W 225, Whiting*(MP)* 379.

8. Every little makes a nickel. *Var.:* Many a little makes a nickel. *Rec. dist.:* U.S., Can. **1st cit.:** ca1225, *Ancrene Riwle,* Camden Soc. (1853); US1732 *Papers of Benjamin Franklin,* ed. Labaree (1959). **20c. coll.:** ODEP 508, Whiting 264, *CODP* 146, Stevenson 1443:13.

9. It's better to have a little than nothing. *Rec. dist.:* Ill., Miss., Ohio.

10. Jack Little sows little, and little he'll reap. *Rec. dist.:* N.Y., S.C.

11. Keep a little for a rainy day. *Rec. dist.:* U.S. *Infm.:* Cf. save.

12. Little and often fills the purse. *Rec. dist.:* Ind., N.Y., S.C. **1st cit.:** 1582 Gasson, *Plays Confuted.* **20c. coll.:** ODEP 469, Stevenson 1443:13.

13. Little by little does the trick. *Rec. dist.:* Ind., N.C., Ont.

14. Little by little one goes far. *Rec. dist.:* Ill., N.Y., N.C. **1st cit.:** US1948 Stevenson, *Home Book of Proverbs.* **20c. coll.:** Stevenson 1444:5.

15. Little is done where many command. *Rec. dist.:* N.J.

16. Little is given, little is expected. *Rec. dist.:* Md. **1st cit.:** US1787 Howell in *Maryland Historical Magazine* (1929). **20c. coll.:** Whiting 265.

17. Little is much if God is in it. *Rec. dist.:* Ont.

18. Little is much when the heart is in it. *Rec. dist.:* Ind.

19. Little said is soonest mended. *Rec. dist.:* U.S., Can. *Infm.:* Cf. least. *1st cit.:* ca1460 *Parliament of Birds* in *Early Popular Poetry,* ed. Hazlitt (1864); US1698 Usher in *William & Mary Coll. Quart.* (1950). *20c. coll.:* ODEP 472, Whiting 257, Stevenson 2190:10, T&W 217, Whiting(MP) 366.

20. Say little; write less; print least. *Rec. dist.:* N.Y., S.C.

21. Too little and too late. *Rec. dist.:* Calif., Colo., Mich., N.Y.

22. Too little and too much spoil everything. *Rec. dist.:* Ill.

23. Use the little to get the big. *Rec. dist.:* Ill. *1st cit.:* US1875 Scarborough, *Chinese Proverbs. 20c. coll.:* Stevenson 925:5.

24. Who possesses little has the first right to it. *Rec. dist.:* Ill.

SEE ALSO He who is AFRAID of doing too much always does too little. / Who ANSWERS suddenly knows little. / Ask much to get a little. / A little DIRT never hurt anyone. / He ENJOYS much who is thankful for a little. / FAITHFUL in little, faithful in much. / It is better to LIE a little than to be unhappy much.

little *(adj.)* **1.** A little man may have a large heart. *Rec. dist.:* N.Y., Ont.

2. A little man sometimes casts a long shadow. *Rec. dist.:* Ill.

3. A little thing in hand is worth more than a great thing in prospect. *Rec. dist.:* Ind.

4. It's the little things in life that count. *Rec. dist.:* U.S.

5. It's the little things that smooth people's roads the most. *Rec. dist.:* N.Y., S.C. *1st cit.:* US1884 Twain, *Huckleberry Finn. 20c. coll.:* Stevenson 1448:10.

6. Little men have sharp wits. *Rec. dist.:* N.Y., S.C.

7. Little things attract light minds. *Rec. dist.:* Ind. *1st cit.:* 1576 Pettie, *Petite Palace of Pleasure;* US1931 Allingham, *Police. 20c. coll.:* ODEP 472, CODP 135, Whiting(MP) 619.

8. Little things worry little minds. *Rec. dist.:* Ind. *1st cit.:* 1764 Goldsmith, *Traveller. 20c. coll.:* ODEP 472.

SEE ALSO A little ABSENCE does much good. / The little ALMS are the good alms. / Little BOATS should stay close to shore. / Wide is the DOOR of the little cottage. / There is no little ENEMY. / Beware of little EXPENSES. / Better a big FISH in a little puddle than a little fish in a big puddle. / Little FISH swim in shallow water. / Men never think their FORTUNE too great nor their wit too little. / Little FRIENDS sometimes prove to be big friends. / There could be no GREAT ones if there were no little. / A little HOUSE well filled, a little land well tilled, and a little wife well willed are great riches. / IF is a little word, yet it is so big you can't get around or over it. / Little LABOR, little gain. / Too little LEAVEN spoils the loaf. / Little MINDS are tamed and subdued by misfortune, but great minds rise above it. / Little PITCHERS have big ears. / Big POSSUM climb little tree. / A little POT is soon hot. / Little ROGUES easily become great ones. / Little STROKES fell great oaks. / Little SUBJECTS decide big ones. / Much TALK, little work. / The TONGUE of the just is a choice silver; the heart of the wicked is little worth. / Little TRAINS go far. / Great TREES keep down little ones. / Little VENTURE, little gain. / It's a whole lot better to be a little WHEEL that is turning than a big wheel standing still.

little *(adv.)* SEE Little by little the BIRD builds his nest. / LOVE me little and love me long.

live *(v.)* **1.** A man cannot live on air. *Rec. dist.:* Miss.

2. All wish to live long but not to be called old. *Rec. dist.:* N.J., N.Y., S.C. *1st cit.:* US1749 Franklin, *PRAlmanac. 20c. coll.:* Stevenson 29:5.

3. As a man lives, so shall he die; as a tree falls, so shall it lie. *Rec. dist.:* N.Y.

4. Better to live well than long. *Var.:* We're here not to live long but to live well. *Rec. dist.:* Ind., Okla., Ont., Tex. *1st cit.:* 1855 Bohn, *Handbook of Proverbs. 20c. coll.:* Stevenson 1412:7.

5. Everyone has to live. *Rec. dist.:* Ark. *1st*

cit.: ca1587 Marlowe and Nashe, *Dido, Queene of Carthage*. *20c. coll.*: ODEP 232.

6. He lives longest who lives best. *Rec. dist.*: Ind. *1st cit.*: 1545 Taverner, *Proverbs of Erasmus*. *20c. coll.*: ODEP 475.

7. He lives twice who lives well. *Rec. dist.*: N.J., Ont. *1st cit.*: 1748 Richardson, *Clarissa*. *20c. coll.*: Stevenson 1412:16.

8. He that lives carnally won't live eternally. *Rec. dist.*: N.Y., S.C. *1st cit.*: US1733 Franklin, *PRAlmanac*. *20c. coll.*: Stevenson 1405:6.

9. It does not matter so much where you live as how well you live there. *Rec. dist.*: N.C.

10. It matters not how long we live, but how. *Rec. dist.*: U.S., Can. *1st cit.*: 1574 Guevara, *Familiar Epistles*, tr. Hellowes (1584). *20c. coll.*: ODEP 479, Stevenson 1412:10.

11. Live and learn; die and forget all. *Vars.*: **(a)** As long as you live you must learn how to live. **(b)** He that lives well is learned enough. **(c)** Learn to live and live to learn. **(d)** Live and learn. **(e)** Live and learn; die and forget. *Rec. dist.*: U.S., Can. *1st cit.*: 1575 Gascoigne, *Glasse of Government*; US1784 *Belknap Papers*, Mass.Hist.Soc. *Collections* (1891). *20c. coll.*: ODEP 473 CODP 136, Whiting 265, Stevenson 1378:1, Whiting*(MP)* 380.

12. Live and let live. *Rec. dist.*: U.S. *1st cit.*: 1622 DeMalynes, *Ancient Law-Merchant*; US1785 *Works of John Adams*. *20c. coll.*: ODEP 473, Whiting 265, CODP 136, Stevenson 1408:7, T&W 226, Whiting*(MP)* 380.

13. Live for the present; plan for the future. *Rec. dist.*: Ill., Oreg.

14. Live freely and die content. *Rec. dist.*: N.C.

15. Live today, for tomorrow may not come. *Var.*: Live today, not tomorrow. *Rec. dist.*: Ind.

16. Live well in the present; the past is gone forever. *Rec. dist.*: N.Y.

17. Live within yourself and you will be your own mourner. *Rec. dist.*: Miss.

18. Man cannot live by bread alone. *Rec. dist.*: U.S., Can. *1st cit.*: 1881 Stevenson, *Virginibus Puerisque*; US1875 Emerson in *North American Review*, May–June. *20c. coll.*: Stevenson 231:8, CODP 144, Whiting*(MP)* 396.

19. No man lives to himself, and no man dies to himself. *Rec. dist.*: N.C., Ont.

20. Only those are fit to live who are not afraid to die. *Rec. dist.*: Ill., R.I. *1st cit.*: US1941 MacArthur, Speech. *20c. coll.*: Stevenson 1419:9.

21. Tell me with whom you live and I will tell you who you are. *Rec. dist.*: N.J., N.Y. *Infm.*: Cf. companion.

22. They that live longest must die at last. *Rec. dist.*: N.Y. *1st cit.*: 1616 Draxe, *Bibliotheca Scholastica in Anglia* (1918). *20c. coll.*: ODEP 474, Stevenson 1411:4.

23. To go slowly and to live a long time are two brothers. *Var.*: Take it easy and live long are brothers. *Rec. dist.*: Ariz., Miss.

24. To live long is to suffer long. *Var.*: He that lives long suffers much. *Rec. dist.*: Ind., N.Y. *1st cit.*: 1620 Cervantes, *Don Quixote*, tr. Shelton. *20c. coll.*: Stevenson 1411:2.

25. We can always live on less when we have more to live on. *Rec. dist.*: Calif., Colo.

26. We only live once. *Rec. dist.*: U.S., Can. *1st cit.*: US1926 Lardner, *Zone of Quiet*. *20c. coll.*: Stevenson 1413:7, Whiting*(MP)* 380.

27. Wish not so much to live long as to live well. *Rec. dist.*: N.Y., S.C. *1st cit.*: 1670 Ray, *English Proverbs*; US1738 Franklin, *PRAlmanac*. *20c. coll.*: Stevenson 1412:10.

SEE ALSO 'Tis more BRAVE to live than to die. / One should live to BUILD, not to boast. / It is not difficult to DIE well, but it is difficult to live well. / They DIE well that live well. / Would you live with EASE, do what you ought and not what you please. / EAT to live; do not live to eat. / He that FIGHTS and runs away may live to fight another day. / FOOLS build houses for wise men to live in. / It is easier to visit FRIENDS than to live with them. / The GOOD that men do lives after them. / All HILLBILLIES don't live in the hills. / Live with a HOG and you'll grunt like one. / He that lives on HOPE has a slender diet. / The happiest place in the world to live is within one's

INCOME. / Live with the LAME and you will limp. / Most good LAWYERS live well, work hard, and die poor. / You can't live down a LIE. / It is better to live like a LION for a day than live like a lamb for a hundred years. / To LOVE is to live, and to live is to love. / You can't live on LOVE alone. / You haven't lived if you haven't LOVED. / He that would live at PEACE and rest must hear and see and say the best. / It is easier to fight for one's PRINCIPLES than to live up to them. / He that is RICH need not live sparingly, and he that can live sparingly need not be rich. / It's better to live RICH than die rich. / Take ROOT and live. / SAVE while you have, give while you live. / He who lives by the SWORD perishes by the sword. / A little too WISE ne'er lived long. / WORK as though you were to live forever.

live *(adj.)* Be a live wire and you won't be stepped on. *Var.:* A live wire is never stepped on. *Rec. dist.:* Miss., Ohio.

SEE ALSO A live COWARD is better than a dead hero. / It is better to be a live RABBIT than a dead tiger.

living **1.** High living, low thinking. *Rec. dist.:* Ont.

2. It takes a heap of living to make a home. *Var.:* It takes a heap o' livin' in a house to make it a home. *Rec. dist.:* U.S., Can.

3. Living in luxury begets lustful desires. *Rec. dist.:* N.Y., N.C.

4. Not living well isn't living at all. *Rec. dist.:* N.Y., S.C. *1st cit.:* US1944 Pratt, *Thunder Mountain.* *20c. coll.:* Stevenson 1412:1.

5. Soft living hardens the head. *Rec. dist.:* Kans.

6. The man who makes an honest living is at peace with his maker. *Rec. dist.:* Ill.

7. They live ill who think of living always. *Rec. dist.:* Mich. *1st cit.:* 1600 Bodenham, *Belvedere.* *20c. coll.:* Stevenson 1412:7.

SEE ALSO DYING is as natural as living. / It's LOVING and giving that makes life worth living. / Never ring a PIG that has to root for a living. / SLAVERY is too high a price to pay for easy living. / Wise use of TIME will make for wiser living. / Learn a TRADE and earn a living.

load *(n.)* **1.** A load becomes light when cheerfully borne. *Var.:* That load which is cheerfully borne becomes pleasant. *Rec. dist.:* Ind., Mich., Utah.

2. Carry your part of the load. *Rec. dist.:* N.C.

3. It's not the load that breaks you down, it's the way you carry it. *Rec. dist.:* Ont.

SEE ALSO A GRUDGE is the heaviest load one can carry. / The willing HORSE carries the load. / Do not burden today's STRENGTH with tomorrow's load.

load *(v.)* *SEE* It's easier to dump the CART than to load it.

loaded *SEE* Loaded WORDS are like loaded dice: they never roll true.

loaf *(n.)* **1.** Cut your own loaf and you'll never be hungry. *Rec. dist.:* N.Y.

2. Half a loaf is better than none. *Vars.:* **(a)** A half loaf is better than no bread at all. **(b)** Half a loaf is better than no bread. **(c)** Half a loaf is better than no loaf at all. *Rec. dist.:* U.S., Can. *1st cit.:* 1546 Heywood, *Dialogue of Proverbs;* US1693 Mather in *Andros Tracts,* ed. Whitmore (1868–74). *20c. coll.:* ODEP 344, Whiting 192, CODP 104, Stevenson 235:12, T&W 267, Whiting(MP) 280.

3. Set not your loaf till the oven's hot. *Rec. dist.:* Wis. *1st cit.:* 1732 Fuller, *Gnomologia.* *20c. coll.:* ODEP 716, Stevenson 1446:3.

SEE ALSO Because KITTENS may be born in an oven, that does not make them loaves of bread. / Too little LEAVEN spoils the loaf. / It's easy to STEAL from a cut loaf.

loaf *(v.)* **1.** A man who can't get up to loaf is too lazy to enjoy it. *Rec. dist.:* W.Va.

2. The man who loafs most gets the fewest loaves. *Rec. dist.:* Ind.

loan *(n.)* A loan oft loses both itself and the friend. *Var.:* Loan often loses both itself and friend. *Rec. dist.:* Ohio, Ont. *1st cit.:* 1600 Shakespeare, *Hamlet.* *20c. coll.:* Stevenson 1385:3.

SEE ALSO HEALTH is a call loan.

loan *(v.)* *SEE* Never loan MONEY to a friend unless you wish to lose him.

loathing Longing is better than loathing. *Rec. dist.:* N.Y., S.C.

lock *(n.)* 1. A lock on a door keeps honest men honest. *Vars.:* **(a)** A lock on the door keeps men honest. **(b)** The lock is not used to keep thieves out but to keep honest men honest. *Rec. dist.:* Ill., Ind.

2. Locks keep out only honest people. *Rec. dist.:* Ill.

SEE ALSO ARMS, women, and locks should be looked at daily. / It is WIT to pick a lock and steal a horse, but wisdom to let it alone.

lock *(v.)* 1. It is too late to lock the stable door when the steed is stolen. *Vars.:* **(a)** Don't lock the chicken house after the chickens are stolen. **(b)** Don't lock the gate after the horses are gone. **(c)** Don't lock the granary after the grain has been stolen. **(d)** It's no use to lock the stable after the horse has been stolen. **(e)** Lock the stable door before the horse is stolen. **(f)** When the horse is stolen they lock the door. *Rec. dist.:* U.S., Can. *1st cit.:* ca1350 *Douce MS 22;* US1745 *Law Papers: Correspondence of Jonathan Law, Governor of Conn., 1741–1750,* Conn.Hist.Soc. *Collections* (1907–14). *20c. coll.:* ODEP 730, Whiting 414, CODP 211, Stevenson 2204:8, T&W 109, Whiting(MP) 182.

locksmith *SEE* LOVE laughs at locksmiths.

log 1. Crooked logs make straight fires. *Rec. dist.:* Tex. *1st cit.:* 1584 Withals, *Dictionary of French and English Tongues.* *20c. coll.:* ODEP 155.

2. Hollow logs often rattle. *Rec. dist.:* Ind.

3. If you turn over a log, you may find a lot of things there besides worms. *Rec. dist.:* Fla.

SEE ALSO There is no WEDGE worse than the one from the same log.

loneliness The surest sign of age is loneliness. *Rec. dist.:* N.Y., S.C. *1st cit.:* US1868 Alcott, *Tablets.* *20c. coll.:* Stevenson 1449:1.

lonely *SEE* One seldom meets a lonely LIE.

lonesome *SEE* Be GOOD and you will be lonesome.

lonesomeness Lonesomeness is the root of all evil. *Rec. dist.:* Wis.

long *(n.)* Long is not forever. *Rec. dist.:* N.Y.

long *(adj.)* 1. Better to have it too long than too short. *Rec. dist.:* Utah.

2. It's a long lane that has no turn. *Vars.:* **(a)** It's a long lane with no turn in it. **(b)** It's a long road that never turns. **(c)** Long is that lane that has no turning. *Rec. dist.:* U.S., Can. *1st cit.:* 1633 *Stationers' Register;* US1778 Paine, *American Crisis* in *Writings of Thomas Paine,* ed. Foner (1945). *20c. coll.:* ODEP 480, Whiting 251, CODP 137, Stevenson 1345:1, T&W 214, Whiting(MP) 360.

3. The longest way around is the shortest way home. *Var.:* The long way around is the sweetest way home. *Rec. dist.:* U.S., Can. *1st cit.:* 1776 Colman, *Spleen;* US1762 *Letter Book of John Watts, 1762–1765,* N.Y.Hist.Soc. *Collections* (1928). *20c. coll.:* CODP 138, Whiting 474, Stevenson 1468:12,

SEE ALSO Long ABSENCE changes friends. / ALWAYS is a long time. / ART is long, life is short. / Eat BREAD and drink water, and you will live a long life. / A DAY to come seems longer than a year that is gone. / The longest DAY will come to an end. / It takes a lean DOG for a long race. / A long FACE makes a long road seem twice as long. / FAME is longer than life. / The longer the FOOT, the higher the man. / GREEDY folks have longer arms. / A woman's HAIR is long, but her tongue is longer. / A long LIFE may not be good enough, but a good life is long enough. / A LITTLE goes a long way. / NEVER is a long time. / Long PAINS are light ones; cruel ones are brief. / Long on PROMISES, short on performance. / The only difference between a RUT and a grave is that a grave is a little longer. / Long SLEEP makes a bare back. / He must have a long SPOON who sups with the devil. / Lightest SUPPERS make long lives. / A long TONGUE has a short hand. / A good TURN goes a long way. / Seldom VISITS make long friends.

long *(adv.)* Long looked for comes at last. *Rec. dist.:* Ind. *1st cit.:* ca1483 *Quatuor Sermones* in *Roxburghe Club Publ.;* US1603 Fones in *Winthrop Papers, 1498–1649* in Mass.Hist.Soc. *Collections* (1863–92). *20c. coll.:* ODEP 430, Whiting 267, Stevenson 722:2.

SEE ALSO DRINK little that you may drink long. / A squeaking GATE hangs the longest. / All wish to LIVE long but not to be called old. / To LIVE long is to suffer long. / Wish not so much to LIVE long as to live well. / OLD young and old long. / QUARRELS never could last long, if on one side only lay the wrong. / REGRETS last longer than repentance. / THINK long, think wrong. / A little too WISE ne'er lives long.

longing Longing is better than loathing. *Rec. dist.:* Ont. *1st cit.:* 1732 Fuller, *Gnomologia.* *20c. coll.:* ODEP 53.

look *(n.)* **1.** A cheerful look makes a dish a feast. *Rec. dist.:* Ill., Kans. *1st cit.:* ca1477 Caxton, *Book of Curteseye.* *20c. coll.:* ODEP 117, Stevenson 329:10.

2. A single look is worth ten thousand words. *Rec. dist.:* Miss. *Infm.:* Cf. picture. *1st cit.:* 1640 Herbert, *Outlandish Proverbs (Jacula Prudentum)* in *Works,* ed. Hutchinson (1941). *20c. coll.:* Stevenson 2611:3.

3. Clothes and looks don't make the person. *Rec. dist.:* N.C. *1st cit.:* US1843 Haliburton, *Old Judge.* *20c. coll.:* T&W 72, Stevenson 368:7, Whiting(MP) 120.

4. Don't judge everyone by his looks. *Rec. dist.:* Ohio.

5. Good looks buy nothing in the market. *Rec. dist.:* N.J.

6. If you've good looks, you don't need any brains. *Rec. dist.:* Wash.

7. It's in the looks that conscious guilt appears. *Rec. dist.:* Ill.

8. Looks aren't everything. *Rec. dist.:* Mich., N.C. *1st cit.:* 1678 Ray, *English Proverbs;* US1839 *John Smith's Letters.* *20c. coll.:* ODEP 646, T&W 228, Whiting(MP) 383.

9. Looks often deceive. *Var.:* One's looks are often deceiving. *Rec. dist.:* U.S., Can. *Infm.:* Cf. appearance. *1st cit.:* 1666 Torriano, *Select Italian Proverbs;* US1759 Franklin, *Papers of Benjamin Franklin,* ed. Labaree (1959). *20c. coll.:* CODP 5, Whiting 10, Stevenson 83:2, Whiting(MP) 13.

10. There's nothing in the looks of a lousy calf. *Rec. dist.:* Ill.

11. You can't get to heaven on your looks. *Rec. dist.:* Miss.

look *(v.)* **1.** A good soldier never looks behind him. *Rec. dist.:* Ohio. *Infm.:* Cf. soldier.

2. He that will not look before him will have to look behind him. *Vars.:* **(a)** Always look forward, and not backward. **(b)** He who does not look ahead remains behind. **(c)** Look before or you'll find yourself behind. *Rec. dist.:* Mich. *1st cit.:* 1640 Herbert, *Outlandish Proverbs (Jacula Prudentum)* in *Works,* ed. Hutchinson (1941); US1735 Franklin, *PRAlmanac.* *20c. coll.:* ODEP 494, Whiting 267, Stevenson 1450:1.

3. If you don't look out for yourself, nobody else will. *Rec. dist.:* Mich., N.Y., S.C., Vt.

4. It's better to be looked over than overlooked. *Rec. dist.:* Ohio.

5. Look and learn. *Rec. dist.:* N.Y.

6. Look and live. *Rec. dist.:* N.C.

7. Look and you shall find. *Rec. dist.:* Ill. *Infm.:* Cf. seek. *1st cit.:* 1579 *Proverbs of Sir James Lopez de Mendoza,* tr. Googe; US1783 *Correspondence of John Jay,* ed. Johnston (1890–93). *20c. coll.:* ODEP 711, Whiting 383, Stevenson 2056:4, Whiting(MP) 552.

8. Look before you leap. *Vars.:* **(a)** Look before you leap and think before you speak. **(b)** Look twice before you jump. **(c)** You better look well before you take the next step. *Rec. dist.:* U.S., Can. *1st cit.:* ca1350, *Douce MS 52;* US1694 *Life and Writings of Francis Makemie,* ed. Schlenther (1971). *20c. coll.:* ODEP 482, Whiting 267, CODP 138, Stevenson 1452:11, T&W 228, Whiting(MP) 383.

9. Look high and fall low. *Var.:* Look high and light low. *Rec. dist.:* Ind. *1st cit.:* 1732 Fuller, *Gnomologia.* *20c. coll.:* Stevenson 1450:6.

10. Look out for others and God will look out for you. *Rec. dist.:* Ont.

11. Look up, not down. *Rec. dist.:* Ill. *1st cit.:* US1871 Hale, *Ten Times One Is Ten.* *20c. coll.:* Stevenson 1726:4.

12. Those who look up see the stars. *Rec. dist.:* Ala., Ga.

SEE ALSO ARMS, women, and locks should

be looked at daily. / A CAT may look at a king. / While drinking from one CUP, look not into another. / To plow a straight FURROW, never look back. / Look to the FUTURE and you will always look up. / Don't HIT before you look. / Don't look a gift HORSE in the mouth. / We are JUDGED by how we look as well as how we act. / Always look for the silver LINING. / A person who looks down his NOSE at people will never see beyond that nose. / A little bit of POWDER and a little bit of paint makes a woman look like what she ain't. / A RAINBOW is big enough for everyone to look at. / What we SEE depends mainly on what we look for. / STOP, look, listen. / THINGS always seem fairer when we look back at them. / A WOMAN is no older than she looks. / You're as YOUNG as you look and as old as you feel.

looker Lookers-on see more than players. *Rec. dist.:* Ont. *1st cit.:* 1530 Palsgrave, *Acolastus,* ed. Carver, E.E.T.S. (1937); US1669 Hubbard in *Saltonstall Papers, 1607–1815,* ed. Moody in Mass.Hist.Soc. *Collections* (1972). *20c. coll.:* ODEP 483, Whiting 267, CODP 138, Stevenson 1453:5.

looking SEE Looking at a HILL won't move it. / If you don't go looking for TROUBLE, trouble won't go looking for you.

looking glass 1. She who loves the looking glass hates the saucepan. *Var.:* The wife who loves the looking glass hates the saucepan. *Rec. dist.:* Ill., Ont.

2. There is no better looking glass than an old friend. *Rec. dist.:* Ind.

3. Your looking glass will tell you what none of your friends will. *Rec. dist.:* Mich.

SEE ALSO When you have committed a CRIME, the whole world is a looking glass.

loop A loose rope builds the best loop. *Rec. dist.:* Okla. *1st cit.:* 1639 Fuller, *Holy War.* *20c. coll.:* CODP 194.

loose SEE Leave a loose THREAD.

Lord 1. Some people depend too little on the Lord, and some people depend too much on Him. *Rec. dist.:* Utah.

2. Speak not the Lord's name in vain. *Rec. dist.:* Mich., N.Y.

3. The Lord chastises His own. *Var.:* Whom the Lord loves He chastises. *Rec. dist.:* Ont. *1st cit.:* 1700 Pomfret, *Verses to a Friend Under Affliction.* *20c. coll.:* Stevenson 976:6.

4. The Lord helps those who help themselves. *Var.:* The Lord looks out for those who look out for themselves. *Rec. dist.:* U.S., Can. *1st cit.:* 1551 Wilson, *Rule of Reason;* US1736 Franklin, *PRAlmanac.* *20c. coll.:* ODEP 310, CODP 93, 11, Whiting 178, Stevenson 979:4, T&W 154, Whiting(MP) 259.

5. The Lord knows when to clip our wings. *Rec. dist.:* Ont.

6. The Lord makes a man, but the wife makes a husband. *Rec. dist.:* N.Y., S.C.

7. The Lord never goes back on His own. *Rec. dist.:* N.C.

8. The Lord never helps him who sits on his ass and waits. *Rec. dist.:* Ark.

9. The Lord provides for the lame and lazy. *Rec. dist.:* Kans.

10. The Lord sends sun at one time, rain at another. *Rec. dist.:* Wis. *1st cit.:* 1542 Boorde, *Compendyons Regyment, or Dyatorye of Health,* E.E.T.S. (1870); US1760 Franklin, *Precautions Used by Those about To Undertake Sea Voyage.* *20c. coll.:* ODEP 312, Stevenson 419:2, T&W 228.

11. The Lord tempers the wind to the shorn lamb. *Rec. dist.:* Mich., N.Y., Ont., S.C. *1st cit.:* 1640 Herbert, *Outlandish Proverbs (Jacula Prudentum)* in *Works,* ed. Hutchinson (1941); US1780 Sewall in *Winslow Papers, 1776–1826,* ed. Raymond (1901). *20c. coll.:* ODEP 312, Whiting 179, Stevenson 908:15, Whiting(MP) 260.

12. The Lord who gave can take away. *Rec. dist.:* Mich. *1st cit.:* US1771 *Diary of Col. Landon Carter of Sabine Hall, 1752–1778,* ed. Greene (1965). *20c. coll.:* Whiting 178, Whiting(MP) 259.

13. The Lord will provide. *Rec. dist.:* U.S., Can.

14. Trust in the Lord, but keep your powder

dry. *Rec. dist.:* Calif., Mich., N.Y., Utah. *1st cit.:* ca1658 Cromwell in Hayes, *Ballads of Ireland* (1855); US1965 Stewart, *Airs Above Ground*. *20c. coll.:* ODEP 842, Whiting(MP) 646.

SEE ALSO FEAR of the Lord is the beginning of wisdom. / He who gives to the POOR lends to the Lord.

lord 1. New lairds make new laws. *Rec. dist.:* N.Y., Ont. *1st cit.:* 1548 Hall, *Chronicle, Henry VI;* US1775 Emerson in Hodgkins, *Letters*. *20c. coll.:* ODEP 564, CODP 161, Whiting 268.

2. There are more lords in the world than brilliant wits. *Rec. dist.:* Mich.

SEE ALSO The good PAYMASTER is lord of another man's purse.

lose 1. Beware of him who has nothing to lose. *Rec. dist.:* Ill., Mich., N.J., N.Y. *1st cit.:* 1580 Lyly, *Euphues and His England*. *20c. coll.:* Stevenson 1457:3.

2. Lose as if you like it; win as if you were used to it. *Rec. dist.:* Ont.

3. Those that have must lose. *Rec. dist.:* Md.

4. 'Tis better to lose with a wise man than to win with a fool. *Var.:* Better to lose with good men than to find gain with bad. *Rec. dist.:* Ont.

5. What you lose today you cannot gain tomorrow. *Rec. dist.:* Ont., Wis.

6. Who loses, rues. *Rec. dist.:* N.C.

7. You cannot lose what you haven't got. *Rec. dist.:* U.S., Can. *1st cit.:* ca1593 Marlowe, *Hero and Leander;* US1936 Farjeon, *Detective Ben*. *20c. coll.:* CODP 139, Whiting(MP) 292, ODEP 485, Stevenson 1456:2.

SEE ALSO A CARD which never appears neither wins nor loses. / Don't CARE loses his corn patch. / He who loses his wealth loses much; he who loses even one friend loses more; but he that loses his COURAGE loses all. / It takes years to make a FRIEND but minutes to lose one. / You never know the value of FRIENDS until you lose them. / GOODWILL, like a good woman, is hard to get and easy to lose. / You never lose by being KIND. / Seek till you find, and you'll never lose your LA-

BOR. / No matter who loses, the LAWYER always wins. / Save your LIFE and lose a minute. / Never loan MONEY to a friend unless you wish to lose him. / The man who loses his OPPORTUNITY loses himself. / Have PATIENCE with a friend rather than lose him forever. / If you leave your PLACE, you lose it. / The SHEEP that bleats loses a mouthful. / If you would lose a troublesome VISITOR, lend him money. / You always WIN if you can lose with a smile. / WOLVES may lose their teeth, but they never lose their nature.

loser 1. A good loser never wins. *Rec. dist.:* Kans.

2. Better to be a good loser than a poor winner. *Var.:* It is better to be a poor loser than a good winner. *Rec. dist.:* Ont.

3. Give losers leave to talk. *Rec. dist.:* Okla., Tex. *1st cit.:* 1533 More, *Works;* US1690 "William Byrd" in *Va.Mag.Hist.* (1918). *20c. coll.:* ODEP 485, Whiting 268, Stevenson 1456:6.

4. Losers are always in the wrong. *Rec. dist.:* Mich. *1st cit.:* 1855 Bohn, *Handbook of Proverbs*. *20c. coll.:* Stevenson 1454:15.

5. The cheerful loser is a winner. *Rec. dist.:* Mich.

SEE ALSO It is a bad BARGAIN when both are losers. / FINDERS keepers, losers weepers. / First WINNER, last loser. / It is just as hard to be a good WINNER as to be a good loser.

losing SEE The losing HORSE blames the saddle.

loss 1. His loss is my gain. *Rec. dist.:* U.S., Can. *1st cit.:* 1733 Barber in *Correspondence of Swift* (1965); US1927 Tully, *Circus*. *20c. coll.:* ODEP 486, CODP 139, Whiting(MP) 400.

2. It is worth a loss to find out what some people are. *Var.:* It is worth a loss financially to find out what some people are. *Rec. dist.:* N.C.

SEE ALSO The loss of TEMPER is the loss of sense.

lost All is not lost that is in danger. *Rec. dist.:* Calif., N.Y., S.C. *1st cit.:* ca1641 Fergusson, *Scottish Proverbs;* US1868 Clift, *Tim Bunker*

Papers. 20c. coll.: ODEP 334, T&W 229, *CODP* 139, Stevenson 928:8, Whiting*(MP)* 384.

SEE ALSO BEAUTY seen is never lost. / BUSINESS neglected is business lost. / EDUCATION is an investment never to be lost nor removed. / EVIL won is evil lost. / A FRIEND is easier lost than found. / FRIENDS are lost by calling often and calling seldom. / The GOOD you do is not lost, though you forget it. / He who HESITATES is lost. / A HOOK's well lost to catch a salmon. / Lost INNOCENCE and wasted time are never recovered. / KINDNESS is lost upon an ungrateful man. / He who LINGERS is lost. / Many a MEAL is lost for want of meat. / MONEY lost is never gained. / MONEY lost, nothing lost; courage lost, much lost; honor lost, more lost; soul lost, all lost. / For the want of a NAIL, the shoe was lost. / A lost OPPORTUNITY never returns. / A man never got lost on a straight ROAD.

lot *(group)* SEE One bad APPLE spoils the lot.

lot *(fate)* Everyone has his lot and a wide world before him. *Rec. dist.:* Ont. *1st cit.:* 1732 Fuller, *Gnomologia. 20c. coll.:* Stevenson 555:10.

SEE ALSO Be CONTENT with your lot. / TEARS and troubles are the lot of all.

lot *(place)* The only lot most men do not grumble at is their burial lot. *Rec. dist.:* Ont.

lot *(quantity)* SEE SHARE a little, help a lot.

lottery SEE MARRIAGE is a lottery.

loud *(adj.)* The louder you are at night, the quieter you'll be in morning. *Rec. dist.:* Kans.

SEE ALSO A loud LAUGH bespeaks the vacant mind.

loud *(adv.)* Presents speak louder than words. *Rec. dist.:* Colo.

SEE ALSO ACTIONS speak louder than words. / The fellow who blows his HORN the loudest is likely in the biggest fog. / KNOWLEDGE talks lowly; ignorance talks loudly. / LIQUOR talks mighty loud when it gets loose from the bottle. / Those who are RIGHT need not talk loudly.

louse A louse not killed is sure to bite again. *Rec. dist.:* Ont.

SEE ALSO Sue a BEGGAR and you'll get a louse. / NITS make lice.

lousy SEE There's nothing in the LOOKS of a lousy calf.

lovable The secret of being loved is being lovable. *Rec. dist.:* N.J., Ont.

love *(n.)* **1.** A small love forgives much, a great love forgives little, and a perfect love forgives all. *Rec. dist.:* Ala., Ga., N.J.

2. Against love and fortune there is no defense. *Rec. dist.:* Ill.

3. Blind love mistakes a harelip for a dimple. *Rec. dist.:* Ill.

4. Brotherly love for brotherly love, but cheese for money. *Rec. dist.:* Kans.

5. Choose your love, then love your choice. *Rec. dist.:* Kans.

6. Everything leaves, but love remains. *Rec. dist.:* Kans.

7. First love, last love, best love. *Rec. dist.:* N.Y., Ont.

8. Follow love and it will flee; flee love and it will follow you. *Rec. dist.:* N.Y. *1st cit.:* ca1400 *Roman de la Rose,* tr. Skeat. *20c. coll.:* ODEP 272, Stevenson 2592:8.

9. Great love from little things may grow. *Rec. dist.:* Ont.

10. He that falls in love with himself will have no rivals. *Rec. dist.:* U.S., Can.

11. He that gives the laws of love is usually a bachelor. *Rec. dist.:* Ill.

12. He who forces love where none is found remains a fool the whole year round. *Rec. dist.:* Ind.

13. He who knows not love has no children. *Rec. dist.:* N.Y.

14. If love interferes with your business, quit your business. *Rec. dist.:* N.C.

15. Love and eggs should be fresh to be enjoyed. *Rec. dist.:* Ind.

16. Love and hate are the two closest emotions. *Rec. dist.:* N.Y.

17. Love and politics don't mix. *Rec. dist.:* N.C.

18. Love and scandal are the best sweeteners of tea. *Rec. dist.:* Wis.

19. Love and smoke cannot be hidden. *Rec. dist.:* U.S., Can. *1st cit.:* ca1300 *Cursor Mundi,* E.E.T.S. (1874–92); US1737 Franklin, *PRAlmanac.* **20c. coll.:** *ODEP* 488, Whiting 269, Whiting*(MP)* 385.

20. Love and the weather can never be depended upon. *Rec. dist.:* Ark.

21. Love asks faith and faith asks firmness. *Rec. dist.:* Miss.

22. Love at first sight is cured by a second look. *Rec. dist.:* Kans.

23. Love can be a blessing or a curse. *Rec. dist.:* Ind.

24. Love can make any place agreeable. *Rec. dist.:* N.J.

25. Love can melt the ice and the snow of the coldest regions. *Rec. dist.:* Calif., N.Y.

26. Love can neither be bought nor sold; its only price is love. *Rec. dist.:* Ont. *1st cit.:* ca1340 Chaucer, *Franklin's Tale.* **20c. coll.:** *ODEP* 489.

27. Love cannot dwell with suspicion. *Rec. dist.:* N.C.

28. Love comes unseen. *Rec. dist.:* N.Y.

29. Love comforts like sunshine after rain. *Rec. dist.:* Wis. *1st cit.:* 1593 Shakespeare, *Venus and Adonis.* **20c. coll.:** Stevenson 1495:5.

30. Love conquers all. *Var.:* Love triumphs over all. *Rec. dist.:* U.S., Can. *1st cit.:* ca1386 Chaucer, *Prologue to Canterbury Tales;* US1929 Quinn, *Phantom.* **20c. coll.:** Stevenson 1472:12, Whiting*(MP)* 385.

31. Love covers many faults. *Rec. dist.:* Mich., N.Y. *1st cit.:* ca1607 Middleton, *Trick to Catch;* US1869 Alcott, *Little Women.* **20c. coll.:** *ODEP* 489, T&W 230, Stevenson 1484:8.

32. Love cures coquetry. *Rec. dist.:* N.Y. *1st cit.:* US1948 Stevenson, *Home Book of Proverbs.* **20c. coll.:** Stevenson 421:5.

33. Love cures the very wound it makes. *Rec. dist.:* N.Y. *1st cit.:* 1539 Publilius Syrus, *Sententiae,* tr. Taverner. **20c. coll.:** Stevenson 1467:6.

34. Love does much, but money does more. *Rec. dist.:* Ala., Ga., Ont. *1st cit.:* ca1534 Gilles, *Duwes.* **20c. coll.:** *ODEP* 490, Stevenson 1482:2.

35. Love enters man through his eyes, woman through her ears. *Rec. dist.:* Ind.

36. Love goes where it's sent. *Rec. dist.:* Ohio, Ont., Utah.

37. Love grows cold when it is not mixed with good works. *Rec. dist.:* Miss.

38. Love has no law but the law of love. *Rec. dist.:* Ill.

39. Love hits everyone. *Rec. dist.:* N.C.

40. Love intoxicates a man; marriage sobers him. *Rec. dist.:* N.Y.

41. Love is a deep well: a man may drink from it often, but he falls into it only once. *Rec. dist.:* N.J.

42. Love is a disease which begins with a fever and ends with a pain. *Rec. dist.:* Ind.

43. Love is a friendship set afire. *Var.:* True love is friendship set on fire. *Rec. dist.:* Ind., Wis.

44. Love is a little sighing and a little lying. *Rec. dist.:* N.Y.

45. Love is a thirst that is never slaked. *Rec. dist.:* N.Y., S.C. *1st cit.:* ca1862 Thoreau, *Early Spring in Massachusetts.* **20c. coll.:** Stevenson 1459:21.

46. Love is a tickling sensation around the heart. *Rec. dist.:* Calif., Ind., N.Y.

47. Love is akin to hate. *Rec. dist.:* Ill.

48. Love is all beautiful. *Rec. dist.:* N.C.

49. Love is an ocean of emotion surrounded by expense. *Rec. dist.:* Kans.

50. Love is better than fame—and money is best of all. *Rec. dist.:* Ill. *1st cit.:* 1860 Taylor, *To J.L.G.* **20c. coll.:** Stevenson 1468:12.

51. Love is blind. *Vars.:* **(a)** Love is blind—and if the blind lead the blind, both shall fall into the ditch. **(b)** Love is blind, but neighbors aren't. **(c)** Love is blind, deaf, and speechless. **(d)** Love is blind; so is hatred. **(e)** Love is deaf as well as blind. *Rec. dist.:* U.S., Can. *1st cit.:* ca1396 Chaucer, *Merchant's Tale;* US1646 Parker in *Thomas Hutchinson Papers,* Publ. Prince Soc. (1865). **20c. coll.:** *ODEP* 490, Whiting 269, *CODP* 140, Stevenson 1439:10, T&W 230, Whiting*(MP)* 386.

52. Love is never without jealousy. *Rec. dist.:* Ill. *1st cit.:* 1576 Pettie, *Petite Palace of Pleasure,* ed. Gollancz (1908). *20c. coll.:* ODEP 491, Stevenson 1464:8.

53. Love is not merely saying, it is doing. *Rec. dist.:* N.C.

54. Love is not time's fool. *Rec. dist.:* Wis.

55. Love is sharper than stones and sticks. *Rec. dist.:* N.C.

56. Love is strong as death; jealousy is cruel as the grave. *Rec. dist.:* N.Y. *1st cit.:* US1644 *Complete Writings of Roger Williams. 20c. coll.:* Whiting 270, Stevenson 1485:3, T&W 230, Whiting*(MP)* 386.

57. Love is strongest in pursuit—friendship in possession. *Rec. dist.:* N.Y.

58. Love is the master of all arts. *Rec. dist.:* Miss.

59. Love is the only fire against which there is no insurance. *Rec. dist.:* Ind.

60. Love is the only service that power cannot command and money cannot buy. *Rec. dist.:* N.J.

61. Love is the salt of life. *Rec. dist.:* Wis. *1st cit.:* ca1721 Sheffield, "Ode on Love" in *Works. 20c. coll.:* Stevenson 1459:18.

62. Love is the thing that lies in a woman's eyes, and lies, and lies, and lies. *Rec. dist.:* Ind.

63. Love is to be honored. *Rec. dist.:* N.C.

64. Love is where you find it. *Rec. dist.:* Ky., N.Y., Tenn.

65. Love knows no boundaries. *Rec. dist.:* Wis.

66. Love knows no jealousy. *Rec. dist.:* Ont.

67. Love knows no obstacles and grows with them. *Rec. dist.:* Ill.

68. Love knows no season. *Rec. dist.:* Calif., Ind.

69. Love lasts seven seconds; the fantasia lasts seven minutes; unhappiness lasts all one's life. *Rec. dist.:* N.Y.

70. Love laughs at locksmiths. *Rec. dist.:* U.S., Can. *1st cit.:* 1593 Shakespeare, *Venus and Adonis;* US1843 Hall, *New Purchase. 20c. coll.:* ODEP 491, T&W 230, CODP 140, Stevenson 1468:8, Whiting*(MP)* 386.

71. Love levels all inequalities. *Rec. dist.:* Mich., N.Y. *1st cit.:* US1909 O. Henry, *Best-Seller. 20c. coll.:* Stevenson 1471:11.

72. Love lives in cottages as well as in courts. *Rec. dist.:* Miss., N.C. *1st cit.:* 1590 Lodge, *Rosalynd, Euphues Golden Legacies;* US1924 Wells, *Furthest Fury. 20c. coll.:* ODEP 492, Whiting*(MP)* 386.

73. Love makes all burdens light. *Rec. dist.:* Ill.

74. Love makes obedience light. *Rec. dist.:* N.C.

75. Love makes the world go round. *Rec. dist.:* U.S., Can. *1st cit.:* 1656 Cowley, *David;* US1906 O. Henry, *Ruler of Men. 20c. coll.:* ODEP 492, Stevenson 1473:1, Whiting*(MP)* 386.

76. Love makes time pass; time makes love pass. *Var.:* Love takes time; time takes love. *Rec. dist.:* N.Y.

77. Love never dies of starvation, but often of indigestion. *Rec. dist.:* Wis.

78. Love never fails. *Rec. dist.:* N.C.

79. Love sees no faults. *Rec. dist.:* N.Y.

80. Love sought is good, but given unsought is better. *Rec. dist.:* N.C. *1st cit.:* 1601 Shakespeare, *Twelfth Night. 20c. coll.:* Stevenson 1468:4.

81. Love takes away the sight, and matrimony restores it. *Rec. dist.:* Ind.

82. Love will creep where it cannot go. *Rec. dist.:* Ill., Tex. *1st cit.:* ca1350 *Douce MS 52. 20c. coll.:* ODEP 424, Stevenson 1469:3.

83. Love will find a way. *Rec. dist.:* U.S., Can. *1st cit.:* ca1607 Deloney, *Gentle Craft;* US1930 Ogburn, *Ra-ta-plan! 20c. coll.:* ODEP 493, Whiting*(MP)* 387, CODP 141, Stevenson 1471:10.

84. Love's anger is fuel to love. *Rec. dist.:* Ill.

85. Mother love is blind. *Rec. dist.:* Ont.

86. Mother's love is best of all. *Rec. dist.:* Wis. *1st cit.:* 1814 *Kennon Letters,* in *Va.Mag.Hist.* (1923–32). *20c. coll.:* Whiting 270.

87. Off with the old love, on with the new. *Rec. dist.:* Wis. *1st cit.:* 1566 Edwards, *Damon* *and Pithias;* US1841 *Journals of Ralph Waldo Emerson,* eds. Emerson and Forbes (1909–14). **20c. coll.:** *ODEP* 586, *T&W* 229, *CODP* 167, Stevenson 1480:5, Whiting*(MP)* 385.

88. Offended love is the most terrible. **Rec. dist.:** N.C.

89. Old love burns low when new love breaks. **Rec. dist.:** N.C. **1st cit.:** US1737 Franklin, *PRAlmanac.* **20c. coll.:** Whiting 270, Stevenson 1481:7, *T&W* 230.

90. Old love does not rust. **Rec. dist.:** N.Y.

91. Old love is easily kindled. **Rec. dist.:** Ind., Ont.

92. One always returns to his first love. **Rec. dist.:** N.C. **1st cit.:** US1948 Stevenson, *Home Book of Proverbs.* **20c. coll.:** Stevenson 1468:11.

93. Puppy love leads to a dog's life. **Rec. dist.:** Ind.

94. Show your love to win love. **Rec. dist.:** N.J. **1st cit.:** ca1510 Barclay, *Mirror of Good Manners.* **20c. coll.:** Stevenson 1476:4.

95. The love light goes out when the gas bill comes in. **Rec. dist.:** Calif.

96. The path of true love never runs smooth. **Var.:** True love never runs smooth. **Rec. dist.:** U.S., Can. **1st cit.:** 1595 Shakespeare, *Midsummer Night's Dream;* US1832 Kennedy, *Swallow Barn,* ed. Hubbell (1929). **20c. coll.:** *ODEP* 148, Whiting 85, *CODP* 44, Stevenson 1475:3, *T&W* 82.

97. The road to love is bumpy. **Rec. dist.:** N.Dak.

98. The slave's love is the master's lifeguard. **Rec. dist.:** N.Y.

99. There are no ugly loves nor handsome prisons. **Rec. dist.:** Ill.

100. To be successful in love, one must know how to begin and when to stop. **Rec. dist.:** Ind., N.J.

101. When love is greatest, words are fewest. **Rec. dist.:** N.J.

102. When want comes in at the door, love flies out of the window. **Vars.:** **(a)** When money flies out the window, love flies out the door. **(b)** When poverty comes in at the door, love goes up the chimney. **(c)** When poverty comes in the door, love goes out the window. **Rec. dist.:** U.S., Can. **1st cit.:** ca1476 Caxton, *Game Chess;* US1790 *Universal Asylum.* **20c. coll.:** *ODEP* 642, Whiting 346, *CODP* 181, Stevenson 1481:3.

103. Where love falls it lies, and even if it be on the manure pile. **Rec. dist.:** Colo.

104. Where there is no love, all faults are seen. **Rec. dist.:** Ind. **1st cit.:** 1659 Howell, *Paroimiografia (English Proverbs).* **20c. coll.:** *ODEP* 490, Stevenson 775:12.

105. You can't control your love. **Rec. dist.:** N.C.

106. You can't live on love alone. **Rec. dist.:** Calif., Mich., N.Y., Wis. **1st cit.:** 1959 Curtis, *No Question of Murder;* US1969 Palmer, *Hildegarde Withers Makes the Scene.* **20c. coll.:** Whiting*(MP)* 388.

SEE ALSO ABSENCE is love's foe: far from the eyes, far from the heart. / ABSENCE kills a little love but makes the big ones grow. / ABSENCE sharpens love; presence strengthens it. / ALL is fair in love and war. / ANGER and love give bad counsel. / A CAREER never takes the place of a home where love reigns. / The best CHAPERONE a girl can have is to be in love with another fellow. / When DOUBT comes in, love goes out. / In DREAMS and in love, nothing is impossible. / FAULTS are thick when love is thin. / FEAR is stronger than love. / FRIENDSHIP is love without his wings. / FRIENDSHIP often ends in love, but love in friendship never. / It's not the HOUSE that makes the home, it's the love that is inside. / IGNORANCE and bungling with love are better than wisdom and skill without. / Without JEALOUSY, there is no love. / LABOR is light where love does pay. / The love of LIBERTY burns brightest in a dungeon. / Where there's MARRIAGE without love, there will be love without marriage. / MARRY first and love will follow. / MONEY is the sinews of love as well as of war. / PITY is akin to love. / Open REBUKE is better than secret love. / Little SILVER, much love. / In the SPRING a young man's fancy lightly turns to thoughts of love. / WAR is the law of violence, peace the law of love. / Love of WIT makes no man rich.

love *(v.)* **1.** He who loves last loves best. *Rec. dist.:* Utah.

2. He who loves much fears much. *Rec. dist.:* Wis.

3. He who loves well chastises well. *Var.:* Love well, whip well. *Rec. dist.:* Ill., Mich. *1st cit.:* US1733 Franklin, *PRAlmanac.* *20c. coll.:* Whiting 271.

4. He who loves well will never forget. *Var.:* He who loves well wishes well. *Rec. dist.:* N.Y. *1st cit.:* ca1380 Chaucer, *Parlement of Foules.* *20c. coll.:* Stevenson 1461:8.

5. If you would be loved, love and be lovable. *Vars.:* **(a)** Think less about being loved and more about being lovable. **(b)** To be loved, love and be lovable. *Rec. dist.:* U.S., Can. *1st cit.:* US1744 Franklin, *PRAlmanac.* *20c. coll.:* Stevenson 1476:11.

6. It is better to love someone you cannot have than have someone you cannot love. *Rec. dist.:* Ind.

7. Love 'em and leave 'em. *Rec. dist.:* U.S. *1st cit.:* 1917 Bridge, *Cheshire Proverbs;* US1933 Duffy, *Seven by Seven.* *20c. coll.:* Stevenson 1461:4.

8. Love all, trust few. *Rec. dist.:* U.S., Can. *1st cit.:* 1602 Shakespeare, *All's Well That Ends Well.* *20c. coll.:* Stevenson 160:18.

9. Love many; hate few; learn to paddle your own canoe. *Rec. dist.:* U.S.

10. Love me little and love me long. *Rec. dist.:* N.Y. *1st cit.:* 1546 Heywood, *Dialogue of Proverbs,* ed. Habernicht (1963); US1790 *Universal Asylum.* *20c. coll.:* ODEP 492, Whiting 271, Stevenson 1477:11, Whiting(MP) 388.

11. Love me, love my dog. *Rec. dist.:* U.S. *1st cit.:* ca1485 *Early English Miscellanies,* Warton Club (1856); US1775 *Warren-Adams Letters,* Mass.Hist.Soc. *Collections* (1917). *20c. coll.:* ODEP 492, Whiting 271, CODP 141, Stevenson 602:6.

12. Love who loves you and respond to who calls you. *Rec. dist.:* N.Y.

13. Love wisely but not too well. *Rec. dist.:* Ind., N.Y. *1st cit.:* 1605 Shakespeare, *Othello.* *20c. coll.:* Stevenson 1475:1.

14. Men who love much will work much. *Rec. dist.:* Ind., N.Y., S.C.

15. They do not love that do not show their love. *Rec. dist.:* N.Y.

16. They love too much that die for love. *Rec. dist.:* Ont.

17. Those whom we love first we seldom wed. *Rec. dist.:* N.Y., S.C.

18. To love and be wise is impossible. *Rec. dist.:* Ariz., N.Y. *1st cit.:* ca1527 Erasmus, *Dicta Sapientum,* tr. Berthelet. *20c. coll.:* CODP 140, Stevenson 1485:7.

19. To love is to live and to live is to love. *Rec. dist.:* N.Y., N.C. *1st cit.:* 1576 Pettie, *Petite Palace of Pleasure,* ed. Gollancz (1908). *20c. coll.:* Stevenson 1474:6.

20. Whom we love best, to them we say least. *Rec. dist.:* Ill., N.Y.

21. You haven't lived if you haven't loved. *Rec. dist.:* Calif., Mich., N.Y. *1st cit.:* 1724 Gay, *Captives.* *20c. coll.:* Stevenson 1474:6.

SEE ALSO Every ASS loves to hear himself bray. / Nobody loves a FAT man. / It is a FOOL who loves a woman from afar. / A true FRIEND is one who knows all your faults and loves you still. / The HEART that loves is always young. / You always HURT the one you love. / MERCHANTS love nobody. / MISERY loves company. / Love your NEIGHBOR as yourself. / Love your NEIGHBOR, but do not pull down the fence. / No one can love his NEIGHBOR on an empty stomach. / A PREACHER loves chicken better than he loves his second cousin. / He who loves the TREE loves the branch. / Love TRUTH for truth's sake.

love letter A love letter sometimes costs more than a three-cent stamp. *Rec. dist.:* Calif., N.Y., S.C.

lovely SEE ORDER is a lovely thing.

lover **1.** A lover may sigh, but he must not puff. *Rec. dist.:* Ill., Wis. *1st cit.:* US1906 O. Henry, *Skylight Room.* *20c. coll.:* Stevenson 1486:7.

2. A lover's anger is short-lived. *Rec. dist.:* Ill.

3. As is the lover, so is the beloved. *Rec. dist.:* Ill.

4. In the eye of the lover, pockmarks are dimples. *Rec. dist.:* Ill.

5. Lovers are fools. *Rec. dist.:* Ind., Ont.

6. Lovers are madmen. *Rec. dist.:* Ind., Ont. *1st cit.:* US1869 Henderson, *Latin Proverbs.* *20c. coll.:* Stevenson 1486:12.

7. Lovers think others blind. *Rec. dist.:* Ill.

8. Lovers, travelers, and poets will give money to be heard. *Rec. dist.:* Ill., N.Y., S.C. *1st cit.:* US1736 Franklin, *PRAlmanac.* *20c. coll.:* Stevenson 1441:3.

9. Once a lover, always a lover. *Rec. dist.:* Ill., Oreg.

10. One can be a lover without sighing. *Rec. dist.:* N.Y.

11. The falling out of lovers is the renewing of love. *Rec. dist.:* Ind. *1st cit.:* 1520 Whitington, *Vulgaria.* *20c. coll.:* ODEP 242, Stevenson 1488:10.

12. The lover is often lost in the husband. *Rec. dist.:* Ill. *1st cit.:* ca1773 Lyttelton, *Advice to a Lady.* *20c. coll.:* Stevenson 1204:2.

13. The sight of lovers feeds those in love. *Rec. dist.:* Ill.

14. There's nothing worse than an old lover. *Rec. dist.:* Ind.

15. True lovers are shy when people are by. *Rec. dist.:* Ind. *1st cit.:* ca1760 Foote, *Lame Lover.* *20c. coll.:* Stevenson 1486:5.

SEE ALSO Telling LIES is a fault in a boy, an art in a lover, an accomplishment in a bachelor, and second nature in a married woman.

loving *(n.)*   **1.** If there is anything better than to be loved, it is loving. *Rec. dist.:* Ky.

2. It takes a lot of loving to make a home. *Rec. dist.:* Miss., N.C., Tenn. *Infm.:* Cf. living.

3. It's loving and giving that make life worth living. *Rec. dist.:* Ont.

4. There is more pleasure in loving than in being in love. *Var.:* There is more pleasure in loving than in being loved. *Rec. dist.:* Ill., N.Y., Wis. *1st cit.:* 1732 Fuller, *Gnomologia.* *20c. coll.:* Stevenson 1463:5.

loving *(adj.)*   SEE A loving HEART is better and stronger than wisdom. / Loving HEARTS

find peace in love; clever heads find profit in it.

low *(v.)*   SEE It isn't the COW that lows the most that will milk the most.

low *(adj.)*   SEE It's a low BUSH that the sun never shines on. / High LIVING, low thinking.

low *(adv.)*   SEE When a man is DOWN, don't kick him lower. / FALLING hurts least those who fly low. / Choose not FRIENDS by outward show, for feathers float while pearls lie low. / LOOK high and light low. / Old LOVE burns low when new love breaks. / STOOP low and it will save you many a bump through life.

lowly *(adj.)*   SEE Cherish some FLOWER, be it ever so lowly.

lowly *(adv.)*   SEE KNOWLEDGE talks lowly; ignorance talks loudly.

loyalty   Loyalty has lost its meaning if its memory is short. *Rec. dist.:* N.J.

luck   **1.** A pocketful of luck is better than a sackful of wisdom. *Rec. dist.:* N.J.

2. Bad luck can't be dated. *Rec. dist.:* Miss.

3. Bad luck comes in threes. *Rec. dist.:* Mich., N.Y., Wash.

4. Bad luck is bad management. *Rec. dist.:* Ind.

5. Bad luck is good luck for someone. *Rec. dist.:* Ont., Oreg.

6. Behind bad luck comes good luck. *Rec. dist.:* Kans. *1st cit.:* 1721 Kelly, *Scottish Proverbs.* *20c. coll.:* Stevenson 1492:11.

7. Don't press luck too far. *Rec. dist.:* U.S., Can. *1st cit.:* US1932 Footner, *Dead Man's Hat.* *20c. coll.:* Whiting(MP) 389.

8. Ef luck's against you, 'tain't no use to squirm and twis'. *Rec. dist.:* Miss.

9. Good luck beats early rising. *Rec. dist.:* Miss., Ont.

10. Good luck disappears like our hair; bad luck lasts like our nails. *Rec. dist.:* Ont.

11. Good luck is a lazy man's explanation of another's success. *Rec. dist.:* Fla.

12. Good luck never comes too late. *Rec. dist.:* Ill.

13. Hard luck can't last one hundred years. *Rec. dist.:* N.Y.

14. If luck is with you, even your ox will give birth to a calf. *Rec. dist.:* N.Y.

15. Luck and glass break easily. *Rec. dist.:* Ont.

16. Luck is a very good word if you put a "p" before it. *Rec. dist.:* Ky., N.C., Ont., Tenn.

17. Luck is always against the man who depends upon it. *Rec. dist.:* N.Y.

18. Luck is better than science. *Rec. dist.:* Calif., Minn., Oreg.

19. Luck is for the few, death for the many. *Rec. dist.:* Wis.

20. Luck is not always a sign of wisdom. *Rec. dist.:* N.Y.

21. Luck is often pluck. *Rec. dist.:* Ill.

22. Never trust to luck. *Rec. dist.:* Mich., N.Dak.

23. No telling which way luck or a half-broke steer is going to run. *Var.:* No telling which way luck is going to run. *Rec. dist.:* Minn.

24. The only sure thing about luck is that it will change. *Var.:* Luck is bound to change. *Rec. dist.:* Ill. *1st cit.:* US1871 Harte, *Outcasts of Poker Flat.* *20c. coll.:* Stevenson 1493:1, T&W 231.

25. There is no luck in laziness. *Rec. dist.:* N.C., Ont. *1st cit.:* US1859 Taliaferro, *Fisher's River.* *20c. coll.:* ODEP 496, T&W 231, Stevenson 1583:4.

26. There's luck in leisure. *Rec. dist.:* N.C., Ont. *1st cit.:* 1683 Meriton, *Yorkshire Dialogue;* US1937 Shellabarger, *While Murder Waits.* *20c. coll.:* ODEP 496, CODP 141, T&W 231, Stevenson 1383:11, Whiting*(MP)* 389.

27. You never can tell the luck of a lousy calf. *Rec. dist.:* Ky., N.C., Ont., Tenn. *1st cit.:* 1769 Blair in *William & Mary Coll. Quart.* (1909). *20c. coll.:* Whiting 271, T&W 231.

28. You never know your luck till the wheel stops. *Rec. dist.:* Oreg.

See also ABILITY, not luck, conquers. /

You don't need BRAINS if you have luck. / DILIGENCE is the mother of good luck. / A stout HEART crushes ill luck. / A sudden LIE has best luck. / Hard WORK conquers the worst of luck.

lucky 1. Better born lucky than rich. *Rec. dist.:* U.S., Can. *1st cit.:* 1639 Clarke, *Paroemiologia;* US1852 Cary, *Clovernook.* *20c. coll.:* CODP 16, T&W 231, Stevenson 1489:11, Whiting*(MP)* 67.

2. He is lucky who forgets what cannot be mended. *Rec. dist.:* Ind.

3. If you're lucky, even your rooster will lay eggs. *Rec. dist.:* N.Y.

4. Lucky at play, unlucky in love. *Rec. dist.:* Ill., Mich. *1st cit.:* 1738 Swift, *Collection of Genteel and Ingenious Conversation;* US1801 Trumbull, *Season in New York 1801: Letters of Harriet and Maria Trunbull,* ed. Morgan (1969). *20c. coll.:* ODEP 496, CODP 142, Stevenson 1493:4, Whiting*(MP)* 92.

5. Lucky men need no counsel. *Rec. dist.:* N.Y. *1st cit.:* 1642 Torriano, *Select Italian Proverbs.* *20c. coll.:* ODEP 496, Stevenson 1489:8.

6. The lucky one must yet learn pain. *Rec. dist.:* N.J.

7. The nigger is luckier than the white man at night. *Rec. dist.:* Ill.

lunatic 1. Lunatics and fools make bad witnesses. *Rec. dist.:* Ill.

2. To a lunatic there is only one sane man in the world—himself. *Rec. dist.:* Ill.

lure *See* It is only the excited FISH that jumps at the lure.

lust *See* LEISURE breeds lust.

luxurious The luxurious live to eat and drink; the wise eat and drink to live. *Rec. dist.:* Mich.

luxury 1. He who wants luxuries, let him pay for them. *Rec. dist.:* Mich.

2. Learn the luxury of doing good. *Rec. dist.:* Wis. *1st cit.:* 1765 Goldsmith, *Traveller.* *20c. coll.:* Stevenson 996:6.

3. Living in luxury begets lustful desires. **_Rec._** **_dist.:_** Mich., N.C.

See also Confession is a luxury of the weak. / Poverty wants some things, luxury many things, avarice all things. / Pride is a luxury a poor man cannot afford.

lye _See_ Flattery is soft soap, and soap is ninety percent lye.

lying Lying is the first step to the prison gates. **_Rec. dist.:_** N.Y.

M

machine A machine running is worth two standing still. *Rec. dist.:* Calif.

mackerel SEE Set a SPRAT to catch a mackerel.

magistrate The magistrate should obey the law; the people should obey the magistrate. *Rec. dist.:* N.Y., S.C. *1st cit.:* US1734 Franklin, *PRAlmanac.* *20c. coll.:* Stevenson 1277:12.

magistry He that buys magistry must sell justice. *Rec. dist.:* Mich. *1st cit.:* 1732 Fuller, *Gnomologia.* *20c. coll.:* Stevenson 269:12.

maid 1. A good maid sometimes makes a bad wife. *Rec. dist.:* Ala., Ga.

2. Maids want nothing but husbands, and when they have them they want everything. *Rec. dist.:* Ont. *1st cit.:* 1678 Ray, *English Proverbs.* *20c. coll.:* ODEP 500, Stevenson 1504:5.

3. Old maids fancy nobody knows how to bring up children but them. *Rec. dist.:* Nebr., N.Y., N.C., S.C. *1st cit.:* 1546 Heywood, *Dialogue of Proverbs,* ed. Habernicht (1863); US1790 *Belknap Papers,* Mass.Hist.Soc. *Collections* (1877–91). *20c. coll.:* ODEP 24, Whiting 16, T&W 233, Stevenson 337:1, Whiting(MP) 392.

4. Praise a maid in the morning and the weather in the evening. *Rec. dist.:* Minn., Wis.

SEE ALSO A DOG's nose and a maid's knee are always cold. / If you can kiss the MISTRESS, never kiss the maid. / The worst STORE is a maid unbestowed. / The last SUITOR wins the maid. / It takes a wise WOMAN to be an old maid.

maiden 1. A maiden that is in love grows bolder without knowing it. *Rec. dist.:* Wis.

2. A neat maiden often makes a dirty wife. *Rec. dist.:* Ont.

3. If one will not, another will, so are all maidens wed. *Rec. dist.:* Ont. *1st cit.:* 1546 Heywood, *Dialogue of Proverbs,* ed. Habernicht (1963). *20c. coll.:* ODEP 890.

4. Maidens should be mild and meek, swift to hear and slow to speak. *Rec. dist.:* Ont. *1st cit.:* 1721 Kelly, *Scottish Proverbs.* *20c. coll.:* ODEP 499, Stevenson 1503:11.

Maine So goes Maine, so goes the nation. *Var.:* As Maine goes, so goes Vermont. *Rec. dist.:* U.S. *1st cit.:* US1956 *Boston Herald,* 6 Sep. *20c. coll.:* Whiting(MP) 392.

majority 1. The majority is often wrong. *Rec. dist.:* N.C.

2. The majority rules. *Rec. dist.:* N.C., Ohio.

3. Under majority rule, heads are counted; under minority rule, heads are cracked. *Rec. dist.:* Ill.

SEE ALSO It is better to be RIGHT than in the majority.

make SEE What MAN makes, man can destroy.

malice 1. Malice drinks its own poison. *Rec. dist.:* Ill., Ind. *1st cit.:* 1572 Harvey, *Marginalia.* *20c. coll.:* ODEP 502, Stevenson 1506:11.

2. Malice has a sharp sight and a strong memory. *Rec. dist.:* Ont. *1st cit.:* 1732 Fuller, *Gnomologia.* *20c. coll.:* Stevenson 1506:7.

3. Malice seldom wants a mark to shoot at. *Rec. dist.:* Ont. *1st cit.:* 1855 Bohn, *Handbook of Proverbs.* *20c. coll.:* Stevenson 1506:2.

4. There is as much malice in a wink as in a word. *Rec. dist.:* N.C., Wis.

5. Though malice may darken truth, it cannot put it out. *Rec. dist.:* Ill. *1st cit.:* 1732 Fuller, *Gnomologia.* *20c. coll.:* Stevenson 1506:5.

6. When there's more malice shown than matter, on the writer falls the satyr. *Rec. dist.:* N.Y., S.C. *1st cit.:* 1678 Ray, *English Proverbs.* *20c. coll.:* ODEP 543, Stevenson 1506:13.

SEE ALSO VANITY backbites more than malice.

malicious The malicious person keeps a viper in his breast. *Rec. dist.:* Ill. *1st cit.:* ca1386 Chaucer, *Summoner's Tale;* US1653 Wigglesworth, *Diary.* *20c. coll.:* ODEP 747, Whiting 464, Stevenson 1506:11, Whiting(MP) 659.

man 1. A brave man is a fool. *Rec. dist.:* Colo.

2. A good man is seldom uneasy, an ill one never easy. *Rec. dist.:* N.Y., S.C. *1st cit.:* US1734 Franklin, *PRAlmanac.* *20c. coll.:* Stevenson 1000:9.

3. A man, a horse, and a dog never weary of each other's company. *Rec. dist.:* Wis.

4. A man among children will long be a child; a child among men will soon be a man. *Rec. dist.:* Wis. *1st cit.:* 1732 Fuller, *Gnomologia.* *20c. coll.:* Stevenson 1512:8.

5. A man can be led, but he can't be driven. *Rec. dist.:* N.C. *1st cit.:* 1928 Crofts, *Sea Mystery;* US1690 Saltonstall in *Winthrop Papers,* Mass.Hist.Soc. *Collections* (1863–92). *20c. coll.:* Whiting(*MP*) 365, Whiting 255.

6. A man can die but once. *Rec. dist.:* Miss., Nebr., N.J., N.Dak. *1st cit.:* ca1425 "Resurrection" in *Towneley Plays;* US1775 Inman in *Letters of James Murray, Loyalist,* eds. Tiffany and Lesley (1901). *20c. coll.:* ODEP 503, Whiting 109, Stevenson 499:4, T&W 102.

7. A man can do a lot of things if he has to. *Rec. dist.:* N.C.

8. A man can do no more than he can. *Rec. dist.:* Colo., Miss., N.Y., N.C. *1st cit.:* 1530 Palsgrave, *Lesclarcissement de la langue Francoyse,* ed. Genin (1852). *20c. coll.:* ODEP 504, Stevenson 1:3.

9. A man can't be hanged for his thoughts. *Rec. dist.:* Calif. *1st cit.:* US1760 W. Franklin in *Papers of Benjamin Franklin,* ed. Labaree (1959). *20c. coll.:* Whiting 198.

10. A man cannot get away from his own shadow. *Rec. dist.:* N.J.

11. A man cannot live to himself alone. *Rec. dist.:* N.Y. *1st cit.:* ca1386 Chaucer, *Tale of Melibee.* *20c. coll.:* Stevenson 55:1.

12. A man chases a woman until she catches him. *Var.:* A man chases a girl until she catches him. *Rec. dist.:* Calif., N.Y.

13. A man convinced against his will is of the same opinion still. *Var.:* Convince a man against his will—he's of the same opinion still. *Rec. dist.:* U.S. *1st cit.:* 1678 Butler, *Hudibras.* *20c. coll.:* CODP 41, Stevenson 1719:10.

14. A man dies; his name remains. *Rec. dist.:* N.J.

15. A man doesn't want a woman smarter than he is. *Rec. dist.:* N.C.

16. A man is a product of his words. *Rec. dist.:* N.Y.

17. A man is as big as the thing that bothers him. *Rec. dist.:* Ohio, Ont.

18. A man is as good as he has to be; a woman is as bad as she dares. *Rec. dist.:* Wash.

19. A man is as old as he feels, a woman as old as she feels like admitting. *Vars.:* (a) A man is as old as he feels, a woman as old as she looks. (b) A man is no older than he feels. *Rec. dist.:* U.S. *1st cit.:* 1871 Lush, *Thames Journal,* 27 Aug.; US1947 Carr, *Sleeping Sphinx.* *20c. coll.:* CODP 144, Whiting(*MP*) 397, ODEP 505.

20. A man is as strong as his will. *Rec. dist.:* Fla.

21. A man is as young as he feels. *Rec. dist.:* N.J., Ohio. *1st cit.:* 1895 *Westminster Gazette,* 27 Nov.; US1947 Carr, *Sleeping Sphinx.* *20c. coll.:* Stevenson 31:1, Whiting(*MP*) 397, ODEP 505.

22. A man is king in his home. *Rec. dist.:* Calif., Ill., N.C. *1st cit.:* 1587 Bridges, *Defence.* *20c. coll.:* ODEP 229, Stevenson 1190:7.

23. A man is known by the company he keeps. *Rec. dist.:* U.S., Can. *1st cit.:* 1591 Smith, *Preparation to Marriage;* US1737 Stephens, *Journal of Proceedings in Georgia* in *Georgia Records* (1906, 1908). *20c. coll.:* ODEP 138, Whiting 81, CODP 40, Stevenson 386:12, T&W 233, Whiting(*MP*) 397.

24. A man is known by the paper he pays for. *Rec. dist.:* N.Y. *1st cit.:* US1928 Shedd, *Salt from My Attic.* *20c. coll.:* Stevenson 386:12.

25. A man is newly married who tells his wife everything. *Rec. dist.:* N.Y., N.C., S.C. *1st cit.:* 1640 Herbert, *Outlandish Proverbs (Jacula Prudentum)* in *Works,* ed. Hutchinson (1941). *20c. coll.:* Stevenson 2498:2.

26. A man is no better than his word. **Rec. dist.:** N.Y.

27. A man is of little use when his wife is a widow. **Rec. dist.:** N.Y.

28. A man is only as good as his weakest moment. **Rec. dist.:** Colo.

29. A man is only half a man without a wife. **Var.:** A man without a wife is but half a man. **Rec. dist.:** Kans., N.Y., N.C., S.C. **1st cit.:** US1755 Franklin, *PRAlmanac.* **20c. coll.:** Stevenson 2496:15.

30. A man is shy in another man's corner. **Rec. dist.:** Miss.

31. A man is what the winds and the tides have made him. **Rec. dist.:** Wis. **1st cit.:** 1591 Shakespeare, *Henry VI.* **20c. coll.:** Stevenson 769:3.

32. A man makes of himself what he will. **Rec. dist.:** Ohio.

33. A man may be deprived of life, but a good name can't be taken from him. **Rec. dist.:** N.Y., N.C., S.C. **1st cit.:** USca1835 Benjamin, *Great Name.* **20c. coll.:** Stevenson 1657:9.

34. A man may be down, but he's never out. **Rec. dist.:** N.C. **1st cit.:** 1951 Saunders, *Sleeping Bacchus;* USca1925 Leffingwell, Slogan of the Salvation Army. **20c. coll.:** Whiting(MP) 184, Stevenson 620:13.

35. A man may be too little to be big. **Rec. dist.:** Colo.

36. A man may smile and smile and still be a villain. **Rec. dist.:** N.Y. **1st cit.:** 1600 Shakespeare, *Hamlet.* **20c. coll.:** Stevenson 2145:3.

37. A man never becomes an orator if he has anything to say. **Rec. dist.:** N.Y., S.C. **1st cit.:** US1901 Dunne, *Gift of Oratory.* **20c. coll.:** Stevenson 1727:12.

38. A man should not stick his nose in his neighbor's pot. **Rec. dist.:** Colo. **1st cit.:** 1545 Cato, *Precepts of Cato,* tr. Burrant; US1809 Irving, *History of New York by D. Knickerbocker.* **20c. coll.:** ODEP 577, Stevenson 1696:10, T&W 264.

39. A man thinks he knows, but a woman knows better. **Rec. dist.:** Ont. **1st cit.:** US1938 Champion, *Racial Proverbs.* **20c. coll.:** Stevenson 1520:1.

40. A man who is not spoken of is not abused. **Rec. dist.:** N.Y.

41. A man who is wise is only as wise as his wife thinks he is. **Rec. dist.:** N.Y., S.C.

42. A man who really amounts to something tries to amount to more. **Rec. dist.:** Calif.

43. A man who wishes to keep a secret should tell nothing in confidence. **Rec. dist.:** Wis.

44. A man without a country is like a man without a soul. **Rec. dist.:** Calif.

45. A man without a religion is a horse without a bridle. **Rec. dist.:** Miss., Wis. **1st cit.:** 1621 Burton, *Anatomy of Melancholy.* **20c. coll.:** ODEP 507, Stevenson 1947:8.

46. A man without a woman is like a ship without a sail. **Rec. dist.:** Colo., Mich., N.Y., S.C.

47. A man without ambition is like a woman without beauty. **Rec. dist.:** N.Y., S.C.

48. A man without books is like a king without money. **Rec. dist.:** Ohio.

49. A man without money is like a ship without a sail. **Rec. dist.:** N.Y.

50. A man without money is no man at all. **Rec. dist.:** N.Y. **1st cit.:** 1592 Delamothe, *Treasure of French Tongue.* **20c. coll.:** ODEP 506.

51. A man without purpose is like a ship without a rudder. **Var.:** The man without a purpose is like a ship without a rudder. **Rec. dist.:** Ohio.

52. A man wrapped up in himself makes a very small bundle. **Var.:** When a man is wrapped up in himself, the package is very small. **Rec. dist.:** U.S., Can.

53. A poor man is always behind. **Rec. dist.:** Colo.

54. A rich man never lacks relatives. **Rec. dist.:** Calif., N.Y. **1st cit.:** 1659 Howell, *Paroimiografia.* **20c. coll.:** ODEP 674, Stevenson 1980:8.

55. A selfish man is always alone. **Rec. dist.:** Calif.

56. A stingy man is always poor. *Rec. dist.:* Calif., N.Y.

57. Act like a man of means, not like a mean man. *Rec. dist.:* Calif., N.Y.

58. All men are born free and equal. *Rec. dist.:* Mass., N.Y., S.C. *1st cit.:* US1779 Adams, Constitution of Massachusetts. *20c. coll.:* Stevenson 705:7.

59. All men are created equal. *Rec. dist.:* U.S., Can. *1st cit.:* US1776 Jefferson, Declaration of Independence. *20c. coll.:* Stevenson 705:7.

60. All men are fools, but all fools are not men. *Rec. dist.:* Calif. *1st cit.:* US1948 Stevenson, *Home Book of Proverbs. 20c. coll.:* Stevenson 848:3.

61. All men must die. *Var.:* All men are mortal. *Rec. dist.:* U.S. *1st cit.:* 1560 Palfreyman, *Mirror for Magistrates;* US1617 Rolfe in *Va.Mag.Hist.* (1902). *20c. coll.: ODEP* 10, Whiting 109, Stevenson 511:8, T&W 102, Whiting(MP) 393.

62. An old man in a house is a good sign. *Rec. dist.:* Colo., N.Y., S.C. *1st cit.:* 1642 Torriano, *Select Italian Proverbs;* US1744 Franklin, *PRAlmanac. 20c. coll.: ODEP* 590, Whiting 280.

63. An old man is twice a boy. *Rec. dist.:* U.S., Can. *1st cit.:* 1539 Taverner, *Proverbs of Erasmus;* US1650 *Works of Anne Bradstreet,* ed. Ellis (1932). *20c. coll.: ODEP* 591, Whiting 70, Stevenson 26:1.

64. An old young man will be a young old man. *Rec. dist.:* U.S. *1st cit.:* 1659 Howell, *Paroimiografia;* US1735 Franklin, *PRAlmanac. 20c. coll.: ODEP* 593, Whiting 280, Stevenson 41:4.

65. Any man can do what another man has done. *Rec. dist.:* Ind., Ont., Wis. *1st cit.:* 1863 Reade, *Hard Cash;* US1856 Durivage, *Three Brides, Love in a Cottage, and Other Tales. 20c. coll.: CODP* 144, T&W 104, *ODEP* 504, Stevenson 539:12, Whiting(MP) 402.

66. As a man is, so he sees. *Rec. dist.:* Ont.

67. As a man lives, so shall he die; as a tree falls, so shall it lie. *Rec. dist.:* U.S., Can. *1st cit.:* 1549 Latimer, *Seven Sermons;* US1762

Works of William Smith, D.D. (1803). *20c. coll.: ODEP* 505, Whiting 452, Stevenson 1419:11.

68. As a man thinks, so he is. *Rec. dist.:* U.S., Can. *1st cit.:* US1948 Stevenson, *Home Book of Proverbs. 20c. coll.:* Stevenson 2305:15.

69. As many men, so many opinions. *Rec. dist.:* U.S., Can. *1st cit.:* ca1390 Chaucer, *Squire's Tale;* USca1656 Bradford, *History of Plymouth Plantation,* ed. Ford (1912). *20c. coll.: CODP* 149, Whiting 280, *ODEP* 525, Stevenson 1722:1, T&W 235, Whiting(MP) 400.

70. As wave follows wave, so new men take old men's places. *Rec. dist.:* N.Y.

71. Beware of men made of clay. *Rec. dist.:* Ont.

72. Beware of no man but yourself. *Rec. dist.:* N.Y. *1st cit.:* 1732 Fuller, *Gnomologia. 20c. coll.:* Stevenson 2058:8.

73. Choose your man as you choose your shoes—for comfort and long wear. *Rec. dist.:* Colo.

74. Don't be a yes-man. *Rec. dist.:* Ont.

75. Don't value a man for the quality he is of, but for the qualities he possesses. *Rec. dist.:* Miss., N.Y., S.C. *1st cit.:* US1734 Franklin, *PRAlmanac. 20c. coll.:* Stevenson 1923:1.

76. Every man can tame a shrew but he that has one. *Rec. dist.:* Ont. *1st cit.:* 1546 Heywood, *Dialogue of Proverbs,* ed. Habernicht (1963). *20c. coll.: ODEP* 687, Stevenson 2102:8.

77. Every man dies as he must. *Rec. dist.:* N.C.

78. Every man drags water to his own mill. *Rec. dist.:* N.Y. *1st cit.:* 1573 Sanford, *Garden of Pleasure. 20c. coll.: ODEP* 201, Stevenson 2459:6.

79. Every man for himself. *Rec. dist.:* U.S. *1st cit.:* ca1390 Chaucer, *Knight's Tale;* US1706 *Correspondence Between William Penn and James Logan, 1700–1705,* ed. Armstrong, Hist. Soc.Penn. *Memoirs* (1870, 1872). *20c. coll.: CODP* 67, Whiting 134, *ODEP* 229, Stevenson 2058:10, T&W 234, Whiting(MP) 394.

80. Every man has a fool up his sleeve. *Rec. dist.:* N.C. *1st cit.:* 1640 Herbert, *Outlandish Proverbs (Jacula Prudentum)* in *Works,* ed.

Hutchinson (1941). *20c. coll.: ODEP* 274, Stevenson 848:3.

81. Every man has a price. *Var.:* Different men sell themselves at different prices. *Rec. dist.:* U.S., Can. *1st cit.:* 1734 Wyndham in *Bee;* US1769 *Papers of Benjamin Franklin,* ed. Smyth (1905–07). *20c. coll.: CODP* 68, Whiting 134, *ODEP* 229, Stevenson 1878:3, T&W 235, Whiting*(MP)* 395.

82. Every man has a right to be conceited. *Rec. dist.:* N.C., Ont. *1st cit.:* 1831 Disraeli, *Young Duke. 20c. coll.:* Stevenson 398:2.

83. Every man has got to kill his own snakes. *Rec. dist.:* Tex. *1st cit.:* US1955 Knight, *They're Going to Kill Me. 20c. coll.:* Whiting*(MP)* 578.

84. Every man has his faults. *Rec. dist.:* Miss., N.Y., Wis. *1st cit.:* 1557 Erasmus, *Merry Dialogue,* ed. de Vocht (1928); US1653 *Apologia of Robert Keayne,* ed. Bailyn (1965). *20c. coll.: ODEP* 229, Whiting 279, Stevenson 773:7, Whiting*(MP)* 399.

85. Every man has one black patch, and some have two. *Rec. dist.:* Ont.

86. Every man in his own way. *Rec. dist.:* Ala., Ga. *1st cit.:* ca1497 Medwall, *Fulgens and Lucres. 20c. coll.: ODEP* 229, Stevenson 2467:12.

87. Every man is a volume if you know how to read him. *Rec. dist.:* Ont. *1st cit.:* 1594 Shakespeare, *Romeo and Juliet. 20c. coll.:* Stevenson 1939:7.

88. Every man is his own enemy. *Rec. dist.:* N.Y. *1st cit.:* 1643 Brown, *Religio Medici. 20c. coll.:* Stevenson 689:8.

89. Every man is occasionally what he ought to be perpetually. *Rec. dist.:* N.J.

90. Every man knows where his own shoe pinches. *Rec. dist.:* Ont. *1st cit.:* ca1386 Chaucer, *Merchant's Tale;* US1709 Prout in *Saltonstall Papers, 1607–1815,* ed. Moody, Mass. Hist.Soc. *Collections* (1972). *20c. coll.: ODEP* 725, Whiting 391, Stevenson 2096:3, T&W 328, Whiting*(MP)* 560.

91. Every man must have his mate. *Rec. dist.:* Ont.

92. Every man must pay his Scot. *Rec. dist.:* N.Y. *Infm.:* "Scot" refers to the bar bill. *1st cit.:* ca1400 *English Gilds,* E.E.T.S. (1870);

US1860 Emerson, "Wealth" in *Conduct of Life. 20c. coll.:* Stevenson 1764:3.

93. Every man must pull his own weight. *Rec. dist.:* N.J.

94. Every man must skin his own skunk. *Rec. dist.:* N.J., N.Y., S.C., Wis. *1st cit.:* US1813 "Portsmouth Oracle" in *Dictionary of Americanisms,* ed. Mathews (1951). *20c. coll.:* Whiting 398, Stevenson 1236:1, T&W 338, Whiting*(MP)* 459.

95. Every man must sow his wild oats. *Rec. dist.:* Mich., Utah. *1st cit.:* 1542 Becon, "Nosegay" in *Early Works;* US1650 *Works of Anne Bradstreet,* ed. Ellis (1932). *20c. coll.: ODEP* 889, Whiting 320, Stevenson 1708:2, T&W 268, Whiting*(MP)* 459.

96. Every man must stand on his own two feet. *Rec. dist.:* Mich., N.Y., Ont. *1st cit.:* 1582 Fioravanti, *Compendium of Rational Secrets,* tr. Hester; US1653 *Apologia of Robert Keayne,* ed. Bailyn (1965). *20c. coll.: ODEP* 770, Whiting 258, Stevenson 1383:4, Whiting*(MP)* 239.

97. Every man should measure himself by his own foot rule. *Rec. dist.:* N.C. *1st cit.:* 1541 Bullinger, *Christian State of Matrimony,* tr. Coverdale. *20c. coll.: ODEP* 521, Stevenson 1552:5.

98. Every man stamps his value upon himself. *Rec. dist.:* Ont.

99. Every man to his own opinion. *Rec. dist.:* N.C.

100. Every man to his own poison. *Rec. dist.:* Calif., Ill., Mich.

101. Every man to his taste. *Var.:* Every man to his own taste. *Rec. dist.:* U.S., Can. *1st cit.:* 1580 Lyly, *Euphues and His England;* US1767 Hulton, *Letters of a Loyalist Lady* (1927). *20c. coll.: CODP* 68, Whiting 135, *ODEP* 230, Stevenson 2281:2, T&W 235, Whiting*(MP)* 395.

102. Every man to his trade. *Rec. dist.:* N.C., Ont. *1st cit.:* 1539 Taverner, *Proverbs of Erasmus;* US1723 Symmes, *Utile Dulci. 20c. coll.: CODP* 69, Whiting 135, *ODEP* 230, Stevenson 2358:6, T&W 235, Whiting*(MP)* 396.

103. Every man will be a poet if he can. *Rec.*

dist.: N.C., S.C. *1st cit.:* US1852 Thoreau, *Journal,* 11 Apr. *20c. coll.:* Stevenson 1818:14.

104. Every man would live long, but no woman would be old. *Rec. dist.:* Ont. *1st cit.:* 1714 Swift, *Thoughts on Various Subjects;* US1749 Franklin, *PRAlmanac. 20c. coll.:* Stevenson 29:5.

105. Every thing comes to a man who does not need it. *Rec. dist.:* N.Y.

106. Every time you forgive a man, you weaken him and strengthen yourself. *Rec. dist.:* N.J., Wis.

107. Give a man enough rope and he will hang himself. *Rec. dist.:* U.S., Can. *1st cit.:* 1639 Fuller, *Holy War;* US1698 Usher in *William & Mary Coll. Quart.* (1950). *20c. coll.:* CODP 194, Whiting 369, ODEP 683, Stevenson 2008:1, T&W 311, Whiting*(MP)* 537.

108. Honest men marry soon, wise men not at all. *Rec. dist.:* Wis. *1st cit.:* 1659 Howell, *Paroimiographia. 20c. coll.:* ODEP 380.

109. If a man empties his purse into his head no one can take it from him. *Rec. dist.:* Wis.

110. If men talked about what they understood, the silence would be unbearable. *Rec. dist.:* Oreg.

111. If what men most admire they would despise, 'twould look as if mankind were growing wise. *Rec. dist.:* N.Y., S.C. *1st cit.:* US1735 Franklin, *PRAlmanac. 20c. coll.:* Stevenson 2534:3.

112. If you must strike a man from behind, slap him on the back. *Rec. dist.:* Colo., Ill., Ind., Wis.

113. It is better for a town to be governed by a good man than by good laws. *Rec. dist.:* Calif., Colo., Utah.

114. It is far easier to know men than to know man. *Rec. dist.:* N.Y. *1st cit.:* US1948 Stevenson, *Home Book of Proverbs. 20c. coll.:* Stevenson 1519:10.

115. It is man that makes truth great, and not truth that makes man great. *Rec. dist.:* Iowa. *1st cit.:* US1948 Stevenson, *Home Book of Proverbs. 20c. coll.:* Stevenson 2386:9.

116. It is the men that make the city. *Rec.*

dist.: N.Y. *1st cit.:* 1489 Caxton, *Fates Arms. 20c. coll.:* ODEP 525, Stevenson 357:3.

117. It's better to be an old man's sweetheart than a young man's slave. *Rec. dist.:* U.S. *1st cit.:* 1546 Heywood, *Dialogue of Proverbs,* ed. Habernicht (1963); US1957 Beam, *Maine Hamlet. 20c. coll.:* CODP 14, Whiting*(MP)* 393, ODEP 51, Stevenson 1542:8.

118. It's the easiest thing in the world for a man to deceive himself. *Rec. dist.:* N.Y., S.C. *1st cit.:* 1640 Herbert, *Outlandish Proverbs (Jacula Prudentum)* in *Works,* ed. Hutchinson (1941); US1746 Franklin, *PRAlmanac. 20c. coll.:* ODEP 175, Stevenson 534:10.

119. Just because a man sings, it's no sign he's happy. *Rec. dist.:* Ohio.

120. Let another man praise you, not your own mouth. *Rec. dist.:* U.S., Can. *1st cit.:* 1484 Caxton, *Fables of Avian;* US1637 *New English Canaan of Thomas Morton,* ed. Adams, Jr., Publ. Prince Soc. (1883). *20c. coll.:* ODEP 507, Whiting 347, Stevenson 1864:2.

121. Look twice at a two-faced man. *Rec. dist.:* Calif., Oreg.

122. Man can't live in this world alone. *Rec. dist.:* U.S. *1st cit.:* US1792 Belknap, *History of New Hampshire* (1813). *20c. coll.:* Whiting 276, Stevenson 1129:5.

123. Man cannot live by bread alone. *Rec. dist.:* U.S., Can. *1st cit.:* 1881 Stevenson, *Virginibus Puerisque;* US1875 Emerson in *North American Review,* May-June. *20c. coll.:* Stevenson 231:8, CODP 144, Whiting*(MP)* 396.

124. Man changes often but gets better seldom. *Rec. dist.:* Ind., N.J. *1st cit.:* US1948 Stevenson, *Home Book of Proverbs. 20c. coll.:* Stevenson 313:7.

125. Man gets and forgets; woman gives and forgives. *Rec. dist.:* N.Y., S.C.

126. Man has his will, but woman has her way. *Rec. dist.:* Calif., Miss., N.Y., N.C., S.C. *1st cit.:* US1858 Holmes, *Autocrat of the Breakfast-Table. 20c. coll.:* Stevenson 2583:2.

127. Man is a bubble. *Rec. dist.:* Calif. *1st cit.:* 1539 Taverner, *Proverbs of Erasmus. 20c. coll.:* ODEP 505, Stevenson 1509:6.

128. Man is a hunter; woman is his game. *Rec. dist.:* Ill. *1st cit.:* 1847 Tennyson, *Princess.* *20c. coll.:* Stevenson 1521:7.

129. Man is a poor stick and a sad squirt. *Rec. dist.:* N.Y., S.C. *1st cit.:* US1922 Sandburg, *Slabs of the Sunburnt West. 20c. coll.:* Stevenson 1509:2.

130. Man is a wolf to man. *Rec. dist.:* N.Y. *1st cit.:* 1545 Cato, *Precepts of Cato,* tr. Burrant. *20c. coll.: ODEP* 505, Stevenson 1518:7.

131. Man is generally led the way which he is inclined to go. *Rec. dist.:* N.Y.

132. Man is greater than the tools he invents. *Rec. dist.:* Miss.

133. Man is his own master. *Rec. dist.:* Calif., N.Y., S.C. *1st cit.:* US1790 *Cary Letters,* ed. Curtis (1891). *20c. coll.:* Whiting 284.

134. Man is his own worst enemy. *Rec. dist.:* Calif., Mich.

135. Man is like a banana: when he leaves the bunch, he gets skinned. *Rec. dist.:* Ohio.

136. Man is made by little things. *Rec. dist.:* Miss.

137. Man is straw, woman fire—and the devil blows. *Rec. dist.:* Ariz. *1st cit.:* ca1303 Mannyng, *Handlyng Synne;* US1809 *Port Folio. 20c. coll.: ODEP* 259, Whiting 277, Stevenson 1520:9, Whiting*(MP)* 397.

138. Man is supreme lord and master of his own ruin and disaster. *Rec. dist.:* Wis.

139. Man is the master of all. *Rec. dist.:* Colo.

140. Man is the measure of all things. *Rec. dist.:* N.Y., Ohio. *1st cit.:* 1547 Baldwin, *Treatise of Morall Phylosophie;* US1948 Beston, *Northern Farm. 20c. coll.: ODEP* 505, Whiting*(MP)* 398, Stevenson 1509:3.

141. Man is the only animal that can be skinned twice. *Rec. dist.:* Calif., Colo.

142. Man is what he eats. *Rec. dist.:* N.Y., S.C. *1st cit.:* US1941 Gray, *Advancing Front of Medicine. 20c. coll.:* Stevenson 661:4.

143. Man marches on; time is. *Rec. dist.:* N.C.

144. Man never acts at variance to his nature. *Rec. dist.:* Ky., Tenn.

145. Man pays, but woman spends. *Rec. dist.:* N.Y.

146. Man proposes, God disposes. *Rec. dist.:* Calif., Nebr., Wash. *1st cit.:* ca1377 Langland, *Piers Plowman;* US1654 Johnson, *Wonder Working Providence of Sions Savior,* ed. Poole (1867). *20c. coll.: ODEP* 506, Whiting 278, *CODP* 144, Stevenson 981:6, T&W 235, Whiting*(MP)* 398.

147. Man reigns, but woman rules. *Rec. dist.:* N.Y.

148. Man stumbles over pebbles but never over mountains. *Rec. dist.:* Miss., N.Y., Ont.

149. Man wants but little here below, nor wants that long. *Rec. dist.:* Miss., N.Y., Ont. *1st cit.:* 1742 Young, *Night Thoughts. 20c. coll.:* Stevenson 2444:8.

150. Man works from sun to sun, but a woman's work is never done. *Rec. dist.:* U.S., Can. *1st cit.:* 1570 Baldwin, *Beware the Cat;* US1722 *Papers of Benjamin Franklin,* ed. Labaree (1959). *20c. coll.: ODEP* 909, Whiting 494, *CODP* 249, Stevenson 2583:9, Whiting*(MP)* 398.

151. Many a man sees a wolf at the door because his wife saw a mink in the window. *Rec. dist.:* Miss.

152. Men and melons are hard to know. *Rec. dist.:* Ind., N.Y., S.C. *1st cit.:* US1733 Franklin, *PRAlmanac. 20c. coll.:* Whiting 279, Stevenson 1519:9.

153. Men apt to promise are apt to forget. *Var.:* A man apt to promise is apt to forget. *Rec. dist.:* U.S., Can. *1st cit.:* 1732 Fuller, *Gnomologia. 20c. coll.:* Stevenson 1895:10.

154. Men are always wooing goddesses and marrying mere mortals. *Rec. dist.:* Wis.

155. Men are best loved furthest off. *Rec. dist.:* Wis. *1st cit.:* ca1547 *Surrey,* ed. Padelford (1928). *20c. coll.: ODEP* 48, Stevenson 591:7.

156. Men are born the slaves of women. *Rec. dist.:* N.Y.

157. Men are but children of a larger growth. *Rec. dist.:* Colo., Wis. *1st cit.:* 1678 Dryden, *All For Love. 20c. coll.:* Stevenson 1516:3.

158. Men are like steel: when they lose their temper, they are no good. *Rec. dist.:* Ohio.

159. Men are like streetcars: there's always another coming along. *Var.:* A man is like a streetcar: if you miss one, there will be another one along in a few minutes. *Rec. dist.:* Ala., Ind., N.J.

160. Men are neither suddenly rich nor suddenly good. *Rec. dist.:* Ont.

161. Men are not to be measured by inches. *Rec. dist.:* Wis. *1st cit.:* 1603 Montaigne, *Essays,* tr. Florio. *20c. coll.: ODEP* 524.

162. Men are what their mothers made them. *Rec. dist.:* N.Y., Ont., S.C. *1st cit.:* US1860 Emerson, "Fate" in *Conduct of Life. 20c. coll.:* Stevenson 1627:4.

163. Men build houses; women build homes. *Rec. dist.:* Ont. *1st cit.:* US1938 Champion, *Racial Proverbs. 20c. coll.:* Stevenson 1520:3.

164. Men grow weaker and wiser. *Rec. dist.:* Ohio.

165. Men, like bullets, go farther when polished. *Rec. dist.:* Ind., Mich., N.Y.

166. Men may blush to hear what they are not ashamed to act. *Rec. dist.:* Ont. *1st cit.:* ca1558 Wedlocke, *Image of Idleness. 20c. coll.: ODEP* 911.

167. Men may meet, though mountains cannot. *Vars.:* (a) Men meet, mountains never. (b) Two men may meet, but never two mountains. *Rec. dist.:* N.Y., S.C. *1st cit.:* 1530 Palsgrave, *Lesclarcissement de la langue Francoyse,* ed. Genin (1852); US1742 Franklin, *PRAlmanac. 20c. coll.: ODEP* 290, Whiting 279, Stevenson 1630:4.

168. Men must work and women must weep. *Rec. dist.:* S.C. *1st cit.:* ca1870 Kingsley, *Three Fishers. 20c. coll.:* Stevenson 2620:4.

169. Men, not gold, make a nation. *Rec. dist.:* Ont.

170. Men often condemn others for what they see no wrong in doing themselves. *Rec. dist.:* N.Y., S.C. *1st cit.:* ca1425 "Judgement" in *Wakefield Plays. 20c. coll.: ODEP* 257.

171. Men seek less to be instructed than applauded. *Rec. dist.:* N.Y., Ont.

172. Men seldom make passes at girls who wear glasses. *Var.:* Men never make passes at girls who wear glasses. *Rec. dist.:* U.S. *1st cit.:* US1926 Parker, "News Item" in *Enough Rope. 20c. coll.:* Stevenson 961:3.

173. Men talk wisely but live foolishly. *Rec. dist.:* Wis.

174. Men walk backwards like crabs and think they are making progress. *Rec. dist.:* Ill. *1st cit.:* 1579 Lyly, *Euphues, Anatomy of Wit. 20c. coll.: ODEP* 152.

175. Men who love much will work much. *Rec. dist.:* Ont.

176. Men's skins have many colors, but human blood is always red. *Rec. dist.:* Kans. *1st cit.:* 1580 Lyly, *Euphues and His England;* US1745 Franklin, *PRAlmanac. 20c. coll.:* Stevenson 202:10, Whiting 36, *ODEP* 69.

177. Men's years and their faults are always more than they are willing to own. *Rec. dist.:* N.Y., S.C. *1st cit.:* 1707 Mapletoft, *Select Proverbs. 20c. coll.: ODEP* 525.

178. Merely to silence a man is not to persuade him. *Rec. dist.:* N.Y., N.C., S.C. *1st cit.:* 1874 Morley, *On Compromise. 20c. coll.:* Stevenson 91:9.

179. Most men would rather say a smart thing than do a good one. *Rec. dist.:* Calif., Wis.

180. Mothers make men. *Rec. dist.:* N.Y.

181. No man can flay a stone. *Rec. dist.:* Tex. *1st cit.:* 1640 Herbert, *Outlandish Proverbs (Jacula Prudentum)* in *Works,* ed. Hutchinson (1941). *20c. coll.: ODEP* 569, Stevenson 2220:6.

182. No man can serve two masters. *Rec. dist.:* U.S. *1st cit.:* ca1330 Wright, *Political Songs,* Camden Soc. (1839); US1713 Steere, *Daniel Catcher and Other Poems. 20c. coll.: ODEP* 569, Whiting 279, *CODP* 162, Stevenson 1546:1, T&W 239, Whiting(MP) 399.

183. No man ever became extremely wicked at once. *Rec. dist.:* Wis. *1st cit.:* ca1580 Sidney, *Arcadia. 20c. coll.: ODEP* 569, Stevenson 2491:8.

184. No man ever got lost on a straight road. *Rec. dist.:* Iowa. *1st cit.:* US1948 Stevenson, *Home Book of Proverbs. 20c. coll.:* Stevenson 1999:1.

185. No man e'er was glorious who was not laborious. *Rec. dist.:* N.Y., S.C. *1st cit.:* US1734

Franklin, *PRAlmanac*. *20c. coll.:* Stevenson 1239:9.

186. No man has a right to all his rights. *Rec. dist.:* Wis.

187. No man has looked upon the morrow's sun. *Rec. dist.:* N.Y., N.C., S.C.

188. No man is above the law, and no man is below it. *Rec. dist.:* N.Y., S.C. *1st cit.:* US1903 Roosevelt, Third Annual Message to Congress, 7 Dec. *20c. coll.:* Stevenson 1363:8.

189. No man is better than he wants to be. *Rec. dist.:* N.Y.

190. No man is dead till he's dead. *Rec. dist.:* N.Y., S.C. *1st cit.:* 1942 Beeding, *Twelve Disguises*. *20c. coll.:* Stevenson 499:6.

191. No man is free who is not master of himself. *Rec. dist.:* N.J. *1st cit.:* US1948 Stevenson, *Home Book of Proverbs*. *20c. coll.:* Stevenson 887:8.

192. No man is hurt by himself. *Rec. dist.:* N.Y. *1st cit.:* 1640 Herbert, *Outlandish Proverbs (Jacula Prudentum)* in *Works*, ed. Hutchinson (1941). *20c. coll.:* ODEP 586.

193. No man is more than his brother if he does not do more than his brother. *Rec. dist.:* Calif.

194. No man is necessary. *Rec. dist.:* U.S., Can. *1st cit.:* US1940 Willkie's campaign theme, used against Roosevelt. *20c. coll.:* Stevenson 1667:5.

195. No man is so old but thinks he may live another day. *Rec. dist.:* Calif., N.C. *1st cit.:* ca1520 *Calisto and Melibea* in *A Select Collection of Old English Plays*, eds. Dodsley and Hazlitt. *20c. coll.:* ODEP 593, Stevenson 25:9.

196. No man is so tall but what he sometimes has to reach. *Rec. dist.:* Wash.

197. No man is wise at all times. *Rec. dist.:* Miss., N.Y., N.C. *1st cit.:* 1481 Caxton, *Reynard*. *20c. coll.:* ODEP 571.

198. No man lives to himself, and no man dies to himself. *Rec. dist.:* N.C., Ohio.

199. No man or nation can go up by heading down. *Rec. dist.:* N.Y., N.C., S.C.

200. Once a man, twice a child. *Rec. dist.:*

U.S., Can. *1st cit.:* 1511 Erasmus, *Moriae Encomium;* US1774 Wendell, *Gentlewoman of Boston,* Am.Antiq.Soc. *Proceedings* (1919). *20c. coll.:* Stevenson 26:1, Whiting 70, T&W 68.

201. One man does not make a team. *Rec. dist.:* Calif.

202. One man in the apartment is worth two on the street. *Rec. dist.:* Wis.

203. One man may be more cunning than another, but not more cunning than everybody else. *Rec. dist.:* N.Y. *1st cit.:* US1745 Franklin, *PRAlmanac*. *20c. coll.:* Stevenson 469:13.

204. Only an old man has patience enough to plant a tree. *Rec. dist.:* Colo.

205. Power flows to the man who knows how. *Rec. dist.:* N.Y. *1st cit.:* US1901 Hubbard, *Philistine*. *20c. coll.:* Stevenson 1857:11.

206. Show me the man that does not make a mistake, and I will show you the man that does not do anything. *Rec. dist.:* N.Y. *1st cit.:* 1868 Magee, Sermon at Peterborough. *20c. coll.:* ODEP 502, CODP 152, Stevenson 1598:6.

207. Six feet under makes all men equal. *Rec. dist.:* N.Y. *1st cit.:* 1563 *Mirror for Magistrates,* ed. Campbell. *20c. coll.:* ODEP 738, Stevenson 1027:12.

208. Some men are merriest when far from home. *Rec. dist.:* Kans.

209. Some men have a short arm for giving and a long arm for getting. *Rec. dist.:* Ariz.

210. Some men, like blisters, only show up when the work is done. *Rec. dist.:* Kans.

211. The best of men are but men after all. *Rec. dist.:* Ont. *1st cit.:* 1680 Aubrey, *Brief Lives*. *20c. coll.:* ODEP 48, CODP 13.

212. The bigger the man, the better the mark. *Rec. dist.:* N.Y. *1st cit.:* 1894 Northall, *Folk Phrases of Four Counties*. *20c. coll.:* ODEP 59.

213. The last man to admit he is wrong is himself. *Rec. dist.:* Calif.

214. The man most down on a thing is he who is least up on it. *Rec. dist.:* N.Y., N.C., S.C.

215. The man that aims at nothing usually

gets it. *Rec. dist.:* Colo., Ohio. *1st cit.:* ca1374 Chaucer, *Troilus and Criseyde.* *20c. coll.:* Stevenson 2418:1.

216. The man that's worthwhile is the man that can smile. *Var.:* The man worthwhile is the man who can smile when everything goes wrong. *Rec. dist.:* Miss., N.Y.

217. The man who believes is the man who achieves. *Rec. dist.:* N.C., Wis.

218. The man who does not know himself is a poor judge of the other fellow. *Rec. dist.:* N.Y.

219. The man who gets in a stew is small potatoes. *Rec. dist.:* Nebr., N.Dak.

220. The man who gets in wet weather is all washed up. *Rec. dist.:* Nebr., Utah.

221. The man who leaves the flock must fight wolves. *Rec. dist.:* Oreg.

222. The man who says it can't be done is liable to be knocked down by someone doing it. *Rec. dist.:* N.J.

223. The man who turns against his own side soon finds both sides against him. *Rec. dist.:* Wis.

224. The poor man pays for all. *Rec. dist.:* N.Y., Okla. *1st cit.:* ca1561 "Poor Man Pays" in *Roxburghe Ballads,* Ballad Soc. (1869–99). *20c. coll.:* ODEP 639.

225. The way to a man's heart is through his stomach. *Rec. dist.:* U.S., Can. *1st cit.:* 1845 Ford, *Handbook for Traveller's in Spain;* US1814 Adams, Letter, 15 Apr., in *Works of John Adams,* ed. Cushing (1904–08). *20c. coll.:* ODEP 871, CODP 242, Stevenson 165:7 and 2217:8, T&W 179, Whiting*(MP)* 673.

226. The worse the man the better the soldier. *Rec. dist.:* N.Y.

227. There are two good men—one dead, the other unborn. *Rec. dist.:* Calif., Wis. *1st cit.:* US1880 Spurgeon, *John Ploughman's Pictures.* *20c. coll.:* Stevenson 998:5.

228. Things turn out for the man who digs. *Rec. dist.:* Calif., Colo.

229. To find out what a man is like, find out what he does in his spare time. *Rec. dist.:* Ala., Ga.

230. Trust every man, but cut the cards. *Rec. dist.:* Vt.

231. What man makes, man can destroy. *Rec. dist.:* N.C.

232. What man has done, man can do. *Rec. dist.:* N.Y., S.C. *1st cit.:* 1863 Reade, *Hard Cash;* US1960 Wees, *Country of Strangers.* *20c. coll.:* Stevenson 539:12, Whiting*(MP)* 402.

233. When a man marries, his life begins. *Rec. dist.:* Kans.

234. When a man marries, his troubles begin; when a man dies, his trouble ends. *Rec. dist.:* Miss., N.Y., N.C., S.C. *1st cit.:* 1843 Halliwell, *Nursery Rhymes of England.* *20c. coll.:* Stevenson 1537:12.

235. When a man takes a wife, he ceases to dread hell. *Rec. dist.:* Calif.

236. When a man's away, abuse him you may. *Rec. dist.:* N.Y.

237. When a man's single, his pockets will jingle. *Rec. dist.:* Colo., Mich., Ohio, Tex.

238. Where one man goes, others will follow. *Rec. dist.:* N.Y.

239. You can't afford to snub a man built on the million dollar plan. *Rec. dist.:* Miss.

240. You can't fool the old man. *Rec. dist.:* Ohio.

241. You can't live with men; neither can you live without them. *Rec. dist.:* Ky., N.Y., Tenn. *1st cit.:* 1711 Addison, *Spectator.* *20c. coll.:* Stevenson 2556:2.

242. You cannot be a true man until you learn to obey. *Rec. dist.:* N.Y.

243. You never know a man until you bed with him a winter and summer. *Rec. dist.:* Calif., Wis.

SEE ALSO A man without AIM is like a clock without hands, as useless if it turns as if it stands. / An ANGRY man opens his mouth and shuts his eyes. / Every man is the ARCHITECT of his own fortune. / BAD men leave their mark wherever they go. / A man is as BIG as the things that make him mad. / A man once BITTEN by a snake will jump at the sight of a rope in his path. / A BLIND man can see his mouth. / A BLIND man is no judge of colors.

/ Don't send a BOY to do a man's job. / A CRAZY man thinks everyone crazy but himself. / A CUNNING man overreaches no one so much as himself. / DEAD men tell no tales. / When a man is DOWN, don't kick him lower. / The more a man DREAMS, the less he believes. / A man takes a DRINK and then the drink takes the man. / A DROWNING man will catch at a straw. / Don't drown yourself to save a DROWNING man. / It is the DULL man who is always sure, and the sure man who is always dull. / Press not the FALLING man too far. / Another man's FOOD is sweeter. / A FOOLISH man despises his mother. / Man's best FRIEND is his dog. / A GREAT man is what he is because he was what he was. / Behind every GREAT man there is a great woman. / No GREAT man ever complains of want of opportunity. / HAPPY is the man that finds wisdom and that gets understanding. / No man is ever HAPPY unless he thinks himself so. / A HASTY man is seldom out of trouble. / Men always HATE most what they envy most. / An HONEST man is the noblest work of God. / A HUNGRY man is an angry man. / A HUNGRY man sees far. / Don't JUDGE a man by his opinion of himself. / Don't JUDGE a man by the coat he wears. / Don't JUDGE a man till his work is done. / Every man JUDGES others by himself. / The less a man KNOWS the more positive he is that he knows everything. / The more a man KNOWS the more he forgives. / A LAZY man will live the longest. / The LAZY man goes to his work like a thief to the gallows. / MANNERS make the man. / Like MASTER, like man. / One man's MEAT is another man's poison. / The MIND of the man is the man. / MUSIC is the poor man's parnassus. / What's one man's NEWS is another man's troubles. / A little NONSENSE now and then is relished by the best of men. / The best laid PLANS of mice and men often go astray. / Many a man thinks he is buying PLEASURE when he is really selling himself a slave to it. / A man is not POOR if he can laugh. / When all are POOR, it doesn't take much to make a rich man. / A man POSSESSES only what he knows he possesses. / PRAISE makes a good man better and a bad man worse. / A QUARRELSOME man has no good neighbors. / The RICHEST man is he who wants least. / Do RIGHT and fear no man; don't write and fear no woman. / Any man can be a SAILOR on a calm sea. / Many a man is a SAILOR who never owned a rowboat. / Eat a peck of SALT with a man before you trust him. / In a calm SEA every man is a pilot. / A SHREWD man feathers his own nest. / With SMALL men no great thing can be accomplished. / SNOW is the poor man's fertilizer. / The STYLE is the man. / SUCCESS has ruined many a man. / Count no man SUCCESSFUL until he is dead. / A man SURPRISED is half beaten. / Poor men's TABLES are soon set. / Nine TAILORS make a man. / When THIEVES fall out, honest men get their due. / The greater your TROUBLES, the greater is your opportunity to show yourself a man. / That must be TRUE which all men say. / It's a lonesome WASHING that has not a man's shirt in it. / WEAK men wait for opportunities; strong men make them. / One man's WEAKNESS is another man's chance. / A man cannot WHISTLE and eat a meal at the same time. / WINE has drowned more men than the sea. / A man shall be commended by his WISDOM. / A WISE man always carries his umbrella. / A WISE man carries his coat on a dry day. / A WISE man changes his mind; a fool never does. / A WISE man is never less alone than when alone. / A WISE man will learn. / A WISE man will make more opportunities than he finds. / It takes a WISE man to find a wise man. / No man is always WISE. / WISE men learn by other men's mistakes; fools insist on learning by their own. / A WOMAN can throw out the window more than a man can bring in at the door. / A WOMAN is as old as she looks, but a man is never old till he quits looking. / A man of WORDS and not of deeds is like a garden full of weeds. / The only WORK that hurts a man is hopeless work. / WORRY kills more men than work. / Beware of the WRATH of a patient man. / A YOUNG man idle, an old man needy. / A YOUNG man looks into the future as an old man into the past.

management Good management is better than good income. *Rec. dist.:* Calif.

mankind Mankind lives on promises. *Rec. dist.:* N.Y., S.C.

SEE ALSO If what MEN most admire they would despise, 'twould look as if mankind were growing wise.

manners 1. Bad manners are a species of bad morals. *Rec. dist.:* Kans.

2. Good manners are made up of petty sacrifices. *Rec. dist.:* Ill.

3. Ill manners produce good laws. *Rec. dist.:* Wis. *1st cit.:* 1539 Taverner, *Proverbs of Erasmus;* US1652 *Complete Writings of Roger Williams* (1963). *20c. coll.:* ODEP 233, Whiting 253, Stevenson 1523:9.

4. Manners are more than meat, and morals more than manners. *Rec. dist.:* Ill. *1st cit.:* ca1628 Carmichaell, *Proverbs in Scots,* ed. Anderson (1957). *20c. coll.:* ODEP 522.

5. Manners make the man. *Rec. dist.:* U.S., Can. *1st cit.:* ca1350, *Douce MS 52;* US1742 Franklin, *PRAlmanac. 20c. coll.:* ODEP 508, Whiting 282, CODP 145, Stevenson 1525:1, Whiting*(MP)* 402.

6. Striking manners are bad manners. *Rec. dist.:* Wis.

7. The test of good manners is being able to put up pleasantly with bad ones. *Rec. dist.:* N.Dak.

SEE ALSO HONORS change manners.

manure *SEE* MONEY is like manure: it's only good when spread around.

many Many are called, but few are chosen. *Var.:* Many are called, but few respond. *Rec. dist.:* U.S., Can. *1st cit.:* US1791 *Diary of William Bentley* (1905–14). *20c. coll.:* Whiting 282, T&W 237, Stevenson 348:4, Whiting*(MP)* 402.

March 1. A warm March will bring a cold April. *Rec. dist.:* Calif., Vt.

2. March is in like a lion, out like a lamb. *Var.:* March comes in like a lion and goes out like a lamb. *Rec. dist.:* U.S., Can. *1st cit.:* ca1620–35 *Telltale;* US1740 Ames, *Almanacs,* ed. Briggs (1891). *20c. coll.:* ODEP 511, Whiting 282, CODP 147, Stevenson 1526:2, T&W 238, Whiting*(MP)* 403.

3. March winds and April showers bring May flowers. *Vars.:* **(a)** March winds and April showers bring forth May flowers. **(b)** March winds bring April showers. *Rec. dist.:* U.S., Can. *1st cit.:* ca1430 Lydgate, *Reason and Sensuality;* US1671 Russell in *Colonial American Poetry,* ed. Silverman (1968). *20c. coll.:* ODEP 17, Whiting 11, CODP 6, Stevenson 1526:1, Whiting*(MP)* 16.

mare 1. He that speaks ill of the mare will buy her. *Rec. dist.:* N.Y., S.C. *1st cit.:* 1599 Minsheu, *Dictionarie in Spanish and English;* US1742 Franklin, *PRAlmanac. 20c. coll.:* ODEP 762, Whiting 283, Stevenson 268:10.

2. The old gray mare ain't what she used to be. *Rec. dist.:* U.S. *1st cit.:* 1546 Heywood, *Dialogue of Proverbs,* ed. Habernicht (1963); US1716 McCliesh in *Letters from Hudson Bay. 20c. coll.:* ODEP 238, Whiting 282, Stevenson 1527:2, T&W 238, Whiting*(MP)* 404

SEE ALSO MONEY makes the mare go.

mark Toe the mark. *Rec. dist.:* U.S., Can. *1st cit.:* 1922 Joyce, *Ulysses;* US1840 Dana, *Two Years Before the Mast* (1911). *20c. coll.:* Whiting*(MP)* 377, T&W 239.

market There's no good market for bad eggs or rotten bananas. *Rec. dist.:* Ill.

SEE ALSO PATIENCE in markets is worth pounds in a year.

marriage 1. A shotgun marriage won't last longer than the honeymoon. *Rec. dist.:* Ill.

2. If more people tried as hard to stay married as they do to get married, fewer marriages would go on the rocks. *Rec. dist.:* Miss.

3. Marriage and hanging go by destiny. *Rec. dist.:* N.C. *1st cit.:* 1519 Horman, *Vulgaria,* ed. James; US1637 *New English Canaan of Thomas Morton,* ed. Adams (1883). *20c. coll.:* ODEP 350, Whiting 283, Stevenson 1536:9, Whiting*(MP)* 405.

4. Marriage is a game best played by two winners. *Rec. dist.:* Calif.

5. Marriage is a lottery. *Rec. dist.:* Ind. *1st cit.:* 1605 Marston, *Dutch Courtesan;* US1939 Sullivan, *Sullivan at Bay. 20c. coll.:* ODEP 513, CODP 147, Stevenson 1532:8, Whiting*(MP)* 405.

6. Marriage is a quick solution to more problems. *Rec. dist.:* Wis.

7. Marriage is a romance novel in which the hero dies in the first chapter. *Rec. dist.:* Calif.

8. Marriage is an institution for the blind. *Rec. dist.:* Calif.

9. Marriage is both heaven and hell. *Var.:* Marriage is heaven or hell. *Rec. dist.:* Calif., Ill.

10. Marriage is like a tub of water: after a while, it is not so hot. *Rec. dist.:* S.Dak.

11. Marriages are made in heaven. *Rec. dist.:* Ill., Kans., S.C., Tex. *1st cit.:* 1566 Painter, *Palace of Pleasure,* ed. Jacobs (1890); US1696 Dunton, *Letters from New England,* Publ. Prince Soc. (1867). *20c. coll.:* ODEP 514, Whiting 284, Stevenson 1523:10, T&W 239, Whiting(MP) 405.

12. Where there's marriage without love, there will be love without marriage. *Rec. dist.:* Calif., Ill., N.Y., Ont., S.C. *1st cit.:* 1642 Fuller, *Holy State;* US1734 Franklin, *PRAlmanac. 20c. coll.:* Stevenson 1539:3.

SEE ALSO Keep your EYES wide open before marriage, half shut afterwards.

marry **1.** Before you marry, 'tis well to tarry. *Var.:* Before you marry, 'tis wise to tarry. *Rec. dist.:* Ala., Ga., Iowa, Ohio.

2. If you marry a beautiful blonde, you marry trouble. *Rec. dist.:* Ill. *1st cit.:* US1936 Herzog, *Jabo Proverbs. 20c. coll.:* Stevenson 1540:3.

3. If you marry for money, you sell your freedom. *Rec. dist.:* Ill., Ont., R.I. *1st cit.:* 1581 Guazzo, *Civile Conversation,* tr. Pettie, T.T. (1925). *20c. coll.:* ODEP 515, Stevenson 1540:6.

4. Marry above your match and you get a master. *Rec. dist.:* N.Y., S.C. *1st cit.:* 1721 Kelly, *Scottish Proverbs;* US1740 Franklin, *PRAlmanac. 20c. coll.:* ODEP 516, Stevenson 1541:7.

5. Marry first and love will follow. *Rec. dist.:* Wis. *1st cit.:* 1600 Shakespeare, *Merry Wives of Windsor. 20c. coll.:* ODEP 515, Stevenson 1540:2.

6. Marry in haste and repent at leisure. *Rec. dist.:* U.S., Can. *1st cit.:* 1566 Tilney, *Duties of Marriage;* US1637 *New English Canaan of Thomas Morton,* ed. Adams (1883). *20c. coll.:*

ODEP 515, Whiting 200, T&W 172, Stevenson 1539:1, Whiting(MP) 289.

7. Marry late or never. *Rec. dist.:* Ill. *1st cit.:* 1616 Draxe, *Bibliotheca Scholastica* in *Anglia* (1918). *20c. coll.:* ODEP 516, Stevenson 1531:6.

8. The day you marry, it is either kill or cure. *Rec. dist.:* Wis.

9. To marry once is a mistake; to marry twice is fatal. *Var.:* To marry once is a duty, twice is folly, thrice is madness. *Rec. dist.:* Calif., Ill.

martyr God's martyr is never the devil's servant. *Rec. dist.:* Ill.

master **1.** A bad master makes a bad servant. *Rec. dist.:* Ill. *1st cit.:* 1706 Stevens, *New Spanish and English Dictionary. 20c. coll.:* ODEP 517.

2. As the master is, so is his dog. *Rec. dist.:* Ill. *1st cit.:* 1926 Fielding, *Footsteps That Stopped;* US1945 Bonnany, *King Is Dead. 20c. coll.:* Whiting(MP) 405.

3. Be master of your anger. *Rec. dist.:* Ill. *1st cit.:* US1948 Stevenson, *Home Book of Proverbs. 20c. coll.:* Stevenson 1907:9.

4. Everyone has his master. *Var.:* Every man has his master. *Rec. dist.:* Ill., Ohio.

5. Like master, like man. *Rec. dist.:* U.S., Can. *1st cit.:* 1530 Palsgrave, *Lesclarcissement de la langue Francoyse,* ed. Genin (1852); US1692 Bulkeley, *Will and Doom,* ed. Hoadly in Conn.Hist.Soc. *Collections* (1895). *20c. coll.:* ODEP 517, Whiting 284, CODP 148, Stevenson 1547:4, T&W 239, Whiting(MP) 405.

6. Masters are made, not born. *Rec. dist.:* Calif., N.Y.

7. To be the master of others, one must first be the master of himself. *Rec. dist.:* Ala., Ga. *1st cit.:* 1597 *Politeuphuia Wits Commonwealth. 20c. coll.:* ODEP 517, Stevenson 2061:1.

8. You are master of the unspoken word; the spoken word is master of you. *Var.:* While the word is yet unspoken, you are master of it; when once it is spoken, it is master of you. *Rec. dist.:* N.Y.

SEE ALSO The EYE of the master does more than his hand. / No MAN can serve two masters. / Let your PURSE be your master. / A good SERVANT makes a good master. / He who has a WIFE has a master.

matches If you play with matches, you will get burned. *Rec. dist.:* Ohio. *1st cit.:* 1582 Whetstone, *Heptameron;* US1884 Thorpe, *Fenton Family.* *20c. coll.:* ODEP 632, CODP 179, Stevenson 811:10, Whiting(MP) 226.

matrimony Matrimony is not a word but a sentence. *Rec. dist.:* N.Y. *1st cit.:* US1940 Thompson, *Body, Boots, and Britches.* *20c. coll.:* Stevenson 1537:10.

maxim A good maxim is never out of season. *Rec. dist.:* Mich., N.C. *1st cit.:* 1855 Bohn, *Handbook of Proverbs.* *20c. coll.:* Stevenson 1906:6.

May What you put off and what you put on, never change till May be gone. *Rec. dist.:* N.J.

maybe Maybes don't fly this time of year. *Rec. dist.:* Ark., Kans. *1st cit.:* 1721 Kelly, *Scottish Proverbs;* US1807 *The Emerald.* *20c. coll.:* ODEP 518, Whiting 285, Whiting(MP) 406.

meal *(repast)* **1.** Many a meal is lost for want of meat. *Rec. dist.:* N.Y., S.C. *1st cit.:* US1740 Franklin, *PRAlmanac.* *20c. coll.:* Stevenson 1550:6.

2. Unquiet meals make ill digestions. *Rec. dist.:* Ill. *1st cit.:* 1593 Shakespeare, *Comedy of Errors.* *20c. coll.:* Stevenson 1550:10.

3. You can't eat a square meal off a round table. *Rec. dist.:* Ohio.

meal *(grain)* **1.** It's easy to bake when the meal is beside you. *Rec. dist.:* Mich., Miss. *1st cit.:* ca1628 Carmichaell, *Proverbs in Scots,* ed. Anderson (1957). *20c. coll.:* ODEP 28.

2. You can't get meal from an empty sack. *Rec. dist.:* N.J.

measles No matter how important you are, you can catch the measles. *Vars.:* **(a)** Even the most important people get measles. **(b)** No matter how sweet you are, you can always take the measles. *Rec. dist.:* Miss., Ohio.

measure *(n.)* **1.** Measure is a treasure. *Rec. dist.:* N.C., Okla. *1st cit.:* ca1200 *Ancrene Riwle,*

Camden Soc. (1894). *20c. coll.:* ODEP 520, Stevenson 1602:4.

2. There is a measure in all things. *Rec. dist.:* Okla., Tex. *1st cit.:* ca1374 Chaucer, *Troilus and Criseyde.* *20c. coll.:* ODEP 520, CODP 149, Stevenson 1602:4.

3. When the measure is full, it runs over. *Rec. dist.:* Ill.

4. Without measure medicine will become poison. *Rec. dist.:* N.Y.

SEE ALSO Just SCALES and full measure injure no men.

measure *(v.)* **1.** Better twice measured than once wrong. *Rec. dist.:* Ohio.

2. Measure twice before you cut once. *Rec. dist.:* Ill., Kans., N.Y., N.C. *1st cit.:* 1591 Florio, *Second Fruites,* ed. Simonini (1953). *20c. coll.:* ODEP 520, Stevenson 1911:10.

SEE ALSO Don't measure my CORN by your bushel.

meat **1.** After meat comes mustard. *Rec. dist.:* U.S., Can. *1st cit.:* 1576 Holyband, *French Littleton.* *20c. coll.:* ODEP 6.

2. All meat is to be eaten, and all maids to be wed. *Rec. dist.:* Ill. *1st cit.:* 1546 Heywood, *Dialogue of Proverbs,* ed. Habernicht (1963). *20c. coll.:* ODEP 10, Stevenson 1554:5.

3. One man's meat is another man's poison. *Var.:* What's one man's meat is another man's poison. *Rec. dist.:* U.S. *1st cit.:* ca1576 Whythorne, *Autobiography,* ed. Osborn (1961); US1776 A. Adams in *Adams Family Correspondence,* ed. Butterfield (1963). *20c. coll.:* ODEP 522, Whiting 280, CODP 149, Stevenson 1554:5, Whiting(MP) 400.

4. They that have no other meat gladly bread and butter eat. *Rec. dist.:* Ill. *1st cit.:* 1639 Clarke, *Paroemiologia.* *20c. coll.:* ODEP 572, Stevenson 235:9.

5. You can't tell how much meat there is in the smokehouse by feeling the roof. *Rec. dist.:* N.Dak.

SEE ALSO The closer to the BONE, the sweeter the meat.

medal Every medal has its reverse. *Rec. dist.:* Ill., Mich. *1st cit.:* 1603 Montaigne, *Essays,* tr.

Florio; US1800 *Writings of Thomas Jefferson,* ed. Bergh (1907). *20c. coll.: ODEP* 522, Stevenson 1555:3.

medicine 1. Medicine can prolong life, but death will seize the doctor, too. *Rec. dist.:* Calif., Ill.

2. Medicines were not meant to live on. *Rec. dist.:* Calif., N.Y. *1st cit.:* 1545 Ascham, *Toxophilus. 20c. coll.: ODEP* 523.

3. There is a medicine for all things except death and taxes. *Rec. dist.:* Ill., Mich., Tex.

SEE ALSO Ready MONEY is ready medicine. / The SICKNESS of the body may be a medicine for the mind. / Eat few SUPPERS and you'll need few medicines.

meek 1. The meek are terrible in their wrath. *Rec. dist.:* Ill.

2. The meek shall inherit the earth. *Var.:* The meek do inherit the earth—six feet by six feet by three feet of it. *Rec. dist.:* U.S., Can. *1st cit.:* US1948 Stevenson, *Home Book of Proverbs. 20c. coll.:* Stevenson 1559:10.

meet SEE EAST is east, and west is west, and never the twain shall meet. / MERRY meet, merry part.

melon Eat your melons and don't ask about the melon bed. *Rec. dist.:* Ill.

SEE ALSO MEN and melons are hard to know.

memory 1. All complain for want of memory, but none for want of judgment. *Rec. dist.:* Calif., Mich., N.Y. *1st cit.:* US1948 Stevenson, *Home Book of Proverbs. 20c. coll.:* Stevenson 1561:8.

2. Memory is the watchman of the brain. *Rec. dist.:* Ill. *1st cit.:* 1605 Shakespeare, *Macbeth. 20c. coll.:* Stevenson 1560:10.

3. No man has a good enough memory to be a successful liar. *Rec. dist.:* Calif., N.C. *1st cit.:* ca1531 Latimer, *Sermons and Remains,* Parker Soc. (1844–45); US1702 Mather, *Magnalia Christi Americana* (1853–55). *20c. coll.: ODEP* 457, Whiting 259, *CODP* 132, Stevenson 1395:6, Whiting(MP) 369.

4. Our memory is always at fault, never our judgment. *Rec. dist.:* Ill. *1st cit.:* US1948 Ste-

venson, *Home Book of Proverbs. 20c. coll.:* Stevenson 1561:8.

5. The memory of a great love is kept green forever. *Rec. dist.:* Ill. *1st cit.:* 1600 Shakespeare, *Hamlet. 20c. coll.:* Stevenson 1562:6.

6. There is no memory which time does not erase. *Rec. dist.:* Calif.

7. You don't trust to memory. *Rec. dist.:* Ark., Kans.

mend 1. It's never too late to mend. *Rec. dist.:* U.S., Can. *1st cit.:* 1590 Greene, *Never Too Late;* US1778 Clinton, *Public Papers of George Clinton, First Governor of New York,* ed. Hastings (1899–1911). *20c. coll.: ODEP* 563, Whiting 252, *CODP* 160, Stevenson 1563:7, T&W 215, Whiting(MP) 362.

SEE ALSO Least SAID, soonest mended.

mending SEE The ROOF doesn't need mending when it's not raining.

merchant 1. A merchant's happiness hangs upon luck. *Rec. dist.:* Ill. *1st cit.:* 1732 Fuller, *Gnomologia. 20c. coll.:* Stevenson 1564:2.

2. Merchants love nobody. *Rec. dist.:* N.Y., S.C. *1st cit.:* US1785 Jefferson, Letter to John Langdon. *20c. coll.:* Stevenson 1564:5.

3. We are merchants today and beggars tomorrow. *Rec. dist.:* Ill.

SEE ALSO Quick RETURNS make rich merchants.

merciful Be merciful to those who show mercy. *Rec. dist.:* Ill. *1st cit.:* ca1377 Langland, *Piers Plowman. 20c. coll.:* Stevenson 1565:9.

mercy It's safer to err on the side of mercy. *Rec. dist.:* Ill.

merit 1. Great merit is coy, as well as great pride. *Rec. dist.:* N.Y., S.C. *1st cit.:* US1752 Franklin, *PRAlmanac. 20c. coll.:* Stevenson 1566:5.

2. Make a merit of necessity. *Rec. dist.:* Mich., N.Y. *1st cit.:* ca1374 Chaucer, *Troilus and Criseyde;* US1678 *Selected Letters of Cotton Mather,* ed. Silverman (1971). *20c. coll.: ODEP* 861, Whiting 465, Stevenson 1668:4, T&W 392, Whiting(MP) 659.

3. Merit is sure to rise to the surface. *Rec.*

dist.: Ill. *1st cit.:* US1948 Stevenson, *Home Book of Proverbs.* *20c. coll.:* Stevenson 1566:3.

4. True merit is like a river: the deeper it is, the less noise it makes. *Rec. dist.:* Ill., Vt.

merry **1.** A merry man is usually a fool. *Rec. dist.:* Ill.

2. Be merry and wise. *Rec. dist.:* N.J. *1st cit.:* 1546 Heywood, *Dialogue of Proverbs,* ed. Habernicht (1963); US1710 Byrd, *Secret Diary of William Byrd of Westover, 1709–1741,* ed. Woodfin (1942). *20c. coll.:* ODEP 527, Whiting 287, Stevenson 1567:5, T&W 241, Whiting*(MP)* 408.

3. Merry meet, merry part. *Rec. dist.:* N.C., Tex. *1st cit.:* 1678 Ray, *English Proverbs.* *20c. coll.:* ODEP 528, Stevenson 1567:7.

SEE ALSO EAT, drink, and be merry, for tomorrow we may die. / The MORE the merrier.

merry-go-round Don't get off the merry-go-round before it stops. *Rec. dist.:* N.J.

messenger SEE KISSES are the messengers of love.

method **1.** Method is the very hinge of business. *Rec. dist.:* Ill.

2. Method will teach you to win time. *Rec. dist.:* Ill.

mickle Many a mickle makes a muckle. *Rec. dist.:* U.S., Can. *1st cit.:* ca1386 Chaucer, *Parson's Tale;* US1793 *Writings of George Washington,* ed. Fitzpatrick (1931–44). *20c. coll.:* ODEP 510, Whiting 287, CODP 146, Whiting*(MP)* 408.

middle *(n.)* Keep in the middle of the road. *Rec. dist.:* U.S. *1st cit.:* ca1870 *Keep in Middle of Road.* *20c. coll.:* Stevenson 1999:1.

SEE ALSO If you play both ENDS against the middle, the middle will soon fold up.

middle *(adj.)* A middle course is the safest. *Rec. dist.:* Ill., N.Y. *1st cit.:* 1732 Pope, "Satires" in *Imitations of Horace;* US1719 Wise, Letter in *Colonial Currency Reprints,* ed. Davis, Publ. Prince Soc. (1910–11). *20c. coll.:* Stevenson 1604:4, Whiting 474.

might **1.** Do what you do with all your might: things half done are never done right.

Rec. dist.: Ill., Ont. *1st cit.:* US1948 Stevenson, *Home Book of Proverbs.* *20c. coll.:* Stevenson 536:11

2. Might makes right. *Vars.:* **(a)** Might beats right. **(b)** Might is not right. **(c)** Might over right and right is might. **(d)** Might overcomes right. *Rec. dist.:* U.S., Can. *1st cit.:* ca1330 Wright, *Political Songs,* Camden Soc. (1839); USca1700 Hubbard, *General History of New England* (1848). *20c. coll.:* ODEP 530, Whiting 288, CODP 150, Stevenson 1572:1, T&W 242, Whiting*(MP)* 409.

mile The first mile is always the hardest. *Rec. dist.:* Calif.

SEE ALSO A MISS is as good as a mile.

milk **1.** A penny's worth of milk brings a dollar's worth of health. *Rec. dist.:* Calif., Wash.

2. Don't cry over spilled milk. *Vars.:* **(a)** Don't grieve over spilt milk. **(b)** 'Tis folly to cry for spilt milk. **(c)** 'Tis no use crying for spilt milk. **(d)** It's no use crying over spilt milk. **(e)** It's no use to cry over spilt milk. **(f)** Never grieve over spilt milk. **(g)** No use crying over spilt milk. **(h)** No use crying over spilt milk—there's enough water in it now. **(i)** No weeping for shed milk. **(j)** There's no use to cry over spilled milk. *Rec. dist.:* U.S., Can. *1st cit.:* 1659 Howell, *Paroimiografia;* US1757 *Papers of Henry Laurens,* ed. Hamer (1968). *20c. coll.:* ODEP 159, Whiting 289, CODP 46, Stevenson 1573:9, T&W 243, Whiting*(MP)* 411.

3. If you give your milk to the cat, you must drink water out of the sink. *Rec. dist.:* Ill.

4. Once milk becomes sour, it can't be made sweet again. *Rec. dist.:* N.Y. *1st cit.:* US1942 Gardner, *D.A. Cooks Goose.* *20c. coll.:* Stevenson 1228:16.

5. You can't pick up spilled milk. *Rec. dist.:* Ala., Ga.

SEE ALSO You cannot sell the COW and have the milk.

mill *(grindstone)* **1.** Enter the mill and you come out floury. *Rec. dist.:* N.J. *1st cit.:* US1948 Stevenson, *Home Book of Proverbs.* *20c. coll.:* Stevenson 389:7.

2. Mills won't grind if you give them no water. *Var.:* Mills will not grind if we give them no water. *Rec. dist.:* N.C., Okla., Tex. *1st cit.:* 1636 Ward, *Sermons.* *20c. coll.:* ODEP 532, Stevenson 1576:1, Whiting(MP) 411.

3. No mill, no meal; no will, no deal. *Rec. dist.:* Ill. *1st cit.:* 1639 Clarke, *Paroemiologia.* *20c. coll.:* ODEP 572, Stevenson 2622:8.

4. The mill cannot grind with the water that is past. *Vars.:* (a) A mill can't grind with the water that is past. (b) The mill will never grind with the water that has passed. *Rec. dist.:* U.S., Can. *1st cit.:* 1616 Draxe, *Bibliotheca Scholastica* in *Anglia* (1918); US1937 Bailey, *Clunk's Claimant.* *20c. coll.:* ODEP 531, Whiting(MP) 411, Stevenson 1575:5.

5. The mills of the gods grind slowly, but they grind exceedingly fine. *Vars.:* (a) The mill of the gods grinds exceedingly fine. (b) The mill of the gods grinds slowly, but it grinds fine. (c) The mills of the gods are slow, but oh so fine. (d) The mills of the gods grind slowly. (e) The mills of the gods grind slowly, but they grind exceedingly small. *Rec. dist.:* U.S., Can. *1st cit.:* 1640 Herbert, *Outlandish Proverbs (Jacula Prudentum)* in *Works,* ed. Hutchinson (1941); US1870 Longfellow, *Poems* (1960). *20c. coll.:* ODEP 314, CODP 151, Stevenson 1575:11, Whiting(MP) 411.

SEE ALSO CORN makes mo' at de mill dan it does in de crib. / Much WATER goes by the mill the miller knows not of.

mill *(monetary unit)* In for a mill, in for a million. *Rec. dist.:* N.Y. *1st cit.:* US1837 *Works of Ralph Waldo Emerson,* ed. Cabot. *20c. coll.:* T&W 244.

millstone The lower millstone grinds as well as the upper. *Rec. dist.:* Ill. *1st cit.:* 1519 Horman, *Vulgaria.* *20c. coll.:* ODEP 532, Stevenson 1577:10.

mind 1. A busy mind breeds no evil. *Rec. dist.:* Ill.

2. A contented mind is a continual feast. *Rec. dist.:* Mich., N.C. *1st cit.:* 1535 Coverdale, *Bible Proverbs;* US1676 Benjamin Tompson, *His Poems,* ed. Hall (1924). *20c. coll.:* ODEP 142, Whiting 290, Stevenson 1582:10.

3. A good mind possesses a kingdom. *Rec. dist.:* Ill. *1st cit.:* 1588 Dyer, "My Mind to Me Kingdom Is." *20c. coll.:* ODEP 533, Stevenson 1581:11.

4. A mind diseased cannot bear anything harsh. *Rec. dist.:* Ill. *1st cit.:* US1948 Stevenson, *Home Book of Proverbs.* *20c. coll.:* Stevenson 1579:10.

5. A proud mind and a light purse are ill met. *Rec. dist.:* N.J. *1st cit.:* ca1430 Lydgate, *Minor Poems.* *20c. coll.:* ODEP 651.

6. A ruffled mind makes a restless pillow. *Rec. dist.:* N.J.

7. A sound mind, a sound body. *Rec. dist.:* Wis. *1st cit.:* 1578 Lemnius, *Touchstone of Complexions,* tr. Newton; US1783 Van Schaack, *Life of Peter Van Schaack* (1842). *20c. coll.:* ODEP 755, Whiting 290, Stevenson 1583:12, Whiting(MP) 412.

8. A willing mind makes a light foot. *Rec. dist.:* Ill., Kans. *1st cit.:* 1640 Herbert, *Outlandish Proverbs (Jacula Prudentum)* in *Works,* ed. Hutchinson (1941). *20c. coll.:* Stevenson 2511:4.

9. A woman's mind is like winter wind. *Rec. dist.:* N.J., N.Y., S.C. *1st cit.:* ca1450 *Sloane MS 38* in *Early English Carols.* *20c. coll.:* ODEP 909.

10. All great minds run in the same channel. *Vars.:* (a) Bright minds run in the same channel. (b) Great minds follow the same track. (c) Great minds run in the same channel, and weak ones in the same gutter. (d) Great minds run in the same channels. *Rec. dist.:* U.S., Can. *1st cit.:* 1594 Shakespeare, *Taming of the Shrew;* US1640 Howes in *Winthrop Papers, 1498–1649,* Mass.Hist.Soc. *Collections* (1929–47). *20c. coll.:* ODEP 326, Whiting 490, Stevenson 2548:13, Whiting(MP) 412.

11. An idle mind is the devil's workshop. *Rec. dist.:* U.S., Can. *1st cit.:* ca1602 Perkins, *Treatise of Callings* in *Works* (1608). *20c. coll.:* ODEP 395, CODP 118.

12. Great minds discuss ideas; average minds discuss events; small minds discuss people. *Rec. dist.:* Colo., Ky.

13. Little minds are tamed and subdued by misfortune, but great minds rise above it. *Rec. dist.:* N.Y., S.C., Utah. *1st cit.:* US1819 Ir-

ving, "Philip of Pokanoket" in *Sketch Book*. **20c. coll.:** Stevenson 1593:5.

14. Little minds, like weak liquors, are soon soured. *Rec. dist.:* Wis. **1st cit.:** 1855 Bohn, *Handbook of Proverbs*. **20c. coll.:** Stevenson 1593:5.

15. Mind is the great lever of all things. *Rec. dist.:* Ill.

16. Mind unemployed is mind unenjoyed. *Rec. dist.:* Ala., Ga., Ill., N.C.

17. Small minds are lured by trifles. *Rec. dist.:* Ill. **1st cit.:** US1948 Stevenson, *Home Book of Proverbs*. **20c. coll.:** Stevenson 2594:4.

18. The mind made up is no mind at all. *Rec. dist.:* Calif.

19. The mind of the man is the man. *Rec. dist.:* Ill. **1st cit.:** 1616 Adams, *Sacrifice of Thankfulness;* US1823 *Austin Papers,* ed. Barker (1924). **20c. coll.:** ODEP 533, Whiting 290, Stevenson 1578:3.

20. Two minds are better than one. *Rec. dist.:* Calif., N.C. **1st cit.:** ca1390 Gower, *Confessio Amantis,* E.E.T.S. (1900). **20c. coll.:** ODEP 851, *CODP* 233, Stevenson 1096:1.

SEE ALSO The PEN is the tongue of the mind. / Out of SIGHT, out of mind.

minute **1.** A minute lost in the morning is never regained all day. *Rec. dist.:* Calif.

2. A minute on the lips is a lifetime on the hips. *Rec. dist.:* Calif., Kans., Miss.

3. Look out for the minutes and the hours will look out for themselves. *Rec. dist.:* Calif., N.Y. **1st cit.:** US1827 *Journals of Ralph Waldo Emerson,* eds. Emerson and Forbes (1909–14). **20c. coll.:** T&W 245, Whiting(MP) 413.

SEE ALSO There's a SUCKER born every minute.

mire **1.** Can't probe mire 'thout getting sullied. *Rec. dist.:* N.Y. **1st cit.:** US1943 Spain, *Death Is Like That.* **20c. coll.:** Stevenson 1585:8.

2. If you stir up the mire, you must bear the smell. *Rec. dist.:* Ill.

3. The more you linger in the mire, the more you foul yourself. *Rec. dist.:* Ill.

mirror **1.** There is no better mirror than an old friend. *Rec. dist.:* Ariz., Ind., Tex. **1st cit.:**

1611 Cotgrave, *Dictionary of French and English Tongues.* **20c. coll.:** ODEP 534, Stevenson 904:4.

2. When you look at yourself in the mirror, you look at a fool. *Rec. dist.:* Ill.

mirth **1.** A cent of mirth is worth a dollar of grief. *Rec. dist.:* Ill. **1st cit.:** 1567 *Trial of Treasure.* **20c. coll.:** ODEP 601, Stevenson 1586:6.

2. Mirth prolongs life. *Rec. dist.:* Ill. **1st cit.:** ca1553 Udall, *Prologue to Ralph Roister Doister.* **20c. coll.:** Stevenson 1586:14.

mischief **1.** A little mischief is a little too much. *Rec. dist.:* Ill.

2. All mischief comes from the opening of the mouth. *Rec. dist.:* Calif.

3. He that mischief hatches, mischief catches. *Rec. dist.:* Ill. **1st cit.:** 1609 Harward, Unpublished manuscript in Library of Trinity College, Cambridge. **20c. coll.:** ODEP 534, Stevenson 1587:12.

4. Mischief comes by the pound and goes by the ounce. *Rec. dist.:* Ill. **1st cit.:** 1573 Sanford, *Garden of Pleasure.* **20c. coll.:** ODEP 534, Stevenson 1587:12.

5. When you plot mischief for others, you're preparing trouble for yourself. *Rec. dist.:* Ill. **1st cit.:** 1484 Aesope, tr. Caxton, E.E.T.S. (1889). **20c. coll.:** Stevenson 1967:4, ODEP 534.

SEE ALSO A little NEGLECT may breed great mischief. / A WORD that is not spoken never does any mischief.

miser **1.** A miser grows rich by seeming poor. *Rec. dist.:* Mich., Miss.

2. A miser is an ass that carries gold and eats thistles. *Rec. dist.:* Ill.

3. A miser's son is a spendthrift. *Rec. dist.:* N.C.

4. A rich miser is poorer than a poor man. *Rec. dist.:* Ill.

5. To ask a miser for a handout is like begging a naked man to give you his clothes. *Rec. dist.:* Ill.

6. To be a miser is to be unhappy. *Rec. dist.:* Fla.

misery 1. A man is twice miserable when he fears his misery before it comes. *Rec. dist.:* Ill.

2. He bears misery best who hides it most. *Rec. dist.:* N.Dak., Ont. *1st cit.:* ca1584 Harvey, *Marginalia. 20c. coll.:* ODEP 535, Stevenson 1591:11.

3. Misery loves company. *Rec. dist.:* U.S., Can. *1st cit.:* ca1349 Rolle, *Meditations on Passion* in *Yorkshire Writers,* ed. Horstmann; US1775 Gilbert, Letter, 4 May, in *Naval Documents of American Revolution,* ed. Clarke. *20c. coll.:* CODP 151, Whiting 291, Stevenson 1592:14, T&W 246, Whiting(MP) 414.

4. Misery makes strange bedfellows. *Rec. dist.:* Ill. *1st cit.:* 1611 Shakespeare, *Tempest;* US1813 *Writings of John Quincy Adams,* ed. Ford (1913–17). *20c. coll.:* ODEP 535, Whiting 292, Stevenson 1591:10, T&W 246.

5. Misery never comes singly. *Var.:* Troubles never come singly. *Rec. dist.:* Colo., Ill. *1st cit.:* ca1300 *King Alisaunder* in *Metrical Romances,* ed. Weber (1810); US1791 Burr, Letter, 27 July, in *Memoirs of Aaron Burr,* ed. Davis (1836). *20c. coll.:* ODEP 535, CODP 151, Whiting 292, Stevenson 1597:4, T&W 246, Whiting(MP) 414.

misfortune 1. Don't rejoice about your neighbor's misfortunes, for the same may happen to you. *Rec. dist.:* Ariz., Ark. Kans. *1st cit.:* 1539 Publilius Syrus, *Sententiae,* tr. Taverner. *20c. coll.:* Stevenson 1596:5.

2. Go fast and you'll catch up with misfortune; walk slow and it will catch up with you. *Rec. dist.:* N.J., N.Dak.

3. Misfortune arrives on horseback but departs on foot. *Rec. dist.:* Ill., N.C., Ont.

4. Misfortunes cause queer bedfellows. *Rec. dist.:* Ill. *1st cit.:* 1611 Shakespeare, *Tempest. 20c. coll.:* ODEP 535, Stevenson 1591:10.

5. Misfortunes make us wise. *Rec. dist.:* N.C., Okla., Ont., Tex. *1st cit.:* 1732 Fuller, *Gnomologia. 20c. coll.:* Stevenson 1595:2.

6. Misfortunes seldom come alone. *Vars.:* **(a)** Misfortune and twins hardly ever come singly. **(b)** Misfortune comes in bunches. **(c)** Misfortunes never come single-handed. **(d)**

The misfortunes never come single. *Rec. dist.:* U.S., Can. *1st cit.:* ca1300 *King Alisaunder* in *Metrical Romances,* ed. Weber (1810); US1722 *Papers of Benjamin Franklin,* ed. Labaree (1959). *20c. coll.:* ODEP 535, Whiting 292, CODP 151, Stevenson 1597:4, T&W 246, Whiting(MP) 414.

7. The greatest misfortune of all is not to be able to bear misfortune. *Rec. dist.:* N.J. *1st cit.:* 1814 Bland, *Proverbs. 20c. coll.:* Stevenson 1593:6.

8. The man born to misfortune will fall on his back and fracture his nose. *Rec. dist.:* Ill.

9. The misfortunes hardest to bear are those which never come. *Vars.:* **(a)** Our worst misfortunes are those which never befall us. **(b)** The misfortunes hardest to bear are those that never befall us. *Rec. dist.:* Ill., N.Y., Ohio, S.C. *1st cit.:* 1885 Hood, *World of Proverbs;* US1817 Jefferson, Letter to Charles Clay. *20c. coll.:* ODEP 921, Stevenson 2378:1.

10. We can always bear our neighbors' misfortunes. *Rec. dist.:* Ill. *1st cit.:* 1773 Goldsmith, *She Stoops to Conquer. 20c. coll.:* ODEP 780, Stevenson 1596:1.

miss *(n.)* A miss is as good as a mile. *Var.:* A near miss is as good as a mile. *Rec. dist.:* U.S., Can. *1st cit.:* 1614 Camden, *Remaines Concerning Britaine;* US1788 *American Museum. 20c. coll.:* CODP 152, Whiting 292, ODEP 535, Stevenson 1597:8, T&W 246, Whiting(MP) 414.

miss *(v.)* You never miss what you never had. *Rec. dist.:* Oreg.

SEE ALSO You never miss the WATER till the well runs dry.

missionary It takes more than crossing an ocean to make a missionary. *Rec. dist.:* Calif., Ill.

mistake 1. Better a mistake avoided than two corrected. *Rec. dist.:* N.Dak.

2. Don't make the same mistake twice. *Rec. dist.:* Ohio.

3. He who makes no mistakes is a fool. *Rec. dist.:* Wis.

4. He who never made a mistake never made

anything. *Var.:* The man who makes no mistakes usually makes nothing. *Rec. dist.:* U.S., Can. *1st cit.:* 1868 Bishop Magee, Sermon at Peterborough; US1941 Halliday, *Bodies*. *20c. coll.:* ODEP 502, Whiting*(MP)* 395, CODP 152, Stevenson 1598:6.

5. He who talks much makes many mistakes. *Var.:* He that speaks much is much mistaken. *Rec. dist.:* Ill. *1st cit.:* 1599 Minsheu, *Dictionary in Spanish and English*. *20c. coll.:* ODEP 803, Stevenson 2277:10.

6. Learn from the mistakes of others. *Var.:* Learn from the mistakes of others and prevent your own. *Rec. dist.:* Ill., Kans. *1st cit.:* ca1374 Chaucer, *Troilus and Criseyde*. *20c. coll.:* ODEP 901.

7. Let not the mistakes of yesterday or the fear of tomorrow spoil today. *Rec. dist.:* Ill.

8. Mistakes are often the best teachers. *Rec. dist.:* Calif. *1st cit.:* ca1860 Froude, "Education" in *Short Studies on Great Subjects*. *20c. coll.:* Stevenson 1599:1.

9. Mistakes don't make haystacks. *Rec. dist.:* Ill.

10. Mistakes will happen. *Var.:* Mistakes will happen in the best-regulated families. *Rec. dist.:* U.S. *1st cit.:* US1835 Crockett, *Account of Col. Crockett's Tour to North and Down East*. *20c. coll.:* T&W 247.

11. One foolish mistake can undo a lifetime of happiness. *Rec. dist.:* Calif.

12. The one and only serious mistake is to be afraid of making mistakes. *Rec. dist.:* N.Y., S.C. *1st cit.:* US1941 Smart, *Wild Geese*. *20c. coll.:* Stevenson 1598:6.

13. There's many a mistake made on purpose. *Rec. dist.:* Ohio, Okla. *1st cit.:* US1853 Haliburton, *Sam Slick's Wise Saws*. *20c. coll.:* T&W 246, Stevenson 1598:7.

14. We learn by our mistakes. *Var.:* We profit by mistakes. *Rec. dist.:* Ohio, Okla.

mister If you want to keep your mister, don't introduce the baby sister. *Rec. dist.:* Wis.

mistress If you can kiss the mistress, never kiss the maid. *Rec. dist.:* Ont., Tex., Wis. *1st cit.:* 1659 Howell, *Paroimiografia;* US1783 *Works*

of John Adams, ed. Adams (1850–56). *20c. coll.:* ODEP 275, Whiting 274, Stevenson 1312:1.

misunderstanding Misunderstanding brings lies to town. *Rec. dist.:* Ill., Mich. *1st cit.:* 1639 Clarke, *Paroemiologia*. *20c. coll.:* ODEP 536, Stevenson 1600:1.

mitten SEE Handle your TOOLS without mittens: the cat in gloves catches no mice.

mob The mob has many heads but no brains. *Rec. dist.:* Ill., Mich. *1st cit.:* 1666 Torriano, *Common Place of Italian Proverbs;* US1747 Franklin, *PRAlmanac*. *20c. coll.:* ODEP 536, Stevenson 1600:9.

moderation 1. Moderation in all things. *Var.:* Everything in moderation. *Rec. dist.:* U.S. *1st cit.:* ca1380 Chaucer, *Troilus and Criseyde;* US1849 Melville, *Mardi*. *20c. coll.:* ODEP 520, T&W 369, Stevenson 1602:4, CODP 152, Whiting*(MP)* 415.

2. Moderation is the best means. *Rec. dist.:* N.Y. *1st cit.:* 1546 Heywood, *Dialogue of Proverbs,* ed. Habernicht (1963). *20c. coll.:* Stevenson 1602:4.

modest Modest dogs miss much meat. *Rec. dist.:* Ill.

modesty 1. Modesty has more charm than beauty. *Rec. dist.:* La.

2. Modesty is a quality in a lover more praised by the woman than liked. *Rec. dist.:* Ill.

3. Modesty is the sweet songbird which no open cage door can tempt to flight. *Rec. dist.:* Ill.

4. Modesty, when she goes, is gone forever. *Var.:* Modesty is like the snow: when it melts it is gone forever. *Rec. dist.:* Ill. *1st cit.:* US1948 Stevenson, *Home Book of Proverbs*. *20c. coll.:* Stevenson 1606:4.

Mohammed Mohammed has to go to the mountain—the mountain will not come to him. *Vars.:* (a) If Mohammed can't come to the mountain, bring the mountain to Mohammed. (b) If the mountain won't come to Mohammed, Mohammed will go to the mountain. (c) Let the mountain come to Mohammed. (d) When the mountain won't come to Mohammed, Mohammed must go to the mountain. *Rec. dist.:* U.S., Can. *1st cit.:* ca1594 Bacon, *Promus;* US1733 *Jonathan Belcher Papers,* Mass.Hist.Soc. *Collections* (1893–94). *20c. coll.:* ODEP 547, Whiting 299, CODP 156, Stevenson 1502:1, T&W 252, Whiting*(MP)* 427.

molasses Molasses attracts more flies than vinegar. *Rec. dist.:* Ill., Ky., Miss., Tenn. *1st cit.:* 1732 Fuller, *Gnomologia;* US1744 Franklin, *PRAlmanac. 20c. coll.:* Stevenson 1158:14, Whiting 159, T&W 140, Whiting*(MP)* 234.

mole 1. Mole don't see w'at his neighbor's doin'. *Rec. dist.:* N.Y., Ont., S.C. *1st cit.:* US1880 Harris, *Plantation Proverbs* in *Uncle Remus, His Songs and His Sayings. 20c. coll.:* Stevenson 1674:3.

2. When seeking the mole, forget not the eagle. *Rec. dist.:* Calif.

molehill SEE Don't make a MOUNTAIN out of a molehill.

moment Spare moments are the gold dust of time. *Rec. dist.:* Ill.

Monday 1. Monday is the key of the week. *Rec. dist.:* Ill.

2. Monday religion is better than Sunday procession. *Rec. dist.:* Kans., N.J., Ohio.

3. So goes Monday, so goes all the week. *Rec. dist.:* Kans., N.J., Ohio.

money 1. All money is clean, even if it's dirty. *Rec. dist.:* Ill.

2. Bad money always comes back. *Rec. dist.:* Ill., Ind., Wis.

3. Bad money drives out good. *Rec. dist.:* N.J., N.Y., S.C. *1st cit.:* 1902 Lean, *Collectanea. 20c. coll.:* ODEP 26, CODP 8, Stevenson 1611:3.

4. Don't marry for money, but don't marry without money. *Rec. dist.:* Mich., Miss. *1st cit.:* 1623 Wodroephe, *Spared Hours of Soldier. 20c. coll.:* ODEP 515, Whiting*(MP)* 416.

5. Don't spend all your money in one place. *Rec. dist.:* N.J., Wis.

6. Don't throw good money after bad. *Vars.:* **(a)** Don't send good money after bad. **(b)** There's no use throwing good money after

bad. *Rec. dist.:* U.S., Can. *1st cit.:* 1706 Stevens, *New Spanish and English Dictionary;* US1690 *Fitzhugh and His Chesapeake World, 1676–1701,* ed. Davis, Va.Hist.Soc. *Documents* (1913). *20c. coll.:* ODEP 819, Whiting 294, Stevenson 1612:13, Whiting*(MP)* 419.

7. Earn money before you spend it. *Rec. dist.:* N.Y., Ont., Wis.

8. Get the money honestly if you can. *Rec. dist.:* N.Y., Ohio. *1st cit.:* US1815 *Reviewers Reviewed. 20c. coll.:* Whiting 293.

9. He that gets money before he gets wit will be a short while master of it. *Rec. dist.:* Ohio.

10. He that is of the opinion money will do everything may well be suspected of doing everything for money. *Rec. dist.:* N.Y. *1st cit.:* US1753 Franklin, *PRAlmanac. 20c. coll.:* Whiting 293, Stevenson 1617:3.

11. He that marries for money earns it. *Var.:* Anytime a man marries for money, he earns it. *Rec. dist.:* Colo., Okla., Wis.

12. It is better to tell your money where to go than to ask it where it went. *Rec. dist.:* Ill.

13. It's a good thing to have money and have things money can buy, and it is a good thing to check up and make sure you haven't lost the things that money can't buy. *Rec. dist.:* N.J.

14. Lend money and you get an enemy. *Rec. dist.:* U.S., Can. *1st cit.:* ca1594 Bacon, *Promus;* US1740 Franklin, *PRAlmanac. 20c. coll.:* ODEP 455, Whiting 293, Whiting*(MP)* 416.

15. Losing comes from winning money. *Rec. dist.:* Ill., Ind.

16. Make money your servant, not your master. *Var.:* Money is a good servant but a bad master. *Rec. dist.:* Ill., N.C. *1st cit.:* ca1626 Bacon, *Aphorismi et Consilia. 20c. coll.:* Stevenson 1610:2.

17. Money and man a mutual friendship show: man makes false money; money makes man so. *Rec. dist.:* Wis. *1st cit.:* US1742 Franklin, *PRAlmanac. 20c. coll.:* Stevenson 1609:9.

18. Money answers all things. *Rec. dist.:* Wis. *1st cit.:* 1630 Adams, *Cosmopolite;* US1719 "Addition" in *Colonial Currency Reprints,* ed.

Davis, Publ. Prince Soc. (1910–11). *20c. coll.:* *ODEP* 538, Whiting 293, Stevenson 1617:1, *Whiting(MP)* 418.

19. Money begets money. *Vars.:* **(a)** Money draws money. **(b)** Money gets money. **(c)** Money makes money. *Rec. dist.:* U.S., Can. *1st cit.:* 1572 Wilson, *Discourse Upon Usury;* US1748 Franklin, "Letter to My Friend A.B." in *Papers of Benjamin Franklin,* ed. Labaree (1959). *20c. coll.:* *ODEP* 538, Stevenson 1615:8, *CODP* 154, *Whiting(MP)* 417.

20. Money borrowed is money spent. *Rec. dist.:* Calif., Colo.

21. Money borrowed is soon sorrowed. *Rec. dist.:* N.Y., Wis.

22. Money burns a hole in the pocket. *Rec. dist.:* U.S., Can. *1st cit.:* ca1530 More, *Works* (1557); US1868 Clift, *Tim Bunker Papers.* *20c. coll.:* *ODEP* 538, T&W 247, Stevenson 1611:5, *Whiting(MP)* 416.

23. Money can't buy happiness. *Vars.:* **(a)** Money will buy everything but real happiness. **(b)** Money won't buy happiness. **(c)** Money won't buy happiness, but it will go a long way in helping you. *Rec. dist.:* U.S., Can. *1st cit.:* 1930 Fletcher, *Heaven Sent Witness;* US1792 Davenport in *William & Mary Coll. Quart.* (1929). *20c. coll.:* *Whiting(MP)* 416, Whiting 198.

24. Money comes like earth scooped up with a needle; it goes like sand washed away by water. *Rec. dist.:* Calif., Colo., N.Y.

25. Money doesn't get dirty. *Rec. dist.:* Calif., Colo.

26. Money doesn't grow on trees. *Rec. dist.:* U.S., Can. *1st cit.:* US1750 Chancellor in *Penn.Mag.Hist.* (1877). *20c. coll.:* Whiting 181, T&W 248.

27. Money doesn't make character. *Rec. dist.:* Calif.

28. Money doesn't make the man. *Rec. dist.:* Colo.

29. Money greases the axle. *Rec. dist.:* Colo.

30. Money greases the machine in the long run. *Rec. dist.:* Colo.

31. Money has little value to its possessor unless it has value to others. *Rec. dist.:* N.J.

32. Money has wings. *Var.:* It seems like hard-earned money has the best wings. *Rec. dist.:* N.Y., S.C. *1st cit.:* 1607–12 Bacon, "Riches" in *Essays,* ed. Arber; US1937 Ingstad, *East of Great Glacier.* *20c. coll.:* *ODEP* 675, *Whiting(MP)* 417.

33. Money helps some people some, but love does more. *Rec. dist.:* Colo., Ont.

34. Money in the purse will always be in fashion. *Rec. dist.:* N.J., Wis. *1st cit.:* 1616 Raleigh, "Advice to Son" in *Remains.* *20c. coll.:* Stevenson 367:7.

35. Money is a bottomless sea in which honor, conscience, and truth may be drowned. *Rec. dist.:* Ill.

36. Money is a universal language speaking any tongue. *Rec. dist.:* Wis. *1st cit.:* 1677 Behn, *Rover.* *20c. coll.:* Stevenson 1617:2.

37. Money is better spent than spared. *Var.:* Better spent than spared. *Rec. dist.:* Calif., N.Y.

38. Money is honey, my little sonny, and a rich man's joke is always funny. *Rec. dist.:* Wis.

39. Money is like manure: it's only good when spread around. *Rec. dist.:* N.C., Ohio. *1st cit.:* 1564 Bullein, *Dialogue Against Fever Pestilence.* *20c. coll.:* Stevenson 1619:2.

40. Money is power. *Rec. dist.:* N.Y., S.C., Wis. *1st cit.:* 1818 Edgeworth, *Letters,* 13 Oct. (1971); US1741 Ames, *Almanacs,* ed. Briggs (1891). *20c. coll.:* *CODP* 153, Whiting 293, Stevenson 1617:9, T&W 248, *Whiting(MP)* 417.

41. Money is round and rolls away. *Rec. dist.:* Wash., Wis. *1st cit.:* 1619 *Helpe to Discourse* (1640); US1880 Spurgeon, *John Ploughman's Pictures.* *20c. coll.:* *ODEP* 539, Stevenson 1614:4.

42. Money is the root of all evil. *Vars.:* **(a)** Money is the source of all evil. **(b)** The lack of money is the root of all evil. **(c)** The love of money is the root of all evil. *Rec. dist.:* U.S., Can. *1st cit.:* ca1000 Aelfric, *Homilies,* ed. Thorpe (1844–46); US1677 Hubbard,

History of Indian Wars in New England, ed. Drake (1865). *20c. coll.: CODP* 153, Whiting 270, *ODEP* 150, Stevenson 1608:1, T&W 230, Whiting*(MP)* 387.

43. Money is the sinews of love as well as of war. *Rec. dist.:* Ill., Ont. *1st cit.:* 1581 Hales, *Discourse of Common Wealth of This Realm of England* (1893); US1690 Winthrop in *Winthrop Papers,* Mass.Hist.Soc. *Collections* (1863–92). *20c. coll.: ODEP* 539, Whiting 293, Stevenson 2451:5, T&W 248, Whiting*(MP)* 417.

44. Money isn't everything in life. *Var.:* Money isn't everything. *Rec. dist.:* U.S., Can. *1st cit.:* 1930 Fletcher, *Heaven Sent Witness;* US1927 O'Neill, *Marco Millions. 20c. coll.:* Whiting*(MP)* 417, *CODP* 153.

45. Money isn't worth a thing except to use in buying something. *Rec. dist.:* N.Y., S.C.

46. Money, like promises, is easier made than kept. *Rec. dist.:* N.Dak., Ont.

47. Money lost is never gained. *Rec. dist.:* Mich., Miss.

48. Money lost, nothing lost; courage lost, much lost; honor lost, more lost; soul lost, all lost. *Rec. dist.:* Calif.

49. Money makes a man laugh. *Rec. dist.:* Wis. *1st cit.:* 1689 Selden, *Table-Talk. 20c. coll.:* Stevenson 1616:7.

50. Money makes the ball roll. *Rec. dist.:* Colo.

51. Money makes the mare go. *Var.:* It takes money to make the mare go. *Rec. dist.:* U.S., Can. *1st cit.:* ca1500 *Early English Carols,* ed. Greene; US1771 *Papers of Sir William Johnson,* ed. Sullivan (1921–65). *20c. coll.: ODEP* 539, Whiting 293, Stevenson 1618:4, T&W 248, Whiting*(MP)* 418.

52. Money makes the pot boil. *Rec. dist.:* Ky., Ont., Tenn., Wis. *1st cit.:* ca1673 D'Avenant, *Playhouse. 20c. coll.: ODEP* 540, Stevenson 1617:8.

53. Money makes the wheels go round. *Rec. dist.:* Colo. *1st cit.:* 1971 Pope-Hennessy, *Anthony Trollope;* US1929 Hope, *Alice in the Delighted States. 20c. coll.:* Whiting*(MP)* 418.

54. Money makes the world go round. *Var.:*

Money runs the world. *Rec. dist.:* Calif., Colo., N.J., N.C., Ont. *1st cit.:* US1929 Hope, *Alice in the Delighted States. 20c. coll.:* Whiting*(MP)* 418.

55. Money mars and money makes. *Rec. dist.:* Wis.

56. Money never comes out of season. *Rec. dist.:* Wis. *1st cit.:* 1591 Shakespeare, *Henry VI. 20c. coll.: ODEP* 540, Stevenson 1609:4.

57. Money reaches its highest value when we have none. *Rec. dist.:* Calif.

58. Money recommends a man everywhere. *Rec. dist.:* Ill. *1st cit.:* ca1500 *Early English Carols,* ed. Greene. *20c. coll.: ODEP* 539, Stevenson 1616:4.

59. Money saved is money earned. *Var.:* Money saved is money got. *Rec. dist.:* N.Y., Ont., S.C., Wis. *1st cit.:* 1640 Herbert, *Outlandish Proverbs (Jacula Prudentum)* in *Works,* ed. Hutchinson (1941); US1699 *College Oration* in *William & Mary Coll. Quart.* (1930) *20c. coll.: ODEP* 619, Whiting 332, Stevenson 1772:8, Whiting*(MP)* 482.

60. Money talks. *Vars.:* (a) Money speaks. (b) Money talks, but all it ever says is goodbye. (c) Money talks, but all it says is goodbye. (d) Money talks, but talk is cheap. *Rec. dist.:* U.S., Can. *1st cit.:* 1666 Torriano, *Common Place of Italian Proverbs;* US1903 *Saturday Evening Post,* 5 Sept. *20c. coll.: CODP* 154, Stevenson 1617:2, Whiting*(MP)* 418.

61. Money when counted, woman when spanked, is OK. *Rec. dist.:* N.Dak.

62. Money will be a slave or a master. *Rec. dist.:* Wis. *1st cit.:* ca1626 Bacon, *Aphorismi et Consilia. 20c. coll.:* Stevenson 1610:2.

63. Money will do anything. *Rec. dist.:* Mich., N.Y. *1st cit.:* 1584 Withals, *Short Dictionary,* ed. Fleming; US1683 *Mather Papers,* Mass. Hist.Soc. *Collections* (1868). *20c. coll.: ODEP* 540, Whiting 293, Stevenson 1618:1, Whiting*(MP)* 418.

64. More money, more sin. *Rec. dist.:* N.J. *1st cit.:* US1849 Thoreau, *Civil Disobedience. 20c. coll.:* Stevenson 1610:4.

65. Never loan money to a friend unless you

wish to lose him. *Rec. dist.:* Ill., Ont., Tex. *1st cit.:* ca1594 Bacon, *Promus;* US1740 Franklin, *PRAlmanac. 20c. coll.:* ODEP 455, Whiting 293, Whiting*(MP)* 416.

66. Never spend your money before you have it. *Rec. dist.:* Kans., N.Y., Ohio, S.C. *1st cit.:* US1817 Jefferson, Letter to Charles Clay. *20c. coll.:* Stevenson 2196:8.

67. Nothing but money is sweeter than honey. *Rec. dist.:* Ill., N.Y., S.C., Wis. *1st cit.:* US1735 Franklin, *PRAlmanac. 20c. coll.:* Whiting 293, Stevenson 1613:9.

68. Nothing like a little money in the sock to give you self-confidence. *Rec. dist.:* N.Y., S.C. *1st cit.:* US1943 Taylor, *Chicken Every Sunday. 20c. coll.:* Stevenson 1611:2.

69. One never gets more than one's money's worth of anything. *Rec. dist.:* N.J.

70. People are funny about money. *Rec. dist.:* Colo., Mich.

71. Put not your trust in money, but put your money in trust. *Rec. dist.:* U.S., Can. *1st cit.:* US1858 Holmes, *Autocrat of the Breakfast-Table. 20c. coll.:* T&W 383, Stevenson 1608:3.

72. Put your money where your mouth is. *Rec. dist.:* U.S.

73. Ready money is ready medicine. *Rec. dist.:* Wis. *1st cit.:* 1565 Cooper, *Thesaurus Linguae Romanae et Britannicae* (1573). *20c. coll.:* ODEP 666, Stevenson 1617:12.

74. Save your money and die rich. *Rec. dist.:* Ohio.

75. The best way to double your money is to fold it and put it back in your pocket. *Vars.:* **(a)** The safest way to double your money is to fold it over and pocket it. **(b)** The safest way to save money is to put it in your pocket. *Rec. dist.:* Colo.

76. The money one gets the wrong way never does one any good. *Rec. dist.:* Calif., Mich.

77. The money paid, the work delayed. *Rec. dist.:* Wis.

78. The value of money lies in what we do with it. *Rec. dist.:* N.J. *1st cit.:* US1737 Franklin, *PRAlmanac. 20c. coll.:* Stevenson 1619:5.

79. There are some things that money can't

buy. *Rec. dist.:* Calif., Mich., N.Y. *1st cit.:* US1925 Gerould, *Midsummer's Mystery. 20c. coll.:* Whiting*(MP)* 416.

80. Those who have money have trouble about it. *Rec. dist.:* N.Y., S.C. *1st cit.:* US1940 Thompson, *Body, Boots, and Britches. 20c. coll.:* Stevenson 1609:8.

81. Those who spend money will never build a porcelain palace. *Rec. dist.:* Ill.

82. When a man says money can do anything, it's a sure sign he hasn't got any. *Rec. dist.:* Ariz. *1st cit.:* 1923 Howe, *Sinner Sermons. 20c. coll.:* Stevenson 1617:3.

83. When money flies out the window, love flies out the door. *Rec. dist.:* Calif., Ill.

84. When money speaks, truth keeps its mouth shut. *Var.:* When money speaks, truth keeps silent. *Rec. dist.:* N.J., N.Y., Wis.

85. When you ain't got no money, well, you needn't come around. *Rec. dist.:* N.Y., S.C. *1st cit.:* US1898 Brewster, Title of Popular Song. *20c. coll.:* Stevenson 1608:6.

86. When you look for money, all you get is sympathy. *Rec. dist.:* Ohio.

87. Who puts up the money does the talking. *Rec. dist.:* Fla.

SEE ALSO A FOOL and his money are soon parted. / TIME is money. / If you would lose a troublesome VISITOR, lend him money.

mongoose There is no need of a mongoose where there are no snakes. *Rec. dist.:* Ill.

monk SEE The HABIT does not make the monk.

monkey **1.** Dress a monkey as you will, it remains a monkey still. *Var.:* A monkey remains a monkey though dressed in a judge's gown. *Rec. dist.:* Ill. *1st cit.:* 1539 Taverner, *Proverbs of Erasmus. 20c. coll.:* Stevenson 77:5.

2. Even a monkey will fall from a tree sometimes. *Rec. dist.:* Miss.

3. Every monkey has his tale. *Rec. dist.:* Miss.

4. Monkey knows what tree to climb. *Rec. dist.:* Ohio.

5. Monkey see, monkey do. *Rec. dist.:* U.S., Can. *1st cit.:* 1934 Hare, *Hand of the Chimpan-*

zee; US1945 Taylor, *Proof of the Pudding. 20c. coll.:* Whiting*(MP)* 420.

6. Monkeys in hard times eat red peppers. *Rec. dist.:* Ky., Ohio, Tenn. *1st cit.:* US1958 *Time,* 3 Nov. *20c. coll.:* Whiting*(MP)* 630.

moon The moon doesn't give a hoot when the dog barks at her. *Rec. dist.:* Ill. *1st cit.:* 1520 Whittington, *Vulgaria;* US1656 Hammond, *Leah and Rachel. 20c. coll.:* ODEP 541, Whiting 114, Stevenson 1621:3, Whiting*(MP)* 178.

morals **1.** Good morals and good manners are sworn friends. *Rec. dist.:* Ill.

2. It is one thing to keep your morals on a high plane; it's another to keep up with them. *Rec. dist.:* Calif.

more **1.** The more you have, the more you want. *Vars.:* **(a)** The more one has, the more one wants. **(b)** The more you get, the more you want. *Rec. dist.:* U.S., Can. *1st cit.:* ca1425 *Castle of Perseverance;* US1761 *Papers of Sir William Johnson,* ed. Sullivan (1921–65). *20c. coll.:* ODEP 543, Whiting 295, CODP 155, Stevenson 444:11.

2. The more you put into a thing, the more you get out. *Rec. dist.:* U.S.

3. The more the merrier. *Rec. dist.:* U.S., Can. *1st cit.:* ca1380 "Pearl" in *Early English Alliterative Poems,* E.E.T.S. (1864–69); US1786 Currie in *Papers of Thomas Jefferson,* ed. Bergh (1907). *20c. coll.:* CODP 155, Whiting 296, ODEP 544, T&W 250, Whiting*(MP)* 424.

morn A foul morn turns into a fine day. *Vars.:* **(a)** A foul morn may turn to a fine day. **(b)** A misty morn may have a fine day. *Rec. dist.:* Ind., Wis. *1st cit.:* 1621 Burton, *Anatomy of Melancholy;* US1677 Hubbard, *History of Indian Wars in New England,* ed. Drake (1865). *20c. coll.:* ODEP 283, Whiting 296, Stevenson 1624:9.

morning Morning hour has gold in its mouth. *Rec. dist.:* Ill. *1st cit.:* 1853 Trench, *On Lessons in Proverbs. 20c. coll.:* Stevenson 1624:6.

See also An HOUR in the morning is worth two in the evening. / A morning's RAIN is like an old woman's dance: it doesn't last long. /

RED sky at night, sailor's delight; red sky in the morning, sailors take warning.

moron Morons will be morons. *Rec. dist.:* Miss.

moss *See* A rolling STONE gathers no moss.

most Make the most of what you have. *Rec. dist.:* Kans.

mother **1.** A mother wants her daughter married well, but her sister doesn't want her married better than she is. *Rec. dist.:* Calif.

2. As is the mother, so is the daughter. *Var.:* Like mother, like daughter. *Rec. dist.:* U.S., Can. *1st cit.:* ca1300 *Cursor Mundi,* E.E.T.S. (1874–92); US1644 *Complete Writings of Roger Williams* (1963). *20c. coll.:* CODP 155, Whiting 297, ODEP 546, Stevenson 1627:9, Whiting*(MP)* 427.

3. If you don't obey your mother, you will obey your stepmother. *Rec. dist.:* Wis.

4. Mother knows best. *Var.:* Mother knows best; father pays less. *Rec. dist.:* U.S. *1st cit.:* 1958 Christie, *Ordeal by Innocence;* US1927 Ferber, *Mother Knows Best. 20c. coll.:* Whiting*(MP)* 427, Stevenson 1626:5.

5. No mother has a homely child. *Rec. dist.:* Wis.

6. Observe the mother and take the daughter. *Rec. dist.:* Wis.

See also Being GOOD is the mother of doing good. / Mother's LOVE is best of all. / NECESSITY is the mother of invention.

mother-in-law The mother-in-law remembers not that she was a daughter-in-law. *Rec. dist.:* Minn., N.C. *1st cit.:* 1594 Withals, *Short Dictionary,* ed. Fleming. *20c. coll.:* ODEP 546, Stevenson 1628:8.

mountain **1.** Don't make a mountain of a molehill. *Var.:* Never make a mountain out of a molehill. *Rec. dist.:* U.S., Can. *1st cit.:* 1548–49 Erasmus, *Apophthegms,* tr. Udall; US1643 Vines in *Winthrop Papers, 1498–1649,* Mass.Hist.Soc. *Collections* (1929–47). *20c. coll.:* ODEP 547, Whiting 300, Stevenson 1630:3, T&W 252, Whiting*(MP)* 428.

2. It is harder to climb the mountain than to climb down. *Rec. dist.:* Wis.

3. One cannot climb mountains by looking at them. *Rec. dist.:* N.J.

4. One must first scale the mountain in order to view the plain. *Rec. dist.:* Wis. *1st cit.:* US1875 Scarborough, *Chinese Proverbs. 20c. coll.:* Stevenson 1631:4.

5. The mountain labored and brought forth a mouse. *Rec. dist.:* Mich., N.Y., N.C., S.C. *1st cit.:* ca1390 Gower, *Confessio Amantis,* E.E.T.S. (1900); US1685 Wisehall in *Hinckley Papers,* Mass.Hist.Soc. *Collections* (1861). *20c. coll.:* ODEP 547, Whiting 299, Stevenson 1629:6, Whiting*(MP)* 428.

6. The mountains are never so far apart but the animals find one another. *Rec. dist.:* Colo.

7. Two men may meet, but never two mountains. *Rec. dist.:* U.S. *1st cit.:* 1530 Palsgrave, *Lesclarcissement de la langue Francoyse,* ed. Genin (1852); US1742 Franklin, *PRAlmanac. 20c. coll.:* ODEP 290, Whiting 279, Stevenson 1630:4.

mouse 1. Better a mouse in the pot than no flesh at all. *Rec. dist.:* N.C. *1st cit.:* 1623 Camden, *Remaines Concerning Britaine. 20c. coll.:* ODEP 50, Stevenson 1632:7.

2. It's a good rule to never send a mouse to catch a skunk, or a pollywog to tackle a whale. *Rec. dist.:* N.Y., S.C. *1st cit.:* USca1861 Lincoln, Remark to D. D. Porter. *20c. coll.:* Stevenson 1552:2.

3. The mouse that has but one hole is soon caught. *Var.:* A smart mouse has more than one hole. *Rec. dist.:* Colo., Ill. *1st cit.:* ca1386 Chaucer, *Prologue to Wife of Bath's Tale;* US1928 Williams, *Crouching Beast. 20c. coll.:* ODEP 548, Whiting*(MP)* 429, Stevenson 1633:1.

SEE ALSO While the CAT's away, the mice will play.

mousetrap 1. Build a better mousetrap and catch a larger rat. *Rec. dist.:* Calif.

2. Build a better mousetrap and the world will beat a path to your door. *Rec. dist.:* Ill., Mich. *1st cit.:* US1871 Emerson in Yule, *Borrowings. 20c. coll.:* Stevenson 1633:6.

3. Don't let the mousetrap smell of blood. *Rec. dist.:* Ill. *1st cit.:* 1659 Howell, *Paroimiografia. 20c. coll.:* ODEP 548, Stevenson 1633:5.

mouth 1. A closed mouth catches no flies. *Rec. dist.:* U.S., Can. *1st cit.:* 1599 Minsheu, *Dictionarie in Spanish and English;* US1742 Franklin, *PRAlmanac. 20c. coll.:* ODEP 127, Whiting 301, Stevenson 1634:8, Whiting*(MP)* 430.

2. A still mouth makes a wise head. *Vars.:* **(a)** A closed mouth makes a wise head. **(b)** A still tongue makes a wise head. *Rec. dist.:* Ill., Wis. *1st cit.:* 1562 Heywood, *Epigrammes;* US1865 Conigland in *Papers of Thomas Ruffin,* ed. Hamilton (1918–20). *20c. coll.:* ODEP 774, Whiting 301, Stevenson 2345:1.

3. Keep your mouth shut and your eyes open. *Rec. dist.:* U.S. *1st cit.:* 1581 Guazzo, *Civile Conversation,* tr. Pettie, T.T. (1925); US1930 Deane, *Mystery. 20c. coll.:* ODEP 419, Whiting*(MP)* 430, Stevenson 1636:4.

4. Large mouth, small manners. *Rec. dist.:* Ill.

5. No mouth speaks louder than the cannon's mouth. *Rec. dist.:* Ill.

6. When you get into deep water, keep your mouth shut. *Rec. dist.:* Mich., Miss.

7. Whosoever keeps his mouth and his tongue keeps his soul from trouble. *Rec. dist.:* Colo., Ill., Utah. *1st cit.:* US1948 Stevenson, *Home Book of Proverbs. 20c. coll.:* Stevenson 1636:6.

SEE ALSO Let another man PRAISE you, and not your own mouth. / A full PURSE makes a mouth speak. / TRUTH may sometimes come out of the devil's mouth.

move Three moves are as bad as a fire. *Rec. dist.:* U.S., Can. *1st cit.:* 1839 Dickens, Letter to Samuel Rogers, 14 Nov.; US1736 Franklin, *PRAlmanac. 20c. coll.:* ODEP 817, Whiting 361, CODP 224, Stevenson 314:2, T&W 306.

much *(n.)* Much never costs little. *Rec. dist.:* Ill., Wis.

SEE ALSO Too much of a GOOD thing is worse than none at all.

much *(adj.)* SEE Too much BED makes a dull head. / Much TALK, little work.

much *(adv.)* SEE LISTEN much and speak little.

mud   1. Do not walk in the mud when there is a dry path. *Rec. dist.:* Ill.

2. He who is in the mud loves to pull another in. *Rec. dist.:* N.Dak.

3. He who plays in the mud is bound to get dirty. *Rec. dist.:* N.J.

4. He who slings mud loses ground. *Var.:* People who sling mud lose ground. *Rec. dist.:* Calif., Colo., N.Y. *1st cit.:* US1940 Thompson, *Body, Boots, and Britches.* *20c. coll.:* Stevenson 1638:7.

5. No mud can soil us but the mud we throw. *Rec. dist.:* N.Y., S.C. *1st cit.:* US1874 Lowell, "To G. W. Curtis." *20c. coll.:* Stevenson 2039:5.

6. You can't touch mud without getting a little on you. *Rec. dist.:* Calif., Ont.

muddy   Muddy water won't do for a mirror. *Rec. dist.:* Ill. *1st cit.:* US1948 Stevenson, *Home Book of Proverbs.* *20c. coll.:* Stevenson 2459:5.

mule   1. Better your own mule than someone else's mule. *Rec. dist.:* Calif.

2. He that rides the mule shoes her. *Rec. dist.:* N.Y., S.C. *1st cit.:* 1541 *Schoolhouse of Women;* US1940 Thompson, *Body, Boots, and Britches.* *20c. coll.:* ODEP 676, Stevenson 2490:4.

3. Mules don't kick according to rules. *Rec. dist.:* Ill., N.Y., S.C.

4. One-eyed mule can't be handled on the blind side. *Rec. dist.:* Miss., N.Y., S.C.

5. When a mule is kicking, he is not pulling; and when he is pulling, he is not kicking. *Rec. dist.:* N.Dak., Ont.

6. When a mule kicks you, consider the source. *Rec. dist.:* Colo.

7. When you see a mule's fixin' to throw you, you jes' git off. *Rec. dist.:* Miss., N.Y.

8. You may lead a mule to water, but you can't make him drink. *Rec. dist.:* U.S., Can. *1st cit.:* ca1175 Lambeth in *Old English Homilies,* E.E.T.S. (1868); US1692 Bulkeley, *Will and Doom,* ed. Hoadly, Conn.Hist.Soc. *Collections* (1895). *20c. coll.:* ODEP 449, Whiting

223, *CODP* 115, Stevenson 1179:9, T&W 191, Whiting*(MP)* 322.

murder   Murder will out. *Rec. dist.:* U.S., Can. *1st cit.:* ca1300 *Cursor Mundi,* E.E.T.S. (1874–92); US1705 Ingles, *Modest Reply to Mr. Blair's Answer* in *Va.Mag.Hist.* (1901). *20c. coll.:* ODEP 551, Whiting 303, *CODP* 157, Stevenson 1641:10, T&W 254, Whiting*(MP)* 434.

SEE ALSO Killing TIME is not murder, it's suicide.

muscle   It takes more muscle to frown than to laugh. *Rec. dist.:* Colo.

muse   The muses starve in a cookshop. *Rec. dist.:* N.Y.

music   1. Music has charm to soothe the savage breast. *Vars.:* **(a)** Music has charms to soothe the savage beast. **(b)** Music has charms to soothe the savage, soften a rock, and split a cabbage. **(c)** Music has charms to soothe the wildest heart. **(d)** Music soothes the savage breast. *Rec. dist.:* U.S., Can. *1st cit.:* 1697 Congreve, *Mourning Bride.* *20c. coll.:* Stevenson 1644:1.

2. Music is the key to the female heart. *Rec. dist.:* Ill.

3. Music will not cure the toothache. *Rec. dist.:* Colo., Ill., Utah. *1st cit.:* 1640 Herbert, *Outlandish Proverbs (Jacula Prudentum)* in *Works,* ed. Hutchinson (1941). *20c. coll.:* ODEP 551, Stevenson 1644:5.

4. Where there is music, there can be no harm. *Rec. dist.:* Calif., Ill. *1st cit.:* US1948 Stevenson, *Home Book of Proverbs.* *20c. coll.:* Stevenson 1643:13.

must   1. Must is a hard nut to crack. *Rec. dist.:* Ill.

2. When you must, you better. *Rec. dist.:* Calif. *1st cit.:* 1597 Shakespeare, *Henry IV, Part I.* *20c. coll.:* Stevenson 1645:8.

mystery   Some mysteries are better left unexplained. *Rec. dist.:* Calif.

N

nail **1.** A nail can go no farther than its head will let it. *Rec. dist.:* Kans.

2. A nail that sticks out is struck. *Rec. dist.:* Ill.

3. Do not hang all on one nail. *Rec. dist.:* Ont.

4. Drive not a second nail till the first be clinched. *Rec. dist.:* Okla. *1st cit.:* 1732 Fuller, *Gnomologia; US*1783 *Journal of Thomas Scattergood. 20c. coll.:* Stevenson 1694:7, Whiting 305.

5. For the want of a nail, the shoe was lost; for want of a shoe, the horse was lost; for want of a horse, the rider was lost. *Rec. dist.:* U.S., Can. *1st cit.:* ca1390 Gower, *Confessio Amantis,* E.E.T.S. (1900); *US*1752 Franklin, *PRAlmanac. 20c. coll.:* ODEP 865, Whiting 469, T&W 256, CODP 241, Stevenson 1644:5, Whiting(MP) 663.

6. One nail drives out another. *Rec. dist.:* Ont. *1st cit.:* ca1200 *Ancrene Riwle,* ed. Morton, Camden Soc. (1853). *20c. coll.:* ODEP 597, CODP 170, Stevenson 1648:8.

SEE ALSO Nothing comes without PAIN except dirt and long nails.

naked **1.** Naked men never lose anything. *Rec. dist.:* Ill.

2. Naked we came, naked we go. *Var.:* Naked into this world we came, and naked will return. *Rec. dist.:* Mich., N.Y. Ont. *1st cit.:* US1875 Scarborough, *Chinese Proverbs. 20c. coll.:* Stevenson 1652:2.

3. There's no use trying to strip a naked man. *Rec. dist.:* W.Va.

name **1.** A good name is rather to be chosen than great riches. *Vars.:* **(a)** A good name is better than fine jewels. **(b)** A good name is better than gold. **(c)** A good name is better than precious ointment. **(d)** A good name is better than precious stones. **(e)** A good name is more precious than rubies. **(f)** A good name is rather to be chosen than great riches and loving favor rather than silver and gold. *Rec. dist.:* U.S., Can. *1st cit.:* ca1350 *How Gode Wyfe Taught Her Daughter; US*1739 *Colonial Records of Georgia,* ed. Chandler, in *Original Papers, 1735–1752* (1910–16). *20c. coll.:* ODEP 322, Whiting 306, Stevenson 1656:8, Whiting(MP) 438.

2. A good name is sooner lost than won. *Rec. dist.:* Ill., N.Dak. *1st cit.:* 1727 Gay, "Fox at Point of Death" in *Fables. 20c. coll.:* Stevenson 1656:1.

3. A good name will shine forever. *Rec. dist.:* N.Dak. *1st cit.:* 1539 Publilius Syrus, *Sententiae,* tr. Taverner. *20c. coll.:* ODEP 322,, Stevenson 1657:1.

4. Big names often stand on small legs. *Rec. dist.:* Miss.

5. Get a good name of early rising, and you may lie abed. *Var.:* He who gets a name for early rising may sleep all day. *Rec. dist.:* U.S., Can. *1st cit.:* 1611 Cotgrave, *Dictionary of French and English Tongues; US*1792 *Universal Asylum. 20c. coll.:* ODEP 554, Whiting 306, Stevenson 1656:3.

6. He who has a bad name is half hanged. *Rec. dist.:* N.J. *1st cit.:* ca1400 *Religious Lyrics of XIVth Century,* ed. Brown (1957). *20c. coll.:* CODP 119, Stevenson 1658:4.

7. If the bullet has your name on it, you'll get it. *Rec. dist.:* Mich. *1st cit.:* 1575 Gascoigne, *Posies; US*1840 Cooper, *Pathfinder. 20c. coll.:* ODEP 90, CODP 27, T&W 47, Whiting(MP) 80.

8. If you have the name, you might as well have the game. *Rec. dist.:* U.S. *1st cit.:* US1836 Haliburton, *Clockmaker. 20c. coll.:* T&W 257, Stevenson 1653:9, Whiting(MP) 438.

9. Names break no bones. *Rec. dist.:* Wash. *1st cit.:* ca1450 *Townley Play of Noah,* eds. England and Pollard, E.E.T.S. (1897). *20c. coll.:* ODEP 353, CODP 107, Stevenson 1654:15.

10. The name lasts longer than the dame. *Rec. dist.:* N.Y.

11. The name may not spoil the man, but the man may spoil the name. *Rec. dist.:* N.Y.

SEE ALSO Give a DOG a bad name and hang him. / FOOLS' names and fools' faces are often seen in public places. / FRAILTY, your name is woman. / GOODWILL, like a good name, is won by many acts and lost by one. / STICKS and stones may break my bones, but names will never hurt me. / An ill WOUND, but not an ill name, may be healed.

narrow *(n.)* SEE WIDE will wear when narrow will tear.

narrow *(adj.)* SEE The narrower the EDGE, the deeper the cut.

narrowness Narrowness of waist shows narrowness of mind. *Rec. dist.:* N.Y.

nation A nation that lives by the dole shall perish by the dole. *Rec. dist.:* Ind.

SEE ALSO PROVERBS are the wisdom of nations.

natural It is natural to want what you can't get. *Rec. dist.:* W.Va.

SEE ALSO DYING is as natural as living.

nature 1. Drive nature out of the door and it will return by the window. *Rec. dist.:* Ill. *1st cit.:* 1539 Taverner, *Proverbs of Erasmus;* US1623 James, *Three Visitors to Early Plymouth. 20c. coll.:* CODP 60, Whiting 306, Stevenson 166:9.

2. Good nature is stronger than tomahawks. *Rec. dist.:* N.Y. *1st cit.:* US1870 Emerson, "Clubs" in *Society and Solitude. 20c. coll.:* Stevenson 1663:1.

3. If nature be deceptive, repair it by industry. *Rec. dist.:* N.Y.

4. Let nature take its course. *Rec. dist.:* Mich., N.Y. *1st cit.:* ca1400 *Beryn,* ed. Furnivall, E.E.T.S. (1909); US1845 Judd, *Margaret. 20c. coll.:* ODEP 556, T&W 258, Stevenson 1662:1, Whiting(MP) 440.

5. Nature abhors a vacuum. *Rec. dist.:* Mich., Ont., Wis. *1st cit.:* ca1550 Smith, *Confutation;* US1766 Ames, *Almanacs,* ed. Briggs (1891). *20c. coll.:* ODEP 55, Whiting 306, CODP 158, Stevenson 1660:7, T&W 258, Whiting(MP) 440.

6. Nature abhors the old. *Rec. dist.:* N.Y., S.C.

7. Nature and love cannot be hid. *Rec. dist.:* Ill.

8. Nature does nothing in vain. *Rec. dist.:* N.J. *1st cit.:* 1481 Caxton, *Mirror of World. 20c. coll.:* ODEP 555, Stevenson 1659:8.

9. Nature ever makes false weight. *Rec. dist.:* Minn.

10. Nature is not made. *Rec. dist.:* N.C.

11. Nature is stronger than education. *Rec. dist.:* Ill.

12. Nature is usually wrong. *Rec. dist.:* N.Y., S.C. *1st cit.:* 1890 Whistler, *Ten O'Clock. 20c. coll.:* Stevenson 98:4.

13. Nature makes women to be won and men to win. *Rec. dist.:* Ill.

14. Nature passes nurture. *Rec. dist.:* Calif., N.Y. *1st cit.:* 1492 *Dialogue of Salomon and Marcolphus,* ed. Duff; US1880 Spurgeon, *John Ploughman's Pictures. 20c. coll.:* ODEP 556, Stevenson 1661:13, Whiting(MP) 440.

15. Nature takes care of everything. *Rec. dist.:* Kans.

16. Nature will out. *Rec. dist.:* N.C., Ont.

17. Wherever nature does least, man does most. *Rec. dist.:* N.C., Wis. *1st cit.:* US1838 Haliburton, *Clockmaker. 20c. coll.:* T&W 258.

18. You cannot break the rules of nature and get by with it. *Rec. dist.:* N.J., N.C.

SEE ALSO CUSTOM is a second nature. / They who cross the SEAS change their skies but not their nature. / SELF-PRESERVATION is the first law of nature. / Every VICE fights against nature.

naught 1. Naught from naught and nothing remains. *Rec. dist.:* N.Y. *1st cit.:* US1845 Cooper, *Chainbearer. 20c. coll.:* T&W 265.

2. Naught is never in danger. *Rec. dist.:* Md. *1st cit.:* 1639 Clarke, *Paroemiologia. 20c. coll.:* Stevenson 1700:7.

3. Naught from naught you can't. *Rec. dist.:* Ont.

4. Naught's a naught and figger's a figger— all for de white man and none for de nigger. *Rec. dist.:* Miss.

Navy Join the Navy and see the world. *Rec. dist.:* U.S. *Infm.:* U.S. Navy recruiting slogan prior to World War II.

nay *See* He that WILL not when he may, when he will he may have nay.

near *(adj.)* **1.** Pretty near ain't quite. *Rec. dist.:* N.Y.

2. So near and yet so far. *Rec. dist.:* Kans., Mich., Miss. *1st cit.:* 1850 Tennyson, *In Memoriam.* *20c. coll.:* Stevenson 3:9.

See also Better a NEIGHBOR near than a brother far.

near *(prep.)* *See* The nearer the CHURCH, the farther from God. / The nearer the GROUND, the sweeter the grass. / Nearest the HEART comes first out. / If you've been near a SKUNK, don't say you haven't been.

nearly **1.** Nearly never did any good. *Rec. dist.:* N.Y., Ont.

2. Nearly never did any harm. *Vars.:* **(a)** Nearly never hurt anybody. **(b)** Nearly never killed a man yet. **(c)** Nearly never killed anyone. *Rec. dist.:* N.Y., Ont.

neat Better be neat and tidy than tight and needy. *Rec. dist.:* N.Y. S.C. *1st cit.:* US1940 Thompson, *Body, Boots, and Britches.* *20c. coll.:* Stevenson 1664:5.

See also A neat MAIDEN often makes a dirty wife.

necessary *See* A necessary LIE is harmless.

necessity **1.** Comply cheerfully where necessity enjoins. *Rec. dist.:* Mich.

2. It is best to prepare for the days of necessity. *Rec. dist.:* Ind.

3. Necessity and opportunity may make a coward valiant. *Rec. dist.:* Ill. *1st cit.:* 1590 Spenser, *Faerie Queene.* *20c. coll.:* ODEP 557.

4. Necessity does everything well. *Rec. dist.:* N.Y., S.C. *1st cit.:* US1844 Emerson "Gifts" in *Essays.* *20c. coll.:* Stevenson 1665:6.

5. Necessity has a greater power than duty. *Rec. dist.:* Ill.

6. Necessity is a good teacher. *Rec. dist.:* Ill.

7. Necessity is a hard master. *Rec. dist.:* Ill.

8. Necessity is the argument of tyrants and the creed of slaves. *Rec. dist.:* Maine.

9. Necessity is the mother of invention. *Rec. dist.:* U.S., Can. *1st cit.:* 1519 Horman, *Vulgaria;* US1681 *William Fitzhugh and His Chesapeake World, 1676–1701,* ed. Davis, Va.Hist.Soc. *Documents* (1963). *20c. coll.:* ODEP 558, Whiting 307, *CODP* 159, Stevenson 1664:5, T&W 258, Whiting*(MP)* 441.

10. Necessity knows no law. *Vars.:* **(a)** Necessity has no law. **(b)** Necessity knows no law, but it is intimately acquainted with many lawyers. *Rec. dist.:* U.S., Can. *1st cit.:* ca1377 Langland, *Piers Plowman;* US1674 *Winthrop Papers, 1498–1649,* Mass.Hist.Soc. *Collections* (1863–92). *20c. coll.:* ODEP 557, Whiting 307, *CODP* 159, Stevenson 1667:9, T&W 258, Whiting*(MP)* 441.

11. Necessity makes a naked woman spin. *Var.:* Necessity teaches a naked woman to spin. *Rec. dist.:* Ohio, Ont.

12. Necessity makes strange bedfellows. *Rec. dist.:* Ill.

13. Necessity never made a good bargain. *Rec. dist.:* N.J., Wis. *1st cit.:* US1735 Franklin, *PRAlmanac.* *20c. coll.:* Whiting 308, Stevenson 1665:10.

14. Necessity sharpens industry. *Rec. dist.:* N.Y.

See also NEEDS must when necessity drives. / Make a VIRTUE of necessity.

neck **1.** Better bend the neck than bruise the forehead. *Rec. dist.:* Ont.

2. Don't stick your neck out. *Var.:* It is never a good idea to stick your neck out. *Rec. dist.:* U.S., Can. *1st cit.:* 1963 Hubbard, *Flush as May;* US1939 Darby, *Murder in House with the Blue Eyes.* *20c. coll.:* Whiting*(MP)* 442, Stevenson 1669:10.

3. He who is to break his neck finds the stairs in the dark. *Rec. dist.:* Ill.

4. Take care of your neck in old age. *Rec. dist.:* Ohio.

See also Everybody thinks the BOIL on his own neck is the biggest. / A HOLE is nothing at all, but you can break your neck in it. /

The HUSBAND is the head of the house, but the wife is the neck and the neck moves the head.

need *(n.)* **1.** Need makes a naked man run. *Rec. dist.:* Wis. *1st cit.:* 1516 Skelton, *Magnyfycence.* *20c. coll.:* ODEP 558.

2. Need makes the old wife trot. *Rec. dist.:* Okla., Tex. *1st cit.:* ca1225 *Trinity MS O,* ed. Förster in *English Studies;* US1708 Taylor, *Poems of Edward Taylor,* ed. Stanford (1940). *20c. coll.:* ODEP 558, Whiting 308, Stevenson 1671:5.

3. Needs must when necessity drives. *Var.:* Needs must when the devil drives. *Rec. dist.:* N.Y., S.C. *1st cit.:* ca1330 *Seven Songs of Rome,* E.E.T.S. (1933); US1660 *Diary of John Hull* in *Archaeologia Americana,* Am.Antiq.Soc. *Transactions* (1875). *20c. coll.:* ODEP 559, Whiting 106, *CODP* 159, Stevenson 1670:15, T&W 260, Whiting*(MP)* 444.

4. One man's need is another man's poison. *Var.:* One man's need is another man's fancy. *Rec. dist.:* Ariz.

5. When in great need, anything will do. *Rec. dist.:* Calif.

SEE ALSO A FRIEND in need is a friend indeed. / Think twice before you speak to a FRIEND in need.

need *(v.)* SEE ADVICE is something the wise don't need and the fools won't take. / You don't need BRAINS if you have luck. / A COW needs her tail more than once in fly time. / A good FACE needs no paint. / It is better to HAVE it and not need it than to need it and not have it. / Eat few SUPPERS and you'll need few medicines. / Good WINE needs no bush.

needed It is a fine thing to make yourself needed. *Rec. dist.:* N.Y.

SEE ALSO To one who understands, few WORDS are needed.

needle **1.** A needle is sharp only at one end. *Var.:* No needle is sharp at both ends. *Rec. dist.:* Ill. *1st cit.:* 1945 Hine, *Confessions of an Uncommon Attorney;* US1875 Scarborough, *Chinese Proverbs.* *20c. coll.:* Whiting*(MP)* 442, Stevenson 1672:5.

2. Needles and pins: when a man marries, his trouble begins. *Var.:* Pins and needles, needles and pins: when a man marries, his trouble begins. *Rec. dist.:* Kans., Ky., Ohio, Tenn. *1st cit.:* 1843 Halliwell, *Nursery Rhymes of England;* US1930 Train, *Adventures of Ephraim Tutt, Attorney and Counsellor-at-Law.* *20c. coll.:* ODEP 559, Whiting*(MP)* 442, Stevenson 1537:12.

3. Where the needle goes, the thread follows. *Var.:* Where the needle goes, the cotton must follow. *Rec. dist.:* Ill., Ont. *1st cit.:* 1640 Herbert, *Outlandish Proverbs (Jacula Prudentum)* in *Works,* ed. Hutchinson (1941). *20c. coll.:* Stevenson 1752:17.

SEE ALSO It is easier for a CAMEL to go through the eye of a needle than it is for a rich man to enter the kingdom of heaven.

needy SEE Better be NEAT and tidy than tight and needy.

neglect *(n.)* **1.** A little neglect may breed great mischief. *Rec. dist.:* U.S. *1st cit.:* US1758 Franklin, "Way to Wealth" in *Papers of Benjamin Franklin,* ed. Labaree (1959). *20c. coll.:* Whiting 309, Stevenson 1672:8.

2. Neglect kills injuries; revenge increases them. *Var.:* Neglect will kill an injury sooner than revenge. *Rec. dist.:* N.Y., Ont., S.C. *1st cit.:* 1607 Jonson, *Volpone;* US1744 Franklin, *PRAlmanac.* *20c. coll.:* ODEP 560, Whiting 309.

3. Present neglect makes future regret. *Rec. dist.:* Ill.

neglect *(v.)* SEE Do not neglect your own in order to weed another's FIELD.

neglected SEE BUSINESS neglected is business lost. / A neglected DUTY returns tomorrow with seven others at its back.

negligence **1.** Great negligence is equal to intentional wrong. *Rec. dist.:* Ill.

2. Gross negligence is a fault; gross fault is a fraud. *Rec. dist.:* Ill.

SEE ALSO A PATCH is the sign of thrift, a hole the sign of negligence.

negligent Nothing is easy to the negligent. *Rec. dist.:* N.Y. *1st cit.:* 1732 Fuller, *Gnomologia.* *20c. coll.:* Stevenson 1672:9.

Negro A Negro that can't sing ain't worth nothing. *Rec. dist.:* N.C.

SEE ALSO SOAP and water will not make a Negro's face white.

neighbor 1. A close neighbor is better than a faraway relative. *Rec. dist.:* N.Y. *1st cit.:* 1545 Taverner, *Proverbs of Erasmus.* *20c. coll.:* ODEP 557.

2. A good neighbor is a fellow who smiles at you over the back fence but doesn't climb it. *Rec. dist.:* Ala., Ga.

3. A good neighbor is a precious thing. *Rec. dist.:* Ill. *1st cit.:* 1732 Fuller, *Gnomologia;* US1790 Jefferson, *Papers,* ed. Boyd (1950). *20c. coll.:* Stevenson 1675:2, Whiting 309.

4. A man that flatters his neighbor spreads a net for his feet. *Rec. dist.:* Ont.

5. A neighbor is a person who knows more about your business than you do. *Rec. dist.:* N.C.

6. As you measure your neighbor he will measure back to you. *Rec. dist.:* Ont.

7. Be better to your neighbors and you will have better neighbors. *Rec. dist.:* Kans.

8. Better a neighbor near than a brother far. *Rec. dist.:* Ill., Oreg. *1st cit.:* ca1340 *Minor Poems of Vernon Manuscript;* US1937 Hart, *700 Chinese Proverbs.* *20c. coll.:* Stevenson 1676:10 and 1675:2.

9. Do not judge your neighbor unless you are in his situation. *Rec. dist.:* N.Y.

10. For neighbors to keep a friendly tone is equal to finding a precious stone. *Rec. dist.:* N.C.

11. Go not unto your neighbor's place too often lest he tire of you. *Rec. dist.:* Ont.

12. He who prays for his neighbor will be heard for himself. *Rec. dist.:* N.C.

13. If your neighbor can't smile, lend him yours. *Rec. dist.:* Utah.

14. It is discouraging to be a good neighbor in a bad neighborhood. *Rec. dist.:* N.Y., S.C.

15. Love your neighbor as yourself. *Vars.:* (a) Fear your neighbor as yourself. (b) Love your neighbor as you love yourself. *Rec. dist.:* U.S., Can. *1st cit.:* 1578 Florio, *Firste Fruites.* *20c. coll.:* Stevenson 1676:6.

16. Love your neighbor, but do not pull down the fence. *Var.:* Love your neighbor, yet pull not down your hedge. *Rec. dist.:* Miss., N.Y., S.C. *1st cit.:* 1640 Herbert, *Outlandish Proverbs (Jacula Prudentum)* in *Works,* ed. Hutchinson (1941); US1754 Franklin, *PRAlmanac.* *20c. coll.:* ODEP 494, Whiting 309, Stevenson 1674:13.

17. Love your neighbor, but leave his wife alone. *Rec. dist.:* Utah.

18. Neighbors are good when they are neighborly. *Rec. dist.:* Ill.

19. No one can love his neighbor on an empty stomach. *Rec. dist.:* N.Y. *1st cit.:* US1912 Wilson, Speech in New York, 23 May. *20c. coll.:* Stevenson 1676:8.

20. No one is rich enough without a neighbor. *Var.:* No one is rich enough to do without a neighbor. *Rec. dist.:* Ill.

21. She who wishes to keep ahead of her neighbor must go to bed at sundown and get up at dawn. *Rec. dist.:* N.Y., S.C.

22. The best neighbors are vacant lots. *Rec. dist.:* N.Y., S.C.

23. To be a good neighbor, take heed to your tongue. *Rec. dist.:* Ont.

24. When the neighbor's house is on fire, beware of your own. *Rec. dist.:* Ill., Mich., N.Y. *1st cit.:* 1519 Horman, *Vulgaria;* US1791 Jefferson, *Papers,* ed. Boyd (1950). *20c. coll.:* ODEP 560, Whiting 310, Stevenson 1675:3.

25. When your neighbor's house declines, beware the possibilities of your own. *Rec. dist.:* Tex.

26. Who has a good neighbor has a good friend. *Rec. dist.:* N.Y.

27. Whoever steals the neighbor's shirt usually dies without his own. *Rec. dist.:* Ont.

28. You must visit your neighbors lest an unused path becomes weedy. *Rec. dist.:* Ont.

SEE ALSO On ANXIETY street there are plenty of neighbors. / Good FENCES make good neighbors. / We are often of greater IMPORTANCE in our own eyes than in the eyes of our neighbor. / A good LAWYER, a bad neighbor.

/ MOLE don't see w'at his neighbor's doin'. / The POOR is hated even of his own neighbors, but the rich have many friends. / A QUARRELSOME man has no good neighbors. / Folks like the TRUTH that hits their neighbors. / If you want to hear the whole TRUTH about yourself, anger your neighbor.

neighborly *SEE* One PATCH is comely, but patch upon patch is beggarly.

neither He who is neither one thing or the other has no friends. *Rec. dist.:* Ont.

nerve One must have an iron cage of nerves to hold a tiger in the breast. *Rec. dist.:* N.C.

nest 1. Feather your own nest. *Vars.:* (a) A shrewd man feathers his own nest. (b) Do not neglect to feather your nest. (c) Feather your nest. *Rec. dist.:* U.S., Can. *1st cit.:* 1553 *Respublica* in *"Lost" Tudor Plays;* US1654 Johnson, *Wonder-Working.* *20c. coll.:* ODEP 252, Whiting 310, Stevenson 790:10, T&W 260, Whiting(MP) 444.

2. God makes a nest for the blind bird. *Var.:* The nest of a blind bird is made by God. *Rec. dist.:* Ill.

3. He that feathers his nest must sleep in it. *Vars.:* (a) If you feather your own nest, sleep in it. (b) If you make your own nest, sleep in it. *Rec. dist.:* Okla.

4. He that has feathered his nest may flee when he likes. *Var.:* He that has feathered his nest may fly when he will. *Rec. dist.:* Tex. *1st cit.:* 1721 Kelly, *Scottish Proverbs.* *20c. coll.:* Stevenson 792:10.

SEE ALSO ANGER is a stone cast at a wasp's nest. / A BIRD may be ever so small, yet it always seeks a nest of its own. / Each BIRD likes his own nest best. / It's an ill BIRD that fouls its own nest. / Little by little the BIRD builds his nest. / There are no BIRDS in last year's nest. / You can't keep the BIRDS from flying over your head, but you can keep them from building a nest in your hair. / Don't go to a BUZZARD's nest to find a dove. / GOD sends every bird its food, but he does not throw it into the nest.

net 1. Don't set the net after the fish have gone by. *Rec. dist.:* N.Y.

2. In vain the net is spread in the sight of any bird. *Rec. dist.:* N.Y., Oreg., S.C. *1st cit.:* 1581 Guazzo, *Civile Conversation,* tr. Pettie, T.T. (1925); US1644 *Complete Writings of Roger Williams.* *20c. coll.:* ODEP 403, Whiting 310, CODP 160, Stevenson 1677:7, Whiting(MP) 444.

SEE ALSO A man in DEBT is caught in a net. / Do not FISH in front of a net. / Don't cry HERRINGS till they are in the net.

nettle Stroke a nettle and it will sting you; grasp it and it is as soft as silk. *Rec. dist.:* Ill. *1st cit.:* 1578 Lyly, *Euphues, Anatomy of Wit;* US1913 Ashurst, *Diary,* ed. Sparks (1962). *20c. coll.:* ODEP 348, Whiting(MP) 444, CODP 160, Stevenson 1677:11.

SEE ALSO KNAVES and nettles are akin: stroke 'em kindly, yet they'll sting.

never *(n.)* Never is a long time. *Vars.:* (a) Never is a long day. (b) Never is a long term. *Rec. dist.:* Ala., Ga. *1st cit.:* ca1390 Chaucer, *Canon's Yeoman's Tale;* US1928 Gilbert, *Mrs. Davenport.* *20c. coll.:* ODEP 562, Whiting(MP) 445, CODP 160, Stevenson 1678:7.

never *(adv.)* 1. Never say die. *Rec. dist.:* U.S., Can. *Infm.:* Never give up. *1st cit.:* 1837 Dickens, *Pickwick Papers;* US1814 *Diary of Benjamin F. Palmer, Privateersman, 1813–1815,* Acorn Club *Publications* (1914). *20c. coll.:* ODEP 563, Whiting 109, Stevenson 500:6, T&W 109.

2. Never say never. *Rec. dist.:* Mich., N.Y. *1st cit.:* 1837 Dickens, *Pickwick Papers.* *20c. coll.:* ODEP 563.

SEE ALSO ALMOST never killed a fly. / ALMOST was never hanged. / One never APPRECIATES what he has until he has lost it. / Better never BEGIN than never make an end. / CAN'T never could. / CHEATERS never prosper. / A bad DEED never dies. / Never say adieu to the DEVIL until you have met. / Never DO anything yourself you can get somebody else to do. / A man may be DOWN, but he is never out. / EAVESDROPPERS never hear any good of themselves. / Never start off on the wrong FOOT. / Never start anything important on FRIDAY. / Be FRIENDLY and you will never want friends. / A broken FRIENDSHIP may be soldered but will never be sound. / GOD never sends mouths but he sends meat. / Sour GRAPES can never make sweet wine. / GRASS never grows in a goose pasture. / He who puts his HAND to the plow should never look back. / Your HAND is never the worse for doing your own work. / Man was never SO HAPPY as when he was doing something. / Never comb a bald HEAD. / A great HEART is never proud. / Faint HEART never won fair lady. / A setting HEN never gets fat. / One who blows a HORN will never blow a vault. / Never believe the IMPOSSIBLE. / Never trust an INDIAN. / Never JUDGE before you see. / A KINDNESS is never lost. / Better come LATE to church than never. / Better LATE than never. / It's never too LATE until it's too late. / It is never too late to LEARN. / He who never LEARNS anything never forgets anything. / LIARS never prosper. / A burned LIGHT will never shine. / The path of true LOVE never runs smooth. / It is better to have LOVED and lost than never to have loved at all. / It's never too late to MEND. / He who never made a MISTAKE never made anything. / NEARLY never did any good. / A watched POT never boils. / It never RAINS but it pours. / Never a RIP without a tear. / The hands of TIME will never turn back. / TOMORROW never comes. / Never bark up the wrong TREE. / Never TROUBLE trouble till trouble troubles you. / An UGLY man never gets a pretty wife. / He that stays in the VALLEY shall never get over the hill. / Never say "WHOOPEE" before you jump. / Never too late to WIN. / Never cry WOLF when not in danger. / WORK never hurt any man.

never-was *SEE* It is better to be a HAS-BEEN than a never-was.

new *(n.)* **1.** Never be the first by whom the new is tried nor yet the last to lay the old aside. *Rec. dist.:* Ala., Ga., Miss. *1st cit.:* 1711 Pope, *Essay on Criticism.* *20c. coll.:* Stevenson 2606:6.

2. The new is what has been forgotten. *Rec. dist.:* N.J. *1st cit.:* ca1785 Bertin, *Epigram.* *20c. coll.:* Stevenson 1680:5.

SEE ALSO Don't trade old FRIENDS for new. / Don't throw away the OLD till you know the new is better. / Use the OLD before getting new.

new *(adj.)* **1.** There's forever something new to be found in friends. *Rec. dist.:* Miss.

2. There's nothing new under the sun. *Rec. dist.:* U.S., Can. *1st cit.:* 1386 Chaucer, *Knight's Tale;* US1650 *Works of Anne Bradstreet,* ed. Ellis (1932). *20c. coll.:* ODEP 580, CODP 164, Whiting 434, Stevenson 1680:8, Whiting(MP) 454.

SEE ALSO New BLOOD tells. / A new BROOM sweeps clean. / No man puts a piece of new CLOTH unto an old garment. / You can't teach an old DOG new tricks. / Make new FRIENDS but keep the old. / New FRIENDS are like silver, but old ones are like gold. / LEARN something new every day. / New LORDS, new laws. / Off with the old LOVE, on with the new. / Old LOVE burns low when new love breaks. / Never sew a new PATCH on an old garment. / Don't throw away your old SHOES before you get new ones.

newborn *SEE* Newborn CALVES don't fear tigers.

news **1.** Bad news travels fast. *Vars.:* **(a)** Bad news travels fast; good news is scarcely heard. **(b)** Good news travels slow. **(c)** Good news travels slowly; bad news travels fast. **(d)** Ill news comes apace. **(e)** Ill news travels fast. *Rec. dist.:* U.S., Can. *1st cit.:* 1539 Taverner, *Proverbs of Erasmus;* USca1656 Bradford, *History of Plymouth Plantation,* ed. Ford (1912). *20c. coll.:* CODP 8, Whiting 311, Stevenson 1683:3, T&W 261, Whiting(MP) 445.

2. He comes too early who brings bad news. *Vars.:* **(a)** Bad news always comes too soon. **(b)** Unwelcome news is always soon enough heard. *Rec. dist.:* Ill., Mich., Wis.

3. He knocks boldly who brings good news. *Rec. dist.:* Ill., Wis. *1st cit.:* 1611 Cotgrave, *Dictionary of French and English Tongues.* *20c. coll.:* ODEP 86, Stevenson 1682:4.

4. He that tells his wife news is but newly married. *Rec. dist.:* N.J., Wis.

5. News is as good as a visit. *Rec. dist.:* Minn.

6. News spreads like wildfire. *Rec. dist.:* Miss., Ohio.

7. No news is good news. *Var.:* All news is not good news. *Rec. dist.:* U.S., Can. *1st cit.:*

1616 James I in *Losely Manuscript;* US1754 *Writings of Samuel Johnson, President of King's College,* ed. Schneider (1929). **20c. coll.:** *ODEP* 572, Whiting 311, *CODP* 163, Stevenson 1682:12, Whiting*(MP)* 445.

8. There's no news like good news. **Rec. dist.:** N.Y.

9. We cannot control the news we get, but we can control the news we start. **Rec. dist.:** N.Y.

10. What's one man's news is another man's troubles. **Rec. dist.:** Ont.

11. Whenever everybody tends to his own business, news is scarce. **Rec. dist.:** N.Y.

newspaper Newspapers are the schoolmaster of the common people. **Rec. dist.:** N.Y., S.C. **1st cit.:** US1887 Beecher, "The Press" in *Proverbs from Plymouth Pulpit.* **20c. coll.:** Stevenson 1684:9.

next *SEE* FLOWERS are always brighter in the next field.

nibble *SEE* OPPORTUNITIES never nibble twice at the same hook.

nice If you can't say something nice about someone, don't say anything. **Var.:** If you can't say something nice, don't say anything. **Rec. dist.:** Iowa, Kans.

nickel **1.** A quick nickel is better than a slow dollar. **Var.:** Many a nickel is better than a slow dollar. **Rec. dist.:** N.Mex.

2. Don't take any wooden nickels. **Rec. dist.:** U.S., Can. **1st cit.:** US1930 Aresby, *Murder at Red Pass.* **20c. coll.:** Whiting*(MP)* 446.

3. Take care of the nickels and the dollars will take care of themselves. **Rec. dist.:** U.S. **1st cit.:** 1724 Chesterfield, Letter, 5 Feb., in *Letters to His Son;* US1936 *New Yorker,* 18 Apr. **20c. coll.:** *ODEP* 798, Whiting*(MP)* 481, *CODP* 176.

nickname **1.** A nickname is the heaviest stone the devil can throw at a man. **Rec. dist.:** Ill.

2. A nickname lasts forever. **Rec. dist.:** N.Y., S.C.

3. Nicknames are stick-names. **Rec. dist.:** Ont.

nigger **1.** A hungry nigger makes a clean dish. **Rec. dist.:** Miss.

2. Hit's a mighty deaf nigger dat don't hear de dinner ho'n. **Rec. dist.:** N.Y., S.C. **1st cit.:** US1880 Harris, *Plantation Proverbs* in *Uncle Remus, His Songs and His Sayings* (1881). **20c. coll.:** Stevenson 578:7.

3. Hungry nigger won't w'ar his maul out. **Rec. dist.:** N.Y., S.C.

4. The only good nigger is a dead nigger. **Rec. dist.:** Ky., Tenn. **Infm.:** Said of any enemy in time of war or conflict, as in the case of American Indians or Japanese.

SEE ALSO NAUGHT's a naught and figger's a figger—all for de white man and none for de nigger.

night **1.** A blustering night, a fair day. **Rec. dist.:** Wis. **1st cit.:** 1609 Shakespeare, *Sonnet 90.* **20c. coll.:** *ODEP* 71, Stevenson 2774:9.

2. Night brings out the stars. **Rec. dist.:** Ohio. **1st cit.:** 1839 Bailey, "Water and Wood" in *Festus.* **20c. coll.:** Stevenson 392:7.

3. Night brings the cows home. **Rec. dist.:** W.Va.

4. The darker the night, the brighter the candle. **Rec. dist.:** Ohio.

5. The longest night must end. **Rec. dist.:** N.Y. **1st cit.:** ca1475 Caxton, *History of Troy.* **20c. coll.:** *ODEP* 482, Stevenson 1686:6.

6. The night has a thousand eyes. **Var.:** The night has a thousand eyes, and the day but one. **Rec. dist.:** Ill., Miss., Wis. **1st cit.:** ca1595 Fergusson, *Scottish Proverbs.* **20c. coll.:** Stevenson 1687:5.

7. The night washes what the day has soaped. **Rec. dist.:** Ill.

8. What is done in the night appears in the day. **Rec. dist.:** Mich. **1st cit.:** ca1390 Gower, *Confessio Amantis,* E.E.T.S. (1900). **20c. coll.:** *ODEP* 199.

SEE ALSO All CATS are black at night. / A bad DAY never has a good night. / Praise a fine DAY at night. / RED sky at night, sailor's delight; red sky in the morning, sailors take warning. / WEEPING may endure for a night, but joy comes in the morning.

nightingale A nightingale won't sing in a cage. *Rec. dist.:* N.Y. *1st cit.:* 1732 Fuller, *Gnomologia*. *20c. coll.:* Stevenson 1688:1.

nine SEE CHARACTER and hard work go together in nine cases out of ten. / POSSESSION is nine points of the law, and self-possession is the other one. / A STITCH in time saves nine. / Nine TAILORS make a man.

nine-tenths SEE Nine-tenths of WISDOM consists in being wise in time.

nip SEE Nip the ACT while in the bud.

nit Nits make lice. *Var.:* Where there are nits, there also are lice. *Rec. dist.:* N.Y., S.C. *1st cit.:* ca1700 *New Dictionary of Canting Crew;* US1755 *New England Quarterly*. *20c. coll.:* ODEP 568, Whiting 313, Stevenson 1135:9, Whiting(*MP*) 449.

nitwit SEE To a nitwit LIFE is one laugh after another.

no *(n.)* **1.** Better say no before marriage than Reno after. *Rec. dist.:* Ind. *Infm.:* Reno, Nev., is noted for the number of divorces performed there.

2. He's no man who can't say no. *Rec. dist.:* Ill.

3. Learn to say no. *Rec. dist.:* Utah.

SEE ALSO When a LADY says no, she means perhaps; when she says perhaps, she means yes; when she says yes, she is no lady.

no *(adj.)* SEE A DEAD man tells no tales. / There are no FAULTS in a thing we want badly. / No GRATITUDE from the wicked. / KINGS can do no wrong. / No MILL, no meal; no will, no deal. / NECESSITY knows no law. / No NEWS is good news. / No SILVER, no servant. / No TERMINATION without determination. / TIME serves no man. / Where there is no WIFE there is no home.

nobility True nobility lies in worth, not birth. *Rec. dist.:* Wis.

SEE ALSO VIRTUE is the best title of nobility. / VIRTUE is the only true nobility.

noble The more noble, the more humble. *Rec. dist.:* Ont. *1st cit.:* 1616 Draxe, *Bibliotheca Scholastica in Anglia* (1918). *20c. coll.:* ODEP 575, Stevenson 1696:2.

SEE ALSO The noblest REVENGE is to forgive. / All WORK is noble.

nobly **1.** It is better to be nobly remembered than to be nobly born. *Rec. dist.:* Ind.

2. The nobly born must nobly do. *Rec. dist.:* Ont.

nobody **1.** Nobody is perfect. *Rec. dist.:* U.S., Can. *1st cit.:* 1931 Hollingworth, *Death Leaves Us Naked;* US1805 Morris, *Diary of French Revolution*, ed. Davenport (1939). *20c. coll.:* Whiting(*MP*) 449.

2. Nobody is trodden on lest he lies down first. *Rec. dist.:* Calif.

SEE ALSO You can't BEAT somebody with nobody. / Everybody's BUSINESS is nobody's business. / Let nobody know your BUSINESS. / Nobody's SWEETHEART is ugly.

nod A nod is as good as a wink to a blind horse. *Rec. dist.:* U.S., Can. *1st cit.:* 1794 Godwin, *Caleb Williams;* US1806 Port Folio. *20c. coll.:* ODEP 575, Whiting 313, CODP 163, Stevenson 1692:3, T&W 263, Whiting(*MP*) 449.

noise SEE An empty BARREL makes the most noise. / The empty BOWL makes the most noise. / Two empty packing BOXES make the most noise, but the squeaky wheel gets the grease. / It's the empty CAR that makes the most noise. / The empty PAIL makes the most noise. / Shallow STREAMS make the most noise. / TIME is a file that wears and makes no noise. / The emptiest VESSEL makes the most noise. / The empty WAGON makes the most noise. / It's not the WHEEL that makes the most noise that does the most harm. / The worst WHEEL of the cart makes the most noise.

noisy SEE It ain't the noisy CART that's easiest upset. / A cat's COURTING is noisy.

none SEE Too much of a GOOD thing is worse than none at all. / They who make the best use of their TIME have none to spare.

nonsense **1.** A little nonsense now and then is relished by the best of men. *Var.:* A little nonsense now and then is relished by the wisest men. *Rec. dist.:* Ill., Ind., N.Y., Wis. *Infm.:* Undated nursery rhyme. *1st cit.:* US1948

Stevenson, *Home Book of Proverbs*. **20c. coll.:** Stevenson 1693:4.

2. Nonsense is often mistaken for sense. *Rec. dist.:* Ill., Ont.

SEE ALSO There is some SENSE in every nonsense.

noon SEE Get up with the DAWN and you can sleep until noon.

noose SEE A HALO only has to fall a few inches to become a noose.

nose **1.** A big nose never spoiled a handsome face. *Rec. dist.:* Ill.

2. A dog's nose is always cold. *Vars.:* **(a)** A dog's nose and a maid's knees are always cold. **(b)** Cold nose, healthy dog. *Rec. dist.:* U.S. *1st cit.:* 1639 Clarke, *Paroemiologia*. **20c. coll.:** *ODEP* 197, Stevenson 603:10.

3. A person who looks down his nose at people will never see beyond that nose. *Rec. dist.:* Ala. *1st cit.:* 1956 Cauldwell, *Firewalkers, a Memoir;* US1940 Stockwell, *Candy Killings*. **20c. coll.:** Whiting*(MP)* 450.

4. Don't cut off your nose to spite your face. *Rec. dist.:* U.S., Can. *1st cit.:* ca1561 *Deceit of Women;* US1784 *Writings of Christopher Gadsden, 1764–1805,* ed. Walsh (1966). **20c. coll.:** *ODEP* 163, Whiting 314, *CODP* 47, Stevenson 1696:11, T&W 263, Whiting*(MP)* 450.

5. He that has a great nose thinks everybody is speaking of it. *Rec. dist.:* Ont. *1st cit.:* 1721 Kelly, *Scottish Proverbs*. **20c. coll.:** *ODEP* 334.

6. Keep your nose clean. *Rec. dist.:* Mich., N.Y., Ohio. *1st cit.:* 1938 Gribble, *Tragedy in E Flat;* US1943 Goldthwaite, *You Did It*. **20c. coll.:** Whiting*(MP)* 451, Stevenson 1694:9.

7. Keep your nose out of other people's business. *Rec. dist.:* U.S. *1st cit.:* US1841 Stephens, *High Life in New York*. **20c. coll.:** T&W 264.

8. Keep your nose to the grindstone. *Rec. dist.:* U.S., Can. *1st cit.:* 1557 Erasmus, *Merry Dialogue,* ed. de Vocht (1928); US1647 Ward, *Simple Cobler of Aggawam in America,* ed. Wroth (1937). **20c. coll.:** *ODEP* 578, Whiting 314, T&W 264, Whiting*(MP)* 451.

9. Keep your nose to yourself and it won't be cut off. *Rec. dist.:* Ill.

10. Let your nose go in front, but don't always follow it. *Rec. dist.:* Ill.

SEE ALSO Your RIGHTS end where my nose begins. / The man who will not SAVE as he goes keeps his nose to the grindstone. / He that is conscious of a STINK in his breeches is jealous of every wrinkle in another's nose.

nothing **1.** Beware of him who has nothing to lose. *Rec. dist.:* Ill.

2. By doing nothing we learn to do ill. *Rec. dist.:* Mich., N.Y., Tex. *1st cit.:* ca1386 Chaucer, *Tale of Melibee*. **20c. coll.:** Stevenson 1213:6, *ODEP* 198.

3. Expect nothing and you won't be disappointed. *Rec. dist.:* Ill., N.C. *1st cit.:* 1727 Pope, Letter, 6 Oct.; US1739 Franklin, *PRAlmanac*. **20c. coll.:** *CODP* 20, Whiting 316, Stevenson 721:6, T&W 265, Whiting*(MP)* 453.

4. From nothing, nothing is made. *Var.:* Where nothing is, nothing can be had. *Rec. dist.:* U.S., Can. *1st cit.:* ca1380 Chaucer, *Boece;* US1716 *Writings of Samuel Johnson, President of King's College,* ed. Schneider (1929). **20c. coll.:** *ODEP* 579, Whiting 316, *CODP* 164, Stevenson 1699:2, T&W 265, Whiting*(MP)* 454.

5. He has hard work indeed who has nothing to do. *Rec. dist.:* N.Y., S.C.

6. He who knows nothing never doubts. *Rec. dist.:* Ala., Ga., Ind. *1st cit.:* 1611 Cotgrave, *Dictionary of French and English Tongues*. **20c. coll.:** *ODEP* 438.

7. Hide nothing from your minister, physician, and lawyer. *Rec. dist.:* N.Y., Wis. *1st cit.:* 1573 Sanford, *Garden of Pleasure;* US1737 Franklin, *PRAlmanac*. **20c. coll.:** *ODEP* 371, Whiting 114, Stevenson 593:10.

8. If a thing is to be done for nothing, do it for yourself. *Rec. dist.:* N.J.

9. If you have nothing, you've got nothing to lose. *Var.:* If you have nothing, you lose nothing. *Rec. dist.:* Ont. *1st cit.:* ca1557 Roper, *Life of More,* ed. Hitchcock; US1814 *Life and Correspondence of Rufus King,* ed. King (1894–1900). **20c. coll.:** *ODEP* 580, Whiting 316, Stevenson 1700:7.

10. Nothing can ever need a lie. *Rec. dist.:* Ill., N.C., Ont.

11. Nothing can last forever. *Rec. dist.:* N.C.

12. Nothing comes out that is not put in. *Var.:* If you put nothing in your purse, you can take nothing out. *Rec. dist.:* Ala., Ga., Tex. *1st cit.:* 1630 Taylor, *Works of John Taylor.* *20c. coll.:* Stevenson 1701:10.

13. Nothing down, nothing up. *Rec. dist.:* N.Y.

14. Nothing enters into a closed hand. *Rec. dist.:* Calif., Colo., Wis. *1st cit.:* 1641 Fergusson, *Scottish Proverbs.* *20c. coll.:* ODEP 579.

15. Nothing happens for nothing. *Rec. dist.:* Ohio. *1st cit.:* ca1380 Chaucer, *Boece;* US1959 Walsh, *Dangerous Passenger.* *20c. coll.:* ODEP 579, Whiting(MP) 453.

16. Nothing is beautiful from every point of view. *Rec. dist.:* Oreg.

17. Nothing is certain but death and taxes. *Rec. dist.:* U.S., Can. *1st cit.:* 1726 Defoe, "Devil" in *History of Apparitions;* US1789 Franklin, Letter to M. Lewis. *20c. coll.:* ODEP 580, Stevenson 2248:16, Whiting 89, CODP 164, Whiting(MP) 158.

18. Nothing is ever as bad as you think it is going to be, and nothing is ever as good as you think it is going to be. *Rec. dist.:* N.Y., Wis.

19. Nothing is gained without work. *Rec. dist.:* Ind., Ont.

20. Nothing is impossible to a willing heart. *Rec. dist.:* N.Y. *1st cit.:* 1509 Hawes, *Passetyne of Pleasure;* US1936 Meynell, *On the Night.* *20c. coll.:* ODEP 580, Whiting(MP) 453, Stevenson 1109:3

21. Nothing is impossible to a willing mind. *Rec. dist.:* Ind., Ky., Tenn.

22. Nothing is perfect. *Rec. dist.:* Mich., N.Y., N.C., Utah.

23. Nothing succeeds like success. *Rec. dist.:* U.S. *1st cit.:* 1868 Helps, *Realman;* US1867 Richardson, *Beyond the Mississippi.* *20c. coll.:* ODEP 581, T&W 359, CODP 165, Stevenson 2236:5, Whiting(MP) 454.

24. Nothing ventured, nothing gained. *Rec. dist.:* U.S., Can. *1st cit.:* ca1374 Chaucer, *Troilus and Criseyde;* US1748 *Letters and Papers of Cadwallader Colden,* N.Y.Hist.Soc. *Collections* (1913–37). *20c. coll.:* ODEP 581, Whiting 316, CODP 165, Stevenson 2418:1, T&W 265, Whiting(MP) 454.

25. Nothing worth having ever comes without a lot of hard work. *Rec. dist.:* N.Y.

26. To do nothing is the way to be nothing. *Rec. dist.:* N.Y.

27. Who accepts nothing has nothing to return. *Rec. dist.:* N.Y., S.C.

28. Who dares nothing need hope for nothing. *Rec. dist.:* Ont.

29. Who does nothing can do nothing wrong. *Rec. dist.:* N.Y., S.C.

30. You get nothing for nothing. *Vars.:* **(a)** Nothing worthwhile is had for nothing. **(b)** You never get anything for nothing. *Rec. dist.:* U.S., Can. *1st cit.:* ca1380 Chaucer, *Boece;* US1959 Walsh, *Dangerous Passenger.* *20c. coll.:* ODEP 579, Whiting(MP) 453, Stevenson 1699:2.

SEE ALSO ANYTHING is better than nothing. / ATTITUDES don't prove nothing. / From the day you were born till you ride in a hearse, there's nothing so BAD but it might have been worse. / There is nothing so BAD in which there is not something good. / BELIEVE only half of what you see and nothing you hear. / A BIT in the morning is better than nothing all day. / COURTESY costs nothing. / CRITICISM is something you can avoid by saying nothing, doing nothing, and being nothing. / To know EVERYTHING is to know nothing. / Twin FOOLS: one doubts nothing, the other, everything. / Speak well of your FRIENDS; of your enemies say nothing. / GAMBLING is getting nothing for something. / Nothing with GOD is accidental. / GOOD that comes too late is good as nothing. / Do nothing by HALVES. / KNAVES imagine nothing can be done without knavery. / A LITTLE is a big per cent on nothing. / There's nothing in the LOOKS of a lousy calf. / A NEGRO that can't sing ain't worth nothing. / There's nothing NEW under the sun. / If you can't put anything on the PILE, take nothing off. / He is RICH who owes nothing. / SOMETHING tastes better than nothing. / You can't make SOMETHING out of nothing. / Men who tell you almost nothing but the TRUTH, tell you almost nothing. / A TRY is better than nothing. / Everybody talks about the WEATHER, but nobody does anything about it. / If you WISH for too much, you will end up with nothing.

notion Everybody to their own notion. *Var.:* Everybody to his own notion. *Rec. dist.:* Miss.

nourish *SEE* What one RELISHES, nourishes.

novelty 1. Men will do anything for novelty. *Rec. dist.:* Ill.

2. Novelty is the great parent of pleasure. *Rec. dist.:* Ill.

3. The novelty of noon is out of date by night. *Rec. dist.:* Ill.

4. 'Tis novelty that sets the people a-gaping. *Rec. dist.:* Ill. *1st cit.:* 1732 Fuller, *Gnomologia. 20c. coll.:* Stevenson 1702:1.

nowhere You can't get nowhere without going. *Rec. dist.:* Calif.

SEE ALSO It's a long ROAD that goes nowhere.

number 'Tis not in numbers but in unity that our great strength lies. *Rec. dist.:* N.Y., S.C.

SEE ALSO There's SAFETY in numbers.

nurse 1. A nurse spoils a good housewife. *Rec. dist.:* Ill. *1st cit.:* 1659 Howell, *English Proverbs. 20c. coll.:* Stevenson 1703:8.

2. Nurses make the worst patients. *Rec. dist.:* N.C.

3. Nurses put one bit in the child's mouth and two in their own. *Rec. dist.:* Ill. *1st cit.:* 1639 Clarke, *Paroemiologia. 20c. coll.:* ODEP 583, Stevenson 1703:5.

4. With seven nurses a child will be without eyes. *Rec. dist.:* N.Y., S.C.

nursery *SEE* The proof of the HOME is the nursery.

nut Sweetest nuts have the hardest shells. *Rec. dist.:* Ont. *1st cit.:* 1566 Beverley, *Ariodanto and Genevra. 20c. coll.:* ODEP 793, Stevenson 82:2.

SEE ALSO He that will eat the KERNEL must crack the nut.

O

oak Great oaks from little acorns grow. *Vars.:* (a) A big oak grew from a little acorn. (b) Big oaks from little acorns grow. (c) Big oaks from little chestnuts grow. (d) From big oaks little acorns grow. (e) From little acorns big oaks grow. (f) From little acorns great oaks grow. (g) From little acorns grow big oaks. (h) From little acorns tall oaks grow. (i) Large oaks from little acorns grow; large aches from little toe corns grow. (j) Little acorns into great oaks grow. (k) Mighty oaks from little acorns grow. (l) Tall oaks from little acorns grow. *Rec. dist.:* U.S., Can. *1st cit.:* ca1374 Chaucer, *Troilus and Criseyde;* US1871 Jones, *Life of Jefferson S. Batkins.* *20c. coll.:* ODEP 584, T&W 268, *CODP* 101, Stevenson 1035:15, Whiting*(MP)* 458.

SEE ALSO Little STROKES fell great oaks. / Easy matter to bend a TWIG; hard matter to bend an oak. / The harder the WIND, the deeper the oak becomes rooted.

oar Don't lean on the oars. *Var.:* Don't rest on your oars. *Rec. dist.:* U.S., Can. *1st cit.:* 1726 Shelvocke, *Voyage Round the World;* US1751 *Wolcott Papers, 1750–1754* in Conn. Hist. Soc. *Collections* (1916). *20c. coll.:* Stevenson 1706:4, Whiting 319, T&W 268, Whiting*(MP)* 458.

oath 1. An unlawful oath is better broken than kept. *Rec. dist.:* Ill. *1st cit.:* 1481 *Reynard, The Fox,* tr. Caxton, ed. Arber (1880). *20c. coll.:* ODEP 585, Stevenson 1707:8.

2. Eggs and oaths are easily broken. *Rec. dist.:* N.Y.

3. He who readily takes oath seldom swears to the truth. *Var.:* He who makes oath seldom swears to the truth. *Rec. dist.:* Ill.

SEE ALSO A true WORD needs no oath.

oats Sow your wild oats and pray for a crop failure. *Rec. dist.:* Calif. *1st cit.:* 1542 Becon, *Early Works;* US1650 *Works of Anne Bradstreet,* ed. Ellis (1932). *20c. coll.:* ODEP 889, Whiting 320, Stevenson 1708:2, T&W 268, Whiting*(MP)* 459.

obedience 1. Obedience is better than sacrifice. *Rec. dist.:* Mich., Minn., N.Y., Ont.

2. Obedience is the first duty of a child. *Rec. dist.:* Ill.

SEE ALSO LOVE makes obedience light.

obey By learning to obey, you will know how to command. *Var.:* If you obey orders, you can give them. *Rec. dist.:* U.S., Can. *1st cit.:* 1574 Guazzo, *Civile Conversation,* tr. Pettie, T.T. (1925); US1734 Franklin, *PRAlmanac.* *20c. coll.:* Stevenson 382:3, Whiting*(MP)* 459.

SEE ALSO He that is BOUND must obey. / LAWS too gentle are seldom obeyed; too severe, seldom executed. / The MAGISTRATE should obey the law; the people should obey the magistrate. / You cannot be a true MAN until you learn to obey. / The VESSEL that will not obey her helm will have to obey the rocks.

object *SEE* The object of WAR is peace.

oblige We can not always oblige, but we can always speak obligingly. *Rec. dist.:* N.J.

obscurity Obscurity often brings safety. *Rec. dist.:* Ohio. *1st cit.:* US1948 Stevenson, *Home Book of Proverbs.* *20c. coll.:* Stevenson 1710:8.

SEE ALSO PURITY is obscurity.

observer When you have no observers, be afraid of yourself. *Rec. dist.:* Mich.

obstacle 1. Obstacles are the stepping-stones to success. *Rec. dist.:* Fla.

2. Obstacles make the goal clearer. *Rec. dist.:* Calif.

3. The greater the obstacle, the more glory in overcoming it. *Var.:* The greater the obstacle, the stronger the desire. *Rec. dist.:* N.C., Ont. *1st cit.:* US1948 Stevenson, *Home Book of Proverbs.* *20c. coll.:* Stevenson 1893:11.

SEE ALSO FORTUNE doesn't lie at the end of the rainbow, it is found behind some obstacle.

obstinacy 1. Obstinacy is most positive when it is most in the wrong. *Rec. dist.:* Ill.

2. Obstinacy is the strength of the weak. *Rec. dist.:* Ill.

obstinate *(n.)* SEE The most WICKED are often the most obstinate.

obstinate *(adj.)* The obstinate man does not hold opinions; his opinions hold him. *Rec. dist.:* Ill. *1st cit.:* ca1680 Butler, *Remaines Concerning Britaine.* *20c. coll.:* Stevenson 1711:6.

occasion SEE The STATESMAN makes the occasion, but the occasion makes the politician. / Soften the WORDS to suit the occasion.

occupation **1.** Absence of occupation is not rest; a mind quite vacant is a mind in distress. *Rec. dist.:* N.C. *1st cit.:* 1781 Cowper, *Retirement.* *20c. coll.:* Stevenson 1712:5.

2. Constant occupation prevents temptation. *Rec. dist.:* N.J., Ont.

occur SEE The thing that often occurs is never much APPRECIATED.

ocean The whole ocean is made up of little drops. *Var.:* Many drops of water make an ocean. *Rec. dist.:* N.Y., Wis.

SEE ALSO The BUZZ of a mosquito can drown out the ocean's roar. / A still RIVER never finds the ocean.

oculist SEE Many are seeking OPPORTUNITIES when they really need an oculist.

odds People usually get at odds with each other when they try to get even. *Rec. dist.:* Ont.

odious SEE COMPARISONS are odious.

odor There is no odor so bad as that which arises from goodness tainted. *Rec. dist.:* N.Y., S.C.

off SEE Off with the old LOVE, on with the new. / Don't cut off your NOSE to spite your face.

offend SEE A good FRIEND never offends.

offender The offender never pardons. *Var.:* Offenders never pardon. *Rec. dist.:* Ont. *1st cit.:* 1640 Herbert, *Outlandish Proverbs (Jacula Prudentum)* in *Works,* ed. Hutchinson (1941). *20c. coll.:* ODEP 586, CODP 167, Stevenson 1712:14.

SEE ALSO The more LAWS, the more offenders.

offense **1.** A good offense is the best defense. *Var.:* The best defense is a good offense. *Rec. dist.:* U.S., Can. *1st cit.:* US1928 Lehman, *Zeppelins.* *20c. coll.:* Whiting(MP) 460.

2. Neither give nor take offense. *Var.:* Neither take offense nor make offense. *Rec. dist.:* Ont. *1st cit.:* US1948 Stevenson, *Home Book of Proverbs.* *20c. coll.:* Stevenson 1713:5.

office **1.** Public office is a public trust. *Rec. dist.:* Ill. *1st cit.:* US1835 Calhoun, Speech, 13 Feb. *20c. coll.:* Stevenson 1714:3.

2. The office makes the man. *Rec. dist.:* N.Y., S.C., Tex. *1st cit.:* 1539 Taverner, *Proverbs of Erasmus.* *20c. coll.:* Stevenson 1713:13.

SEE ALSO He that has a TRADE has an estate, and he that has a calling has an office of profit and honor.

official **1.** An honest official has no fat subordinates. *Rec. dist.:* Ill. *1st cit.:* US1938 Champion, *Racial Proverbs.* *20c. coll.:* Stevenson 1714:1.

2. Officials have good jobs waiting for them in the next world. *Rec. dist.:* N.Y.

often SEE FRIENDS are lost by calling often and calling seldom. / Thoughtless FRIENDS are often a nuisance. / Weak HEADS are often headstrong. / LITTLE and often fills the purse. / LOOKS often deceive. / A neat MAIDEN often makes a dirty wife. / A PITCHER that goes to the well too often is liable to be broken.

oil *(n.)* **1.** A spoonful of oil on the troubled waters goes farther than a quart of vinegar. *Rec. dist.:* Utah. *1st cit.:* ca731 Bede, *Ecclesiastical History;* US1786 Rush, *Letters,* ed. Butterfield (1951). *20c. coll.:* ODEP 587, Whiting 321, Stevenson 1715:10 T&W 269, Whiting(MP) 460.

2. If there is no oil in the lamp, the wick is wasted. *Rec. dist.:* Ill. *1st cit.:* US1875 Scarborough, *Chinese Proverbs.* *20c. coll.:* Stevenson 2284:9.

3. Oil and water don't mix. *Vars.:* **(a)** Oil and vinegar don't mix. **(b)** Oil and water cannot mix. **(c)** Oil and water will not mix. **(d)** Water and oil do not mix. *Rec. dist.:* U.S., Can. *1st cit.:* US1783 Jones, *Letters of Joseph Jones of Virginia, 1773–1787,* ed. Ford (1889). *20c. coll.:* Whiting 321, T&W 269, Whiting(MP) 460.

4. Put the oil where the squeak is. *Rec. dist.:* Ill., Miss.

5. To pour oil on the fire is not the way to quench it. *Rec. dist.:* N.Y. *1st cit.:* 1581 Guazzo, *Civile Conversation,* tr. Pettie, T.T. (1925); US1645 Jenner in *Winthrop Papers, 1498–1649,* Mass.Hist.Soc. *Collections* (1929–47). *20c. coll.:* ODEP 582, Whiting 321, Stevenson 1716:3, T&W 269, Whiting(MP) 460.

6. When the oil is exhausted, the lamp dies out. *Rec. dist.:* Ind. *1st cit.:* 1573 Gascoigne, *Dan Bartholomew of Bath. 20c. coll.:* ODEP 587, Stevenson 1716:3.

7. When you strike oil, quit boring. *Rec. dist.:* Ky., Tenn.

SEE ALSO A BUSINESS with an income at its heels always furnishes oil for its own wheels.

oil *(v.)* Oil not, neither will you spin. *Rec. dist.:* Calif.

oilfield Oilfields get in your blood. *Rec. dist.:* Tex.

ointment 1. Golden ointment is no cure for a wound of the heart. *Rec. dist.:* Ill.

2. Precious ointments come in small boxes. *Rec. dist.:* Ohio.

SEE ALSO Dying FLIES spoil the sweetness of the ointment.

old *(n.)* 1. Don't throw away the old till you know the new is better. *Var.:* Never part with the old until you are sure the new is better. *Rec. dist.:* Ont.

2. Look for the old so as to learn the new. *Rec. dist.:* N.Y.

3. The old forget; the young don't know. *Rec. dist.:* Ohio.

4. Use the old before getting new. *Rec. dist.:* Ont.

SEE ALSO NATURE abhors the old. / The YOUNG are slaves to novelty, the old to customs. / The YOUNG may die; the old must die.

old *(adj.)* 1. A man is as old as his arteries. *Rec. dist.:* W.Va. *1st cit.:* 1950 Jepson, *Hungry*

Spider; US1925 Campbell, *Lazy Colon. 20c. coll.:* Whiting(MP) 397.

2. An old man in the house is a good sign. *Rec. dist.:* N.Y., S.C. *1st cit.:* 1642 Torriano, *Select Italian Proverbs. 20c. coll.:* ODEP 590.

3. An old young man will be a young old man. *Rec. dist.:* N.Y., S.C. *1st cit.:* 1659 Howell, *Paroimiografia. 20c. coll.:* ODEP 593, Stevenson 41:4.

4. Few persons know how to be old. *Rec. dist.:* S.C. *1st cit.:* US1948 Stevenson, *Home Book of Proverbs. 20c. coll.:* Stevenson 29:9.

5. Grow old gracefully. *Rec. dist.:* N.Y.

6. Growing old is no more than a bad habit which a busy man has no time to form. *Rec. dist.:* N.Y.

7. Never too old to mend. *Rec. dist.:* N.Y.

8. Old age comes uncalled. *Rec. dist.:* Miss.

9. Old age is honorable. *Rec. dist.:* Miss.

10. Old age is the night of life, as night is the old age of day. *Rec. dist.:* Maine.

11. Old age makes us wiser and more foolish. *Rec. dist.:* Miss.

12. Old age writes in sand; youth carves in stone. *Rec. dist.:* Mich.

13. Old in body, young in spirit. *Rec. dist.:* N.C.

14. Old men are twice children. *Var.:* Once an old man, twice a child. *Rec. dist.:* Ind., Mich., N.Y. *1st cit.:* 1527 Longland, *Sermones. 20c. coll.:* ODEP 591.

15. Old young and old long. *Rec. dist.:* Okla., Tex. *1st cit.:* 1539 Taverner, *Proverbs of Erasmus;* US1735 Franklin, *PRAlmanac. 20c. coll.:* ODEP 590, Stevenson 41:4.

16. The best time to prepare for old age is when you are young. *Rec. dist.:* N.Y., S.C.

17. The old one crows; the young one learns. *Rec. dist.:* N.Y., S.C. *1st cit.:* ca1350 *Douce MS 52. 20c. coll.:* ODEP 538.

18. Though old and wise, be still advised. *Rec. dist.:* Colo. *1st cit.:* 1640 Herbert, *Outlandish Proverbs (Jacula Prudentum)* in *Works,* ed. Hutchinson (1941). *20c. coll.:* ODEP 538.

19. We get too soon old and too late smart. *Rec. dist.:* N.Y., S.C.

20. Wear out the old things first. *Rec. dist.:* Ont.

21. You are as old as you feel. *Var.:* A man is as old as he feels. *Rec. dist.:* Calif., Mich., N.Y. *1st cit.:* 1907 *Illustrated London News,* 25 May; US1926 Fletcher, *Green Ink. 20c. coll.:* ODEP 505, Whiting*(MP)* 397.

22. You are never older than you think you are. *Rec. dist.:* Ill., Minn.

23. You're not too old to learn. *Var.:* Never too old to learn. *Rec. dist.:* U.S., Can. *1st cit.:* ca1530 Barclay, *Eclogues,* E.E.T.S. (1927); US1783 Williams, *Journal of Penrose,* ed. Dickason (1969). *20c. coll.:* ODEP 563, Whiting 257, *CODP* 161, Stevenson 36:5.

SEE ALSO Young ANGEL, old devil; young devil, old angel. / New ARTS destroy the old. / When they're BIG enough, they're old enough. / The DAUGHTER of a spry old woman makes a poor housekeeper. / The good old DAYS were once the present, too. / You can't teach an old DOG new tricks. / There are more old DRINKERS than old doctors. / EDUCATION is the best provision for old age. / The older the FIDDLE, the better the tune. / The older the FOOL, the harder he falls. / There is no FOOL like an old fool. / Old FOXES are not easily caught. / Trust not a new FRIEND nor an old enemy. / Don't trade old FRIENDS for new. / New FRIENDS are like silver, but old ones are like gold. / Old FRIENDS are best. / Old women's GOLD is not ugly. / There never was a GOOSE so old and gray but what a gander would wander her way. / It is a thousand times easier to contract a new HABIT than to get rid of an old one. / There's no HEAD like an old head. / An old HEN never grows young. / A HORSE is as old as his teeth. / An old HORSE for a hard road. / An old HORSE slips quicker than a young one. / You can't teach an old HORSE new tricks. / A young IDLER, an old beggar. / On an old KETTLE there isn't much to mend. / There's no LIAR like an old liar. / All wish to LIVE long but not to be called old. / Old LOVE burns low when new love breaks. / Old LOVE is easily kindled. / There's nothing worse than an old LOVER. / New LOVES and old wines are best. / NEED makes the old wife trot. / PAINS to get, care to keep, and fear to lose is the best way to make an easy bed for old age. / Never sew a new PATCH on an old garment. / The young RAVENS are beaked like the old. / The old ROCKING CHAIR will get you. / Lie on ROSES when young; lie on thorns when old. / Young SAINT, old devil. / Old SHOES wear best. / SPARE when you are young and spend when you are old. / Waste not fresh TEARS over old griefs. / A young TREE is easier twisted than an old tree. / TRUTH never grows old. / There is many a good TUNE played on the old fiddle. / A young TWIG is easier twisted than an old tree. / A WOMAN is as old as she looks, but a man is never old till he quits looking. / That WOMAN is young that does not look a day older than she says she is. / A YOUNG man looks into the future as an old man into his past. / The YOUNG folks think the old folks are fools, but the old folks know the young folks are fools. / You're as YOUNG as you look, and as old as you feel. / Every dissipation of YOUTH has to be paid for with a draft on old age. / In YOUTH we run into difficulties; in old age difficulties run into us. / When a YOUTH is saved, a life is saved; when an old person is saved, only a soul is saved. / YOUTH is a blunder, manhood a struggle, old age a regret.

omelette You can't have an omelette unless you break the egg. *Var.:* You cannot make an omelette without breaking eggs. *Rec. dist.:* Mich., Miss., N.Y. *1st cit.:* 1859 Thompson, *Audi Alteram Partem;* US1926 Niles, *Black Haiti. 20c. coll.:* ODEP 594, Whiting*(MP)* 461, *CODP* 168, Stevenson 1230:6.

once SEE It is better to ASK twice than to go wrong once. / If anyone BETRAYS you once, it's his fault; if he betrays you twice, it's your fault. / Once BURNED, twice shy. / CHRISTMAS comes but once a year. / A COW needs her tail more than once in fly time. / Once a CROOK, always a crook. / A man can only DIE once. / Once a DRUNKARD, always a drunkard. / Once a FOOL, always a fool. / HEAR twice before you speak once. / Better once in HEAVEN than ten times at the gate. / You can fool an old HORSE once, but you can't fool him twice. /

Once a KNAVE, always a knave. / We only LIVE once. / Once a MAN, twice a child. / OPPORTUNITY knocks but once. / One cannot be in two PLACES at once. / Once a THIEF, always a thief. / You are only YOUNG once. / YOUTH comes but once in a lifetime.

one 1. It requires more than one to make a bargain. *Rec. dist.:* N.Y., S.C.

2. One today is worth two tomorrows. *Rec. dist.:* Ohio.

3. One with the law is a majority. *Var.:* One on God's side is a majority. *Rec. dist.:* N.Y., S.C.

4. When one will not, two cannot quarrel. *Rec. dist.:* Mich.
    SEE ALSO ALL for one, one for all. / The BIG ones don't always get away. / Human BLOOD is all one color. / Beware of the man of one BOOK. / The BUYER needs a thousand eyes; the seller wants but one. / When one DOOR closes, another one opens. / One ENEMY is too much for a man, and a hundred friends are too few. / The EVILS you do two by two you pay for one by one. / Two EYES can see more than one. / One EYEWITNESS is better than ten hearsays. / One at a time is good FISHING. / One FOOL is enough in a house. / One FOOT is better than crutches. / There is more than one FROG in the puddle. / HATE is a burning fire that may consume the one who hates. / Two HEADS are better than one. / An overdose of HILARITY does no one any good. / No one is INFALLIBLE. / Make one in a thousand an INTIMATE. / A JOURNEY of a thousand miles begins with one step. / KNOWLEDGE and wisdom are far from being one. / A LIE stands on one leg, and truth on two. / LIFE is just one damned thing after another. / Two MINDS are better than one. / The MOUSE that has but one hole is soon caught. / The OLD one crows; the young one learns. / Every man has one black PATCH, and some have two. / One PLOWS, another sows—who will reap, no one knows. / What one man SOWS another man reaps. / One STEP astray is one step away. / One SWALLOW does not make a summer. / At the TABLE it becomes no one to be bashful. / One THING at a time. / One TONGUE is sufficient

for a woman. / Two can live cheaper than one.

one-eyed SEE In the land of the BLIND, the one-eyed are kings. / One-eyed MULE can't be handled on the blind side.

only *(adj.)* SEE The only good INDIAN is a dead Indian. / The only LOT most men do not grumble at is their burial lot.

onward Onward ever, downward never. *Rec. dist.:* Ill.

open *(v.)* SEE An ANGRY man opens his mouth and shuts his eyes. / To open a BOOK brings profit. / Good CLOTHES open all doors. / When one DOOR closes, another one opens. / When you open a DOOR you do not know how many rooms lie beyond. / A man without a smiling FACE must not open a shop. / It is better to be thought a FOOL than to open your mouth and let the world know it. / SEEK and you shall find; knock and it shall be opened unto you. / It is easy to open a SHOP, but hard to keep it open. / One SIN opens the door for another.

open *(adj.)* SEE A DOOR must be open or shut. / Keep your EARS open: even a rattlesnake will warn before he bites. / Keep your EYES wide open before marriage and half shut afterwards. / False FRIENDS are worse than open enemies. / When the HOUSE is open the honest man sins. / Open REBUKE is better than secret love. / Not to oversee WORKMEN is to leave them with your purse open.

operate SEE SUCCESS is operated on a self-service basis.

opinion 1. Don't let another's opinion sway your judgment. *Rec. dist.:* Ont. *1st cit.:* 1580 Lyly, *Euphues and His England,* ed. Arber (1868). *20c. coll.:* Stevenson 1720:2.

2. Everyone to his own opinions. *Var.:* Every man to his own opinion. *Rec. dist.:* Ill., N.C. *1st cit.:* 1576 Pettie, *Petite Palace of Pleasure.* *20c. coll.:* Stevenson 1721:8.

3. It's difference of opinion that makes a horse race. *Rec. dist.:* Ind., Oreg. *1st cit.:* US1893 Twain, *Pudd'nhead Wilson's Calendar.* *20c. coll.:* Stevenson 1719:4.

4. Public opinion is a second conscience. *Rec. dist.:* Ill.

5. Those who never retract their opinions love themselves more than they love truth. *Rec. dist.:* Ill. *1st cit.:* US1948 Stevenson, *Home Book of Proverbs.* *20c. coll.:* Stevenson 1718:13.

6. We think very few people sensible, except those who are of our opinion. *Rec. dist.:* Ill.

SEE ALSO As many MEN, as many opinions. / He that is of the opinion MONEY will do everything may well be suspected of doing everything for money. / A man convinced against his WILL is of the same opinion still.

opportunity 1. A lost opportunity never returns. *Rec. dist.:* N.J. *1st cit.:* 1678 Ray, *English Proverbs.* *20c. coll.:* Stevenson 1722:2.

2. A man must make his opportunity as often as he finds it. *Rec. dist.:* Ont.

3. Don't wait for opportunities—make them. *Rec. dist.:* Md. *1st cit.:* 1597 Bacon, "Of Ceremonies and Respects" in *Essays.* *20c. coll.:* Stevenson 1722:3.

4. If opportunity knocks, let her in. *Rec. dist.:* N.Y.

5. Keep yourself from the opportunity and God will keep you from the sin. *Rec. dist.:* N.C., S.C.

6. Many are seeking opportunities when they really need an oculist. *Rec. dist.:* N.C.

7. Opportunities are few to the man who cannot make up his mind. *Rec. dist.:* N.Y., S.C.

8. Opportunities do not wait. *Rec. dist.:* Ill.

9. Opportunities look for you when you are worth finding. *Rec. dist.:* Ont.

10. Opportunities neglected are lost. *Rec. dist.:* Mich., Ont.

11. Opportunities never nibble twice at the same hook. *Var.:* Opportunity never nibbles at the same hook twice. *Rec. dist.:* Ont.

12. Opportunity doesn't knock the door down. *Rec. dist.:* N.Y.

13. Opportunity is bald on the back of her head; seize her as she passes. *Rec. dist.:* N.C.

14. Opportunity is the thief of virtue. *Rec. dist.:* N.Y.

15. Opportunity is where you find it. *Rec. dist.:* Calif.

16. Opportunity knocks but once. *Vars.:* **(a)** Opportunity knocks but once, but temptation hammers incessantly. **(b)** Opportunity only knocks once, and there is no latch on the outside—it must be opened from within. *Rec. dist.:* U.S., Can. *1st cit.:* 1567 Fenton, *Bandello;* US1809 *Port Folio.* *20c. coll.:* ODEP 282, Whiting 166, *CODP* 171, Stevenson 1722:2, Whiting*(MP)* 464.

17. Opportunity knocks for every man, but a woman gets a ring. *Rec. dist.:* Calif.

18. Opportunity makes a thief. *Rec. dist.:* N.Y., S.C. *1st cit.:* ca1220 *Hali Meidenhad,* E.E.T.S. (1866); US1734 *Letter* in *Colonial Currency Reprints, 1682–1751.* *20c. coll.:* ODEP 600, Whiting 322, *CODP* 171, Stevenson 1725:7, Whiting*(MP)* 464.

19. Opportunity never knocks for persons not worth a rap. *Rec. dist.:* Calif., Colo.

20. Opportunity sooner or later comes to all who work and wish. *Rec. dist.:* N.Y., N.C.

21. Take advantage of the little opportunities and you won't need to wait for a big one. *Rec. dist.:* N.C. *1st cit.:* 1539 Taverner, *Proverbs of Erasmus;* US1623 Winthrop in *Winthrop Papers, 1498–1649,* Mass.Hist.Soc. *Collections* (1929–47). *20c. coll.:* ODEP 822, Stevenson 2324:3, Whiting 443, T&W 375, Whiting *(MP)* 630.

22. Take opportunity by the forelock. *Rec. dist.:* Ont.

23. The man who loses his opportunity loses himself. *Rec. dist.:* N.C.

24. The opportunity is often lost by deliberating. *Rec. dist.:* Mich., N.Y.

25. The opportunity of a lifetime is seldom so labeled. *Rec. dist.:* Colo.

26. We should never lose a good opportunity. *Rec. dist.:* Calif.

SEE ALSO CALAMITY is virtue's opportunity. / No GREAT man ever complains of want of opportunity. / The QUARREL of friends is the opportunity of their foes. / The greater your TROUBLES, the greater is your opportunity to show yourself a man. / WEAK men wait for opportunities; strong men make them. / A WISE man will make more opportunity than he finds.

opposite Opposites attract each other. *Var.:* Opposites attract. *Rec. dist.:* Miss., N.J., Ohio. *1st cit.:* 1930 Cox, *Vane Mystery;* US1918 Watson and Rees, *Mystery of the Downs.* **20c. coll.:** Whiting*(MP)* 464.

opposition 1. Don't be afraid of opposition. *Rec. dist.:* Ont.

2. Opposition is the life of trade. *Rec. dist.:* Ont.

oppression Oppression will make a wise man mad. *Rec. dist.:* Mich. *1st cit.:* 1616 Breton, *Crossing of Proverbs.* **20c. coll.:** ODEP 600, Stevenson 1726:1.

optimist The optimist's cup is half full; the pessimist's cup is half empty. *Rec. dist.:* Oreg.

optimistic *SEE* An optimistic ATTITUDE is half of success.

orange 1. Half an orange tastes as sweet as a whole one. *Rec. dist.:* Ill. *1st cit.:* US1938 Champion, *Racial Proverbs.* **20c. coll.:** Stevenson 236:1.

2. The orange that is squeezed too hard yields a bitter juice. *Rec. dist.:* Ill. *1st cit.:* 1732 Fuller, *Gnomologia.* **20c. coll.:** ODEP 600, Stevenson 1727:6.

orator 1. An orator without judgment is a horse without a bridle. *Rec. dist.:* N.Y., S.C.

2. He is a good orator who convinces himself. *Rec. dist.:* Wis. *1st cit.:* 1707 Mapletoft, *Select Proverbs.* **20c. coll.:** ODEP 323, Stevenson 1727:8.

SEE ALSO Be not your TONGUE your own shame's orator.

order *(command)* 1. Be humble and obey; you will be giving orders someday. *Var.:* If you obey orders, you can give them. *Rec. dist.:* Kans. *1st cit.:* 1574 Guazzo, *Civile Conversation,* tr. Pettie, T.T. (1925); US1734 Franklin, *PRAlmanac.* **20c. coll.:** Stevenson 382:3, Whiting 320, T&W 78, Whiting*(MP)* 459.

2. Orders are orders. *Rec. dist.:* Mich., N.Y. *Infm.:* Orders must not be challenged. *1st cit.:*

US1930 Levinrew, *Murder on the Palisades.* **20c. coll.:** Whiting*(MP)* 465.

order *(tidiness)* 1. Order and method render things easy. *Rec. dist.:* Mich., N.Y., S.C.

2. Order is a lovely thing. *Rec. dist.:* N.Y., S.C. *1st cit.:* USca1910 Branch, *Monk in Kitchen.* **20c. coll.:** Stevenson 1729:1.

3. Order is heaven's first law. *Rec. dist.:* Ill., Ont.

4. Order makes for peace. *Rec. dist.:* Ont.

SEE ALSO First determine whether your own BACKYARD is in order.

orderly *SEE* In an orderly HOUSE all things are always ready.

organ As the organ, so the tone. *Rec. dist.:* Ont.

organism Each organism knows best where it itches. *Rec. dist.:* N.Y.

originate *SEE* It is easy to REPEAT, but hard to originate.

orphan *SEE* Late CHILDREN, early orphans.

other *(pn.)* 1. A man is not deceived by others, he deceives himself. *Rec. dist.:* Ont. *1st cit.:* 1693 Congreve, *Old Batchelour;* US1738 Franklin, *PRAlmanac.* **20c. coll.:** Stevenson 534:9.

2. All that you say about others, say not to them. *Rec. dist.:* Ont.

3. Be sure that there are others worse off than yourself. *Rec. dist.:* Ont.

4. Don't talk about others, for they may be able to talk about you. *Rec. dist.:* Colo., Ohio.

5. If we can tell others what to do, we should know what to do ourselves. *Rec. dist.:* Ind.

6. Think of others before you think of yourself. *Rec. dist.:* Okla.

SEE ALSO He who ABUSES others must not be peeved by the actions of others. / BE that which you would make others. / BELITTLE others and be little. / If you wish to see the BEST of others, show the best of yourself. / When we lift the BURDENS of others, we are developing strength to bear our own. / Do not take CREDIT that is due to others. / If you CURSE others, you will be cursed. / Some DAYS are darker than others. / We are never more DISCONTENTED with others than when we are discontented with ourselves. / Do unto others as you would have them do unto you. / A neglected DUTY returns tomorrow with seven others at its back. / When you are not at EASE with others, others are not at ease with you. / EAT to please yourself, but dress to please others. / EXPERIENCE is a dear school, but fools learn in no other. / In seeking FAME and profit, depend only on yourself, and not others. / Find FAULT in yourself before finding faults in others. / By others' FAULTS wise men correct their own. / Go hide the FAULTS of others and God will veil your own. / People should cure their own FAULTS before finding faults in others. / He has sorry FOOD who feeds on the faults of others. / A FOOL laughs when others laugh. / Build not up a FORTUNE on the labor of others. / Those who betray their FRIENDS must not expect others to keep faith with them. / The GOOD you do to others will always come back to you. / Most of our HAPPINESS in this world consists in possessing what others can't get. / HELP others as they help you. / Three HELPING each other is as good as six. / Better to bear the ILLS we have than fly to others we know not of. / INJURE others, injure yourself. / Don't JUDGE others by yourself. / Be KIND in all you do and say, that others may be kind to you. / If you have KNOWLEDGE, you should let others light their candles by it. / LIARS begin by imposing on others, but end by deceiving themselves. / LOOK out for others, and God will look out for you. / OPPOSITES attract each other. / The best PLAN is to profit by the folly of others. / The proud hate PRIDE in others. / Don't expect others to keep a SECRET you cannot keep yourself. / Never TRUST a man who doesn't trust others. / He is not WELL-BRED that cannot bear the ill-breeding in others. / If you WILL, others will let you. / Learn WISDOM by the follies of others. / Who laughs at others, WOES finds.

other *(adj.)* SEE Other men's FAILURES can never save you. / The GRASS is always greener on the other side of the fence. / He that can't bear with other people's PASSIONS, cannot

govern his own. / One half the WORLD does not know how the other half lives.

ought SEE Do what you ought, come what may.

ounce He that will steal an ounce will steal a pound. *Rec. dist.:* Ont.

SEE ALSO An ounce of CARE is worth a pound of cure. / A pound of CURE will not pay an ounce of debt. / An ounce of HELP is worth a pound of pity. / In a thousand pounds of LAW there is not one ounce of love. / An ounce of PREVENTION is worth a pound of cure. / An ounce of WISDOM is worth a pound of wit. / An ounce of WIT that is bought is worth a pound that is taught.

ourselves We are born not for ourselves alone. *Var.:* We are not made for ourselves alone. *Rec. dist.:* N.Y. *1st cit.:* ca1525 Barclay, *Mirror of Good Manners. 20c. coll.:* ODEP 75.

SEE ALSO CHANCE contrives better than we ourselves. / No one can DISGRACE us but ourselves. / We cannot do EVIL to others without doing it to ourselves. / We shall never gather HAPPINESS if we try to retain it for ourselves. / If we can tell OTHERS what to do, we should know what to do ourselves.

out There are more out than in. *Rec. dist.:* N.Y.

SEE ALSO You can't get BLOOD out of a turnip. / You can take a BOY out of the country, but you can't take the country out of the boy. / Out of DEBT, out of danger. / You can run into DEBT but you have to crawl out. / A man may be DOWN, but not out. / What the EBB takes out, the flood brings in. / You can take the FARMER out of the country, but you can't take the country out of the farmer. / A FIRE is never out until the last spark is extinguished. / The GAME's not over until the last man strikes out. / You can take the GIRL out of the country, but you can't take the country out of the girl. / A HASTY man is seldom out of trouble. / Nearest the HEART comes first out. / Be sure a LIE will find you out. / You get out of LIFE what you put into it. / MARCH is in like a lion, out like a lamb. / MURDER will out. / NATURE will out. / The PLEASURE of doing good is the only one that will not wear out. / If you put nothing in your PURSE, you can take nothing out. / When the RUM is in, the wit is out. / Out of SIGHT, out of mind. / Out of TIME, out of mind. / Better a TOOTH out than always aching. / It's easier to stay out than to get out of TROUBLE. / The best way to get out of TROUBLE is not to get in it. / The TRUTH will out. / When WINE is in, wit is out.

outbid Be not too hasty to outbid others. *Rec. dist.:* Ont. *1st cit.:* 1664 Codrington, *Select Proverbs.* *20c. coll.:* ODEP 357.

outcome *See* Much OUTCRY, little outcome.

outcry Much outcry, little outcome. *Rec. dist.:* Ont.

outlook When the outlook isn't good, try the uplook. *Var.:* If the outlook is not good, try the uplook. *Rec. dist.:* Ill., Ont.

output *See* INCOME is measured by output.

outside 1. I'd rather be on the outside looking in than on the inside a-looking out. *Var.:* You can be on the outside looking in or on the inside cashing in. *Rec. dist.:* N.Y., S.C. *1st cit.:* US1906 Synder, Song Title. *20c. coll.:* Stevenson 1534:7.

2. There's more room outside than inside. *Rec. dist.:* Ont.

See also If you are INSIDE, you can't be outside. / Those KNOCKING are always on the outside. / Outside SHOW is poor substitute for inner worth. / Don't be VOGUE on the outside and vague on the inside.

outsider The outsider sees the most of the game. *Rec. dist.:* Ill.

outward *(adj.)* *See* The outward FORMS the inward man reveal—we guess the pulp before we cut the peel.

outward *(adv.)* *See* There's no ELBOW that bends outward.

outwit *See* CUNNING often outwits itself.

oven *See* Because KITTENS may be born in an oven, that does not make them loaves of bread.

over *See* If you can't GO over or under, go through. / WATER will be water the world

over. / When a WOMAN throws a man over, he usually lands on his knees to another woman.

overcoat *See* There is no good ARGUING with the inevitable; the only argument available with the east wind is to put on your overcoat.

overcome He who overcomes others is strong; he who overcomes himself is mightier still. *Rec. dist.:* Ill.

See also Who overcomes by FORCE has overcome but half his foe.

overcoming *See* The greater the OBSTACLE, the more glory in overcoming it.

overcurious The overcurious are not overwise. *Rec. dist.:* Iowa.

overdone Overdone is worse than underdone. *Rec. dist.:* Ont.

overdose *See* An overdose of HILARITY does no one any good.

overestimate *See* Do not let your VANITY make you overestimate your powers.

overfeeding More die of overfeeding than underfeeding. *Rec. dist.:* Ont.

overfill *See* You can't overfill fortune's SACKS.

overhear *See* What you HEAR never sounds half so important as what you overhear.

overload *See* Don't overload GRATITUDE: if you do, she'll kick.

overreach *See* A CUNNING man overreaches no one so much as himself.

oversee *See* Not to oversee WORKMEN is to leave them with your purse open.

oversleeping Oversleeping will never make your dreams come true. *Rec. dist.:* Colo.

overthrow *See* An unhappy man's CART is easy to overthrow. / The best CART may overthrow.

overwork *(n.)* *See* No WORK is worse than overwork.

overwork *(v.)* *See* Don't overwork a willing HORSE.

owe **1.** A man who doesn't owe anything is pretty well off, even if he hasn't got anything. *Rec. dist.:* N.Dak.

2. Owe no man anything. *Rec. dist.:* Ind. *1st cit.:* US1948 Stevenson, *Home Book of Proverbs.* *20c. coll.:* Stevenson 531:11.

SEE ALSO PAY what you owe.

owing Sleep without owing and wake without owing. *Rec. dist.:* N.Y., Ont., S.C.

owl **1.** The owl of ignorance lays the egg of pride. *Rec. dist.:* Ill.

2. The owl thinks all her young ones beauties. *Rec. dist.:* Ill. *1st cit.:* 1576 Fulwell, *Ars Adulanti.* *20c. coll.:* ODEP 604, Stevenson 1732:6.

3. You can't stay up with the midnight owl and expect to get up with the barnyard fowl. *Rec. dist.:* Ont.

own *(pn.)* SEE Mind no BUSINESS but your own. / The DEVIL protects his own. / Before you flare up at anyone's FAULTS, take time to count ten of your own. / Forgive everyman's FAULTS except your own. / We tax our FRIENDS with faults, but see not our own. / When your neighbor's HOUSE is on fire, beware of your own. / The LORD chastises his own. / The LORD never goes back on his own. / When ROGUES fall out, honest men come by their own.

own *(adj.)* SEE He who follows his own ADVICE must take the consequences. / Paddle your own CANOE. / Sweep in front of your own DOOR first. / Be not lenient to your own FAULTS. / Stand on your own two FEET. / A FOOL laughs at his own folly. / You can't beat a man at his own GAME. / Every man should cultivate his own GARDEN. / Always swing on your own GATE. / If you cook your own GOOSE you will have to eat it. / Toot your own HORN lest the same be never tooted. / Everyone to his own OPINIONS. / The PAINTER never paints his own house. / The PAPERHANGER never papers his own house. / The POT boils best on its own hearth. / Few RICH men own their own property—their property owns them. / Hoe your own ROW. / A SAINT has no

value in his own house. / Everyone to his own TASTE. / This above all: to your own self be TRUE. / Every TUB sits on its own bottom. / VIRTUE is its own reward. / One's own WILL is good food.

owner If the owner keeps his eye on the horse, it will fatten. *Rec. dist.:* N.Y., S.C. *1st cit.:* 1530 Whitford, *Werke for Householders;* US1686 Dunton, *Letters from New England* (1867). *20c. coll.:* ODEP 517, Whiting 284, Stevenson 1548:6, T&W 239.

SEE ALSO The OX knows his owner, and the ass his master's crib.

ox **1.** An ox is taken by the horns, and a man by the tongue. *Rec. dist.:* Wis. *1st cit.:* 1593 Eliot, *Ortho-Epia Gallica.* *20c. coll.:* ODEP 604, Stevenson 2612:9.

2. Don't muzzle the ox when he treads out the corn. *Vars.:* **(a)** Don't muzzle the ox that treads out the corn. **(b)** You shall not muzzle the ox when he treads out the corn. *Rec. dist.:* Ill. *1st cit.:* 1583 Babington, *Exposition of Commandments;* US1713 Chalkley, "Forcing" in *Works of Thomas Chalkley* (1766). *20c. coll.:* ODEP 552, Whiting 324, Stevenson 2612:9, Whiting(MP) 468.

3. It all depends on whose ox is gored. *Rec. dist.:* U.S. *1st cit.:* US1867 Richardson, *Beyond the Mississippi.* *20c. coll.:* T&W 273, Stevenson 291:3, Whiting(MP) 468.

4. It doesn't matter if the ox is blind; load the wagon and apply the line. *Rec. dist.:* Ala., Ga.

5. Take heed of an ox before, an ass behind, and a monk on all sides. *Rec. dist.:* Mich. *1st cit.:* 1640 Herbert, *Outlandish Proverbs (Jacula Prudentum)* in *Works,* ed. Hutchinson (1941). *20c. coll.:* ODEP 604, Stevenson 1911:11.

6. Tell an ox by his horns, but a man by his word. *Rec. dist.:* Ont. *1st cit.:* 1595 Fergusson, *Scottish Proverbs.* *20c. coll.:* Stevenson 2612:9.

7. The fat ox in the stall gives no thought to the hungry as they pass by. *Rec. dist.:* Ont.

8. The ox knows his owner, and the ass his master's crib. *Rec. dist.:* Calif. *1st cit.:* US1948 Stevenson, *Home Book of Proverbs.* *20c. coll.:* Stevenson 1734:1.

9. When the ox is down, many are the butchers. *Rec. dist.:* Calif., Colo. *1st cit.:* 1670 Ray, *English Proverbs.* *20c. coll.:* Stevenson 750:3.

10. When the ox is in the ditch, pull him out. *Rec. dist.:* Ky., Tenn.

11. Where no oxen are, the crib is clean. *Rec. dist.:* Minn.

SEE ALSO It makes a lot of difference whose BULL gores the ox. / The FINGERS of the housewife do more than a yoke of oxen. / It's better to be the beak of a HEN than the tail of an ox. / If LUCK is with you, even your ox will give birth to a calf. / He who greases his WHEELS, helps his oxen.

oyster He was a bold man who first ate an oyster. *Rec. dist.:* N.Y. *1st cit.:* 1655 Moffett, *Health's Improvement.* *20c. coll.:* ODEP 72, Stevenson 1735:10.

SEE ALSO While the KINGFISHER and the oyster are struggling the fisherman gets both.

P

pace 'Tis the pace that kills. *Rec. dist.:* Okla., Tex. *1st cit.:* 1850 Thackeray, *Pendennis;* US1855 Hammett, *Wonderful Adventures of Captain Priest. 20c. coll.:* ODEP 606, T&W 274, CODP 174, Stevenson 1736:9, Whiting(*MP*) 479.

SEE ALSO An early START and a steady pace make the slowest win the race.

pack *(n.)* SEE To carry CARE into your bed is to sleep with a pack on your back. / Every HORSE thinks his pack heaviest. / Let every PEDDLER carry his own pack. / Throw a STONE in a pack of dogs, and the one that's hit will holler.

pack *(v.)* SEE Many can pack CARDS that cannot play.

package You can't tell what's in a package by the cover. *Vars.:* **(a)** You can never tell a package by its wrapper. **(b)** You can never tell what's in a package by its cover. **(c)** You can't tell what's in a package by its wrapper. *Rec. dist.:* Ill.

SEE ALSO DIAMONDS come in small packages. / DYNAMITE comes in small packages.

packsaddle SEE An ASS covered with gold is more respected than a horse with a packsaddle.

packthread SEE A mad BULL is not to be tied up with a packthread.

paddle SEE Paddle your own CANOE.

padlock A bad padlock invites a picklock. *Var.:* A weak padlock invites a picklock. *Rec. dist.:* Ark., N.J., Ont. *1st cit.:* 1732 Fuller, *Gnomologia. 20c. coll.:* Stevenson 1725:4.

SEE ALSO WEDLOCK is a padlock.

pail The empty pail makes the most noise. *Rec. dist.:* Ont. *Infm.:* Cf. barrel, cask. *1st cit.:* ca1430 Lydgate, *Pilgrimage of Man,* E.E.T.S. (1891); US1676 *Complete Writings of Roger Williams* (1963). *20c. coll.:* CODP 64, Whiting 59, ODEP 220, Stevenson 676:17, T&W 391.

pain *(n.)* **1.** An hour of pain is as long as a day of pleasure. *Rec. dist.:* Ill. *1st cit.:* 1732 Fuller, *Gnomologia. 20c. coll.:* Stevenson 1738:12.

2. Even pain is not painful. *Rec. dist.:* Ont.

3. Great pain and a little gain make a man soon weary. *Rec. dist.:* Mich. *1st cit.:* ca1500 *Early English Carols,* ed. Greene; US1851 Melville, *Moby Dick* in *Works* (1922). *20c. coll.:* ODEP 334, T&W 274, Stevenson 924:6.

4. Great pains cause us to forget the small ones. *Rec. dist.:* Ill.

5. Is there anything men take more pains about than to make themselves unhappy? *Rec. dist.:* N.Y., S.C.

6. Long pains are light ones; cruel ones are brief. *Var.:* Great pains shortly spread their force, and long-continued pains are not severe. *Rec. dist.:* N.Y., S.C.

7. No pains, no gains; no sweat, no sweet. *Rec. dist.:* U.S., Can. *1st cit.:* 1577 Grange, *Golden Aphroditis;* US1745 Franklin, *PRAlmanac. 20c. coll.:* ODEP 572, Whiting 171, Stevenson 1739:10, T&W 149, Whiting(*MP*) 247.

8. Nothing brings more pain than too much pleasure. *Rec. dist.:* N.Y., S.C. *1st cit.:* US1738 Franklin, *PRAlmanac. 20c. coll.:* Stevenson 1739:4.

9. Nothing comes without pain except dirt and long nails. *Rec. dist.:* Miss. *1st cit.:* 1561 Becon, *Sick Man's Salve. 20c. coll.:* ODEP 581.

10. One pain kills another. *Rec. dist.:* Ont.

11. One's pain is lessened by another's anguish. *Rec. dist.:* Miss. *1st cit.:* 1594 Shakespeare, *Romeo and Juliet. 20c. coll.:* Stevenson 1042:8.

12. Pain is no evil unless it conquers us. *Rec. dist.:* U.S. *1st cit.:* ca1860 Kingsley, *St. Maura. 20c. coll.:* Stevenson 1738:1.

13. Pain past is pleasure. *Rec. dist.:* N.C., Ont. *1st cit.:* 1732 Fuller, *Gnomologia. 20c. coll.:* Stevenson 1738:9.

14. Pain wastes the body, pleasures the understanding. *Rec. dist.:* Ill. *1st cit.:* US1735 Franklin, *PRAlmanac.* *20c. coll.:* Stevenson 1738:11.

15. Pains are the wages of ill pleasures. *Rec. dist.:* Ill. *1st cit.:* 1732 Fuller, *Gnomologia.* *20c. coll.:* Stevenson 1739:2.

16. Pains to get, care to keep, and fear to lose is the best way to make an easy bed for old age. *Rec. dist.:* N.Y., S.C.

17. Save pains by taking pains. *Rec. dist.:* Ont.

18. Take pains or the pains will take you. *Rec. dist.:* Ont.

19. The honest man takes pains and then enjoys the pleasure; the knave takes pleasure and then suffers the pains. *Rec. dist.:* N.Y. *1st cit.:* US1755 Franklin, *PRAlmanac.* *20c. coll.:* Stevenson 1157:18.

20. There is no pain so great that time will not soften. *Rec. dist.:* Ill. *1st cit.:* ca1374 Chaucer, *Troilus and Criseyde.* *20c. coll.:* ODEP 824, Stevenson 2330:2.

See also A DOCTOR eases your pain; God cures it. / Hope of GAIN lessens pain. / There are no GAINS without pains. / If you do ILL, the joy fades, not the pains; if well, the pain does fade, the joy remains. / Gild a JOY and heal a pain. / The LUCKY one must yet learn pain. / He that preaches PATIENCE never knew pain. / PRIDE feels no pain. / The PROUD have all the pain—none of the pleasures of the vain. / SORROW for the husband is like a pain in the elbow—sharp and short.

pain *(v.)* What pains us trains us. *Rec. dist.:* Ala., Ga.

painful *See* Next to INGRATITUDE, the most painful thing to bear is gratitude. / The painful PREACHER, like a candle bright, consumes himself in giving others light.

paint *(n.)* A girl who's wearing paint has a better chance than one who ain't. *Rec. dist.:* Ill.

See also You can't judge a CAR by its paint job. / A good FACE needs no paint. / A little bit of POWDER and a little bit of paint makes a woman look like what she ain't. / The good-looking WOMAN needs no paint.

paint *(v.)* *See* HOPE paints her palace on the hilltop.

painter The painter never paints his own house. *Rec. dist.:* Ont.

painting Look at paintings and fish from a distance. *Rec. dist.:* Ill. *1st cit.:* 1640 Herbert, *Outlandish Proverbs (Jacula Prudentum)* in *Works,* ed. Hutchinson (1941); US1753 Franklin, *PRAlmanac.* *20c. coll.:* ODEP 607, Stevenson 592:1.

See also The BLIND man's wife needs no painting.

pair *See* Every COUPLE is not a pair. / Young COURAGE and old caution are a strong pair. / A pair of good EARS will drain dry a hundred tongues. / A willing HEART carries a weary pair of feet a long way. / One good pair of SOLES is better than two tops.

palace You cannot make a cheap palace. *Rec. dist.:* N.Y., S.C. *1st cit.:* US1857 Emerson, *Journals.* *20c. coll.:* Stevenson 327:5.

See also HOPE paints her palace on the hilltop. / A HUT is a palace to a poor man. / If the KING is in the palace, nobody looks at the walls. / If there is PEACE in your heart, your home is like a palace.

pale *See* The palest INK is better than the finest memory.

palm **1.** Let him who deserves the palm carry it. *Rec. dist.:* Ont. *1st cit.:* 1722 Jortin, *Lusus Poetici: Ad Ventos;* US1776 Tilghman, *Memoir of Lt. Col. Tilghman,* (1876). *20c. coll.:* Stevenson 1741:14, Whiting 325, T&W 275.

2. The palm is given to virtue. *Rec. dist.:* Mich.

pampering Pampering a child is like a bear's hug: it may crush it to death. *Rec. dist.:* Ill.

pan **1.** A thin pan gwine get hot quicker than a thick one, an' cold the same way. *Rec. dist.:* S.C.

2. A watched pan is long in boiling. *Rec. dist.:* Ark., Ohio. *1st cit.:* 1848 Gaskell, *Mary Barton;* US1933 Palmer, *Puzzle of the Pepper Tree.* *20c. coll.:* ODEP 869, Whiting(MP) 507, Stevenson 1839:6.

3. Don't leap from the frying pan into the

fire. *Vars.:* **(a)** Don't jump from the frying pan into the fire. **(b)** If you jump out of the frying pan, you'll jump on the stove. *Rec. dist.:* U.S., Can. *1st cit.:* 1528 More, *Dialogue Concerning Heresies;* US1681 *James Claypoole's Letter Book,* ed. Balderston (1967). *20c. coll.:* Stevenson 814:1, Whiting 170, *ODEP* 292, T&W 147, Whiting*(MP)* 244.

See also It does not take an ATHLETE to jump from the frying pan into the fire.

pants **1.** Got the same pants to get glad in as you had to get sad in. *Rec. dist.:* Utah.

2. Pants don't make the man. *Rec. dist.:* Calif., N.Y.

See also INSPIRATION for writing is mostly the application of the seat of pants to the seat of chair. / The TAILOR'S sons wear patched pants.

papa It's papa who pays. *Rec. dist.:* Ky., Tenn.

paper **1.** A man is known by the paper he pays for. *Rec. dist.:* N.Y., S.C. *1st cit.:* US1928 Shedd, *Salt from My Attic. 20c. coll.:* Stevenson 386:12.

2. Paper and ink and little justice. *Rec. dist.:* Calif.

3. Paper bleeds little. *Rec. dist.:* N.J., N.Y., S.C. *1st cit.:* US1940 Hemingway, *For Whom the Bell Tolls. 20c. coll.:* Stevenson 1743:4.

4. Paper does not blush. *Rec. dist.:* Ill., N.Y., S.C. *1st cit.:* 1577 Grange, *Golden Aphroditis. 20c. coll.:* Stevenson 1771:4.

5. Paper is patience: you can put anything on it. *Var.:* Paper is patient. *Rec. dist.:* Wis.

See also Write on one SIDE of the paper but on both sides of the subject. / A white WALL is the fool's writing paper: he writes his name there.

paperhanger The paperhanger never papers his own house. *Rec. dist.:* Ont.

paradise *See* HOME is the father's kingdom, the children's paradise, the mother's world. / It is better to sit with a WISE man in prison than with a fool in paradise.

parcel *See* The WRAPPING sells the parcel.

pardon *(n.)* Keep your pardon for others. *Rec. dist.:* Ont.

See also Those that have much BUSINESS must have much pardon.

pardon *(v.)* **1.** He who will not pardon others must not himself expect pardon. *Rec. dist.:* Ill.

2. Pardon others often, yourself seldom. *Var.:* Pardon all men but never yourself. *Rec. dist.:* U.S., Can. *1st cit.:* 1574 Guazzo, *Civile Conversation,* tr. Pettie, T.T. (1925). *20c. coll.:* Stevenson 1744:4.

3. They never pardon who have done the wrong. *Rec. dist.:* Ill. *1st cit.:* 1640 Herbert, *Outlandish Proverbs (Jacula Prudentum) in Works,* ed. Hutchinson (1941). *20c. coll.:* *ODEP* 586, Stevenson 1244:5.

See also The OFFENDER never pardons.

pardoning Pardoning the bad is injuring the good. *Rec. dist.:* Ill. *1st cit.:* 1732 Fuller, *Gnomologia. 20c. coll.:* *ODEP* 609, Stevenson 1744:9.

parent **1.** If the parents are good, the children follow in their footsteps. *Rec. dist.:* N.J. *1st cit.:* 1574 Guazzo, *Civile Conversation,* tr. Pettie, T.T. (1925). *20c. coll.:* Stevenson 336:6.

2. Parents are God's most gifted ministers. *Rec. dist.:* Ind.

3. Parents are patterns. *Rec. dist.:* N.J.

4. The art of being a parent consists of sleeping when the baby isn't looking. *Rec. dist.:* N.Y., S.C.

See also ACCIDENT is commonly the parent of dishonor. / ADVERSITY is the parent of virtue. / FATE gives you parents; choice gives us friends. / INDUSTRY is the parent of success.

Paris Paris was not built in a day. *Rec. dist.:* N.Y.

See also Good AMERICANS, when they die, go to Paris.

parish A mad parish must have a mad priest. *Rec. dist.:* Ill. *1st cit.:* 1642 Torriano, *Select Italian Proverbs. 20c. coll.:* *ODEP* 498.

parley *See* VIRTUE which parleys is near a surrender.

parliament *See* IDLENESS and pride tax with a heavier hand than kings and parliaments.

parlor All that is said in the parlor should not be heard in the hall. *Rec. dist.:* Mich. *1st* *cit.:* 1721 Kelly, *Scottish Proverbs.* **20c. coll.:** *ODEP* 692, Stevenson 1315:4.

SEE ALSO A PIG in the parlor is still a pig.

parrot The parrot has fine feathers, but he doesn't go to the dance. *Rec. dist.:* N.Y., S.C.

parson Never spare the parson's wine nor the baker's pudding. *Rec. dist.:* N.Y., S.C. *1st cit.:* US1733 Franklin, *PRAlmanac.* **20c. coll.:** Whiting 327, Stevenson 1746:4.

part *(n.)* **1.** It is easy to take a man's part, but the matter is to maintain it. *Rec. dist.:* Mich.

2. One part to sow, and part to eat, and part to pay the lord with. *Rec. dist.:* Ont.

3. The hardest part of the job is the beginning. *Rec. dist.:* Oreg. *1st cit.:* 1537 Whitford, *Work for Householders.* **20c. coll.:** Stevenson 152:2.

SEE ALSO DISCRETION is the better part of valor. / A real man is he whose GOODNESS is a part of himself. / HONOR and shame from no condition rise. Act well your part; there all the honor lies. / Carry your part of the LOAD.

part *(v.)* SEE A FOOL and his money are soon parted. / He's no FOOL who parts with what he cannot keep to get what he shall not lose. / The best of FRIENDS must part. / MERRY meet, merry part. / Never part with the OLD until you are sure the new is better.

parting Parting is such sweet sorrow. *Rec. dist.:* U.S., Can. *1st cit.:* 1594 Shakespeare, *Romeo and Juliet.* **20c. coll.:** Stevenson 1747:5.

SEE ALSO LIFE is just one parting after another.

partridge **1.** If you breed a partridge, you'll get a partridge. *Rec. dist.:* N.Y., S.C.

2. The partridge loves peas, but not those that go into the pot with it. *Rec. dist.:* Ill.

SEE ALSO An INDIAN, a partridge, and a spruce tree can't be tamed.

party **1.** Always leave the party when you are still having a good time. *Rec. dist.:* Okla.

2. There isn't much to talk about at some parties until after one or two couples leave. *Rec. dist.:* Miss.

SEE ALSO FOOLS give parties; sensible people go to them. / All free GOVERNMENTS are party governments. / IGNORANCE leads men into a party, and shame keeps them from getting out again. / True PATRIOTISM is of no party.

pass *(n.)* SEE BOYS seldom make passes for girls who wear glasses.

pass *(v.)* This, too, will pass. *Var.:* Solemn words and these are they: Even this shall pass away. *Rec. dist.:* U.S., Can. *1st cit.:* 1852 FitzGerald, *Polonius;* US1951 McCloy, *Through a Glass Darkly.* **20c. coll.:** Stevenson 1709:13, Whiting(MP) 475.

SEE ALSO If the BERMUDAS let you pass, you must beware of Hatteras. / No DAY passes without some grief. / He who cannot FORGIVE others breaks the bridge over which he must pass himself. / A FORTUNE never passes the second generation. / Any GOOD that we do should be done now, for we pass this way but once. / The MILL cannot grind with the water that is past. / NATURE passes nurture. / The fat OX in the stall gives no thought to the hungry as they pass by. / A THIEF passes for a gentleman when stealing has made him rich. / The WORLD turns aside to let any man pass who knows whither he is going.

passion **1.** A man in passion rides a mad horse. *Vars.:* **(a)** A man in passion rides a horse that runs away with him. **(b)** A man in passion rides a wild horse. *Rec. dist.:* N.Y., S.C. *1st cit.:* 1732 Fuller, *Gnomologia;* US1749 Franklin, *PRAlmanac.* **20c. coll.:** Stevenson 1748:6.

2. All the passions are extinguished with old age; self-love never dies. *Rec. dist.:* Ind. *1st cit.:* US1948 Stevenson, *Home Book of Proverbs.* **20c. coll.:** Stevenson 40:7.

3. Control your passion or it will control you. *Vars.:* **(a)** Govern your passions; or they will govern you. **(b)** Govern your passions; otherwise they will govern you. **(c)** He is a governor that governs his passions, and he is a servant that serves them. *Rec. dist.:* Colo., N.J., N.Y., S.C. *1st cit.:* 1831 Hone, *Year-Book.* **20c. coll.:** Stevenson 1749:7.

4. He that can't bear with other people's passions cannot govern his own. *Rec. dist.:* N.Y., S.C. *1st cit.:* US1747 Franklin, *PRAlmanac.* *20c. coll.:* Stevenson 1749:7.

5. He that overcomes his passions overcomes his greatest enemies. *Rec. dist.:* Ill.

6. He that shows a passion tells his enemy where he may hit him. *Rec. dist.:* Mich., Wis.

7. If passion drives, let reason hold the reins. *Rec. dist.:* N.Y., Ohio, S.C. *1st cit.:* US1749 Franklin, *PRAlmanac.* *20c. coll.:* Stevenson 1749:7.

8. No man can guess in cold blood what he may do in a passion. *Rec. dist.:* Ill. *1st cit.:* 1855 Bohn, *Handbook of Proverbs.* *20c. coll.:* Stevenson 1749:2.

9. Passion is ever the enemy of truth. *Rec. dist.:* Mich.

10. Passion is like an unruly horse, and prudence its blind driver. *Rec. dist.:* Mich.

11. Passions spin the plot. *Rec. dist.:* N.Y., S.C. *1st cit.:* US1933 Fisher, *Passion Spins the Plot.* *20c. coll.:* Stevenson 1749:13.

12. Set bounds to your passion by reason. *Rec. dist.:* Mich.

13. The end of passion is the beginning of repentance. *Rec. dist.:* N.Y., S.C. *1st cit.:* 1623 Feltham, *Resolves;* US1749 Franklin, *PRAlmanac.* *20c. coll.:* ODEP 221, Stevenson 1749:6.

14. The passions are like fire and water: good servants but bad masters. *Rec. dist.:* Ill. *1st cit.:* US1948 Stevenson, *Home Book of Proverbs.* *20c. coll.:* Stevenson 1749:12.

15. The worst passions have their root in the best. *Rec. dist.:* N.Y., S.C. *1st cit.:* US1837 Thoreau, *Autumn.* *20c. coll.:* Stevenson 1750:5.

16. When passion enters in at the foregate, wisdom goes out at the postern. *Rec. dist.:* Ill. *1st cit.:* 1732 Fuller, *Gnomologia.* *20c. coll.:* Stevenson 1749:4.

17. Where passion is high, there reason is low. *Rec. dist.:* Ill.

18. You can't ration passion. *Rec. dist.:* Ill.

See also ABSENCE cools moderate passions but inflames violent ones. / Never confuse ASTHMA with passion. / None can be free who is a SLAVE to his passions.

past *(n.)* 1. Many people will forget the past for a present. *Rec. dist.:* N.Dak.

2. May the best of your past be the worst of your future. *Rec. dist.:* Ont.

3. Our past has gone into history. *Rec. dist.:* N.Y., S.C. *1st cit.:* US1901 McKinley, Speech, Memphis, 30 Apr. *20c. coll.:* Stevenson 1751:9.

4. Study the past if you would divine the future. *Rec. dist.:* Ont., Oreg. *1st cit.:* 1640 Herbert, *Outlandish Proverbs (Jacula Prudentum)* in *Works,* ed. Hutchinson (1941); US1775 Henry, Speech in Virginia House of Delegates, 23 Mar. *20c. coll.:* Stevenson 1751:17.

5. The past always looks better than it was; it's only pleasant because it isn't here. *Rec. dist.:* N.Y., S.C. *1st cit.:* US1898 Dunne, *Family Union.* *20c. coll.:* Stevenson 1751:1.

6. The past at least is secure. *Rec. dist.:* N.Y., S.C. *1st cit.:* US1830 Webster, speech U.S. Senate, 26 Jan. *20c. coll.:* Stevenson 1751:9.

7. While you glory in the past, be busy in the present lest you be caught unprepared in the future. *Rec. dist.:* Miss.

See also Planning your FUTURE saves you from regretting your past. / You can never plan the FUTURE by the past. / A man's best REPUTATION for his future is his record of the past. / A YOUNG man looks into the future as an old man into his past.

past *(adj.)* *See* The RIVER past, and God forgotten.

past *(prep.)* *See* Past SHAME, past grace.

pasture 1. Change of pasture makes fat calves. *Rec. dist.:* Colo. *1st cit.:* 1542 Bullinger, *Christian State of Matrimony,* tr. Coverdale. *20c. coll.:* ODEP 114, Stevenson 314:4.

2. Good pastures make fat sheep. *Rec. dist.:* Ont.

3. The other man's pasture always looks the greenest. *Vars.:* (a) Distant pastures always look greener. (b) Faraway pastures look green. (c) Grass is greener in other pastures. (d) The greenest pasture is just over the fence. (e) The next pasture is always the greenest. (f) The other side of the pasture is always greener. *Rec. dist.:* U.S., Can. *1st cit.:* US1936 Kenny, *This Is Murder.* *20c. coll.:* Whiting(MP) 475.

SEE ALSO BREED is stronger than pasture. / GRASS never grows in a goose pasture.

pat A pat on the back will build character if applied low enough, hard enough, and often enough. *Rec. dist.:* Colo.

patch *(n., cloth)* **1.** A patch is better than a hole. *Var.:* A homely patch is better than a hole. *Rec. dist.:* Ont. *1st cit.:* 1605 Camden, *Remains.* *20c. coll.:* Stevenson 368:1.

2. A patch is the sign of thrift, a hole the sign of negligence. *Rec. dist.:* Ont.

3. A patch on your coat and money in your pocket is better and more creditable than a writ on your back and no money to take it off. *Rec. dist.:* N.Y., S.C. *1st cit.:* US1756 Franklin, *PRAlmanac.* *20c. coll.:* Stevenson 368:8.

4. Better have a patch on your back than a rip on your back. *Rec. dist.:* Ohio.

5. Don't put new patches on old garments. *Var.:* Never sew a patch on an old garmet. *Rec. dist.:* Miss., Ont.

6. Every man has one black patch, and some have two. *Rec. dist.:* Ont.

7. One patch is comely, but patch upon patch is beggarly. *Vars.:* **(a)** Patch beside patch is neighborly; patch upon patch is beggarly. **(b)** Patch by patch is good husbandry, but patch upon patch is beggarly. **(c)** Patch by patch is neighborly; patch on top of patch is beggarly. *Rec. dist.:* U.S., Can. *1st cit.:* 1639 Berkeley MS 1885; US1840 Dana, *Two Years Before the Mast* (1911). *20c. coll.:* ODEP 612, T&W 276, Stevenson 1752:9.

8. Patches are honorable. *Rec. dist.:* Ont.

9. The best patch is of the same cloth. *Rec. dist.:* Ill. *1st cit.:* 1732 Fuller, *Gnomologia.* *20c. coll.:* Stevenson 368:1.

SEE ALSO Worn-out GARMENTS have the newest patches. / The HOLE and the patch should be commensurate.

patch *(n., land)* *SEE* Don't care lost his corn patch.

patch *(v.)* *SEE* Patch GRIEF with proverbs.

patched *SEE* The TAILOR's sons wear patched pants. / Better WHOLE than patched with gold.

path **1.** A beaten path is a safe one. *Var.:* The beaten path is the best. *Rec. dist.:* N.J., Okla.

2. A trodden path bears no grass. *Rec. dist.:* Ont. *1st cit.:* 1659 Howell, *Paroimiografia;* US1769 Woodmason, *Carolina Backcountry on Eve of Revolution: Journal of Charles Woodmason,* ed. Hooker (1953). *20c. coll.:* ODEP 331, Whiting 186, Stevenson 1753:9.

3. Every path has a puddle. *Var.:* Every path has its puddle. *Rec. dist.:* U.S., Can. *1st cit.:* 1640 Herbert, *Outlandish Proverbs (Jacula Prudentum)* in *Works,* ed. Hutchinson (1941). *20c. coll.:* ODEP 612, Stevenson 1753:11.

4. Every path leads two ways. *Rec. dist.:* Ont.

5. On an unknown path every foot is slow. *Rec. dist.:* Miss.

6. Stay on the straight and narrow path. *Vars.:* **(a)** Follow the straight and narrow path. **(b)** Keep the straight and narrow path. **(c)** Keep to the straight and narrow path. **(d)** Walk the straight and narrow path. *Rec. dist.:* U.S., Can. *1st cite:* 1943 Strange, *Look Your Last.* *20c. coll.:* Stevenson 1753:8.

7. The longer the path, the sweeter the way home. *Rec. dist.:* Ind.

8. The middle path is safest. *Var.:* The middle path is the safe path. *Rec. dist.:* Mich., N.Dak. *1st cit.:* US1948 Stevenson, *Home Book of Proverbs.* *20c. coll.:* Stevenson 1604:4.

9. You can't follow two paths. *Rec. dist.:* Ont.

SEE ALSO The paths of GLORY lead but to death. / Let not the GRASS grow on the path of friendship. / Build a better MOUSETRAP and the world will beat a path to your door. / Do not walk in the MUD when there is a dry path. / You must visit your NEIGHBORS lest an unused path becomes weedy.

pathway *SEE* There is no pathway of FLOWERS leading to glory.

patience **1.** A moment's patience is a ten-years' comfort. *Rec. dist.:* Ill.

2. A poor man without patience is like a lamp without oil. *Rec. dist.:* Ill.

3. All commend patience, but none can endure to suffer. *Rec. dist.:* Ill. *1st cit.:* US1948 Stevenson, *Home Book of Proverbs.* *20c. coll.:* Stevenson 1757:12.

4. Have patience with a friend rather than lose him forever. *Rec. dist.:* Ill.

5. He that can have patience can have what he will. *Rec. dist.:* N.Y., N.C., S.C. *1st cit.:* US1736 Franklin, *PRAlmanac. 20c. coll.:* Whiting 328, Stevenson 1755:5.

6. He that preaches patience never knew pain. *Rec. dist.:* N.Y.

7. One learns patience by suffering. *Rec. dist.:* S.C.

8. Only those who have the patience to do simple things perfectly will acquire the skill to do difficult things easily. *Rec. dist.:* Utah.

9. Patience conquers. *Rec. dist.:* Colo. *1st cit.:* ca1377 Langland, *Piers Plowman. 20c. coll.:* Stevenson 1756:5.

10. Patience cures many an old complaint. *Rec. dist.:* Ill., N.Y., S.C.

11. Patience devours the devil. *Rec. dist.:* Ill.

12. Patience in market is worth pounds in a year. *Rec. dist.:* N.Y., S.C. *1st cit.:* US1753 Franklin, *PRAlmanac. 20c. coll.:* Stevenson 1755:5.

13. Patience is a flower that grows not in every garden. *Rec. dist.:* Ill. *1st cit.:* 1616 Draxe, *Bibliotheca Scholastica* in *Anglia* (1918); US1869 Spurgeon, *John Ploughman's Talks. 20c. coll.:* ODEP 612, Stevenson 1755:6.

14. Patience is a plaster for all sores. *Rec. dist.:* Ill., N.Dak., Ont. *1st cit.:* ca1390 Gower, *Confessio Amantis. 20c. coll.:* ODEP 612, Stevenson 1755:2.

15. Patience is a remedy for every sorrow. *Vars.:* **(a)** Patience is a remedy for every disease. **(b)** Patience is a remedy for every trouble. **(c)** Patience is the best remedy for every trouble. *Rec. dist.:* Ala., Ga., Ill., N.Y., S.C. *1st cit.:* ca1536 Erasmus, *Dicta Sapientum. 20c. coll.:* ODEP 612, Stevenson 1756:11.

16. Patience is a virtue. *Vars.:* **(a)** Patience is a virtue; catch it if you can: seldom in a woman and never in a man. **(b)** Patience is a virtue few possess. **(c)** Patience is a virtue which few possess—some have a little, others have less. **(d)** Patience is the best virtue. *Rec. dist.:* U.S., Can. *1st cit.:* ca1377 Langland, *Piers Plowman;*

US1724 *Works of Thomas Chalkley* (1766). *20c. coll.:* ODEP 613, Whiting 328, CODP 174, Stevenson 1754:2, T&W 276, Whiting(MP) 476.

17. Patience is bitter, but its fruit is sweet. *Var.:* Patience is a tree whose root is bitter, but its fruit is very sweet. *Rec. dist.:* Ont. *1st cit.:* US1948 Stevenson, *Home Book of Proverbs. 20c. coll.:* Stevenson 1757:5.

18. Patience is the better part of valor. *Rec. dist.:* Ky., Tenn.

19. Patience is the key of paradise. *Rec. dist.:* Ill. *1st cit.:* US1938 Champion, *Racial Proverbs. 20c. coll.:* Stevenson 1755:3.

20. Patience is the mother of virtue. *Rec. dist.:* Ont.

21. Patience is the wisest recipe for success. *Rec. dist.:* Ont.

22. Patience surpasses knowledge. *Rec. dist.:* U.S., Can.

23. Patience under old injuries invites new ones. *Rec. dist.:* Mich. *1st cit.:* 1616 Adams, *Divine Herbal. 20c. coll.:* ODEP 613.

24. Patience wears out stones. *Var.:* Patience pierces the rock. *Rec. dist.:* Ill., Ont.

25. Patience, time, and money overcome everything. *Rec. dist.:* Ill. *1st cit.:* 1640 Herbert, *Outlandish Proverbs (Jacula Prudentum)* in *Works,* ed. Hutchinson (1941). *20c. coll.:* ODEP 613.

26. Poor are they who have not patience. *Var.:* How poor they are not to have patience. *Rec. dist.:* N.Y., Ont. *1st cit.:* 1605 Shakespeare, *Othello. 20c. coll.:* Stevenson 1757:6.

27. They that have patience may accomplish anything. *Rec. dist.:* Utah.

SEE ALSO Where FORCE fails, skill and patience will prevail. / PAPER is patience: you can put anything on it. / The REMEDY for hard times is to have patience. / TIME and patience change the mulberry leaf to satin. / TRIBULATION works patience.

patient *(n.)* **1.** A good doctor treats both the patient and the disease. *Rec. dist.:* N.Y., S.C.

2. An intemperate patient makes a cruel doctor. *Rec. dist.:* Mich. *1st cit.:* 1539 Publilius

Syrus, *Sententiae*, tr. Taverner. *20c. coll.:* Stevenson 596:10.

SEE ALSO DOCTORS make the worst patients. / NURSES make the worst patients.

patient *(adj.)* He that is patient finds his foe at his feet. *Rec. dist.:* Ind.

SEE ALSO Beware the ANGER of a patient man. / Beware the FURY of a patient man. / Many patient SHEEP will enter one stall. / Beware of the WRATH of a patient man.

patriot 1. A mahogany patriot is a critter that rides like a beggar a-horseback. *Rec. dist.:* N.Y., N.C., S.C.

2. A mahogany patriot is a false patriot. *Rec. dist.:* N.Y., N.C., S.C. *Infm.:* A term from the time of the American Revolution.

patriotism 1. Patriotism is the last refuge of a scoundrel. *Rec. dist.:* N.J. *1st cit.:* 1775 *Apophthegms of Johnson* in Boswell, *Life of Johnson. 20c. coll.:* Stevenson 1757:16.

2. Patriotism knows neither latitude nor longitude; it is not climatic. *Rec. dist.:* N.Y., S.C. *1st cit.:* US1888 Storrs, *Political Oratory. 20c. coll.:* Stevenson 1758:3.

3. True patriotism is of no party. *Rec. dist.:* N.J. *1st cit.:* 1762 Smollett, *Adventures of Sir Launcelot Greaves. 20c. coll.:* Stevenson 1758:3.

patronage Without patronage art is like a windmill without wind. *Rec. dist.:* Ill.

SEE ALSO The GREAT are often selfish in their patronage of those who help them.

pattern SEE PARENTS are patterns.

Paul SEE Rob PETER to pay Paul.

pauper SEE A young DRUNKARD, an old pauper.

pause At a great pennyworth, pause a while. *Rec. dist.:* N.Y., S.C. *Infm.:* Cf. bargain. *1st cit.:* 1640 Herbert, *Outlandish Proverbs (Jacula Prudentum)* in *Works,* ed. Hutchinson (1941); US1739 Franklin, *PRAlmanac. 20c. coll.:* ODEP 317, Whiting 333, Stevenson 121:13.

paw SEE POSSUM's tail good as a paw.

pay *(n.)* SEE THANKS is poor pay on which to keep a family.

pay *(v.)* 1. Don't pay for a dead horse. *Rec. dist.:* N.Y., S.C. *1st cit.:* 1638 Brome, *Anti-*

podes in *Works* (1873); US1732 Byrd, *Progress to the Mines. 20c. coll.:* ODEP 916, Whiting 224, Stevenson 1174:1, T&W 192, Whiting(MP) 325.

2. Don't pay for a dead man's shoes. *Rec. dist.:* Calif., N.Y. *1st cit.:* 1530 Palsgrave, *Lesclarcissement de la langue Francoyse,* ed. Genin (1852); US1714 Winthrop in *Winthrop Papers,* Mass.Hist.Soc. *Collections* (1863–92). *20c. coll.:* ODEP 171, Whiting 281, Stevenson 2096:2, T&W 234, Whiting(MP) 402.

3. He that pays aforehand has never his work well done. *Var.:* He that pays for work before it's done, has but a pennyworth for two pence. *Rec. dist.:* N.Y., S.C. *1st cit.:* 1591 Florio, *Second Fruites,* ed. Simonini (1953); US1786 *Writings of George Washington,* ed. Fitzpatrick (1931–44). *20c. coll.:* ODEP 614, Whiting 329, Stevenson 1762:1, Whiting(MP) 476.

4. It is better to pay and have a little left than to have much and be always in debt. *Rec. dist.:* Wis. *1st cit.:* 1642 Torriano, *Select Italian Proverbs. 20c. coll.:* ODEP 56.

5. Pay as you go. *Var.:* Pay as you go and nothing you'll owe. *Rec. dist.:* Ill., Mich., Ont., Utah. *1st cit.:* 1855 Bohn, *Handbook of Proverbs;* US1851 Polly, *Peablossom's Wedding,* ed. Burke. *20c. coll.:* Stevenson 1761:7, T&W 277.

6. Pay what you owe. *Vars.:* (a) Pay what you owe and what you're worth you'll know. (b) Pay what you owe and you'll know what you own. *Rec. dist.:* Calif., Ill., N.Y., Ont., S.C. *1st cit.:* 1706 Stevens, *New Spanish and English Dictionary;* US1739 Franklin, *PRAlmanac. 20c. coll.:* ODEP 615, Stevenson 529:4.

7. Soon paid is well paid. *Rec. dist.:* Ill.

SEE ALSO It pays to ADVERTISE. / ADVICE that ain't paid for ain't no good. / A BARGAIN is usually worth no more than you pay for it. / Better to pay the BUTCHER than the doctor. / COURTESY pays compound interest. / CRIME doesn't pay. / If you want to DANCE, you must pay the fiddler. / Pay your DEBTS or lose your friends. / Folks who never DO any more than they get paid for never get paid for any more than they do. / Some pay their DUES when due, some others when overdue, and some never do. / The EVILS you do two by two you pay for one by one. / You GET what you pay for. / Be slow to take a GIFT; most men give to be paid back. / Everything that is worth HAVING must be paid for. / It pays to be IGNORANT. / INDUSTRY pays debts, while despair increases them. / You pay for every LESSON you learn. / Every MAN must pay his Scot. / Rob PETER to pay Paul. / He who pays the PIPER may call the tune. / Pay the PIPER his due. / You have to pay the PRICE for being a good man. / They who borrow TROUBLE must pay a high rate of interest. / Don't pay too much for your WHISTLE. / WORK is work if you're paid to do it, an' it's pleasure if you pay to be allowed to do it. / WORRYING doesn't mend nor pay. / Every dissipation of YOUTH has to be paid for with a draft on old age.

payer SEE ADVISERS are not payers.

paymaster 1. A good paymaster is never in want of workmen. *Rec. dist.:* Ill.

2. A good paymaster needs no security. *Rec. dist.:* Calif. *1st cit.:* 1620 Cervantes, *Don Quixote,* tr. Shelton. *20c. coll.:* ODEP 323, Stevenson 1763:9.

3. Of a bad paymaster get what you can, though it be but a straw. *Rec. dist.:* Mich.

4. The good paymaster is lord of another man's purse. *Var.:* A good payer is master of another's purse. *Rec. dist.:* N.Y., S.C. *1st cit.:* 1640 Herbert, *Outlandish Proverbs (Jacula Prudentum)* in *Works,* ed. Hutchinson (1941); US1736 Franklin, *PRAlmanac. 20c. coll.:* ODEP 323, Whiting 329, Stevenson 1762:6.

payment SEE Wrong COUNT is no payment. / TITHING is simply payment of an honest debt. / Sweet's the WINE, but sour's the payment.

pea 1. Every pea helps to fill the sack. *Rec. dist.:* Miss.

2. It ain't far from peas to pudding, but it shore is a long way back. *Rec. dist.:* Ky., Tenn.

3. Too many peas spoil the soup. *Rec. dist.:* Ont.

peace 1. A bad peace is better than a good quarrel. *Rec. dist.:* Ont. *1st cit.:* 1545 Gardiner,

Letters, ed. Muller; US1748 *Wolcott Papers, 1750–1754,* Conn.Hist.Soc. *Collections* (1916). *20c. coll.:* ODEP 416, Whiting 329, Stevenson 2452:6.

2. A disarmed peace is weak. *Rec. dist.:* Ill. *1st cit.:* 1640 Herbert, *Outlandish Proverbs (Jacula Prudentum)* in *Works,* ed. Hutchinson (1941). *20c. coll.:* ODEP 189, Stevenson 1766:1.

3. A harvest of peace is produced from a seed of contentment. *Rec. dist.:* Ill.

4. Better keep peace than make peace. *Var.:* It is better to keep peace than to make peace. *Rec. dist.:* Ala., Ga., Ill., N.J.

5. He that would live at peace and rest must hear and see and say the best. *Rec. dist.:* N.Y., S.C. *1st cit.:* ca1450 *Proverbs of Good Counsel* in *Book of Precedence,* E.E.T.S. (1869); US1736 Franklin, *PRAlmanac. 20c. coll.:* ODEP 474, Whiting 329, Stevenson 1764:7.

6. If there is peace in your heart, your home is like a palace. *Rec. dist.:* Ont.

7. If you desire peace, be ever prepared for war. *Vars.:* (a) If you desire peace, prepare for war. (b) Prepare for war in time of peace. (c) We should provide in peace what we need in war. *Rec. dist.:* Colo., Ill., S.C., Utah. *1st cit.:* 1548 Hall, *Chronicle of Edward IV;* US1755 Grant in *Documents Relating to Indian Affairs* in *Colonial Records of South Carolina,* ed. McDowell (1958–70). *20c. coll.:* ODEP 616, Whiting 329, CODP 175, Stevenson 1873:1, Whiting(MP) 477.

8. No man can live at peace unless his neighbor lets him. *Rec. dist.:* Ill. *1st cit.:* 1639 Clarke, *Paroemiologia. 20c. coll.:* ODEP 20, Stevenson 1674:10.

9. Nothing can bring you peace but yourself. *Rec. dist.:* Minn., N.Y., N.Dak., S.C. *1st cit.:* US1841 Emerson, "Self Reliance" in *Essays. 20c. coll.:* Stevenson 1766:3.

10. Peace and honor are the sheaves of virtue's harvest. *Rec. dist.:* Mich.

11. Peace at any price. *Rec. dist.:* Okla. *1st cit.:* 1839 Clarendon, *History of Rebellion. 20c. coll.:* Stevenson 1765:1.

12. Peace feeds, war wastes; peace breeds, war consumes. *Rec. dist.:* Ill.

13. Peace flourishes when reason rules. *Rec. dist.:* Ill.

14. Peace has her victories no less renowned than war. *Rec. dist.:* Ill., N.Y., N.C., S.C. *1st cit.:* 1652 Milton, "To Lord General Cromwell" in *Sonnets. 20c. coll.:* Stevenson 2452:3.

15. Peace has won finer victories than war. *Rec. dist.:* Ont.

16. Peace is found only in the graveyard. *Rec. dist.:* Ont.

17. Peace is goodwill in action. *Rec. dist.:* Wash.

18. Peace rules the day when reason rules the mind. *Rec. dist.:* Colo. *1st cit.:* ca1759 Collins, *Hassan. 20c. coll.:* Stevenson 1765:7.

19. Peace with a cudgel in hand is war. *Rec. dist.:* Ill.

20. The garment of peace never fades. *Rec. dist.:* Ill.

21. The real and lasting victories are those of peace and not of war. *Rec. dist.:* N.Y. *1st cit.:* US1860 Emerson, "Worship" in *Conduct of Life. 20c. coll.:* Stevenson 2452:3.

22. The sheep who talks peace with a wolf will soon be mutton. *Rec. dist.:* Ill.

23. Who holds his peace and gathers stones will find a time to throw them. *Rec. dist.:* Ont. *1st cit.:* 1599 Minsheu, *Dictionarie in Spanish and English. 20c. coll.:* ODEP 377.

SEE ALSO He is HAPPIEST, be he peasant or king, who finds peace in his home. / HOPE and fear, peace and strife, make up the troubled web of life. / INVINCIBLE in peace and invisible in war. / ORDER makes for peace. / The tree of SILENCE bears the fruit of peace. / Whoever has a strong SWORD has peace. / Be at war with your VICES, at peace with your neighbors, and let every new-year find you a better man. / Hotter WAR, sooner peace. / The object of WAR is peace. / There never was a good WAR or a bad peace. / WAR is the law of violence, peace the law of love. / WEALTH and power do not give peace of mind. / A WISE man is one who keeps his peace. / WOMEN leave peace behind 'em when they go.

peacemaker SEE KINDNESS is a great peacemaker. / SILENCE is a great peacemaker.

peach **1.** Everything is not all peaches and cream. *Rec. dist.:* Wis.

2. The ripest peach hangs highest on the tree. *Var.:* The ripest peach is highest on the tree. *Rec. dist.:* Colo., N.Y., S.C., Wyo. *1st cit.:* US1892 Riley, *Ripest Peach. 20c. coll.:* Stevenson 1767:9.

3. There is nothing peachier than a peach. *Rec. dist.:* N.Y., S.C. *1st cit.:* US1935 Nash, *Ocean, Keep Right on Rolling. 20c. coll.:* Stevenson 1767:7.

SEE ALSO The ROSE has its thorn, the peach its worm.

pear **1.** Go to the pear tree for pears, not an elm. *Rec. dist.:* N.C. *1st cit.:* 1612 Cervantes, *Don Quixote,* tr. Shelton; US1807 *Port Folio* (1809). *20c. coll.:* ODEP 20, Whiting 330, Stevenson 1228:10, Whiting(MP) 478.

2. The man who plants pears is a-planting for his heirs. *Rec. dist.:* Mich., N.Y. *1st cit.:* 1640 Herbert, *Outlandish Proverbs (Jacula Prudentum)* in *Works,* ed. Hutchinson (1941). *20c. coll.:* CODP 240, ODEP 630, Stevenson 1768:3.

pearl **1.** A pearl is often hidden in an ugly shell. *Rec. dist.:* Miss. *1st cit.:* 1599 Shakespeare, *As You Like It. 20c. coll.:* Stevenson 1157:4.

2. Don't cast your pearls before swine. *Rec. dist.:* U.S., Can. *1st cit.:* 1340 *Ayenbite of Inwit,* E.E.T.S. (1866); US1640 Howe in *Winthrop Papers, 1498–1649,* Mass.Hist.Soc. *Collections* (1929–47). *20c. coll.:* ODEP 617, Whiting 330, CODP 176, Stevenson 1768:13, T&W 278, Whiting(MP) 478.

3. He who would search for pearls must dive below. *Rec. dist.:* Utah. *1st cit.:* 1678 Dryden, "Prologue" to *All For Love. 20c. coll.:* Stevenson 706:14.

4. Many a pearl is still hidden in its oyster. *Rec. dist.:* Calif.

5. String your pearls on a strong cord. *Var.:* String all your pearls on a strong cord. *Rec. dist.:* Ill.

SEE ALSO Choose not FRIENDS by outward show, for feathers float while pearls lie low. / Every GRAIN is not a pearl.

pebble **1.** A pebble and a diamond are alike to a blind man. *Rec. dist.:* N.Y. *1st cit.:* 1732 Fuller, *Gnomologia. 20c. coll.:* Stevenson 198:2.

2. One loose pebble can start a landslide. *Rec. dist.*: Ill.

3. There are more pebbles on the beach than one. *Vars.*: **(a)** Don't think you are the only pebble on the beach. **(b)** You're not the only pebble on the beach. *Rec. dist.*: U.S. *1st cit.*: 1896 Braistead, *You're Not the Only Pebble on Beach;* US1924 Van Vechten, *Tattooed Countess.* *20c. coll.*: Stevenson 1769:5, Whiting*(MP)* 478.

SEE ALSO Better a DIAMOND with a flaw than a pebble. / There's a FISH in every sea and a pebble on every beach.

peck *(n.)* The blind man's peck should be well measured. *Rec. dist.*: N.Y. *1st cit.*: 1832 Henderson, *Scottish Proverbs.* *20c. coll.*: ODEP 618, Stevenson 198:4.

SEE ALSO We must all eat a peck of DIRT before we die. / Eat a peck of SALT with a man before you trust him.

peck *(v.)* *SEE* When a man's COAT is threadbare, it is easy to peck a hole in it. / The RAVENS don't peck one another's eyes out.

pedantry Pedantry is a vice in all professions. *Rec. dist.*: Mich.

peddler Let every peddler carry his own pack. *Rec. dist.*: Ont., Tex. *1st cit.*: 1611 Cotgrave, *Dictionary of French and English Tongues.* *20c. coll.*: ODEP 618, Stevenson 1236:1.

pedestal Many have lived on a pedestal who will never have a statue when dead. *Rec. dist.*: Utah.

pedigree **1.** Pedigree won't sell a lame horse. *Rec. dist.*: Ont.

2. Seek not a good man's pedigree. *Rec. dist.*: Mich. *1st cit.*: 1732 Fuller, *Gnomologia.* *20c. coll.*: Stevenson 63:10.

SEE ALSO HONOR is of an old immaculate pedigree.

peek A peek in the hand is worth three finesses. *Var.*: A peek in the hand is worth two finesses. *Rec. dist.*: Fla., Mich.

peel *SEE* Little TATERS is hard to peel.

peg **1.** A peg is driven out by a peg, a nail by a nail. *Rec. dist.*: Ill. *1st cit.*: ca1200 *Ancrene Riwle,* ed. Morton. *20c. coll.*: ODEP 597, CODP 170, Stevenson 1648:8.

2. You can't put a round peg in a square hole. *Vars.*: **(a)** You can't drive a square peg into a round hole. **(b)** You can't put square pegs in round holes. *Rec. dist.*: U.S., Can. *1st cit.*: 1804 Sydney Smith, Lecture in *Sketches of Moral Philosophy;.* US1897 Twain, *Following Equator.* *20c. coll.*: ODEP 685, Stevenson 1770:6, Whiting*(MP)* 479.

SEE ALSO All WORDS are pegs to hang ideas on.

pen *(enclosure)* Don't build the pen before the litter comes. *Rec. dist.*: Miss.

SEE ALSO PIGS dunno w'at a pen's fer.

pen *(writing)* **1.** The pen conveys one's meaning a thousand miles. *Rec. dist.*: Ind.

2. The pen is mightier than the sword. *Var.*: The pen is noisier than the sword. *Rec. dist.*: U.S., Can. *1st cit.*: 1571 Tigurinus, *Institution of Christian Prince;* US1938 Saltmarsh, *Clouded Moon.* *20c. coll.*: ODEP 618, Whiting*(MP)* 480, CODP 176, Stevenson 1771:9.

3. The pen is the tongue of the mind. *Vars.*: **(a)** The pen is the tongue of the hand. **(b)** The pen is the tongue of the soul. *Rec. dist.*: U.S. *1st cit.*: 1620 Cervantes, *Don Quixote,* tr. Shelton. *20c. coll.*: Stevenson 1771:1.

4. The pen of the tongue should be dipped in the ink of the heart. *Rec. dist.*: Mich.

SEE ALSO Of all cold WORDS of tongue or pen, the worst are these: I knew him when. / Of all the WORDS of tongue or pen, the saddest are these: it might have been.

pence **1.** Better short of pence than short of sense. *Rec. dist.*: Ont.

2. Take care of the pence and the pounds will take care of themselves. *Rec. dist.*: Ohio, Okla., Ont., Tex. *1st cit.*: 1750 Lord Chesterfield, Letter, 5 Feb., in *Letters to His Son;* US1820 Loomis, "Proverbs in Farmer's Almanac" in *Western Folklore* (1956). *20c. coll.*: ODEP 798, T&W 279, CODP 176, Stevenson 1772:4, Whiting*(MP)* 481.

pencil Don't write before your pencil is sharpened. *Rec. dist.*: Ont.

penny **1.** A bad penny always comes back. *Vars.*: **(a)** A bad penny always returns. **(b)** A bad penny always turns up. *Rec. dist.*: U.S., Can. *1st cit.*: 1824 Scott, *Redgauntlet;* US1766

A. Adams in *Adams Family Correspondence,* ed. Butterfield (1963). *20c. coll.:* ODEP 26, Whiting 332, Stevenson 1773:10, T&W 280, Whiting*(MP)* 481.

2. A hard-earned penny is a well-earned penny. *Rec. dist.:* N.Y.

3. A penny in the hand is worth two in the pot. *Rec. dist.:* Ky., Tenn.

4. A penny saved is a penny earned. *Vars.:* (a) A penny saved is a penny earned; a penny spent is a penny ruined. (b) A penny saved is a penny made. (c) A penny saved is as good as twopence earned. (d) He who saves a penny earns a penny. (e) Penny saved, a penny made. *Rec. dist.:* U.S., Can. *1st cit.:* 1640 Herbert, *Outlandish Proverbs (Jacula Prudentum)* in *Works,* ed. Hutchinson (1941); US1699 College oration in *William & Mary Coll. Quart.* *20c. coll.:* ODEP 619, Whiting 332, CODP 176, Stevenson 1772:8, T&W 279, Whiting*(MP)* 482.

5. A penny today is worth two tomorrow. *Rec. dist.:* Colo.

6. A single penny fairly got is worth a thousand that are not. *Rec. dist.:* Calif.

7. An honest penny is worth a stolen dollar. *Rec. dist.:* Colo.

8. Count your pennies and the dollars. *Rec. dist.:* N.Y.

9. In for a penny, in for a pound. *Rec. dist.:* U.S. *Infm.:* Put everything you've got into any endeavor. *1st cit.:* 1695 Ravenscroft, *Canterbury Guests;* US1785 *Writings of George Washington,* ed. Fitzpatrick (1931–44). *20c. coll.:* ODEP 402, Whiting 332, CODP 120, Stevenson 1773:6, T&W 280 Whiting*(MP)* 481.

10. One cannot have a good penny with bad wares. *Rec. dist.:* Ont.

11. One penny is better than none. *Rec. dist.:* Ont.

12. Pennies make dollars. *Rec. dist.:* Ky., Miss., Tenn.

13. Penny and penny laid up will be many. *Rec. dist.:* N.C., Tex. *1st cit.:* 1591 Stepney, *Spanish Schoolmaster.* *20c. coll.:* ODEP 619, Stevenson 1772:4.

14. Penny goes after penny till Peter hasn't any. *Rec. dist.:* Ont.

15. Penny-wise, pound-foolish. *Var.:* Don't be penny-wise and dollar-foolish. *Rec. dist.:* U.S., Can. *1st cit.:* 1621 Burton, *Anatomy of Melancholy;* US1747 Franklin, *PRAlmanac.* *20c. coll.:* Stevenson 1771:15, Whiting 332, ODEP 620, CODP 177, T&W 280, Whiting*(MP)* 482.

16. Save your pennies for a rainy day. *Rec. dist.:* Wis.

17. Take care of your pennies and the dollars will take care of themselves. *Vars.:* (a) Count your pennies and the dollars will take care of themselves. (b) Look after the pennies and the pounds will take care of themselves. (c) Save the pennies and they make the dimes and the dollars take care of themselves. (d) Save the pennies—the dollars will take care of themselves. (e) Save your pennies and the dollars will take care of themselves. (f) Take care of the nickels and the dollars will take care of themselves. (g) Take care of the pence and the pounds will take care of themselves. *Rec. dist.:* U.S., Can. *1st cit.:* 1750 Lord Chesterfield, Letter, 5 Feb., in *Letters to Son;* US1820 Loomis, "Proverbs in Farmer's Almanac" in *Western Folklore* (1956). *20c. coll.:* ODEP 798, T&W 279, CODP 176, Stevenson 1772:4, Whiting*(MP)* 481.

18. 'Tis a well-spent penny that saves a groat. *Var.:* That penny's well spent that saves a groat. *Rec. dist.:* N.Y., S.C., Tex. *1st cit.:* 1591 Davies of Hereford, *O Utinam;* US1749 Franklin, *PRAlmanac.* *20c. coll.:* ODEP 619, Whiting 333, Stevenson 1774:4.

19. Two pennies will creep together. *Var.:* Put two pennies in your purse and they'll creep together. *Rec. dist.:* Ill., Miss., N.Y. *1st cit.:* ca1595 Fergusson, *Scottish Proverbs.* *20c. coll.:* Stevenson 1615:2.

20. Who will not keep a penny shall never have many. *Var.:* Who will not keep a penny never shall have any. *Rec. dist.:* Ont. *1st cit.:* 1541 Bullinger, *Christian State of Matrimony,* tr. Coverdale. *20c. coll.:* ODEP 417, Stevenson 1772:6.

21. You can tell a bad penny by its ring. *Rec. dist.:* Ill.

SEE ALSO That which catches the EYE also catches the penny. / WIFE make your own candle, spare penny to handle.

pennyworth **1.** At a great pennyworth, pause a while. *Rec. dist.:* N.Y., S.C. *Infm.:* Cf. bargain. *1st cit.:* 1640Herbert, *Outlandish Proverbs (Jacula Prudentum)* in *Works,* ed. Hutchinson (1941); US1739 Franklin, *PRAlmanac. 20c. coll.:* ODEP 317, Whiting 333, Stevenson 121:13. **2.** Many have been ruined by buying good pennyworths. *Rec. dist.:* N.Y., S.C. *1st cit.:* 1732 Fuller, *Gnomologia;* US1747 Franklin, *PRAlmanac. 20c. coll.:* ODEP 317, Whiting 333, Stevenson 268:5.

people **1.** Always be nice to people on the way up the ladder 'cause you may meet them on the way down. *Rec. dist.:* N.Y.

2. As people think, so they are. *Rec. dist.:* Ont.

3. Beware of those people who list their possessions. *Rec. dist.:* Ill.

4. Blunt people come to the point quickly. *Rec. dist.:* N.J.

5. Changeable people are not easily satisfied. *Rec. dist.:* Ont., Utah.

6. Don't judge other people by yourself. *Rec. dist.:* Ont.

7. Few people can cuss and think at the same time. *Rec. dist.:* Ill.

8. Give some people everything you have and they still want the moon for a cow pasture. *Rec. dist.:* N.Mex., N.Y.

9. It is with narrow-souled people as with narrow-necked bottles: the less they have in them, the more noise they make in pouring out. *Rec. dist.:* N.Y., S.C.

10. It takes all kinds of people to make the world. *Rec. dist.:* Ind., Ky., Okla., Tenn. *1st cit.:* 1620 Cervantes, *Don Quixote,* tr. Shelton; US1855 Haliburton, *Nature and Human Nature. 20c. coll.:* ODEP 11, T&W 280, CODP 3.

11. Let the people rule. *Rec. dist.:* N.Y., S.C. *1st cit.:* US1829 Jackson, Slogan while president of the United States. *20c. coll.:* Stevenson 1775:8.

12. Many people will sell their souls for money. *Rec. dist.:* N.C.

13. Never trust people who pretend to be different from what they really are. *Rec. dist.:* Ont.

14. People are more easily led than driven. *Rec. dist.:* N.Y., S.C. *1st cit.:* 1928 Crofts, *Sea Mystery;* US1690 Saltonstall in *Winthrop Papers,* Mass.Hist.Soc. *Collections* (1863–92). *20c. coll.:* Whiting(MP) 365, Whiting 255.

15. People are not always feeling their pulse to see if they are happy. *Rec. dist.:* Miss.

16. People are not sorry for what they do wrong, but are sorry when they are caught. *Rec. dist.:* N.C.

17. People don't see things on their own doorsteps. *Rec. dist.:* N.C.

18. People in hell want ice water. *Rec. dist.:* Ind., Ky.

19. People take you at your own valuation. *Rec. dist.:* Ont.

20. People usually get at odds with each other when they try to get even. *Rec. dist.:* Ont.

21. People who advertise their troubles never seem to get rid of their stock. *Rec. dist.:* Ariz.

22. People who get to the top are not afraid of uphill work. *Rec. dist.:* Calif.

23. People who have nothing to do on earth ought to be in it. *Rec. dist.:* Minn.

24. People who know little talk much; people who know much talk little. *Rec. dist.:* Utah. *1st cit.:* 1659 Howell, *Paroimiografia;* US1875 Scarborough, *Chinese Proverbs. 20c. coll.:* ODEP 437, Stevenson 2279:4.

25. People who put off little things never put over big things. *Rec. dist.:* N.C.

26. People who work on holidays will always be poor. *Rec. dist.:* N.H.

27. People who wouldn't think of talking with their mouths full often speak with their heads empty. *Rec. dist.:* Ont.

28. People with wax heads shouldn't walk in the sun. *Rec. dist.:* N.Y., S.C. *1st cit.:* 1640

Herbert, *Outlandish Proverbs (Jacula Pruden-tum)* in *Works,* ed. Hutchinson (1941); US1749 Franklin, *PRAlmanac.* **20c. coll.:** *ODEP* 360, Whiting 203, Stevenson 1095:7.

29. Small people do small things. *Rec. dist.:* N.C. *Infm.:* Small means petty.

30. Small people get their exercise by jumping at conclusions. *Rec. dist.:* Miss., N.C.

31. Some people are born in the objective case. *Rec. dist.:* Miss.

32. Some people can't see beyond the tip of their nose. *Rec. dist.:* Ont. *1st cit.:* ca1594 Bacon, *Promus;* US1744 *Journal of William Black* in *Pa.Mag.Hist.* (1877). **20c. coll.:** *ODEP* 709, Whiting 232, Stevenson 1696:3, T&W 264, Whiting*(MP)* 452.

33. Some people don't have the sense of a bedbug. *Rec. dist.:* Miss.

34. Take people as you find them. *Rec. dist.:* Ont. *1st cit.:* 1548 Hall, *Chronicle of Lancastre and York.* **20c. coll.:** *ODEP* 799.

35. There are more people married now than are doing well. *Rec. dist.:* Ind.

36. There are three kinds of people: the wills, the won'ts, and the can'ts. *Rec. dist.:* N.C.

37. There are two kinds of people in the world: the kind who have the ideas and the kind who do something about them. *Rec. dist.:* Colo.

38. There are two kinds of people on earth today: the people who lift and the people who lean. *Rec. dist.:* N.Y., S.C. *1st cit.:* USca1890 Wilcox, *Lifting and Leaning.* **20c. coll.:** Stevenson 999:4.

39. Three types of people in the world: those who have wishbones, those who have funny bones, and those who have backbones. *Rec. dist.:* Miss.

40. Two people draw four, and four draw eight. *Rec. dist.:* N.Y.

41. You can fool some of the people all the time, all the people some of the time, but you can't fool all the people all the time, *Vars.:* **(a)** You can fool all of the people part of the time, and part of the people all the time, but you can't fool all the people all of the time. **(b)**

You can fool some of the people all the time, but you can't fool all the people some of the time. *Rec. dist.:* U.S., Can. *1st cit.:* US1856 Lincoln, Speech at Bloomington, Ill., 29 May. **20c. coll.:** Stevenson 534:1.

42. You can please some of the people all the time, or all the people some of the time, but never all of the people all of the time. *Rec. dist.:* Ala., Ga.

43. You have to winter and summer with people to know them. *Rec. dist.:* Ont. *1st cit.:* 1955 Coles, *Man in the Green Hat;* US1713 Wise, *Churches Quarrel Espoused,* ed. Cook (1966). **20c. coll.:** Whiting*(MP)* 690, Whiting 489, T&W 407.

44. You meet the strangest people in the strangest places. *Rec. dist.:* Ohio.

45. You're not the only people on the beach. *Rec. dist.:* Calif. *Infm.:* Cf. pebble.

SEE ALSO AMBITION is not the voice of little people. / If there were no BAD people, there would be no good lawyers. / People are willing to BELIEVE alarming things to keep from believing what they don't want to. / BLONDES aren't the only people who are light-headed. / FAT people are jolly people. / People count up the FAULTS of those who keep them waiting. / People should cure their own FAULTS before finding faults in others. / FOOLS give parties; sensible people go to them. / People who wear GLASSES shouldn't have too long a nose. / Some people are so GOOD that they are no good. / All GOVERNMENTS depend on the good will of the people. / LIFE is too short to fool with dishonest people. / LOCKS keep out only honest people. / It is worth a LOSS to find out what some people are. / The MAGISTRATE should obey the law; the people should obey the magistrate. / Like PRIEST, like people. / A READING people will be a knowing people. / Some people would rather be RIGHT than pleasant. / It's not the SKIRT that breaks people; it's the chiffon ruffles. / Some people have TACT; others tell the truth. / People who have TOOLS are able to make a great many things. / Where there is no VISION, the people perish. / The VOCATION of every man and woman is to serve people. / The VOICE of the people is the voice of God. / There are only two people who fix WATCHES: a fool and a watchmaker. / The world is full of WILLING people—some willing to work and the rest willing to let them. / The WORLD is what people make it.

percept Percepts without concepts are blind. *Rec. dist.:* Wis.

perfect **1.** None of us are perfect. *Vars.:* **(a)** Don't make fun of others: we're not all perfect. **(b)** Not one is perfect. *Rec. dist.:* Ark. *1st cit.:* 1931 Hollingworth, *Death Leaves Us Naked;* US1929 Biggers, *Black Camel.* *20c. coll.:* Whiting*(MP)* 449.

2. Nothing is perfect. *Rec. dist.:* N.C.
SEE ALSO HAPPINESS is not perfect until it is shared. / PRACTICE makes perfect.

perfection *SEE* TRIFLES make perfection, but perfection is no trifle.

perform Perform whatever you promise. *Rec. dist.:* Mich. *1st cit.:* US1948 Stevenson, *Home Book of Proverbs.* *20c. coll.:* Stevenson 1897:14.
SEE ALSO It is one thing to PROMISE, another to perform.

performance An acre of performance is worth the whole world of promise. *Rec. dist.:* Miss., Wis. *1st cit.:* 1593 Harvey, *Pierce's Supererogation.* *20c. coll.:* ODEP 621, Stevenson 1897:13.
SEE ALSO Long on PROMISES, short on performance.

performer Performers are needed much more than reformers. *Rec. dist.:* Utah.

perfume *SEE* A BLONDE needs just enough perfume for you to know that she's around. / FLATTERY, like perfume, should be smelled, not swallowed. / HAPPINESS is a perfume that you cannot pour on others without spilling a little on yourself.

peril **1.** No one is bound to expose himself to peril. *Rec. dist.:* Mich.

2. The moment of peril is the moment for courage. *Rec. dist.:* W.Va.

perish *SEE* He that loves DANGER shall perish therein. / Better be POOR and live than rich and perish. / Where there is no VISION, the people perish.

perseverance **1.** Perseverance is failing nineteen times and succeeding the twentieth. *Rec. dist.:* Ont.

2. Perseverance is the keynote to success. *Var.:* Perseverance is the keynote to bring success. *Rec. dist.:* Ill.

3. Perserverance is the mother of invention. *Rec. dist.:* Calif.

4. Perseverance will accomplish all things. *Var.:* Perseverance conquers all things. *Rec. dist.:* Miss., N.Dak., Ont. *1st cit.:* 1732 Fuller, *Gnomologia;* US1865 Richardson, *Secret Service.* *20c. coll.:* Stevenson 434:12, T&W 281.

persevere To persevere is to win. *Rec. dist.:* Ont.

persimmon There was never a persimmon except there was a possum to eat it. *Rec. dist.:* Tex.
SEE ALSO The longest POLE gets the persimmon.

persistence Persistence will accomplish more than force. *Rec. dist.:* Ont.

person **1.** A churchgoing person is apt to be a law-abiding person. *Rec. dist.:* Ont.

2. A person is what he is under pressure. *Rec. dist.:* N.C.

3. A person who stoops to get even is rarely able to stand upright again. *Rec. dist.:* Ont. *1st cit.:* US1845 *Dictionary of Americanisms,* ed. Matthews (1951). *20c. coll.:* T&W 122.

4. Be kind to a person going up 'cause you will meet him coming down. *Rec. dist.:* Ohio.

5. If you want to know what a person is, have a business deal with him. *Rec. dist.:* N.Dak.

6. Many a person thinks he is hard-boiled when he is only half-baked. *Rec. dist.:* N.Dak.

7. You can tell a lot about a person by the way he walks. *Rec. dist.:* N.C.
SEE ALSO An AMATEUR is a person who plays a game for the fun of it. / An AMBITIOUS person is always dangerous. / A DIPLOMAT is a person who can tell you to the devil so pleasantly that you are raring to go. / The HAPPIEST person is the person who thinks the most interesting thoughts. / You may HATE

the things a person does, but never hate the person. / A NEIGHBOR is a person who knows more about your business than you do. / Few persons know how to be OLD. / A PET person and a pet pig are the worst pets of all. / A RICH person ought to have a strong stomach.

perspiration SEE GENIUS is one percent inspiration and ninety-nine percent perspiration.

persuade Would you persuade, speak of interest, not of reason. *Rec. dist.:* N.Y., S.C. *1st cit.:* US1734 Franklin, *PRAlmanac.* *20c. coll.:* Stevenson 1781:13.

persuasion Persuasion is better than force. *Vars.:* **(a)** Gentle persuasion is better than force. **(b)** Gentle persuasion often succeeds where force fails. **(c)** Take by persuasion, not by force. *Rec. dist.:* Calif. *1st cit.:* 1869 Henderson, *Latin Proverbs.* *20c. coll.:* Stevenson 1781:15.

persuasive SEE Some people think that the louder they SHOUT, the more persuasive their argument is.

pessimist A pessimist is a person who has lived with an optimist. *Rec. dist.:* Calif., Ill.

pest SEE The unbidden GUEST is always a pest.

pester It pays to pester. *Rec. dist.:* Nebr.

pet A pet person and a pet pig are the worst pets of all. *Rec. dist.:* Miss.

Peter Rob Peter to pay Paul. *Rec. dist.:* U.S., Can. *1st cit.:* ca1380 Wyclif, *Select English Works;* US1657 *Thomas Hutchinson Papers,* Publ. Prince Soc. (1865, reprint 1967). *20c. coll.:* ODEP 680, Whiting 333, Stevenson 1783:8, T&W 281, Whiting(MP) 485.

petticoat SEE For when LADIES wear the breeches, their petticoats ought to be long enough to hide 'em.

petty SEE A GENTLEMAN is broad and fair, the vulgar are biased and petty. / Good MANNERS are made up of petty sacrifices.

philosopher **1.** Many talk like philosophers and live like fools. *Rec. dist.:* Ill., Ont. *1st cit.:* 1855 Bohn, *Handbook of Proverbs.* *20c. coll.:* Stevenson 2540:2.

2. One true philosopher is worth a thousand linguists. *Rec. dist.:* Mich.

SEE ALSO All men are FOOLS, but the wisest of fools are called philosophers.

philosophy Philosophy means being able to explain why you are happy when you are poor. *Rec. dist.:* Minn.

phone SEE It isn't a HOME without a phone.

physic SEE TEMPERANCE is the best physic.

physician **1.** A physician is a man who pours drugs of which he knows little into a body of which he knows less. *Rec. dist.:* Wis. *1st cit.:* 1847 Helps, *Friends in Council.* *20c. coll.:* Stevenson 598:2.

2. A physician of anger is reason. *Rec. dist.:* Minn.

3. A young physician should have three graveyards. *Rec. dist.:* Ill.

4. From the physician and the lawyer keep not the truth hidden. *Rec. dist.:* Wis. *1st cit.:* 1573 Sanford, *Garden of Pleasure;* US1737 Franklin, *PRAlmanac.* *20c. coll.:* ODEP 371, Whiting 114, Stevenson 593:10.

5. He's the best physician that knows the worthlessness of most medicines. *Rec. dist.:* N.Y. *1st cit.:* US1733 Franklin, *PRAlmanac.* *20c. coll.:* Stevenson 598:2.

6. Physician, heal thyself. *Rec. dist.:* N.J., Ont. *1st cit.:* ca1412 Hoccleve, *De Regimine Principum;* US1703 Taylor, *Christographia,* ed. Grabo (1962). *20c. coll.:* ODEP 622, Whiting 334, *CODP* 177, Stevenson 599:4, Whiting(MP) 486.

7. Physicians kill more than they cure. *Rec. dist.:* N.Y., S.C. *1st cit.:* 1621 Burton, *Anatomy of Melancholy.* *20c. coll.:* ODEP 622, Stevenson 599:9.

8. The best physicians are Dr. Diet, Dr. Quiet, and Dr. Merryman. *Rec. dist.:* Ill., N.Y., S.C. *1st cit.:* 1558 Bulleyn, *Government of Health;* US1761 Ames, *Almanacs,* ed. Briggs (1891). *20c. coll.:* ODEP 622, Whiting 114, *CODP* 56, Stevenson 598:5, Whiting(MP) 172.

9. The physician is an angel when employed and a devil when he demands. *Rec. dist.:* Ill.

1st cit.: 1820 Scott, *Abbot.* **20c. coll.:** ODEP 622.

10. When you call the physician, call the lawyer to make your will. *Rec. dist.:* Ill.

11. Who has a physician has an executioner. *Rec. dist.:* N.Y.

SEE ALSO May HOPE be the physician when calamity is the disease. / Old WIVES and children make fools of physicians.

pick **1.** Always pick on someone your own size. *Rec. dist.:* Mich., N.Y., Ont.

2. It will never get well if you pick it. *Rec. dist.:* Ill., N.J. *1st cit.:* US1933 Mencken, "What Is Going on in the World" in *American Mercury,* Nov. **20c. coll.:** Stevenson 1789:2.

3. Pick where you scratch. *Rec. dist.:* Ohio.

SEE ALSO HAPPINESS grows at our own firesides and is not to be picked in strangers' gardens. / You can't pick up spilled MILK. / Don't go through the WOODS and pick up a crooked stick.

picking **1.** One at a time is good picking. *Rec. dist.:* Ont.

2. Pickin' up is better than totin', but puttin' down beats the world. *Rec. dist.:* Ala., Ga.

pickle SEE HUNGER is the best pickle.

picture **1.** A beautiful picture is a silent teacher. *Rec. dist.:* Colo., Vt.

2. A picture is a poem without words. *Rec. dist.:* Mich. *1st cit.:* US1948 Stevenson, *Home Book of Proverbs.* **20c. coll.:** Stevenson 1789:14.

3. Every picture has a negative. *Rec. dist.:* Calif., Colo.

4. One picture is worth ten thousand words. *Var.:* A picture is worth a thousand words. *Rec. dist.:* Calif., Colo., N.Y., Ont., Utah. *1st cit.:* US1921 *Printers' Ink,* 8 Dec. **20c. coll.:** CODP 177, Stevenson 2611:3.

5. Screening a picture doesn't take the trash out. *Rec. dist.:* Ont.

SEE ALSO A man's ACTIONS are motion pictures of his beliefs. / A great ARTIST can paint a great picture on a small canvas. / LIFE is a picture, so paint it well. / Mean SOULS, like mean pictures, are often found in good-looking frames.

pie **1.** A good pie wants no bread. *Rec. dist.:* Mich.

2. Apple pie without cheese is like a kiss without a squeeze. *Var.:* Apple pie without cream is like sleep without a dream. *Rec. dist.:* U.S., Can. *1st cit.:* ca1750 Old English rhyme. **20c. coll.:** Stevenson 331:8.

3. Don't eat your pies before they are made. *Rec. dist.:* Ill.

4. Every pie has its own piecrust. *Rec. dist.:* Calif., N.Y.

5. It's poor pie that doesn't grease its own tin. *Rec. dist.:* Calif.

6. You made your pie; now eat it. *Rec. dist.:* Colo.

SEE ALSO Give a bit of your CAKE to one who is going to eat pie. / Too many FINGERS spoil the pie. / PROMISES are like piecrust: they are made to be broken.

piece Save the pieces to pay the rent. *Rec. dist.:* N.Y., Ont., S.C.

SEE ALSO By a small SAMPLE we may judge the whole piece.

piety **1.** Hypocritical piety is double iniquity. *Rec. dist.:* Mich.

2. True piety elevates the spirit, ennobles the heart, and strengthens the courage. *Rec. dist.:* Ill.

pig **1.** A pig in the parlor is still a pig. *Var.:* Put a pig in the parlor and he is still a pig. *Rec. dist.:* N.Y., S.C. *1st cit.:* US1964 Swann, *Brass Key.* **20c. coll.:** Stevenson 1790:14, Whiting(MP) 488.

2. A pig used to dirt turns up its nose at rice boiled in milk. *Rec. dist.:* N.Y., S.C. *1st cit.:* US1948 Stevenson, *Home Book of Proverbs.* **20c. coll.:** Stevenson 1790:14.

3. De pig dat runs off wid de year er corn gits little mo' dan de cob. *Rec. dist.:* N.Y., S.C.

4. Don't buy a pig in a poke. *Rec. dist.:* U.S. *1st cit.:* ca1300 *Proverbs of Hending,* ed. Schleichin *Anglia* (1927); US1732 *South Carolina Gazette* in *William & Mary. Coll. Quart.* **20c. coll.:** ODEP 95, Whiting 335, Stevenson 1791:10, T&W 284, Whiting(MP) 489.

5. Even a blind pig occasionally picks up an acorn. *Rec. dist.:* Colo., Ill., Ky.

6. Feed a pig and you'll have a hog. *Rec. dist.:* Okla., Tex. *1st cit.:* 1732 Fuller, *Gnomologia.* *20c. coll.:* Stevenson 1791:4.

7. Give to a pig when it grunts and a child when it cries, and you will have a fine pig and a bad child. *Rec. dist.:* Minn.

8. If a pig had wings he might fly. *Rec. dist.:* Ont. *1st cit.:* 1862 Hislop, *Proverbs of Scotland;* US1934 Vines, *Green Thicket World.* *20c. coll.:* ODEP 625, Whiting(MP) 489.

9. Never ring a pig that has to root for a living. *Rec. dist.:* N.Y., S.C. *1st cit.:* US1940 Thompson, *Body, Boots, and Britches.* *20c. coll.:* Stevenson 1793:4.

10. Pigs are pigs. *Var.:* Pigs is pigs. *Rec. dist.:* Colo., N.Y., S.C. *1st cit.:* 1822 Lamb, Letter to S.T. Coleridge, 9 Mar. *20c. coll.:* Stevenson 1792:2.

11. Pigs dunno w'at a pen's fer. *Rec. dist.:* N.Y., S.C.

12. Pigs grow fat where lambs would starve. *Rec. dist.:* Ont.

13. Runt pig is best hog in litter. *Rec. dist.:* N.Y., S.C.

14. The biggest pig eats the most. *Rec. dist.:* Ohio.

15. The leanest pigs squeal the most. *Rec. dist.:* Ont.

16. The pig dreams of acorns, and the goose of maize. *Rec. dist.:* Calif.

17. The pig furthest from the trough squeals loudest. *Rec. dist.:* Fla.

18. The still pig gets all the slop. *Var.:* It isn't the pig who squeals loudest that gets the swill. *Rec. dist.:* Calif. *1st cit.:* ca1225 *Trinity MS;* US1855 Haliburton, *Nature and Human Nature.* *20c. coll.:* ODEP 774, Stevenson 2176:4, T&W 284, Whiting(MP) 584.

19. The trouble is there are too many pigs for the teats. *Rec. dist.:* Okla. *1st cit.:* US1861 Lincoln, referring to rush of would-be office-holders to Washington after his inauguration. *20c. coll.:* Stevenson 1714:4.

20. Wash a pig, scent a pig; a pig still is a pig. *Rec. dist.:* Ont.

21. When you see a pig, you should kick it. *Rec. dist.:* P.E.I. *Infm.:* Some people should be treated like an unruly pig.

22. You can lead a pig to water, but you can't make him drink. *Rec. dist.:* Ont. *Infm.:* Cf. horse.

23. You can't fatten a pig on one ear of corn. *Rec. dist.:* Ky.

SEE ALSO You can't make a CIGAR out of a pig's tail. / Above all things keep CLEAN: it is not necessary to be a pig in order to raise one. / The FROST will bring the pig home. / Can't make a HOG without a pig to start with. / A PET person and a pet pig are the worst pets of all. / Don't RAIN eve'y time de pig squeal. / A barren SOW was never good to pigs. / The VOICE of a pig can't be disguised. / You can't make a WHISTLE out of a pig's tail.

pigskin Too much attention to the pigskin doesn't help the sheepskin. *Rec. dist.:* Mich., N.Y.

pile If you can't put anything on the pile, take nothing off. *Rec. dist.:* Ont.

SEE ALSO Where LOVE falls it lies, and even if it be on the manure pile.

pill **1.** Bitter pills may have blessed effects. *Rec. dist.:* Mich. *1st cit.:* ca1374 Chaucer, *Troilus and Criseyde;* US1630 *Winthrop Papers, 1498–1649,* Mass.Hist.Soc. *Collections* (1929–47). *20c. coll.:* ODEP 63, Whiting 337, Stevenson 1795:4.

2. Pills are to be swallowed, not chewed. *Rec. dist.:* Ohio, Ont. *1st cit.:* 1566 Painter, *Palace of Pleasure,* ed. Jacobs (1890). *20c. coll.:* Stevenson 1795:3.

SEE ALSO Every DOCTOR thinks his pills the best.

pillow SEE The dawn of ANTICIPATION forms a most soothing pillow for a restless head. / A clean CONSCIENCE is a good pillow.

pilot **1.** A pilot is not chosen for his riches but his knowledge. *Rec. dist.:* Ill.

2. Don't try to be the best pilot in the world, just the oldest. *Rec. dist.:* N.Mex.

3. Every man is a pilot in a calm sea. *Var.:* In a calm sea every man is a pilot. *Rec. dist.:* U.S., Can. *1st cit.:* ca1592 Greene, *James IV.* *20c. coll.:* ODEP 99, Stevenson 1795:13.

4. There are old pilots and there are bold pilots, but there are no old, bold pilots. *Rec. dist.:* Ill., N.J.

pin **1.** A pin a day is a groat a year. *Rec. dist.:* Mich. *1st cit.:* 1712 Addison, *Spectator;* US1737 Franklin, *PRAlmanac.* *20c. coll.:* ODEP 626, Whiting 338, Stevenson 1796:3.

2. Don't come to me for safety pins. *Rec. dist.:* Ont.

3. He that will not stoop for a pin will never be worth a pound. *Rec. dist.:* Calif. *1st cit.:* 1609 Harward, Unpublished manuscript in library of Trinity College, Cambridge. *20c. coll.:* ODEP 777, CODP 178, Stevenson 1796:7.

4. He that will steal a pin will steal a better thing. *Rec. dist.:* N.J., Tex. *1st cit.:* 1537 Whitford, *Werke for Householders.* *20c. coll.:* ODEP 772, Stevenson 1797:2.

5. If you begin with a common pin, you will end with a silver bowl. *Rec. dist.:* Calif.

6. See a pin, pick it up, all day you'll have good luck. *Rec. dist.:* U.S. *1st cit.:* 1659 Howell, *Paroimiografia;* US1965 Untermeyer, *Private Collection: Memoir.* *20c. coll.:* ODEP 626, Whiting(MP) 493.

7. 'Tis a sin to steal a pin as much as it is a potato. *Var.:* If he'll steal a pin, he'll steal a potato. *Rec. dist.:* Colo. *1st cit.:* 1875 Cheales, *Proverbial Folk-Lore;* US1956 Disney, *Unappointed Rounds.* *20c. coll.:* CODP 204, Whiting(MP) 568, Stevenson 2211:6.

8. Unreturned pins break friendship. *Rec. dist.:* Va.

SEE ALSO Folks that tend BABIES mustn't have pins about them. / We have HEADS on us for the same reason pins do—to keep us from going too far. / NEEDLES and pins: when a man marries his trouble begins.

pinch *(n.)* One pinch of salt sets the whole pot to boiling. *Rec. dist.:* N.Y.

SEE ALSO Never trust a FRIEND who deserts you in a pinch.

pinch *(v.)* *SEE* Everyone knows where his SHOE pinches. / The pretty SHOE often pinches the foot. / Wear my SHOES and you'll know where they pinch.

pinnacle A man on a pinnacle has no place to go but down. *Rec. dist.:* Ont.

pint A pint's a pound the world around. *Rec. dist.:* U.S., Can. *1st cit.:* US1792 *Diary of William Bentley* (1905–14). *20c. coll.:* Whiting 338.

pipe No longer pipe, no longer dance. *Rec. dist.:* N.Y. *1st cit.:* 1605 Camden, *Remains;* US1702 Mather, *Magnalia Christi Americana* (1853–55). *20c. coll.:* Stevenson 1799:1, Whiting 339, ODEP 569.

SEE ALSO He DANCES well to whom fortune pipes.

piper **1.** He who pays the piper may call the tune. *Vars.:* **(a)** He who calls the tune must pay the piper. **(b)** He who pays the piper calls the tune. *Rec. dist.:* U.S., Can. *1st cit.:* 1895 *London Daily News,* 18 Dec.; US1779 *Diary of Grace Galloway* in *Pa.Mag.Hist.* (1931). *20c. coll.:* ODEP 615, Whiting 339, CODP 175, Stevenson 1798:10, T&W 287, Whiting(MP) 495.

2. No piper can please all ears. *Rec. dist.:* Ill.

3. Pay the piper his due. *Var.:* You must pay the piper. *Rec. dist.:* Calif., Colo., N.Y. *1st cit.:* 1638 Taylor, *Taylor's Feast;* US1779 *Diary of Grace Galloway* in *Pa.Mag.Hist.* (1931). *20c. coll.:* ODEP 615, Whiting 339, Stevenson 1798:9, T&W 287, Whiting(MP) 495.

pippin *SEE* Plant the crab TREE where you will, it will never bear pippins.

pirate When the pirate promises masses and wax, the vessel is in a bad plight. *Rec. dist.:* Mich.

pit If you dig a pit for someone else, you fall into it yourself. *Var.:* Whoso digs a pit, he shall fall therein. *Rec. dist.:* Ont. *1st cit.:* 1509 Barclay, *Ship of Fools;* US1608 Wingfield, *Discourse* in *Transactions and Collections of American Antiquarian Society* (1860). *20c. coll.:* ODEP 187, Whiting 339, Stevenson 1799:10, Whiting(MP) 496.

pitch (n.) **1.** He who touches pitch will get black. *Vars.:* **(a)** He that handles pitch shall foul his fingers. **(b)** They that touch pitch will be defiled. **(c)** Touch pitch and you'll be defiled. **(d)** Whoso touches pitch, his hand is defiled. **(e)** You can't handle pitch without being defiled. **(f)** You can't touch pitch without being defiled. **(g)** You can't touch pitch without soiling the fingers. **(h)** You cannot handle pitch without blackening your fingers. *Rec. dist.:* U.S., Can. *1st cit.:* ca1303 Mannyng, *Handlyng Synne,* E.E.T.S. (1901); US1707 *Life and Writings of Francis Makemie,* ed. Schlenther (1971). *20c. coll.:* ODEP 834, Whiting 340, CODP 228, Stevenson 1799:12, T&W 287, Whiting(MP) 497.

2. If you throw enough pitch, some of it is sure to stick. *Rec. dist.:* N.Y., S.C. *1st cit.:* 1656 Trepan; US1703 *Correspondence Between William Penn and James Logan, 1700–1705,* ed. Armstrong, Hist.Soc.Penn. *Memoirs* (1870–72). *20c. coll.:* ODEP 189, Whiting 109, CODP 54, Stevenson 277:7, T&W 287.

pitch (v.) He who pitches too high will not get through his song. *Rec. dist.:* Ont.

pitcher **1.** A pitcher that goes to the well too often is liable to be broken. *Vars.:* **(a)** A pitcher that goes oft to the well is broken at last. **(b)** A pitcher that goes to the well too often is broken at last. **(c)** The pitcher can go to the well too often. **(d)** The pitcher may go once too often to the well. **(e)** The pitcher that goes often to the well comes home broken at last. **(f)** The pitcher that goes often to the well shall at last be broken. **(g)** The pitcher went once too often to the well. *Rec. dist.:* U.S., Can. *1st cit.:* 1340 *Ayenbite of Inwit,* E.E.T.S. (1866); USca1731 Cook, *History of Col. Nathaniel Bacon's Rebellion,* Am.Antiq.Soc. *Proceedings* (1934). *20c. coll.:* ODEP 628, Whiting 340, CODP 178, Stevenson 1801:1, T&W 288, Whiting(MP) 498.

2. Little pitchers have big ears. *Vars.:* **(a)** Little pitchers have great ears. **(b)** Little pitchers have long ears. **(c)** Pitchers have ears. **(d)** Small pitchers have wide ears. *Rec. dist.:* U.S. *1st cit.:* 1546 Heywood, *Dialogue of Proverbs,* ed. Habernicht (1963); US1943 Head, *Smell of Money.* *20c. coll.:* ODEP 471, Stevenson 1800:5, CODP 135, Whiting(MP) 498.

3. Little pitchers pour less. *Rec. dist.:* Ont.

See also Great TALKERS are like broken pitchers: everything runs out of them.

pity (n.) **1.** Don't waste pity on a scamp. *Rec. dist.:* Ariz.

2. It is as great a pity to see a woman weep as to see a goose go barefoot. *Rec. dist.:* Ont. *1st cit.:* ca1540 Bale, *Kynge Johan.* *20c. coll.:* ODEP 708, Stevenson 1010:2.

3. Pity and need make all flesh kin. *Rec. dist.:* Ill.

4. Pity is akin to love. *Rec. dist.:* U.S. *1st cit.:* 1601 Shakespeare, *Twelfth Night;* US1787 Humphreys in *American Museum.* *20c. coll.:* ODEP 628, Whiting 269, CODP 178, Stevenson 1801:9, Whiting(MP) 498.

5. Pity melts the mind to love. *Rec. dist.:* N.Y., S.C. *1st cit.:* 1697 Dryden, *Alexander's Feast.* *20c. coll.:* Stevenson 1801:9.

See also An ounce of HELP is worth a pound of pity.

pity (v.) *See* A BACHELOR is to be admired; a spinster is to be pitied. / Better be ENVIED than pitied. / He is my FRIEND that helps me and not he that pities me. / Tell not your WOES to him that doesn't pity you.

place **1.** A place for everything and everything in its place. *Vars.:* **(a)** Have a place for everything and everything in its place. **(b)** To everything its place: it saves time and many bad words. *Rec. dist.:* U.S., Can. *1st cit.:* 1640 Herbert, *Outlandish Proverbs (Jacula Prudentum)* in *Works,* ed. Hutchinson (1941); US1855 Haliburton, *Nature and Human Nature.* *20c. coll.:* ODEP 628, CODP 179, Stevenson 1803:6, T&W 288, Whiting(MP) 499.

2. Any old place I can hang my hat is home sweet home to me. *Var.:* Any place I hang my hat is home sweet home. *Rec. dist.:* N.Y., S.C. *1st cit.:* US1901 Title of a popular song by William Jerome. *20c. coll.:* Stevenson 1151:9.

3. Everything is good in its place. *Rec. dist.:* Ill.

4. Give place to your betters. *Rec. dist.:* Mich.

5. He who thinks his place is below him will certainly be below his place. *Rec. dist.:* Miss. *1st cit.:* 1902 Hulme, *Proverb Lore.* *20c. coll.:* Stevenson 1803:3.

6. High places have their precipices. *Rec. dist.:* Ill. *1st cit.:* 1732 Fuller, *Gnomologia.* *20c. coll.:* ODEP 372, Stevenson 1032:14.

7. If you leave your place, you lose it. *Rec. dist.:* Ont.

8. One cannot be in two places at once. *Var.:* You can't be in two places at the same time. *Rec. dist.:* U.S., Can. *1st cit.:* 1509 Barclay, *Ship of Fools;* US1961 Reilly, *Certain Sleep.* *20c. coll.:* ODEP 851, Whiting(MP) 499.

9. The higher the place, the harder the fall. *Rec. dist.:* Calif. *1st cit.:* ca1230 Hali Meidenhad; US1952 DuBois, *Cavalier's Corpse.* *20c. coll.:* ODEP 372, Whiting(MP) 307.

SEE ALSO The toughest BRONCS is always them you've rode some other place. / FOOLS' names and fools' faces are often seen in public places. / A FOX is not caught twice in the same place. / The HAPPIEST place in the world to live is within one's income. / HEAVEN is a place prepared for those prepared for it. / There's no place like HOME. / LIGHTNING never strikes in the same place twice. / Don't spend all your MONEY in one place. / Go not unto your NEIGHBOR's place too often, lest he tire of you. / A PRISON ain't just a place—it's being somewheres you don't want to be. / There is a TIME and place for everything. / WOMAN's place is in the home. / If you intend to WORK, there is no better place than where you are; if you do not intend to work, you cannot get along anywhere.

plague **1.** Men may die of the plague though the spots never appear. *Rec. dist.:* Ill.

2. The plague and the hero are both of a trade. *Rec. dist.:* N.Y., S.C. *1st cit.:* US1748 Franklin, *PRAlmanac.* *20c. coll.:* Stevenson 1138:1.

plain *(n.)* SEE The WALL has ears and the plain has eyes.

plain *(adj.)* SEE BEAUTY, like truth, is never so glorious as when it goes plainest. / The morning DAYLIGHT appears plainer when you put out your candle. / VIRTUE is like a rich stone, best plain set.

plaintiff The plaintiff must prove. *Rec. dist.:* Mich.

plan *(n.)* **1.** Sunday plans never stand. *Rec. dist.:* Ont.

2. The best-laid plans of mice and men often go astray. *Vars.:* **(a)** The best-laid plans of mice and men will always come to some bad end. **(b)** The best-laid schemes o' mice an' men gang aft agley. *Rec. dist.:* U.S., Can. *1st cit.:* 1786 Burns, *Poems.* *20c. coll.:* CODP 13, Stevenson 2040:2.

3. The best plan is to profit by the folly of others. *Rec. dist.:* Ont.

4. You can't afford to snub a man built on the million-dollar plan. *Rec. dist.:* Calif.

SEE ALSO A little IMPATIENCE spoils great plans.

plan *(v.)* **1.** Plan and propose and God will dispose. *Rec. dist.:* Ont.

2. Plan your work and work your plan. *Rec. dist.:* Ill., N.C., Ont.

SEE ALSO It is one thing to plan a DEED, another to carry it out. / DREAMS are what you hope for; reality is what you plan for. / You can never plan the FUTURE by the past. / The darkest HOUR in any man's life is when he sits down to plan to get money without earning it. / Live for the PRESENT; plan for the future.

plane Every plane has its pilot. *Rec. dist.:* N.J.

planning Planning your future saves you from regretting your past. *Rec. dist.:* Ont.

plant SEE You can't have the ear unless you plant the CORN. / One GENERATION plants the trees; another sits in their shade. / He who plants KINDNESS gathers joy. / The man who plants PEARS is a planting for his heirs. / PLOW before you plant. / He that plants TREES loves others besides himself.

plaster Make the plaster as large as the sore. *Rec. dist.:* Ont. *1st cit.:* 1546 Bale, *Examination of Anne Askew;* US1701 *Diary of Samuel Sew-*

all, 1674–1729, Mass.Hist.Soc. *Collections* (1878–82). *20c. coll.: ODEP* 630, Whiting 341.

plate A cracked plate always lasts longer than a new one. *Var.:* A cracked plate may last as long as a sound one. *Rec. dist.:* Ont.

SEE ALSO Enjoy your ICE CREAM while it's on your plate.

platter The platter kills more than the sword. *Rec. dist.:* Ill. *1st cit.:* ca1384 Wyclif, *Works,* ed. Arnold; US1754 Ames, *Almanacs,* ed. Briggs (1891). *20c. coll.: ODEP* 306, Whiting 177, Stevenson 965:10.

play *(n.)* **1.** Cheating play never thrives. *Rec. dist.:* N.J. *1st cit.:* 1855 Bohn, *Handbook of Proverbs. 20c. coll.:* Stevenson 328:1.

2. Free sitters always grumble most at the play. *Rec. dist.:* Ont. *1st cit.:* US1937 Hart, *700 Chinese Proverbs. 20c. coll.:* Stevenson 1808:1.

3. Good play is fair play. *Rec. dist.:* N.C., Okla., Tex. *1st cit.:* US1805 Brackenridge, *Modern Chivalry,* ed. Newlin (1937). *20c. coll.:* Whiting 341.

4. Tit for tat's fair play. *Rec. dist.:* Ont. *1st cit.:* US1941 Partridge, *Dictionary of Clichés. 20c. coll.:* Stevenson 2332:7.

SEE ALSO One ACTOR cannot make a play. / TURNABOUT is fair play. / All WORK and no play makes Jack a dull boy. / WORK before play.

play *(v.)* **1.** It is not clever to play, but to stop playing. *Var.:* It is not clever to gamble, but to stop playing. *Rec. dist.:* Ill., N.C.

2. Play close to the chest. *Rec. dist.:* Mich., Miss.

3. Play while you play; work while you work. *Vars.:* **(a)** When you play, play hard; when you work, don't play at all. **(b)** Work while you work; play while you play. That is the way to be happy and gay. *Rec. dist.:* U.S., Can. *1st cit.:* US1924 Bailey, *Mr. Fortune's Practice. 20c. coll.:* Whiting(MP) 702.

SEE ALSO From BEAVERS, bees should learn to mend their ways. A bee works; a beaver works and plays. / If you play with the BULL, you will get a horn in the arse. / He who

plays with a CAT must expect to be scratched. / While the CAT's away, the mice will play. / If you play both ENDS against the middle, the middle will soon fold up. / You cannot play a FIDDLE without a fiddlestick. / Don't play with FIRE. / It is a cunning part to play the FOOL well. / A GAME is not won until it has been played. / If you play with a PUPPY, he will lick your mouth. / You can't play wid TAR an' git none of it on yo' hands. / They who play with edge TOOLS must expect to be cut. / WORK while you work and play while you play.

player Though most be players, some must be spectators. *Rec. dist.:* N.J.

SEE ALSO CARDS and dice is like all in life; dey ever falls well for bold players. / The CARDS beat all the players, be they ever so skillful. / LOOKERS-ON see more than players.

playing It is well to leave off playing when the game is at the best. *Rec. dist.:* Mich., N.Y. *1st cit.:* ca1350 *Douce MS 52. 20c. coll.: ODEP* 453, Stevenson 931:7.

plaything SEE Every AGE wants its playthings. / Old BOYS have their playthings as well as young ones; the difference is only in the price.

plea A false plea is the basest of all things. *Rec. dist.:* Ont.

pleasant SEE A pleasant GRIN will let you in where a knocker was never known. / The PAST always looks better than it was; it's only pleasant because it isn't here.

please **1.** He labors in vain who tries to please everybody. *Vars.:* **(a)** He who tries to please everybody labors in vain. **(b)** He who tries to please everybody pleases nobody. **(c)** Please all and you will please none. **(d)** Those who seek to please everybody please nobody. **(e)** Try to please everybody and you please nobody. *Rec. dist.:* U.S., Can. *1st cit.:* ca1500 *15c. School Book,* ed. Nelson. *20c. coll.: ODEP* 633, Stevenson 1810:10.

2. He that would please all and himself too takes more in hand than he is like to do. *Rec. dist.:* Ill., N.Y., S.C. *1st cit.:* US1733 Franklin, *PRAlmanac. 20c. coll.:* Stevenson 1810:8.

3. Please ever; tease never. *Rec. dist.:* Ont.

4. What pleases you in others will please them in you. *Rec. dist.:* Wis.

5. You can't please everybody. *Var.:* You cannot please the whole world and his wife. *Rec. dist.:* U.S., Can. *1st cit.:* 1472 Paston, Letter of 16 May in *Paston Letters* (1971); US1742 *Colonial Records of Georgia,* ed. Chandler, in *Original Papers, 1735–1752* (1910–16). *20c. coll.:* CODP 179, Whiting 134, ODEP 633, Stevenson 1810:5.

SEE ALSO Would you live with EASE, do what you ought and not what you please. / EAT to please yourself, but dress to please others. / You can please some of the PEOPLE all the time, or all the people some of the time, but never all of the people all of the time.

pleasing SEE Pleasing WORDS and bad deeds deceive both the wise and the simple.

pleasure **1.** A man of pleasure is a man of pains. *Rec. dist.:* Ill. *1st cit.:* ca1526 Erasmus, *Dicta Sapientum. 20c. coll.:* ODEP 633, Stevenson 1813:5.

2. Do not bite at the bait of pleasure till you know there is no hook beneath it. *Rec. dist.:* N.Y., S.C. *1st cit.:* US1786 Jefferson, Letter to Maria Cosway. *20c. coll.:* Stevenson 1814:12.

3. Don't find pleasure without conscience. *Rec. dist.:* Ind.

4. Flee the pleasure that will bite tomorrow. *Rec. dist.:* Ill. *1st cit.:* 1573 Sanford, *Garden of Pleasure. 20c. coll.:* ODEP 271, Stevenson 1814:5.

5. Fly pleasure and it will follow you. *Var.:* Fly pleasures and they'll follow you. *Rec. dist.:* N.Y., Ont., S.C. *1st cit.:* ca1400 Chaucer, *Romance of the Rose;* US1738 Franklin, *PRAlmanac. 20c. coll.:* ODEP 272, Whiting 341, Stevenson 1812:7.

6. Many a man thinks he is buying pleasure when he is really selling himself a slave to it. *Rec. dist.:* N.Y., S.C. *1st cit.:* US1750 Franklin, *PRAlmanac. 20c. coll.:* Stevenson 1814:6.

7. No pleasure without pain. *Rec. dist.:* Ill. *1st cit.:* ca1526 Erasmus, *Dicta Sapientum. 20c. coll.:* ODEP 633, Stevenson 1739:5.

8. One man's pleasure is another man's poison. *Rec. dist.:* Calif. *Infm.:* Cf. meat.

9. Pleasure first and business after. *Rec. dist.:* Ill. *1st cit.:* 1924 Bailey, *Mr. Fortune's Pleasure;* US1941 Wentworth, *Weekend with Death. 20c. coll.:* Whiting(MP) 82, Stevenson 263:1.

10. Pleasure in excess is criminal. *Rec. dist.:* Mich.

11. Pleasure is seldom found where it is most eagerly sought. *Rec. dist.:* Mich. *1st cit.:* 1758 Johnson, *Idler. 20c. coll.:* Stevenson 1812:7.

12. Pleasure is the source of pain; pain is the source of pleasure. *Rec. dist.:* Ill. *1st cit.:* ca1450 *Reliquiae Antiquae. 20c. coll.:* Stevenson 1739:5.

13. Pleasure has a way of engrossing us until it becomes work. *Rec. dist.:* Okla.

14. Pleasures are like poppies spread. *Rec. dist.:* Ont. *1st cit.:* 1791 Burns, "Tam O'Shanter." *20c. coll.:* Stevenson 1814:11.

15. Self-sought pleasure rarely satisfies for long. *Rec. dist.:* Ont.

16. Short pleasure often brings long repentance. *Rec. dist.:* Ill. *1st cit.:* 1468 *Coventry Plays,* Shakespeare Soc. *20c. coll.:* ODEP 728, Stevenson 1815:5.

17. The best pleasures of all last but a time. *Rec. dist.:* N.C. *1st cit.:* 1702 Farquhar, *Twin Rivals;* US1858 Field, *Drama in Pokerville* in Porter, *Major Thorpe's Scenes in Arkansaw. 20c. coll.:* Stevenson 1812:16, T&W 290.

18. The itch of pleasure does not itch at all. *Rec. dist.:* Ont.

19. The pleasure of doing good is the only one that will not wear out. *Rec. dist.:* Ill., Oreg., Wis.

20. The pleasure of what we enjoy is lost by coveting more. *Rec. dist.:* N.Y. *1st cit.:* 1732 Fuller, *Gnomologia. 20c. coll.:* Stevenson 444:7.

21. The pleasures of youth make the pains of old age. *Rec. dist.:* Calif., Colo.

22. There is more pleasure in loving than in being in love. *Rec. dist.:* Wis. *1st cit.:* 1732 Fuller, *Gnomologia. 20c. coll.:* Stevenson 1463:5.

23. There is not half the pleasure in possessing an object as in the effort to attain it. *Rec. dist.:* N.Y. *1st cit.:* 1597 Shakespeare, *Merchant of Venice.* *20c. coll.:* Stevenson 1832:3.

24. We have no rose without its thorn, no pleasure without alloy. *Rec. dist.:* N.Y., S.C. *1st cit.:* 1430–40 Lydgate, *Prologue to Bochas;* US1786 Jefferson, Letter to Maria Cosway. *20c. coll.:* ODEP 684, Stevenson 2010:2, Whiting 371, Whiting(MP) 538.

25. When pleasure is the business of life, it ceases to be pleasure. *Rec. dist.:* N.Y., S.C. *1st cit.:* US1853 Haliburton, *Sam Slick's Wise Saws.* *20c. coll.:* Stevenson 1813:10.

26. Who pleasure gives shall joy receive. *Rec. dist.:* N.Y., S.C. *1st cit.:* US1734 Franklin, *PRAlmanac.* *20c. coll.:* Stevenson 1812:2.

SEE ALSO A BABE in the house is a wellspring of pleasure. / BUSINESS before pleasure. / Where BUSINESS and pleasure clash, then let the business go smash. / DISEASES are the tax on pleasures. / GRIEF often treads upon the heels of pleasure. / PAIN past is pleasure. / PAIN wastes the body, pleasures the understanding. / A WISE man writes for pleasure; a fool reads because he is curious. / WORK is work if you're paid to do it, an' it's pleasure if you pay to be allowed to do it.

plenty **1.** Plenty ought to be enough. *Rec. dist.:* Ky., Tenn.

2. Too much plenty makes mouth dainty. *Vars.:* **(a)** Plenty makes daintiness. **(b)** Plenty makes dainty. *Rec. dist.:* N.Y., S.C. *1st cit.:* ca1641 Fergusson, *Scottish Proverbs,* ed. Beveridge, S.T.S. (1924); US1749 Franklin, *PRAlmanac.* *20c. coll.:* ODEP 634, Stevenson 1815:9.

SEE ALSO There's plenty of HUNTING but little finding. / IDLENESS is never enjoyable unless there is plenty to do. / PRIDE breakfasted with plenty, dined with poverty, and supped with infamy.

plodding Plodding wins the race. *Rec. dist.:* Ont. *Infm.:* Cf. slow. *1st cit.:* 1859 Smiles, *Self-Help;* US1936 Dean, *What Gentleman Strangles a Lady?* *20c. coll.:* ODEP 744, Whiting(MP) 575, Stevenson 1930:8.

plot **1.** A mischievous plot may produce a good end. *Rec. dist.:* Ill.

2. A tragic plot may produce a comic conclusion. *Rec. dist.:* Ill.

SEE ALSO PASSIONS spin the plot.

plow *(n.)* **1.** A dull-edged plow furrows your brow. *Rec. dist.:* Ohio.

2. Don't get your plow in too deep. *Var.:* Don't set your plow too deep. *Rec. dist.:* Ill., Miss.

3. Don't lay down the plow until you are at the end of the furrow. *Rec. dist.:* Wash.

4. Don't put the plow before the horse. *Rec. dist.:* Ont. *1st cit.:* ca1340 Michel, *Ayenbite of Inwit.* *20c. coll.:* Stevenson 290:9.

5. Every fellow likes his own plow best. *Rec. dist.:* Ont.

6. He that by the plow would thrive, himself must either hold or drive. *Rec. dist.:* Ariz., Ohio, Utah. *1st cit.:* 1678 Ray, *English Proverbs;* US1747 Franklin, *PRAlmanac.* *20c. coll.:* ODEP 635, Whiting 341, Stevenson 1816:7, T&W 290.

7. It's the man behind the plow who does the work. *Rec. dist.:* Ont.

8. Put your hand to the plow. *Vars.:* **(a)** He who puts his hand to the plow should never look back. **(b)** Lay your hand to the plow. **(c)** When you put your hand to the plow, do not look back. *Rec. dist.:* Ill., Miss., Ont. *1st cit.:* 1596 *History of Scotland,* tr. Dalrymple; US1741 Douglas, Second letter in *Colonial Currency,* ed. Davis, Publ. Prince Soc. (1910–11). *20c. coll.:* Stevenson 1817:1, Whiting 196, Whiting(MP) 285.

9. The man who pulls the plow gets the plunder. *Rec. dist.:* N.Y., S.C.

10. The plow doesn't go before the oxen. *Rec. dist.:* Vt. *1st cit.:* US1948 Stevenson, *Home Book of Proverbs.* *20c. coll.:* Stevenson 290:9.

11. The plow is mightier than the sword. *Rec. dist.:* Ill.

plow *(v.)* **1.** One plows, another sows—who will reap, no one knows. *Rec. dist.:* Ohio.

2. Plow before you plant. *Rec. dist.:* Ohio.

3. Plow deep while sluggards sleep, and you shall have corn to sell and to keep. *Vars.*: **(a)** Plow deep and you will have plenty of corn. **(b)** Plow deep while sluggards sleep. *Rec. dist.*: U.S., Can. *1st cit.*: 1659 Howell, *Paroimiografia;* US1756 Franklin, *PRAlmanac.* *20c. coll.*: ODEP 634, Whiting 400, Stevenson 1239:15, Whiting(MP) 575.

4. Plow or not plow, you must pay the rent. *Rec. dist.*: Mich. *1st cit.*: 1846 Denham, *Proverbs.* *20c. coll.*: Stevenson 1816:9.

plowing SEE TOMORROW may be carriage driver's day fer plowing.

plowman An innocent plowman is of more worth than a vicious prince. *Var.*: A plowman on his legs is higher than a gentleman on his knees. *Rec. dist.*: Ill., N.Y., S.C. *1st cit.*: US1734 Franklin, *PRAlmanac.* *20c. coll.*: Stevenson 1816:13.

pluck *(n.)* Pluck is better than luck. *Vars.*: **(a)** A pound of pluck is worth a ton of luck. **(b)** An ounce of pluck is worth a pound of luck. **(c)** Pluck is more essential than luck. *Rec. dist.*: N.C., Ont., W.Va.

pluck *(v.)* SEE FEATHER by feather a goose is plucked. / If you would enjoy the FRUIT, pluck not the flower.

plum The higher the plum tree, the riper the plums. *Rec. dist.*: Mich. *1st cit.*: 1579 Gosson, *Ephemerides.* *20c. coll.*: ODEP 373.
SEE ALSO Make your PUDDING according to your plums.

pocket There are no pockets in shrouds. *Vars.*: **(a)** Shrouds have no pockets. **(b)** The shroud has no pockets. *Rec. dist.*: N.J., N.Y., P. E.I., S.C. *1st cit.*: 1853 Trench, *Lessons in Proverbs* (1894); USca1897 Miller, *Dead Millionaire.* *20c. coll.*: ODEP 443, Stevenson 1985:5, CODP 203, Whiting(MP) 501.
SEE ALSO Wear your LEARNING like your watch, in a private pocket. / Put your PRIDE in your pocket. / Your WOODEN overcoat won't have any pockets.

poet **1.** All men are poets at heart. *Var.*: Every man will be a poet if he can. *Rec. dist.*: N.Y., S.C. *1st cit.*: US1836 Emerson, *Literary Ethics.* *20c. coll.*: Stevenson 1818:14.

2. Nobody loves a poet. *Rec. dist.*: N.Y., S.C. *1st cit.*: US1919 Babbitt, *Rousseau and Romanticism.* *20c. coll.*: Stevenson 1819:5.

3. Poets and pigs are appreciated only after their death. *Rec. dist.*: Ill.

4. Poets are the fathers of lies. *Rec. dist.*: Ill. *1st cit.*: US1948 Stevenson, *Home Book of Proverbs.* *20c. coll.*: Stevenson 1823:5.

5. The poet is born, not made. *Var.*: A good poet is made as well as born. *Rec. dist.*: Ill., Mass., Ont., Tex. *1st cit.*: 1581 Guazzo, *Civile Conversation,* tr. Pettie, T.T. (1925); US1812 Hitchcock, *Social Monitor.* *20c. coll.*: ODEP 636, Whiting 334, Stevenson 1820:8, Whiting(MP) 502.
SEE ALSO LOVERS, travellers, and poets will give money to be heard.

poetry **1.** Poetry is the devil's drink. *Rec. dist.*: Oreg. *1st cit.*: 1605 Bacon, *Advancement of Learning.* *20c. coll.*: Stevenson 1821:11.

2. Poetry solaces sorrow. *Rec. dist.*: Mich.
SEE ALSO POVERTY, poetry, and new titles of honor make men ridiculous.

point SEE Nothing is BEAUTIFUL from every point of view. / The shortest DISTANCE between two points is a straight line. / TACT is the art of making a point without making an enemy.

poise **1.** One woman's poise is another woman's poison. *Rec. dist.*: Wis.

2. Poise and self-confidence make up a large part of good looks. *Rec. dist.*: N.C.

poison *(n.)* **1.** One who takes poison swallows its dish as well. *Rec. dist.*: Ill.

2. Poison quells poison. *Var.*: It takes poison to kill poison. *Rec. dist.*: Ill., Ohio. *1st cit.*: ca1377 Langland, *Piers Plowman.* *20c. coll.*: Stevenson 1825:2, ODEP 597.
SEE ALSO One man's MEAT is another man's poison.

poison *(v.)* SEE One sickly SHEEP infects the flock and poisons all the rest.

poke *(n.)* SEE Don't buy a PIG in a poke.

poke *(v.)* SEE Seldom poke another's FIRE, or you may rouse his burning ire.

poker *See* It's the SHOVEL that laughs at the poker.

pole The longest pole gets the persimmon. *Var.:* The longest pole knocks the highest persimmon. *Rec. dist.:* Ala., Ga., Miss. *1st cit.:* US1863 *Dictionary of Americanisms,* ed. Matthews (1951). *20c. coll.:* T&W 291.

polecat A polecat is a polecat, no matter what you call it. *Rec. dist.:* Miss.

policy 1. Policy often effects what force cannot. *Rec. dist.:* Mich. *1st cit.:* ca1547 Redford, *Wit and Science;* US1797 Brackenridge, *Modern Chivalry,* ed. Newlin (1937). *20c. coll.:* ODEP 637, Whiting 342, Stevenson 1826:8.

2. The worst of all policies in hard times is to sit down and fold your hands. *Rec. dist.:* Miss.

See also HONESTY is the best policy.

polish *(n.)* 1. It depends on what you're made of whether you take on a polish or get worn down. *Rec. dist.:* Utah.

2. Polish on the heels of shoes is a truer test of thoroughness than shine on the toes. *Rec. dist.:* Miss.

polish *(v.)* *See* A GEM is not polished without rubbing, nor is a man perfect without trials.

polite Truly polite is always polite. *Rec. dist.:* Ill.

politeness 1. Politeness costs nothing and gains everything. *Rec. dist.:* U.S., Can. *1st cit.:* 1659 Torriano, *Dictionary in English and Italian,* ed. Florio; US1765 Timberlake, *Memoirs, 1756–1765,* ed. Williams (1927). *20c. coll.:* ODEP 486, Whiting 342, CODP 37, Stevenson 1827:3, Whiting(MP) 504.

2. Politeness is inward kindness outwardly expressed. *Rec. dist.:* Miss.

3. Politeness is the just medium between ceremony and rudeness. *Rec. dist.:* Mich.

4. Politeness is to do and say the kindest thing in the kindest way. *Rec. dist.:* Ill., N.C. *1st cit.:* USca1910 Lewisohn, *Politeness. 20c. coll.:* Stevenson 1827:2.

5. Politeness is to goodness what words are to thought. *Rec. dist.:* Ind.

6. Too much politeness is a form of cunning. *Rec. dist.:* Ill.

7. True politeness consists in treating others just as you love to be treated yourself. *Rec. dist.:* Ill.

political *See* An empty STOMACH is not a good political adviser.

politically Nothing is politically right which is morally wrong. *Rec. dist.:* Ill.

politician 1. A politician is a fellow who gives you the key to the city after he's taken everything worth having. *Rec. dist.:* N.Dak.

2. A politician is an animal who can sit on a fence and yet keep both ears to the ground. *Rec. dist.:* Ky., Tenn.

3. Sooner or later all politicians die of swallowing their own lies. *Var.:* All political parties die at last of swallowing their own lies. *Rec. dist.:* N.Y., S.C. *1st cit.:* US1940 Boothe, *Europe in the Spring. 20c. coll.:* Stevenson 1747:10.

See also The STATESMAN makes the occasion, but the occasion makes the politician.

politics 1. In politics a man must learn to rise above principle. *Rec. dist.:* Md., N.Y., S.C.

2. Never contend with anyone about his politics. *Rec. dist.:* Mich.

3. Politics is a rotten egg; if broken open it stinks. *Rec. dist.:* Ill.

4. Politics is the mother of graft. *Rec. dist.:* Ala., Ga.

5. Politics makes strange bedfellows. *Var.:* Politics has strange bedfellows. *Rec. dist.:* U.S. *1st cit.:* 1611 Shakespeare, *Tempest;* US1839 *Diary of Philip Hone, 1828–1851,* ed. Nevins (1927). *20c. coll.:* ODEP 535, Whiting 343, CODP 180, Stevenson 1829:7, T&W 291, Whiting(MP) 504.

6. Those who mess with politics are bound to catch smut. *Rec. dist.:* Ala., Ga.

See also LOVE and politics don't mix.

pollywog *See* It's a good rule to never send a MOUSE to catch a skunk or a pollywog to tackle a whale.

pomp Pomp ruins families and leads to the corruption of manners. *Rec. dist.:* Mich.

pond *SEE* It's a poor FROG who doesn't play with his own pond.

pony A chompy pony ain't a-fixin' to push no cattle. *Rec. dist.:* N.Mex.

pool A standing pool soon stagnates. *Var.:* Standing pools gather filth. *Rec. dist.:* Ont., Tex. *1st cit.:* 1579 Gosson, *School Abuse. 20c. coll.:* ODEP 771, Stevenson 2460:11.

SEE ALSO Set a FROG on a golden stool; away it hops to reach the pool.

poor *(n.)* **1.** Even the strongest may be punished when they oppress the poor. *Rec. dist.:* Utah.

2. He who gives to the poor lends to the Lord. *Var.:* Who give to the poor lends to God. *Rec. dist.:* Calif., Ont. *1st cit.:* US1948 Stevenson, *Home Book of Proverbs. 20c. coll.:* Stevenson 1845:12.

3. Remember the poor: it costs nothing. *Rec. dist.:* N.Y., S.C. *1st cit.:* US1893 Twain, *Pudd'nhead Wilson's Calendar. 20c. coll.:* Stevenson 1846:1.

4. Rob not the poor because he is poor. *Rec. dist.:* Ohio. *1st cit.:* US1948 Stevenson, *Home Book of Proverbs. 20c. coll.:* Stevenson 1842:8.

5. The poor are rich when they are satisfied. *Rec. dist.:* N.Y. *1st cit.:* 1623 Wodroephe, *Spared Hours of a Soldier;* US1749 Franklin, *PRAlmanac. 20c. coll.:* Stevenson 414:7.

6. The poor have little; beggars none; the rich too much; enough, not one. *Rec. dist.:* N.Y., S.C.

7. The poor is hated even of his own neighbors, but the rich have many friends. *Rec. dist.:* Ont., Oreg. *1st cit.:* US1948 Stevenson, *Home Book of Proverbs. 20c. coll.:* Stevenson 1855:5.

8. The poor must dance as the rich pipe. *Rec. dist.:* N.Y.

9. The poor you have with you always. *Rec. dist.:* Ohio. *1st cit.:* US1948 Stevenson, *Home Book of Proverbs. 20c. coll.:* Stevenson 1845:7.

10. What is the matter with the poor is poverty. *Rec. dist.:* Ont.

SEE ALSO He who closes his DOOR to the poor will find the gates of heaven closed. / If LIFE were a thing that money could buy, the rich would live and the poor would die. / The PRODIGALITY of the rich is the providence of the poor. / The RICH and poor meet together: the Lord is the maker of them all. / The RICH ride in chaises; the poor walk with God.

poor *(adj.)* **1.** A man is not poor if he can laugh. *Rec. dist.:* Miss., Ont.

2. A poor man has no friends. *Rec. dist.:* N.Y., S.C. *1st cit.:* ca1386 Chaucer, *Tale of the Man of Law;* US1779 *Diary of Grace Galloway* in *Pa.Mag.Hist.* (1931). *20c. coll.:* Stevenson 1847:8, Whiting 343.

3. A poor man is better than a liar. *Rec. dist.:* Ont. *1st cit.:* US1948 Stevenson, *Home Book of Proverbs. 20c. coll.:* Stevenson 1395:4.

4. A poor man wears his clothes three ways: new, old, and patched. *Rec. dist.:* N.Y.

5. Better be poor and live than rich and perish. *Rec. dist.:* Ont.

6. Better be poor than wicked. *Rec. dist.:* Okla., Tex.

7. Better poor with honor than rich with shame. *Rec. dist.:* Calif.

8. For one poor man there are a hundred indignant. *Rec. dist.:* N.Y., S.C. *1st cit.:* US1746 Franklin, *PRAlmanac. 20c. coll.:* Stevenson 1844:7.

9. He becomes poor that deals with a slack hand, but the hand of diligence makes rich. *Var.:* He becomes poor that deals with a slack hand. *Rec. dist.:* Ind., Ont. *1st cit.:* US1948 Stevenson, *Home Book of Proverbs. 20c. coll.:* Stevenson 577:6.

10. He is not poor that has little, but he that desires more. *Var.:* It is not the man who has too little, but the man who craves more, that is poor. *Rec. dist.:* N.Y. *1st cit.:* 1547 Baldwin, *Treatise of Morall Phylosophie. 20c. coll.:* ODEP 639, Stevenson 1842:10.

11. He is poor whom God hates. *Rec. dist.:* N.Y. *1st cit.:* 1611 Cotgrave, *Dictionary of French and English Tongues. 20c. coll.:* ODEP 639, Stevenson 978:13.

12. It is better poor and free than to be rich and a slave. *Rec. dist.:* Ont.

13. It is easy to pass a poor man's door. *Rec. dist.:* P.E.I.

14. It is harder to be poor without murmuring than to be rich without arrogance. *Rec. dist.:* Calif.

15. It's a poor family that has neither a whore nor a thief in it. *Rec. dist.:* N.Y., S.C. *1st cit.:* 1566 Wager, *Mary Magdalene.* *20c. coll.:* ODEP 639, Stevenson 757:6.

16. It's hell to be poor. *Rec. dist.:* N.Y.

17. No matter what else you have, you are poor if you lack friends. *Rec. dist.:* N.C.

18. Poor folks are contented with duck soup. *Rec. dist.:* Calif.

19. Poor folks are glad of porridge. *Rec. dist.:* Ont. *1st cit.:* 1576 Fulwell, *Ars Adulandi.* *20c. coll.:* ODEP 638, Stevenson 1844:9.

20. Poor folks have poor ways. *Var.:* Poor people have poor ways. *Rec. dist.:* Colo.

21. The poor man pays all. *Var.:* The poor man pays for all. *Rec. dist.:* Ind., Okla. *1st cit.:* ca1561 "Poor Man Pays" in *Roxburghe Ballads,* Ballad Soc. (1869–99). *20c. coll.:* ODEP 639, Stevenson 1847:4.

22. The poorest man is he whose only wealth is money. *Rec. dist.:* N.Y.

23. There is no use being poor and looking poor. *Rec. dist.:* Ont.

24. To be poor without being free is the worst state into which a man can fall. *Rec. dist.:* Mich.

25. When all are poor, it don't take much to make a rich man. *Rec. dist.:* N.Y., S.C. *1st cit.:* US1853 Haliburton, *Sam Slick's Wise Saws.* *20c. coll.:* Stevenson 1854:7.

SEE ALSO Noble ANCESTRY makes a poor dish at the table. / CONTENT makes poor men rich; discontent makes rich men poor. / It's no DISGRACE to be poor, but it may as well be. / It's a poor DOG that won't wag his own tail. / What is a poor man's FOLLY is a rich man's gain. / Rich GIFTS wax poor when givers prove unkind. / GREED often makes one poor. / Don't worry about the old HORSE being poor—just feed him. / A HUT is a palace to a poor man. / A poor LABORER is better than a rich loafer. / LIME and lime without manure makes the farmer rich and the son poor. / Better to be a good LOSER than a poor winner. / Poor are they who have not PATIENCE. / It's poor PIE that doesn't grease its own tin. / POVERTY consists in feeling poor. / PROMISES will not make you poor. / It's a poor RULE that won't work both ways. / Poor men's TABLES are soon set. / A nice WIFE and a back door oft do make a rich man poor.

Pope It is hard to live in Rome and strive against the Pope. *Rec. dist.:* Mich. *1st cit.:* ca1628 Carmichaell, *Proverbs in Scots,* ed. Anderson (1957). *20c. coll.:* ODEP 737, CODP 204, Stevenson 1830:8.

popular Popular opinion is the greatest lie in the world. *Rec. dist.:* Ill. *1st cit.:* 1732 Fuller, *Gnomologia.* *20c. coll.:* Stevenson 1720:14.

SEE ALSO ADVICE is not a popular thing to give.

popularity 1. Popularity is glory's small change. *Rec. dist.:* Oreg. *1st cit.:* US1948 Stevenson, *Home Book of Proverbs.* *20c. coll.:* Stevenson 1830:14.

2. There is no gain in subtracting from your character to add to your popularity. *Rec. dist.:* Ind.

porch Sweep off your own back porch first. *Rec. dist.:* Iowa.

porcupine 1. Don't pet a porcupine unless you are looking for trouble. *Rec. dist.:* Ont.

2. The porcupine, whom one must handle gloved, may be respected, but it is never loved. *Rec. dist.:* N.Y., S.C. *1st cit.:* US1924 Guiterman, *Poet's Proverbs.* *20c. coll.:* Stevenson 319:2.

porridge 1. Cold porridge is easily heated. *Rec. dist.:* Ont. *1st cit.:* 1670 Ray, *English Proverbs.* *20c. coll.:* ODEP 592, Stevenson 1831:4.

2. The less porridge, the more spoons. *Rec. dist.:* Ill.

SEE ALSO POOR folks are glad of porridge.

port Any port in a storm. *Var.:* Any old port in a storm. *Rec. dist.:* U.S., Can. *1st cit.:* 1749

Cleland, *Memoirs of Woman of Pleasure;* US1775 Warren in *Warren-Adams Letters,* Mass.Hist.Soc. *Collections* (1917). *20c. coll.:* CODP 4, Whiting 343, ODEP 15, Stevenson 1831:8, T&W 292, Whiting*(MP)* 505.

position 1. A humble position often brings safety. *Rec. dist.:* Ont.

2. With higher positions there comes added responsibilities. *Rec. dist.:* N.C.

positive *(n.)* 1. Accentuate the positive. *Rec. dist.:* Ohio.

2. The most positive are often the most mistaken. *Var.:* Positive men are most often in error. *Rec. dist.:* Ill., Mich. *1st cit.:* 1732 Fuller, *Gnomologia. 20c. coll.:* Stevenson 308:18.

SEE ALSO Two YESES make a positive.

positive *(adj.)* *SEE* Only a FOOL is positive.

possess 1. A man possesses only what he knows he possesses. *Rec. dist.:* Ont.

2. Possess it yourself and give it to another. *Rec. dist.:* N.Dak.

3. To be content, look backward on those who possess less than yourself, not forward on those who possess more. *Rec. dist.:* N.Y., S.C. *1st cit.:* US1757 Franklin, *PRAlmanac. 20c. coll.:* Stevenson 413:6.

SEE ALSO Too few know when they possess ENOUGH, and fewer know how to enjoy it. / So long as we can lose any HAPPINESS we possess some. / Don't value a man for the QUALITY he is of, but for the qualities he possesses.

possession 1. Great possessions are great cares. *Rec. dist.:* Ill. *1st cit.:* 1639 Clarke, *Paroemiologia. 20c. coll.:* Stevenson 1834:1.

2. Possession is nine points of the law, and self-possession is the other one. *Vars.:* **(a)** Possession is eleven points of the law, and they say there are but twelve. **(b)** Possession is nine points of the law. **(c)** Possession is nine-tenths of the law. *Rec. dist.:* U.S., Can. *1st cit.:* ca1596 *Edward III;* USca1700 Hubbard, *General History of New England* (1848). *20c. coll.:* ODEP 640, Whiting 343, CODP 181, Stevenson 1831:13, T&W 292, Whiting*(MP)* 505.

SEE ALSO He who lives in DESIRE or fear can never enjoy his possessions. / KNOWLEDGE conquered by labor becomes a possession. / WEALTH consists not of having great possessions but in having few wants.

possibility Possibilities are infinite. *Rec. dist.:* Mich. *1st cit.:* 1732 Fuller, *Gnomologia. 20c. coll.:* Stevenson 1837:5.

possible *SEE* It is not possible to found a lasting POWER upon injustice.

possum 1. Big possum climb little tree. *Rec. dist.:* N.Y., S.C. *1st cit.:* US1880 Harris, *Uncle Remus, His Songs and His Sayings. 20c. coll.:* Stevenson 1037:1.

2. Possum's tail good as a paw. *Rec. dist.:* N.Y., S.C.

3. The big possum walks just before the dawn. *Rec. dist.:* Miss.

4. You can never get all the possums up the same tree. *Rec. dist.:* Tex.

SEE ALSO There was never a PERSIMMON except there was a possum to eat it.

post 1. A standing post gathers no sense. *Rec. dist.:* Ont.

2. One locust-wood post will wear out two fence-post holes. *Rec. dist.:* N.Y.

SEE ALSO A false REPORT rides post. / Muddy ROADS call de milepost a liar.

posture Good posture means better health. *Rec. dist.:* Ont.

pot 1. A little pot is soon hot. *Rec. dist.:* U.S. *1st cit.:* 1546 Heywood, *Dialogue of Proverbs,* ed. Habernicht (1963); US1820 Irving, *Bracebridge Hall. 20c. coll.:* ODEP 471, T&W 293, CODP 135, Stevenson 1840:2.

2. A watched pot never boils. *Var.:* A watched pot is long in boiling. *Rec. dist.:* U.S. *1st cit.:* 1848 Gaskell, *Mary Barton;* US1933 Palmer, *Puzzle of the Pepper Tree. 20c. coll.:* ODEP 869, Whiting*(MP)* 507, CODP 242, Stevenson 1839:6.

3. Borrowed pots are apt to leak. *Rec. dist.:* Ill.

4. Every pot has its cover. *Var.:* There isn't a pot you can't fit a cover to. *Rec. dist.:* N.Y.

5. Every pot must stand upon its own bottom. *Rec. dist.:* N.Y. *1st cit.:* 1564 Bullein, *Dialogue Against Fever,* E.E.T.S. (1888); US1750 Fairservice, "Plain Dealing" in *Mag.Hist.* (1919). *20c. coll.:* ODEP 845, Whiting 456, CODP 232, Stevenson 2397:4, T&W 384, Whiting(MP) 649.

6. He who stirs the soup pot eats first. *Rec. dist.:* N.Y., S.C. *1st cit.:* US1942 Delehanty, *Arise From Sleep. 20c. coll.:* Stevenson 662:3.

7. Never leave the mark of the pot upon the ashes. *Rec. dist.:* Tex.

8. Pint pots are soon filled. *Rec. dist.:* W.Va.

9. Put the big pot in the little one, kill a pumpkin, and churn. *Vars.:* **(a)** Put the big pot in the little one. **(b)** Put the big pot in the little one and make hash out of the skillet. **(c)** Put the big pot in the little one and make soup out of the legs. **(d)** Put the big pot in the little pot and make soup out of the lid. **(e)** We'll put the big pot in the little one and fry the skillet. *Rec. dist.:* U.S. *1st cit.:* US1930 Dobie, *Coronado's Children. 20c. coll.:* Whiting(MP) 507.

10. The busy man has few idle visitors; to the boiling pot the flies come not. *Rec. dist.:* Ind. *1st cit.:* 1640 Herbert, *Outlandish Proverbs (Jacula Prudentum)* in *Works,* ed. Hutchinson (1941). *20c. coll.:* ODEP 72, Stevenson 836:5.

11. The cracked pot lasts the longest. *Rec. dist.:* N.Y.

12. The emptier the pot, the quicker it boils. *Rec. dist.:* Colo., Minn.

13. The pot boils best on its own hearth. *Rec. dist.:* Ont.

14. The pot calls the kettle black. *Vars.:* **(a)** A kettle can't throw up black to the pot. **(b)** No pot can call the kettle black. **(c)** The kettle can't say to the pot, "You're black." **(d)** The pot accuses the kettle of being black. **(e)** The pot can't call the kettle black. **(f)** The pot shouldn't call the kettle black. **(g)** The skillet can't call the pot black. *Rec. dist.:* U.S. *1st cit.:* 1620 Cervantes, *Don Quixote,* tr. Shelton; US1807 Salmagundi in *Works of Washington Irving* (1873). *20c. coll.:* ODEP 421, Whiting 344, T&W 293, Stevenson 1840:14, Whiting(MP) 506.

15. There's a pot of gold at the end of the rainbow. *Rec. dist.:* Ind., Miss. *1st cit.:* 1836 Cooper, *Glossary of Provincialisms in Sussex;* US1943 Teale, *Dune Boy. 20c. coll.:* ODEP 221, Whiting(MP) 507, Stevenson 1933:6.

16. You can't rub on a black pot without getting black on you. *Rec. dist.:* Ohio.

SEE ALSO When the BEANS get too thick, the pot burns. / BEAUTY doesn't make the pot boil. / Good BROTH may be made in an old pot. / Look for the HANDLE when the pot's in the fire. / Too many HANDS in the pot make poor soup. / If you have no HONEY in your pot, have some in your mouth. / A PENNY in the hand is worth two in the pot. / Fair WORDS make the pot boil.

potato 1. A hot potato is hard to cool. *Rec. dist.:* Ill.

2. Don't eat your father's seed potatoes. *Rec. dist.:* Ont.

3. If you plant potatoes you can't reap tomatoes. *Rec. dist.:* Ont.

4. It's no good planting a boiled potato. *Rec. dist.:* Ill.

5. Small potatoes are few in a hill. *Rec. dist.:* N.C. *1st cit.:* US1836 Col. Crockett's Exploits in Texas. *20c. coll.:* T&W 294, Stevenson 1842:1, Whiting(MP) 508.

6. The poor potatoes are all in one hill. *Rec. dist.:* Ky., Tenn.

7. When the going is rough, big potatoes come to the top. *Rec. dist.:* Oreg.

potter Every potter praises his own pot, and more if it be broken. *Rec. dist.:* Mich. *1st cit.:* 1855 Bohn, *Handbook of Proverbs. 20c. coll.:* Stevenson 1836:6.

SEE ALSO The CLAY replies not to the potter. / We are CLAY in the hands of the potter.

poultry SEE The sleeping FOX catches no poultry.

pound Forever and ever it takes a pound to fight a pound. *Rec. dist.:* N.Y., S.C. *1st cit.:* US1849 Emerson, *Lectures and Biographical Studies: Aristocracy. 20c. coll.:* Stevenson 392:14.

SEE ALSO An ounce of CARE is worth a pound of cure. / A pound of CURE will not pay an ounce of debt. / An ounce of HELP is worth a pound of pity. / In a thousand pounds of LAW there is not one ounce of love. / One pound of LEARNING requires ten pounds of common sense to use it. / He that will steal an OUNCE will steal a pound. / PATIENCE in market is worth pounds in a year. / A PINT'S a pound the world around. / An ounce of PREVENTION is worth a pound of cure. / An ounce of WISDOM is worth a pound of wit. / An ounce of WIT that is bought is worth a pound that is taught.

pour *SEE* It never RAINS but it pours.

pout Pout and you bear life alone. *Rec. dist.:* Ont.

poverty 1. Both poverty and prosperity come from spending money—prosperity from spending it wisely. *Rec. dist.:* Minn.

2. It easier to praise poverty than to bear it. *Rec. dist.:* Ariz., Ill. *1st cit.:* 1666 Torriano, *Common Place of Italian Proverbs. 20c. coll.:* ODEP 212, Stevenson 1843:5.

3. Neither great poverty nor great riches will hear reason. *Rec. dist.:* Ont.

4. Of all poverty, that of the mind is the most deplorable. *Rec. dist.:* Mich.

5. Poverty and hunger have many apt pupils. *Rec. dist.:* Ont.

6. Poverty and love are hard to hide. *Rec. dist.:* Ill.

7. Poverty and shame shall be to him that refuses instructions, but he that regards reproof shall be honored. *Var.:* Poverty and shame shall be to him that refuses instruction. *Rec. dist.:* Ind., Ont.

8. Poverty comes from God, but not dirt. *Rec. dist.:* N.Y.

9. Poverty consists in feeling poor. *Rec. dist.:* N.Y., S.C. *1st cit.:* US1870 Emerson, *Domestic Life. 20c. coll.:* Stevenson 1842:10.

10. Poverty gives a man strange bedfellows. *Vars.:* **(a)** Poverty makes a man acquainted with strange bedfellows. **(b)** Poverty makes strange bedfellows. *Rec. dist.:* Ill., Tex. *1st cit.:* 1611 Shakespeare, *Tempest;* US1838 Halibur-

ton, *Clockmaker. 20c. coll.:* CODP 2, T&W 294, Stevenson 1845:5.

11. Poverty has no kin. *Rec. dist.:* Ala., Ga., Ill. *1st cit.:* ca1386 Chaucer, *Tale of Man of Law. 20c. coll.:* Stevenson 1847:8.

12. Poverty is no crime. *Rec. dist.:* N.Y., Oreg. *1st cit.:* 1591 Florio, *Second Fruites,* ed. Simonini (1953). *20c. coll.:* ODEP 642, CODP 182.

13. Poverty is no disgrace. *Rec. dist.:* Nebr. *1st cit.:* 1591 Florio, *Second Fruites,* ed. Simonini (1953). *20c. coll.:* ODEP 642, CODP 182, Stevenson 1845:3.

14. Poverty is no sin. *Var.:* Poverty is no sin, but it is terribly inconvenient. *Rec. dist.:* Ill., N.J., S.C. *1st cit.:* 1591 Florio, *Second Fruites,* ed. Simonini (1953). *20c. coll.:* ODEP 642, Stevenson 1848:3.

15. Poverty is not a shame, but being ashamed of it is. *Rec. dist.:* Ill., N.J. *1st cit.:* 1732 Fuller, *Gnomologia;* US1749 Franklin, *PRAlmanac. 20c. coll.:* ODEP 642, Stevenson 1845:4.

16. Poverty is the mother of all the arts. *Rec. dist.:* Ill. *1st cit.:* ca1526 Erasmus, *Dicta Sapientum. 20c. coll.:* ODEP 642, Stevenson 1846:12.

17. Poverty is the mother of crime; want of sense is the father. *Rec. dist.:* N.C. *1st cit.:* US1948 Stevenson, *Home Book of Proverbs. 20c. coll.:* Stevenson 1847:7.

18. Poverty is the mother of invention. *Rec. dist.:* Ont. *1st cit.:* 1519 Horman, *Vulgaria. 20c. coll.:* ODEP 558.

19. Poverty is the sixth sense. *Rec. dist.:* N.J.

20. Poverty makes a hog gentle. *Rec. dist.:* Ont.

21. Poverty makes good fellowship. *Rec. dist.:* Tex.

22. Poverty may be a cure for dyspepsia, but most people prefer the dyspepsia. *Rec. dist.:* Ky.

23. Poverty of mind is often concealed under the barb of splendor. *Rec. dist.:* Mich.

24. Poverty parts friends. *Rec. dist.:* Ill. *1st cit.:* ca1386 Chaucer, *Tale of Melibee. 20c. coll.:* Stevenson 1847:3.

25. Poverty, poetry, and new titles of honor make men ridiculous. *Rec. dist.:* N.Y., S.C.

26. Poverty shows us who our friends are and who are our enemies. *Rec. dist.:* Ill.

27. Poverty wants some things, luxury many things, avarice all things. *Var.:* Poverty wants many things, but covetousness all. *Rec. dist.:* N.Y., S.C. *1st cit.:* 1539 Publilius Syrus, *Sententiae,* tr. Taverner; US1735 Franklin, *PRAlmanac.* *20c. coll.:* ODEP 643, Whiting 346.

28. Poverty with security is better than plenty in the midst of fear and uncertainty. *Rec. dist.:* Ont. *1st cit.:* 1477 *Dictes and Sayenges of Philosophirs,* tr. Rivers. *20c. coll.:* Stevenson 1855:2.

29. There is no virtue that poverty does not destroy. *Rec. dist.:* Ill. *1st cit.:* 1573 Sanford, *Garden of Pleasure.* *20c. coll.:* ODEP 862, Stevenson 1848:1.

30. Unsullied poverty is always happy, while impure wealth brings with it many sorrows. *Rec. dist.:* Ont.

31. What is the matter with the poor is poverty. *Rec. dist.:* Ont.

32. When poverty comes in the door, love flies out the window. *Vars.:* **(a)** When poverty comes in at the door, love flies out at the window. **(b)** When poverty comes in at the door, love goes up the chimney. **(c)** When poverty comes in the door, love goes out the window. **(d)** When poverty comes to the door, love flies out the window. **(e)** When poverty enters the door, love flies out the window. **(f)** When poverty flies in one window, love flies out the other. *Rec. dist.:* U.S. *1st cit.:* ca1476 Caxton, *Game Chess;* US1790 *Columbian Mag.* *20c. coll.:* ODEP 642, Whiting 346, CODP 181, Stevenson 1481:3, Whiting(MP) 508.

SEE ALSO DEBT is the worst kind of poverty. / OLD age and poverty are two heavy burdens, either is enough. / OLD age and poverty are wounds that can't be healed. / PRIDE breakfasted with plenty, dined with poverty, and supped with infamy. / SLOTH breeds poverty. / SLOTH is the mother of poverty.

powder **1.** A little bit of powder and a little bit of paint makes a woman look like what she ain't. *Vars.:* **(a)** A little bit of powder and a little bit of paint makes an ugly woman look like what she ain't. **(b)** A little powder and a little paint can make you look like what you ain't. **(c)** Powder and paint make a girl look what she ain't. *Rec. dist.:* U.S., Can.

2. Face powder may win a man, but it takes baking powder to hold him. *Rec. dist.:* Kans.

3. Keep your powder dry. *Vars.:* **(a)** Put your trust in God and keep your powder dry. **(b)** Trust in God and keep your powder dry. *Rec. dist.:* U.S., Can. *1st cit.:* ca1658 Cromwell in Hayes, *Ballads of Ireland;* US1965 Stewart, *Airs.* *20c. coll.:* ODEP 842, CODP 231, Stevenson 1857:7, Whiting(MP) 646.

power **1.** As water finds its level, so power goes. *Rec. dist.:* N.Y., S.C.

2. Do things and you shall have the power. *Rec. dist.:* N.Y.

3. If you want to be the power behind the throne, stay behind the throne three or four times. *Rec. dist.:* N.Y., S.C. *1st cit.:* 1770 Pitt, Speech, 2 Mar.; US1874 Twain, *Life on the Mississippi.* *20c. coll.:* ODEP 643, Stevenson 2314:2.

4. It is not possible to found a lasting power upon injustice. *Rec. dist.:* Ont.

5. Never underestimate the power of women. *Rec. dist.:* N.C.

6. O would some power the gift give us to see ourselves as others see us. *Rec. dist.:* Ill., Ind., Ont. *1st cit.:* ca1785 Burns, "To a Louse." *20c. coll.:* Stevenson 2065:6.

7. Power can achieve more by gentle means than by violence. *Rec. dist.:* Ill.

8. Power corrupts, and absolute power corrupts absolutely. *Rec. dist.:* N.Y., S.C. *1st cit.:* 1887 Acton, Letter in *Life and Letters of Mandel Creighton* (1904). *20c. coll.:* CODP 182, Stevenson 1858:14.

9. Power discovers the real disposition of a man. *Rec. dist.:* Mich.

10. Power flows to him who knows how. *Rec. dist.:* N.Y., S.C. *1st cit.:* US1901 Hubbard, *Philistine.* *20c. coll.:* Stevenson 1857:11.

11. Power itself has not one-half the might of gentleness. *Rec. dist.:* Mich.

12. Sudden power is apt to be insolent, sudden liberty saucy; that behaves best which has grown gradually. *Rec. dist.:* N.Y., S.C. *1st cit.:* US1753 Franklin, *PRAlmanac.* *20c. coll.:* Stevenson 1858:9.

SEE ALSO It is only in ACTION that you have the power to grow. / BEAUTY is power; a smile is its sword. / A FRIEND in power is a friend lost. / A good INTENTION clothes itself with sudden power. / KNOWLEDGE itself is power. / MONEY is power. / To have what you want is RICHES, but to be able to do without is power. / Do not pray for TASKS equal to your powers; pray for power equal to your tasks. / Do not let your VANITY make you overestimate your powers. / Sell not VIRTUE to purchase wealth nor liberty to purchase power. / WEALTH and power do not give peace of mind. / WEALTH means power, it means leisure, it means ability. / Let your WILL roar when your power can but whisper.

powerful He is powerful who governs his passions. *Rec. dist.:* N.Y., S.C.

SEE ALSO A KING is never powerful that has not power on the sea.

practice *(n.)* **1.** Practice makes perfect. *Rec. dist.:* U.S., Can. *1st cit.:* 1563 Wilson, *Arte of Rhetorique* (1909); US1761 *Diary and Autobiography of John Adams,* ed. Butterfield (1966). *20c. coll.:* ODEP 856, Whiting 346, CODP 182, Stevenson 1859:10, T&W 295, Whiting(MP) 509.

2. Underhand practices fail in the end. *Rec. dist.:* Mich.

SEE ALSO KNOWLEDGE directs practice, and practice increases knowledge. / KNOWLEDGE is a treasure, but practice is the key to it.

practice *(v.)* Practice what you preach. *Rec. dist.:* U.S., Can. *1st cit.:* ca1377 Langland, *Piers Plowman;* US1702 Mather, *Magnalia Christi Americana,* (1853). *20c. coll.:* ODEP 643, Whiting 346, CODP 182, Stevenson 1870:2, T&W 295, Whiting(MP) 510.

SEE ALSO HONESTY is more praised than practiced. / There are some who PREACH beautifully, but practice not their beautiful doctrine. / Many have quarreled about RELIGION that never practiced it.

praise *(n.)* **1.** A little praise goes a long ways. *Rec. dist.:* Calif.

2. A puff of wind and popular praise weigh alike. *Rec. dist.:* Ill.

3. Every man likes his own praise best. *Rec. dist.:* Ill.

4. Faint praise is disparagement. *Rec. dist.:* Mich. *1st cit.:* 1732 Fuller, *Gnomologia.* *20c. coll.:* Stevenson 1864:8.

5. If you wish praise, die; if you wish blame, marry. *Rec. dist.:* N.Y.

6. Praise from a wife is praise indeed. *Rec. dist.:* N.Y., S.C.

7. Praise is the reflection of virtue. *Rec. dist.:* Ohio. *1st cit.:* 1551 Wilson, *Rule of Reason.* *20c. coll.:* ODEP 644, Stevenson 1860:5.

8. Praise makes a good man better and a bad man worse. *Rec. dist.:* U.S. *1st cit.:* 1659 Pecke, *Parnassi Puerperium.* *20c. coll.:* ODEP 644, Stevenson 1861:9.

9. Praise undeserved is scandal in disguise. *Var.:* Praise undeserv'd is satire in disguise. *Rec. dist.:* Colo. *1st cit.:* 1733 Pope, *Imitations of Horace.* *20c. coll.:* Stevenson 1860:10.

10. Praise without profit puts little in the pocket. *Rec. dist.:* Mich.

11. Proper praise sticks. *Rec. dist.:* N.Y., S.C.

12. The sweetest of all sounds is praise. *Rec. dist.:* Calif. *1st cit.:* US1948 Stevenson, *Home Book of Proverbs.* *20c. coll.:* Stevenson 1863:1.

13. The worst praise is self-praise. *Rec. dist.:* N.J.

14. There is something sweeter than receiving praise: the feeling of having deserved it. *Rec. dist.:* Wis.

15. They that value not praise will never do anything worthy of it. *Rec. dist.:* Ont.

SEE ALSO BLAME is safer than praise. / BLAME-ALL and praise-all are two blockheads. / SELF-PRAISERS rob themselves of the praise they seek. / Deepest WOUNDS are often inflicted by praise.

praise *(v.)* **1.** Let another man praise you, and not your own mouth. *Vars.:* **(a)** Let another man praise you, and not your own mouth; a stranger, and not your own lips. **(b)** Let another man praise you, not yourself. **(c)** Let another man praise you. *Rec. dist.:* U.S.

1st cit.: 1484 Caxton, *Fables of Avian;* US1817 *Writings of John Quincy Adams,* ed. Ford (1913–17). *20c. coll.: ODEP* 507, Whiting 347, *CODP* 200, Stevenson 1864:2.

2. Praise publicly; blame privately. *Rec. dist.:* Oreg. *1st cit.:* ca1526 Erasmus, *Dicta Sapientum. 20c. coll.: ODEP* 4, Stevenson 1864:10.

3. Usually we praise only to be praised. *Rec. dist.:* N.C. *1st cit.:* US1948 Stevenson, *Home Book of Proverbs. 20c. coll.:* Stevenson 1861:6.

SEE ALSO Praise the BRIDGE that carries you over. / Never praise your CIDER or your horse. / Praise a fine DAY at night. / Praise a FOOL and you make him useful. / HONESTY is praised and left to starve. / Praise the SEA, but keep on land. / Great SERMONS lead the people to praise the preacher; good preaching leads the people to praise the Saviour.

prancing Those that do the most prancing make the least progress. *Rec. dist.:* Ont.

prating SEE A prating FOOL shall fall.

pray **1.** He prays the best who loves best all things both great and small. *Rec. dist.:* N.C.

2. He that would learn to pray, let him go to the sea. *Rec. dist.:* Ont. *1st cit.:* 1576 Gascoigne, *Steele Glas. 20c. coll.: ODEP* 451, Stevenson 2048:6.

3. None can pray well but he that lives well. *Rec. dist.:* Ill., Okla.

4. Pray and work and you will be happy. *Rec. dist.:* Ont.

5. 'Tis easy to sigh but 'tis better to pray. *Rec. dist.:* Ont.

6. When going to sea, pray once; when going to war, pray twice; when going to be married, pray thrice. *Rec. dist.:* Minn.

7. When it's hard to pray, pray the hardest. *Rec. dist.:* N.C.

SEE ALSO When the DEVIL comes, it is too late to pray. / Pray to GOD, but keep hammering. / He who prays for his NEIGHBOR will be heard for himself. / WORK as if everything depended on you; pray as if everything depended on God.

prayer **1.** It's not the length of the prayer that is the most important. *Rec. dist.:* N.C.

2. More things are wrought by prayer than this world dreams of. *Rec. dist.:* Minn., Ont. *1st cit.:* 1842 Tennyson, *Morte d'Arthur. 20c. coll.:* Stevenson 1865:6.

3. Nightly prayer makes the day to shine. *Rec. dist.:* Ill.

4. Prayer and provender hinder no man's journey. *Var.:* Prayer and provender never hinder a journey. *Rec. dist.:* Mich., N.Y., Ont. *1st cit.:* 1599 Minsheu, *Dictionarie in Spanish and English;* US1744 Franklin, *PRAlmanac. 20c. coll.: ODEP* 645, Whiting 347, Stevenson 1866:15.

5. Prayer changes things. *Rec. dist.:* Ill.

6. Prayer hinders no work. *Rec. dist.:* N.Y., S.C.

7. Prayer is a cry of hope. *Rec. dist.:* Ind.

8. Prayer is a wish turned upward. *Rec. dist.:* Calif.

9. Prayer is food for the soul. *Rec. dist.:* Ind.

10. Prayer is the pillow of religion. *Rec. dist.:* Ill.

11. Prayer is the voice of faith. *Rec. dist.:* Ill.

12. Prayer should be the key of the day and the lock of the night. *Rec. dist.:* Ill. *1st cit.:* 1620 Feltham, *Resolves. 20c. coll.: ODEP* 645.

13. Prayer-worn knees and a rusty hoe never need a crop of corn. *Rec. dist.:* Calif.

14. Say your prayers as if you were going to die tomorrow; do your work as if you were going to live forever. *Rec. dist.:* Ont. *1st cit.:* US1757 Franklin, *PRAlmanac. 20c. coll.:* Stevenson 2618:15.

15. Some people who moan about prayers being answered don't seem to realize the answer may be no. *Rec. dist.:* Ala., Ga.

16. The prayer of the innocent is never unheard. *Rec. dist.:* Ont.

SEE ALSO COURAGE is fear that has said its prayers.

praying **1.** He who is always praying has a dangerous life. *Rec. dist.:* N.C.

2. Praying keeps us from sinning; sinning keeps us from praying. *Rec. dist.:* Utah.

preach 1. He preaches best who loves the most. *Rec. dist.*: Ind.

2. He preaches well who lives well. *Var.*: He who lives well is the best preacher. *Rec. dist.*: Ill., N.J. *1st cit.*: 1620 Cervantes, *Don Quixote,* tr. Shelton. *20c. coll.*: ODEP 645, Stevenson 1870:1.

3. There are some who preach beautifully but practice not their beautiful doctrine. *Rec. dist.*: N.Y.
SEE ALSO None preaches better than the ANT, and she says nothing. / If the BEARD were all, the goat might preach. / When the FOX preaches, beware of the geese. / It is easy for a man in HEALTH to preach patience to the sick. / PRACTICE what you preach.

preacher 1. A preacher loves chicken better than he loves his second cousin. *Rec. dist.*: W.Va.

2. A preacher's son is often bad. *Rec. dist.*: Nebr.

3. He is a good preacher who follows his own preaching. *Var.*: It is a good preacher that follows his own instructions. *Rec. dist.*: N.J., Ont. *1st cit.*: 1597 Shakespeare, *Merchant of Venice*. *20c. coll.*: Stevenson 1871:4.

4. Preacher, be advised by your own sermons. *Rec. dist.*: N.C. *1st cit.*: 1902 Hulme, *Proverb Lore*. *20c. coll.*: Stevenson 1870:6.

5. Preachers can talk but never teach unless they practice what they preach. *Rec. dist.*: Ill., N.Y., S.C. *1st cit.*: ca1377 Langland, *Piers Plowman*. *20c. coll.*: ODEP 643, Stevenson 1870:2.

6. The painful preacher, like a candle bright, consumes himself in giving others light. *Rec. dist.*: N.Y., S.C. *1st cit.*: US1742 Franklin, *PRAlmanac*. *20c. coll.*: Stevenson 1869:5.

7. When de preacher comes in, de chickens cry. *Rec. dist.*: Ill.

8. Woe to those preachers who listen not to themselves. *Rec. dist.*: N.J., Ont. *1st cit.*: 1902 Hulme, *Proverb Lore*. *20c. coll.*: Stevenson 1870:6.
SEE ALSO Great SERMONS lead the people to praise the preacher; good preaching leads the people to praise the Saviour.

preaching It is bad preaching to deaf ears. *Rec. dist.*: N.Y.

precedent A precedent embalms a principle. *Rec. dist.*: Ill. *1st cit.*: 1788 Scott in Stowell, *Opinion*. *20c. coll.*: Stevenson 1362:6.

precept Precepts may lead, but examples draw. *Rec. dist.*: Mich. *1st cit.*: 1855 Bohn, *Handbook of Proverbs*. *20c. coll.*: Stevenson 718:4.
SEE ALSO EXAMPLE is better than precept.

precious *SEE* The BRAVE man holds honor far more precious than life. / True FRIENDS are like diamonds, precious and rare; false ones like autumn leaves, found everywhere. / For NEIGHBORS to keep a friendly tone, is equal to finding a precious stone.

precipitation Precipitation will ruin the best-laid designs. *Rec. dist.*: Mich.

prefer *SEE* There are many who prefer to DESPISE and belittle that which is beyond their reach. / FRIENDS are to be preferred to relatives.

prejudice 1. It is never too late to give up our prejudices. *Rec. dist.*: N.Y., Okla., S.C. *1st cit.*: US1854 Thoreau, *Walden*. *20c. coll.*: Stevenson 1873:1.

2. Never let the prejudice of the eye determine the heart. *Rec. dist.*: Ill.

3. No tree takes so deep a root as prejudice. *Rec. dist.*: N.Y.

4. Prejudice is being down on what we are not up on. *Vars.*: (a) Prejudice is being down on anything you are not up on. (b) Prejudice is being down on what you're not up on. *Rec. dist.*: Colo., Ill., N.Dak.

5. Prejudice is the child of ignorance. *Rec. dist.*: N.Y. *1st cit.*: ca1821 Hazlitt, "On Prejudice" in *Essays*.
20c. coll.: Stevenson 1872:10.

6. Prejudice is the reason of fools. *Rec. dist.*: Ill.

7. When we destroy an old prejudice, we have need of a new one. *Rec. dist.*: Ill.
SEE ALSO ACQUAINTANCES soften prejudices. / When the JUDGMENT is weak the prejudice is strong. / OPINIONS grounded on

prejudice are always sustained with the greatest violence.

premier *See* SCHOOLS hide future premiers.

preparation There's nothing like too much preparation to dull the sharp edge of a man's honin'. *Rec. dist.:* Miss.

See also Great SUCCESS is always preceded by great preparation. / In peace or in war your SUCCESS of tomorrow depends upon the preparation you are making today.

prepare *See* The FUTURE belongs to those who prepare for it. / In fair WEATHER prepare for foul.

presence Whose presence does no good, their absence does no harm. *Rec. dist.:* Ohio.

See also ABSENCE of body is better than presence of mind in time of danger. / CONSCIENCE is God's presence in man.

present *(n., gift)* Presents speak louder than words. *Rec. dist.:* N.Y., S.C.

See also A FRIEND is a present you give yourself.

present *(n., time)* **1.** Live for the present; plan for the future. *Rec. dist.:* Ill., Oreg.

2. There's never a time like the present. *Var.:* There is no time like the present. *Rec. dist.:* U.S., Can. *1st cit.:* 1562 Legh, *Accidence of Armoury;* US1764 A. Adams in *Adams Family Correspondence,* ed. Butterfield (1963). *20c. coll.:* ODEP 824, Whiting 439, CODP 226, Stevenson 1874:11, T&W 373, Whiting(MP) 626.

3. Think of the present and not of the past. *Rec. dist.:* Calif.

See also The good old DAYS were once the present, too. / Don't mortgage the FUTURE for the present. / While you glory in the PAST, be busy in the present lest you be caught unprepared in the future.

present *(adj.)* Enjoy the present moment and don't grieve for tomorrow. *Rec. dist.:* Ill. *1st cit.:* US1948 Stevenson, *Home Book of Proverbs.* *20c. coll.:* Stevenson 1875:2.

See also FRIENDS, though absent, are still present. / A man without thought of the FUTURE must soon have present sorrow.

preserve *See* DIGNITY is one thing that can't be preserved in alcohol.

president It's not a president's business to catch flies. *Rec. dist.:* Ill.

press *(n.)* Freedom of the press is like a flaming sword. *Rec. dist.:* Wis.

press *(v.)* *See* Press not a FALLING man too hard.

presume *See* All are presumed GOOD until they are found in a fault.

presumption Presumption has ruined multitudes. *Rec. dist.:* Mich. *1st cit.:* 1732 Fuller, *Gnomologia;* US1747 Franklin, *PRAlmanac.* *20c. coll.:* Stevenson 554:1.

pretender Pretenders should be put to the test. *Rec. dist.:* Mich.

pretense **1.** If you want a pretense to whip a dog, it is enough to say he ate up the frying pan. *Rec. dist.:* Ill. *1st cit.:* 1706 Stevens, *New Spanish and English Dictionary.* *20c. coll.:* ODEP 864, Stevenson 608:5.

2. The mask of pretense often becomes reality. *Rec. dist.:* Ill.

pretension The world is his who can see through pretension. *Rec. dist.:* N.Y., S.C. *1st cit.:* US1837 Emerson, *American Scholar.* *20c. coll.:* Stevenson 2630:3.

prettiness Prettiness dies quickly. *Rec. dist.:* N.Dak., Ont. *1st cit.:* 1610 Bretnor, *Almanac* in *Elizabethan and Jacobean Studies,* ed. Crow (1959). *20c. coll.:* ODEP 646, Stevenson 1876:8.

pretty *(n.)* Pretty is as pretty does. *Rec. dist.:* U.S. *1st cit.:* 1929 Hayes, *Crime;* US1853 Haliburton, *Sam Slick's Wise Saws.* *20c. coll.:* Whiting(MP) 510, T&W 296, Stevenson 539:2.

pretty *(adj.)* *See* WOMEN are wacky, women are vain: they'd rather be pretty than have a good brain.

prevail *See* Where FORCE fails, skill and patience will prevail. / RIGHT will prevail. / TRUTH is mighty and will prevail.

prevent Prevent rather than repent. *Rec. dist.:* Ill.

See also A STUMBLE may prevent a fall.

prevention An ounce of prevention is worth a pound of cure. *Var.:* Prevention is better than cure. *Rec. dist.:* U.S., Can. *1st cit.:* ca1240 Bracton, *De Legibus;* US1772 Scammell in *Documentary History of Maine Containing Baxter Manuscripts,* ed. Baxter (1869–1916). *20c. coll.:* ODEP 646, Whiting 347, *CODP* 183, Stevenson 1877:4, T&W 272, Whiting*(MP)* 465.

price 1. Don't buy at too dear a price. *Rec. dist.:* Miss.

2. You have to pay the price for being a good man. *Rec. dist.:* N.Y., S.C. *1st cit.:* US1923 Davis, *Icebound. 20c. coll.:* Stevenson 997:8.

SEE ALSO Good ADVICE is beyond price. / Old BOYS have their playthings as well as young ones; the difference is only in the price. / There is no GOOD that does not cost a price. / LOVE can neither be bought nor sold; its only price is love. / Every MAN has a price. / PEACE at any price. / REVENGE is dearly bought at the price of liberty. / SLAVERY is too high a price to pay for an easy living. / Eternal VIGILANCE is the price of supremacy.

prick 1. A stiff prick knows no conscience. *Rec. dist.:* Colo. *Infm.:* A prick refers to the penis. *1st cit.:* 1933 O'Flaherty, *Martyr;* US1935 Farrell, *Judgement Day. 20c. coll.:* Whiting*(MP)* 511.

2. Don't kick against pricks. *Var.:* It is hard to kick against the pricks. *Rec. dist.:* U.S., Can. *1st cit.:* ca1300 *Cursor Mundi;* US1637 *John Wheelwright, His Writings,* ed. Bell, Publ. Prince Soc. (1876). *20c. coll.:* ODEP 421, Whiting 347, Stevenson 1293:10, T&W 296, Whiting*(MP)* 511.

3. Early pricks turn to thorns. *Var.:* It early pricks that will be a thorn. *Rec. dist.:* Ont., Tex. *1st cit.:* ca1350 *Douce MS 52. 20c. coll.:* ODEP 211, Stevenson 2303:9.

prickle SEE Gather THISTLES, except prickles.

pride 1. A man's pride in what he knows decreases as his knowledge grows. *Rec. dist.:* Ont.

2. A woman's pride is as strong as a man's stubbornness. *Rec. dist.:* Ont.

3. Better stand alone in conscious pride than err with millions on your side. *Rec. dist.:* N.C.

1st cit.: 1761 Churchill, *Night. 20c. coll.:* Stevenson 706:9.

4. Declaiming against pride is not always a sign of humility. *Var.:* It is not a sign of humility to disclaim against pride. *Rec. dist.:* N.Y., S.C. *1st cit.:* 1732 Fuller, *Gnomologia;* US1749 Franklin, *PRAlmanac. 20c. coll.:* ODEP 175, Stevenson 1197:4.

5. Fond pride of dress is sure a very curse; ere fancy you consult, consult your purse. *Rec. dist.:* Ind. *1st cit.:* US1940 Thompson, *Body, Boots, and Britches. 20c. coll.:* Stevenson 367:7.

6. If pride leads the van, beggary brings up the rear. *Rec. dist.:* N.Y., S.C. *1st cit.:* US1735 Franklin, *PRAlmanac. 20c. coll.:* Stevenson 1881:16.

7. It is pride, not nature, that craves much. *Rec. dist.:* Ill., Ont.

8. Never say no from pride or yes from weakness. *Rec. dist.:* Minn.

9. Pride and poverty go hand in hand. *Rec. dist.:* Calif.

10. Pride and the gout are seldom cured throughout. *Rec. dist.:* N.Y., S.C. *1st cit.:* US1747 Franklin, *PRAlmanac. 20c. coll.:* Stevenson 1879:10.

11. Pride breakfasted with plenty, dined with poverty, and supped with infamy. *Rec. dist.:* N.Y., S.C. *1st cit.:* US1757 Franklin, *PRAlmanac. 20c. coll.:* Whiting 348, ODEP 646, Stevenson 1879:7.

12. Pride comes before a fall. *Vars.:* (a) Empty pride usually takes a fall. (b) Pride goes before a downfall. (c) Pride goes before a fall. (d) Pride goes before a fall, a haughty spirit before destruction. (e) Pride goes before destruction. *Rec. dist.:* U.S., Can. *1st cit.:* ca1350 *Douce MS 52;* US1725 Wolcott, *Poetical Meditations. 20c. coll.:* ODEP 647, Whiting 348, *CODP* 183, Stevenson 1882:7, T&W 296, Whiting*(MP)* 511.

13. Pride costs more than hunger, thirst, or cold. *Rec. dist.:* Ky., N.Y., Okla., Tenn. *1st cit.:* 1831 Hone, *Year-book. 20c. coll.:* Stevenson 1880:8.

14. Pride feels no pain. *Rec. dist.:* Ont. *1st cit.:*

1614 Adams, *Fatal Banquet. 20c. coll.: ODEP* 647, *CODP* 183, Stevenson 1878:5.

15. Pride goes before, and shame follows after. *Var.:* When pride comes, then comes shame. *Rec. dist.:* U.S. *1st cit.:* ca1350 *Douce MS 52;* US1758 Franklin, *PRAlmanac. 20c. coll.: ODEP* 647, Whiting 348, Stevenson 1882:6, Whiting *(MP)* 511.

16. Pride goes forth on horseback grand and gay, and comes back on foot and begs its way. *Rec. dist.:* Ind., Ont. *1st cit.:* US1870 Longfellow, *Bell of Atri. 20c. coll.:* Stevenson 1882:5.

17. Pride in prosperity turns to misery in adversity. *Rec. dist.:* Ill. *1st cit.:* 1732 Fuller, *Gnomologia. 20c. coll.:* Stevenson 1879:12.

18. Pride is a luxury a poor man cannot afford. *Rec. dist.:* N.Y., S.C. *1st cit.:* US1941 Shattuck, *Snark Was a Boojum. 20c. coll.:* Stevenson 1852:14.

19. Pride is as loud a beggar as want, and a great deal more saucy. *Rec. dist.:* Mich. *1st cit.:* 1732 Fuller, *Gnomologia;* US1750 Franklin, *PRAlmanac. 20c. coll.: ODEP* 647, Stevenson 1880:4, Whiting 348.

20. Pride is at the bottom of all great mistakes. *Rec. dist.:* N.C. *1st cit.:* ca1860 Ruskin, "Conception of God" in *The True and Beautiful. 20c. coll.:* Stevenson 1879:15.

21. Pride is neither too hot nor too cold. *Rec. dist.:* Ohio.

22. Pride is painful. *Rec. dist.:* Ont. *1st cit.:* 1629 Adams, *Sermons* (1861). *20c. coll.:* Stevenson 1878:5.

23. Pride must pinch. *Var.:* Pride must be pinched. *Rec. dist.:* N.C., Ont. *1st cit.:* 1894 Northall, *Folk Phrases. 20c. coll.: ODEP* 647, Stevenson 1878:5.

24. Pride often apes humility. *Rec. dist.:* Ill. *1st cit.:* 1799 Coleridge, *Devil's Thoughts. 20c. coll.: ODEP* 647, Stevenson 1883:2.

25. Pride often borrows the cloak of humility. *Rec. dist.:* Ill. *1st cit.:* 1732 Fuller, *Gnomologia. 20c. coll.:* Stevenson 1883:4.

26. Pride that dines on vanity sups on contempt. *Rec. dist.:* Ind. *1st cit.:* US1752 Franklin, *PRAlmanac. 20c. coll.:* Whiting 348, *ODEP* 646, Stevenson 1879:7.

27. Pride will keep you warm. *Rec. dist.:* Md.

28. Pride's an ill horse to ride. *Rec. dist.:* Ont.

29. Put your pride in your pocket. *Rec. dist.:* Ohio. *1st cit.:* US1837 *Diary of Philip Hone, 1828–1851,* ed. Nevins (1927). *20c. coll.:* Whiting 348, Stevenson 1881:6, T&W 296, Whiting *(MP)* 511.

30. Sheer pride and sloth, the roots of every vice. *Rec. dist.:* N.C.

31. The proud hate pride in others. *Rec. dist.:* Ill.

32. There is no pride like that of a beggar grown rich. *Rec. dist.:* Ill. *1st cit.:* US1948 Stevenson, *Home Book of Proverbs. 20c. coll.:* Stevenson 1852:12.

SEE ALSO IDLENESS and pride tax with a heavier hand than kings and parliaments. / We are taxed twice as much by our IDLENESS, three times as much by our pride, and four times as much by our folly. / IGNORANCE and pride grow on the same wood. / Great MERIT is coy, as well as great pride.

priest 1. Like priest, like people. *Rec. dist.:* Ont. *1st cit.:* 1561 Pilkington, *Burning of Paul's Church;* USca1700 Hubbard, *General History of New England* (1848). *20c. coll.: ODEP* 647, Whiting 348, *CODP* 177, Stevenson 1884:11.

2. One son becomes a priest, nine generations are sure of heaven. *Rec. dist.:* Ind.

3. Only those become priests who cannot earn a living. *Rec. dist.:* Ind.

prince SEE Many will entreat the FAVOR of the prince. / An innocent PLOWMAN is of more worth than a vicious prince.

principle 1. Better poisoned in one's blood than to be poisoned in one's principles. *Rec. dist.:* Ill.

2. In politics a man must learn to rise above principle. *Rec. dist.:* Ill., N.Y., S.C.

3. It is easier to fight for one's principles than to live up to them. *Rec. dist.:* Ala., Ga., Okla.

4. Never sacrifice principles to please anyone. *Rec. dist.:* Mich.

5. Principle is a passion for truth and right. *Rec. dist.:* Ill.

6. 'Tis against some men's principle to pay interest, and seems against others' interest to pay the principal. *Rec. dist.:* N.Y., S.C.

printing press The printing press is the mother of errors. *Rec. dist.:* Ill.

prison A prison ain't just a place—it's being somewheres you don't want to be. *Rec. dist.:* N.Y., S.C. *1st cit.:* US1923 Davis, *Icebound.* *20c. coll.:* Stevenson 1888:1.

SEE ALSO There are no ugly LOVES nor handsome prisons. / Stone WALLS do not a prison make, nor iron bars a cage. / It is better to sit with a WISE man in prison than with a fool in paradise.

privilege 1. It is a woman's privilege to change her mind. *Var.:* To change the mind is a lady's privilege. *Rec. dist.:* Mich., N.Y., S.C. *1st cit.:* 1616 Draxe, *Bibliotheca Scholastica* in *Anglia* (1918); US1748 Ames, *Almanacs,* ed. Briggs (1891). *20c. coll.:* ODEP 909, Whiting 494, Stevenson 2578:9, T&W 410, Whiting(MP) 694.

2. Usurp not the privileges of another. *Rec. dist.:* Mich.

SEE ALSO Equal RIGHTS for all, special privileges for none.

probability 1. A thousand probabilities do not make one truth. *Rec. dist.:* Ill., Mich., Ont. *1st cit.:* 1707 Mapletoft, *Select Proverbs.* *20c. coll.:* ODEP 648.

2. Lest men suspect your tale untrue, keep probability in view. *Rec. dist.:* Ill. *1st cit.:* 1727 Gay, "Painter Who Pleased Nobody" in *Fables. 20c. coll.:* Stevenson 1890:7.

3. Probabilities direct the conduct of the wise man. *Rec. dist.:* Ill.

probe SEE Can't probe MIRE 'thout getting sullied.

problem A problem, when solved, is simple. *Var.:* This problem, when solved, will be simple. *Rec. dist.:* N.Y., Ont.

SEE ALSO MARRIAGE is a quick solution to more problems.

process SEE LIFE is one long process of getting tired.

procrastination 1. Procrastination is the root of all evil. *Rec. dist.:* Fla.

2. Procrastination is the thief of time. *Rec. dist.:* U.S., Can. *1st cit.:* 1742 Young, *Night Thoughts;* US1784 Morris in *Papers of Alexander Hamilton,* eds. Syrett and Cooke (1961). *20c. coll.:* ODEP 648, Whiting 349, *CODP* 184, Stevenson 1890:16, T&W 296, Whiting(MP) 512.

prodigal *(n.)* The prodigal robs his heir; the miser robs himself. *Rec. dist.:* Ill. *1st cit.:* 1732 Fuller, *Gnomologia. 20c. coll.:* Stevenson 1891:6.

prodigal *(adj.)* SEE A miserly FATHER makes a prodigal son.

prodigality The prodigality of the rich is the providence of the poor. *Rec. dist.:* N.Y., S.C.

produce SEE A closed BOOK does not produce a learned man. / An hour's INDUSTRY will do more to produce cheerfulness than a month's moaning.

product SEE A BARGAIN is not a bargain unless you can use the product. / A LADY is known by the product she endorses.

profession SEE Monday RELIGION is better than Sunday profession.

proficient Start young at what you wish to become proficient in. *Rec. dist.:* Ont.

profit *(n.)* **1.** Great profits on small capital are after all small. *Rec. dist.:* N.C. *1st cit.:* US1875 Scarborough, *Chinese Proverbs. 20c. coll.:* Stevenson 1892:14.

2. In all labor there is profit. *Rec. dist.:* Ont. *1st cit.:* US1948 Stevenson, *Home Book of Proverbs. 20c. coll.:* Stevenson 1331:3.

3. Much profit, much risk. *Rec. dist.:* Wash. *1st cit.:* US1875 Scarborough, *Chinese Proverbs. 20c. coll.:* Stevenson 1892:13.

4. No one was ever ruined by taking a profit. *Rec. dist.:* Ill.

5. Nothing can sit still and make a profit except a hen. *Rec. dist.:* Kans.

6. Small profits are not to be despised. *Rec. dist.:* Mich.

7. Those who take the profits should also bear the expense. *Rec. dist.:* N.Y.

8. Today's profits are yesterday's goodwill ripened. *Rec. dist.:* N.J., Utah.

9. Who busies himself where no profit is found remains a fool the whole year round. *Rec. dist.:* N.Y.

SEE ALSO To open a BOOK brings profit. / JUSTICE goes out the window when profit comes in.

profit *(v.)* **1.** He profits most who serves best. *Var.:* The science of business is the science of service, and he profits most who serves best. *Rec. dist.:* U.S., Can. *Infm.:* This is the motto of Rotary International. *1st cit.:* US1915 Sheldon, *Science of Business.* *20c. coll.:* Stevenson 2078:9.

2. The best plan is to profit by the folly of others. *Rec. dist.:* Ont.

SEE ALSO Many receive ADVICE, but only the wise profit from it. / ANGER profits nobody.

profitable Nothing is profitable which is dishonest. *Rec. dist.:* Mich., N.Y.

profusion Profusion is the charm of hospitality. *Rec. dist.:* Ill.

progress *(n.)* **1.** All progress of the best kind is slow. *Rec. dist.:* Ont.

2. Every step of progress that the world has made has been from scaffold to scaffold and from stake to stake. *Rec. dist.:* Ont.

3. Progress never stands still. *Rec. dist.:* Ill.

SEE ALSO He who rises EARLY makes progress in his work. / Those that do the most PRANCING make the least progress.

progress *(v.)* You either progress or go backwards; you cannot stand still. *Rec. dist.:* N.C.

promise *(n.)* **1.** A bad promise is better broken than kept. *Var.:* Bad promises are better broken than kept. *Rec. dist.:* N.Y., N.C., Ont., S.C. *1st cit.:* US1769 Brooke, *History of Emily Montague,* ed. Dwight (1822). *20c. coll.:* Whiting 320, Stevenson 1895:6.

2. A promise is a debt. *Rec. dist.:* Ill. *1st cit.:* ca1330 Wright, *Political Songs,* Camden Soc.

(1839); US1931 Burnham, *Murder of Lala Lee.* *20c. coll.:* Stevenson 1896:10, Whiting(MP) 513, *ODEP* 649.

3. A promise is a promise. *Rec. dist.:* Ont., S.C.

4. A promise is only made to be broken. *Rec. dist.:* N.C.

5. A promise made is a debt unpaid. *Rec. dist.:* Ill., Ind. *1st cit.:* ca1330 Wright, *Political Songs,* Camden Soc. (1839); US1958 *Bangor Daily News,* 14 July. *20c. coll.:* Stevenson 1896:10, Whiting(MP) 513.

6. All promises are either broken or kept. *Rec. dist.:* Okla. *1st cit.:* 1590 Dee, *Diary.* *20c. coll.:* *ODEP* 649, Stevenson 1895:8.

7. Few promises are best and fair performance. *Rec. dist.:* N.Y., S.C.

8. Long on promises, short on performance. *Rec. dist.:* N.Mex. *1st cit.:* 1548 Hall, *Chronicle of Lancastre and York;* US1664 *Works of Anne Bradstreet,* ed. Ellis (1932). *20c. coll.:* *ODEP* 649, Whiting 349, Stevenson 1897:6, Whiting(MP) 513

9. Many promises lessen confidence. *Rec. dist.:* N.C. *1st cit.:* US1948 Stevenson, *Home Book of Proverbs.* *20c. coll.:* Stevenson 1895:13.

10. Never make a promise when you know at the beginning you can't keep it. *Var.:* Never make a promise if you don't intend to keep it. *Rec. dist.:* N.C. *1st cit.:* US1748 Washington, *Copy Book.* *20c. coll.:* Stevenson 1895:14.

11. People who do not keep their promises are sure to suffer for it sooner or later. *Rec. dist.:* Ont.

12. Promise is a pretty word; if fulfilled, it's good. *Rec. dist.:* Ill. *1st cit.:* US1628 *Winthrop Papers,* Mass.Hist.Soc. *Collections* (1863–92). *20c. coll.:* Whiting 497.

13. Promises are like piecrust: they are made to be broken. *Vars.:* **(a)** Promises are like good piecrusts: easily broken. **(b)** Promises are like piecrusts. **(c)** Promises are like piecrust: easy made and easy broken. **(d)** Some promises are like good piecrust: short and easy to break. *Rec. dist.:* U.S. *1st cit.:* 1599 Shakespeare, *King Henry V;* US1789 *American Museum.* *20c. coll.:*

ODEP 649, Whiting 349, *CODP* 184, Stevenson 1896:8, Whiting*(MP)* 512.

14. Promises are most given when least said. *Rec. dist.:* Utah.

15. Promises don't fill the belly. *Rec. dist.:* Ill. *1st cit.:* US1800 Spurgeon, *John Ploughman's Pictures.* *20c. coll.:* Stevenson 1896:6.

16. Promises fill no sack. *Rec. dist.:* Ohio.

17. Promises will not make you poor. *Var.:* Promises will not make you poor; giving is what breaks you. *Rec. dist.:* Calif.

18. Trust not fine promises. *Rec. dist.:* Ill.

19. Who makes no promises has none to perform. *Rec. dist.:* Ill.

20. You can't live on promises. *Rec. dist.:* N.C.

SEE ALSO Straight FOLKS never make broken promises. / A small GAIN is worth more than a large promise. / A GIFT is better than a promise. / MANKIND lives on promises. / MONEY, like promises, is easier made than kept. / An acre of PERFORMANCE is worth the whole world of promise.

promise *(v.)* **1.** Be slow to promise and quick to perform. *Var.:* Be slow to make a promise but swift to keep it. *Rec. dist.:* Ill., Mich. *1st cit.:* 1548 Hall, *Chronicle of Lancastre and York;* US1664 *Works of Anne Bradstreet,* ed. Ellis (1932). *20c. coll.:* ODEP 649, Whiting 349, Stevenson 1897:6, Whiting*(MP)* 513.

2. Expect nothing from him who promises a great deal. *Vars.:* **(a)** Expect nothing from him whom is lavish of his promises. **(b)** He that promises too much means nothing. *Rec. dist.:* Ill., Mich. *1st cit.:* ca1589 Greene, *Honorable Historie of Friar Bacon and Frier Bongay.* *20c. coll.:* ODEP 649.

3. It is one thing to promise, another to perform. *Rec. dist.:* Ill., Ont. *1st cit.:* 1548 Hall, *Chronicle of Lancastre and York;* US1664 *Works of Anne Bradstreet,* ed. Ellis (1932). *20c. coll.:* ODEP 649, Whiting 349, Stevenson 1897:6, Whiting*(MP)* 513.

4. Men apt to promise are apt to forget. *Rec. dist.:* N.Y., Ont. *1st cit.:* 1732 Fuller, *Gnomologia.* *20c. coll.:* Stevenson 1895:10.

5. Promise little but do much. *Rec. dist.:* Ill., Mich., Ont. *1st cit.:* US1948 Stevenson, *Home Book of Proverbs.* *20c. coll.:* Stevenson 1897:3.

6. Promising means nothing; giving is the real thing. *Rec. dist.:* Ariz.

7. The more you promise, the less you will have to deliver. *Rec. dist.:* Ill.

promiser No greater promisers than those who have nothing to give. *Rec. dist.:* N.Y.

promontory See one promontory, one mountain, one sea, one river, and see all. *Var.:* See one promontory, one mountain, one sea, one river, and you have seen them all. *Rec. dist.:* Ill.

promotion *SEE* The WISE shall inherit glory, but shame shall be the promotion of fools.

pronounce *SEE* WRITE with the learned; pronounce with the vulgar.

proof **1.** The proof of the home is the nursery. *Rec. dist.:* N.Y., S.C. *1st cit.:* US1906 *Poor Richard Jr.'s Almanac.* *20c. coll.:* Stevenson 1153:2.

2. The proof of the pudding is in the eating. *Vars.:* **(a)** The proof is in the pudding. **(b)** The proof of the pudding is the chewing of the bag. **(c)** The proof of the pudding lies in its eating. *Rec. dist.:* U.S., Can. *1st cit.:* ca1300 *King Alisaunder;* US1769 *Papers of Lloyd Family of Lloyd's Neck, L.I., N.Y.,* ed. Barck, N.Y.Hist.Soc. *Collections* (1926–27). *20c. coll.:* ODEP 650, Whiting 350, *CODP* 184, Stevenson 1898:6, T&W 297, Whiting*(MP)* 513.

property **1.** Few rich men own their own property—their property owns them. *Rec. dist.:* N.Y., S.C. *1st cit.:* US1896 Ingersoll, Speech, New York, 29 Oct. *20c. coll.:* Stevenson 1899:6.

2. Such as waste their own property will not be careful of that of others. *Rec. dist.:* Mich.

prophesy **1.** Don't prophesy unless you know. *Rec. dist.:* Ont. *1st cit.:* US1862 Lowell, *Mason and Slidell.* *20c. coll.:* Stevenson 1902:3.

2. Prophesy as you like, but always hedge. *Rec. dist.:* N.Y., S.C.

prophet A prophet is without honor in his own country. *Vars.:* **(a)** A prophet is not without honor, save his own. **(b)** A prophet is not without honor, save in his own country and in his own house. **(c)** A prophet is with honor save in his own country. **(d)** No man is a prophet in his own country. *Rec. dist.:* U.S., Can. *1st cit.:* ca1485 Malory, *Works,* tr. Caxton (1967); US1632 Howes in *Winthrop Papers, 1498–1649,* Mass.Hist.Soc. *Collections* (1929–47). *20c. coll.:* CODP 184, Whiting 350, ODEP 650, Stevenson 1901:7, T&W 297, Whiting(MP) 513.

SEE ALSO JESTERS do oft prove prophets.

proportion SEE A man is RICH in proportion to the number of things which he can afford to let alone.

propose SEE MAN proposes, God disposes.

proposition SEE LIFE is a queer proposition.

prosper SEE CHEATERS never prosper. / FOOLS never prosper. / Ill-gotten GOODS prosper not long. / LIARS never prosper. / Better suffer for TRUTH than prosper by falsehood.

prosperity **1.** Do not in prosperity what may be repented of in adversity. *Rec. dist.:* Mich.

2. He that swells in prosperity will be sure to shrink in adversity. *Rec. dist.:* Ill., Mich. *1st cit.:* 1732 Fuller, *Gnomologia;* US1775 *Historical Memoirs of Williamm Smith, 1763–1776,* ed. Sabine (1956). *20c. coll.:* Stevenson 1904:7, Whiting 202.

3. In time of prosperity, friends will be plenty; in time of adversity, not one in twenty. *Rec. dist.:* N.Y., S.C. *1st cit.:* ca1500 15c. *School Book,* ed. Nelson. *20c. coll.:* ODEP 650, Stevenson 907:5.

4. Prosperity destroys fools and endangers the wise. *Rec. dist.:* Ill. *1st cit.:* 1732 Fuller, *Gnomologia. 20c. coll.:* Stevenson 1902:10.

5. Prosperity discovers vice; adversity, virtue. *Rec. dist.:* N.Y., S.C. *1st cit.:* 1732 Fuller, *Gnomologia;* US1751 Franklin, *PRAlmanac. 20c. coll.:* Stevenson 1903:12, Whiting 350.

6. Prosperity is not without its troubles. *Rec. dist.:* Ont.

7. Prosperity is the surest breeder of insolence. *Rec. dist.:* N.Y., S.C. *1st cit.:* US1867 Twain, Letter to Alta California, 23 Feb. *20c. coll.:* Stevenson 1903:9.

8. Prosperity makes friends; adversity tries them. *Rec. dist.:* Ill. *1st cit.:* ca1500 15c. *School Book,* ed. Nelson; US1827 *Letters from John Pintard, 1816–1833,* N.Y.Hist.Soc. *Collections* (1940–41). *20c. coll.:* ODEP 650, Whiting 350, Stevenson 907:6.

9. Too much prosperity makes most men fools. *Rec. dist.:* Ind.

SEE ALSO ADVERSITY is the prosperity of the great. / CALAMITY and prosperity are the touchstones of integrity. / A FRIEND cannot be known in prosperity; an enemy cannot be hidden in adversity. / He who knows no LAZINESS will know prosperity.

protect SEE The DEVIL protects his own.

protest SEE Against CRITICISM a man can neither protest nor defend; he must act in spite of it.

proud *(n.)* The proud have all the pain—none of the pleasures of the vain. *Rec. dist.:* Ont.

proud *(adj.)* **1.** A proud man is always a foolish man. *Rec. dist.:* Ill.

2. A proud woman brings distress on her family. *Rec. dist.:* Ill.

3. As sore places meet most rubs, proud folks meet most affronts. *Rec. dist.:* N.Y., S.C. *1st cit.:* US1734 Franklin, *PRAlmanac. 20c. coll.:* Stevenson 1879:7.

4. Never be too proud to turn back. *Rec. dist.:* N.J.

SEE ALSO A great HEART is never proud. / A proud MIND and a light purse are ill met.

proudness De proudness in a man don't count w'en his head's cold. *Rec. dist.:* N.Y., S.C.

prove **1.** He that proves too much proves nothing. *Rec. dist.:* Ill. *1st cit.:* 1732 Fuller, *Gnomologia. 20c. coll.:* Stevenson 1898:9.

2. Never try to prove that nobody doubts. *Rec. dist.:* Ill.

SEE ALSO Little FRIENDS sometimes prove to be big friends. / GOLD is proven by touch. / HOPE proves a man deathless. / JESTERS do oft prove prophets. / Believe every man a LIAR until he proves himself true.

proverb 1. Mad folks and proverbs reveal many truths. *Rec. dist.*: Ill.

2. Proverbs are the daughters of daily experience. *Rec. dist.*: Ala., N.Y.

3. Proverbs are the wisdom of nations. *Rec. dist.*: Wis. *1st cit.*: ca1626 Bacon, *Novum Organum.* *20c. coll.*: Stevenson 1906:5.

SEE ALSO Patch GRIEF with proverbs.

provide SEE The LORD will provide.

providence 1. A special providence takes care of idiots and stick-and-dirt chimneys. *Rec. dist.*: Miss. *1st cit.*: 1861 Hughes, *Tom Brown at Oxford;* US1906 Lincoln, *Mr. Pratt.* *20c. coll.*: ODEP 365, Whiting(MP) 513.

2. Don't tempt providence. *Rec. dist.*: S.C. *1st cit.*: 1910 Shaw, *Misalliance.* *20c. coll.*: Stevenson 1909:8.

3. Don't wait for providence to send you a worm. *Rec. dist.*: Ont.

4. Providence assists not the idle. *Rec. dist.*: Ill.

5. Providence for the worst; the best will save itself. *Rec. dist.*: Mich.

6. Providence helps those who help themselves. *Rec. dist.*: Ont. *1st cit.*: 1545 Taverner, *Proverbs of Erasmus;* US1736 Franklin, *PRAlmanac.* *20c. coll.*: ODEP 310, Whiting 178, Stevenson 979:11, T&W 154, Whiting(MP) 260.

7. Providence requires three things of us before it will help us: a stout heart, a strong arm, and a stiff upper lip. *Rec. dist.*: N.Y., S.C. *1st cit.*: US1853 Haliburton, *Sam Slick's Wise Saws.* *20c. coll.*: Stevenson 1909:3.

8. Providence tempers the wind to the shorn lamb. *Rec. dist.*: Ont. *Infm.*: Cf. God, Lord. *1st cit.*: 1640 Herbert, *Outlandish Proverbs (Jacula Prudentum)* in *Works,* ed. Hutchinson (1941); US1780 Sewall in *Winslow Papers,* ed. Raymond (1901). *20c. coll.*: ODEP 312, Whiting 179, CODP 312, Stevenson 890:15, T&W 154, Whiting(MP) 260.

9. We must follow, not force, providence. *Rec. dist.*: Ill.

SEE ALSO When FOOLS make mistakes, they lay the blame on providence. / The PRODIGALITY of the rich is the providence of the poor.

provoke SEE It is better to bear a single INJURY in silence than to provoke a thousand by flying into a rage. / One SIN another does provoke.

prudence 1. A grain of prudence is worth a pound of craft. *Rec. dist.*: Ill., N.C. *1st cit.*: 1548 Hall, *Chronicle of Lancastre and York;* US1771 *Diary and Autobiography of John Adams,* ed. Butterfield (1961). *20c. coll.*: ODEP 601, Whiting 323, CODP 172, Stevenson 1909:17.

2. From prudence comes peace; from peace, abundance. *Rec. dist.*: Mich.

prudent He is prudent who is patient. *Rec. dist.*: N.Dak., N.Y.

prune Remember that no matter how young a prune is, he's always wrinkled. *Rec. dist.*: Nebr.

public *(n.)* 1. He who serves a public has but a scurvy master. *Rec. dist.*: Tex. *1st cit.*: 1855 Bohn, *Handbook of Proverbs.* *20c. coll.*: Stevenson 1913:5.

2. The public has more interest in the punishment of an injury than he who receives it. *Rec. dist.*: Mich.

3. The public is the only critic whose opinion is worth anything at all. *Rec. dist.*: N.Y., S.C.

SEE ALSO Don't air your dirty LINENS in public.

public *(adj.)* 1. Public men should have public minds. *Rec. dist.*: Mich.

2. Public office is a public trust. *Rec. dist.*: Okla. *1st cit.*: US1835 Calhoun, Speech, 13 Feb. *20c. coll.*: Stevenson 1714:3.

pudding 1. Better some of the pudding than none of the pie. *Rec. dist.*: Ill. *1st cit.*: 1670 Ray, *English Proverbs.* *20c. coll.*: ODEP 55, Stevenson 236:3.

2. Make your pudding according to your plums. *Var.*: Make the pudding according to your plums. *Rec. dist.*: Ill., Ont.

SEE ALSO Never spare the PARSON's wine nor the baker's pudding. / The PROOF of the pudding is in the eating. / It's not improbable that a man may receive more solid SATISFACTION from pudding while he is alive than from praise after he is dead.

puddle SEE Better a big FISH in a little puddle than a little fish in a big puddle. / There is more than one FROG in the puddle. / Every PATH has a puddle. / Better be a big TOAD in a small puddle than a small toad in a big puddle.

puff SEE A LOVER may sigh, but he must not puff. / Puff not against the WIND.

pull It is easier to pull down than to build up. *Rec. dist.:* Ill. *1st cit.:* 1577 Stanihurst in Holinshed, *Chronicles of Ireland.* *20c. coll.:* ODEP 653, CODP 185.
SEE ALSO A CROW does not pull out the eye of another crow. / A HORSE can't pull while kicking. / Don't whip the HORSE that is pulling. / Love your NEIGHBOR, but do not pull down the fence. / The man who pulls the PLOW gets the plunder. / If you have STRINGS, pull them.

pullet Pullet can't roost too high fer de owl. *Rec. dist.:* N.Y., S.C. *1st cit.:* US1880 Harris, *Plantation Proverbs* in *Uncle Remus: His Songs and His Sayings.* *20c. coll.:* Stevenson 1131:10.
SEE ALSO Empty SMOKE-HOUSE makes de pullet holler.

pulling Pulling down another means getting below him. *Rec. dist.:* N.J.

pulse SEE PEOPLE are not always feeling their pulse to see if they are happy.

pumpkin 1. Every pumpkin is known by its stem. *Rec. dist.:* Ill.

2. You can raise a pumpkin in a few weeks, but it takes years to raise an oak tree. *Rec. dist.:* N.C.

pun It often happens that a bad pun goes further than a better one. *Rec. dist.:* Colo., Ind.

punctuality 1. Punctuality begets confidence and is the sure path to honor and respect. *Rec. dist.:* Mich.

2. Punctuality is the art of guessing correctly how late the other party is going to be. *Rec. dist.:* N.Dak.

3. Punctuality is the first rung on the ladder of success. *Rec. dist.:* N.C.

4. Punctuality is the soul of business. *Rec. dist.:* N.Y., S.C. *1st cit.:* 1911 Crossing, *Folk Rhymes of Devon;* US1853 Haliburton, *Sam Slick's Wise Saws.* *20c. coll.:* CODP 185, ODEP 654.

5. Punctuality is the thief of time. *Rec. dist.:* N.Y., S.C. *1st cit.:* 1891 Wilde, *Picture of Dorian Gray.* *20c. coll.:* Stevenson 1916:11.

punish He who punishes one chastises a hundred. *Var.:* Who punishes one threatens a hundred. *Rec. dist.:* Ill., N.Y., Wis.
SEE ALSO ANGER punishes itself. / Men are punished by their SINS, not for them. / The WORM was punished for early rising.

punishment 1. Many without punishment, none without sin. *Rec. dist.:* Ill. *1st cit.:* 1616 Draxe, *Bibliotheca Scholastica* in *Anglia* (1918). *20c. coll.:* ODEP 654, Stevenson 773:7.

2. Punishment and reward act like the bridle and spur. *Rec. dist.:* Mich.

3. Punishment comes slowly, but it comes. *Rec. dist.:* Ill.

4. Punishment deferred commonly falls the heavier. *Rec. dist.:* Mich.

5. Punishment is a close attendant to guilt. *Rec. dist.:* Ill.

6. Punishment is always a two-edged sword. *Rec. dist.:* N.Y., S.C. *1st cit.:* US1916 Burleigh and Bierstadt, *Punishment.* *20c. coll.:* Stevenson 1918:6.

7. The punishment should fit the crime. *Rec. dist.:* Ill., N.Y. *1st cit.:* 1885 Gilbert, *The Mikado.* *20c. coll.:* Stevenson 1916:13.
SEE ALSO Every SIN carries its own punishment.

pupil To learn, a pupil must meet the teacher halfway. *Rec. dist.:* N.Y.

puppy *(n.)* 1. If you play with a puppy, he will lick your mouth. *Var.:* Play with a puppy, he'll lick you in the face. *Rec. dist.:* Ala., Ga.

2. It is bad for puppies to play with cub bears. *Rec. dist.:* Ill.

3. Who play wid de puppy get bit wid de fleas. *Rec. dist.:* Wis.

SEE ALSO The hasty BITCH brings forth blind puppies. / Every DOG thinks her puppies are the cutest.

puppy *(adj.)* SEE Puppy LOVE leads to a dog's life.

purchase SEE Sell not VIRTUE to purchase wealth nor liberty to purchase power.

purchaser Let the purchaser buy at his own risk. *Rec. dist.:* Ont. *1st cit.:* 1523 Fitzherbert, *Boke of Husbandry;* US1758 Eliot, *Essays on Field Husbandry in New England, 1748–1762,* eds. Carmen and Tugwell (1934). *20c. coll.:* ODEP 96, Stevenson 268:13, Whiting 52, CODP 28, Whiting(MP) 86.

pure SEE His HEART cannot be pure whose tongue is not clean. / Let your HEART keep pure and the world will, too. / If you foul the SPRING, you can't expect the stream to be pure.

purity Purity is obscurity. *Rec. dist.:* N.Y., S.C. *1st cit.:* US1940 Nash, *On a Wicked World.* *20c. coll.:* Stevenson 1919:9.

purpose 1. Before you work for some purpose, you must have a purpose. *Rec. dist.:* N.C.

2. Have a purpose for everything you undertake to do. *Rec. dist.:* N.C.

3. Many good purposes lie in the churchyard. *Rec. dist.:* Miss.

4. Many men fail because they lack purpose. *Rec. dist.:* N.Y., S.C.

SEE ALSO AMBITION is the incentive that makes purpose great and achievement greater. / AUTHORITY can serve no good purpose unless it is rightly exercised. / The DEVIL can cite scripture for his purpose. / There's many a MISTAKE made on purpose.

purse 1. A full purse has many friends. *Var.:* A full purse never lacks friends. *Rec. dist.:* Ala., Ga., Tex. *1st cit.:* ca1500 *Early English Carols,* ed. Greene. *20c. coll.:* ODEP 293, Stevenson 1613:1.

2. A full purse makes a mouth speak. *Var.:* A full purse makes the mouth run over. *Rec. dist.:* Miss., Wis. *1st cit.:* 1670 Ray, *English Proverbs.* *20c. coll.:* Stevenson 1921:7.

3. A heavy purse makes a light heart. *Rec. dist.:* Ill., Ind. *1st cit.:* ca1514 Barclay, *Eclogues,* E.E.T.S. (1927). *20c. coll.:* ODEP 366, Stevenson 1921:6.

4. A light purse is a heavy curse. *Rec. dist.:* N.Y., S.C. *1st cit.:* 1732 Fuller, *Gnomologia;* US1745 Franklin, *PRAlmanac.* *20c. coll.:* Stevenson 1921:18, Whiting 352.

5. A light purse makes a heavy heart. *Var.:* Light purse, heavy heart. *Rec. dist.:* N.Y., S.C., Ont. *1st cit.:* ca1514 Barclay, *Eclogues,* E.E.T.S. (1927); US1733 Franklin, *PRAlmanac.* *20c. coll.:* ODEP 463, Whiting 352, Stevenson 1921:6.

6. A weasel-skinned purse is never empty. *Rec. dist.:* Ont.

7. An empty purse fills the face with wrinkles. *Rec. dist.:* Miss. *1st cit.:* 1616 Draxe, *Bibliotheca Scholastica in Anglia* (1918). *20c. coll.:* ODEP 219, Stevenson 1921:16.

8. As the purse is emptied, the heart is filled. *Rec. dist.:* N.Y. *1st cit.:* 1600 Dekker, *Old Fortunatus.* *20c. coll.:* ODEP 219.

9. Ask your purse what you should buy. *Rec. dist.:* U.S., Can. *1st cit.:* 1732 Fuller, *Gnomologia.* *20c. coll.:* Stevenson 1921:18.

10. Better an empty purse than an empty head. *Rec. dist.:* Ill., Nebr.

11. If a man empties his purse into his head, no one can take it from him. *Rec. dist.:* Ala., Ga.

12. If you put nothing in your purse, you can take nothing out. *Rec. dist.:* Ohio, Okla. *1st cit.:* 1642 Torriano, *Select Italian Proverbs.* *20c. coll.:* ODEP 656, Stevenson 1921:18.

13. Let your purse be your master. *Rec. dist.:* Okla., Tex. *1st cit.:* 1616 Withals, *Short Dictionary.* *20c. coll.:* ODEP 655, Stevenson 1921:12.

14. Wrinkled purses make wrinkled faces. *Rec. dist.:* Ont.

15. You can't make a silk purse out of a sow's ear. *Vars.:* **(a)** You can't make a purse out of a sow's ear. **(b)** You can't make a silk out a pig's ear. **(c)** You cannot make a silk purse from a sow's ear. *Rec. dist.:* U.S. *1st cit.:* ca1514 Barclay, *Eclogues,* E.E.T.S. (1927);

US1804 Brackenridge, *Modern Chivalry,* ed. Newlin (1937). *20c. coll.:* ODEP 733, Whiting 352, *CODP* 204, Stevenson 2176:7, T&W 298, Whiting*(MP)* 515.

SEE ALSO A BAG full of flour and a purse full of money are the best relatives in the world. / Be ready with your BONNET but slow with your purse. / Better have a FRIEND on the road than gold or silver in your purse. / When two FRIENDS have a common purse, one sings and the other weeps. / INDUSTRY keeps the body healthy, the mind clear, the heart whole, and the purse full. / MONEY in the purse will always be in fashion. / The good PAYMASTER is lord of another man's purse. / Not to oversee WORKMEN is to leave them with your purse open.

purse strings   The purse strings are the most common ties of friendship. *Rec. dist.:* Ill. *1st cit.:* 1732 Fuller, *Gnomologia.* *20c. coll.:* Stevenson 903:2.

pursue   SEE The GUILTY flee when no man pursues.

pursuing   SEE HAPPINESS is never found by pursuing it. / We LEARN by doing, achieve by pursuing.

pursuit   Lowly pursuits become lowly men. *Rec. dist.:* N.Y.

push *(n.)*   SEE When a man is going DOWN-HILL, everyone gives him a push.

push *(v.)*   SEE The DOOR to success is labeled "push." / A chompy PONY ain't a-fixin' to push no cattle.

pushing   Just pushing ahead will open the door to success much quicker than pulling. *Rec. dist.:* Miss.

put   Put up or shut up. *Var.:* Either put up or shut up. *Rec. dist.:* U.S., Can. *1st cit.:* 1970 Fraser, *Royal Flash;* US1924 Wells, *Farthest Fury.* *20c. coll.:* Whiting*(MP)* 516, Stevenson 2111:4.

SEE ALSO Don't put the CART before the horse. / You GET out of the world just what you put into it. / He who puts up with INSULT invites injury. / What you put into someone's LIFE will someday come back into your own. / You get out of LIFE what you put into it. / NOTHING comes out that is not put in. / You can't put a round PEG in a square hole. / If you put nothing in your PURSE, you can take nothing out. / Don't put off to TOMORROW what you can do today.

putting   SEE Puttin' FEATHERS on a buzzard don't make it no eagle. / Puttin' a HANDLE on the gourd don't make it no dipper. / PICKIN' up is better than totin', but puttin' down beats the world. / Always TAKING out of the meat tub and never putting in soon comes to the bottom.

Q

quack Quacks use their skill to make sound men sick and ill men dead. *Rec. dist.:* Ill.

quackery Quackery has no such friend as credulity. *Rec. dist.:* Ill.

quality 1. Don't value a man for the quality he is of, but for the qualities he possesses. *Rec. dist.:* Ill., N.Y. *1st cit.:* US1724 Franklin, *PRAlmanac.* *20c. coll.:* Stevenson 1923:1.

2. It is better to believe that a man possesses good qualities than to assert that he does not. *Rec. dist.:* Ind.

3. Men of great qualities do not always succeed in life. *Rec. dist.:* Mich.

4. Quality is better than quantity. *Var.:* It is quality rather than quantity which counts. *Rec. dist.:* Okla., Ont. *1st cit.:* 1604 Grymeston, *Miscellanea.* *20c. coll.:* ODEP 658, Stevenson 1923:2.

5. Quality shows. *Rec. dist.:* N.C.
SEE ALSO The quality of MERCY is not strained.

quantity SEE QUALITY is better than quantity.

quarrel *(n.)* 1. Adjusting quarrels proves goodwill; preventing them is nobler still. *Rec. dist.:* Ind.

2. An old quarrel is easily renewed. *Rec. dist.:* Ill.

3. Deep as are the quarrels, deep becomes the love. *Rec. dist.:* N.Y.

4. From one quarrel come a hundred sins. *Rec. dist.:* Ill.

5. He that can make a fire well can end a quarrel. *Rec. dist.:* Ont.

6. He who forgives ends the quarrel. *Rec. dist.:* N.Y.

7. He who returns the first blow is the man who begins the quarrel. *Rec. dist.:* Ohio.

8. If you don't have the first quarrel, you will never have the second. *Rec. dist.:* Utah.

9. It takes two to make a quarrel. *Vars.:* (a) It takes two to have a quarrel but only one to start it. (b) It takes two to make a quarrel, but one can end it. *Rec. dist.:* U.S., Can. *1st cit.:* 1706 Stevens, *New Spanish and English Dictionary;* US1845 Judd, *Margaret, A Tale of the Real and Ideal.* *20c. coll.:* ODEP 852, T&W 389, CODP 234, Stevenson 1924:1, Whiting*(MP)* 653.

10. Never interfere with family quarrels. *Rec. dist.:* N.C.

11. Never let the sun go down on a quarrel. *Rec. dist.:* N.Y.

12. Never pick a quarrel, even when it's right. *Var.:* Never pick a quarrel, even when it's ripe. *Rec. dist.:* Ill.

13. No quarrel ever stirred before the second word. *Var.:* The second word makes the quarrel. *Rec. dist.:* N.Y., Ohio, Ont. *1st cit.:* US1924 Guiterman, *Poet's Proverbs.* *20c. coll.:* Stevenson 1923:14.

14. Quarrels are easily begun but with difficulty ended. *Rec. dist.:* Ill.

15. Quarrels never could last long if on one side only lay the wrong. *Var.:* Quarrels do not last long if the wrong is only on one side. *Rec. dist.:* Calif., N.Y. *1st cit.:* US1741 Franklin, *PRAlmanac.* *20c. coll.:* Stevenson 1923:15.

16. The quarrel of friends is the opportunity of their foes. *Rec. dist.:* Ont.

17. There is no quarrel between the good and the bad, but only between the bad and the bad. *Rec. dist.:* N.Y.

18. There is nothing so foolish as an idle quarrel. *Rec. dist.:* Ont.

19. Those who in quarrels interpose must often wipe a bloody nose. *Rec. dist.:* Colo. *1st cit.:* 1727 Gay, "Mastiff" in *Fables;* US1740 Franklin, *PRAlmanac.* *20c. coll.:* Stevenson 1923:12, Whiting 353.

20. Who seeks a quarrel finds it near at hand. *Rec. dist.:* Ind.

quarrel *(v.)* 1. Be not the first to quarrel nor the last to make up. *Rec. dist.:* Ont.

2. Never quarrel with your bread and butter. *Rec. dist.:* Ill. *1st cit.:* 1738 Swift, *Collection of Genteel and Ingenious Conversation.* *20c. coll.:* ODEP 658.

3. When two quarrel, both are to blame. *Rec. dist.:* Ill., Mich.

SEE ALSO CHILDREN and princes will quarrel for trifles. / Many have quarreled about RELIGION that never practiced it. / Never quarrel with a WOMAN. / A bad WORKMAN quarrels with his tools.

quarreling Quarreling is the weapon of the weak. *Rec. dist.:* Ill.

quarrelsome 1. A quarrelsome disposition makes few friends. *Rec. dist.:* Ill.

2. A quarrelsome man has no good neighbors. *Rec. dist.:* N.Y. *1st cit.:* US1746 Franklin, *PRAlmanac.* *20c. coll.:* Stevenson 1923:11.

quart You can't get a quart out of a thimble. *Rec. dist.:* N.Y., Ont. *1st cit.:* 1896 Hicks-Breach, in *Daily News,* 23 July; US1978 Ginley, *Bogmail.* *20c. coll.:* ODEP 659, Whiting(MP) 518, CODP 187.

queen *SEE* KINGS and queens must die, as well as you and I.

queer 1. Everybody's queer but you and me, and even you are a little queer. *Rec. dist.:* Ky., N.Y., N.Dak., Tenn. *Infm.:* Attributed to Robert Owen in 1828, when he severed business relations with William Allen.

2. To a queer man all the world is queer save himself. *Rec. dist.:* Ill.

SEE ALSO LIFE is a rather queer proposition after all.

quench *SEE* FIRE is not to be quenched with tow. / To pour OIL on the fire is not the way to quench it.

question *(n.)* **1.** Ask me no questions and I'll tell you no lies. *Vars.:* **(a)** Ask me no questions and I'll tell you no lies; give me some peaches and I'll make you some pies. **(b)** Ask me not questions and I'll tell you no fibs. **(c)** Ask me not questions and I'll tell you no lies; give me some apples and I'll bake you a pie. *Rec. dist.:* U.S., Can. *1st cit.:* 1773 Goldsmith, *She Stoops to Conquer;* US1775 Adams in *Warren-Adams Letters,* Mass.Hist.Soc. Collections (1917). *20c. coll.:* ODEP 20, Whiting 353, CODP 7, Stevenson 1394:2, T&W 300, Whiting(MP) 519.

2. Ask questions and learn. *Var.:* If you don't ask questions, you'll never learn anything. *Rec. dist.:* Ala., Ga., N.C.

3. Never answer a question until it is asked. *Var.:* It is enough to answer questions when they are asked. *Rec. dist.:* Ill., Ont. *1st cit.:* 1492 *Dialogue of Salomon & Marcolphus,* ed. Duff. *20c. coll.:* ODEP 561, Stevenson 1926:9.

4. No question is ever settled. *Rec. dist.:* Ill., N.Y. *Infm.:* Attributed to Abraham Lincoln referring to the slavery question, but in the form, "No question is ever settled until it is settled right." *1st cit.:* US1886 Wilcox, *Settle the Question Right.* *20c. coll.:* Stevenson 1926:1.

5. Questions are never indiscreet; answers sometimes are. *Rec. dist.:* N.Y. *1st cit.:* 1895 Wilde, *An Ideal Husband.* *20c. coll.:* Stevenson 1926:12.

6. Silly question, silly answer. *Var.:* Ask a silly question, you'll get a silly answer. *Rec. dist.:* U.S., Can. *1st cit.:* 1584 Lyly, *Campaspe;* US1858 Hammett, *Piney Woods Tavern.* *20c. coll.:* ODEP 659, T&W 300, Stevenson 851:3, Whiting(MP) 519.

7. 'Tis better to ask some of the questions than to know all the answers. *Rec. dist.:* Ind.

8. 'Tis not every question that deserves an answer. *Rec. dist.:* Ill., Tex. *1st cit.:* 1875 Cheales, *Proverbial Folk-Lore.* *20c. coll.:* Stevenson 1926:8.

9. To a man full of questions, make no answer at all. *Rec. dist.:* Ill.

10. Weighty questions ask for deliberate answers. *Rec. dist.:* N.Y. *1st cit.:* US1735 Franklin, *PRAlmanac.* *20c. coll.:* Stevenson 1926:9.

SEE ALSO Give a civil ANSWER to a civil question. / There's no ANSWER to a fool's question. / A FOOL can ask more questions in a minute than a wise man can answer in an hour.

question *(v.)* **1.** He who questions nothing learns nothing. *Rec. dist.:* Ill. *1st cit.:* 1732 Fuller, *Gnomologia.* *20c. coll.:* Stevenson 1925:6.

2. To question a wise man is the beginning of wisdom. *Rec. dist.:* Ill.

3. Yours is not to question why; yours is but to do or die. *Rec. dist.:* Calif., Colo., Mich., N.Y. *1st cit.:* 1621 Robinson, *Adagia in Latine and English;* US1819 Pierce, *Rebelliad.* **20c. coll.:** ODEP 192, Whiting 113, Stevenson 537:5, T&W 104, Whiting*(MP)* 171.

quick *(n.)* We must live by the quick, not by the dead. *Rec. dist.:* N.Y. *1st cit.:* 1576 Pettie, *Petite Palace of Pleasure;* USca1800 Jefferson, *Writings.* **20c. coll.:** Stevenson 1418:4.

quick *(adj.)* **1.** Be quick but never hurry, for hurry brings disaster. *Rec. dist.:* N.Y. *1st cit.:* 1751 Chesterfield, *Letters,* 28 July. **20c. coll.:** Stevenson 1202:19.

2. Quick at meat, quick at work. *Rec. dist.:* Ont. *1st cit.:* 1611 Cotgrave, *Dictionary of French and English Tongues.* **20c. coll.:** ODEP 660, Stevenson 1927:3.

SEE ALSO CANDY is dandy, but liquor is quicker. / The quickest GENEROSITY is the best. / The HAND is quicker than the eye. / A quick NICKEL is better than a slow dollar. / Quick RETURNS make rich merchants.

quickly What is quickly done is quickly undone. *Rec. dist.:* Ill. *1st cit.:* 1647 Gracian, *Oraculo Manual.* **20c. coll.:** Stevenson 535:8.

SEE ALSO He ACTS well who acts quickly. / Small EVILS hatch quickly. / Beware of those who get FAMILIAR quickly. / GOOD and quickly seldom meet. / A short HORSE is quickly curried.

quicksand *SEE* Even an ASS will not fall twice in the same quicksand.

quiet *(n.)* There's always a quiet after a storm. *Var.:* There is always quietness after a storm. *Rec. dist.:* N.Y. *1st cit.:* ca1200 *Ancrene Riwle;* USca1680 *Voyages of Radisson,* ed. Scull, Publ. Prince Soc. (1885). **20c. coll.:** ODEP 6, Whiting 418, *CODP* 2, Stevenson 2222:2, T&W 54.

quiet *(adj.)* **1.** Anything for a quiet life. *Rec. dist.:* Ont. *1st cit.:* ca1621 Middleton, *Anything for a Quiet Life.* **20c. coll.:** ODEP 15.

2. Keep quiet and let people think you're ignorant; don't speak and remove all doubt. *Rec. dist.:* Calif., Colo., Miss., N.Y.

3. Quiet people, whether wise or dull, get the benefit of the doubt. *Rec. dist.:* Ill.

SEE ALSO The quiet HOG drinks the most swill. / The best PHYSICIANS are Dr. Diet, Dr. Quiet, and Dr. Merryman.

quietness **1.** Better a dry morsel with quietness than a house full of sacrifice with strife. *Rec. dist.:* Ind., Ont. *1st cit.:* US1948 Stevenson, *Home Book of Proverbs.* **20c. coll.:** Stevenson 1928:4.

2. Next to love, quietness. *Rec. dist.:* Ont. *1st cit.:* 1678 Ray, *English Proverbs.* **20c. coll.:** ODEP 493, Stevenson 1928:5.

quill A goose quill is more dangerous than a lion's claw. *Var.:* A goose's quill is more dangerous than a lion's claw. *Rec. dist.:* Mich., N.Y. *Infm.:* A "goose quill" refers to a pen.

quit **1.** Don't quit till the hearse comes around. *Rec. dist.:* Miss.

2. Never quit until the last one. *Rec. dist.:* Ind.

3. When you're through, quit. *Rec. dist.:* N.C.

SEE ALSO If LOVE interferes with your business, quit your business. / A WINNER never quits, and a quitter never wins.

quitter God almighty hates a quitter. *Var.:* God hates a quitter. *Rec. dist.:* Ill., Mich., N.Y. *Infm.:* Remark made by Fessenden at Republican National Convention in St. Louis, June 1896, referring to J. Manley. *1st cit.:* US1896 Fessenden in Robinson, *Life of T. B. Reed* (1930). **20c. coll.:** Stevenson 448:10.

SEE ALSO A WINNER never quits, and a quitter never wins.

quotation Quotation confesses inferiority. *Rec. dist.:* N.Y. *1st cit.:* US1875 Emerson, *Quotation and Originality.* **20c. coll.:** Stevenson 1929:1.

R

rabbit 1. Brer Rabbit trusts no mistake. *Rec. dist.:* S.C.

2. Don't stay with the rabbits but run with the hounds. *Rec. dist.:* Ont. *1st cit.:* ca1440 *Jacob's Well,* E.E.T.S. (1900); US1755 *Colonial Virginia Satirist,* ed. Davis, Am. Phil.Soc. *Transactions* (1967). *20c. coll.:* ODEP 689, Whiting 225, CODP 195, Stevenson 1077:10, Whiting*(MP)* 288.

3. First catch your rabbit and then make your stew. *Var.:* Don't make your stew until you catch the rabbit. *Rec. dist.:* Ont. *1st cit.:* 1801 *Spirit of Farmers' Museum;* US1922 Fox, *Ethel Opens the Door. 20c. coll.:* CODP 81, Whiting*(MP)* 287, ODEP 262, Stevenson 1075:14.

4. It is better to be a live rabbit than a dead tiger. *Rec. dist.:* Ala., Ga.

5. There is always something to keep the rabbit's tail short. *Var.:* Anything to keep the rabbit's tail short. *Rec. dist.:* N.Y., N.C., Ont., S.C.

6. You can't tell how far a rabbit can jump by the length of its ears. *Rec. dist.:* Ill.

7. You get the rabbit from the hind legs. *Rec. dist.:* N.Y., S.C. *Infm.:* Sneak up on your prey from behind.
See also Cows can't catch no rabbits. / If the DOG hadn't stopped to lift his leg he would have caught the rabbit. / It's safer to be a HOUND than a rabbit. / WHISKEY make rabbit hug lion.

race 1. No race is won or lost until the line is crossed. *Rec. dist.:* Ind.

2. The race is not always to the swift. *Vars.:* (a) The race is not always to the swift, but that is where to look. (b) The race is not always to the swift, nor the battle to the strong. (c) The race is not to the swift. (d) The races are not always to the swift. (e) To the swifter the race is lost. *Rec. dist.:* U.S., Can. *1st cit.:* 1581 Elliot, *Report of Taking E. Campion;* US1671 Pray in *Winthrop Papers,* Mass.Hist.Soc. *Collections* (1863–92). *20c. coll.:* ODEP 661, Whiting 355, CODP 188, Stevenson 1930:2, T&W 301, Whiting*(MP)* 521.

3. You must run to win the race. *Rec. dist.:* Ind. *1st cit.:* 1732 Fuller, *Gnomologia. 20c. coll.:* ODEP 661, Stevenson 1930:6.
See also A lean HORSE wins the race. / It's a difference of OPINION that makes a horse race. / SLOW and easy wins the race. / A good START is half the race.

racehorse 1. Don't judge a man's knowledge of racehorses by the clothes he wears. *Rec. dist.:* Oreg.

2. You can't make a racehorse out of a mule. *Rec. dist.:* Okla.
See also A skinny WOMAN is like a racehorse: fast and fun, but no good for work.

rack Stand to the rack, fodder or no fodder. *Rec. dist.:* S.C. *Infm.:* Stay at your task or assigned position. *1st cit.:* US1834 Crockett, *Life of David Crockett. 20c. coll.:* T&W 301.
See also Use your HEAD for something besides a hat rack.

racket *See* ROOSTER makes more racket dan de hen w'at lay de aig.

radio Always turn the radio on before you listen to it. *Rec. dist.:* N.Dak.

rag Every rag meets its mate. *Rec. dist.:* N.Y.

rage 1. Provoke not the rage of a patient man. *Rec. dist.:* Mich.

2. Rage is brief insanity. *Rec. dist.:* Ont. *1st cit.:* ca1200 *Ancrene Riwle,* Camden Soc. (1853); US1652 *Complete Writings of Roger Williams* (1963). *20c. coll.:* ODEP 13, Whiting 9, Stevenson 68:11.
See also FEAR is a fine spur; so is rage. / It is better to bear a single INJURY in silence than to provoke a thousand by flying into a rage.

rail 1. One broken rail will wreck a train. *Rec. dist.:* N.C.

2. The bottom rail gets on top every fifty years. *Rec. dist.:* N.Y., S.C.

railroad Even railroads have curves. *Rec. dist.:* Miss. *Infm.:* A saying used by the West Milwaukee Railroad Shop to remind the engineers on the trains to slow down on the curves.

rain *(n.)* **1.** A little rain stills a great wind. *Var.:* A small rain may allay a great storm. *Rec. dist.:* Ill., N.Y., N.C., S.C. *1st cit.:* ca1200 *Ancrene Riwle,* Camden Soc. (1853). *20c. coll.:* ODEP 662, Stevenson 1933:2, Whiting*(MP)* 523.

2. A morning's rain is like an old woman's dance: it doesn't last long. *Rec. dist.:* Miss., S.C. *1st cit.:* 1640 Herbert, *Outlandish Proverbs (Jacula Prudentum)* in *Works,* ed. Hutchinson (1941). *20c. coll.:* Stevenson 1932:2.

3. A small rain lays a great dust. *Vars.:* **(a)** Small rain lays great dust. **(b)** Small rain will lay a great dust. *Rec. dist.:* Ill., Miss., Ont. *1st cit.:* 1670 Ray, *English Proverbs. 20c. coll.:* ODEP 662, Stevenson 1932:12.

4. After rain comes sunshine. *Vars.:* **(a)** After the rain, the sun. **(b)** Sunshine always follows rain. *Rec. dist.:* Ill., N.Y. *1st cit.:* 1484 Caxton, *Aesope;* US1869 Spurgeon, *John Ploughman's Talks. 20c. coll.:* Stevenson 1933:3.

5. All who travel in the rain get wet. *Rec. dist.:* N.J.

6. If there were no rain, there'd be no hay to make when the sun shines. *Rec. dist.:* Ky., Tenn.

7. Into each life some rain must fall. *Var.:* Into every life a little rain must fall. *Rec. dist.:* U.S., Can. *1st cit.:* 1960 Wodehouse, *Jeeves in Offing;* US1935 Ashbrook, *Most Immoral Murder. 20c. coll.:* Whiting*(MP)* 370.

8. It is pleasant to look on the rain when one stands dry. *Rec. dist.:* Ill.

9. More rain, more grass. *Rec. dist.:* Ind.

10. More rain, more rest. *Vars.:* **(a)** More rain, more rest; fine weather not the best. **(b)** Some rain, some rest. **(c)** Some rain, some rest; fine weather isn't always best. *Rec. dist.:* N.Y., Okla., Ont., S.C. *1st cit.:* 1864 "Cornish Proverbs" in *Notes & Queries. 20c. coll.:* ODEP 544, Stevenson 1932:11.

11. Rain before seven, clear before eleven.

Vars.: **(a)** Rain before seven, fine before eleven. **(b)** Rain before seven, quit before eleven. **(c)** Thunder before seven, rain before eleven; rain before seven, stop before eleven. *Rec. dist.:* U.S., Can. *1st cit.:* 1853 "Rain before Seven" in *Notes & Queries;* US1950 Gould, *Yankee Boyhood. 20c. coll.:* ODEP 662, Whiting*(MP)* 523, *CODP* 188, Stevenson 1933:1.

12. Rain falls alike on the just and unjust. *Rec. dist.:* Ky., Miss., N.Y., Ont., Tenn. *1st cit.:* US1948 Stevenson, *Home Book of Proverbs. 20c. coll.:* Stevenson 1284:9.

13. Rain in May makes the hay. *Rec. dist.:* Wis.

14. Rain never melted anyone. *Rec. dist.:* Ont. *1st cit.:* 1738 Swift, *Collection of Genteel and Ingenious Conversation;* US1870 Bridgman, *Robert Lynne. 20c. coll.:* Stevenson 1931:15.

15. Rain one day, shine the next. *Rec. dist.:* Wis.

16. Rain won't stand on a tin roof. *Rec. dist.:* N.C.

17. The rain that rains on everybody else can't keep you dry. *Rec. dist.:* Ont.

SEE ALSO EVENING red and morning gray will send the sailor on his way, but evening gray and morning red will bring rain down upon his head. / Even a FOOL carries his coat in the rain. / The LORD sends sun at one time, rain at another. / LOVE comforts like sunshine after rain. / Take the SUNSHINE with the rain. / Three THINGS drive a man out of his home: smoke, rain, and a scolding wife. / The UMBRELLA goes up when the rain comes down.

rain *(v.)* **1.** Don't rain eve'y time de pig squeal. *Rec. dist.:* N.Y., S.C.

2. It never rains but it pours. *Vars.:* **(a)** Every time it rains, it pours. **(b)** When it rains, it pours. *Rec. dist.:* U.S., Can. *1st cit.:* 1726 Arbuthnot, *It Cannot Rain but it Pours;* US1755 *Papers of Benjamin Franklin,* ed. Labaree (1959). *20c. coll.:* ODEP 663, Whiting 356, *CODP* 188, Stevenson 1930:10, T&W 303, Whiting*(MP)* 523.

SEE ALSO It never THUNDERS but it rains. / If you leave your UMBRELLA at home, it is sure to rain.

rainbow 1. A rainbow is big enough for everyone to look at. *Rec. dist.:* N.Y., S.C. *1st cit.:* US1940 Case, *Do Not Disturb. 20c. coll.:* Stevenson 1933:4.

2. Rainbow at night, sailor's delight; rainbow at morning, sailors take warning. *Vars.:* (a) Rainbow at night, sailor's delight; rainbow in the morning, the sailor's warning. (b) Rainbow at night, shepherd's delight; rainbow in morning, shepherds take warning. (c) Rainbow in the morning, sailor take warning; rainbow at night, sailor's delight. *Rec. dist.:* U.S., Can. *1st cit.:* 1555 Digges, *Prognostication;* US1893 Inwards, *Weather-Lore: Collection of Proverbs. 20c. coll.:* ODEP 662, Stevenson 1933:7, Whiting*(MP)* 524.

raincrow Raincrow don't sing no chune, but you c'n 'pen' on 'im. *Rec. dist.:* Miss., N.Y. *Infm.:* Standard version reads: "Raincrow don't sing no tune, but you can depend on him." The raincrow predicts rain.

rainy Save for a rainy day. *Vars.:* (a) Put by for a rainy day. (b) Put something away for a rainy day. (c) Save it for a rainy day. (d) Save your money for a rainy day. (e) Save your pennies for a rainy day. *Rec. dist.:* U.S., Can. *1st cit.:* ca1566 Bugbears; US1753 *Papers of Benjamin Franklin,* ed. Labaree (1959). *20c. coll.:* ODEP 663, Whiting 96, Stevenson 491:8, T&W 92, Whiting*(MP)* 154.

raising Letting grow and raising are different. *Rec. dist.:* Ky., Tenn.

rake *(scoundrel)* A reformed rake makes the best husband. *Rec. dist.:* N.Y., N.C., S.C. *1st cit.:* 1924 Munro (pseud. Saki), *Square Egg;* US1797 Foster, *Coquette,* ed. Brown (1939). *20c. coll.:* Whiting*(MP)* 524, Whiting 356.

rake *(tool)* Keep the rake near the scythe, and the cart near the rake. *Rec. dist.:* Colo., N.Y. *Infm.:* Be prepared. *1st cit US1841 Emerson, "Prudence" in Essays. 20c. coll.:* Stevenson 1934:5.

ram Don't look for a ram with five feet. *Rec. dist.:* Ill.

rank The rank and file are usually slow on the uptake, but they can be quick on the letdown. *Rec. dist.:* W.Va.

ransom The ransom of a man's life is his riches. *Rec. dist.:* Ind.

rap *SEE* If you will not hear REASON, she will surely rap your knuckles.

rare *SEE* True FRIENDS are like diamonds, precious and rare; false ones like autumn, leaves found everywhere. / SILENCE is a rare jewel. / A VIRTUOUS woman is rarer than a precious jewel.

rascal There isn't a rascal or a thief that doesn't have his devotion. *Rec. dist.:* Calif.

SEE ALSO One begins by being a DUPE; one ends by being a rascal. / The FOOLS do more hurt in the world than the rascals.

rascality Rascality has limits; stupidity has not. *Rec. dist.:* Ont.

rash *SEE* A rash FRIEND is worse than a foe.

rat 1. Don't corner a rat. *Rec. dist.:* Ky., Tenn.

2. Even a rat, when cornered, will turn and fight. *Var.:* A cornered rat will fight like a demon. *Rec. dist.:* Ind., Oreg. *1st cit.:* 1928 Adams, *Empty Bed;* US1867 Harris, *Sut Lovingood. 20c. coll.:* T&W 303, Whiting*(MP)* 525.

3. It takes a rat to catch a rat. *Rec. dist.:* Okla.

4. Rats desert a sinking ship. *Vars.:* (a) Only a rat leaves a sinking ship. (b) Rats always leave a sinking ship. *Rec. dist.:* U.S., Can. *1st cit.:* 1579 Lupton, *Thousand Notable Things;* US1755 *Papers of Benjamin Franklin,* ed. Labaree (1959). *20c. coll.:* ODEP 664, Whiting 357, Stevenson 1936:11, Whiting*(MP)* 526.

5. Rats know the way of rats. *Rec. dist.:* Ill. *1st cit.:* US1938 Champion, *Racial Proverbs. 20c. coll.:* Stevenson 2300:1.

6. The rat which has but one hole is soon caught. *Rec. dist.:* Colo., Mich., N.Y. *1st cit.:* ca1386 Chaucer, *Prologue to Wife of Bath's Tale;* US1821 Dalton, *Travels in U.S., 1819–1820,* ed. Appleby. *20c. coll.:* ODEP 548, Whiting 357.

SEE ALSO A bad CAT deserves a bad rat. / Sell your GOODS at market price; keep it not for rats and mice. / Don't throw WATER on a drowned rat.

rate *SEE* They who borrow TROUBLE must pay a high rate of interest.

rattle *See* An empty CART rattles loudest.

rattlesnake *See* Never shake HANDS with a rattlesnake.

raven 1. The raven eludes a blackness. *Rec. dist.:* Ill.

2. The ravens don't peck one another's eyes out. *Rec. dist.:* N.Y.

3. The young ravens are beaked like the old. *Rec. dist.:* Ill. *1st cit.:* 1659 Howell, *Paroimiografia.* *20c. coll.:* Stevenson 1627:8.

raw *See* Raw LEATHER will stretch.

razor If you don't have a razor, you are sure to be shaved. *Rec. dist.:* Utah.
See also A lot of a CHILD's welfare can be done with a razor strap.

reach *(n.)* 1. A man's reach must exceed his grasp. *Vars.:* (a) A man's reach ought to exceed his grasp. (b) A man's reach should be beyond his grasp. (c) A man's reach should exceed his grasp. *Rec. dist.:* Ont. *1st cit.:* 1855 Browning, *Andrea del Sarto.* *20c. coll.:* Stevenson 100:13.

2. Do not despise that which is beyond reach. *Var.:* There are many who pretend to despise that which is beyond their reach. *Rec. dist.:* Ont.

3. From life to death is man's reach. *Rec. dist.:* Ill.

4. Out of reach is not worth having. *Rec. dist.:* N.C.

reach *(v.)* *See* Winter GRAPE sour whedder you kin reach 'im or not. / Don't get off the LADDER before you reach the ground.

reaction *See* ACTIONS and reactions are equal.

read 1. He that can read and meditate will not find his evenings long or life tedious. *Rec. dist.:* Ill.

2. Read carefully; sign cautiously. *Rec. dist.:* Ont.

3. Read much, but not too many books. *Rec. dist.:* Ill. *1st cit.:* 1711 Pope, *Essay on Criticism.* *20c. coll.:* Stevenson 1937:9.

4. Read much, speak little, and write less. *Rec. dist.:* Ill.

5. The man who reads is the man who leads. *Rec. dist.:* Miss.

6. 'Tis not how much but how well we read. *Rec. dist.:* Wis.

7. To read and not to understand is to pursue and not to take. *Rec. dist.:* Mich.
See also It is a tie between men to have read the same BOOK. / The man who doesn't read good BOOKS has no advantage over the man who can't read them. / You are known by the BOOKS you read. / Every MAN is a volume if you know how to read him.

reader 1. Seldom readers are slow readers. *Rec. dist.:* Ont.

2. 'Tis the good reader that makes the book good. *Rec. dist.:* N.Y., S.C. *1st cit.:* US1870 Emerson, "Success" in *Society and Solitude.* *20c. coll.:* Stevenson 1938:8.
See also FLATTERERS are clever mind readers: they tell us exactly what we think.

reading 1. A reading people will be a knowing people. *Rec. dist.:* Miss.

2. Extensive reading is a priceless treasure. *Rec. dist.:* Ind.

3. Reading makes a full man, conference a ready man, writing an exact man. *Var.:* Reading makes a full man, meditation a profound man, discourse a clear man. *Rec. dist.:* Ill., N.Y. *1st cit.:* 1597 Bacon, "Of Studies" in *Essays;* US1738 Franklin, *PRAlmanac.* *20c. coll.:* Stevenson 1937:10.
See also Easy WRITING makes hard reading.

ready 1. In an orderly house all things are always ready. *Var.:* All is soon ready in an orderly house. *Rec. dist.:* Ont.

2. It's better to be ready and not to go than not to be ready and go. *Rec. dist.:* N.J.
See also READING makes a full man, conference a ready man, writing an exact man. / Where the WILL is ready the feet are light.

real *See* Real HAPPINESS is found not in doing the things you like to do, but in liking the things you have to do.

reality 1. Reality never surpasses imagination. *Rec. dist.:* Ont.

2. There are stranger things in reality than can be found in romances. *Rec. dist.:* N.Y., S.C.

SEE ALSO DREAMS are what you hope for; reality is what you plan for.

realization SEE ANTICIPATION is twice the joy of realization. / EXPECTATION always surpasses realization.

realm SEE KINGS and realms pass away, but time goes on forever.

reap SEE Sow the WIND and reap the whirlwind.

reaper **1.** A bad reaper never got a good sickle. *Rec. dist.:* Wis.

2. A good reaper deserves a good sickle. *Rec. dist.:* Utah.

reason **1.** A man without reason is a beast in season. *Rec. dist.:* Ill. *1st cit.:* 1659 Howell, *Paroimiografia.* *20c. coll.:* ODEP 507, Stevenson 1940:3.

2. Better die than turn your back on reason. *Rec. dist.:* Ind.

3. Hear reason or she'll make you feel her. *Rec. dist.:* Colo.

4. Hearken to reason or she will not be heard. *Rec. dist.:* N.Y.

5. If you will not hear reason, she will surely rap your knuckles. *Var.:* Hearken to reason or she will be heard. *Rec. dist.:* N.Y., S.C. *1st cit.:* 1611 Cotgrave, *Dictionary of French and English Tongues;* US1745 Franklin, *PRAlmanac.* *20c. coll.:* ODEP 363, Stevenson 1940:8.

6. Reason is the life of the law. *Rec. dist.:* Ont. *1st cit.:* 1628 Coke, *Institutes of Lawes of England.* *20c. coll.:* Stevenson 1359:11.

7. Reason succeeds where force fails. *Rec. dist.:* Ont.

8. There is reason in all things. *Rec. dist.:* Ont. *1st cit.:* 1602 Marston, *Antonio and Mellida;* US1859 Smith, *My Thirty Years Out of the Senate.* *20c. coll.:* ODEP 666, T&W 305, Stevenson 1940:4, Whiting*(MP)* 528.

9. 'Tis in vain to speak reason where it will not be heard. *Rec. dist.:* Ill.

10. Without a good reason for doing a thing, we have a fine reason for leaving it alone. *Rec. dist.:* Ind.

SEE ALSO ANGER is never without reason. / The FEAR's greater than the reason for it. / FORTUNE knows neither reason nor law. / If PASSION drives, let reason hold the reins. / Would you PERSUADE, speak of interest, not of reason. / Neither great POVERTY or great riches will hear reason.

rebellion **1.** Rebellion to tyrants is obedience to God. *Rec. dist.:* N.Y. *1st cit.:* USca1770 Franklin in Randolph, *Life of Jefferson.* *20c. coll.:* Stevenson 1943:2.

2. The only justification of rebellion is success. *Rec. dist.:* N.Y. *1st cit.:* US1878 Reed, Speech in House of Representatives, 12 Apr. *20c. coll.:* Stevenson 1943:4.

rebuke *(n.)* **1.** Open rebuke is better than secret love. *Vars.:* **(a)** Open rebuke is better than secret hatred. **(b)** Open rebuke is better than secret scorn. *Rec. dist.:* Ill., Wis. *1st cit.:* US1948 Stevenson, *Home Book of Proverbs.* *20c. coll.:* Stevenson 1958:14.

2. Rebuke ought not to have a grain more of salt than of sugar. *Rec. dist.:* Ill. *1st cit.:* 1580 Lyly, *Euphues and His England.* *20c. coll.:* Stevenson 1958:14.

rebuke *(v.)* SEE Reprove not a SCORNER lest he hate you; rebuke a wise man and he will love you.

recall SEE TIME and words can never be recalled.

recede Nothing recedes like success. *Rec. dist.:* Calif.

SEE ALSO Not to ADVANCE is to recede.

receive SEE It is better to GIVE than to receive. / Who PLEASURE gives shall joy receive.

receiver **1.** No receiver, no thief; no penny, no paternoster. *Rec. dist.:* N.Y. *1st cit.:* ca1386 Chaucer, *Cook's Tale;* US1656 Hammond, *Leah and Rachel.* *20c. coll.:* ODEP 573, Whiting 358, Stevenson 2300:6.

2. The receiver is as bad as the thief. *Rec. dist.:* U.S., Can. *1st cit.:* ca1390 Chaucer, *Cook's Tale;* US1716 "Considerations" in *Colonial Currency Reprints,* ed. Davis, Publ. Prince Soc.

(1910–11). **20c. coll.:** *CODP* 189, Whiting 358, *ODEP* 667, Stevenson 2300:8.

recipe *See* PATIENCE is the wisest recipe for success.

reckon *See* Don't reckon without your HOST.

reckoning Short reckonings make long friends. **Rec. dist.:** Ky., Mich., Ont. *1st cit.:* 1537 Whitford, *Werke for Householders;* US1776 Paine, *Common Sense.* **20c. coll.:** *ODEP* 728, Whiting 359, *CODP* 202, Stevenson 1943:12, T&W 305.

See also Merry is the FEAST making till we come to the reckoning. / The fairer the HOST-ESS, the fouler the reckoning.

recognition Recognition for everything comes eventually. **Rec. dist.:** N.Y.

recognize *See* GOOD is recognized when it goes, and evil when it comes. / Half the battle of TEMPTATION is recognizing it.

recommendation *See* SELF-PRAISE is no recommendation.

recompense *See* The SUN never repents of the good it does, nor does it ever demand a recompense.

reconciled *See* Beware of ENEMIES reconciled and meat twice boiled.

record *See* A man's best REPUTATION for his future is his record of the past.

recover *See* Lost INNOCENCE and wasted time are never recovered. / A SLIP of the foot you may soon recover, but a slip of the tongue you may never get over.

red Red sky at night, sailor's delight; red sky in the morning, sailors take warning. **Var.:** A red sun at night is a sailor's delight. **Rec. dist.:** U.S., Can. *1st cit.:* ca1454 Pecock, *Follower to Donet,* E.E.T.S. (1918); US1852 Cary, *Clovernook.* **20c. coll.:** *CODP* 189, T&W 122, *ODEP* 741, Stevenson 2474:11, Whiting(*MP*) 573.

See also EVENING red and morning gray will send the sailor on his way, but evening gray and morning red will bring rain down upon his head. / The redder the FRUIT, the higher it hangs.

redress *See* A FAULT confessed is half redressed.

reed 1. A beaten soldier fears a reed. **Rec. dist.:** Ind.

2. Reeds will bend, but iron will not. **Rec. dist.:** N.C.

3. The reed does blow at every blast. **Rec. dist.:** Ont. *1st cit.:* ca1374 Chaucer, *Troilus and Criseyde;* US1776 *St. Clair Papers,* ed. Smith (1882). **20c. coll.:** *ODEP* 584, Whiting 359, *CODP* 189, Stevenson 1705:3.

4. Where there are reeds, there is water. **Rec. dist.:** Ont. *1st cit.:* ca1700 *Dictionary of Canting Crew.* **20c. coll.:** *ODEP* 669, Stevenson 1944:7.

See also HOPE is a slender reed for a stout man to lean on.

reflection Reflection insures safety, but rashness is followed by regrets. **Rec. dist.:** Ill. *1st cit.:* US1948 Stevenson, *Home Book of Proverbs.* **20c. coll.:** Stevenson 1083:10.

See also PRAISE is the reflection of virtue.

reform *(n.)* 1. All social reforms must begin with ourselves. **Rec. dist.:** Ind.

2. Reforms are generally most unpopular where most needed. **Rec. dist.:** Ill.

reform *(v.)* The greatest need to reform is among the reformers. **Rec. dist.:** Ont.

reformed *See* A reformed RAKE makes the best husband.

refusal *See* He who BEGS timidly, courts refusal.

regard *See* Where there is HUNGER law is not regarded, and where law is not regarded there will be hunger.

region High regions are never without storms. **Rec. dist.:** Mich.

regret *(n.)* 1. Regret causes an aching which is worse than pain. **Rec. dist.:** W.Va.

2. Regret is a terrible weakness. **Rec. dist.:** Ohio.

3. Regrets last longer than repentance. **Rec. dist.:** N.Y., S.C. *1st cit.:* US1940 *Meditations in Wall Street.* **20c. coll.:** Stevenson 1946:9.

See also Careless HURRY may cause endless regret. / One wrong THOUGHT may cause a lifelong regret. / YOUTH is a blunder, manhood a struggle, old age a regret.

regret *(v.)* SEE FRET today, regret tomorrow.

regretting SEE FORGETTING is regretting. / PLANNING your future saves you from regretting your past.

rehearsing SEE Bad HEARING makes bad rehearsing. / A man in SUFFERING finds relief in rehearsing his ills.

reign He who reigns within himself is more than a king. *Rec. dist.:* Ont. *1st cit.:* US1887 Beecher, *Proverbs from Plymouth Pulpit.* *20c. coll.:* Stevenson 2061:4.
   SEE ALSO The KING reigns but does not rule.

rein SEE If PASSION drives, let reason hold the reins.

rejoice 1. Rejoice today and repent tomorrow. *Rec. dist.:* N.J.

2. Rejoice with them that rejoice; weep with them that weep. *Var.:* Rejoice with those that do rejoice. *Rec. dist.:* Mich., Ont. *1st cit.:* ca1386 Chaucer, *Tale of Melibee;* US1883 Wilcox, "Solitude" in *N.Y. Sun,* 25 Feb. *20c. coll.:* Stevenson 2266:10, *CODP* 129.
   SEE ALSO It's a poor HEART that never rejoices.

rekindle SEE Old FIRES are easily rekindled.

relation SEE BARGAINING has neither friends nor relations.

relationship Relationship is a poor ship to sail on. *Rec. dist.:* Ont.

relative 1. A lot of relatives, a lot of trouble. *Rec. dist.:* Ill.

2. God gives us relatives; thank God we can choose our friends. *Vars.:* (a) God gave us our relatives; we can choose our friends. (b) God gives us our relatives, but we can pick our teeth. *Rec. dist.:* U.S., Can. *1st cit.:* US1844 Stephens, *High Life in New York.* *20c. coll.:* T&W 305, Stevenson 1296:2.

3. If you have nothing, go to your relatives. *Rec. dist.:* Ont.

4. Relatives are best with a wall between. *Rec. dist.:* Ont.

5. Relatives are friends from bitter necessity. *Rec. dist.:* Ill.

6. Relatives take the greatest liberties and give the least assistance. *Rec. dist.:* Calif., Colo.

7. With a relative eat and drink, but transact no business with him. *Rec. dist.:* Calif.
   SEE ALSO A BAG full of flour and a purse full of money are the best relatives in the world. / FRIENDS are to be preferred to relatives. / Where there is a VOICE there is a relative.

relax Relax and enjoy it. *Rec. dist.:* N.Y. *1st cit.:* 1969 Catling, *Freddy Hill;* US1957 Goldman, *Temple of Gold.* *20c. coll.:* Whiting*(MP)* 530.

reliable SEE WORK don't never set aroun' hollerin' fer ol' reliable to come to do it.

relief SEE A man in SUFFERING finds relief in rehearsing his ills.

religion 1. A man without religion is a horse without a bridle. *Rec. dist.:* Ill., Miss. *1st cit.:* 1621 Burton, *Anatomy of Melancholy.* *20c. coll.:* *ODEP* 507, Stevenson 1947:8.

2. A woman without religion is a flower without perfume. *Rec. dist.:* Ill.

3. Each one holds his own religion for the best. *Rec. dist.:* Ill. *1st cit.:* 1587 Bridges, *Defence;* US1742 Franklin, *PRAlmanac.* *20c. coll.:* *ODEP* 411, Whiting 360.

4. He that has not religion for his pillow is without a resting place. *Rec. dist.:* Mich.

5. If religion was a thing we all could buy, the rich would live and the poor would die. *Rec. dist.:* Ill.

6. It matters not what religion an ill man is of. *Rec. dist.:* N.Y. *1st cit.:* 1732 Fuller, *Gnomologia.* *20c. coll.:* *ODEP* 670, Stevenson 1947:17.

7. Many have quarreled about religion that never practiced it. *Rec. dist.:* N.Y. *1st cit.:* US1753 Franklin, *PRAlmanac.* *20c. coll.:* Stevenson 1947:16.

8. Monday religion is better than Sunday profession. *Rec. dist.:* Ont.

9. Religion adapted to the wise alone leaves most of the sheep unshepherded. *Rec. dist.:* Ill.

10. Religion is the best armor in the world, but the worst cloak. *Rec. dist.:* N.Y. *1st cit.:*

1732 Fuller, *Gnomologia*. *20c. coll.*: Stevenson 1947:17.

11. Religion should be a rule of life, not a casual incident of it. *Rec. dist.*: Wis. *1st cit.*: 1616 Breton, *Crossing of Proverbs*. *20c. coll.*: ODEP 670, Stevenson 1947:4.

12. There is no bargain-counter religion. *Rec. dist.*: N.C.

13. You're not supposed to keep religion— it's supposed to keep you. *Rec. dist.*: N.C.

relish *(n.)* The cost often spoils the relish. *Rec. dist.*: Ill.

relish *(v.)* What one relishes, nourishes. *Rec. dist.*: Ky., N.Y., S.C., Tenn. *1st cit.*: US1734 Franklin, *PRAlmanac*. *20c. coll.*: Stevenson 84:10.

SEE ALSO A little NONSENSE now and then is relished by the best of men.

rely SEE A great TALKER may be no fool, but he is one who relies on him.

remark **1.** Heated remarks never thaw icy hearts. *Rec. dist.*: Ont.

2. Most people make many remarks without saying anything remarkable. *Rec. dist.*: Ill.

remedy **1.** A good remedy for anger is delay. *Rec. dist.*: Kans. *1st cit.*: 1539 Publilius Syrus, *Sententiae*, tr. Taverner. *20c. coll.*: Stevenson 70:3.

2. For every evil under the sun, there is a remedy or there is none. If there be one, seek and find it; if there be none, never mind it. *Vars.*: **(a)** For every ill beneath the sun, there is a remedy or none. **(b)** For every ill beneath the sun, there is some remedy or none. If there be one, go find it; if not, never mind it. *Rec. dist.*: N.C., Ont., W.Va., Wis. *1st cit.*: ca1843 *Maxims and Morals*. *20c. coll.*: Stevenson 1950:10, ODEP 228.

3. Sometimes the remedy is worse than the disease. *Var.*: The remedy is worse than the disease. *Rec. dist.*: N.Y., Oreg. *1st cit.*: 1582 Mulcaster, *The Elementary*, ed. Campagnac (1925); US1633 Howes in *Winthrop Papers, 1498–1649*, Mass.Hist.Soc. *Collections* (1929–47). *20c. coll.*: ODEP 671, Whiting 360, Stevenson 1952:6.

4. The remedy for hard times is to have patience. *Rec. dist.*: Ill. *1st cit.*: 1613 Overbury, *News from Lower End of Table*; US1682 *James Claypoole's Letter Book*, ed. Balderston (1967). *20c. coll.*: Stevenson 1756:9, Whiting 360, ODEP 670.

5. There is a remedy for all things but death. *Rec. dist.*: N.Y. *1st cit.*: ca1430 Lydgate, *Daunce of Machabree*; US1788 *Prose of Philip Freneau*, ed. Marsh (1955). *20c. coll.*: ODEP 670, Whiting 361, CODP 190, Stevenson 1950:10.

6. There is a remedy for everything, could men find it. *Var.*: There is a remedy for everything, could we but hit upon it. *Rec. dist.*: Ill., N.J., N.C., Tex. *1st cit.*: 1573 Gascoigne, *Adventures*. *20c. coll.*: ODEP 670, Stevenson 1950:10.

7. Things without remedy should be without regard. *Rec. dist.*: Ind. *1st cit.*: 1605 Shakespeare, *Macbeth*. *20c. coll.*: Stevenson 1950:9.

SEE ALSO Desperate EVILS require desperate remedies.

remember SEE When BEFRIENDED, remember it; when you befriend, forget it. / What we LEARN early we remember late. / Tell the TRUTH all the time and you won't have to remember what you said.

remembrance The remembrance of past dangers is pleasant. *Rec. dist.*: Mich. *1st cit.*: ca1375 Barbour, *Acts and Life of Robert Bruce*. *20c. coll.*: ODEP 671, Stevenson 1953:2.

SEE ALSO There is GLADNESS in remembrance.

reminiscence SEE One man's REMORSE is another man's reminiscence.

remorse **1.** One man's remorse is another man's reminiscence. *Rec. dist.*: N.Y. *1st cit.*: US1940 Nash, *Clean Conscience Never Relaxes*. *20c. coll.*: Stevenson 1954:11.

2. Remorse is a sign that it wasn't as pleasant as expected. *Rec. dist.*: N.Y. *1st cit.*: US1940 *Meditations in Wall Street*. *20c. coll.*: Stevenson 1954:11.

3. Remorse is the echo of a lost virtue. *Rec. dist.*: Ill.

4. Remorse is the thing we ought to feel and don't. *Rec. dist.*: N.Y. *1st cit.*: US1940 *Medi-*

tations in Wall Street. **20c. coll.:** Stevenson 1954:11.

remove *(n.)* Three removes are as bad as a fire. *Rec. dist.:* Mich., Tex. *1st cit.:* 1839 Dickens, Letter to Samuel Rogers, 14 Nov.; US1736 Franklin, *PRAlmanac.* **20c. coll.:** *ODEP* 817, Stevenson 314:2, Whiting 361, *CODP* 224, T&W 306.

remove *(v.)* SEE EDUCATION is an investment never to be lost nor removed. / It is better to remain SILENT and to be thought a fool than to speak and remove all doubt.

render SEE Render unto CAESAR the things which are Caesar's.

rent **1.** One owes nothing till the rent becomes due. *Rec. dist.:* Mich.

2. Short rents make careless tenants. *Rec. dist.:* Ont.
    SEE ALSO Save the PIECES to pay the rent.

repay SEE An act of KINDNESS is well repaid. / Repay KINDNESS with kindness.

repeat **1.** It is easy to repeat, but hard to originate. *Rec. dist.:* N.Y., S.C. *1st cit.:* US1842 Thoreau, *Winter.* **20c. coll.:** Stevenson 1729:13.

2. Nobody will repeat it if you do not say it. *Rec. dist.:* Ont.
    SEE ALSO HISTORY repeats itself.

repent **1.** We never repent of having eaten or drunk too little. *Rec. dist.:* N.Y. *1st cit.:* US1817 Jefferson, Letter to Charles Clay. **20c. coll.:** Stevenson 661:1

2. We often repent of what we have said, but never of what we have not. *Rec. dist.:* N.Y., S.C.
    SEE ALSO Not to repent of a FAULT is to justify it. / MARRY in haste and repent at leisure. / REJOICE today and repent tomorrow. / The SUN never repents of the good it does, nor does it ever demand a recompense.

repentance **1.** Late repentance is seldom worth much. *Rec. dist.:* Ill. *1st cit.:* 1552 Latimer, *Works.* **20c. coll.:** *ODEP* 443, Stevenson 1956:12.

2. Repentance is never too late. *Rec. dist.:* U.S., Can. *1st cit.:* ca1230 *Ancrene Wisse,* ed.

Tolkien, E.E.T.S. (1960). **20c. coll.:** *ODEP* 563, Stevenson 1956:4.

3. That may be soon done which brings long repentance. *Rec. dist.:* Ill.

4. When all is consumed, repentance comes too late. *Rec. dist.:* Ont. *1st cit.:* 1670 Ray, *English Proverbs;* US1788 *American Museum.* **20c. coll.:** *ODEP* 672, Whiting 361, Stevenson 1956:15.
    SEE ALSO Sudden FRIENDSHIP, sure repentance. / The end of PASSION is the beginning of repentance. / Short PLEASURE often brings long repentance. / REGRETS last longer than repentance.

repetition Repetition is the mother of learning. *Var.:* Repetition is the mother of skill. *Rec. dist.:* Ind., S.C.

reply *(n.)* Never give a hasty reply. *Rec. dist.:* N.Y.

reply *(v.)* SEE The CLAY replies not to the potter.

report *(n.)* A false report rides post. *Rec. dist.:* Ont. *1st cit.:* 1659 Howell, *Paroimiografia (English Proverbs).* **20c. coll.:** Stevenson 1957:16.

report *(v.)* SEE It takes less time to avoid an ACCIDENT than it does to report it.

reproach The sting of a reproach is the truth of it. *Rec. dist.:* Ill. *1st cit.:* 1732 Fuller, *Gnomologia.* **20c. coll.:** *ODEP* 774, Stevenson 1958:4.

reproof A smart reproof is better than smooth deceit. *Rec. dist.:* Ill. *1st cit.:* ca1386 Chaucer, *Tale of Melibee.* **20c. coll.:** Stevenson 1958:8.
    SEE ALSO CONTEMPT of a man is the sharpest reproof.

reprove **1.** Reprove mildly and correct with caution. *Rec. dist.:* Mich.

2. Reprove others but correct yourself. *Rec. dist.:* Ill.
    SEE ALSO Reprove your FRIEND privately; commend him publicly.

reputation **1.** A good reputation covers a multitude of sins. *Rec. dist.:* Ill.

2. A good reputation is more valuable than money. *Rec. dist.:* Ky., Tenn. *1st cit.:* ca1350 *How Gode Wyfe Taught Her Daughter;* US1739

Colonial Records of Georgia, ed. Chandler, in *Original Papers, 1735–1752* (1910–16). *20c. coll.:* ODEP 322, Whiting 306, Stevenson 1656:8, Whiting*(MP)* 438.

3. A good reputation stands still; a bad one runs. *Rec. dist.:* N.J.

4. A great reputation is a great charge. *Rec. dist.:* N.Y. *1st cit.:* 1732 Fuller, *Gnomologia.* *20c. coll.:* Stevenson 1959:13.

5. A man that outlives his reputation soon becomes miserable. *Rec. dist.:* Mich.

6. A man's best reputation for his future is his record of the past. *Rec. dist.:* Ont.

7. A wounded reputation is seldom cured. *Var.:* A broken reputation is never mended. *Rec. dist.:* Mich., N.C. *1st cit.:* 1855 Bohn, *Handbook of Proverbs.* *20c. coll.:* Stevenson 1959:10.

8. Beware of him that regards not his reputation. *Rec. dist.:* Mich.

9. Reputation is hard to make and easy to lose. *Rec. dist.:* N.C.

10. Reputation is what you are in the light; character is what you are in the dark. *Rec. dist.:* Ill.

11. The greater a man's reputation, the greater the criticism. *Rec. dist.:* Ill.

12. The way to gain a good reputation is to endeavor to be what you desire to appear. *Rec. dist.:* N.C.

SEE ALSO CHARACTER is what we are; reputation is what others think we are. / If you take care of your CHARACTER, your reputation will take care of itself. / GLASS, china, and reputations are easily cracked and never well mended.

resembling *SEE* Resembling the GREAT in some ways does not make us equally great.

resentment Quick resentments are often fatal. *Rec. dist.:* Ont.

resolute A resolute man cares nothing about difficulties. *Rec. dist.:* Ind.

SEE ALSO WORK is afraid of a resolute man.

resolution It's better not to make a New Year's resolution than to make one and break it. *Rec. dist.:* N.C.

resolve 1. He that resolves to mend hereafter resolves to mend not. *Rec. dist.:* N.Y. *1st cit.:* US1745 Franklin, *PRAlmanac.* *20c. coll.:* Stevenson 1956:9.

2. Whatsoever is well resolved on should be quickly performed. *Rec. dist.:* Mich.

resort *SEE* FLATTERY is the last resort of fools.

respect *(n.)* *SEE* It is a rare thing to win an ARGUMENT and the other fellow's respect.

respect *(v.)* **1.** One who cannot respect himself cannot respect another. *Rec. dist.:* Ont.

2. Respect a man—he will do the more. *Rec. dist.:* Ill. *1st cit.:* 1659 Howell, *Paroimiografia.* *20c. coll.:* ODEP 672, Stevenson 1962:15.

SEE ALSO There is no man so BAD but he secretly respects the good. / Respect your ELDERS.

respected To be respected is to be rich in spirit. *Rec. dist.:* Ala., Ga.

SEE ALSO An ASS covered with gold is more respected than an ass covered with a pack saddle. / A man's COUNTRY is where the things he loves are most respected.

responsibility 1. Some people grow with responsibility; others just swell. *Rec. dist.:* Colo., W.Va.

2. The more responsibilities a man assumes, the more likely he is to rise up to meet them. *Rec. dist.:* Ill.

rest *(n., leisure)* **1.** He that can take rest is greater than he that can take cities. *Rec. dist.:* Ill. *1st cit.:* US1737 Franklin, *PRAlmanac.* *20c. coll.:* Stevenson 1963:7.

2. Men tire themselves in pursuit of rest. *Rec. dist.:* Ill.

3. No rest for the weary. *Var.:* No rest for the weary, and less for the wicked. *Rec. dist.:* U.S., Can. *1st cit.:* 1931 Graeme, *Murder of Some Importance;* US1938 Bush, *Tudor Queen.* *20c. coll.:* Whiting*(MP)* 530, Stevenson 2491:6.

4. No rest for the wicked. *Rec. dist.:* Ill., Mich., N.C. *1st cit.:* 1931 Graeme, *Murder of Some Importance;* US1938 Bush, *Tudor Queen.* *20c. coll.:* Whiting*(MP)* 530, Stevenson 2491:6.

5. Rest is a good thing. *Rec. dist.:* N.Y.

6. Rest is the sweet sauce of labor. *Rec. dist.:* Ill., Ont. *1st cit.:* US1948 Stevenson, *Home Book of Proverbs.* *20c. coll.:* Stevenson 1964:1.

7. Too much rest is rust. *Rec. dist.:* Ont. *1st cit.:* US1948 Stevenson, *Home Book of Proverbs.* *20c. coll.:* Stevenson 2020:6.

SEE ALSO AMBITION has no rest. / When the BELLY is full, the bones are at rest. / From LABOR there shall come forth rest. / More RAIN, more rest. / Look not on TEMPTATION and your mind will be at rest.

rest *(n., remainder)* SEE Ill behooves the best of us to CRITICIZE the rest of us. / One sickly SHEEP infects the flock and poisons the rest.

rest *(v.)* **1.** If you rest, you rust. *Rec. dist.:* Ind., Ont. *1st cit.:* US1948 Stevenson, *Home Book of Proverbs.* *20c. coll.:* Stevenson 2020:6.

2. Rest, rust, rot. *Rec. dist.:* Md.

3. The best way to rest is to get away from the rest. **Rec. dist.:** Ont.

SEE ALSO After DINNER rest awhile; after supper walk a mile.

restraint SEE It is only ROGUES who feel the restraint of law.

result SEE IGNORANCE is the result of neglected opportunities. / SATISFACTION is a result of a job well done.

retain SEE It costs less to retain the BUSINESS of an old customer than it does to get two new ones. / We shall never gather HAPPINESS if we try to retain it for ourselves.

retirement Retirement is a prison to the fool, but a paradise to the wise. *Rec. dist.:* Mich.

retribution Swift is heaven's retribution. *Rec. dist.:* Ill.

return *(n.)* Quick returns make rich merchants. *Rec. dist.:* Mich.

return *(v.)* SEE He who returns the first BLOW is the man who begins the quarrel. / Send a FOOL to the market, and a fool he'll return. / Who accepts NOTHING has nothing to return.

reveal SEE Mad FOLKS and proverbs reveal many truths.

revenge **1.** If you want revenge, then dig two graves. *Rec. dist.:* Oreg.

2. Revenge is dearly bought at the price of liberty. *Rec. dist.:* Ont. *1st cit.:* 1668 La Fontaine, *Fables,* tr. Wright. *20c. coll.:* Stevenson 1973:7.

3. Revenge is like biting a dog because he bit you. *Rec. dist.:* Oreg.

4. Revenge is sweet. *Rec. dist.:* U.S., Can. *1st cit.:* 1566 Painter, *Palace of Pleasure,* ed. Jacobs (1890); USca1656 Bradford, *History of Plymouth Plantation,* ed. Ford (1912). *20c. coll.:* ODEP 673, Whiting 362, *CODP* 190, Stevenson 1973:4, T&W 306, Whiting(MP) 530.

5. The noblest revenge is to forgive. *Rec. dist.:* Tex. *1st cit.:* 1547 Baldwin, *Treatise of Morall Phylosophie;* US1752 Franklin, *PRAlmanac.* *20c. coll.:* ODEP 858, Stevenson 1973:8.

6. There is small revenge in words, but words may be great. *Var.:* There's small revenge in words, but words may be greatly revenged. *Rec. dist.:* Ill., N.Y. *1st cit.:* US1735 Franklin, *PRAlmanac.* *20c. coll.:* Stevenson 2600:4.

SEE ALSO FORGIVENESS is better than revenge. / NEGLECT kills injuries; revenge increases them. / To forget a WRONG is the best revenge.

revive SEE As the SUN rises, man's hope revives.

revolution **1.** Every revolution was first a thought in one man's mind. *Rec. dist.:* N.Y. *1st cit.:* US1841 Emerson, "History" in *Essays.* *20c. coll.:* Stevenson 1974:10.

2. Revolutions are not made by men in spectacles. *Rec. dist.:* N.Y. *1st cit.:* US1871 Holmes, *Young Practitioner.* *20c. coll.:* Stevenson 1974:8.

3. Revolutions are vices when they fail; they are virtues when successful. *Rec. dist.:* Ill.

reward *(n.)* **1.** Expect no reward for serving the wicked. *Rec. dist.:* N.C., Ont.

2. The hope of reward sweetens labor. *Rec. dist.:* Ont. *1st cit.:* US1948 Stevenson, *Home Book of Proverbs.* *20c. coll.:* Stevenson 1975:10.

3. The reward is in the doing. *Rec. dist.:* Ill. *1st cit.:* US1948 Stevenson, *Home Book of Proverbs.* *20c. coll.:* Stevenson 1975:7.

4. The reward of a good deed is to have done it. *Var.:* The best reward of a kindly deed is the knowledge of having done it. **Rec. dist.:** Ind., N.C., S.C. **1st cit.:** 1607 Shakespeare, *Coriolanus;* US1844 Emerson, *New England Reformers.* **20c. coll.:** Stevenson 1975:7.

5. The reward of good deeds endures. **Rec. dist.:** Mich.

6. The reward of good works is like dates—sweet and ripening late. **Rec. dist.:** N.Y.

7. Though late, a due reward succeeds. **Rec. dist.:** Ont.

SEE ALSO HAPPINESS is the best reward. / HONOR is the reward of virtue. / VIRTUE is its own reward.

reward *(v.)* SEE He that rewards FLATTERY begs it. / HOPE inspires; work wins; success rewards.

rib SEE Birchen TWIGS break no ribs.

rich *(n.)* **1.** The rich and poor meet together: the Lord is the maker of them all. **Rec. dist.:** Wis. **1st cit.:** US1948 Stevenson, *Home Book of Proverbs.* **20c. coll.:** Stevenson 1855:4.

2. The rich get richer, and the poor have children. **Rec. dist.:** N.Y.

3. The rich ride in chaises; the poor walk with God. **Rec. dist.:** Mich., Miss.

SEE ALSO The PRODIGALITY of the rich is the providence of the poor.

rich *(adj.)* **1.** A man is rich in proportion to the number of things which he can afford to let alone. **Rec. dist.:** N.Y., S.C. **1st cit.:** US1854 Thoreau, *Walden.* **20c. coll.:** Stevenson 1981:7.

2. A rich man can no more enter the kingdom of heaven than a camel can pass through the eye of a needle. **Var.:** It is easier for a camel to go through the eye of a needle than it is for a rich man to enter the kingdom of heaven. **Rec. dist.:** Ind. **1st cit.:** 1534 Lupset, *Treatise on Dying Well;* US1776 *Journal and Letter of Francis Asbury,* ed. Ford (1967). **20c. coll.:** ODEP 559, Stevenson 278:9, Whiting 54, T&W 54, Whiting(MP) 89.

3. A rich man for dogs and a poor man for babies. **Rec. dist.:** N.Y.

4. A rich man has the world by the tail. **Rec. dist.:** Ind. **1st cit.:** ca1630 *Roxburghe Ballads,*

Ballad Soc. (1869–99). **20c. coll.:** Stevenson 1982:14.

5. A rich man is either a rogue or a rogue's heir. **Rec. dist.:** Ill.

6. A rich man is happy while he is alive but sorry when he dies. **Rec. dist.:** N.C.

7. A rich man is never ugly in the eye of a girl. **Rec. dist.:** Ill.

8. A rich man knows not his friends. **Rec. dist.:** Ill. **1st cit.:** 1640 Herbert, *Outlandish Proverbs (Jacula Prudentum)* in *Works,* ed. Hutchinson (1941). **20c. coll.:** ODEP 674, Stevenson 1983:5.

9. A rich man's foolish sayings pass for wise ones. **Rec. dist.:** Ill.

10. A rich man's wooing is seldom long of doing. **Rec. dist.:** Ill.

11. A rich person ought to have a strong stomach. **Rec. dist.:** N.Y. **1st cit.:** US1882 Whitman, *Specimen Days.* **20c. coll.:** Stevenson 1980:9.

12. All ask if a man be rich, not if he be good. **Rec. dist.:** Ill.

13. Few rich men own their own property—their property owns them. **Rec. dist.:** N.Y. **1st cit.:** US1896 Ingersoll, Speech in New York, 29 Oct. **20c. coll.:** Stevenson 1899:6.

14. He alone is rich who makes proper use of his riches. **Rec. dist.:** Ill.

15. He is not rich who is not satisfied. **Rec. dist.:** Ill., N.Dak. **1st cit.:** 1732 Fuller, *Gnomologia;* US1755 Franklin, *PRAlmanac.* **20c. coll.:** ODEP 675, Stevenson 1981:4.

16. He is rich who does not desire more. **Rec. dist.:** Miss., N.C. **1st cit.:** ca1526 Erasmus, *Dicta Sapientum,* tr. Berthelet; US1755 Franklin, *PRAlmanac.* **20c. coll.:** ODEP 675, Stevenson 1981:4.

17. He is rich who owes nothing. **Rec. dist.:** Ind. **1st cit.:** 1640 Herbert, *Outlandish Proverbs (Jacula Prudentum)* in *Works,* ed. Hutchinson (1941). **20c. coll.:** Stevenson 530:7.

18. He that is rich need not live sparingly, and he that can live sparingly need not be rich. **Rec. dist.:** N.Y. **1st cit.:** US1734 Franklin, *PRAlmanac.* **20c. coll.:** Stevenson 1982:2.

19. He that's ordained to be rich shall be rich. *Rec. dist.:* N.C.

20. If rich, be not elated; if poor, be not dejected. *Rec. dist.:* Mich.

21. It's better to live rich than die rich. *Rec. dist.:* Ill.

22. Labor not to be rich. *Rec. dist.:* N.C. *1st cit.:* US1948 Stevenson, *Home Book of Proverbs.* *20c. coll.:* Stevenson 1977:2.

23. Many of us wish we were as rich as people think we are. *Rec. dist.:* Ohio.

24. Rich men have no faults. *Rec. dist.:* Ont. *1st cit.:* 1732 Fuller, *Gnomologia.* *20c. coll.:* Stevenson 1982:5.

25. Rich people have mean ways, and poor people poor ways. *Rec. dist.:* Tex.

26. Richest is he who wants least. *Rec. dist.:* Ont. *1st cit.:* ca1387 Usk, *Testament of Love* in *Works of Chaucer and Others,* ed. Skeat (1905). *20c. coll.:* ODEP 674.

27. The richest man is he who wants least. *Rec. dist.:* Ont. *1st cit.:* ca1387 Usk, *Testament of Love* in *Works of Chaucer and Others,* ed. Skeat (1905). *20c. coll.:* ODEP 674.

28. The richest man carries nothing away with him but his shroud. *Rec. dist.:* Ill. *1st cit.:* 1604 Shakespeare, *Measure for Measure.* *20c. coll.:* Stevenson 1985:3.

SEE ALSO ADVERSITY makes a man wise, but not rich. / CONTENT makes poor men rich; discontent makes rich men poor. / He who never FAILS will never grow rich. / They are rich who have FRIENDS. / Rich GIFTS wax poor when givers prove unkind. / Fat HENS make rich soup. / It is better to be an HONEST man than a rich one. / A poor LABORER is better than a rich loafer. / LIME and lime without manure makes the farmer rich and the son poor. / A MISER grows rich by seeming poor. / No one is rich enough without a NEIGHBOR. / Better be POOR and live than rich and perish. / It is better POOR and free than rich and a slave. / The POOR have little; beggars none; the rich too much; enough, not one. / When all are POOR, it don't take much to make a rich man. / Quick RETURNS make rich merchants. / It is not WEALTH but wisdom that

makes a man rich. / Love of WIT makes no man rich. / A snow YEAR, a rich year.

riches 1. Enough is great riches. *Rec. dist.:* Ill. *1st cit.:* ca1387 Usk, *Testament of Love* in *Works of Chaucer and Others,* ed. Skeat (1905). *20c. coll.:* ODEP 674, Stevenson 1980:13.

2. Gathering of riches is a pleasant torment. *Rec. dist.:* Mich.

3. It is better to choose great riches than a good name, as name can't buy anything. *Rec. dist.:* R.I.

4. Moderate riches will carry you; if you have more, you must carry them. *Rec. dist.:* N.C. *1st cit.:* ca1386 Chaucer, *Tale of Melibee;* US1744 Franklin, *PRAlmanac.* *20c. coll.:* Stevenson 1983:10.

5. No riches to sobriety. *Rec. dist.:* N.Y.

6. Riches and cares are inseparable. *Rec. dist.:* Ill. *1st cit.:* ca1526 Erasmus, *Dicta Sapientum,* tr. Berthelet; US1744 Franklin, *PRAlmanac.* *20c. coll.:* ODEP 675, Stevenson 1983:10.

7. Riches and honor are like floating clouds. *Rec. dist.:* N.Y.

8. Riches and virtue do not often keep each other company. *Rec. dist.:* Ill. *1st cit.:* 1621 Burton, *Anatomy of Melancholy;* US1800 Jefferson, Letter to J. Moore. *20c. coll.:* Stevenson 1978:15.

9. Riches are for spreading. *Rec. dist.:* Ont. *1st cit.:* 1597 Bacon, "Of Expence" in *Essays.* *20c. coll.:* Stevenson 1984:1.

10. Riches have wings. *Rec. dist.:* N.Y., Okla., S.C., Tex. *1st cit.:* 1607–12 Bacon, "Riches" in *Essays,* ed. Arber; US1730 Chalkley, "Youth" in *Works of Thomas Chalkley,* (1766). *20c. coll.:* ODEP 675, Whiting 363, Stevenson 1977:3.

11. Riches, like manure, do no good until they are spread. *Rec. dist.:* Ont. *1st cit.:* 1564 Bullein, *Dialogue Against Fever,* E.E.T.S. (1888). *20c. coll.:* ODEP 675.

12. Riches make friends, and adversity proves them. *Rec. dist.:* Ohio. *1st cit.:* 1597 Ling, *Politeuphuia.* *20c. coll.:* Stevenson 907:6.

13. Riches serve a wise man but command a fool. *Rec. dist.:* Ill., Ont. *1st cit.:* ca1606 Charron, *Wisdom*, tr. Lennard (1640); US1669 Penn, *No Cross, No Crown*. **20c. coll.**: *ODEP* 676, Stevenson 1978:6.

14. The abuse of riches is worse than the want of them. **Rec. dist.**: Ill.

15. The ransom of a man's life is his riches. **Rec. dist.**: Ind.

16. There is no royal road to riches. **Rec. dist.**: Ont.

17. To have what you want is riches, but to be able to do without is power. **Rec. dist.**: Ill.

SEE ALSO CHILDREN are poor men's riches. / CONTENTMENT is better than riches. / Out of DEBT is riches enough. / FORTUNE can take away riches but not courage. / HAPPINESS is more than riches. / A little HOUSE well fill'd, a little land well till'd, and a little wife well will'd, are great riches. / KNOWLEDGE is better than riches. / A good NAME is rather to be chosen than great riches. / VIRTUE and riches seldom settle on one man.

riddance Good riddance to bad rubbish. **Vars.**: **(a)** Bad rubbish is good riddance. **(b)** Good riddance of bad rubbish. **Rec. dist.**: U.S., Can. **1st cit.**: 1848 Dickens, *Dombey and Son;* US1771 *Essex Gazette* in *Olden Times Series,* ed. Brooks (1886). **20c. coll.**: *ODEP* 323, Whiting 363, Whiting*(MP)* 531.

ride SEE He that makes himself an ASS must not complain if men ride him. / From the day you were born till you ride in a hearse, there's nothing so BAD but it might have been worse. / Give a BEGGAR a horse and he'll ride it to death. / The toughest BRONCS is always them you've rode some other place. / DEATH rides with the drinking driver. / When FORTUNE smiles, we ride in chase, and when she frowns, we walk away. / If you can't get a HORSE, ride a cow. / When two ride one HORSE, one must sit behind. / He that rides the MULE shoes her. / PRIDE's an ill horse to ride. / The RICH ride in chaises; the poor walk with God. / THINGS are in the saddle and ride mankind. / He who rides the TIGER can never dismount. / If WISHES were horses, beggars might ride.

rider A long rider sits deep. **Rec. dist.**: Okla.
SEE ALSO Black CARE rarely sits behind a rider whose pace is fast enough. / TIME is the rider that breaks youth.

ridicule (*n.*) **1.** Ridicule is a weak weapon. **Rec. dist.**: Ill.

2. Ridicule is the test of truth. **Rec. dist.**: Ala., Ga. **1st cit.**: 1709 Shaftesbury, *Essay on Freedom of Wit and Humour*. **20c. coll.**: Stevenson 1987:6.

ridicule (*v.*) Never ridicule what you cannot comprehend. **Rec. dist.**: Ill.

riding There's more to riding than a pair of boots. **Rec. dist.**: Ill.

rifle In the hands of a good shot every rifle is deadly. **Rec. dist.**: Ill.

right (*n.*) **1.** A right cannot arise from a wrong. **Var.**: A right cannot arise from wrong. **Rec. dist.**: N.C., Ont.

2. Do right and fear no man; don't write and fear no woman. **Rec. dist.**: Ill., Ind., N.Y. **1st cit.**: ca1450 *Proverbs of Good Counsel* in *Book of Precedence,* E.E.T.S. (1869); US1918 McLuke, Epigram in *Cincinnati Enquirer*. **20c. coll.**: *CODP* 56, Stevenson 1989:4.

3. Do right and fear not. **Rec. dist.**: Ont.

4. Equal rights for all, special privileges for none. **Rec. dist.**: N.Y. **1st cit.**: US1801 Jefferson, First inaugural address. **20c. coll.**: Stevenson 1287:13.

5. Public rights are to be preferred to private. **Rec. dist.**: Mich.

6. Rather be beaten in right than succeed in wrong. **Rec. dist.**: N.J.

7. Right is more precious than peace. **Rec. dist.**: Ont. **1st cit.**: US1917 Wilson, Presidential war message to Congress. **20c. coll.**: Stevenson 1990:5.

8. Right makes might. **Rec. dist.**: Ga., Ky., Tenn. **1st cit.**: ca1330 Wright, *Political Songs,* Camden Soc. (1839); USca1700 Hubbard, *General History of New England* (1848). **20c. coll.**: *ODEP* 530, Whiting 288, *CODP* 150, Stevenson 1572:1, T&W 242, Whiting*(MP)* 409.

9. Right will last, and wrong cannot endure. **Rec. dist.**: N.C.

10. Right will prevail. *Vars.:* **(a)** Right always wins. **(b)** The wrong shall fail, the right prevail. *Rec. dist.:* Ill., Ind., Iowa, Ky., Tenn.

11. Right wrongs nobody. *Var.:* Right is right, and right wrongs no man. *Rec. dist.:* N.Y., Ont. *1st cit.:* 1832 Henderson, *Scottish Proverbs.* *20c. coll.:* ODEP 678, Stevenson 1991:9.

12. Right's right and wrong's wrong. *Rec. dist.:* N.Y., N.C., Ohio. *1st cit.:* 1819 Crabbe, *Tales of the Hall.* *20c. coll.:* Stevenson 1989:9.

13. The greatest right in the world is the right to be wrong. *Rec. dist.:* N.Y. *1st cit.:* US1917 Weinberger, "First Casualties in War" in *N.Y. Evening Post,* 10 Apr. *20c. coll.:* Stevenson 1992:3.

14. To do a great right, do a little wrong. *Rec. dist.:* Ala., Ga.

15. Your rights end where my nose begins. *Rec. dist.:* Miss.

SEE ALSO MIGHT makes right. / He that climbs the tall TREE has a right to the fruit. / Two WRONGS do not make a right.

right *(v.)* SEE WRONG will right itself in time.

right *(adj.)* **1.** Be sure you are right, then go ahead. *Rec. dist.:* U.S., Can. *1st cit.:* US1834 Crockett, *Life of David Crockett.* *20c. coll.:* T&W 307, Stevenson 1989:10.

2. It is better to be right than in the majority. *Rec. dist.:* Ala., Ga. *1st cit.:* 1691 Norris, *Practical Discourses;* US1849 Thoreau, *Civil Disobedience.* *20c. coll.:* Stevenson 1505:3.

3. No one is always right. *Rec. dist.:* Utah.

4. Not everything legally right is morally right. *Rec. dist.:* Utah.

5. Some people would rather be right than pleasant. *Rec. dist.:* Ont.

6. Those who are right need not talk loudly. *Rec. dist.:* Ont.

SEE ALSO The CUSTOMER is always right. / None but a FOOL is always right. / The LAME man who keeps the right road outstrips the runner who keeps the wrong one. / Better to LIMP on the right road than to speed on the wrong one. / The right ROAD is the shortest road. / Always put the SADDLE on the right horse. / Strike when the TIME is right. / There is your WAY, my way, and the right way.

right *(adv.)* **1.** Always do right; it will gratify some people and astonish the rest. *Rec. dist.:* N.J. *1st cit.:* US1893 Twain, *Pudd'nhead Wilson's Calendar.* *20c. coll.:* Stevenson 1989:4.

2. Always go right and you'll never go wrong. *Rec. dist.:* Ill.

3. He who lives right lives forever. *Rec. dist.:* Ill., Ind.

4. If you can't do a thing right, don't do it at all. *Rec. dist.:* Ohio.

5. If you want something done right, do it yourself. *Rec. dist.:* U.S., Can. *1st cit.:* US1880 Spurgeon, *John Ploughman's Pictures.* *20c. coll.:* Stevenson 2063:5.

6. It's easy to die right, but it's hard to live right. *Rec. dist.:* N.C.

SEE ALSO Whatever you DO, do with all your might, for things done by halves are never done right. / Things done by HALVES are never done right.

rind Under the coarsest rind, the sweetest meat. *Rec. dist.:* N.Y., S.C. *1st cit.:* US1856 Thoreau, *Early Spring in Massachusetts.* *20c. coll.:* Stevenson 394:3.

ring *(n.)* SEE No HOG ever grunted the ring out of its nose. / SPRING time is ring time.

ring *(v.)* SEE A BELL, once rung, cannot be rerung.

rinse Catch it in the rinse if you can't in the wash. *Var.:* What won't come out in the wash will come out in the rinse. *Rec. dist.:* Ill., N.C.

riot Nothing is learned in a riot. *Rec. dist.:* N.C.

rip *(n.)* Never a rip without a tear. *Rec. dist.:* Calif., N.Y.

SEE ALSO Better have a PATCH on your back than a rip on your back.

rip *(v.)* SEE Do not rip up old SORES.

ripe **1.** Quick ripe, quick rotten. *Var.:* Early ripe, early rotten. *Rec. dist.:* Ill., Ind. *1st cit.:* ca1377 Langland, *Piers Plowman;* US1699 Ward, "Trip to New England" in Winship, *Boston in 1682 and 1699* (1905). *20c. coll.:* ODEP 752, Whiting 364, CODP 207, Stevenson 1994:6, T&W 307.

2. When you're ripe, you're rotten. *Rec. dist.:* Ohio.

SEE ALSO The time to pick BERRIES is when they're ripe. / FOXES, when they cannot reach the grapes, say they are not ripe. / FRIENDSHIP, like persimmons, is good only when ripe. / The ripest PEACH is highest on the tree.

ripen SEE TIME ripens all things.

ripping You learn as much ripping as sewing. *Rec. dist.:* Ont.

ripple SEE A ripple of LAUGHTER is worth a flood of tears.

rise **1.** Because you rise earlier does not mean it will be daylight. *Rec. dist.:* N.Y. *1st cit.:* 1591 Stepney, *Spanish Schoolemaster. 20c. coll.:* ODEP 678, Stevenson 1995:9.

2. He that rises late must trot all day. *Var.:* He that rises late must trot all day, and shall scarce overtake his business at night. *Rec. dist.:* Ill., Mich., N.Y. *1st cit.:* 1659 Howell, *Paroimiografia (Spanish Proverbs); US*1742 Franklin, *PRAlmanac. 20c. coll.:* ODEP 679, Stevenson 1995:9.

SEE ALSO Early to BED and early to rise makes a man healthy, wealthy, and wise. / The COCK crows at sunrise to tell us to rise. / One may sooner FALL than rise. / You can't rise with the LARK if you've been on one the night before. / In POLITICS a man must learn to rise above principle. / It is better to SIT still than to rise to fall. / He who sits on a hot STOVE shall rise again. / Defer not till TOMORROW to be wise; tomorrow's sun to you may never rise. / TRUTH, crushed to earth, will rise again.

rising **1.** He who gets a name for early rising may sleep all day. *Rec. dist.:* Ill. *1st cit.:* 1611 Cotgrave, *Dictionary of French and English Tongues; US*1805 Taggart, *Letters,* ed. Haynes, Am.Antiq.Soc. *Proceedings* (1923). *20c. coll.:* ODEP 554, Whiting 306.

2. Our greatest glory consists not in never falling, but in rising every time we fall. *Var.:* True greatness is not in never falling, but in rising when you fall. *Rec. dist.:* Ill., Miss., Ont.

SEE ALSO FALLING is easier than rising. / Good LUCK beats early rising. / The WORM was punished for early rising.

risk *(n.)* **1.** No risk, no gain. *Rec. dist.:* Ill., Miss. *1st cit.:* 1839 Tupper, "Of Wealth" in *Proverbial Philosophy; US*1832 *Correspondence of Andrew Jackson,* ed. Bassett (1926–33). *20c. coll.:* Stevenson 925:8, Whiting 364.

2. Swift risks are often attended with precipitate falls. *Rec. dist.:* Ill.

SEE ALSO Let the PURCHASER buy at his own risk.

risk *(v.)* It is better to risk than to delay overmuch. *Rec. dist.:* Mich.

risky SEE BEER on whiskey, mighty risky; whiskey on beer, never fear.

rival SEE He that falls in LOVE with himself will have no rivals.

river **1.** A river runs its course. *Rec. dist.:* Miss.

2. A running river never freezes. *Rec. dist.:* Ont.

3. A still river never finds the ocean. *Rec. dist.:* Ont.

4. All rivers run to the sea. *Vars.:* **(a)** Follow the river and you will get to the sea. **(b)** The greatest rivers must run into the sea. *Rec. dist.:* Ill., Okla., Ont. *1st cit.:* ca1530 Barclay, *Eclogues,* E.E.T.S. (1874); *US*1760 *Papers of Benjamin Franklin,* ed. Labaree (1959). *20c. coll.:* ODEP 679, Whiting 364, Stevenson 1998:2.

5. Deep rivers move with silent majesty; shallow brooks are noisy. *Rec. dist.:* Mich., Utah, Wis. *1st cit.:* 1574 Guazzo, *Civile Conversation,* tr. Pettie, T.T. (1925). *20c. coll.:* Stevenson 2464:9.

6. Don't cross your rivers before you get to them. *Rec. dist.:* Ont. *1st cit.:* 1930 Walling, *Man With the Squeaky Voice; US*1938 Champion, *Racial Proverbs. 20c. coll.:* Whiting(MP) 74, Stevenson 2377:12.

7. Look at the river before you cross with the ferry. *Rec. dist.:* Miss.

8. Swift rivers travel far. *Rec. dist.:* N.C.

9. The river past, and God forgotten. *Rec. dist.:* Ont. *1st cit.:* 1640 Herbert, *Outlandish Proverbs (Jacula Prudentum)* in *Works,* ed. Hutchinson (1941). *20c. coll.:* Stevenson 485:6.

10. The time to go down the river is when the water is up. *Rec. dist.:* N.Y.

11. When a river does not make a noise, it is either empty or very full. *Rec. dist.:* Mich. *1st cit.:* 1574 Guazzo, *Civile Conversation,* tr. Pettie, T.T. (1925). *20c. coll.:* Stevenson 2464:9.

12. Where there's a river there's a bridge. *Rec. dist.:* N.C.

SEE ALSO Little STREAMS make big rivers.

road 1. A man never got lost on a straight road. *Var.:* No one was ever lost on a straight road. *Rec. dist.:* Mont., N.C., Oreg.

2. All roads lead to Rome. *Rec. dist.:* U.S., Can. *1st cit.:* ca1391 Chaucer, *Prologue to Astrolabe;* US1924 Fletcher, *King. 20c. coll.:* ODEP 679, Whiting(MP) 532, CODP 192, Stevenson 2003:5.

3. Be sure you know the road before you act as guide. *Rec. dist.:* Ont.

4. Don't cross the road till you come to it. *Rec. dist.:* Ill.

5. Every road has a turning. *Var.:* Every road has its turning. *Rec. dist.:* Ark., Ind., Kans., Ohio, Ont.

6. Every road has hills to be climbed. *Rec. dist.:* Ont.

7. Follow the straight road. *Rec. dist.:* N.Y. *1st cit.:* US1948 Stevenson, *Home Book of Proverbs. 20c. coll.:* Stevenson 1991:1.

8. He who wishes to know the road through the mountains must ask those who have already trodden it. *Var.:* If you wish to know the road ahead, inquire of those who have traveled it. *Rec. dist.:* Ind., Ohio.

9. It is a long road that does not end. *Var.:* It is a long road that has no ending. *Rec. dist.:* Ky., Tenn. *1st cit.:* US1854 Shillaber, *Mrs. Partington. 20c. coll.:* T&W 308.

10. It's a long road that goes nowhere. *Rec. dist.:* Ont.

11. It's a long road that has no turning. *Vars.:* (a) It is a long road that has no bend. (b) It is a long road which does not have any turnings. (c) It's a long road that has no turn. (d) It's a long road that knows no turn. (e) It's a long road that never turns. (f) It's a long road without a turning. (g) There is never a road so long without a turn in it. (h) There's no road that has no turning. (i) 'Tis a long road that has no turning. *Rec. dist.:* U.S. *1st cit.:* 1633 *Stationer's Register,* 8 July (1877); US1778 Paine, *American Crisis* in *Writings of Thomas Paine,* ed. Foner (1945). *20c. coll.:* ODEP 480, Whiting 251, CODP 138, Stevenson 1345:1, T&W 214, Whiting(MP) 360.

12. Keep in the middle of the road. *Var.:* Keep in the center of the road. *Rec. dist.:* N.Y. *1st cit.:* USca1870 *Keep in Middle of Road. 20c. coll.:* Stevenson 1999:1.

13. Keep the common road and you are safe. *Rec. dist.:* Ont. *1st cit.:* 1732 Fuller, *Gnomologia. 20c. coll.:* Stevenson 1991:1.

14. Muddy roads call de milepost a liar. *Rec. dist.:* Tex.

15. No flowery road leads to glory. *Var.:* No path of flowers leads to glory. *Rec. dist.:* Wis. *1st cit.:* 1678 La Fontaine, *Fables,* tr. Wright. *20c. coll.:* Stevenson 962:15.

16. No road is long with good company. *Rec. dist.:* Ill. *1st cit.:* 1653 Walton, *Compleat Angler. 20c. coll.:* Stevenson 385:1.

17. Take the beaten road. *Var.:* Take the beaten path. *Rec. dist.:* Mich.

18. The beaten road is the safest. *Rec. dist.:* N.Y.

19. The downward road is easy. *Rec. dist.:* Ont. *1st cit.:* 1684 Bunyan, *Pilgrim s Progress. 20c. coll.:* Stevenson 746:13.

20. The lame man who keeps the right road outstrips the runner who keeps the wrong one. *Rec. dist.:* N.C.

21. The longest road is sometimes the shortest way home. *Var.:* The long road may be the quickest way home. *Rec. dist.:* Ky., Ont., Tenn. *1st cit.:* 1580 Lyly, *Euphues and His England;* US1762 *Letter Book of John Watts, 1762–1765,* N.Y.Hist.Soc. *Collections* (1928). *20c. coll.:* ODEP 245, Whiting 474, CODP 138, Stevenson 2468:12, T&W 396, Whiting(MP) 669.

22. The middle road is the safer. *Var.:* The middle road is the safest. *Rec. dist.:* N.C., Ont. *1st cit.:* 1732 Fuller, *Gnomologia;* US1719

Wise, Letter in *Colonial Currency Reprints,* ed. Davis, Publ. Prince Soc. (1910–11). *20c. coll.:* Stevenson 1999:1, Whiting 474.

23. The other track on the road is always the smoothest. *Rec. dist.:* Ont.

24. The right road is the shortest road. *Rec. dist.:* Ind.

25. The road of by-and-by leads to the town of never. *Rec. dist.:* Miss., N.C.

26. The road of life is lined with many milestones. *Rec. dist.:* N.C.

27. The road to hell is paved with good intentions. *Rec. dist.:* U.S., Can. *1st cit.:* 1574 Guevara, *Familiar Epistles,* tr. Hellowes (1584); US1890 James, *Principles of Psychology.* *20c. coll.:* CODP 192, ODEP 367, Stevenson 1128:8.

28. There is no royal road to learning. *Rec. dist.:* Okla., Ont., Tex. *1st cit.:* 1857 Trollope, *Barchester Towers;* US1824 *Journals of Ralph Waldo Emerson,* eds. Emerson and Forbes (1909–14). *20c. coll.:* ODEP 686, T&W 308, CODP 194, Stevenson 1379:4, Whiting*(MP)* 532.

See also A long FACE makes a long road seem twice as long. / Better have a FRIEND on the road than gold or silver in your purse. / An old HORSE for a hard road.

roar *See* Let your WILL roar when your power can but whisper.

roasted *See* If you want roasted BANANAS, you must burn your fingers first.

rob *See* Another's CARES will not rob you of sleep. / The back DOOR robs the house. / JAYBIRDS don't rob their own nests. / Rob PETER to pay Paul. / Rob not the POOR because he is poor. / The TABLE robs more than the thief.

robber There is no worse robber than a bad book. *Rec. dist.:* Ill. *1st cit.:* 1853 Trench, *Lessons in Proverbs.* *20c. coll.:* Stevenson 218:8.

robbery *See* A fair EXCHANGE is no robbery.

robe Long robe, little science. *Rec. dist.:* Ill.

robin It takes more than a robin to make spring. *Var.:* One robin doesn't make a spring. *Rec. dist.:* U.S. *Infm.:* Cf. swallow.

rock *(n.)* **1.** Rocks are thrown only at fruit-bearing trees. *Rec. dist.:* Ohio.

2. The bigger the rock, the bigger the splash. *Rec. dist.:* Ohio.

3. You can get used to anything except a rock in your shoe. *Rec. dist.:* Fla., Ind.

See also If FROGS had wings, they wouldn't bump their asses on rocks. / A HEAD that is as hard as rock will burst into pieces. / A SOUL built of solid rock will not falter.

rock *(v.)* *See* The HAND that rocks the cradle is the hand that rules the world.

rocking chair The old rocking chair will get you. *Rec. dist.:* Miss., S.C.

See also WORRY is like a rocking chair: both give you something to do, but neither gets you anywhere.

rod **1.** Bend the rod while it's hot. *Rec. dist.:* Ont.

2. Spare the rod and spoil the child. *Vars.:* **(a)** He who spares his rod hates his son. **(b)** He who spares the rod spoils the child. *Rec. dist.:* U.S., Can. *1st cit.:* ca1000 Aelfric, *Homilies* (1843); US1740 Byrd, *Letters in Va.Mag.Hist.* (1929). *20c. coll.:* ODEP 759, Whiting 366, CODP 209, Stevenson 344:8, T&W 309, Whiting*(MP)* 534.

See also A WHIP for a fool and a rod for a school.

rogue **1.** A rogue's throat smells of hemp. *Rec. dist.:* Mich.

2. If you pity rogues, you are no great friend of honest men. *Rec. dist.:* Ill.

3. It is only rogues who feel the restraint of law. *Rec. dist.:* N.Y. *1st cit.:* ca1870 Holland, "Perfect Liberty" in *Gold-Foil.* *20c. coll.:* Stevenson 1363:2.

4. It takes a rogue to catch a rogue. *Rec. dist.:* Ont. *1st cit.:* 1774 Tucker, *Light of Nature Pursued;* US1676 Walker in *First Century of American Verse,* ed. Jantz (1962). *20c. coll.:* Whiting 367, Stevenson 2003:1, T&W 309.

5. Little rogues easily become great ones. *Rec. dist.:* N.Y. *1st cit.:* US1754 Franklin, *PRAlmanac.* *20c. coll.:* Stevenson 2002:11.

6. No rogue like the godly rogue. *Rec. dist.:*

N.Y., S.C. *1st cit.:* 1732 Fuller, *Gnomologia.* *20c. coll.:* ODEP 682, Stevenson 2002:12.

7. Nobody calls himself a rogue. *Rec. dist.:* Ill., Ont. *1st cit.:* 1855 Bohn, *Handbook of Proverbs.* *20c. coll.:* Stevenson 2002:8.

8. Once a rogue, always a rogue. *Rec. dist.:* Ont.

9. One rogue does not betray another. *Rec. dist.:* Ill.

10. One rogue knows another. *Rec. dist.:* Ill.

11. When rogues fall out, honest men come by their own. *Rec. dist.:* Ill., Tex. *1st cit.:* 1546 Heywood, *Dialogue of Proverbs,* ed. Habernicht (1963); US1742 Franklin, *PRAlmanac.* *20c. coll.:* ODEP 810, Whiting 368, Stevenson 2298:2.

SEE ALSO The INFORMER is the worse rogue of the two.

roll *SEE* The man who flings a STONE up a mountainside may have it rolled back upon himself. / Loaded WORDS are like loaded dice: they never roll true. / You can't keep up with the WORLD by letting it roll by.

rolling *SEE* A rolling STONE gathers no moss. / Watch out for the rolling STONE.

romance *SEE* There are stranger things in REALITY than can be found in romances.

Romans *SEE* When in ROME, do as the Romans.

Rome **1.** Rome was not built in a day. *Rec. dist.:* U.S., Can. *1st cit.:* 1545 Erasmus, *Adages,* tr. Taverner; US1646 *Thomas Hutchinson Papers,* Publ. Prince Soc. (1865). *20c. coll.:* ODEP 683, Whiting 368, CODP 193, Stevenson 2004:10, T&W 310, Whiting*(MP)* 535.

2. See Rome and die. *Rec. dist.:* N.C.

3. When in Rome, do as the Romans. *Vars.:* **(a)** If you go to Rome, do as the Romans do. **(b)** When in Rome, do as the Romans do. **(c)** When you are at Rome, do as Rome. **(d)** When you are at Rome, do as Rome does. *Rec. dist.:* U.S., Can. *1st cit.:* ca1530 Hill, *Commonplace Book,* E.E.T.S. (1907); USca1680 *Voyages of Radisson,* ed. Scull, Publ. Prince Soc. (1885). *20c. coll.:* ODEP 683, Whiting

368, *CODP* 193, Stevenson 2005:1, T&W 310, Whiting*(MP)* 536.

SEE ALSO All ROADS lead to Rome.

roof **1.** An empty house needs no roof. *Rec. dist.:* N.C.

2. No roof can cover two families. *Rec. dist.:* N.Y. *1st cit.:* US1940 Thompson, *Body, Boots, and Britches.* *20c. coll.:* Stevenson 757:12.

3. Thatch your roof before rainy weather; dig your well before you are thirsty. *Rec. dist.:* Ill. *1st cit.:* US1875 Scarborough, *Chinese Proverbs.* *20c. coll.:* Stevenson 866:1.

4. The roof doesn't need mending when it's not raining. *Rec. dist.:* Miss.

SEE ALSO Never take a SHINGLE off the roof. / Just because there's SNOW on the roof, that doesn't mean the fire's out inside. / TROUBLE: two women under one roof.

room **1.** Always room for one more. *Rec. dist.:* U.S., Can.

2. The biggest room in the world is the room for improvement. *Var.:* There's always room for improvement. *Rec. dist.:* Miss.

3. There's always room at the top. *Rec. dist.:* U.S., Can. *1st cit.:* 1914 Bennet, *Price of Love;* US1900 W. James lette of 2 Apr. *20c. coll.:* CODP 193, Whiting*(MP)* 536.

4. There's more room outside than inside. *Rec. dist.:* Ont.

5. Where there is room in the heart, there is room in the house. *Rec. dist.:* Ont.

SEE ALSO A bad BROOM leaves a dirty room. / When you open a DOOR you do not know how many rooms lie beyond. / A fair FIRE makes a room gay. / A HOUSE without books is like a room without windows. / A LAZY man is no better than a dead one, but he takes up more room.

roost *(n.)* It is ill with the roost when the hens crow and the cock must remain silent. *Rec. dist.:* Tex.

roost *(v.)* *SEE* BUZZARDS fly high but roost on the ground. / CHICKENS will always come home to roost. / CURSES, like chickens, come home to roost.

rooster   **1.** He that's a good rooster will crow in any hen yard. *Rec. dist.:* N.Mex.

2. Hungry rooster never cackles when he scratches up a worm. *Var.:* Hungry rooster don't cackle w'en he fin' a wum. *Rec. dist.:* Miss. *1st cit.:* US1880 Harris, *Plantation Proverbs* in *Uncle Remus, His Songs and His Sayings. 20c. coll.:* Stevenson 1199:18.

3. Rooster makes more racket dan de hen w'at lay de aig. *Rec. dist.:* Ala., Ga. *1st cit.:* US1880 Harris, *Plantation Proverbs* in *Uncle Remus, His Songs and His Sayings. 20c. coll.:* Stevenson 375:2.

4. The rooster can crow, but it's the hen that delivers the goods. *Rec. dist.:* Miss. *1st cit.:* US1880 Harris, *Plantation Proverbs* in *Uncle Remus, His Songs and His Sayings. 20c. coll.:* Stevenson 375:2.

5. The rooster crows to let us know, if we are wise, it's time to rise. *Rec. dist.:* Ont.

SEE ALSO If you're LUCKY, even your rooster will lay eggs.

root *(n.)*   Take root and live. *Rec. dist.:* Ind. *Infm.:* "Take root" refers to settling down and homesteading.

SEE ALSO Kind HEARTS are the gardens, kind thoughts the roots, kind words the flowers, kind deeds the fruits. / MONEY is the root of all evil. / PATIENCE is bitter, but its fruit is sweet. / WOMEN are the root of all evil.

root *(v.)*   Root, hog, or die. *Rec. dist.:* U.S. *Infm.:* This is the refrain of the folk song "The Bull-Wackers Epic." *1st cit.:* US1834 Crockett, *Life of David Crockett. 20c. coll.:* T&W 184, Stevenson 1147:9, Whiting*(MP)* 310.

SEE ALSO Never ring a PIG that has to root for a living.

rooted   *SEE* The harder the WIND, the deeper the oak becomes rooted.

rope   **1.** Give a man rope enough and he'll hang himself. *Vars.:* **(a)** Give a calf all the rope it wants and it will hang itself. **(b)** Give a calf enough rope and he will hang himself. **(c)** Give a thief enough rope and he will hang himself. **(d)** Give him enough rope and he will hang himself. **(e)** Give him rope and he'll hang himself. *Rec. dist.:* U.S., Can. *1st cit.:*

1639 Fuller, *Holy War;* US1698 Usher in *William & Mary Coll. Quart.* (1950). *20c. coll.:* ODEP 683, Whiting 369, *CODP* 194, Stevenson 2008:1, T&W 311, Whiting*(MP)* 537.

2. Never talk of rope in the house of a man who has been hanged. *Var.:* Never mention a rope in the house of a man who has been hanged. *Rec. dist.:* Calif., Colo. *1st cit.:* 1599 Minsheu, *Dictionary in Spanish and English;* US1855 Haliburton, *Nature and Human Nature. 20c. coll.:* ODEP 684, T&W 311, Whiting*(MP)* 538.

3. Pull gently at a weak rope. *Rec. dist.:* Ohio.

SEE ALSO Let him which ain't SINFUL haul first on the rope. / A man once bitten by a SNAKE will jump at the sight of a rope in his path.

rose   **1.** A rose becomes more beautiful between two thorns. *Rec. dist.:* Ind. *1st cit.:* 1580 Lyly, *Euphues and His England,* ed. Arber (1868). *20c. coll.:* Stevenson 2010:2.

2. A rose by another name would smell as sweet. *Vars.:* **(a)** A rose by any other name would be confusing. **(b)** A rose of any other color would smell the same. *Rec. dist.:* U.S., Can. *1st cit.:* 1594 Shakespeare, *Romeo and Juliet. 20c. coll.:* Stevenson 1655:6.

3. A rose is a rose is a rose is a rose. *Rec. dist.:* N.Y. *1st cit.:* US1922 Stein, *Sacred Emily* in *Geography and Plays. 20c. coll.:* Stevenson 2009:5.

4. If you make a bed of roses, you will have to sleep on the thorns also. *Rec. dist.:* N.C. *1st cit.:* 1635 Quarles, *Emblems. 20c. coll.:* Stevenson 2009:14.

5. If you would gather roses, do not sow rotten seeds. *Rec. dist.:* Ont.

6. Lie on roses when young; lie on thorns when old. *Rec. dist.:* Ont. *1st cit.:* 1732 Fuller, *Gnomologia. 20c. coll.:* ODEP 460, Stevenson 2010:1.

7. No rose without thorns. *Vars.:* **(a)** All roses have thorns. **(b)** Every rose has a thorn. **(c)** Every rose has its thorn. **(d)** Roses have thorns. **(e)** There are no roses without thorns. **(f)** We have no rose without its thorn, no pleasure without alloy. **(g)** You can't have your rose without a thorn. *Rec. dist.:* U.S., Can. *1st cit.:* 1430 Lydgate, *Prologue to Bochas;* US1734 Franklin, *PRAlmanac.* *20c. coll.:* ODEP 684, Whiting 371, Stevenson 2010:2, Whiting(*MP*) 538.

8. The greatest rose possesses the sharpest thorn. *Rec. dist.:* Ont.

9. The rose has its thorn, the peach its worm. *Rec. dist.:* N.Y. *1st cit.:* US1853 Haliburton, *Sam Slick's Wise Saws.* *20c. coll.:* Stevenson 2010:2.

10. When gathering roses, look out for thorns. *Rec. dist.:* Ont. *1st cit.:* US1938 Champion, *Racial Proverbs.* *20c. coll.:* Stevenson 2009:7.

11. You cannot pluck roses without fear of thorns nor enjoy a fair wife without danger of horns. *Rec. dist.:* Wis. *1st cit.:* US1734 Franklin, *PRAlmanac.* *20c. coll.:* Stevenson 2497:4.

SEE ALSO LIFE is no bed of roses. / Always a THORN among the roses. / You get a THORN with every rose. / He who sows THORNS shall not gather roses.

rosebuds **1.** Gather rosebuds while ye may. *Var.:* Gather ye rosebuds while ye may. *Rec. dist.:* U.S., Can. *1st cit.:* 1592 Spenser, *Faerie Queene.* *20c. coll.:* Stevenson 2325:3.

2. Watched rosebuds open slowly. *Rec. dist.:* N.J., N.Y.

rot SEE REST, rust, rot. / The RUST rots the steel which use preserves.

rote SEE By rote RULE goes many a fool.

rotten SEE The rottenest BOUGH cracks first. / Quick RIPE, quick rotten. / A rotten TREE bears no fruit.

rough *(n.)* Take the rough with the smooth. *Rec. dist.:* Ont. *1st cit.:* ca1400 Beryn, *Tale of Beryn,* E.E.T.S. (1909); US1775 Macpherson in Read, *Life and Correspondence of Joseph Read* (1870). *20c. coll.:* ODEP 685, Whiting 372, Stevenson 2010:12, Whiting(*MP*) 539.

rough *(adj.)* When the going is rough, big potatoes come to the top. *Rec. dist.:* Oreg.

SEE ALSO Much RUST needs a rough file. / A good SAILOR likes a rough sea.

round *(n.)* SEE He that climbs a LADDER must begin at the first round.

round *(adj.)* SEE MONEY is round, and rolls away. / You can't put a round PEG in a square hole.

rouse SEE Seldom poke another's FIRE, or you may rouse his burning ire.

roving SEE It's the roving BEE that gathers honey.

row *(n.)* Hoe your own row. *Var.:* Be sure you hoe the right row. *Rec. dist.:* U.S., Can. *1st cit.:* 1929 Loder, *Between Twelve and One;* US1844 Stephens, *High Life in New York.* *20c. coll.:* T&W 312, Stevenson 2011:1, Whiting(*MP*) 539.

SEE ALSO More CORN grows in crooked rows.

row *(v.)* SEE Every person should row his own BOAT. / He that's carried down the STREAM need not row.

rowing When you stop rowing, you start downstream. *Rec. dist.:* Utah.

royal SEE There is no royal ROAD to learning.

royalty Royalty consists not in great pomp but in great virtues. *Rec. dist.:* Mich.

rub SEE There's just one way to rub a CAT's fur. / Never rub your EYE but with your elbow.

rubber Cheap rubber will stretch. *Rec. dist.:* Ky., Tenn.

rubbing An inch of rubbing saves scrubbing. *Rec. dist.:* N.C.

SEE ALSO A GEM is not polished without rubbing; nor is a man perfect without trials.

rubbish **1.** A dealer in rubbish sounds the praise of rubbish. *Rec. dist.:* Ill.

2. Rubbish accumulates; mountains arise. *Rec. dist.:* Ill.

3. Rubbish is only matter out of place. *Rec. dist.:* Ill.

SEE ALSO Good RIDDANCE to bad rubbish.

rubies SEE WISDOM is better than rubies.

rudeness Rudeness will repel when courtesy would attract friends. *Rec. dist.:* Ill.

rue SEE Who LOSES, rues.

ruffle SEE It's not the SKIRT that breaks people; it's the chiffon ruffles.

rugged SEE A rugged STONE grows smooth from hand to hand.

ruin *(n.)* **1.** Going to ruin is silent work. *Rec. dist.:* Ill.

2. Ruin is most fatal when it begins at the bottom. *Rec. dist.:* Ill.

3. When a man lays the foundation of his own ruin, others will build on it. *Rec. dist.:* Ill.
    SEE ALSO RULE or ruin. / Destroy the SEED of evil or it will grow up to your ruin.

ruin *(v.)* Many have been ruined by buying good pennyworths. *Rec. dist.:* N.Y. *1st cit.:* 1732 Fuller, *Gnomologia;* US1747 Franklin, *PRAlmanac.* *20c. coll.:* ODEP 687, Stevenson 268:5.
    SEE ALSO ABUNDANCE of money ruins youth. / ABUNDANCE, like want, ruins many. / Live only for this DAY, and you ruin tomorrow. / Nothing ruins a DUCK but his bill. / SUCCESS has ruined many a man. / WAR is a business that ruins those who succeed in it.

rule *(n.)* **1.** A general rule must be generally understood. *Rec. dist.:* N.C.

2. As a rule, man's a fool: when it's hot he wants it cool, and when it's cool he wants it hot, always wanting what is not. *Rec. dist.:* Ind.

3. Better no rule than a cruel rule. *Rec. dist.:* Ind., Ont.

4. By rote rule goes many a fool. *Rec. dist.:* Ont.

5. It's a poor rule that won't work both ways. *Rec. dist.:* U.S., Can. *1st cit.:* US1837 *Letters of James Fenimore Cooper,* ed. Beard (1960–68). *20c. coll.:* Whiting 373, Stevenson 2013:12, T&W 313, Whiting(MP) 541.

6. Keep the rule and the rule will keep you. *Rec. dist.:* Ont.

7. Preach not your musty rule. *Rec. dist.:* N.C.

8. Rules were made to be broken. *Rec. dist.:* U.S., Can. *1st cit.:* 1953 Clarke, *Expedition to Earth;* US1960 Farmer, *Strange Relations.* *20c. coll.:* Whiting(MP) 541.

9. Submit to the rule you yourself laid down. *Rec. dist.:* Ill.

10. The first rule of the house is to bore nobody. *Rec. dist.:* Ont.

11. The only rule that works both ways is the golden rule. *Rec. dist.:* N.C.

12. There is only one rule for being a good talker: learn how to listen. *Rec. dist.:* Ont. *1st cit.:* 1820 Colton, *Lacon.* *20c. coll.:* Stevenson 1441:1.

13. There's no rule without an exception. *Var.:* There is no general rule without exception. *Rec. dist.:* U.S. *1st cit.:* 1579 *News from North;* US1840 Cooper, *Pathfinder.* *20c. coll.:* ODEP 687, T&W 313, CODP 71, Stevenson 2014:1.
    SEE ALSO There is an EXCEPTION to every rule. / MULES don't kick according to rules. / You cannot break the rules of NATURE and get by with it. / RELIGION should be a rule of life, not a casual incident of it.

rule *(v.)* **1.** He who would rule must hear and be deaf, see and be blind. *Rec. dist.:* Ill.

2. It is better to rule by love than by fear. *Rec. dist.:* N.Y.

3. Rule or ruin. *Rec. dist.:* Ohio. *1st cit.:* 1681 Dryden, *Absalom and Achitophel.* *20c. coll.:* Stevenson 2013:2.
    SEE ALSO CHANCES rule men and not men chances. / The HAND that rocks the cradle is the hand that rules the world. / The KING reigns but does not rule. / The MAJORITY rules. / Let the PEOPLE rule.

ruler A customary ruler is the devil's bagpipe which the world does run after. *Rec. dist.:* N.Y.

rum **1.** He that spills the rum loses that only; he that drinks it often loses that and himself. *Rec. dist.:* N.Y. *1st cit.:* US1750 Franklin, *PRAlmanac.* *20c. coll.:* Stevenson 2017:11.

2. When the rum is in, the wit is out. *Rec. dist.:* U.S., Can. *1st cit.:* ca1386 Chaucer, *Par-*

doner's Tale; US1813 Eaton, *Life of Late Gen. William Eaton.* **20c. coll.:** ODEP 895, Whiting 488, CODP 247, Stevenson 2523:7, T&W 406, Whiting*(MP)* 688.

3. When you incline to drink rum, fill the glass half with water. *Rec. dist.:* Ind.

rumor Anyone can start a rumor, but none can stop one. *Rec. dist.:* N.C. *1st cit.:* US1948 Stevenson, *Home Book of Proverbs.* **20c. coll.:** Stevenson 2017:17.

run *(n.)* A good run is better than a bad stand. *Var.:* A good run is better than a stiff fight. *Rec. dist.:* Ill., Ky., N.J., Tenn. *1st cit.:* US1943 Heberden, *Murder Goes Astray.* **20c. coll.:** Stevenson 800:8, Whiting*(MP)* 541.

run *(v.)* **1.** He who expects to run must crawl first. *Rec. dist.:* Iowa.

2. It is useless to run; better to start on time. *Rec. dist.:* Ala., Ga., Ont.

3. Never run after a worrier or a bus: another one is sure to be along soon. *Var.:* Never run after a woman or a streetcar: there'll be another along in a few minutes. *Rec. dist.:* N.Y.

4. One can run only as fast as his legs will carry him. *Rec. dist.:* Ont.

5. They stumble that run fast. *Rec. dist.:* Ont. *1st cit.:* 1594 Shakespeare, *Romeo and Juliet.* **20c. coll.:** Stevenson 2142:7.

6. You cannot run and bark at the same time. *Rec. dist.:* Miss.

7. You must run to win the race. *Rec. dist.:* Ind. *1st cit.:* 1732 Fuller, *Gnomologia.* **20c. coll.:** Stevenson 1930:6.

See also Business is like a car: it will not run by itself, except downhill. / You can run into DEBT but you have to crawl out. / Two DOGS fight over a bone while the third runs away with it. / When a man is DOWN everyone runs over him. / He who FIGHTS and runs away will live to fight another day. / Long runs the FOX, but at last is caught. / The GUILTY one always runs. / Run with the HOGS and they will rub dirt on you. / The path of true LOVE never runs smooth. / No telling which way LUCK or a half-broke steer is going to run. / Don't stay with the RABBITS but run with the hounds. / If all the TROUBLES were

hung on bushes, we would take our own and run. / You have to learn to WALK before you can run. / Still WATER runs deep.

runner **1.** A good runner is never caught. *Rec. dist.:* Ohio.

2. It's better to be a good runner than a bad stander. *Rec. dist.:* N.Y. *1st cit.:* US1943 Heberden, *Murder Goes Astray.* **20c. coll.:** Stevenson 800:8, Whiting*(MP)* 541.

See also The LAME man who keeps the right road outstrips the runner who keeps the wrong one.

running *(n.)* **1.** It's no use running; you should start on time. *Rec. dist.:* Ont.

2. Running is better than standing. *Rec. dist.:* N.J., N.Y.

See also Don't try running WATER up a hill.

running *(adj.)* *See* One can't shoe a running HORSE. / Running WATER washes clean.

runt The runt makes the best sow. *Var.:* Runt pig is best hog in litter. *Rec. dist.:* Ont. *1st cit.:* 1678 Ray, *English Proverbs.* **20c. coll.:** Stevenson 1792:11.

rush *See* Don't rush the CATTLE. / FOOLS rush in where angels fear to tread.

Russian Scratch a Russian and you find a Tartar. *Rec. dist.:* Ont. *1st cit.:* 1855 Thackeray, *Newcomes;* US1823 *Diary of James Gallatin, 1813–1827,* ed. Gallatin (1916). **20c. coll.:** ODEP 706, Whiting 374, CODP 198, Stevenson 2019:13, Whiting*(MP)* 542.

rust *(n.)* **1.** Much rust needs a rough file. *Rec. dist.:* Ont. *1st cit.:* US1948 Stevenson, *Home Book of Proverbs.* **20c. coll.:** Stevenson 160:11.

2. Rust wastes more than use. *Rec. dist.:* Ill., Ohio.

3. Take away the rust from the silver and there'll come forth a pure vessel. *Rec. dist.:* Ont.

4. The rust rots the steel which use preserves. *Rec. dist.:* Ont. *1st cit.:* 1576 Patricius, *Civil Policy.* **20c. coll.:** ODEP 406, Stevenson 2020:1

See also SLOTH, like rust, consumes faster

than labor wears, while the used key is always bright. / The WHEEL that turns gathers no rust.

rust *(v.)* More people rust out than wear out. *Rec. dist.:* Ky., Tenn.

SEE ALSO If you REST, you rust. / REST, rust, rot. / A SPADE and a thought should never be allowed to rust. / It is better to WEAR out than to rust out.

rut The only difference between a rut and a grave is that a grave is a little longer. *Var.:* The only difference between a rut and a grave is their dimensions. *Rec. dist.:* Calif., Colo., N.Y.

S

Sabbath The Sabbath was made for man, and not man for the Sabbath. *Rec. dist.:* N.C. *1st cit.:* US1948 Stevenson, *Home Book of Proverbs. 20c. coll.:* Stevenson 2021:2.

sable Sables feel proud in the absence of ermine. *Rec. dist.:* N.Y.

sack **1.** A broken sack won't hold corn. *Rec. dist.:* Ind. *1st cit.:* 1573 Sanford, *Garden of Pleasure. 20c. coll.:* ODEP 88, Stevenson 2021:4.

2. A sack is best tied before it is full. *Rec. dist.:* Ill. *1st cit.:* 1580 Munday, *Zelauto;* US1811 *Port Folio 20c. coll.:* ODEP 59, Whiting 375, Stevenson 1912:1.

3. An empty sack won't stand alone. *Vars.:* **(a)** An empty sack cannot stand upright. **(b)** An empty sack is hard to stand up direct. **(c)** An empty sack will never stand upright. **(d)** An empty sack won't stand up. **(e)** Empty sacks cannot stand straight. **(f)** It is hard for an empty sack to stand upright. **(g)** It's hard for an empty sack to stand alone. *Rec. dist.:* U.S., Can. *1st cit.:* 1642 Torriano, *Select Italian Proverbs;* US1740 Franklin, *PRAlmanac. 20c. coll.:* ODEP 220, Whiting 18, CODP 64, Stevenson 2021:14, T&W 14.

4. Everyone thinks his sack heaviest. *Rec. dist.:* Ont. *1st cit.:* 1573 Gascoigne, *Hundreth Sundrie Flowres. 20c. coll.:* ODEP 231, Stevenson 256:7.

5. The standing sack fills quicker. *Rec. dist.:* Ont.

6. There comes nothing out of the sack but what was in it. *Rec. dist.:* Okla. *1st cit.:* 1581 Cartigny, *Voyage of Wandering Knight;* US1869 Spurgeon, *John Ploughman's Talks. 20c. coll.:* ODEP 136, Stevenson 2021:6.

7. You can't overfill fortune's sacks. *Rec. dist.:* Ont.

SEE ALSO You may know by the HANDFUL the whole sack. / Every PEA helps to fill the sack.

sacrifice *SEE* As often as we do GOOD, we sacrifice. / OBEDIENCE is better than sacrifice.

sad *SEE* A sad SAINT is a sorry saint. / The sweetest SONGS are those that tell of saddest thoughts. / Of all the WORDS of tongue or pen, the saddest are these: it might have been.

saddle **1.** Always put the saddle on the right horse. *Rec. dist.:* Ill., Ont., Tex. *1st cit.:* 1607 Dekker and Webster, *Westward Hoe;* US1692 Bulkeley, *Will and Doom,* ed. Hoadly, Conn.Hist.Soc. *Collections* (1895). *20c. coll.:* ODEP 690, Whiting 375, Stevenson 2022:2, T&W 315, Whiting(MP) 543.

2. High-powered saddles ain't half as rare as high-powered hombres in 'em. *Rec. dist.:* N.Mex.

3. If the saddle squeaks, it ain't bought. *Rec. dist.:* Okla.

SEE ALSO The losing HORSE blames the saddle.

sadness *SEE* In HAPPINESS, iron is bright; in sadness, gold is dull.

safe **1.** It is better to be safe than sorry. *Var.:* Better safe than sorry. *Rec. dist.:* U.S., Can. *1st cit.:* 1837 Lover, *Rory O'More;* US1932 Plum, *Murder at the Hunting Club. 20c. coll.:* CODP 15, Stevenson 2022:9, Whiting(MP) 543.

2. The way to be safe is never to feel secure. *Rec. dist.:* U.S. *1st cit.:* 1641 Quarles, *Enchiridion;* US1732 Franklin, *PRAlmanac. 20c. coll.:* Stevenson 2055:7.

SEE ALSO BLAME is safer than praise. / It is easy to be BRAVE from a safe distance. / He who rings the CHURCH bells is safe. / GOD promises a safe landing, but not a calm passage. / The safest HELMET is virtue. / It's safer to be a HOUND than a rabbit. / The beaten ROAD is the safest. / He that is too SECURE is not safe. / It is better to be on the safe SIDE. / Be SILENT and safe: silence never betrays you. / The little STATION is the safest. / The safe WAY is the right way.

safely *SEE* ANTS live safely till they have gotten wings. / By FALLING we learn to go safely. / Stick to the HORSE that carried you safely across.

safety 1. Safety first. *Rec. dist.:* U.S., Can. *1st cit.:* 1915 *Motto of Industrial Council for Industrial Safety;* US1937 Gardner, *Dangerous Dowager.* *20c. coll.:* ODEP 691, Whiting*(MP)* 543, Stevenson 2023:11.

2. The only safety is in God. *Rec. dist.:* Mich.

3. There's safety in numbers. *Var.:* There is safety in numbers. *Rec. dist.:* U.S., Can. *1st cit.:* ca1550 Knox in Black, *Reign of Elizabeth;* US1929 Chancellor, *Dark God.* *20c. coll.:* ODEP 691, Whiting*(MP)* 544, Stevenson 2022:11.

SEE ALSO In SKATING over thin ice, our safety is our speed. / WISDOM promises godliness and safety.

sail *(n.)* 1. As the sail is set, so goes the ship. *Rec. dist.:* Ont.

2. Cut your sail according to your cloth. *Rec. dist.:* Nebr.

3. Don't carry too much sail. *Rec. dist.:* Ont.

4. Hoist up the sail while the gale does last. *Rec. dist.:* Ont. *1st cit.:* 1583 Melbancke, *Philotimus.* *20c. coll.:* ODEP 376, Stevenson 2024:12.

5. Keep your sails trimmed. *Rec. dist.:* N.Y.

6. Make not your sail too large for your ship. *Rec. dist.:* Mich., Ont. *1st cit.:* 1565 Calfhill, *Treatise of Cross;* US1946 Crispin, *Holy Disorders.* *20c. coll.:* ODEP 692, Stevenson 2024:9, Whiting*(MP)* 544.

SEE ALSO RELATIONSHIP is a poor ship to sail on. / A SHIP under sail and a big-bellied woman are the handsomest two things that can be. / As the WIND blows, set your sails.

sail *(v.)* He that will not sail till all dangers are over must not put to sea. *Rec. dist.:* Ill. *1st cit.:* 1592 Delamothe, *Treasure of French Tongue.* *20c. coll.:* ODEP 692, Stevenson 2024:4.

sailing It is safest sailing within reach of shore. *Rec. dist.:* Ill.

sailor 1. A good sailor likes a rough sea. *Rec. dist.:* Ont.

2. Any man can be a sailor on a calm sea. *Rec. dist.:* Calif., N.Y., Ont., S.C. *1st cit.:* ca1592 Greene, *James IV.* *20c. coll.:* ODEP 99.

3. Good sailors never die. *Rec. dist.:* Mich., N.Y., S.C.

4. Many a man is a sailor who never owned a rowboat. *Rec. dist.:* N.Y., S.C.

5. Sailors get their money like horses, but spend it like asses. *Rec. dist.:* Wis. *1st cit.:* 1751 Smollett, *Peregrine Pickle.* *20c. coll.:* ODEP 692, Stevenson 2026:7.

saint 1. A sad saint is a sorry saint. *Rec. dist.:* Ont.

2. A saint has no value in his own house. *Rec. dist.:* Ont.

3. All are not saints that go to church. *Var.:* They are not all saints that use holy water. *Rec. dist.:* U.S., Can. *1st cit.:* ca1576 Whythorne, *Autobiography,* ed. Osborn (1961). *20c. coll.:* ODEP 9, Stevenson 2026:13.

4. Saint abroad and devil at home. *Rec. dist.:* Ill., N.Y., S.C. *1st cit.:* 1541 *Schoolhouse of Women;* US1880 Spurgeon, *John Ploughman's Pictures.* *20c. coll.:* ODEP 693, Stevenson 1211:2.

5. Young saint, old devil. *Var.:* A young saint, an old sinner. *Rec. dist.:* U.S., Can. *1st cit.:* ca1400 *Middle English Sermons,* ed. Ross, E.E.T.S. (1940); USca1675 *John Saffin, His Book,* ed. Hazard (1928). *20c. coll.:* ODEP 928, Whiting 377, Stevenson 45:7, Whiting*(MP)* 545.

SEE ALSO COLLEGES hate geniuses, just as convents hate saints. / An open DOOR may tempt a saint. / The greater the SINNER, the greater the saint. / Scratch a SLUGGARD and find a saint. / When the VOYAGE is over, the saint is forgot.

sake SEE ART for art's sake. / Love TRUTH for truth's sake.

salary Draw your salary before spending it. *Rec. dist.:* N.Y., S.C. *1st cit.:* 1901 Ade, "People's Choice" in *Forty Modern Fables.* *20c. coll.:* Stevenson 2196:8.

salesman A green salesman will sell more than a blue one. *Rec. dist.:* Miss.

salt 1. Don't rub salt in the wound. *Rec. dist.:* Mich., N.J., N.Y., S.C. *1st cit.:* US1940 Strange, *Picture.* *20c. coll.:* Whiting*(MP)* 546, Stevenson 2646:5.

2. Earn your salt. *Rec. dist.:* Ill., Ohio. *1st cit.:* 1830 Marryat, *King's Own;* US1776 McKesson in *Public Papers of George Clinton, First Governor of New York,* ed. Hastings (1899–1911). *20c. coll.:* ODEP 922, Whiting 378, T&W 316, Whiting*(MP)* 546.

3. Eat a peck of salt with a man before you trust him. *Rec. dist.:* N.Y., N.C., S.C., Tex. *1st cit.:* ca1500 *15c. School Book,* ed. Nelson; US1769 Woodmason, *Carolina Backcountry on Eve of Revolution, Journal of Charles Woodmason,* ed. Hooker (1952). *20c. coll.:* ODEP 40, Whiting 331, Stevenson 2031:1.

4. Give neither salt nor advice till asked for it. *Rec. dist.:* N.Y., S.C. *1st cit.:* 1707 Mapletoft, *Select Proverbs.* *20c. coll.:* ODEP 303.

5. One pinch of salt sets the whole pot to boiling. *Rec. dist.:* Ont.

6. Season all you hear with salt. *Rec. dist.:* N.C. *1st cit.:* 1599 Rainolds, *Overthrow Stage Plays;* US1645 *John Wheelwright, His Writings,* ed. Bell, Publ. Prince Soc. (1876). *20c. coll.:* ODEP 330, Whiting 184, Stevenson 2030:1.

SEE ALSO Salt the COW to get the calf. / LOVE is the salt of life.

salute As you salute, you will be saluted. *Rec. dist.:* Ill., Mich.

salve There's a salve for every sore. *Var.:* Every sore has its salve. *Rec. dist.:* Ohio, Ont. *1st cit.:* 1541 *Schoolhouse of Women;* US1652 Bradford, *Dialogue of Third Conference,* ed. Deane (1870). *20c. coll.:* ODEP 698, Whiting 378, Stevenson 2032:10.

same *SEE* LIGHTNING never strikes in the same place twice. / You can never get all the POSSUMS up the same tree. / You should never TRUST a man, but if you do, never trust the same one twice.

sample By a small sample we may judge the whole piece. *Rec. dist.:* Ont. *1st cit.:* 1584 Withals, *Short Dictionary;* US1799 Carey, *Porcupiniad.* *20c. coll.:* ODEP 690, Whiting 378.

sand **1.** A little sand keeps you from slipping. *Var.:* A little sand in your tracks keeps you from slipping. *Rec. dist.:* Calif., Ind.

2. A person has to have a lot of sand to do something. *Rec. dist.:* N.C. *Infm.:* In this case, sand means courage.

3. If you play with sand, you'll get dirty. *Rec. dist.:* N.C.

4. There is more than one grain of sand on the seashore. *Rec. dist.:* Calif.

SEE ALSO AGE writes in the sand. / Never cast an ANCHOR in shifting sand. / You can't put your FOOTPRINTS in the sand of time by sitting down. / No HILL too steep, no sand too deep. / MONEY comes like earth scooped up with a needle; it goes like sand washed away by water. / WALLS of sand are sure to crumble.

sands The sands of time never run smooth. *Rec. dist.:* Ohio.

Santa Claus No one will kill Santa Claus. *Vars.:* **(a)** Nobody kills Santa Claus. **(b)** Nobody shoots Santa Claus. *Rec. dist.:* N.J. *1st cit.:* US1933 Newspaper interview with Alfred E. Smith, New York, 30 Nov. *20c. coll.:* Stevenson 2033:8.

sapling **1.** How the sapling bends, so grows the tree. *Rec. dist.:* Ohio. *1st cit.:* 1732 Pope, *Epistles to Several Persons;* US1796 *Writings of George Washington,* ed. Fitzpatrick (1931–44). *20c. coll.:* CODP 232, Whiting 459, Stevenson 2351:7, T&W 387.

2. You may bend a sapling, but never a tree. *Rec. dist.:* Ont. *1st cit.:* 1543 Hardyng, *English Chronicle in Metre.* *20c. coll.:* ODEP 46, Stevenson 2371:5.

sarcasm Sarcasm is the language of the devil. *Rec. dist.:* Ill. *1st cit.:* 1836 Carlyle, *Sartor Resartus.* *20c. coll.:* Stevenson 2033:9.

Satan **1.** Get behind me, Satan, and push hard. *Vars.:* **(a)** Get behind me, Satan. **(b)** Get behind me, Satan, and push. *Rec. dist.:* Ark., Ind., Mich., Wis.

2. Satan has some mischief still for idle hands to do. *Rec. dist.:* N.H., Ont. *1st cit.:* ca1386 Chaucer, *Tale of Melibee;* US1808 A. Adams in Mass.Hist.Soc. *Proceedings* (1936–41). *20c. coll.:* ODEP 180, Whiting 104, CODP 51, Stevenson 1216:2, T&W 318, Whiting*(MP)* 162.

3. Speak of Satan and you'll see his horns.

Rec. dist.: Mich., Ont. *1st cit.:* 1591 Lyly, *Endimion;* US1728 Byrd, *Histories of Dividing Line Betwixt Virginia and North Carolina,* ed. Boyd (1929). *20c. coll.:* ODEP 804, Whiting 106, CODP 220, Stevenson 568:9, T&W 98, Whiting(MP) 165.

satiety 1. Satiety causes disgust; abundance begets indifference. *Rec. dist.:* Ill. *1st cit.:* US1948 Stevenson, *Home Book of Proverbs.* *20c. coll.:* Stevenson 2034:1.

2. Satiety comes of riches, contumely of satiety. *Rec. dist.:* Mich. *1st cit.:* US1948 Stevenson, *Home Book of Proverbs.* *20c. coll.:* Stevenson 2034:1.

satin Beneath satin and silk there is much suffering. *Rec. dist.:* Ont.

satisfaction 1. It's not improbable that a man may receive more solid satisfaction from pudding while he is alive than from praise after he is dead. *Rec. dist.:* N.Y. *1st cit.:* 1728 Pope, *Dunciad;* US1750 Franklin, *PRAlmanac.* *20c. coll.:* ODEP 644, Stevenson 1915:3.

2. Satisfaction is a result of a job well done. *Rec. dist.:* Ind.

3. Satisfaction is the best payment. *Rec. dist.:* N.Y. *1st cit.:* 1597 Shakespeare, *Merchant of Venice.* *20c. coll.:* Stevenson 1763:7.

satisfy *SEE* Man is never satisfied with the WEATHER.

Saturday Saturday begun is never done. *Rec. dist.:* N.C.

SEE ALSO Saturday's CLEANING will not last through Sunday, but Sunday's will last all week. / Saturday's FLITTING is short sitting.

sauce 1. Make not your sauce till you have caught the fish. *Rec. dist.:* Ont. *1st cit.:* 1732 Fuller, *Gnomologia.* *20c. coll.:* Stevenson 333:1.

2. What is sauce for the goose is sauce for the gander. *Var.:* A sauce for the goose is sauce for the gander. *Rec. dist.:* U.S., Can. *1st cit.:* 1670 Ray, *English Proverbs;* US1757 *Colonial Virginia Satirist,* ed. Davis, Am.Phil.Soc. *Transactions* (1967). *20c. coll.:* ODEP 699, Whiting 379, CODP 197, Stevenson 2035:4, T&W 318, Whiting(MP) 548.

SEE ALSO APPETITE furnishes the best sauce. / REST is the sweet sauce of labor.

saucer The cracked saucer lasts longest. *Rec. dist.:* Ont.

sausage 1. A long sausage and a short grace. *Rec. dist.:* Ont.

2. Every sausage knows if it is mek outer cow or dawg. *Rec. dist.:* N.Y., S.C.

save 1. He who saves in little things can be liberal in great ones. *Rec. dist.:* Ind.

2. He who would save should begin with his mouth. *Rec. dist.:* Ill.

3. Let him save himself who can. *Rec. dist.:* Ont.

4. Save and have. *Rec. dist.:* Calif.

5. Save today, safe tomorrow. *Rec. dist.:* Okla.

6. Save when you are young to spend when you are old. *Rec. dist.:* Ohio.

7. Save while you have; give while you live. *Rec. dist.:* Ont.

8. The man who will not save as he goes keeps his nose to the grindstone. *Rec. dist.:* Ont. *1st cit.:* US1758 Franklin, "Way to Wealth" in *Papers of Benjamin Franklin,* ed. Labaree (1959). *20c. coll.:* Whiting 314, Stevenson 1694:7.

SEE ALSO For AGE and want, save while you may, for no morning sun lasts all day. / Short ANSWERS save trouble. / Save the APPLES for when you are hungry. / Use your BRAIN and save your heels. / Save a DOLLAR and keep your worries away. / Don't DROWN yourself to save a drowning man. / Other men's FAILURES can never save you. / One HAND scatters what the other saves. / He who HESITATES is sometimes saved. / The only way to save an HOUR is spend it wisely. / Save your LIFE and lose a minute. / MONEY saved is money earned. / A PENNY saved is a penny earned. / Save for a RAINY day. / SOULS are not saved in bundles. / A STITCH in time saves nine. / STOOP low and it will save you many a bump through life. / Few have earned large SUCCESS who didn't save part of their small earnings. / He who wants to TRAVEL far saves his horse. / When a YOUTH is saved, a life is saved; when an old person is saved, only a soul is saved.

saving 1. All things are cheap to the saving, dear to the wasteful. *Rec. dist.:* N.Y., S.C. *1st* *cit.:* US1734 Franklin, *PRAlmanac.* **20c. coll.:** Stevenson 2036:2.

2. If you would be wealthy, think of saving as well as getting. *Var.:* Think of saving as well as of getting. *Rec. dist.:* Ill., Ind. *1st cit.:* US1743 Franklin, *PRAlmanac.* **20c. coll.:** Whiting 379, Stevenson 2036:2.

3. Of saving comes having. *Var.:* From saving comes having. *Rec. dist.:* Ind., Ky., Tenn., Tex. *1st cit.:* ca1450 *Reliquiae Antiquae;* US1739 Franklin, *PRAlmanac.* **20c. coll.:** Stevenson 2036:11, Whiting 379, ODEP 700.

4. There's more in saving than there is in earning. *Rec. dist.:* S.C.

SEE ALSO No ALCHEMY likes saving.

Savior SEE Great SERMONS lead the people to praise the preacher; good preaching leads the people to praise the Savior.

saw *(n.)* A dull saw cuts deepest. *Rec. dist.:* N.Y.

saw *(v.)* SEE You can't saw WOOD with a hammer.

say **1.** All that you say about others, say not to them. *Rec. dist.:* Ont.

2. Don't say it—write it. *Rec. dist.:* Ont.

3. If you don't say anything, you won't be called upon to repeat it. *Rec. dist.:* Colo., N.Y.

4. It is easier said than done. *Vars.:* **(a)** A thing is easier said than done. **(b)** Easier said than done. **(c)** Things are easier said than done. *Rec. dist.:* U.S., Can. *1st cit.:* ca1450 *Religious and Love Poems,* ed. Furnivall, E.E.T.S.(1866); US1712 *Selected Letters of Cotton Mather,* ed. Silverman (1971). **20c. coll.:** ODEP 212, Whiting 380, Stevenson 2037:14, T&W 319, Whiting(MP) 544.

5. It is not what you say, but how you say it. *Rec. dist.:* N.C.

6. It's not what you said; it's what you didn't say. *Rec. dist.:* N.C.

7. Learn to say before you sing. *Rec. dist.:* Tex. *1st cit.:* 1639 Clarke, *Paroemiologia.* **20c. coll.:** ODEP 451, Stevenson 2163:7.

8. Least said, soonest mended. *Vars.:* **(a)** Least said is easiest mended. **(b)** Least said is soonest mended. **(c)** Least said, sooner mended. **(d)** Less said, soonest mended. **(e)** Little said is soonest mended. **(f)** Little said, soon amended. **(g)** The least said is the easiest mended. **(h)** The least said is the soonest mended. **(i)** The less said, the easiest mended. *Rec. dist.:* U.S., Can. *1st cit.:* ca1460 "Parliament of Birds" in *Early Popular Poetry,* ed. Hazlett (1864); US1698 Usher in *William & Mary Coll. Quart.* (1950). **20c. coll.:** ODEP 472, Whiting 257, CODP 131, Stevenson 2190:10, T&W 217, Whiting(MP) 366.

9. Less said, more done. *Rec. dist.:* N.Y.

10. Nothing is said now that has not been said before. *Rec. dist.:* N.C. *1st cit.:* 1621 Burton, *Anatomy of Melancholy.* **20c. coll.:** Stevenson 1804:6.

11. Said first and thought after makes many a disaster. *Rec. dist.:* Ky., Tenn. *1st cit.:* US1940 Thompson, *Body, Boots, and Britches.* **20c. coll.:** Stevenson 2307:5.

12. Say little; write less; print least. *Rec. dist.:* Ont. *1st cit.:* 1666 Torriano, *Common Place of Italian Proverbs.* **20c. coll.:** ODEP 701.

13. Say well is good, but do well is better. *Rec. dist.:* N.Y., N.C., S.C. *1st cit.:* 1536 Elyot, "Remedy for Sedition" in *Boke of Governor,* ed. Croft. **20c. coll.:** ODEP 702, Stevenson 2038:6.

14. Say what you mean and mean what you say. *Rec. dist.:* N.Y. *1st cit.:* US1948 Stevenson, *Home Book of Proverbs.* **20c. coll.:** Stevenson 2193:3.

15. The more you say, the less you shine. *Rec. dist.:* N.Y.

16. They say is a tough old liar. *Vars.:* **(a)** The biggest liar in the world is they say. **(b)** They say so is half a lie. *Rec. dist.:* Calif., N.Y., Ont. *1st cit.:* 1666 Torriano, *Common Place of Italian Proverbs;* US1869 Spurgeon, *John Ploughman's Talks.* **20c. coll.:** ODEP 809, Stevenson 2018:8.

17. Watch what you say, when, and to whom. *Rec. dist.:* Ohio.

18. What can't be said is often whistled. *Rec. dist.:* Calif., Colo., N.Y.

19. What is said is said, and no sponge can wipe it out. *Rec. dist.:* Ala., Ga.

20. What people say behind your back is your standing in the community. *Rec. dist.:* N.Y.

21. What's said can never be resaid. *Rec. dist.:* N.C. *1st cit.:* 1933 Brady, *Fair Murder;* US1856 Whitcher, *Widow Bedott Papers.* *20c. coll.:* Whiting(MP) 549, T&W 319.

SEE ALSO If you say A, they'll make you say B. / Judge a DUTCHMAN by what he means, not by what he says. / A FOOL always talks most when he has the least to say. / If you can't say something GOOD about someone, don't say anything at all. / Say no ILL of the year till it be past. / You can THINK what you like, but don't say it. / That must be TRUE which all men say. / It is better to say a good WORD about a bad fellow than a bad word about a good fellow.

saying 1. If it isn't worth saying, don't say it at all. *Rec. dist.:* N.Y. *1st cit.:* ca1377 Langland, *Piers Plowman;* US1764 *Papers of Benjamin Franklin,* ed. Labaree (1959). *20c. coll.:* ODEP 814, Whiting 380, Stevenson 2187:11, Whiting(MP) 549.

2. Many a true saying is uttered through false teeth. *Rec. dist.:* Colo.

3. Saying and doing are two different things. *Vars.:* **(a)** Between saying and doing there is a long road. **(b)** Saying and doing are two things. *Rec. dist.:* U.S. *1st cit.:* 1546 Heywood, *Dialogue of Proverbs,* ed. Habernicht (1963); US1697 Chalkley, "God's Great Love" in *Works of Thomas Chalkley* (1766). *20c. coll.:* ODEP 702, Whiting 380, Stevenson 2037:9.

4. Saying so don't make it so. *Rec. dist.:* Mich., N.Y.

5. Sayings go cheap. *Rec. dist.:* N.Y. *1st cit.:* ca1628 Carmichaell, *Proverbs in Scots,* ed. Anderson (1927). *20c. coll.:* ODEP 702.

SEE ALSO DOING is better than saying. / It is not with saying "HONEY, honey" that sweetness comes into the mouth. / LOVE is not merely saying, it is doing. / Be SILENT if you have nothing worth saying. / Big TALKING, but little saying.

scabbard *SEE* One SWORD keeps another in its scabbard.

scabbed *SEE* One scabbed SHEEP will mar a flock.

scald *SEE* Cool WORDS scald not a tongue.

scale *(n.)* Just scales and full measure injure no men. *Rec. dist.:* Ind.

scale *(v.)* *SEE* One must first scale the MOUNTAIN in order to view the plain.

scandal 1. A scandal is something that has to be bad to be good. *Rec. dist.:* N.Dak.

2. In scandal as in robbery, the receiver is as bad as the thief. *Rec. dist.:* N.Y. *1st cit.:* 1623 Wodroephe, *Spared Hours of a Soldier;* US1716 "Considerations" in *Colonial Currency Reprints,* ed. Davis, Publ. Prince Soc. (1910–11). *20c. coll.:* ODEP 667, Whiting 358, Stevenson 2039:3.

3. Scandal grows with the telling. *Rec. dist.:* Ill., Ont.

4. Scandal will rub out like dirt when it is dry. *Rec. dist.:* Mich. *1st cit.:* 1732 Fuller, *Gnomologia.* *20c. coll.:* Stevenson 2039:5.

5. Silence scandal by silence. *Rec. dist.:* Ont.

SEE ALSO Self BRAG, half scandal. / SELF-PRAISE is half scandal.

scar He jests at scars who never felt a wound. *Rec. dist.:* N.J., N.Y., N.C., S.C. *1st cit.:* 1594 Shakespeare, *Romeo and Juliet.* *20c. coll.:* Stevenson 2647:7.

SEE ALSO A gaping CUT always leaves a scar. / The wrinkled SKIN easily conceals a scar. / It is the unshed TEARS that make the scar. / WARS bring scars.

scare A good scare is worth more to a man than good advice. *Rec. dist.:* N.Y., S.C. *1st cit.:* 1911 Howe, *Country Town Sayings.* *20c. coll.:* Stevenson 21:5.

scared 1. I'd rather be scared a minute than be a corpse the rest of my life. *Rec. dist.:* N.Y.

2. Skeert ain't kilt nobody yit. *Rec. dist.:* Miss.

scarlet *SEE* An APE is an ape, a varlet is a varlet, though they be clad in silk and scarlet.

scary *SEE* A scary HORSE needs a stout bridle.

scatter Scatter with one hand; gather with two. *Rec. dist.:* N.Y., Ont. *1st cit.:* 1659 Howell, *Paroimiografia (English Proverbs)*. **20c. coll.:** *ODEP* 703, Stevenson 2197:5.

SEE ALSO One HAND scatters what the other saves.

scattering *SEE* A close GATHERING gets a wide scattering.

scenery You can't admire scenery on an empty stomach. **Rec. dist.:** Ont.

scent *SEE* Wash a PIG, scent a pig; a pig still is a pig.

schemes The best-laid schemes o' mice an' men gang aft agley. **Rec. dist.:** U.S., Can. **1st cit.:** 1786 Burns, "To a Mouse" in *Poems*. **20c. coll.:** *CODP* 13, Stevenson 2040:2.

scholar 1. A mere scholar, a mere ass. **Rec. dist.:** N.Y. **1st cit.:** 1606 Marston, *What You Will*. **20c. coll.:** *ODEP* 526, Stevenson 2040:6.

2. Every good scholar is not a good schoolmaster. **Rec. dist.:** Mich. **1st cit.:** 1732 Fuller, *Gnomologia*. **20c. coll.:** Stevenson 2040:11.

3. Great scholars are not the shrewdest men. **Rec. dist.:** Ill.

4. He who robs a scholar robs the public. **Rec. dist.:** Ill. **1st cit.:** 1670 Ray, *English Proverbs*. **20c. coll.:** Stevenson 2000:3.

5. Scholars are their country's treasure and the richest ornaments of the feast. **Rec. dist.:** N.Y.

6. Scholars are wont to sell their birthright for a mess of learning. **Rec. dist.:** N.Y., S.C. **1st cit.:** US1849 Thoreau, *Week on Concord and Merrimack Rivers*. **20c. coll.:** Stevenson 2041:2.

school 1. No school ever rises above its administration. **Rec. dist.:** Wis.

2. Schools hide future premiers. **Rec. dist.:** Ind.

3. We learn not for school but for life. **Rec. dist.:** Ont. **1st cit.:** US1948 Stevenson, *Home Book of Proverbs*. **20c. coll.:** Stevenson 1378:1.

4. You can send a man to school, but you can't make him learn. **Vars.:** (a) Send a boy to school, but you can't make him think. (b) You can send a student to school, but you can't make him think. **Rec. dist.:** Colo., N.Y.

SEE ALSO ADVERSITY is the true school of the mind. / EXPERIENCE is a dear school, but fools learn in no other. / Don't tell TALES out of school. / A WHIP for a fool and a rod for a school.

schoolhouse *SEE* EDUCATION doesn't come by bumping your head against the school house.

schoolmaster *SEE* NEWSPAPERS are the schoolmaster of the common people.

schoolroom *SEE* The mother's HEART is the child's schoolroom.

science 1. Much science, much sorrow. **Rec. dist.:** Ill. **1st cit.:** 1607 *Politeuphuia*. **20c. coll.:** *ODEP* 549, Stevenson 1376:11.

2. Science is nothing but good sense and reason. **Rec. dist.:** Ind. **1st cit.:** US1948 Stevenson, *Home Book of Proverbs*. **20c. coll.:** Stevenson 2041:8.

3. Science moves on. **Rec. dist.:** N.C.

scissors Dull scissors can't cut straight. **Rec. dist.:** Ky., Tenn.

scoffer The scoffer is only trying to hide his own conscience. **Rec. dist.:** Ill.

scold He scolds most that can hurt the least. **Rec. dist.:** Ill.

scone *SEE* Turn your BACK and someone will steal your scone.

scoop *SEE* MONEY comes like earth scooped up with a needle; it goes like sand washed away by water. / The SEA cannot be scooped up in a tumbler.

scorner 1. He that teaches a scorner does an injury to himself. **Rec. dist.:** Ont.

2. Reprove not a scorner lest he hate you; rebuke a wise man and he will love you. **Var.:** Rebuke a scorner and he will hate you; rebuke a wise man and he will love you. **Rec. dist.:** N.Y. **1st cit.:** US1948 Stevenson, *Home Book of Proverbs*. **20c. coll.:** Stevenson 1958:13.

scot Every man must pay his scot. **Rec. dist.:** N.J., N.Y., S.C. **Infm.:** "Scot" means the tavern bill. **1st cit.:** US1860 Emerson, "Wealth" in *Conduct of Life*. **20c. coll.:** Stevenson 1764:3.

scratch 1. Scratch a tender spot and it will soon be a sore. **Rec. dist.:** Ont.

2. Scratch where it itches. *Var.:* Scratch it where it itches. *Rec. dist.:* U.S., Can. *1st cit.:* 1574 Guazzo, *Civile Conversation,* tr. Pettie, T.T. (1925); US1938 Nash, *Taboo to Boot.* *20c. coll.:* Stevenson 2045:8, ODEP 706.

SEE ALSO He who plays with a CAT must expect to be scratched. / CHARACTER is the diamond that scratches every other stone. / Remember, a HEN can scratch for a dozen chicks as easily as for one. / Where the HEN scratches, there she expects to find a bug. / Hungry ROOSTER never cackles when he scratches up a worm. / Scratch a SLUGGARD and find a saint.

scratching There is a difference between scratching your leg and tearing it all to hell. *Rec. dist.:* Oreg.

SEE ALSO EATING and scratching, it's all in the beginning.

scripture Scripture, like nature, lays down no definitions. *Rec. dist.:* Ill.

SEE ALSO The DEVIL can cite scripture for his purpose.

scrubbing *SEE* An inch of RUBBING saves scrubbing.

scuttle *SEE* He who scuttles the SHIP he arrives in may have to swim when he leaves.

scythe *SEE* Keep the RAKE near the scythe, and the cart near the rake.

sea **1.** Calm seas do not make good sailors. *Var.:* Smooth seas make poor sailors. *Rec. dist.:* N.Y.

2. In a calm sea every man is a pilot. *Var.:* Every man is pilot when the sea is calm. *Rec. dist.:* U.S., Can. *1st cit.:* ca1592 Greene, *James IV. 20c. coll.:* ODEP 99, Stevenson 1795:13.

3. Never go to the sea when a storm is coming. *Rec. dist.:* Ont.

4. Praise the sea, but keep on land. *Rec. dist.:* Ont., Tex. *1st cit.:* 1591 Florio, *Second Fruites,* ed. Simonini (1953). *20c. coll.:* ODEP 644, Stevenson 1912:3.

5. The sea cannot be scooped up in a tumbler. *Rec. dist.:* Ont. *1st cit.:* ca1534 Giles, *Duwes;* US1702 Taylor, *Christographia,* ed. Grabo (1962). *20c. coll.:* ODEP 707, Whiting 382.

6. The sea is full of other fish. *Var.:* There are other fish in the sea. *Rec. dist.:* Ind. *1st cit.:* ca1573 Harvey, *Letter-Book;* US1933 Nash, *Look of Silver Lining. 20c. coll.:* CODP 83, Stevenson 816:9.

7. The sea refuses no river. *Rec. dist.:* Ill. *1st cit.:* 1601 Lyly, *Love's Met. 20c. coll.:* ODEP 707, Stevenson 2049:14.

8. They who cross the seas change their skies but not their natures. *Rec. dist.:* Wis. *1st cit.:* 1581 Averell, *Charles and Julia;* US1766 Kent in *Papers of Benjamin Franklin,* ed. Labaree (1959). *20c. coll.:* ODEP 114, Whiting 382.

9. When the sea is crossed, the saint is generally forgotten. *Rec. dist.:* Mich. *1st cit.:* US1948 Stevenson, *Home Book of Proverbs. 20c. coll.:* Stevenson 485:6.

10. Wherever there's a sea, there's a ship. *Rec. dist.:* Calif., N.Y., Ont.

SEE ALSO The sea is full of other FISH. / There are better FISH in the sea than have ever been caught. / There's a FISH in every sea and a pebble on every beach. / Anyone can hold the HELM when the sea is calm. / A KING is never powerful that has not power on the sea. / To go to LAW is to go to sea. / He that would learn to PRAY, let him go to sea. / All RIVERS run to the sea. / A good SAILOR likes a rough sea. / WINE has drowned more men than the sea.

sealed *SEE* A sealed DOOR invites a thief.

seaman The good seaman is known in bad weather. *Rec. dist.:* N.J. *1st cit.:* US1767 Parker in *Papers of Benjamin Franklin,* ed. Labaree (1959). *20c. coll.:* Stevenson 2051:1, Whiting 383.

seamstress A bad seamstress uses a long thread. *Rec. dist.:* Ont.

search *(n.)* Nothing's so hard but a search will find it out. *Rec. dist.:* Ont. *1st cit.:* 1648 Herrick, *Seeke and Finde. 20c. coll.:* Stevenson 2056:5.

search *(v.)* *SEE* HAPPINESS is for those who make it and not for those who search for it.

season There's a season for all things. *Rec. dist.:* Ind., N.Y., Ont. *1st cit.:* 1968 Joseph,

Hole in the Zero; USca1682 "Wall and Garden" in *Mass. Election Sermons, 1670–1775,* ed. Plumstead (1968). ***20c. coll.:*** Whiting*(MP)* 551, Whiting 383, Stevenson 2051:1.

SEE ALSO LOVE knows no season. / A good MAXIM is never out of season. / MONEY never comes out of season.

seasoned SEE KNOWLEDGE and timber shouldn't be much used until they are seasoned.

seat 1. If your seat is hard to sit upon, stand up. ***Rec. dist.:*** Ont.

2. There are no reserved seats in the halls of fame or the chapels of faith. ***Rec. dist.:*** Ill.

seated SEE It is better to be LAME than always seated.

second *(n.)* Seconds are the gold dust of time. ***Rec. dist.:*** Ill.

second *(adj.)* You can't steal second base while your foot is on first. ***Rec. dist.:*** Ill.

SEE ALSO CUSTOM is a second nature. / You can't take a second DRINK unless you have taken a first. / HARMONY is often obtained by playing second fiddle. / No QUARREL ever stirred before the second word. / The second WIFE always sits on the right knee.

secrecy Secrecy is the soul of all great designs. ***Rec. dist.:*** Ill.

secret *(n.)* **1.** A man who wishes to keep a secret should tell nothing in confidence. ***Rec. dist.:*** Wis.

2. A secret is either too good to keep or too bad not to tell. ***Rec. dist.:*** Ohio.

3. A secret shared is no secret. ***Rec. dist.:*** N.Y. ***1st cit.:*** 1929 Pryde, *Secret Room;* US1926 Merritt, *Ship of Ishtar.* ***20c. coll.:*** Whiting*(MP)* 551.

4. A secret should be a secret. ***Var.:*** Keep a secret a secret. ***Rec. dist.:*** Ont.

5. A secret's a secret until it's told. ***Vars.:*** **(a)** A secret ceases to be a secret when once told. **(b)** Secrets, when told, are not secrets. ***Rec. dist.:*** Ohio, Ont., Utah.

6. Don't expect others to keep a secret you cannot keep yourself. ***Rec. dist.:*** Md., Ont. ***1st cit.:*** ca1386 Chaucer, *Tale of Melibee;* US1795 Cathcart, *Diplomatic Journal of James L. Cathcart,* Am.Antiq.Soc. *Proceedings* (1954). ***20c. coll.:*** Stevenson 2053:4, Whiting 383, ODEP 146.

7. If it is a secret, don't tell it to a woman. ***Rec. dist.:*** Ill. ***1st cit.:*** 1474 Caxton, *Game of Chess.* ***20c. coll.:*** Stevenson 2054:6.

8. If you reveal your secret, you yield your liberty. ***Var.:*** To whom you reveal your secrets you yield your liberty. ***Rec. dist.:*** Ill. ***1st cit.:*** 1574 Guazzo, *Civile Conversation,* tr. Pettie, T.T. (1925); US1737 Franklin, *PRAlmanac.* ***20c. coll.:*** Stevenson 2052:2.

9. If you want to keep a secret, keep it to yourself. ***Var.:*** If you wish another to keep your secret first keep it yourself. ***Rec. dist.:*** Ill., N.Y., Ont. ***1st cit.:*** ca1386 Chaucer, *Tale of Melibee;* US1863 *Journals of Ralph Waldo Emerson,* eds. Emerson and Forbes (1909–14). ***20c. coll.:*** Stevenson 2053:4.

10. It is no secret that is known to three. ***Rec. dist.:*** N.Y.

11. It is not wise to seek a secret, and honest not to reveal it. ***Rec. dist.:*** Ont. ***1st cit.:*** US1747 Franklin, *PRAlmanac.* ***20c. coll.:*** Stevenson 2051:13.

12. None are so fond of secrets as those who do not mean to keep them. ***Rec. dist.:*** Ill. ***1st cit.:*** 1820 Colton, *Lacon.* ***20c. coll.:*** Stevenson 2051:9.

13. Secrets are never long-lived. ***Rec. dist.:*** Mich.

14. Tell your secret to your servant and you make him your master. ***Rec. dist.:*** Ill. ***1st cit.:*** 1581 Guazzo, *Civile Conversation,* tr. Pettie, T.T. (1925). ***20c. coll.:*** ODEP 808, Stevenson 2052:2.

15. The great secret of life is to hear lessons and not teach them. ***Rec. dist.:*** N.Y., S.C.

16. The only secret a woman can keep is her age. ***Rec. dist.:*** Ky., Tenn. ***1st cit.:*** 1732 Fuller, *Gnomologia.* ***20c. coll.:*** Stevenson 2054:10.

17. The secret of being loved is being lovable. ***Rec. dist.:*** Ont.

18. The secret of life is not to do what you

like but to like what you do. *Rec. dist.:* N.Y., Wis.

19. The secret of success in conversation is to be able to disagree without being disagreeable. *Rec. dist.:* N.Y.

20. The secret to being lovable is to be unselfish. *Rec. dist.:* Ont.

21. Two can keep a secret if one is dead. *Var.:* It takes two to keep a secret. *Rec. dist.:* U.S., Can. *1st cit.:* ca1558 Wedlocke, *Image of Idleness;* US1735 Franklin, *PRAlmanac. 20c. coll.:* ODEP 417, Whiting 437, CODP 224, Stevenson 2053:3, Whiting(MP) 654.

SEE ALSO WINE is the discoverer of secrets. / Any WOMAN can keep a secret, but she generally needs one other woman to help her. / Blessed is the WOMAN who can keep a secret and the man who will not tell his wife.

secret *(adj.)* Nothing is so secret but time and truth will reveal it. *Rec. dist.:* Mich.

secure He that is too secure is not safe. *Var.:* The way to be safe is never to feel secure. *Rec. dist.:* U.S., Can. *1st cit.:* 1585 Prime, *Sermon in St. Mary's Oxon.;* US1748 Franklin, *PRAlmanac. 20c. coll.:* ODEP 872, Stevenson 2055:7.

security **1.** Security is man's downfall. *Rec. dist.:* Ill.

2. There's security in numbers. *Rec. dist.:* N.C. *1st cit.:* ca1550 Knox in Black, *Reign of Elizabeth;* US1914 Dreiser, *Titan. 20c. coll.:* ODEP 691, CODP 196, Stevenson 2022:11.

SEE ALSO There is no LIBERTY without security, and no security without unity. / A good PAYMASTER needs no security. / POVERTY with security is better than plenty in the midst of fear and uncertainty.

see **1.** Better seen than heard. *Vars.:* **(a)** Be seen, not heard. **(b)** Better to be seen than heard. *Rec. dist.:* N.C., Ont.

2. Blessed are they that have not seen and yet have believed. *Rec. dist.:* U.S., Can. *1st cit.:* US1948 Stevenson, *Home Book of Proverbs. 20c. coll.:* Stevenson 162:9.

3. He who cannot see well should go softly. *Rec. dist.:* Mich.

4. See yourself as others see you. *Rec. dist.:*

N.C., Ont. *1st cit.:* ca1785 Burns, "To a Louse." *20c. coll.:* Stevenson 2065:6.

5. Seldom seen, soon forgotten. *Rec. dist.:* N.Y., Okla. *1st cit.:* ca1350 *Douce MS 52. 20c. coll.:* ODEP 712, Stevenson 2108:5.

6. What we see depends mainly on what we look for. *Rec. dist.:* N.C.

7. What you don't see you won't get hung for. *Rec. dist.:* N.Y., S.C. *1st cit.:* US1940 Saxby, *Death in the Sun. 20c. coll.:* Stevenson 2107:8.

SEE ALSO BELIEVE only half of what you see and nothing you hear. / Never BUY anything before you see it. / De howlin' DOG know w'at he sees. / See no EVIL, hear no evil, speak no evil. / What the EYE doesn't see, the heart doesn't grieve for. / To see an old FRIEND is as agreeable as a good meal. / HEAR, see, and be silent. / A HUNGRY man sees far. / As a MAN is, so he sees. / MOLE don't see w'at his neighbor's doin'. / MONKEY see, monkey do. / Those who look up see the STARS. / We see THINGS not as they are but as we are. / A WISE man sees twice as much as he talks about. / As YOUNG folks see, the young folks do; as they hear, they say.

seed **1.** Destroy the seed of evil or it will grow up to your ruin. *Rec. dist.:* Fla., Ind.

2. The seeds of great things are often small. *Rec. dist.:* Ill. *1st cit.:* 1555 *Decades of the New World,* tr. Eden. *20c. coll.:* Stevenson 1035:15.

SEE ALSO If you want to raise CORN, plant corn seed, not cotton seed. / Don't eat your father's seed POTATOES. / If you would gather ROSES, do not sow rotten seeds.

seeing **1.** Seeing is believing. *Var.:* What we see we believe. *Rec. dist.:* U.S., Can. *1st cit.:* 1609 Harward, Unpublished manuscript in library of Trinity College, Cambridge; US1732 *Jonathan Belcher Papers,* Mass.Hist.Soc. Collections. (1893–94). *20c. coll.:* ODEP 710, Whiting 27, CODP 199, Stevenson 2105:12, T&W 321, Whiting(MP) 551.

SEE ALSO The EYE is not satisfied with seeing.

seek **1.** Seek and you shall find; knock and it shall be opened unto you. *Vars.:* **(a)** Seek and you shall find. **(b)** The one who seeks is the one who finds. *Rec. dist.:* U.S., Can. *1st cit.:* 1530 Palsgrave, *Lesclarcissement de la langue Francoyse;* US1783 *Correspondence of John Jay,* eds. Betts and Bear (1966). *20c. coll.: CODP* 199, Whiting 383, Stevenson 2056:4, Whiting*(MP)* 552.

2. Who seeks what he should not finds what he would not. *Rec. dist.:* Ill. *1st cit.:* 1666 Torriano, *Common Place of Italian Proverbs. 20c. coll.:* Stevenson 2056:6.

SEE ALSO Who seeks ADVENTURE finds blows. / Seek not to be CONSOLED but to console. / He that seeks TROUBLE never misses. / WATER seeks its own level.

seem *SEE* THINGS are not always what they seem. / True WORTH is in being, not in seeming; in doing, not in dreaming.

seldom *SEE* FRIENDS are lost by calling often and calling seldom. / One seldom meets a lonely LIE.

self 1. Deny self for self's sake. *Rec. dist.:* N.Y. *1st cit.:* US1735 Franklin, *PRAlmanac. 20c. coll.:* Stevenson 2058:1.

2. Self is the best servant. *Rec. dist.:* N.C.

3. Self loves itself best. *Rec. dist.:* Ont.

self-conceit 1. Self-conceit is harder to cure than cancer. *Rec. dist.:* N.Y.

2. Self-conceit often leads to self-destruction. *Rec. dist.:* Ont.

self-confidence Self-confidence is the first requisite of great undertakings. *Rec. dist.:* Ill.

SEE ALSO POISE and self-confidence make up a large part of good looks.

self-conquest Self-conquest is the greatest of all victories. *Rec. dist.:* Wis.

self-deceit Self-deceit is the easiest of any. *Rec. dist.:* Mich.

self-defense Self-defense is nature's oldest law. *Rec. dist.:* Ill. *1st cit.:* 1613 Dallington, *Aphorisms;* US1689 Danforth in *Thomas Hutchinson Papers,* Publ. Prince Soc. (1815). *20c. coll.: ODEP* 712, Whiting 383, Stevenson 2062:3.

self-exaltation Self-exaltation is the fool's paradise. *Rec. dist.:* Mich.

self-help Self-help is the best help. *Rec. dist.:* Ont.

self-interest 1. Self-interest is the beginning of wisdom. *Rec. dist.:* Ky., Tenn.

2. Self-interest is the rule, self-sacrifice the exception. *Rec. dist.:* Mich.

selfishness Selfishness is harder to kill than a cat. *Rec. dist.:* Ind.

self-loser *SEE* SELF-SEEKERS are self-losers.

self-praise 1. Self-praise is half slander. *Rec. dist.:* Ill.

2. Self-praise is no recommendation. *Rec. dist.:* N.Y., S.C. *1st cit.:* 1852 Dickens, *Bleak House;* US1778 Windee in *Public Papers of George Clinton,* ed. Hastings (1899–1911). *20c. coll.:* Stevenson 1863:5, Whiting 347, *ODEP* 507, *CODP* 200, Whiting*(MP)* 552.

3. Self-praise, no honor. *Rec. dist.:* Ont.

4. Self-praise stinks. *Rec. dist.:* Calif. *1st cit.:* Caxton, *Fables of Avian;* US1943 Scully, *Rogues. 20c. coll.: ODEP* 507, Whiting*(MP)* 552.

self-preservation Self-preservation is the first law of nature. *Rec. dist.:* U.S., Can. *1st cit.:* 1613 Dallington, *Aphorisms;* US1689 Danforth in *Thomas Hutchinson Papers,* Publ. Prince Soc. (1865). *20c. coll.: ODEP* 712, Whiting 383, *CODP* 200, Stevenson 2068:15, T&W 322, Whiting*(MP)* 552.

self-respect Never lose your self-respect: if that be lost, all is lost. *Rec. dist.:* Mich.

self-restraint Few are those who err on the side of self-restraint. *Rec. dist.:* Ill., N.Y. *1st cit.:* US1948 Stevenson, *Home Book of Proverbs. 20c. coll.:* Stevenson 2060:7.

self-seekers Self-seekers are self-losers. *Rec. dist.:* Ont.

sell Sell honestly, but not honesty. *Rec. dist.:* Ont.

SEE ALSO Never sell AMERICA short. / You cannot sell the COW and have the milk. / PEDIGREE won't sell a lame horse. / PLOW deep while sluggards sleep, and you shall have corn to sell and to keep. / Buy the TRUTH, but never sell it. / Sell not VIRTUE to purchase wealth nor liberty to purchase power.

seller *See* The BUYER needs a thousand eyes; the seller wants but one.

selling *See* A JEW can make a living by selling shoestrings. / Many a man thinks he is buying PLEASURE when he is really selling himself a slave to it.

send *See* If you would have your BUSINESS done, go; if not, send. / Send a FOOL to the market, and a fool he'll return. / If you want a thing done, GO; if not, send. / It's a good rule to never send a MOUSE to catch a skunk, or a pollywog to tackle a whale.

sense 1. A handful of common sense is worth a bushel of learning. *Rec. dist.:* Kans.

2. Better sense in the head than cents in the pocket. *Rec. dist.:* Ill.

3. Bought sense is the best sense. *Rec. dist.:* Ohio. *1st cit.:* ca1495 Medwall, *Nature;* US1787 *American Museum.* *20c. coll.:* ODEP 78, Whiting 490, Stevenson 2546:3.

4. Common sense is always worth more than cunning. *Rec. dist.:* Kans.

5. Common sense is not so common. *Rec. dist.:* N.Y., Utah.

6. Common sense is the rarest thing in the world and the most valuable. *Rec. dist.:* Md.

7. Common sense is very uncommon with a lot of people. *Rec. dist.:* Kans.

8. Horse sense is the result of stable thinking. *Rec. dist.:* Ohio.

9. It is hard to talk sense, but harder to find listeners if you do. *Rec. dist.:* Ill.

10. No sense, no feeling. *Var.:* Where there's no sense there's no feeling. *Rec. dist.:* Fla., Ind., Ont. *1st cit.:* 1939 Marsh, *Number of People;* US1949 Queen, *Cat of Many Tails.* *20c. coll.:* Whiting(MP) 552.

11. Sense comes with age. *Rec. dist.:* N.Y.

12. There is some sense in every nonsense. *Rec. dist.:* Ont.

13. Where sense is wanting, everything is wanting. *Rec. dist.:* Ill. *1st cit.:* US1754 Franklin, *PRAlmanac.* *20c. coll.:* Whiting 384, Stevenson 2070:12.

See also The GUIDE of life is common sense.

/ Better short of PENCE than short of sense. / Much SPEECH, less sense. / The loss of TEMPER is the loss of sense.

sensuality Sensuality is the grave of the soul. *Rec. dist.:* Ill.

sentence *See* MATRIMONY is not a word but a sentence.

seriously Blessed is he who takes himself seriously. *Rec. dist.:* Ohio.

sermon 1. Great sermons lead the people to praise the preacher; good preaching leads the people to praise the Saviour. *Rec. dist.:* N.Y., S.C. *1st cit.:* US1876 Finney, *Memoirs.* *20c. coll.:* Stevenson 2072:11.

2. Sermons should be weighty but not heavy. *Rec. dist.:* Ont.

3. The best sermon is a good life. *Rec. dist.:* Ind. *1st cit.:* US1948 Stevenson, *Home Book of Proverbs.* *20c. coll.:* Stevenson 2072:10.

See also The BELL sends others to church but itself never minds the sermon.

serpent How sharper than a serpent's tooth it is to have a thankless child. *Rec. dist.:* Nebr. *1st cit.:* 1605 Shakespeare, *King Lear.* *20c. coll.:* Stevenson 342:1.

servant 1. A good servant makes a good master. *Rec. dist.:* Tex. *1st cit.:* 1592 Delamothe, *Treasure of French Tongue.* *20c. coll.:* ODEP 714.

2. A good servant must have good wages. *Rec. dist.:* Ill. *1st cit.:* 1732 Fuller, *Gnomologia.* *20c. coll.:* Stevenson 2076:3.

3. A good servant never lacks a master. *Rec. dist.:* Ill.

4. A good servant should have the back of an ass, the tongue of a sheep, and the snout of a swine. *Rec. dist.:* Ind. *1st cit.:* 1589 Wright, *Display of Dutie.* *20c. coll.:* ODEP 715, Stevenson 2075:8.

5. A true servant will deceive his master never. *Rec. dist.:* N.C.

6. If you would have a faithful servant that you would like, serve yourself. *Var.:* If you would have a faithful servant and one that you like, serve yourself. *Rec. dist.:* Ill., Utah.

1st cit.: 1659 Torriano, *Vocabolario Italiano &* *Inglese;* US1737 Franklin, *PRAlmanac.* *20c. coll.:* ODEP 715, *CODP* 200, Whiting 385, Stevenson 2077:12.

SEE ALSO Neither beg of him who has been a BEGGAR nor serve him who has been a servant. / FIRE is a good servant but a bad master. / The GNAT is small, to be sure, but she is not the servant of the cow. / He is a GOVERNOR that governs his passions, and he is a servant that serves them. / Everyone has his MASTER. / Make MONEY your servant, not your master. / No SILVER, no servant.

serve **1.** He who serves is not free. *Rec. dist.:* Mich.

2. Serve yourself if you would be well served. *Rec. dist.:* Ont. *1st cit.:* 1659 Torriano, *Vocabolario Italiano & Inglese.* *20c. coll.:* ODEP 715, *CODP* 200, Whiting 385, Stevenson 2077:12.

3. They also serve who only stand and wait. *Var.:* He also serves who stands and waits. *Rec. dist.:* U.S., Can. *1st cit.:* ca1650 Milton, *On His Blindness.* *20c. coll.:* Stevenson 2078:4.

SEE ALSO FIRST come, first served. / He PROFITS most who serves best. / RICHES serve a wise man but command a fool. / TIME serves no man. / YOUTH will be served.

service **1.** Faithful service should be long remembered. *Rec. dist.:* Ont.

2. Service is not spelled "serves." *Rec. dist.:* Utah.

3. The big word is service. *Rec. dist.:* Ohio.

4. The most acceptable service of God is doing good to man. *Rec. dist.:* N.Y., S.C.

set *SEE* A fine DIAMOND may be ill set. / Let not the SUN set on your anger. / Never let the SUN set on work undone. / Poor men's TABLES are soon set.

setting *SEE* A setting HEN never gets fat.

settle *SEE* No QUESTION is ever settled.

seven *SEE* A DEAD person is wept for for seven days; a fool, all his life.

severe *SEE* LAWS too gentle are seldom obeyed; too severe, seldom executed.

severity *SEE* KINDNESS effects more than severity.

shade If you are hotheaded, keep in the shade. *Rec. dist.:* Ont.

SEE ALSO Morning VOWS are often lost in the midnight shade.

shadow **1.** Beware lest you lose the substance by grasping the shadow. *Var.:* He who grabs at the shadow may lose the substance. *Rec. dist.:* Ont. *1st cit.:* 1548 Hall, *Chronicle of Lancastre and York;* US1632 Peirce in Bradford, *History of Plymouth Plantation.* *20c. coll.:* ODEP 110, Whiting 385, Stevenson 2616:2, Whiting(MP) 553.

2. No man sees the shadow who faces the sun. *Rec. dist.:* Ont.

3. Once standing upright, don't worry if your shadow is crooked. *Rec. dist.:* N.Y.

SEE ALSO A beaten DOG is afraid of the stick's shadow. / Coming EVENTS cast their shadows before. / The smallest HAIR throws its shadow. / Don't measure your IMPORTANCE by your morning shadow. / Better to be SMALL and shine than to be great and cast a shadow. / A crooked STICK will have a crooked shadow. / A single SUNBEAM drives away many shadows. / Stand in the SUNSHINE and the shadow will fall behind.

shady *SEE* A shady BUSINESS never yields a sunny life.

shake *SEE* The TAIL cannot shake the dog.

shallow *SEE* Little FISH swim in shallow water. / Deep RIVERS move with silent majesty; shallow brooks are noisy. / Shallow STREAMS make the most noise.

shame *(n.)* **1.** He who has no shame has no honor. *Rec. dist.:* Mich., N.Y., N.C. *1st cit.:* 1732 Fuller, *Gnomologia.* *20c. coll.:* Stevenson 2083:11.

2. Past shame, past grace. *Rec. dist.:* Ont. *1st cit.:* ca1547 Redford, *Wit and Science.* *20c. coll.:* ODEP 611, Stevenson 2083:9.

3. Shame generally follows vice. *Rec. dist.:* Mich. *1st cit.:* ca1300 Havelock, *The Dane,* E.E.T.S. (1868); US1664 *Works of Anne Bradstreet,* ed. Ellis (1932). *20c. coll.:* ODEP 592, Whiting 396.

SEE ALSO Where the HEART is past hope, the face is past shame. / IGNORANCE leads men into a party, and shame keeps them from getting out again. / PRIDE goes before, and shame follows after. / SIN is easier to stand than shame. / Old SINS breed new shame.

shame *(v.)* SEE Speak the TRUTH and shame the devil. / TRUTH may be blamed, but never shamed.

share 1. Share a little, help a lot. *Rec. dist.:* Ont.

2. Share and share alike. *Rec. dist.:* U.S., Can. *1st cit.:* 1571 Edwards, *Damon and Pithias.* *20c. coll.:* ODEP 720.

SEE ALSO HAPPINESS is not perfect until it is shared. / A JOY that's shared is a joy made double. / You may share the LABORS of the great, but you will not share the spoil.

sharp SEE Dull KNIFE cuts cheese thinner than a sharp one. / LOVE is sharper than stones and sticks. / MALICE has a sharp sight and a strong memory. / A NEEDLE is sharp only at one end. / The devil's TONGUE is sharpest on the backlash. / The TONGUE is the only tool that grows sharper with use. / The sweetest WINE makes the sharpest vinegar.

shave SEE A BARBER learns to shave by shaving fools. / A HANDSAW is a good thing, but not to shave with.

sheep 1. A lazy sheep thinks its wool heavy. *Rec. dist.:* Ohio. *1st cit.:* 1727 Gay, "Hare and Friends" in *Fables.* *20c. coll.:* ODEP 449, Stevenson 2086:4.

2. Each one thinks his sheep is the blackest. *Rec. dist.:* N.C.

3. Every sheep with its like. *Rec. dist.:* Tex.

4. He that makes himself a sheep shall be eaten by the wolves. *Var.:* Make yourself a sheep and the wolves will eat you. *Rec. dist.:* Mich., Ohio. *1st cit.:* 1583 Melbancke, *Philotimus;* US1733 *Writings of Benjamin Franklin,* ed. Smyth (1905–07). *20c. coll.:* ODEP 502, Whiting 387, Stevenson 2088:8.

5. Many patient sheep will enter one stall. *Rec. dist.:* Ohio.

6. Might as well be hanged for a sheep as a lamb. *Var.:* As good be hanged for a sheep as a goat. *Rec. dist.:* U.S., Can. *1st cit.:* 1678 Ray,

English Proverbs; US1787 A. Adams in *Diary and Autobiography of John Adams,* ed. Butterfield (1966). *20c. coll.:* ODEP 350, Whiting 386, CODP 106, Stevenson 1067:4, T&W 324, Whiting*(MP)* 554.

7. One scabbed sheep will mar a flock. *Rec. dist.:* Ont. *1st cit.:* ca1350 *Douce MS 52;* US1624 Sherley in Bradford, *History of Plymouth Plantation,* ed. Ford (1912). *20c. coll.:* ODEP 702, Whiting 387, Stevenson 2086:7, T&W 423.

8. One sheep follows another. *Rec. dist.:* Okla. *1st cit.:* 1599 Heywood, *Edward IV, Part 1* (1874); US1792 *Writings of Christopher Gadsden, 1764–1805,* ed. Walsh (1966). *20c. coll.:* ODEP 721, Whiting 388, Stevenson 2087:1, Whiting*(MP)* 555.

9. One sickly sheep infects the flock and poisons all the rest. *Rec. dist.:* Ont.

10. The she-goat brings no sheep into the world. *Rec. dist.:* N.Y., S.C.

11. The sheep that bleats loses a mouthful. *Rec. dist.:* N.Y., N.C. *1st cit.:* 1599 Minsheu, *Dialogues in Spanish.* *20c. coll.:* ODEP 66, CODP 20, Stevenson 2087:4.

12. There's a black sheep in every family. *Vars.:* **(a)** Black sheep dwell in every fold. **(b)** There is a black sheep in every flock. *Rec. dist.:* U.S., Can. *1st cit.:* 1816 Scott, *Old Mortality;* US1779 Eustace in *Lee Papers,* N.Y.Hist.Soc. *Collections* (1871–74). *20c. coll.:* ODEP 65, Whiting 387, Stevenson 2087:5, Whiting*(MP)* 555.

SEE ALSO Anybody that would take a DARE would kill a sheep and eat the hair. / Better a SHREW than a sheep. / There's many a THREAD twixt sheep and shirt. / It never troubles the WOLF how many the sheep may be. / The WOLF eats sheep now and then, but thousands are devoured by men.

sheet 1. Don't cut the sheet to mend a dishcloth. *Rec. dist.:* Minn.

2. One clean sheet will not soil another. *Rec. dist.:* N.Y., S.C.

SEE ALSO Better wear out SHOES than sheets.

shell SEE Half an EGG is better than the shell. / He that will have the KERNEL must crack the shell.

shield SEE VIRTUE is a thousand shields. / Use your WIT as a shield, not as a sword.

shift A bad shift is better than none. **Rec. dist.:** N.C., Ont. **1st cit.:** 1551 Wilson, *Rule of Reason.* **20c. coll.:** ODEP 26, Stevenson 2090:7.

shin Never be breaking your shin on a stool that is not in your way. **Rec. dist.:** Miss. **1st cit.:** ca1628 Carmichaell, *Proverbs in Scots,* ed. Anderson (1957); US1833 *Correspondence of Andrew Jackson,* ed. Bassett (1926–33). **20c. coll.:** ODEP 461, Whiting 389.

shine *(n.)* SEE POLISH on the heels of shoes is a truer test of thoroughness than shine on the toes.

shine *(v.)* SEE Happy is the BRIDE the sun shines on. / It's a low BUSH that the sun never shines on. / Make HAY while the sun shines. / There is no LIE, spun so fine, through which the truth won't shine. / A burned LIGHT will never shine. / The LIGHT that shines farthest shines brightest at home. / If there were no RAIN, there'd be no hay to make when the sun shines. / The more you SAY, the less you shine. / Better to be SMALL and shine than to be great and cast a shadow. / A good SOLDIER never shines the heels of his shoes. / Behind the clouds, the SUN is shining. / Somewhere the SUN is shining; somewhere a little rain is falling. / The SUN shines on the evil as well as the good.

shingle 1. Never take a shingle off the roof. **Rec. dist.:** Ind.

2. There's no shingle so thin that it doesn't have two sides. **Rec. dist.:** Miss.

ship 1. A bad ship never casts anchor in port. **Rec. dist.:** Oreg., Wash.

2. A great ship asks for deeper water. **Vars.:** **(a)** Big ships require deep waters. **(b)** Great ships need deep waters. **(c)** Great ships require deep waters. **Rec. dist.:** Ont., Tex., Utah. **1st cit.:** 1640 Herbert, *Outlandish Proverbs (Jacula Prudentum)* in *Works,* ed. Hutchinson (1941). **20c. coll.:** ODEP 724, Stevenson 2091:1.

3. A ship under sail and a big-bellied woman are the handsomest two things that can be seen. **Rec. dist.:** N.Y., S.C. **1st cit.:** 1609 Harward, Unpublished manuscript in library of Trinity College, Cambridge; US1735 Franklin, *PRAlmanac.* **20c. coll.:** ODEP 724, Whiting 390.

4. An anchored ship doesn't carry much cargo. **Rec. dist.:** N.C.

5. Don't give up the ship. **Rec. dist.:** U.S., Can. **1st cit.:** US1814 *Diary of F. Palmer, Privateersman, 1813–1815,* Acorn Club *Publications* (1914). **20c. coll.:** Whiting 389, Stevenson 2091:6, T&W 327, Whiting(MP) 551.

6. Don't spoil the ship for half a penny's worth of tar. **Rec. dist.:** Ill. **1st cit.:** 1623 Camden, *Remaines Concerning Britaine;* US1928 McFee, *Pilgrims of Adversity.* **20c. coll.:** ODEP 723, Whiting(MP) 557, CODP 201, Stevenson 2085:12.

7. Every ship needs a captain. **Rec. dist.:** Colo.

8. He who scuttles the ship he arrives in may have to swim when he leaves. **Rec. dist.:** Ont.

9. In calm waters every ship has a good captain. **Rec. dist.:** Calif. **1st cit.:** ca1592 Greene, *James IV.* **20c. coll.:** ODEP 99.

10. Judge not of a ship as she lies on the stocks. **Rec. dist.:** Mich., Ont. **Infm.:** "On the stocks" refers to being in dry dock under repair.

11. Ships don't come in, they are brought in. **Rec. dist.:** N.Y. **Infm.:** Tugs bring large ships in to the pier.

12. Small ships should stay near the shore; larger ships may venture more. **Rec. dist.:** N.Y. **1st cit.:** US1751 Franklin, *PRAlmanac.* **20c. coll.:** Whiting 38, Stevenson 1035:5.

SEE ALSO BOOKS are ships that pass through the vast seas of time. / Two CAPTAINS will sink a ship. / Small LEAKS sink big ships. / RATS desert a sinking ship. / As the SAIL is set, so goes the ship. / Make not your SAIL too large for your ship. / Wherever there's a SEA, there's a ship. / A SLIP of the lip might sink a ship. / TIME is a ship that never anchors. / Slow WIND also brings the ship to harbor.

shipwreck 1. Each man makes his own shipwreck. **Rec. dist.:** Ill. **1st cit.:** US1948 Stevenson, *Home Book of Proverbs.* **20c. coll.:** Stevenson 2092:9.

2. He who has suffered shipwreck fears to sail

upon the seas. *Rec. dist.:* Ill. *1st cit.:* 1648 Herrick, *Shipwreck.* *20c. coll.:* Stevenson 727:4.

3. Let another's shipwreck be your sea work. *Rec. dist.:* Mich. *Infm.:* Salvage another's shipwreck. *1st cit.:* 1640 Quarles, *Enchiridion.* *20c. coll.:* ODEP 724, Stevenson 2092:7.

shirk SEE SIN, sorrow, and work are the things that men can't shirk.

shirt **1.** Close sits my shirt, but closer my skin. *Rec. dist.:* Okla. *1st cit.:* ca1570 *Ballads,* Percy Soc. *20c. coll.:* ODEP 556, CODP 158, Stevenson 322:4.

2. The shirt is nearer than the coat. *Rec. dist.:* Ill. *1st cit.:* 1461 *Paston Letters,* ed. Gairdner. *20c. coll.:* ODEP 556, Stevenson 2057:7.

3. Whoever steals the neighbor's shirt usually dies without his own. *Rec. dist.:* Ont.

4. You can't take the shirt off a naked man. *Rec. dist.:* Calif., N.Y. *1st cit.:* 1492 *Dialogue of Salomon and Marcolphus,* ed. Duff. *20c. coll.:* ODEP 554.

SEE ALSO There's many a THREAD twixt sheep and shirt. / It's a lonesome WASHING that has not a man's shirt in it.

shirtsleeve **1.** From shirtsleeves to shirtsleeves in three generations. *Rec. dist.:* U.S., Can. *Infm.:* A fortune may be lost in three generations. *1st cit.:* 1928 Sayers, *Dawson Pedigree;* US1907 Butler, *True and False Democracy.* *20c. coll.:* Whiting(MP) 558, CODP 201, Stevenson 62:8.

2. Shirtsleeves make the best uniform. *Rec. dist.:* Ont.

shoe *(n.)* **1.** A black shoe makes a blithe heart. *Rec. dist.:* N.Y., Ont. *1st cit.:* 1659 Howell, *Paroimiografia (English Proverbs).* *20c. coll.:* Stevenson 2095:7.

2. Better cut the shoe than pinch the foot. *Rec. dist.:* Tex. *1st cit.:* 1580 Lyly, *Euphues and His England.* *20c. coll.:* ODEP 52, Stevenson 2094:15.

3. Better wear out shoes than sheets. *Rec. dist.:* Ill., Ohio, Ont. *1st cit.:* 1663 Stampoy, *Scotch Proverbs.* *20c. coll.:* ODEP 57, Stevenson 1239:14.

4. Cheap shoes squeak. *Rec. dist.:* Calif., Mich., N.Y.

5. Don't pay for dead men's shoes. *Rec. dist.:* Ky., Tenn.

6. Don't put the shoe on unless it fits. *Rec. dist.:* Ohio.

7. Don't throw away your old shoes before you get new ones *Rec. dist.:* Ont.

8. Every shoe fits not every foot. *Var.:* You can't put the same shoe on every foot. *Rec. dist.:* Mich., Ont., Tex. *1st cit.:* 1587 Bridges, *Defence of Government of Church of England.* *20c. coll.:* ODEP 725, Stevenson 2095:6.

9. Everyone knows where his shoe pinches. *Vars.:* **(a)** None knows where the shoe pinches like the one who wears the shoe. **(b)** The wearer best knows where the shoe pinches. *Rec. dist.:* U.S., Can. *1st cit.:* ca1386 Chaucer, *Merchant's Tale;* US1709 Prout in *Saltonstall Papers, 1607–1815,* ed. Moody, Mass.Hist.Soc. *Collections* (1972). *20c. coll.:* ODEP 725, Whiting 391, Stevenson 2096:1, T&W 328, Whiting(MP) 560.

10. He that waits for dead men's shoes may go a long time barefoot. *Rec. dist.:* Mich., Nebr., Tex. *1st cit.:* 1530 Palsgrave, *Lesclarcissement de langue Francoyse,* ed. Genin (1852); US1714 Winthrop in *Winthrop Papers,* Mass.Hist.Soc. *Collections* (1929–47). *20c. coll.:* ODEP 171, Whiting 281, CODP 119, Stevenson 2096:2, T&W 234.

11. He who makes shoes goes barefoot. *Rec. dist.:* Utah. *1st cit.:* 1621 Burton, *Anatomy of Melancholy.* *20c. coll.:* Stevenson 2097:12.

12. I work for young shoes, not old shoes. *Rec. dist.:* N.J. *Infm.:* Said by young girls who refuse to marry old men.

13. If the shoe fits, put it on. *Var.:* If the shoe fits, wear it. *Rec. dist.:* U.S., Can. *1st cit.:* US1773 N.Y. *Gazette* in *Newspaper Extracts Relating to New Jersey,* eds. Nelson and Honeyman (1894–1923). *20c. coll.:* Whiting 390, Stevenson 2097:1, T&W 328, Whiting(MP) 560.

14. New shoes are like new friends—hard to get used to. *Rec. dist.:* Oreg.

15. Old shoes are easy, old friends are best. *Rec. dist.:* Ont. *1st cit.:* 1825 Brockett, *Glossary of North Country Words;* US1764 *Letters of Benjamin Rush,* ed. Butterfield (1951). *20c. coll.:* ODEP 213, Whiting 391, T&W 328.

16. Old shoes wear best. *Rec. dist.:* Fla., Miss., N.Y.

17. The devil's shoes never squeak. *Rec. dist.:* W.Va.

18. The pretty shoe often pinches the foot. *Var.:* The fairest-looking shoe may pinch the foot. *Rec. dist.:* Ill., Wis.

19. The squeaking shoe isn't paid for. *Var.:* Shoes that are not paid for always squeak. *Rec. dist.:* Colo., Ohio, Ont. *1st cit.:* 1825 Brockett, *Glossary of North Country Words. 20c. coll.:* Stevenson 2094:6.

20. There is never an old shoe but there is a sock to fit it. *Rec. dist.:* P.E.I.

21. There was never a shoe but had its mate. *Rec. dist.:* N.Y., S.C.

22. We never feel the shoe until it pinches our own foot. *Rec. dist.:* Ont. *1st cit.:* US1846 *Journals of Ralph Waldo Emerson,* eds. Emerson and Forbes (1909–14). *20c. coll.:* T&W 328.

23. Wear my shoes and you'll know where they pinch. *Rec. dist.:* Ont. *1st cit.:* 1609 Rowlands, *Whole Crew of Kind Gossips;* US1709 Prout in *Saltonstall Papers, 1607–1815,* ed. Moody, Mass.Hist.Soc. *Collections* (1972). *20c. coll.:* Stevenson 2096:3, Whiting 391, T&W 329.

See also There's a FOOT for every old shoe. / Don't criticize a man's GAIT until you are in his shoes. / The bigger a man's HEAD gets, the easier it is to fill his shoes. / More than one way to shoe a HORSE. / For the want of a NAIL, the shoe was lost; for want of a shoe, the horse was lost; for want of a horse, the rider was lost. / You can't walk and look at the STARS if you have a stone in your shoe.

shoe *(v.)* *See* He that rides the MULE shoes her.

shoemaker **1.** Shoemaker, stick to your last. *Var.:* Shoemaker, stick to your shoes. *Rec. dist.:* U.S., Can. *1st cit.:* 1539 Taverner, *Prov-*

erbs of Erasmus; US1647 Ward, *Simple Cobler of Aggawam in America,* ed. Wroth (1937). *20c. coll.:* ODEP 130, Whiting 78, CODP 39, Stevenson 2098:4, T&W 329.

2. The shoemaker's child goes barefoot. *Rec. dist.:* U.S., Can. *1st cit.:* 1546 Heywood, *Dialogue of Proverbs,* ed. Habernicht (1963); US1965 Ransome, *Alias His Wife. 20c. coll.:* ODEP 543, Whiting(MP) 561, CODP 202, Stevenson 2097:12.

shoestring *See* A JEW can make a living by selling shoestrings.

shoot *(n.)* The shoot at length becomes a tree. *Rec. dist.:* Ont.

shoot *(v.)* **1.** He who shoots may hit at last. *Rec. dist.:* Ill. *1st cit.:* 1551 More, *Utopia,* tr. Robinson. *20c. coll.:* ODEP 727, Stevenson 2099:5.

2. If you can't shoot it down, run it down. *Rec. dist.:* Calif.

See also The ARCHER that shoots badly has a lie already. / MALICE seldom wants a mark to shoot at.

shop **1.** A good shop needs no sign. *Var.:* A good shop wants no sign. *Rec. dist.:* Ill.

2. It is easy to open a shop but hard to keep it open. *Rec. dist.:* Ont. *1st cit.:* US1872 Doolittle, *Chinese Vocabulary. 20c. coll.:* Stevenson 2100:7.

3. Keep your shop and your shop will keep you. *Rec. dist.:* U.S., Can. *1st cit.:* 1605 Chapman, Jonson, and Marston, *Eastward Hoe;* US1652 Davis, *Hints of Contemporary Life in Writings of T. Shepard,* Col.Soc.Mass. *Publications* (1908). *20c. coll.:* ODEP 419, Whiting 392, CODP 124, Stevenson 2100:5.

shore *See* Little BOATS should stay close to shore.

shorn *See* GOD tempers the wind to the shorn lamb. / Many go out for WOOL and come home shorn.

short *See* Never sell AMERICA short. / The shortest ANSWER is doing. / Short ANSWERS save trouble. / ART is long, life is short. / Short-tailed DOG wag his tail same as a long 'un. / Easy got, easy gain: short joy, long pain. / Those have a short LENT who owe money to be paid at Easter. / LIFE is short and sweet. / LIFE is short, and time is swift. / LIFE is too short to be little. / LIFE is too short to fool with dishonest people. / Long on PROMISES, short on performance. / A long SAUSAGE and a short grace. / A long TONGUE has a short hand. / A short VISIT is best.

shortcut A shortcut is often a wrong cut. *Rec. dist.:* N.Y., Oreg.

See also Don't go round the WORLD for a shortcut.

shot 1. One shot meat; two shots maybe; three shots no good. *Rec. dist.:* N.Mex.

2. You can get only one shot at a shell bird. *Rec. dist.:* P.E.I.

shoulder 1. Put your shoulder to the wheel. *Rec. dist.:* U.S., Can. *1st cit.:* 1621 Burton, *Anatomy of Melancholy;* US1776 *American Crisis* in *Writings of Thomas Paine,* ed. Foner (1945). *20c. coll.:* ODEP 729, Whiting 393, Stevenson 2101:7, T&W 331, Whiting(*MP*) 563.

2. Who lets another sit on his shoulder will soon have him on his head. *Rec. dist.:* Ill.

See also The BURDEN is light on the shoulders of another. / A CHIP on the shoulder is a good indication of wood higher up. / You musn't expect a man's HEAD on a boy's shoulders. / There is no putting old HEADS on young shoulders.

shout 1. Do not shout until you are out of the woods. *Rec. dist.:* Ont. *1st cit.:* 1792 D'Arblay (a.k.a. Burney), *Diary* (1876); US1770 *Papers of Benjamin Franklin,* ed. Labaree (1959). *20c. coll.:* ODEP 345, Whiting 495, *CODP* 105, Stevenson 2591:2, T&W 411, Whiting(*MP*) 696.

2. Some people think that the louder they shout, the more persuasive their argument is. *Rec. dist.:* N.C.

shovel It's the shovel that laughs at the poker. *Rec. dist.:* Ill.

show (*n.*) 1. Outside show is poor substitute for inner worth. *Rec. dist.:* Ont.

2. Outside show, inside woe. *Rec. dist.:* Colo.

3. The show must go on. *Rec. dist.:* U.S., Can. *1st cit.:* US1867 *Dictionary of Americanisms,* ed. Matthews (1951). *20c. coll.:* T&W 331, Stevenson 1808:6.

4. Trust not to outward show. *Rec. dist.:* Mich.

See also DURABILITY is better than show. / Choose not FRIENDS by outward show, for feathers float while pearls lie low.

show (*v.*) It's the way you show up at the showdown that counts. *Rec. dist.:* Ill.

See also Show me your COMPANIONS, and I'll tell you who you are. / Show me your HAND and I'll tell you your trade. / LAUGH and show your ignorance. / Show me a LIAR and I'll show you a thief.

shower 1. A bee was never caught in a shower. *Rec. dist.:* N.Y. *1st cit.:* 1893 Inwards, *Weather Lore.* *20c. coll.:* Stevenson 145:6.

2. A heavy shower is soon over. *Rec. dist.:* Ill. *1st cit.:* 1859 Henderson, *Latin Proverbs.* *20c. coll.:* Stevenson 2222:8.

3. A sunshining shower never lasts half an hour. *Vars.:* **(a)** A sunshining shower won't last half an hour. **(b)** A sunshiny shower won't last half an hour. **(c)** Sunshiny showers, will rain tomorrow. *Rec. dist.:* U.S., Can. *1st cit.:* 1846 Denham, *Proverbs.* *20c. coll.:* Stevenson 1932:4.

4. April showers bring May flowers. *Rec. dist.:* U.S., Can. *1st cit.:* ca1430 Lydgate, *Reason and Sensuality;* US1671 Russell in *Colonial American Poetry,* ed. Silverman (1962). *20c. coll.:* ODEP 17, Whiting 11, CODP 6, Stevenson 1526:1, Whiting(*MP*) 16.

5. Small showers last long, but sudden storms are short. *Rec. dist.:* Ont.

See also Little DROPS produce a shower. / No SUN, no showers, no summer flowers. / SUNSHINE and showers make up life's hours.

shrew 1. Better a shrew than a sheep. *Rec. dist.:* Tex. *Infm.:* It is better for a person to be aggressive than passive. *1st cit.:* 1562 Legh, *Accidence of Armoury.* *20c. coll.:* ODEP 730, Stevenson 2102:10.

2. Every man can tame a shrew but he that has her. *Vars.:* **(a)** Every man can tame a shrew but he that has one. **(b)** Everyone can tame a shrew but him that has her. *Rec. dist.:* Ill., Mich. *1st cit.:* 1546 Heywood, *Dialogue of Proverbs,* ed. Habernicht (1963). *20c. coll.:* ODEP 678, Stevenson 2102:8.

shrewd A shrewd man feathers his own nest. *Rec. dist.:* Ont. *1st cit.:* 1553 *Respublica* in *Lost Tudor Plays* (1907); US1654 Johnson, *Wonder-Working Providence of Sion's Savior in New England,* ed. Poole (1867). *20c. coll.:* ODEP 252, Whiting 310, Stevenson 792:10, T&W 260, Whiting(*MP*) 444.

shrink *See* He that swells in PROSPERITY will be sure to shrink in adversity.

shroud A shroud has no pockets. *Vars.:* (a) Shrouds have no pockets. (b) There are no pockets in a shroud. *Rec. dist.:* U.S., Can. *1st cit.:* 1853 Trench, *Lessons in Proverbs* (1894); USca1897 Miller, *Dead Millionaire.* *20c. coll.:* ODEP 443, Stevenson 1985:5, *CODP* 203, Whiting(*MP*) 501.

shut *See* A DOOR must be open or shut. / When the DOOR is shut, the work improves. / Keep your EYES wide open before marriage, half shut afterwards. / PUT up or shut up. / STAND up, speak up, and shut up. / You can shut the door on a THIEF, but you can do nothing about a liar.

shy A man is shy in another man's corner. *Rec. dist.:* Miss.

See also Once BITTEN, twice shy. / Once BURNED, twice shy. / Once CAUGHT, twice shy.

sick 1. The sick man sleeps when the debtor cannot. *Rec. dist.:* Ill.

2. The sickest is not the nearest to the grave. *Rec. dist.:* S.C.

See also It is easy for a man in HEALTH to preach patience to the sick. / HOPE deferred makes the heart sick.

sickle Don't thrust your sickle into another's corn. *Rec. dist.:* N.C. *1st cit.:* 1387 Higden, *Polychronicon,* tr. Trevisa. *20c. coll.:* ODEP 732, Stevenson 2102:13.

See also A bad REAPER never got a good sickle.

sickly *See* FOOLS die young and look sickly.

sickness 1. Sickness comes in haste and goes at leisure. *Rec. dist.:* Ill. *1st cit.:* 1654 Whitlock, *Zootomia.* *20c. coll.:* Stevenson 586:11.

2. Sickness is felt, but health not at all. *Rec. dist.:* Mich., Ont. *1st cit.:* 1732 Fuller, *Gnomologia.* *20c. coll.:* Stevenson 2103:10.

3. Sickness tells us what we are. *Rec. dist.:* Ont. *1st cit.:* 1732 Fuller, *Gnomologia.* *20c. coll.:* ODEP 732, Stevenson 2103:11.

4. The chamber of sickness is the chapel of devotion. *Rec. dist.:* N.Y. *1st cit.:* 1616 Draxe, *Bibliotheca Scholastica* in *Anglia* (1918). *20c. coll.:* ODEP 113, Stevenson 2103:5.

5. The sickness of the body may prove the health of the mind. *Rec. dist.:* Ill. *1st cit.:* 1624 Hewes, *Perfect Survey.* *20c. coll.:* ODEP 113, Stevenson 2104:1.

side 1. Always look on the bright side. *Var.:* Look on the bright side, or polish up the dark one. *Rec. dist.:* U.S., Can. *1st cit.:* 1726 Wesley, *Sermons,* ed. Sugden (1921); US1942 Wentworth, *Pursuit of Parcel.* *20c. coll.:* ODEP 482, Stevenson 1726:7.

2. Don't get up on the wrong side of the bed. *Rec. dist.:* U.S., Can. *1st cit.:* 1540 Palsgrave, *Acolastus,* ed. Carver, E.E.T.S. (1937); US1847 Melville, *Omoo in Works* (1923). *20c. coll.:* ODEP 678, T&W 21, Stevenson 141:11.

3. Everyone has his weak side. *Rec. dist.:* Ala., Ga. *1st cit.:* 1692 *Aesop's Fables,* tr. L'Estrange. *20c. coll.:* ODEP 873, Stevenson 773:7.

4. It is better to be on the safe side. *Rec. dist.:* Ont. *1st cit.:* 1528 More, *Dialogue of Comfort and Against Tribulation.* *20c. coll.:* Stevenson 2104:12, *CODP* 14, ODEP 691, Whiting (*MP*) 564.

5. There are three sides to every story—your side, my side, and the right side. *Rec. dist.:* Ill. *1st cit.:* 1711 Addison, *Spectator;* US1802 *Diary and Autobiography of John Adams,* ed. Butterfield (1966). *20c. coll.:* Stevenson 1926:3, Whiting 393, ODEP 852, *CODP* 234, Whiting(*MP*) 564.

6. There are two sides to everything. *Vars.:* (a) There are always two sides to a fence. (b) There are two sides to every question. (c) There are two sides to every story. (d) There

were always two sides to every argument—his and the wrong side. *Rec. dist.:* Ill. *1st cit.:* 1742 Ralph, *Other Side of the Question;* US1802 *Diary and Autobiography of John Adams,* ed. Butterfield (1961). *20c. coll.:* ODEP 852, Whiting 393, *CODP* 234, Stevenson 1926:3, Whiting*(MP)* 564.

7. There's a good and bad side of everything. *Rec. dist.:* S.C.

8. Write on one side of the paper but on both sides of the subject. *Rec. dist.:* Calif.

SEE ALSO A FRIEND by your side can keep you warmer than the richest furs. / The GRASS is always greener on the other side of the fence. / QUARRELS never could last long if on one side only lay the wrong. / There's no SHINGLE so thin that it doesn't have two sides.

sideshow Don't let the sideshow run away with the circus. *Rec. dist.:* Calif.

siesta *SEE* A lame GOAT takes no siesta.

sigh It's easy to sigh, but it's better to pray. *Rec. dist.:* Ont.

SEE ALSO A LOVER may sigh, but he must not puff.

sight Out of sight, out of mind. *Rec. dist.:* U.S., Can. *1st cit.:* ca1275 *Proverbs of Alfred,* tr. Skeat; US1629 Winthrop in *Winthrop Papers, 1498–1649,* Mass.Hist.Soc. *Collections* (1929–47). *20c. coll.:* ODEP 602, Whiting 394, *CODP* 172, Stevenson 2106:14, T&W 333, Whiting*(MP)* 566.

SEE ALSO CHARM strikes the sight, but merit wins the soul. / JUDGE not of men or things at first sight. / LOVE at first sight is cured by a second look.

sign *(n.)* **1.** All signs fail in dry weather. *Rec. dist.:* U.S., Can. *1st cit.:* 1893 Inwards, *Weather Lore;* US1729 Ames, *Almanacs,* ed. Briggs (1891). *20c. coll.:* Stevenson 2475:5, Whiting 394, T&W 333, Whiting*(MP)* 567.

2. Don't always believe in signs. *Rec. dist.:* Ont.

3. The surest sign of age is loneliness. *Rec. dist.:* N.Y. *1st cit.:* US1868 Alcott, *Tablets.* *20c. coll.:* Stevenson 1449:1.

SEE ALSO GRATITUDE is the sign of noble souls. / An OLD man in the house is a good

sign. / A PATCH is the sign of thrift, a hole the sign of negligence.

sign *(v.)* *SEE* READ carefully; sign cautiously.

silence **1.** Nothing is more useful to a man than silence. *Rec. dist.:* Wis. *1st cit.:* US1948 Stevenson, *Home Book of Proverbs.* *20c. coll.:* Stevenson 2110:5.

2. Silence and reflection cause dejection. *Rec. dist.:* Ill.

3. Silence gives consent. *Rec. dist.:* U.S., Can. *1st cit.:* ca1300 Pope Boniface VIII, *Book of Decretals;* US1648 Winthrop in *Winthrop Papers, 1498–1649,* Mass.Hist.Soc. *Collections* (1929–47). *20c. coll.:* Stevenson 2112:3, Whiting 394, ODEP 733, *CODP* 203, T&W 333, Whiting*(MP)* 567.

4. Silence in time of suffering is best. *Rec. dist.:* Ont.

5. Silence is a fine jewel for a woman, but it is little worn. *Rec. dist.:* Ill. *1st cit.:* 1539 Taverner, *Proverbs of Erasmus.* *20c. coll.:* ODEP 733, *CODP* 203, Stevenson 2581:3.

6. Silence is a friend that betrays no man. *Rec. dist.:* N.Y.

7. Silence is a great peacemaker. *Rec. dist.:* Ont.

8. Silence is a rare jewel. *Rec. dist.:* N.C.

9. Silence is a still noise. *Rec. dist.:* N.Y., S.C. *1st cit.:* US1874 Shaw (pseud. Josh Billings), *Encyclopedia of Wit and Wisdom.* *20c. coll.:* Stevenson 2108:14.

10. Silence is equivalent to confession. *Rec. dist.:* N.Y. *1st cit.:* US1948 Stevenson, *Home Book of Proverbs.* *20c. coll.:* Stevenson 2112:5.

11. Silence is golden. *Rec. dist.:* U.S., Can. *1st cit.:* 1865 White, *Eastern England;* US1923 Nevinson, *Changes.* *20c. coll.:* *CODP* 203, Whiting*(MP)* 586, Stevenson 2111:7.

12. Silence is not always a sign of wisdom, but babbling is ever a folly. *Rec. dist.:* N.Y., S.C. *1st cit.:* 1620 J.C., *Two Merry Milk-Maids.* *20c. coll.:* ODEP 898.

13. Silence is often the key to success. *Rec. dist.:* Ont.

14. Silence is sometimes the severest criticism. *Rec. dist.:* N.Y.

15. Silence is the best answer to the stupid. *Rec. dist.:* Ill.

16. Silence is the best policy. *Rec. dist.:* Calif., N.Y., S.C. *1st cit.:* US1931 Eppley, *Murder in the Cellar.* *20c. coll.:* Whiting*(MP)* 567.

17. Silence is the fittest reply to folly. *Rec. dist.:* Ill. *1st cit.:* US1948 Stevenson, *Home Book of Proverbs.* *20c. coll.:* Stevenson 2108:12.

18. Silence is the ornament of the ignorant. *Rec. dist.:* Ill. *1st cit.:* US1948 Stevenson, *Home Book of Proverbs.* *20c. coll.:* Stevenson 2111:2.

19. Silence is the virtue of a fool. *Rec. dist.:* Ill. *1st cit.:* 1605 Bacon, *De Augmentis Scientiarum.* *20c. coll.:* Stevenson 2108:11.

20. Silence is wisdom when speaking is folly. *Rec. dist.:* Ill. *1st cit.:* 1620 J.C., *Two Merry Milk-Maids;* US1790 *New Letters of Abigail Adams,* ed. Mitchell (1947). *20c. coll.:* ODEP 898, Whiting 395, Stevenson 2113:16, Whiting*(MP)* 567.

21. The tree of silence bears the fruit of peace. *Rec. dist.:* Ont.

SEE ALSO It is not the father's ANGER but his silence his son dreads. / It is better to bear a single INJURY in silence than to provoke a thousand by flying into a rage. / Silence SCANDAL by silence. / More have repented of SPEECH than of silence. / No WISDOM like silence.

silent **1.** Be silent and safe: silence never betrays you. *Rec. dist.:* Ohio. *1st cit.:* ca1880 O'Reilly, *Rules of Road.* *20c. coll.:* Stevenson 2111:1.

2. Be silent if you have nothing worth saying. *Rec. dist.:* Ont., Tex.

3. He that knows not when to be silent knows not when to speak. *Rec. dist.:* Mich. *1st cit.:* US1948 Stevenson, *Home Book of Proverbs.* *20c. coll.:* Stevenson 2113:5.

4. He who knows how to keep silent knows a great deal. *Rec. dist.:* Ill.

5. It is better to remain silent and be thought of as a fool than to speak and prove the same. *Rec. dist.:* U.S., Can. *1st cit.:* USca1862 Lincoln, Epigram in *Golden Book* (1931). *20c. coll.:* Stevenson 2111:2.

SEE ALSO Beware of a silent DOG and silent water. / A silent FOOL is a wise fool. / Deep RIVERS move with silent majesty; shallow brooks are noisy.

silk **1.** All that rustles is not silk. *Rec. dist.:* Ill.

2. Silks and satins, scarlet and velvet put out the kitchen fire. *Rec. dist.:* U.S., Can. *1st cit.:* 1640 Herbert, *Outlandish Proverbs (Jacula Prudentum)* in *Works,* ed. Hutchinson (1941); US1746 Franklin, *PRAlmanac.* *20c. coll.:* ODEP 733, Whiting 395, Stevenson 2114:8.

SEE ALSO We're all ADAM's children; silk makes the difference. / An APE is an ape, a varlet is a varlet, though they be clad in silk and scarlet. / Though the FOX wear silk, he is still a fox. / You can't make a silk PURSE out of a sow's ear. / Beneath SATIN and silk there is much suffering.

silly *SEE* Fine CLOTHES may disguise, silly words will disclose a fool. / Silly QUESTION, silly answer.

silver **1.** All complain of want of silver but none of want of sense. *Rec. dist.:* Ill.

2. If you haven't silver in your purse, you should have silk on your tongue. *Rec. dist.:* Ill. *1st cit.:* 1611 Cotgrave, *Dictionary of French and English Tongues.* *20c. coll.:* ODEP 734, Stevenson 2115:2.

3. Little silver, much love. *Rec. dist.:* Wis.

4. No silver, no servant. *Rec. dist.:* N.J. *1st cit.:* 1616 Draxe, *Bibliotheca Scholastica in Anglia* (1918). *20c. coll.:* ODEP 573, Stevenson 161:7.

5. Silver has a silver sound. *Rec. dist.:* Ill. *1st cit.:* 1594 Shakespeare, *Romeo and Juliet.* *20c. coll.:* ODEP 734, Stevenson 2115:4.

6. When you go to buy, don't show your silver. *Rec. dist.:* N.J. *1st cit.:* US1937 Hart, *Seven Hundred Chinese Proverbs.* *20c. coll.:* Stevenson 268:7.

SEE ALSO A CAT with a silver collar is none the better mouser. / Every CLOUD has a silver lining. / Better have a FRIEND on the road than gold or silver in your purse. / GENIUS without education is like silver in the mine. / Take away the RUST from the silver and there'll come forth a pure vessel. / SPEECH is silver; silence is golden. / Every man is not born with a silver SPOON in his mouth. / The TONGUE of the just is a choice silver; the heart of the wicked is little worth. / A WORD fitly spoken is like apples of gold in pictures of silver. / WORDS are silver and silence is gold.

simple 1. Simple things in life are best. *Rec. dist.*: Minn.

2. The simple are easily deceived. *Rec. dist.*: Ont.

SEE ALSO Pleasing WORDS and bad deeds deceive both the wise and the simple.

simplicity 1. Simplicity is truth's most becoming garb. *Rec. dist.*: Calif.

2. The expression of truth is simplicity. *Rec. dist.*: Calif.

sin *(n.)* 1. A sin confessed is half forgiven. *Rec. dist.*: Ill., N.Y., N.C., S.C. *1st cit.*: ca1612 Harrington, *Epigrams. 20c. coll.*: Stevenson 400:1.

2. Commit a sin thrice and you will think it allowable. *Rec. dist.*: Ill.

3. Condemn the sin, not the sinner. *Rec. dist.*: N.Y.

4. Every man has his besetting sin. *Rec. dist.*: Ill. *1st cit.*: 1883 Drummond, *Natural Law in Spiritual World. 20c. coll.*: Stevenson 2117:3.

5. Every sin carries its own punishment. *Rec. dist.*: Okla., Tex. *1st cit.*: 1616 Draxe, *Bibliotheca Scholastica* in *Anglia* (1918). *20c. coll.*: ODEP 735, Stevenson 2120:10.

6. He that swims in sin will sink in sorrow. *Rec. dist.*: Ill., N.Y. *1st cit.*: 1563 Googe, *Eclogs,* ed. Arber. *20c. coll.*: ODEP 795, Stevenson 2117:11.

7. Innumerable sins bring countless sorrows. *Rec. dist.*: Mich.

8. It is a sin for any man to do less than his best. *Rec. dist.*: Wis.

9. It is not a sin to sell dear, but it is to make ill measure. *Rec. dist.*: N.Y., S.C. *1st cit.*: 1721 Kelly, *Scottish Proverbs. 20c. coll.*: ODEP 736.

10. Let him that is without sin cast the first stone. *Rec. dist.*: U.S., Can. *1st cit.*: US1948 Stevenson, *Home Book of Proverbs. 20c. coll.*: Stevenson 2118:4.

11. Men are punished by their sins, not for them. *Rec. dist.*: N.Y., S.C. *1st cit.*: US1901 Hubbard, *Philistine. 20c. coll.*: Stevenson 2120:10.

12. Old sins breed new shame. *Rec. dist.*: Tex. *1st cit.*: ca1300 *Havelock, The Dane,* E.E.T.S. (1868). *20c. coll.*: ODEP 592, Stevenson 2120:11, Whiting*(MP)* 568.

13. Old sins have long shadows. *Rec. dist.*: Calif., N.Y. *1st cit.*: 1940 Christie, *Sad Cypress;* US1925 Vane, *Scar. 20c. coll.*: CODP 168, Whiting*(MP)* 568, Stevenson 2120:6.

14. One sin another does provoke. *Var.*: One sin opens the door for another. *Rec. dist.*: N.Y., Wis. *1st cit.*: ca1425 *Castle of Perseverance. 20c. coll.*: ODEP 735, Stevenson 2118:12.

15. Sin and happiness cannot dwell together. *Rec. dist.*: Ind.

16. Sin concealed needs two forgivings. *Rec. dist.*: Ill.

17. Sin has many tools, but a lie is the handle which fits them all. *Rec. dist.*: U.S., Can. *1st cit.*: US1858 Holmes, *Autocrat of Breakfast-Table. 20c. coll.*: Stevenson 1394:5.

18. Sin is easier to stand than shame. *Rec. dist.*: N.Y., S.C.

19. Sin is the seed, and death is the harvest. *Rec. dist.*: Ill.

20. Sin may be clasped so close we cannot see its face. *Rec. dist.*: Miss., Ont.

21. Sin, sorrow, and work are the things that men can't shirk. *Rec. dist.*: N.Y., S.C.

22. The sins of fathers are visited on the children. *Rec. dist.*: Ill. *1st cit.*: 1596 Shakespeare, *King John. 20c. coll.*: Stevenson 2117:5.

23. The sins of the offenders are the strength of the tyrants. *Rec. dist.*: N.Y.

24. Whosoever commits sin is the servant of sin. *Rec. dist.*: N.Y.

25. Your sins will find you out. *Vars.*: **(a)** Be sure, your sins will find you out. **(b)** Whichever way you turn about, be sure, your sins will find you out. *Rec. dist.*: U.S., Can. *1st cit.*: 1942 Bailey, *Nobody's Vineyard;* US1941 Howie, *Murder for Christmas. 20c. coll.*: Stevenson 2119:1, Whiting*(MP)* 569.

SEE ALSO Keep yourself from the OPPORTUNITY and God will keep you from the sin. / The less the TEMPTATION, the greater the sin.

sin *(v.)* **1.** He who has sinned has already punished himself. *Rec. dist.:* N.Y., S.C. *1st cit.:* US1948 Stevenson, *Home Book of Proverbs. 20c. coll.:* Stevenson 2120:10.

2. Sin in haste; repent at leisure. *Rec. dist.:* U.S., Can.

3. They that sin are enemies to themselves. *Rec. dist.:* N.Y., S.C. *1st cit.:* US1948 Stevenson, *Home Book of Proverbs. 20c. coll.:* Stevenson 2120:10.

SEE ALSO When the HOUSE is open, the honest man sins.

sincerity **1.** Sincerity gives wings to power. *Rec. dist.:* Ill.

2. Sincerity is the mortar of friendship. *Rec. dist.:* Oreg.

sinful Let him who ain't sinful haul first on the rope. *Rec. dist.:* Ala., Ga., N.Mex.

sing **1.** He who sings drives away his cares. *Var.:* He that sings frightens away his ills. *Rec. dist.:* Ill. *1st cit.:* US1948 Stevenson, *Home Book of Proverbs. 20c. coll.:* Stevenson 2164:3.

2. He who sings in summer will weep in winter. *Rec. dist.:* N.Y.

3. Who cannot sing may whistle. *Rec. dist.:* Ont., Wis.

SEE ALSO Every BIRD likes to hear himself sing. / The BIRD that can sing and won't sing should be made to sing. / When two FRIENDS have a common purse, one sings and the other weeps. / It is better to hear the LARK sing than the mouse cheep. / Learn to SAY before you sing.

singer Live with a singer if you would learn to sing. *Rec. dist.:* Ill.

singing Singing on the street, disappointment you will meet. *Rec. dist.:* Ill.

single *SEE* TROUBLE never comes single-handed.

sink *(n.)* *SEE* WAR is the sink of all injustice.

sink *(v.)* Sink or swim. *Var.:* Sink, swim, or die. *Rec. dist.:* U.S., Can. *1st cit.:* ca1368

Chaucer, *Compleynt Unto Pity;* US1652 *Complete Writings of Roger Williams* (1963). *20c. coll.:* ODEP 737, Whiting 396, Stevenson 2262:4, T&W 335, Whiting(MP) 569.

SEE ALSO Two CAPTAINS will sink a ship. / Many DROPS of water will sink a ship. / Small LEAKS sink big ships. / A SLIP of the lip might sink a ship. / When WINE sinks, words swim.

sinking *SEE* RATS desert a sinking ship.

sinner **1.** Once a sinner, always a sinner. *Rec. dist.:* Ont.

2. The greater the sinner, the greater the saint. *Rec. dist.:* N.Y., S.C. *1st cit.:* 1772 Graves, *Spiritual Quixote;* US1768 Woodmason, *Carolina Backcountry on Eve of Revolution,* ed. Hooker (1953). *20c. coll.:* ODEP 336, Whiting 397, *CODP* 101, Stevenson 2026:9, T&W 335.

sip *SEE* He that sips many ARTS drinks none.

sire *SEE* TIME is the sire of fame.

sister *SEE* If you want to keep your MISTER, don't introduce the baby sister.

sit **1.** He sits not sure that sits too high. *Rec. dist.:* Ont. *1st cit.:* 1611 Cotgrave, *Dictionary of French and English Tongues. 20c. coll.:* ODEP 738, Stevenson 2122:7.

2. It is better to sit still than to rise to fall. *Rec. dist.:* Ont. *1st cit.:* ca1410 *Towneley Plays,* E.E.T.S. (1897). *20c. coll.:* ODEP 55, Stevenson 2122:10.

3. Sit before you fall. *Rec. dist.:* Ont.

SEE ALSO If you get burnt you got to sit on the BLISTER. / After DINNER sit awhile; after supper walk a mile. / An unbidden GUEST knows not where to sit. / A man on a galloping HORSE will never sit it. / Better to sit IDLE than to work idle. / Every KETTLE has to sit on its own bottom. / Don't STAND when you can sit, and don't sit when you can lie down. / Even if you are on the right TRACK, you won't get over if you sit there. / You can't keep TROUBLE from coming in, but you needn't give it a chair to sit in. / The second WIFE always sits on the right knee. / It is better to sit with a WISE man in prison than with a fool in paradise.

sitting 'Tis as cheap sitting as standing. *Var.:* It's as cheap sitting as standing. *Rec. dist.:* N.C., Ont. *1st cit.:* 1666 Torriano, *Common Place of Italian Proverbs;* US1840 Haliburton, *Clockmaker.* *20c. coll.:* ODEP 116, T&W 335, CODP 35, Stevenson 327:9, Whiting*(MP)* 569.

SEE ALSO You can't put your FOOTPRINTS in the sands of time by sitting down.

situation There are no hopeless situations; there are only hopeless men. *Rec. dist.:* N.Y. *1st cit.:* US1940 Boothe, *Europe in Spring.* *20c. coll.:* Stevenson 1166:2.

size **1.** Do not judge a thing by its size. *Rec. dist.:* Ont.

2. It doesn't depend upon size, or a cow would catch a rabbit. *Rec. dist.:* Ill. *Infm.:* Success does not depend on size. *1st cit.:* 1883 Burne, *Shropshire Folk-Lore.* *20c. coll.:* Stevenson 445:5.

SEE ALSO You can't tell a FROG by the size of his jump.

skating **1.** In skating over thin ice, our safety is our speed. *Rec. dist.:* Ont. *1st cit.:* US1841 Emerson, "Prudence" in *Essays.* *20c. coll.:* Stevenson 1211:8.

2. More belongs to skating than a pair of skates. *Rec. dist.:* Ont.

skeleton **1.** No man is qualified to remove the skeleton from his own closet. *Rec. dist.:* N.Y., S.C.

2. There's a skeleton in every family closet. *Vars.:* **(a)** There is a skeleton in every closet. **(b)** There is a skeleton in every home. **(c)** There is a skeleton in every house. **(d)** There's a skeleton in every family. **(e)** There's a skeleton in everybody's closet. *Rec. dist.:* U.S., Can. *1st cit.:* 1845 Thackeray, *Punch in the East;* US1876 Nash, *New England Life.* *20c. coll.:* ODEP 739, T&W 336, Stevenson 2123:9, Whiting*(MP)* 571.

skepticism Skepticism is slow suicide. *Rec. dist.:* N.Y.

skill **1.** If skill could be acquired by watching, dogs would be butchers. *Rec. dist.:* Ariz.

2. Skill and assurance are an invincible cou-

ple. *Rec. dist.:* Ill. *1st cit.:* 1640 Herbert, *Outlandish Proverbs (Jacula Prudentum)* in *Works,* ed. Hutchinson (1941). *20c. coll.:* ODEP 740, Stevenson 2124:7.

3. Skill is better than strength. *Rec. dist.:* N.Y. *1st cit.:* 1869 Henderson, *Latin Proverbs.* *20c. coll.:* Stevenson 2124:5.

SEE ALSO Few things are impossible to DILIGENCE and skill. / Where FORCE fails, skill and patience will prevail. / IGNORANCE and bungling with love are better than wisdom and skill without.

skillet Tote your own skillet. *Rec. dist.:* Ala., Ga., Miss., Tex.

skillful SEE The CARDS beat all the players, be they ever so skillful.

skin *(n.)* **1.** The skin you love to touch isn't nearly so handy around the house as dishpan hands. *Rec. dist.:* Ind.

2. The wrinkled skin easily conceals a scar. *Rec. dist.:* N.J.

SEE ALSO BEAUTY is only skin deep. / Lend your HORSE and you may have back his skin.

skin *(v.)* SEE There's more than one way to skin a CAT without tearing the hide. / Every man must skin his own SKUNK. / Don't skin your WOLVES before you get them.

skirt It's not the skirt that breaks people; it's the chiffon ruffles. *Rec. dist.:* N.Y., S.C. *1st cit.:* US1906 Knowles, *Cheerful Year Book.* *20c. coll.:* Stevenson 625:10.

skunk **1.** A skunk is ready to give you a scent anytime. *Rec. dist.:* Minn.

2. A skunk smells its own hole first. *Rec. dist.:* Mich., N.Y., Ont.

3. Every man must skin his own skunk. *Var.:* Skin your own skunks. *Rec. dist.:* U.S. *1st cit.:* US1813 *Portsmouth Oracle,* 20 Nov. *20c. coll.:* Whiting 398, Stevenson 1236:1, T&W 338.

4. If you've been near a skunk, don't say you haven't been. *Rec. dist.:* N.Mex.

5. You can't keep from getting soiled if you fight with a skunk. *Rec. dist.:* Ohio.

SEE ALSO It's a good rule to never send a MOUSE to catch a skunk, or a pollywog to tackle a whale.

sky 1. Every sky has its cloud. *Rec. dist.*: Ill., Wash.

2. If the sky falls we shall catch larks. *Rec. dist.*: Mich., Ont. *1st cit.*: ca1445 *Peter Idley's Instructions to His Son;* US1778 *New Jersey Gazette* in *Newspaper Extracts Relating to New Jersey,* ed. Stryker (1901–17). *20c. coll.*: *CODP* 205, Whiting 398, *ODEP* 740, Stevenson 2126:9, Whiting(*MP*) 573.

SEE ALSO They who cross the SEAS change their skies but not their natures.

slack SEE He becomes POOR that deals with a slack hand, but the hand of diligence makes rich.

slander 1. Slander expires at a good woman's door. *Rec. dist.*: Ill.

2. Slander flings stones at itself. *Rec. dist.*: N.Y. *1st cit.*: 1732 Fuller, *Gnomologia. 20c. coll.*: Stevenson 2128:15.

3. Slander is sharper than the sword. *Var.*: Slander's sting is sharper than a sword. *Rec. dist.*: Iowa, Wis. *1st cit.*: 1609 Shakespeare, *Cymbeline. 20c. coll.*: Stevenson 2129:8.

4. Slander that is raised is ill to fell. *Rec. dist.*: Ont. *1st cit.*: ca1460 *How Gode Wyfe Taught Her Daughter. 20c. coll.*: Stevenson 2128:12.

SEE ALSO He that hides HATRED with lying lips and he that utters slander is a fool. / Guard your TONGUE; slander sometimes comes home to roost.

slap SEE If you must strike a MAN from behind, slap him on the back.

slave 1. As the slave departs, the man returns. *Rec. dist.*: Ill. *1st cit.*: 1799 Campbell, *Pleasures of Hope. 20c. coll.*: Stevenson 2130:8.

2. Better starve free than be a slave. *Vars.*: (a) Better starve free than be a fat slave. (b) It is better poor and free than rich and a slave. *Rec. dist.*: Ont.

3. Better the devil's than a woman's slave. *Rec. dist.*: Ill. *1st cit.*: 1624 Massinger, *Parliament of Love. 20c. coll.*: Stevenson 2555:3.

4. Do not be a slave to fashion. *Rec. dist.*: N.Y., Ont.

5. He is a slave to the greatest slave who serves none but himself. *Rec. dist.*: Mich.

6. He is still a slave whose limbs alone are freed. *Rec. dist.*: Ill.

7. He that is one man's slave is free from none. *Rec. dist.*: Ill. *1st cit.*: 1606 Chapman, *Gentleman Usher. 20c. coll.*: Stevenson 2130:8.

8. None can be free who is a slave to his passions. *Rec. dist.*: Ill. *1st cit.*: 1732 Fuller, *Gnomologia. 20c. coll.*: Stevenson 1749:15.

9. The blow that liberates the slave sets the master free. *Rec. dist.*: Ill. *1st cit.*: US1895 Roche, *Gettysburg. 20c. coll.*: Stevenson 2131:3.

SEE ALSO Better an old man's DARLING than a young man's slave. / FEAR is the virtue of slaves. / The right HAND is slave to the left. / The real HOUSEWIFE is at once a slave and a lady. / MONEY will be a slave or a master. / NECESSITY is the argument of tyrants and the creed of slaves. / Many a man thinks he is buying PLEASURE when he is really selling himself a slave to it.

slavery 1. Slavery enchains a few; more enchain themselves to slavery. *Rec. dist.*: Ill. *1st cit.*: US1948 Stevenson, *Home Book of Proverbs. 20c. coll.*: Stevenson 2131:9.

2. Slavery is a weed that grows in every soil. *Rec. dist.*: Ill. *1st cit.*: 1775 Burke, *Conciliation with the Colonies. 20c. coll.*: Stevenson 2130:6.

3. Slavery is too high a price to pay for an easy living. *Rec. dist.*: Ont.

4. The sign of slavery is to have a price and to be bought for it. *Rec. dist.*: Ill. *1st cit.*: 1866 Ruskin, "War" in *Crown of Wild Olives. 20c. coll.*: Stevenson 2131:8.

SEE ALSO A great FORTUNE is slavery. / Lean LIBERTY is better than fat slavery.

sleep (*n.*) 1. Let your midday sleep be short or none at all. *Rec. dist.*: Wis. *1st cit.*: ca1460 Russell, *Book of Nature. 20c. coll.*: Stevenson 2135:8.

2. Long sleep makes a bare back. *Rec. dist.*: Miss.

3. One hour's sleep before midnight is worth three after. *Rec. dist.*: Wis. *1st cit.*: 1640 Herbert, *Outlandish Proverbs (Jacula Prudentum)* in *Works,* ed. Hutchinson (1941). *20c. coll.*: *ODEP* 389, *CODP* 115, Stevenson 2133:12.

4. The sleep of a laboring man is sweet. *Rec. dist.:* N.C. *1st cit.:* 1678 Bunyan, "Author's Apology" in *Pilgrim's Progress. 20c. coll.:* Stevenson 2133:3.

5. Too much sleep is a burden. *Rec. dist.:* N.Y.

sleep *(v.)* **1.** He sleeps well who is not conscious that he sleeps ill. *Rec. dist.:* Minn. *1st cit.:* 1732 Fuller, *Gnomologia. 20c. coll.:* Stevenson 2136:3.

2. He who sleeps late has short days. *Rec. dist.:* Wis. *1st cit.:* 1732 Fuller, *Gnomologia. 20c. coll.:* Stevenson 2136:9.

3. Sleep over it or you may weep over it. *Rec. dist.:* N.J., Ont.

4. Some sleep five hours; nature requires seven, laziness nine, and wickedness eleven. *Rec. dist.:* Minn.

SEE ALSO AFFAIRS sleep soundly when fortune is present. / Sleep with your ANGER. / To carry CARE into your bed is to sleep with a pack on your back. / An ENEMY does not sleep. / Sleep without OWING and wake without owing. / PLOW deep while sluggards sleep, and you shall have corn to sell and to keep. / Sleep without SUPPING and wake without owing.

sleeping *(n.)* There shall be sleeping enough in the grave. *Vars.:* **(a)** There will be sleeping enough in the grave. **(b)** Up, sluggard, and waste not life; in the grave there will be sleeping enough. *Rec. dist.:* U.S., Can. *1st cit.:* 1954 Fleming, *Live and Let Die;* US1741 Franklin, *PRAlmanac. 20c. coll.:* Whiting(MP) 574, Whiting 399, ODEP 742, Stevenson 2133:6.

sleeping *(adj.)* SEE Sleeping CATS catch no mice. / A sleeping DOG never bites. / The sleeping FOX catches no poultry. / Don't wake a sleeping LION.

sleeve SEE Keep your broken ARM in your sleeve. / Pin not your FAITH on another's sleeve. / Every man has a FOOL in his sleeve. / Don't wear your HEART on your sleeve. / From SHIRTSLEEVES to shirtsleeves in three generations. / SHIRTSLEEVES make the best uniform.

sleight 'Tis sleight, not strength, that gives the greatest lift. *Rec. dist.:* N.Y. *1st cit.:* 1607 Middleton, *Michaelmas Terme. 20c. coll.:* Stevenson 2228:1.

slender SEE HOPE is a slender reed for a stout man to lean on.

slice You never miss a slice from a cut loaf. *Rec. dist.:* N.Y. *1st cit.:* 1593 Shakespeare, *Titus Andronicus;* US1960 Albee, *By the Sea. 20c. coll.:* ODEP 724, Whiting(MP) 574, CODP 205.

slide One can't slide uphill. *Rec. dist.:* Ky., Tenn. *1st cit.:* US1854 Thoreau, *Slavery in Massachusetts. 20c. coll.:* Stevenson 1624:1.

slight SEE He that will slight my HORSE will buy my horse. / WOMEN forgive injuries but never forget slights.

slip *(n.)* **1.** A slip of the foot and you may soon recover, but a slip of the tongue you may never get over. *Rec. dist.:* N.Y., S.C., Wis. *1st cit.:* 1732 Fuller, *Gnomologia;* US1747 Franklin, *PRAlmanac. 20c. coll.:* Stevenson 2342:4.

2. A slip of the lip might sink a ship. *Vars.:* **(a)** A slip of the lip may sink a ship. **(b)** A slip of the lip will sink a ship. **(c)** Slips of the lips will sink ships. *Rec. dist.:* Mich., N.Y., Ont.

3. A slip of the tongue is not fault of the mind. *Rec. dist.:* Ill., Ont., S.C. *1st cit.:* US1854 Shillaber, *Life and Sayings of Mrs. Partington. 20c. coll.:* T&W 339, Stevenson 2342:4.

4. Better a slip with the foot than with the tongue. *Var.:* Better slip with the foot than with the tongue. *Rec. dist.:* U.S., Can. *1st cit.:* 1573 Sanford, *Garden of Pleasure;* US1734 Franklin, *PRAlmanac. 20c. coll.:* ODEP 55, Whiting 162, Stevenson 2342:4.

5. Every slip is not a fall. *Rec. dist.:* Tex. *1st cit.:* 1732 Fuller, *Gnomologia. 20c. coll.:* Stevenson 2139:3.

6. There is many a slip twixt cup and lip. *Vars.:* **(a)** Many a slip twixt the cup and the lip. **(b)** Many's the slip between cup and lip. **(c)** There's many a slip betwixt the cup and the lip. **(d)** There's many a slip twixt the cup and the lip. *Rec. dist.:* U.S., Can. *1st cit.:* 1539 Taverner, *Proverbs of Erasmus;* US1758 Writ-

ings of George Washington, ed. Fitzpatrick (1931–44). **20c. coll.:** *ODEP* 160, Whiting 399, *CODP* 147, Stevenson 2139:5, T&W 339, Whiting*(MP)* 575.

slip *(v.)* SEE An old HORSE slips quicker than a young one. / If the KNOT is loose, the string will slip.

slippery SEE The DOORSTEP of a great house is slippery.

slipping SEE A little SAND keeps you from slipping.

sloth **1.** Sloth breeds poverty. **Rec. dist.:** Ill.

2. Sloth is the mother of poverty. **Var.:** Sloth is the key to poverty. **Rec. dist.:** Ill., N.Y., Ont. **1st cit.:** 1669 *Politeuphuia,* ed. Ling. **20c. coll.:** Stevenson 2141:6.

3. Sloth is the mother of vice. **Rec. dist.:** Ill., N.C. **1st cit.:** ca1205 Layamon, *Brut,* Soc. Antiquaries (1847); USca1680 *Voyages of Radisson,* ed. Scull, Publ. Prince Soc. (1885). **20c. coll.:** *ODEP* 396, Whiting 231, *CODP* 118, Stevenson 1214:3, T&W 198, Whiting*(MP)* 334.

4. Sloth, like rust, consumes faster than labor wears, while the used key is always bright. **Rec. dist.:** Ill., N.Y. **1st cit.:** US1744 Franklin, *PRAlmanac.* **20c. coll.:** Whiting 399, *ODEP* 743, Stevenson 2141:1.

5. Sloth makes all things difficult, but industry makes all things easy. **Vars.:** **(a)** All things are easy to industry, all things difficult to sloth. **(b)** Sloth makes all things difficult, but industry all things easy. **Rec. dist.:** N.Y., Okla., S.C. **1st cit.:** US1734 Franklin, *PRAlmanac.* **20c. coll.:** Whiting 399, Stevenson 2141:1.

6. Sloth wears out the body while it corrodes the mind. **Rec. dist.:** Mich.
SEE ALSO TORPOR and sloth, torpor and sloth, these are the cooks that unseason the broth.

slow **1.** If you go mo' slow, you'll go mo' fast. **Rec. dist.:** Miss., N.Y.

2. Slow and easy wins the race. **Vars.:** **(a)** Slow and steady wins the race. **(b)** Slow but certain wins the race. **Rec. dist.:** Ind., N.Y., S.C. **1st cit.:** 1859 Smiles, *Self-Help;* US1936

Dean, *What Gentleman Strangles a Lady?* **20c. coll.:** *ODEP* 744, Whiting*(MP)* 575.

3. Slow but sure. **Rec. dist.:** U.S. **1st cit.:** 1562 Legh, *Accidence of Armoury;* US1759 Ames in *Dedham Historical Register* (1890–1903). **20c. coll.:** *ODEP* 743, Whiting 400, *CODP* 205, Stevenson 2142:7, T&W 339, Whiting*(MP)* 575.

4. Slow things are sure things. **Rec. dist.:** Calif., Colo.
SEE ALSO He that is slow to ANGER is better than the mighty. / The FEET are slow when the head wears snow. / Be slow in choosing a FRIEND, but slower in changing him. / A quick NICKEL is better than a slow dollar. / On an unknown PATH every foot is slow. / Seldom READERS are slow readers. / Slow are the STEPS of those who leave their hearts behind. / Too SWIFT arrives as tardy as too slow. / Slow WIND also brings the ship to harbor.

slowly SEE Make HASTE slowly. / The WAGON of God drives slowly and well.

slowpoke Slowpokes get busy when the hour gets late. **Rec. dist.:** Ont.

sluggard **1.** Scratch a sluggard and find a saint. **Rec. dist.:** N.Y., S.C. **1st cit.:** US1940 Nash, *Plea for League of Sleep.* **20c. coll.:** Stevenson 2143:7.

2. Sluggards cause their own misfortune. **Rec. dist.:** Mich.

3. Sluggards work best when the sun's in the west. **Rec. dist.:** N.C.
SEE ALSO PLOW deep while sluggards sleep, and you shall have corn to sell and to keep.

slumber SEE TRUTH is found in strange places and often slumbers even in a joke.

slumberer The slumberers are the prey of the wakeful. **Rec. dist.:** Ill.

smack One smack is worth a dozen scats. **Rec. dist.:** Ont. **Infm.:** A "smack" is a blow.

small *(n.)* Many small makes a great. **Rec. dist.:** Ky., Tenn. **1st cit.:** ca1386 Chaucer, *Pardoner's Tale.* **20c. coll.:** *ODEP* 510, Stevenson 1443:13.

small *(adj.)* **1.** Better to be small and shine than to be great and cast a shadow. *Rec. dist.:* Ont.

2. If you feel you're too small to do big things, then do big things in a small way. *Rec. dist.:* Ont.

3. No matter how small you are, you are too big to be dishonest. *Rec. dist.:* Nebr.

4. With small men no great thing can be accomplished. *Rec. dist.:* Ala., Ga.

SEE ALSO In great ACTION men show themselves as they ought to be, in small action as they are. / Big BUCKETS can be filled at small streams. / DYNAMITE comes in small packages. / Wink at small FAULTS. / Lose a small FISH to catch a big one. / Sma' FISH are better than nae fish. / A small GIFT usually gets small thanks. / GREAT men never feel great; small men never feel small. / Small HEAD, big ideas. / Small LEAKS sink big ships. / Great PROFITS on small capital are after all small. / Small SHOWERS last long, but sudden storms are short.

smallpox *SEE* AFFECTATION is a greater enemy to the face than smallpox.

smart Most men would rather say a smart thing than do one. *Rec. dist.:* Ind.

SEE ALSO You have to be smarter than the DOG to teach him tricks. / We get too soon OLD and too late smart.

smell *(n.)* The strength of a smell depends on the distance of its travel. *Rec. dist.:* Ind.

smell *(v.)* They that smell least smell best. *Rec. dist.:* Ont. *1st cit.:* 1529 Hyrde, *Instruction of a Christian Woman.* *20c. coll.:* ODEP 745, Stevenson 2144:6.

SEE ALSO FLATTERY, like perfume, should be smelled, not swallowed. / A FOX does not smell his own stench. / A ROSE by another name would smell as sweet. / A SKUNK smells its own hole first.

smile *(n.)* **1.** A smile costs nothing but gives much. *Rec. dist.:* Miss., N.Y.

2. A smile goes a long way. *Var.:* A smile can go a long way. *Rec. dist.:* Ill., Ohio.

3. A smile is the same in any language—easily understood. *Rec. dist.:* Miss., N.Y.

4. A smile is worth a million dollars. *Rec. dist.:* Ont., S.C.

5. A smile is worth its face value. *Rec. dist.:* Ont.

6. A smile will sway the universe. *Rec. dist.:* Oreg.

7. A smile will take a lot of the kick out of a disappointment. *Rec. dist.:* Minn.

8. A tender smile is sorrow's only balm. *Rec. dist.:* N.J.

9. Bear it with a smile. *Rec. dist.:* Calif.

10. Better the last smile than the first laughter. *Rec. dist.:* Ill. *1st cit.:* 1546 Heywood, *Dialogue of Proverbs.* *20c. coll.:* ODEP 56, Stevenson 2145:8.

11. No one needs a smile quite so much as he who has none to give away. *Rec. dist.:* N.C.

12. One smile is worth a thousand tears. *Rec. dist.:* Calif.

13. Smiles turn swiftly to tears. *Rec. dist.:* Wis.

14. The one with a smile always wins. *Rec. dist.:* Ont.

15. There are daggers behind men's smiles. *Rec. dist.:* N.Y., S.C. *1st cit.:* ca1390 Chaucer, *Knight's Tale;* US1807 *Correspondence of Andrew Jackson,* ed. Bassett (1926–33). *20c. coll.:* ODEP 444, Whiting 143, Stevenson 2145:3.

16. You are not fully dressed until you put on a smile. *Rec. dist.:* Colo.

SEE ALSO BEAUTY is power: a smile is its sword. / DECEIT is a lie which wears a smile. / A FACE without a smile is like a lantern without a light. / The VOICE with a smile always wins. / You always WIN if you can lose with a smile.

smile *(v.)* **1.** A man who can smile when he feels like cussin' has the qualities of a winner. *Rec. dist.:* W.Va.

2. He who cannot smile ought not own a shop. *Rec. dist.:* Ont.

3. He who smiles when he walks away will live to fight another day. *Rec. dist.:* Minn.

4. Smile and the world smiles with you. *Vars.:* **(a)** Smile and the world smiles with you; kick and you kick alone: for a cheerful grin will let you in where the kicker was never known. **(b)** Smile and the world smiles with you; weep and you weep alone. *Rec. dist.:* U.S., Can. *1st cit.:* 1979 *Daily Telegraph,* 3 Nov.; US1883 Wilcox, "Solitude" in *N.Y. Sun,* 25 Feb. *20c. coll.: CODP* 129, Stevenson 2266:10.

5. The man that's worthwhile is the man that can smile. *Var.:* The man worthwhile is the man who can smile when everything is wrong. *Rec. dist.:* Miss.

SEE ALSO When FORTUNE smiles, take the advantage. / When FORTUNE smiles, we ride in chase, and when she frowns, we walk away. / A good NEIGHBOR is a fellow who smiles at you over the back fence but doesn't climb it. / A man may smile and smile and still be a VILLAIN.

smiling Keep smiling when things are at their worst. *Rec. dist.:* Miss.

SEE ALSO A man without a smiling FACE must not open a shop.

smite *SEE* It's the THUNDER that frights but the lightning that smites.

smock *SEE* The LAUNDRESS washes her own smock first.

smoke *(n.)* **1.** A warm smoke is better than a cold fog. *Rec. dist.:* P.E.I.

2. It's no use crabbing at the smoke when the barn's burning down. *Rec. dist.:* Oreg.

3. Smoke follows beauty. *Rec. dist.:* Ill., Ky., N.Y., Tenn. *1st cit.:* ca1640 Smyth, *Berkeley MS. 20c. coll.: ODEP* 746, Stevenson 2174:3.

4. There is no fire without some smoke. *Var.:* Where there is fire there is smoke. *Rec. dist.:* U.S., Can. *1st cit.:* ca1375 Barbour, *Bruce,* ed. Skeat, E.E.T.S. (1889); US1773 Bradford in *Papers of James Madison,* eds. Hutchinson and Rachel (1962). *20c. coll.: ODEP* 573, Whiting 401, *CODP* 206, Stevenson 812:1, T&W 340, Whiting*(MP)* 576.

5. Where there is smoke, there is fire. *Vars.:* **(a)** If there's smoke, there is fire. **(b)** No smoke without a fire. **(c)** There can't be smoke without a fire. **(d)** There's no smoke without fire. **(e)** Where much smoke is, there must be some fire. **(f)** Where there is so much smoke,

there must be some fire. **(g)** Where there's much smoke, there's bound to be a little fire. **(h)** Where there's smoke, there's bound to be fire. **(i)** Where there's smoke, there's fire. *Rec. dist.:* U.S., Can. *1st cit.:* ca1375 Barbour, *Bruce,* ed. Skeat, E.E.T.S. (1889); US1773 Bradford in *Papers of James Madison,* eds. Hutchinson and Rachel (1962). *20c. coll.: ODEP* 573, Whiting 401, *CODP* 206, Stevenson 812:1, T&W 340, Whiting*(MP)* 576.

SEE ALSO He that makes a FIRE of straw has much smoke but little warmth. / You can hide the FIRE, but not the smoke. / LOVE and smoke cannot be hidden. / Three THINGS drive a man out of his home: smoke, rain, and a scolding wife.

smoke *(v.)* It is better to smoke in this world than in the next. *Rec. dist.:* Ont.

SEE ALSO If BOYS were meant to smoke, they'd have chimneys on their heads. / LADIES don't smoke.

smokehouse Empty smokehouse makes de pullet holler. *Rec. dist.:* N.Y., S.C.

smooth *SEE* The path of true LOVE never runs smooth. / Take the ROUGH with the smooth. / A rugged STONE grows smooth from hand to hand. / Smooth WORDS make smooth ways.

smuggler An old smuggler makes a good custom's officer. *Rec. dist.:* Minn.

snake **1.** A man once bitten by a snake will jump at the sight of a rope in his path. *Rec. dist.:* Tex. *1st cit.:* 1678 Ray, *Adagia Hebraica. 20c. coll.: ODEP* 62, Stevenson 727:5.

2. A snake crawls on its own stomach, but a flea crawls on everybody else. *Rec. dist.:* Ky., Tenn.

3. It takes a snake to catch a snake. *Rec. dist.:* Oreg.

4. When you see a snake, never mind where he came from. *Rec. dist.:* Ont.

SEE ALSO Mend the first BREAK, kill the first snake, and conquer everything you undertake.

snare He who lays a snare for another, himself falls into it. *Rec. dist.:* Ont. *1st cit.:* 1509 Barclay, *Ship of Fools,* ed. Jamieson in *Ec-*

logues, E.E.T.S. (1874); US1646 Winslow, *Hypocrisie Unmasked,* ed. Chapin (1916). **20c. coll.:** ODEP 187, Whiting 402, Stevenson 1969:6, Whiting*(MP)* 578.

snatch *See* ABILITY will see a chance and snatch it; who has a match will find a place to strike it.

sneer **1.** A sneer cannot be answered. *Rec. dist.:* Ill.

2. Sneers are poor weapons at the best. *Rec. dist.:* Ill.

snobbery Snobbery is the pride of those not sure of their own position. *Rec. dist.:* Minn.

snow *(n.)* **1.** A fall of snow in May is worth a ton of hay. *Rec. dist.:* Ont. **1st cit.:** 1893 Inwards, *Weather Lore.* **20c. coll.:** Stevenson 1550:3.

2. A snow year, a rich year. *Rec. dist.:* Ont. **1st cit.:** 1580 Monardes, *Joyful News of the New Found World,* tr. Frampton. **20c. coll.:** ODEP 748, Stevenson 2151:9.

3. Just because there's snow on the roof, that doesn't mean the fire's out inside. *Rec. dist.:* U.S.

4. Snow is the poor man's fertilizer. *Rec. dist.:* Ill. **1st cit.:** US1798 Allen, *Natural and Political History of State of Vermont,* Vt.Hist.Soc. *Collections* (1890). **20c. coll.:** Whiting 404, T&W 342, Whiting*(MP)* 580.

See also The FEET are slow when the head wears snow. / THAW shows up what the snow has hidden.

snow *(v.)* *See* No APRIL is so good that it won't snow on a farmer's hat.

snowball *See* A LIE is like a snowball: the farther you roll it, the bigger it becomes.

snub *See* You can't afford to snub a MAN built on the million dollar plan.

soap **1.** Never stint soap and water. *Rec. dist.:* Ont.

2. Soap and water will not make a Negro's face white. *Rec. dist.:* Miss., Ont. **1st cit.:** US1870 Emerson, "Works and Days" in *Society and Solitude.* **20c. coll.:** Stevenson 1672:11.

3. You can't eat soap and wash with it. *Rec. dist.:* Ont.

See also FLATTERY is soft soap, and soft soap is ninety percent lye.

soar Soar not too high to fall, but stoop to rise. *Rec. dist.:* Utah. **1st cit.:** 1623 Massinger, *Duke of Milan.* **20c. coll.:** Stevenson 2536:12.

soberness What soberness conceals, drunkenness reveals. *Var.:* Drunkenness reveals what soberness conceals. *Rec. dist.:* Mich., Wis. **1st cit.:** ca1386 Chaucer, *Man of Law's Tale.* **20c. coll.:** ODEP 749, Stevenson 636:3.

sock *See* Nothing like a little MONEY in the sock to give you self-confidence. / There is never an old SHOE but there is a sock to fit it.

soft *See* A soft ANSWER turns away wrath. / FLATTERY is soft soap, and soft soap is ninety percent lye. / A soft WORD is often worth more than a house and a lot. / Soft WORDS break no bones.

soften *See* Soften the WORDS to suit the occasion.

softly He who treads softly goes far. *Var.:* He that goes softly goes safely. *Rec. dist.:* N.J. **1st cit.:** 1576 Holyband, *Frenche Littelton.* **20c. coll.:** ODEP 750, Stevenson 1083:1.

soil *(n.)* **1.** Any soil will do to bury in. *Rec. dist.:* Wash. **1st cit.:** US1875 Scarborough, *Chinese Proverbs.* **20c. coll.:** Stevenson 1027:7.

2. Soil and friendship must be cultivated. *Rec. dist.:* Calif.

soil *(v.)* *See* No MUD can soil us but the mud we throw. / One clean SHEET will not soil another.

sold *See* Well BOUGHT is half sold.

soldier **1.** A beaten soldier fears a reed. *Rec. dist.:* Ind.

2. A good soldier never looks back. *Var.:* A good soldier never looks behind him. *Rec. dist.:* Mich., Ohio, Ont.

3. A good soldier never shines the heels of his shoes. *Rec. dist.:* N.Y., S.C. **1st cit.:** US1940 Thompson, *Body, Boots, and Britches.* **20c. coll.:** Stevenson 2156:10.

4. A live soldier is better than a dead hero. *Rec. dist.:* Mich., N.Y., Ont.

5. A soldier will remember his friend. *Rec. dist.:* Minn.

6. A soldier, fire, and water soon make room for themselves. *Rec. dist.:* Mich. *1st cit.:* 1640 Herbert, *Outlandish Proverbs (Jacula Prudentum)* in *Works,* ed. Hutchinson (1941); US1809 *Port Folio. 20c. coll.:* ODEP 869, Whiting 405.

7. All are not soldiers who go to war. *Rec. dist.:* Ill. *1st cit.:* US1948 Stevenson, *Home Book of Proverbs. 20c. coll.:* Stevenson 81:3.

8. He is not a good soldier who fights with his tongue. *Rec. dist.:* Ill.

9. Many soldiers are brave at the table who are cowards in the field. *Rec. dist.:* Mich.

10. Old soldiers never die. *Var.:* Old soldiers never die—they just smell that way. *Rec. dist.:* U.S., Can. *1st cit.:* 1920 Foley, *Old Soldiers Never Die* (song title); US1952 Wilson, *Hemlock and After. 20c. coll.:* CODP 168, Whiting*(MP)* 581.

sole One pair of good soles is better than two tops. *Rec. dist.:* Miss.

solitude Solitude is at times the best society. *Var.:* Solitude is sometimes the best society. *Rec. dist.:* Ill. *1st cit.:* 1667 Milton, *Paradise Lost. 20c. coll.:* Stevenson 2160:6.

some Better some than none. *Rec. dist.:* Ont. *1st cit.:* 1546 Heywood, *Dialogue of Proverbs,* ed. Habernicht (1963). *20c. coll.:* Stevenson 236:1.

SEE ALSO You can fool some of the PEOPLE all the time, all the people some of the time, but you can't fool all the people all the time.

somebody You can't beat somebody with nobody. *Rec. dist.:* Ill. *1st cit.:* US1923 Sullivan, *Our Times. 20c. coll.:* Stevenson 1829:6.

SEE ALSO Never DO anything yourself you can get somebody else to do. / The more you LEAN on somebody else, the leaner your chances of success.

someplace There's always someplace else to go. *Rec. dist.:* Colo.

something **1.** A second-rate something is better than a first-rate nothing. *Rec. dist.:* Colo.

1st cit.: 1546 Heywood, *Dialogue of Proverbs,* ed. Habernicht (1963). *20c. coll.:* Stevenson 236:1.

2. Better something than nothing. *Var.:* Something is better than nothing. *Rec. dist.:* Calif., Wis. *1st cit.:* 1546 Heywood, *Dialogue of Proverbs,* ed. Habernicht (1963); US1842 Irving, *Attorney. 20c. coll.:* ODEP 751, T&W 345, CODP 207, Stevenson 236:1, Whiting*(MP)* 582.

3. Don't make something out of nothing. *Var.:* You can't make something out of nothing. *Rec. dist.:* Mich., N.Y., Okla.

4. Don't start something you can't finish. *Rec. dist.:* Mich., N.Y., N.C., S.C.

5. Something tastes better than nothing. *Rec. dist.:* Wis.

6. When you get something for nothing, someone is getting nothing for something. *Rec. dist.:* Calif., Colo.

7. You don't get something for nothing. *Rec. dist.:* U.S., Can. *1st cit.:* 1845 Disraeli, *Sybil;* US1869 Barnum, *Struggles and Triumphs of P. T. Barnum. 20c. coll.:* Stevenson 2161:7, T&W 344, Whiting*(MP)* 582.

8. You get out of something only what you put in. *Rec. dist.:* Calif., Colo., Mich., N.Y.

SEE ALSO There is nothing so BAD in which there is not something good. / If you want something done and done well, DO it yourself. / GAMBLING is getting nothing for something. / Be not simply GOOD; be good for something. / The quickest way to show IGNORANCE is to talk about something you know nothing about.

somewhere SEE Somewhere the SUN is shining; somewhere a little rain is falling.

son **1.** A foolish son is the calamity of his father, and the contentions of a wife are a continual dropping. *Rec. dist.:* U.S., Can. *Infm.:* "Dropping" refers to the dripping of water, which wears away the stone. *1st cit.:* US1948 Stevenson, *Home Book of Proverbs. 20c. coll.:* Stevenson 772:9.

2. A good son is the light of the family. *Rec. dist.:* Ill.

3. A good son makes a good husband. *Rec. dist.:* N.Y.

4. A son's a son till he gets him a wife; a daughter's a daughter all of her life. *Rec. dist.:* U.S., Can. *1st cit.:* 1670 Ray, *English Proverbs;* US1788 *Writings of Benjamin Franklin,* ed. Smyth (1905–07). *20c. coll.: ODEP* 751, Whiting 405, *CODP* 207, Stevenson 2162:12.

5. A wise son hears his father's instructions. *Rec. dist.:* Ont.

6. A wise son makes a glad father, but a foolish son is the heaviness of his mother. *Rec. dist.:* U.S., Can. *1st cit.:* US1732 *Jonathan Belcher Papers,* Mass.Hist.Soc. *Collections* (1893–94). *20c. coll.:* Whiting 406, Stevenson 772:9.

7. He that gathers in the summer is a wise son. *Rec. dist.:* Ill.

8. It is a wise son that knows his own father. *Rec. dist.:* N.Y. *1st cit.:* 1584 Withals, *A Short Dictionary for Young Beginners;* US1723 *New-England Courant,* ed. Miller (1956). *20c. coll.: ODEP* 899, Whiting 70, *CODP* 247, Stevenson 770:8, T&W 68, Whiting*(MP)* 111.

9. Marry your son when you please and your daughter when you can. *Rec. dist.:* Ind., N.Y. *1st cit.:* 1640 Herbert, *Outlandish Proverbs (Jacula Prudentum)* in *Works,* ed. Hutchinson (1941); US1734 Franklin, *PRAlmanac. 20c. coll.: ODEP* 516, Whiting 405, Stevenson 2162:10.

10. The son is father to the man. *Rec. dist.:* Ky., Tenn. *Infm.:* Cf. child.

11. Who has no son has no satisfaction. *Rec. dist.:* Ill.

SEE ALSO It is not the father's ANGER but his silence his son dreads. / The son of the CAT pursues the rat. / Like FATHER, like son. / You cannot choose your FATHER, but you choose your father's son. / A PREACHER'S son is often bad.

song **1.** A good song is none the worse for being sung twice. *Rec. dist.:* N.Y.

2. A song will outlive sermons in the memory. *Rec. dist.:* Ill.

3. In whose heart there is no song, to him the miles are many and long. *Rec. dist.:* Ont.

4. Lightsome songs make a merry gait. *Rec. dist.:* Ont.

5. New songs are eagerly sung. *Rec. dist.:* Ill. *1st cit.:* US1948 Stevenson, *Home Book of Proverbs. 20c. coll.:* Stevenson 1681:3.

6. Sweet song has betrayed many. *Rec. dist.:* Ill.

7. The fellow who works for a song has trouble meeting his notes. *Rec. dist.:* Wis.

8. The sweetest songs are sung in sorrow. *Rec. dist.:* N.Y., Ont.

9. The sweetest songs are those that tell of saddest thoughts. *Rec. dist.:* Ont.

SEE ALSO He who PITCHES too high will not get through his song. / The SOUND makes the song. / WINE, women, and song will get a man wrong.

soon **1.** Better three hours too soon than a minute too late. *Rec. dist.:* Ont. *1st cit.:* US1871 Jones, *Life of Jefferson S. Batkins. 20c. coll.:* T&W 345.

2. The sooner the better. *Rec. dist.:* U.S., Can. *1st cit.:* ca1475 *Mankind,* ed. Brand (1918); US1640 Gostin in *Winthrop Papers,* Mass. Hist.Soc. *Collections* (1929–47). *20c. coll.: ODEP* 753, Whiting 406, Stevenson 2167:1, T&W 345, Whiting*(MP)* 583.

sore Do not rip up old sores. *Var.:* Don't rip up old sores and cast up old scores. *Rec. dist.:* Ont. *1st cit.:* 1553 Udall, *Ralph Roister Doister;* US1733 *Jonathan Belcher Papers,* Mass.Hist.Soc. *Collections* (1893–94). *20c. coll.: ODEP* 678, Whiting 407, Stevenson 2167:10.

SEE ALSO PATIENCE is a plaster for all sores.

sorrow **1.** Don't nurse your sorrows. *Rec. dist.:* Ont.

2. Fat sorrow is better than lean sorrow. *Rec. dist.:* Ont. *1st cit.:* 1662 Rogers, *Rich Fool;* US1867 Richardson, *Beyond the Mississippi, 1857–67. 20c. coll.: ODEP* 247, T&W 345, Stevenson 2168:3.

3. Jesting lies bring serious sorrows. *Rec. dist.:* N.Y. *1st cit.:* 1855 Bohn, *Handbook of Proverbs. 20c. coll.:* Stevenson 1267:4.

4. Light sorrows speak; great ones are dumb. *Rec. dist.:* Ill. *1st cit.:* 1565 Cooper, *Thesaurus*

Linguae Romanae et Britannicae (1573). **20c. coll.:**
ODEP 744, Stevenson 1041:9.

5. Make not two sorrows of one. **Rec. dist.:**
Ont. **1st cit.:** ca1430 Lydgate, "Chorle and
Bird" in *Minor Poems,* Percy Soc. **20c. coll.:**
ODEP 852, Stevenson 2169:6.

6. Our sorrows are less if in our anguish we
find a partner in distress. **Rec. dist.:** N.C. **1st
cit.:** 1540 Palsgrave, *Acolastus,* ed. Carver,
E.E.T.S. (1937). **20c. coll.:** *ODEP* 338, Stevenson 1042:8.

7. Rejoice not in another's sorrow. **Rec. dist.:**
N.C.

8. Sorrow for the husband is like a pain in the
elbow—sharp and short. **Rec. dist.:** N.Y.

9. Sorrow is better than laughter. **Rec. dist.:**
Ont. **1st cit.:** US1948 Stevenson, *Home Book
of Proverbs.* **20c. coll.:** Stevenson 2168:6.

10. Sorrow is only grain deep. **Rec. dist.:** Ind.

11. Sorrow never comes singly. **Rec. dist.:** Ont.
1st cit.: ca1300 *King Alisaunder,* ed. Smithers,
E.E.T.S. (1952); US1722 *Papers of Benjamin
Franklin,* ed. Labaree (1959). **20c. coll.:** *ODEP*
535, Whiting 292, *CODP* 151, Stevenson
1596:9, T&W 246, Whiting*(MP)* 414.

12. Sorrow remains when joy is but a blast.
Rec. dist.: N.Y.

13. Sorrow treads upon the heels of mirth.
Rec. dist.: Ont. **1st cit.:** US1853 Haliburton,
Sam Slick's Wise Saws. **20c. coll.:** Stevenson
2168:7.

14. Sorrows remembered sweeten present joy.
Rec. dist.: Ill. **1st cit.:** ca1375 Barbour, *Bruce,*
ed. Skeat, E.E.T.S. (1977). **20c. coll.:** *ODEP*
671, Stevenson 1953:3.

15. There's no sorrow on this earth that can't
be cured in heaven. **Var.:** Earth has no sorrow
that heaven cannot heal. **Rec. dist.:** N.Y., N.C.
1st cit.: ca1852 Moore, *Come, Ye Disconsolate.*
20c. coll.: Stevenson 2168:5.

16. When sorrow is asleep, wake it not. **Rec.
dist.:** Ill. **1st cit.:** 1595 Shakespeare, *Midsummer
Night's Dream.* **20c. coll.:** *ODEP* 754, Stevenson 2170:2.

SEE ALSO Suppressing a moment of ANGER
may save a day of sorrow. / BORROW and

borrow adds up to sorrow. / He that speaks
without CARE shall remember with sorrow. /
EARTH has no sorrow that heaven cannot heal.
/ JOY is kin to sorrow. / JOYS are our wings;
our sorrows, our spurs. / Our greatest JOYS
and our greatest sorrows grow on the same
vine. / An ounce of WIT is worth a pound of
sorrow.

sorrowing SEE He that goes A-BORROWING
goes a-sorrowing.

sorry SEE Better LATE than sorry. / A RICH
man is happy while he is alive but sorry when
he dies. / It is better to be SAFE than sorry. /
A sad SAINT is a sorry saint.

soul 1. A penny soul never 'came twopence.
Rec. dist.: N.J. **1st cit.:** 1844 *Chambers' Journal
of Popular Literature.* **20c. coll.:** *ODEP* 619.

2. A soul built of solid rock will not falter.
Rec. dist.: Ind.

3. As cold water to a thirsty soul, so is good
news from a far country. **Rec. dist.:** N.Y.,
S.C. **1st cit.:** US1758 Kirkpatrick in *Letters to
Washington,* ed. Hamilton (1898–1902). **20c.
coll.:** Whiting 311, Stevenson 1682:11.

4. Don't trade your soul for a mess of pot-
tage. **Rec. dist.:** Minn. **1st cit.:** ca1557 *Jacob and
Esau;* USca1700 Hubbard, *General History of
New England* (1848). **20c. coll.:** *ODEP* 713,
Whiting 33, Stevenson 188:4, Whiting*(MP)*
52.

5. Great souls have will; feeble ones only
have wishes. **Rec. dist.:** Ont.

6. Great souls suffer in silence. **Rec. dist.:** Minn.
1st cit.: US1948 Stevenson, *Home Book of
Proverbs.* **20c. coll.:** Stevenson 2239:4.

7. If you've lost your soul, you've lost all.
Rec. dist.: N.C.

8. Keep your soul and your shop will keep
you. **Rec. dist.:** Tex.

9. Many people will sell their souls for money.
Rec. dist.: N.C.

10. Mean souls, like mean pictures, are often
found in good-looking frames. **Rec. dist.:** Ont.

11. Souls are not saved in bundles. **Rec. dist.:**
N.Y., S.C. **1st cit.:** 1640 Herbert, *Outlandish
Proverbs (Jacula Prudentum)* in *Works,* ed.

Hutchinson (1941); US1860 Emerson, "Worship" in *Conduct of Life*. *20c. coll.: ODEP* 115, Stevenson 2032:2.

12. The soul is a temple. *Rec. dist.:* N.C.

13. To the hungry soul, every bitter thing is sweet. *Rec. dist.:* Minn.

SEE ALSO BEAUTY comes from the soul. / There's no BEAUTY like the beauty of the soul. / A deformed BODY may have a beautiful soul. / Though the BODY may be imprisoned, the soul can be free. / BREVITY is the soul of wit. / CHARM strikes the sight, but merit wins the soul. / An honest CONFESSION is good for the soul. / DUTY done is the soul's fireside. / The EYES are the windows of the soul. / When the FIRE burns in the soul, the tongue cannot be silent. / GRATITUDE is the sign of noble soul. / A HOUSE without woman and firelight is like a body without soul or spirit. / PRAYER is food for the soul. / PUNCTUALITY is the soul of business. / Who keeps his TONGUE will keep his soul. / When a YOUTH is saved, a life is saved; when an old person is saved, only a soul is saved.

sound *(n.)* The sound makes the song. *Rec. dist.:* Ont.

sound *(v.)* SEE A cracked BELL can never sound well.

sound *(adj.)* SEE A sound HEART is the life of the flesh, but envy the rottenness of the bones.

soup SEE Fat HENS make rich soup. / Too many PEAS spoil the soup. / He who stirs the soup POT eats first.

sour *(n.)* **1.** Too much sour spoils the sweet. *Rec. dist.:* Ont.

2. You must take the sour with the sweet. *Rec. dist.:* Ont. *1st cit.:* 1509 Barclay, *Ship of Fools,* ed. Jamieson in *Eclogues,* E.E.T.S. (1894); US1709 *Diary of Samuel Sewall, 1674–1729,* Mass.Hist.Soc. *Collections* (1878–82). *20c. coll.: ODEP* 794, Whiting 407, Stevenson 2260:9, Whiting(MP) 584.

SEE ALSO He deserves not SWEET that will not taste of sour. / SWEETS to the sweet and sour to the sour.

sour *(adj.)* SEE Handsome APPLES are sometimes sour. / Sour GRAPES can never make

sweet wine. / Once MILK becomes sour, it can't be made sweet again. / Little MINDS, like weak liquors, are soon soured. / Sweet's the WINE, but sour's the payment.

source Consider the source. *Rec. dist.:* Ala., Ga., Mich., N.Y. *1st cit.:* 1673 Temple, *Observations Upon the Netherlands;* US1928 Shedd, *Salt from My Attic. 20c. coll.:* Stevenson 2174:18.

SEE ALSO The FOUNTAIN is clearest at its source. / A STREAM never rises higher than its source. / The STREAM is always purer at its source.

sow *(n.)* **1.** A barren sow was never good to pigs. *Rec. dist.:* Ala., Ga. *1st cit.:* ca1595 Fergusson, *Scottish Proverbs. 20c. coll.:* Stevenson 2175:8, *ODEP* 31.

2. If you like the sow, you like her litter. *Rec. dist.:* Miss.

3. Little knows the fat sow what the lean one thinks. *Rec. dist.:* Okla. *1st cit.:* ca1350 *Douce MS 52. 20c. coll.: ODEP* 471, Stevenson 2175:11.

4. The silent sow gets all the swill. *Rec. dist.:* Ont. *1st cit.:* ca1225 *Trinity MS,* ed. Förester in *English Studies;* US1962 *Bangor Daily News,* 25 June. *20c. coll.: ODEP* 774, Whiting(MP) 584, Stevenson 2176:4.

5. You need not grease a fat sow. *Rec. dist.:* Ont. *1st cit.:* ca1549 Heywood, *Dramatic Works,* ed. Shepherd (1874); US1937 Winston, *It's a Far Cry. 20c. coll.: ODEP* 332, Whiting(MP) 584.

SEE ALSO You can't make a silk PURSE out of a sow's ear. / The RUNT makes the best sow.

sow *(v.)* **1.** What one man sows another man reaps. *Rec. dist.:* N.Y. *1st cit.:* 1577 Holinshed, *Chronicles;* US1664 *Wyllys Papers 1590–1796,* Conn.Hist.Soc. *Collections* (1924). *20c. coll.: ODEP* 597, Whiting 408, Stevenson 2178:7.

2. You shall reap what you sow. *Vars.:* **(a)** As they sow, so let them reap. **(b)** As you have sown, so shall you reap. **(c)** As you sow you shall reap. **(d)** As you sow, so shall you reap. **(e)** Men must reap the things they sow. **(f)** We reap just what we sow and nothing else. **(g)** What man sows he must reap. **(h)** What you sow you shall reap. **(i)** Whatsoever a man sows, that shall he reap. **(j)** Whoever sows a deed will reap it no matter how long it is. **(k)** You reap what you sow. **(l)** You will reap what you sow. *Rec. dist.:* U.S., Can. *1st cit.:* ca900 Cynewulf, *Christian Anglo-Saxon Poetic Records,* ed. Knapp; US1679 *Fitzhugh and His Chesapeake World,* ed. Davis, Va.Hist.Soc. Documents (1963). *20c. coll.:* ODEP 757, Whiting 408, CODP 208, Stevenson 2179:4, Whiting(*MP*) 585.

SEE ALSO If the BRAIN sows not corn, it plants thistles. / He who sows COURTESY reaps friendship. / FOOLISHNESS grows by itself—no need to sow it. / He that sows INIQUITY shall reap vanity. / Sow your wild OATS and pray for a crop failure. / They that sow in TEARS shall reap in joy. / He that sows THORNS should never go barefoot. / Sow a THOUGHT and reap an act.

sowing No sowing, no reaping. *Rec. dist.:* Calif.

SEE ALSO You can't raise GRAIN by sowing grass. / WEEDS need no sowing.

spade A spade and a thought should never be allowed to rust. *Rec. dist.:* Ont.

spare *(v.)* **1.** Better spare at the brim than at the bottom. *Rec. dist.:* N.Y., S.C. *1st cit.:* 1523 Fitzherbert, *Boke of Husbandry;* US1869 Spurgeon, *John Ploughman's Talks.* *20c. coll.:* ODEP 55, Stevenson 2181:11.

2. Better spared than ill spent. *Rec. dist.:* N.Y. *1st cit.:* 1616 Draxe, *Bibliotheca Scholastica in Anglia* (1918). *20c. coll.:* ODEP 55, Stevenson 2181:10.

3. It is too late to spare when the bottom is bare. *Rec. dist.:* Ill. *1st cit.:* 1539 Taverner, *Proverbs of Erasmus.* *20c. coll.:* ODEP 759, Stevenson 2182:3.

4. Spare and have is better than spend and crave. *Rec. dist.:* N.Y., S.C. *1st cit.:* US1758 Franklin, *PRAlmanac.* *20c. coll.:* Whiting 409, Stevenson 2182:12.

5. Spare well and spend well. *Rec. dist.:* N.Y. *1st cit.:* 1541 Bullinger, *Christian State of Matrimony,* tr. Coverdale. *20c. coll.:* ODEP 759, CODP 209, Stevenson 2181:9.

6. Spare when you are young and spend when you are old. *Var.:* He that spares when he is young may spend when he is old. *Rec. dist.:* Mich., N.Y., Okla., Tex. *1st cit.:* 1541 Bullinger, *Christian State of Matrimony,* tr. Coverdale. *20c. coll.:* ODEP 759, CODP 209, Stevenson 2181:8.

7. Too late to spare when all is spent. *Rec. dist.:* Ont. *1st cit.:* 1539 Taverner, *Proverbs of Erasmus.* *20c. coll.:* ODEP 759.

SEE ALSO He that has a thousand FRIENDS has not a friend to spare. / If you have an HOUR to spare, don't spend it with someone who hasn't. / He that has KNOWLEDGE spares his words. / Spare the ROD and spoil the child. / They who make the best use of their TIME have none to spare.

spare *(adj.)* *SEE* To find out what a MAN is like, find out what he does in his spare time.

sparingly *SEE* He that is RICH need not live sparingly, and he that can live sparingly need not be rich.

spark **1.** A little spark kindles a great fire. *Rec. dist.:* Fla., Mich., Tex. *1st cit.:* 1412 Lydgate, *Troy Book,* ed. Bergen, E.E.T.S. (1906); US1624 *Letters of John Davenport,* ed. Calden (1927). *20c. coll.:* ODEP 759, Whiting 409, Stevenson 806:9, Whiting(*MP*) 586.

2. Even a spark is fire. *Rec. dist.:* Ill.

3. Sparks become flame. *Rec. dist.:* Ill. *1st cit.:* 1412 Lydgate, *Troy Book,* ed. Bergen, E.E.T.S. (1906). *20c. coll.:* ODEP 759, Stevenson 807:2.

SEE ALSO A FIRE is never out until the last spark is extinguished.

sparrow Two sparrows upon one ear of corn are not likely to agree. *Rec. dist.:* Mich. *1st cit.:* 1599 Minsheu, *Dictionarie in Spanish and English.* *20c. coll.:* ODEP 852, Stevenson 1997:10.

spatter *SEE* If you fool with a tumble-turd BUG, you are apt to be spattered.

speak **1.** Do not speak badly of yourself and expect people to respect you. *Rec. dist.:* Ont.

2. He cannot speak well that cannot hold his tongue. *Rec. dist.:* Tex. *1st cit.:* 1545 *Precepts of Cato,* tr. Burrant; US1758 Ames, *Almanacs,* ed. Briggs (1891). *20c. coll.:* ODEP 761, Whiting 409, Stevenson 2349:4.

3. He that speaks much is much mistaken. *Var.:* He who speaks much errs much. *Rec. dist.:* Colo., Mich. *1st cit.:* US1736 Franklin, *PRAlmanac.* *20c. coll.:* Stevenson 2185:9.

4. He who does not speak well is not heard. *Rec. dist.:* Colo.

5. He who speaks and has nothing to say says it cleverly. *Rec. dist.:* N.J.

6. He who speaks not till the last may profit by the follies of the rash. *Rec. dist.:* Ariz., N.C.

7. If you cannot speak well of a person, don't speak of him at all. *Rec. dist.:* Wash. *1st cit.:* US1876 Nash, *New England Life.* *20c. coll.:* T&W 399.

8. Many speak much who cannot speak well. *Rec. dist.:* Ill., Ont. *1st cit.:* 1597 *Politeuphuia Wits Commonwealth.* *20c. coll.:* ODEP 761.

9. Never speak to deceive nor listen to betray. *Rec. dist.:* Mich.

10. Never trust a man who speaks well of everybody. *Rec. dist.:* N.C.

11. Speak fair, think what you will. *Rec. dist.:* Calif. *1st cit.:* 1598 Barckley, *Discourse of Felicity of Man.* *20c. coll.:* ODEP 760, Stevenson 2189:3.

12. Speak fitly or be silent wisely. *Rec. dist.:* N.Y. *1st cit.:* 1611 Cotgrave, *Dictionary of French and English Tongues.* *20c. coll.:* ODEP 760, Stevenson 2113:3.

13. Speak gently: it is better to rule by love than by fear. *Rec. dist.:* Ont.

14. Speak little; do much. *Rec. dist.:* Miss. *1st cit.:* US1755 Franklin, *PRAlmanac.* *20c. coll.:* Whiting 265, Stevenson 2614:13.

15. Speak little; speak well. *Rec. dist.:* Ont.

16. Speak neither well nor ill of yourself. *Rec. dist.:* Ill.

17. Speak not rather than speak ill. *Rec. dist.:* Ohio.

18. Speak now or forever hold your peace. *Rec. dist.:* U.S. *1st cit.:* US1948 Stevenson, *Home Book of Proverbs.* *20c. coll.:* Stevenson 2193:7.

19. Speak so that even he who runs must understand. *Rec. dist.:* Iowa.

20. Speak softly and carry a big stick. *Rec. dist.:* U.S. *1st cit.:* US1901 T. Roosevelt, Address at Minnesota State Fair, 2 Sept. *20c. coll.:* Stevenson 1874:5.

21. Speak up or shut up. *Rec. dist.:* Ont. *1st cit.:* US1948 Stevenson, *Home Book of Proverbs.* *20c. coll.:* Stevenson 2193:6.

22. Speak well of everyone if you speak of them at all. *Rec. dist.:* Okla.

23. Speak what you feel, not what you ought to. *Rec. dist.:* Colo. *1st cit.:* US1948 Stevenson, *Home Book of Proverbs.* *20c. coll.:* Stevenson 2193:8.

24. Speak when you are spoken to; come when you are called. *Vars.:* **(a)** Don't speak unless spoken to. **(b)** Speak only when you are spoken to. *Rec. dist.:* U.S., Can. *1st cit.:* 1586 La Primaudaye, *French Academy,* tr. Bowes. *20c. coll.:* ODEP 761, Stevenson 336:8.

SEE ALSO Speak not evil of the ABSENT; it is unjust. / ACTIONS speak louder than words. / Speak of ANGELS and you'll hear the rustling of their wings. / It is an ill CAUSE that none dare speak in. / CHILDREN and fools speak the truth. / Speak well of the DEAD. / He who speaks EVIL hears worse. / See no EVIL, hear no evil, speak no evil. / Some folks speak from EXPERIENCE; others, from experience, don't speak. / Only FOOLS speak or fiddle at the table. / He's my FRIEND who speaks well behind my back. / A GOSSIP speaks ill of all and all of her. / HEAR twice before you speak once. / Don't speak ILL of yourself; others will do it for you. / He that speaks ILL of the mare will buy her. / Everyone speaks for his own INTEREST. / PRESENTS speak louder than words. / Speak of SATAN and you'll see his horns. / STAND up, speak up, and shut up. / One may THINK what he dare not speak. / THINK much; speak little; write less. / THINK twice; speak once. / Speak your THOUGHTS lest someone steal them. / The TONGUE can speak a word whose speed outsteps the steed. / Speak the TRUTH and shame the devil.

speaking Speaking without thinking is shooting without aiming. *Rec. dist.:* Ill.

SEE ALSO SILENCE is wisdom when speaking is folly.

specialist Specialists are people who know more and more about less and less until they know everything about nothing. *Rec. dist.:* Miss.

specimen The poorest specimen of fish is he who is selfish. *Rec. dist.:* N.Y.

spectacles Through green spectacles the world is green. *Rec. dist.:* Ill.

speculate *SEE* You never ACCUMULATE if you don't speculate.

speech 1. Courteous speech is worth much and costs little. *Rec. dist.:* Ill.

2. Mild speech enchains the heart. *Rec. dist.:* Ill.

3. More have repented speech than silence. *Rec. dist.:* Ill. *1st cit.:* 1579 *Proverbs of Sir James Lopez de Mendoza,* tr. Googe. *20c. coll.:* ODEP 672, Stevenson 2114:2.

4. Much speech, less sense. *Rec. dist.:* Colo., Ont.

5. Speech is silver; silence is golden. *Var.:* Speaking is silver, silence is golden. *Rec. dist.:* U.S., Can. *1st cit.:* 1836 Carlyle, *Sartor Resartus;* US1848 Lowell, *Biglow Papers.* *20c. coll.:* ODEP 763, Stevenson 2112:14, CODP 210, T&W 346, Whiting*(MP)* 586.

6. Speech is the gift of all but the thought of few. *Rec. dist.:* Ont. *1st cit.:* 1855 Bohn, *Handbook of Proverbs.* *20c. coll.:* Stevenson 2183:1.

7. Speech is the index of the mind. *Rec. dist.:* Ont. *1st cit.:* 1545 *Precepts of Cato,* tr. Burrant. *20c. coll.:* ODEP 763, Stevenson 2183:5.

8. Speech was given a man to conceal his thoughts. *Rec. dist.:* Oreg. *1st cit.:* 1759 Goldsmith, *The Bee.* *20c. coll.:* Stevenson 2307:7.

speed 1. Speed does not take heed. *Rec. dist.:* Mich., Ont.

2. Speed gets you nowhere if you're headed in the wrong direction. *Rec. dist.:* Colo.

3. They walk with speed who walk alone. *Rec. dist.:* N.J.

SEE ALSO In SKATING over thin ice, our safety is our speed. / Less TALK, more speed. / The TONGUE can speak a word whose speed outsteps the steed.

spell If you can't spell something, you don't know it. *Rec. dist.:* N.C.

spend 1. He who spends more than he should shall not have to spend when he would. *Rec. dist.:* N.Y., S.C. *1st cit.:* 1664 Codrington, *Select Proverbs.* *20c. coll.:* ODEP 764, Stevenson 2197:1.

2. Spend and God will send. *Var.:* Give and spend, and God will send. *Rec. dist.:* Ind., N.C., Tex. *1st cit.:* ca1350 *Douce MS 52.* *20c. coll.:* ODEP 763, Stevenson 2182:4.

3. Whatever you have, spend less. *Rec. dist.:* N.J. *1st cit.:* 1776 Boswell, *Life of Johnson.* *20c. coll.:* Stevenson 2196:14.

4. Who spends before he thinks, will beg before he dies. *Rec. dist.:* Ill. *1st cit.:* 1597 *Politeuphuia Wits Commonwealth.* *20c. coll.:* ODEP 764, Stevenson 2195:9.

SEE ALSO The only way to save an HOUR is spend it wisely. / When the HUSBAND earns well, the wife spends well. / Them as LENDS, spends. / Don't spend all your MONEY in one place. / Earn MONEY before you spend it. / Never spend your MONEY before you have it. / SPARE well and spend well.

spender Great spenders are bad lenders. *Vars.:* **(a)** Great spenders are often bad lenders. **(b)** Great spenders are poor lenders. *Rec. dist.:* Miss., Ont., Wis. *1st cit.:* 1626 Breton, *Soothing of Proverbs;* USca1700 Hubbard, *General History of New England* (1848). *20c. coll.:* ODEP 764, Whiting 409, Stevenson 2195:4.

spendthrift *SEE* A MISER'S son is a spendthrift.

spent *SEE* 'Tis a well-spent PENNY that saves a groat. / Too late to SPARE when all is spent.

spice He that has the spice may season as he pleases. *Rec. dist.:* Mich. *1st cit.:* 1640 Herbert, *Outlandish Proverbs (Jacula Prudentum)* in *Works,* ed. Hutchinson (1941). *20c. coll.:* ODEP 764, Stevenson 1982:2.

SEE ALSO COMPETITION is the spice of business. / HUMOR is the spice of life. / VARIETY is the spice of life.

spider A spider spins his web strand by strand. *Rec. dist.:* Ont.

spigot 1. Some spare at the spigot and let out at the bunghole. *Var.:* Save at the spigot and waste at the bung. *Rec. dist.:* U.S., Can. *1st cit.:* 1642 Torriano, *Select Italian Proverbs;* US1780 *New-York Gazette* in *Newspaper Extracts Relating to New Jersey,* ed. Stryker (1894–1923). *20c. coll.:* ODEP 759, Whiting 409, CODP 208, Stevenson 2182:1, T&W 347, Whiting(MP) 587.

spill See HAPPINESS is a perfume that you cannot pour on others without spilling a little on yourself. / He that spills the RUM loses that only; he that drinks it often loses that and himself.

spilled See Don't CRY over spilt milk. / Spilled WATER cannot be gathered up.

spin See PASSIONS spin the plot. / A SPIDER spins his web strand by strand.

spirit 1. A broken spirit dries the bones. *Rec. dist.:* N.Y.

2. A child's spirit is easily broken and difficult to heal. *Rec. dist.:* N.Y.

3. Be sure you raise no more spirits than you can conjure down. *Rec. dist.:* Mich. *1st cit.:* 1631 Jonson, *New Inn;* US1714 Pennington, *Apostle of New Jersey, John Talbot, 1645–1727* (1938). *20c. coll.:* ODEP 663, Whiting 106, Stevenson 2199:6, T&W 562.

4. He that rules his spirit is better than he that takes a city. *Rec. dist.:* N.Y.

5. It's the spirit that counts. *Rec. dist.:* N.C.

6. The spirit is willing but the flesh is weak. *Rec. dist.:* U.S., Can. *1st cit.:* 1608 Armin, *Nest Ninnies;* US1816 Smith, *Life of Elias Smith.* *20c. coll.:* ODEP 765, Whiting 410, Stevenson 2198:14.

See ALSO Old in BODY, young in spirit. / A DIVIDED man makes an unhappy spirit.

spit 1. Do not spit into the well you may have to drink out of. *Rec. dist.:* Ariz.

2. Who spits against the wind spits in his own face. *Rec. dist.:* Wis. *1st cit.:* 1557 Guevara, *Dialogue of Princes,* tr. North; US1757 *Papers of Benjamin Franklin,* ed. Labaree (1959). *20c. coll.:* ODEP 766, Whiting 485, Stevenson 2199:8, T&W 405, Whiting(MP) 686.

3. Wish in one hand and spit in the other. *Var.:* Spit in one hand and wish in the other, and see which one gets full quickest. *Rec. dist.:* N.Y. *1st cit.:* US1941 Charles, *Vice Czar Murders.* *20c. coll.:* Stevenson 1059:2.

spite See Don't cut off your NOSE to spite your face.

splash You splash me, I splash you. *Rec. dist.:* Ont.

See ALSO Throw a STONE in the mud and it splashes in your face.

split See No man can ride a BRONCO if he ain't split up the middle.

spoil (n.) See You may share the LABORS of the great, but you will not share the spoil. / To the VICTOR belong the spoils.

spoil (v.) See One bad APPLE spoils the lot. / Too many COOKS spoil the broth. / The COST often spoils the relish. / You can't spoil a rotten EGG. / Too many FINGERS spoil the pie. / Dying FLIES spoil the sweetness of the ointment. / It's the little FOXES that spoil the vines. / Too many HANDS spoil the pie. / A little IMPATIENCE spoils great plans. / Too little LEAVEN spoils the loaf. / The NAME may not spoil the man, but the man may spoil the name. / Spare the ROD and spoil the child. / Don't spoil the SHIP for half a penny's worth of tar. / Make a SPOON or spoil a horn. / Untimeous SPURRING spoils the steed. / Even SUGAR itself may spoil a good dish. / Too much SWEET spoils the best coffee.

spoiled See COFFEE boiled is coffee spoiled.

spoke The longer the spoke, the greater the tire. *Var.:* The longer the spoke, the longer the wheel. *Rec. dist.:* Ont., Utah.

spoken That is well spoken that is well taken. *Rec. dist.:* Ont.

See ALSO "IF" is the longest word ever spoken. / A WORD that is not spoken never does any mischief. / Spoken WORDS are like flown birds: neither can be recalled.

sponge See What is SAID is said, and no sponge can wipe it out.

spoon **1.** As a spoon can't taste the flavor of the soup, a fool in the company of the wise learns nothing. *Rec. dist.:* Ill.

2. Every man is not born with a silver spoon in his mouth. *Rec. dist.:* U.S. *1st cit.:* 1639 Clarke, *Paroemiologia;* US1780 Thaxter in *Adams Family Correspondence,* ed. Butterfield (1963). *20c. coll.:* ODEP 76, Whiting 410, CODP 217, Stevenson 559:1, T&W 348. Whiting*(MP)* 588.

3. He must have a long spoon who sups with the devil. *Vars.:* **(a)** He must have a long spoon who must sup with the devil. **(b)** He needs a long spoon who would sup with the devil. **(c)** He that eats with the devil without a long spoon, his fare will be ill. **(d)** If you are going to sup with the devil, find a long spoon. **(e)** Takes a long spoon to eat wid de devil. *Rec. dist.:* U.S., Can. *1st cit.:* ca1390 Chaucer, *Squire's Tale;* US1834 Waddell in *Papers of Thomas Ruffin,* ed. Hamilton (1918–20). *20c. coll.:* ODEP 480, Whiting 410, CODP 217, Stevenson 559:1, Whiting*(MP)* 165.

4. Make a spoon or spoil a horn. *Var.:* Spoil the horn and make a spoon. *Rec. dist.:* Ont. *1st cit.:* 1818 Scott, *Rob Roy. 20c. coll.:* ODEP 500, Stevenson 2201:9.

5. When de spoon want anything, it better go ter de bowl. *Rec. dist.:* N.Y.

spoonful *See* A spoonful of LAUGHING equals a spoonful of crying.

sport **1.** A good sport always wins. *Rec. dist.:* N.C.

2. It is a poor sport that is not worth a candle. *Rec. dist.:* Tex.

3. It is a sport to a fool to do mischief, but a man of understanding has wisdom. *Rec. dist.:* Ont. *1st cit.:* US1948 Stevenson, *Home Book of Proverbs. 20c. coll.:* Stevenson 1587:8.

spot Scratch a tender spot and it will soon be a sore. *Rec. dist.:* Ont.
See also A LEOPARD cannot change his spots. / You can't tell a LEOPARD by its spots.

sprat Set a sprat to catch a mackerel. *Var.:* Risk a sprat to catch a whale. *Rec. dist.:* Ont. *1st cit.:* 1810 Poole, *Hamlet Travestie;* US1797

Cobbett, *Porcupine's Works. 20c. coll.:* ODEP 768, Whiting 441, Stevenson 818:10, T&W 348, Whiting*(MP)* 589.

spread *See* MONEY is like manure: it's only good when spread around. / A man that flatters his NEIGHBOR spreads a net for his feet. / NEWS spreads like wildfire.

spring *(n., season)* **1.** A dry spring, a rainy summer. *Rec. dist.:* Utah.

2. If there's spring in winter and winter in spring, the year won't be good for anything. *Rec. dist.:* Wis. *1st cit.:* 1659 Howell, *Paroimiografia (Spanish Proverbs). 20c. coll.:* Stevenson 2203:1.

3. In the spring a young man's fancy lightly turns to thoughts of love. *Vars.:* **(a)** In spring a young man's fancy lightly turns to what he's been thinking about all winter. **(b)** In spring a young man's fancy turns to what a young woman has been thinking the whole year. **(c)** In the spring a young man's fancy lightly turns to thoughts of home. **(d)** In the spring a young man's fancy turns to thoughts of baseball. **(e)** In the spring a young man's fancy turns to what a girl's been thinking. **(f)** Spring turns a young man's fancy to thoughts of love. *Rec. dist.:* U.S., Can. *1st cit.:* 1842 Tennyson, *Locksley Hall. 20c. coll.:* Stevenson 2203:3.
See also Many CHANGES can take place on a spring day. / Long FALL, late spring. / It takes more than a ROBIN to make spring. / A misty WINTER brings a pleasant spring; a pleasant winter, a misty spring.

spring *(n., water)* **1.** From a pure spring, pure water flows. *Rec. dist.:* Ill., Ont.

2. If you foul the spring, you can't expect the stream to be pure. *Var.:* Pure water flows from a clean spring. *Rec. dist.:* Ill., Ont.

3. Muddy springs will have muddy streams. *Rec. dist.:* Utah. *1st cit.:* US1938 Champion, *Racial Proverbs. 20c. coll.:* Stevenson 2174:16.

spring *(v.)* *See* FEAR always springs from ignorance. / HOPE springs eternal in the human breast. / Taste the JOY that springs from labor. / TROUBLE springs from idleness.

springhouse De springhouse may freeze, but niggers'll keep de shuckpen warm. *Rec. dist.:* N.Y.

springtime Springtime is ring time. *Rec. dist.:* Ont.

spur *(n.)* **1.** A spur in the head is worth two in the feet. *Rec. dist.:* Ont. *1st cit.:* 1668 Skippon, *Diary;* US1832 Kennedy, *Swallow Barn,* ed. Hubbell (1919). *20c. coll.:* ODEP 768, T&W 349, Stevenson 2203:11.

2. The spur in front will not drive you as fast as the spur that is behind. *Rec. dist.:* N.Y., S.C.

3. The spur won't hurt when the hide is thick. *Rec. dist.:* N.Y., S.C. *1st cit.:* US1853 Haliburton, *Sam Slick's Wise Saws.* *20c. coll.:* T&W 349, Stevenson 2203:9.

SEE ALSO The APPLAUSE that pleases the weak mind is but a spur to the strong one. / FEAR is a fine spur; so is rage. / JOYS are our wings; our sorrows, our spurs.

spur *(v.)* SEE Don't spur a willing HORSE. / You needn't KICK before you're spurred.

spurring Untimeous spurring spoils the steed. *Rec. dist.:* Ont. *1st cit.:* 1581 Guazzo, *Civile Conversation,* tr. Pettie, T.T. (1925). *20c. coll.:* ODEP 855, Stevenson 1084:11.

squall Look for squalls, but don't make them. *Rec. dist.:* Ill. *1st cit.:* US1802 *Papers of John Steele,* ed. Wagstaff (1924). *20c. coll.:* Whiting 411.

square SEE You can't put a round PEG in a square hole.

squeak *(n.)* SEE Put the OIL where the squeak is.

squeak *(v.)* SEE If the SADDLE squeaks, it ain't bought.

squeaking SEE The squeaking SHOE isn't paid for. / A squeaking WHEEL never wears out. / The WHEEL that does the squeaking is the one that gets the grease.

squeaky SEE Two empty packing BOXES make the most noise, but the squeaky wheel gets the grease.

squeal SEE Don't RAIN eve'y time de pig squeal.

squirt SEE MAN is a poor stick and a sad squirt.

stab A stab in the back is worse than a kick in the face. *Rec. dist.:* Ill.

stability There is stability in heaven. *Rec. dist.:* Mich.

stable **1.** It's no use to lock the stable after the horse has been stolen. *Rec. dist.:* U.S., Can. *1st cit.:* ca1350 Douce MS 52; US1745 *Correspondence During Law's Governorship of Connecticut, 1741–1750,* Conn.Hist.Soc. *Collections* (1907–14). *20c. coll.:* ODEP 730, Whiting 414, CODP 211, Stevenson 2204:8, T&W 109, Whiting(MP) 182.

2. The stable wears out a horse more than the road. *Rec. dist.:* Ill.

3. Uphill bear him; downhill spare him; on the level let him trot; in stable forget him not. *Rec. dist.:* Ill. *1st cit.:* 1721 Kelly, *Scottish Proverbs.* *20c. coll.:* ODEP 855.

staff **1.** Keep the staff in your own hand. *Rec. dist.:* Ont. *1st cit.:* 1710 Palmer, *Moral Essays on English, Scotch, and Foreign Proverbs;* US1776 Rutledge in *Letters of Members of Continental Congress,* ed. Burnett (1921). *20c. coll.:* ODEP 418, Whiting 412, Stevenson 1235:2.

2. Never trust a broken staff. *Var.:* Trust not a broken staff. *Rec. dist.:* Tex. *1st cit.:* 1580 Gifford, *Posie of Gilloflowers,* ed. Grosart. *20c. coll.:* Stevenson 2205:3.

SEE ALSO BREAD is the staff of life.

stag SEE When the TIGER is dead, the stag dances on his grave.

stage SEE All the WORLD's a stage.

stagnate SEE A standing POOL soon stagnates.

stain The stain of wine is like a stain of blood. *Rec. dist.:* Ill.

stair They who enter by the back stairs may expect to be shown out at the window. *Rec. dist.:* Utah.

SEE ALSO He who is to break his NECK finds the stairs in the dark.

stake An ill stake stands the longest. *Rec. dist.*: N.C. *1st cit.*: 1546 Heywood, *Dialogue of Proverbs,* ed. Habernicht (1963). *20c. coll.*: ODEP 770, Stevenson 2491:9.

stall SEE The fat OX in the stall gives no thought to the hungry as they pass by.

stamp *(n.)* The postage stamp's usefulness lies in the ability to stick. *Rec. dist.*: Utah.

SEE ALSO A love LETTER sometimes costs more than a three-cent stamp.

stamp *(v.)* SEE Every man stamps his VALUE upon himself.

stand *(n.)* SEE A good RUN is better than a bad stand.

stand *(v.)* 1. Don't stand when you can sit, and don't sit when you can lie down. *Rec. dist.*: Ind.

2. Stand up, speak up, and shut up. *Rec. dist.*: Ky., Tenn.

3. When you think you stand, take heed—you may fall. *Var.*: Let him that thinks he stands take heed lest he fall. *Rec. dist.*: Ky., Miss., Tenn. *1st cit.*: USca1656 Bradford, *History of Plymouth Plantation,* ed. Ford (1912). *20c. coll.*: Whiting 413.

SEE ALSO It's not where we stand but in what DIRECTION we are moving. / Stand on your own two FEET. / A HOUSE divided against itself cannot stand. / A KINGDOM divided against itself cannot stand. / A LIE stands on one leg, truth on two. / Every POT must stand upon its own bottom. / An empty SACK won't stand alone. / Let every TUB stand on its own bottom. / UNITED we stand; divided we fall.

standing SEE Be not AFRAID; be only afraid of standing still. / The standing SACK fills quicker. / 'Tis as cheap SITTING as standing.

star 1. Aim for the stars. *Vars.*: (a) Aim at the stars, but keep your feet on the ground. (b) Aim at the stars if you fall to the stumps. (c) Aim for a star even though you hit a cow on the hillside. *Rec. dist.*: Colo., N.Y., Utah.

2. Don't let the stars get in your eyes. *Rec. dist.*: Colo.

3. Follow your own star. *Rec. dist.*: Ill. *1st cit.*:

US1948 Stevenson, *Home Book of Proverbs.* *20c. coll.*: Stevenson 2207:2.

4. Stars are not seen by sunshine. *Rec. dist.*: N.Y., Ont. *1st cit.*: 1732 Fuller, *Gnomologia.* *20c. coll.*: Stevenson 2207:11.

5. There will always be stars if you look to see them. *Rec. dist.*: N.Dak.

6. Those who look up see the stars. *Rec. dist.*: Ala., Ga.

7. When it gets dark, the stars come out. *Rec. dist.*: Ohio.

8. You can't live on a star. *Rec. dist.*: N.C.

9. You can't walk and look at the stars if you have a stone in your shoe. *Rec. dist.*: Ill.

SEE ALSO If you can't be the SUN, be a star. / Hitch your WAGON to a star.

stare The fewer to stare, the better the fare. *Rec. dist.*: Ont. *1st cit.*: 1530 Palsgrave, *Lesclarcissement de la langue Francoyse.* *20c. coll.*: Stevenson 1566:13.

stargazer Stargazers are poor pathfinders. *Rec. dist.*: Colo.

stark SEE The lazy LAD makes a stark old man.

start *(n.)* 1. A good start is half the race. *Var.*: A good start means a good end. *Rec. dist.*: Ill., N.Y., Ont.

2. An early start and a steady pace make the slowest win the race. *Rec. dist.*: Ont.

3. Bad start, good ending. *Rec. dist.*: Oreg. *1st cit.*: ca1300 *Proverbs of Hendying;* US1755 *Writings of George Washington,* ed. Fitzpatrick (1931–44). *20c. coll.*: ODEP 317, Whiting 27, CODP 97, Stevenson 153:9, Whiting(MP) 41.

start *(v.)* 1. Don't start anything you can't finish. *Vars.*: (a) Don't start what you can't finish. (b) Never start what you cannot finish. *Rec. dist.*: U.S., Can. *1st cit.*: 1477 *Dictes and Sayenges of Philosophirs,* tr. Rivers; US1921 O'Neill, *Anna Christie.* *20c. coll.*: Stevenson 154:4.

2. Start sooner, go slower, and live longer. *Rec. dist.*: Ky., Tenn.

SEE ALSO It takes two to start an ARGUMENT.

/ Never start anything important on FRIDAY. / A JOB started right is a job half done. / Start in TIME to be in time. / TROUBLE starts when you start feeling sorry for yourself.

started Getting started is half of the fight. *Rec. dist.:* N.Y.

SEE ALSO Getting THINGS done is largely a matter of getting things started.

starve *SEE* Feed a COLD and starve a fever. / A three years' DROUGHT will not starve a cook. / HONESTY is praised and left to starve. / PIGS grow fat where lambs would starve. / Better starve free than be a SLAVE.

statesman The statesman makes the occasion, but the occasion makes the politician. *Rec. dist.:* N.Y., S.C. *1st cit.:* US1852 Hilliard, Eulogy for Daniel Webster, 30 Nov. *20c. coll.:* Stevenson 2210:6.

station 1. De littler de station, de bigger de agent. *Rec. dist.:* Miss.

2. The little station is the safest. *Rec. dist.:* Ont.

stave Thirteen staves and never a hoop will not make a barrel. *Rec. dist.:* N.Y. *1st cit.:* US1796 Paine, Letter to George Washington, 30 Nov. *20c. coll.:* Stevenson 2407:9.

stay Some people stay longer in an hour than others stay in a week. *Rec. dist.:* Miss.

SEE ALSO Little BOATS should stay close to shore. / Stay on the straight and narrow PATH. / Don't stay with the RABBITS but run with the hounds. / It's easier to stay out than to get out of TROUBLE. / He who stays in the VALLEY will never get over the hill.

steadily *SEE* A full CUP must be carried steadily.

steal 1. He who steals will always fail. *Rec. dist.:* N.Y.

2. It's easy to steal from a cut loaf. *Rec. dist.:* Ont. *1st cit.:* 1593 Shakespeare, *Titus Andronicus.* *20c. coll.:* ODEP 724, CODP 205.

3. Steal all you can with your eyes but never with your hands. *Rec. dist.:* N.Y.

SEE ALSO Better to BEG than to steal, but better to work than to beg. / A howlin' COYOTE ain't stealin' no chickens. / He that

steals an EGG will steal a chicken. / If you LIE, you steal. / He that will steal an OUNCE will steal a pound. / He that will steal a PIN will steal a better thing. / Whoever steals the neighbor's SHIRT usually dies without his own. / Speak your THOUGHTS lest someone steal them. / It is WIT to pick a lock and steal a horse, but wisdom to let it alone.

stealing *SEE* You go to HELL for lying the same as stealing.

steam The steam that blows the whistle never turns the wheel. *Rec. dist.:* Iowa, Ky.

steel *SEE* The TONGUE is not steel, but it cuts.

steep *SEE* No HILL too steep, no sand too deep.

steer *SEE* No telling which way LUCK or a half-broke steer is going to run.

step *(n.)* 1. A step in time saves nine. *Rec. dist.:* Ky., Minn., Tenn. *1st cit.:* 1732 Fuller, *Gnomologia.* *20c. coll.:* Stevenson 2216:6.

2. Don't stare at the steps of success—step up the stairs. *Rec. dist.:* Ill.

3. Don't take two steps and slide back three. *Rec. dist.:* Ky., Tenn.

4. If you are out of step with everyone else, you had better look. *Rec. dist.:* N.C.

5. It's the first step that costs. *Rec. dist.:* Ohio. *1st cit.:* ca1596 Munday, *Sir Thomas More;* US1786 *Patrick Henry: Life, Correspondence and Speeches,* ed. Henry (1891). *20c. coll.:* ODEP 773, Whiting 414, *CODP* 82, Stevenson 2212:3, Whiting(MP) 593.

6. Make one wrong step and down you go. *Rec. dist.:* Ont.

7. One step astray is one step away. *Rec. dist.:* Ohio.

8. Slow are the steps of those who leave their hearts behind. *Rec. dist.:* Ont.

9. Step by step, one goes a long way. *Rec. dist.:* Colo. *1st cit.:* 1611 Cotgrave, *Dictionary of French and English Tongues; 20c. coll.:* ODEP 773.

10. The first step is the hardest. *Rec. dist.:* Ont. *1st cit.:* ca1596 Munday, *Sir Thomas More.*

20c. coll.: ODEP 773, *CODP* 82, Stevenson 2212:3.

11. The hardest step is over the threshold. *Rec. dist.:* Ill. *1st cit.:* 1659 Howell, *Paroimiografia (Italian Proverbs).* *20c. coll.:* Stevenson 2212:6.

12. There is a slippery step at every man's door. *Rec. dist.:* Ky., Tenn.

SEE ALSO A JOURNEY of a thousand miles begins with one step.

step *(v.)* SEE Be a live WIRE and you won't be stepped on.

stepmother There are as many good step-mothers as white ravens. *Rec. dist.:* Ill. *1st cit.:* 1640 Herbert, *Outlandish Proverbs (Jacula Prudentum)* in *Works,* ed. Hutchinson (1941). *20c. coll.:* Stevenson 2213:4.

SEE ALSO If you don't obey your MOTHER, you will obey your stepmother.

stepping-stone SEE FAILURES are the stepping-stones to success. / Make your STUMBLING BLOCKS stepping-stones.

stew *(n.)* SEE First catch your RABBIT and then make your stew.

stew *(v.)* Let him stew in his own brew. *Vars.:* **(a)** Let him stew in his own kettle. **(b)** Let him stew in his own soup. **(c)** Let them stew in their own juice. **(d)** Let them stew in their own juice who unwise deeds perform. *Rec. dist.:* Ont. *1st cit.:* ca1300 *Coer de Lion, Richard* in Weber, *Metrical Romances* (1811); US1733 *Jonathan Belcher Papers,* Mass.Hist.Soc. *Collections* (1893–94). *20c. coll.:* ODEP 292, Whiting 187, Stevenson 1282:7, Whiting*(MP)* 346.

stick *(n.)* **1.** A crooked stick makes a straight fire. *Rec. dist.:* N.Y. *1st cit.:* 1584 Withals, *Short Dictionary.* *20c. coll.:* ODEP 155, Stevenson 458:8.

2. A crooked stick will have a crooked shadow. *Rec. dist.:* Miss., Ont. *1st cit.:* 1640 Herbert, *Outlandish Proverbs (Jacula Prudentum)* in *Works,* ed. Hutchinson (1941). *20c. coll.:* ODEP 769, Stevenson 458:11.

3. A straight stick is crooked in the water. *Rec. dist.:* N.Dak., Ohio. *1st cit.:* 1589 Nashe,

Anatomy of the Absurd; USca1700 *Poems of Edward Taylor,* ed. Stanford (1960). *20c. coll.:* ODEP 778, Whiting 469, Stevenson 2213:9.

4. Don't count your sticks till the lumber's on the pile. *Rec. dist.:* Colo.

5. Little sticks kindle large fires. *Rec. dist.:* N.Y. *1st cit.:* ca1303 Mannyng, *Handlyng Synne,* ed. Furnivall, E.E.T.S. (1901). *20c. coll.:* ODEP 472, Stevenson 807:5.

6. One stick is easier broken than a bunch. *Rec. dist.:* N.C. *1st cit.:* US1677 Hubbard, *History of Indian Wars in New England,* ed. Drake (1865). *20c. coll.:* Whiting 49.

7. Sticks and stones may break my bones, but names will never hurt me. *Vars.:* **(a)** Sticks and stones may break my bones, but words can never hurt me. **(b)** Sticks and stones may break my bones, but words can never touch me. **(c)** Sticks and stones may break your bones, but words will never hurt you. **(d)** Sticks and stones will break my bones, but words will never hurt me. *Rec. dist.:* N.Y. *1st cit.:* 1894 Northall, *Folk Phrases of Four Counties;* US1936 Gibbons, *Miss Linsey.* *20c. coll.:* ODEP 773, Whiting*(MP)* 594, *CODP* 212, Stevenson 2609:6.

8. When you pick up a stick at one end, you also pick up the other end. *Rec. dist.:* Ind., Wash.

9. You can't make a crooked stick lay straight. *Rec. dist.:* Vt.

SEE ALSO He who has a mind to beat a DOG will easily find a stick. / To kill an old DOG you must hide your stick. / LOVE is sharper than stones and sticks. / SPEAK softly and carry a big stick.

stick *(v.)* **1.** Stick in until you stick out. *Rec. dist.:* Ont.

2. Stick together or get stuck separately. *Rec. dist.:* N.Y. *1st cit.:* US1942 Rawson, *No Coffin for the Corpse.* *20c. coll.:* Stevenson 1067:11.

SEE ALSO Don't stick out your HAND further than you can draw it back. / Stick to the old HORSE that carried you safely across. / SHOEMAKER, stick to your last.

stiff *(n.)* SEE "IF" is a big stiff.

stiff *(adj.)* SEE Keep a stiff upper LIP.

still *See* Still HEAD, wise heart. / The still PIG gets all the slop. / A still RIVER never finds the ocean. / SILENCE is a still noise. / TIME never stands still. / A still TONGUE makes a wise head. / No WEATHER's ill if the wind be still.

sting *See* If a BEE stings you once, it's the bee's fault; if a bee stings you twice, it's your own damn fault. / FALSEHOOD is a nettle that stings those who meddle with it. / KNAVES and nettles are akin: stroke 'em kindly, yet they'll sting.

stingy 1. A stingy man gives an egg to get a chicken. *Rec. dist.:* Miss. *1st cit.:* 1869 Henderson, *Latin Proverbs.* *20c. coll.:* Stevenson 952:12. 2. If you're not stingy, you're not wealthy, and if you're not wealthy, you're not stingy. *Rec. dist.:* Ill., Ont.

stink 1. He that is conscious of a stink in his breeches is jealous of every wrinkle in another's nose. *Rec. dist.:* N.Y. *1st cit.:* US1751 Franklin, *PRAlmanac.* *20c. coll.:* Stevenson 780:4.
2. The more you stir a stink, the louder it smells. *Vars.:* **(a)** Stir up stink and it will make more stink. **(b)** The more you stir dirt, the worse it stinks. **(c)** The more you stir it, the worse it stinks. *Rec. dist.:* U.S., Can. *1st cit.:* 1546 Heywood, *Dialogue of Proverbs,* ed. Habernicht (1963); US1689 Mather, "Vindication" in *Andros Tracts,* ed. Whitmore, Publ. Prince Soc. (1868–74). *20c. coll.:* ODEP 775, Whiting 458, Stevenson 2216:1, Whiting(MP) 650.
See also Let every CAT cover up his own stink.

stipend You'll have to preach according to your stipend. *Rec. dist.:* Ont.

stir *See* He who stirs the soup POT eats first. / No QUARREL ever stirred before the second word. / The more you stir a STINK, the louder it smells.

stitch 1. A dropped stitch is soon a hole. *Rec. dist.:* Ill.
2. A stitch in time saves nine. *Vars.:* **(a)** A stitch in time saves nine, and sometimes ninety-nine. **(b)** Stitch in time saves nine. *Rec. dist.:* U.S., Can. *1st cit.:* 1732 Fuller, *Gnomologia;*

US1797 Baily, *Journal of Tour of North America in 1796–1797* (1856). *20c. coll.:* ODEP 775, Whiting 415, *CODP* 213, Stevenson 2216:6, T&W 354, Whiting(MP) 595.
See also CHARACTER, like embroidery, is made stitch by stitch. / HITCHES lead to stitches. / He that doesn't tie a KNOT may lose his first stitch.

stockings *See* A GIRL with cotton stockings never sees a mouse.

stocks *See* Judge not of a SHIP as she lies on the stocks.

stolen *See* Better to give me nothing than stolen ALMS. / Stolen HOURS are the sweetest. / Stolen KISSES are the best. / Stolen WATERS are sweet.

stomach 1. An empty stomach is not a good political adviser. *Rec. dist.:* N.Y. *1st cit.:* US1931 Einstein, *Cosmic Religion.* *20c. coll.:* Stevenson 1201:1.
2. An empty stomach may sometimes vomit. *Rec. dist.:* N.C.
3. Full stomach, contented heart. *Rec. dist.:* N.Mex.
4. Full stomachs make empty heads. *Rec. dist.:* Ind.
5. If it were not for the stomach, the back would wear gold. *Rec. dist.:* Ill. *1st cit.:* 1732 Fuller, *Gnomologia;* US1750 Franklin, *PRAlmanac.* *20c. coll.:* Stevenson 166:5.
6. Lazy folks' stomachs don't get tired. *Rec. dist.:* Ill., Ont. *1st cit.:* US1880 Harris, *Plantation Proverbs* in *Uncle Remus, His Songs and His Sayings.* *20c. coll.:* Stevenson 2217:18.
7. Stuff not your stomach with sweets if you choose to keep your sweet tooth. *Rec. dist.:* Ont.
8. The stomach carries the feet. *Rec. dist.:* Ill. *1st cit.:* 1612 Cervantes, *Don Quixote,* tr. Shelton. *20c. coll.:* Stevenson 2216:11.
9. When the stomach is full the heart is glad. *Rec. dist.:* N.Y.
10. You can win a man through his stomach. *Rec. dist.:* N.C. *1st cit.:* 1845 Ford, *Hand-book for Travellers in Spain;* US1814 Adams, Letter, 15 Apr., in *Works of John Adams,* ed. Cushing

(1904–08). **20c. coll.:** *ODEP* 871, *CODP* 242, Stevenson 165:7 and 2217:8, T&W 179, Whiting*(MP)* 673.

SEE ALSO An ARMY travels on its stomach. / Big EYES mean small stomachs. / A HUNGRY stomach has no ears. / The way to a MAN's heart is through his stomach. / No one can love his NEIGHBOR on an empty stomach. / A RICH person ought to have a strong stomach. / You can't admire SCENERY on an empty stomach.

stone 1. A little stone may upset a large cart. *Rec. dist.:* Ind. *1st cit.:* 1869 Henderson, *Latin Proverbs.* **20c. coll.:** Stevenson 1442:5.

2. A rolling stone gathers no moss. *Vars.:* (a) A rolling stone gathers no moss but picks up a high polish. (b) A rolling stone gathers no moss, but still water becomes stagnant. *Rec. dist.:* U.S., Can. *1st cit.:* ca1377 Langland, *Piers Plowman;* US1721 Wise, *Word of Comfort to Melancholy Country.* **20c. coll.:** *ODEP* 682, Whiting 416, *CODP* 193, Stevenson 2218:6, T&W 355, Whiting*(MP)* 597.

3. A rugged stone grows smooth from hand to hand. *Rec. dist.:* Ohio. *1st cit.:* 1640 Herbert, *Outlandish Proverbs (Jacula Prudentum) in Works,* ed. Hutchinson (1941). **20c. coll.:** *ODEP* 687, Stevenson 2220:2.

4. A small stone in shoe causes large pain in foot. *Rec. dist.:* Ind.

5. A stone that may fit in the wall is never left by the way. *Rec. dist.:* Ohio. *1st cit.:* 1852 Trench, *On Lessons in Proverbs.* **20c. coll.:** Stevenson 2220:16.

6. Don't throw stones at glass houses. *Var.:* Don't throw stones from glass houses. *Rec. dist.:* U.S., Can. *1st cit.:* ca1374 Chaucer, *Troilus and Criseyde;* US1710 Dummer in *William & Mary Coll. Quart.* (1967). **20c. coll.:** *ODEP* 360, Whiting 225, *CODP* 92, Stevenson 1193:2, T&W 194, Whiting*(MP)* 484.

7. Don't throw stones at your neighbors if your own windows are glass. *Rec. dist.:* Miss.

8. He who sits on stone rests twice. *Rec. dist.:* Ont. *1st cit.:* ca1595 Fergusson, *Scottish Proverbs,* ed. Beveridge, S. T.S. (1924). **20c. coll.:** Stevenson 2219:2.

9. It is disgraceful to stumble against the same stone twice. *Rec. dist.:* Ont. *1st cit.:* 1539 Taverner, *Proverbs of Erasmus.* **20c. coll.:** *ODEP* 783, Stevenson 723:8.

10. No man can flay a stone. *Rec. dist.:* Tex. *1st cit.:* 1640 Herbert, *Outlandish Proverbs (Jacula Prudentum) in Works,* ed. Hutchinson (1941). **20c. coll.:** *ODEP* 569, Stevenson 2220:6.

11. No stone ever falls alone. *Rec. dist.:* Wash.

12. One stone alone cannot grind corn. *Rec. dist.:* N.Y.

13. One stone does not make a wall. *Rec. dist.:* Oreg.

14. The man who flings a stone up a mountainside may have it rolled back upon himself. *Rec. dist.:* N.C.

15. Throw a stone in a pack of dogs, and the one that's hit will holler. *Rec. dist.:* Ill.

16. Throw a stone in the mud and it splashes in your face. *Rec. dist.:* Ont.

17. Watch out for the rolling stone. *Rec. dist.:* Ohio.

18. Who holds his peace and gathers stones will find a time to throw them. *Rec. dist.:* N.Y. *1st cit.:* 1599 Minsheu, *Dictionarie in Spanish and English.* **20c. coll.:** *ODEP* 377.

SEE ALSO ANGER is a stone cast at a wasp's nest. / CHARACTER is the diamond that scratches every other stone. / Constant DRIPPING wears away a stone. / People who live in GLASS houses shouldn't throw stones. / He that has a HEAD of glass must not throw stones at another. / LOVE is sharper than stones and sticks. / PATIENCE wears out stones. / Let him that is without SIN cast the first stone. / You can't walk and look at the STARS if you have a stone in your shoe. / STICKS and stones may break my bones, but names will never hurt me. / It's a steady STREAM that wears a stone. / Stone WALLS do not a prison make nor iron bars a cage.

stool 1. Between two stools we come to the ground. *Rec. dist.:* U.S., Can. *1st cit.:* ca1390 Gower, *Confessio Amantis;* US1729 Alexander in *Letters and Papers of Cadwallader Colden,* N.Y.Hist.Soc. *Collections* (1917–37). **20c. coll.:**

ODEP 57, Whiting 417, *CODP* 17, Stevenson 2221:4, T&W 356, Whiting*(MP)* 599.

SEE ALSO Set a FROG on a golden stool, away it hops to reach the pool. / Never be breaking your SHIN on a stool that is not in your way. / The UNINVITED should bring their own stool.

stoop **1.** Stoop low and it will save you many a bump through life. *Var.:* You must learn to stoop as you go through life. *Rec. dist.:* N.C., Ohio. *1st cit.:* US1724 Mather, Remark to Benjamin Franklin. *20c. coll.:* Stevenson 169:4.

2. Stoop to conquer. *Var.:* We must stoop to conquer. *Rec. dist.:* Ill., N.J., N.Y. *1st cit.:* 1773 Goldsmith, *She Stoops to Conquer. 20c. coll.:* Stevenson 403:8.

stop Stop, look, listen. *Rec. dist.:* Ind., Mich., N.J., N.Y. *1st cit.:* US1912 Upton, Warning on railroad crossing signs. *20c. coll.:* Stevenson 2455:5.

SEE ALSO Those who tell one FIB will hardly stop at two.

store **1.** He who has a store should attend to it. *Var.:* He who has a store should attend to it; if he does not, he should sell. *Rec. dist.:* Calif.

2. The worst store is a maid unbestowed. *Rec. dist.:* Ont. *1st cit.:* 1659 Howell, *Paroimiografia. 20c. coll.:* ODEP 921, Stevenson 1503:6.

storehouse The tongue's great storehouse is the heart. *Rec. dist.:* Ont.

storm **1.** After the storm comes the calm. *Vars.:* **(a)** After a storm, the sun always shines. **(b)** There's always quietness after a storm. *Rec. dist.:* U.S., Can. *1st cit.:* ca1200 *Ancrene Riwle;* USca1680 *Voyages of Radisson,* ed. Scull, Publ. Prince Soc. (1885). *20c. coll.:* ODEP 6, Whiting 418, *CODP* 2, Stevenson 2222:2, T&W 54.

2. Don't worry over a storm in a teapot. *Rec. dist.:* Ont. *1st cit.:* 1678 Ormonde, Letter to Earl of Arlington in *History MS Commentary, Ormonde MS;* US1836 Crockett, *Col. Crockett's Exploits and Adventures in Texas. 20c. coll.:* ODEP 778, T&W 367, Stevenson 2221:10, Whiting*(MP)* 614.

3. It's always calm before the storm. *Var.:*

There is always a calm before a storm. *Rec. dist.:* U.S., Can. *1st cit.:* ca1200 *Ancrene Riwle;* US1754 *Works of William Smith, D.D.* (1803). *20c. coll.:* ODEP 6, Whiting 54, Stevenson 2222:2, T&W 54.

4. Ride in the whirlwind and direct the storm. *Rec. dist.:* Ont. *1st cit.:* 1705 Addison, *Campaign. 20c. coll.:* Stevenson 2484:14.

5. Storms make oaks take deeper root. *Rec. dist.:* Ont. *1st cit.:* 1640 Herbert, *Outlandish Proverbs (Jacula Prudentum)* in *Works,* ed. Hutchinson (1941). *20c. coll.:* Stevenson 2369:10.

6. The harder the storm, the sooner it's over. *Rec. dist.:* N.C. *1st cit.:* 1872 Kilvert, *Diary,* 9 June. *20c. coll.:* ODEP 721, *CODP* 201, Stevenson 2222:8.

SEE ALSO Every CLOUD is not a sign of a storm. / Any PORT in a storm. / High REGIONS are never without storms. / Never go to the SEA when a storm is coming. / Small SHOWERS last long, but sudden storms are short. / A vow made in the storm is forgotten in the calm. / WIND precedes a storm.

stormy SEE The calmest HUSBANDS make the stormiest wives.

story **1.** Don't believe that story true that ought not to be true. *Rec. dist.:* N.Y.

2. It's a good story that fills the belly. *Rec. dist.:* Calif., N.Y.

3. No story of success ever starts with if and but. *Rec. dist.:* Ont.

4. One story is good till another is told. *Rec. dist.:* Ont. *1st cit.:* 1593 Greene, *Works;* US1769 *Writings of Samuel Adams,* ed. Cushing (1904–08). *20c. coll.:* Stevenson 2271:12, Whiting 418, Whiting*(MP)* 599.

SEE ALSO There are three SIDES to every story—your side, my side, and the right side. / There are always two TALES to a story.

stove He who sits on a hot stove shall rise again. *Vars.:* **(a)** He who sits on a hot stove gets burned in the end. **(b)** He who sits on a red-hot stove will rise. *Rec. dist.:* Ky., Tenn., Wis.

See also A COOK is no better than her stove.

stovewood Distant stovewood is good stovewood. *Rec. dist.:* Tex.

straight *See* Straight FOLKS never make broken promises. / A HORSE never goes straight up a hill. / The shortest distance between two points is a straight LINE. / Stay on the straight and narrow PATH. / A man never got lost on a straight ROAD. / A crooked STICK makes a straight fire. / A straight STICK looks crooked in water.

strange *See* POLITICS makes strange bedfellows. / TRUTH is stranger than fiction.

stranger 1. Be slow to take when strangers haste to give. *Rec. dist.:* Mich.

2. It is better to be beaten by your own man than kissed by a stranger. *Rec. dist.:* Wis.

strap The tighter the burden strap, 'tis most likely to break. *Rec. dist.:* Ont.

See also A lot of a CHILD's welfare can be done with a razor strap.

straw 1. A straw shows which way the wind blows. *Var.:* Straws show which way the wind is blowing. *Rec. dist.:* U.S., Can. *1st cit.:* 1689 Selden, "Libels" in *Table-Talk;* US1774 Galloway, *Letters of Members of Continental Congress,* ed. Burnett (1921). *20c. coll.:* ODEP 779, Whiting 419, *CODP* 214, Stevenson 2225:3, T&W 357, Whiting*(MP)* 601.

2. People who live in straw houses shouldn't throw bombs. *Rec. dist.:* Ill.

3. The last straw will break the camel's back. *Rec. dist.:* U.S., Can. *1st cit.:* 1655 Bramhall, *Defence of True Liberty of Human Actions;* US1866 Smith, *Bill Arp, So Called.* *20c. coll.:* ODEP 443, T&W 54, *CODP* 128, Stevenson 2226:2, Whiting*(MP)* 600.

See also A DROWNING man will catch at a straw.

strawberry 1. Anything is good with strawberries and cream. *Rec. dist.:* Oreg.

2. One man's strawberries are another man's hives. *Rec. dist.:* N.Y. *1st cit.:* US1945 Cooley, *Eat and Get Slim.* *20c. coll.:* Stevenson 1825:15.

stream 1. A dry stream carries no water. *Rec. dist.:* Kans.

2. A stream never rises higher than its source. *Rec. dist.:* Ont. *1st cit.:* 1578 Proctor, *Gorgious Gallery of Inventions,* ed. Rollins. *20c. coll.:* ODEP 779, *CODP* 215, Stevenson 2227:3.

3. Don't change horses in the middle of the stream. *Rec. dist.:* U.S., Can. *1st cit.:* 1889 Butler, *C.G. Gordon;* US1864Collected Works of Abraham Lincoln, eds. Bassler and Dunlap (1953). *20c. coll.:* *CODP* 34, Stevenson 1178:10, T&W 191, Whiting*(MP)* 325.

4. He that's carried down the stream need not row. *Rec. dist.:* Tex. *1st cit.:* 1732 Fuller, *Gnomologia.* *20c. coll.:* ODEP 103, Stevenson 2227:4.

5. It's a steady stream that wears a stone. *Rec. dist.:* Ont. *1st cit.:* ca1250 *Ancrene Wisse* (1962); US1702 Mather, *Magnalia Christi Americana* (1853–55). *20c. coll.:* *CODP* 42, Whiting 121, Stevenson 2463:1, T&W 111, Whiting*(MP)* 186.

6. It's easy going with the stream. *Rec. dist.:* N.J. *1st cit.:* 1579 Calvin, "Timothy" in *Calvin's Sermons.* *20c. coll.:* Stevenson 2227:4.

7. Little streams make big rivers. *Var.:* Little streams grow into mighty rivers. *Rec. dist.:* Ohio, Ont. *1st cit.:* 1885 Mawr, *Analogous Proverbs.* *20c. coll.:* Stevenson 1035:15.

8. Never cross the stream before you come to it. *Rec. dist.:* Ont. *1st cit.:* 1599 Porter, *Two Angry Women of Abington;* US1850 Longfellow, *Journal,* 29 Apr., in *Life of Henry Wadsworth Longfellow* (1886). *20c. coll.:* Stevenson 2377:12, *CODP* 45, ODEP 156, T&W 43.

9. Shallow streams make the most noise. *Var.:* Shallow streams make more noise. *Rec. dist.:* Idaho, Ont. *1st cit.:* 1576 Sidney, *Lady of May.* *20c. coll.:* ODEP 719.

10. Strive not against the stream. *Var.:* No striving against the stream. *Rec. dist.:* Okla., Tex. *1st cit.:* ca1275 *Proverbs of Alfred,* tr. Skeat; US1685 *Diary of Samuel Sewall, 1674–1729,* Mass.Hist.Soc. *Collections* (1878–82). *20c. coll.:* ODEP 782, Whiting 420, Stevenson 2226:7.

11. The stream is always purer at its source.

Rec. dist.: Okla. *1st cit.:* 1590 Spenser, *Faerie Queene. 20c. coll.:* Stevenson 2147:17.

12. We must run with the stream. *Rec. dist.:* Mich. *1st cit.:* 1593 Nashe, *Christ's Tears. 20c. coll.:* Stevenson 2227:4.

SEE ALSO Big BUCKETS can be filled at small streams. / LIFE is a bubble on the stream.

street 1. An easy street is hard to find. *Rec. dist.:* N.J.

2. Easy street never leads anywhere. *Rec. dist.:* Ohio.

3. Easy street often turns out to be nothing more than a blind alley. *Var.:* Easy street is always a dead-end street or a blind alley. *Rec. dist.:* N.Y.

4. On anxiety street there are plenty of neighbors. *Rec. dist.:* Ont.

SEE ALSO An ANGEL on the street, a devil at home. / GRASS doesn't grow on a busy street. / HAIR never grows on a busy street.

streetcar Don't get on the streetcar before it stops. *Rec. dist.:* Ont.

strength 1. Do not burden today's strength with tomorrow's load. *Rec. dist.:* Ont.

2. In unity there is strength. *Vars.:* **(a)** In union there is stength. **(b)** In unity is strength; what we have we hold. **(c)** There is strength in union. **(d)** 'Tis not in numbers but in unity that our great strength lies. **(e)** Union gives strength. *Rec. dist.:* U.S., Can. *1st cit.:* ca1526 Erasmus, *Dicta Sapientum,* tr. Berthelet; US1654 *Complete Writings of Roger Williams* (1963). *20c. coll.:* ODEP 854, Whiting 461, CODP 236, Stevenson 2407:6, T&W 390, Whiting(MP) 656.

3. It is not strength but art that obtains the prize. *Rec. dist.:* N.Y., Ont. *1st cit.:* 1720 *Iliad,* tr. Pope. *20c. coll.:* Stevenson 2228:1.

4. The strength will with the burden grow. *Rec. dist.:* N.Y., S.C. *1st cit.:* US1865 Taylor, *Abraham Lincoln. 20c. coll.:* Stevenson 2228:7.

5. There is strength in numbers. *Rec. dist.:* Calif., Mich., N.Y. *1st cit.:* ca1759 Collins, *Ode to Simplicity. 20c. coll.:* Stevenson 1703:4.

6. We all have strength enough to bear the misfortunes of others. *Rec. dist.:* N.Y. *1st cit.:* 1706 Pope, *Thoughts on Various Subjects;* US1740 Franklin, *PRAlmanac. 20c. coll.:* Stevenson 1596:8, ODEP 780.

7. Where there is great strength, there ain't apt to be much gumption. *Rec. dist.:* N.Y. *1st cit.:* US1853 Haliburton, *Sam Slick's Wise Saws. 20c. coll.:* Stevenson 2227:5.

SEE ALSO Good ACTIONS give strength to ourselves and inspire good actions in others. / If you faint in the days of ADVERSITY, your strength is small. / Using our BRAINS is often wiser than depending on our strength. / When we lift the BURDENS of others, we are developing strength to bear our own. / A WOMAN'S strength is in her tongue.

stretch SEE Don't stretch out your ARM farther than the sleeve will reach.

strife Strife makes friendship stronger. *Rec. dist.:* Oreg.

SEE ALSO HATRED stirs up strife. / HOPE and fear, peace and strife, make up the troubled web of life. / WOMEN and dogs cause too much strife.

strike SEE If you must strike a man from behind, slap him on the BACK. / Strike my DOG and you strike me. / Strike while your EMPLOYER has a big contract. / The GAME's not over until the last man strikes out. / Strike while the IRON is hot. / LIGHTNING never strikes in the same place twice.

striking SEE Striking MANNERS are bad manners.

string *(n.)* **1.** If you have strings, pull them. *Rec. dist.:* Miss. *1st cit.:* 1929 Elam, *George Borrow. 20c. coll.:* Whiting(MP) 603.

2. It's good to have two strings to one's bow. *Rec. dist.:* N.Y., Tex. *1st cit.:* ca1477 Caxton, *Jason;* US1650 *Works of Anne Bradstreet,* ed. Ellis (1932). *20c. coll.:* ODEP 852, Whiting 421, Stevenson 2230:4, T&W 358, Whiting(MP) 603.

3. String cannot be made from stone. *Rec. dist.:* N.J.

4. The tighter the string, the sooner it will break. *Rec. dist.:* N.Dak. *1st cit.:* ca1594 Bacon, *Promus. 20c. coll.:* ODEP 781.

string *(v.)* SEE String your PEARLS on a strong cord.

stripe SEE You can tell a ZEBRA by his stripes.

strive **1.** Strive and succeed. *Rec. dist.:* Ohio.

2. Strive though you fail. *Rec. dist.:* Ohio.

3. Who may not strive may yet fulfill the harder task of standing still. *Rec. dist.:* Pa.

stroke **1.** Different strokes for different folks. *Rec. dist.:* U.S.

2. Little strokes fell great oaks. *Vars.:* **(a)** Small strokes cut down the oaks. **(b)** Small strokes fell big oaks. *Rec. dist.:* U.S., Can. *1st cit.:* ca1370 Chaucer, *Romance of Rose;* US1750 Franklin, *PRAlmanac.* *20c. coll.:* ODEP 782, Whiting 421, *CODP* 135, Stevenson 1705:5, Whiting*(MP)* 603.

3. One stroke fells not an oak. *Var.:* An oak is not felled at one stroke. *Rec. dist.:* Tex. *1st cit.:* ca1370 Chaucer, *Romance of Rose.* *20c. coll.:* ODEP 584, *CODP* 135, Stevenson 1705:5.

strong *(n.)* The strong and the weak cannot keep company. *Rec. dist.:* Ind.

SEE ALSO Tain't the BIGGEST en de strongest dat does de mostest in dis world.

strong *(adj.)* **1.** He that is not strong should be cunning. *Rec. dist.:* Minn. *1st cit.:* 1736 Bailey, "Wile" in *Dictionary.* *20c. coll.:* Stevenson 470:4.

2. The strong man and the waterfall channel their own path. *Rec. dist.:* N.Y. *1st cit.:* 1871 Smiles, *Character.* *20c. coll.:* Stevenson 2228:9.

3. To be strong is to be happy. *Rec. dist.:* N.Y. *1st cit.:* US1851 Longfellow, *Golden Legend.* *20c. coll.:* Stevenson 1070:5.

SEE ALSO The weaker the ARGUMENT, the stronger the words. / A strong BODY makes the mind strong. / The weaker the BODY, the stronger the mind. / BREED is stronger than pasture. / A good CAUSE makes a stout heart and a strong arm. / A CHAIN is no stronger than its weakest link. / KINDNESS is stronger than force. / MALICE has a sharp sight and a strong memory. / Good NATURE is stronger than tomahawks. / A RICH person ought to have a strong stomach. / Some TASKS require a strong back and a weak mind. / Your WISHBONE is stronger than your backbone.

struggle SEE While the KINGFISHER and the oyster are struggling, the fisherman gets both.

stubble There is stubble only where the harvest has been. *Rec. dist.:* Ill. *1st cit.:* US1948 Stevenson, *Home Book of Proverbs.* *20c. coll.:* Stevenson 44:6.

student **1.** If the student hasn't learned, the teacher hasn't taught. *Rec. dist.:* Calif.

2. You can lead a student to college, but you cannot make him think. *Rec. dist.:* Wis.

studious SEE LEARNING to the studious and riches to the careful.

study *(n.)* Diligent study makes for a full cup of life's pleasures. *Rec. dist.:* N.Y.

SEE ALSO ACTION without study is fatal; study without action is fatal.

study *(v.)* **1.** It's not the number of hours you study that counts, but how you study. *Rec. dist.:* N.C.

2. Let him study who wishes to get knowledge. *Rec. dist.:* R.I.

3. Study long and study wrong. *Rec. dist.:* S.C.

4. The more we study, the more we discover our ignorance. *Rec. dist.:* Ill., Miss., Ont.

5. The more you study, the more you forget. *Rec. dist.:* Iowa.

SEE ALSO Study the PAST if you would divine the future.

stumble *(n.)* A stumble may prevent a fall. *Rec. dist.:* Miss., N.Y. *1st cit.:* 1732 Fuller, *Gnomologia.* *20c. coll.:* ODEP 783, Stevenson 747:1.

stumble *(v.)* **1.** To stumble once is better than to be always tottering. *Rec. dist.:* Ont.

2. Wisely and slowly—they stumble that run fast. *Rec. dist.:* Ont. *1st cit.:* 1594 Shakespeare, *Romeo and Juliet.* *20c. coll.:* Stevenson 2142:7.

3. You will not stumble while on your knees. *Rec. dist.:* N.Y.

SEE ALSO WALK too fast and stumble over nothing.

stumbling block 1. Don't be stumbling blocks but stepping-stones. *Rec. dist.:* Miss.

2. Make your stumbling blocks stepping-stones. *Rec. dist.:* N.Y., S.C.

3. The only difference between stumbling blocks and stepping-stones is the way you use them. *Rec. dist.:* Ont., Wis.

stupidity *SEE* RASCALITY has limits; stupidity has not.

sturgeon *SEE* Every FISH is not a sturgeon.

style 1. A bad style is better than a lewd story. *Rec. dist.:* Mich.

2. Style is the dress of thoughts. *Rec. dist.:* N.Y. *1st cit.:* 1711 Pope, *Essay on Criticism.* *20c. coll.:* Stevenson 2235:8.

3. The style is the man. *Vars.:* **(a)** The style is the man himself. **(b)** The style is the man; the hand is the gentleman. *Rec. dist.:* N.Y., S.C. *1st cit.:* 1621 Burton, *Anatomy of Melancholy;* USca1852 Ballou, *Sermons.* *20c. coll.:* ODEP 783, Stevenson 2235:2, *CODP* 216.

SEE ALSO COURTESY is one habit that never goes out of style. / No matter how FASHIONS change, a ruffled temper will never be in style.

subject 1. Little subjects decide big ones. *Rec. dist.:* Ohio.

2. You may talk too much on the best of subjects. *Rec. dist.:* N.Y. *1st cit.:* US1745 Franklin, *PRAlmanac.* *20c. coll.:* Stevenson 2277:2.

SEE ALSO Write on one SIDE of the paper but on both sides of the subject.

substance Beware lest you lose the substance by grasping the shadow. *Vars.:* **(a)** Never give up the substance for the shadow. **(b)** Take not the shadow for the substance. *Rec. dist.:* Ont. *1st cit.:* 1548 Hall, *Chronicle of Lancastre and York;* US1632 Peirce in Bradford, *History of Plymouth Plantation,* ed. Ford (1912). *20c. coll.:* ODEP 110, Whiting 385, Stevenson 2079:12.

succeed 1. If at first you don't succeed, try, try again. *Vars.:* **(a)** If at first you don't succeed, keep on sucking till you do succeed. **(b)** If at first you don't succeed, keep on sucking till you do suck a seed. *Rec. dist.:* U.S., Can. *1st cit.:* 1847 Marryat, *Children of New Forest;*

US1840 Palmer, *Teacher's Manual.* *20c. coll.:* Stevenson 2397:3, *CODP* 216, Whiting(MP) 604.

2. Succeed or die trying. *Rec. dist.:* Calif.

SEE ALSO If you miss the first BUTTONHOLE, you will not succeed in buttoning up your coat. / The same GAME does not often succeed twice. / Always LATE, never succeed. / REASON succeeds where force fails. / STRIVE and succeed. / Nothing succeeds like SUCCESS. / Second TRIALS often succeed. / WAR is a business that ruins those who succeed in it.

succeeding *SEE* YIELDING is sometimes the best way of succeeding.

success 1. The key to success is the ability to apply the seat of the pants to the seat of a chair. *Rec. dist.:* Colo., N.Y.

2. A man is really a success when flattery gives him a headache instead of a big head. *Rec. dist.:* Wis.

3. A selfish success is a successful failure. *Rec. dist.:* Fla.

4. Confidence in success is almost success. *Rec. dist.:* Wis.

5. Deserve success and it will come. *Var.:* Deserve success if you wish to command it. *Rec. dist.:* Ont.

6. Few have earned large success who didn't save part of their small earnings. *Rec. dist.:* N.Y.

7. Getting what you go after is called success, but liking it while you are getting it is happiness. *Rec. dist.:* Wis.

8. Great success is always preceded by great preparation. *Rec. dist.:* Kans., Ky., Tenn.

9. In peace or in war, your success of tomorrow depends upon the preparation you are making today. *Rec. dist.:* Wis.

10. In success be moderate. *Rec. dist.:* Ill. *1st cit.:* US1734 Franklin, *PRAlmanac.* *20c. coll.:* Stevenson 2236:6.

11. Just pushing ahead will open the door to success much quicker than pulling. *Rec. dist.:* Miss.

12. Meet success like a gentleman and disaster like a man. *Rec. dist.:* N.Y.

13. Men buy success by giving up a lot of things they want for what they want most of all. *Rec. dist.:* Ind.

14. No story of success ever starts with if and but. *Rec. dist.:* Ont.

15. Nothing succeeds like success. *Rec. dist.:* U.S., Can. *1st cit.:* 1868 Helps, *Realmah;* US1867 Richardson, *Beyond the Mississippi.* *20c. coll.:* ODEP 581, T&W 359, CODP 165, Stevenson 2236:5, Whiting*(MP)* 453.

16. One thing better than success is to be worthy of success. *Rec. dist.:* Fla.

17. Success at first often undoes men at last. *Rec. dist.:* Ill.

18. Success comes in cans, failures in can'ts. *Rec. dist.:* N.C.

19. Success comes in rising every time you fall. *Rec. dist.:* Wis.

20. Success comes to those who are too busy to look for it. *Rec. dist.:* Utah.

21. Success covers a multitude of blunders. *Rec. dist.:* Ill.

22. Success has ruined many a man. *Var.:* Success leads men astray to their ruin. *Rec. dist.:* Ill., Ind., N.Y. *1st cit.:* US1752 Franklin, *PRAlmanac. 20c. coll.:* Stevenson 2236:15.

23. Success is a chain of gold—but it is a chain. *Rec. dist.:* Ind.

24. Success is a matter of using one's time well. *Rec. dist.:* N.C.

25. Success is first a dream. *Rec. dist.:* Calif.

26. Success is never blamed. *Rec. dist.:* Calif. *1st cit.:* 1732 Fuller, *Gnomologia. 20c. coll.:* Stevenson 2236:1.

27. Success is never final. *Rec. dist.:* Utah.

28. Success is operated on a self-service basis. *Rec. dist.:* Ohio.

29. Success is the child of audacity. *Rec. dist.:* Ill. *1st cit.:* 1846 Disraeli, *Iskander. 20c. coll.:* Stevenson 2237:3.

30. Success is the size of a hole a man can leave when he dies. *Rec. dist.:* Calif.

31. Success is two percent inspiration and ninety-eight percent perspiration. *Rec. dist.:* Mich., Vt. *Infm.:* Cf. genius.

32. Success is where you find it. *Rec. dist.:* Fla.

33. Success makes a fool seem wise. *Rec. dist.:* Wis. *1st cit.:* 1707 Mapletoft, *Select Proverbs. 20c. coll.:* ODEP 784, Stevenson 2236:14.

34. Success makes fools admired, makes villains honest. *Rec. dist.:* Ill.

35. Success makes success as money makes money. *Rec. dist.:* Ill. *1st cit.:* 1967 Richardson, *Courtesans;* US1927 Martin, *Mosaic. 20c. coll.:* Whiting*(MP)* 605.

36. Success never needs an excuse. *Rec. dist.:* Ill.

37. Success often costs more than it is worth. *Rec. dist.:* Ill.

38. Success ruins a fool. *Rec. dist.:* Ala., Ga. *1st cit.:* 1732 Fuller, *Gnomologia. 20c. coll.:* Stevenson 845:7.

39. Success soon pales. *Rec. dist.:* Ill.

40. The door of the room to success always swings on the hinges of opposition. *Rec. dist.:* Wis.

41. The door to success is labeled push. *Rec. dist.:* Wis.

42. The first element of success is the will to succeed. *Rec. dist.:* Wis.

43. The more you lean on somebody else, the leaner your chances of success. *Rec. dist.:* Ill.

44. The secret of success is constancy to purpose. *Rec. dist.:* N.Y. *1st cit.:* 1872 Disraeli, Speech in London, 24 June. *20c. coll.:* Stevenson 1920:6.

45. The success of the wicked entices many more. *Rec. dist.:* Ill. *1st cit.:* US1948 Stevenson, *Home Book of Proverbs. 20c. coll.:* Stevenson 2492:5.

46. The worst use that can be made of success is to boast of it. *Rec. dist.:* Ill.

47. There is no such thing as success in bad business. *Rec. dist.:* Minn.

48. When we think we may fail, we are often near success. *Rec. dist.:* Ont.

49. You can't be a howling success by simply howling. *Rec. dist.:* Iowa.

50. You won't find many rules for success that work unless you do. *Rec. dist.:* Colo.

SEE ALSO ACTION is the basis of success. / A bold ATTEMPT is half success. / An optimistic ATTITUDE is half of success. / CHARACTER is the cornerstone of success. / DILIGENCE is the mistress of success. / Earnest EFFORT leads to success. / FAILURE teaches success. / If we blame others for our FAILURES, we should also give them credit for our successes. / INDUSTRY is the parent of success. / Good LUCK is a lazy man's explanation of another's success. / PUNCTUALITY is the first rung on the ladder of success. / The only justification of REBELLION is success. / SYSTEM spoils success.

successful **1.** Count no man successful until he is dead. *Rec. dist.:* N.Y. *1st cit.:* US1941 Updegraff, *Hills Look Down.* *20c. coll.:* Stevenson 527:2.

2. Successful people are the ones who admit they haven't accomplished everything. *Rec. dist.:* Minn.

3. Successful people do what failures put off until tomorrow. *Rec. dist.:* Oreg.

SEE ALSO Better to be FAITHFUL than successful. / To be successful in LOVE, one must know how to begin and when to stop.

succor Succor never comes too late. *Rec. dist.:* Ill., N.J.

sucker **1.** Never give a sucker an even break. *Rec. dist.:* U.S., Can. *Infm.:* Attributed to Texas Guinan, a popular jazz singer and nightclub owner, ca1920. *1st cit.:* US1925 *Collier's,* 26 Nov. *20c. coll.:* CODP 216, Whiting*(MP)* 605.

2. Suckers will bite. *Rec. dist.:* Ky., Tenn.

3. There's a sucker born every minute. *Vars.:* **(a)** A sucker is born every minute. **(b)** A sucker is born every minute, and two to take him. **(c)** Another sucker is born everyday. **(d)** In the West a sucker is born every minute, but in New York they appear in chunks of roe. *Rec. dist.:* U.S. *1st cit.:* USca1850 Barnum, Maxim. *20c. coll.:* Stevenson 2237:13.

suction Keep out of the suction of those who drift backward. *Rec. dist.:* N.Dak.

sudden SEE Sudden FRIENDSHIP, sure repentance. / A sudden LIE has best luck.

suddenly SEE Who ANSWERS suddenly, knows little.

sue SEE Sue a BEGGAR, and you'll get a louse.

suffer SEE They COMPLAIN most who suffer least. / It is better to suffer an INJURY than to inflict one. / It is better to suffer INJUSTICE than to do it. / To LIVE long is to suffer long. / People who do not keep their PROMISES are sure to suffer for it sooner or later. / Better suffer for TRUTH than prosper by falsehood. / It is better to suffer WRONG than to do wrong.

suffering A man in suffering finds relief in rehearsing his ills. *Rec. dist.:* N.C.

SEE ALSO COURAGE comes through suffering. / Beneath SATIN and silk there is much suffering. / SILENCE in time of suffering is best.

sufficient SEE A WORD to the wise is sufficient.

sugar **1.** Even sugar itself may spoil a good dish. *Rec. dist.:* Tex.

2. If you want sugar, ask for it; don't go scratching around the bowl. *Rec. dist.:* Colo.

3. The sugar of life is often bittersweet. *Rec. dist.:* N.Y.

4. Use sugar more than vinegar. *Rec. dist.:* Ont.

suggestion It is easier to make a suggestion than to carry it out. *Rec. dist.:* Calif.

suit *(n.)* That suit is best that best fits me. *Vars.:* **(a)** That suit is best that fits me. **(b)** That suit is best which fits me. *Rec. dist.:* Okla., Tex. *1st cit.:* 1639 Clarke, *Paroemiologia.* *20c. coll.:* ODEP 786, Stevenson 625:5.

suit *(v.)* SEE Suit the ACTION to the word. / What you can't GET is just what suits you.

suitor The last suitor wins the maid. *Rec. dist.:* Ont. *1st cit.:* 1611 Cotgrave, *Dictionary of French and English Tongues.* *20c. coll.:* ODEP 786, Stevenson 2591:9.

summer Hot summer, cold winter. *Rec. dist.:* N.J., Ohio.

See also The CUCKOO of summer is the scald crow of winter. / A summer's FOG will roast a hog. / He that gathers in summer is a wise SON. / No SUN, no showers, no summer flowers. / One SWALLOW does not make a summer. / WINTER eats what summer gets.

sun **1.** After the clouds, the sun shines. *Rec. dist.:* N.Y. *1st cit.:* ca1374 Chaucer, *Troilus and Criseyde.* *20c. coll.:* Stevenson 2244:7.

2. As the sun rises, man's hope revives. *Rec. dist.:* Ala., Ga.

3. Behind the clouds, the sun is shining. *Vars.:* **(a)** Somewhere behind the clouds the sun is shining. **(b)** The sun is always shining behind the clouds. *Rec. dist.:* Calif., Minn. *1st cit.:* US1841 Longfellow, *Rainy Day.* *20c. coll.:* Stevenson 2245:2.

4. February sun is dearly won. *Rec. dist.:* Ont.

5. If you can't be the sun, be a star. *Rec. dist.:* Ont.

6. In every country the sun rises in the morning. *Rec. dist.:* N.Y., Tex. *1st cit.:* 1640 Herbert, *Outlandish Proverbs (Jacula Prudentum)* in *Works,* ed. Hutchinson (1941). *20c. coll.:* ODEP 787, Stevenson 2249:8.

7. Let not the sun set on your anger. *Var.:* Let not the sun go down upon your wrath. *Rec. dist.:* U.S., Can. *1st cit.:* 1642 Fuller, "Of Anger" in *Holy State.* *20c. coll.:* Stevenson 2649:8.

8. Never let the sun set on work undone. *Rec. dist.:* Miss., N.Y., Wash.

9. Never shut out the January sun. *Rec. dist.:* Ont.

10. No sun, no showers, no summer flowers. *Rec. dist.:* Ont.

11. Somewhere the sun is shining; somewhere a little rain is falling. *Rec. dist.:* N.Y. *1st cit.:* US1906 Harris, *Somewhere.* *20c. coll.:* Stevenson 2244:7.

12. Sun follows the rain. *Rec. dist.:* Ind. *1st cit.:* ca1374 Chaucer, *Troilus and Criseyde;* USca1870 Miller, *For Princess Maud.* *20c. coll.:* Stevenson 2244:7.

13. The morning sun never lasts a day. *Rec.*

dist.: Ind., Tex. *1st cit.:* 1640 Herbert, *Outlandish Proverbs (Jacula Prudentum)* in *Works,* ed. Hutchinson (1941). *20c. coll.:* ODEP 544, Whiting 424, Stevenson 2243:7.

14. The same sun that will melt butter will harden clay. *Rec. dist.:* N.C. *1st cit.:* 1551 Cranmer, *Answer to Gardiner.* *20c. coll.:* ODEP 365, Stevenson 1116:13.

15. The sun doesn't shine on both sides of the hedge at once. *Rec. dist.:* Ariz. *1st cit.:* 1879 Jeffries, *Wild Life in South Country.* *20c. coll.:* ODEP 786.

16. The sun is not less bright for sitting on a dunghill. *Rec. dist.:* Mich. *1st cit.:* ca1303 Mannyng, *Handlyng Synne,* ed. Furnivall, E.E.T.S. (1901). *20c. coll.:* ODEP 787, Stevenson 2242:6.

17. The sun never hurt an honest man's face. *Rec. dist.:* Minn.

18. The sun never repents of the good he does, nor does he ever demand a recompense. *Rec. dist.:* N.Y. *1st cit.:* US1735 Franklin, *PRAlmanac.* *20c. coll.:* Stevenson 2243:3.

19. The sun never sets on the British Isles. *Rec. dist.:* N.Y. *1st cit.:* 1829 Wilson, *Noctes Ambrosianae;* US1898 Dunne, *On Victorian Era.* *20c. coll.:* Stevenson 693:5.

20. The sun shines on all the world. *Rec. dist.:* N.J. *1st cit.:* 1552 Latimer, *Sermons.* *20c. coll.:* ODEP 787, Stevenson 2244:1.

21. The sun shines on the evil as well as the good. *Var.:* The sun shines on the just and the unjust. *Rec. dist.:* Ill. *1st cit.:* 1552 Latimer, *Sermons;* US1805 *Memoirs of John Quincy Adams,* ed. Adams (1874–77). *20c. coll.:* ODEP 787, Whiting 424, Stevenson 2244:1.

22. The sun will shine through the darkest clouds. *Rec. dist.:* N.Y. *1st cit.:* 1546 Heywood, *Dialogue of Proverbs,* ed. Habernicht (1963). *20c. coll.:* Stevenson 2244:7.

23. Though the sun shine, leave not your cloak at home. *Rec. dist.:* N.Y. *1st cit.:* ca1390 Chaucer, *Proverbs.* *20c. coll.:* ODEP 12.

24. When the sun goes red to bed, 'twill rain tomorrow, it is said. *Var.:* If the sun goes pale to bed, 'twill rain tomorrow, it is said. *Rec.*

dist.: U.S., Can. *1st cit.*: 1838 Bray, *Traditions of Devon.* *20c. coll.*: Stevenson 2243:10.

25. When the sun is in the west, lazy folks work best. *Rec. dist.*: N.Y., Ont.

26. While the sun is shining, it is day. *Rec. dist.*: N.Y. *1st cit.*: 1528 Tyndale, *Obedience of a Christian Man.* *20c. coll.*: ODEP 170.

27. You can't see the sun when you're crying. *Rec. dist.*: N.Y.

See ALSO For AGE and want, save while you may, for no morning sun lasts all day. / Happy is the BRIDE the sun shines on. / It's a low BUSH that the sun never shines on. / One CLOUD is enough to eclipse all the sun. / The FLAME of a setting sun tells you there are better days to come. / Make HAY while the sun shines. / He that has a HEAD of wax must not walk in the sun. / The LORD sends sun at one time, rain at another. / There's nothing NEW under the sun. / If there were no RAIN, there'd be no hay to make when the sun shines. / No man sees the SHADOW who faces the sun. / Defer not till TOMORROW to be wise: tomorrow's sun to you may never rise. / Back the WIND and front the sun.

sunbeam A single sunbeam drives away many shadows. *Rec. dist.*: Ont.

Sunday Sunday oils the wheels of the week. *Rec. dist.*: Ont.

sunny **1.** Keep your sunny side up. *Rec. dist.*: Mich., N.Y., Ont.

2. Look on the sunny side of life. *Rec. dist.*: Mich., N.Y. *1st cit.*: 1726 Wesley, *Sermons* in *Works* (1872); US1942 Wentworth, *Pursuit of a Parcel.* *20c. coll.*: ODEP 482, Stevenson 1726:7.

sunrise The sunrise never failed us yet. *Rec. dist.*: Ont. *1st cit.*: US1872 Thaxter, *Sunrise Never Failed Us Yet.* *20c. coll.*: Stevenson 2243:8.

See ALSO The COCK crows at sunrise to tell us to rise.

sunset See LAUGH before breakfast, cry before sunset.

sunshine **1.** After sunshine come showers; after pleasure comes sorrow. *Rec. dist.*: Va. *1st cit.*: 1709 Dykes, *English Proverbs.* *20c. coll.*: Stevenson 2244:7.

2. All sunshine makes a desert. *Rec. dist.*: Calif.

3. Stand in the sunshine and the shadow will fall behind. *Rec. dist.*: Ont., W.Va.

4. Sunshine and showers make up life's hours. *Rec. dist.*: Ont.

5. Sunshine follows rain. *Rec. dist.*: U.S., Can. *1st cit.*: ca1374 Chaucer, *Troilus and Criseyde;* USca1870 Miller, *For Princess Maud.* *20c. coll.*: Stevenson 2244:7.

6. Take the sunshine with the rain. *Rec. dist.*: Ont.

7. We never appreciate the sunshine and the rainbow until the storm clouds hang low. *Rec. dist.*: N.C.

See ALSO Fresh AIR and sunshine and plenty of grace slam the door in the doctor's face. / STARS are not seen by sunshine.

sup **1.** He who sups late sups well. *Rec. dist.*: N.Y.

2. Hot sup, hot swallow. *Rec. dist.*: Ont. *1st cit.*: ca1400 *Latin MS 394,* ed. Pantin, in *Bulletin of J. Rylands Library.* *20c. coll.*: ODEP 388.

superior *(n.)* Yield to your superiors. *Rec. dist.*: Mich. *1st cit.*: 1574 Guazzo, *Civile Conversation,* tr. Pettie, T.T. (1925). *20c. coll.*: Stevenson 159:4.

superior *(adj.)* See He who can take ADVICE is sometimes superior to those who give it.

supper **1.** Better lose a supper than have a hundred physicians. *Rec. dist.*: Ill.

2. Eat few suppers and you'll need few medicines. *Rec. dist.*: Miss., N.Y., S.C. *1st cit.*: ca1546 Heywood, *Dialogue of Proverbs,* ed. Habernicht (1963); US1742 Franklin, *PRAlmanac.* *20c. coll.*: ODEP 252, Whiting 425, Stevenson 2248:10.

3. He that steals the old man's supper does him no wrong. *Rec. dist.*: Utah. *1st cit.*: 1640 Herbert, *Outlandish Proverbs (Jacula Prudentum)* in *Works,* ed. Hutchinson (1941); US1737 Franklin, *PRAlmanac.* *20c. coll.*: ODEP 924, Whiting 276, Stevenson 27:1.

4. Lightest suppers make long lives. *Rec. dist.*:

Ont. *1st cit.:* ca1550 *Reliquiae Antiquae,* ed. Halliwell. *20c. coll.:* Stevenson 573:3.

5. Suppers kill more than the greatest doctors can cure. *Rec. dist.:* Vt. *1st cit.:* 1640 Herbert, *Outlandish Proverbs (Jacula Prudentum)* in *Works,* ed. Hutchinson (1941). *20c. coll.:* ODEP 789, Stevenson 2248:12.

SEE ALSO After DINNER sit awhile; after supper walk a mile. / HOPE is a good breakfast, but it is a bad supper.

supperless Better go to bed supperless than rise in debt. *Var.:* Rather go to bed supperless than run in debt for a breakfast. *Rec. dist.:* Wash. *1st cit.:* 1654 Fuller, "Grand Assizes" in *Sermons;* US1739 Franklin, *PRAlmanac.* *20c. coll.:* ODEP 53, Whiting 24, Stevenson 528:8.

supping Sleep without supping and wake without owing. *Rec. dist.:* N.Y. *1st cit.:* 1640 Herbert, *Outlandish Proverbs (Jacula Prudentum)* in *Works,* ed. Hutchinson (1941); US1757 Franklin, *PRAlmanac.* *20c. coll.:* ODEP 742, Stevenson 528:2.

support *SEE* Don't fan the FLAME that supports the fire.

sure **1.** Better sure than sorry. *Rec. dist.:* U.S., Can. *1st cit.:* 1695 Ravenscroft, *Canterbury Guests;* US1927 Birmingham, *Gold, Gore, and Gehenna.* *20c. coll.:* ODEP 51, Whiting(MP) 607, CODP 15, Stevenson 2249:10.

2. There is nothing sure under the sun. *Rec. dist.:* Ill.

SEE ALSO It is the DULL man who is always sure and the sure man who is always dull. / Sudden FRIENDSHIP, sure repentance. / Be sure you are RIGHT, then go ahead. / Be sure you know the ROAD before you act as guide. / SLOW but sure.

surety He that is surety for another is never sure himself. *Rec. dist.:* Mich. *1st cit.:* 1539 Taverner, *Proverbs of Erasmus;* US1813 Dow, *History of Cosmopolite, or Lorenzo Dow's Journal* (1848). *20c. coll.:* ODEP 790, Whiting 425, Stevenson 2250:8.

surgeon **1.** A good surgeon must have an eagle's eye, a man's heart, and a lady's hand. *Rec. dist.:* Ill., Ind., N.Y. *1st cit.:* 1585 Robson,

Choice Change. *20c. coll.:* ODEP 790, Stevenson 2251:7.

2. Call not a surgeon before you are wounded. *Rec. dist.:* Calif.

surprise Surprises never cease. *Rec. dist.:* Ont.

surprised A man surprised is half beaten. *Rec. dist.:* Ont. *1st cit.:* 1573 Sanford, *Garden of Pleasure.* *20c. coll.:* ODEP 503, Stevenson 2251:9.

surrender Every compromise is surrender and invites new demands. *Rec. dist.:* N.Y. *1st cit.:* US1849 Emerson, *American Civilization.* *20c. coll.:* Stevenson 396:15.

SEE ALSO VIRTUE which parleys is near a surrender.

suspect *SEE* The less we KNOW, the more we suspect.

suspicion **1.** Suspicion always haunts the guilty party. *Rec. dist.:* N.Y. *1st cit.:* 1591 Shakespeare, *Henry VI, Part III;* US1782 Diary of William Pynchon of Salem, ed. Oliver (1890). *20c. coll.:* ODEP 249, Whiting 425, Stevenson 2298:11.

2. Suspicion breeds phantoms. *Rec. dist.:* Ill.

3. Suspicion is no less an enemy to virtue than to happiness. *Rec. dist.:* Mich. *1st cit.:* 1750 Johnson, *Rambler.* *20c. coll.:* Stevenson 2252:9.

4. Suspicion may be no fault, but showing it may be a great one. *Rec. dist.:* Ont. *1st cit.:* 1732 Fuller, *Gnomologia.* *20c. coll.:* Stevenson 2252:5.

SEE ALSO CAESAR's wife must be above suspicion. / CREDIT is suspicion asleep. / Too much FORCE breeds suspicion. / LOVE cannot dwell with suspicion.

sustain *SEE* He who derives the ADVANTAGE ought to sustain the burden.

swallow *(n.)* One swallow does not make a summer. *Vars.:* **(a)** One swallow does not make a spring. **(b)** One swallow makes not a spring, nor one woodchuck a winter. *Rec. dist.:* U.S., Can. *1st cit.:* 1539 Taverner, *Proverbs of Erasmus;* US1652 *Complete Writings of Roger Williams* (1963). *20c. coll.:* ODEP 791,

Whiting 425, *CODP* 218, Stevenson 2253:5, T&W 362, Whiting*(MP)* 607.

swallow *(v.)* A man must not swallow more than he can digest. *Rec. dist.:* N.C.

See also DEFEAT isn't bitter if you don't swallow it. / FLATTERY, like perfume, should be smelled, not swallowed. / IDLENESS is the Dead Sea that swallows all virtues. / PILLS are to be swallowed, not chewed. / Sooner or later all POLITICIANS die of swallowing their own lies. / Hot SUP, hot swallow.

swan The swan sings when death comes. *Rec. dist.:* Tex. *1st cit.:* ca1380 Chaucer, *Parliament of Foules;* US1634 Wood, *New-England's Prospects,* Publ. Prince Soc. (1865). *20c. coll.:* ODEP 791, Whiting 425, Stevenson 2254:5, T&W 362, Whiting*(MP)* 607.

See also Every mother's DUCK is a swan. / Every man thinks his own GEESE swans.

swap *See* Short TALK in a hoss swap.

sway *See* Don't let another's OPINION sway your judgment.

swear He who swears, swears in vain. *Rec. dist.:* Ill.

sweat *(n.)* No sweat, no sweet. *Rec. dist.:* Ill. *1st cit.:* 1576 Pettie, *Petite Palace of Pleasure,* ed. Gollancz (1908). *20c. coll.:* ODEP 794, Stevenson 2257:12.

See also No PAINS, no gains; no sweat, no sweet. / Use more WIT and less sweat.

sweat *(v.)* Sweat and be saved. *Rec. dist.:* N.J.

sweep *See* Sweep in front of your own DOOR first.

sweet *(n.)* **1.** Every sweet has its bitter. *Rec. dist.:* N.Y. *1st cit.:* ca1400 *Beryn,* ed. Furnivall, E.E.T.S. (1909); US1797 Tomlin in *Va.Mag.Hist.* (1922). *20c. coll.:* ODEP 793, Whiting 426, Stevenson 2260:9, T&W 362.

2. He deserves not sweet that will not taste of sour. *Rec. dist.:* Okla., Tex. *1st cit.:* 1533–34 Udall, *Flowers for Latine Speakyng out of Terence;* US1707 *Diary of Samuel Sewall, 1674–1729,* Mass.Hist.Soc. *Collections* (1878–82). *20c. coll.:* ODEP 177, Whiting 407, Stevenson 2259:4.

3. One man's sweet is another man's sour. *Rec. dist.:* N.Y. *1st cit.:* 1869 Henderson, *Latin Proverbs. 20c. coll.:* Stevenson 1825:14.

4. Sweets to the sweet and sour to the sour. *Rec. dist.:* Mich., N.Y., Ohio. *1st cit.:* 1600 Shakespeare, *Hamlet;* US1869 Alcott, *Little Women. 20c. coll.:* Stevenson 2259:2, T&W 362, Whiting*(MP)* 608.

5. Too much sweet spoils the best coffee. *Rec. dist.:* Miss.

6. We know the sweet when we have tasted the bitter. *Rec. dist.:* N.Y., Va. *1st cit.:* ca1374 Chaucer, *Troilus and Criseyde. 20c. coll.:* Stevenson 2259:4.

See also Every BITTER has its sweet. / The BITTER must come before the sweet. / You have to take the BITTER with the sweet. / No PAINS, no gains; no sweat, no sweet. / Too much SOUR spoils the sweet. / Stuff not your STOMACH with sweets if you choose to keep your sweet tooth.

sweet *(adj.)* Sweet are the slumbers of the virtuous. *Rec. dist.:* Mich.

See also The APPLES on the other side of the wall are the sweetest. / The loudest BELL does not always have the sweetest tone. / The blacker the BERRY, the sweeter the juice. / That which was BITTER to endure may be sweet to remember. / The closer to the BONE, the sweeter the meat. / The FLOWER of sweetest smell is shy and lowly. / The handsomest FLOWER is not the sweetest. / Another man's FOOD is sweeter. / Forbidden FRUIT is the sweetest. / Sour GRAPES can never make sweet wine. / The sweetest GRAPES hang highest. / The nearer the GROUND, the sweeter the grass. / HONEY is sweet, but bees sting. / Once MILK becomes sour, it can't be made sweet again. / Nothing but MONEY is sweeter than honey. / Sweetest NUTS have the hardest shells. / The longer the PATH, the sweeter the way home. / PATIENCE is bitter, but its fruit is sweet. / REVENGE is sweet. / The SLEEP of a laboring man is sweet. / The sweetest SONGS are sung in sorrow. / Old TUNES are sweetest; old friends are surest. / The sweetest WINE makes the sharpest vinegar.

sweeten *See* The HOPE of reward sweetens labor.

sweetheart **1.** Everybody's sweetheart is nobody's wife. *Rec. dist.:* Oreg.

2. It's better to be an old man's sweetheart than a young man's slave. *Rec. dist.:* U.S. *1st cit.:* 1546 Heywood, *Dialogue of Proverbs,* ed. Habernicht (1963). *20c. coll.:* ODEP 51, CODP 14, Stevenson 1542:8.

3. Nobody's sweetheart is ugly. *Rec. dist.:* Miss., Ohio, Ont.

sweetness *See* Dying FLIES spoil the sweetness of the ointment. / It is not with saying "HONEY, honey" that sweetness comes into the mouth.

swell *See* Jump when the WAVE is on the swell.

swift *(n.)* Too swift arrives as tardy as too slow. *Rec. dist.:* Ont. *1st cit.:* 1594 Shakespeare, *Romeo and Juliet. 20c. coll.:* Stevenson 1084:1.
See also The RACE is not always to the swift.

swift *(adj.)* *See* LIFE is short, and time is swift. / MAIDENS should be mild and meek, swift to hear and slow to speak.

swill If you get mixed up in swill, you'll be eaten up by the swine. *Rec. dist.:* N.Dak.
See also The silent SOW gets all the swill.

swim Don't try to swim where there is no water. *Rec. dist.:* W.Va.
See also Never venture out of your DEPTH till you can swim. / A dead FISH can float downstream, but it takes a live one to swim upstream. / Little FISH swim in shallow water. / He that swims in SIN shall sink in sorrow. / When WINE sinks, words swim.

swine One swine recognizes another. *Rec. dist.:* Ill.
See also Don't cast your PEARLS before swine.

switch A forgotten switch may cause a wreck. *Rec. dist.:* Ont.

sword **1.** He who lives by the sword shall perish by the sword. *Rec. dist.:* U.S., Can. *1st cit.:* 1601 Munday, *Death of Robert, Earl of Huntington;* US1652 *Complete Writings of Roger Williams* (1963). *20c. coll.:* CODP 137, Whiting 427, Stevenson 2265:3, T&W 363, Whiting(MP) 608.

2. Never stir the fire with a sword. *Rec. dist.:* N.Y. *1st cit.:* 1523 Erasmus, *Adagia,* tr. Taverner. *20c. coll.:* Stevenson 2265:6.

3. No sword bites so fiercely as an evil tongue. *Rec. dist.:* N.J., N.Y., S.C.

4. One sword keeps another in its scabbard. *Vars.:* **(a)** One sword drawn keeps the other in the scabbard. **(b)** One sword often keeps another in the scabbard. **(c)** One sword often keeps another in the sheath. *Rec. dist.:* Calif., Mich., N.Y. *1st cit.:* 1625 Purchas, *Pilgrims* (1905–07); US1747 *Papers of Benjamin Franklin,* ed. Labaree (1959). *20c. coll.:* ODEP 796, Whiting 427, Stevenson 1874:4.

5. The sword outlasts the scabbard. *Rec. dist.:* Mich., N.Y. *1st cit.:* 1817 Byron, "We'll Go No More A-Roving." *20c. coll.:* ODEP 65, Stevenson 2173:1, Whiting(MP) 609.

6. Whoever has a strong sword has peace. *Rec. dist.:* Ill.
See also Foul AIR slays like a sword. / GLUTTONY kills more than the sword. / The PEN is mightier than the sword. / PUNISHMENT is always a two-edged sword. / The TONGUE destroys a greater horde than does the sword. / The TONGUE is sharper than the sword. / TRUTH is mightier than the sword. / WIT without descretion is a sword in the hand of a fool.

sympathy **1.** Sympathy is akin to love. *Rec. dist.:* Ky., Tenn.

2. Sympathy is two hearts tugging at one load. *Rec. dist.:* Ont.

3. Sympathy killed a cat. *Rec. dist.:* N.C.

system **1.** A little system prevents a lot of bungling. *Rec. dist.:* Calif.

2. System spoils success. *Rec. dist.:* Ont.

T

table 1. At a round table, there is no dispute of place. *Rec. dist.:* Calif. *1st cit.:* 1611 Cotgrave, *Dictionary of French and English Tongues. 20c. coll.:* ODEP 685, Stevenson 2267:9.

2. At the table it becomes no one to be bashful. *Rec. dist.:* Wis.

3. Poor men's tables are soon set. *Rec. dist.:* N.Y. *1st cit.:* 1616 Draxe, *Bibliotheca Scholastica* in *Anglia* (1918). *20c. coll.:* ODEP 639, Stevenson 1844:3.

4. Rich men's tables have few crumbs. *Rec. dist.:* N.Y.

5. The table robs more than the thief. *Rec. dist.:* Okla. *1st cit.:* 1640 Herbert, *Outlandish Proverbs (Jacula Prudentum)* in *Works,* ed. Hutchinson (1941). *20c. coll.:* ODEP 796, Stevenson 2267:4.

6. When one has a good table, he is always right. *Rec. dist.:* Minn. *1st cit.:* US1948 Stevenson, *Home Book of Proverbs. 20c. coll.:* Stevenson 2267:8.

SEE ALSO Lay your CARDS on the table. / Don't EAT before you set the table. / The FATHER is the guest who best becomes the table. / Only FOOLS speak or fiddle at the table.

tablecloth If I can't be a tablecloth, I won't be a dishrag. *Rec. dist.:* Ill., Ind. *1st cit.:* 1678 Ray, *English Proverbs. 20c. coll.:* ODEP 190.

tact 1. For success in life, tact is more important than talent. *Rec. dist.:* Miss.

2. Social tact is making your company feel at home even though you wish they were. *Rec. dist.:* Ill.

3. Some people have tact; others tell the truth. *Var.:* Some people have tact, and others tell the truth. *Rec. dist.:* Ill., Ont.

4. Tact is removing the sting of a bee without being stung. *Rec. dist.:* Minn.

5. Tact is the art of making a point without making an enemy. *Rec. dist.:* Miss.

tail 1. Don't get your tail in a twist. *Rec. dist.:* Ont.

2. Don't get your tail over the line. *Rec. dist.:* Ont.

3. Make not the tail broader than the wings. *Rec. dist.:* Mich. *1st cit.:* 1597 Bacon, "Followers" in *Essays. 20c. coll.:* ODEP 797.

4. Tail goes with the hide. *Rec. dist.:* Miss., Ont., Wis. *1st cit.:* 1721 Kelly, *Scottish Proverbs;* US1959 Cushman, *Goodbye, Old Dry. 20c. coll.:* ODEP 797, Whiting(MP) 611, Stevenson 2268:6.

5. The tail cannot shake the dog. *Var.:* The tail cannot wag the dog. *Rec. dist.:* Calif., Mich., N.Y. *1st cit.:* 1936 Greg, *Murder of Estelle Cantor. 20c. coll.:* Whiting(MP) 611.

SEE ALSO It's better to be the BEAK of a hen than the tail of an ox. / When wrestlin' a BEAR, never grab for his tail. / A BIRD never flies so far that his tail doesn't follow. / Little BOYS are made of rats and snails and puppy-dog tails. / An old COW needs her tail more than once. / Cows don't know the good of the tail until fly time. / A DOG is loved by old and young, he wags his tail and not his tongue. / Short-tailed DOG wag his tail same as a long 'un. / An EEL held by the tail is not yet caught. / If you can get over the HORSE, you can get over the tail. / No KITE ever flew so high but what its tail followed it. / There is always something to keep the RABBIT's tail short. / A RICH man has the world by the tail. / You can't tell how far a TOAD will jump by the length of its tail.

tailor 1. A long thread, a lazy tailor. *Vars.:* (a) A long thread bespeaks a lazy tailor. (b) Lazy tailor uses long thread. *Rec. dist.:* N.Y., N.C. *1st cit.:* US1938 Champion, *Racial Proverbs. 20c. coll.:* Stevenson 2140:8.

2. Nine tailors make a man. *Var.:* Two tailors go to a man. *Rec. dist.:* N.Y., S.C., Tex. *1st cit.:* ca1600 *Tarlton's Jests,* Shakespeare Soc.; US1647 Ward, *Simple Cobler of Aggawam in*

America, ed. Wroth (1937). *20c. coll.: ODEP* 567, Whiting 430, *CODP* 162, Stevenson 2269:7, T&W 365, Whiting*(MP)* 611.

3. The tailors and barbers go halves with God Almighty. *Rec. dist.:* N.Y., S.C.

4. The tailor's sons wear patched pants. *Rec. dist.:* Wis.

5. The tailor's wife is worst clad. *Var.:* The tailor's wife is worse clad. *Rec. dist.:* Tex.

SEE ALSO A THREAD is always on the tailor.

tainted SEE There is no ODOR so bad as that which arises from goodness tainted.

take 1. Take all you want, but eat all you take. *Rec. dist.:* Ind., Mich.

2. Take it or leave it. *Rec. dist.:* U.S., Can. *1st cit.:* 1576 Lambarde, *Perambulation of Kent;* US1939 Cameron, *Murder's Coming. 20c. coll.: ODEP* 799, Whiting*(MP)* 612.

3. Take what you want, says God, but pay for it. *Rec. dist.:* Ont.

4. You can't take it with you. *Rec. dist.:* U.S., Can. *1st cit.:* 1841 Marryat, *Masterman Ready;* US1855 Jones, *Winkles. 20c. coll.: ODEP* 799, T&W 365, Stevenson 1984:15, Whiting*(MP)* 612.

SEE ALSO It always takes two to make a BARGAIN. / You have to take the BITTER with the sweet. / You can take a BOY out of the country, but you can't take the country out of the boy. / Do not take CREDIT that is due to others. / Take each DAY as it comes. / Don't DISH it out if you can't take it. / First man takes a DRINK; then drink takes a drink; then drink takes a man. / It takes a FOOL to know a fool. / It takes the FOOLISH to confound the wise. / Don't take your HAND off the plow. / Take things always by their smooth HANDLE. / Giv' em an INCH, they'll take a mile. / It is better to take many INJURIES than to give one. / Better LEAVE than take. / Live your LIFE, do your work, then take your hat. / LOVE takes away the sight, and matrimony restores it. / Don't take any wooden NICKELS. / Neither give nor take OFFENSE. / It takes two to make a QUARREL. / SPEED does not take heed. / Don't wait till you get TIME—take time. / Take TIME when time is, for time will

away. / He that takes a WIFE takes care. / It takes a wise WOMAN to be an old maid. / YOUTH and white paper take any impression.

take-it-easy Take-it-easy and live-long are brothers. *Rec. dist.:* Miss.

taking 1. Always taking out of the meat tub and never putting in soon comes to the bottom. *Rec. dist.:* Ind., N.Y., S.C. *1st cit.:* 1659 Howell, *Paroimiografia. 20c. coll.: ODEP* 12.

2. Take while the taking is good. *Rec. dist.:* Mich., N.Y., Ohio, S.C.

SEE ALSO Some are always GIVING, others are always taking.

tale 1. A good tale ill told is a bad one. *Var.:* Many a good tale is spoiled in the telling. *Rec. dist.:* La., Ont. *1st cit.:* ca1532 Fortescue, *Fortescue Papers. 20c. coll.: ODEP* 802, Stevenson 2272:12.

2. A good tale is not the worse for being told twice. *Rec. dist.:* N.J., Okla., Tex. *1st cit.:* 1577 Stanyhurst in Holinshed, *Description of Ireland. 20c. coll.: ODEP* 802, *CODP* 220, Stevenson 2272:12.

3. A tale grows better in the telling. *Rec. dist.:* Oreg.

4. A tale out of season is as music in mourning. *Rec. dist.:* Mich.

5. Don't tell tales out of school. *Vars.:* **(a)** Don't carry tales out of school. **(b)** Tell no tales out of school. *Rec. dist.:* U.S., Can. *1st cit.:* 1530 Tyndale, *Practyse of Prelates;* US1786 *Anarchaid,* ed. Humphreys, Scholars' Facsimiles and Reprints (1967). *20c. coll.: ODEP* 803, Whiting 430, *CODP* 220, Stevenson 2272:13, T&W 365, Whiting*(MP)* 612.

6. Every monkey has his tale. *Rec. dist.:* Miss.

7. It ought to be a good tale that is twice told. *Rec. dist.:* Ill., Ohio, Ont.

8. Lest men suspect your tale untrue, keep probability in view. *Rec. dist.:* Ill.

9. One tale is good till another is told. *Rec. dist.:* Ont. *1st cit.:* 1593 Greene, *Mamillia;* US1769 *Writings of Samuel Adams,* ed. Cushing (1913–17). *20c. coll.: ODEP* 579, Whiting 418, Stevenson 2271:12, Whiting*(MP)* 612.

10. There are always two tales to a story. **Rec. dist.:** Ont.

11. There is many a true tale told in jest. **Rec. dist.:** Okla.

12. You can't go so far but what your tales will follow you. **Rec. dist.:** Ill.

See also A short ANECDOTE is often a tall tale. / DEAD men tell no tales. / A still TONGUE tells no tales.

tale bearer 1. Put no faith in tale bearers. **Var.:** Listen not to tale bearers. **Rec. dist.:** Mich., Miss. **1st cit.:** ca1450 *Proverbs of Wisdom.* **20c. coll.:** ODEP 656, Stevenson 2274:11.

2. Tale bearers are commonly a sort of half-witted men. **Rec. dist.:** Ill.

3. The tale hearer is as bad as the tale bearer. **Rec. dist.:** Ont. **1st cit.:** 1777 Sheridan, *School for Scandal.* **20c. coll.:** Stevenson 2128:8.

4. The words of a tale bearer are as wounds. **Rec. dist.:** Ohio.

talent 1. Hide not your talents: they for use are given. **Rec. dist.:** Ont. **1st cit.:** US1750 Franklin, *PRAlmanac.* **20c. coll.:** Stevenson 2275:2.

2. Real talent never makes a fool of itself. **Rec. dist.:** Ariz.

3. Talent is developed in solitude; character, in the stream of life. **Rec. dist.:** Minn.

See also GENIUS does what it must—talent what it may. / INDUSTRY will improve great talents if you have them.

talk *(n.)* 1. Big talk will not boil the pot. **Var.:** Talking will not make the pot boil. **Rec. dist.:** Ill.

2. Idle talk burns the porridge. **Rec. dist.:** Calif.

3. Less talk, more speed. **Rec. dist.:** Ont.

4. Long talk, short walk. **Rec. dist.:** Miss. **Infm.:** Said by boys who take girls on long walks for romantic reasons.

5. Loose talk costs lives. **Rec. dist.:** Calif. **Infm.:** A warning against spies, used during World War II.

6. Much talk, little work. **Rec. dist.:** La. **1st cit.:** 1509 Barclay, *Ship of Fools,* ed. Jamieson in *Eclogues,* E.E.T.S. (1874); US1733 Frank-

lin, *PRAlmanac.* **20c. coll.:** ODEP 804, Whiting 431, Stevenson 2038:2, T&W 366, Whiting(MP) 612.

7. Short talk in a hoss swap. **Rec. dist.:** Miss.

8. Talk brings on talk. **Rec. dist.:** Ill.

9. Talk does not cook rice. **Var.:** Promisin' talk don't cook rice. **Rec. dist.:** Ill., N.Y., S.C.

10. Talk is cheap. **Vars.:** **(a)** Talk is cheap, but it takes money to buy land. **(b)** Talk is cheap, but it takes money to buy liquor. **(c)** Talk is cheap, but it takes money to buy whiskey. **(d)** Talk is cheap—takes money to buy land. **Rec. dist.:** U.S. **1st cit.:** US1843 Haliburton, *Attache or Sam Slick in England.* **20c. coll.:** T&W 365, Whiting(MP) 612.

11. Talk is easy, but work is hard. **Rec. dist.:** Ont.

12. Ten measures of talk were sent down from heaven, and women took nine. **Rec. dist.:** Ont.

13. Where there is so much talk, there is little thought. **Rec. dist.:** Ky., Tenn.

See also A BIRD is known by his note and a man by his talk. / By WORK you get money, by talk you get knowledge.

talk *(v.)* 1. Don't sit around and talk about what you are going to do—do it. **Rec. dist.:** Minn.

2. He that talks to himself talks to a fool. **Rec. dist.:** Ill., Ind. **1st cit.:** 1721 Kelly, *Scottish Proverbs.* **20c. coll.:** ODEP 804, Stevenson 2278:1.

3. He who talks hears only what he knows; he who listens may learn something. **Rec. dist.:** Oreg.

4. He who talks much errs much. **Vars.:** **(a)** Much talking, much erring. **(b)** Talk much and err much. **Rec. dist.:** Calif., Ill. **1st cit.:** 1599 Minsheu, *Dialogues in Dictionarie in Spanish and English.* **20c. coll.:** ODEP 803.

5. He who talks much says many foolish things. **Rec. dist.:** Ont. **1st cit.:** 1727 Gay, *Fables.* **20c. coll.:** Stevenson 417:11.

6. He who talks the most knows the least. **Rec. dist.:** Calif.

7. Look out for the man that does not talk

and the dog that does not bark. *Rec. dist.:* Miss.

8. One who talks the loudest says the least. *Rec. dist.:* Calif.

9. People who talk about others are talked about by others. *Rec. dist.:* Calif.

10. Sweet-talk to the old lady to get to the daughter. *Rec. dist.:* Miss.

11. Talk good, talk on; talk bad, stop. *Rec. dist.:* Ala., Ga.

12. Talk less; listen more. *Rec. dist.:* Ill., Ont.

13. Talk softly but carry a big stick. *Rec. dist.:* Mich., N.Y., S.C. *1st cit.:* US1901 Theodore Roosevelt, Address at Minnesota State Fair, 2 Sept. *20c. coll.:* Stevenson 1874:5.

14. There isn't much to talk about at some parties until one or two couples leave. *Rec. dist.:* Miss.

15. You may talk too much on the best of subjects. *Rec. dist.:* N.Y., S.C.

SEE ALSO Never ARGUE with a man who talks loud; you couldn't convince him of anything. / A CHILD learns to talk in about two years, but it takes about sixty years for him to learn to keep his mouth shut. / Talk of the DEVIL and his imp appears. / To make ENEMIES, talk; to make friends, listen. / A FOOL always talks most when he has the least to say. / A FOOL talks when he should be listening. / A FOOL talks while a wise man thinks. / If you talk with a HOG, don't expect anything but a grunt. / Each LIAR loves to hear himself talk. / Give LOSERS leave to talk. / MONEY talks. / Don't talk about OTHERS, for they may be able to talk about you. / Those who are RIGHT need not talk loudly. / Everybody talks about the WEATHER, but nobody does anything about it. / Most WORRY is half over when you sit down and talk it over.

talker **1.** A great talker may be no fool, but he is one that relies on him. *Rec. dist.:* Ill. *1st cit.:* US1753 Franklin, *PRAlmanac. 20c. coll.:* Stevenson 2277:2.

2. Big talker, little doer. *Vars.:* **(a)** Great talkers are not good doers. **(b)** Great talkers, little doers. **(c)** The greatest talkers are the least doers. *Rec. dist.:* U.S., Can. *1st cit.:* 1509 Bar-

clay, *Ship of Fools,* ed. Jamieson in *Eclogues,* E.E.T.S. (1874); US1753 Franklin, *PRAlmanac. 20c. coll.:* ODEP 804, Whiting 431, Stevenson, 2038:2, T&W 366, Whiting(MP) 612.

3. Great talkers are like broken pitchers: everything runs out of them. *Var.:* Great talkers are like leaky pitchers: everything runs out of them. *Rec. dist.:* Mich., Ohio. *1st cit.:* 1855 Bohn, *Handbook of Proverbs. 20c. coll.:* Stevenson 2275:8.

talking **1.** Big talking, but little saying. *Rec. dist.:* Ont. *1st cit.:* 1709 Dykes, *English Proverbs;* US1940 *Meditations in Wall Street. 20c. coll.:* Stevenson 2037:4.

2. By talking, people understand one another. *Rec. dist.:* N.Y.

3. People who wouldn't think of talking with their mouths full often speak with their heads empty. *Rec. dist.:* Ont.

4. Talking pays no toll. *Rec. dist.:* Ont., R.I. *1st cit.:* 1640 Herbert, *Outlandish Proverbs (Jacula Prudentum)* in *Works,* ed. Hutchinson (1941). *20c. coll.:* ODEP 804, Stevenson 2277:9.

5. Talking will not make the pot boil. *Rec. dist.:* Ky., Tenn.

tall SEE Great OAKS from little acorns grow. / He that climbs the tall TREE has a right to the fruit.

talons SEE It is better to keep a WOLF out of the fold than to trust drawing his teeth and talons after he shall have entered.

tame SEE AGE and marriage tame man and beast. / An INDIAN, a partridge, and a spruce tree can't be tamed. / Every man can tame a SHREW but he that has her.

tar **1.** The tar of my country is better than the honey of others. *Rec. dist.:* Ariz.

2. You can't play wid tar an' git none of it on yo' hands. *Rec. dist.:* N.Y. *Infm.:* Cf. pitch.

SEE ALSO Don't spoil the SHIP for half a penny's worth of tar.

tardy SEE Too SWIFT arrives as tardy as too slow.

tare If men had not slept, the tare had not been sown. *Rec. dist.:* Mich., N.Y.

target *SEE* The WORLD is an easy target till you come to shoot at it.

tart *SEE* A tart TEMPER never mellows with age.

Tartar *SEE* Scratch a RUSSIAN and you find a Tartar.

task **1.** A task that is pleasant is soon finished. *Rec. dist.:* Ont.

2. A task that's worth doing at all is worth doing well. *Var.:* Any task worth doing is worth doing well. *Rec. dist.:* U.S., Can. *1st cit.:* 1746 Chesterfield, *Letters to His Son;* US1780 A. Adams in *Adams Family Correspondence,* ed. Butterfield (1956). *20c. coll.:* ODEP 921, Whiting 113, Stevenson 536:3, T&W 104.

3. A task well begun is half done. *Vars.:* (a) A good beginning is half the task. (b) A task well begun is a task half done. *Rec. dist.:* U.S., Can. *1st cit.:* ca1500 *15c. School Book,* ed. Nelson; US1931 Taylor, *Cape Cod Mystery.* *20c. coll.:* ODEP 877, Whiting(MP) 41, Stevenson 152:10.

4. Do not pray for tasks equal to your powers; pray for power equal to your tasks. *Rec. dist.:* Ont.

5. Never leave a task until it is done. *Vars.:* (a) Always finish a task begun. (b) If a task is once begun, never leave it till it's done. (c) If a task is once begun, never leave it till it's done. Be the labor great or small, do it well or not at all. (d) When a task is first begun, never leave it till it's done. *Rec. dist.:* U.S., Can. *1st cit.:* 1477 *Dictes and Sayenges of Philosophirs,* tr. Rivers. *20c. coll.:* Stevenson 154:4.

6. Some tasks require a strong back and a weak mind. *Rec. dist.:* Colo., Oreg., Wis.

SEE ALSO It is a task to LEARN, but it is much harder to unlearn.

taste *(n.)* **1.** Everyone to his own taste. *Vars.:* (a) Each to his own taste. (b) Every man to his taste. (c) Everybody to his own taste. (d) Everyone is entitled to his own taste. *Rec. dist.:* U.S., Can. *1st cit.:* 1580 Lyly, *Euphues and His England;* US1767 Hulton, *Letters of a Loyalist Lady* (1927). *20c. coll.:* ODEP 230, Whiting 135, CODP 68, Stevenson 2281:2, T&W 235, Whiting(MP) 395.

2. No accounting for taste. *Vars.:* (a) There is no accounting for taste. (b) There is no accounting for tastes. *Rec. dist.:* U.S., Can. *1st cit.:* 1599 Minsheu, *Dialogues* in *Dictionarie in Spanish and English;* US1808 Barker, *Tears and Smiles.* *20c. coll.:* ODEP 2, Whiting 2, Stevenson 2282:5, T&W 2, Whiting(MP) 3.

3. Taste and desire cannot be disputed. *Rec. dist.:* N.Y.

4. Tastes cannot be controlled. *Rec. dist.:* N.Y., S.C. *1st cit.:* US1784 Jefferson, *Notes on Money Unit.* *20c. coll.:* Stevenson 2282:1.

5. Tastes differ. *Rec. dist.:* Ont. *1st cit.:* 1868 Collins, *Moonstone;* US1803 Davis, *Travels in America 1798–1802.* *20c. coll.:* ODEP 805, Whiting 432, CODP 220, Stevenson 2281;7, Whiting(MP) 613.

6. There is no disputing concerning tastes. *Vars.:* (a) Taste and desire cannot be disputed. (b) There is no disputing of our tastes. *Rec. dist.:* U.S., Can. *1st cit.:* ca1667 Taylor, *Reflections on Ridicule;* US1786 Hazard in *Belknap Papers,* Mass.Hist.Soc. *Collections* (1877). *20c. coll.:* Stevenson 2282:5, Whiting 111.

7. 'Tis the taste that tells the tale. *Rec. dist.:* Calif.

SEE ALSO The COST takes away the taste. / The taste o' the DEVIL is better'n his broth. / You don't have to eat a whole TUB of butter to get the taste.

taste *(v.)* Wish not to taste what does not to you fall. *Rec. dist.:* Ont.

SEE ALSO Stolen FRUIT tastes the sweetest. / SOMETHING tastes better than nothing. / He deserves not SWEET that will not taste of sour. / We know the SWEET when we have tasted the bitter.

tater Little taters is hard to peel. *Rec. dist.:* N.Y., S.C. *Infm.:* "Taters" refers to potatoes.

tater vine Tater vine growin' w'ile you sleep. *Rec. dist.:* N.Y., S.C.

tattler A tattler is worse than a thief. *Rec. dist.:* Ont. *1st cit.:* 1678 Ray, *English Proverbs;* US1875 Scarborough, *Chinese Proverbs.* *20c. coll.:* Stevenson 1012:11.

tavern The going out of the tavern is the best part of the journey. *Rec. dist.:* Mich.

tax *(n.)* SEE Nothing is CERTAIN except death and taxes. / DEATH and taxes are two things we can't beat.

tax *(v.)* SEE We tax our FRIENDS with faults, but see not our own. / IDLENESS and pride tax with a heavier hand that kings and parliaments. / We are taxed twice as much by our IDLENESS, three times as much by our pride, and four times as much by our folly.

taxation Taxation without representation is tyranny. *Rec. dist.:* N.Y., S.C. *1st cit.:* 1761 Pratt, Speech, House of Lords; US1761 Otis, Argument on illegality of writs of assistance before the Superior Court of Massachusetts. *20c. coll.:* Stevenson 2283:6.

tea SEE ANYTIME is tea time. / LOVE and scandal are the best sweeteners of tea.

teach 1. He that teaches a scorner does an injury to himself. *Rec. dist.:* Ont.

2. He that teaches himself has a fool for a teacher. *Rec. dist.:* Ind., Wis. *1st cit.:* ca1637 Jonson, *Timber;* US1741 Franklin, *PRAlmanac. 20c. coll.:* ODEP 806, Whiting 162, Stevenson 2284:6.

3. What Johnny will not teach himself, Johnny will not learn. *Rec. dist.:* Ont.

4. While I teach, I learn. *Vars.:* **(a)** He who teaches often learns himself. **(b)** Men learn while they teach. **(c)** One learns by teaching. **(d)** Teaching others teaches yourself. **(e)** To teach another is to learn yourself. *Rec. dist.:* U.S., Can. *1st cit.:* ca1386 Chaucer, *Prologue to Canterbury Tales;* US1905 Henry, *Service of Love. 20c. coll.:* Stevenson 2285:1.

5. Who teaches me for a day is my father for a lifetime. *Rec. dist.:* Ind.

SEE ALSO Teach your CHILD to hold his tongue; he'll learn fast enough to speak. / CHILDREN can teach old folks. / He who can, DOES; those who can't, teach. / You can't teach an old DOG new tricks. / You have to be smarter than the DOG to teach him tricks. / FAILURE teaches success. / You can't teach an old HORSE new tricks. / The great SECRET of life is to hear lessons and not teach them. / THIEVES cannot teach honesty. / YEARS teach more than books.

teacher 1. He is the best teacher who follows his own instructions. *Rec. dist.:* Calif., Ill. *1st cit.:* ca1377 Langland, *Piers Plowman;* US1733 Franklin, *PRAlmanac. 20c. coll.:* Stevenson 1870:2.

2. If the learner hasn't learned, the teacher hasn't taught. *Rec. dist.:* W.Va.

3. Some teachers are time servers. *Rec. dist.:* Miss.

SEE ALSO EXPERIENCE is a hard master, but a good teacher. / EXPERIENCE is the best teacher. / As the HEART makes the home, the teacher makes the child. / TIME is the best teacher. / VICES are learned without a teacher.

teaching 1. Teaching should be full of ideas, not stuffed with facts. *Rec. dist.:* Ill.

2. To know how to suggest is the art of teaching. *Rec. dist.:* Ill.

teakettle A shallow teakettle boils the loudest. *Rec. dist.:* Calif.

team A man is only as good as the worst on his team. *Rec. dist.:* N.C.

SEE ALSO One HAIR of a woman draws more than a team of horses.

teapot SEE Don't worry over a STORM in a teapot.

tear *(n.)* 1. A woman's tears are her strongest weapons. *Rec. dist.:* N.J. *1st cit.:* 1605 Shakespeare, *King Lear. 20c. coll.:* Stevenson 2290:4.

2. It is the unshed tears that make the scars. *Rec. dist.:* Md.

3. More tears are shed in playhouses than in churches. *Rec. dist.:* Ill.

4. Nothing dries sooner than tears. *Rec. dist.:* Okla., Tex. *1st cit.:* 1563 Wilson, *Arte of Rhetorique;* US1867 Harte, *Lost Galleon. 20c. coll.:* ODEP 579, Stevenson 2286:10.

5. Only mothers' tears are worth their salt. *Rec. dist.:* Ind.

6. Shed tears boldly: weeping is nature's mark to know an honest heart by. *Rec. dist.:* Ill.

7. Tears and troubles are the lot of all. *Rec. dist.:* Ont.

8. Tears are often the telescope through which men see far into heaven. *Rec. dist.:* Ala., Ga., N.Y., S.C. *1st cit.:* US1887 Beecher, *Proverbs from Plymouth Pulpit.* **20c. coll.:** Stevenson 2287:1.

9. Tears are the natural penalties of pleasure. *Rec. dist.:* Ill.

10. Tears are the silent language of grief. *Rec. dist.:* Ill.

11. Tears bring nobody back from the grave. *Rec. dist.:* Ill.

12. Tears for the bride rain falls on. *Rec. dist.:* Wis.

13. Tears hinder sorrow from becoming despair. *Rec. dist.:* Ill.

14. Tears of joy are the dew in which the sun of righteousness is mirrored. *Rec. dist.:* Mich.

15. The tear of sympathy brings its own relief. *Rec. dist.:* Mich.

16. The tears of the congregation are the praises of the minister. *Rec. dist.:* Mich.

17. They that sow in tears shall reap in joy. *Rec. dist.:* Ont. *1st cit.:* US1948 Stevenson, *Home Book of Proverbs.* **20c. coll.:** Stevenson 2180:1.

18. Waste not fresh tears over old griefs. *Rec. dist.:* Ont.

19. Your tears will be bottled up in heaven. *Rec. dist.:* Ill.

SEE ALSO CANDOR once went further boldly and in smiles, but it crept home in tatters and tears. / After LAUGHTER, tears. / A RIPPLE of laughter is worth a flood of tears. / SMILES turn swiftly to tears. / Some swim in WEALTH, but sink in tears.

tear *(v.)* *SEE* WIDE will wear, but narrow will tear.

tease *SEE* PLEASE ever; tease never.

teaspoon *SEE* A WOMAN can throw more out the back door in a teaspoon than a man can bring in the front door in a shovel.

teats *SEE* The trouble is there are too many PIGS for the teats.

teeter *SEE* The longer the BOARD, the better the teeter.

telescope *SEE* TEARS are often the telescope through which men see far into heaven.

tell **1.** Don't tell all you know nor all you can. *Rec. dist.:* Ill., Minn. *1st cit.:* 642 Torriano, *Select Italian Proverbs.* **20c. coll.:** ODEP 807, Stevenson 158:4.

2. Tell not all you know, and tell only what you know right well. *Rec. dist.:* Va.

SEE ALSO New BLOOD tells. / Tell everybody your BUSINESS and the devil will do it for you. / CLASS will tell. / DAISIES won't tell. / DEAD men tell no tales. / You can never tell a DOG by his bark. / FIND out all you can and tell as little as possible. / Tell me who your FRIENDS are and I will tell you what kind of a man you are. / Tell me with whom you GO, and I'll tell you what you do. / GOD knows, but he won't tell. / Show me your HAND and I'll tell you your trade. / It is as bad to believe a LIE as to tell one. / Tell a LIE and find the truth. / LIES do harm only to them that tells 'em. / Ask me no QUESTIONS and I'll tell you no lies. / A SECRET's a secret until it's told. / Don't tell TALES out of school. / TIME will tell. / You can't tell how far a TOAD will jump by the length of its tail. / Tell me with whom you TRAVEL and I'll tell you who you are. / You can never tell till you've TRIED. / Always tell the TRUTH, but don't always be telling the truth. / Tell the TRUTH if it kills you. / You can tell a lot about a person by the way he WALKS. / Tell a WOMAN and you tell the world.

teller *SEE* TRUTH never hurt the teller.

telling *SEE* In telling AGE of another multiply by two; in telling your own age divide by two. / SCANDAL grows with the telling.

temper *(n.)* **1.** A lost temper needs no advertising. *Rec. dist.:* Minn.

2. A sunny temper gilds the edge of life's blackest clouds. *Rec. dist.:* Minn.

3. A tart temper never mellows with age. *Rec. dist.:* Ill., Wis.

4. Command your temper lest it command

you. *Var.:* Control your temper or it will control you. *Rec. dist.:* Mich., Ont.

5. If your temper is good, keep it; if it is bad, don't lose it. *Rec. dist.:* Minn.

6. Keep your temper: nobody else wants it. *Rec. dist.:* N.J. Ont., Utah.

7. No matter how fashions change, a ruffled temper will never be in style. *Rec. dist.:* Miss.

8. Short tempers often go with long tongues. *Rec. dist.:* Ont.

9. Tempers, like faces, generally appear best at a distance. *Rec. dist.:* Mich.

10. The loss of temper is the loss of sense. *Rec. dist.:* Ont.

11. Your temper is too valuable a possession to lose. *Rec. dist.:* Utah.

SEE ALSO An EXAGGERATION is a truth that has lost its temper. / When alone, we have our own THOUGHTS to watch; when in the family, our tempers; when in society, our tongues.

temper *(v.)* SEE GOD tempers the wind to the shorn lamb. / The LORD tempers the wind to the shorn lamb.

temperance Temperance is the best physic. *Rec. dist.:* Ill., Ont. *1st cit.:* 1520 *Vulgaria,* tr. Whittington; US1797 Miller in *Life and Correspondence of James Iredell,* ed. McRee (1857–58). *20c. coll.:* *ODEP* 808, Whiting 432, Stevenson 2291:9.

tempt SEE The open DOOR tempts a saint. / Don't tempt PROVIDENCE. / TRUST not, tempt not.

temptation 1. Don't stop to argue with temptation—you will be sorry. *Rec. dist.:* Kans.

2. Half the battle of temptation is recognizing it. *Rec. dist.:* N.C.

3. Look not on temptation and your mind will be at rest. *Rec. dist.:* Ind.

4. Resist temptation till you conquer it. *Rec. dist.:* Utah.

5. Temptation is a blessing in disguise. *Rec. dist.:* N.C.

6. Temptation is the devil looking through the keyhole, but sin is opening the door. *Rec. dist.:* N.C.

7. Temptation is the fire that brings up the scum of the heart. *Rec. dist.:* Ala., Ga.

8. Temptation is the proving ground of man's soul. *Rec. dist.:* N.C.

9. Temptations, like misfortunes, are sent to test our moral strength. *Rec. dist.:* Ill.

10. The best way to resist temptation is to give in to it. *Rec. dist.:* Calif.

11. The less the temptation, the greater the sin. *Rec. dist.:* Calif., Tex.

12. We can resist everything except temptation. *Rec. dist.:* Ill. *1st cit.:* 1892 Wilde, *Lady Windermere's Fan.* *20c. coll.:* Stevenson 2292:14.

13. Who avoids temptation avoids sin. *Rec. dist.:* Calif.

SEE ALSO Constant OCCUPATION prevents temptation. / TERROR is a great temptation. / It's good to be without VICES, but it is not good to be without temptations.

ten SEE If you're ANGRY count to ten. / There are ten COMMANDMENTS of life, but man wishes someone would tell his wife there are only ten. / Don't waste ten DOLLARS looking for a dime. / Better once in HEAVEN than ten times at the gate. / A VOLUNTEER is worth ten pressed men.

tenant SEE Better an empty HOUSE than a bad tenant. / Short RENTS make careless tenants. / Aching TEETH are ill tenants.

tend SEE He who tends his own BUSINESS has a good one. / The DEVIL always tends to his own business.

tendency Evil tendencies are early shown. *Rec. dist.:* Ark.

tender SEE Brave HEARTS are tender hearts.

termination No termination without determination. *Rec. dist.:* Wis.

terrible SEE Offended LOVE is the most terrible.

terror Terror is a great temptation. *Rec. dist.:* Ala., Ga.

test *(n.)* 1. The greatest test of true bravery is fear to offend. *Rec. dist.:* N.Y.

2. The test of the pudding is in the eating. *Rec. dist.:* N.Y. *Infm.:* Cf. proof.

3. To go downhill is easy; the uphill climb is the test. *Rec. dist.:* Kans.

SEE ALSO FIRE is the test of gold. / POLISH on the heels of shoes is a truer test of thoroughness than shine on the toes.

test *(v.)* Test before trusting. *Rec. dist.:* Ont. *Infm.:* Cf. try. *1st cit.:* ca1450–1500 *Gode Wyfe Wolde a Pilgrimage.* *20c. coll.:* ODEP 845.

SEE ALSO GOLD is tested by fire, men by gold.

Texas 1. God made West Texas when he was a small boy wanting a sandbox. *Rec. dist.:* Tex.

2. If I owned Texas and hell, I would rent out Texas and live in hell. *Rec. dist.:* N.Y., S.C. *1st cit.:* US1855 Statement by Gen. Sheridan at Fort Clark, Tex. *20c. coll.:* Stevenson 1127:5.

text 1. A text out of context is pretext. *Rec. dist.:* Ky., Tenn.

2. Stick to your text if you die preaching. *Rec. dist.:* N.J., N.Y., S.C.

thank SEE THINK and thank.

thankful SEE A thankful HEART is not only the greatest virtue but the parent of all other virtues.

thanks 1. Thanks is poor pay on which to keep a family. *Var.:* Thanks is poor pay. *Rec. dist.:* Miss., N.Y. *1st cit.:* 1666 Torriano, *Select Italian Proverbs;* US1934 Rathbone, *Brass Knocker.* *20c. coll.:* ODEP 593, Whiting*(MP)* 615.

2. Thanks killed the cat. *Rec. dist.:* Ky. *1st cit.:* US1962 *Bangor Daily News,* 10 Aug. *20c. coll.:* Whiting*(MP)* 615.

3. The more you do, the less thanks you get. *Rec. dist.:* Ont.

4. You can't put thanks into your pocket. *Rec. dist.:* Ill.

SEE ALSO My DAME fed her hens on thanks, but they laid no eggs. / A small GIFT usually gets small thanks.

Thanksgiving 1. Thanksgiving is good; thanks-living is better. *Rec. dist.:* Ont.

2. While Thanksgiving has its foundation on Plymouth Rock, Christmas rests upon the Rock of Ages. *Rec. dist.:* Miss.

thatched SEE Better WHOLE than thatched with gold.

thaw *(n.)* Thaw shows up what the snow has hidden. *Rec. dist.:* Ont.

thaw *(v.)* SEE Heated REMARKS never thaw icy hearts.

theater SEE LIFE is a theater where the worst people sometimes get the best seats.

thick Too thick won't stick. *Rec. dist.:* N.J., Ont.

SEE ALSO When the BEANS get too thick, the pot burns. / FAULTS are thick where love is thin. / Thin ICE and thick ice look the same from a distance. / The SPUR won't hurt when the hide is thick.

thicker SEE BLOOD is thicker than water.

thief 1. A thief is worse than a liar. *Rec. dist.:* Ont.

2. A thief knows a thief as a wolf knows a wolf. *Rec. dist.:* Ill. *1st cit.:* 1539 Taverner, *Proverbs of Erasmus.* *20c. coll.:* ODEP 810, Stevenson 1430:1.

3. A thief passes for a gentleman when stealing has made him rich. *Rec. dist.:* Oreg. *1st cit.:* 1732 Fuller, *Gnomologia.* *20c. coll.:* ODEP 810.

4. All are not thieves that dogs bark at. *Rec. dist.:* N.Y., Oreg. *1st cit.:* 1755 Peacham, *Garden of Eloquence;* US1832 Kennedy, *Swallow Barn.* *20c. coll.:* ODEP 811, T&W 368, Stevenson 2297:5.

5. All thieves come to some bad end. *Rec. dist.:* Ill.

6. An old thief makes a good sheriff. *Rec. dist.:* Calif.

7. Give a thief enough rope and he'll hang himself. *Rec. dist.:* Ont. *1st cit.:* 1639 Fuller, *Holy War.* *20c. coll.:* ODEP 683.

8. He is not a thief until he is caught. *Rec. dist.:* Wis.

9. It takes a thief to catch a thief. *Var.:* Set a thief to catch a thief. *Rec. dist.:* U.S., Can. *1st* *cit.:* 1654 Gayton, *Pleasant Notes Upon Don Quixote;* US1819 Brackenridge, *Voyage to South America in 1817 and 1818.* **20c. coll.:** *ODEP* 810, Whiting 453, *CODP* 222, Stevenson 2300:3, T&W 368, Whiting*(MP)* 616.

10. Men do not despise a thief if he steals to satisfy his soul when it is hungry. *Rec. dist.:* Ont. *1st cit.:* US1948 Stevenson, *Home Book of Proverbs.* **20c. coll.:** Stevenson 2299:1.

11. Once a thief, always a thief. *Rec. dist.:* Ohio, Okla. *1st cit.:* 1706 Stevens, *New Spanish and English Dictionary.* **20c. coll.:** *ODEP* 594, Stevenson 2298:6.

12. Save a thief from the gallows and he'll be the first to cut your throat. *Rec. dist.:* Calif., Tex. *1st cit.:* ca1440 Lydgate, *Fall of Princes;* US1845 Judd, *Margaret.* **20c. coll.:** *ODEP* 700, T&W 368, Stevenson 2299:9.

13. The big thieves hang the little thieves. *Rec. dist.:* N.J. *1st cit.:* 1607 Estienne, *World of Wonders,* tr. R.C.; US1748 Franklin, *PRAlmanac.* **20c. coll.:** *ODEP* 335, Stevenson 2297:2.

14. The end of the thief is the gallows. *Rec. dist.:* N.Y. *1st cit.:* 1626 Breton, *Soothing of Proverbs.* **20c. coll.:** *ODEP* 810.

15. The thief is sorry to be hanged, not to be a thief. *Rec. dist.:* Minn.

16. The thief thinks that everyone else is a thief. *Var.:* A thief thinks every other man will steal. *Rec. dist.:* Ill., Miss.

17. There is no thief like a bad book. *Var.:* There is no worse robber than a bad book. *Rec. dist.:* Ill.

18. Thieves cannot teach honesty. *Rec. dist.:* Ont.

19. We hang little thieves and take off our hats to great ones. *Rec. dist.:* Calif. *1st cit.:* 1639 Clarke, *Paroemiologia;* US1748 Franklin, *PRAlmanac.* **20c. coll.:** *CODP* 135, Stevenson 2297:2.

20. When thieves fall out, honest men get their due. *Rec. dist.:* Calif. *1st cit.:* 1546 Heywood, *Dialogue of Proverbs,* ed. Habernicht (1963); US1742 Franklin, *PRAlmanac.* **20c. coll.:** *ODEP* 810, Stevenson 2298:2, Whiting 368, Whiting*(MP)* 616.

21. You can catch a thief but never a liar. *Rec. dist.:* Ind., Ont., Pa.

22. You can jail a thief but never a liar. *Rec. dist.:* Ont.

23. You can shut the door on a thief, but you can do nothing about a liar. *Rec. dist.:* N.Y.

24. You can watch a thief, but you can't watch a liar. *Vars.:* **(a)** You can watch a thief, but you can't trust a liar. **(b)** You can watch the thief but not the liar. *Rec. dist.:* Ont.

SEE ALSO One day a BEGGAR, the next a thief. / The BEGGAR may sing before the thief. / COURTESY is for gentlemen and necessary for thieves. / A sealed DOOR invites a thief. / Small FAULTS indulged in are little thieves that let in greater. / The HOLE invites the thief. / There is HONOR even among thieves. / He who holds the LADDER is as bad as the thief. / The LAZY man goes to his work like a thief to the gallows. / A LIAR is worse than a thief. / OPPORTUNITY makes a thief. / PROCRASTINATION is the thief of time. / PUNCTUALITY is the thief of time. / There isn't a RASCAL or a thief that doesn't have his devotion. / The RECEIVER is as bad as the thief. / A TATTLER is worse than a thief.

thimble SEE You can't get a QUART out of a thimble.

thimbleful SEE A thimbleful of EXPERIENCE is worth a tubful of knowledge.

thin SEE FAULTS are thick where love is thin. / Where the HEDGE is thin, men will see through it. / In skating over thin ICE our safety is in our speed. / Thin ICE and thick ice look the same from a distance. / Thin ICE carries no weight.

thing **1.** A little thing in hand is worth more than a great thing in prospect. *Var.:* A little thing in the hand is worth a great thing in prospect. *Rec. dist.:* Ind., Ont.

2. A man can do a lot of things if he has to. *Rec. dist.:* N.C.

3. A thing done right today means less trouble tomorrow. *Rec. dist.:* Ont.

4. All things are possible to him that believes. *Rec. dist.:* Calif., Pa.

5. All things come to him who waits. **Rec. dist.:** U.S., Can. **1st cit.:** 1530 Barclay, *Eclogues*, E.E.T.S. (1927); US1863 Longfellow, "Student's Tale" in *Tales of Wayside Inn*. **20c. coll.:** *ODEP* 231, Stevenson 2440:10, Whiting*(MP)* 205.

6. Certainly there are lots of things in life that money won't buy, but have you ever tried to buy them without money? **Rec. dist.:** N.Y.

7. Do a thing and have done with it. **Rec. dist.:** Ont.

8. Do not ignore the things of today. **Rec. dist.:** Ont.

9. Don't do the same thing twice. **Rec. dist.:** Ind.

10. Each thing has its right place if you know how to place it. **Rec. dist.:** Minn.

11. First one thing and then another. **Vars.:** **(a)** If it's not one thing, it's another. **(b)** If it's not one thing, it's two. **(c)** It's one thing or another. **Rec. dist.:** Miss., Ont., S.C. **1st cit.:** ca1374 Chaucer, *Troilus and Criseyde;* USca1906 O'Malley, Epigram in Hubbard, *Thousand and One Epigrams*. **20c. coll.:** Stevenson 2301:9, Whiting*(MP)* 619.

12. Four things cannot be brought back: a word spoken, an arrow discharged, the divine decree, and past time. **Rec. dist.:** Ill.

13. Getting things done is largely a matter of getting things started. **Rec. dist.:** Ont.

14. Great things have a small beginning. **Var.:** Great things often come from small beginnings. **Rec. dist.:** Calif., N.Y., S.C. **1st cit.:** 1609 Harward, Unpublished manuscript in Trinity College Library, Cambridge; USca1656 Bradford, *History of Plymouth Plantation*, ed. Ford (1912). **20c. coll.:** *ODEP* 42, Whiting 27, Stevenson 1035:15, Whiting*(MP)* 619.

15. He who would do a great thing well must first have done the simplest thing perfectly. **Rec. dist.:** Ont.

16. If things were to be done twice, all would be wise. **Rec. dist.:** Ohio, Okla. **1st cit.:** 1640 Herbert, *Outlandish Proverbs (Jacula Prudentum)* in *Works,* ed. Hutchinson (1941); US1758

Ames, *Almanacs,* ed. Briggs (1891). **20c. coll.:** *ODEP* 499, Whiting 435.

17. In the end, the things that count are the things that you can't count. **Rec. dist.:** N.J.

18. It ain't the things you don't know that makes you ignorant as much as it is the things you know that ain't so. **Rec. dist.:** N.Y., S.C.

19. It is due each man to find one thing he can do well. **Rec. dist.:** N.C.

20. It's the little things in life that count. **Rec. dist.:** U.S. **1st cit.:** 1892 Doyle, *Case of Identity*. **20c. coll.:** Stevenson 1443:2.

21. Just let things rock along. **Rec. dist.:** Miss.

22. Keep a thing seven years and it's bound to come in handy. **Var.:** Keep a thing seven years and you will find a use for it. **Rec. dist.:** Okla., Ont., Tex. **1st cit.:** 1566 Painter, *Palace of Pleasure,* ed. Jacobs (1890); US1863 Reade, *Hard Cash*. **20c. coll.:** *CODP* 124, Stevenson 1291:5, Whiting*(MP)* 619.

23. Of a little thing, a little displeases. **Rec. dist.:** Mich. **1st cit.:** 1640 Herbert, *Outlandish Proverbs (Jacula Prudentum)* in *Works,* ed. Hutchinson (1941). **20c. coll.:** *ODEP* 472, Stevenson 1443:9. Whiting*(MP)* 619.

24. One thing at a time. **Vars.:** **(a)** One thing at a time, and that done well, is a very good thing, as any can tell. **(b)** One thing at a time is good going. **Rec. dist.:** Calif., Mich., N.Y., Ont. **1st cit.:** 1772 Wesley, *Letters;* US1702 *Correspondence Between William Penn and James Logan, 1700–1705,* ed. Armstrong, Hist.Soc.Penn. *Memoirs* (1870). **20c. coll.:** *ODEP* 598, Whiting 434, Stevenson 1780:2,

25. Small things affect light minds. **Rec. dist.:** Calif. **1st cit.:** 1576 Pettie, *Petite Palace of Pleasure,* ed. Gollancz (1908); US1880 Spurgeon, *John Ploughman's Pictures*. **20c. coll.:** *ODEP* 472, *CODP* 135, Stevenson 1443:6, Whiting*(MP)* 619.

26. Take care of the little things and the big things will take care of themselves. **Rec. dist.:** Ill., Ont.

27. Take things as they are, not as you'd have them be. **Rec. dist.:** U.S., Can. **1st cit.:** 1509 Barclay, *Ship of Fools,* ed. Jamieson in *Ec-*

logues, E.E.T.S. (1876); US1795 *Correspondence of John Jay,* ed. Johnston (1893). *20c. coll.: ODEP* 801, Whiting 434, Stevenson 415:4, Whiting*(MP)* 621.

28. The best things come in small packages. *Var.:* Valuable things come in small packages. *Rec. dist.:* U.S., Can. *1st cit.:* 1659 Howell, *Paroimiografia (French Proverbs);* US1931 Jacobs, *Snug Harbor. 20c. coll.: CODP* 13, Whiting*(MP)* 618.

29. The thing that often occurs is never much appreciated. *Rec. dist.:* N.Y.

30. The things most people want to know are usually none of their business. *Rec. dist.:* Calif.

31. There are more things than are thought of in heaven and earth. *Rec. dist.:* N.Y.

32. Things always seem fairer when we look back at them. *Rec. dist.:* Ont.

33. Things are as they are and not what they ought to be. *Rec. dist.:* Ohio.

34. Things are in the saddle and ride mankind. *Rec. dist.:* N.Y., S.C. *1st cit.:* US1846 Emerson, *Ode. 20c. coll.:* Stevenson 1497:6.

35. Things are not always what they seem. *Var.:* Things are not what they seem. *Rec. dist.:* Okla., Ont., S.C., Utah. *1st cit.:* 1932 Fletcher, *Man in the Fur Coat;* US1930 Woodrow, *Moonhill. 20c. coll.:* Whiting*(MP)* 620.

36. Things are tough all over. *Rec. dist.:* Calif., Mich., N.Y.

37. Things done cannot be undone. *Rec. dist.:* U.S., Can. *1st cit.:* 1546 Heywood, *Dialogue of Proverbs,* ed. Habernicht (1963); US1782 *Diary and Autobiography of John Adams,* ed. Butterfield (1961). *20c. coll.: ODEP* 199, Whiting 113, Stevenson 543:15, T&W 104.

38. Things hardly attained are long retained. *Rec. dist.:* N.J. *Infm.:* "Hardly" means with difficulty or with much effort.

39. Things have their laws as well as men. *Rec. dist.:* N.Y., S.C.

40. Things ill gained are ill lost. *Rec. dist.:* Minn. *1st cit.:* ca1386 Chaucer, *Reynard,* ed. Arber. *20c. coll.: ODEP* 399.

41. Three things drive a man out of his home: smoke, rain, and a scolding wife. *Rec. dist.:*

Ky., Tenn. *1st cit.:* ca1386 Chaucer, *Tale of Melibee. 20c. coll.: ODEP* 817, Stevenson 2311:3, Whiting*(MP)* 620.

42. We may not be able to do great things, but we can do little things in a big way. *Rec. dist.:* Minn.

43. We see things not as they are but as we are. *Rec. dist.:* Ont.

44. You may hate the things a person does, but never hate the person. *Rec. dist.:* N.Mex. *1st cit.:* 1533 Tyndale, *Enchiridion. 20c. coll.: ODEP* 358.

SEE ALSO The BEST things in life are free. / A man is as BIG as the things that make him mad. / Do not BOAST of a thing until it is done. / The BUSIEST thing in the world is idle curiosity. / All things CHANGE, and we change with them. / It is an ill thing to be DECEIVED but worse to deceive. / Few things are impossible to DILIGENCE and skill. / If you can't DO a thing right, don't do it all. / If you want a thing well done, DO it yourself. / Whatever you DO, do with your might; things done by halves are never done right. / A thing worth DOING is worth thing well. / The only thing we have to FEAR is fear itself. / Put FIRST things first. / FORBID a thing and that we do. / He who is neither one thing or the other has no FRIENDS. / You don't GET more out of a thing that you put into it. / The GREAT man makes the great thing. / Real HAPPINESS is found not in doing the things you like to do, but in liking the things you have to do. / In an orderly HOUSE all things are always ready. / INITIATIVE is doing the right thing without being told. / JUDGE not of men or things at first sight. / It's the LITTLE things in life that count. / LITTLE things worry little minds. / Great LOVE from little things may grow. / There is a MEASURE in all things. / MODERATION is all things. / MONEY answers all things. / Wear out the OLD things first. / There is REASON in all things. / He who SAVES in little things can be liberal in great ones. / If you feel you're too SMALL to do big things, then do big things in a small way. / Keep SMILING when things are at their worst. / He who

TALKS much says many foolish things. / It is only at low TIDE we find things worth picking up. / TIME devours all things. / TIME ends all things. / TIME ripens all things. / The TONGUE is a little thing, but it fills the universe with trouble. / VIRTUE conquers all things. / The WANT of a thing is more than the worth of it. / WANT a thing long enough and you won't. / It's not the WORTH of the thing but the want that makes its value. / The WORTH of a thing is best known by its want. / The WORTH of a thing is what it will bring. / Count that thing WRONG which would be wrong if everybody did it.

think 1. As a man thinks, so he is. *Vars.:* (a) As a man thinks in his heart, so is he. (b) As people think, so they are. *Rec. dist.:* Ala., Ga. *1st cit.:* US1948 Stevenson, *Home Book of Proverbs.* *20c. coll.:* Stevenson 2305:15.

2. If you don't think well of yourself, no one else will. *Rec. dist.:* Ont.

3. One may think what he dare not speak. *Rec. dist.:* Ont., Wis. *1st cit.:* 1597 Shakespeare, *Merchant of Venice.* *20c. coll.:* ODEP 812, Stevenson 2307:10.

4. Quick to think, slow to speak. *Rec. dist.:* Ont.

5. Think all you speak, but speak not all you think. *Rec. dist.:* Calif.

6. Think and thank. *Rec. dist.:* Ont.

7. Think before you leap. *Rec. dist.:* Okla.

8. Think deep and not loud. *Rec. dist.:* Ill.

9. Think long, think wrong. *Rec. dist.:* Ohio.

10. Think more and talk less. *Rec. dist.:* Ky., Tenn. *1st cit.:* ca1430 Lydgate, *Minor Poems.* *20c. coll.:* ODEP 701.

11. Think much; speak little; write less. *Rec. dist.:* Vt.

12. Think—then act. *Vars.:* (a) Think before you act; think twice before you speak. (b) Think twice before you act. *Rec. dist.:* U.S., Can. *1st cit.:* 1557 Edgeworth, *Sermons Repertory;* US1895 Hubbard, *Philistine.* *20c. coll.:* ODEP 263, Stevenson 2307:4, CODP 223, Whiting(MP) 621.

13. Think twice; speak once. *Vars.:* (a) Al-

ways think before you speak. (b) If you think twice before you speak once, you will speak twice the better for it. (c) Think before you speak. (d) Think twice and say nothing. (e) Think twice before you speak. (f) Think twice before you speak once. *Rec. dist.:* U.S., Can. *1st cit.:* 1623 Painter, *Chaucer New Painted;* US1970 Neely, *Walter Syndrome.* *20c. coll.:* ODEP 263, Whiting(MP) 621, CODP 223, Stevenson 2307:5.

14. Those who dare to think by themselves can make others think with them. *Rec. dist.:* Ill.

15. We grow like what we think, so let us think of the good, the true, and the beautiful. *Rec. dist.:* N.Y.

16. What others think of us is not as important as what we think of ourselves. *Rec. dist.:* Minn.

17. What we think doesn't cause as much trouble as what we say. *Rec. dist.:* Minn.

18. Where all think alike, no one thinks very much. *Rec. dist.:* Ont.

19. You are what you think, not what you think you are. *Rec. dist.:* Minn.

20. You can think what you like, but don't say it. *Rec. dist.:* Ont.

SEE ALSO AGE should think and youth should do. / Nothing is ever as BAD as you think it is going to be, and nothing is ever as good as you think it is going to be. / On a good BARGAIN think twice. / They who drink BEER think beer. / They CAN because they think they can. / Multitudes CAN'T because they think they can't. / You can send a man to CONGRESS but you cannot make him think. / A CRAZY man thinks everyone crazy but himself. / What I must DO is all that concerns me, not what people think. / Every DOG thinks her puppies are the cutest. / EVIL to him who evil thinks. / FLATTERERS are clever mind readers, they tell us exactly what we think. / A FOOL talks while a wise man thinks. / Every man thinks his own GEESE swans. / The GIRL that thinks no man is good enough for her is right, but she's left. / The HAPPIEST person is the person who thinks the most interesting thoughts. / No man is ever HAPPY unless he thinks himself so. / Every HORSE thinks his pack heaviest. / A drop of INK may make a million think. / A MAN thinks he knows, but a woman knows better. / Think of OTHERS before you think of yourself. / He who thinks his PLACE is below him will certainly be below his place. / Little knows the fat SOW what the lean one thinks. / SPEAK fair, think what you will. / When you think you STAND, take heed— you may fall. / You can lead a STUDENT to college, but you cannot make him think. / Those can WIN who think they can. / When about to put your WORDS in ink, 'twill do no harm to stop and think. / YOUNG men think old men are fools; old men know young men are fools.

thinker 1. It is the quick thinkers who become leaders. *Rec. dist.:* Ill.

2. The profound thinker always suspects that he is superficial. *Rec. dist.:* Ill.

3. There are two classes of thinkers: the shallow ones who fall short of the truth and the abstruse ones who go beyond it. *Rec. dist.:* Ill.

4. Thinkers are as scarce as gold. *Rec. dist.:* Ill.

SEE ALSO ILL doers are ill thinkers.

thinking 1. It is for want of thinking most men are undone. *Rec. dist.:* N.Y.

2. Thinking is poor wit. *Rec. dist.:* Ont.

3. Thinking is the important thing in life. *Rec. dist.:* N.C.

4. Thinking is very far from knowing. *Rec. dist.:* N.Y. *1st cit.:* 1706 Stevens, *New Spanish and English Dictionary;* US1835 Longstreet, *Georgia Scenes.* *20c. coll.:* ODEP 813, T&W 369, Stevenson 2304:2.

SEE ALSO DRINKING and thinking don't mix. / Nothing is EVIL but thinking makes it so. / HORSE-SENSE is just stable thinking. / High LIVING, low thinking.

thinner *SEE* Dull KNIFE cuts cheese thinner than a sharp one.

thirst *SEE* Thousands DRINK themselves to death before one dies of thirst. / LOVE is a thirst that is never slaked.

thirsty *SEE* Dig the WELL before you are thirsty.

thirty The person you're to be thirty years from now is in your hands now. *Rec. dist.:* Miss.

thistle Gather thistles, except prickles. *Rec. dist.:* Ont. *1st cit.:* 1583 Prime, *Fruitful and Brief Discourse.* *20c. coll.:* ODEP 758, Stevenson 2177:9.

SEE ALSO FIGS do not grow on thistles.

thorn 1. A thorn is small, but he who has felt it doesn't forget it. *Rec. dist.:* Ind.

2. Always a thorn among the roses. *Rec. dist.:* U.S., Can. *1st cit.:* 1430–40 Lydgate, *Prologue to Bochas;* US1734 Franklin, *PRAlmanac.* *20c. coll.:* ODEP 684, Whiting 371, Stevenson 2010:2.

3. He that sows thorns should never go barefoot. *Vars.:* (a) Barefooted men should not tread on thorns. (b) He that sows thorns should never go barefooted. (c) He who scatters thorns should not go barefooted. *Rec. dist.:* Miss., Ont. *1st cit.:* ca1594 Bacon, *Promus;* US1736 Franklin, *PRAlmanac.* *20c. coll.:* ODEP 30, Whiting 435, Stevenson 2303:7.

4. He who sows thorns shall not gather roses. *Rec. dist.:* Miss., Ont. *1st cit.:* US1948 Stevenson, *Home Book of Proverbs.* *20c. coll.:* Stevenson 2009:6.

5. He who sows thorns will never reap grapes. *Rec. dist.:* Tex. *1st cit.:* 1537 Turner, *Old Learning and New.* *20c. coll.:* ODEP 331.

6. It early pricks that will be a thorn. *Vars.:* (a) Early pricks turn to thorns. (b) That which will become a thorn grows sharp early. *Rec. dist.:* Pa., Tex. *1st cit.:* ca1350 Douce MS 52. *20c. coll.:* ODEP 211, Stevenson 2303:9.

7. Under the thorn grow the roses. *Rec. dist.:* N.Y.

8. You get a thorn with every rose, but aren't the roses sweet? *Rec. dist.:* N.Y., Ont., S.C.

SEE ALSO Even if the ASS is laden with gold, he will seek his food among the thorns. / A thorn of EXPERIENCE is worth a wilderness of advice. / You can't gather FIGS from thorns. / A ROSE becomes more beautiful between two thorns. / The greatest ROSE possesses the sharpest thorn. / Lie on ROSES when young; lie on thorns when old. / When gathering ROSES, look out for thorns.

thought *(n.)* **1.** A kind thought is never lost. *Rec. dist.:* Calif., Mich., N.Y., S.C.

2. A man can't be hanged for his thoughts. *Rec. dist.:* Mich., N.Y., Ont.

3. A thought once awakened does not slumber. *Rec. dist.:* Utah.

4. All thoughts of a turtle are turtle, and of a rabbit, rabbit. *Rec. dist.:* N.Y., S.C. *1st cit.:* US1870 Emerson, *Natural History of Intellect.* *20c. coll.:* Stevenson 2304:16.

5. Be careful of your thoughts: they may become words at any time. *Rec. dist.:* Calif.

6. Entertain no thoughts which you would blush at in words. *Rec. dist.:* Mich.

7. Even as your thought, so let your speech be fair. *Rec. dist.:* Ont.

8. First thoughts are best thoughts. *Var.:* Second thoughts are best. *Rec. dist.:* Ont. *1st cit.:* 1852 Fitzgerald, "Second Thoughts" in *Polonius;* US1926 Fletcher, *Massingham.* *20c. coll.:* Stevenson 2308:11, Whiting*(MP)* 622.

9. Great thoughts, like great deeds, need no trumpet. *Rec. dist.:* Calif., Ill., N.Y., S.C.

10. He who quells an angry thought is greater than a king. *Rec. dist.:* Ill., N.Y.

11. My own thoughts are my companions. *Rec. dist.:* N.Y.

12. One courageous thought will put to flight a host of troubles. *Rec. dist.:* Ont.

13. One wrong thought may cause a lifelong regret. *Rec. dist.:* Ill.

14. Second thoughts are best. *Rec. dist.:* Ont. *1st cit.:* 1577 Holinshed, *Chronicles of England;* US1687 *Complete Writings of Roger Williams* (1963). *20c. coll.:* ODEP 708, Whiting 436, *CODP* 198, Stevenson 2308:10, Whiting*(MP)* 622.

15. Sow a thought and reap an act. *Rec. dist.:* Ill., N.Y., S.C. *1st cit.:* US1870 Emerson, "Art" in *Society and Solitude.* *20c. coll.:* Stevenson 2306:11.

16. Speak your thoughts lest someone steal them. *Rec. dist.:* Ala., Ga.

17. The fingers of your thought mold your face carelessly. *Rec. dist.:* Fla.

18. The thought is father to the deed. *Rec. dist.:* N.Y. *1st cit.:* US1948 Stevenson, *Home Book of Proverbs.* *20c. coll.:* Stevenson 2306:11.

19. The thoughts of the heart—these are the wealth of a man. *Rec. dist.:* Ont.

20. They are never alone who are accompanied by noble thought. *Rec. dist.:* N.Y., Okla., S.C. *1st cit.:* ca1580 Sidney, *Arcadia;* US1854 Thoreau, *Walden.* *20c. coll.:* Stevenson 2306:2.

21. Thought is for the old, and action for the young. *Rec. dist.:* Calif., Ind.

22. Thought without action will have no result at all. *Rec. dist.:* Calif.

23. Thoughts unexpressed may some day fall back dead, but God Himself can't kill them once they're said. *Rec. dist.:* N.C.

24. When alone, we have our own thoughts to watch; when in the family, our tempers; when in society, our tongues. *Var.:* When alone, we have our thoughts to watch. *Rec. dist.:* Ont., Wis.

25. Women's thoughts are always afterthoughts. *Rec. dist.:* Ill.

26. You can't keep thoughts from entering your head, but you can keep from hoarding them there. *Rec. dist.:* Ariz.

27. Your thoughts go no further than your vocabulary. *Rec. dist.:* Ala., Ga.

SEE ALSO ACTION is itself the best remedy for morbid thoughts. / CONSERVATION is the mirror of a man's thoughts. / A man without thought of the FUTURE must soon have present sorrow. / Kind HEARTS are the gardens, kind thoughts the roots, kind words the flowers, kind deeds the fruits. / LANGUAGE is the dress of thought. / POLITENESS is to goodness what words are to thought. / Every REVOLUTION was first a thought in one man's mind. / A SPADE and a thought should never be allowed to rust. / SPEECH is the gift of all but the thought of few. / STYLE is the dress of thoughts. / The WISH is father to the thought.

thought (*v.*) *See* It is better to be thought a FOOL than to open your mouth and let the world know it. / There are more THINGS than are thought of in heaven and earth. / An ounce of WIT that's bought is worth a pound that's thought.

thoughtful It is better to be thoughtful than thoughtless. *Rec. dist.:* Ill.

thoughtless *See* Thoughtless FRIENDS are often a nuisance.

thousand It's the first thousand that comes hardest. *Rec. dist.:* Ill.

See also The BUYER needs a thousand eyes; the seller wants but one. / A COWARD dies a thousand deaths. / He that has a thousand FRIENDS has not a friend to spare. / One good HEAD is better than a thousand stong hands. / Deviate an INCH, lose a thousand miles. / It is wiser to bear a single INJURY in silence than to provoke a thousand by flying into a rage. / Make one in a thousand an INTIMATE. / A JOURNEY of a thousand miles begins with one step. / The PEN conveys one's meaning a thousand miles. / One PICTURE is worth ten thousand words. / A thousand WORDS won't fill a bushel.

thread 1. A long thread, a lazy tailor. *Vars.:* **(a)** A long thread bespeaks a lazy tailor. **(b)** Lazy tailor uses long thread. *Rec. dist.:* Ont. *1st cit.:* US1938 Champion, *Racial Proverbs.* *20c. coll.:* Stevenson 2140:8.

2. A thread is always on the tailor. *Rec. dist.:* N.Y.

3. A thread too finespun will easily break. *Rec. dist.:* Ark. *1st cit.:* 1640 Herbert, *Outlandish Proverbs (Jacula Prudentum)* in *Works,* ed. Hutchinson (1941). *20c. coll.:* ODEP 815, Stevenson 2309:6.

4. Leave a loose thread. *Rec. dist.:* Ont. *Infm.:* Always leave a loose thread when you stop sewing to mark your place.

5. The thread follows the needle. *Var.:* Where the needle goes, the thread follows. *Rec. dist.:* Ky., Ont., Tenn. *1st cit.:* 1902 Hulme, *Proverb Lore;* US1937 Hart, *Chinese Proverbs.* *20c. coll.:* Stevenson 2309:8.

6. The thread is cut where the thread is thin-nest. *Rec. dist.:* Wash. *1st cit.:* 1640 Herbert, *Outlandish Proverbs (Jacula Prudentum)* in *Works,* ed. Hutchinson (1941). *20c. coll.:* Stevenson 2309:7.

7. There's many a thread 'twixt sheep and shirt. *Rec. dist.:* Ont.

See also A gentle HEART is tied with an easy thread. / Always tie a KNOT in the end of your thread and you will never lose the first stitch. / For a WEB begun, God sends thread.

threadbare *See* When a man's COAT is threadbare, it is easy to pick a hole in it.

threaten He threatens who is afraid. *Rec. dist.:* Ohio. *1st cit.:* US1782 Franklin, *PRAlmanac.* *20c. coll.:* Whiting 437, Stevenson 2310:8.

threatened Threatened folks live the longest: they take numerous precautions. *Var.:* Threatened folks live long. *Rec. dist.:* Ill., Mich. *1st cit.:* 1534 Byrne, *Lisle Letters.* *20c. coll.:* CODP 224, ODEP 815.

three *See* One BOY's a boy; two boys, a half a boy; three boys, no boy at all. / When you point one FINGER at someone else, you point three at yourself. / FISH and visitors stink in three days. / What HAPPENS twice happens thrice. / To a wise HEAD—two or three words. / A LOVE LETTER sometimes costs more than a three-cent stamp. / Three types of PEOPLE in the world: those who have wishbones, those who have funny bones, and those who have backbones. / There are three SIDES to every story—your side, my side, and the right side. / Three THINGS drive a man out of his home: smoke, rain, and a scolding wife. / Two is company; three is a crowd.

thrift 1. Most people consider thrift a fine virtue in ancestors. *Rec. dist.:* N.Y.

2. Practice thrift or else you'll drift. *Rec. dist.:* Ont.

3. Thrift is to a man what chastity is to a woman. *Rec. dist.:* N.Y., S.C. *1st cit.:* ca1937 Howe, Aphorism in *Saturday Review of Literature,* 13 May 1944. *20c. coll.:* Stevenson 2313:6.

See also A PATCH is the sign of thrift, a hole the sign of negligence.

thrifty A thrifty father rarely has a thrifty son. *Rec. dist.:* Miss.

SEE ALSO A thrifty FATHER rarely has thrifty sons.

thrive **1.** Better late thrive than never do well. *Rec. dist.:* N.Y.

2. He that would thrive must rise at five; he that has thrived may rise at seven. *Rec. dist.:* Minn. *1st cit.:* ca1590 Harvey, *Marginalia.* *20c. coll.:* Stevenson 2313:11.

SEE ALSO He that by the PLOW would thrive, himself must either hold or drive.

throat *SEE* A fool's TONGUE is long enough to cut his throat. / Let not your TONGUE cut your throat.

through *SEE* If you can't GO over or under, go through.

throw *(n.)* *SEE* The best throw of the DICE is to throw them away.

throw *(v.)* Don't throw away what others may use. *Rec. dist.:* Okla.

SEE ALSO Don't throw out the BABY with the bathwater. / Don't throw out old CLOTHES before you get new ones. / You'll have to throw the old COW a nubbin before you can ever catch the calf. / He who lives in a GLASS house shouldn't throw stones. / GOD sends every bird its food, but he does not throw it into the west. / He that has a HEAD of glass shold not throw stones at another. / No MUD can soil us but the mud we throw. / When you see a MULE's fixin' to throw you, you jes git off. / Don't throw away the OLD till you know the new is better. / Who holds his PEACE and gathers stones will find a time to throw them. / If you throw enough PITCH, some of it is sure to stick. / A WOMAN can throw out on a spoon more than a man can bring in on a shovel.

thrust *SEE* Some are born GREAT, some achieve greatness, and some have greatness thrust upon them.

thunder *(n.)* **1.** A winter's thunder is a summer's hunger. *Vars.:* **(a)** Winter's thunder makes summer's hunger. **(b)** Winter's thunder: rich man's food and poor man's hunger. *Rec. dist.:* Ont. *1st cit.:* 1605 Camden, *Remaines Concerning Britaine.* *20c. coll.:* Stevenson 2315:9.

2. It's the thunder that frights but the lightning that smites. *Rec. dist.:* Ont.

3. Thunder in February means frost in April. *Vars.:* **(a)** Thunder in February, rain in July. **(b)** Thunder in March, corn to parch. *Rec. dist.:* Miss.

4. Thunder in the fall, no winter at all. *Rec. dist.:* Ont.

5. Thunder without rain is like words without deeds. *Rec. dist.:* Ill.

6. When the thunder is very loud, there's very little rain. *Rec. dist.:* Ill.

thunder *(v.)* **1.** If it thunders before seven, it will rain before eleven. *Rec. dist.:* Ill.

2. It never thunders but it rains. *Rec. dist.:* Wis. *1st cit.:* ca1386 Chaucer, *Prologue to Wife of Bath's Tale;* US1775 Ames, *Almanacs,* ed. Briggs (1891). *20c. coll.:* Stevenson 2316:1, Whiting 437, ODEP 820.

Thursday *SEE* Every DAY is not Friday; there is also Thursday.

ticket **1.** If you don't have a ticket, you don't ride. *Rec. dist.:* Mich.

2. No tickee, no washee. *Rec. dist.:* Mich., N.Y., Tex. *Infm.:* If you don't have your ticket, you don't get your wash. *1st cit.:* US1931 Taylor, *The Proverb.* *20c. coll.:* Stevenson 1612:11, Whiting(MP) 625.

tide **1.** Every tide has its ebb. *Rec. dist.:* Ill., Tex. *1st cit.:* ca1412 Lydgate, *Troy Book,* E.E.T.S. (1935). *20c. coll.:* ODEP 269, Stevenson 2317:9, Whiting(MP) 625.

2. Every tide must turn. *Rec. dist.:* Tex. *1st cit.:* 1659 Howell, *Paroimiografia (English Proverbs).* *20c. coll.:* ODEP 821.

3. It is only at low tide we find things worth picking up. *Rec. dist.:* Ill.

4. There is a tide in the affairs of men which, taken at the flood, leads on to fortune. *Rec. dist.:* Ohio. *1st cit.:* 1599 Shakespeare, *Julius Caesar;* US1784 *Diary of Chief Justice William Smith, 1784–1793,* ed. Upton, Champlain Soc. Publications (1963). *20c. coll.:* ODEP 821, Whiting 438, Stevensons 2318:2.

5. Wait for the rising tide. *Rec. dist.:* Ohio.

6. Wait for the turn of the tide. *Rec. dist.:* Ont.

SEE ALSO TIME and tide wait for no man.

tidy SEE Better be NEAT and tidy than tight and needy.

tie Do not be in a hurry to tie what you cannot untie. *Rec. dist.:* Miss.

SEE ALSO The COW must graze where she is tied. / A gentle HEART is tied with an easy thread. / He that don't tie a KNOT may lose his first stitch.

tiger **1.** Clipping a tiger's claws never makes him lose his taste for blood. *Rec. dist.:* Ill.

2. He who rides the tiger can never dismount. *Rec. dist.:* N.J., Ont. *1st cit.:* 1902 Colquhoun, *Mastery of Pacific;* US1875 Scarborough, *Chinese Proverbs.* *20c. coll.:* ODEP 677, CODP 191, Stevenson 2318:6, Whiting(MP) 625.

3. Tigers and deer do not stroll together. *Rec. dist.:* Ind.

4. When the tiger is dead, the stag dances on his grave. *Rec. dist.:* N.Y.

5. When the tiger salaams, the end of the world arrives. *Rec. dist.:* N.C.

6. While keeping a tiger from the front door, the wolf enters from the back. *Rec. dist.:* Wis.

SEE ALSO One must have an iron CAGE of nerves to hold a tiger in the breast. / New born CALVES don't fear tigers. / The COURAGE of the tiger is one and of the horse another. / It is better to be a live RABBIT than a dead tiger.

tight *(n.)* SEE WIDE will wear, but tight will tear.

tight *(adj.)* SEE If you make a bad BARGAIN, hug it the tighter. / Best draw a tight CINCH.

till Mind your till, and till your mind. *Rec. dist.:* Ill. *Infm.:* The first "till" refers to a cash drawer, the second to plowing.

tillage SEE A FIELD becomes exhausted by constant tillage.

timber Dey's jes' ez good a timber in de woods ez w'at been bought. *Rec. dist.:* Tex.

time **1.** A moment of time is a moment of mercy. *Rec. dist.:* Mich.

2. A short time is long for the unprepared. *Rec. dist.:* Minn.

3. All that time is lost which might be better employed. *Rec. dist.:* Wash.

4. Always is a long time. *Rec. dist.:* Ill.

5. An inch of time is an inch of gold. *Var.:* One inch of time is one inch of gold. *Rec. dist.:* Ont., Wis. *1st cit.:* 1872 Doolittle, *Chinese Proverbs.* *20c. coll.:* Stevenson 2319:6.

6. Appoint a time for everything, and do everything in its time. *Rec. dist.:* Mich.

7. As good have no time as make no good use of it. *Rec. dist.:* Ohio.

8. Begin in time to finish without hurry. *Rec. dist.:* Ont.

9. Better on time than late. *Rec. dist.:* Ohio.

10. Don't fiddle your time away. *Rec. dist.:* Miss.

11. Don't spend your time in vain regrets. *Rec. dist.:* Minn.

12. Don't wait till you get time—take time. *Rec. dist.:* Ont.

13. Don't waste five-dollar time on a five-cent job. *Rec. dist.:* Miss.

14. Employ the time well if you mean to gain leisure. *Rec. dist.:* Ind., N.Y., Ont., S.C. *1st cit.:* US1740 Franklin, *PRAlmanac.* *20c. coll.:* Stevenson 2326:4.

15. Everything has its time. *Rec. dist.:* Calif., Mich., N.Y. *1st cit.:* ca1390 Chaucer, *Prologue to Clerk's Tale;* US1623 Altham in James, *Three Visitors to Early Plymouth.* *20c. coll.:* ODEP 823, Whiting 439, CODP 226, Stevenson 2328:5, T&W 374, Whiting(MP) 627.

16. He that gains time gains all things. *Rec. dist.:* Ill. *1st cit.:* 1573 Sanford, *Garden of Pleasure.* *20c. coll.:* ODEP 823.

17. He who has time does not wait for time. *Rec. dist.:* Ont. *1st cit.:* 1573 Sanford, *Garden of Pleasure.* *20c. coll.:* ODEP 822.

18. He who knows most grieves most for wasted time. *Rec. dist.:* Ont.

19. If you want to pass time quickly, just give your note for ninety days. *Rec. dist.:* Calif.

20. Improve time and time will improve you. *Rec. dist.:* Utah.

21. In time, on time, everytime, and all the time, excepting when ahead of time, and that's a little better time. *Rec. dist.:* Okla.

22. It's time enough to bid the devil good morning when you meet him. *Rec. dist.:* Kans. *1st cit.:* 1872 Blake, Article in London *Daily News,* 5 Aug. *20c. coll.:* Stevenson 557:13.

23. Kill time and time will kill you. *Rec. dist.:* Va.

24. Killing time is not murder, it's suicide. *Rec. dist.:* Ont.

25. Let time that makes you homely make you sage. *Rec. dist.:* Ill.

26. Little by little time goes by, short if you sing, long if you sigh. *Rec. dist.:* N.J.

27. Lost time is never found. *Var.:* Lost time is never found again, and what we call time enough always proves little enough. *Rec. dist.:* U.S., Can. *1st cit.:* ca1374 Chaucer, *Troilus and Criseyde;* US1738 *Colonial Records of Georgia,* ed. Chandler, in *Original Papers, 1735–1752* (1910–16). *20c. coll.:* ODEP 824, Whiting 442, Stevenson 2326:11, Whiting(MP) 629.

28. Never waste time. *Rec. dist.:* Ill.

29. Noiseless falls the foot of time. *Rec. dist.:* Minn. *1st cit.:* 1802 Juvenal, *Satires,* tr. Gifford. *20c. coll.:* Stevenson 2323:6.

30. Nothing is more injurious than unoccupied time. *Rec. dist.:* Minn.

31. Nothing is more precious than time, yet nothing is less valued. *Rec. dist.:* N.Y., Ont., S.C. *1st cit.:* US1775 Ames, *Almanacs,* ed. Briggs (1891). *20c. coll.:* Whiting 441.

32. Out of time, out of mind. *Rec. dist.:* N.C. *1st cit.:* 1414 *Rolls of Parliament. 20c. coll.:* Stevenson 2322:6.

33. Start in time to be in time. *Rec. dist.:* Ohio.

34. Strike when the time is right. *Rec. dist.:* Okla.

35. Take time by the forelock. *Var.:* Catch time by the forelock; he is bald behind. *Rec. dist.:* U.S., Can. *1st cit.:* 1539 Taverner, *Proverbs of Erasmus;* US1623 Winthrop in *Winthrop Papers, 1498–1649,* Mass.Hist.Soc. *Collections* (1929–47). *20c. coll.:* ODEP 822, Whiting 443, Stevenson 2324:3, T&W 375, Whiting(MP) 630.

36. Take time when time is, for time will away. *Rec. dist.:* Ont. *1st cit.:* 1545 Skelton, *On Time;* US1758 Franklin, *PRAlmanac. 20c. coll.:* ODEP 825, Stevenson 2324:6.

37. The best way to kill time is to work it to death. *Rec. dist.:* Calif., Ill., Utah.

38. The hands of time will never turn back. *Rec. dist.:* Ont.

39. The only value of time is its use. *Rec. dist.:* Ill.

40. The sands of time never run smooth. *Rec. dist.:* Ohio.

41. The stairway of time ever echoes with the wooden shoe going up, the polished shoe coming down. *Rec. dist.:* N.Y., S.C.

42. The third time is a charm. *Rec. dist.:* U.S., Can. *1st cit.:* 1721 Kelly, *Scottish Proverbs;* US1832 Ames, *Nautical Reminiscences. 20c. coll.:* ODEP 813, Whiting 440, CODP 223, Stevenson 2312:2, T&W 374, Whiting(MP) 627.

43. There is a time and place for everything. *Vars.:* **(a)** There is a time for all things. **(b)** There is a time for everything. *Rec. dist.:* U.S., Can. *1st cit.:* ca1390 Chaucer, *Prologue to Clerk's Tale;* US1623 Altham in James, *Three Visitors to Early Plymouth. 20c. coll.:* ODEP 823, Whiting 439, CODP 225, Stevenson 2329:1, T&W 374, Whiting(MP) 627.

44. There is a time to fish and a time to dry nets. *Rec. dist.:* Calif., Ill.

45. There must be a first time for everything. *Rec. dist.:* U.S., Can. *1st cit.:* ca1390 Chaucer, *Prologue to Clerk's Tale;* US1792 Hamilton, *Papers of Alexander Hamilton,* eds. Syrett and Cooke (1961). *20c. coll.:* CODP 226, Whiting 440, Whiting(MP) 627.

46. There's a time for business. *Rec. dist.:* N.C.

47. There's always time to do what you want to do. *Rec. dist.:* Calif., Ill.

48. There's no time like the present. *Vars.:* **(a)** Now is the best time for everything. **(b)** Now is the time. *Rec. dist.:* U.S., Can. *1st cit.:* 1562 Legh, *Accidence of Armoury;* US1764 A. Adams in *Adams Family Correspondence,* ed. Butterfield (1966). *20c. coll.:* ODEP 824, Whiting 439, CODP 226, Stevenson 1874:11, T&W 373, Whiting(MP) 626.

49. They who make the best use of their time have none to spare. *Rec. dist.:* Ont. *1st cit.:* 1732 Fuller, *Gnomologia.* *20c. coll.:* ODEP 49.

50. Time and patience change the mulberry leaf to satin. *Rec. dist.:* Ont. *1st cit.:* 1659 Howell, *New Sayings;* US1705 Ingles, *Modest Reply to Mr. Commissary Ward's Answer* in *Va.Mag.Hist.* (1901). *20c. coll.:* ODEP 822, Whiting 440.

51. Time and tide wait for no man. *Var.:* Time waits for no man. *Rec. dist.:* U.S., Can. *1st cit.:* ca1386 Chaucer, *Prologue to Clerk's Tale;* USca1656 Bradford, *History of Plymouth Plantation,* ed. Ford (1912). *20c. coll.:* ODEP 822, Whiting 438, CODP 225, Stevenson 2322:12, T&W 373, Whiting(MP) 628.

52. Time and trouble circle the world. *Rec. dist.:* Ohio.

53. Time and words can never be recalled. *Rec. dist.:* Ont. *1st cit.:* 1732 Fuller, *Gnomologia.* *20c. coll.:* Stevenson 2319:14.

54. Time brings everything to light. *Vars.:* **(a)** Time will reveal all things. **(b)** Time will show. *Rec. dist.:* U.S., Can. *1st cit.:* 1530 Palsgrave, *Lesclarcissement de la langue Francoyse,* ed. Genin (1852); US1612 Strachey, *Historie of Travaile into Virginia Britannia,* ed. Wright, Hakluyt Soc. (1953). *20c. coll.:* ODEP 823, Whiting 440, Stevenson 2330:4.

55. Time brings everything to those who can wait for it. *Rec. dist.:* Ill.

56. Time changes ever, but the heart of man never. *Rec. dist.:* Ont.

57. Time changes everything. *Var.:* Time changes all things. *Rec. dist.:* Calif., Ky., Tenn. *1st cit.:* US1937 Marquand, *Late George Apley.* *20c. coll.:* Whiting(MP) 628.

58. Time changes the oak into a coffin. *Rec. dist.:* Ill.

59. Time consumes the strongest. *Rec. dist.:* Ohio.

60. Time devours all things. *Rec. dist.:* Ont. *1st cit.:* 1549 Thomas, *History of Italy.* *20c. coll.:* ODEP 823, Stevenson 2327:5.

61. Time ends all things. *Rec. dist.:* Vt. *1st cit.:* US1786 Ames, *Almanacs,* ed. Briggs (1891). *20c. coll.:* Whiting 440.

62. Time erases all sorrows. *Rec. dist.:* Wis. *1st cit.:* ca1374 Chaucer, *Troilus and Criseyde;* US1786 Carr in *Papers of Thomas Jefferson,* ed. Boyd (1950). *20c. coll.:* ODEP 824, Whiting 441, Stevenson 2329:3.

63. Time flies. *Vars.:* **(a)** Time flies like the wind. **(b)** Time flies—say not so. Time stops—we go. *Rec. dist.:* U.S., Can. *1st cit.:* ca1386 Chaucer, *Prologue to Clerk's Tale;* US1710 Paine in *Mayflower Descendant* (1910). *20c. coll.:* ODEP 823, Whiting 440, CODP 226, Stevenson 2323:1, T&W 374, Whiting(MP) 628.

64. Time flies like an arrow, and time lost never returns. *Rec. dist.:* Ill. *1st cit.:* 1710 Ekken, *Ten Kun,* tr. Hoshino; US1943 Gardiner, *Case of Buried Clock.* *20c. coll.:* Stevenson 2322:10.

65. Time goes slow for those who watch it. *Rec. dist.:* Calif.

66. Time hangs heavy on idle hands. *Rec. dist.:* Ind.

67. Time has a wallet. *Rec. dist.:* Ind. *1st cit.:* 1601 Shakespeare, *Troilus and Cressida.* *20c. coll.:* Stevenson 2321:8.

68. Time heals all wounds. *Vars.:* **(a)** Time cures all ills. **(b)** Time dresses the greatest wounds. **(c)** Time heals all. **(d)** Time is a great healer. **(e)** Time will bring healing. **(f)** Time will heal. *Rec. dist.:* U.S., Can. *1st cit.:* ca1374 Chaucer, *Troilus and Criseyde;* US1830 McLemore in *Correspondence of Andrew Jackson,* ed. Bassett (1926–33). *20c. coll.:* ODEP 823, Whiting 442, CODP 226, Stevenson 2329:2, Whiting(MP) 628.

69. Time is a cunning workman. *Rec. dist.:* Ont.

70. Time is a file that wears and makes no noise. *Rec. dist.:* Ill., Ont. *1st cit.:* 1666 Torriano, *Select Italian Proverbs.* **20c. coll.:** *ODEP* 823, Stevenson 2328:1.

71. Time is a hard taskmaster. *Rec. dist.:* Ill.

72. Time is an herb that cures all diseases. *Rec. dist.:* Minn.

73. Time is a ship that never anchors. *Rec. dist.:* Ont.

74. Time is a true friend to sorrow. *Rec. dist.:* Ill.

75. Time is capital: invest it wisely. *Rec. dist.:* Calif.

76. Time is like money: once spent, it can never be spent again. *Rec. dist.:* Calif.

77. Time is money. *Rec. dist.:* U.S., Can. *1st cit.:* 1572, Wilson, *Discourse upon Usury;* US1736 Franklin, *PRAlmanac.* **20c. coll.:** *ODEP* 823, Whiting 441, *CODP* 226, Stevenson 2318:8, T&W 374, Whiting*(MP)* 629.

78. Time is not the click of the clock, it is the everlasting now. *Rec. dist.:* W.Va.

79. Time is shorter than you think. *Rec. dist.:* Okla.

80. Time is the best doctor. *Rec. dist.:* N.Y.

81. Time is the best teacher. *Var.:* Time is a great teacher. *Rec. dist.:* U.S., Can. *1st cit.:* 1799 Burke, Letter to Sir H. Langrishe, 26 May. **20c. coll.:** Stevenson 2318:7.

82. Time is of the essence. *Var.:* Time is the important thing. *Rec. dist.:* N.Y., S.C., Wis. *1st cit.:* US1629 Fones in *Winthrop Papers, 1498–1649,* in Mass.Hist.Soc. *Collections* (1863–92). **20c. coll.:** Whiting 441, T&W 374, Whiting*(MP)* 629.

83. Time is the rider that breaks youth. *Rec. dist.:* N.Y., S.C. *1st cit.:* 1640 Herbert, *Outlandish Proverbs (Jacula Prudentum)* in *Works,* ed. Hutchinson (1941). **20c. coll.:** *ODEP* 824, Stevenson 2327:7.

84. Time is the sire of fame. *Rec. dist.:* Mich., N.Y.

85. Time is, time was, and time is past. *Rec. dist.:* Ill. *1st cit.:* ca1589 Greene, *Honorable Historie of Frier Bacon and Frier Bongay.* **20c. coll.:** *ODEP* 824, Stevenson 2321:1.

86. Time leaps; wisdom crowds. *Rec. dist.:* N.Dak.

87. Time makes turncoats of us all. *Rec. dist.:* Ill.

88. Time marches on. *Rec. dist.:* Calif., Mich., N.Y.

89. Time never stands still. *Rec. dist.:* Mich., N.Y., Ont.

90. Time passes quickly; make good use of it. *Rec. dist.:* Calif.

91. Time ripens all things. *Rec. dist.:* Ont. *1st cit.:* 1578 Florio, *Firste Fruites.* **20c. coll.:** Stevenson 2330:10.

92. Time saved at a cost of an accident is no saving. *Rec. dist.:* Ill.

93. Time serves no man. *Rec. dist.:* N.Y.

94. Time was made for slaves. *Rec. dist.:* Calif. *1st cit.:* 1850 Buckstone, *Billie Taylor.* **20c. coll.:** Stevenson 2319:1.

95. Time wasted getting even could be saved by getting ahead. *Rec. dist.:* N.J.

96. Time wasted is time lost. *Var.:* Time wasted is never regained. *Rec. dist.:* Ala., Ga., Iowa.

97. Time will pass. *Rec. dist.:* Calif.

98. Time will tell. *Vars.:* **(a)** Only time will tell. **(b)** Time alone will tell. **(c)** Time has tales to tell. **(d)** Time will disclose all things. **(e)** Time will tell tales. *Rec. dist.:* U.S., Can. *1st cit.:* 1530 Palsgrave, *Lesclarcissement de la langue Francoyse,* ed. Genin (1852); US1609 Strachey, *Historie of Travaile into Virginia Britannia,* ed. Wright, Hakluyt Soc. (1953). **20c. coll.:** *ODEP* 823, Whiting 440, *CODP* 277, T&W 375, Whiting*(MP)* 630.

99. Time works for those who work. *Rec. dist.:* Calif., Ont.

100. Time works wonders. *Rec. dist.:* Calif., Ill., N.Y. *1st cit.:* 1588 Marten, *Exhortation to Defend Country;* US1871 Jones, *Life of Jefferson S. Batkins.* **20c. coll.:** *ODEP* 825, T&W 375, *CODP* 227, Stevenson 2329:4.

101. Use time as though you knew its value. *Rec. dist.:* Ont.

102. We mustn't waste time, for that's the stuff life's made of. *Var.:* Don't squander time, for time is what life is made of. *Rec. dist.:* N.Y.

103. Well-arranged time is the surest mark of a well-arranged mind. *Rec. dist.:* Ill.

104. What we call time enough always proves little enough. *Rec. dist.:* N.Y., N.Dak. *1st cit.:* 1910 Joyce, *English as We Speak It;* US1747 Franklin, *PRAlmanac.* *20c. coll.:* Stevenson 2319:12, Whiting 440.

105. Wise use of time will make for wiser living. *Rec. dist.:* N.C.

106. You can't throw down time and pick it up again. *Rec. dist.:* Minn.

107. You sit your time like many a good goose. *Rec. dist.:* Ont.

SEE ALSO It takes less time to avoid an ACCIDENT than it does to report it. / AIM high, time flies. / Time to catch BEARS is when they're out. / BOOKS are ships that pass through the vast seas of time. / When you's BROKE, dat's de time to ack stylish, so folks won't know you're broke. / Don't try to sit on two CHAIRS at the same time. / COURAGE is a virtue the young cannot spare; to lose it is to grow old before their time. / You'll be a long time DEAD. / DEATH is but death, and all in time shall die. / You may DELAY, but time will not. / A creaking DOOR lasts a long time. / ENJOY yourself; there is less time than you think. / One at a time is good FISHING. / You can't put your FOOTPRINTS in the sands of time by sitting down. / Have FUN while you live because you're going to be dead a long time. / The time to give up the GAME is when it is at its best. / He doubles his GIFT who gives in time. / Have a GOOD time, but if you can't be good, be careful. / If it HAPPENS twice it will happen three times. / Work hard in HARVEST time. / Better once in HEAVEN than ten times at the gate. / Don't waste time looking at the HILL, climb it. / HUSBANDS are like automobiles: if you take care of them, you don't have to be getting new ones all the time. / LEISURE is the time for doing something useful. / LIFE is not so short but that there is always time for courtesy. / LIFE is short, and time is swift. / LOVE is not time's fool. / To find out what a MAN is like, find out what he does in his spare time. / You can please some of the PEOPLE all the time, or all the people some of the time, but never all of the people all of the time. / The worst of all POLICIES in hard times is to sit down and fold your hands. / PROCRASTINATION is the thief of time. / PUNCTUALITY is the thief of time. / The man who hasn't time to READ hasn't time to succeed. / The time to go down to the RIVER is when the water is up. / The ROOSTER crows to let us know, if we are wise, it's time to rise. / It is useless to RUN; better to start on time. / You cannot RUN and bark at the same time. / SECONDS are the gold dust of time. / A STITCH in time saves nine. / SUCCESS is a matter of using one's time well. / Some TEACHERS are time servers. / One THING at a time. / Four THINGS cannot be brought back: a word spoken, an arrow discharged, the divine decree, and past time. / Tell the TRUTH all the time and you won't have to remember what you said. / Nine-tenths of WISDOM consists in being wise in time. / WRONG will right itself in time.

times **1.** Keep ahead of the times. *Rec. dist.:* Utah.

2. Other times, other customs. *Var.:* Other times, other manners. *Rec. dist.:* Ill. *1st cit.:* 1576 Pettie, *Petite Palace of Pleasure,* ed. Gollancz (1908); US1919 Thayer, *Mystery on 13th Floor.* *20c. coll.:* Stevenson 1524:3, Whiting(MP) 626, ODEP 600.

3. These are the times that try men's souls. *Rec. dist.:* N.Y., S.C. *1st cit.:* US1776 Paine, *The Crisis* in *Complete Writings of Thomas Paine,* ed. Foner (1945). *20c. coll.:* Stevenson 2331:8.

4. Times are tough when the skies aren't smoky. *Rec. dist.:* Pa.

5. Times change, and people change their ideas. *Rec. dist.:* Calif. *1st cit.:* ca1596 Spenser, *Mutabilitie;* US1943 Grafton, *Rat Began to Gnaw Rope.* *20c. coll.:* Stevenson 315:5.

6. Times change, and we change with them. *Rec. dist.:* Ohio, N.Y. *1st cit.:* 1579 Lyly, *Euphues, Anatomy of Wit;* US1934 Sharpe, *Murder of Honest Broker.* *20c. coll.:* ODEP 825, Whiting(MP) 628, CODP 227, Stevenson 315:5.

timid *(n.)* The timid are never free. *Rec. dist.:* Mich.

timid *(adj.)* When you spit in a timid man's eye, he says it is raining. *Rec. dist.:* Ill.

SEE ALSO Timid DOGS bark most. / A timid HORSEMAN does not stay mounted long.

tin SEE Some people go to a lot of trouble to hide their LIGHT under a bushel when a tin cup would suffice for the job.

tinker SEE If "ifs" and "ands" were pots and pans, there were little need for tinkers.

tire *(n.)* SEE The longer the SPOKE, the greater the tire.

tire *(v.)* He who does not tire, tires adversity. *Rec. dist.:* Miss.

SEE ALSO Go not unto your NEIGHBOR's place too often lest he tire of you.

tired SEE If you GROWL all day it is no wonder you are dog tired at night.

tithing Tithing is simply payment of an honest debt. *Rec. dist.:* N.C.

title He has a better title who was first in point of time. *Rec. dist.:* Ill.

SEE ALSO The man who WALKS takes title to the world around him.

toad 1. A toad in a puddle is better than a puddle in a toad. *Rec. dist.:* Ont. *Infm.:* Something possible is better than the impossible.

2. Better be a big toad in a small puddle than a small toad in a big puddle. *Rec. dist.:* Mich., N.Y., Ont., S.C. *1st cit.:* US1871 Jones, *Life of Jefferson S. Batkins.* *20c. coll.:* T&W 376.

3. You can't tell how far a toad will jump by the length of its tail. *Var.:* You cannot tell how far a toad can jump by looking at him. *Rec. dist.:* Ill., Mich.

SEE ALSO You can't get FEATHERS off a toad.

tobacco 1. Don't chew your tobacco twice. *Rec. dist.:* U.S. *Infm.:* Don't repeat what you have just said.

2. It's allers best for a man to chaw his own tobakker. *Rec. dist.:* Tex. *1st cit.:* US1858 Hammett, *Piney Woods Tavern.* *20c. coll.:* T&W 376.

today 1. Do today's right; don't fuss about tomorrow's. *Rec. dist.:* Calif.

2. Don't do anything today that you may be sorry for tomorrow. *Rec. dist.:* Calif.

3. Here today, gone tomorrow. *Var.:* Hyar t'day an' thar t'morrer. *Rec. dist.:* U.S., Can. *1st cit.:* 1549 Calvin, *Life and Convictions of a Christian Man;* US1650 *Works of Anne Bradstreet,* ed. Ellis (1932). *20c. coll.:* ODEP 370, Whiting 444, Stevenson 1336:4, T&W 182, Whiting(MP) 633.

4. Live today, for tomorrow may not come. *Vars.:* (a) Be gay today, for tomorrow you may die. (b) Live today, for tomorrow you may die. (c) Live today, not tomorrow. (d) Live today: tomorrow may be too late. *Rec. dist.:* Ark., Okla., Utah.

5. Never do today what you can put off until tomorrow. *Vars.:* (a) Don't do today what you can put off till tomorrow, for tomorrow pays time and a half. (b) Don't do today what you can put off until tomorrow. (c) Don't put off today what you can't put off tomorrow. (d) Never do today what can be done tomorrow. (e) Never do today what you can get somebody else to do tomorrow. (f) Never do today what you can put off till tomorrow. *Rec. dist.:* U.S., Can. *1st cit.:* 1849 *Punch;* USca1785 Burr, Maxim in Parton, *Life of Aaron Burr.* *20c. coll.:* Stevenson 2340:7, T&W 377, Whiting(MP) 636.

6. One today is worth two tomorrows. *Rec. dist.:* U.S., Can. *1st cit.:* 1641 Quarles, *Enchiridion;* US1757 Franklin, *PRAlmanac.* *20c. coll.:* ODEP 827, Whiting 444, Stevenson 2336:1.

7. Plan today for tomorrow. *Rec. dist.:* Fla.

8. Take care of today and tomorrow will take care of itself. *Vars.:* (a) Live today well and tomorrow will take care of itself. (b) Look out for today; tomorrow will take care of itself. *Rec. dist.:* Ky., Ohio, Ont., Tenn., Utah.

9. Today is not the same as tomorrow. *Rec. dist.:* Fla.

10. Today is the tomorrow that you worried about yesterday. *Var.:* Today is the tomorrow you dreamed about yesterday. *Rec. dist.:* Calif., N.J., Okla., Utah.

11. Today is yesterday's pupil. *Var.:* Today is the pupil of yesterday. *Rec. dist.:* Miss., N.Y., N.C. *1st cit.:* 1601 Wheeler, *Treatise of Com-*

merce; US1751 Franklin, *PRAlmanac*. **20c. coll.:** *ODEP* 827, Stevenson 2336:6.

12. Today is yesterday's tomorrow. **Rec. dist.:** N.Y., S.C., Utah. **1st cit.:** 1745 Young, *Night Thoughts*. **20c. coll.:** Stevenson 2336:7.

13. Today must borrow nothing of tomorrow. **Rec. dist.:** Ill.

14. Today will never come again. **Rec. dist.:** Wis.

15. What a wonderful world this would be if we all did as well today as we expect to do tomorrow. **Rec. dist.:** Ont.

16. What's done today you don't need to do tomorrow. **Rec. dist.:** Ont.

SEE ALSO The BOY of today will be the man of tomorrow. / BREAD today is better than cake tomorrow. / DRIVE safe today, and drive tomorrow. / Better an EGG today than a hen tomorrow. / FEAST today makes fast tomorrow. / FRET today, regret tomorrow. / A GIFT today is treasure tomorrow. / One HOUR today is worth two tomorrow. / Do not IGNORE the things of today. / First IMPROVE yourself today, then your friends tomorrow. / Today LIFE is our school; tomorrow our school is life. / What you LOSE today you cannot gain tomorrow. / Let not the MISTAKES of yesterday nor the fear of tomorrow spoil today. / SAVE today, safe tomorrow. / In peace or in war, your SUCCESS of tomorrow depends upon the preparation you are making today. / Don't be afraid of TOMORROW; look what could happen today. / Never put off until TOMORROW what you can do today. / We never see TOMORROW till it becomes today. / What you don't USE today, save for tomorrow. / He is a WISE man who knows more today than he did yesterday. / The WORRIES of today are minor matters of tomorrow.

toe **1.** Don't tread on other people's toes. **Rec. dist.:** Mich., N.Y., Ont. **1st cit.:** US1834 Davis, *Letters of Major J. Downing*. **20c. coll.:** T&W 376, Whiting(MP) 634.

2. Never tread on a sore toe. **Rec. dist.:** N.J., Ont. **1st cit.:** 1855 Bohn, *Handbook of Proverbs*. **20c. coll.:** Stevenson 1910:13.

3. One who keeps on his toes is never down at the heels. **Rec. dist.:** Ind.

4. Toes that are tender will be stepped on. **Rec. dist.:** Vt. **1st cit.:** US1835 Crockett, *Account of Col. Crockett's Tour to North and Down East*. **20c. coll.:** T&W 376.

SEE ALSO Take no more on your HEELS than you can kick off with your toe. / POLISH on the heels of shoes is a truer test of thoroughness than shine on the toes.

together *SEE* ALL things work together for good. / BIRDS of a feather flock together. / The FAMILY who prays together, stays together. / GOSSIPING and lying go together. / GRATITUDE and greed go not together. / Let us all HANG together or hang separately. / STICK together or get stuck separately. / It's always fair WEATHER when good friends get together.

toil **1.** Blessed are the horned hands of toil. **Rec. dist.:** N.Y., Ont.

2. The blessing of the earth is toil. **Rec. dist.:** N.Y.

SEE ALSO The BLESSING of earth is toil. / HONOR lies in honest toil.

toiler Toilers are crowned with success. **Rec. dist.:** Wis.

tolerance **1.** It is only one step from tolerance to forgiveness. **Rec. dist.:** Ill.

2. Tolerance is a two-way street. **Rec. dist.:** Minn.

3. Tolerance is the last study in the school of wisdom. **Rec. dist.:** Oreg.

toll *SEE* TALKING pays no toll.

tomahawk *SEE* Good NATURE is stronger than tomahawks.

tomorrow **1.** Boast not of tomorrow, for you know not what a day may bring forth. **Var.:** Boast not yourself of tomorrow, for you know not what a day may bring forth. **Rec. dist.:** Minn., N.C. **1st cit.:** 1535 Coverdale, *Proverbs*. **20c. coll.:** Stevenson 2338:8.

2. Defer not till tomorrow to be wise: tomorrow's sun to you may never rise. **Rec. dist.:** Ont.

3. Don't be afraid of tomorrow; look what could happen today. **Rec. dist.:** Miss.

4. Don't spend too much on tomorrow—it isn't yours yet. **Rec. dist.:** Tex.

5. Don't wish for tomorrow—you're wishing your life away. *Rec. dist.:* N.Dak.

6. Let tomorrow take care of itself. *Rec. dist.:* Okla.

7. Never put off until tomorrow what you can do today. *Vars.:* **(a)** Defer not till tomorrow what may be done today. **(b)** Don't leave until tomorrow what can be done the day after. **(c)** Don't put off for tomorrow what you can do today. **(d)** Don't put off till tomorrow what you can do today. **(e)** Don't put off till tomorrow what you can put off till next week. **(f)** Don't put off to tomorrow what you can do today. **(g)** Don't put off until tomorrow what you can do today. **(h)** Never leave for tomorrow what you can do today. **(i)** Never leave that for tomorrow which you can do today. **(j)** Never leave until tomorrow what you can do today. **(k)** Never put off till tomorrow what should be done today. *Rec. dist.:* U.S., Can. *1st cit.:* ca1386 Chaucer, *Tale of Melibee;* US1690 Winthrop in *Winthrop Papers,* Mass.Hist.Soc. *Collections* (1863–92). *20c. coll.:* ODEP 656, Whiting 446, CODP 186, Stevenson 2346:6, T&W 377, Whiting(MP) 636.

8. Never spend tomorrow counting yesterday's empty bottles. *Rec. dist.:* Calif., Ky.

9. There is always a tomorrow. *Rec. dist.:* Ky., Tenn.

10. Tomorrow is a new day. *Var.:* Tomorrow is another day. *Rec. dist.:* Calif., Ill., Ont. *1st cit.:* ca1520 Rastell, *Calisto & Meliboea;* US1913 Biggers, *Seven Keys to Baldpate. 20c. coll.:* ODEP 829, Whiting(MP) 636, CODP 227, Stevenson 2340:4.

11. Tomorrow is untouched. *Rec. dist.:* Ont. *1st cit.:* 1846 Denham, *Proverbs Relating to Weather. 20c. coll.:* Stevenson 2338:8.

12. Tomorrow may be the carriage driver's day for plowing. *Rec. dist.:* N.Y.

13. Tomorrow never comes. *Vars.:* **(a)** Tomorrow may never come. **(b)** Tomorrow never gets here: when it gets here, it's today. *Rec. dist.:* U.S., Can. *1st cit.:* 1539 Taverner, *Proverbs of Erasmus;* US1756 Franklin, *PRAlmanac. 20c. coll.:* ODEP 829, Whiting 446,

CODP 228, Stevenson 2339:1, Whiting(MP) 636.

14. We never see tomorrow till it becomes today. *Rec. dist.:* Ill.

SEE ALSO A BORE is a guy who is here today and here tomorrow. / BREAD today is better than cake tomorrow. / Live only for this DAY, and you ruin tomorrow. / Drunken DAYS have their tomorrows. / A neglected DUTY returns tomorrow with seven others at its back. / EAT, drink, and be merry, for tomorrow we may die. / An EGG today is better than a hen tomorrow. / EGGS now are better than chickens tomorrow. / FEAST today makes fast tomorrow. / FRET today, regret tomorrow. / A GIFT today is a treasure tomorrow. / First IMPROVE yourself today, then improve your friends tomorrow. / Today's JOYS may be tomorrow's woes. / What you LOSE today you cannot gain tomorrow. / Do not burden today's STRENGTH with tomorrow's load. / In peace or in war, your SUCCESS of tomorrow depends upon the preparation you are making today. / A THING done right today means less trouble tomorrow. / Here TODAY, gone tomorrow. / Plan TODAY for tomorrow. / TODAY must borrow nothing of tomorrow. / What's done TODAY you don't need to do tomorrow. / What a wonderful WORLD this would be if we all did as well today as we expect to do tomorrow.

tone SEE The loudest BELL does not always have the sweetest tone. / As the ORGAN, so the tone.

tongs Don't keep all your tongs in one fire. *Rec. dist.:* Ont.

tongue **1.** A fool's tongue is long enough to cut his throat. *Rec. dist.:* Ill., Miss. *1st cit.:* 1678 Ray, *English Proverbs. 20c. coll.:* Stevenson 844:12, ODEP 277.

2. A long tongue has a short hand. *Var.:* A long tongue is a sign of a short hand. *Rec. dist.:* Ont. *1st cit.:* 1640 Herbert, *Outlandish Proverbs (Jacula Prudentum)* in *Works,* ed. Hutchinson (1941); US1880 Spurgeon, *John Ploughman's Pictures. 20c. coll.:* ODEP 481, Stevenson 2344:8.

3. A still tongue makes a wise head. *Var.:*

Still tongue, wise head. *Rec. dist.*: U.S., Can. *1st cit.*: 1562 Heywood, *Sixth Hundreth Epigrammes;* US1796 Barton, *Disappointment.* *20c. coll.*: *ODEP* 774, Whiting 446, *CODP* 213, Stevenson 2345:1, T&W 378, Whiting*(MP)* 637.

4. A still tongue tells no tales. *Rec. dist.*: Ont.

5. A wholesome tongue is a tree of life. *Rec. dist.*: Ont.

6. A woman's tongue is one that will never wear out. *Rec. dist.*: Ohio, Ont., Wis.

7. Be not your tongue your own shame's orator. *Rec. dist.*: N.Y.

8. Confine your tongue, lest it confine you. *Rec. dist.*: Mich., Ont.

9. Don't let your tongue run away with your brains. *Rec. dist.*: Wis. *1st cit.*: 1732 Fuller, *Gnomologia.* *20c. coll.*: Stevenson 2343:6.

10. Don't throw your tongue into high gear till you get your brain in motion. *Rec. dist.*: Minn.

11. Guard your tongue; slander sometimes comes home to roost. *Rec. dist.*: Ont.

12. He who cannot hold his tongue is unworthy of having one. *Rec. dist.*: Mich.

13. He who has not a good tongue needs to have good hands. *Rec. dist.*: Ont.

14. He who holds his tongue is strong. *Rec. dist.*: Wis. *1st cit.*: US1948 Stevenson, *Home Book of Proverbs.* *20c. coll.*: Stevenson 2349:9.

15. He who uses his tongue will reach his destination. *Rec. dist.*: R.I.

16. Hold your tongue. *Vars.*: **(a)** Hold your tongue; don't let it go. **(b)** Hold your tongue in an ill time. **(c)** Hold your tongue with your teeth. *Rec. dist.*: Ill., Ky., Ont., Tenn. *1st cit.*: 1616 Draxe, *Bibliotheca Scholastica in Anglia* (1918). *20c. coll.*: *ODEP* 377, Stevenson 2349:2.

17. In company, guard your tongue; in solitude, your heart. *Rec. dist.*: Miss.

18. Keep a good tongue in your head. *Var.*: Keep a civil tongue in your head. *Rec. dist.*: Mich., N.Y. *1st cit.*: 1542 Erasmus, *Apophthegms,* tr. Udall. *20c. coll.*: *ODEP* 829.

19. Keep your tongue from evil and your lips from speaking guile. *Rec. dist.*: N.Y. *1st cit.*:

US1948 Stevenson, *Home Book of Proverbs.* *20c. coll.*: Stevenson 2346:10.

20. Keep your tongue within your teeth. *Var.*: Keep your tongue in your mouth. *Rec. dist.*: Nebr., Okla., Tex. *1st cit.*: ca1561 *Deceit of Woman.* *20c. coll.*: *ODEP* 418, Stevenson 2348:12.

21. Let not your tongue cut your throat. *Rec. dist.*: Ky., Okla., Tenn. *1st cit.*: 1855 Bohn, *Handbook of Proverbs.* *20c. coll.*: Stevenson 2342:1.

22. Make use of your tongue, and you will find out. *Rec. dist.*: N.Y.

23. Man's tongue is soft and bone does lack, yet a stroke therewith may break a man's back. *Rec. dist.*: Wis. *1st cit.*: ca1225 *Trinity MS O* in *English Studies;* USca1700 Hubbard, *General History of New England* (1878). *20c. coll.*: *ODEP* 829, Whiting 447, Stevenson 2348:5.

24. No one ever repented holding his tongue. *Rec. dist.*: Vt.

25. One tongue is enough for two women. *Rec. dist.*: Ont. *1st cit.*: 1732 Fuller, *Gnomologia.* *20c. coll.*: Stevenson 2580:15.

26. One tongue is sufficient for a woman. *Rec. dist.*: Ohio. *1st cit.*: 1659 N.R., *Proverbs English, French, Dutch, Italian and Spanish.* *20c. coll.*: *ODEP* 598, Stevenson 2580:15.

27. Remember, your tongue is in a wet place: it's likely to slip. *Rec. dist.*: Ala., Ga.

28. Talk of the rack, what is it to a woman's tongue? *Rec. dist.*: N.Y. *1st cit.*: 1888 Mackaye, *Paul Kauvar.* *20c. coll.*: Stevenson 2580:11.

29. The boneless tongue, so small and weak, can crush and kill. *Rec. dist.*: Ont. *1st cit.*: US1938 Champion, *Racial Proverbs.* *20c. coll.*: Stevenson 2348:4.

30. The devil's tongue is sharpest on the backlash. *Rec. dist.*: N.Mex.

31. The tongue can speak a word whose speed outsteps the steed. *Rec. dist.*: Ont.

32. The tongue destroys a greater horde than does the sword. *Rec. dist.*: Ont.

33. The tongue is a little thing, but it fills the universe with trouble. *Rec. dist.*: Miss., Wis.

34. The tongue is an unruly member. *Rec. dist.:* N.Y.

35. The tongue is not steel, but it cuts. *Var.:* The tongue is not steel, yet it cuts. *Rec. dist.:* N.J., Ohio, Vt. *1st cit.:* ca1386 Chaucer, *Maunciple's Tale.* *20c. coll.:* ODEP 829, Stevenson 2347:9.

36. The tongue is sharper than the sword. *Rec. dist.:* Ont. *1st cit.:* ca1386 Chaucer, *Maunciple's Tale.* *20c. coll.:* Stevenson 2347:10.

37. The tongue is the only tool that grows sharper with use. *Vars.:* **(a)** A woman's tongue is the only sharp-edged tool that grows keener with constant use. **(b)** A woman's tongue is the only sharp-edged tool that grows keener with use. **(c)** A woman's tongue is the only sharp-edged tool that grows sharper with use. *Rec. dist.:* Wis. *1st cit.:* US1819 Irving, *Rip Van Winkle.* *20c. coll.:* Stevenson 2347:9.

38. The tongue of the just is a choice silver; the heart of the wicked is little worth. *Var.:* The tongue of the just is as choice silver. *Rec. dist.:* Ind., Ont.

39. The tongue offends, and the ears get the cuffing. *Rec. dist.:* N.Y., S.C. *1st cit.:* US1757 Franklin, *PRAlmanac.* *20c. coll.:* Whiting 447, Stevenson 655:6.

40. The tongue returns to the aching tooth. *Rec. dist.:* N.Y., S.C. *1st cit.:* 1586 Guazzo, *Civile Conversation,* tr. Pettie, T.T. (1925); US1746 Franklin, *PRAlmanac.* *20c. coll.:* ODEP 829, Whiting 447, Stevenson 2353:6, Whiting(MP) 638.

41. The tongue speaks wisely when the soul is wise. *Rec. dist.:* Wis.

42. The tongue wounds more than the arrow. *Rec. dist.:* Oreg.

43. The tongue's great storehouse is the heart. *Rec. dist.:* Ont.

44. Tongue double brings trouble. *Rec. dist.:* Miss., Utah. *1st cit.:* 1484 Avian, tr. Caxton; US1733 Franklin, *PRAlmanac.* *20c. coll.:* Stevenson 2344:3, Whiting 447.

45. Turn your tongue seven times before speaking. *Rec. dist.:* Vt. *1st cit.:* US1948 Stevenson, *Home Book of Proverbs.* *20c. coll.:* Stevenson 2307:4.

46. Wagging tongue indicates brains that don't think. *Rec. dist.:* Wis.

47. Who keeps his tongue will keep his soul. *Rec. dist.:* Ont.

48. Your tongue can undo all you be. *Rec. dist.:* Ont.

49. Your tongue is your ambassador. *Rec. dist.:* Ind. *1st cit.:* 1580 Lyly, *Euphues and His England,* ed. Arber (1868). *20c. coll.:* Stevenson 2346:1.

SEE ALSO A BAWL becomes a beller when the tongue is stickin' out. / Teach your CHILD to hold his tongue; he'll learn fast enough to speak. / DEATH and life are in the power of the tongue. / A DOG has friends because he wags his tail instead of his tongue. / Have a long EAR and a short tongue. / A pair of good EARS will drain dry a hundred tongues. / Though FEET should slip, never let the tongue. / When FIRE burns within the soul, the tongue cannot be silent. / FOOLS cannot hold their tongues. / Often we hold FRIENDS by holding our tongues. / An empty HEAD, like a bell, has a long tongue. / What the HEART thinks, the tongue speaks. / Who has a clean HEART has also a clean tongue. / To be a good NEIGHBOR, take heed to your tongue. / The PEN is the tongue of the mind. / A SLIP of the foot and you may soon recover, but a slip of the tongue you may never get over. / A SLIP of the tongue is not fault of the mind. / Better a SLIP with the foot than with the tongue. / He cannot SPEAK well that cannot hold his tongue. / No SWORD bites so fiercely as an evil tongue. / It is very well that the TEETH are before the tongue. / Short TEMPERS often go with long tongues. / When alone, we have our own THOUGHTS to watch; when in the family, our tempers; when in society, our tongues. / WISE men keep guard on their tongue. / A WOMAN fights with her tongue. / Cool WORDS scald not a tongue. / Of all the WORDS of tongue or pen, the saddest are these: it might have been. / Your WORK expresses you more correctly than your tongue.

tonic SEE WORK is a fine tonic.

tool **1.** A tool is but the extension of a man's hand. *Rec. dist.:* N.Y., S.C. *1st cit.:* 1833 Carlyle, *Sartor Resartus;* US1887 Beecher, *Prov-*

erbs *from Plymouth Pulpit. 20c. coll.:* Stevenson 2350:2.

2. Handle your tools without mittens: the cat in gloves catches no mice. *Var.:* Handle your tools without mittens. *Rec. dist.:* Ill., N.Y., S.C. *1st cit.:* US1758 Franklin, *PRAlmanac. 20c. coll.:* Stevenson 2350:3.

3. Of what good are tools if allowed to rust? *Rec. dist.:* Miss.

4. People who have tools are able to make a great many things. *Rec. dist.:* Okla.

5. They who play with edged tools must expect to be cut. *Var.:* Do not play with edged tools. *Rec. dist.:* Mich., Ont., Tex. *1st cit.:* ca1568 Ascham, *Scholemaster* in *Works,* ed. Wright; US1765 *Letter Book of John Watts, 1762–1765,* N.Y.Hist.Soc. *Collections* (1928). *20c. coll.:* ODEP 120, Whiting 447, Stevenson 2350:7, T&W 378, Whiting(MP) 638.

6. Time spent in sharpening one's tools is not wasted. *Rec. dist.:* Oreg.

7. When the tool is dull, put forth more strength. *Rec. dist.:* Ont.

SEE ALSO CARDS are the devil's tools. / A lazy CARPENTER fights with his tools. / CHILDREN and fools shouldn't play with sharp tools. / DISCOURAGEMENT is the devil's most valuable tool. / Idle HANDS are the devil's tools. / MAN is greater than the tools he invents. / If you deny the TRADE, you should give up the tools. / VOCABULARY is the tool of wise men. / A bad WORKMAN quarrels with his tools. / A poor WORKMAN loses his tools. / A WORKMAN is no better than his tools.

toot *SEE* Toot your own HORN; no one will toot it for you.

tooth **1.** A tooth in the mouth is worth two in the plate. *Rec. dist.:* Minn.

2. Aching teeth are ill tenants. *Rec. dist.:* Minn., Ont. *1st cit.:* 1659 Howell, *Paroimiografia (French Proverbs). 20c. coll.:* ODEP 2, Stevenson 2354:3.

3. All teeth showing is not laughter. *Rec. dist.:* N.Y.

4. Be true to your teeth or they'll be false to you. *Var.:* Don't be false to your teeth or they'll be false to you. *Rec. dist.:* Ont.

5. Better a tooth out than always aching. *Rec. dist.:* Okla. *1st cit.:* 1659 Howell, *Paroimiografia (English Proverbs). 20c. coll.:* Stevenson 2354:1.

6. It is very well that the teeth are before the tongue. *Rec. dist.:* Ont.

7. Never show your teeth unless you can bite. *Rec. dist.:* Calif., Ohio. *1st cit.:* 1639 Fuller, *Holy War;* US1752 *Papers of Sir William Johnson,* ed. Sullivan (1921–65). *20c. coll.:* ODEP 62, Whiting 447.

8. You can look at teeth and not be bitten. *Rec. dist.:* Ont.

9. You can't tell which tooth bit you if you back into a buzzard. *Rec. dist.:* Wis.

SEE ALSO ADAM ate the apple, and our teeth still ache. / An EYE for an eye, a tooth for a tooth. / A man may dig a GRAVE with his teeth. / The HOPE for the poor is like tough meat for one who has no teeth. / A HORSE is as old as his teeth. / When the HUSBANDS have eaten sour grapes, their wives' teeth are set on edge. / Many a true SAYING is uttered through false teeth. / Stuff not your STOMACH with sweets if you choose to keep your sweet tooth. / Follow not TRUTH too near the heels lest it dash out your teeth. / WOLVES may lose their teeth, but they never lose their nature.

toothpick *SEE* The DOG chews no orange toothpicks, yet his teeth are white.

top Don't blow your top. *Rec. dist.:* U.S., Can. *Infm.:* Control your anger. *1st cit.:* US1940 Steel, *Dead of Night. 20c. coll.:* Whiting(MP) 640.

SEE ALSO An ANGEL on top but a devil underneath. / CREAM always comes to the top. / The best FRUIT is on top of the tree. / The bottom RAIL gets on top every fifty years. / There's always ROOM at the top. / One pair of good SOLES is better than two tops.

torment *SEE* HOPE is the worst of evils, for it prolongs the torment of man.

tormentor *SEE* The COVETOUS man is his own tormentor.

tornado A tornado never hits the junction of two rivers. *Rec. dist.:* Kans.

torpor Torpor and sloth, torpor and sloth, these are the cooks that unseason the broth.

Rec. dist.: N.Y., S.C. *1st cit.:* US1939 Nash, *Procrastination Is All of the Time.* *20c. coll.:* Stevenson 2141:3.

tote Tote while totin's good. *Rec. dist.:* Miss. *Infm.:* "Tote" refers to carrying.
   SEE ALSO Tote your own SKILLET.

toting SEE PICKIN' up is better than totin', but puttin' down beats the world.

totter SEE Everything does not FALL that totters.

tottering SEE To STUMBLE once is better than to be always tottering.

touch *(n.)* SEE GOLD is proven by touch.

touch *(v.)* SEE He who touches PITCH will get black.

touchstone SEE CALAMITY and prosperity are the touchstones of integrity. / CALAMITY is the touchstone of a brave mind.

tough SEE The toughest BRONCS is always them you've rode some other place. / The tougher the FIGHT, the sweeter the triumph. / The HOPE of the poor is like tough meat for one who has no teeth.

tourist SEE The VAGABOND, when rich, is called a tourist.

tow SEE FIRE is not to be quenched with tow.

tower 1. The highest towers begin from the ground. *Var.:* The highest towers rise from the ground. *Rec. dist.:* N.Y., S.C. *1st cit.:* US1875 Scarborough, *Chinese Proverbs.* *20c. coll.:* Stevenson 63:9.

2. Towers are measured by their shadows and great men by their slanderers. *Rec. dist.:* Ill. *1st cit.:* 1853 Trench, *On Lessons in Proverbs.* *20c. coll.:* Stevenson 1033:3.

town SEE Send the CHILDREN to town and you'll have to go yourself. / Go to the COUNTRY to hear the news of the town. / If ENVY were a rash, the whole town would be ill. / You can't have a family FUSS without the whole town knowing about it. / The ROAD of by-and-by leads to the town of never.

track *(n.)* 1. Don't get off the beaten track. *Rec. dist.:* Ont.

2. Even if you are on the right track, you won't get over if you sit there. *Rec. dist.:* Ont.

3. The other track on the road is always the smoothest. *Rec. dist.:* Ont.
   SEE ALSO You can't grow GRASS on the beaten track.

track *(v.)* He who likes to track likes to cheat. *Rec. dist.:* Ohio.

tractor A tractor doesn't eat its head off in the barn when it isn't working. *Rec. dist.:* Wash.

trade *(n.)* 1. A man of many trades begs his bread on Sunday. *Rec. dist.:* N.Y., S.C. *1st cit.:* 1606 *Return from Parnassus.* *20c. coll.:* ODEP 510, Stevenson 2357:2.

2. Every man to his trade. *Rec. dist.:* N.C., Ont. *1st cit.:* 1539 Taverner, *Proverbs of Erasmus;* US1723 Symmes, *Utile Dulci.* *20c. coll.:* ODEP 230, Whiting 135, CODP 69, Stevenson 2358:6, T&W 380, Whiting(MP) 396.

3. He that has a trade has an estate, and he that has a calling has an office of profit and honor. *Vars.:* (a) He that has a trade has a share everywhere. (b) He that has a trade has an office of profit and honor. *Rec. dist.:* Ill., N.C., S.C. *1st cit.:* 1539 Taverner, *Proverbs of Erasmus;* US1742 Franklin, *PRAlmanac.* *20c. coll.:* ODEP 835, Whiting 450, Stevenson 2358:4.

4. If you deny the trade, you should give up the tools. *Rec. dist.:* Ont.

5. In trade, competition prevents imposition. *Rec. dist.:* Ill.

6. Learn a trade and earn a living. *Rec. dist.:* Ont. *1st cit.:* 1559 *Worke of Ioannes Ferrarius,* tr. Bavarde. *20c. coll.:* ODEP 452.

7. Two of a trade seldom agree. *Var.:* Two of a trade can never agree. *Rec. dist.:* Calif., Mich., N.Y., Ohio, Ont. *1st cit.:* 1604 Dekker, *Honest Whore;* US1770 Tyler, *Verse of Royall Tyler,* ed. Peladeau (1968). *20c. coll.:* ODEP 851, Stevenson 2357:5, CODP 233, Whiting(MP) 655.
   SEE ALSO COMPETITION is the life of trade. / DEPENDENCE is a poor trade. / Show me your HAND and I'll tell you your trade. / KNAVERY is the worst trade. / OPPOSITION is the life of

trade. / The PLAGUE and the hero are both of a trade. / There are TRICKS in all trades.

trade (v.) SEE Don't trade old FRIENDS for new.

trail It's a long trail that has no turning. **Var.:** It is a long trail that has no ending. **Rec. dist.:** Fla., Md.

train (n.) **1.** A train gets to its destination on time by staying on the track. **Rec. dist.:** Minn.

2. Every train has a caboose. **Rec. dist.:** Pa.

3. Little trains go far. **Rec. dist.:** Ont.

SEE ALSO A MAN is like a train, he's at his best when he's on the level.

train (v.) SEE What PAINS us trains us. / Get 'em YOUNG and train 'em.

training Training is everything. The peach was once a bitter almond; cauliflower is but cabbage with a college education. **Rec. dist.:** N.Y., S.C.

SEE ALSO To the wise, YOUTH is a time for training.

traitors SEE Our DOUBTS are traitors.

trample SEE If one FAILS the whole world tramples on him. / A truely GREAT man will neither trample on a worm nor sneak to an emperor.

transgressor The way of the transgressor is hard. **Rec. dist.:** Ont. **1st cit.:** US1948 Stevenson, *Home Book of Proverbs.* **20c. coll.:** Stevenson 2468:1.

translation Translation is at best an echo. **Rec. dist.:** Ill. **1st cit.:** 1851 Borrow, *Lavengro.* **20c. coll.:** Stevenson 2360:1.

trap **1.** The fox condemns the trap, not himself. **Rec. dist.:** Ont.

2. Watch out for the trap if it hasn't been sprung. **Rec. dist.:** N.Dak.

trappings Trappings do not make the horse; clothes do not make the man. **Rec. dist.:** N.Y.

trash **1.** All trash goes before the broom. **Var.:** All trash goes out with the broom. **Rec. dist.:** Ky., N.C., Tenn.

2. Don't blow trash in my backyard. **Rec. dist.:** Ky., Tenn.

3. Fool with trash, it will blow in your eyes. **Rec. dist.:** N.C.

4. Trash always comes to the top. **Rec. dist.:** Ky., Tenn.

SEE ALSO Screening a PICTURE doesn't take the trash out.

travel (n.) **1.** Travel broadens the mind. **Rec. dist.:** Ind. **1st cit.:** 1933 Powell, *Venusberg.* **20c. coll.:** CODP 229, Whiting(MP) 641.

2. Travel is the best school. **Rec. dist.:** Minn.

SEE ALSO The strength of a SMELL depends on the distance of its travel.

travel (v.) **1.** He that travels far knows much. **Rec. dist.:** Ind. **1st cit.:** 1620 Cervantes, *Don Quixote,* tr. Shelton. **20c. coll.:** ODEP 836, Stevenson 2360:6.

2. He travels fastest who travels alone. **Vars.:** **(a)** He travels fast who travels alone. **(b)** He who travels fast travels alone. **(c)** Who travels alone travels fastest. **Rec. dist.:** U.S., Can. **1st cit.:** 1888 Kipling, *Story of Gadsby;* US1854 Thoreau, *Walden.* **20c. coll.:** CODP 229, Stevenson 307:8.

3. He who wants to travel far saves his horse. **Rec. dist.:** Ont.

4. Little by little, one travels far. **Rec. dist.:** Calif., Minn.

5. Tell me with whom you travel and I'll tell you who you are. **Rec. dist.:** Calif.

6. Travel in the light; rest in the night. **Rec. dist.:** Okla.

SEE ALSO An ARMY travels on its stomach. / The FOOL wanders, the wise man travels. / He that can travel well afoot keeps a good HORSE. / He that RISES late must trot all day.

traveler **1.** A traveler never gets lost on a straight road. **Rec. dist.:** Ky., Tenn.

2. An American traveler abroad always comes home an ardent patriot. **Rec. dist.:** Ill.

3. Lovers, travelers, and poets will give money to be heard. **Rec. dist.:** N.Y.

4. We are all graveyard travelers, and when

you worry, you're just whipping up your horse. *Rec. dist.:* Ky., Tenn.

traveling Traveling is one way of lengthening life, at least in appearance. *Rec. dist.:* N.Y., S.C.

SEE ALSO If an ASS goes traveling, he'll not come home a horse.

treacherous Men are oftener treacherous through weakness than design. *Rec. dist.:* Ill.

treachery Treachery, cautious at the start, betrays itself in the end. *Rec. dist.:* Ill.

SEE ALSO CUNNING and treachery often proceed from want of capacity.

tread He who treads softly goes far. *Rec. dist.:* Ont. *1st cit.:* ca1350 *Douce MS 52.* *20c. coll.:* ODEP 238.

SEE ALSO If a man once FALLS all will tread on him. / FOOLS rush in where angels fear to tread. / Tread in my FOOTSTEPS if you can straddle far enough. / GRIEF often treads upon the heels of pleasure. / Tread not on thin ICE. / You shall not muzzle the OX when he treads out the corn. / SORROW treads upon the heels of mirth. / Never tread on a sore TOE. / Don't tread on other people's TOES.

treason Treason is never successful, for when it is successful, men do not call it treason. *Rec. dist.:* Ill. *1st cit.:* ca1612 Harington, "Of Treason" in *Epigrams.* *20c. coll.:* Stevenson 2365:13.

treasure **1.** Lay not up for yourselves treasures upon earth. *Rec. dist.:* N.Y.

2. Measure your treasure by the pleasure it brings. *Rec. dist.:* Wash.

3. Treasures of wickedness profit nothing. *Rec. dist.:* Mich.

4. Where your treasure is, there will your heart be also. *Var.:* Where the treasure is, there the heart will be also. *Rec. dist.:* Ky. N.Y., Ont., Tenn. *1st cit.:* 1597 Payne, *Royall Exchange;* US1630 *Winthrop Papers, 1498–1649,* Mass. Hist.Soc. *Collections* (1927–47). *20c. coll.:* Stevenson 2367:11, Whiting 451, T&W 381, Whiting(MP) 642.

SEE ALSO Little CHESTS may hold great treasures. / A FATHER'S a treasure, a brother's a comfort, a friend is both. / A rich FRIEND is a

treasure. / A GIFT today is a treasure tomorrow. / KNOWLEDGE is a treasure, but practice is the key to it. / MEASURE is a treasure. / Extensive READING is a priceless treasure. / VIRTUOUS men are king's treasures. / A true WIFE is her husband's heart's treasure.

treat *SEE* BUSINESS goes where it is invited and stays where it is well treated. / HOME is the place where we are treated the best and grumble the most. / As JAMES treats God, so God treats James.

tree **1.** A crooked tree throws only a crooked shadow. *Rec. dist.:* N.Y.

2. A crooked tree will never straighten its branches. *Rec. dist.:* N.Mex.

3. A family tree is valuable when it produces good timber and not just a bunch of nuts. *Rec. dist.:* Ohio.

4. A fig tree looking on a fig tree becomes fruitful. *Rec. dist.:* Ont.

5. A great tree has a great fall. *Rec. dist.:* Tex. *1st cit.:* 1732 Fuller, *Gnomologia.* *20c. coll.:* Stevenson 2368:8.

6. A rotten tree bears no fruit. *Rec. dist.:* Ont.

7. A tall tree makes a squirrel saucy. *Rec. dist.:* Ark.

8. A tree is as strong as its roots. *Rec. dist.:* Calif.

9. A tree is known by its fruit. *Vars.:* **(a)** As the tree, so the fruit. **(b)** Judge a tree by its fruit. **(c)** Judge a tree by the fruit it bears. **(d)** Such as the tree is, so is the fruit. **(e)** Such as the tree is, such is the fruit. **(f)** You can judge a tree by the fruit it bears. *Rec. dist.:* U.S., Can. *1st cit.:* ca1389 Chaucer, *Parson's Tale;* US1634 Wood, *New-England's Prospects,* Publ. Prince Soc. (1865). *20c. coll.:* ODEP 837, Whiting 452, CODP 229, Stevenson 2310:9, T&W 381, Whiting(MP) 643.

10. A tree often transplanted neither grows nor thrives. *Rec. dist.:* Wis. *1st cit.:* 1609 Harward, Unpublished manuscript in Trinity College Library, Cambridge; US1737 Franklin, *PRAlmanac.* *20c. coll.:* ODEP 838, Whiting 452, Stevenson 314:1.

11. A tree with beautiful blossoms does not always yield the best fruit. *Rec. dist.:* Ill.

12. A young tree is easier twisted than an old tree. *Var.:* An old tree is harder twist than a twig. *Rec. dist.:* Ont.

13. An old tree is hard to straighten. *Rec. dist.:* N.J., Ont.

14. An older tree knows more than a growing one. *Rec. dist.:* Wash.

15. As a tree falls, so shall it lie. *Vars.:* (a) As the tree falls, so let it lie. (b) Where the tree falls, there it shall lie. *Rec. dist.:* U.S., Can. *1st cit.:* 1549 Latimer, *Seven Sermons,* ed. Arber; US1762 Smith, *Works of William Smith, D.D.* (1803). *20c. coll.:* ODEP 505, Whiting 452, CODP 229, Stevenson 2368:6.

16. As the tree is bent, so the tree is inclined. *Vars.:* (a) As the tree is bent, so grows the tree. (b) As the tree is bent, so is the vine. *Rec. dist.:* Calif., Ohio, Ont.

17. Bend the tree while it is young. *Rec. dist.:* Ala., Ga.

18. Big trees grow from little acorns. *Var.:* Great trees from little acorns grow. *Rec. dist.:* Calif. *Infm.:* Cf. oak.

19. Go to a pear tree for pears, not to an elm. *Rec. dist.:* N.C.

20. Good trees grow straight. *Rec. dist.:* Calif.

21. Great trees keep down little ones. *Rec. dist.:* Okla., Tex. *1st cit.:* 1732 Fuller, *Gnomologia. 20c. coll.:* ODEP 335, Stevenson 1035:10.

22. He that climbs the tall tree has a right to the fruit. *Rec. dist.:* Ont.

23. He that plants trees loves others besides himself. *Rec. dist.:* Mich., Okla., Tex. *1st cit.:* 1732 Fuller, *Gnomologia. 20c. coll.:* ODEP 630, Stevenson 2370:1.

24. He who loves the tree loves the branch. *Rec. dist.:* Ohio.

25. It is the good apple tree that has the most clubs under it. *Rec. dist.:* Miss.

26. It takes all kinds of trees to make a forest. *Rec. dist.:* Ont.

27. Large trees give more shade than fruit. *Rec. dist.:* Ind. *1st cit.:* 1640 Herbert, *Outlandish Proverbs (Jacula Prudentum)* in *Works,* ed. Hutchinson (1941); US1866 Emerson, *Journals. 20c. coll.:* ODEP 335, Stevenson 2370:4.

28. Move an old tree and it will wither and die. *Vars.:* (a) Old trees cannot easily be transplanted. (b) Old trees must not be transplanted. (c) Remove an old tree and it will wither. *Rec. dist.:* N.J. Ont. *1st cit.:* 1523 Barclay, *Mirror of Good Manners. 20c. coll.:* ODEP 671, Stevenson 2367:14.

29. Never bark up the wrong tree. *Rec. dist.:* U.S., Can. *1st cit.:* US1832 Hall, *Legend of the West. 20c. coll.:* T&W 381, ODEP 30, Whiting 452, Stevenson 122:12, Whiting(MP) 643.

30. Never climb a crooked tree. *Rec. dist.:* Ont.

31. One never knows how the tree is bent until it has lost its leaves. *Rec. dist.:* Wis.

32. One tree can make a million matches, and one match can destroy a million trees. *Var.:* One tree will make a million matches; one match may burn a million trees. *Rec. dist.:* N.Y.

33. Our crosses are hewn from different trees, but we all must have our calvaries. *Rec. dist.:* N.Y., S.C. *1st cit.:* US1948 Stevenson, *Home Book of Proverbs. 20c. coll.:* Stevenson 460:8.

34. Plant the crab tree where you will, it never will bear pippins. *Rec. dist.:* Ill. *1st cit.:* 1579 Lyly, *Euphues, Anatomy of Wit. 20c. coll.:* ODEP 152, Stevenson 2368:8.

35. Tall trees catch much wind. *Rec. dist.:* N.Dak.

36. The bigger the tree, the harder she falls. *Rec. dist.:* Ohio. *1st cit.:* ca1374 Chaucer, *Troilus and Criseyde. 20c. coll.:* ODEP 373, Stevenson 748:13.

37. The taller the tree, the harder the bark; the taller the girl, the harder the spark. *Rec. dist.:* Minn. *Infm:* "Spark" refers to kissing.

38. The tree that grows the straightest lives the longest. *Rec. dist.:* Ill.

39. When the tree is fallen, everyone goes to it with his hatchet. *Rec. dist.:* Tex. *1st cit.:* 1586 Guazzo, *Civile Conversation,* tr. Pettie, T.T. (1925). *20c. coll.:* ODEP 837, Stevenson 750:7.

SEE ALSO An APPLE never falls far from the tree. / Little AXE cuts down big tree. / The first BLOW does not fell the tree. / Best CLUBS are found under a hickory tree. / You can't get all your COONS up one tree. / A DOG, a woman, a hickory tree: the more you beat them the better they will be. / There are many kinds of fruit that grow on the tree of life, but none so sweet as FRIENDSHIP. / Domestic FRUIT will not grow on a wild tree. / Good FRUIT never comes from a bad tree. / He that would have the FRUIT must climb the tree. / The FRUIT never falls very far from the tree. / You cannot eat the FRUIT while the tree is in blossom. / One GENERATION plants the trees, another sits in their shade. / Just because there are no LEAVES on the trees doesn't mean there's no life in the limbs. / As a MAN lives, so shall he die; as a tree falls, so shall it lie. / Even a MONKEY will fall from a tree sometimes. / Big POSSUM climb little tree. / You can never get all the POSSUMS up the same tree. / You may bend a SAPLING, but never a tree. / The SHOOT at length becomes a tree. / A wholesome TONGUE is a tree of life. / A young TWIG is easier twisted than an old tree. / As the TWIG is bent, so grows the tree. / A WEDGE from itself splits the oak tree. / The WIND blows easily through a leafless tree. / There's nothing that keeps its YOUTH but a tree and truth.

trial **1.** Nothing beats a trial but a failure. *Rec. dist.:* W.Va.

2. Old trials are better borne than new ones. *Rec. dist.:* Ont.

3. Second trials often succeed. *Rec. dist.:* Ont.

4. Trials break little men but make great ones. *Rec. dist.:* N.Y.

SEE ALSO A GEM is not polished without rubbing, nor is a man perfect without trials. / VIRTUE rejoices in trial.

tribulation Tribulation works patience. *Rec. dist.:* Ill.

tribute SEE Millions for DEFENSE, but not a cent for tribute.

trick There are tricks in all trades. *Rec. dist.:* U.S., Can. *1st cit.:* 1632 Parker, *Knavery in all*

Trades; US1857 Bennett, *Border Rover*. **20c. coll.:** ODEP 431, T&W 380, CODP 230, Stevenson 2372:4, Whiting(MP) 643.

SEE ALSO Can't learn an old DOG new tricks. / LITTLE by little does the trick.

trickery SEE BEAUTY is yet the pleasing trickery that cheats half the world.

trifle **1.** It's a trifle that makes fools laugh. *Rec. dist.:* Ill.

2. Trifles lead to serious matters. *Rec. dist.:* Mich. *1st cit.:* US1948 Stevenson, *Home Book of Proverbs*. **20c. coll.:** Stevenson 2373:11.

3. Trifles make perfection, but perfection is no trifle. *Rec. dist.:* Ill., Miss., N.Y. *1st cit.:* US1948 Stevenson, *Home Book of Proverbs*. **20c. coll.:** Stevenson 2374:1.

trim He who trims himself to suit everyone soon whittles himself away. *Rec. dist.:* Minn.

SEE ALSO Keep your SAILS trimmed.

trip A thousand-mile trip begins with one step. *Rec. dist.:* Ill.

triumph Don't sing your triumph before you have conquered. *Rec. dist.:* N.J. *1st cit.:* 1545 Taverner, *Proverbs of Erasmus*. **20c. coll.:** ODEP 839.

SEE ALSO The tougher the FIGHT, the sweeter the triumph.

trivial Trivials make perfection, but perfection isn't trivial. *Rec. dist.:* Calif. *1st cit.:* US1948 Stevenson, *Home Book of Proverbs*. **20c. coll.:** Stevenson 2374:1.

SEE ALSO What mighty CONTESTS rise from trivial things.

trodden SEE A trodden PATH bears no grass.

trot SEE NEED makes the old wife trot. / He who RISES late may trot all day and not overtake his business.

trouble *(n.)* **1.** Do not ever meet trouble halfway. *Var.:* Never meet trouble halfway. *Rec. dist.:* Minn., N.J. *1st cit.:* 1598 Shakespeare, *Much Ado About Nothing*; US1923 Powys, *Black Bryony*. **20c. coll.:** ODEP 523, Whiting(MP) 645, CODP 149.

2. Don't borrow trouble. *Vars.:* **(a)** Don't go around looking for trouble. **(b)** Don't invite trouble. **(c)** Don't look for trouble. **(d)** Never borrow the other fellow's troubles. *Rec. dist.:* U.S., Can. *1st cit.:* 1719 Defoe, *Farther Adventures of Robinson Crusoe;* US1776 Ashbury, *Journal of Francis Ashbury,* ed. Potts (1958). *20c. coll.:* Stevenson 2377:7, Whiting 454, T&W 382, Whiting*(MP)* 645.

3. Don't tell your troubles to others—most of 'em don't care. *Rec. dist.:* Minn.

4. Everybody has his troubles. *Rec. dist.:* Wash.

5. He that seeks trouble never misses. *Vars.:* **(a)** He that seeks trouble always finds it. **(b)** Look for trouble and you're sure to find it. **(c)** Look for trouble and you're sure to get it. *Rec. dist.:* Calif., Mich., Wis. *1st cit.:* ca1460 *Political Religious and Love Poems,* E.E.T.S. (1866); US1942 Thayer, *Murder Is Out.* *20c. coll.:* ODEP 711, Stevenson 2378:4.

6. If all the troubles were hung on bushes, we would take our own and run. *Rec. dist.:* N.Y.

7. If you don't go looking for trouble, trouble won't go looking for you. *Rec. dist.:* Ont.

8. It seems sometimes that the biggest things in the world are our troubles, the smallest things blessings. *Rec. dist.:* Vt.

9. It takes only a little trouble to get in a lot of it. *Rec. dist.:* N.C.

10. It's easier to stay out of trouble than to get out of trouble. *Rec. dist.:* Ala., Ga., Ill., Ont.

11. Keep your eye peeled for trouble. *Var.:* Keep your eye skinned for trouble. *Rec. dist.:* Tex.

12. Laugh your troubles away. *Rec. dist.:* Ont.

13. Man is born unto trouble. *Rec. dist.:* Minn. *1st cit.:* US1876 Twain, *Tom Sawyer.* *20c. coll.:* Stevenson 2376:4.

14. Most trouble starts from misunderstandings. *Rec. dist.:* N.C.

15. Never trouble trouble till trouble troubles you. *Vars.:* **(a)** Do not trouble trouble until trouble troubles you. **(b)** Don't trouble trouble till trouble troubles you. **(c)** Never bother trouble lest trouble troubles you. **(d)** Never get mixed up in someone else's trouble until it troubles you. **(e)** Never trouble trouble till trouble troubles you, for if you trouble trouble, trouble is sure to trouble you. *Rec. dist.:* U.S., Can. *1st cit.:* 1884 *Folk-Lore Journal;* US1776 Ashbury, *Journal of Francis Ashbury,* ed. Potts (1958). *20c. coll.:* CODP 230, Whiting 454, Stevenson 2377:7, Whiting*(MP)* 645.

16. Of all your troubles great and small, the greatest are those that don't happen at all. *Rec. dist.:* Ont.

17. One hasn't anything without trouble. *Rec. dist.:* N.Y.

18. Pack up your troubles. *Rec. dist.:* Miss., N.J.

19. Taking trouble is the best way to avoid trouble. *Rec. dist.:* Ill.

20. Tell your troubles to the policeman. *Var.:* Tell your troubles to the wall. *Rec. dist.:* Mich., Ohio, Ont.

21. The best way to get out of trouble is not to get in it. *Rec. dist.:* Miss.

22. The greater your troubles, the greater is your opportunity to show yourself a man. *Rec. dist.:* Miss.

23. The size of your troubles generally depends on whether they are coming or going. *Rec. dist.:* Oreg.

24. They who borrow trouble must pay a high rate of interest. *Rec. dist.:* Ont.

25. Those who make trouble for others often fall into it themselves. *Rec. dist.:* Ont.

26. Trouble: two women under one roof. *Rec. dist.:* Ont.

27. Trouble arises when you least expect it. *Rec. dist.:* Calif.

28. Trouble is merely opportunity in work clothes. *Rec. dist.:* Ind., Minn.

29. Trouble loves company. *Rec. dist.:* Minn.

30. Trouble never comes single-handed. *Vars.:* **(a)** Trouble comes in bunches. **(b)** Trouble comes in bunches like grapes. **(c)** Trouble comes in twos. **(d)** Trouble never comes single. **(e)** Trouble never comes singly. **(f)** Troubles always come in bunches. **(g)** Troubles never come singly. *Rec. dist.:* U.S. *1st cit.:* US1875 Scarborough, *Chinese Proverbs.* *20c. coll.:* Stevenson 1275:11.

31. Trouble shared is trouble halved. *Rec. dist.:* N.Y., S.C. *1st cit.:* 1931 Sayers, *Five Red Herrings.* *20c. coll.:* *CODP* 230, Stevenson 2375:14, Whiting(*MP*) 646.

32. Trouble springs from idleness. *Rec. dist.:* Ont. *1st cit.:* US1756 Franklin, *PRAlmanac.* *20c. coll.:* Whiting 454.

33. Trouble starts when you start feeling sorry for yourself. *Rec. dist.:* Okla.

34. We milk trouble drier than we do enjoyment. *Rec. dist.:* N.Y.

35. When we can't make light of our troubles, we can keep them dark. *Vars.:* **(a)** If we can't make light of our troubles, keep them in the dark. **(b)** If you cannot make light of your troubles, keep them in the dark. **(c)** When we can't make light of our troubles, we can keep them in the dark. *Rec. dist.:* Ala., Ga., Miss., Ohio, Okla.

36. W'en trouble cum, frien' run. *Rec. dist.:* S.C.

37. You can't escape trouble by running away from it. *Rec. dist.:* Wash.

38. You can't keep trouble from coming in, but you needn't give it a chair to sit in. *Rec. dist.:* Miss., Ohio, Vt.

SEE ALSO Little CHILDREN, little troubles, big children, big troubles. / He that has a CHOICE has trouble. / COMPANY in distress makes trouble less. / A clear CONSCIENCE can bear any trouble. / The DIFFERENCE between you and other people is that their money looks bigger and their troubles smaller. / One advantage of a college EDUCATION is that it makes one capable of getting into more intelligent trouble. / Even a FISH wouldn't get in trouble if he kept his mouth shut. / A HASTY man is seldom out of trouble. / LIFE's jes pushin' 'side yo' troubles and lookin' for de light. / Those who have MONEY have trouble about it. / What's one man's NEWS is another man's troubles. / PATIENCE is the best remedy for every trouble. / Don't pet a PORCUPINE unless you are looking for trouble. / TEARS and troubles are the lot of all. / One courageous THOUGHT will put to flight a host of troubles. / TIME and trouble circle the world. / The TONGUE is a little thing, but it fills the universe with trouble. / TONGUE double brings trouble. / If a man could have all his WISHES, he would double his trouble. / The fellow who WORKS for a song has trouble meeting his notes. / WORRY is interest paid on trouble before it falls due.

trouble *(v.)* Never trouble another for what you can do yourself. *Var.:* Never trouble another lest trouble trouble you. *Rec. dist.:* Ohio, S.C., Wash.

SEE ALSO It never troubles the WOLF how many the sheep may be.

troubled SEE Never FISH in troubled waters.

troublesome SEE Grief for a dead WIFE and a troublesome guest continues to the threshold, and there is at rest.

trough Dirty troughs will serve dirty sows. *Rec. dist.:* Ill.

trousers **1.** Never wear your best trousers when you go out to fight for freedom. *Rec. dist.:* Ont.

2. Trousers help trousers; skirts help skirts. *Rec. dist.:* Ill.

trout **1.** A live trout is better than a dead whale. *Rec. dist.:* Wis. *1st cit.:* US1941 Sassoon, "Aliveness in Literature" in *Saturday Review of Literature.* *20c. coll.:* Stevenson 1418:3.

2. You can't catch trout with dry trousers. *Var.:* You cannot catch trout with dry breeches. *Rec. dist.:* Ill., Ohio. *1st cit.:* US1948 Stevenson, *Home Book of Proverbs.* *20c. coll.:* Stevenson 1228:11.

true *(n.)* SEE We grow like what we THINK, so let us think of the good, the true, and the beautiful.

true *(adj.)* **1.** Dare to be true: nothing can need a lie. *Rec. dist.:* Ont.

2. That must be true which all men say. *Rec. dist.:* Mich., N.Y., Tex. *1st cit.:* 1520 Whittington, *Vulgaria,* E.E.T.S. (1932). *20c. coll.:* *ODEP* 841, Stevenson 1721:3.

3. This above all: to your own self be true. *Vars.:* **(a)** To your own self be true, and it must follow, as the night the day, you cannot then be false to any man. **(b)** To your own self be true. You cannot then be false to any man. *Rec. dist.:* U.S., Can. *1st cit.:* 1600 Shakespeare, *Hamlet.* *20c. coll.:* Stevenson 2379:9.

SEE ALSO True BLUE will never stain. / Blue EYES, true eyes. / FLOWERS of true friendship never fade. / A true FRIEND is one who knows all your faults and loves you still. / The truth although severe is a true FRIEND. / They are rich who have true FRIENDS. / True GREATNESS is not in never falling, but in rising when you fall. / True HAPPINESS comes from within. / True HAPPINESS consists of making others happy. / Believe every man a LIAR until he proves himself true. / True LOVERS are shy when people are by. / You cannot be a true MAN until you learn to obey. / A true SERVANT will deceive his master never. / There is many a true TALE told in jest. / VIRTUE is the only true nobility. / A true WIFE is her husband's better half. / A true WORD needs no oath. / There's many a true WORD said in jest. / Loaded WORDS are like loaded dice: they never roll true.

trump When in doubt, lead trumps. *Rec. dist.:* Mich., N.Y. Oreg. *Infm.:* Refers to bridge, a card game, but it also means to take bold action.

trumpet SEE Brave ACTIONS never want a trumpet.

trumpeter It is not the trumpeters that fight the battles. *Rec. dist.:* N.Y., S.C. *1st cit.:* US1887 Beecher, *Proverbs from Plymouth Pulpit.* *20c. coll.:* Stevenson 2381:10.

trust *(n.)* **1.** Betray no trust; divulge no secret. *Rec. dist.:* Mich.

2. Sudden trust brings sudden repentance. *Rec. dist.:* Mich. *1st cit.:* 1669 *Politeuphuia,* ed. Ling. *20c. coll.:* Stevenson 2383:4.

SEE ALSO Put your trust in GOD and keep your powder dry. / A LIE stands on one leg, trust on two. / Put not your trust in MONEY, but put your money in trust.

trust *(v.)* **1.** Do not trust too much in an enchanting face. *Rec. dist.:* Calif.

2. In matters concerning yourself, trust first your head; in matters concerning others, trust first your heart. *Rec. dist.:* N.Dak.

3. Never trust a man who doesn't trust others. *Rec. dist.:* Md.

4. Never trust a man who speaks well of everybody. *Rec. dist.:* N.C. *1st cit.:* ca1905 Collins, *Aphorisms.* *20c. coll.:* Stevenson 2383:3.

5. Those who trust us educate us. *Rec. dist.:* Minn.

6. To trust oneself is good—not to trust oneself is better. *Rec. dist.:* N.Dak.

7. Trust every man, but always cut the cards. *Rec. dist.:* Calif.

8. Trust not him that has once broken faith. *Rec. dist.:* N.C. *1st cit.:* 1591 Shakespeare, *Henry VI.* *20c. coll.:* Stevenson 2382:3.

9. Trust not, tempt not. *Rec. dist.:* N.Y.

10. Trust yourself only and another shall not betray you. *Rec. dist.:* N.Y., S.C. *1st cit.:* 1732 Fuller, *Gnomologia;* US1739 Franklin, *PRAlmanac.* *20c. coll.:* Stevenson 2383:7.

11. You should never trust a man, but if you do, never trust the same one twice. *Rec. dist.:* N.Y.

SEE ALSO Never trust the ADVICE of a man in difficulties. / Men's FACES are not to be trusted. / Never trust a FRIEND who deserts you in a pinch. / You can't trust your best FRIEND. / Trust in GOD and do something. / He that trusts in his own HEART is a fool. / Be JUST to all, but trust not all. / He who sows his LAND trusts in God. / LOVE many, trust few. / Eat a peck of SALT with a man before you trust him. / Never trust a broken STAFF. / TRY before you trust. / It is better to keep a WOLF out of the fold than to trust to drawing his teeth and talons after he shall have entered.

trusted To be trusted is a greater compliment than to be loved. *Rec. dist.:* N.Y.

trusting There is no trusting to the countenance. *Rec. dist.:* Mich.

truth **1.** A truth that's told with bad intent beats all the lies you can invent. *Rec. dist.:* Ill., Minn.

2. All fails where truth fails. *Rec. dist.:* Calif.

3. Always tell the truth, but don't always be telling the truth. *Vars.:* **(a)** All truth is not to be told at all times. **(b)** All truths must not be told at all times. **(c)** The truth cannot always be told. **(d)** The truth is not to be spoken at all times. **(e)** The truth is not told at all times. *Rec. dist.:* Mich., Okla., Utah, Wis. *1st cit.:* ca1350 *Douce MS 52;* US1748 "Word" in *Colonial Currency Reprints, 1682–1757,* ed. Davis, Publ. Prince Soc. (1910–11). *20c. coll.:* ODEP 371, Whiting 455, Stevenson 2393:8, T&W 383, Whiting*(MP)* 648.

4. Always tell your doctor and your lawyer the truth. *Var.:* From the physician and the lawyer keep not the truth hidden. *Rec. dist.:* Nebr., Wis. *1st cit.:* 1573 Sanford, *Garden of Pleasure;* US1737 Franklin, *PRAlmanac. 20c. coll.:* ODEP 371, Whiting 114, Whiting*(MP)* 647.

5. Better suffer for truth than prosper by falsehood. *Rec. dist.:* Miss. *1st cit.:* US1948 Stevenson, *Home Book of Proverbs. 20c. coll.:* Stevenson 2396:7.

6. Buy the truth, but never sell it. *Rec. dist.:* Ont. *1st cit.:* US1948 Stevenson, *Home Book of Proverbs. 20c. coll.:* Stevenson 2391:1.

7. Doubt him who serves the truth of a thing. *Rec. dist.:* Mich.

8. Folks like the truth that hits their neighbors. *Rec. dist.:* Wis.

9. Follow not truth too near the heels lest it dash out your teeth. *Rec. dist.:* Ont. *1st cit.:* 1614 Raleigh, *History of World. 20c. coll.:* ODEP 272, Stevenson 2387:15.

10. Half the truth is often a great lie. *Vars.:* **(a)** A half-truth is often a great lie. **(b)** Half a truth is worse than a whole lie. **(c)** Half-truth is often a great lie. *Rec. dist.:* U.S., Can. *1st cit.:* 1859 Tennyson, *Grandmother;* US1758 Franklin, *PRAlmanac. 20c. coll.:* ODEP 344, Whiting 192, CODP 104, Stevenson 2396:8.

11. He who follows truth too closely will have dirt kicked in his face. *Rec. dist.:* N.C.

12. If we tell untruths, no one will believe us even when we do speak the truth. *Var.:* If we tell untruths, no one will believe us when we speak the truth. *Rec. dist.:* Ont.

13. If you want the truth, ask a child. *Var.:* If you want the truth, go to a child or a fool. *Rec. dist.:* Ky., Tenn.

14. If you want to hear the whole truth about yourself, anger your neighbor. *Rec. dist.:* Ont.

15. It is not truth that makes man great, but man that makes truth great. *Rec. dist.:* Minn.

16. It is truth that makes a man angry. *Rec. dist.:* Vt.

17. It takes two to speak truth: one to speak and another to hear. *Var.:* It takes two to speak truth. *Rec. dist.:* Ill., N.Y.

18. Live truth instead of professing it. *Rec. dist.:* Minn.

19. Love truth for truth's sake. *Rec. dist.:* Ont.

20. Many a truth is spoken in jest. *Vars.:* **(a)** A truth is often told in a joke. **(b)** Much truth is spoken in jest. **(c)** Truth is often spoken as a jest. *Rec. dist.:* Ala., Calif., Ga., Ont. *Infm.:* Cf. word. *1st cit.:* ca1386 Chaucer, *Monk's Prologue;* US1728 Byrd, *Histories of Dividing Line Betwixt Virginia and North Carolina,* ed. Boyd (1929). *20c. coll.:* ODEP 841, Whiting 496, CODP 230, Stevenson 1267:5, T&W 413, Whiting*(MP)* 699.

21. Men who tell you almost nothing but the truth tell you almost nothing. *Rec. dist.:* N.Y.

22. Speak every man truth with his neighbor. *Rec. dist.:* Ont.

23. Speak the truth and shame the devil. *Vars.:* **(a)** Come tell the truth and shame the devil. **(b)** It takes the truth to shame the devil. **(c)** Speak the truth and embarrass the devil. **(d)** Tell the truth and shame the devil. *Rec. dist.:* U.S., Can. *1st cit.:* 1548 Patten, *Expedition into Scotland;* US1796 *Diary of Elihu Hubbard Smith, 1771–1789,* ed. Cronin (1973). *20c. coll.:* ODEP 807, Whiting 455, CODP 221, Stevenson 2389:5, T&W 98, Whiting*(MP)* 647.

24. Speak the truth bravely, cost as it may; hiding the wrong act is not the way. *Rec. dist.:* Wis. *1st cit.:* US1948 Stevenson, *Home Book of Proverbs. 20c. coll.:* Stevenson 2386:4.

25. Tell the truth all the time and you won't have to remember what you said. *Var.:* If you tell the truth, you don't have to remember anything. *Rec. dist.:* Ala., Calif., Ga., Ont.

26. Tell the truth if it kills you. *Rec. dist.:* Miss.

27. The expression of truth is simplicity. *Rec. dist.:* N.C. *1st cit.:* US1948 Stevenson, *Home Book of Proverbs.* *20c. coll.:* Stevenson 2384:7.

28. The greater the truths, the greater the libel. *Rec. dist.:* N.Y., S.C. *1st cit.:* 1828 Lyton, *Pelham;* US1950 Crispin, *Sudden.* *20c. coll.:* ODEP 336, Whiting*(MP)* 647, CODP 101, Stevenson 1387:1.

29. The greatest truths are the simplest, and so are the greatest men. *Rec. dist.:* N.Y., N.C., Wis.

30. The man who fears no truths has nothing to fear from lies. *Rec. dist.:* N.Y.

31. The truth always pays. *Rec. dist.:* Ky., Tenn. *1st cit.:* US1928 Cole, *Man from the River.* *20c. coll.:* Whiting*(MP)* 649.

32. The truth doesn't hurt unless it ought to. *Rec. dist.:* Calif., Ohio.

33. The truth hurts. *Vars.:* (a) It's the truth that hurts. (b) The truth always hurts. (c) The truth hurts, and so would you if you were stretched so much. (d) The truth often hurts. *Rec. dist.:* U.S., Can. *1st cit.:* US1956 Taylor, *I Have.* *20c. coll.:* Whiting*(MP)* 648.

34. The truth is better than a lie. *Rec. dist.:* N.C.

35. The truth itself is not believed from those who often have deceived. *Rec. dist.:* Ind., Ohio.

36. The truth never shocked a man. *Rec. dist.:* Ill.

37. The truth of the soul is in the spirit. *Rec. dist.:* Utah.

38. The truth shall make you free. *Var.:* Know the truth and the truth shall set you free. *Rec. dist.:* Calif., Ont., S.C. *1st cit.:* ca1784 Cowper, *The Task.* *20c. coll.:* Stevenson 2388:7.

39. The truth will out. *Vars.:* (a) The truth will come to light. (a) Time brings truth to light. *Rec. dist.:* U.S., Can. *1st cit.:* 1439 Lydgate, *Life of St. Alban* (1974); US1780 Gordon, *Letters of Rev. William Gordon, Historian of the American Revolution,* Mass.Hist.Soc. Collections (1929–30). *20c. coll.:* CODP 231, Whiting 456, ODEP 845, Stevenson 2391:11, T&W 384, Whiting*(MP)* 649.

40. There is no standard for truth: we cannot even agree on the meaning of words. *Rec. dist.:* Ill.

41. To define a truth is to limit its scope. *Rec. dist.:* Ill.

42. To withhold the truth is to bury gold. *Rec. dist.:* Oreg.

43. Truth always brings division between right and wrong. *Rec. dist.:* N.C.

44. Truth and oil always come to the top. *Rec. dist.:* Ill. *1st cit.:* 1620 Cervantes, *Don Quixote,* tr. Shelton. *20c. coll.:* ODEP 843, Stevenson 2392:11.

45. Truth and roses have thorns about them. *Vars.:* (a) Truth and roses have thorns. (b) Truths, like roses, have thorns about them. *Rec. dist.:* Calif., Ill., N.Y., S.C., Wis. *1st cit.:* 1707 Mapletoft, *Select Proverbs.* *20c. coll.:* ODEP 845, Stevenson 2386:6.

46. Truth creeps out of the ground. *Rec. dist.:* Ont.

47. Truth, crushed to earth, will rise again. *Rec. dist.:* Ill., N.Y. *1st cit.:* 1915 Anspacher, *Unchastened Woman;* USca1879 Bryant, *Battle Field.* *20c. coll.:* Stevenson 708:5.

48. Truth fears no colors. *Var.:* Truth needs no colors. *Rec. dist.:* Ill., Vt. *Infm.:* Truth fears no enemy. *1st cit.:* 1592 Nashe, *Strange News;* US1741 Stephens, *Journal of Proceedings in Georgia* in *Georgia Records* (1906). *20c. coll.:* ODEP 843, Whiting 456, Stevenson 2388:4.

49. Truth fears nothing but concealment. *Rec. dist.:* N.C.

50. Truth finds foes where it makes none. *Rec. dist.:* Ill. *1st cit.:* ca1530 Terence, *Andria.* *20c. coll.:* ODEP 843, Stevenson 2311:5.

51. Truth gives a short answer, but lies go round about. *Rec. dist.:* Calif.

52. Truth has no confines. *Rec. dist.:* Ariz.

53. Truth, harsh though it be, is a faithful friend. *Vars.:* (a) Truth, although severe, is a true friend. (b) Truth, though severe, is a faithful friend. *Rec. dist.:* Ill., Oreg., Wis.

54. Truth is a rare commodity. *Rec. dist.:* Calif.

55. Truth is a useful idea. *Rec. dist.:* Minn.

56. Truth is found in strange places and often slumbers even in a joke. *Var.:* Truth struggles in strange places and often slumbers in a joke. *Rec. dist.:* Ind., Minn.

57. Truth is heavy; therefore few wear it. *Rec. dist.:* Ont.

58. Truth is mightier than the sword. *Rec. dist.:* Ont.

59. Truth is mighty and will prevail. *Vars.:* **(a)** The truth will always prevail. **(b)** Truth is mighty and it will prevail. **(c)** Truth will prevail. *Rec. dist.:* U.S., Can. *1st cit.:* ca1390 Gower, *Confessio Amantis;* US1715 *Diary of Cotton Mather,* ed. Ford, Mass.Hist.Soc. *Collections* (1911–12). *20c. coll.:* ODEP 844, Whiting 455, Stevenson 2392:10.

60. Truth is simple, requiring neither study nor art. *Rec. dist.:* N.C. *1st cit.:* 1535 Joye, *Apologie to Tyndale,* ed. Arber. *20c. coll.:* ODEP 843.

61. Truth is stranger than fiction. *Vars.:* **(a)** Truth is greater than fiction. **(b)** Truth is stronger than fiction. *Rec. dist.:* U.S., Can. *1st cit.:* 1823 Byron, *Don Juan;* US1845 Mayo, *Kaloolah. 20c. coll.:* ODEP 844, T&W 384, Stevenson 2393:7, Whiting*(MP)* 648.

62. Truth is the basis of all excellence. *Rec. dist.:* Mich.

63. Truth is the daughter of time. *Rec. dist.:* Ill. *1st cit.:* Gardiner, Letter to Cromwell in *Letters,* ed. Muller. *20c. coll.:* ODEP 844, Stevenson 2387:7.

64. Truth is the gate of justice. *Rec. dist.:* Ill.

65. Truth is the spring of heroic virtue. *Rec. dist.:* Ill.

66. Truth is too heavy for most people to bear. *Rec. dist.:* Ill.

67. Truth is truth, though spoken by an enemy. *Rec. dist.:* Fla., Ill.

68. Truth is truth to the end of reckoning. *Rec. dist.:* Ill., N.Y. *1st cit.:* ca1566 Curio, *Pasquin in Trance,* tr. W. P. *20c. coll.:* ODEP 844, Stevenson 2387:9.

69. Truth keeps to the bottom of her well. *Var.:* Truth lies at the bottom of a well. *Rec. dist.:* Ill., N.Y., S.C. *1st cit.:* 1547 Baldwin, *Treatise of Moral Philosophie;* US1779 *Journal and Letters of Samuel Curwen,* ed. Ward (1844). *20c. coll.:* ODEP 844, Whiting 456, *CODP* 231, Stevenson 2393:10, T&W 384, Whiting*(MP)* 648.

70. Truth may be blamed, but never shamed. *Rec. dist.:* U.S., Can. *1st cit.:* ca1450 *Coventry Mystery Play,* Shakespeare Soc.; US1767 Ames, *Almanacs,* ed. Briggs (1891). *20c. coll.:* ODEP 844, Whiting 456.

71. Truth may sometimes come out of the devil's mouth. *Rec. dist.:* Ill. *1st cit.:* 1592 Shakespeare, *Richard III. 20c. coll.:* ODEP 183, Stevenson 2387:4.

72. Truth never grows old. *Rec. dist.:* Ill., Ont. *1st cit.:* 1732 Fuller, *Gnomologia. 20c. coll.:* Stevenson 2391:6.

73. Truth never hurt the teller. *Vars.:* **(a)** The truth never hurt. **(b)** The truth never hurts anyone. *Rec. dist.:* Minn., Miss. *1st cit.:* 1872 Browning, *Fifine at Fair.* US1934 Bush, *Dead Shepherd. 20c. coll.:* Stevenson 2389:8, Whiting*(MP)* 648.

74. Truth never perishes. *Rec. dist.:* Wis.

75. Truth seeks no corners. *Rec. dist.:* Ill., Tex. *1st cit.:* 1564 Bullein, *Dialogue Against Fever,* E.E.T.S. (1888); US1644 *Complete Writings of Roger Williams* (1963). *20c. coll.:* ODEP 845, Whiting 456, Stevenson 2389:7.

76. Truth shall conquer all. *Rec. dist.:* Ont.

77. Truth tastes bitter. *Var.:* Truth is bitter. *Rec. dist.:* Calif., Ill. *1st cit.:* US1948 Stevenson, *Home Book of Proverbs. 20c. coll.:* Stevenson 2388:9.

78. When in doubt, tell the truth. *Rec. dist.:* Ill. *1st cit.:* US1894 Twain, *Notebook. 20c. coll.:* Stevenson 2391:18.

79. Where doubt is, truth is. *Rec. dist.:* Ill.

80. Without truth there can be no virtue. *Rec. dist.:* Ont.

SEE ALSO BEAUTY is truth, truth beauty. / The first CASUALTY when war comes is truth. / CHILDREN and fools speak the truth. / CONSCIENCE is only another name for truth. / An EXAGGERATION is a truth that has lost its temper. / FAITH is inward truth daring the unknown. / One truth we gain from living through the years, FEAR brings more pain then does the pain it fears. / FLATTERY begets friends but the truth begets emnity. / FLATTERY brings friends, truth friendship. / The truth is not simply that we may form HABITS, but that we are forming them. / A HOUR perhaps divides the false and truth. / The IDEAL is but the truth at a distance. / There's nothing so kingly as KINDNESS and nothing so royal as truth. / When KNAVES fall out, honest men get their goods; when priests dispute we come at the truth. / LANGUAGE is the vehicle of truth. / A LIE can go a mile before the truth can put its boots on. / A LIE can go around the world and back while the truth is lacing up its boots. / A LIE runs until it is overtaken by the truth. / A LIE stands on one leg, truth on two. / If you tell a LIE an' stick to it, dat's as good as de truth anyhow. / Never tell a LIE till the truth doesn't fit. / Tell a LIE and find the truth. / There is no LIE, spun so fine, through which the truth won't shine. / When MONEY speaks, truth keeps its mouth shut. / RIDICULE is the test of truth. / One doesn't need so many WORDS to tell the truth.

try *(n.)* A try is better than nothing. *Rec. dist.:* Ont.

try *(v.)* **1.** He who never tries anything will never win. *Rec. dist.:* Ariz.

2. I'll try it is a soldier; I will is a king. *Rec. dist.:* Ont.

3. It is better to have tried and died than never to have lived. *Var.:* It is better to try and fail than fail to try. *Rec. dist.:* Ont.

4. Try anything once. *Rec. dist.:* Ohio.

5. Try before you trust. *Rec. dist.:* Ohio. *1st cit.:* ca1450–1500 *Gode Wife Wolde a Pilgrimage;* US1741 Ames, *Almanacs,* ed. Briggs (1891). *20c. coll.:* ODEP 845, Whiting 456.

6. Try did wonders. *Rec. dist.:* Calif.

7. Try it before you buy it. *Rec. dist.:* Wash.

8. You can never tell till you've tried. *Rec. dist.:* N.J., Ohio. *1st cit.:* 1539 Publilius Syrus, *Sententiae,* tr. Taverner; US1941 Howie,

Murder for Christmas. **20c. coll.:** Stevenson 2396:14.

SEE ALSO ADVERSITY tries virtue. / I CAN'T never did anything, I'll try has done wonders. / Never say CAN'T, say I'll try. / Try your FRIEND before you have need of him. / GOLD must be tried by fire. / Try the ICE before you venture upon it. / Never be the first by whom the NEW is tried nor yet the last to lay the old aside. / If at first you don't SUCCEED, try, try again.

trying No one was ever blamed for trying. *Rec. dist.:* Ohio.

SEE ALSO There is no FAILURE except in no longer trying.

tub 1. Every tub smells of the wine it holds. *Rec. dist.:* Ill., Ont. *1st cit.:* 1509 Barclay, *Ship of Fools,* ed. Jamieson in *Eclogues,* E.E.T.S. (1874). *20c. coll.:* Stevenson 1561:9.

2. Let every tub stand on its own bottom. *Vars.:* (a) Every tub has to stand on its own bottom. (b) Every tub must set on its own bottom. (c) Every tub must sit on its own bottom. (d) Every tub must stand on its own bottom. (e) Every tub ought to stand on its own bottom. (f) Every tub sets on its own bottom. (g) Every tub should rest on its own bottom. (h) Every tub should stand on its own bottom. (i) Every tub should stand on its own bottom, but be not overconfident. (j) Every tub sits on its own bottom. (k) Every tub stands on its own bottom. *Rec. dist.:* U.S., Can. *1st cit.:* 1564 Bullein, *Dialogue Against Fever,* E.E.T.S. (1888); US1750 Fairservice, "Plain Dealing" in *Mag.Hist.* **20c. coll.:** ODEP 845, Whiting 456, *CODP* 232, Stevenson 2397:4, T&W 384, Whiting(MP) 649.

3. You don't have to eat a whole tub of butter to get the taste. *Rec. dist.:* Wash.

SEE ALSO MARRIAGE is like a tub of water: after a while, it is not so hot.

tugging *SEE* SYMPATHY is two hearts tugging at one load.

tug-of-war *SEE* When GREEK meets Greek, then comes a tug-of-war.

tuition *SEE* EXPERIENCE is the best teacher, but it charges high tuition fees.

tumble *(n.)* The hardest tumble a man can take is the fall off his own bluff. *Rec. dist.:* N.Y.

tumble *(v.)* He who tumbles isn't much of a traveler. *Rec. dist.:* Ky.

tumult Keep yourself from the tumult of the mob. *Rec. dist.:* Mich.

tune 1. Any tune is music when you feels like dancin'. *Rec. dist.:* Wis.

2. Old tunes are sweetest; old friends are surest. *Rec. dist.:* Ont.

3. There is many a good tune played on the old fiddle. *Vars.:* **(a)** Many a good tune is played on a fiddle. **(b)** The best tunes come from old fiddles. **(c)** You can play fine tunes on an old fiddle. *Rec. dist.:* U.S., Can. *1st cit.:* 1903 Butler, *Way of All Flesh;* US1933 Patrick, *S.S. Murder.* **20c. coll.:** ODEP 325, Whiting(MP) 649, CODP 99, Stevenson 2398:1.

4. Who dances to the tune must pay the piper. *Vars.:* **(a)** He who calls the tune must pay the piper. **(b)** He who pays the piper calls the tune. **(c)** Who dances to the tune must pay the fiddler. *Rec. dist.:* Nebr., Ont. *1st cit.:* 1638 Taylor, *Taylor's Feast;* US1797 Callender, *American Annual Register.* **20c. coll.:** ODEP 615, Whiting 339, CODP 175, Stevenson 1789:9, T&W 287, Whiting(MP) 495.

SEE ALSO The older the FIDDLE, the better the tune.

turn *(n.)* 1. A good turn goes a long way. *Rec. dist.:* N.Y.

2. Do a good turn daily. *Rec. dist.:* Ohio.

3. Never do anyone an ill turn. *Rec. dist.:* Ont.

4. One bad turn deserves another. *Rec. dist.:* Calif. *1st cit.:* 1509 Barclay, *Ship of Fools,* ed. Jamieson in *Eclogues,* E.E.T.S. (1874). **20c. coll.:** Stevenson 2401:2, Whiting(MP) 651.

5. One good turn deserves another. *Rec. dist.:* U.S., Can. *1st cit.:* ca1400 *Latin MS 394,* tr. Pantin, in *Bulletin of J. Rylands Library;* US1717 Wise, *Vindication.* **20c. coll.:** ODEP 325, Whiting 458, CODP 99, Stevenson 2401:1, T&W 386, Whiting(MP) 651.

6. One never loses by doing a good turn. *Var.:* You will never lose a turn by doing good. *Rec. dist.:* Ont. *1st cit.:* 1666 Torriano, *Select Italian Proverbs.* **20c. coll.:** ODEP 486, Stevenson 2400:4.

7. Your turn today, mine tomorrow. *Rec. dist.:* Fla.

SEE ALSO It's a long LANE that has no turn. / There is never a ROAD so long without a turn in it. / Never take the WHIP when a word will do the turn. / Every WORM has his turn.

turn *(v.)* It is better to turn back than to turn astray. *Var.:* It is better to turn back than to go astray. *Rec. dist.:* Ill., N.J.

SEE ALSO A soft ANSWER turns away wrath. / It is better to turn BACK than to go astray. / One should turn his COAT according to the weather. / GET what you can, and what you get, hold, 'Tis the stone that will turn all your lead into gold. / Even a RAT, when cornered, will turn and fight. / In the SPRING a young man's fancy lightly turns to thoughts of love. / Every TIDE must turn. / The hands of TIME will never turn back.

turnabout Turnabout is fair play. *Rec. dist.:* U.S., Can. *1st cit.:* 1755 *Life of Capt. Dudley Bradstreet,* ed. Taylor; US1777 Drayton in Gibbes, *Documentary History of American Revolution.* **20c. coll.:** ODEP 846, Whiting 458, CODP 232, Stevenson 2399:7, T&W 386, Whiting(MP) 651.

turning *SEE* It's a long LINE that has no turning. / Every ROAD has a turning. / It's a long ROAD that has no turning.

turnip *SEE* You can't get BLOOD out of a turnip.

turtle *SEE* All THOUGHTS of a turtle are turtle, and of a rabbit, rabbit.

twenty *SEE* Not HANDSOME at twenty, not strong at thirty, not rich at forty, not wise at fifty—never will be.

twenty-one *SEE* It takes twenty-one YEARS for one woman to make a man of her son; it takes twenty-one seconds for another woman to make a fool of him.

twice SEE It is better to ASK twice than to go wrong once. / On a good BARGAIN think twice. / If a BEE stings you once, it's the bee's fault; if a bee stings you twice, it's your own damn fault. / If anyone BETRAYS you once, it's his fault; if he betrays you twice, it's your fault. / You can't eat the same BREAD twice. / Once BURNED, twice shy. / He CONQUERS twice who overcomes himself. / That which is well DONE is twice done. / Nobody is twice a DUNCE. / He that EATS and saves sets the table twice. / A long FACE makes a long road seem twice as long. / A FAULT once denied is twice committed. / He who cuts his own FIREWOOD has it warm him twice. / A FISH never nibbles at the same hook twice. / Only a FOOL makes the same mistake twice. / A FOX is not caught twice in the same place. / The same GAME does not often succeed twice. / He who GIVES quickly gives twice. / What HAPPENS twice, happens thrice. / HEAR twice before you speak once. / You can fool an old HORSE once, but you can't fool him twice. / We are taxed twice as much by our IDLENESS, three as much times by our pride, and four times as much as by our folly. / An old MAN is twice a boy. / Once a MAN, twice a child. / A good TALE is not the worse for being told twice. / Don't do the same THING twice. / THINK twice; speak once. / Don't chew your TOBACCO twice. / You should never TRUST a man, but if you do, never trust the same one twice. / A WISE man sees twice as much as he talks about.

twig 1. A young twig is easier twisted than an old tree. *Rec. dist.:* Tex.

2. As the twig is bent, so grows the tree. *Vars.:* (a) As the twig is bent, so goes the tree. (b) As the twig is bent, so grows the child. (c) As the twig is bent, so is the tree inclined. (d) As the twig is bent, so it will grow. (e) As the twig is bent, so the branch is broken. (f) As the twig is bent, so the oak will grow. (g) As the twig is bent, so the tree inclines. (h) As the twig is bent, so the tree is inclined. (i) As the twig is bent, so the tree is inclined to grow. (j) As the twig is bent, so the tree will grow. (k) As the twig is bent, so will grow the tree. (l) As the twig is bent, the

child will grow. (m) As the twig is bent, the tree will grow. *Rec. dist.:* U.S., Can. *1st cit.:* 1530 Palsgrave, *Lesclarcissement de la langue Francoyse,* ed. Genin (1852); US1796 *Writings of George Washington,* ed. Fitzpatrick (1931–44). *20c. coll.:* CODP 232, Whiting 459, Stevenson 2371:4, T&W 387, Whiting(MP) 652.

3. Bend the twig while it is still green. *Rec. dist.:* Ohio, Tex. *1st cit.:* ca1595 Fergusson, *Scottish Proverbs.* *20c. coll.:* Stevenson 2371:4.

4. Best to bend it while a twig. *Rec. dist.:* Ohio. *1st cit.:* 1543 Hardyng, *English Chronicle in Metre.* *20c. coll.:* ODEP 46, Stevenson 2371:4.

5. Birchen twigs break no ribs. *Rec. dist.:* Ont. *1st cit.:* 1583 Babington, *Exposition of Commandments.* *20c. coll.:* ODEP 59.

6. Easy matter to bend a twig; hard matter to bend an oak. *Rec. dist.:* Tex.

7. The young twig is easily bent. *Rec. dist.:* Ont. *1st cit.:* 1580 Lyly, *Euphues and His England.* *20c. coll.:* Stevenson 2371:5.

SEE ALSO As the WIND blows, so bends the twig.

twin SEE Twin FOOLS, one doubts nothing, the other, everything.

twist SEE A young TREE is easier twisted than an old tree.

twitter SEE As the old BIRD sings, so the young ones twitter.

two 1. Two can live cheaper than one. *Vars.:* (a) Two can live as cheap as one. (b) Two can live as cheap as one if one's a horse and the other is a sparrow. (c) Two can live as cheaply as one only if one doesn't eat. (d) Two can live as cheaply as one. *Rec. dist.:* U.S., Can. *1st cit.:* US1921 Lardner, *Big Town.* *20c. coll.:* Whiting(MP) 654.

2. Two in distress make trouble less. *Rec. dist.:* N.Y.

3. Two is company; three is a crowd. *Vars.:* (a) One, company; two, crowd; three, too many; four's allowed. (b) Two is a couple, three a crowd; five on the sidewalk is not allowed. (c) Two is a couple, three is a crowd, four is too many, and five is not allowed. (d) Two is company, three's a crowd, four is a

regiment, and five's not allowed. **(e)** Two's a company, three's a crowd; four on the sidewalk is not allowed. **(f)** Two's a party, three's a crowd. **(g)** Two's company, but three's a crowd. *Rec. dist.:* U.S., Can. *1st cit.:* 1706 Stevens, *New Spanish and English Dictionary;* US1860 Haliburton, *Season-Ticket.* *20c. coll.:* ODEP 851, T&W 388, CODP 233, Stevenson 386:1, Whiting*(MP)* 654.

SEE ALSO It takes two to start an ARGUMENT. / It always takes two to make a BARGAIN. / A BIRD in the hand is better than two in the bush. / Hit take two BIRDS fer to make a nes'. / Two BLACKS don't make a white. / One BOY's a boy; two boys, a half a boy; three boys, no boy at all. / Two DOGS fight for a bone, and a third runs away with it. / A DOLLAR in the bank is worth two in the hand. / Of two EVILS choose the least. / The EVILS you do by two and two, you pay for one by one. / Four EYES see more than two. / Never carry two FACES under one hood. / FALSE with one can be false with two. / He who does one FAULT at first, and lies to hide it, makes it two. / Stand on your own two FEET. / It takes two to FIGHT. / Ring on the FINGER is worth two on the phone. / Arguing with a FOOL shows there are two. / One FOOT is better than two crutches. / It takes two to make a FUSS. / When you get one GIRL you better try two, cause there ain't no telling what one'll do. / Scatter with one HAND, gather with two. / A HANDKERCHIEF dropped is worth two in the hand. / Four HANDS can do more than two. / Two HANDS are better than one. / To a wise HEAD—two or three words. / Two HEADS are better than one. / You can't have two HILLS without a valley. / No two people can ride the same HORSE, unless one rides behind. / One HOUR today is worth two tomorrow. / One HOUR's sleep before midnight is worth two hours after. / Late HOURS are bad for one but they're alright for two. / A very little HOUSE for one family will do, but I never knew a house built for two. / It is easier to feed two HUNGRY people than one with a coming appetite. / One good HUSBAND is worth two good wives, for the scarcer things are the more they're valued. / Of two ILLS, choose the least. / A LIE stands on one leg, truth on two. / Two MINDS are better than one. / Every man has one black PATCH, and some have two. / One cannot be in two PLACES at once. / It takes two to make a QUARREL. / One SHOT meat; two shots maybe; three shots no good. / A SPUR in the head is worth two in the feet. / One TODAY is worth two tomorrows. / Two of a TRADE seldom agree. / There are two kinds of WOMEN: those who take what you are and those who take what you have. / Two WRONGS do not make a right.

typist The first essential of a typist is a good eraser. *Rec. dist.:* Fla.

tyranny Tyranny breeds deceit. *Rec. dist.:* N.C.

SEE ALSO DEMOCRACY is better than tyranny. / TAXATION without representation is tyranny.

tyrant 1. A tyrant never knows true friendship nor perfect liberty. *Rec. dist.:* Ill.

2. A tyrant never wants a plea. *Rec. dist.:* Calif.

3. A tyrant's breath is another's death. *Rec. dist.:* Ill. *1st cit.:* 1855 Bohn, *Handbook of Proverbs.* *20c. coll.:* Stevenson 2404:4.

4. There is no tyrant like an ex-slave. *Rec. dist.:* Calif.

SEE ALSO Any EXCUSE will serve a tyrant. / GOLD is an unseen tyrant. / REBELLION to tyrants is obedience to God.

U

ugliness Ugliness is the guardian of women. *Rec. dist.:* Ill.

SEE ALSO BEAUTY is loved without knowing anything, ugliness hated without being to blame.

ugly **1.** An ugly baby makes a beautiful adult. *Rec. dist.:* N.C.

2. An ugly man never gets a pretty wife. *Rec. dist.:* N.C.

3. An ugly woman dreads the mirror. *Rec. dist.:* Ill.

4. If all the world were ugly, deformity would be no monster. *Rec. dist.:* Ill.

5. If you despise that which is ugly, you do not know that which is beautiful. *Rec. dist.:* Ill.

6. No woman is ugly if she is well dressed. *Rec. dist.:* Ill.

7. The ugliest woman can look in the mirror and think she is beautiful. *Rec. dist.:* N.C.

8. Ugly is to the bone; beauty lasts only a day. Ugly holds its own—you never can tell. *Rec. dist.:* N.Y., Wis. *1st cit.:* 1881 Evans, *Leicestershire Words.* *20c. coll.:* Stevenson 140:5.

SEE ALSO Old woman's GOLD is not ugly. / There are not ugly LOVES, nor handsome prisons. / Nobody's SWEETHEART is ugly.

ulcer An ulcer and a bird do not choose where to appear. *Rec. dist.:* Ill.

umbrage Umbrage should never be taken where offense is not intended. *Rec. dist.:* Mich.

umbrella **1.** If you leave your umbrella at home, it is sure to rain. *Rec. dist.:* Mich., N.Y., S.C. *1st cit.:* US1907 Burgess, *Are You a Bromide?* *20c. coll.:* Stevenson 2405:10.

2. The umbrella goes up when the rain comes down. *Rec. dist.:* Ont.

3. Two under an umbrella makes the third a wet fellow. *Rec. dist.:* Fla.

SEE ALSO COMPROMISE makes a good umbrella but a poor roof. / A WISE man always carries his umbrella.

un-American *SEE* IMPOSSIBLE is un-American.

unanimity Unanimity makes humble help strong. *Rec. dist.:* N.Y.

unbelieving *SEE* BELIEVING has a core of unbelieving.

unbestowed *SEE* The worst STORE is a maid unbestowed.

unbidden *SEE* An unbidden GUEST knows not where to sit.

unborn A boy is better unborn than untaught. *Vars.:* **(a)** Better be unborn than unbred. **(b)** Better be unborn than untaught, for ignorance is the root of misfortune. *Rec. dist.:* U.S., Can. *1st cit.:* ca1275 *Proverbs of Alfred,* ed. Skeat; US1933 Phillpotts, *Captain's Curio.* *20c. coll.:* ODEP 56, Whiting(MP) 656, Stevenson 2286:6.

uncalled *SEE* OLD age comes uncalled.

uncertain *SEE* Where the LAW is uncertain there is no law.

uncertainty *SEE* POVERTY with security is better than plenty in the midst of fear and uncertainty.

unchaste **1.** The unchaste woman can never become chaste again. *Rec. dist.:* Ill.

2. The unchaste woman will hesitate at no wickedness. *Rec. dist.:* Ill.

under *SEE* There is nothing NEW under the sun.

underdone *SEE* OVERDONE is worse than underdone.

understand **1.** A man doesn't learn to understand anything unless he loves it. *Rec. dist.:* Ont.

2. A person should not meddle with what he does not understand. *Rec. dist.:* Ont.

3. He that understands amiss, concludes worse. *Rec. dist.:* Mich.

4. He who understands most is the other men's master. *Rec. dist.:* Wis.

5. To one who understands, few words are needed. *Rec. dist.:* Calif.

6. To really understand a man we must judge him in misfortune. *Rec. dist.:* N.Y.

7. To understand is to forgive. *Rec. dist.:* Ont. *1st cit.:* 1941 Heyer, *Envious Casca.* *20c. coll.:* Stevenson 2406:15.

8. Whatever you cannot understand you cannot possess. *Var.:* What a man does not understand he does not possess. *Rec. dist.:* Wis. *1st cit.:* US1948 Stevenson, *Home Book of Proverbs.* *20c. coll.:* Stevenson 2406:8.

9. You can't make other people understand what you are trying to explain if you don't understand it yourself. *Rec. dist.:* N.C.

SEE ALSO To ACT is easy, but to understand is hard. / People CONDEMN what they do not understand. / Men DESPISE what they do not understand. / Don't find FAULT with what you don't understand.

understanding 1. Be not disturbed at being misunderstood; be disturbed at not understanding. *Rec. dist.:* Minn.

2. The understanding is always the dupe of the heart. *Rec. dist.:* Ill.

3. Understanding is the faculty of reflection. *Rec. dist.:* Mich.

SEE ALSO A FOOL has no understanding but that his heart may discover itself. / PAIN wastes the body, pleasures the understanding. / Happy is the man that finds WISDOM and that gets understanding. / Through WISDOM is a house builded, and by understanding it is established.

understood *SEE* A SMILE is the same in any language—easily understood.

undertake 1. Undertake no more than you can perform. *Rec. dist.:* N.Y.

2. Who undertakes too much seldom succeeds. *Rec. dist.:* Oreg.

undertaker *SEE* EXPERIENCE is the best teacher; only the undertaker can issue a diploma.

undertaking 1. Every undertaking is only begun with difficulty. *Rec. dist.:* N.Y.

2. In your every undertaking, consider some day you will have to die. *Rec. dist.:* Kans.

undeserved *SEE* PRAISE undeserved is scandal in disguise.

undo *SEE* Your TONGUE can undo all you be.

undone *SEE* What is DONE cannot be undone. / It is for want of THINKING most men are undone.

undutiful *SEE* An undutiful DAUGHTER will prove an unmanageable wife.

uneasy *SEE* FOOLS are never uneasy. / A GOOD man is seldom uneasy, an ill one never easy.

unemployed *SEE* MIND unemployed is mind unenjoyed.

unequal There is no unequal before natural law. *Rec. dist.:* Ill.

unexpected It's always the unexpected that happens. *Vars.:* **(a)** It is the unexpected that always happens. **(b)** The unexpected always happens. **(c)** The unexpected often happens. *Rec. dist.:* U.S., Can. *1st cit.:* 1886 Hardy, *How To Be Happy Though Married.* *20c. coll.:* ODEP 854, CODP 236, Stevenson 721:15, Whiting(MP) 656.

unfeminine *SEE* STUPIDITY in a woman is unfeminine.

unfortunate 1. Deride not the unfortunate. *Rec. dist.:* Mich.

2. However unfortunate we are, there are always people worse off than we. *Rec. dist.:* Kans.

3. None know the unfortunate, and the fortunate do not know themselves. *Rec. dist.:* Ill. *1st cit.:* US1747 Franklin, *PRAlmanac.* *20c. coll.:* Stevenson 871:10.

ungrateful To do good to the ungrateful is like throwing water into the sea. *Rec. dist.:* N.Y. *1st cit.:* 1732 Fuller, *Gnomologia.* *20c. coll.:* Stevenson 1243:2.

SEE ALSO KINDNESS is lost upon an ungrateful man.

unhappiness *SEE* Always stop to think whether your FUN will cause another's unhappiness.

unhappy *See* An unhappy man's CART is easy to overthrow. / It is better to LIE a little than to be unhappy much.

unholiness Unholiness is the deformity of the mind. *Rec. dist.:* Mich.

uniform *See* SHIRTSLEEVES make the best uniform.

uninvited The uninvited should bring their own stool. *Rec. dist.:* Ala., Ga. *1st cit.:* ca1350 *Douce MS 52. 20c. coll.:* ODEP 853.

union In union there is strength. *Vars.:* **(a)** In union is strength—what we have we hold. **(b)** 'Tis not in numbers but in union that our great strength lies. **(c)** Union is strength. *Rec. dist.:* U.S., Can. *1st cit.:* ca1526 Erasmus, *Dicta Sapientum,* tr. Berthelet; US1654 *Complete Writings of Roger Williams* (1963). *20c. coll.:* ODEP 854, Whiting 461, CODP 236, Stevenson 2407:6, T&W 390, Whiting(MP) 656.

unique *See* Every GREAT man is unique.

united United we stand; divided we fall. *Var.:* By uniting we stand; by dividing we fall. *Rec. dist.:* U.S., Can. *1st cit.:* US1768 Dickinson, *Liberty Song in Boston Gazette,* 18 July. *20c. coll.:* CODP 236, Whiting 461, Stevenson 59:9, Whiting(MP) 656.

unity **1.** There's unity in diversity. *Rec. dist.:* Ill.

2. Unity is the essence of amity. *Rec. dist.:* Mich.
   See also There is no LIBERTY without security, and no security without unity.

universal *See* IGNORANCE is universal.

universe God dictated the universe but never signed it. *Rec. dist.:* Ill.
   See also The TONGUE is a little thing, but it fills the universe with trouble.

university The true university is a collection of books. *Rec. dist.:* N.C. *1st cit.:* 1840 Carlyle, *On Heroes and Hero-Worship. 20c. coll.:* Stevenson 1390:10.

unjust Envy not the unjust man, and do not follow his way. *Rec. dist.:* S.C.
   See also RAIN falls alike on the just and unjust. / The SUN shines on the just and the unjust.

unkind *See* Rich GIFTS wax poor when givers prove unkind.

unkindness Unkindness has no remedy at law. *Rec. dist.:* Mich. *1st cit.:* 1678 Ray, *English Proverbs;* USca1852 Ballou, *Sermons. 20c. coll.:* Stevenson 2409:2.

unkissed *See* UNKNOWN, unkissed.

unknowingly *See* Our greatest DEEDS we do unknowingly.

unknown **1.** Everything that is unknown is taken to be grand. *Rec. dist.:* Minn. *1st cit.:* 1814 Bland, *Proverbs. 20c. coll.:* Stevenson 592:3.

2. To be unknown is better than to be ill known. *Rec. dist.:* Ont.

3. Unknown, unkissed. *Rec. dist.:* Okla. *1st cit.:* 1374 Chaucer, *Troilus and Criseyde;* US1658 Filmer in *Va.Mag.Hist.* (1960). *20c. coll.:* ODEP 854, Whiting 461.

4. Unknown, unmissed. *Rec. dist.:* Ont.
   See also The BAD which is well known is better than the good unknown. / FAITH is inward truth daring the unknown.

unlearn *See* It is a task to LEARN, but it is much harder to unlearn.

unlock *See* A little KEY may unlock a box wherein lies a bunch of keys.

unlucky *See* LUCKY at play, unlucky in love.

unmarried *See* It's a woman's BUSINESS to get married as soon as possible, and a man's to keep unmarried as long as he can.

unminded Unminded, unmoaned. *Rec. dist.:* Ont. *1st cit.:* 1546 Heywood, *Dialogue of Proverbs,* ed. Habernicht (1963). *20c. coll.:* ODEP 855, Stevenson 5:9.

unmissed *See* UNKNOWN, unmissed.

unoccupied *See* Nothing is more INJURIOUS than unoccupied time.

unpunished *See* A false WITNESS shall not go unpunished.

unquiet *See* Unquiet MEALS make ill digestion.

unrest *See* Rest comes from unrest and unrest from rest.

unrighteousness Unrighteousness has its punishment here as well as hereafter. *Rec. dist.:* Mich.

unrued *See* Unseen, unrued.

unruly *See* The tongue is an unruly member.

unscramble *See* You can't unscramble eggs.

unseen Unseen, unrued. *Rec. dist.:* N.Y.
   See also Gold is an unseen tyrant.

unselfish *See* The secret to being lovable is to be unselfish.

unspoken *See* An unkind word is better left unspoken. / While the word is yet unspoken, you are master of it; when once it is spoken, it is master of you.

untaught Better untaught than ill taught. *Var.:* Better untaught than badly taught. *Rec. dist.:* Ill., Miss. *1st cit.:* 1678 Ray, *English Proverbs.* *20c. coll.:* ODEP 857, Stevenson 2286:2.
   See also A boy is better unborn than untaught.

untimeous *See* Untimeous spurring spoils the steed.

untouched *See* Tomorrow is untouched.

untruth Nothing can overtake an untruth if it has a minute's start. *Rec. dist.:* Ill.

up **1.** Everything that goes up must come down. *Vars.:* **(a)** All that goes up comes down. **(b)** All that goes up is bound to come down. **(c)** All that goes up must come down. **(d)** That which goes up must come down. **(e)** What goes up comes down. **(f)** What goes up must come down. **(g)** Whatever goes up must come down. *Rec. dist.:* U.S., Can. *1st cit.:* US1939 Wilder, *By Shores of Silver Lake.* *20c. coll.:* CODP 236.

2. Things have to go up—they can't go any further down. *Rec. dist.:* Calif.

3. How could we measure the ups in life if it weren't for the downs? *Rec. dist.:* Miss.

4. We all have our ups and downs. *Rec. dist.:* U.S., Can. *1st cit.:* 1940 Beeding, *Heads Off at*

Midnight; US1761 Husband in *Eighteenth Century Tracts Concerning North Carolina,* ed. Boyd, N.C.Hist.Comm., *Publications* (1917). *20c. coll.:* Stevenson 1904:10, Whiting 461, Whiting *(MP)* 657.
   See also Don't be down on something before you are up on it. / Use it up; make it do; wear it out. / Water always flows down, not up.

upright *See* He that walks uprightly walks surely, but he that perverts his ways shall be known.

uprightness Uprightness ever gathers the fruits of its own rearing. *Rec. dist.:* Mich.

upstream *See* Driftwood never goes upstream. / A dead fish can float downstream, but it takes a live one to swim upstream.

us *See* After us the deluge.

usage Usage is the best interpreter of things. *Rec. dist.:* Ill.

use *(n.)* Make use of your friends by being of use to them. *Rec. dist.:* Minn.
   See also Abuse does not take away use. / Sweet are the uses of adversity. / Most of the learning in use is of no great use. / They who make the best use of their time have none to spare.

use *(v.)* **1.** Use it but don't abuse it. *Var.:* Use but don't abuse it. *Rec. dist.:* Calif., Ill., Mich., N.Y.

2. Use it up; make it do; wear it out. *Var.:* Use it up, wear it out, make it do, or go without. *Rec. dist.:* Ohio.

3. Use what you would not lose. *Var.:* What you do not use, you will not lose. *Rec. dist.:* Calif., Mich., N.Y., Oreg.

4. What you don't use today, save for tomorrow. *Rec. dist.:* Wash.
   See also If you have a good excuse do not use it. / Don't use your feet, use your head. / Money isn't worth a thing except to use in buying something. / To walk one must use his feet. / Use the world, desire heaven.

used *See* The used key is always bright.

useful 1. Be useful as well as ornamental. *Rec. dist.:* Ky., Tenn.

2. Be useful where you live. *Rec. dist.:* Ky., Tenn.

3. Combine the useful with the pleasant. *Rec. dist.:* Mich.

4. The useful and the beautiful are never separated. *Rec. dist.:* N.C. *1st cit.:* US1844 Emerson, "Poet" in *Essays.* *20c. coll.:* Stevenson 139:2.

SEE ALSO Nothing is more useful to a man than SILENCE. / The most useful TRUTHS are the plainest.

usefulness Usefulness and baseness cannot exist in the same thing. *Rec. dist.:* Mich. *1st cit.:* US1948 Stevenson, *Home Book of Proverbs.* *20c. coll.:* Stevenson 2412:1.

SEE ALSO HAPPINESS is a wayside flower growing upon the highways of usefulness.

useless *SEE* The AIM is useless without the way. / An IDLER is a watch that wants both hands, as useless if it goes as if it stands. / It is useless to RUN, better to start on time.

usher *SEE* White LIES are but the ushers to black ones.

using *SEE* SUCCESS is a matter of using one's time well.

usury Usury is the daughter of avarice. *Rec. dist.:* Mich.

utility 1. Practical utility is the mother of justice and equity. *Rec. dist.:* N.C.

2. Utility is preferable to grandeur. *Rec. dist.:* Mich.

utter *SEE* A FOOL utters all his mind, but a wise man keeps it in till afterwards.

utterance Tune your own utterance to your own ear. *Rec. dist.:* N.Y.

V

vacant *See* A loud LAUGH bespeaks the vacant mind. / Absence of OCCUPATION is not rest; a mind quite vacant is a mind in distress.

vacuum A vacuum is always filled. *Rec. dist.:* Ont.

See also NATURE abhors a vacuum.

vagabond The vagabond, when rich, is called a tourist. *Rec. dist.:* Ont.

vagrant 1. A vagrant is everywhere at home. *Rec. dist.:* Ill.

2. The true vagrant is the only king above all comparison. *Rec. dist.:* Ill.

vague *See* Don't be VOGUE on the outside and vague on the inside.

vain 1. If we are vain and love to be flattered, we shall become foolish. *Rec. dist.:* N.Y.

2. Vain is the help of man. *Rec. dist.:* Minn. *1st cit.:* US1948 Stevenson, *Home Book of Proverbs. 20c. coll.:* Stevenson 1130:6.

See also After the ACTING, wishing is in vain. / An old DOG does not bark in vain. / FAVOR is deceitful and beauty is vain. / A word of KINDNESS is seldom spoken in vain. / In vain the NET is spread in the sight of any bird. / He labors in vain who tries to PLEASE everybody.

valet *See* No man is a HERO to his valet.

valiant *See* COWARDS die many a death, but the valiant die but one.

valley 1. Always a valley before a hill. *Rec. dist.:* Ont. *1st cit.:* 1614 Webster, *Duchess of Malfi. 20c. coll.:* Stevenson 395:3.

2. He that stays in the valley shall never get over the hill. *Var.:* He that stays in the valley will never get over the hill. *Rec. dist.:* U.S., Can. *1st cit.:* 1616 Draxe, *Bibliotheca Scholastica* in *Anglia* (1918); US1702 Mather, *Magnalia Christi Americana* (1853–55). *20c. coll.:* ODEP 772, Whiting 463, Stevenson 100:14.

3. They who are content to remain in the valley will get no news from the mountains. *Rec. dist.:* N.C.

See also ACT so in the valley that you need

not fear those who stand on the hill. / There is no HILL without a valley.

valor Valor can do but little without discretion. *Rec. dist.:* Mich. *1st cit.:* 1672 Codrington, *Select Proverbs. 20c. coll.:* ODEP 858, Stevenson 584:7.

See also DIPLOMACY is a better part of valor. / DISCRETION is the better part of valor.

valuable *See* A good REPUTATION is more valuable than money. / Common SENSE is the rarest thing in the world and the most valuable.

value *(n.)* 1. Every man stamps his value upon himself. *Rec. dist.:* Ont.

2. If you'd know the value of money, go and borrow some. *Rec. dist.:* U.S., Can. *1st cit.:* 1640 Herbert, *Outlandish Proverbs (Jacula Prudentum)* in *Works,* ed. Hutchinson (1941); US1754 Franklin, *PRAlmanac. 20c. coll.:* Stevenson 222:14, Whiting 463, ODEP 435.

3. Like a postage stamp, a man's value depends upon his ability to stick to a thing till he gets there. *Rec. dist.:* Miss.

4. Set not too high a value on your own abilities. *Rec. dist.:* N.Y.

See also It is better to have one FRIEND of great value than many with no value. / You never know the value of FRIENDS until you lose them. / A SAINT has no value in his own house. / The only value of TIME is its use. / Use TIME as though you knew its value.

value *(v.)* *See* Value your FRIENDS above your opinions. / Don't value a GEM by what it's set in. / HEALTH is not valued till sickness comes. / Don't value a man for the QUALITY he is of, but for the qualities he possesses. / Nothing is more precious than TIME, yet nothing is less valued.

vanity 1. Do not let your vanity make you overestimate your powers. *Rec. dist.:* Kans., N.Y., Ont.

2. Every man has as much vanity as he is deficient in understanding. *Rec. dist.:* Mich.

3. Vanity backbites more than malice. *Rec.*

dist.: N.Y. *1st cit.:* US1745 Franklin, *PRAlmanac. 20c. coll.:* Stevenson 2415:1.

4. Vanity dies hard. *Rec. dist.:* Ariz.

5. Vanity is the sixth sense. *Rec. dist.:* Ill. *1st cit.:* 1837 Carlyle, *French Revolution. 20c. coll.:* Stevenson 2415:17.

6. Vanity of vanities, all is vanity. *Var.:* Vanity, vanity, all is vanity. *Rec. dist.:* Mich., N.Y. *1st cit.:* US1940 Nash, *Ha! Original Sin! 20c. coll.:* Stevenson 2415:3.

7. Virtue would not go far if a little vanity walked not with it. *Rec. dist.:* N.Y.

SEE ALSO Foolish CURIOSITY and vanity often lead to misfortune. / He that sows INIQUITY shall reap vanity.

vanquisher Vanquishers are kings, the vanquished thieves. *Rec. dist.:* Ill.

variety Variety is the spice of life. *Vars.:* (a) Variety is the spice of collecting. (b) Variety is the spice of love. (c) Variety's the very spice of life. *Rec. dist.:* U.S., Can. *1st cit.:* ca1783 Cowper, *The Task;* US1778 *Heath Papers,* Mass.Hist.Soc. *Collections* (1878–1904). *20c. coll.:* CODP 238, Whiting 463, ODEP 858, Stevenson 2416:1, T&W 391, Whiting(MP) 658.

varlet SEE An APE is an ape, a varlet is a varlet, though they be clad in silk and scarlet.

varnish SEE CULTURE is one thing and varnish is another.

vault SEE One who blows a HORN will never blow a vault.

vegetable Vegetables from your neighbor's garden are always the best. *Rec. dist.:* Ill.

veil SEE Go hide the FAULTS of others and God will veil your own.

velvet SEE SILKS and satins, scarlet and velvet, put out the kitchen fire.

venerable SEE AGE is venerable in a man and would be in a woman if she ever became old.

vengeance 1. A woman's vengeance has no bounds. *Rec. dist.:* Ill. *1st cit.:* 1622 Fletcher, *Spanish Curate. 20c. coll.:* Stevenson 2562:9.

2. Cover the desire for vengeance with an appearance of calm. *Rec. dist.:* N.C.

venture 1. Boldly ventured is half won. *Rec. dist.:* Ill.

2. He that does not venture must not complain of bad luck. *Rec. dist.:* Ill.

3. He that ventures too far loses all. *Rec. dist.:* Ill. *1st cit.:* 1611 Cotgrave, *Dictionary of French and English Tongues. 20c. coll.:* Stevenson 2418:2.

4. Nothing ventured, nothing gained. *Vars.:* (a) Never venture, never gain. (b) Nothing venture, nothing have. (c) Nothing venture, nothing lose. (d) Nothing venture, nothing win. (e) Nothing ventured, nothing done. (f) Nothing ventured, nothing made. (g) Nothing ventured, nothing won. *Rec. dist.:* U.S., Can. *1st cit.:* ca1374 Chaucer, *Troilus and Criseyde;* US1748 Ayscough in *Letters and Papers of Cadwallader Colden,* N.Y.Hist.Soc. *Collections* (1917–37). *20c. coll.:* ODEP 581, Whiting 316, CODP 165, Stevenson 2418:1, T&W 265, Whiting(MP) 454.

SEE ALSO He that would catch a FISH must venture his bait. / Venture a small FISH to catch a great one. / Try the ICE before you venture upon it. / VESSELS large may venture more, but little boats should keep to shore.

verdict 1. One wise man's verdict outweighs all the fools'. *Rec. dist.:* Ill.

2. When a man tries himself, the verdict is in his favor. *Rec. dist.:* N.Y.

Vermont Vermont has two seasons—winter and the Fourth of July. *Rec. dist.:* Vt.

vessel *(container)* 1. A bad vessel is seldom broken. *Rec.: dist.:* N.Y. *1st cit.:* 1640 Herbert, *Outlandish Proverbs (Jacula Prudentum)* in *Works,* ed. Hutchinson (1941). *20c. coll.:* Stevenson 2491:9.

2. A cracked vessel is known by its sound, a cracked mind by the tongue's speech. *Rec. dist.:* Ill.

3. Do not look upon the vessel but upon that which it contains. *Var.:* Don't look upon the vessel but that which it contains. *Rec. dist.:* Ill., Ont. *1st cit.:* 1678 Ray, *Adagia Hebraica. 20c. coll.:* Stevenson 78:7.

4. Empty vessels are easily carried. *Rec. dist.:* Ont.

5. The emptiest vessel makes the most noise. *Vars.:* **(a)** Empty vessels give the greatest sound. **(b)** Empty vessels make the most noise. **(c)** Empty vessels make the most sounds. **(d)** The empty vessel makes the greatest sound. *Rec. dist.:* U.S., Can. *1st cit.:* 1547 Baldwin, *Treatise of Morall Philosophie;* US1645 *Collected Writings of Roger Williams* (1963). *20c. coll.:* ODEP 220, Whiting 464, *CODP* 64, Stevenson 676:17, T&W 391, Whiting*(MP)* 658.

6. The vessel only holds its fill. *Rec. dist.:* Minn. *1st cit.:* 1732 Fuller, *Gnomologia. 20c. coll.:* ODEP 859.

7. Too much in the vessel bursts the lid. *Rec. dist.:* Ill.
   SEE ALSO Take away the RUST from the silver and there'll come forth a pure vessel.

vessel *(ship)* **1.** Do not ship all in one vessel. *Rec.: dist.:* Iowa.

2. The vessel that will not obey her helm will have to obey the rocks. *Rec. dist.:* Ont.

3. Vessels large may venture more, but little boats should keep to shore. *Rec. dist.:* Ill., N.Y. *1st cit.:* 1678 Ray, *English Proverbs;* US1751 Franklin, *PRAlmanac. 20c. coll.:* Stevenson 2100:15, Whiting 38.

vest He who eats the fastest often feeds his vest. *Rec. dist.:* Ont.

vicar It is by the vicar's skirts that the devil climbs into the belfry. *Rec. dist.:* N.Y. *1st cit.:* 1659 Howell, *Paroimiografia (Spanish Proverbs);* US1840 Longfellow, *Spanish Student. 20c. coll.:* ODEP 180, Stevenson 562:3.

vice **1.** A vice lives and thrives by concealment. *Rec. dist.:* Ohio. *1st cit.:* US1948 Stevenson, *Home Book of Proverbs. 20c. coll.:* Stevenson 2321:11.

2. Be at war with your vices, at peace with your neighbors, and let every new year find you a better man. *Rec. dist.:* N.Y. *1st cit.:* US1755 Franklin, *PRAlmanac. 20c. coll.:* Stevenson 159:1.

3. Every vice fights against nature. *Rec. dist.:* Mich.

4. He who plunges into vice resembles a man who rolls from the tip of a precipice. *Rec. dist.:* Wis.

5. I'd rather have a comfortable vice than a virtue that bores. *Rec. dist.:* Ky., Tenn.

6. No vice is complete by itself. *Var.:* No vice goes alone. *Rec. dist.:* Ill.

7. Vice knows she's ugly, so puts on her mask. *Var.:* Vice would be frightful if it did not wear a mask. *Rec. dist.:* N.Y. *1st cit.:* 1732 Fuller, *Gnomologia;* US1746 Franklin, *PRAlmanac. 20c. coll.:* Stevenson 2420:7.

8. Vice makes virtue look well to its anchors. *Var.:* Vice makes virtue shine. *Rec. dist.:* N.Y. *1st cit.:* US1853 Haliburton, *Sam Slick's Wise Saws. 20c. coll.:* Stevenson 2422:10.

9. Vice makes virtue shine. *Rec. dist.:* Ill., N.J. *1st cit.:* 1732 Fuller, *Gnomologia. 20c. coll.:* Stevenson 2422:7.

10. Vice must never plead prescript. *Rec. dist.:* Mich.

11. Vice should not correct sin. *Rec. dist.:* N.Y. *1st cit.:* 1672 Walker, *Paroemiologia Anglo-Latina;* US1692 Penn, *Some Fruits of Solitude. 20c. coll.:* Stevenson 2421:12.

12. Vices are learned without a teacher. *Rec. dist.:* Ill. *1st cit.:* 1666 Torriano, *Common Place of Italian Proverbs. 20c. coll.:* Stevenson 2421:10.

13. Vices often become virtues; hatred is respectable in wartime. *Rec. dist.:* Ill.

14. What maintains one vice would bring up two children. *Rec. dist.:* Ill. *1st cit.:* US1747 Franklin, *PRAlmanac. 20c. coll.:* ODEP 500, Whiting 464.

15. When our vices leave us, we flatter ourselves that we leave them. *Rec. dist.:* N.J., N.Y. *1st cit.:* US1948 Stevenson, *Home Book of Proverbs. 20c. coll.:* Stevenson 2420:10.
   SEE ALSO With the old ALMANAC and the old year, leave your vices, though ever so dear. / Through tattered CLOTHES small vices do appear. / GOSSIP is vice enjoyed vicariously. / There is an HYPOCRISY in vice as well as religion. / PROSPERITY discovers vice, adversity, virtue. / SLOTH is the mother of vice. / Men do not vary much in VIRTUE; their vices only are different. / VIRTUE consists in fleeing

vice. / VIRTUE is a mean between two vices. / VIRTUE is never aided by a vice. / Great virtues do not excuse small vices. / VIRTUES all agree, but vices fight one another.

vicious SEE To a vicious DOG a short chain. / An innocent PLOWMAN is of more worth than a vicious prince.

victor 1. One trouble with the world is that there are always more victors than spoils. *Rec. dist.:* N.Y.

2. To the victor belong the spoils. *Vars.:* (a) The victor gets the spoils. (b) To the victor go the spoils. *Rec. dist.:* U.S., Can. *1st cit.:* US1832 Marcy, Speech given as senator from New York. *20c. coll.:* Stevenson 2200:7.

victory 1. A man learns little from victory but much from defeat. *Rec. dist.:* N.C.

2. All victory ends in the defeat of death. *Rec. dist.:* N.C.

3. In victory the hero seeks the glory, not the prey. *Rec. dist.:* Ill.

4. It is more difficult to look upon victory than upon battle. *Rec. dist.:* Ill. *1st cit.:* US1633 *Saltonstall Papers,* ed. Moody in Mass.Hist.Soc. *Collections* (1972). *20c. coll.:* Whiting 464.

5. Love victory but despise the pride of triumph. *Rec. dist.:* Ill.

6. Pursue not a victory too far: you may provoke the foe to desperate resistance. *Rec. dist.:* Ill.

7. The real and lasting victories are those of peace and not of war. *Rec. dist.:* N.Y. *1st cit.:* 1652 Milton, "To Lord General Cromwell" in *Sonnets;* US1860 Emerson, "Worship" in *Conduct of Life. 20c. coll.:* Stevenson 2452:3.

8. There is never a victory without a battle. *Rec. dist.:* Ky., Tenn.

9. Victory belongs to the most persevering. *Rec. dist.:* Ill.

SEE ALSO The ARMY knows how to gain a victory but not how to make proper use of it. / The harder the BATTLE, the sweeter the victory.

view The higher we rise, the broader the view. *Rec. dist.:* Ill., Ohio.

SEE ALSO Nothing is BEAUTIFUL from every point of view.

vigilance 1. Eternal vigilance is the price of celibacy. *Rec. dist.:* N.Y. *1st cit.:* US1906 *Poor Richard Jr.'s Almanac. 20c. coll.:* Stevenson 308:2.

2. Eternal vigilance is the price of good navigation. *Rec. dist.:* Md., Mich. **Infm.:** This proverb appears on the wall in Luce Hall, the seamanship and navigation building at the U.S. Naval Academy, Annapolis, Md.

3. Eternal vigilance is the price of supremacy. *Rec. dist.:* Tex.

vigilant Be ever vigilant, but never suspicious. *Rec. dist.:* Tex.

SEE ALSO A careless WATCH invites the vigilant foe.

village 1. Don't live in a village whose mayor is a doctor. *Rec. dist.:* Ill.

2. That village is in a bad fix whose physician has the gout. *Rec. dist.:* Ill.

villain 1. A man may smile and smile and still be a villain. *Vars.:* (a) One may smile and smile and be a villain still. (b) One may smile and smile and be a villain. *Rec. dist.:* Utah. *1st cit.:* ca1386 Chaucer, *Knight's Tale;* US1943 Stein, *Case of Absent Minded Professor. 20c. coll.:* Stevenson 2145:3.

2. A villain may disguise himself, but he will not deceive the wise. *Rec. dist.:* Ariz.

3. Villains may prosper for a time, but their end is ignominy. *Rec. dist.:* Mich.

vine 1. Big vines, small potatoes. *Vars.:* (a) Big vines, small berries. (b) Big vines, small tomatoes. *Rec. dist.:* Wash.

2. When the vine is ripe, the fruit will fall. *Rec. dist.:* Kans.

SEE ALSO It's the little FOXES that spoil the vines. / Our greatest JOYS and our greatest sorrows grow on the same vine.

vinegar 1. Beware of vinegar made of sweet wine. *Rec. dist.:* Ill. *1st cit.:* 1573 Sanford, *Garden of Pleasure;* US1754 Franklin, *PRAlmanac. 20c. coll.:* ODEP 860, Stevenson 68:1.

2. Vinegar catches no flies. *Rec. dist.:* Miss., N.Y. *1st cit.:* 1732 Fuller, *Gnomologia. 20c. coll.:* Stevenson 1158:14.

See also OIL and vinegar don't mix. / Use SUGAR more than vinegar. / The sweetest WINE makes the sharpest vinegar. / Tart WORDS make no friends: a spoonful of honey will catch more flies than a gallon of vinegar.

violence 1. Nothing good comes of violence. *Rec. dist.:* Ill.

2. Violence breeds hatred, and hatred dissension. *Rec. dist.:* N.Y.

3. Violence does even justice unjustly. *Rec. dist.:* Ill.

See also WAR is the law of violence; peace, the law of love.

virtue 1. A fair woman without virtue is like stale wine. *Rec. dist.:* Ill. *1st cit.:* 1855 Bohn, *Handbook of Proverbs*. *20c. coll.:* Stevenson 2560:6.

2. Assume a virtue if you have it not. *Rec. dist.:* N.J. *1st cit.:* 1600 Shakespeare, *Hamlet*. *20c. coll.:* Stevenson 2433:5.

3. Great virtues do not excuse small vices. *Rec. dist.:* N.J.

4. If you have virtue, acquire also the graces and beauties of virtue. *Rec. dist.:* N.Y. *1st cit.:* US1738 Franklin, *PRAlmanac*. *20c. coll.:* Stevenson 2429:15.

5. It is in virtue that happiness consists, for virtue is the state of mind which tends to make the whole life harmonious. *Rec. dist.:* N.Y. *1st cit.:* 1733 Pope, *Essay on Man;* US1738 Franklin, *PRAlmanac*. *20c. coll.:* Stevenson 2434:6.

6. It is well to remember people's virtues and not their deficiencies. *Rec. dist.:* N.C.

7. Make not the rewards of virtue the gifts of favor. *Rec. dist.:* Mich.

8. Make a virtue of necessity. *Rec. dist.:* U.S., Can. *1st cit.:* ca1374 Chaucer, *Troilus and Criseyde;* USca1678 Mather, *Collected Letters of Cotton Mather*, ed. Silverman (1971). *20c. coll.:* ODEP 861, Whiting 465, Stevenson 1668:4, T&W 392, Whiting(MP) 659.

9. Men do not vary much in virtue; their vices only are different. *Rec. dist.:* N.Y., S.C. *1st cit.:* US1911 Hubbard, *Epigrams*. *20c. coll.:* Stevenson 2422:2.

10. Much virtue in herbs, little in men. *Rec. dist.:* N.Y. *1st cit.:* 1640 Herbert, *Outlandish Proverbs (Jacula Prudentum)* in *Works,* ed. Hutchinson (1941); US1755 Franklin, *PRAlmanac*. *20c. coll.:* Stevenson 2430:7.

11. People shouldn't be too good and exaggerate their own virtues. *Rec. dist.:* Ala., Ga.

12. Search others for their virtues, yourself for your vices. *Rec. dist.:* Mich. *1st cit.:* US1738 Franklin, *PRAlmanac*. *20c. coll.:* Stevenson 159:1.

13. Seek virtue, and of that possessed, to providence resign the rest. *Rec. dist.:* N.Y. *1st cit.:* US1740 Franklin, *PRAlmanac*. *20c. coll.:* Stevenson 2429:15.

14. Sell not virtue to purchase wealth nor liberty to purchase power. *Rec. dist.:* N.Y. *1st cit.:* US1738 Franklin, *PRAlmanac*. *20c. coll.:* Stevenson 2429:15.

15. There is no virtue in giving to others what is useless to oneself. *Rec. dist.:* Ark.

16. To be proud of virtue is to poison yourself with the antidote. *Rec. dist.:* N.Y.

17. Unless virtue guide us, our choice must be wrong. *Rec. dist.:* N.Y. *1st cit.:* US1693 Penn, *Some Fruits of Solitude*. *20c. coll.:* Stevenson 348:5.

18. Virtue and honesty are cheap at any price. *Rec. dist.:* N.Y.

19. Virtue and riches seldom settle on one man. *Rec. dist.:* N.Y.

20. Virtue and vice cannot dwell under the same roof. *Rec. dist.:* N.Y.

21. Virtue debases itself by justifying itself. *Rec. dist.:* N.Y.

22. Virtue dies at twelve o'clock at night. *Rec. dist.:* N.C.

23. Virtue flourishes in misfortune. *Rec. dist.:* N.Y.

24. Virtue is a mean between two vices. *Rec. dist.:* Wis. *1st cit.:* 1557 Edgeworth, *Sermons Fruitful, Godly, and Learned*. *20c. coll.:* ODEP 861, Stevenson 2421:14.

25. Virtue is a thousand shields. *Rec. dist.:* Ont.

26. Virtue is everlasting wealth. *Rec. dist.:* Miss.

27. Virtue is found in the mean. *Rec. dist.:* Ill.

28. Virtue is its own reward. *Rec. dist.:* U.S., Can. *1st cit.:* 1509 Barclay, *Ship of Fools,* ed. Jamieson in *Eclogues,* E.E.T.S. (1874); US1732 Franklin, *Papers of Benjamin Franklin,* ed. Labaree (1950). *20c. coll.:* ODEP 861, Whiting 466, CODP 238, Stevenson 2435:1, T&W 392, Whiting(*MP*) 659.

29. Virtue is like a rich stone, best plain set. *Rec. dist.:* N.J., Ont. *1st cit.:* ca1594 Bacon, *Promus.* *20c. coll.:* ODEP 861, Stevenson 2428:13.

30. Virtue is never aided by a vice. *Rec. dist.:* Ont.

31. Virtue is the best title of nobility. *Rec. dist.:* Ont. *1st cit.:* 1591 Ariosto, *Orlando Furioso* in *English Heroical Verse,* tr. Harington. *20c. coll.:* ODEP 861, Stevenson 1690:5.

32. Virtue is the only true nobility. *Rec. dist.:* Ill., Ont., Tex. *1st cit.:* 1651 Shute, "Sarah and Hagar" in *Sermons.* *20c. coll.:* Stevenson 1690:5.

33. Virtue is the safest helmet. *Var.:* The safest helmet is virtue. *Rec. dist.:* Mich., Ont.

34. Virtue never grows old. *Rec. dist.:* Ill. *1st cit.:* 1611 Cotgrave, *Dictionary of French and English Tongues.* *20c. coll.:* ODEP 861, Stevenson 2423:8.

35. Virtue rejoices in trial. *Rec. dist.:* Ont. *1st cit.:* US1948 Stevenson, *Home Book of Proverbs.* *20c. coll.:* Stevenson 2431:11.

36. Virtue survives the grave. *Rec. dist.:* Ont.

37. Virtue which parleys is near a surrender. *Rec. dist.:* Ill., Mich., Tex. *1st cit.:* 1721 Bailey, *Dictionary.* *20c. coll.:* Stevenson 2429:11.

38. Virtue will triumph. *Rec. dist.:* Ill.

39. Virtues all agree, but vices fight one another. *Rec. dist.:* Ill. *1st cit.:* 1732 Fuller, *Gnomologia.* *20c. coll.:* Stevenson 2422:7.

40. Without virtue, happiness cannot be. *Rec. dist.:* N.Y. *1st cit.:* US1790 Jefferson, *Writings of Thomas Jefferson,* ed. Bergh (1907). *20c. coll.:* Stevenson 2434:4.

SEE ALSO AFFLICTION is the wholesome sort of virtue. / BEAUTY without virtue is a rose without fragrance. / BLOOD is inherited and virtue acquired. / BLUSHING is virtue's color. / CHARITY is a virtue of the heart and not of the hand. / COURAGE is a virtue the young cannot spare; to lose it is to grow old before the time. / FEAR is the virtue of slaves. / FRANKNESS is not a virtue. / HONOR is the reward of virtue. / PATIENCE is a virtue. / PATIENCE is the mother of virtue. / PROSPERITY discovers vice, adversity, virtue. / Without TRUTH there can be no virtue. / VICE makes virtue look well to its anchors.

virtuous **1.** A virtuous woman commands her husband by obeying him. *Rec. dist.:* Ill.

2. A virtuous woman is rarer than a precious jewel. *Rec. dist.:* N.C.

3. Virtuous men are kings' treasures. *Rec. dist.:* Ont.

vision **1.** We call loudly for a man of vision, and when we get one we call him a visionary. *Rec. dist.:* Wis.

2. Where there is no vision, the people perish. *Rec. dist.:* Ill., Wis. *1st cit.:* US1948 Stevenson, *Home Book of Proverbs.* *20c. coll.:* Stevenson 2435:9.

SEE ALSO FAITH is the vision of the heart.

visit *(n.)* **1.** A short visit is best. *Var.:* Short visits and seldom are best. *Rec. dist.:* U.S., Can. *1st cit.:* US1733 Franklin, *PRAlmanac.* *20c. coll.:* Stevenson 2436:3.

2. Make your visits short and you are always welcome. *Rec. dist.:* Ky., Tenn.

3. Short visits make long friends. *Rec. dist.:* Tex. *1st cit.:* US1733 Franklin, *PRAlmanac.* *20c. coll.:* Stevenson 2436:3, T&W 392.

4. Visits should be short, like a winter's day. *Rec. dist.:* Ill. *1st cit.:* US1733 Franklin, *PRAlmanac.* *20c. coll.:* Stevenson 2436:3.

visit *(v.)* The best way to visit the poor is to help the poor. *Rec. dist.:* Ala., Ga.

SEE ALSO It is easier to visit FRIENDS than to live with them.

visitor **1.** If you would lose a troublesome visitor, lend him money. *Rec. dist.:* N.Y. *1st cit.:* US1744 Franklin, *PRAlmanac.* *20c. coll.:* Stevenson 1384:11.

2. Visitors, if they did not visit, would do nothing. *Rec. dist.:* Ill.

SEE ALSO The BUSY man has few idle visitors; to the boiling pot the flies come not. / FISH and visitors smell in three days.

vivacity 1. The vivacity that increases with years is not far from folly. *Rec. dist.:* Ill. *1st cit.:* US1948 Stevenson, *Home Book of Proverbs.* *20c. coll.:* Stevenson 29:8.

2. Vivacity in youth is often mistaken for genius, and solidity for dullness. *Rec. dist.:* Ill.

3. Vivacity is the gift of woman. *Rec. dist.:* Ill.

4. Vivacity is the health of the spirit. *Rec. dist.:* Ill.

vocabulary Vocabulary is the tool of wise men. *Rec. dist.:* Wis.

SEE ALSO ACCIDENT is a word not to be found in the divine vocabulary. / Your THOUGHTS go no further than your vocabulary.

vocation The vocation of every man and woman is to serve people. *Rec. dist.:* N.C.

vogue Don't be vogue on the outside and vague on the inside. *Rec. dist.:* Miss.

voice 1. A fool's voice is known by a multitude of words. *Rec. dist.:* N.Y. *1st cit.:* ca1303 Mannyng, *Handlyng Synne.* *20c. coll.:* Stevenson 844:12.

2. A sweet voice is often a devil's arrow that reaches the heart. *Rec. dist.:* Ill.

3. A voice gentle and low is an excellent thing in woman. *Rec. dist.:* S.C. *1st cit.:* 1605 Shakespeare, *King Lear.* *20c. coll.:* Stevenson 2437:10.

4. Listen to the still, small voice within. *Rec. dist.:* Md., N.Y., S.C. *1st cit.:* US1841 Thoreau, *Winter.* *20c. coll.:* Stevenson 1105:12.

5. The voice is the guardian of the mind. *Rec. dist.:* Ill.

6. The voice is the music of the heart. *Rec. dist.:* Ill.

7. The voice of a pig can't be disguised. *Rec. dist.:* Nev., N.Y.

8. The voice of the people is the voice of God. *Rec. dist.:* Ill., N.Y. *1st cit.:* ca1412 Hoc-

cleve, *Regement of Princes,* E.E.T.S. (1897); USca1734 "Wall and Garden" in *Mass. Election Sermons,* ed. Plumstead (1968). *20c. coll.:* ODEP 862, Whiting 466, CODP 238, Stevenson 1766:8, T&W 392, Whiting(*MP*) 659.

9. The voice of the pigeon on the spit is not like the voice of the pigeon in the tree. *Rec. dist.:* Ill.

10. The voice of truth is easily known. *Rec. dist.:* W.Va.

11. The voice with a smile always wins. *Rec. dist.:* Ont.

12. Where there is a voice, there is a relative. *Rec. dist.:* Ohio.

SEE ALSO AMBITION is not the voice of little people. / From a CROW's beak comes a crow's voice. / Give every man your EAR but few your voice.

volume 1. Every man is a volume if you know how to read him. *Rec. dist.:* Ont.

2. The volume of nature is the book of knowledge. *Rec. dist.:* Mich.

voluntary SEE A voluntary BURDEN is no burden. / DRUNKENNESS is voluntary madness.

volunteer A volunteer is worth ten pressed men. *Rec. dist.:* N.Y. *1st cit.:* 1705 Seymour in Hearne, *Remarks and Collections.* *20c. coll.:* ODEP 862, Stevenson 2158:6, CODP 238.

voluptuousness 1. Voluptuousness blindfolds the eyes of the mind. *Rec. dist.:* Mich.

2. Voluptuousness, like justice, is blind, but that is the only resemblance between them. *Rec. dist.:* Ill.

vote A straw vote only shows which way the hot air blows. *Rec. dist.:* N.Y. *1st cit.:* US1930 O. Henry in Pattee, *New American Literature.* *20c. coll.:* Stevenson 2438:6.

vow 1. A vow made in the storm is forgotten in the calm. *Var.:* Vows made in storms are forgotten in calms. *Rec. dist.:* Ill., Mich., N.Y., S.C. *1st cit.:* 1530 Palsgrave, *Lesclarcissement de la langue Francoyse.* *20c. coll.:* ODEP 862, Stevenson 2439:2.

2. Morning vows are often lost in the midnight shades. *Rec. dist.:* N.Y.

voyage 1. In the voyage of life, may content be our fellow passenger. *Rec. dist.:* N.Y.

2. When the voyage is over, the saint is forgot. *Rec. dist.:* N.Y. *1st cit.:* 1611 Cotgrave, *Dictionary of French and English Tongues. 20c. coll.:* ODEP 167, Stevenson 485:6.

vulgar *(n.)* To endeavor to work upon the vulgar with fine sense is like attempting to hew blocks with a razor. *Rec. dist.:* Ill.

SEE ALSO GENTLEMEN cherish worth; the vulgar cherish dirt. / WRITE with the learned; pronounce with the vulgar.

vulgar *(adj.)* Vulgar minds growl beneath their load; the brave bear theirs without repining. *Rec. dist.:* Ill.

SEE ALSO Follow the WISE few rather than the vulgar many.

vulture *SEE* Where the CORPSE is, there the vultures gather. / The feast of vultures and a waste of life is WAR.

W

wade Do not wade in unknown waters. *Vars.:* **(a)** It's not safe to wade in unknown water. **(b)** Never wade in unknown waters. *Rec. dist.:* Ill., N.Y., N.C. *1st cit.:* ca1523 *Manifest Detection,* Percy Soc. *20c. coll.:* ODEP 863, Stevenson 2459:1.

wag SEE A DOG is loved by old and young; he wags his tail and not his tongue. / Short-tailed DOG wag his tail same as a long 'un.

wage The wages of sin is death. *Rec. dist.:* Calif., Nebr., N.Y., Wis. *1st cit.:* US1875 Eddy, *Science and Health.* *20c. coll.:* Stevenson 2119:6.

wager A wager is a fool's argument. *Var.:* Fools for arguments use wagers. *Rec. dist.:* Ill., Wis. *1st cit.:* 1664 Butler, *Hudibras.* *20c. coll.:* Stevenson 90:11.

wagging SEE A wagging-tailed DOG never bites.

wagon **1.** Get off the wagon or quit dragging both feet. *Rec. dist.:* Ill.

2. Hitch your wagon to a star. *Rec. dist.:* U.S., Can. *1st cit.:* 1935 Flynn, *Edge of Terror;* US1870 Emerson, "Civilization" in *Society and Solitude.* *20c. coll.:* Whiting(MP) 661, ODEP 375, Stevenson 2207:3.

3. The empty wagon makes the most noise. *Vars.:* **(a)** An empty wagon always rattles. **(b)** An empty wagon always rattles the loudest. **(c)** An empty wagon makes the most noise. **(d)** An empty wagon rattles loudest. **(e)** An empty wagon rumbles loud. **(f)** Only the empty wagon rattles. *Rec. dist.:* U.S. *1st cit.:* ca1430 Lydgate, *Pilgrimage of Man,* E.E.T.S. (1899); US1853 Hammet, *Stray Yankee in Texas.* *20c. coll.:* CODP 64, T&W 391, ODEP 20, Stevenson 676:17, Whiting(MP) 661.

4. The wagon of God drives slowly and well. *Rec. dist.:* Ont.

SEE ALSO If you don't believe in COOPERATION, watch what happens to a wagon when one wheel comes off.

wait **1.** Everything comes to him who waits. *Vars.:* **(a)** All good things come to those who wait. **(b)** All things come to him who hustles while he waits. **(c)** All things come to him who waits—if he hustles while he's waiting. **(d)** All things come to the other fellow if you will only sit down and wait. **(e)** Everything comes to the man who waits. **(f)** Everything comes to them who wait. **(g)** Everything comes to those who can wait. **(h)** Everything comes to those who wait. *Rec. dist.:* U.S., Can. *1st cit.:* ca1530 Barclay, *Eclogues,* E.E.T.S. (1927); US1863 Longfellow, "Student's Tale" in *Tales of Wayside Inn.* *20c. coll.:* ODEP 231, Stevenson 2440:10, CODP 3, Whiting(MP) 205.

2. Wait and you will be rewarded. *Rec. dist.:* N.Dak. *1st cit.:* 1647 Gracian, *Oraculo Manual;* US1849 Thoreau, "Monday" in *Week on Concord and Merrimack Rivers.* *20c. coll.:* Stevenson 2440:7.

SEE ALSO Wait till we see how the CAT jumps. / DEATH waits for no one. / FORTUNE is like price: if you can wait long enough, the price will fall. / Learn to LABOR and to wait. / The LORD never helps him who sits on his ass and waits. / They also SERVE who only stand and wait. / Don't wait till you get TIME—take time. / TIME and tide wait for no man.

wake SEE An alarm CLOCK will wake a man, but he has to get up by himself. / Don't wake a sleeping LION. / When SORROW is asleep, wake it not.

walk **1.** He that walks uprightly walks surely, but he that perverts his ways shall be known. *Var.:* Upright walking is sure walking. *Rec. dist.:* Ont.

2. The man who walks takes title to the world around him. *Rec. dist.:* N.Y.

3. Those who walk down alone walk the least. *Rec. dist.:* Ky., Tenn.

4. To walk one must use his feet. *Rec. dist.:* Colo., N.Y.

5. Walk too fast and stumble over nothing. *Rec. dist.:* Miss.

6. You can tell a lot about a person by the way he walks. *Rec. dist.:* N.C.

7. You have to learn to walk before you can run. *Rec. dist.:* U.S., Can. *1st cit.:* ca1350 *Douce MS 52;* US1794 *Writings of George Washington,* ed. Fitzpatrick (1925). *20c. coll.:* ODEP 120, Whiting 468, *CODP* 240, Stevenson 2440:13, Whiting*(MP)* 138.

SEE ALSO No one can walk BACKWARDS into the future. / One must CRAWL before he walks. / He who DRINKS and walks away, lives to drink another day. / When FORTUNE smiles, we ride in chase, and when she frowns, we walk away. / Don't walk on thin ICE. / It doesn't matter how high you JUMP provided you walk straight when you get down. / The big POSSUM walks just before the dawn. / The RICH ride in chaises; the poor walk with God.

walking SEE A WOMAN is known by her walking and drinking.

wall **1.** A wall between preserves love. *Rec. dist.:* Ill. *1st cit.:* 1710 Palmer, *Moral Essays on English, Scotch, and Foreign Proverbs. 20c. coll.:* Stevenson 1674:13.

2. A white wall is the fool's writing paper: he writes his name there. *Var.:* White walls are fools' writing papers. *Rec. dist.:* Ont., Wis. *1st cit.:* 1573 Sanford, *Garden of Pleasure;* US1733 Franklin, *PRAlmanac. 20c. coll.:* ODEP 885, Stevenson 847:2.

3. Everyone gives a push to a tumbling wall. *Rec. dist.:* N.J.

4. He who climbs to the top of a wall should not kick over his ladder, as he might wish sometime to climb down again. *Rec. dist.:* Ont. *1st cit.:* 1655 Fuller, *Church-History of Britain. 20c. coll.:* Stevenson 1340:3.

5. Stone walls do not a prison make, nor iron bars a cage. *Rec. dist.:* N.Y. *1st cit.:* 1642 Lovelace, *To Althea from Prison. 20c. coll.:* Stevenson 1888:5.

6. The great wall stands; the builder is gone. *Rec. dist.:* Ind.

7. The wall has ears and the plain has eyes. *Var.:* Walls have ears. *Rec. dist.:* U.S., Can. *1st cit.:* 1573 Gascoigne, *Supposes* in *Works,*

ed. Cunliffe (1907); US1791 S.P.L., "Thoughts on Proverbs" in *Universal Asylum. 20c. coll.:* ODEP 864, Whiting 469, *CODP* 240, Stevenson 654:8, T&W 393, Whiting*(MP)* 663.

8. Walls of sand are sure to crumble. *Rec. dist.:* Ont.

SEE ALSO True FRIENDS, like ivy and the wall, both stand together and together fall. / If the KING is in the palace, nobody looks at the walls. / RELATIVES are best with a wall between. / The WEAKEST goes to the wall.

wallet Don't fling away de empty wallet. *Rec. dist.:* N.Y. *1st cit.:* US1880 Harris, *Plantation Proverbs* in *Uncle Remus, His Songs and Sayings. 20c. coll.:* Stevenson 1921:16.

SEE ALSO The BEGGAR's wallet has no bottom.

wander SEE The FOOL wanders; the wise man travels. / There never was a GOOSE so gray but some gander will wander her way.

want *(n.)* **1.** Halving your wants quadruples your wealth. *Rec. dist.:* Ont.

2. Hundreds would never have known want if they had not at first known waste. *Rec. dist.:* N.C. *1st cit.:* 1576 Edwardes, *Paradise of Dainty Devices* in *British Bibliography* (1812); US1767 Ames, *Almanacs,* ed. Briggs (1891). *20c. coll.:* ODEP 869, Whiting 471, Stevenson 2457:9, T&W 394, Whiting*(MP)* 664.

3. Many wants attend those who have many ambitions. *Rec. dist.:* N.Y.

4. The want of a thing is more than the worth of it. *Rec. dist.:* N.Y., S.C. *1st cit.:* 1586 Whetstone, *English Myrror;* US1720 Colman, "Distressed Society" in *Colonial Currency Reprints,* ed. Davis, Publ. Prince Soc. (1910–11). *20c. coll.:* ODEP 642, Whiting 469, Stevenson 2639:5.

5. Want is the mother of industry. *Rec. dist.:* Ill. *1st cit.:* ca1526 Erasmus, *Dicta Sapientum,* tr. Berthelet; US1720 Colman, "Distressed State" in *Colonial Currency Reprints,* ed. Davis, Publ. Prince Soc. (1910–11). *20c. coll.:* ODEP 642, Whiting 469, Stevenson 2443:6.

6. Want makes strife between man and wife. *Rec. dist.:* Ill. *1st cit.:* 1732 Fuller, *Gnomologia. 20c. coll.:* Stevenson 1850:1.

7. Want of rest is worse than want of wealth. *Rec. dist.:* Ill.

8. Want will be your master. *Rec. dist.:* Ill. *1st cit.:* 1738 Swift, *Collection of Genteel and Ingenious Conversation.* *20c. coll.:* ODEP 865, Stevenson 2443:12.

9. We lessen our wants by lessening our desires. *Rec. dist.:* N.Y. *1st cit.:* US1948 Stevenson, *Home Book of Proverbs.* *20c. coll.:* Stevenson 2443:9.

SEE ALSO ABUNDANCE, like want, ruins many. / For AGE and want, save while you may, for no morning lasts all day. / No GREAT man ever complains of want of opportunity. / HASTE makes waste, and waste makes want. / Many a MEAL is lost for want of meat. / For the want of a NAIL, the shoe was lost. / It is for want of THINKING most men are undone. / Willful WASTE makes woeful want. / WEALTH consists not of having great possessions but in having few wants. / WEALTH, like want, ruins many.

want *(v.)* **1.** He that wants should not be bashful. *Rec. dist.:* N.J.

2. It ain't what you wants in dis world, it's what you gits. *Rec. dist.:* Miss. *1st cit.:* US1940 Gardiner, *D.A. Goes to Trial.* *20c. coll.:* Stevenson 2444:2.

3. It's not what you want that makes you fat, but what you get. *Rec. dist.:* Miss., Tex.

4. Man wants but little here below, nor wants that long. *Rec. dist.:* N.Y. *1st cit.:* 1742 Young, *Night Thoughts.* *20c. coll.:* Stevenson 2444:8.

5. Since we cannot get what we want, let us like what we can get. *Rec. dist.:* Ont.

6. "Take what you want," says God, "but pay for it." *Rec. dist.:* Mich. *1st cit.:* US1841 Emerson, "Compensation" in *Essays.* *20c. coll.:* Stevenson 1761:13.

7. Want a thing long enough and you won't. *Rec. dist.:* Ohio.

SEE ALSO If you want to be ALLURING, don't chase your young man. / We ain't what we want to BE, and we ain't what we are gonna be, but we ain't what we waz. / The more you EAT, the more you want. / There is no FAULT in a thing we want badly. / As a rule,

man's a FOOL: when it's hot, he wants it cool; when it's cool, he wants it hot—always wanting what is not. / It's easy to make a FROG jump into water when that's what he wants to do. / A PRISON ain't just a place—it's being somewheres you don't want to be. / The RICHEST man is he who wants least. / WASTE not, want not.

war **1.** A great war leaves the country with three armies: an army of cripples, an army of mourners, and an army of thieves. *Rec. dist.:* Pa.

2. Be at war with your vices, at peace with your neighbors, and let every new year find you a better man. *Rec. dist.:* N.Y. *1st cit.:* US1755 Franklin, *PRAlmanac.* *20c. coll.:* Stevenson 159:1.

3. Don't win the war before it's won. *Rec. dist.:* N.J.

4. He who preaches up war is a fit chaplain of the devil. *Rec. dist.:* Miss. *1st cit.:* 1659 Howell, *New Sayings.* *20c. coll.:* ODEP 645, Stevenson 2449:6.

5. Hotter war, sooner peace. *Rec. dist.:* Md. *1st cit.:* US1820 Wright, *Views of Society and Manners in America,* ed. Baker (1963). *20c. coll.:* Whiting 469.

6. In wars, laws have no authority. *Rec. dist.:* Mich. *1st cit.:* 1651 Hobbes, *Leviathan.* *20c. coll.:* Stevenson 2449:1.

7. That war is just which is necessary. *Rec. dist.:* Ill. *1st cit.:* 1597 Shakespeare, *Henry IV, Part I.* *20c. coll.:* Stevenson 2447:7.

8. The fear of war is worse than war itself. *Rec. dist.:* N.Y. *1st cit.:* US1948 Stevenson, *Home Book of Proverbs.* *20c. coll.:* Stevenson 2449:8.

9. The feast of vultures and a waste of life is war. *Rec. dist.:* Ont.

10. The object of war is peace. *Rec. dist.:* N.Y. *1st cit.:* 1399 Gower, *In Praise of Peace;* US1826 Kent, *Commentaries on American Law.* *20c. coll.:* ODEP 866, Stevenson 2452:2.

11. The sooner the war, the quicker peace. *Rec. dist.:* Ont.

12. There never was a good war or a bad

peace. *Rec. dist.*: Ont. *1st cit.*: US1775 *Writings of Benjamin Franklin,* ed. Smyth (1905–07). *20c. coll.*: Whiting 329, Stevenson 2452:6.

13. War begets no good offspring. *Rec. dist.*: N.J.

14. War is a business that ruins those who succeed in it. *Rec. dist.*: N.Y.

15. War is death's feast. *Rec. dist.*: Ill. *1st cit.*: 1611 Cotgrave, *Dictionary of French and English Tongues.* *20c. coll.*: ODEP 866, Stevenson 2446:1.

16. War is hell. *Rec. dist.*: U.S., Can. *1st cit.*: 1591 Shakespeare, *Henry VI, Part II;* US1880 Sherman, Address to Grand Army of Republic Convention at Columbus, Ohio, 11 Aug. *20c. coll.*: Stevenson 2449:10.

17. War is sweet to them that know it not. *Rec. dist.*: N.J. *1st cit.*: 1539 Taverner, *Proverbs of Erasmus.* *20c. coll.*: ODEP 866, Stevenson 2448:1.

18. War is the law of violence, peace the law of love. *Rec. dist.*: Ill.

19. War is the sink of all injustice. *Rec. dist.*: Ont.

20. War seldom enters but where wealth allures. *Rec. dist.*: Ill. *1st cit.*: 1687 Dryden, *Hind and Panther.* *20c. coll.*: Stevenson 2450:3.

21. Wars bring scars. *Rec. dist.*: Miss. *1st cit.*: 1639 Clarke, *Paroemiologia;* US1745 Franklin, *PRAlmanac.* *20c. coll.*: ODEP 868, Whiting 470, Stevenson 2445:12.

SEE ALSO ALL is fair in love and war. / The first CASUALTY when war comes is truth. / All DELAYS are dangerous in war. / Who has LAND has war. / MONEY is the sinews of love as well as of war. / If you desire PEACE, be ever prepared for war. / PEACE has won finer victories than war.

ware **1.** Forbidden wares sell twice as dear. *Rec. dist.*: Ill. *1st cit.*: ca1650 Denham, *Natura Naturata.* *20c. coll.*: Stevenson 1894:1.

2. Pleasing ware is half sold. *Rec. dist.*: Mich. *1st cit.*: 1611 Cotgrave, *Dictionary of French and English Tongues.* *20c. coll.*: ODEP 633, Stevenson 2454:6.

SEE ALSO If FOOLS went not to market, bad

wares would not be sold. / GLASSES and lasses are brittle ware.

war-horse An old war-horse delights in battle. *Rec. dist.*: Ill.

warm **1.** He that is warm thinks all are so. *Rec. dist.*: Mich. *1st cit.*: 1640 Herbert, *Outlandish Proverbs (Jacula Prudentum)* in *Works,* ed. Hutchinson (1941). *20c. coll.*: ODEP 867, Stevenson 2454:11.

2. Warm and wet for oats and corn, cool and dry for wheat and rye. *Rec. dist.*: Ill.

3. You can't get warm on another's fur coat. *Rec. dist.*: N.Y.

SEE ALSO A FRIEND by your side can keep you warmer than the richest furs. / A cold HAND, a warm heart. / PRIDE will keep you warm. / The colder the WIND, the warmer the hearth. / He is WISE enough that can keep himself warm.

warmth SEE He that makes a FIRE of straw has much smoke but little warmth.

warning The warnings of age are the weapons of youth. *Rec. dist.*: N.Y.

SEE ALSO RAINBOW at night, sailor's delight; rainbow at morning, sailors take warning. / RED sky at night, sailor's delight; red sky in the morning, sailors take warning.

warp SEE Elm BOARDS will warp around your neck before you can get them from the mill.

warrior **1.** Great warriors, like earthquakes, are remembered for the injury they have accomplished. *Rec. dist.*: N.Y.

2. The warrior lives an honorable life even in poverty. *Rec. dist.*: Ill.

wary SEE There's no ARREST for the wary.

wash *(n.)* **1.** It will all come out in the wash. *Var.*: It all comes out in the wash, but don't get caught in the ringer. *Rec. dist.*: U.S., Can. *1st cit.*: 1620 Cervantes, *Don Quixote,* tr. Shelton; US1910 O. Henry, *Little Local Color.* *20c. coll.*: ODEP 135, Stevenson 2455:13, Whiting(MP) 664.

2. What won't come out in the wash will come out in the rinse. *Rec. dist.*: Wis.

SEE ALSO No TICKEE, no washee.

wash *(v.)* SEE Don't build your CASTLES in the air. It's liable to rain and wash them away. / Wash a DOG, comb a dog, still a dog. / The LAUNDRESS washes her own smock first. / When you are washing WINDOWS, do the corners first and the center will take care of itself.

washing 1. It's a lonesome washing that has not a man's shirt in it. *Rec. dist.:* Miss.

2. The woman who likes washing can always find water. *Rec. dist.:* Ill.

SEE ALSO A clean HAND needs no washing.

wasp More wasps are caught by honey than by vinegar. *Rec. dist.:* Ont. *1st cit.:* 1666 Torriano, *Select Italian Proverbs;* US1744 Franklin, *PRAlmanac.* *20c. coll.:* CODP 113, Whiting 159, Stevenson 1158:14, T&W 140, Whiting(MP) 234.

waste *(n.)* Willful waste makes woeful want. *Var.:* Willful waste makes wasteful want. *Rec. dist.:* U.S., Can. *1st cit.:* 1576 Edwardes, *Paradise of Dainty Devices* in *British Bibliography* (1812); US1767 Ames, *Almanacs,* ed. Briggs (1891). *20c. coll.:* ODEP 869, Whiting 471, Stevenson 2457:9, T&W 394, Whiting(MP) 664.

SEE ALSO A FAVOR ill placed is great waste. / HASTE makes waste. / Without a HEDGE a vineyard is laid waste. / HURRY makes waste. / Hundreds would never have known WANT if they had not at first known waste. / The feast of vultures and a waste of life is WAR.

waste *(v.)* 1. Those who waste will want. *Rec. dist.:* Ill.

2. Waste and want; save and have. *Rec. dist.:* Ill.

3. Waste not, want not. *Var.:* Waste not and you'll want not—willful waste makes woeful want. *Rec. dist.:* U.S., Can. *1st cit.:* 1772 Wesley, *Letters,* ed. Telford (1931); US1932 Smith, *Topper Takes Trip.* *20c. coll.:* ODEP 869, Whiting(MP) 664, CODP 242, Stevenson 2457:2.

SEE ALSO Don't waste ten DOLLARS looking for a dime. / Don't waste time looking at the HILL—climb it. / RUST wastes more than use. / Waste not fresh TEARS over old griefs. / TIME wasted is time lost.

wasted SEE Talk not of wasted AFFECTION; affection is never wasted. / Lost INNOCENCE and wasted time are never recovered.

watch *(n., guard)* A careless watch invites the vigilant foe. *Rec. dist.:* Ont. *1st cit.:* 1591 Shakespeare, *Henry VI, Part I.* *20c. coll.:* ODEP 325, Stevenson 2458:4.

watch *(n., timepiece)* There are only two people who fix watches: a fool and a watchmaker. *Rec. dist.:* Ind.

SEE ALSO An IDLER is a watch that wants both hands, as useless if it goes as if it stands. / Wear your LEARNING like your watch, in a private pocket.

watch *(v.)* SEE Watch the BUTCHER when he weighs the roast; otherwise you'll buy his hand. / The man who watches the CLOCK generally remains one of the hands. / HARM watch, harm catch. / You can watch a THIEF, but you can't watch a liar. / Don't set a WOLF to watch the sheep.

watched SEE A watched FIRE never burns. / A watched KETTLE never boils. / A watched POT never boils.

watching A good person doesn't need watching and a bad one isn't worth watching. *Rec. dist.:* Ont.

SEE ALSO If SKILL could be acquired by watching, dogs would be butchers. / ZEAL is like fire, it needs feeding and watching.

water 1. All water that goes up has to come down. *Rec. dist.:* Ill.

2. As water runs towards the shore, so does money toward the rich. *Rec. dist.:* Wis.

3. Don't get into deep water until you learn how to swim. *Rec. dist.:* Ky., Tenn. *1st cit.:* 1855 Bohn, *Handbook of Proverbs.* *20c. coll.:* CODP 225, Stevenson 1912:10.

4. Don't throw away your dirty water until you get clean. *Vars.:* (a) Cast not out the foul water till you have clean. (b) Don't throw away dirty water until you bring in clean, for dirty water can put out fire. *Rec. dist.:* Ill., Miss., Okla. *1st cit.:* ca1475 *Modern Philology* (1940); US1869 Spurgeon, *John Ploughman's Talks.* *20c. coll.:* CODP 225, Stevenson 1911:9, ODEP 106, Whiting(MP) 668.

5. Don't throw water on a drowned rat. *Rec. dist.*: S.C. *1st cit.*: ca1628 Carmichaell, *Proverbs in Scots,* ed. Anderson (1957); US1702 Mather, *Magnalia Christi Americana* (1853–55). *20c. coll.*: ODEP 643, Whiting 473.

6. Don't try running water up a hill. *Rec. dist.*: Ont.

7. Every man drags water to his own mill. *Rec. dist.*: Ont. *1st cit.*: 1573 Sanford, *Garden of Pleasure.* *20c. coll.*: ODEP 201, Stevenson 1576:7.

8. Much water goes by the mill the miller knows not of. *Rec. dist.*: Okla. *1st cit.*: 1546 Heywood, *Dialogue of Proverbs,* ed. Habernicht (1963). *20c. coll.*: ODEP 870, Stevenson 1576:8.

9. Pure water is better than bad wine. *Rec. dist.*: Ill., Ont.

10. Running water washes clean. *Rec. dist.*: Okla.

11. Spilled water cannot be gathered up. *Rec. dist.*: Ind., Ont. *1st cit.*: US1875 Scarborough, *Chinese Proverbs.* *20c. coll.*: Stevenson 2426:3.

12. Still water runs deep. *Vars.*: (a) Cool water runs deep. (b) Still water flows deep. (c) Still water runs deep and dirty. (d) Still water runs deepest. (e) Still waters run deep. *Rec. dist.*: U.S., Can. *1st cit.*: ca1400 "Cato Morals" in *Cursor Mundi,* E.E.T.S. (1874); US1768 *Works of William Smith, D.D.* (1803). *20c. coll.*: CODP 213, Whiting 471, ODEP 775, Stevenson 1894:3, T&W 394, Whiting*(MP)* 666.

13. Stolen waters are sweet. *Rec. dist.*: Ill., N.Y. *1st cit.*: ca1548 *Wyll of Deuyll;* USca1700 Hubbard, *General History of New England* (1848). *20c. coll.*: ODEP 775, Whiting 417, CODP 213–14, Stevenson 1894:3, Whiting*(MP)* 666.

14. Stump water won't cure de gripes. *Rec. dist.*: N.Y.

15. The water isn't boiled until the kettle sings. *Rec. dist.*: Wis.

16. Those who drink but water will have no liquor to buy. *Rec. dist.*: N.Y. *1st cit.*: US1853 Haliburton, *Sam Slick's Wise Saws.* *20c. coll.*: Stevenson 246:5.

17. Water always flows down, not up. *Rec. dist.*: Ont.

18. Water cannot be divided by a stroke. *Rec. dist.*: Ill.

19. Water gone over a dam never returns. *Rec. dist.*: N.Dak. *1st cit.*: US1797 Appleton in Am.Antiq.Soc. *Proceedings* (1923). *20c. coll.*: Whiting 473, Whiting*(MP)* 667, Stevenson 2461:2.

20. Water is the only drink for a wise man. *Rec. dist.*: Wis. *1st cit.*: US1854 Thoreau, *Walden.* *20c. coll.*: Stevenson 2465:5.

21. Water seeks its own level. *Vars.*: (a) Water finds its own level. (b) Water seeks its level. (c) Water will find its own level. *Rec. dist.*: U.S., Can. *1st cit.*: 1955 Parry, *Sea of Glass;* US1778 Morris in *Public Papers of George Clinton, First Governor of New York,* ed. Hastings (1899–1911). *20c. coll.*: Whiting 473, T&W 395, Whiting*(MP)* 668.

22. Water that has passed cannot make the mill go. *Vars.*: (a) No grist is ground with the water that is passed. (b) The mill will never grind with the water that has passed. (c) The water that is past doesn't turn the wheel. (d) You can't grind wheat with the water that's passed the mill. (e) You cannot turn a wheel with water that has passed. *Rec. dist.*: Mich., N.Y. *1st cit.*: 1616 Draxe, *Bibliotheca Scholastica* in *Anglia* (1918). *20c. coll.*: ODEP 531, CODP 151, Stevenson 1575:5, Whiting*(MP)* 668.

23. Water will be water the world over. *Rec. dist.*: Miss.

24. Water will rust the stomach. *Rec. dist.*: Ill.

25. When the water's high, the boat's high. *Rec. dist.*: Ohio.

26. When you get into deep water, keep your mouth shut. *Rec. dist.*: Miss.

27. You go where you can get ice water. *Rec. dist.*: Ky., Tenn.

28. You never miss the water till the well runs dry. *Var.*: We only know the worth of water when the well is dry. *Rec. dist.*: U.S., Can. *1st cit.*: ca1628 Carmichaell, *Collection of Scottish Proverbs,* ed. Anderson (1957); US1746 Franklin, *PRAlmanac.* *20c. coll.*: ODEP 435,

Stevenson 2459:2, *CODP* 152, Whiting(MP) 666.

SEE ALSO BLOOD is thicker than water. / Sit still in the BOAT that carries you across deep water. / Cast your BREAD upon the water; it will return to you a hundredfold. / Eat BREAD and drink water, and you will live a long life. / Scalded CATS fear even cold water. / COURTESY is like oil on troubled waters. / Cast no DIRT in the well that gives you water. / Beware of a silent DOG and silent water. / Many DROPS of water will sink a ship. / A DUCK never flies so high but that it has to come down for water. / Can't carry FIRE in one hand and water in the other. / FIRE and water do not mix. / The best FISHING is in the deepest water. / It's easy to make a FROG jump into water when that's what he wants to do. / FROGS do not croak in running water. / No GRIST is ground with the water that is passed. / Don't wash your HAIR before you get the water. / Don't stick your HAND in boiling water to see if it is hot. / People in HELL want ice water, too. / You can lead a HORSE to water but you can't make him drink. / MARRIAGE is like a tub of water: after a while, it is not so hot. / The MILL cannot grind with the water that is past. / OIL and water don't mix. / Where there are REEDS, there is water. / The time to go down the RIVER is when the water is up. / A great SHIP asks for deeper water. / Never stint SOAP and water. / SOAP and water will not make a Negro's face white. / A dry STREAM carries no water. / A dry WELL pumps no water. / The deeper the WELL, the colder the water.

wave Jump when the wave is on the swell. *Rec. dist.:* Calif.

SEE ALSO Where there's a WIND there's a wave.

waver SEE WEALTH makes wit waver.

wax SEE If your HEAD is wax, do not walk in the sun.

way 1. Anyone can have his own way if there's not someone in it. *Rec. dist.:* Ont.

2. Better one safe way than a hundred on which you cannot reckon. *Rec. dist.:* Utah.

3. Every man in his own way. *Rec. dist.:*

U.S., Can. *1st cit.:* ca1497 Medwall, *Fulgens and Lucres.* *20c. coll.:* ODEP 229.

4. Everyone enjoys himself in his own way. *Rec. dist.:* Ont.

5. He is in the way of life that keeps instruction, but he that refuses errs. *Rec. dist.:* Ont.

6. He knows the way best who went there last. *Rec. dist.:* Wis.

7. He that goes a great way for a wife is either cheated or means to cheat. *Rec. dist.:* Ark. *1st cit.:* 1732 Fuller, *Gnomologia.* *20c. coll.:* Stevenson 250l:9.

8. He who learns the hard way will never forget. *Rec. dist.:* N.Dak.

9. If your ways are bad, everybody will dislike you. *Rec. dist.:* Okla.

10. It is the ordinary way of the world to keep folly at the helm and wisdom under the hatches. *Rec. dist.:* Ont.

11. It's all in the way you look at it. *Rec. dist.:* Calif., Mich., N.Y., Tex.

12. It's not so much where you are as which way you are going. *Rec. dist.:* Okla.

13. Never too late to mend your ways. *Rec. dist.:* U.S., Can. *1st cit.:* 1590 Greene, *Never Too Late;* US1729 *Papers of Benjamin Franklin,* ed. Labaree (1959). *20c. coll.:* ODEP 563, Whiting 252, Stevenson 1563:7, T&W 215, Whiting(MP) 362.

14. None goes his way alone. *Rec. dist.:* Okla.

15. That's the way with a woman. *Rec. dist.:* Ark., Mich.

16. The best way out is always through. *Rec. dist.:* Ill. *1st cit.:* US1930 Frost, *Servant to Servants.* *20c. coll.:* Stevenson 2468:12.

17. The longest way around is the shortest way home. *Vars.:* (a) The farther way about is the nearest way home. (b) The farthest way around is the shortest way. (c) The longest way round is the sweetest way home. *Rec. dist.:* U.S., Can. *1st cit.:* 1580 Lyly, *Euphues and His England;* US1762 *Letter Book of John Watts, 1762–65,* N.Y.Hist.Soc. *Collections* (1928). *20c. coll.:* ODEP 245, Whiting 474, CODP 138, Stevenson 2468:12, T&W 396, Whiting(MP) 669.

18. The middle way is the best. *Rec. dist.:* N.Y. *1st cit.:* 1732 Pope, "Satires" in *Imitations of Horace;* US1719 Wise, Letter in *Colonial Currency Reprints,* ed. Davis, Publ. Prince Soc. (1910–11). *20c. coll.:* Stevenson 1604:4, Whiting 474.

19. The safe way is the right way. *Rec. dist.:* Ont.

20. The way of a fool is right in his own eyes. *Rec. dist.:* Ill.

21. The way to hell is paved with good intentions. *Vars.:* **(a)** Hell is lined with good intentions. **(b)** Hell is paved with good intentions. **(c)** The pathway to hell is paved with good intentions. **(d)** The road to hell is paved with good intentions. *Rec. dist.:* U.S., Can. *1st cit.:* 1574 Guevara, *Familiar Epistles,* tr. Hellowes (1584); US1809 *Port Folio. 20c. coll.:* CODP 192, Whiting 209, ODEP 367, Stevenson 1128:8, Whiting*(MP)* 673.

22. There are more ways to the wood than one. *Rec. dist.:* Okla. *1st cit.:* 1533 Udall, *Floures for Latine Speakyng;* US1651 *Complete Writings of Roger Williams* (1963). *20c. coll.:* ODEP 872, Whiting 474, Stevenson 2467:5, Whiting*(MP)* 670.

23. There is more than one way to skin a cat. *Rec. dist.:* U.S., Can. *1st cit.:* 1678 Ray, *English Proverbs;* US1839 *John Smith's Letters. 20c. coll.:* ODEP 872, T&W 396, CODP 242, Stevenson 297:5, Whiting*(MP)* 670.

24. There is no easy way. *Rec. dist.:* S.C.

25. There is your way, my way, and the right way. *Rec. dist.:* Mich., N.Y., Okla.

26. Whatever way the wind does blow, some hearts are glad to have it so. *Rec. dist.:* N.Y.

27. Willful ways make woeful want. *Rec. dist.:* N.Y.

SEE ALSO The best way to keep ACTS in memory is to refresh them with new ones. / APPEARANCES go a great ways. / It's a bad BARGAIN that can't run both ways. / A willful BEAST must have his own way. / There's more than one way to skin a CAT without tearing the hide. / Stroke the FEATHERS the right way. / The way to gain a FRIEND is to be one. / There is more than one way to cook a GOOSE.

/ A willing HEART carries a weary pair of feet a long way. / The way to a man's HEART is through his ego. / A LITTLE goes a long way. / LOVE will find a way. / POOR folks have poor ways. / PRIDE goes forth on horseback grand and gay, and comes back on foot and begs its way. / RICH people have mean ways, and poor people poor ways. / The way to be SAFE is never to feel secure. / Never be breaking your SHIN on a stool that is not in your way. / A STRAW shows which way the wind blows. / The best way to kill TIME is to work it to death. / Speak the TRUTH bravely, cost as it may; hiding the wrong act is not the way. / A good TURN goes a long way. / Where there's a WILL there's a way. / To him that WILLS, ways are not wanting. / WOMAN will have both her word and her way. / A kind WORD goes a long way. / Smooth WORDS make smooth ways. / The best way to get rid of WORK is to do it. / YIELDING is sometimes the best way of succeeding.

wayside *SEE* Fair FLOWERS are never left standing by the wayside. / HAPPINESS is a wayside flower growing upon the highways of usefulness.

weak *(n.)* **1.** Even the weakest may find means to avenge a wrong. *Rec. dist.:* N.C.

2. The weak may be joked out of everything but their weakness. *Rec. dist.:* Ont.

3. The weakest goes to the wall. *Rec. dist.:* Mich., N.Y., Tex. *1st cit.:* ca1500 *Coventry Plays,* E.E.T.S. (1902); US1686 Dunton, *Letters from New England,* Publ. Prince Soc. (1867). *20c. coll.:* ODEP 873, Whiting 475, CODP 243, Stevenson 2469:14, Whiting*(MP)* 673.

4. You cannot strengthen the weak by weakening the strong. *Rec. dist.:* Utah.

SEE ALSO CONFESSION is a luxury of the weak. / The STRONG and the weak cannot keep company.

weak *(adj.)* **1.** Don't hit someone who looks weak. *Rec. dist.:* Mich., N.Y.

2. Everyone has his weak side. *Rec. dist.:* Ala., Ga., Mich., N.Y. *1st cit.:* 1678 Ray, *English Proverbs. 20c. coll.:* Stevenson 2469:2, ODEP 873.

3. They are the weakest, however strong, who have no confidence in their own ability. *Rec. dist.:* Wis.

4. Weak men had best be witty. *Rec. dist.:* Ill. *1st cit.:* 1639 Clarke, *Paroemiologia. 20c. coll.:* ODEP 873, Stevenson 2469:2.

5. Weak men wait for opportunities; strong men make them. *Rec. dist.:* N.C.

6. Where it is weakest, there the thread breaks. *Rec. dist.:* Ill. *1st cit.:* 1640 Herbert, *Outlandish Proverbs (Jacula Prudentum) in Works,* ed. Hutchinson (1941). *20c. coll.:* ODEP 815, Stevenson 2309:7.

SEE ALSO The weaker the ARGUMENT, the stronger the words. / Some tasks require a strong BACK and a weak mind. / The weaker the BODY, the stronger the mind. / A CHAIN is no stronger than its weakest link. / The weakest FRUIT drops earliest to the ground. / GENERATIONS grow weaker and wiser. / Weak HEADS are often head-strong. / IDLENESS is only the refuge of weak minds, the holiday of fools. / The SPIRIT is willing but the flesh is weak. / WILLOWS are weak, but they bind other wood.

weaken SEE It's a great LIFE if you don't weaken. / To widen your LIFE without deepening it is only to weaken it.

weakness One man's weakness is another man's chance. *Rec. dist.:* Wis.

wealth **1.** A man of wealth is a slave to his possessions. *Rec. dist.:* Ill.

2. A man's true wealth is the good he does in the world. *Var.:* A man's good wealth is the good he does in the world. *Rec. dist.:* Ont.

3. Command your wealth, else it will command you. *Rec. dist.:* Ill. *1st cit.:* 1732 Fuller, *Gnomologia. 20c. coll.:* Stevenson 2472:11.

4. He who loses wealth loses much; he who loses even one friend loses more; but he that loses his courage loses all. *Rec. dist.:* Ill. *1st cit.:* US1948 Stevenson, *Home Book of Proverbs. 20c. coll.:* Stevenson 1540:6.

5. He who marries for wealth sells his liberty. *Rec. dist.:* Iowa, Ont., Wis. *1st cit.:* 1581 Guazzo, *Civile Conversation,* tr. Pettie, T.T. (1925). *20c. coll.:* ODEP 515, Stevenson 1540:6.

6. Inherited wealth is a big handicap to happiness; it is a certain death to ambition as cocaine is to morality. *Rec. dist.:* N.Y. *1st cit.:* US1905 Vanderbilt, Newspaper interview. *20c. coll.:* Stevenson 2473:9.

7. It is not wealth but wisdom that makes a man rich. *Rec. dist.:* N.Y. *1st cit.:* ca1275 *Proverbs of Alfred. 20c. coll.:* ODEP 898, Stevenson 2537:6.

8. Sudden wealth is dangerous. *Rec. dist.:* Ont.

9. The first wealth is health. *Rec. dist.:* N.Y. *1st cit.:* US1860 Emerson, "Power" in *Conduct of Life. 20c. coll.:* Stevenson 1100:5.

10. Wealth and content are not always bedfellows. *Rec. dist.:* N.Y. *1st cit.:* US1749 Franklin, *PRAlmanac. 20c. coll.:* Whiting 476, Stevenson 2472:10.

11. Wealth and power do not give peace of mind. *Rec. dist.:* N.C.

12. Wealth can buy no health. *Rec. dist.:* Ind.

13. Wealth consists not of having great possessions but of having few wants. *Rec. dist.:* Ont.

14. Wealth does not always improve us. *Rec. dist.:* Ont.

15. Wealth is best known by want. *Rec. dist.:* Ill. *1st cit.:* 1631 Dekker, *Penny-wise, Pound-foolish. 20c. coll.:* ODEP 873, Stevenson 2471:3.

16. Wealth is like rheumatism: it falls on the weakest parts. *Rec. dist.:* Ill. *1st cit.:* 1633 Herbert, "Confession" in *Works,* ed. Hutchinson (1941). *20c. coll.:* ODEP 873, Stevenson 2473:6.

17. Wealth is not his that has it but his that enjoys it. *Rec. dist.:* Okla., Ont. *1st cit.:* 1659 Howell, *Paroimiografia (Italian Proverbs);* US1736 Franklin, *PRAlmanac. 20c. coll.:* Stevenson 2471:4, Whiting 476.

18. Wealth, like want, ruins many. *Rec. dist.:* Ont. *1st cit.:* 1766 *Goody Two-Shoes. 20c. coll.:* ODEP 2.

19. Wealth makes many friends. *Rec. dist.:* Ill. *1st cit.:* ca1386 Chaucer, *Tale of Melibee;* US1804 Brackenridge, *Modern Chivalry, 1792–1815,* ed. Newlin (1937). *20c. coll.:* ODEP 674, Whiting 476, Stevenson 906:3.

20. Wealth makes wit waver. *Rec. dist.:* Ont.

1st cit.: ca1595 Fergusson, *Scottish Proverbs.* *20c. coll.:* Stevenson 2473:2, ODEP 873.

21. Wealth makes worship. *Rec. dist.:* N.Y. *1st cit.:* 1616 Breton, *Crossing of Proverbs. 20c. coll.:* ODEP 874, Stevenson 2472:3.

22. Wealth may not produce civilization, but civilization produces money. *Rec. dist.:* N.Y. *1st cit.:* US1887 Beecher, *Proverbs from Plymouth Pulpit. 20c. coll.:* Stevenson 360:5.

23. Wealth means power; it means leisure; it means ability. *Rec. dist.:* N.Y. *1st cit.:* US1820 Tudor, *Letters on Eastern States. 20c. coll.:* Whiting 476.

24. Wealth unused may as well not exist. *Rec. dist.:* Ont.
SEE ALSO Where GENIUS, wealth and strength fails perseverance will succeed. / GOLD is wealth in fancy only. / Where there is GOLD there is wealth. / Folks spend their HEALTH to acquire wealth and later spend their wealth in an effort to regain their health. / HEALTH is wealth. / The THOUGHTS of the heart—these are the wealth of a man. / Sell not VIRTUE to purchase wealth, nor liberty to purchase power. / VIRTUE is everlasting wealth. / Halving your WANTS quadruples your wealth. / A good WIFE and health are a man's best wealth.

wealthy If you would be wealthy, think of saving as well as getting. *Rec. dist.:* Ky., Tenn. *1st cit.:* US1743 Franklin, *PRAlmanac. 20c. coll.:* Stevenson 2036:2.
SEE ALSO Early to BED and early to rise makes a man healthy, wealthy, and wise.

wean SEE A blattin' CALF is soon weaned.

weapon What weapon has the lion but himself? *Rec. dist.:* N.Y.
SEE ALSO A man of COURAGE is never in need of weapons. / KINDNESS is the noblest weapon to conquer with. / A woman's TEARS are her strongest weapons.

wear (*n.*) SEE CARE saves wear.

wear (*v.*) It is better to wear out than to rust out. *Var.:* Better to wear out than to rust out. *Rec. dist.:* U.S., Can. *1st cit.:* 1557 Edgeworth, *Sermons;* US1702 Mather, *Magnalia Christi Americana* (1853–55). *20c. coll.:* ODEP 56,
Whiting 476, *CODP* 17, Stevenson 2020:3, T&W 397, Whiting*(MP)* 673.
SEE ALSO If the CAP fits, wear it. / EAT it up, wear it out, make it do, or do without. / Your EXPRESSION is the most important thing you can wear. / The FEET are slow when the head wears snow. / Though the FOX wear silk he is still a fox. / The best of FRIENDS wear out with wrong use. / If the GLOVE fits, wear it. / Don't wear your HEART on your sleeve. / What you wear in your HEART shows in your face. / Wear your LEARNING like your watch, in a private pocket. / Old SHOES wear best. / TIME is a file that wears and makes no noise. / TRUTH is heavy; therefore few wear it. / Don't wear out your WELCOME. / WIDE will wear when narrow will tear.

wearer The wearer best knows where the shoe pinches. *Var.:* None knows where the shoe pinches like the one who wears the shoe. *Rec. dist.:* Miss., Tex. *1st cit.:* ca1386 Chaucer, *Merchant's Tale;* US1766 *Beekman Mercantile Papers, 1746–1799,* ed. White (1956). *20c. coll.:* ODEP 725, Whiting 391, Stevenson 2096:3, T&W 328, Whiting*(MP)* 560.

wearing Everything is the worse for wearing. *Rec. dist.:* N.Y. *1st cit.:* 1516 Skelton, *Magnyfycence;* US1815 Humphreys, *Yankey in England. 20c. coll.:* ODEP 232, Whiting 502, Stevenson 2473:12, T&W 415, Whiting*(MP)* 705.

weather 1. Calm weather in June sets corn in tune. *Rec. dist.:* Wis. *1st cit.:* 1573 Tusser, *Hundredth Good Pointes of Husbandrie. 20c. coll.:* ODEP 99.

2. Change of weather is a discourse of fools. *Rec. dist.:* Wis. *1st cit.:* 1659 Howell, *Paroimiografia (Spanish Proverbs). 20c. coll.:* ODEP 114, Stevenson 2474:8.

3. Everybody talks about the weather, but nobody does anything about it. *Rec. dist.:* U.S. *1st cit.:* USca1890 Warner, Editorial in *Courant,* Hartford, Conn. *20c. coll.:* Stevenson 2474:8.

4. For weather go to heaven, but for company go to hell. *Rec. dist.:* Ind. *1st cit.:* US1948 Stevenson, *Home Book of Proverbs. 20c. coll.:* Stevenson 1120:5.

5. God's weather is good weather. *Rec. dist.:* Ont.

6. In fair weather prepare for foul. *Rec. dist.:* Ont. *1st cit.:* 1732 Fuller, *Gnomologia.* *20c. coll.:* ODEP 240, Stevenson 2474:9.

7. It's always cool weather when the chinquapin blooms. *Rec. dist.:* Miss.

8. It's always fair weather when good friends get together. *Rec. dist.:* U.S., Can. *1st cit.:* US1894 Hovey, *Stein Song.* *20c. coll.:* Stevenson 2474:9.

9. Man is never satisfied with the weather. *Rec. dist.:* N.C.

10. Never waste time complaining about Arkansas weather: it will soon change. *Vars.:* (a) If you don't like Oklahoma weather, wait a minute. (b) If you don't like the weather in Chicago, wait a few minutes. (c) If you don't like the weather, wait five minutes. *Rec. dist.:* Ark., Mich. *Infm.:* Varied in form depending upon the location.

11. No weather's ill if the wind be still. *Var.:* Never mind the weather if the wind don't blow. *Rec. dist.:* Tex. *1st cit.:* 1594 Shakespeare, *Love's Labour's Lost.* *20c. coll.:* ODEP 875, Stevenson 2516:1.

See also The ALMANAC writer makes the almanac, but God makes the weather. / We may achieve CLIMATE, but weather is thrust upon us. / After CLOUDS, clear weather. / The higher the CLOUDS, the fairer the weather. / One should turn his COAT according to the weather. / A FIELD has three needs: good weather, good seed, and a good husbandman. / All SIGNS fail in dry weather. / Every WIND has its weather. / Only YANKEES and fools predict the weather.

weather-wise Some are weather-wise, some are otherwise. *Var.:* Those that are weather-wise are rarely otherwise. *Rec. dist.:* N.Y. *1st cit.:* 1601 Jonson, *Poetaster;* US1735 Franklin, *PRAlmanac.* *20c. coll.:* ODEP 751, Whiting 477, Stevenson 2474:5.

weave *See* To have IDEAS is to gather flowers, to think is to weave them into garlands. / What a tangled WEB we weave when first we practice to deceive.

web 1. For a web begun, God sends thread. *Rec. dist.:* Ont.

2. What a tangled web we weave when first we practice to deceive. *Rec. dist.:* Ariz., N.J., Ohio. *1st cit.:* 1808 Scott, *Marmion.* *20c. coll.:* Stevenson 534:5.

See also HOPE and fear, peace and strife, make up the troubled web of life.

wed Earlier wed, sooner dead. *Rec. dist.:* Ont. *1st cit.:* 1615 "Cold Year, 1614" in *Old Book Collector's Miscellany,* ed. Hindley. *20c. coll.:* ODEP 211, Stevenson 1530:8.

See also Always to COURT and never to wed is the happiest life that ever was led. / Those whom we LOVE first we seldom wed. / If one will not, another will, so are all MAIDENS wed.

wedding One wedding makes another. *Rec. dist.:* Calif., N.Y. *1st cit.:* ca1634 Parker, *Wooing Maid;* US1818 *Cary Letters,* ed. Curtis (1891). *20c. coll.:* ODEP 875, Whiting 477, CODP 243, Stevenson 1536:6, T&W 398, Whiting(MP) 675.

wedge 1. A wedge of itself splits the oak. *Rec. dist.:* N.Y., S.C. *1st cit.:* US1940 Thompson, *Body, Boots, and Britches.* *20c. coll.:* Stevenson 690:6.

2. There is no wedge worse than the one from the same log. *Rec. dist.:* Wis.

wedlock 1. Humble wedlock is better than proud virginity. *Rec. dist.:* Mich.

2. The chain of wedlock is so heavy that it takes two to carry it, and sometimes three. *Rec. dist.:* N.Y.

3. Wedlock is a padlock. *Rec. dist.:* Ill., Tex. *1st cit.:* 1678 Ray, *English Proverbs.* *20c. coll.:* ODEP 876, Whiting(MP) 675, Stevenson 1538:5.

weed 1. An armful of weeds is worth an ear of corn. *Rec. dist.:* Ill. *Infm.:* Weeds can be used for fodder for the hogs instead of corn.

2. Ill weeds always grow apace; folly runs a rapid race. *Rec. dist.:* Ill., Ont. *1st cit.:* ca1470 *Harleian MS,* ed. Förester in *Anglia;* USca1714 "Wall and Garden" in *Mass. Election Sermons, 1670–1775,* ed. Plumstead (1968). *20c. coll.:*

ODEP 401, Whiting 478, *CODP* 120, Stevenson 2476:12.

3. The weed of crime bears bitter fruit. *Var.:* The weed of crime grows bitter fruit. *Rec. dist.:* N.Y., Oreg.

4. Weeds need no sowing. *Var.:* Weeds want no sowing. *Rec. dist.:* Ala., Ga., Ohio. *1st cit.:* 1659 Gent, *Proverbs English, French, Dutch, Italian and Spanish. 20c. coll.:* ODEP 876, Stevenson 2476:7.

SEE ALSO A lot of good COTTON stalks get chopped up for associating with weeds. / The FROST hurts not the weeds. / A good GARDEN always has weeds. / A man of WORDS and not of deeds is like a garden full of weeds.

weedy SEE You must visit your NEIGHBORS lest an unused path becomes weedy.

week SEE COMPANY on Monday, company all week. / Who goes for a DAY into the forest should take bread for a week. / Some people STAY longer in an hour than others stay in a week.

weep We weep when we are born, not when we die. *Rec. dist.:* N.Y. *1st cit.:* 1576 Kerton, *Mirror of Man's Life;* USca1880 Aldrich, *Metempsychosis. 20c. coll.:* ODEP 876, Stevenson 523:14.

SEE ALSO When two FRIENDS have a common purse, one sings and the other weeps. / REJOICE with them that rejoice; weep with them that weep. / SLEEP over it or you may weep over it.

weeper SEE FINDERS keepers, losers weepers.

weeping Weeping may endure for a night, but joy comes in the morning. *Rec. dist.:* Ont. *1st cit.:* US1948 Stevenson, *Home Book of Proverbs. 20c. coll.:* Stevenson 1275:7.

weigh Weigh right if you sell dear. *Rec. dist.:* Mich., Miss. *1st cit.:* 1573 Sanford, *Garden of Pleasure. 20c. coll.:* ODEP 877.

SEE ALSO Watch the BUTCHER when he weighs the roast; otherwise you'll buy his hand. / WORDS and deeds are not weighed in the same balance.

weight **1.** No one knows the weight of another's burden. *Rec. dist.:* N.Y. *1st cit.:* 1640

Herbert, *Outlandish Proverbs (Jacula Prudentum)* in *Works,* ed. Hutchinson (1941). *20c. coll.:* ODEP 438, Stevenson 257:5.

2. The weight of knowledge is never measured. *Rec. dist.:* Ky., Tenn.

3. Weight broke the wagon down. *Var.:* Weight broke the bridge down. *Rec. dist.:* Colo., N.Y., Okla., Tex.

4. Weight can break a bridge. *Rec. dist.:* Ill.

SEE ALSO An HONEST man is worth his weight in gold. / Thin ICE carries no weight.

welcome *(n.)* **1.** Don't wear out your welcome. *Var.:* Do not wear your welcome out. *Rec. dist.:* U.S., Can. *1st cit.:* 1546 Heywood, *Dialogue of Proverbs,* ed. Habernicht (1963); US1960 Millar, *Ferguson Affair. 20c. coll.:* ODEP 877, Stevenson 2478:12, Whiting*(MP)* 676.

2. Welcome is the best dish on the table. *Rec. dist.:* Ky., Tenn. *1st cit.:* ca1430 Lydgate, *Isopes,* E.E.T.S. (1911). *20c. coll.:* ODEP 877, Stevenson 2478:8.

3. Welcome is the best of cheer. *Var.:* Welcome is the best cheer. *Rec. dist.:* Tex., Wis. *1st cit.:* ca1430 Lydgate, *Isopes,* E.E.T.S. (1911). *20c. coll.:* ODEP 877, Stevenson 2478:8.

SEE ALSO Small CHEER and great welcome make a merry feast. / His WORTH is warrant for his welcome.

welcome *(v.)* SEE When all FRUIT fails, welcome haws.

welcome *(adj.)* You're twice welcome: welcome when you come and welcome when you go. *Rec. dist.:* Ont. *1st cit.:* 1546 Heywood, *Dialogue of Proverbs,* ed. Habernicht (1963). *20c. coll.:* ODEP 877.

SEE ALSO A constant GUEST is never welcome.

well *(n.)* **1.** A dry well pumps no water. *Rec. dist.:* Kans.

2. A well without a bucket is no good. *Rec. dist.:* Miss.

3. Dig the well before you are thirsty. *Vars.:* **(a)** Dig a well before it rains. **(b)** Dig the well before you get thirsty. *Rec. dist.:* Ill., Miss. *1st cit.:* US1948 Stevenson, *Home Book of Proverbs. 20c. coll.:* Stevenson 866:1.

4. Do not spit into the well: you may have to drink out of it. *Rec. dist.:* Ariz. *1st cit.:* 1593 Shakespeare, *Titus Andronicus.* *20c. coll.:* ODEP 189, Stevenson 1241:13.

5. Drawn wells are seldom dry. *Rec. dist.:* Okla., Tex. *1st cit.:* 1597 Gerard, *Herbal, or General History of Plants.* *20c. coll.:* ODEP 202, Stevenson 2479:4.

6. It is too late to close the well after the goat has fallen in. *Rec. dist.:* Ont.

7. The deeper the well, the colder the water. *Rec. dist.:* Ill.

SEE ALSO You can't tell the DEPTH of the well by the length of the handle on the pump. / Cast no DIRT in the well that gives you water. / The JUG goes to the well until it breaks. / A PITCHER that goes to the well too often is liable to be broken. / You never miss the WATER till the well runs dry.

well *(adv.)* **1.** He is not well bred that cannot bear ill breeding in others. *Var.:* He is not well bred that cannot bear the ill breeding in others. *Rec. dist.:* Ill., Ont.

2. Many a man has done well at the last hour. *Rec. dist.:* N.C.

3. Well married, a man is winged; ill matched, he is shackled. *Rec. dist.:* N.Y. *1st cit.:* US1887 Beecher, *Proverbs from Plymouth Pulpit.* *20c. coll.:* Stevenson 1537:11.

SEE ALSO He ACTS well who acts quickly. / ALL'S well that ends well. / BELIEVE well and have well. / He is not well BRED that cannot bear ill breeding in others. / Do it well or not at all. / If we like to DO a thing, we do it well. / If you want something DONE and done well, do it yourself. / Once DONE well is twice done. / He who GREASES well drives well. / When the HUSBAND earns well, the wife spends well. / If you do ILL, the joy fades, not the pains; if well, the pain does fade, the joy remains. / It costs more to do ILL than well. / If you want a JOB well done, give it to a busy man. / Well LATHERED, half shaved. / LAUGH and be well. / Wish not so much to LIVE long as to live well. / Not LIVING well isn't living at all. / NECESSITY does everything well. / Many SPEAK much who cannot speak well. / SPEAK little; speak well. / SPEAK well of every-

one if you speak of them at all. / That is well SPOKEN that is well taken. / He who would do a great THING well must first have done the simplest thing perfectly. / It is due each man to find one THING he can do well. / If you don't THINK well of yourself no one else will. / Employ the TIME well if you mean to gain leisure.

well *(interj.)* "Well" is a deep subject. *Rec. dist.:* Miss.

well-doing Never be weary of well-doing. *Rec. dist.:* Ont. *1st cit.:* 1609 Harward, Unpublished manuscript in library of Trinity College, Cambridge. *20c. coll.:* ODEP 562, Stevenson 996:5.

wench Every wench has her sweetheart, and the dirtiest the most. *Rec. dist.:* Ill.

west SEE EAST is east, and west is west, and never the twain shall meet. / Too far EAST is west. / East or west, HOME is best.

wet *(v.)* SEE The CAT that would eat fish must wet her feet.

wet *(adj.)* SEE Wet APRIL brings milk to the cows and sheep. / Remember, your TONGUE is in a wet place: it's likely to slip. / WARM and wet for oats and corn, cool and dry for wheat and rye.

whale SEE Every little FISH would become a whale. / It's a good rule to never send a MOUSE to catch a skunk or a pollywog to tackle a whale.

wheat SEE WARM and wet for oats and corn, cool and dry for wheat and rye.

wheel **1.** A squeaking wheel never wears out. *Rec. dist.:* Ont.

2. Always look on the hindwheels. *Rec. dist.:* Ont.

3. He who greases his wheels helps his oxen. *Rec. dist.:* Tex. *1st cit.:* 1666 Torriano, *Common Place of Italian Proverbs;* US1677 Hubbard, *History of Indian Wars in New England,* ed. Drake (1865). *20c. coll.:* ODEP 332, Whiting 479, T&W 400, Stevenson 1613:6, Whiting(MP) 678.

4. It's a whole lot better to be a little wheel that is turning than a big wheel standing still. *Rec. dist.:* Ohio.

5. It's not the wheel that makes the most noise that does the most harm. *Rec. dist.:* Ont.

6. The wheel comes full circle. *Rec. dist.:* Ill. *1st cit.:* 1605 Shakespeare, *King Lear;* US1942 Holding, *Kill Joy.* *20c. coll.:* Stevenson 2483:7, Whiting*(MP)* 678.

7. The wheel of fortune is forever in motion. *Rec. dist.:* Ill. *1st cit.:* 1760 Goldsmith, *Citizen of the World;* US1748 *Papers of Benjamin Franklin,* ed. Labaree (1959). *20c. coll.:* Stevenson 877:4, Whiting 165, T&W 144, Whiting*(MP)* 240.

8. The wheel that does the squeaking is the one that gets the grease. *Vars.:* **(a)** A squeaky wheel gets all the grease. **(b)** It's the squeaking wheel that gets the oil. **(c)** It's the wheel that squeaks that gets the oil. **(d)** The squeaking wheel gets the grease. **(e)** The squeaky wheel gets the oil. **(f)** The wheel that squeaks most gets the most grease. **(g)** The wheel that squeaks the loudest gets the grease. **(h)** The wheel that squeaks the loudest is the one that gets the grease. **(i)** The wheel that squeaks the loudest is the wheel that gets the grease. *Rec. dist.:* U.S., Can. *1st cit.:* ca1937 Bartlett, *Familiar Quotations;* US1952 Marshall, *Jane Hadden.* *20c. coll.:* CODP 211, Whiting*(MP)* 678, Stevenson 2483:6.

9. The wheel that turns gathers no rust. *Rec. dist.:* Ont.

10. The wheels of the gods grind slowly. *Rec. dist.:* Ind. *1st cit.:* 1640 Herbert, *Outlandish Proverbs (Jacula Prudentum)* in *Works,* ed. Hutchinson (1941); US1870 Longfellow, *Poems* (1960). *20c. coll.:* ODEP 314, CODP 151, Stevenson 1575:11, Whiting*(MP)* 411.

11. The worst wheel of the cart makes the most noise. *Vars.:* **(a)** The worst wheel of a cart creaks most. **(b)** The worst wheel on the wagon makes the most noise. *Rec. dist.:* U.S., Can. *1st cit.:* ca1400 *Latin MS,* tr. Pantin, in *Bulletin of J. Rylands Library;* US1737 Franklin, *PRAlmanac.* *20c. coll.:* ODEP 921, Whiting 479, Stevenson 2483:8, Whiting*(MP)* 678.

SEE ALSO Two empty packing BOXES make the most noise, but the squeaky wheel gets the grease. / A BUSINESS with an income at its heels always furnishes oil for its own wheels.

/ If you think COOPERATION is unnecessary, just try running your car a while on three wheels. / FEET were made before wheels. / Put your SHOULDER to the wheel.

wheelbarrow *SEE* BUSINESS is like a wheelbarrow: it stands still until somebody pushes it.

whetstone *SEE* The WORLD is a whetstone and man a knife.

whine *SEE* Better to WHISTLE than whine.

whip *(n.)* **1.** A little less whip and more control. *Rec. dist.:* Ohio.

2. A whip for a fool and a rod for a school. *Var.:* A whip for the horse; a bridle for the ass; a rod for the fool's back. *Rec. dist.:* Ont., Oreg. *1st cit.:* 1605 Rowley, *When You See Me.* *20c. coll.:* ODEP 883, Stevenson 2484:10.

3. Never take the whip when a word will do the turn. *Rec. dist.:* N.Y. *1st cit.:* 1721 Kelly, *Scottish Proverbs;* US1928 Odlum, *Rainbow Round My Shoulder.* *20c. coll.:* Stevenson 1551:7.

4. No whip cuts so sharply as the lash of conscience. *Rec. dist.:* Ill.

5. One whip is good enough for a good horse; for a bad one, not a thousand. *Rec. dist.:* Ill.

whip *(v.)* *SEE* Don't whip the HORSE that is pulling.

whirlwind Ride in the whirlwind and direct the storm. *Rec. dist.:* Ont. *1st cit.:* 1705 Addison, *The Campaign;* US1801 Polk in *John Gray Blount Papers,* eds. Keith and Masterson (1952–65). *20c. coll.:* Stevenson 2484:14, Whiting 480.

SEE ALSO Sow the WIND and reap the whirlwind.

whiskey **1.** When the whiskey is in, the wit is out. *Rec. dist.:* Ont. *1st cit.:* ca1386 Chaucer, *Pardoner's Tale;* US1813 *Life of Late Gen. William Eaton.* *20c. coll.:* ODEP 895, Whiting 488, CODP 247, Stevenson 2523:7, T&W 406, Whiting*(MP)* 688.

2. Whiskey and gasoline don't mix. *Vars.:* **(a)** Gasoline and whiskey don't mix. **(b)** Gasoline and whiskey usually mix with blood on the highway. *Rec. dist.:* Calif., Ill., Mich., N.Y.

3. Whiskey make rabbit hug lion. *Rec. dist.:* N.Y. *1st cit.:* US1928 Odlum, *Rainbow Round My Shoulder.* *20c. coll.:* Stevenson 2485:3.

4. Whiskey—a good servant but a bad master. *Rec. dist.:* Md.

SEE ALSO BEER on whiskey, mighty risky; whiskey on beer, never fear. / Save your BOTTLES; it may rain whiskey.

whisper *(n.)* SEE What a WOMAN has to say above a whisper isn't worth listening to.

whisper *(v.)* SEE Let your WILL roar when your power can but whisper.

whispered SEE ADVICE whispered is worthless.

whispering Where there is whispering, there is lying. *Rec. dist.:* Okla. *1st cit.:* 1584 Withals, *Short Dictionary.* *20c. coll.:* ODEP 884, Stevenson 2485:11.

whistle *(n.)* 1. Don't pay too much for your whistle. *Rec. dist.:* U.S., Can. *1st cit.:* 1854 Surtees, *Handley Cross;* US1779 Franklin, "The Whistle" in *Writings of Benjamin Franklin,* ed. Smyth (1905–07). *20c. coll.:* Stevenson 2486:5, Whiting 480, ODEP 615, T&W 407, Whiting(MP) 680.

2. You can't make a whistle out of a pig's tail. *Rec. dist.:* Colo.

SEE ALSO The STEAM that blows the whistle will never turn the wheel.

whistle *(v.)* 1. A man cannot whistle and eat a meal at the same time. *Rec. dist.:* Miss. *1st cit.:* 1574 Guazzo, *Civile Conversation,* tr. Pettie, T.T. (1925). *20c. coll.:* Stevenson 1230:2.

2. Better to whistle than whine. *Rec. dist.:* Ohio.

3. Whistle while you work. *Rec. dist.:* U.S., Can. *Infm.:* Name of a popular song in Walt Disney's *Snow White and Seven Dwarfs,* his first feature-length cartoon of 1937.

SEE ALSO When a GIRL whistles, the angels cry. / Who cannot SING may whistle.

whistling 1. A whistling girl and a crowing hen always come to the same bad end. *Vars.:* (a) A whistling gal and a crowing hen always come to a bad end. (b) A whistling girl and a cackling hen come to no good end. (c) A whistling girl and a crowing hen never come to any good end. (d) A whistling girl and a crowing hen will always come to some bad end. (e) A whistling girl and a crowing hen will come to no good end. (f) A whistling maid and a crawing hen is neither guid nor cannie aboot any poor man's house. (g) A whistling woman and a crowing hen always come to the same bad end. (h) Whistling girls and cackling hens always come to some bad ends. (i) Whistling girls and crowing hens always come to some bad end. (j) Whistling girls and crowing hens are not the kind that catch the men. (k) Whistling girls and crowing hens are the two worst things a farmer can keep. (l) Whistling girls or crowing hens are neither fit for God or men. (m) Whistling maids and crowing hens are two unlucky things. *Rec. dist.:* U.S., Can. *1st cit.:* 1721 Kelly, *Scottish Proverbs;* US1930 Botkin, *Folk-Say, Regional Miscellany.* *20c. coll.:* ODEP 155, Whiting(MP) 305, CODP 245, Stevenson 2505:5.

2. A whistling girl and a flock of sheep are the best property a man can keep. *Vars.:* (a) A whistling girl and a flock of sheep are the very best things a farmer can keep. (b) A whistling girl and a good fat sheep are the two best things a farmer can keep. (c) A whistling girl and a good flock of sheep are the best things a farmer can keep. (d) A whistling girl and a jumping sheep are the two worst things a farmer should keep. (e) A whistling girl and an old black sheep are two of the best things a farmer can keep. *Rec. dist.:* U.S.

white *(n.)* SEE BLACK is black and white is white. / Two BLACKS don't make a white.

white *(adj.)* SEE BERRIES white, take flight; berries red, never dread. / The whiter the BREAD, the sooner you're dead. / A CROW is no whiter for being washed. / A FOOL's head never grows white. / If all FOOLS wore white caps, we'd all look like geese. / White HANDS cannot hurt. / No LIES are white; they are all black. / White LIES are but the ushers to black ones. / NAUGHT's a naught and figger's a figger—all for de white man and none for de nigger. / SOAP and water will not make a Negro's face white.

who 1. It's not who you know or what you know; it's what you know on whom. *Rec. dist.:* Calif., Colo., N.Y.

2. Never mind who was your grandfather—what are you? *Rec. dist.:* Ont.

SEE ALSO It's not what you KNOW, but whom you know.

whole *(n.)* Half is sometimes better than the whole. *Rec. dist.:* Oreg. *1st cit.:* 1550 Latimer, *Sermons.* *20c. coll.:* Stevenson 1056:2.

whole *(adj.)* Better whole than patched with gold. *Rec. dist.:* Miss.

SEE ALSO Give him a FINGER and he will take a hand. / You may know by the HANDFUL the whole sack. / Eat whole HOG or die.

whoopee Never say "whoopee" before you jump. *Rec. dist.:* Ont.

whore 1. Once a whore, always a whore. *Rec. dist.:* Ill. *1st cit.:* 1613 Parrot, *Laquei Ridiculosi;* US1824 Marshall, *History of Kentucky.* *20c. coll.:* CODP 169, ODEP 594, Stevenson 2489:14.

2. Spit in a whore's face and she'll say it's raining. *Rec. dist.:* Ill.

3. Whores' curses are blessings. *Rec. dist.:* Ill. *1st cit.:* 1855 Bohn, *Handbook of Proverbs.* *20c. coll.:* Stevenson 2489:1.

why Every why has a wherefore. *Rec. dist.:* U.S., Can. *1st cit.:* 1573 Gascoigne, *Works,* ed. Cunliffe (1907–10); US1763 Franklin, *Papers of Benjamin Franklin,* ed. Labaree (1959). *20c. coll.:* ODEP 886, Whiting 481, Stevenson 2490:10, T&W 401, Whiting(MP) 682.

wicked *(n.)* 1. Expect no reward for serving the wicked. *Rec. dist.:* Ont.

2. No gratitude from the wicked. *Rec. dist.:* Ont. *1st cit.:* 1612 Cervantes, *Don Quixote,* tr. Shelton. *20c. coll.:* Stevenson 1243:3.

3. The most wicked are often the most obstinate. *Rec. dist.:* N.J.

4. The wicked flee when no man pursues. *Var.:* The wicked flee when no man pursues, but the righteous are as bold as a lion. *Rec. dist.:* Ill., Mich., N.Y. *1st cit.:* 1869 Henderson, *Latin Proverbs;* US1771 *Trial of Atticus Before Justice Beau, for Rape* in *Satiric Comedies,*

eds. Meserve and Reardon (1969). *20c. coll.:* Stevenson 2491:1, Whiting 482.

5. The wicked flourish as the green bay tree. *Rec. dist.:* S.C. *1st cit.:* 1548 *Book of Common Prayer.* *20c. coll.:* Stevenson 2492:4.

6. The wicked grow worse, and good men better, for trouble. *Rec. dist.:* N.Y.

7. The wicked shall fall by his own wickedness. *Rec. dist.:* Ont.

8. Unenviable is the state of the wicked, however prosperous they may appear. *Rec. dist.:* Mich.

9. When the wicked bear rule, the people mourn. *Rec. dist.:* Ont.

SEE ALSO No REST for the wicked. / The TONGUE of the just is a choice silver; the heart of the wicked is little worth.

wicked *(adj.)* 1. A wicked man is afraid of his own memory. *Rec. dist.:* Ill.

2. A wicked man is his own hell. *Rec. dist.:* Ill. *1st cit.:* 1604 Marlowe, *Dr Faustus.* *20c. coll.:* ODEP 887, Stevenson 2491:3.

3. No man ever became extremely wicked at once. *Rec. dist.:* Wis. *1st cit.:* ca1580 Sidney, *Arcadia.* *20c. coll.:* Stevenson 2491:8.

SEE ALSO A wicked COMPANION invites us all to hell. / Better be POOR than wicked.

wickedness 1. Shun wickedness. *Rec. dist.:* Mich.

2. Wickedness with beauty is the devil's hook ready baited. *Rec. dist.:* N.Y. *1st cit.:* 1732 Fuller, *Gnomologia.* *20c. coll.:* Stevenson 2491:3.

wide *(n.)* Wide will wear when narrow will tear. *Var.:* Wide will wear, but narrow will tear. *Rec. dist.:* Ill. *1st cit.:* 1609 Harward, Unpublished manuscript in library of Trinity College, Cambridge. *20c. coll.:* ODEP 887, Stevenson 627:4.

wide *(adj.)* SEE Wide is the DOOR of the little cottage. / A close GATHERING gets a wide scattering.

widen SEE To widen your LIFE without deepening it is only to weaken it.

widow 1. Befriend the widow and fatherless. *Rec. dist.:* Mich.

2. He that marries a widow and four children marries four thieves. *Rec. dist.:* N.Y. *1st cit.:* ca1576 Whythorne, *Autobiography,* ed. Osborne (1961). *20c. coll.:* ODEP 514, Stevenson 2494:14.

3. Never marry a widow unless her first husband was hanged. *Rec. dist.:* Wis. *1st cit.:* 1721 Kelly, *Scottish Proverbs. 20c. coll.:* ODEP 515, Stevenson 2494:12.

wife **1.** A good wife and health are a man's best wealth. *Rec. dist.:* N.Y. *1st cit.:* 1591 Smith, *Preparative to Marriage;* US1746 Franklin, *PRAlmanac. 20c. coll.:* ODEP 326, Whiting 482, Stevenson 2503:1.

2. A good wife is a perfect lady in the living room, a good cook in the kitchen, and a harlot in the bedroom. *Rec. dist.:* N.Y. *1st cit.:* US1942 Sale, *Passing Strange. 20c. coll.:* Stevenson 1207:11, Whiting(MP) 682.

3. A good wife makes a good husband. *Rec. dist.:* Ind. *1st cit.:* 1546 Heywood, *Dialogue of Proverbs,* ed. Habernicht (1963). *20c. coll.:* Stevenson 1206:6, ODEP 326.

4. A kind wife makes a faithful husband. *Rec. dist.:* Mich.

5. A lazy wife and a large barn bring luck to any man. *Rec. dist.:* N.Y.

6. A light wife makes a heavy husband. *Rec. dist.:* N.Y. *1st cit.:* 1597 Shakespeare, *Merchant of Venice. 20c. coll.:* Stevenson 2504:8.

7. A nice wife and a back door oft do make a rich man poor. *Rec. dist.:* N.Y. *1st cit.:* ca1450 *Proverbs of Good Counsel. 20c. coll.:* ODEP 565, Stevenson 2501:3.

8. A no-account wife takes advice from everyone but her husband. *Rec. dist.:* Miss.

9. A quiet wife is mighty pretty. *Rec. dist.:* Ill.

10. A true wife is her husband's better half. *Rec. dist.:* Miss.

11. A true wife is her husband's flower of beauty. *Rec. dist.:* Miss.

12. A true wife is her husband's heart's treasure. *Rec. dist.:* Miss.

13. A wife is a young man's slave and an old man's darling. *Rec. dist.:* Ill. *1st cit.:* 1546 Hey-

wood, *Dialogue of Proverbs,* ed. Habernicht (1963); US1940 Rhode, *Death. 20c. coll.:* ODEP 51, *CODP* 14, Stevenson 1542:8, Whiting(MP) 393.

14. Choose a wife on a Saturday rather than on a Sunday. *Vars.:* **(a)** If you want a neat wife, choose her on a Saturday. **(b)** Who will have a handsome wife, let him choose her upon Saturday and not upon Sunday, when she is in her fine clothes. *Rec. dist.:* N.J., N.Y., S.C. *Infm.:* Judge a woman by her everyday clothes, not her Sunday best clothes. *1st cit.:* 1659 Howell, *Paroimiografia (Spanish Proverbs);* US1737 Franklin, *PRAlmanac. 20c. coll.:* ODEP 122, Whiting 482, Stevenson 2502:3.

15. Discreet wives have sometimes neither eyes nor ears. *Rec. dist.:* Mich. *1st cit.:* 1594 Shakespeare, *Romeo and Juliet. 20c. coll.:* ODEP 189, Stevenson 2496:16.

16. Fat wives make lean husbands. *Rec. dist.:* Ont.

17. Good wives and good plantations are made by good husbands. *Rec. dist.:* N.Y. *1st cit.:* US1736 Franklin, *PRAlmanac. 20c. coll.:* Stevenson 1206:6.

18. Grief for a dead wife and a troublesome guest continues to the threshold, and there is at rest. *Rec. dist.:* N.Y. *1st cit.:* US1734 Franklin, *PRAlmanac. 20c. coll.:* Stevenson 2507:1.

19. He knows little who will tell his wife all he knows. *Rec. dist.:* Wis. *1st cit.:* 1642 Fuller, *Holy State. 20c. coll.:* Stevenson 2498:2.

20. He that has a good wife has an angel by his side; he that has a bad one has a devil at his elbow. *Rec. dist.:* La., Mich., N.Y.

21. He that has not got a wife is not yet a complete man. *Rec. dist.:* N.Y. *1st cit.:* US1744 Franklin, *PRAlmanac. 20c. coll.:* Stevenson 2496:15.

22. He that takes a wife takes care. *Rec. dist.:* N.Y. *1st cit.:* ca1495 Medwall, *Nature;* US1736 Franklin, *PRAlmanac. 20c. coll.:* ODEP 888, Whiting 482, Stevenson 2503:6.

23. He that tells his wife news is but newly married. *Rec. dist.:* N.J. *1st cit.:* ca1275 *Proverbs of Alfred,* ed. Skeat. *20c. coll.:* ODEP 808, Stevenson 2498:2.

24. He who has a fair wife needs more than two eyes. *Rec. dist.:* N.Y. *1st cit.:* 1545 *Precepts of Cato,* tr. Burrant. *20c. coll.:* ODEP 240.

25. He who hasn't anything to do pulls his wife's eyes out. *Rec. dist.:* N.Y.

26. He who loves his wife should watch her. *Rec. dist.:* Ark.

27. If your wife is small, bend down to take her counsel. *Rec. dist.:* N.Y. *1st cit.:* US1948 Stevenson, *Home Book of Proverbs.* *20c. coll.:* Stevenson 2495:2.

28. It is cheaper to find a wife than to feed a wife. *Rec. dist.:* Ill.

29. Lots of men get women, but few get wives. *Rec. dist.:* Ky., Tenn.

30. Most men get as good a wife as they deserve. *Rec. dist.:* N.Y. *1st cit.:* US1948 Stevenson, *Home Book of Proverbs.* *20c. coll.:* Stevenson 2499:2.

31. Ne'er seek a wife till you know what to do with her. *Rec. dist.:* Ont.

32. Never praise your wife until you have been married ten years. *Rec. dist.:* Ark.

33. Next to no wife, a good wife is best. *Rec. dist.:* N.J. *1st cit.:* ca1497 Medwall, *Fulgens and Lucres.* *20c. coll.:* ODEP 888, Stevenson 2497:2.

34. Old wives and bairns make fools of physicians. *Var.:* Old wives and children make fools of physicians. *Rec. dist.:* N.Y. *1st cit.:* 1721 Kelly, *Scottish Proverbs.* *20c. coll.:* Stevenson 595:9.

35. Rule a wife and have a wife. *Rec. dist.:* Ky., Tenn.

36. The first wife is matrimony; the second, company; the third, heresy. *Rec. dist.:* Ont. *1st cit.:* 1569 Howell, *Paroimiografia (Spanish Proverbs).* *20c. coll.:* ODEP 263, Stevenson 2500:10.

37. The happiest wife is not she that gets the best husband but she that makes the best of that which she gets. *Rec. dist.:* N.Y. *1st cit.:* US1913 Rowland, *Sayings of Mrs. Solomon.* *20c. coll.:* Stevenson 1207:7.

38. The second wife always sits on the right knee. *Rec. dist.:* N.Y. *1st cit.:* US1940 Thompson, *Body, Boots, and Britches.* *20c. coll.:* Stevenson 1543:7.

39. The wife can throw more out the back window in a spoon than a man can bring in the front door with a shovel. *Vars.:* **(a)** A wife can throw out with a spoon faster than a husband can bring in with a shovel. **(b)** The wife can throw more out the back door than the husband can bring in the front. *Rec. dist.:* Ill., Ky., Tenn. *1st cit.:* US1831 *Journals of Ralph Waldo Emerson,* eds. Emerson and Forbes (1909–14). *20c. coll.:* T&W 409, Stevenson 2564:8, Whiting(MP) 694.

40. They all know what to do with a bad wife but he who's got one. *Rec. dist.:* Utah. *1st cit.:* 1621 Burton, *Anatomy of Melancholy.* *20c. coll.:* ODEP 687, Stevenson 2497:8.

41. Where there is no wife there is no home. *Rec. dist.:* Ont.

42. Who finds a wife finds a good thing. *Rec. dist.:* N.Y. *1st cit.:* US1948 Stevenson, *Home Book of Proverbs.* *20c. coll.:* Stevenson 2503:1.

43. Who is the wife of one cannot eat the rice of two. *Rec. dist.:* Ind.

44. Wife make your own candle, spare penny to handle. *Rec. dist.:* N.Y. *1st cit.:* US1940 Thompson, *Body, Boots, and Britches.* *20c. coll.:* Stevenson 282:1.

SEE ALSO An old BACHELOR is fussy because he has never had a wife to fuss at him. / From the BLACK man keep your wife; with a red man beware your knife. / The BLIND man's wife needs no painting. / When a man's a FOOL, his wife will rule. / Take a FRIEND for what he does, a wife for what she has, and goods for what they are worth. / Three faithful FRIENDS: an old wife, an old dog, and ready money. / A little HOUSE well filled, a little land well tilled, and a little wife well willed are great riches. / A deaf HUSBAND and a blind wife are always a happy couple. / Motherless HUSBAND makes happy wife. / The HUSBAND is the head of the house, but the wife is the neck and the neck moves the head. / When the HUSBAND earns well, the wife spends well. / The calmest HUSBANDS make the stormiest wives. / Go down the LADDER for a wife; go up the ladder for a friend. / A good MAID sometimes makes a bad wife. / A neat MAIDEN often makes a dirty wife. / A MAN who is wise is only as wise as his wife thinks he is. / A MAN without a wife is but half a man. / When a MAN takes a wife, he ceases to dread hell. / NEED makes the old wife trot. / You cannot pluck ROSES without fear of thorns nor enjoy a fair wife without danger of horns. / The TAILOR's wife is worst clad. / An UGLY man never gets a pretty wife. / He that goes a great WAY for a wife is either cheating or means to cheat. / Many a man sees a WOLF at the door because his wife saw a mink in the window.

wild SEE The wilder the COLT, the better the horse. / Domestic FRUIT will not grow on a wild tree.

will *(n., document)* **1.** Where there's a will, there's a lawsuit. *Rec. dist.:* Miss.

2. Where there's a will, there's relatives. *Rec. dist.:* Ohio.

SEE ALSO A fat KITCHEN makes a lean will.

will *(n., volition)* **1.** A man convinced against his will is of the same opinion still. *Vars.:* **(a)** A man convinced against his will is of his own opinion still. **(b)** A woman convinced against her will is of the same opinion still. **(c)** Persuade a man against his will—he's of the same opinion still. *Rec. dist.:* U.S., Can. *1st cit.:* 1678 Butler, *Hudibras.* *20c. coll.:* ODEP 139, CODP 41, Stevenson 1719:10.

2. A man's will is his heaven. *Rec. dist.:* Ont.

3. A will of your own will help you to succeed better than the will of a rich relative. *Rec. dist.:* N.Y.

4. Let your will roar when your power can but whisper. *Rec. dist.:* N.Y. *1st cit.:* ca1650 Fuller, *Introductio ad Prudentiam.* *20c. coll.:* Stevenson 2508:11.

5. One's own will is good food. *Rec. dist.:* Ont.

6. We may do as we will if we have the will. *Rec. dist.:* Utah. *1st cit.:* US1859 Smiles, *Self-Help.* *20c. coll.:* Stevenson 2510:6.

7. Where the will is ready the feet are light.

Rec. dist.: Ont. *1st cit.:* 1640 Herbert, *Outlandish Proverbs (Jacula Prudentum)* in *Works,* ed. Hutchinson (1941). *20c. coll.:* ODEP 890, Stevenson 2511:4.

8. Where there's a will there's a way. *Rec. dist.:* U.S., Can. *1st cit.:* 1640 Herbert, *Outlandish Proverbs (Jacula Prudentum)* in *Works,* ed. Hutchinson (1941); US1838 Conant, *Earnest Man.* *20c. coll.:* ODEP 891, T&W 402, CODP 245, Stevenson 2510:12, Whiting(MP) 683.

9. Will is character in action. *Rec. dist.:* Ill.

SEE ALSO MAN has his will, but woman has her way.

will *(v.)* **1.** He that will not when he may, when he will he may have nay. *Rec. dist.:* U.S., Can. *1st cit.:* ca1000 *Anglo-Saxon Homily* in *Early English Proverbs,* ed. Skeat. *20c. coll.:* ODEP 890, CODP 245, Stevenson 1724:2, Whiting(MP) 684.

2. If you will, others will let you. *Var.:* If you will, you can. *Rec. dist.:* Ont.

3. To him that wills, ways are not wanting. *Rec. dist.:* N.Y. *1st cit.:* 1692 South, *Twelve Sermons.* *20c. coll.:* ODEP 891.

SEE ALSO What will BE will be. / Bury CAN'T and you'll find will. / If one will not, another will, so are all MAIDENS wed. / SPEAK fair, think what you will. / I'll TRY it is a soldier; I will is a king.

willful SEE Willful WASTE makes woeful want. / Willful WAYS make woeful want.

willing The world is full of willing people—some willing to work and the rest willing to let them. *Rec. dist.:* Okla.

SEE ALSO The FATES lead the willing man; the unwilling they drag. / Don't overwork a willing HORSE. / The willing HORSE carries the load. / The willing HORSE gets the whip. / A willing MIND makes a light foot.

willow **1.** Bend the willow while it's young. *Rec. dist.:* Ont.

2. Willows are weak, but they bind other wood. *Rec. dist.:* Ont. *1st cit.:* 1640 Herbert, *Outlandish Proverbs (Jacula Prudentum)* in *Works,* ed. Hutchinson (1941); US1754 Franklin,

PRAlmanac. **20c. coll.:** *ODEP* 891, Whiting 484, Stevenson 2511:10.

win **1.** Never too late to win. **Rec. dist.:** Ont.

2. Those can win who think they can. **Rec. dist.:** Calif., Colo., N.Y., Wis.

3. Who never wins can rarely lose; who never climbs as rarely falls. **Rec. dist.:** N.Y.

4. You always win if you can lose with a smile. **Var.:** You always win if you lose with a smile. **Rec. dist.:** Ont.

5. You win a few and you lose a few. **Rec. dist.:** U.S., Can. **1st cit.:** 1897 Kipling, *Captains Courageous.* **20c. coll.:** *CODP* 246.

SEE ALSO The more ARGUMENTS you win, the less friends you will have. / A CARD which never appears neither wins nor loses. / He that would the DAUGHTER win would with the mother begin. / No FIGHT, no win. / Let them LAUGH that win. / No matter who loses, the LAWYER always wins. / LIFE's a gamble: you win or lose. / LOSE as if you like it; win as if you were used to it. / SLOW and easy wins the race. / The last SUITOR wins the maid. / He who never TRIES anything will never win. / The VOICE with a smile always wins. / A WINNER never quits, and a quitter never wins. / 'Tis better to lose with a WISE man than to win with a fool.

wind **1.** A little wind kindles a big flame. **Rec. dist.:** Fla., Ind. **1st cit.:** 1586 Guazzo, *Civile Conversation,* tr. Pettie, T.T. (1925). **20c. coll.:** *ODEP* 472, Stevenson 2514:12.

2. An ill wind blows no good. **Vars.:** **(a)** It is an ill wind that blows no one any good. **(b)** It is an ill wind that blows nobody any good. **(c)** It's an ill wind that blows no good. **(d)** It's an ill wind that blows nobody good. **(e)** Never an ill wind blows but that it doesn't do someone some good. **Rec. dist.:** U.S., Can. **1st cit.:** 1546 Heywood, *Dialogue of Proverbs,* ed. Habernicht (1963); US1739 *Letters of James Murray, Loyalist,* ed. Tiffany (1901). **20c. coll.:** *ODEP* 401, Whiting 486, *CODP* 120, Stevenson 2512:4, T&W 403, Whiting(MP) 685.

3. As the wind blows, set your sails. **Rec. dist.:** Minn., N.Y. **1st cit.:** 1574 Baret, *Alvearie.* **20c. coll.:** Stevenson 2025:1, *ODEP* 893.

4. As the wind blows, so bends the twig. **Var.:** As the wind blows, so the tree lists. **Rec. dist.:** Okla.

5. Back the wind and front the sun. **Rec. dist.:** U.S., Can. **Infm.:** Chief Sherer of Marquette, Mich. Coast Guard Station notes this is an old mariners' rule for running from a storm or gale: the wind brings the bad weather and the sun indicates good weather. It is also used to mean "run from trouble."

6. Every wind has its weather. **Rec. dist.:** Calif., Colo., N.Y.

7. If we go with the wind, we shall soon be gone with the wind. **Rec. dist.:** Ont.

8. If wind blows on you through a hole, say your prayers and mind your soul. **Rec. dist.:** N.Y. **1st cit.:** US1736 *Papers of Benjamin Franklin,* ed. Labaree (1959). **20c. coll.:** *ODEP* 133, Whiting 485, Stevenson 2513:10.

9. If you sail with a bad wind, you must needs understand tacking. **Rec. dist.:** Ont.

10. It's a bad wind that never changes. **Rec. dist.:** Fla. **1st cit.:** US1830 Ames, *Mariner's Sketches.* **20c. coll.:** Whiting 485.

11. Look and see which way the wind blows before you commit yourself. **Rec. dist.:** Ark. **1st cit.:** 1546 Heywood, *Dialogue of Proverbs,* ed. Habernicht (1963); US1642 Jordan in *Documentary History of Maine, Containing Trelawny Papers,* ed. Baxter (1884). **20c. coll.:** *ODEP* 436, Whiting 487, Stevenson 2515:1, T&W 404.

12. No wind can do him good who steers for no port. **Var.:** No wind is of service to him who is bound for nowhere. **Rec. dist.:** Ont. **1st cit.:** 1613 Overbury, *News from Sea;* US1917 Seitz, *In Praise of War.* **20c. coll.:** Stevenson 2515:5.

13. Puff not against the wind. **Rec. dist.:** Tex. **1st cit.:** 1509 Barclay, *Ship of Fools,* ed. Jamieson in *Eclogues,* E.E.T.S. (1874). **20c. coll.:** *ODEP* 653, Stevenson 2514:7.

14. Slow wind also brings the ship to harbor. **Rec. dist.:** Ont. **1st cit.:** 1580 Lyly, *Euphues and His England.* **20c. coll.:** Stevenson 2092:1.

15. Sow the wind and reap the whirlwind. **Var.:** If you sow the wind you reap the whirlwind. *Rec. dist.*: U.S., Can. *1st cit.*: 1583 Prime, *Fruitful and Brief Discourse;* US1853 Curtis, *Potiphar Papers.* *20c. coll.*: ODEP 757, T&W 404, CODP 208, Stevenson 2179:1, Whiting*(MP)* 687.

16. The colder the wind, the warmer the hearth. *Rec. dist.*: Ont.

17. The harder the wind, the deeper the oak becomes rooted. *Rec. dist.*: N.C. *1st cit.*: 1640 Herbert, *Outlandish Proverbs (Jacula Prudentum)* in *Works,* ed. Hutchinson (1941). *20c. coll.*: Stevenson 2369:10.

18. The same wind which extinguishes a small love kindles a great one. *Rec. dist.*: Ill.

19. The wind blows easily through a leafless tree. *Rec. dist.*: Ala., Ga.

20. The wind is fresh and free. *Rec. dist.*: Ont.

21. Whatever way the wind does blow, some hearts are glad to have it so. *Rec. dist.*: Ont.

22. Where there's a wind there's a wave. *Rec. dist.*: N.Y., Ont.

23. Who spits against the wind spits in his own face. *Rec. dist.*: Wis. *1st cit.*: 1557 North, *Dialogue of Princes;* US1757 Franklin, *Papers of Benjamin Franklin,* ed. Labaree (1959). *20c. coll.*: ODEP 766, Whiting 485, Stevenson 2199:8, T&W 405, Whiting*(MP)* 686.

24. Wind and tide wait for no man. *Rec. dist.*: N.Y.

25. Wind before rain, take your topsail down; rain before wind, put them up again. *Rec. dist.*: U.S., Can. *1st cit.*: 1853 *Notes and Queries.* *20c. coll.*: ODEP 662.

26. Wind precedes a storm. *Rec. dist.*: Wis. *1st cit.*: 1539 Taverner, *Proverbs of Erasmus.* *20c. coll.*: ODEP 820, Stevenson 2516:4.

27. You can't hinder the wind from blowing. *Rec. dist.*: N.Y. *1st cit.*: US1776 *Writings of George Washington,* ed. Fitzpatrick (1931–44). *20c. coll.*: Whiting 488.

SEE ALSO ANGER is a wind that blows out the light of the mind. / Leave your CARES to the wind. / GOD tempers the wind to the shorn lamb. / MARCH winds and April showers bring May flowers. / No WEATHER's ill if the wind be still.

window **1.** He whose windows are of glass should never throw stones. *Var.*: Don't throw stones at your neighbors if your own windows are glass. *Rec. dist.*: N.Y. *1st cit.*: ca1374 Chaucer, *Troilus and Criseyde;* US1710 Dummer in *William & Mary Coll. Quart.* (1967). *20c. coll.*: ODEP 360, Whiting 225, CODP 92, Stevenson 1193:4, T&W 194.

2. When you are washing windows, do the corners first and the center will take care of itself. *Rec. dist.*: Ill.

SEE ALSO The EYES are the windows of the soul. / A HOME without books is like a house without windows. / JUSTICE goes out the window when profit comes in. / When want comes in at the door, LOVE flies out of the window.

wine **1.** Don't pour new wine in old bottles. *Var.*: Don't put new wine in old bottles. *Rec. dist.*: U.S., Can. *1st cit.*: 1912 Strachey, *Landmarks in French Literature.* *20c. coll.*: CODP 161, Stevenson 2519:4.

2. Drink wine and have the gout; drink none and have it too. *Rec. dist.*: Ont. *1st cit.*: 1584 Cogan, *Haven of Health.* *20c. coll.*: ODEP 203, Stevenson 1013:2.

3. Good is the man who refrains from wine. *Rec. dist.*: N.C.

4. Good wine needs no bush. *Rec. dist.*: U.S., Can. *1st cit.*: ca1426 Lydgate, *Pilgrimage of Man,* E.E.T.S. (1899); US1666 Alsop, *Character of Province of Maryland,* ed. Mereness (1902). *20c. coll.*: ODEP 326, Whiting 488, CODP 99, Stevenson 2518:2, T&W 405, Whiting*(MP)* 688.

5. If wine tells truth, and so have said the wise, it makes me laugh to think how brandy lies. *Rec. dist.*: N.Y. *1st cit.*: US1850 Holmes, *Banker's Secret.* *20c. coll.*: Stevenson 2525:3.

6. In wine there is truth. *Rec. dist.*: U.S., Can. *1st cit.*: 1545 Erasmus, *Adages,* tr. Taverner; US1755 Franklin, *PRAlmanac.* *20c. coll.*: ODEP 896, Whiting 488, CODP 231, Stevenson 2524:3, T&W 384, Whiting*(MP)* 688.

7. Never spare the parson's wine nor the baker's pudding. *Rec. dist.*: N.Y. *1st cit.*: US1733 Franklin, *PRAlmanac.* *20c. coll.*: Whiting 327, Stevenson 580:5.

8. Sweet's the wine, but sour's the payment. *Rec. dist.:* Ont.

9. Take counsel in wine, but resolve afterwards in water. *Rec. dist.:* N.Y. *1st cit.:* US1733 Franklin, *PRAlmanac.* *20c. coll.:* Stevenson 2522:4.

10. The sweetest wine makes the sharpest vinegar. *Rec. dist.:* Tex. *1st cit.:* 1566 Painter, *Palace of Pleasure,* ed. Jacobs (1890). *20c. coll.:* Stevenson 2519:8, *ODEP* 860, *CODP* 219.

11. The wine of life comes not from battles but from bottles. *Rec. dist.:* N.C.

12. When wine is in, wit is out. *Rec. dist.:* U.S., Can. *1st cit.:* ca1386 Chaucer, *Pardoner's Tale;* US1813 Eaton, *Life of Gen. William Eaton.* *20c. coll.:* *ODEP* 895, Whiting 488, *CODP* 247, Stevenson 2523:7, T&W 406, Whiting(MP) 688.

13. When wine sinks, words swim. *Rec. dist.:* Md., Ont. *1st cit.:* 1721 Kelly, *Scottish Proverbs.* *20c. coll.:* *ODEP* 896, Stevenson 2524:1.

14. Wine and women don't mix. *Rec. dist.:* Ala., Ga.

15. Wine and youth are flax upon fire. *Rec. dist.:* Ont. *1st cit.:* 1580 Lyly, *Euphues and His England.* *20c. coll.:* Stevenson 2521:2.

16. Wine has drowned more men than the sea. *Rec. dist.:* N.Y., Tex. *1st cit.:* 1669 Ling, *Politeuphuia;* US1763 Ames, *Almanacs,* ed. Briggs (1891). *20c. coll.:* Stevenson 2523:4, Whiting 489.

17. Wine is a mocker. *Rec. dist.:* N.C. *1st cit.:* US1948 Stevenson, *Home Book of Proverbs.* *20c. coll.:* Stevenson 2523:2.

18. Wine is the discoverer of secrets. *Rec. dist.:* Ind. *1st cit.:* 1616 Raleigh, *Instructions to His Son.* *20c. coll.:* Stevenson 2524:1.

19. Wine makes all sorts of creatures at the table. *Rec. dist.:* N.Y. *1st cit.:* 1640 Herbert, *Outlandish Proverbs (Jacula Prudentum) in Works,* ed. Hutchinson (1941). *20c. coll.:* *ODEP* 896.

20. Wine on beer brings good cheer; beer on wine is not so fine. *Rec. dist.:* Wis. *1st cit.:* 1586 Evans, *Withals Dictionary Revised.* *20c. coll.:* Stevenson 146:12.

21. Wine's fine with a line. *Rec. dist.:* Wis.

22. Wine, women, and song will get a man wrong. *Rec. dist.:* N.C. *1st cit.:* 1580 Lyly, *Euphues and His England.* *20c. coll.:* *ODEP* 632, Stevenson 2526:4.

SEE ALSO BEER before wine, you'll feel fine; wine before beer, you'll feel queer. / It is better to have BREAD left over than run short of wine. / Sour GRAPES can never make sweet wine. / INTOXICATION is not the wine's fault, but the man's. / JOY is the best wine. / Every TUB smells of the wine it holds. / Beware of VINEGAR made of sweet wine. / Pure WATER is better than bad wine.

wing **1.** Unused wings cannot soar. *Rec. dist.:* Ont.

2. You cannot fly with one wing. *Rec. dist.:* Ont. *1st cit.:* 1721 Kelly, *Scottish Proverbs.* *20c. coll.:* *CODP* 19, Stevenson 179:1.

SEE ALSO Speak of ANGELS and you'll hear the rustling of their wings. / ANTS live safely till they have gotten wings. / FRIENDSHIP is love without its wings. / If FROGS had wings, they wouldn't bump their asses on rocks. / JOYS are our wings; our sorrows, our spurs. / LIARS have short wings. / The LORD knows when to clip our wings. / If a PIG had wings he might fly. / RICHES have wings.

winged *SEE* WELL married, a man is winged; ill matched, he is shackled.

wink *(n.)* *SEE* There is as much MALICE in a wink as in a word. / A NOD is as good as a wink to a blind horse.

wink *(v.)* *SEE* Wink at small FAULTS.

winker All winkers are not blind. *Rec. dist.:* Utah. *1st cit.:* ca1570 *Ancient Ballads,* ed. Huth. *20c. coll.:* Stevenson 2527:10.

winner **1.** A winner never quits, and a quitter never wins. *Var.:* A quitter never wins, and a winner never quits. *Rec. dist.:* U.S., Can.

2. All the world loves a winner. *Rec. dist.:* Calif., N.J., N.Y.

3. First winner, last loser. *Rec. dist.:* Ont.

4. It is just as hard to be a good winner as to be a good loser. *Rec. dist.:* N.C.

SEE ALSO A KNOCKER never wins and a

winner never knocks. / A good LOSER never wins. / Better to be a good LOSER than a poor winner. / The cheerful LOSER is a winner.

winter *(n.)* **1.** A green winter, a full grave-yard. *Var.:* A green winter makes a fat church yard. *Rec. dist.:* U.S., Can. *1st cit.:* 1635 Swan, *Speculum Mundi.* *20c. coll.:* ODEP 337, CODP 102, Stevenson 2530:4.

2. A hard winter makes a good crop year. *Rec. dist.:* N.Y.

3. A misty winter brings a pleasant spring; a pleasant winter, a misty spring. *Rec. dist.:* Miss.

4. After a rainy winter follows a fruitful spring. *Rec. dist.:* Ark.

5. Snowy winter, plentiful harvest. *Rec. dist.:* N.Y. *1st cit.:* US1733 Franklin, *PRAlmanac.* *20c. coll.:* Whiting 489.

6. 'Tis a hard winter when one wolf eats another. *Rec. dist.:* Okla. *1st cit.:* 1579 Lyly, *Euphues and His England;* US1806 Tracy in *Life and Correspondence of Rufus King,* ed. King (1894–1900). *20c. coll.:* ODEP 353, Whiting 489, Stevenson 2553:5.

7. Winter comes but once a year, and when it comes, it brings the doctor good cheer. *Rec. dist.:* N.Y. *1st cit.:* US1948 Stevenson, *Home Book of Proverbs.* *20c. coll.:* Stevenson 2530:4.

8. Winter eats what summer gets. *Vars.:* **(a)** Winter discovers what summer conceals. **(b)** Winter finds out what summer lays up. *Rec. dist.:* Ill., Mich. *1st cit.:* ca1450 *Gode Wyfe Wolde a Pylgrimage;* US1744 Ames, *Almanacs,* ed. Briggs (1891). *20c. coll.:* ODEP 897, Whiting 489, Stevenson 2530:7.

9. Winter weather and women's thoughts change often. *Rec. dist.:* Ill. *1st cit.:* ca1450 *Songs and Carols.* *20c. coll.:* Stevenson 316:4.

SEE ALSO The CUCKOO of summer is the scald crow of winter. / A winter's THUNDER is a summer's hunger. / THUNDER in the fall, no winter at all.

winter *(v.)* You have to winter and summer with people to know them. *Var.:* You don't know a person until you winter and summer with him. *Rec. dist.:* N.Y. *1st cit.:* US1713 Wise, *Churches Quarrel Espoused,* ed. Cook

(1966). *20c. coll.:* Whiting 489, T&W 407, Whiting(MP) 690.

wipe SEE What is SAID is said, and no sponge can wipe it out.

wire Be a live wire and you won't be stepped on. *Var.:* A live wire never gets stepped on. *Rec. dist.:* N.Y., Ont. *Infm.:* "Live wire" refers to an active person.

wisdom **1.** A man shall be commended by his wisdom. *Rec. dist.:* Ont.

2. A man with wisdom is better off than a stupid man with any amount of charm and superstition. *Rec. dist.:* W.Va.

3. An ounce of wisdom is worth a pound of wit. *Rec. dist.:* U.S., Can. *1st cit.:* 1548 Hall, *Chronicle of Lancastre and York;* US1771 *Diary and Autobiography of John Adams,* ed. Butterfield (1961). *20c. coll.:* ODEP 601, Whiting 323, CODP 172, Stevenson 2534:8, T&W 271, Whiting(MP) 465.

4. Bought wisdom is best if you don't pay too dear for it. *Rec. dist.:* Ohio.

5. Happy is the man that finds wisdom and that gets understanding. *Rec. dist.:* Wis.

6. If wisdom's ways you wisely seek, five things observe with care: of whom you speak, to whom you speak, how, when, and where. *Rec. dist.:* N.J., N.Y.

7. It needs great wisdom to play the fool. *Rec. dist.:* Ill. *1st cit.:* 1574 Guazzo, *Civile Conversation,* tr. Pettie, T.T. (1925); US1921 Thorne, *Sheridan Road Mystery.* *20c. coll.:* Stevenson 859:4, Whiting(MP) 690.

8. Learn wisdom by the follies of others. *Rec. dist.:* Ill., Ont. *1st cit.:* 1855 Bohn, *Handbook of Proverbs.* *20c. coll.:* Stevenson 2541:6.

9. Nine-tenths of wisdom consists in being wise in time. *Rec. dist.:* N.Y. *1st cit.:* US1917 Roosevelt, Speech, Lincoln, Nebr., 14 June. *20c. coll.:* Stevenson 2540:4.

10. No wisdom like silence. *Rec. dist.:* N.Y. *1st cit.:* 1620 J.C., *Two Merry Milkmaids.* *20c. coll.:* ODEP 898, Stevenson 2110:5.

11. The doors of wisdom are never shut. *Rec. dist.:* Ill. *1st cit.:* US1755 Franklin, *PRAlmanac.* *20c. coll.:* Stevenson 2534:3.

12. Through wisdom is a house built, and by

understanding is it established. *Rec. dist.:* Ont. *1st cit.:* US1948 Stevenson, *Home Book of Proverbs. 20c. coll.:* Stevenson 2538:1.

13. When wisdom fails, luck helps. *Rec. dist.:* Ill.

14. Wisdom brings knowledge. *Rec. dist.:* Ont.

15. Wisdom doesn't always speak in Greek and Latin. *Rec. dist.:* Ill. *1st cit.:* 1732 Fuller, *Gnomologia. 20c. coll.:* Stevenson 2533:6.

16. Wisdom goes not always by years. *Rec. dist.:* N.Y. *1st cit.:* 1732 Fuller, *Gnomologia. 20c. coll.:* Stevenson 2534:4.

17. Wisdom in a poor man is a diamond set in lead. *Rec. dist.:* Ill. *1st cit.:* 1732 Fuller, *Gnomologia. 20c. coll.:* Stevenson 2536:8.

18. Wisdom is better than rubies. *Vars.:* **(a)** Wisdom is better than riches. **(b)** Wisdom is better than wealth. *Rec. dist.:* U.S., Can. *1st cit.:* 1590 Greene, *Never Too Late;* US1702 Taylor, *Christographia,* ed. Grabo (1963). *20c. coll.:* Stevenson 2537:10, Whiting 490.

19. Wisdom is ever a blessing; education is sometimes a curse. *Rec. dist.:* N.Y. *1st cit.:* US1928 Shedd, *Salt from My Attic. 20c. coll.:* Stevenson 669:2.

20. Wisdom is the principal thing; therefore get wisdom, and with all your getting get understanding. *Rec. dist.:* N.Y. *1st cit.:* US1948 Stevenson, *Home Book of Proverbs. 20c. coll.:* Stevenson 2538:1.

21. Wisdom is too high for a fool. *Rec. dist.:* Ont.

22. Wisdom never lies. *Rec. dist.:* Ill.

23. Wisdom of many and the wit of one. *Rec. dist.:* Ont. *1st cit.:* ca1850 Russell, Apothegm in Macintosh, *Memoirs. 20c. coll.:* Stevenson 1906:1.

24. Wisdom promises godliness and safety. *Rec. dist.:* Ont.

SEE ALSO With AGE comes wisdom. / AUTHORITY without wisdom is like a heavy axe without an edge: fitter to bruise than to polish. / From the mouths of BABES come words of wisdom. / CUNNING is the dwarf of wisdom. / EXPERIENCE is the father of wisdom and memory the mother. / EXPERIENCE teaches

wisdom unto fools. / FEAR of the Lord is the beginning of wisdom. / It is the ordinary way of the world to keep FOLLY at the helm and wisdom under the hatches. / It is as sport to a FOOL to do mischief, but a man of understanding has wisdom. / FOOLS despise wisdom and instruction. / IGNORANCE and bungling with love are better than wisdom and skill without. / A common JESTER may have wit but not wisdom. / KNOWLEDGE and wisdom are far from being one. / KNOWLEDGE comes, but wisdom lingers. / A pocketful of LUCK is better than a sackful of wisdom. / PROVERBS are the wisdom of nations. / SELF-INTEREST is the beginning of wisdom. / SILENCE is not always a sign of wisdom, but babbling is ever a folly. / SILENCE is wisdom when speaking is folly. / It is not WEALTH but wisdom that makes a man rich. / The WISE man hides his wisdom; the fool displays his foolishness. / The WISE seek wisdom; the fool has found it. / If you have WIT and learning, add to it wisdom and modesty. / It is WIT to pick a lock and steal a horse, but wisdom to let it alone. / A flow of WORDS is no proof of wisdom. / Not by YEARS but by disposition is wisdom acquired.

wise *(n.)* **1.** The lips of the wise disperse knowledge. *Rec. dist.:* Ont.

2. The wise and the fool have their fellows. *Rec. dist.:* Ont. *1st cit.:* 1659 Howell, *Paroimiografia (English Proverbs). 20c. coll.:* Stevenson 857:9.

3. The wise is only once betrayed. *Rec. dist.:* N.J.

4. The wise seek wisdom; the fool has found it. *Rec. dist.:* Ill.

5. The wise shall inherit glory, but shame shall be the promotion of fools. *Var.:* The wise shall inherit glory. *Rec. dist.:* Ont. *1st cit.:* US1948 Stevenson, *Home Book of Proverbs. 20c. coll.:* Stevenson 858:1.

6. When the wise is angry, he is wise no longer. *Rec. dist.:* Ont.

SEE ALSO ADVICE is something the wise don't need and the fools won't take. / The BRAVE and the wise can both pity and excuse when cowards and fools show no mercy. / It takes the FOOLISH to confound the wise. / A WORD to the wise is sufficient.

wise *(adj.)* **1.** A little too wise ne'er lives long. *Rec. dist.:* Ala., Ga. *1st cit.:* 1607 Middleton, *Phoenix.* *20c. coll.:* ODEP 832, Stevenson 525:5.

2. A man who is wise is only as wise as his wife thinks he is. *Rec. dist.:* Wis.

3. A wise man always carries his umbrella. *Rec. dist.:* Ky., Tenn.

4. A wise man carries his coat on a dry day. *Rec. dist.:* N.Mex.

5. A wise man changes his mind; a fool never does. *Vars.:* **(a)** A wise man changes his mind often, but a fool never does. **(b)** A wise man changes his mind, but a fool never does. **(c)** A wise man often changes his mind; a fool never does. **(d)** A wise man will change his mind, but a fool never will. **(e)** Wise men change their minds; fools never do. *Rec. dist.:* U.S., Can. *1st cit.:* ca1386 Chaucer, *Tale of Melibee;* US1871 Jones, *Life of Jefferson S. Batkins.* *20c. coll.:* ODEP 900, T&W 236, Stevenson 857:14, Whiting(*MP*) 402.

6. A wise man has wise children. *Rec. dist.:* Kans.

7. A wise man is never less alone than when alone. *Rec. dist.:* Miss. *1st cit.:* ca1555 *Songs and Ballads, Philip and Mary,* Roxbury Club. *20c. coll.:* ODEP 900.

8. A wise man is nobody's fool. *Rec. dist.:* Ky., Tenn.

9. A wise man is one who keeps his peace. *Var.:* It's a wise man who holds his peace. *Rec. dist.:* Ind.

10. A wise man is strong. *Rec. dist.:* N.Y. *1st cit.:* US1948 Stevenson, *Home Book of Proverbs.* *20c. coll.:* Stevenson 2538:1.

11. A wise man knows his own ignorance; a fool thinks he knows. *Rec. dist.:* Ont.

12. A wise man learns by the experiences of others; an ordinary man learns by his own experience; a fool learns by nobody's experiences. *Rec. dist.:* N.Y.

13. A wise man sees twice as much as he talks about. *Rec. dist.:* N.C.

14. A wise man thinks twice before he speaks. *Rec. dist.:* Ind.

15. A wise man will learn. *Rec. dist.:* Ont.

16. A wise man will make more opportunities than he finds. *Var.:* Wise men make more opportunities than they find. *Rec. dist.:* Ind., N.Y. *1st cit.:* 1732 Fuller, *Gnomologia.* *20c. coll.:* Stevenson 2534:4.

17. A wise man will saw wood and say nothing. *Rec. dist.:* Colo.

18. A wise man without work is a bee without honey. *Rec. dist.:* Calif.

19. A wise man writes for pleasure; a fool reads because he is curious. *Rec. dist.:* Ont.

20. A wise woman never outsmarts her husband. *Rec. dist.:* N.Y.

21. Any wise man can be fooled by a foolish woman. *Rec. dist.:* N.Y.

22. Be wise today; 'tis madness to defer. *Rec. dist.:* Ont. *1st cit.:* 1742 Young, *Night Thoughts.* *20c. coll.:* Stevenson 2535:4.

23. Follow the wise few rather than the vulgar many. *Rec. dist.:* Ill.

24. Go where he will, a wise man is always at home. *Rec. dist.:* N.Y. *1st cit.:* US1867 Emerson, *Woodnotes.* *20c. coll.:* Stevenson 2533:13.

25. He is a wise man who knows more today than he did yesterday. *Rec. dist.:* Mich., N.Y.

26. He is not wise who is not wise for himself. *Rec. dist.:* Okla. *1st cit.:* ca1532 *Tales and Quick Answers.* *20c. coll.:* ODEP 902, Stevenson 2539:7.

27. He is wise enough that can keep himself warm. *Rec. dist.:* N.Y. *1st cit.:* 1537 *Thersites.* *20c. coll.:* ODEP 899, Stevenson 2534:11.

28. He is wise who speaks little. *Vars.:* **(a)** He is a wise man who speaks little. **(b)** He is wise who talks but little. *Rec. dist.:* Ill., Ont.

29. He that walks with a wise man shall be wise, but a companion of fools shall be destroyed. *Rec. dist.:* N.Y. *1st cit.:* US1948 Stevenson, *Home Book of Proverbs.* *20c. coll.:* Stevenson 387:4.

30. He who thinks he is wise is a fool; he who

knows he is a fool is wise. *Rec. dist.:* Ind. *1st cit.:* 1599 Shakespeare, *As You Like It.* *20c. coll.:* Stevenson 855:7.

31. It is better to sit with a wise man in prison than with a fool in paradise. *Rec. dist.:* Ont.

32. It takes a wise man to be a fool. *Var.:* It takes a wise man to act the goat. *Rec. dist.:* Ont. *1st cit.:* ca1500 *Proverbs at Wressell,* British Museum MS 18 in *Antiquarian Repertory* (1809). *20c. coll.:* ODEP 900, Stevenson 859:4.

33. It takes a wise man to find a wise man. *Rec. dist.:* N.Y. *1st cit.:* US1948 Stevenson, *Home Book of Proverbs.* *20c. coll.:* Stevenson 2539:4.

34. It's a wise man who knows his own limitations. *Rec. dist.:* Ind.

35. Many seem wise when they are only windy. *Rec. dist.:* Ont.

36. No man is always wise. *Rec. dist.:* Ill., N.Y. *1st cit.:* 1481 Caxton, *Reynard the Fox.* *20c. coll.:* ODEP 571, Stevenson 2537:8.

37. None but the wise man can employ leisure well. *Rec. dist.:* Ont.

38. None so wise but the fool overtakes him. *Rec. dist.:* Tex. *1st cit.:* 1640 Herbert, *Outlandish Proverbs (Jacula Prudentum)* in *Works,* ed. Hutchinson (1941). *20c. coll.:* ODEP 899, Stevenson 857:12.

39. Some are wise and some are otherwise. *Rec. dist.:* Ont. *1st cit.:* 1601 Jonson, *Poetaster.* *20c. coll.:* ODEP 751, Stevenson 2535:7.

40. Something said by a wise man may be made fun of by a fool. *Rec. dist.:* Ont.

41. The wise man hides his wisdom; the fool displays his foolishness. *Rec. dist.:* N.Y.

42. The wise man said, "It can't be done"; the fool came and did it. *Rec. dist.:* Ky., Tenn.

43. The wisest man is he who does not fancy he is wise at all. *Rec. dist.:* Ont. *1st cit.:* US1948 Stevenson, *Home Book of Proverbs.* *20c. coll.:* Stevenson 2534:9.

44. The wisest man may always learn something from the humblest peasant. *Rec. dist.:* Ind.

45. 'Tis better to lose with a wise man than to win with a fool. *Rec. dist.:* N.Y.

46. To a wise head, two or three words. *Rec. dist.:* N.Y.

47. Who is wise is he that learns from everyone. *Rec. dist.:* Miss. *1st cit.:* US1948 Stevenson, *Home Book of Proverbs.* *20c. coll.:* Stevenson 2531:12.

48. Wise is he who knows himself and has the strength of will not to have another drink when he has had his fill. *Rec. dist.:* Ill.

49. Wise men care not for what they cannot have. *Rec. dist.:* N.Y. *1st cit.:* 1640 Herbert, *Outlandish Proverbs (Jacula Prudentum)* in *Works,* ed. Hutchinson (1941). *20c. coll.:* ODEP 900, Stevenson 2534:10.

50. Wise men excuse others; fools excuse themselves. *Rec. dist.:* Ind.

51. Wise men keep guard on their tongue. *Rec. dist.:* Ont.

52. Wise men lay up knowledge. *Rec. dist.:* Ont.

53. Wise men learn by other men's mistakes; fools insist on learning by their own. *Rec. dist.:* Calif., Colo., Ill., Mich., N.Y. *1st cit.:* ca1374 Chaucer, *Troilus and Criseyde;* US1743 Franklin, *PRAlmanac.* *20c. coll.:* ODEP 901, Whiting 199, Stevenson 724:13.

SEE ALSO If what men most ADMIRE they would despise, 'twould look like mankind were growing wise. / ADVERSITY makes a man wise, but not rich. / Consider the ANT, you sluggard, and be wise. / Early to BED and early to rise makes a man healthy, wealthy, and wise. / Using our BRAINS is often wiser than depending on our strength. / It is a wise CHILD that knows its own father. / After CROSSES and losses, men grow humbler and wiser. / The CUNNING man steals a horse; the wise man lets him alone. / After the DANGER everyone is wise. / A DRUNKEN man will get sober, but a fool never gets wise. / It's a wise FATHER who knows his own son. / A FISHERMAN, once stung, will be wiser. / A FOOL can ask more questions in a minute than a wise man can answer in an hour. / A FOOL might be counted wise if he kept his mouth shut. / A FOOL says I can't. A wise man says I'll try. / A FOOL talks while a wise man thinks. / A silent FOOL is a wise fool. / He is a FOOL who cannot be angry, but he is wise who will not. / The FOOL wanders; the wise man travels. / FOOLS are wise men in the affairs of women. / FOOLS build houses for wise men to live in. / FOOLS make feasts and wise men eat them. / GREAT men are not always wise. / You are never too wise to LEARN. / MISFORTUNES make us wise. / PENNY-WISE, pound-foolish. / RICHES serve a wise man, but command a fool. / A wise SON makes a glad father, but a foolish son is the heaviness of his mother. / Wise use of TIME will make for wiser living. / A still TONGUE makes a wise head. / VOCABULARY is the tool of wise men. / It takes a wise WOMAN to be an old maid.

wisely Not wisely but too well. *Rec. dist.:* N.Y. *1st cit.:* 1605 Shakespeare, *Othello*. *20c. coll.:* Stevenson 1475:1.

SEE ALSO The only way to save an HOUR is spend it wisely. / MEN talk wisely but live foolishly.

wish *(n.)* **1.** If a man could have all his wishes, he would double his trouble. *Rec. dist.:* Ala., Ga. *1st cit.:* US1752 Franklin, *PRAlmanac*. *20c. coll.:* Stevenson 2542:4.

2. If wishes were horses, beggars might ride. *Vars.:* **(a)** If wishes were fishes, we'd have some fried; if wishes were horses, beggars might ride. **(b)** If wishes were horses, beggars could ride. **(c)** If wishes were horses, beggars would ride. **(d)** If wishes were horses, we would all take a ride. *Rec. dist.:* U.S., Can. *1st cit.:* ca1628 Carmichaell, *Proverbs in Scots,* ed. Anderson (1957); US1930 Ogburn, *Ra-ta-plan! 20c. coll.:* ODEP 903, *CODP* 248, Stevenson 2542:1, Whiting*(MP)* 690.

3. The wish is father of the thought. *Var.:* The wish is father to the thought. *Rec. dist.:* Ont. *1st cit.:* ca1386 Chaucer, *Tale of Melibee;* US1783 *Life of Peter Van Schaak* (1842). *20c. coll.:* ODEP 43, Whiting 490, CODP 248, Stevenson 2542:16, T&W 407, Whiting*(MP)* 690.

4. Wishes never fill the bag. *Rec. dist.:* Tex. *1st cit.:* 1666 Torriano, *Common Place of Italian Proverbs*. *20c. coll.:* ODEP 903, Stevenson 2543:1.

SEE ALSO Great SOULS have will; feeble ones only have wishes. / WORDS reveal wishes.

wish *(v.)* **1.** Don't wish about what you wish you had; wish about what you've got. *Rec. dist.:* Iowa.

2. Don't wish too hard: you might just get what you wish for. *Rec. dist.:* Calif., Colo., N.Y.

3. If you wish for too much, you will end up with nothing. *Rec. dist.:* Ont.

4. Wish not for that which you cannot obtain. *Rec. dist.:* Mich.

5. Wish not to taste what does not to you fall. *Rec. dist.:* Ont.

SEE ALSO Better to HAVE than to wish. / INDUSTRY need not wish. / Wish not so much to LIVE long as to live well. / She who wishes to keep ahead of her NEIGHBOR must go to bed at sundown and get up at dawn. / He who wishes to know the ROAD through the mountains must ask those who have already trodden it.

wishbone Your wishbone is stronger than your backbone. *Rec. dist.:* Ohio.

wishing *SEE* After the ACTING, wishing is in vain. / LIFE consists in wishing you had if you didn't and wishing you hadn't if you did.

wit **1.** A sarcastic wit is a human pole cat. *Rec. dist.:* Ont.

2. An ounce of wit is worth a pound of sorrow. *Rec. dist.:* N.Y. *1st cit.:* ca1680 Baxter, *Of Self-Denial*. *20c. coll.:* Stevenson 2543:6.

3. An ounce of wit that is bought is worth a pound that is taught. *Rec. dist.:* Miss., N.Y. *1st cit.:* 1732 Fuller, *Gnomologia;* US1745 Franklin, *PRAlmanac. 20c. coll.:* ODEP 601, Whiting 323, Stevenson 2546:3.

4. Bought wit is best. *Rec. dist.:* Calif., Colo., Mich., N.Y. *1st cit.:* ca1495 Medwall, *Nature;* US1787 *American Museum. 20c. coll.:* ODEP 78, Whiting 490, Stevenson 2546:3, T&W 407, Whiting*(MP)* 690.

5. Good wits commonly agree. *Var.:* Good wits commonly jump. *Rec. dist.:* N.Y. *1st cit.:* 1594 Shakespeare, *Taming of the Shrew;* US1640 Howes in *Winthrop Papers, 1498–1649,* Mass.

Hist.Soc. *Collections* (1929–47). *20c. coll.: ODEP* 326, Whiting 490, Stevenson 2548:13.

6. If you have wit and learning, add to it wisdom and modesty. *Rec. dist.:* N.Y. *1st cit.:* US1738 Franklin, *PRAlmanac. 20c. coll.:* Stevenson 2547:10.

7. It is wit to pick a lock and steal a horse, but wisdom to let it alone. *Rec. dist.:* Tex. *1st cit.:* 1659 Howell, *Paroimiografia (French Proverbs). 20c. coll.: ODEP* 904, Stevenson 2547:12.

8. Little wit in the head makes much work for the feet. *Var.:* A little wit in the head makes muckle travel to the feet. *Rec. dist.:* Ill., Ont. *1st cit.:* 1641 Fergusson, *Scottish Proverbs. 20c. coll.: ODEP* 473, Stevenson 2544:9.

9. Love of wit makes no man rich. *Rec. dist.:* Ont. *1st cit.:* 1732 Fuller, *Gnomologia. 20c. coll.:* Stevenson 2544:12.

10. Mother wit is better than book education. *Rec. dist.:* Miss. *1st cit.:* US1846 Hooper, *Some Adventures of Captain Simon Suggs. 20c. coll.:* T&W 251.

11. The wit of conversation consists more in finding it in others than showing a great deal yourself. *Rec. dist.:* N.Y. *1st cit.:* US1756 Franklin, *PRAlmanac. 20c. coll.:* Stevenson 418:2.

12. Use more wit and less sweat. *Rec. dist.:* Ont.

13. Use your wit as a shield, not as a sword. *Vars.:* **(a)** Use your wit as a shield, not as a dagger. **(b)** Use your wits as a buckler, not as a sword. *Rec. dist.:* Ill., Mich., N.J. *1st cit.:* 1855 Bohn, *Handbook of Proverbs. 20c. coll.:* Stevenson 2544:2.

14. Wit is the salt of conversation, not the food. *Rec. dist.:* N.Y. *1st cit.:* 1819 Hazlitt, *Lectures on English Comic Writers. 20c. coll.:* Stevenson 2545:12.

15. Wit without discretion is a sword in the hand of a fool. *Rec. dist.:* Calif.

See also BREVITY is the soul of wit. / An ounce of DISCRETION is worth a pound of wit. / HUMOR is wit with a rooster's tail feathers stuck in its cap. / IDLENESS turns the edge of wit. / THINKING is poor wit. / WEALTH makes wit waver. / An ounce of WISDOM is worth a pound of wit. / WORDS may show a man's wit, but actions his meaning.

witch Don't swap the witch for the devil. *Rec. dist.:* Ky., Tenn.

wither *See* HEARTS don't break, they bend and wither. / Move an old TREE and it will wither and die.

witness **1.** A false witness shall not go unpunished. *Rec. dist.:* Ont.

2. You shall not bear false witness against your neighbor. *Rec. dist.:* Ill.

See also True BRAVERY is without witness. / Whenever a man commits a CRIME, God finds a witness.

woe **1.** Tell not your woes to him that doesn't pity you. *Rec. dist.:* Ont.

2. Who laughs at others, woes finds. *Rec. dist.:* Ill.

See also Today's JOYS may be tomorrow's woes.

woeful *See* Willful WASTE make woeful want. / Willful WAYS make woeful want.

wolf **1.** A wolf may change his mind but never his fur. *Rec. dist.:* Ont.

2. Don't set a wolf to watch the sheep. *Rec. dist.:* Calif. *1st cit.:* 1513 More, *Richard III. 20c. coll.: ODEP* 907, Stevenson 2088:10.

3. Don't skin your wolves before you get them. *Rec. dist.:* Colo.

4. He who marries a wolf often looks toward the forest. *Rec. dist.:* Wis.

5. It is better to keep a wolf out of the fold than to trust drawing his teeth and talons after he shall have entered. *Rec. dist.:* N.Y., Va. *1st cit.:* US1782 Jefferson, *Notes on Virginia. 20c. coll.:* Stevenson 425:7.

6. It is difficult to take a wolf by the ears. *Rec. dist.:* Mich. *1st cit.:* ca1386 Chaucer, *Tale of Melibee;* US1650 *Works of Anne Bradstreet,* ed. Ellis (1932). *20c. coll.: ODEP* 906, Whiting 492, Stevenson 2551:8, Whiting(MP) 692.

7. It is easy to fool the young wolf. *Rec. dist.:* Ont.

8. It never troubles the wolf how many the sheep may be. *Rec. dist.:* Wis. *1st cit.:* 1625

Bacon, "Of True Greatnesse of Kingdoms and Estates" in *Essays*. *20c. coll.:* ODEP 840, Stevenson 2089:3.

9. Keep the wolf from the door. *Rec. dist.:* U.S. *1st cit.:* ca1470 Hardyng, *Chronicle;* US1702 Mather, *Magnalia Christi Americana* (1853–55). *20c. coll.:* Stevenson 2553:4, Whiting 492, ODEP 418, T&W 408, Whiting*(MP)* 692.

10. Many a man sees a wolf at the door because his wife saw a mink in the window. *Rec. dist.:* Miss.

11. Never cry wolf when not in danger. *Rec. dist.:* U.S., Can. *1st cit.:* 1629 *Aesop's Fables,* tr. L'Estrange; US1803 *Writings of Thomas Jefferson,* ed. Bergh (1907). *20c. coll.:* ODEP 158, Whiting 492, Stevenson 2553:2, Whiting*(MP)* 692.

12. The wolf eats sheep now and then, but thousands are devoured by men. *Rec. dist.:* N.Y. *1st cit.:* US1740 Franklin, *PRAlmanac.* *20c. coll.:* Stevenson 2087:11.

13. Who keeps company with a wolf learns to howl. *Vars.:* (a) He who goes with wolves will learn to howl. (b) Live with the wolves and you will learn to howl. (c) Live with wolves and you shall learn to howl. (d) When you are with the wolves you must howl with them. *Rec. dist.:* U.S., Can. *1st cit.:* 1579 Tomson, "2 Timothy 3" in *Sermons of Calvin.* *20c. coll.:* ODEP 419, Stevenson 2554:7.

14. Wolves may lose their teeth, but they never lose their nature. *Rec. dist.:* Ont. *1st cit.:* 1616 Draxe, *Bibliotheca Scholastica* in *Anglia* (1918); US1755 Franklin, *PRAlmanac.* *20c. coll.:* ODEP 907, Whiting 492, Stevenson 2553:1.

15. Wolves never prey upon wolves. *Rec. dist.:* Utah. *1st cit.:* 1576 Pettie, *Petite Palace of Pleasure,* ed. Gollancz (1908); US1733 Franklin, *PRAlmanac.* *20c. coll.:* Stevenson 2553:5, Whiting 144, ODEP 353, T&W 408, Whiting*(MP)* 693.

16. Wolves of the same litter run in the same pack. *Rec. dist.:* Colo.

SEE ALSO A bad DOG never sees the wolf. / GREED killed the wolf. / HUNGER fetches the wolf out of the woods. / While keeping a TIGER from the front door, a wolf enters in at the back.

woman **1.** A gracious woman retains honor. *Var.:* A gracious woman retains honor, and strong men retain riches. *Rec. dist.:* Ont.

2. A skinny woman's like a racehorse: fast and fun, but no good for work. *Rec. dist.:* N.Mex.

3. A two-faced woman and a jealous man is the cause of trouble since the world began. *Rec. dist.:* Wis.

4. A virtuous woman is a source of honor to her husband; a vicious one causes him disgrace. *Rec. dist.:* Ill.

5. A woman, a cat, and a chimney should never leave the house. *Rec. dist.:* Tex.

6. A woman, a dog, and a walnut tree: the more you beat them, the better they be. *Vars.:* (a) A woman, a dog, and a hickory tree: the more you beat them, the more they beg (b) A woman, a dog, and a walnut tree: the harder you beat 'em, the better they be. (c) A woman, a dog, and a walnut tree: the worse you treat them, the better they will be. *Rec. dist.:* U.S., Can. *1st cit.:* 1581 Guazzo, *Civile Conversation,* tr. Pettie, T.T. (1925); US1836 Haliburton, *Clockmaker* (1838). *20c. coll.:* ODEP 758, T&W 408, CODP 248, Stevenson 2558:5, Whiting*(MP)* 694.

7. A woman and a cherry are painted for their own harm. *Rec. dist.:* Mich. *1st cit.:* 1659 Howell, *Paroimiografia (Spanish Proverbs).* *20c. coll.:* ODEP 907, Stevenson 738:4.

8. A woman can throw out the window more than a man can bring in at the door. *Vars.:* (a) A sloppy, wasteful woman will waste and carry out more in her apron than an ambitious man can haul in a wagon. (b) A woman can throw more out the back door in a teaspoon than a man can bring in the front door in a shovel. (c) A woman can throw more out the window than a man can bring in through the door. (d) A woman can throw out more with a spoon than a man can bring in with a shovel. (e) A woman cannot throw out on a spoon more than a man can bring in on a shovel. *Rec. dist.:* U.S., Can. *1st cit.:* US1831 *Journals* *of Ralph Waldo Emerson,* eds. Emerson and Forbes (1909–14). *20c. coll.:* T&W 409, Stevenson 2564:8, Whiting*(MP)* 694.

9. A woman can't drive her husband, but she can lead him. *Rec. dist.:* N.Y.

10. A woman conceals what she knows not. *Rec. dist.:* Okla., Tex. *1st cit.:* ca1386 Chaucer, *Tale of Melibee. 20c. coll.:* ODEP 908, Stevenson 2054:10.

11. A woman fights with her tongue. *Rec. dist.:* Ont.

12. A woman is a dish for the gods. *Rec. dist.:* N.J.

13. A woman is as old as she looks, but a man is never old till he quits looking. *Rec. dist.:* Ont., Tex.

14. A woman is known by her walking and drinking. *Rec. dist.:* N.Y.

15. A woman is no older than she looks. *Var.:* A woman is no older than she looks, and a man than he feels. *Rec. dist.:* Ala., Ga., Tex.

16. A woman is only a woman. *Var.:* A woman is only a woman; a good cigar is a smoke. *Rec. dist.:* Calif., Mich., Oreg.

17. A woman is the greatest contradiction of all. *Rec. dist.:* Ill.

18. A woman knows a bit more than Satan. *Rec. dist.:* Ill. *1st cit.:* 1559 Bercher, *Nobility of Women. 20c. coll.:* Stevenson 2570:4.

19. A woman laughs when she can but cries whenever she wishes. *Rec. dist.:* N.J. *1st cit.:* 1570 Baldwin, *Beware the Cat;* US1712 Byrd, *Secret Diary of William Byrd of Westover, 1709–1712,* eds. Wright and Tinling (1941). *20c. coll.:* ODEP 911, Whiting 494, Stevenson 2558:6.

20. A woman never forgets her sex. She would rather talk with a man than an angel any day. *Rec. dist.:* Wis. *1st cit.:* US1872 Holmes, *Poet at the Breakfast-Table. 20c. coll.:* Stevenson 1204:4.

21. A woman over thirty who will tell her exact age will tell anything. *Rec. dist.:* N.Y.

22. A woman remembers a kiss long after a man has forgotten. *Rec. dist.:* N.Y.

23. A woman should hang on to her youth, but not while he's driving. *Rec. dist.:* N.Dak.

24. A woman who looks much in the glass spins but little. *Rec. dist.:* Wis. *1st cit.:* 1623 Dawe, *Vox Graculi. 20c. coll.:* ODEP 911.

25. A woman's hair is her crowning glory. *Rec. dist.:* N.Y. *1st cit.:* US1948 Stevenson, *Home Book of Proverbs. 20c. coll.:* Stevenson 1052:4.

26. A woman's hair is long; her tongue is longer. *Rec. dist.:* Oreg.

27. A woman's in pain, a woman's in woe, a woman is ill when she likes to be so. *Rec. dist.:* N.Dak.

28. A woman's place is in the home. *Vars.:* **(a)** A woman's place is in the hay. **(b)** Woman's sphere is in the home. *Rec. dist.:* U.S., Can. *1st cit.:* 1897 Grand, *Beth Book;* US1844 Stephens, *High Life in New York. 20c. coll.:* CODP 249, Stevenson 2586:4, T&W 409, Whiting*(MP)* 695.

29. A woman's strength is in her tongue. *Rec. dist.:* Ohio. *1st cit.:* 1659 Howell, *Paroimiografia (English Proverbs). 20c. coll.:* Stevenson 2580:5.

30. A woman's whole life is a history of the affections. *Rec. dist.:* N.Y.

31. A woman's work is never done. *Var.:* Man's work lasts till set of sun; woman's work is never done. *Rec. dist.:* U.S., Can. *1st cit.:* 1570 Baldwin, *Beware the Cat;* US1722 Franklin, *PRAlmanac. 20c. coll.:* ODEP 909, Whiting 494, CODP 249, Stevenson 2583:9.

32. A worthy woman is the crown of her husband. *Rec. dist.:* N.Y. *1st cit.:* US1948 Stevenson, *Home Book of Proverbs. 20c. coll.:* Stevenson 2503:1.

33. All women and cats are black in darkness. *Rec. dist.:* Wis. *1st cit.:* US1745 Franklin, Letter, 25 June. *20c. coll.:* Stevenson 488:2.

34. All women look the same after the sun goes down. *Rec. dist.:* Ill. *1st cit.:* US1948 Stevenson, *Home Book of Proverbs. 20c. coll.:* Stevenson 488:2.

35. An aversion to women is like an aversion to life. *Rec. dist.:* N.Y.

36. Any woman can keep a secret, but she generally needs one other woman to help her. *Rec. dist.:* Miss.

37. As great a pity to see a woman weep as to see a goose go barefoot. *Rec. dist.:* Ont. *1st cit.:* 1523 Fitzherbert, *Boke of Husbandry.* *20c. coll.:* ODEP 708, Stevenson 2290:6.

38. Blessed is the woman who can keep a secret and the man who will not tell his wife. *Rec. dist.:* Miss.

39. Every woman keeps a corner in her heart where she is always twenty-one. *Rec. dist.:* Ill., N.Y.

40. God help the man who won't marry until he finds a perfect woman, and God help him still more if he finds her. *Rec. dist.:* Ill.

41. Goodwill, like a good woman, is hard to get and easy to lose. *Rec. dist.:* N.Y., N.Mex.

42. Handle with care women and glass. *Rec. dist.:* Ont. *1st cit.:* 1535 Berners, *Golden Book;* US1810 *Port Folio.* *20c. coll.:* ODEP 907, Whiting 493, Stevenson 2557:10.

43. Is a woman ever satisfied? No, if she were she wouldn't be a woman. *Rec. dist.:* N.J.

44. It is a woman's privilege to change her mind. *Rec. dist.:* Mich., N.Y., S.C. *1st cit.:* 1616 Draxe, *Bibliotheca Scholastica* in *Anglia* (1918); US1748 Ames, *Almanacs,* ed. Briggs (1891). *20c. coll.:* ODEP 909, Whiting 494, Stevenson 2578:9, T&W 410, Whiting(MP) 694.

45. It is better to dwell in the corner of a housetop than with a brawling woman in a wide house. *Rec. dist.:* Ala., Ga. *1st cit.:* US1948 Stevenson, *Home Book of Proverbs.* *20c. coll.:* Stevenson 2581:2.

46. It takes a smart woman to be a fool. *Rec. dist.:* Md.

47. It takes a wise woman to be an old maid. *Rec. dist.:* N.Y.

48. It takes two old women to make a cheese: one to hold and the other to squeeze. *Rec. dist.:* Maine.

49. Let the women wear the breeches. *Rec. dist.:* Miss. *1st cit.:* 1564 Bullein, *Dialogue Against Fever Pestilence;* US1666 Alsop, *Char-acter of the Province of Maryland,* ed. Mereness (1902). Stevenson 2505:4, Whiting 45, ODEP 874, T&W 42, Whiting(MP) 72.

50. Lots of men get women, but few get wives. *Rec. dist.:* Ky., Tenn.

51. Never quarrel with a woman. *Rec. dist.:* Ind. *1st cit.:* US1875 Scarborough, *Chinese Proverbs.* *20c. coll.:* Stevenson 2567:6.

52. Never run after a woman or a streetcar: there'll be another along in a few minutes. *Rec. dist.:* Mich., N.Y., Pa.

53. No woman should ever be quite accurate about her age: it looks so calculating. *Rec. dist.:* N.Y.

54. Once a woman has given you her heart, you can never get rid of the rest of her. *Rec. dist.:* Ill. *1st cit.:* 1696 Vanbrugh, *Relapse.* *20c. coll.:* Stevenson 2585:8.

55. One hair of a woman draws more than a team of horses. *Rec. dist.:* Ont. *1st cit.:* 1591 Florio, *Second Fruites.* *20c. coll.:* Stevenson 138:8.

56. Plain women are as safe as churches. *Rec. dist.:* Ill.

57. Tell a woman and you tell the world. *Rec. dist.:* Ont. *1st cit.:* 1700 Dryden, *Wife of Bath.* *20c. coll.:* Stevenson 2054:8.

58. Tell a woman she's a beauty and the devil will tell her ten times. *Rec. dist.:* Ill. *1st cit.:* 1732 Fuller, *Gnomologia.* *20c. coll.:* Stevenson 136:11.

59. That woman is young that does not look a day older than she says she is. *Rec. dist.:* Miss.

60. The best-dressed woman usually arrives with the least. *Var.:* The best-dressed woman usually arrives last with the least. *Rec. dist.:* Ont.

61. The fewer the women, the less the trouble. *Rec. dist.:* Ill.

62. The good-looking woman needs no paint. *Rec. dist.:* Ill.

63. The level of the woman is the level of the world. *Rec. dist.:* N.C.

64. The longest five years in a woman's life is

between twenty-nine and thirty. *Rec. dist.:* Ont.

65. The only secret a woman can keep is that of her age. *Rec. dist.:* Ill. *1st cit.:* 1732 Fuller, *Gnomologia. 20c. coll.:* Stevenson 2054:10.

66. The ugliest woman can look in the mirror and think she is beautiful. *Rec. dist.:* N.C. *1st cit.:* US1948 Stevenson, *Home Book of Proverbs. 20c. coll.:* Stevenson 2584:10.

67. The woman that deliberates is lost. *Rec. dist.:* N.J. *1st cit.:* 1713 Addison, *Cato;* US1858 Holmes, *Autocrat of the Breakfast-Table. 20c. coll.:* ODEP 909, T&W 409, Stevenson 2561:1.

68. The woman who'll kiss and tell is small as the little end of nothing. *Rec. dist.:* N.Y.

69. The woman you keep keeps you. *Rec. dist.:* Ill.

70. The world is full of wicked women. *Rec. dist.:* Ohio.

71. There are two kinds of women: those who take what you are and those who take what you have. *Rec. dist.:* N.J., N.C.

72. There is nothing better than a good woman and nothing worse than a bad one. *Rec. dist.:* N.Y. *1st cit.:* US1948 Stevenson, *Home Book of Proverbs. 20c. coll.:* Stevenson 2574:8.

73. There was never a conflict without a woman. *Rec. dist.:* Wis. *1st cit.:* 1639 Clarke, *Paroemiologia. 20c. coll.:* ODEP 867, Stevenson 2587:1.

74. There's hardly a strife in which a woman has not been a prime mover. *Rec. dist.:* Ill., Oreg. *1st cit.:* 1658 *Wit Restor'd. 20c. coll.:* Stevenson 2587:6.

75. Two things govern the world—women and gold. *Rec. dist.:* Oreg.

76. Two women in the same house can never agree. *Var.:* Two women cannot live under one roof. *Rec. dist.:* Ont. *1st cit.:* ca1417 *Reliquiae Antiquae* (1841 ed.); US1793 *Writings of George Washington,* ed. Fitzpatrick (1931–44). *20c. coll.:* Stevenson 1997:14, Whiting 493, Whiting(MP) 693.

77. What a woman has to say above a whisper isn't worth listening to. *Rec. dist.:* N.J.

78. When a woman is speaking, listen to what she says with her eyes. *Rec. dist.:* N.Y.

79. When a woman throws a man over, he usually lands on his knees to another woman. *Rec. dist.:* Miss.

80. Wherever there is a woman, there is gossip. *Rec. dist.:* W.Va.

81. While there's a world, it's a woman that will govern it. *Rec. dist.:* Ill. *1st cit.:* 1690 Vanbrugh, *Provok'd Wife. 20c. coll.:* Stevenson 2583:8.

82. Woman brings to man the greatest blessing and the greatest plague. *Rec. dist.:* Ill. *1st cit.:* US1948 Stevenson, *Home Book of Proverbs. 20c. coll.:* Stevenson 2574:6.

83. Woman: God bless her by that name, for it is a far nobler name than lady. *Rec. dist.:* N.Y. *1st cit.:* US1931 Walsh, *Golden Treasury of Medieval Literature. 20c. coll.:* Stevenson 2558:10.

84. Woman is a mystery to men, but women are wise to each other. *Rec. dist.:* Ill.

85. Woman will have both her word and her way. *Vars.:* (a) Man has his will, but woman has her way. (b) Woman must have her way. *Rec. dist.:* Ill., N.Y. *1st cit.:* 1733 Gay, "Song" in *Achilles. 20c. coll.:* Stevenson 2583:2.

86. Women and dogs cause too much strife. *Rec. dist.:* Miss., N.Y. *1st cit.:* 1541 *Schoolhouse of Women. 20c. coll.:* ODEP 910, Stevenson 2569:1.

87. Women and dogs set men together by the ears. *Rec. dist.:* Ill., N.Y. *1st cit.:* 1639 Clarke, *Paroemiologia Anglo-Latina. 20c. coll.:* ODEP 910, Stevenson 2569:1.

88. Women and elephants never forget. *Rec. dist.:* Ill. *1st cit.:* 1910 Munro (pseud. Saki), "Reginald on Besetting Sins" in *Reginald;* US1930 Parker, *Ballade of Unfortunate Mammals. 20c. coll.:* Stevenson 675:8.

89. Women are always in extremes. *Rec. dist.:* Ill., N.Y. *1st cit.:* ca1526 Erasmus, *Dicta Sapientum,* tr. Berthelet. *20c. coll.:* ODEP 908, Stevenson 2585:4.

90. Women are ambulating blocks for millinery. *Rec. dist.:* Miss.

91. Women are as fickle as April weather. *Rec. dist.:* Ill.

92. Women are like books: too much gilding makes men suspicious that the binding is the most important part.

93. Women are necessary evils. *Rec. dist.:* Ill. *1st cit.:* 1547 Baldwin, *Treatise of Morall Phylosophie;* US1721 Wise, *Word of Comfort to Melancholy Country. 20c. coll.:* ODEP 910, Whiting 494, Stevenson 2572:9.

94. Women are saints in church, angels in the street, devils in the kitchen, and apes in bed. *Rec. dist.:* Ill. *1st cit.:* 1559 Bercher, *Nobility of Women. 20c. coll.:* Stevenson 2574:2.

95. Women are strong when they arm themselves with their weaknesses. *Rec. dist.:* Ill. *1st cit.:* US1948 Stevenson, *Home Book of Proverbs. 20c. coll.:* Stevenson 2560:1.

96. Women are the devil's nets. *Rec. dist.:* Ill. *1st cit.:* 1520 *Calisto and Melibea. 20c. coll.:* ODEP 910, Stevenson 2574:1.

97. Women are the root of all evil. *Rec. dist.:* Wis. *1st cit.:* US1948 Stevenson, *Home Book of Proverbs. 20c. coll.:* Stevenson 2570:4.

98. Women are wacky, women are vain: they'd rather be pretty than have a good brain. *Rec. dist.:* N.Y. *1st cit.:* US1940 Fishback, *Lip Service. 20c. coll.:* Stevenson 136:7.

99. Women at lust are a contradiction. *Rec. dist.:* N.C.

100. Women, cows, and hens should not run. *Rec. dist.:* N.C.

101. Women forgive injuries but never forget slights. *Rec. dist.:* N.Y. *1st cit.:* US1843 Haliburton, *Old Judge. 20c. coll.:* Stevenson 2561:2.

102. Women leave peace behind 'em when they go. *Rec. dist.:* N.Y. *1st cit.:* US1906 O. Henry, *Between Rounds. 20c. coll.:* Stevenson 2561:3.

103. Women sometimes exaggerate a little, and this is an important point to be remembered by men and women. *Rec. dist.:* Wis.

104. Women will have the last word. *Rec.* *dist.:* Ill., N.Y. *1st cit.:* 1541 *Schoolhouse of Women;* US1728 Byrd, *Histories of Dividing Line Betwixt Virginia and North Carolina,* ed. Boyd, (1929). *20c. coll.:* ODEP 911, Whiting 494, Stevenson 2581:6, T&W 409, Whiting(MP) 694.

105. Women would be more charming if one could fall into their arms without falling into their hands. *Rec. dist.:* Wis. *Infm.:* Bierce's favorite toast. *1st cit.:* US1929 Grattan, *Bitter Bierce. 20c. coll.:* Stevenson 2558:10.

106. You can never pin a woman down to an answer. *Rec. dist.:* N.C.

107. You get a woman mad and her blood good and hot, better let her blood cool for she'll sho' hurt you. *Rec. dist.:* S.C.

108. You never can tell about women, but if you can, you shouldn't. *Rec. dist.:* Ont.

SEE ALSO A man without AMBITION is like a woman without looks. / ARMS, women, and locks should be looked at daily. / A BARN, a fence, and a woman always need mending. / CHILDREN, chickens, and women never have enough. / Women's CLOCKS will walk with every wind. / The CONVERSATION of a woman is worth all the libraries in the world. / The DAUGHTER of a spry old woman makes a poor housekeeper. / A FIRE scorches from near, a beautiful woman from near and from afar. / It is a FOOL who loves a woman from afar. / FOOLS are wise men in the affairs of women. / FRAILTY, your name is woman. / GOLD, women, and linen should be chosen by daylight. / Old women's GOLD is not ugly. / Behind every GREAT man there is a great woman. / HELL knows no wrath like a woman scorned. / The HELL of women is old age. / A HOUSE without woman and firelight is like a body without soul or spirit. / HOUSE goes mad when women gad. / No HOUSE was ever big enough for two women. / Men build HOUSES; women build homes. / Getting KISSES out of a woman is like getting olives out of a bottle: the first may be devilish difficult, but the rest come easy. / A LADY is a woman who makes it easy for a man to be a gentleman. / A MAN doesn't want a woman smarter than he is. / A MAN is as old as he feels, a woman as old as she feels like admitting. / A MAN thinks he knows, but a woman knows better. / MAN gets and forgets; woman gives and forgives. / A little bit of POWDER and a little bit of paint makes a woman look like what she ain't. / Do RIGHT and fear no man; don't write and fear no woman. / A SHIP under sail and a big-bellied woman are the handsomest two things that can be seen. / Ten measures of TALK were sent down from heaven, and women took nine. / THRIFT is to a man what chastity is to a woman. / One TONGUE is enough for two women. / A VIRTUOUS woman is rarer than a precious jewel. / WINE and women don't mix. / WINE, women, and song will get a man wrong. / A WISE woman never outsmarts her husband. / Any WISE man can be fooled by a foolish woman.

wonder *(n.)* **1.** No wonder is greater than any other wonder, and if once explained, ceases to be a wonder. *Rec. dist.:* Ill.

2. Wonders will never cease. *Rec. dist.:* U.S., Can. *1st cit.:* 1776 Boaden, *Private Correspondence of D. Garrick* (1823); US1766 *Letters of Copley and Pelham*, Mass.Hist.Soc. *Collections* (1914). *20c. coll.:* ODEP 912, Whiting 291, CODP 249, Stevenson 2587:9, T&W 410, Whiting*(MP)* 696.
SEE ALSO The larger the island of KNOWLEDGE, the longer the shoreline of wonder.

wonder *(v.)* SEE The FOOL wonders; the wise man asks.

wood **1.** Chop your own wood and it will warm you twice. *Rec. dist.:* Ill., Okla. *1st cit.:* US1819 Kinloch, *Letters from Geneva and France.* *20c. coll.:* Whiting 495, Whiting*(MP)* 696.

2. Crooked wood makes an even fire. *Rec. dist.:* Mich. **Infm.:** Cf. stick. *1st cit.:* 1584 Withals, *Short Dictionary.* *20c. coll.:* ODEP 155, Stevenson 458:8.

3. Do not shout until you are out of the woods. *Vars.:* **(a)** Don' crow till ya git out o' de woods—dey might be uh beah behin' de las' tree. **(b)** Don't yell before you're out of the woods. **(c)** Never crow till you're out of the woods. *Rec. dist.:* Ont. *1st cit.:* 1792 D'Ar-

blay, *Diary;* US1770 *Papers of Benjamin Franklin,* ed. Labaree (1959). *20c. coll.:* ODEP 345, Whiting 495, CODP 105, Stevenson 2591:2, T&W 411, Whiting*(MP)* 696.

4. Don't go through the woods and pick up a crooked stick. *Var.:* Don't go all the way through the woods and then pick up a crooked stick. *Rec. dist.:* N.Y., Ont. *1st cit.:* US1937 Gordon, *Garden of Adonis.* *20c. coll.:* Whiting*(MP)* 697.

5. Green wood makes a hot fire. *Rec. dist.:* Tex. *1st cit.:* 1477 *Dictes and Sayenges of Philosophirs,* tr. Rivers. *20c. coll.:* ODEP 337, Stevenson 2590:1.

6. Sometimes one can't see the wood for the trees. *Rec. dist.:* U.S., Can. *1st cit.:* 1546 Heywood, *Dialogue of Proverbs,* ed. Habernicht (1963); US1813 Adams in *Adams-Jefferson Letters,* ed. Cappon (1959). *20c. coll.:* ODEP 710, Whiting 495, Stevenson 2590:11, Whiting*(MP)* 697.

7. There are more ways to the wood than one. *Rec. dist.:* Okla. *1st cit.:* 1533 Udall, *Floures for Latine Speakyng;* US1651 *Complete Writings of Roger Williams* (1963). *20c. coll.:* ODEP 872, Whiting 474, Stevenson 2467:5, Whiting*(MP)* 670.

8. Wood half-burnt is easily kindled. *Rec. dist.:* Okla. *1st cit.:* 1557 Cavendish, *Life of Cardinal Wolsey.* *20c. coll.:* ODEP 913, Stevenson 2589:11.

9. You can always cut more wood off, but you cannot put it on again. *Rec. dist.:* Mich., N.J.

10. You can't saw wood with a hammer. *Rec. dist.:* Ont. *1st cit.:* US1814 *Diary of F. Palmer, Privateersman, 1813–1815,* Acorn Club *Publications* (1914). *20c. coll.:* Whiting 495.
SEE ALSO A CHIP on the shoulder is a good indication of wood higher up. / IGNORANCE and pride grow on the same wood. / Dey's jes' ez good a TIMBER in de woods ez w'at been bought. / A WISE man will saw wood and say nothing.

wooden **1.** Do not take any wooden nickels. *Var.:* Don't buy any wooden nutmegs. *Rec. dist.:* Ill., Mich., N.Y., Okla., Tex. *1st* *cit.*: US1930 Aresbys, *Murder.* **20c. coll.**: Whiting*(MP)* 446.

2. Your wooden overcoat won't have any pockets. **Rec. dist.**: N.Y. **1st cit.**: 1853 Trench, *Lessons in Proverbs* (1894); US1940 Thompson, *Body, Boots, and Britches.* **20c. coll.**: ODEP 443, Stevenson 1985:5, *CODP* 203.

woodpecker If woodpecker want sweet meat, he haffa don't mind jar 'e head. **Rec. dist.**: S.C.

woodsman You can tell a woodsman by his chips. **Rec. dist.**: Miss.

wooing Happy's the wooing that's not long a-doing. **Rec. dist.**: Mich., Miss. **1st cit.**: 1576 *Parade of Devil's Devices* in *British Bibliography* (1812); US1734 Franklin, *PRAlmanac.* **20c. coll.**: ODEP 913, Whiting 496, Stevenson 2592, Whiting*(MP)* 697.

wool 1. Bad is the wool that cannot be dyed. **Rec. dist.**: Ont. **1st cit.**: 1680 *Philostratus,* tr. Blount. **20c. coll.**: Stevenson 2596:1.

2. Many go out for wool and come home shorn. **Vars.**: **(a)** Many go for wool and come home shorn themselves. **(b)** Many who go for wool come back shorn. **Rec. dist.**: Miss., Okla., Wis. **1st cit.**: 1599 Minsheu, *Dialogues in Spanish;* US1855 Haliburton, *Nature and Human Nature.* **20c. coll.**: ODEP 913, T&W 412, *CODP* 249, Stevenson 2595:5, Whiting*(MP)* 698.

word 1. A flow of words is no proof of wisdom. **Rec. dist.**: N.Y.

2. A gentle word will make the argument stand. **Rec. dist.**: Ill.

3. A good word costs no more than a bad one. **Rec. dist.**: N.J., N.Y. **1st cit.**: 1579 *Proverbs of Sir James Lopez de Mendoza,* tr. Googe; US1803 Davis in *Barbary Wars* (1939–44). **20c. coll.**: ODEP 327, Whiting 496, Stevenson 2610:3, T&W 413.

4. A good word for a bad one is worth much and costs little. **Var.**: Pleasant words are valued and do not cost much. **Rec. dist.**: Mich., N.J., N.Y., Ont. **1st cit.**: 1640 Herbert, *Outlandish Proverbs (Jacula Prudentum)* in *Works,* ed. Hutchinson (1941). **20c. coll.**: Stevenson 2610:4.

5. A kind word goes a long way. **Vars.**: **(a)** A kind word is never thrown away. **(b)** A kind word never hurt anyone. **Rec. dist.**: U.S., Can. **1st cit.**: 1732 Fuller, *Gnomologia;* US1852 Cary, *Clovernook.* **20c. coll.**: Stevenson 2610:4, T&W 412, Whiting*(MP)* 699.

6. A man of words and not of deeds is like a garden full of weeds. **Rec. dist.**: Ill. **1st cit.**: 1659 Howell, *Paroimiografia (English Proverbs);* US1758 *Letters of Benjamin Franklin and Jane Mecom,* ed. Van Doran, Am.Phil.Soc. *Memoirs* (1950). **20c. coll.**: ODEP 915, Whiting 278, Stevenson 2615:9.

7. A man that breaks his word bids others be false to him. **Rec. dist.**: Calif., Mich. **1st cit.**: 1548 Hall, *Chronicle of Lancastre and York.* **20c. coll.**: ODEP 83.

8. A soft word is often worth more than a house and a lot. **Rec. dist.**: N.Y.

9. A thousand words won't fill a bushel. **Rec. dist.**: Ill., Ohio. **1st cit.**: 1641 Fergusson, *Scottish Proverbs;* US1758 Franklin, "Way to Wealth" in *Papers of Benjamin Franklin,* ed. Labaree (1959). **20c. coll.**: ODEP 916, Whiting 496, Stevenson 2608:3.

10. A true word needs no oath. **Rec. dist.**: N.J. **1st cit.**: US1948 Stevenson, *Home Book of Proverbs.* **20c. coll.**: Stevenson 2613:3.

11. A word before is worth two behind. **Var.**: A word before is worth two after. **Rec. dist.**: N.Dak., Ont. **1st cit.**: ca1641 Fergusson, *Scottish Proverbs.* **20c. coll.**: ODEP 914, Stevenson 2600:1.

12. A word fitly spoken is like apples of gold in pictures of silver. **Var.**: A word spoken at the right time is worth a piece of gold; silence at the right time is worth two. **Rec. dist.**: U.S. **1st cit.**: US1948 Stevenson, *Home Book of Proverbs.* **20c. coll.**: Stevenson 2603:1.

13. A word hurts more than a wound. **Rec. dist.**: Ohio, Ont. **1st cit.**: ca1200 *Ancrene Riwle;* US1875 Scarborough, *Chinese Proverbs.* **20c. coll.**: Stevenson 2605:9.

14. A word of kindness is seldom spoken in vain. **Rec. dist.**: Ont.

15. A word that is not spoken never does any mischief. **Rec. dist.**: N.Y. **1st cit.**: US1895 Dana,

Making of a Newspaper Man. **20c. coll.:** Stevenson 2597:2.

16. A word to the wise is sufficient. **Vars.: (a)** A word is enough to the wise. **(b)** A word to the wise is enough. **(c)** A word to the wise is enough, and many words won't fill a bushel. **Rec. dist.:** U.S., Can. **1st cit.:** ca1275 *Proverbs of Alfred;* US1645 *John Wheelwright, His Writings,* ed. Bell, Publ. Prince Soc. (1876). **20c. coll.:** ODEP 914, Whiting 498, CODP 250, Stevenson 2611:7, T&W 412, Whiting(MP) 701.

17. All words are pegs to hang ideas on. **Rec. dist.:** N.Y. **1st cit.:** US1887 Beecher, *Proverbs from Plymouth Pulpit.* **20c. coll.:** Stevenson 2601:1.

18. An honest man's word is as good as his bond. **Vars.: (a)** A man's word is as good as his gold. **(b)** A Quaker's word is as good as his bond. **Rec. dist.:** U.S., Can. **1st cit.:** ca1400 Chaucer, *Book of Duchess;* US1777 *Diary of Col. Landon Carter of Sabine Hall, 1752–1778,* ed. Greene (1965). **20c. coll.:** ODEP 380, Whiting 497, T&W 413, Stevenson 2613:3, Whiting(MP) 699.

19. An idle word is never well spoken. **Rec. dist.:** Ont.

20. An unkind word is better left unspoken. **Rec. dist.:** Ont.

21. Big words seldom go with good deeds. **Rec. dist.:** Calif., Ill., La. **1st cit.:** US1948 Stevenson, *Home Book of Proverbs.* **20c. coll.:** Stevenson 2615:7.

22. Blessed are they that hear the word of God and keep it. **Rec. dist.:** N.Y., R.I., S.C.

23. By your words you shall be condemned. **Rec. dist.:** Utah.

24. Cool words scald not a tongue. **Rec. dist.:** N.Y., Tex. **1st cit.:** ca1549 Heywood, *Dialogue of Proverbs,* ed. Habernicht (1963); US1767 Ames, *Almanacs,* ed. Briggs (1891). **20c. coll.:** ODEP 241, Whiting 496, Stevenson 2608:6.

25. Every word has a meaning. **Rec. dist.:** N.Y.

26. Fair words butter no cabbage. **Var.:** Sweet words butter no parsnips. **Rec. dist.:** N.Y., Tex. **1st cit.:** 1639 Clarke, *Paroemiologia;*

US1840 Haliburton, *Letter-Bag of the Great Western.* **20c. coll.:** ODEP 241, T&W 413, CODP 80, Stevenson 2608:1, Whiting(MP) 698.

27. Fair words make the pot boil. **Rec. dist.:** Ont. **1st cit.:** 1721 Kelly, *Scottish Proverbs.* **20c. coll.:** ODEP 241, Stevenson 2609:1.

28. Fancy words do not make a scholar. **Rec. dist.:** Ill.

29. Few words are best. **Rec. dist.:** Okla., Tex. **1st cit.:** ca1600 *Boxburghe Ballads;* US1822 *Last Poems of Philip Freneau,* ed. Pattee (1902–07). **20c. coll.:** Stevenson 2605:2, Whiting 496, T&W 413.

30. Few words, many deeds. **Rec. dist.:** Tex. **1st cit.:** 1592 Delamothe, *Treasure of French Tongue;* US1776 *Public Papers of George Clinton, First Governor of New York,* ed. Hastings (1899–1911). **20c. coll.:** ODEP 254, Whiting 496, Stevenson 2615:8.

31. If a man's word is no good, neither is his note. **Rec. dist.:** Colo.

32. Immodest words are in all cases indefensible. **Rec. dist.:** Mich. **1st cit.:** 1684 Dillon, *On Translated Verse.* **20c. coll.:** Stevenson 710:6.

33. In a multitude of words there wants not sin. **Var.:** In the multitude of words there wants not sin, but he that refrains his lips is wise. **Rec. dist.:** N.C. **1st cit.:** US1948 Stevenson, *Home Book of Proverbs.* **20c. coll.:** Stevenson 2602:8.

34. It is better to say a good word about a bad fellow than a bad word about a good fellow. **Rec. dist.:** Ont.

35. Kind words and few are a woman's ornament. **Rec. dist.:** Wis.

36. Kind words are the music of the world. **Rec. dist.:** N.Y.

37. Kind words never die. **Rec. dist.:** Okla., Ont.

38. Loaded words are like loaded dice: they never roll true. **Rec. dist.:** Wis.

39. More words than one go to a bargain. **Rec. dist.:** Tex. **1st cit.:** 1580 Munday, *Zelauto;* US1806 *Port Folio.* **20c. coll.:** ODEP 544, Whiting 498, Stevenson 120:15.

40. No truer word, save God's, was ever spoken than that the largest heart is soonest broken. *Rec. dist.:* Ill. *1st cit.:* ca1846 Landor, *Epigrams.* *20c. coll.:* Stevenson 1114:9.

41. Of all cold words of tongue or pen, the worst are these: I knew him when. *Rec. dist.:* N.Y. *1st cit.:* USca1940 Guiterman, *Prophets in Their Own Country.* *20c. coll.:* Stevenson 1946:13.

42. Of all the words of tongue or pen, the saddest are these: it might have been. *Rec. dist.:* U.S., Can. *1st cit.:* US1854 Whittier, *Maud Muller.* *20c. coll.:* Stevenson 1946:13.

43. One hard word brings another. *Rec. dist.:* Ont. *1st cit.:* ca1549 Heywood, *Dialogue of Proverbs,* ed. Habernicht (1963). *20c. coll.:* ODEP 401, Stevenson 2601:5.

44. Our words have wings but fly not where we would. *Rec. dist.:* Ill. *1st cit.:* 1868 Eliot, *Spanish Gypsy.* *20c. coll.:* Stevenson 2600:10.

45. Pleasing words and bad deeds deceive both the wise and the simple. *Rec. dist.:* Calif., N.Y. *1st cit.:* 1578 Florio, *Firste Fruites.* *20c. coll.:* Stevenson 2614:12.

46. Smooth words make smooth ways. *Rec. dist.:* Calif.

47. Soft words break no bones. *Var.:* Soft words break no hearts. *Rec. dist.:* Ont., Tex. *1st cit.:* ca1450 *Towneley Play of Noah,* E.E.T.S. (1897); US1801 Brackenridge, *Gazette Publications.* *20c. coll.:* ODEP 353, Whiting 496, CODP 107, Stevenson 2607:7, Whiting(MP) 699.

48. Soft words win a hard heart. *Rec. dist.:* Ont.

49. Soften the words to suit the occasion. *Rec. dist.:* Ont.

50. Speak kind words and you will hear kind answers. *Rec. dist.:* Ill.

51. Spoken words are like flown birds: neither can be recalled. *Rec. dist.:* N.Y. *1st cit.:* US1948 Stevenson, *Home Book of Proverbs.* *20c. coll.:* Stevenson 2597:2.

52. Tart words make no friends: a spoonful of honey will catch more flies than a gallon of vinegar. *Rec. dist.:* Wis. *1st cit.:* US1744 Franklin, *PRAlmanac.* *20c. coll.:* Stevenson 2609:5.

53. The hard words cut the heart. *Rec. dist.:* Ont. *1st cit.:* ca1200 *Ancrene Riwle.* *20c. coll.:* ODEP 915.

54. The second word makes the quarrel. *Var.:* No quarrel ever stirred before the second word. *Rec. dist.:* N.Y., Ohio, Ont. *1st cit.:* US1938 Champion, *Racial Proverbs.* *20c. coll.:* Stevenson 2598:9.

55. The words of a talebearer are as wounds. *Rec. dist.:* Ohio.

56. The written word remains. *Rec. dist.:* Ont. *1st cit.:* US1948 Stevenson, *Home Book of Proverbs.* *20c. coll.:* Stevenson 2602:4.

57. There's many a true word said in jest. *Var.:* Many a true word has been spoken in jest. *Rec. dist.:* U.S., Can. *1st cit.:* ca1386 Chaucer, *Monk's Tale;* US1728 Byrd, *Histories of Dividing Line Betwixt Virginia and North Carolina,* ed. Boyd (1929). *20c. coll.:* ODEP 841, Whiting 496, CODP 230, Stevenson 1267:5, T&W 413, Whiting(MP) 699.

58. To one who understands, few words are needed. *Rec. dist.:* Calif., Ont.

59. Weigh well your words before you give them breath. *Rec. dist.:* N.C. *1st cit.:* 1605 Shakespeare, *Othello.* *20c. coll.:* Stevenson 2602:5.

60. When about to put your word in ink, 'twill do no harm to stop and think. *Rec. dist.:* Ill., Miss.

61. While the word is yet unspoken, you are master of it; when once it is spoken, it is master of you. *Vars.:* (a) Before the word is spoken you must govern it; after it is spoken it will govern you. (b) Of the unspoken word you are master; the spoken word is master of you. (c) You are master of the unspoken word; the spoken word is master of you. *Rec. dist.:* Miss., N.C., Utah. *1st cit.:* 1477 *Dictes and Sayenges of Philosophirs,* tr. Rivers. *20c. coll.:* Stevenson 2597:2, ODEP 914.

62. Words and deeds are not weighed in the same balance. *Rec. dist.:* Ont.

63. Words are silver and silence is gold. *Rec. dist.:* Ont. *Infm.:* Cf. speech.

64. Words are the only things that last forever. *Rec. dist.:* Ill. *1st cit.:* 1821 Hazlitt, "On Thought and Action" in *Table Talk.* *20c. coll.:* Stevenson 2602:4.

65. Words fall lightly as the snow; they're easily and thoughtlessly said, yet hard words can enter the heart and lie there as heavy as lead. *Rec. dist.:* Ill.

66. Words, like feathers, are carried away by the wind. *Rec. dist.:* Ill. *1st cit.:* ca1570 *Pedlar's Prophecy.* *20c. coll.:* ODEP 915, Stevenson 2611:1.

67. Words, like glass, darken whatever they do not help to see. *Rec. dist.:* Ill.

68. Words may show a man's wit, but actions his meaning. *Rec. dist.:* N.Y.

69. Words must be weighed, not counted. *Rec. dist.:* Ill., Ont. *1st cit.:* 1855 Bohn, *Handbook of Proverbs.* *20c. coll.:* Stevenson 2602:5.

70. Words never filled a belly. *Rec. dist.:* N.Y. *1st cit.:* 1564 Edwards, *Damon and Pithias;* US1766 Parker in *Papers of Benjamin Franklin,* ed. Labaree (1959). *20c. coll.:* ODEP 241, Whiting 499, Stevenson 2608:2.

71. Words once spoken you can never recall. *Rec. dist.:* U.S., Can. *1st cit.:* ca1386 Chaucer, *Maunciple's Tale;* US1792 *Universal Asylum.* *20c. coll.:* ODEP 914, Whiting 498, Stevenson 2592:2, Whiting(MP) 701.

72. Words reveal wishes. *Rec. dist.:* Ont.

73. You can tell by his words what a fool has in his head. *Rec. dist.:* Ont.

74. You can't argue with the printed word. *Rec. dist.:* Ky., Tenn.

SEE ALSO ACCIDENT is a word not to be found in the divine vocabulary. / ACTIONS and words are the windows through which the heart is seen. / Suit the ACTIONS to the word. / The weaker the ARGUMENT, the stronger the words. / Fine CLOTHES may disguise, silly words will disclose a fool. / DEEDS are fruits; words are but leaves. / DEEDS speak louder than words. / FEELINGS are useless without words. / To a wise HEAD, two or three words. / Kind HEARTS are the gardens, kind thoughts the roots, kind words the flowers, kind deeds the fruits. / IF is a little word, yet it is so big you can't get around or over it. / IF is the longest word ever spoken. / He that has KNOWLEDGE spares his words. / There is as much MALICE in a wink as in a word. / MATRIMONY is not a word but a sentence. / Tell an OX by his horns, but a man by his word. / One PICTURE is worth ten thousand words. / PRESENTS speak louder than words. / There's small REVENGE in words, but words may be greatly revenged. / TIME and words can never be recalled. / WOUNDS made by words are hard to heal. / WRANGLERS never want words.

work *(n.)* **1.** A man can't do no mo' dan jes' so much work in one day. *Rec. dist.:* Miss.

2. A work ill done must be done twice. *Rec. dist.:* Okla. *1st cit.:* 1659 Howell, *Paroimiografia (English Proverbs).* *20c. coll.:* Stevenson 538:6.

3. All work and no play makes Jack a dull boy. *Vars.:* **(a)** All work and no play isn't much fun. **(b)** All work and no play makes Jack a dull boy; all work and no spree makes Jill a dull she. **(c)** All work and no play makes Jack a rich man. **(d)** All work and no play makes Johnny a dull boy. *Rec. dist.:* U.S., Can. *1st cit.:* 1659 Howell, *Paroimiografia (English Proverbs);* US1804 Brackenridge, *Modern Chivalry, 1792–1815,* ed. Newlin (1937). *20c. coll.:* ODEP 916, Whiting 499, CODP 250, Stevenson 1258:7, T&W 413, Whiting(MP) 701.

4. All work is noble. *Rec. dist.:* Ont. *1st cit.:* 1843 Carlyle, *Past and Present.* *20c. coll.:* Stevenson 2619:6.

5. By work you get money, by talk you get knowledge. *Rec. dist.:* N.Y. *1st cit.:* US1853 Haliburton, *Sam Slick's Wise Saws.* *20c. coll.:* Stevenson 2277:7.

6. Chase your work or your work will chase you. *Var.:* Drive your work—do not let it drive you. *Rec. dist.:* Ark., N.Dak., Utah.

7. Do work well or not at all. *Rec. dist.:* Ark.

8. Do your own work and know yourself. *Rec. dist.:* Mich.

9. Hard work conquers the worst of luck. *Rec. dist.:* Ill.

10. Hard work is not easy, and dry bread is not greasy. *Rec. dist.:* N.C.

11. Hard work is the best investment a man

can make. *Rec. dist.:* N.Y. *1st cit.:* USca1925 Schwab, *Ten Commandments of Success.* *20c. coll.:* Stevenson 2619:7.

12. He has hard work indeed who has nothing to do. *Rec. dist.:* Ont. *1st cit.:* US1798 *Journal and Letters of Francis Asbury,* ed. Potts (1958). *20c. coll.:* Whiting 499.

13. If you want work well done, select a busy man. *Rec. dist.:* Colo.

14. It is slow work to be born again. *Rec. dist.:* Utah.

15. It's all in a day's work. *Rec. dist.:* Kans. *1st cit.:* 1738 Swift, *Collection of Genteel and Ingenious Conversation* (1911). *20c. coll.:* ODEP 917, Stevenson 2621:12.

16. Never look at half-done work. *Rec. dist.:* Ont. *1st cit.:* 1721 Kelly, *Scottish Proverbs.* *20c. coll.:* CODP 85, Stevenson 848:6.

17. No man does as much work today as he is going to do tomorrow. *Rec. dist.:* Ill.

18. No work is worse than overwork. *Rec. dist.:* Ont.

19. Nothing is gained without work. *Rec. dist.:* Ont. *1st cit.:* 1709 Addison, *Tatler.* *20c. coll.:* Stevenson 1331:5.

20. Nothing worth having ever comes without a lot of hard work. *Rec. dist.:* N.C. *1st cit.:* 1709 Addison, *Tatler.* *20c. coll.:* Stevenson 1331:5.

21. One does his best work when working alone. *Rec. dist.:* Ill.

22. Plan your work and work your plan. *Rec. dist.:* Ont.

23. The best way to get rid of work is to do it. *Rec. dist.:* Calif., Colo., N.J., N.Y.

24. The only work that hurts a man is hopeless work. *Rec. dist.:* Miss.

25. The works of man will perish. *Rec. dist.:* Mich.

26. There is no man born into the world whose work is not born with him. *Vars.:* **(a)** No man is born in the world that his work is not born with him. **(b)** No one man is born that his work is not with him. *Rec. dist.:* N.Y., N.C.

27. Too light for heavy work and too heavy for light work. *Rec. dist.:* Md.

28. Work beats worry. *Rec. dist.:* Md.

29. Work before play. *Rec. dist.:* U.S., Can.

30. Work consists of whatever a body is obliged to do, and play consists of whatever a body is not obliged to do. *Rec. dist.:* N.Y. *1st cit.:* US1876 Twain, *Tom Sawyer.* *20c. coll.:* Stevenson 2622:2.

31. Work don't never set aroun' hollerin' fer ol' reliable to come to do it. *Rec. dist.:* Miss.

32. Work is a fine tonic. *Rec. dist.:* Ont.

33. Work is a habit; so is laziness. *Rec. dist.:* Ont.

34. Work is afraid of a resolute man. *Rec. dist.:* N.Y. *1st cit.:* US1937 Hart, *Chinese Proverbs.* *20c. coll.:* Stevenson 2619:3.

35. Work is fine fire for frozen fingers. *Rec. dist.:* Ill.

36. Work is not hard unless you prefer doing something else. *Rec. dist.:* Ohio.

37. Work is not the curse, but drudgery is. *Rec. dist.:* N.Y. *1st cit.:* US1887 Beecher, *Proverbs from Plymouth Pulpit.* *20c. coll.:* Stevenson 2621:2.

38. Work is the only capital that never misses dividends. *Rec. dist.:* N.Y. *1st cit.:* US1906 *Poor Richard Jr.'s Almanac.* *20c. coll.:* Stevenson 2622:2.

39. Work is work if you're paid to do it, an' it's pleasure if you pay to be allowed to do it. *Rec. dist.:* N.Y. *1st cit.:* US1901 Dunne, *Golf.* *20c. coll.:* Stevenson 2622:2.

40. Work keeps you out of mischief. *Rec. dist.:* N.C.

41. Work makes life pleasant. *Rec. dist.:* Ill.

42. Work never hurt any man. *Vars.:* **(a)** Hard work never hurt anybody. **(b)** Work will never kill any man. *Rec. dist.:* U.S., Can. *1st cit.:* 1879 Craik, *Young Mrs. Jardine;* US1923 Davis, *Icebound.* *20c. coll.:* ODEP 917, Stevenson 2619:7, Whiting(MP) 702.

43. Work was made for a Negro and a mule; a mule has enough sense to turn his back on it. *Rec. dist.:* Ill.

44. Work well begun is half ended. *Rec. dist.:* U.S., Can. *1st cit.:* 1908 MacLaren, *Acts.* *20c. coll.:* Stevenson 152:10.

45. Work well done makes pleasure more fun. *Rec. dist.:* Ala., Ga.

46. Your work expresses you more correctly than your tongue. *Rec. dist.:* S.C.

SEE ALSO No BEES, no honey; no work, no money. / A BOY can't do a man's work. / CHARACTER and hard work go together in nine cases out of ten. / COOPERATION isn't letting the other fellow do all the work. / There is no greater CURE for misery than hard work. / The DICTIONARY is the only place where success comes before work. / The EYE of the master does more than his hand. / FAITH without works is vain hope. / GENIUS begins great works; labor alone finishes them. / Your HAND is never the worse for doing your own work. / Many HANDS make light work. / HELL is full of good meanings, but heaven is full of good works. / LOVE grows cold when it is not mixed with good works. / The MONEY paid, the work delayed. / He that PAYS aforehand has never his work well done. / It's the man behind the PLOW who does the work. / Never let the SUN set on work undone. / A WISE man without work is a bee without honey. / Little WIT in the head makes much work for the feet. / Nothing worries WORRY like work. / WORRY kills more men than work.

work (*v.*)   **1.** If you are willing to work, you can write your name anywhere you choose. *Rec. dist.:* Ont.

2. If you intend to work, there is no better place than where you are; if you do not intend to work, you cannot get along anywhere. *Rec. dist.:* Ont.

3. It may be hard to work, but it must be harder to want. *Rec. dist.:* Ill.

4. The fellow who works for a song has trouble meeting his notes. *Rec. dist.:* Wis.

5. The harder you work, the more luck you have. *Rec. dist.:* Ont.

6. Those who will not work shall not eat. *Rec. dist.:* Ind., N.J. *1st cit.:* ca1386 Chaucer, *Tale of Melibee;* US1719 Chalkley, *Journal in Works of Thomas Chalkley* (1766). *20c. coll.:* Stevenson 2623:6, Whiting 499, *ODEP* 917, *CODP* 250, T&W 414, Whiting*(MP)* 702.

7. To work is to pray. *Rec. dist.:* Ont.

8. Unless you work hard, you cannot succeed. *Rec. dist.:* Ont.

9. Work as if everything depended on you; pray as if everything depended on God. *Rec. dist.:* Miss.

10. Work as though you were to live forever. *Rec. dist.:* Miss. *1st cit.:* US1757 Franklin, *PRAlmanac.* *20c. coll.:* Stevenson 2618:15.

11. Work, for the night is coming. *Rec. dist.:* Wis. *1st cit.:* 1834 Carlyle, *Sartor Resartus;* USca1860 Coghill, *Work Song.* *20c. coll.:* Stevenson 1685:6.

12. Work hard in harvest time. *Rec. dist.:* Ind.

13. Work while you work and play while you play. *Rec. dist.:* Ky., Okla., Tenn. *1st cit.:* US1924 Bailey, *Mr. Fortune's Practice.* *20c. coll.:* Whiting*(MP)* 702.

SEE ALSO Better to BEG than to steal, but better to work than to beg. / Work for your BREAD if you get your cheese for nothing. / CAN'T is a sluggard, too lazy to work. / People who DREAM all night don't work all day. / You can make your DREAMS come true if you wake up and work. / A man EATS so he works. / Be an EMPLOYEE and work eight hours; be a boss and your work is never done. / The GRUMBLER does not work; the worker does not grumble. / Better sit IDLE than work for nought. / Most good LAWYERS live well, work hard, and die poor. / A LAZY man works the hardest. / Men who LOVE much will work much. / MAN works from sun to sun, but a woman's work is never done. / PLAY while you play; work while you work. / TIME works for those who work. / WHISTLE while you work.

working   It is working that makes a workman. *Rec. dist.:* Ont. *1st cit.:* 1732 Fuller, *Gnomologia.* *20c. coll.:* Stevenson 2623:9.

SEE ALSO Good HUMOR is the suspenders that keep our working clothes on.

workingman   At the workingman's house, hunger looks in but dares not enter. *Rec. dist.:* N.Y. *1st cit.:* US1737 Franklin, *PRAlmanac.* *20c. coll.:* Stevenson 2623:8.

workman   **1.** A bad workman quarrels with his tools. *Rec. dist.:* U.S., Can. *1st cit.:* 1568 Gelli, *Fearful Fancies of Florentine,* tr. Barker;

US1875 Scarborough, *Chinese Proverbs.* **20c. coll.:** *ODEP* 26, Stevenson 2624:6, *CODP* 9.

2. A poor workman loses his tools. *Rec. dist.:* Ont. **1st cit.:** 1611 Cotgrave, *Dictionary of French and English Tongues.* **20c. coll.:** Stevenson 2624:6.

3. A workman is known by his chips. *Rec. dist.:* N.Y. **1st cit.:** 1869 Hazlitt, *Proverbs.* **20c. coll.:** Stevenson 2624:1.

4. A workman is no better than his tools. *Var.:* A workman may be known by his tools. *Rec. dist.:* Okla., Ont. **1st cit.:** 1577 *Art of Angling;* US1847 Davies, *Diary.* **20c. coll.:** *ODEP* 917, Stevenson 2624:8, Whiting*(MP)* 702.

5. A workman is worthy of his hire. *Rec. dist.:* Ind., N.C. **1st cit.:** ca1390 Chaucer, *Summoner's Tale;* US1644 *Complete Writings of Roger Williams* (1963). **20c. coll.:** *CODP* 128, Whiting 249, *ODEP* 439, Stevenson 1339:9, T&W 212, Whiting*(MP)* 357.

6. As is the workman, so is the work. *Vars.:* **(a)** The work praises the workman. **(b)** The workman is known by his work. *Rec. dist.:* U.S., Can. **1st cit.:** 1490 Vincentius, *Works,* tr. Caxton (1529). **20c. coll.:** *ODEP* 917, Stevenson 2623:7.

7. Good workmen need good tools. *Rec. dist.:* Ont.

8. Not to oversee workmen is to leave them with your purse open. *Rec. dist.:* Mich., N.Y. **1st cit.:** 1732 Fuller, *Gnomologia;* US1751 Franklin, *PRAlmanac.* **20c. coll.:** Stevenson 1548:3, Whiting 500.

9. The workman who would do good work must first sharpen his tools. *Rec. dist.:* W.Va.

10. Workmen are easier found than masters. *Rec. dist.:* Ill.

SEE ALSO TIME is a cunning workman. / It is WORKING that makes a workman.

workshop SEE An idle BRAIN is the devil's workshop. / An idle MIND is the devil's workshop.

world **1.** All of the world is crazy except me and you, and sometimes even you are a bit odd. *Var.:* All the world is queer save you and me, and sometimes even you are a little queer. *Rec. dist.:* Ill., Wis.

2. All the world's a stage. *Var.:* The world is a stage and all the people in it actors. *Rec. dist.:* U.S., Can. **1st cit.:** ca1530 Lucian, *Necromantia,* tr. unknown; US1857 Holmes, *Prologue.* **20c. coll.:** *ODEP* 918, Stevenson 2627:1.

3. Don't go round the world for a shortcut. *Rec. dist.:* Ont.

4. He conquers the world who conquers himself. *Rec. dist.:* Ala., Ga.

5. In spite of colleges and schools, the world remains a ship of fools. *Rec. dist.:* N.Y.

6. In this world it isn't what we take up that counts but what we give. *Rec. dist.:* Utah.

7. It is only an uncivilized world which would worship civilization. *Rec. dist.:* N.Y. **1st cit.:** US1940 *Meditations in Wall Street.* **20c. coll.:** Stevenson 360:6.

8. It's a small world. *Rec. dist.:* Mich., Miss., N.Y. **1st cit.:** 1886 Sala, *America Revisited;* US1905 Peabody, *To Be Young Was Very Heaven.* **20c. coll.:** *ODEP* 918, Stevenson 2632:3, Whiting*(MP)* 703.

9. Let him that will move the world first move himself. *Rec. dist.:* Ont.

10. One half the world does not know how the other half lives. *Vars.:* **(a)** Half the world does not know how the other half lives. **(b)** Half the world knows not how the other half lives. **(c)** One half the world does not know what the other half is doing. *Rec. dist.:* Mich., N.Y., Wis. **1st cit.:** 1607 Hall, *Holy Observations;* US1755 Franklin, *PRAlmanac.* **20c. coll.:** *ODEP* 344, Whiting 192, *CODP* 104, Stevenson 2629:3, T&W 414, Whiting*(MP)* 280.

11. The world does not grow better by force or by the policeman's club. *Rec. dist.:* N.Y. **1st cit.:** US1911 Gaynor, *Letters and Speeches.* **20c. coll.:** Stevenson 1918:6.

12. The world is a ladder for some to go up and some down. *Rec. dist.:* Ill. **1st cit.:** 1481 Caxton, *Reynard the Fox.* **20c. coll.:** *ODEP* 918, Stevenson 2625:3.

13. The world is a net: the more we stir in it, the more we are entangled. *Rec. dist.:* Ill. **1st cit.:** 1732 Fuller, *Gnomologia.* **20c. coll.:** Stevenson 2627:5.

14. The world is a whetstone and man a knife. *Rec. dist.:* N.Y.

15. The world is an easy target till you come to shoot at it. *Rec. dist.:* Ont.

16. The world is dying for a little bit of love. *Rec. dist.:* N.C.

17. The world is his who can see through its pretension. *Rec. dist.:* N.Y. *1st cit.:* US1837 Emerson, *American Scholar.* *20c. coll.:* Stevenson 2630:3.

18. The world is his who has the money to go over it. *Rec. dist.:* N.Y. *1st cit.:* US1860 Emerson, "Wealth" in *Conduct of Life.* *20c. coll.:* Stevenson 2630:3.

19. The world is made up of two classes, the hunters and the hunted. *Rec. dist.:* N.Y.

20. The world is too much with us. *Rec. dist.:* Ont.

21. The world is too narrow for two fools to quarrel in. *Rec. dist.:* Ill.

22. The world is what people make it. *Rec. dist.:* N.Y. *1st cit.:* US1939 Habas, *Morals for Moderns.* *20c. coll.:* Stevenson 2626:8.

23. The world is your cow, but you have to do the milking. *Rec. dist.:* N.Y. *1st cit.:* US1940 Thompson, *Body, Boots, and Britches.* *20c. coll.:* Stevenson 2630:3.

24. The world owes us a living. *Var.:* The world owes me a living. *Rec. dist.:* Ont., Wis. *1st cit.:* US1946 Quentin, *Puzzle for Fools.* *20c. coll.:* Whiting(MP) 704.

25. The world runs by compromises. *Rec. dist.:* N.C.

26. The world turns aside to let any man pass who knows whither he is going. *Rec. dist.:* N.Y.

27. The world: we live in it, but leave it we must. *Rec. dist.:* Ont.

28. This is a world of action and not one for moping and droning in. *Rec. dist.:* Miss.

29. Use the world, desire heaven. *Rec. dist.:* Ont.

30. What a wonderful world this would be if we all did as well today as we expect to do tomorrow. *Rec. dist.:* Ont.

31. You can't keep up with the world by letting it roll by. *Rec. dist.:* N.Y.

32. You cannot please the whole world and his wife. *Rec. dist.:* N.Y., Ont. *1st cit.:* US1948 Stevenson, *Home Book of Proverbs.* *20c. coll.:* Stevenson 2631:5.

33. You get out of the world just what you put into it. *Rec. dist.:* Ont., Wis.

SEE ALSO Tain't the BIGGEST en de strongest dat does de mostest in dis world. / The CEMETERIES are filled with people who thought the world couldn't get along without them. / What you give in CHARITY in this world you take with you after death. / CROWS are black the world over. / The FOLLIES of a fool are known to the world and not to himself; the follies of a wise man are known to himself but not to the world. / The FOOLS do more hurt in this world than the rascals. / A true FRIEND is one that steps in when the rest of the world steps out. / Men of GENIUS often bring great misery to the world. / The HAND that rocks the cradle is the hand that rules the world. / Stand on your HEAD and the world will be upside down. / Every HOME is a world in itself. / HOME is the father's kingdom, the children's paradise, the mother's world. / HOPE is the light of the world. / Alter IDEAS and you alter the world. / It takes all KINDS of people to make a world. / KNAVES and fools divide the world. / LAUGH and the world laughs with you; cry and you cry alone. / A LIE can go around the world and back while the truth is lacing up its boots. / LOVE makes the world go around. / An acre of PERFORMANCE is worth the whole world of promise. / The greatest RIGHT in the world is the right to be wrong. / Common SENSE is the rarest thing in the world and the most valuable. / SMILE and the world smiles with you. / It is better to SMOKE in this world than in the next. / It ain't what you WANTS in dis world, it's what you gits. / WATER will be water the world over. / A man's true WEALTH is the good he does in the world. / All the world loves a WINNER. / A two-faced WOMAN and a jealous man is the cause of trouble since the world began. / Tell a WOMAN and you tell the world. / The level of the WOMAN is the level of the world. / Kind WORDS are the music of the world. / Man's true WORTH is the good he does in the world.

worm 1. A worm is about the only thing that does not fall down. *Var.:* Don't worry when you stumble; remember, a worm is about the only thing that won't fall down. *Rec. dist.:* Ky., Miss.

2. Every worm has his turn. *Rec. dist.:* N.Y. *1st cit.:* 1546 Heywood, *Dialogue of Proverbs,* ed. Habernicht (1963); US1703 Taylor, *Christographia,* ed. Grabo (1962). *20c. coll.:* ODEP 837, Whiting 501, *CODP* 251, Stevenson 2634:1, T&W 414, Whiting(MP) 705.

3. He who makes a worm of himself should not holler when trampled upon. *Var.:* He who makes himself a worm should not holler when trampled on. *Rec. dist.:* Ill.

4. The worm is always wrong when it argues with the chicken. *Rec. dist.:* Pa.

5. The worm was punished for early rising. *Rec. dist.:* N.Y. *1st cit.:* US1860 Saxe, *Early Rising. 20c. coll.:* Stevenson 1996:1.

6. The worm will turn. *Vars.:* **(a)** Even a worm will turn. **(b)** Every worm turns sometime. **(c)** Step on a worm and it is sure to turn. **(d)** The trampled worm will turn. **(e)** Tread on a worm and it will turn. *Rec. dist.:* U.S., Can. *1st cit.:* 1546 Heywood, *Dialogue of Proverbs,* ed. Habernicht (1963); US1703 Taylor, *Christographia. 20c. coll.:* ODEP 837, Whiting 501, *CODP* 251, Stevenson 2634:1, T&W 414, Whiting(MP) 705.
SEE ALSO The early BIRD catches the worm. / Don't wait for PROVIDENCE to send you a worm. / Hungry ROOSTER never cackles when he scratches up a worm. / The ROSE has its thorn, the peach its worm.

worry (*n.*) 1. Most worry is half over when you sit down and talk it over. *Rec. dist.:* Ont.

2. Nothing worries worry like work. *Rec. dist.:* Ont.

3. The worries of today are the minor matters of tomorrow. *Rec. dist.:* Ill.

4. They who live in worry invite death in a hurry. *Rec. dist.:* Ill.

5. Worry is interest paid on trouble before it falls due. *Var.:* Worry is the interest paid by those who borrow trouble. *Rec. dist.:* Ont., W.Va. *1st cit.:* US1924 Lyon in *Judge Magazine,* 1 Mar. *20c. coll.:* Stevenson 2635:7.

6. Worry is like a rocking chair: both give you something to do, but neither gets you anywhere. *Var.:* Worry is like a rocking chair: it's something to do but doesn't get you anywhere. *Rec. dist.:* Wash., Wis.

7. Worry kills more men than work. *Rec. dist.:* Ind. *1st cit.:* 1879 Craik, *Young Mrs. Jardine. 20c. coll.:* ODEP 917, *CODP* 250, Stevenson 2635:3.

8. Worry never crossed a bridge. *Rec. dist.:* N.C.

worry (*v.*) 1. If you can do nothing about it, don't worry; if you can do something about it, do it—don't worry. *Rec. dist.:* Ont.

2. If you worry, you die; if you don't worry, you die anyway. *Rec. dist.:* Calif., Mich., N.Y.
SEE ALSO The BEE that makes the honey doesn't stand around the hive, and the man who makes the money has to worry, work, and strive. / KINGS and bears often worry their keeper. / LITTLE things worry little minds.

worrying 1. Worrying doesn't mend nor pay. *Rec. dist.:* Ont.

2. Worrying is often stewing without doing. *Rec. dist.:* N.Y.
SEE ALSO A BUDGET is a method of worrying before you spend as well as afterward.

worse 1. Be sure that there are others worse off than yourself. *Rec. dist.:* Ont.

2. If worse comes to worst, make the best of it. *Vars.:* **(a)** Let the worse come to the worst. **(b)** The worse comes to the worst. *Rec. dist.:* Ohio.
SEE ALSO BAD is called good when worse happens. / From the day you were born till you ride in a hearse, there's nothing so BAD but it might have been worse. / A dog's BARK is worse than his bite. / It is an ill thing to be DECEIVED, but worse to deceive. / He who speaks EVIL hears worse. / Go FARTHER and fare worse. / Your HAND is never the worse for doing your own work. / More HASTE, worse speed. / A LIAR is worse than a thief. /

PRAISE makes a good man better and a bad man worse. / Sometimes the REMEDY is worse than the disease. / There is no worse ROBBER than a bad book. / A good TALE is none the worse for being twice told.

worship *(n.)*   SEE WEALTH makes worship.

worship *(v.)*   It is only when men begin to worship that they begin to grow. *Rec. dist.:* N.C. *1st cit.:* US1922 Coolidge, Speech, Fredericksburg, Va., 6 July. *20c. coll.:* Stevenson 2636:6.

SEE ALSO It is only an uncivilized WORLD which would worship civilization.

worshiper   Beware of front-seat worshipers. *Rec. dist.:* Ont.

worst *(n.)*   **1.** Always figure for the worst and the best is bound to happen. *Rec. dist.:* N.Y., Tex., Wis. *1st cit.:* 1546 Heywood, *Dialogue of Proverbs,* ed. Habernicht (1963). *20c. coll.:* Stevenson 2637:6.

2. Blessed is he who expects the worst, for he shall not be disappointed. *Rec. dist.:* N.Y. *1st cit.:* US1941 MacInnes, *Above Suspicion.* *20c. coll.:* Stevenson 2637:4.

3. Figure on the worst but hope for the best. *Var.:* Provide for the worst: the best will save itself. *Rec. dist.:* U.S., Can. *1st cit.:* 1528 More, *Works of Thomas More* (1557); US1771 Rowland, *Peter Chester,* Mass.Hist.Soc. *Collections* (1925). *20c. coll.: ODEP* 250, Whiting 502, *CODP* 114, Stevenson 2637:4, Whiting(*MP*) 705.

4. The worst is yet to come. *Var.:* Cheer up— the worst is yet to come. *Rec. dist.:* U.S., Can. *1st cit.:* 1860 Tennyson, *Sea Dreams.* *20c. coll.:* Stevenson 2638:2.

5. The worst of a thing is what it will bring. *Rec. dist.:* Tex.

6. When the worst comes, the worst is going. *Var.:* When things are at the worst, they will mend. *Rec. dist.:* N.J. *1st cit.:* 1582 Whetstone, *Heptameron of Civil Discourses.* *20c. coll.: ODEP* 811, *CODP* 223, Stevenson 2638:1.

SEE ALSO FIRST gets the worst. / A man is only as GOOD as the worst on his team. / The worst of all POLICIES in hard times is to sit down and fold your hands. / Keep SMILING when things are at their worst.

worst *(adj.)*   SEE DEBT is the worst poverty. / DOCTORS make the worst patients. / FIRST is worst, second the same, last is best of all the game. / HOPE is the worst of evils, for it prolongs the torment of man. / KNAVERY is the worst trade. / NURSES make the worst patients. / The worst PASSIONS have their root in the best. / The TAILOR's wife is worst clad. / The worst WHEEL of the cart makes the most noise. / Of all cold WORDS of tongue or pen, the worst are these: I knew him when.

worst *(adv.)*   SEE HOME is where you act the worst and are treated the best.

worth *(n.)*   **1.** He whose own worth does speak need not speak his own worth. *Rec. dist.:* Ont. *1st cit.:* 1642 Fuller, "Self-Praising" in *Holy State.* *20c. coll.:* Stevenson 1864:4.

2. His worth is warrant for his welcome. *Rec. dist.:* Ont.

3. It is not what he has nor even what he does which directly expresses the worth of a man, but what he is. *Rec. dist.:* Ala., Ga.

4. It's not the worth of the thing but the want that makes its value. *Rec. dist.:* Va. *1st cit.:* 1616 Draxe, *Bibliotheca Scholastica* in *Anglia* (1918). *20c. coll.:* Stevenson 2639:5.

5. Man's true worth is the good he does in the world. *Rec. dist.:* N.Y.

6. The worth of a thing is best known by its want. *Var.:* The worth of a thing is best known by the lack of the thing. *Rec. dist.:* Ill., N.Y. *1st cit.:* 1586 Whetstone, *English Myrror;* US1765 Timberlake, *Memoirs 1756–1765,* ed. Williams (1927). *20c. coll.: ODEP* 922, Whiting 469, Stevenson 2639:5.

7. The worth of a thing is what it will bring. *Rec. dist.:* Ill. *1st cit.:* 1569 Agrippa, *Vanity of Arts and Sciences,* tr. Sanford (1575). *20c. coll.: ODEP* 922, *CODP* 251, Stevenson 2638:3.

8. True worth is in being, not in seeming; in doing, not in dreaming. *Rec. dist.:* N.Mex., N.Y. *1st cit.:* US1849 Cary, *Nobility.* *20c. coll.:* Stevenson 2638:4.

9. Worth has been underrated ever since wealth was overvalued. *Rec. dist.:* Mich. *1st cit.:* 1732 Fuller, *Gnomologia.* *20c. coll.:* Stevenson 2638:6.

10. Worth makes the man and want of it the

fellow. *Rec. dist.:* Wis. *1st cit.:* 1733 Pope, *Essay on Man.* *20c. coll.:* Stevenson 1379:10.

SEE ALSO Outside SHOW is poor substitute for inner worth.

worth *(prep.)* What is worth most is often valued least. *Rec. dist.:* Ark.

SEE ALSO A BIRD in the hand is worth two in the bush. / Anything worth DOING is worth doing well. / A DOLLAR in the bank is worth two in the hand. / If you want to know what a DUCAT is worth, borrow one. / An EGG today is worth a hen tomorrow. / A thorn of EXPERIENCE is worth a wilderness of advice. / Take a FRIEND for what he does, a wife for what she has, and goods for what they are worth. / A small GAIN is worth more than a large promise. / A HAIR on the head is worth two in the brush. / Anything worth HAVING is worth keeping. / If it is worth HAVING, it is worth working for. / HEALTH is worth more than learning. / An HOUR in the morning is worth two in the evening. / One good IDEA put to use is worth a hundred buzzing around in the back of your head. / A JOB worth doing is worth doing well. / A LAUGH is worth a thousand groans in any market. / A ripple of LAUGHTER is worth a flood of tears. / PATIENCE in market is worth pounds in a year. / An acre of PERFORMANCE is worth the whole world of promise. / One PICTURE is worth ten thousand words. / An ounce of PREVENTION is worth a pound of cure. / If it isn't worth SAYING, don't say it at all. / A good SCARE is worth more to a man than good advice. / One hour's SLEEP before midnight is worth three after. / A SPUR in the head is worth two in the feet. / A little THING in the hand is worth a great thing in prospect. / One TODAY is worth two tomorrows. / A VOLUNTEER is worth ten pressed men. / An ounce of WIT is worth a pound of sorrow. / An ounce of WIT that is bought is worth a pound that is taught. / A soft WORD is often worth more than a house and a lot. / A WORD before is worth two behind.

worthlessness SEE He's the best PHYSICIAN that knows the worthlessness of most medicines.

worthy SEE Every ASS thinks himself worthy to stand with the king's horses. / The LABORER is worthy of his hire. / They that value not PRAISE will never do anything worthy of it. / A WORKMAN is worthy of his hire.

would I would if I could, but I can't. *Rec. dist.:* N.Y.

SEE ALSO He who would not when he could is not ABLE when he would.

wound *(n.)* 1. A green wound is soon healed. *Rec. dist.:* Ont. *1st cit.:* ca1532 Fortescue, *Fortescue Papers.* *20c. coll.:* ODEP 337, Stevenson 2647:3.

2. All honor's wounds are self-inflicted. *Rec. dist.:* N.Y. *1st cit.:* USca1900 Carnegie, Epigram in Hendrick, *Life of Carnegie.* *20c. coll.:* Stevenson 1160:13.

3. An ill wound, but not an ill name, may be healed. *Var.:* An ill wound is cured, but not an ill name. *Rec. dist.:* N.Y. *1st cit.:* 1640 Herbert, *Outlandish Proverbs (Jacula Prudentum)* in *Works,* ed. Hutchinson (1941); US1753 Franklin, *PRAlmanac.* *20c. coll.:* ODEP 401, Whiting 502, Stevenson 1658:3.

4. Deepest wounds are often inflicted by praise. *Rec. dist.:* Ala., Ga.

5. Faithful are the wounds of a friend. *Rec. dist.:* Ont. *1st cit.:* 1862 Rossetti, *House to House.* *20c. coll.:* Stevenson 912:5.

6. Old wounds soon bleed. *Rec. dist.:* Ont.

7. Reopen not a wound once healed. *Rec. dist.:* Ont. *1st cit.:* 1553 Udall, *Ralph Roister Doister;* US1727 Dummer in *Documentary History of State of Maine Containing Baxter Manuscripts,* ed. Baxter (1869–1916). *20c. coll.:* ODEP 678, Whiting 502, Stevenson 2646:5, Whiting(MP) 705.

8. The private wound is deepest. *Rec. dist.:* Ill. *1st cit.:* 1579 Lyly, *Euphues, Anatomy of Wit.* *20c. coll.:* ODEP 923, Stevenson 2648:7.

9. Though the wound be healed, the scar remains. *Rec. dist.:* Mich. *1st cit.:* ca1542 Wyatt, *Being in Prison.* *20c. coll.:* ODEP 923, Stevenson 752:6.

10. Wounds made by words are hard to heal. *Rec. dist.:* Miss. *1st cit.:* ca1650 Sidney, "Letter to His Son, Sir Philip Sidney" in Symonds, *Life of Sidney* (1878). *20c. coll.:* Stevenson 2605:9.

SEE ALSO TIME heals all wounds. / A WORD hurts more than a wound.

wound (*v.*) *SEE* The TONGUE wounds more than the arrow.

wrangler Wranglers never want words. *Rec. dist.:* Ont. *1st cit.:* 1616 Draxe, *Bibliotheca Scholastica* in *Anglia* (1918). *20c. coll.:* ODEP 923, Stevenson 2648:10.

wrapped A man wrapped up in himself makes a small package. *Vars.:* **(a)** A man wrapped up in himself makes a mighty small package. **(b)** When a man is wrapped up in himself, the package is small. *Rec. dist.:* Calif., Colo., N.Y.

wrapping The wrapping sells the parcel. *Rec. dist.:* Ont.

wrath **1.** Beware of the wrath of a patient man. *Rec. dist.:* Miss.

2. The wrath of brothers is the wrath of devils. *Rec. dist.:* N.C. *1st cit.:* 1732 Fuller, *Gnomologia.* *20c. coll.:* Stevenson 247:7.

SEE ALSO A soft ANSWER turns away wrath. / HELL knows no wrath like a woman scorned.

wreck *SEE* A forgotten SWITCH may cause a wreck.

wrench **1.** Don't buy a left-hand monkey wrench. *Rec. dist.:* Ont.

2. Don't throw a monkey wrench in the works. *Rec. dist.:* U.S., Can. *1st cit.:* US1920 Johnson, "Shooting Stars" in *Everybody's Magazine,* May. *20c. coll.:* Stevenson 1497:3, Whiting(MP) 422.

wrinkle *SEE* The HEART has no wrinkles. / A good LIFE keeps away wrinkles. / An empty PURSE fills the face with wrinkles.

wrinkled *SEE* Wrinkled PURSES make wrinkled faces.

write **1.** Don't say it, write it. *Rec. dist.:* Ont.

2. Don't write and fear no woman. *Var.:* Do right and fear no man; don't write and fear no woman. *Rec. dist.:* N.Y. *1st cit.:* USca1918 McLuke, Epigram in *Cincinnati Enquirer.* *20c. coll.:* Stevenson 1989:4.

3. Don't write before your pencil is sharpened. *Rec. dist.:* Ont.

4. He who would write and can't write can

surely review. *Rec. dist.:* N.Y. *1st cit.:* US1848 Lowell, *Fable for Critics.* *20c. coll.:* Stevenson 455:11.

5. If you don't write, you're wrong. *Rec. dist.:* Ohio.

6. Never write what you dare not sign. *Var.:* Never write what you would not say. *Rec. dist.:* Calif., N.Y., Ont., S.C.

7. Write with the learned; pronounce with the vulgar. *Rec. dist.:* N.Y. *1st cit.:* 1678 Ray, *English Proverbs;* US1738 Franklin, *PRAlmanac.* *20c. coll.:* Stevenson 2652:3.

SEE ALSO A good BIOGRAPHY is never written until after the person is dead. / It is well that our FAULTS are not written on our faces. / Write on one SIDE of the paper but on both sides of the subject. / THINK much; speak little; write less. / A WISE man writes for pleasure; a fool reads because he is curious. / If you are willing to WORK, you can write your name anywhere you choose.

writing **1.** Easy writing makes hard reading. *Rec. dist.:* Ont. *1st cit.:* ca1816 Sheridan, *Clio's Protest.* *20c. coll.:* Stevenson 2654:3.

2. Never sign a writing till you have read it. *Rec. dist.:* Mich.

3. The art of writing is the art of applying the seat of the pants to the seat of the chair. *Rec. dist.:* N.Y.

SEE ALSO READING makes a full man, conference a ready man, writing an exact man.

written *SEE* The written WORD remains.

wrong (*n.*) **1.** Don't compromise with wrong because it is safe. *Rec. dist.:* Ill.

2. It costs more to revenge wrongs than to bear them. *Rec. dist.:* Ont.

3. It is better to suffer wrong than to do wrong. *Rec. dist.:* Ohio, Utah. *1st cit.:* 1639 Clarke, *Paroemiologia;* US1859 Stephens, *Fashion and Famine.* *20c. coll.:* Stevenson 2656:13, T&W 415.

4. Little wrongs breed great evils. *Rec. dist.:* Ill.

5. Man only from himself can suffer wrong. *Rec. dist.:* N.Y. *1st cit.:* US1742 Franklin, *PRAlmanac.* *20c. coll.:* Stevenson 2656:11.

6. People do wrong, though there is much more to be gained by doing right. **Rec. dist.:** Ill.

7. The smaller the wrong, the greater the guilt. **Rec. dist.:** Ind.

8. The wrong shall fail, the right prevail. **Rec. dist.:** Ohio.

9. There is as much in knowing how not to do wrong as there is in knowing how to do right. **Rec. dist.:** Ill.

10. To forget a wrong is the best revenge. **Rec. dist.:** Tex. **1st cit.:** 1732 Fuller, *Gnomologia.* **20c. coll.:** Stevenson 2656:14.

11. To tell your wrong is worse than keeping your mouth shut. **Rec. dist.:** N.C.

12. Two wrongs do not make a right. **Var.:** Two wrongs won't right a wrong. **Rec. dist.:** U.S., Can. **1st cit.:** 1875 Cheales, *Proverbial Folk-Lore;* US1783 Rush, *Letters,* ed. Butterfield (1951). **20c. coll.:** ODEP 853, Whiting 502, *CODP* 235, Stevenson 1991:4, T&W 415, Whiting*(MP)* 706.

13. Wrong will right itself in time. **Rec. dist.:** Ont.

14. Wrongs may try a good man, but cannot imprint on him a false stamp. **Rec. dist.:** Mich.

15. You may sometimes be much in the wrong in owning your being in the right. **Rec. dist.:** N.Y., S.C. **1st cit.:** US1754 Franklin, *PRAlmanac.* **20c. coll.:** Stevenson 1991:8.

SEE ALSO The ABSENT are always in the wrong. / KINGS can do no wrong. / RIGHT's right and wrong's wrong. / To do a great RIGHT, do a little wrong.

wrong *(v.)*   SEE RIGHT wrongs nobody.

wrong *(adj.)*   Count that thing wrong which would be wrong if everybody did it. **Rec. dist.:** Ohio.

SEE ALSO The LAME man who keeps the right road outstrips the runner who keeps the wrong one. / The MAJORITY is often wrong. / NATURE is usually wrong. / The greatest RIGHT in the world is the right to be wrong. / A SHORTCUT is often the wrong cut. / Never bark up the wrong TREE. / The WORM is always wrong when it argues with the chicken.

wrong *(adv.)*   1. Don't scold anyone for doing things wrong if you do them that way yourself. **Rec. dist.:** Wis.

2. If a thing is done wrong, it is far better that it had not been done at all. **Rec. dist.:** Ill.

SEE ALSO It is better to ASK twice than to go wrong once. / Who does NOTHING can do nothing wrong. / The man worthwhile is the man who can SMILE when everything goes wrong. / WINE, women, and song will get a man wrong.

Y

Yankee Only Yankees and fools predict the weather. *Rec. dist.:* Miss.

yard A yard is an index to the interior of the house. *Rec. dist.:* N.C.

yarn Tend to your own little ball of yarn. *Rec. dist.:* Ill.

year **1.** A bad year is kinder than the poor man's neighbor. *Rec. dist.:* N.C.

2. A cherry year, a merry year; a plum year, a dumb year. *Rec. dist.:* Wash. *1st cit.:* 1644 *Poor Robin's Almanac* in Lean, *Collectanea.* *20c. coll.:* ODEP 117, CODP 35, Stevenson 331:11.

3. A snow year, a rich year. *Rec. dist.:* N.Y., Vt. *1st cit.:* 1580 Monardes, *Joyful News Out of the New Found World,* tr. Frampton. *20c. coll.:* ODEP 748, Stevenson 2151:9.

4. After a wet year, a cold one. *Rec. dist.:* Utah.

5. It will be all the same in a hundred years. *Var.:* It will be all the same a hundred years hence. *Rec. dist.:* Calif., Kans., N.Mex., Ont. *1st cit.:* 1611 Cotgrave, *Dictionary of French and English Tongues;* US1775 Schaw, *Journal of Lady of Quality, 1774–1776,* ed. Andrews (1934). *20c. coll.:* ODEP 10, Whiting 504, Stevenson 2658:2, T&W 416, Whiting(MP) 707.

6. Men's years and their faults are always more than they are willing to own. *Rec. dist.:* Ont. *1st cit.:* 1707 Mapletoft, *Select Proverbs.* *20c. coll.:* ODEP 525, Stevenson 773:5.

7. Not by years but by disposition is wisdom acquired. *Rec. dist.:* N.Y.

8. Our years roll on. *Rec. dist.:* Mich. *1st cit.:* ca1845 Barham, *Eheu Fugaces.* *20c. coll.:* Stevenson 2323:2.

9. The fewer the years, the fewer the tears. *Rec. dist.:* Ill., N.Y. *1st cit.:* 1732 Fuller, *Gnomologia.* *20c. coll.:* Stevenson 2287:3.

10. The first hundred years are the hardest. *Var.:* The first one hundred years are the hardest. *Rec. dist.:* U.S., Can. *1st cit.:* US1928 Thomas, *Raiders.* *20c. coll.:* Whiting(MP) 707.

11. The years teach much that the days never knew. *Var.:* The years teach much which the days never knew. *Rec. dist.:* Minn., N.Y., Wash. *1st cit.:* US1844 Emerson, "Experience" in *Essays.* *20c. coll.:* Stevenson 2658:13.

12. We do not count a man's years until he has nothing else to count. *Rec. dist.:* N.Y., Utah.

13. Years know more than books. *Var.:* Years teach more than books. *Rec. dist.:* Miss., N.Y., Wis. *1st cit.:* 1640 Herbert, *Outlandish Proverbs (Jacula Prudentum)* in *Works,* ed. Hutchinson (1941). *20c. coll.:* ODEP 925, Stevenson 2658:15.

SEE ALSO After a hundred years we shall all be BALD. / CHRISTMAS comes but once a year. / A DAY to come seems longer than a year that is gone. / It will all be the same after you are DEAD a hundred years. / We live in DEEDS, not years. / A three years' DROUGHT will not starve a cook. / With the old year leave your FAULTS, however dear. / It takes years to make a FRIEND but minutes to lose one. / Say no ILL of the year till it be past. / The bottom RAIL gets on top every fifty years. / Keep a THING seven years and it's bound to come in handy. / WINTER comes but once a year, and when it comes, it brings the doctor good cheer.

yearning SEE There are three INGREDIENTS in the good life, learning, earning, and yearning.

yell Don't yell before you're out of the woods. *Rec. dist.:* Ont. *Infm.:* Cf. holler.

yes Two yeses make a positive. *Rec. dist.:* Kans.

SEE ALSO When a LADY says no, she means perhaps; when she says perhaps, she means yes; when she says yes, she is no lady.

yesterday **1.** No man can call again yesterday. *Rec. dist.:* Ill., N.Y., Ont. *1st cit.:* 1516 Skelton, *Magnyfycence.* *20c. coll.:* ODEP 926, Stevenson 2660:6.

2. Yesterday is gone, forget it; tomorrow isn't here, don't worry about it; today is here, use it. *Rec. dist.:* Ind., Minn.

3. Yesterday is gone; today is going; tomorrow you may be gone. *Rec. dist.*: N.Y.

4. Yesterday is past; tomorrow may never come; this day is ours. *Rec. dist.*: N.Y.

5. Yesterday's errors, let yesterday cover. *Rec. dist.*: Fla.

SEE ALSO TODAY is yesterday's pupil. / He is a WISE man who knows more today than he did yesterday.

yet SEE Don't spend too much on TOMOR-ROW—it isn't yours yet.

yield It is better to yield than to come to misfortune through stubbornness. *Rec. dist.*: N.Y.

SEE ALSO A shady BUSINESS never yields a sunny life.

yielding 1. Yielding an inch would be giving an ell. *Rec. dist.*: N.Y.

2. Yielding is sometimes the best way of succeeding. *Rec. dist.*: N.Y.

3. Yielding stills all war. *Rec. dist.*: Ill.

yoke SEE The FINGERS of the housewife do more than a yoke of oxen.

young (*n.*) 1. The young are slaves to novelty, the old to customs. *Rec. dist.*: N.Y.

2. The young do not know what age is, and the aged forget what youth was. *Rec. dist.*: Ill.

3. The young know everything, the middle-aged suspect everything, and the old believe everything. *Rec. dist.*: Kans.

4. The young may die; the old must die. *Var.*: The young may go; the old must go. *Rec. dist.*: U.S., Can. *1st cit.*: 1534 More, *Dialogue of Comforte* in *Works* (1557). *20c. coll.*: ODEP 927, CODP 253, Stevenson 525:1.

5. When we are out of sympathy with the young, our work in the world is over. *Rec. dist.*: Ill.

SEE ALSO The AGED knows; the young supposes. / Each old CROW thinks her young are the blackest.

young (*adj.*) 1. A young man idle, an old man needy. *Vars.*: (a) An idle youth, a needy eye. (b) Young idler, an old beggar. *Rec. dist.*: Mich., Ohio. *1st cit.*: 1564 Bullein, *Dialogue;*

US1940 Thompson, *Body, Boots, and Britches*. *20c. coll.*: ODEP 395, Stevenson 41:3.

2. A young man looks into the future as an old man into his past. *Rec. dist.*: Ill.

3. A young trooper should have an old horse. *Rec. dist.*: Calif., N.Y., Tex.

4. A young whore, an old saint. *Rec. dist.*: N.Y. *1st cit.*: 1670 Ray, *English Proverbs*. *20c. coll.*: Stevenson 2490:3.

5. A young woman married to an old man must behave like an old woman. *Rec. dist.*: Ill.

6. As young folks see, the young folks do; as they hear, they say. *Rec. dist.*: Ont.

7. Get 'em young and train 'em. *Var.*: Catch them while they're young. *Rec. dist.*: N.Y., Wis.

8. Go it while you're young. *Rec. dist.*: N.H. *1st cit.*: US1848 Lincoln, Letter to W. H. Herndon, 11 July. *20c. coll.*: Stevenson 2662:4.

9. If the young man would and the old man could, there would be nothing undone. *Rec. dist.*: Ill. *1st cit.*: 1642 Torriano, *Select Italian Proverbs*. *20c. coll.*: ODEP 927.

10. Start young at what you wish to become proficient in. *Rec. dist.*: Ont.

11. The way never to grow old and grey headed is to die young. *Rec. dist.*: N.Y.

12. The young folks think the old folks are fools, but the old folks know the young folks are fools. *Var.*: Young men think old men are fools; old men know young men are fools. *Rec. dist.*: U.S., Can. *1st cit.*: ca1576 Whythorne, *Autobiography*, ed. Osborne (1961); US1840 Haliburton, *Clockmaker*. *20c. coll.*: ODEP 927, T&W 236, CODP 253, Stevenson 43:5, Whiting(MP) 402.

13. When young folks talk to old folks, they should know what they're about. *Rec. dist.*: W.Va.

14. You are only young once. *Rec. dist.*: U.S., Can. *1st cit.*: US1941 Wentworth, *In the Balance*. *20c. coll.*: Stevenson 2664:13, Whiting(MP) 708.

15. You're as young as you feel. *Rec. dist.*: N.Dak. *1st cit.*: 1855 Collins, *How Old Are You?* *20c. coll.*: Stevenson 31:1.

16. You're as young as you look and as old as you feel. *Rec. dist.:* N.Y., Ont.

17. Young heads are giddy and young hearts are warm. *Rec. dist.:* N.Y. *1st cit.:* 1784 Cowper, *Tirocinium.* *20c. coll.:* Stevenson 2662:7.

18. Young man married is a young man marred. *Rec. dist.:* N.C. *1st cit.:* 1546 Heywood, *Dialogue of Proverbs,* ed. Habernicht (1963); US1945 Campbell, *With Bated Breath.* *20c. coll.:* ODEP 513, Whiting(MP) 402, Stevenson 1532:3.

19. Young people can do what the old ones can't because the young ones don't know it can't be done. *Rec. dist.:* Tenn.

SEE ALSO Young ANGEL, old devil; young devil, old angel. / Old in BODY, young in spirit. / A rich BRIDE goes young to the church. / As the old COCK crows, the young cock learns. / Better an old man's DARLING than a young man's slave. / Beware of the young DOCTOR and the old barber. / Whom the GODS love die young. / The GOOD die young. / To a young HEART everything is fun. / An old HEN never grows young. / An old HORSE slips quicker than a young one. / LADIES young and fair have the gift to know it. / An OLD young man will be a young old man. / OLD young and old long. / The OLD one crows, the young one learns. / Lie on ROSES when young; lie on thorns when old. / Young SAINT, old devil. / SAVE when you're young to spend when you are old. / SPARE when you are young and spend when you are old. / A young TREE is easier twisted than an old tree. / Bend the TREE while it is young. / A young TWIG is easier twisted than an old tree. / Bend the WILLOW while it's young.

yours What's yours is mine, and what's mine is yours. *Rec. dist.:* Calif., Mich., N.Y. *1st cit.:* 1576 Pettie, *Petite Palace of Pleasure;* US1792 Heth in *Papers of Alexander Hamilton,* eds. Syrett and Cooke (1961). *20c. coll.:* ODEP 533, Whiting 505, Stevenson 1834:8, T&W 245, Whiting(MP) 708.

yourself **1.** Be yourself. *Rec. dist.:* Kans., Ont.

2. Conquer yourself. *Rec. dist.:* N.Y.

3. Don't count yourself too many. *Rec. dist.:* N.C.

4. Don't kid yourself. *Rec. dist.:* Mich., N.Y., Ont.

5. Look at yourself in the mirror. *Rec. dist.:* N.C.

6. Never excuse yourself to yourself. *Rec. dist.:* Ont. *1st cit.:* 1595 Shakespeare, *Midsummer Night's Dream.* *20c. coll.:* Stevenson 720:5.

7. Serve yourself if you would be well served. *Rec. dist.:* Ont. *1st cit.:* 1659 Torriano, *Vocabolario Italiano & Inglese;* US1737 Franklin, *PRAlmanac.* *20c. coll.:* ODEP 715, Whiting 385, CODP 200, Stevenson 2077:12.

8. Through yourself you know others. *Rec. dist.:* Minn.

9. What you do yourself is half done. *Rec. dist.:* Ill.

10. Wherever you go, you can never get rid of yourself. *Var.:* Wherever you must go, you must live with yourself. *Rec. dist.:* N.C., Ont., S.C.

11. You have to live with yourself. *Rec. dist.:* N.C.

SEE ALSO If you wish to see the BEST in others, show the best of yourself. / If you want something done and done well, DO it yourself. / Never DO anything yourself you can get somebody else to do. / DOUBT whom you will, but never yourself. / Find FAULTS in yourself before finding faults in others. / HELP yourself and heaven will help you. / If you don't HELP yourself, nobody will. / INJURE others, injure yourself. / Don't JUDGE others by yourself.

youth **1.** A growing youth has a wolf in his stomach. *Var.:* A growing boy has a wolf in his stomach. *Rec. dist.:* Colo., Ill. *1st cit.:* 1611 Cotgrave, *Dictionary of French and English Tongues.* *20c. coll.:* ODEP 340, Stevenson 2661:10.

2. A man whose youth has no follies will in his maturity have no power. *Rec. dist.:* Ill.

3. Application in youth makes old age comfortable. *Rec. dist.:* Mich. *1st cit.:* 1700 Goldsmith, *Deserted Village.* *20c. coll.:* Stevenson 41:3.

4. Every dissipation of youth has to be paid for with a draft on old age. *Rec. dist.:* Wis.

5. He that corrects not youth controls not age. *Rec. dist.:* Ill.

6. If only youth had the experience and old age had the strength. *Rec. dist.:* Kans.

7. If youth but knew and age but could do. *Rec. dist.:* Ill., Oreg. *1st cit.:* 1611 Cotgrave, *Dictionary of French and English Tongues.* *20c. coll.:* Stevenson 42:7.

8. In youth we believe many things that are not true; in old age we doubt many truths. *Rec. dist.:* Ill.

9. In youth we run into difficulties; in old age difficulties run into us. *Rec. dist.:* N.Y.

10. It is less painful in youth than in age to be ignorant. *Rec. dist.:* Mich.

11. Reckless youth makes rueful age. *Rec. dist.:* N.Y., Tex. *1st cit.:* ca1520 Dunbar, *Works,* S.T.S. (1884). *20c. coll.:* ODEP 667, Stevenson 42:4.

12. The mark must be made in youth. *Rec. dist.:* Ind. *1st cit.:* 1579 Lyly, *Euphues, Anatomy of Wit,* ed. Arber (1868). *20c. coll.:* Stevenson 2665:4.

13. The youth of the soul is everlasting, and eternity is youth. *Rec. dist.:* Ill.

14. There's no such word as can't in the lexicon of youth. *Rec. dist.:* dist.: N.Y.

15. There's nothing that keeps its youth but a tree and truth. *Rec. dist.:* Ont.

16. To the wise, youth is a time for training. *Rec. dist.:* Ont.

17. When a youth is saved, a life is saved; when an old person is saved, only a soul is saved. *Rec. dist.:* N.C.

18. You cannot mate youth with age unless age has a big bankroll. *Rec. dist.:* Ill.

19. Youth and age can never agree. *Rec. dist.:* U.S., Can. *1st cit.:* ca1390 Chaucer, *Miller's Tale;* US1789 Morris, *Diary of French Revolution,* ed. Davenport (1930). *20c. coll.:* ODEP 929, Whiting 505, Stevenson 43:2.

20. Youth and white paper take any impression. *Rec. dist.:* Ill. *1st cit.:* 1579 Lyly, *Euphues,*

Anatomy of Wit, ed. Arber (1868). *20c. coll.:* ODEP 929, Stevenson 2665:4.

21. Youth comes but once in a lifetime. *Rec. dist.:* N.Y. *1st cit.:* US1839 Longfellow, *Hyperion.* *20c. coll.:* Stevenson 2664:13.

22. Youth is a blunder, manhood a struggle, old age a regret. *Rec. dist.:* Kans. *1st cit.:* 1844 Disraeli, *Coningsby.* *20c. coll.:* Stevenson 42:5.

23. Youth is a wonderful thing; too bad it has to be wasted on children. *Var.:* Youth is such a lovely thing; it is too bad it's wasted on the young. *Rec. dist.:* N.Y., Wis.

24. Youth is full of vitamins; age is full of germs. *Rec. dist.:* N.Y. *1st cit.:* US1939 Burgess, *Look Eleven Years Younger.* *20c. coll.:* Stevenson 40:9.

25. Youth is not a time of life, it is a state of mind. *Rec. dist.:* Wis. *1st cit.:* US1922 Ullman, *From the Summit of Four Score Years.* *20c. coll.:* Stevenson 2665:3.

26. Youth longs and manhood strives, but age remembers. *Rec. dist.:* N.Y. *1st cit.:* US1879 Holmes, *Iron Gate.* *20c. coll.:* Stevenson 43:11.

27. Youth must store up; age must use. *Rec. dist.:* Ill.

28. Youth supplies us with colors, age with canvas. *Rec. dist.:* N.Y. *1st cit.:* US1852 Thoreau, *Winter,* 26 Jan. *20c. coll.:* Stevenson 40:9.

29. Youth will be served. *Var.:* Youth must be served. *Rec. dist.:* Colo., Ill., Kans., Ont. *1st cit.:* 1851 Borrow, *Lavengro;* US1930 Benet, *Young Blood.* *20c. coll.:* ODEP 929, Stevenson 2663:6, CODP 253, Whiting(MP) 708.

30. Youth will have its fling. *Var.:* Youth will have its swing. *Rec. dist.:* Ill., Tex. *1st cit.:* 1562 Legh, *Accidence of Armoury;* US1921 Herbert, *House.* *20c. coll.:* ODEP 929, Whiting (MP) 708, Stevenson 2663:6.

SEE ALSO ABUNDANCE of money ruins youth. / AGE needs a critic, youth a model. / AGE should think and youth should do. / BEAUTY is the bloom of youth. / IDLENESS in youth makes way for a painful and miserable old age. / WINE and youth are flax upon fire.

Z

zeal **1.** Zeal is blind when it encroaches on the rights of others. *Rec. dist.:* Mich., N.Y.

2. Zeal is like fire: it needs both feeding and watching. *Var.:* Zeal is like fire: it needs feeding and watching. *Rec. dist.:* N.Y. *1st cit.:* 1732 Fuller, *Gnomologia.* *20c. coll.:* Stevenson 2666:5.

3. Zeal is only for wise men but is mostly found in fools. *Rec. dist.:* Calif., N.Y., Wis. *1st cit.:* 1732 Fuller, *Gnomologia.* *20c. coll.:* Stevenson 2665:10.

4. Zeal without knowledge is a fire without light. *Rec. dist.:* N.Y., N.C., S.C. *1st cit.:* 1732 Fuller, *Gnomologia.* *20c. coll.:* ODEP 930, Stevenson 2666:5.

5. Zeal without knowledge is the sister of folly. *Rec. dist.:* N.Y. *1st cit.:* 1611 Davies of Hereford, *Scourge of Folly.* *20c. coll.:* ODEP 930, Stevenson 2666:5.

zebra You can tell a zebra by its stripes. *Var.:* You know a zebra by its stripes. *Rec. dist.:* Calif., Mich., N.Y.

zero Zero times zero is equal to zero. *Rec. dist.:* Calif., Mich.
SEE ALSO FAME one day, zero the next.

BIBLIOGRAPHY

This bibliography is divided into eight sections, the first five of which are limited to studies or collections of proverbs that have appeared as English-language books. Included are sections on bibliographies, proverb journals, important studies on proverbs, international proverb collections that include Anglo-American proverbs, and Anglo-American proverb collections. The last three sections list important essays that deal with American proverbs, small regional and ethnic American proverb collections, and studies of proverbs in American literature.

The most comprehensive investigation of American proverbs available is Wolfgang Mieder's *American Proverbs: A Study of Texts and Contexts* (New York: Peter Lang, 1989). The fifteen chapters of this book deal with the proverb in general, American proverbs in particular, proverbs of immigrants, proverbs current in various states, proverbs of Native Americans, African-American proverbs, Benjamin Franklin's "proverbs," proverbs in prose literature, proverb poems, proverbs in popular songs, wellerisms, proverb parodies, proverbs in comics and cartoons, and proverbs in advertisements; the final chapter discusses the modern American proverb "Different strokes for different folks." Each chapter includes an interpretative essay, a bibliography, and numerous texts in context. A large bibliography, three indexes, and forty illustrations are also included.

BIBLIOGRAPHIES

Bartlett, John. *Catalogue of a Choice and Valuable Collection of Rare Books of Proverbs and Emblems, Dance of Death, etc., Including Many Books Printed in the Sixteenth and Seventeenth Centuries and Curiously Illustrated Works.* Boston: Little, Brown & Co., 1888.

Bonser, Wilfrid. *Proverb Literature: A Bibliography of Works Relating to Proverbs.* London: William Glaisher, 1930. Reprint. Nendeln, Liechtenstein: Kraus Reprint, 1967.

De Caro, Francis A., and William K. McNeil. *American Proverb Literature: A Bibliography.* Bloomington, Ind.: Folklore Forum, Indiana University, 1971.

Mieder, Wolfgang. *International Bibliography of Explanatory Essays on Individual Proverbs and Proverbial Expressions.* Bern: Peter Lang, 1977.

Mieder, Wolfgang. *Proverbs in Literature: An International Bibliography.* Bern: Peter Lang, 1978.

Mieder, Wolfgang. *International Proverb Scholarship: An Annotated Bibliography.* New York: Garland Publishing, 1982.

Mieder, Wolfgang. *Investigations of Proverbs, Proverbial Expressions, Quotations and Clichés. A Bibliography of Explanatory Es-*

says Which Appeared in "Notes and Queries" (1849–1983). Bern: Peter Lang, 1984.

Mieder, Wolfgang. "International Bibliography of New and Reprinted Proverb Collections." Annual bibliography in Proverbium: Yearbook of International Proverb Scholarship, 1984ff.

Mieder, Wolfgang. "International Proverb Scholarship: An Updated Bibliography." Annual bibliography in Proverbium: Yearbook of International Proverb Scholarship, 1984ff.

Mieder, Wolfgang. International Proverb Scholarship: An Annotated Bibliography. Supplement I (1800–1981). New York: Garland Publishing, 1990.

Stirling-Maxwell, Sir William. An Essay Towards a Collection of Books Relating to Proverbs, Emblems, Apophthegms, Epitaphs and Ana, Being a Catalogue of Those at Keir. London: Privately printed, 1860.

Urdang, Laurence, and Frank R. Abate. Idioms and Phrases Index. 3 vols. Detroit: Gale Research Co., 1983.

PROVERB JOURNALS

Proverbium: Bulletin d'information sur les recherches parémiologiques, 1–25 (1965–1975), 1–1008. Ed. by Matti Kuusi et al. (Helsinki). Reprint (2 vols.). Ed. by Wolfgang Mieder. Bern: Peter Lang, 1987.

Proverbium Paratum: Bulletin d'information sur les recherches parémiologiques, 1–4 (1980–1989), 1–460. Ed. by Vilmos Voigt et al. (Budapest).

Proverbium: Yearbook of International Proverb Scholarship, 1984ff. Ed. by Wolfgang Mieder et al. (Burlington, Vt.).

STUDIES

Alster, Bendt. Studies in Sumerian Proverbs. Copenhagen: Akademisk Forlag, 1975.

Barakat, Robert A. A Contextual Study of Arabic Proverbs. Helsinki: Suomalainen Tiedeakatemia, 1980.

Blackwood, Andrew J. In All Your Ways: A Study of Proverbs. Grand Rapids: Baker Book House, 1979.

Boas, George. Vox Populi: Essays in the History of an Idea. Baltimore: Johns Hopkins University Press, 1969.

Bridges, Charles. An Exposition of the Book of Proverbs. London: Seeley, Jackson, & Halliday, 1859. Reprinted with the title Proverbs: A Commentary on Proverbs. Edinburgh: The Banner of Truth Trust, 1977.

Bryant, Margaret M. Proverbs and How to Collect Them. Greensboro, N.C.: American Dialect Society, 1945.

Carnes, Pack, ed. Proverbia in Fabula: Essays on the Relationship of the Fable and the Proverb. Bern: Peter Lang, 1988.

Cheales, Allan Benjamin. Proverbial Folklore. London: Simpkin, Marshall & Co., 1874. Reprint. Darby, Pa.: Folcroft Library Editions, 1976.

Dundes, Alan. Life is Like a Chicken Coop Ladder: A Portrait of German Culture Through Folklore. New York: Columbia University Press, 1984.

Dundes, Alan, and Claudia A. Stibbe. The Art of Mixing Metaphors: A Folkloristic Interpretation of the "Netherlandish Proverbs" by Pieter Bruegel the Elder. Helsinki: Suomalainen Tiedeakatemia, 1981.

Elmslie, William Alexander. Studies in Life from Jewish Proverbs. London: James Clarke, 1917.

Fontaine, Carole R. Traditional Sayings in the Old Testament: A Contextual Study. Sheffield: The Almond Press, 1982.

Frank, Grace, and Dorothy Miner. Proverbes en Rimes: Text and Illustrations of the Fifteenth Century from a French Manuscript in the Walters Art Gallery, Baltimore. Baltimore: Johns Hopkins University Press, 1937.

Gordon, Edmund I. Sumerian Proverbs: Glimpses of Everyday Life in Ancient Mesopotamia. Philadelphia: University of Pennsylvania Press, 1959.

Grauls, Jan. The Proverbs of Pieter Bruegel the Elder (1527–1569). Antwerp: Gevaert, 1938.

Griffis, William. Proverbs of Japan: A Little Picture of the Japanese Philosophy of Life as Mirrored in Their Proverbs. New York: Japan Society, 1924.

Guershoon, Andrew. *Certain Aspects of Russian Proverbs.* London: Frederick Muller, 1941.

Hasan-Rokem, Galit. *Proverbs in Israeli Folk Narratives: A Structural Semantic Analysis.* Helsinki: Suomalainen Tiedeakatemia, 1982.

Hood, Edwin Paxton. *The World of Proverb and Parable.* London: Hodder & Stoughton, 1885.

Houghton, Herbert. *Moral Significance of Animals as Indicated in Greek Proverbs.* Amherst, Mass.: Carpenter & Morehouse, 1915.

Hulme, F. Edward. *Proverb Lore: Being a Historical Study of the Similarities, Contrasts, Topics, Meanings, and Other Facets of Proverbs, Truisms, and Pithy Sayings, as Expressed by the Peoples of Many Lands and Times.* London: Elliot Stock, 1902. Reprint. Detroit: Gale Research Co., 1968.

Huzii, Otoo. *Japanese Proverbs.* Tokyo: Japanese Government Railways, 1940.

Kidner, Frank Derek. *The Proverbs: An Introduction and Commentary.* London: Tyndale Press, 1964.

Krikmann, Arvo. *On Denotative Indefiniteness of Proverbs.* Tallinn: Academy of Sciences of the Estonian SSR, Institute of Language and Literature, 1974.

Krikmann, Arvo. *Some Additional Aspects of Semantic Indefiniteness of Proverbs.* Tallinn: Academy of Sciences of the Estonian SSR, Institute of Language and Literature, 1974.

Kuusi, Matti. *Towards an International Type-System of Proverbs.* Helsinki: Suomalainen Tiedeakatemia, 1972.

Levy, Isaac Jack. *Prolegomena to the Study of the Refranero Sefardi.* New York: Las Americas Publications, 1968.

McKane, William. *Proverbs: A New Approach.* London: SCM Press, 1970.

Mahgoub, Fatma Mohammed. *A Linguistic Study of Cairene Proverbs.* Bloomington: Indiana University Press, 1968.

Marvin, Dwight Edwards. *The Antiquity of Proverbs: Fifty Familiar Proverbs and Folk Sayings with Annotations and Lists of Connected Forms, Found in All Parts of the World.* New York: G. P. Putnam's Sons, 1922.

Marzal, Angel. *Gleanings from the Wisdom of Mari.* Rome: Biblical Institute Press, 1976.

Matisoff, James A. *Blessings, Curses, Hopes, and Fears: Psycho-Ostensive Expressions in Yiddish.* Philadelphia: Institute for the Study of Human Issues, 1979.

Mieder, Wolfgang. *Tradition and Innovation in Folk Literature.* Hanover, N.H.: University Press of New England, 1987.

Mieder, Wolfgang. *American Proverbs: A Study of Texts and Contexts.* New York: Peter Lang, 1989.

Mieder, Wolfgang, ed. *Selected Writings on Proverbs by Archer Taylor.* Helsinki: Suomalainen Tiedeakatemia, 1975.

Mieder, Wolfgang, and Alan Dundes, eds. *The Wisdom of Many: Essays on the Proverb.* New York: Garland Publishing, 1981.

Norrick, Neal R. *How Proverbs Mean: Semantic Studies in English Proverbs.* Amsterdam: Mouton, 1985.

Parker, A. A. *The Humour of Spanish Proverbs.* London: The Hispanic & Luso-Brazilian Councils, 1963.

Penfield, Joyce. *Communicating with Quotes: The Igbo Case.* Westport, Conn.: Greenwood Press, 1983.

Permiakov, Grigorii L'vovich. *From Proverb to Folk-Tale: Notes on the General Theory of Cliché.* Moscow: "Nauka" Publishing House, 1979.

Pfeffer, J. Alan. *The Proverb in Goethe.* New York: Columbia University Press, 1948.

Phillips, Margaret Mann. *The "Adages" of Erasmus: A Study with Translations.* Cambridge: Cambridge University Press, 1964.

Plopper, Clifford H. *Chinese Proverbs: 1. The Relationship of Friends as Brought out by the Proverbs; 2. Economics as Seen Through the Proverbs.* Peking: North China Union Language School, 1932.

Plopper, Clifford H. *The Religious Life of the Chinese as Disclosed in Their Proverbs.* Shanghai: China Press, 1926. Reprint. New York: Paragon Book Reprint Corp., 1969.

Robinson, Benjamin Willard. *The Sayings of*

Jesus, Their Background and Interpretation. New York: Harper, 1930.

Scott, R. B. Y. *The Anchor Bible: Proverbs, Ecclesiastes. Introduction, Translation, and Notes.* Garden City, N.Y.: Doubleday, 1965.

Smith, Arthur Henderson. *Proverbs and Common Sayings from the Chinese.* Shanghai: American Presbyterian Mission Press, 1914. Reprint. New York: Paragon Book Reprint Corp. and Dover Publications, 1965.

Smith, Charles G. *Shakespeare's Proverb Lore: His Use of the Sententiae of Leonard Culman and Publilius Syrus.* Cambridge, Mass.: Harvard University Press, 1963.

Taylor, Archer. *Comparative Studies in Folklore: Asia-Europe-America.* Taipei: The Orient Cultural Service, 1972.

Taylor, Archer. *The Proverb.* Cambridge, Mass.: Harvard University Press, 1931. Reprint. Hatboro, Pa.: Folklore Associates, 1962. Reprint, with an introduction and bibliography by Wolfgang Mieder. Bern: Peter Lang, 1985.

Thiselton-Dyer, T. F. *Folklore of Women: As Illustrated by Legendary and Traditionary Tales, Folk-Rhymes, Proverbial Sayings, Superstitions, etc.* London: Elliot Stock, 1905. Reprint. Williamstown, Mass.: Corner House Publishers, 1975.

Thompson, John Mark. *The Form and Function of Proverbs in Ancient Israel.* The Hague: Mouton, 1974.

Trench, Richard Chenevix. *On the Lessons in Proverbs: Being the Substance of Lectures Delivered to Young Men's Societies at Portsmouth and Elsewhere.* New York: Redfield, 1853. Reprint as *Proverbs and Their Lessons.* London: Macmillan, 1869. Reprint. London: George Routledge, 1905.

Whiting, Bartlett Jere. *Chaucer's Use of Proverbs.* Cambridge, Mass.: Harvard University Press, 1934. Reprint. New York: AMS Press, 1973.

Whiting, Bartlett Jere. *Proverbs in the Earlier English Drama with Illustrations from Contemporary French Plays.* Cambridge, Mass.: Harvard University Press, 1938. Reprint. New York: Octagon Book, 1969.

Wilson, F. P. *The Proverbial Wisdom of Shakespeare.* New York: Modern Humanities Research Association, 1961. Reprint. Norwood, Pa.: Norwood Editions, 1978.

Wood, James. *Wisdom Literature: An Introduction.* London: Gerald Duckworth, 1967.

Yankah, Kwesi. *The Proverb in the Context of Akan Rhetoric: A Theory of Proverb Praxis.* Bern: Peter Lang, 1989.

Young, Blamire. *The Proverbs of Goya: Being an Account of "Los Proverbios", Examined and Now for the First Time Explained.* New York: Houghton Mifflin, 1923.

INTERNATIONAL PROVERB COLLECTIONS

Bechtel, John H. *Proverbs: Maxims and Phrases Drawn from All Lands and Times.* London: Gay & Bird, 1906.

Bland, Robert. *Proverbs, Chiefly Taken from the Adagia of Erasmus, with Explanations and Examples from the Spanish, French and English Languages.* 2 vols. London: T. Egerton, 1814.

Bohn, Henry G. *A Polyglot of Foreign Proverbs, Comprising French, Italian, German, Dutch, Spanish, Portuguese, and Danish, with English Translations & a General Index.* London: Henry G. Bohn, 1857. Reprint. Detroit: Gale Research Co., 1968.

Bush, William. *1800 Selected Proverbs of the World, Ancient, Medieval and Modern.* Boston: Meador, 1838.

Champion, Selwyn Gurney. *Racial Proverbs: A Selection of the World's Proverbs Arranged Linguistically with Authoritative Introductions to the Proverbs of 27 Countries and Races.* London: George Routledge & Sons, 1938. Reprint. London: Routledge & Kegan, 1963.

Champion, Selwyn Gurney. *The Eleven Religions and Their Proverbial Lore.* New York: E. P. Dutton, 1945.

Champion, Selwyn Gurney. *War Proverbs and Maxims from East and West.* London: Probsthain, 1945.

Christy, Robert. *Proverbs, Maxims and Phrases of All Ages.* New York: G. P. Putnam's Sons, 1887. Reprint. Norwood, Pa.: Norwood Editions, 1977.

Codrington, Robert. *A Collection of Many Select and Excellent Proverbs out of Several Languages*. London: W. Lee, 1664.

Cohen, Israel. *Dictionary of Parallel Proverbs in English, German and Hebrew*. Tel Aviv: Machbarot Lesifrut Publishers, 1961.

Conklin, George W. *The World's Best Proverbs*. Philadelphia: Mackay, 1906.

Davidoff, Henry. *A World Treasury of Proverbs from Twenty-Five Languages*. New York: Random House, 1946. Also published as *Speakers' and Writers' Treasury of Proverbs*. New York: Grosset & Dunlap, 1946.

Dennys, E. M. *Proverbs and Quotations of Many Nations*. London: Simpkin, Marshall & Co., 1890.

Fergusson, Rosalind. *The Facts on File Dictionary of Proverbs*. New York: Facts on File, 1983. Also published as *The Penguin Dictionary of Proverbs*. New York: Penguin Books, 1983.

Fuller, Thomas. *Gnomologia; Adages and Proverbs; Wise Sentences and Witty Sayings, Ancient and Modern, Foreign and British*. London: B. Barker, 1732.

Glusky, Jerzy. *Proverbs. A Comparative Book of English, French, German, Italian, Spanish and Russian Proverbs with a Latin Appendix*. New York: Elsevier Publishing Co., 1971.

Guinzbourg, Lt. Colonel Victor S. M. de. *Wit and Wisdom of the United Nations: Proverbs and Apothegms on Diplomacy*. New York: Privately printed, 1961.

Guinzbourg, Lt. Colonel Victor S. M. de. *Supplement: Wit and Wisdom of the United Nations or The Modern Machiavelli*. New York: Privately printed, 1965.

Guzzetta-Jones, Angeline, Joseph Antinoro-Polizzi, and Carl Zollo. *We Remember . . . A Collection of 200 Years of Golden Sayings of Some of the Ethnic Groups that Made America Great*. Rochester, N.Y.: Flower City Printing Co., 1975.

Houghton, Patricia. *A World of Proverbs*. Poole, U.K.: Blandford, 1981.

Howell, James. *Lexicon Tetraglotton. An English-French-Italian-Spanish Dictionary with the Choicest Proverbs*. London: Bee, 1660.

Hunt, Cecil. *Hand-Picked Proverbs, Selected from the Storehouse of the World's Wisdom*. London: Methuen, 1940.

Jones, H. P. *Dictionary of Foreign Phrases and Classical Quotations Comprising 14,000 Idioms, Proverbs, Maxims and Mottoes*. Edinburgh: Deacon, 1929.

Kelen, Emery. *Proverbs of Many Nations*. New York: Lothrop, Lee & Shepard, 1966.

Kelly, Walter K. *A Collection of the Proverbs of All Nations. Compared, Explained, and Illustrated*. Andover, Mass.: Warren F. Draper, 1879. Reprint. Darby, Pa.: Folcroft Library Editions, 1972. Reprint. Philadelphia: R. West, 1978.

King, William Francis Henry. *Classical and Foreign Quotations, Law Terms and Maxims, Proverbs, Mottoes, Phrases, and Expressions in French, German, Greek, Italian, Spanish and Portuguese*. New York: T. Whitaker, 1888. Reprint. Detroit: Gale Research Co., 1968.

Konstandt, Oscar. *One Hundred Proverbs with Their Equivalents in German, French, Italian and Spanish*. Great Malvern, U.K.: Edelweiss House, 1958.

Lawson, James Gilchrist. *The World's Best Proverbs and Maxims*. New York: Grosset & Dunlap, 1926.

Long, James. *Eastern Proverbs and Emblems Illustrating Old Truths*. London: Trübner, 1881.

Mair, James Allan, *A Handbook of Proverbs. English, Scottish, Irish, American, Shakespearean and Scriptural*. London: Routledge, 1873.

Mapletoft, John. *Select Proverbs, Italian, Spanish, French, English, Scottish, British, etc. Chiefly Moral. The Foreign Languages Done into English*. London: Monckton, 1707.

Marvin, Dwight Edwards. *Curiosities in Proverbs: A Collection of Unusual Adages, Maxims, Aphorisms, Phrases and Other Popular Dicta from Many Lands*. New York: G. P. Putnam's Sons, 1916. Reprint. Darby, Pa.: Folcroft Library Editions, 1980.

Mawr, E. B. *Analogous Proverbs in Ten Languages*. London: Elliot Stock, 1885.

Middlemore, James. *Proverbs, Sayings and*

Comparisons in Various Languages. London: Isbister, 1889.

Mieder, Wolfgang. *The Prentice-Hall Encyclopedia of World Proverbs.* Englewood Cliffs, N.J.: Prentice-Hall, 1986.

Mieder, Wolfgang. *Love: Proverbs of the Heart.* Shelburne, Vt.: The New England Press, 1989.

Mieder, Wolfgang. *Not By Bread Alone: Proverbs of the Bible.* Shelburne, Vt.: The New England Press, 1990.

O'Leary, C. F. *The World's Best Proverbs and Proverbial Phrases.* St. Louis: Herder, 1907.

Opdyke, George Howard. *The World's Best Proverbs and Short Quotations.* Chicago: Laird, 1920.

Orton, James. *Proverbs Illustrated by Parallel, or Related Passages, to which are Added Latin, French, Spanish and Italian Proverbs with Translations.* Philadelphia: E. H. Butler, 1852.

Ray, John. *Proverbial Sayings, or a Collection of the Best English Proverbs by John Ray, Scots Proverbs by Allan Ramsay, Italian Proverbs by Orlando Pescetti, Spanish Proverbs by Ferdinand Nunez. With the Wise Sayings and Maxims of the Ancients.* London, 1800.

Roback, Abraham A. *A Dictionary of International Slurs.* Cambridge, Mass.: Sci-Art Publishers, 1944. Reprint. Waukesha, Wis.: Maledicta Press, 1979.

Rosenzweig, Paul. *The Book of Proverbs: Maxims from East and West.* New York: Philosophical Library, 1965.

Shearer, William John. *Wisdom of the World in Proverbs of All Nations.* New York: Macmillan, 1904.

Stevenson, Burton. *The Macmillan (Home) Book of Proverbs, Maxims and Familiar Phrases.* New York: Macmillan, 1948.

Wade, John (pseud. Thomas Fielding). *Select Proverbs of All Nations with an Analysis of the Wisdom of the Ancients.* London: Berger, 1824.

Walker, J. *Handy Book of Proverbs.* New York: Crowell, 1910.

Ward, Caroline. *National Proverbs in the Principal Languages of Europe.* London: Parker, 1842.

ANGLO-AMERICAN PROVERB COLLECTIONS

Abel, Alison M. *Make Hay While the Sun Shines: A Book of Proverbs.* London: Faber, 1977.

Aik, Kam Chuan. *Dictionary of Proverbs.* Singapore: Federal Publications, 1988.

Angland, Joan Walsh. *A Pocketful of Proverbs.* New York: Harcourt, Brace & World, 1964.

Apperson, G. L. *English Proverbs and Proverbial Phrases: A Historical Dictionary.* London: J. M. Dent, 1929. Reprint. Detroit: Gale Research Co., 1969.

Barber, John Warner. *The Book of 1000 Proverbs.* New York: American Heritage Press, 1971.

Bartlett, John. *Familiar Quotations: A Collection of Passages, Phrases and Proverbs Traced to Their Sources in Ancient and Modern Literature.* Boston: Little, Brown & Co., 1855 (15th ed., 1980).

Bartlett, John Russell. *Dictionary of Americanisms.* Boston: Little, Brown & Co., 1877.

Baz, Petros D. *A Dictionary of Proverbs.* New York: Philosophical Library, 1963.

Bear, John. *The World's Worst Proverbs.* Los Angeles: Price, Stern, Sloan Publishers, 1976.

Benham, William Gurney. *Putnam's Complete Book of Quotations, Proverbs and Household Words.* New York: G. P. Putnam's Sons, 1926.

Boatner, Maxine, John Gates, and Adam Makkai. *A Dictionary of American Idioms.* Woodbury, N.Y.: Barron's Educational Series, 1975.

Bohn, Henry. *A Hand-Book of Proverbs Comprising an Entire Republication of Ray's Collection of English Proverbs, with His Additions from Foreign Languages.* London: H. G. Bohn, 1855.

Bourdillon, Francis. *The Voice of the People: Some Proverbs and Common Sayings Examined and Applied.* London: The Religious Tract Society, 1896.

Breton, Nicholas. *Crossing of Proverbs.* London: Wright, 1616.

Brewer, Ebenezer C. *Dictionary of Phrase and Fable.* New York: Harper & Row, 1870 (centenary edition revised by Ivor H. Evans, 1970).

Brown, Raymond Lamont. *A Book of Proverbs*. Newton Abbot, U.K.: David & Charles, 1970.

Browning, David C. *Everyman's Dictionary of Quotations and Proverbs*. London: Dent, 1951. Reprinted as *Dictionary of Quotations and Proverbs*. London: Octopus Books, 1982.

Carmichaell, James. *The James Carmichaell Collection of Proverbs in Scots*. Ed. by M. L. Anderson. Edinburgh: Edinburgh University Press, 1957.

Cheviot, Andrew. *Proverbs, Proverbial Expressions, and Popular Rhymes of Scotland*. London: Alexander Gardner, 1896. Reprint. Detroit: Gale Research Co., 1969.

Chiu, Kwong Ki. *A Dictionary of English Phrases with Illustrative Sentences*. New York: A. S. Barnes, 1881. Reprint. Detroit: Gale Research Co., 1971.

Collins, Vere Henry. *A Book of Proverbs, with Origins and Explanations*. London: Longman, 1959.

Colombo, John Robert. *Colombo's Little Book of Canadian Proverbs, Graffiti, Limericks & Other Vital Matters*. Edmonton, Alberta: Hurtig, 1975.

Curran, Peter. *Proverbs in Action*. Hove, U.K.: Editype, 1972.

Dent, Robert W. *Shakespeare's Proverbial Language: An Index*. Berkeley: University of California Press, 1981.

Dent, Robert W. *Proverbial Language in English Drama Exclusive of Shakespeare, 1495–1616: An Index*. Berkeley: University of California Press, 1984.

Downey, William Scott. *Proverbs*. New York: Edward Walker, 1858.

Drakeford, John W. *A Proverb a Day Keeps the Troubles Away*. Nashville: Broadman Press, 1976.

Ewart, Neil. *Everyday Phrases: Their Origins and Meanings*. Poole, U.K.: Blandford, 1983.

Feibleman, James Kern. *New Proverbs for Our Day*. New York: Horizon Press, 1978.

Fergusson, David. *Fergusson's Scottish Proverbs from the Original Print of 1641, Together with a Larger Manuscript Collection of about the Same Period Hitherto Unpublished*. Ed. by Erskine Beveridge. Edinburgh: Scottish Text Society, 1924.

Funk, Charles Earle. *"A Hog on Ice" and Other Curious Expressions*. New York: Harper & Row, 1948. Reprint. New York: Warner Paperbacks. 1972. Reprint. New York: Harper Colophon Books, 1985.

Funk, Charles Earle. *"Heavens to Betsy!" and Other Curious Sayings*. New York: Harper & Row, 1955: Reprint. New York: Warner Paperbacks, 1972. Reprint. New York: Harper and Row, 1986.

Gray, Marvin L. *I Heard Somewhere: A Book of Contemporary American Proverbs*. New York: Pageant Press, 1961.

Hargrave, Bash. *Origin and Meanings of Popular Phrases and Names*. London: T. Werner Laurie, 1925. Reprint. Detroit: Gale Research Co., 1968.

Hazlitt, W. Carew. *English Proverbs and Proverbial Phrases*. London: Reever and Turner, 1869. Reprint. Detroit: Gale Research Co., 1969.

Henderson, Andrew. *Scottish Proverbs*. Edinburgh: Oliver & Boyd, 1832; Reprint. Glasgow: Thomas D, Morison, 1881. Reprint. Detroit: Gale Research Co., 1969.

Henderson, George Surgeon. *The Popular Rhymes, Sayings, and Proverbs of the County of Berwick*. Newcastle-on-Tyne: For the author, 1856. Reprint. Darby, Pa.: Folcroft Library Editions, 1977.

Herbert, George. *Outlandish Proverbs*. London: Humphrey Blunden, 1640. Reprint. London: T. Garthwait, 1651. Reprinted in F. E. Hutchinson, ed., *The Works Of George Herbert*. Oxford: Clarendon Press, 1941.

Heywood, John. *A Dialogue Conteinyng the Number in Effect of all the Proverbes in the Englishe Tongue*. London: Berthelet, 1549. Reprinted as *The Proverbs of John Heywood*. Ed. by Julian Sharman. London: George Bell, 1874. Reprint. Darby, Pa.: Folcroft Library Editions, 1972. The newest scholarly edition is Rudolph E. Habernicht, ed., *John Heywood's "A Dia-*

logue of Proverbs." Berkeley: University of California Press, 1963.

Hislop, Alexander. *The Proverbs of Scotland with Explanatory and Illustrative Notes and a Glossary*. Edinburgh: Alexander Hislop & Co., 1868. Reprint. Detroit: Gale Research Co., 1968.

Holt, Alfred H. *Phrase and Word Origins: A Study of Familiar Expressions*. New York: Dover, 1961.

Hyamson, Albert M. *A Dictionary of English Phrases*. New York: E. P. Dutton, 1922. Reprint. Detroit: Gale Research Co., 1970.

Inwards, Richard. *Weather Lore: A Collection of Proverbs, Sayings and Rules Concerning the Weather*. London: Elliot Stock, 1898.

Jauss, Anne Marie. *Wise and Otherwise: The Do's and Don'ts of Sundry Proverbs*. New York: McKay, 1953.

Jensen, Irving Lester. *Proverbs*. Chicago: Moody Press, 1982.

Johnson, Albert. *Common English Proverbs*. London: Longman, Green & Co., 1954.

Kandel, Howard. *The Power of Positive Pessimism: Proverbs for Our Times*. Los Angeles: Price, Stern, Sloan Publishers, 1964.

Kelly, James. *A Complete Collection of Scotish [sic] Proverbs, Explained and Made Intelligible to the English Reader*. London: William and John Innys, 1721. Reprint. Darby, Pa.: Folcroft Library Editions, 1976.

Kin, David. *Dictionary of American Maxims*. New York: Philosophical Library, 1955.

Kin, David. *Dictionary of American Proverbs*. New York: Philosophical Library, 1955.

Lean, Vincent Stuckey. *Lean's Collectanea. Collections of Proverbs (English and Foreign), Folklore, and Superstitions, also Compilations Towards Dictionaries of Proverbial Phrases and Words, Old and Disused*. Ed. by T. W. Williams. 4 vols. Bristol, U.K.: J. W. Arrowsmith, 1902–4. Reprint. Detroit: Gale Research Co., 1969.

Lurie, Charles N. *Everyday Sayings: Their Meanings Explained, Their Origins Given*. London: G. P. Putnam's Sons, 1928. Reprint. Detroit: Gale Research Co., 1968.

Makkai, Adam. *Handbook of Commonly Used American Idioms*. Woodbury, N.Y.: Barron's Educational Series, 1984.

Marcha, E. F. *Handy Book of English Proverbs*. Toledo, Ohio: E. F. Marcha, 1905.

Mathews, Mitford M. *A Dictionary of Americanisms on Historical Principles*. Chicago: University of Chicago Press, 1951.

Mieder, Wolfgang. *Salty Wisdom: Proverbs of the Sea*. Shelburne, Vt.: The New England Press, 1990.

Nares, Robert. *A Glossary of Words, Phrases, Names and Allusions in the Works of English Authors, Particularly of Shakespeare and His Contemporaries*. London: George Routledge, 1905. Reprint. Detroit: Gale Research Co., 1966.

Nelson, Thomas H. *Modern Proverbs*. Grand Rapids: Zondervan, 1937.

Partridge, Eric. *A Dictionary of Catch Phrases*. New York: Stein and Day, 1977.

Partridge, Eric. *A Dictionary of Clichés*. London: George Routledge, 1940.

Partridge, Eric. *A Dictionary of Slang and Unconventional English*. New York: Macmillan, 1937 (7th ed., 1970).

Peterson, Gail. *Proverbs to Live By*. Kansas City, Kans.: Hallmark Cards, 1968.

Pullar-Strecker, Herbert. *Proverbs for Pleasure: Uncommon Sayings Collected, Arranged and Annotated*. New York: Philosophical Library, 1955.

Rayner, John L. *Proverbs and Maxims*. London: Cassell, 1910.

Read, Allen Walker. *Classic American Graffiti*. Paris: Privately printed, 1935. Reprint. Waukesha, Wis.: Maledicta Press, 1977.

Rees, Nigel. *Sayings of the Century: The Stories Behind the Twentieth Century's Quotable Sayings*. London: George Allen & Unwin, 1984.

Rees, Nigel. *Why Do We Say. . . ? Words and Sayings and Where They Come From*. Poole, U.K.: Blandford, 1987.

Reid, John Calvin. *Proverbs to Live By*. Glendale, Calif.: Regal Books, 1977.

Rhys, Ernest. *The Dictionary of Best Known Quotations and Proverbs*. New York: Garden City Publishing Co., 1939.

Ridout, Ronald, and Clifford Whiting. *En-*

glish Proverbs Explained. London: Pan Books, 1969.

Rogers, James. The Dictionary of Clichés. New York: Facts on File, 1985.

Sewell, Helen. Words to the Wise: A Book of Proverbs for Boys and Girls. New York: Dodd, 1932.

Simpson, John A. The Concise Oxford Dictionary of Proverbs. Oxford: Oxford University Press, 1982.

Skeat, Walter. Early English Proverbs: Chiefly of the Thirteenth and Fourteenth Centuries. Oxford: Clarendon Press, 1910. Reprint. Darby, Pa.: Folcroft Library Editions, 1974.

Skeat, Walter, ed. The Proverbs of Alfred. Oxford: Clarendon Press, 1907. Reprint. Darby, Pa.: Folcroft Library Editions, 1974.

Spurgeon, Charles Haddon. The Salt-Cellars, Being a Collection of Proverbs. New York: A. C. Armstrong, 1889. Reprinted as Spurgeon's Proverbs and Sayings with Notes. Grand Rapids: Baker Book House, 1975.

Stark, Judith. Priceless Proverbs from the Tongue of the Young. Los Angeles: Price, Stern, Sloan, 1982.

Stevenson, Burton. The Macmillan (Home) Book of Proverbs, Maxims and Familiar Phrases. New York: Macmillan, 1948.

Swainson, C. A Handbook of Weather Folk-Lore, Being a Collection of Proverbial Sayings Relating to the Weather, with Explanatory and Illustrative Notes. London: William Blackwood, 1873. Reprint. Detroit: Gale Research Co., 1974.

Taylor, Archer, and Bartlett Jere Whiting. A Dictionary of American Proverbs and Proverbial Phrases, 1820–1880. Cambridge, Mass.: Harvard University Press, 1958.

Taylor, Joseph. Antiquitates Curiosae: The Etymology of Many Remarkable Old Sayings, Proverbs, and Singular Customs. London: T. and J. Allman, 1818.

Tilley, Morris Palmer. A Dictionary of the Proverbs in England in the Sixteenth and Seventeenth Centuries. Ann Arbor: University of Michigan Press, 1950.

Tonn, Maryjane Hooper. Proverbs to Live by. Milwaukee: Ideals Publishing Corp., 1977.

Trusler, John. Proverbs Exemplified, and Illustrated by Pictures from Real Life. London: Literary Press, 1790. Reprint. New York: Johnson Reprint Corp., 1970.

Urdang, Laurence, and Nancy LaRoche. Picturesque Expressions: A Thematic Dictionary. Detroit: Gale Research Co., 1980. Reprint enlarged with the help of Walter W. Hunsinger. Detroit: Gale Research Co., 1985.

Urdang, Laurence, and Ceila Dame Robbins. Slogans. Detroit: Gale Research Co., 1984.

Urdang, Laurence, Ceila Dame Robbins, and Frank R. Abate. Mottoes. Detroit: Gale Research Co., 1986.

Whiting, Bartlett Jere. Early American Proverbs and Proverbial Phrases. Cambridge, Mass.: Harvard University Press, 1977.

Whiting, Bartlett Jere. Modern Proverbs and Proverbial Sayings. Cambridge, Mass.: Harvard University Press, 1989.

Whiting, Bartlett Jere. Proverbs, Sentences, and Proverbial Phrases from English Writings Mainly Before 1500. Cambridge, Mass.: Harvard University Press, 1968.

Wilkerson, David. Pocket Proverbs: Wisdom to Live by. Ventura, Calif.: Regal Books, 1983.

Wilson, F. P. The Oxford Dictionary of English Proverbs. 3d ed. Oxford: Oxford University Press, 1970 (1st ed. 1935 by William George Smith).

STUDIES OF AMERICAN PROVERBS

Albig, William. "Proverbs and Social Control." Sociology and Social Research 15 (1931): 527–35.

Arora, Shirley L. "A Critical Bibliography of Mexican American Proverbs." Aztlan 13 (1982): 71–80.

Arora, Shirley L. " 'No Tickee, No Shirtee': Proverbial Speech and Leadership in Academe." In Inside Organizations: Understanding the Human Dimension, edited by Michael Owen Jones, Michael Dane Moore, and Richard Christopher Snyder, 179–89. Newbury Park, Calif.: Sage Publishers, 1988.

Arora, Shirley L. "On the Importance of Rotting Fish: A Proverb and Its Audience." *Western Folklore* 48 (1989): 271–88.

Arora, Shirley L. "Proverbs in Mexican American Tradition." *Aztlan* 13 (1982): 43–69.

Baker, Ronald L. " 'Hogs Are Playing with Sticks—Bound To Be Bad Weather': Folk Belief or Proverb?" *Midwestern Journal of Language and Folkore* 1 (1975): 65–67.

Barbour, Frances M. "Embellishment of the Proverb." *Southern Folklore Quarterly* 28 (1964): 291–98.

Barbour, Frances M. "Some Uncommon Sources of Proverbs." *Midwest Folklore* 13 (1963): 97–100.

Bassin, Alexander. "Proverbs, Slogans and Folk Sayings in the Therapeutic Community: A Neglected Therapeutic Tool." *Journal of Psychoactive Drugs* 16 (1984): 51–56.

Bauman, Richard, and Neil McCabe. "Proverbs in an LSD Cult." *Journal of American Folklore* 83 (1970): 318–24.

Briggs, Charles L. "Proverbs." In *Competence in Performance: The Creativity of Tradition in Mexicano Verbal Art,* 101–35, 380 (notes). Philadelphia: University of Pennsylvania Press, 1988.

Briggs, Charles L. "The Pragmatics of Proverb Performances in New Mexican Spanish." *American Anthropologist* 87 (1985): 793–810.

Bronner, Simon J. ". . . 'Feeling's the Truth'." *Tennessee Folklore Society Bulletin* 48 (1982): 117–24.

Bronner, Simon J. "The Haptic Experience of Culture." *Anthropos* 77 (1982): 351–62.

Brooke, Pamela. "Picture Talk: Proverbs, Similes, and Other Folk Speech." *Instructor* 3 (March 1987): 92–94.

Browne, Ray B. " 'The Wisdom of Many': Proverbs and Proverbial Expressions." In *Our Living Traditions: An Introduction to American Folklore,* edited by Tristram Potter Coffin, 192–203. New York: Basic Books, 1968.

Brunvand, Jan Harold. "Proverbs and Proverbial Phrases." In *The Study of American Folklore: An Introduction,* 38–47. New York: W. W. Norton and Co., 1968.

Bryant, Margaret M. "Collecting Proverbs." *Badger Folklore* 1 (1948): 15–17.

Bryant, Margaret M. "Proverbial Lore in American Life and Speech." *Western Folklore* 10 (1951): 134–42.

Bryant, Margaret M. *Proverbs and How to Collect Them.* Greensboro, N.C.: American Dialect Society, 1945.

Bryant, Margaret M. "Proverbs: Proverb Lore in American Life and Speech." *New York Folklore Quarterly* 8 (1952): 221–26.

Bryant, Margaret M. "Sayings of the Masses: How You Can Help Preserve Them." *Southern Folklore Quarterly* 10 (1946): 129–36.

Bryant, Margaret M. "The People's Sayings: How You Can Help Record Them." *New York Folklore Quarterly* 1 (1945): 50–56.

Bynum, Joyce. "Folk Speech—A Dying Art." *ETC. A Review of General Semantics* 44 (1987): 308–11.

Bynum, Joyce. "More About Proverbs." *ETC. A Review of General Semantics* 44 (1987): 192–95.

Bynum, Joyce. "Proverbs." *ETC. A Review of General Semantics* 44 (1987): 88–91.

Chu, Mike Shan Yuan. *An Approach to American Idioms.* Ph.D. diss. University of Nebraska, 1985.

Claudel, Calvin André. "Proverbs and Folk Expressions." *Bluegrass Literary Review* 1 (1980): 29–32.

Cohen, Gerald Leonard. *Studies in Slang.* 2 vols. Bern: Peter Lang, 1985 and 1989.

Daniel, Jack L. "Towards an Ethnography of Afroamerican Proverbial Usage." *Black Lines* 2 (1973): 3–12.

Daniel, Jack L., Geneva Smitherman-Donaldson, and Milford A. Jeremiah. "Makin' a Way outa No Way: The Proverb Tradition in the Black Experience." *Journal of Black Studies* 17 (1987): 482–508.

Davidson, Levette J. "Folk Speech and Folk Sayings." In *A Guide to American Folklore,* edited by L. J. Davidson, 42–52. Denver: University of Denver Press, 1951.

De Caro, Frank A. "Riddles and Proverbs." In *Folk Groups and Folklore Genres: An Introduction,* edited by Elliott Oring, 175–97. Logan: Utah State University Press, 1986.

De Caro, Frank A. "Talk is Cheap: The Nature of Speech According to American Proverbs." *Proverbium: Yearbook of International Proverb Scholarship* 4 (1987): 17–37.

Dundes, Alan. "On the Structure of the Proverb." *Proverbium* 25 (1975): 961–73. Also in Alan Dundes. *Analytic Structures in Folklore,* 103–18. The Hague: Mouton, 1975. Reprint. Wolfgang Mieder and Alan Dundes, eds. *The Wisdom of Many: Essays on the Proverb,* 43–64. New York: Garland Publishing, 1981.

Dundes, Alan. "Seeing is Believing." *Natural History,* no. 5 (May 1972): 8–14 and 86. Also in Alan Dundes. *Interpreting Folklore,* 86–92. Bloomington: Indiana University Press, 1980.

Dundes, Alan. "The Crowing Hen and the Easter Bunny: Male Chauvinism in American Folklore." In *Folklore Today: A Festschrift for Richard M. Dorson,* edited by Linda Dégh, Henry Glassie, and Felix J. Oinas, 123–38. Bloomington: Indiana University Press, 1976.

Folly, Dennis W. "Getting the Butter from the Duck: Proverbs and Proverbial Expressions in an Afro-American Family." In *A Celebration of American Family Folklore: Tales and Traditions from the Smithsonian Collection,* edited by Steven J. Zeitlin, Amy J. Kotkin, and Holly C. Baker, 232–41, 290–91 (notes). New York: Pantheon, 1982.

Gardner, Emelyn, and Wayland D. Hand. "Instructions to Collectors of Proverbial Lore." *California Folklore Quarterly* 4 (1945): 87–89.

Georges, Robert A. "Proverbial Speech in the Air." *Midwestern Journal of Language and Folklore* 7 (1981): 39–48.

Halpert, Herbert. "Some Forms of a Proverbial Rhyme ('When You Buy Meat, You Buy Bones; Buy Land, You Buy Stones')." *Journal of American Folklore* 64 (1951): 317–19.

Harder, Kelsie B. "Proverbs and Proverbial Sayings." *Publications of the American Dialect Society* 71 (1983): 60–66.

Hudson, Catherine. "Traditional Proverbs as Perceived by Children from an Urban Environment." *Journal of the Folklore Society of Greater Washington [D.C.]* 3 (1972): 17–24.

Jente, Richard. "The American Proverb." *American Speech* 7 (1931–1932): 342–48.

Jordan, Rosan A. "Five (Mexican American) Proverbs in Context." *Midwestern Journal of Language and Folklore* 8 (1982): 109–15.

Joyner, Charles. "Proverbs." In *Encyclopedia of Southern Culture,* edited by Charles Reagan Wilson and William Ferris, 516–17. Chapel Hill: University of North Carolina Press, 1989.

Kimmerle, Marjorie M. "A Method of Collecting and Classifying Folk Sayings." *Western Folklore* 6 (1947): 351–66.

Kingsbury, Stewart A. "On Handling 250,000+ Citation Slips for American Dialect Society (ADS) Proverb Research." *Proverbium: Yearbook of International Proverb Scholarship* 1 (1984): 195–205.

Kirshenblatt-Gimblett, Barbara. "A Playful Note: 'The Good Old Game of Proverbs.' " *Proverbium* 22 (1973): 860–61.

Leary, James P. " 'The Land Won't Burn': An Esoteric American Proverb and Its Significance." *Midwestern Journal of Language and Folklore* 1 (1975): 27–32.

Lewis, Mary Ellen B. "The Feminists Have Done It: Applied Folklore (Women and Proverbs)." *Journal of American Folklore* 87 (1974): 85–87.

Loomis, C. Grant. "Proverbs in Business." *Western Folklore* 23 (1964): 91–94.

Loomis, C. Grant. "Traditional American Wordplay: The Epigram and Perverted Proverbs." *Western Folklore* 8 (1949): 348–57.

Luomala, Katharine. "A Bibliographical Survey of Collections of Hawaiian Sayings."

Proverbium: Yearbook of International Proverb Scholarship 2 (1985): 279–306.

Mieder, Barbara, and Wolfgang Mieder. "Tradition and Innovation: Proverbs in Advertising." *Journal of Popular Culture* 11 (1977): 308–19. Also in *The Wisdom of Many: Essays on the Proverb,* edited by W. Mieder and Alan Dundes, 309–22. New York: Garland Publishing, 1981.

Mieder, Wolfgang. *American Proverbs: A Study of Texts and Contexts.* New York: Peter Lang, 1989.

Mieder, Wolfgang. " 'A Picture is Worth a Thousand Words': From Advertising Slogan to American Proverb." *Southern Folklore* 47 (1990): 207–25.

Mieder, Wolfgang. "A Proverb a Day Keeps No Chauvinism Away." *Proverbium: Yearbook of International Proverb Scholarship* 2 (1985): 273–77.

Mieder, Wolfgang. "Popular Views of the Proverb." *Proverbium: Yearbook of International Proverb Scholarship* 2 (1985): 109–43.

Mieder, Wolfgang. "Proverbial Slogans Are the Name of the Game." *Kentucky Folklore Record* 24 (1978): 49–53.

Mieder, Wolfgang. "Proverbs in American Popular Songs." *Proverbium: Yearbook of International Proverb Scholarship* 5 (1988): 85–101.

Mieder, Wolfgang. "Proverbs of the Native Americans: A Prize Competition." *Western Folklore* 48 (1989): 256–60.

Mieder, Wolfgang. "The Proverb in the Modern Age: Old Wisdom in New Clothing." In *Tradition and Innovation in Folk Literature,* 118–56, 248–55 (notes). Hanover, N.H.: University Press of New England, 1987.

Mieder, Wolfgang. "The Use of Proverbs in Psychological Testing." *Journal of the Folklore Institute* 15 (1978): 45–55.

Mieder, Wolfgang. *Tradition and Innovation in Folk Literature.* Hanover, N.H.: University Press of New England, 1987.

Mieder, Wolfgang. " 'Wine, Women and Song': From Martin Luther to American T-Shirts." *Kentucky Folklore Record* 29 (1983): 89–101. Also in *Folk Groups and*

Folklore Genres: A Reader, edited by Elliott Oring, 279–90. Logan: Utah State University Press, 1989.

Miller, Edd, and Jesse J. Villarreal. "The Use of Clichés by Four Contemporary Speakers (Winston Churchill, Anthony Eden, Franklin D. Roosevelt, and Henry Wallace)." *Quarterly Journal of Speech* 31 (1945): 151–55.

Monteiro, George. "Proverbs in the Re-Making." *Western Folklore* 27 (1968): 128.

Nierenberg, Jess. "Proverbs in Graffiti: Taunting Traditional Wisdom." *Maledicta* 7 (1983): 41–58.

Page, Mary H., and Nancy D. Washington. "Family Proverbs and Value Transmission of Single Black Mothers." *Journal of Social Psychology* 127 (1987): 49–58.

Powers, Marsh K. "Proverbs as Copy-Patterns." *Printers' Ink* 164 (August 17, 1933): 24–26.

Roberts, John W. "Slave Proverbs: A Perspective." *Callaloo* 1 (1978): 129–40.

Rogers, Tim B. "The Use of Slogans, Colloquialisms, and Proverbs in the Treatment of Substance Addiction: A Psychological Application of Proverbs." *Proverbium: Yearbook of International Proverb Scholarship* 6 (1989): 103–12.

Rogow, Arnold, Gloria Carey, and Calista Farrell. "The Significance of Aphorisms in American Culture." *Sociology and Social Research* 41 (1957): 417–20.

Senger, Matthias W. "The Fate of an Early American School Book: Leonhard Culmann's 'Sententiae Pueriles.' " *Harvard Library Bulletin* 32 (1984): 256–73.

Sperber, Hans. " 'Fifty-Four Forty or Fight': Facts and Fictions." *American Speech* 32 (1957): 5–11.

Stitt, J. Michael. "Conversational Genres at a Las Vegas '21' Table." *Western Folklore* 45 (1986): 278–89.

Taylor, Archer. "How Nearly Complete Are the Collections of Proverbs?" *Proverbium* 14 (1969): 369–71.

Taylor, Archer. "Investigations of English Proverbs, Proverbial and Conventional Phrases, Oaths and Clichés." *Journal of American Folklore* 65 (1952): 255–65.

Taylor, Archer. " 'One for the Cutworm.' " *Western Folklore* 17 (1958): 52–53.

Taylor, Archer. *Selected Writings on Proverbs by Archer Taylor*. Edited by Wolfgang Mieder. Helsinki: Suomalainen Tiedeakatemia, 1975.

Taylor, Archer. *The Proverb*. Cambridge, Mass.: Harvard University Press, 1931. Reprint. Hatboro, Pa.: Folklore Associates, 1962. Reprint, with an introduction and bibliography by Wolfgang Mieder. Bern: Peter Lang, 1985.

Whiting, Bartlett Jere. "Some Current Meanings of 'Proverbial.' " *Harvard Studies and Notes in Philology and Literature* 16 (1934): 229–52.

Whiting, Bartlett Jere. "William Johnson of Natchez: Free Negro (and His Proverbs)." *Southern Folklore Quarterly* 16 (1952): 145–53.

REGIONAL AND ETHNIC AMERICAN PROVERB COLLECTIONS

Adams, Owen S. "Traditional Proverbs and Sayings from California." *Western Folklore* 6 (1947): 59–64.

Adams, Owen S. "More California Proverbs." *Western Folklore* 7 (1948): 136–44.

Allen, Harold B. "Hunting for Minnesota Proverbs." *Minnesota History* 27 (1946): 33–36.

Atkinson, Mary Jordan. "Familiar Sayings of Old-Time Texas." In *Texas Folk and Folklore*, edited by Mody C. Boatright, Wilson M. Hudson, and Allen Maxwell, 213–18. Dallas: Southern Methodist University Press, 1954.

Austin, Mary. "Sayings." *Virginia Quarterly Review* 9 (1933): 574–77.

Ayalti, Hanan J. *Yiddish Proverbs*. New York: Schocken Books, 1963 (5th ed., 1975).

Baldwin, L. Karen. "A Sampling of Housewives' Proverbs and Proverbial Phrases from Levittown, Pennsylvania." *Keystone Folklore Quarterly* 10 (1965): 127–48.

Barbour, Frances M. *Proverbs and Proverbial Phrases of Illinois*. Carbondale: Southern Illinois University Press, 1963.

Barnes-Harden, Alene L. "Proverbs, Folk Expressions and Superstitions." In *African American Verbal Arts: Their Nature and Communicative Interpretation (A Thematic Analysis)*, 57–80. Ph.D. diss. State University of New York at Buffalo, 1980.

Barrick, Mac E. "Early Proverbs from Carlisle, Pennsylvania (1788–1821)." *Keystone Folklore Quarterly* 13 (1968): 193–217.

Barrick, Mac E. "Proverbs." In *German-American Folklore*, 36–46. Little Rock: August House, 1987.

Barrick, Mac E. "Proverbs and Sayings from Cumberland County (Pennsylvania)." *Keystone Folklore Quarterly* 8 (1963): 139–203.

Basso, Keith H. " 'Wise Words' of the Western Apache: Metaphor and Semantic Theory." In *Meaning in Anthropology*, edited by K. H. Basso and Henry A. Selby, 93–121. Albuquerque: University of New Mexico Press, 1976. Reprinted in shortened form in *Folk Groups and Folklore Genres: A Reader*, edited by Elliott Oring, 291–301 (96–107 of original). Logan: Utah State University Press, 1989.

Baughman, Ernest W. "Folk Sayings and Beliefs." *New Mexico Folklore Record* 9 (1954–1955): 23–27.

Blair, Marion E. "The Prevalence of Older English Proverbs in Blount County, Tennessee." *Tennessee Folklore Society Bulletin* 4 (1938): 1–24.

Blue, John S. *Hoosier Tales and Proverbs*. Rensselaer, Ind.: J. S. Blue, 1982.

Boas, Franz. "Metaphor." In *Primitive Art*, 320–25. Oslo: H. Aschehoug, 1927.

Boswell, George. "Folk Wisdom in Northeastern Kentucky." *Tennessee Folklore Society Bulletin* 33 (1967): 10–17.

Botkin, B. A. "Folk-Say." In *A Treasury of New England Folklore*, edited by B. A. Botkin, 494–95, 510–11, 520. New York: American Legacy Press, 1947 (rev. 1965).

Boudreaux, Anna Mary. "Proverbs, Metaphors and Sayings of the Kaplan Area." *Louisiana Folklore Miscellany* 3 (1970): 16–24.

Bradley, F. W. "South Carolina Proverbs."

Southern Folklore Quarterly 1 (1937): 57–101.

Brewer, J. Mason. "Old Time Negro Proverbs." In *Spur-of-the-Cock,* edited by J. Frank Dobie, 101–5. Austin: Texas Folk-Lore Society, 1933. Reprinted in *Texas Folk and Folklore,* edited by Mody C. Boatright, Wilson M. Hudson, and Allen Maxwell, 219–23. Dallas: Southern Methodist University Press, 1954. Reprinted in *Mother Wit from the Laughing Barrel: Readings in the Interpretation of African Folklore,* edited by Alan Dundes, 246–50. Englewood Cliffs, N.J.: Prentice-Hall, 1973.

Brewer, J. Mason. "Proverbs." In *American Negro Folklore,* 311–25. Chicago: Quadrangle Books, 1968.

Brewster, Paul G. "Folk 'Sayings' from Indiana." *American Speech* 14 (1939): 261–68, and 16 (1941): 21–25.

Brunvand, Jan Harold. *A Dictionary of English Proverbs and Proverbial Phrases from Books Published by Indiana Authors before 1890.* Bloomington: Indiana University Press, 1961.

Bynum, Joyce. "Syriac Proverbs from California." *Western Folklore* 31 (1972): 87–101.

Clements, William M. "Rapports locaux: Proverbs in the Indiana University Folklore Archives." *Proverbium* 14 (1969): 410–11.

Coad, Oral S. "Proverb Collecting in New Jersey." *New York Folklore Quarterly* 3 (1947): 320–22.

Cobos, Rubén. *Southwestern Spanish Proverbs / Refranes españoles del sudoeste.* Cerrillos, N. Mex.: San Marcos Press, 1973.

Coffin, Tristram, and Hennig Cohen. "Proverbs." In *Folklore in America,* edited by T. Coffin and H. Cohen, 141–51. Garden City, N.Y.: Doubleday, 1966.

Coghlan, Evelyn. "Ethnic Folklore in New Jersey." *New Jersey Folklore* 1 (1976): 3–27.

Corum, Ann Kondo. *Folk Wisdom from Hawaii or Don't Take Bananas on a Boat.* Honolulu: The Bess Press, 1985.

Cox, Ernest. "Rustic Imagery in Mississippi

Proverbs." *Southern Folklore Quarterly* 11 (1947): 263–67.

Eddins, A.W. "Grandma's Sayings." In *Texas Folk and Folklore,* edited by Mody C. Boatright, Wilson M. Hudson, and Allen Maxwell, 218–19. Dallas: Southern Methodist University Press, 1954.

Eisiminger, Sterling. "A Glossary of Ethnic Slurs in American English." *Maledicta* 3 (1979): 153–74.

Emrich, Duncan. "Proverbs and Proverbial Speech." In *Folklore on the American Land,* 60–89. Boston: Little, Brown and Co., 1982.

Fogel, Edwin Miller. *Proverbs of the Pennsylvania Germans.* Lancaster, Pa.: The Pennsylvania-German Society, 1929.

Gabel, Marie. "Proverbs of Volga German Settlers in Ellis County." *Heritage of Kansas* 9 (1976): 55–58.

Gard, Robert E., and L. G. Sorden. "Proverbs and Plain Talk." In *Wisconsin Lore,* 315–34. New York: Duell, Sloan and Pearce, 1962.

Glazer, Mark. *A Dictionary of Mexican American Proverbs.* Westport, Conn.: Greenwood Press, 1987.

Glazer, Mark. *Flour From Another Sack & Other Proverbs, Folk Beliefs, Tales, Riddles & Recipes: A Collection of Folklore from the Lower Rio Grande Valley of Texas.* Edinburg, Tex.: Pan American University Press, 1982.

Glick, David. *Proverbs of the Pennsylvania Dutch.* Smoketown, Pa.: Brookshire, 1972.

Guzzetta-Jones, Angeline, Joseph Antinoro-Polizzi, and Carl Zollo. *We Remember . . . A Collection of 200 Years of Golden Sayings of Some of the Ethnic Groups that Made America Great.* Rochester, N.Y.: Flower City Printing Co., 1975.

Hall, Joseph S. *Sayings from Old Smokey: Some Traditional Phrases, Expressions, and Sentences Heard in the Great Smokey Mountains and Nearby Areas.* Asheville, N.C.: The Cataloochee Press, 1972.

Hand, Wayland D. "Perverted Proverbs (from California)." *Western Folklore* 27 (1968): 263–64.

Hardie, Margaret. "Proverbs and Proverbial

Expressions in the United States East of the Missouri and North of the Ohio Rivers." *American Speech* 4 (1929): 461–72.

Harmon, Marion F. "Old Sayings." In *Negro Wit and Humor*, 121–22. Louisville: Harmon Publishing Co., 1914.

Hendricks, George D. "Texas Folk Proverbs." *Western Folklore* 21 (1962): 92.

Hines, Donald M. *Frontier Folksay: Proverbial Lore of the Inland Pacific Northwest Frontier*. Norwood, Pa.: Norwood Editions, 1977.

Hughes, Muriel J. "Vermont Proverbs and Proverbial Sayings." *Vermont History* 28 (1960): 113–42, 200–230.

"Indian Proverbs." *Journal of American Folklore* 19 (1906): 173–74.

Judd, Henry P. *Hawaiian Proverbs and Riddles*. Honolulu: Bernice P. Bishop Museum, 1930. Reprint. Millwood, N.Y.: Kraus Reprint, 1978.

Kloberdanz, Timothy J. "Proverbs and Proverbial Expressions among the Germans from Russia." *Journal of the American Historical Society of Germans from Russia* 2 (1979): 29–31.

Koch, Mary. "Volga German Proverbs and Proverbial Expressions from the Colony of Dreispitz." *Journal of the American Historical Society of Germans from Russia* 2 (1979): 32–37.

Koch, William E. "Proverbs and Riddles." In *Kansas Folklore*, edited by Samuel J. Sackett and W. E. Koch, 90–103. Lincoln: University of Nebraska Press, 1961.

Kumove, Shirley. *Words Like Arrows: A Treasury of Yiddish Folk Sayings*. Toronto: University of Toronto Press, 1984. Reprint. New York: Warner Books, 1986.

Mason, John Alfred. "Aphorisms from the Quarters." In *Uncle Gabe Tucker; or Reflections, Song, and Sentiment in the Quarters*, 131–47. Philadelphia: Lippincott, 1883. Reprinted in J. Mason Brewer, *American Negro Folklore*, 315–23. Chicago: Quadrangle Books, 1968.

Malone, Kemp. "Negro Proverbs from Maryland." *American Speech* 4 (1929): 285.

McNeil, William K. "Folklore from Big Flat, Arkansas, Part III: Proverbs and Proverbial Phrases." *Mid-American Folklore* 12 (1984): 27–30.

Mead, Jane Thompson. "Proverbs: Sayings from Westfield, Chautauqua Co." *New York Folklore Quarterly* 10 (1954): 226–27.

Mieder, Wolfgang. *American Proverbs: A Study of Texts and Contexts*. New York: Peter Lang, 1989.

Mieder, Wolfgang. *As Sweet as Apple Cider: Vermont Expressions*. Shelburne, Vt.: The New England Press, 1988.

Mieder, Wolfgang. *Talk Less and Say More: Vermont Proverbs*. Shelburne, Vt.: The New England Press, 1986.

Mieder, Wolfgang. *Yankee Wisdom: New England Proverbs*. Shelburne, Vt.: The New England Press, 1989.

Monteiro, George. "Proverbs and Proverbial Phrases of the Continental Portuguese." *Western Folklore* 22 (1963): 19–45.

Morison, O. "Tsimshian Proverbs." *Journal of American Folklore* 2 (1889): 285–86.

"Parodied Proverbs from Idaho." *Western Folklore* 24 (1965): 289–90.

Pearce, Helen. "Folk Sayings in a Pioneer Family of Western Oregon." *California Folklore Quarterly* 5 (1946): 229–42.

Pearce, T. M. "The English Proverb in New Mexico." *California Folklore Quarterly* 5 (1946): 350–54.

Pérez, Soledad. "Dichos from Austin." In *Texas Folk and Folklore*, edited by Mody C. Boatright, Wilson M. Hudson, and Allen Maxwell, 223–29. Dallas: Southern Methodist University Press, 1954.

Person, Henry. "Proverbs and Proverbial Lore from the State of Washington." *Western Folklore* 17 (1958): 176–85.

"Perverted Proverbs (from California)." *Western Folklore* 20 (1961): 200.

Polve, Adella. "Utah Folksay." *Utah Humanities Review* 1 (1947): 300–301.

Pound, Louise. "Proverbs and Phrases (from Massachusetts)." *Journal of American Folklore* 5 (1892): 60.

"Proverbs and Sayings (from New York)." *New York Folklore Quarterly* 2 (1946): 219–20.

Randolph, Vance, and George P. Wilson.

"Sayings and Wisecracks." In *Down in the Holler: A Gallery of Ozark Folk Speech,* 172–222. Norman: University of Oklahoma Press, 1953.

Richmond, Winthrop Edson. "The Collection of Proverbs in Indiana." *Hoosier Folklore* 5 (1946): 150–56.

Rogers, E. G. "Popular Sayings of Marshall County." *Tennessee Folklore Society Bulletin* 15 (1949): 70–75.

Skelton, Ferne, ed. *Pioneer Proverbs: Wit and Wisdom from Early America.* Collected by Mary Turner. High Point, N.C.: Hutcraft, 1971.

Shoemaker, Henry. *Scotch-Irish and English Proverbs and Sayings of the West Branch Valley of Central Pennsylvania.* Reading, Pa.: Reading Eagle Press, 1927.

Smith, Morgan, and A. W. Eddins. "Wise Saws from Texas." In *Straight Texas,* edited by J. Frank Dobie and Mody C. Boatright, 239–44. Dallas: Southern Methodist University Press, 1937.

Smitherman, Geneva. "Some Well-Known Black Proverbs and Sayings." In *Talkin and Testifyin: The Language of Black America,* 245–46. Detroit: Wayne State University Press, 1986.

Snapp, Emma Louise. "Proverbial Lore in Nebraska." *University of Nebraska Studies in Language, Literature and Criticism,* 13 (1933): 51–112.

Spaulding, Henry. "Proverbs, Folk Talk and Superstitions." In *Encyclopedia of Black Folklore and Humor,* edited by H. Spaulding, 530–41. Middle Village, N.Y.: Jonathan David Publishers, 1972.

Taylor, Archer. "Notes on North Carolina Proverbs." *North Carolina Folklore* 12 (1964): 13–14.

Taylor, Archer. "A Few Additional Nineteenth-Century American Proverbs." *North Carolina Folklore* 13 (1965): 37–38.

Taylor, Archer, and C. Grant Loomis. "California Proverbs and Sententious Sayings." *Western Folklore* 10 (1951): 248–49.

Thompson, Harold W. "Proverbs." *Body, Boots, and Britches,* 481–504. Philadelphia: J. B. Lippincott, 1940.

Thompson, Harold W. "Proverbs and Sayings." *New York Folklore Quarterly* 5 (1949): 230–35, 296–300.

Thurston, Helen M. "Sayings and Proverbs from Massachusetts." *Journal of American Folklore* 19 (1906): 122.

Wakefield, Edward. "Wisdom of Gombo (Creole Proverbs from Louisiana)." *Nineteenth Century* 30 (1891): 575–82.

White, Vallie Tinsley. "Proverbs and Picturesque Speech from Claiborne Parish, Louisiana." *Louisiana Folklore Miscellany* 2 (1962): 85–87.

Whiting, Bartlett Jere. "Lowland Scots and Celtic Proverbs in North Carolina." *Journal of Celtic Studies* 1 (1949): 116–27.

Whiting, Bartlett Jere. "Proverbs and Proverbial Sayings (from North Carolina)." In *The Frank C. Brown Collection of North Carolina Folklore* (vol. 1), edited by Newman Ivey White, 329–501. Durham, N.C.: Duke University Press, 1952.

Wilgus, D. K. "Proverbial Material from the Western Kentucky Folklore Archive." *Kentucky Folklore Record* 6 (1960): 47–49.

Work, Monroe N. "Geechee and Other Proverbs (from the Sea Islands)." *Journal of American Folklore* 32 (1919): 441–42.

PROVERBS IN AMERICAN LITERATURE

Abrahams, Roger D., and Barbara A. Babcock. "The Literary Use of Proverbs." *Journal of American Folklore* 90 (1977): 414–29.

Abrams, W. Amos. " 'Time Was': Its Lore and Language." *North Carolina Folklore* 19 (1971): 40–46.

Anderson, John Q. "Emerson and the Language of the Folk." In *Folk Travelers: Ballads, Tales, and Talk,* edited by Mody C. Boatright, Wilson M. Hudson, and Allen Maxwell, 152–59. Dallas: Southern Methodist University Press, 1953.

Anderson, John Q. "Folklore in the Writings of 'The Louisiana Swamp Doctor.' " *Southern Folklore Quarterly* 19 (1955): 243–51.

Arner, Robert D. "Folk Metaphors in Edward Taylor's 'Meditation.' " *Seventeenth Century News* 31 (1973): 6–9.

Arner, Robert D. "Proverbs in Edward Taylor's 'Gods Determinations.' " *Southern Folklore Quarterly* 37 (1973): 1–13.

Babcock, C. Merton. "Melville's Proverbs of the Sea." *Western Folklore* 11 (1952): 254–65.

Babcock, C. Merton. "Melville's World's Language." *Southern Folklore Quarterly* 16 (1952): 177–82.

Babcock, C. Merton. "Some Expressions from Herman Melville." *Publications of the American Dialect Society* 3 (1959): 3–13.

Baker, Ronald Lee. "Robinson's Use of Proverbs and Proverbial Phrases." *Folklore in the Writings of Rowland E. Robinson*, 253–92. Ph.D. diss., Indiana University, 1969.

Barbour, Frances M. *A Concordance to the Sayings in Franklin's "Poor Richard."* Detroit: Gale Research Co., 1974.

Barker, Addison. " 'Good Fences Make Good Neighbors.' " *Journal of American Folklore* 64 (1951): 421.

Barnes, Daniel R. "Telling It Slant: Emily Dickinson and the Proverb." *Genre* 12 (1979): 219–41.

Barrick, Mac E. "Proverbs and Sayings from Gibbsville, Pennsylvania: John O'Hara's Use of Proverbial Materials." *Keystone Folklore Quarterly* 12 (1967): 55–80.

Barrick, Mac E. "Ruxton's Western Proverbs." *Western Folklore* 34 (1975): 215–25.

Blackwell, Louise. "Eudora Welty: Proverbs and Proverbial Phrases in 'The Golden Apples.' " *Southern Folklore Quarterly* 30 (1966): 332–41.

Boswell, George W. "Folkways in Faulkner." *Mississippi Folklore Register* 1 (1967): 83–90.

Brookes, Stella Brewer. "Proverbs and Folk-Say." In *Joel Chandler Harris—Folklorist*, 97–110. Athens: University of Georgia Press, 1950 (3d ed., 1972).

Brunvand, Jan Harold. *A Dictionary of Proverbs and Proverbial Phrases from Books Published by Indiana Authors Before 1890.* Bloomington: Indiana University Press, 1961.

Cameron, Kenneth Walter. "Emerson's Arabian Proverbs." *Emerson Society Quarterly* 13 (1958): 50.

Cameron, Kenneth Walter. "Emerson, Thoreau, 'Elegant Extracts,' and Proverb Lore." *Emerson Society Quarterly* 6 (1957): 28–39.

Carion, Flavia de. *Some Florida Proverbs and Their Literary Background.* Master's thesis, University of Florida, 1948.

Carnes, Pack. "The American Face of Aesop: Thurber's Fables and Tradition." *Moderna Språk* 79 (1986): 3–17. Reprinted in *Proverbia in Fabula: Essays on the Relationship of the Fable and the Proverb,* edited by Pack Carnes, 311–31. Bern: Peter Lang, 1988.

Clark, Joseph D. "Burke Davis as Folklorist." *North Carolina Folklore* 19 (1971): 59–65.

Clarke, Mary Washington. *Jesse Stuart's Kentucky.* New York: McGraw-Hill, 1968.

Clarke, Mary Washington. "Proverbs, Proverbial Phrases, and Proverbial Comparisons in the Writings of Jesse Stuart." *Southern Folklore Quarterly* 29 (1965): 142–63.

Coues, R. W. "Odd Terms in a Writer of Letters." *Dialect Notes* 6 (1928–1939): 1–6.

D'Avanzo, Mario L. "Emerson's 'Days' and Proverbs." *American Transcendental Quarterly* 1 (1969): 83–85.

De Caro, Francis A. "Proverbs and Originality in Modern Short Fiction." *Western Folklore* 37 (1978): 30–38.

Everman, Welch D. "Harry Mathews's 'Selected Declarations of Dependence': Proverbs and the Forms of Authority." *Review of Contemporary Fiction* 7 (1987): 146–53.

Figh, Margaret Gillis. "Folklore and Folk Speech in the Works of Marjorie Kinnan Rawlings." *Southern Folklore Quarterly* 11 (1947): 201–9.

Figh, Margaret Gillis. "Folklore in the 'Rufus Sanders' Sketches." *Southern Folklore Quarterly* 19 (1955): 185–95.

Figh, Margaret Gillis. "Tall Talks and Folk Sayings in Bill Arp's Works." *Southern Folklore Quarterly* 13 (1949): 206–12.

Flanagan, John T. "Folklore in the Novels of Conrad Richter." *Midwest Folklore* 2 (1952): 5–14.

French, Florence Healy. "Cooper's Use of Proverbs in the Anti-Rent Novels." *New York Folklore Quarterly* 26 (1970): 42–49.

French, Florence Healy. "Cooper the Tinkerer." *New York Folklore Quarterly* 26 (1970): 229–39.

Frizzell, John Henry. *Proverbial Philosophy in American Literature.* Master's thesis, Pennsylvania State University, 1912.

Gallacher, Stuart A. "Franklin's 'Way to Wealth': A Florilegium of Proverbs and Wise Sayings." *Journal of English and Germanic Philology* 48 (1949): 229–51.

Gallagher, Edward J. "The Rhetorical Strategy of Franklin's 'Way to Wealth.' " *Eighteenth Century Studies* 6 (1973): 475–85.

Galvin, Brendan. "Theodore Roethke's Proverbs." *Concerning Poetry* 5 (1972): 35–47.

Glassie, Henry. "The Use of Folklore in 'David Harum.' " *New York Folklore Quarterly* 23 (1967): 163–85.

Grimes, Geoffrey Allan. " 'Muels,' 'Owls,' and Other Things: Folk Material in the Tobacco Philosophy of Josh Billings." *New York Folklore Quarterly* 26 (1970): 283–96.

Harder, Kelsie B. "Proverbial Snopeslore." *Tennessee Folklore Society Bulletin* 24 (1958): 89–95.

Kroll, Harry Harrison. "How I Collect Proverbial Materials for My Novels." *Tennessee Folklore Society Bulletin* 23 (1957): 1–5.

LaRosa, Ralph Charles. *Emerson's Proverbial Rhetoric: 1818–1838.* Ph.D. diss., University of Wisconsin, 1969.

LaRosa, Ralph Charles. "Emerson's 'Sententiae' in 'Nature' (1836)." *Emerson Society Quarterly,* no. 58 (1970): 153–57.

LaRosa, Ralph Charles. "Invention and Imitation in Emerson's Early Lectures." *American Literature* 44 (1972): 13–30.

LaRosa, Ralph Charles. "Necessary Truths: The Poetics of Emerson's Proverbs." In *Literary Monographs.* Vol. 8, *Mid-Nineteenth Century Writers: Eliot, De Quincey, Emerson,* edited by Eric Rothstein and Joseph Anthony Wittreich, 129–92, 210–16 (notes). Madison: University of Wisconsin Press, 1976.

Loomis, C. Grant. "Emerson's Proverbs." *Western Folklore* 17 (1958): 257–62.

Loomis, C. Grant. "Folk-Language in William McLeod Raine's 'West.' " *Tennessee Folklore Society Bulletin* 24 (1958): 131–48.

Loomis, C. Grant. "Henry David Thoreau as Folklorist." *Western Folklore* 16 (1957): 90–106.

Loomis, C. Grant. "Random Proverbs in Popular Literature." *Western Folklore* 16 (1957): 133–35.

McNeil, William K. "Proverbs Used in New York Autograph Albums 1820–1900." *Southern Folklore Quarterly* 33 (1969): 352–59.

Meister, Charles W. "Franklin as a Proverb Stylist." *American Literature* 24 (1952–1953): 157–66.

Mieder, Wolfgang. "A Sampler of Anglo-American Proverb Poetry." *Folklore Forum* 13 (1980): 39–53.

Mieder, Wolfgang. " 'Behold the Proverbs of a People': A Florilegium of Proverbs in Carl Sandburg's Poem 'Good Morning, America.' " *Southern Folklore Quarterly* 35 (1971): 160–68.

Mieder, Wolfgang. "Proverbs in Carl Sandburg's Poem 'The People, Yes.' " *Southern Folklore Quarterly* 37 (1973): 15–36.

Mieder, Wolfgang. "The Proverb and Anglo-American Literature." *Southern Folklore Quarterly* 38 (1974): 49–62.

Mieder, Wolfgang. *Tradition and Innovation in Folk Literature.* Hanover, N.H.: University Press of New England, 1987.

Mieder, Wolfgang. "Traditional and Innovative Proverb Use in Lyric Poetry." *Proverbium Paratum* 1 (1980): 16–27.

Moldenhauer, Joseph J. "The Rhetorical Function of Proverbs in 'Walden.' " *Journal of American Folklore* 80 (1967): 151–59.

Monteiro, George. " 'Good Fences Make

Good Neighbors': A Proverb and a Poem." *Revista de Etnografia* 16, no. 31 (1972): 83–88.

Monteiro, George. "Louisa May Alcott's Proverb Stories." *Tennessee Folklore Society Bulletin* 42 (1976): 103–7.

Monteiro, George. "Straight and Crooked Lines: The Literary Uses of a Proverb." *Estudios Anglo-Americanos* 5–6 (1981–1982): 113–17.

Monteiro, George. "The Literary Uses of a Proverb." *Folklore* (London) 87 (1976): 216–18.

Montgomery, Evelyn. "Proverbial Materials in 'The Politician Out-Witted' and Other Comedies of Early American Drama 1789–1829." *Midwest Folklore* 11 (1961–1962): 215–24.

Newcomb, Robert. *The Sources of Benjamin Franklin's Sayings of Poor Richard.* Ph.D. diss., University of Maryland, 1957.

Owen, Guy. "The Use of Folklore in Fiction." *North Carolina Folklore* 19 (1971): 73–79.

Reaver, J. Russell. "Thoreau's Ways with Proverbs." *American Transcendental Quarterly* 1 (1969) 2–7.

Reaver, J. Russell. "Emerson's Use of Proverbs." *Southern Folklore Quarterly* 28 (1963): 280–99.

Roberts, Leonard. "Additional Notes on Archer Taylor's 'On Troublesome Creek.' " *Kentucky Folklore Record* 8 (1962): 142–44.

Russell, Thomas Herbert, ed. *The Sayings of Poor Richard: Wit, Wisdom and Humor of Benjamin Franklin in the Proverbs and Maxims of Poor Richard's Almanacks for 1733 to 1758.* Chicago: Veterans of Foreign Wars of the United States, 1926.

Sackett, Samuel J. "Edgar Watson Howe as Proverb Maker." *Journal of American Folklore* 85 (1972): 73–77.

Steele, Thomas J. "Orality and Literacy in Matter and Form: Ben Franklin's 'Way to Wealth.' " *Oral Tradition* 2 (1987): 273–85.

Stephens, Robert O. "Macomber and That Somali Proverb." In *Fitzgerald-Hemingway Annual 1977,* edited by Margaret

Duggan and Richard Layman, 137–47. Detroit: Gale Research Co., 1977.

Sullivan, Patrick. "Benjamin Franklin, the Inveterate (and Crafty) Public Instructor: Instruction on Two Levels in 'The Way to Wealth.' " *Early American Literature* 21 (1986–1987): 248–59.

Taylor, Archer. "Americanisms in 'The Log of a Cowboy.' " *Western Folklore* 18 (1959): 39–41.

Taylor, Archer. "Poe, Dr. Lardner, and 'Three Sundays in a Week.' " *American Notes and Queries* 3 (1943–1944): 153–55.

Taylor, Archer. "Proverbial Comparisons and Similes in 'On Troublesome Creek.' " *Kentucky Folklore Record* 8 (1962): 87–96.

Taylor, Archer. "Proverbial Materials in Edward Eggleston, 'The Hoosier Schoolmaster.' " In *Studies in Folklore in Honor of Stith Thompson,* edited by W. Edson Richmond, 262–70. Bloomington: Indiana University Press, 1957.

Taylor, Archer. "Proverbial Materials in Two Novels by Harry Harrison Kroll." *Tennessee Folklore Society Bulletin* 22 (1956): 39–52.

Taylor, Archer. "Proverbial Materials in Two More Novels by Harry Harrison Kroll." *Tennessee Folklore Society Bulletin* 22 (1956): 73–84.

Taylor, Archer. "Proverbs and Proverbial Phrases in the Writings of Mary N. Murfree." *Tennessee Folklore Society Bulletin* 24 (1958): 11–50.

Taylor, Archer. "Some Americanisms in James Hall, 'Legends of the West' (Philadelphia 1833)." *Western Folklore* 18 (1959): 331.

Taylor, Archer. "Some Proverbial Expressions from Bayard Taylor's 'Story of Kennett.' " *Keystone Folklore Quarterly* 6 (1961): 23–24.

Tolman, Ruth B. "Proverbs and Sayings in Eighteenth-Century Almanacs." *Western Folklore* 21 (1962): 35–42.

Van Doren, Carl. *Benjamin Franklin.* Esp. 106–15, 149–51, 266–68. New York: Viking Press, 1938.

Walker, Warren S. *Folk Elements in the Novels of James Fenimore Cooper.* Ph.D. diss., Cornell University, 1951.

Walker, Warren S. "Proverbs in the Novels of James Fenimore Cooper." *Midwest Folklore* 3 (1953): 99–107.

Washington, Mary Louise. *The Folklore of the Cumberlands as Reflected in the Writings of Jesse Stuart.* Ph.D. diss., University of Pennsylvania, 1960.

Webber, Eunice Lucille. *Proverbs and Proverbial Phrases in Volumes I–IV of the Works of Benjamin Franklin.* Master's thesis, Stetson University, 1942.

West, Harry C. "Negro Folklore in Pierce's Novels." *North Carolina Folklore* 19 (1971): 66–72.

West, Harry C. "Simon Suggs and His Similes." *North Carolina Folklore* 16 (1968): 53–57.

West, Victor R. "Folklore in the Works of Mark Twain." *University of Nebraska Studies in Language, Literature, and Criticism* 10 (1930): 1–87.

Whiting, Bartlett Jere. "Proverbial Sayings from 'Fisher's River, North Carolina.' " *Southern Folklore Quarterly* 11 (1947): 173–85.

Whiting, Bartlett Jere. "Proverbs in Cotton Mather's 'Magnalia Christi Americana.' " *Neuphilologische Mitteilungen* 73 (1972): 477–84.

Wilhelm, Albert E. "Robert Frost's Proverbial Promises: Indian Responses to 'Stopping by Woods.' " *Motif: International Newsletter of Research in Folklore and Literature* 4 (October 1982): 7.

Willis, Lonnie L. *Folklore in the Published Writings of Henry David Thoreau: A Study and a Compendium-Index.* Ph.D. diss., University of Colorado, 1966.

Yates, Irene. "A Collection of Proverbs and Proverbial Sayings from South Carolina Literature." *Southern Folklore Quarterly* 11 (1947): 187–99.